AUSTRALIA'S EVOLVING DEMOCRACY

A New Democratic Audit

Edited by
**Mark Evans,
Patrick Dunleavy
and John Phillimore**

Published by

LSE Press

10 Portugal Street

London

WC2A 2HD

press.lse.ac.uk

Text © The authors, 2024

Images © listed individually in source captions

First published 2024

Cover design by Diana Jarvis

Print and digital versions typeset by PDQ Media

ISBN (Paperback): 978-1-911712-30-5

ISBN (PDF): 978-1-911712-31-2

ISBN (EPUB): 978-1-911712-32-9

ISBN (Mobi): 978-1-911712-33-6

DOI: https://doi.org/10.31389/lsepress.ada

This work is licensed under the Creative Commons Attribution-NonCommercial 4.0 International (CC BY-NC 4.0) Licence (unless stated otherwise within the content of the work). To view a copy of this licence, visit https://creativecommons.org/licenses/by-nc/4.0/ or send a letter to Creative Commons, 444 Castro Street, Suite 900, Mountain View, California, 94041, USA. This licence allows for copying and distributing the work, providing author attribution is clearly stated and that you are not using the material for commercial purposes.

Third-party images featured in this book are not covered by the book's Creative Commons licence. Details of the copyright ownership are given in the individual image source information.

The full text of this book has been peer-reviewed to ensure high academic standards. For our full publishing ethics policies, see https://press.lse.ac.uk

Suggested citation: Evans, Mark; Dunleavy, Patrick and Phillimore, John (2024) *Australia's Evolving Democracy: A New Democratic Audit*, London: LSE Press. **https://doi.org/10.31389/lsepress.ada** Licence: CC BY-NC 4.0

To read the free, open access version of this book online, visit https://doi.org/10.31389/lsepress.ada or scan this QR code with your mobile device:

Contents

Editors 6
Contributors 7
Preface 11
How to read this book 15
Acknowledgements 17
List of figures 19
Glossary 25

PART I FOUNDATIONS 31

1. Situating Australian democracy 33
   Patrick Dunleavy, Mark Evans, Harry Hobbs and Patrick Weller

2. Human rights and civil liberties 53
   Mark Evans and Stan Grant

3. The Constitution 70
   Harry Hobbs

4. The 2023 Voice to Parliament referendum 84
   Mark Evans and Michelle Grattan

PART II NATIONAL POLITICS 95

5. Elections and voting 97
   Patrick Dunleavy and Mark Evans

6. Political parties 120
   Patrick Dunleavy and Mark Evans

7. Interest groups and corporate power 143
   Patrick Dunleavy

8. Mainstream media 166
   Patrick Dunleavy

9. Social media 191
   Max Halupka

10. Gender equality and rights 206
    Pia Rowe

PART III FEDERAL GOVERNMENT ... 229

11 Parliament – the House of Representatives ... 231
   Sarah Moulds

12 Parliament – the Senate ... 253
   Brenton Prosser, Mary Walsh and John Hawkins

13 Prime Minister, Cabinet and government ... 275
   Mark Evans and Patrick Dunleavy

14 The Australian Public Service ... 301
   John Halligan and Mark Evans

15 Government policy-making ... 326
   John Butcher

16 How democratic is Australian federalism? ... 346
   John Phillimore and Alan Fenna

PART IV STATE AND LOCAL POLITICS ... 365

17 New South Wales ... 367
   Mark Evans

18 Victoria ... 392
   Tom Daly and James Murphy

19 Queensland ... 415
   Cosmo Howard and Pandanus Petter

20 South Australia ... 432
   Rob Manwaring, Josh Holloway and Andrew Parkin

21 Western Australia ... 453
   John Phillimore, Martin Drum, Sarah Murray, Peter Wilkins, Narelle Miragliotta and Benjamin Reilly

22 Tasmania ... 478
   Lachlan Johnson, Richard Eccleston and Mike Lester

23 Northern Territory ... 497
   Rolf Gerritsen

24 Australian Capital Territory ... 514
   Brendan McCaffrie

25 Local democracy in metropolitan regions and big cities ... 529
   Graham Sansom and Su Fei Tan

26 Systems of local government ... 544
   Su Fei Tan and Graham Sansom

PART V CHALLENGES AND CHANGE 557

27 Political institutions in the Anthropocene 559
    Pierrick Chalaye and John S. Dryzek
28 Democratic resilience and change 574
    Patrick Dunleavy and Mark Evans

Index 603

Editors

Mark Evans (FIPPA, FRS) is Deputy Vice Chancellor Research at Charles Sturt University and was formerly Director of Democracy 2025 at the Museum of Australian Democracy in Canberra from 2018 to 2022. Prior to this, he was Executive Director of the Institute for Governance and Policy Analysis at the University of Canberra (2009–18) and editor of the international journal *Policy Studies* (2004 to 2021). His research focuses on evaluating domestic and international evidence on how to improve democratic governance and practice. His most recent books include *Saving Democracy* (Bloomsbury Press, 2022, co-authored with Gerry Stoker) and *From Turnbull to Morrison: The Trust Divide* (Melbourne University Press, 2019, with Michelle Grattan and Brendan McCaffrie).

Patrick Dunleavy is Emeritus Professor of Political Science and Public Policy at the London School of Economics and Political Science (LSE). He worked in the Department of Government at LSE from 1979 to 2020. He is also Emeritus Professor of Government at the University of Canberra, where he was Centenary Professor 2015–2020. A Fellow of the British Academy and the Academy of Social Sciences, he also served as founding editor-in-chief at LSE Press from 2020–2023. He was director of the UK Democratic Audit from 2013 to 2020. His recent books include *The UK's Changing Democracy: The 2018 Democratic Audit* (open access from LSE Press, 2018, co-edited) and *Maximizing the Impacts of Academic Research* (Palgrave, now Bloomsbury Press, 2021, co-authored with Jane Tinkler). **p.dunleavy@lse.ac.uk**

John Phillimore is Executive Director of the John Curtin Institute of Public Policy at Curtin University, Western Australia. He has written widely on federalism, public policy and public administration, and is a regular commentator on Australian and Western Australian politics. In 2021 Professor Phillimore was appointed to the Ministerial Expert Committee on Electoral Reform in Western Australia. Its recommendations led to the reform of the state's voting system for the Legislative Council. **J.Phillimore@curtin.edu.au**

Contributors

John Butcher is Adjunct Research Fellow at the John Curtin Institute of Public Policy. John has worked as an academic researcher, as a policy analyst for government in the areas of disability and housing policy, and as a performance analyst in the Australian National Audit Office (ANAO). He has published extensively on the evolving relationship between government and the not-for-profit sector. His recent work includes *Collaboration for Impact: Lessons from the Field* (ANU Press, 2020, co-authored with David J. Gilchrist).

Pierrick Chalaye is a Postdoctoral Fellow at the Institute TRansitions Energétiques et Environnementales (TREE), University of Pau (France). He completed his PhD in comparative environmental politics/policy at the University of Canberra (Australia) in 2021 and has since been working on environmental and energy politics and deliberative democratic theory.

Tom Daly is Associate Professor and Deputy Director in the Melbourne School of Government at the University of Melbourne. He is also Deputy Secretary-General of the International Association of Constitutional Law (IACL). He has published widely on democratic decline and its manifestations comparatively, especially in Brazil and South America, and its legal and constitutional implications.

Martin Drum is Professor of Politics and International Relations and Executive Dean (Arts, Sciences, Law and Business) at Notre Dame University in Australia. He has taught and researched on a range of issues, including public policy, voting, elections and Australian politics. Professor Drum was appointed to the Ministerial Expert Committee on Electoral Reform in 2022. Its recommendations led to the reform of the voting system for the Legislative Council in Western Australia.

John S. Dryzek is Centenary Professor at the Centre for Deliberative Democracy and Global Governance at the University of Canberra. His recent books include *The Politics of the Anthropocene* (Oxford University Press, 2019, co-authored with Jonathan Pickering) and *Democratizing Global Justice: Deliberating Global Goals* (Cambridge University Press, 2021, co-authored with Ana Tanasoca).

Richard Eccleston is Director of the Tasmanian Policy Exchange at the University of Tasmania. He is a specialist in social and economic policy and has worked on a wide range of policy issues, analysing and developing practical evidence-based solutions to some of the most significant policy challenges facing our community. In recent years Richard has worked with a range of governments and led projects on a wide range of topics from tax reform, housing affordability, regional governance and development to climate and energy policy. He has been a Fulbright Senior Scholar based in Washington DC and was the Founding Director of the Institute for Social Change at the University of Tasmania.

Alan Fenna is Professor of Politics in the John Curtin Institute of Public Policy at Curtin University, Western Australia. He publishes extensively on Australian and comparative federalism as well as constitutionalism and public policy. He is the author, most recently, of *The Constitution of Western Australia: An Exploration* (Springer, 2023, co-authored with Sarah Murray).

Rolf Gerritsen is Adjunct Professor in the Northern Institute at Charles Darwin University, where he was previously Professorial Research Fellow. His research has focused on political economy, regional development and historical anthropology.

Stan Grant Junior (FASSA) is one of Australia's most distinguished philosophical thinkers and journalists. He is currently Distinguished Professor of Theology and Chair of the Yindyamarra Trust at Charles Sturt University. He was formerly Senior International Correspondent for CNN in Asia and the Middle East. Stan has been awarded three Walkley awards, two Peabody awards, four Asia TV awards, an Australian TV Logie award, International Indigenous Trailblazer award, two Australian Academy of Cinema Television awards, and an Australian Heritage Literature award, among many others. His latest books include *Australia Day* (Harper Collins, 2019), *With the Falling of the Dusk* (HarperCollins, 2023) and *The Queen is Dead* (HarperCollins, 2023).

Michelle Grattan (AO, FASSA) is one of Australia's most respected political journalists. She has been a member of the Canberra parliamentary press gallery for more than 40 years, during which time she has covered all the most significant stories in Australian politics. She was the former editor of *The Canberra Times*, was Political Editor of *The Age* and has been with the *Australian Financial Review* and *The Sydney Morning Herald*. Michelle currently has a dual role with an academic position at the University of Canberra and as Associate Editor (Politics) and Chief Political Correspondent at *The Conversation*. She is the author, co-author and editor of several books including *Australian Prime Ministers* (New Holland, 2016), *From Turnbull to Morrison: The Trust Divide* (Melbourne University Press, 2019) and *The Morrison Government* (UNSW Press, 2023). She was made an Officer of the Order of Australia (AO) in 2004 for her long and distinguished service to Australian journalism.

John Halligan is Emeritus Professor of Public Administration and Governance in the Centre for Environmental Governance at the University of Canberra. His recent books include *Performance Management in the Public Sector* (Routledge, 2015, 2nd ed, co-authored with Wouter Van Dooren and Geert Bouckaert); *Reforming Public Management and Governance: Impacts and Lessons from Anglophone Countries* (Elgar, 2020); and *Advising Governments in the Westminster Tradition: Policy Advisory Systems in Australia, Britain, Canada and New Zealand* (co-authored, Cambridge University Press, 2020).

Max Halupka is Senior Lecturer in the Canberra School of Politics, Economics and Society at the University of Canberra. His research publications focus mainly on social media (especially as a new field for political activism or 'clicktivism'), political trust and democracy, e-government and public administration systems.

John Hawkins is Deputy Head in the Canberra School of Politics, Economy and Society at the University of Canberra. His research covers banking policies and restructuring, financial policy-making, central banks, the Australian Parliament and political history. He was previously secretary to the Senate Economics Committee.

Harry Hobbs is Associate Professor in the Faculty of Law and Justice at the University of New South Wales. His research articles are in constitutional law, indigenous legal issues (especially in Australia), human rights law, transitional justice and international criminal law.

Josh Holloway is Lecturer in Government in the College of Business, Government and Law, at Flinders University. His research articles focus on centre-left parties, especially the comparative analysis of social democratic parties, green parties, and democracy and democratic resilience.

Cosmo Howard is Associate Professor in the School of Government and International Relations and Centre for Governance and Public Policy at Griffith University. His research focuses on inequality and the role of expertise in policy-making and he currently holds two Australian Research Council Discovery Projects. One traces the evolution of the discourse of the 'fair go' in Australian and New Zealand public policy, and the second compares the politics of expertise during COVID-19 in Australia, Sweden, the UK and the USA.

Lachlan Johnson is Research Fellow (Public Policy) in the Tasmanian Policy Exchange at the University of Tasmania. His recent articles cover tax policy and avoidance/evasion issues, economic and regional development, knowledge industries and Tasmania's economy.

Mike Lester is a researcher at the University of Tasmania. He was previously a journalist for 20 years and is now a public relations consultant in Tasmania. He has co-written articles for the *Australasian Parliamentary Review* and commented on Tasmania's politics for the *Australian Journal of Politics and History*.

Rob Manwaring is Associate Professor in the College of Business, Government and Law at Flinders University. He has written numerous journal articles on social democracy, comparative labour parties and centre-left parties internationally, as well as South Australia's politics. His books include *Why the Left Loses: The Decline of the Centre-Left in Comparative Perspective* (Policy Press, 2017, co-authored with Paul Kennedy).

Brendan McCaffrie is Senior Lecturer at the University of New South Wales (UNSW) in Canberra. He was previously Director of the MPA Program at the Canberra School of Politics, Economics and Society, University of Canberra. He has published extensively on executive government, prime ministers and Canberra Cabinets, and on Australian Capital Territory (ACT) government.

Narelle Miragliotta is an Associate Professor in Politics and International Relations at Murdoch University, Australia. She has research interests in different facets of Australian and liberal democratic political institutions, including constitutions, parliaments, political parties and elections and electoral systems.

Sarah Moulds is an Associate Professor in Law at the University of South Australia. Her recent articles focus on COVID-19 legislation in Australia and Parliament. She has been actively engaged in local, national and international conversations about emergency law-making in response to the COVID-19 pandemic, and the role parliaments can and should play in holding governments to account. Sarah is also editor of the *Australian Parliamentary Review*.

James Murphy is a Lecturer in Australian Politics at the University of Melbourne. He studies subnational Australian politics, especially Victorian state politics, as well as policy advocacy campaigns. He completed his doctoral thesis on the politics of Melbourne's East–West Link at Swinburne in 2019, published as *The Making and Unmaking of the East-West Link* (Melbourne University Press, 2022). For the last seven years, he has taught politics, history and public policy at various higher education institutions.

Sarah Murray is a Professor at the University of Western Australia Law School. She is an expert in constitutional law, electoral law and court innovation. She is a former commissioner at the Law Reform Commission of Western Australia, co-chair of the International Society of Public Law AUS–NZ Chapter and a co-convenor of the WA Chapter of the Electoral Regulation and Research Network. She is co-author of *The Constitution of Western Australia: An Exploration* (Springer, 2023, co-authored with Alan Fenna). Sarah was appointed to the Ministerial Expert Committee on Electoral Reform in 2022. Its recommendations led to the reform of the voting system for the Legislative Council in Western Australia.

Andrew Parkin is Emeritus Professor in Political Science in the College of Business, Government and Law at Flinders University. He has published chiefly in public policy and administration, Australian government and politics, international relations and applied political philosophy.

Pandanus Petter is a Postdoctoral Research Fellow at Australian National University's School of Politics and International Relations. His research focuses on representative democracy and responsiveness with a particular focus on members of parliament in Westminster jurisdictions and Queensland state politics. At the time of writing, he was a member of the research team for an ARC funded project at Griffith University on the Antipodean idea of the 'fair go' studying discourses of inequality in Australian and New Zealand public policy.

Brenton Prosser is Professor of Public Policy and Leadership at the University of New South Wales (UNSW) in Canberra. He is a former Chief-of-Staff to a crossbench Senator and senior political adviser in the South Australian upper house. His research interests include minority government, policy and public trust, while his journal articles cover social policy, social disadvantage, democracy and leadership.

Benjamin Reilly is currently Adjunct Senior Fellow at the East–West Centre in Hawaii, USA. He was formerly Professor of Political Science and held leadership positions at the University of Western Australia, Murdoch University and the Australian National University. He has also worked for the United Nations, International IDEA and other international organisations. His research focuses on the comparative politics of democracy and democratic reform.

Pia Rowe is Research Fellow at the '50/50 by 2030' Foundation at the University of Canberra. Her research articles focus on gender equality and issues, social media and collaborative consumption, trust and democracy, and the sociology of households.

Graham Sansom is Adjunct Professor at the University of Technology Sydney (UTS) Institute for Public Policy and Governance. He was previously Professor and Director of the Australian Centre of Excellence for Local Government. His publications cover local, metropolitan and regional governance across Australia and internationally.

Su Fei Tan is Principal Project Officer at the New South Wales Office of Local Government and previously worked at the University of Technology Sydney (UTS) Centre for Local Government. Her journal articles cover Australian local government, metropolitan governance and topics in gender and development.

Mary Walsh is Associate Dean Education in the Faculty of Business, Government and Law and member of the School of Politics, Economics and Society at the University of Canberra. She is a political theorist with research interests in Hannah Arendt, Australian politics and public policy. Her most recent publications include work on 'Freedom from democracy' in the journal *Democratic Theory*, and a chapter in defence of former Australian Prime Minister Julia Gillard in *Gender Politics: Navigating Political Leadership in Australia* (edited by Zareh Ghazarian and Katrina Lee-Koo).

Patrick Weller is Professor Emeritus in the School of Government and International Relations at Griffith University. He has authored numerous journal articles and books on political science, mainly on prime ministers and cabinet government, on policy-making and comparative executive politics. His most recent books include *Comparing Cabinets: Dilemmas of Collective Government* (Oxford University Press, 2021, co-authored with Dennis C. Grube and R.A.W. Rhodes) and *Comparing Westminster* (Oxford University Press, 2009, co-authored with R.A.W. Rhodes and John Wanna).

Peter Wilkins is Adjunct Professor at the John Curtin Institute of Public Policy at Curtin University in Western Australia (WA). He served as WA's Deputy Ombudsman and prior to this as Assistant Auditor General Performance Review. He is a National Fellow and WA Fellow of the Institute of Public Administration Australia.

Preface

Founded 123 years ago, Australia's political system has coped well with unprecedented environmental variety and development, and transformative economic and population changes. An intricate, balanced, liberal democracy has been progressively created which has increasingly attracted admirers, especially as some major historic wrongs against minorities have recently been fully rectified or substantially ameliorated.

Australia's evolving liberal democracy also stands now in stark contrast with two far more studied countries, the USA and the UK (the historic examples on which its Constitution draws extensively). These long-established major democracies have both changed radically. The USA is now widely classed as a 'backsliding' liberal democracy because many key political actors have resiled from essential norms and practices (Levitsky and Ziblatt, 2023). Shady 'voter suppression' tactics have once again been used in many Republican states and the party's 2024 presidential candidate, Donald Trump, repeatedly denied that previous national elections were fairly conducted. In the UK, governance apparently tipped into a vortex of decline after Brexit. From 2015 to 2024, prime ministers (PMs), cabinets and ministers rotated rapidly as four failed governments succeeded each other in short order, and wider policy systems failed, producing severely dysfunctional public service outcomes (Bevan, 2023).

By contrast, Australia has not recently shown destabilising increases in rancorous partisan polarisation, nor has it seen any major declines in governance capabilities (despite a few small wobbles on both fronts). However, there have been recurring problems with political corruption, threats to the separation of powers, unequal rights for minority groups, unconstrained media/big business power, and bursts of increased polarisation (for example, during the 2023 Voice referendum). So Australian democracy (like every democracy in the world) has significant issues and problems, explored in the chapters of this book.

Yet Australia also stands out as an evolving liberal democracy within a severely darkening world picture. An overtly autocratic-gangster regime in Russia and renewed strong authoritarianism in China have rapidly destroyed the always brittle, US-dominated 'peace' of the post-Cold War period. And, partly as a result of the Western powers' actions at that time, violent power politics on an age-old pattern (Kelly, 2022) has quickly become the dominant theme of international relations once again. The decisions made by Western nations (on Iraq in 2003 and on Gaza in 2023–2024) that contributed to the demise of hopes for a more ethical international order highlighted in acute ways how apparently limited democratic failings at home can quickly magnify into policy decisions creating cumulative damage. The survival and flourishing of liberal states still taking a normative approach to the international system is likely to be vital for future global peace and stability. For example, critics argue that domestic political forces pushing governments to look West have meant that Australian foreign policy has been less influential in its near neighbourhood, as with its limited role in ASEAN, the Association of Southeast Asian Nations.

Australia's stable evolution of an apparently more 'balanced' model suggests that its political system is worth careful study and analysis. Yet understanding Australian politics has not been made easy, due to two factors. First, Australian government is *sui generis* in many respects and combines many elements that are often separate in other systems. Major British legacies are the 'Westminster system' of parliamentary dominance, plus the strong centralisation of tax-raising powers. Yet there is also very strong federalism and a USA-influenced Senate, whose members (and those of state upper houses) are nonetheless elected by proportional representation (see

Chapter 1). Second, Australian political scientists have tended to cover political phenomena in rather a detheorised (almost apolitical) way. The literature can be inaccessible because it focuses on 'high' politics and sometimes fails to explain distinctively Australian 'low politics' and practices for international (often, even for inter-state) readers. Issues can be covered in ways that may seem remote from citizens' concerns about the health of their democracy.

In this book, we seek to reconsider Australia's political system as a whole, using the framework for auditing democratic institutions originally developed in the 1990s by the political philosopher David Beetham and the journalist, writer and social movement guru Stuart Weir. Beetham's pioneering work (1995; 1999) and the UK Democratic Audit (DA) books for the UK with Weir (Beetham and Weir, 1999; Beetham; Ngan and Weir, 2002), together with two later DA UK editions produced by by Liverpool and LSE teams (Wilks-Heeg, Blick and Crone, 2012; Dunleavy, Park and Taylor, 2018), all developed an influential template for this work. A variant of the approach was also applied in Australia (Sawer, Aljorenson and Larkin, 2009). (See note 1 in Chapter 1 below for a full listing of previous DA books.) In its modern form, the approach involves asking searching yet normatively based questions about the empirical operations and democratic quality of the many different institutions that go to make up a working liberal democracy. It seeks to make detailed qualitative assessments against explicit democratic criteria specifically adapted to each institution. For each detailed aspect, we ask:

- What should we normatively expect of this particular major institution or micro-institution (which might be an organisation, or a set of norms, conventions or practices) in order to optimise democratic control?
- How can we best capture citizens' complex views and feed them into policy processes in ways maximising social welfare, enhancing political equality and building citizens' satisfaction with and commitment to democracy?

Normally the answers given here are nuanced and draw attention to very subtle and variable phenomena. Our rich explanatory account draws out both existing areas of democratic strength and opportunities for further progress, on the one hand, and areas of flawed operations or future threats, on the other – a pros-and-cons framework. There is always much to be said on both sides, but we give a carefully balanced summary of these SWOT elements in every chapter, designed to help readers to make up their own minds about key issues. The chapters also explain key problems or disputed areas in more detail. The five main parts in the book seek to cover (almost) all the democratically relevant aspects of contemporary Australian politics, with 26 chapters covering single-institution or single-polity aspects and two overview chapters at the beginning and end of the book.

Part I establishes the institutional background. Aimed especially at international readers, or those new to studying Australian politics, the opening chapter introduces some distinctive features of elections and of executive governance that have developed over time and that are shared across the federal and state levels. The next two chapters consider different fundamental aspects for any liberal democracy, the protection of human rights and civil liberties and the Australian constitution, both of which are again distinctive. A brief chapter also covers the Voice referendum in late 2023, a recent failure on a long journey to reset the relations with First Nations peoples.

Part II considers the major 'input politics' processes as they operate at national level – the critical transmission mechanisms by which citizens and enterprises seek to get governing elites to defend their interests, advance their priorities and shape civil society. Naturally, Australia's frequent national elections play the central role here, but so too do the political parties as they compete for votes and develop policies and candidates. Between elections, interest groups, the mainstream media (press and broadcasters) and now social media, all exercise immense influence on policy development. A final aspect of civil society and input politics of great salience has been the development of gender equality in Australia.

Part III turns to the core democratic institutions at national level: the two houses of Parliament and their integral relationship with the federal 'core executive' consisting of the PM, Cabinet and the wider government. The House of Representatives and the Senate are elected in radically different ways, and their pathways of development have increasingly diverged in the recent era. Legislators in both houses face some considerable difficulties in holding ministers and the PM to account, but have also developed distinctive micro-institutions to combat these limitations, such as a uniquely intensive question time in the lower chamber and a powerful committee system in the Senate. Yet the PM, ministers and central departments constitute a strong executive, with many budgetary and administrative powers under current legislation. Governments have the capacity to pass new laws relatively easily, so long as they have a secure House majority. The Australian public service (the APS, the federal civil service) has been one of the most admired central bureaucracies in Anglosphere countries. It plays a key role in both delivering services and policy-making. Policy-making driven by a manifesto doctrine that ministers should keep their promises to voters also has to negotiate many hurdles of administrative and micro-political feasibility. This part of the book ends by considering the inter-governmental relations between the Commonwealth government at national level and the state and territory governments that depend on federal government transfers to finance much of their budgets and policies.

Part IV shifts focus to the six state governments and two territories. These are each separate polities, with their own political, electoral and party dynamics and some distinctive institutions that share a common 'Australian' character. Yet they also illustrate how detailed design differences at the micro-institutional level can make key differences to how democracy operates. Each state is discussed in a separate chapter, beginning with the three eastern seaboard states, whose large populations and strong economies dominate – New South Wales, Victoria and Queensland. The next three states – South Australia, Western Australia and Tasmania – are smaller in population terms, and (in different ways) primary industries like agriculture and mining are more important in their economies. The two territories – Northern Territory and the Australian Capital Territory (ACT, including Canberra) – are not states. Both have legislatures with a single house and their own governments, but they also still operate under some measure of federal government 'tutelage'. The part concludes by looking first at urban politics in Australia's distinctively big cities, and then at the wider local government system operating across regional and 'shire' Australia.

Part V concludes the book by considering two key sets of challenges confronting the contemporary political system. First, Australia is a country where 'the environment' is constantly present and strongly shapes public consciousness. Across the country's massive territorial area, climate change in the Anthropocene era presents enormous challenges, often largely ducked by governments before the change of federal government in 2022. The final chapter shows how Australia's evolving political system has increasingly stood out as a well-balanced, flexible and secure liberal democracy – albeit in a middle-ranking position and despite some large problems, such as declining public trust. Some key problems remain in adapting partisan political rhetoric and partisan dynamics to modern, complex conditions and demands on governments. But there are grounds for optimism in past progress and current conditions.

In a book this wide-ranging, some mistakes may have crept in, and there may be issues or arguments that we have not appreciated. We aim to revise and update this book when we can, so your comments, corrections, criticism or suggestions can really help us. Please email, tweet or message us on any of the addresses provided below. And if you have enjoyed reading the book and want to advance open social science too, why not give us a re-tweet, a 'like' on Facebook or LinkedIn, or some other form of positive mention on social media? We hope you enjoy the book.

Finally, we would like to dedicate this book to David Beetham (1938 to 2022), Professor of Politics from the University of Leeds, and Stuart Weir (1938 to 2024), one of the co-founders of Charter 88 and Professor at Essex University. David was a noted human rights campaigner, an engaged political philosopher and community activist, and the original theorist behind the democratic audit, which he co-founded with Stuart. Stuart was a brilliant journalist, campaigner, author and intellectual. We hope that this book lives up to their legacy.

Mark Evans, Patrick Dunleavy and John Phillimore

Mark Evans (Charles Sturt University)
email: dvcre@csu.edu.au
X (Twitter): **@MarkEvansACT**
LinkedIn: https://uk.linkedin.com/in/mark-evans-9025148

Patrick Dunleavy (London School of Economics)
Email: p.dunleavy@lse.ac.uk
X (Twitter): **@PJDunleavy**
LinkedIn: https://www.linkedin.com/in/patrick-dunleavy-46b87b40/

John Phillimore (Curtin University)
email: J.Phillimore@curtin.edu.au

References

$ *here indicates a paywall link*
Beetham, David (ed) (1995) *Defining and Measuring Democracy*, London: Sage.
Beetham, David (1999) 'The Idea of Democratic Audit in Comparative Perspective', *Parliamentary Affairs*, vol. 52, no. 4, pp.567–81. $ https://doi.org/10.1093/pa/52.4.567
Beetham, David and Weir, Stuart (1999) *Political Power and Democratic Control in Britain*, London: Routledge. $ https://www.routledge.com/Political-Power-and-Democratic-Control-in-Britain/Beetham-Weir/p/book/9780415096447
Beetham, David; Ngan, Pauline; and Weir, Stuart (2002) *Democracy Under Blair: A Democratic Audit of the United Kingdom*, London: Politico's.
Bevan, Gwyn (2023) *How Did Britain Come to This? A Century of Failures of Systemic Governance*, London: LSE Press. https://press.lse.ac.uk/site/books/m/10.31389/lsepress.hdb/
Dunleavy, Patrick; Park, Alice; and Taylor, Ros (eds) (2018) *The UK's Changing Democracy: The 2018 Democratic Audit*, London: LSE Press. OA at: https://doi.org/10.31389/book1
Kelly, Paul (2021) *Conflict, War and Revolution: The Problem of Politics in International Political Thought*, London: LSE Press. https://press.lse.ac.uk/site/books/m/10.31389/lsepress.cwr/
Levitsky, Steven; and Ziblatt, Daniel (2023) *Tyranny of the Minority: Why American Democracy Reached the Breaking Point*, New York: Penguin/Random House. $ https://www.penguinrandomhouse.com/books/706046/tyranny-of-the-minority-by-steven-levitsky-and-daniel-ziblatt/
Sawer, Marian; Aljorenson, Norman; and Larkin, Phil (2009) *Australia – The State of Democracy*, Canberra: Federation Press. [Out of print]
Wilks-Heeg, Stuart; Blick, Andrew; and Crone, Stephen (2012) *How Democratic Is the UK? The 2012 Audit,* Liverpool: Democratic Audit. https://demaudituk.wpengine.com/wp-content/uploads/2013/07/auditing-the-uk-democracy-the-framework.pdf

How to read this book

This book is designed to make understanding Australia's democratic political system easily accessible for international readers, people new to analysing Australian politics (including students, of course) and citizens and general readers. We start each chapter by considering several recent developments immediately relevant for democratic operations in that issue area or polity. Next, we give our main summary of strengths, weakness, opportunities and threats in the SWOT section, showing both aspects of that issue or polity where democratic operations have gone well, and also those where any problems or issues remain. The SWOT sections are short and accessible, and the pros and cons format is designed to help readers make up their own minds. After this section, there are normally two or three more detailed accounts of particular issues, illustrating how the operations of micro-institutions shape democratic quality in that area. At the end of the chapter, the conclusion is just a short, top-and-tail finishing section. It may sometimes cue you to an author's overall judgement. But in no case does it replace our main audit summary section, which is the balanced coverage of all main points in the SWOT. The final chapter (28) alone has a different pattern, drawing out some more general conclusions.

As committed open access (OA) authors, our book is permanently downloadable free from LSE Press, either in the three formats available for the whole book (PDF, e-book and Kindle reader) or in the PDF format available for each individual chapter. The whole book is also published as a paperback (but LSE Press must charge at a non-profit rate for this). So we anticipate that the vast majority of readers will use digital formats. To add to the benefits of doing so, the majority of references included in the book are to OA sources, so that readers can immediately check them out if they are interested. These OA reference links have background URLs – so just click on them to go immediately to the cited OA source. In addition, the DOI webpage number or permanent URL links for all OA sources are included in the end-of-chapter references lists.

A few of our older references unfortunately still lie behind paywalls, and in these cases, the citation in the text has no background URL. However, in the end-of-chapter references we indicate paywall sources by the $ sign and again provide a link to the DOI webpages or an equivalent stable URL wherever possible. Hopefully, readers with university library access (like students and academics) may be able to access paywall journal articles. Unfortunately, for paywall or paper-only books, our DOI or URL links mostly lead only to the publisher's webpage. But even this possibility, or looking up the volume on Google Books, can normally help readers to see a bit more information, such as chapter headings or some 'snippet' content. That can help readers decide if it will be worth trying to find the source and read more.

For any potentially evanescent content from our references – such as government or parliamentary reports, consultants reports, think tank publications and all other 'grey literature' sources, as well as blogs and newspaper or magazine articles – we use the PermaLink system from Harvard Law Library (see https://guides.library.harvard.edu/perma). When a reader downloads either the whole book or any chapter here, the system also downloads with it a cloud of its special permanent connections for any of the above kinds of materials cited there. Previously, such sources were vulnerable to becoming inaccessible over time, creating 'link rot' problems. We now hope that this will not occur with this book and we record our appreciation to Harvard Law School Library for this free system.

Reusing materials from this book

As part of our commitment to open science, this book has a Creative Commons licence of the type No Derivatives (CC BY-NC 4.0) (see https://creativecommons.org/share-your-work/cclicenses/), which means that 'reusers can copy and distribute the material in any medium or format in unadapted form only, for non-commercial purposes only, and only so long as attribution is given to the creator'. So, academics, students and ordinary citizens are completely free to re-use all our materials in any non-commercial publications of their own, and in teaching, blogging and so forth, without seeking further permission from us, *so long as* each use has a readable acknowledgement of this text as the source *and* our text or figures have not been altered in any way. This licence covers all the charts, tables and diagrams that we have produced for the book, as well as text. Unfortunately, it does not cover some small instances of copyright graphics for which we sought permission in a figure, noted as such below it.

For permissions for any commercial re-use of any part of the book (going beyond using short extracts for academic discussion or review), please contact LSE Press at the London School of Economics at LSEPublishing@lse.ac.uk

Citing the book

Please cite the whole book as follows:

Evans, Mark; Dunleavy, Patrick; and Phillimore, John (eds) (2024) *Australia's Evolving Democracy: A New Democratic Audit.* London: LSE Press. https://doi.org/10.31389/lsepress.ada

If you want to cite an individual chapter of the book, information on how to do this is given at the bottom of the first page of each chapter. The general format (using Chapter 3 as an example) is:

Hobbs, Harry, (2024) 'The Constitution', in Mark Evans, Patrick Dunleavy and John Phillmore (eds) *Australia's Evolving Democracy: A New Democratic Audit*, London: LSE Press, Chapter 3, https://doi.org/10.31389/lsepress.ada.c

Because the whole book is published from the outset by LSE Press in digital formats where users can set their own font sizes and pagination (using the e-Pub or Kindle book downloads), page number references will not work for every book user. To be maximally helpful for all readers, we recommend including a micro-quotation of five or six words from our book within your own text, and then linking to the DOI web address file for the relevant book chapter – readers can then search using Control+F (or equivalent key in their software) to find the exact quoted words and the relevant text in context. However, if you wish to still use page numbers in references they will of course work for readers using PDF files or paper versions of the book, where page breaks are stable.

Acknowledgements

This work has been a large-scale collective endeavour and our deepest thanks go to our 28 author-contributors who have stuck with the project and always responded so fully to our requests. Their unstinting generosity in committing time and expertise to the project, and their encouragement for the editors throughout, puts us heavily in their debt. We are deeply grateful to them and to their many different universities who supported the work through their time. Mark Evans and Patrick Dunleavy both came to the Australian Democratic Audit (ADA) project with a long history of contact with the Democratic Audit in Britain, and we thank all the authors of predecessor volumes in the UK and Australia for the expertise in conducting audits that they developed and from which we have borrowed.

The 2024 Australian Democratic Audit owes its existence to the establishment of the initiative *Democracy 2025: Strengthening Democratic Practice* as a collaboration between the Museum of Australian Democracy (MoAD) at Old Parliament House, Canberra, and the Institute for Governance and Policy Analysis (IGPA) at the University of Canberra. In 2018 Mark Evans founded Democracy 2025 with Daryl Karp AM, the director of the MoAD from 2013 to 2022. She helped shape and sustain the ADA project through to its start and early years. We are most grateful to Daryl for all her help, encouragement, advice and financial support, and to other MoAD staff involved at various times. Patrick Dunleavy's stint as Centenary Professor at the University of Canberra (2015–2020) also helped to get the book launched. Once the book project's scope was defined we were extremely lucky to be able to engage John Phillimore as the lead editor for the very extensive parts of the analysis covering state politics and sub-national government – his expertise and commitment proved invaluable. John thanks the authors of the state and territory chapters for their diligence and patience in steering their chapters through several iterations to completion.

More recently the Senate Inquiry into nationhood, national identity and democracy influenced the shape of the project and endorsed Democracy 2025's recommendations for a permanent independent Democratic Audit of Australia, which we hope to see implemented. The book project has recently been financially assisted by Charles Sturt University, to which we are also very grateful. We also thank the many different Australian universities who supported our contributing authors' work on the audit through funding their research time. We thank LSE Press and their staff, the incomparable Elaine Tuffery of Just Content, and other copy editors for their assistance in realising a complex project.

In addition, we thank many other Australian academics for their valuable advice and unstinting assistance on countless issues falling within their specialisms and for helpful comments by anonymous reviewers of the book, which produced many small changes. We are most grateful to Dr Sarah Cameron of Griffith University for her advice on many aspects of Australian voting and elections. For their generous permission to re-use original materials in figures, we are indebted to Professor Simon Jackman of Sydney University (see Figure 4.1), Antony Green of ABC News (see Figure 4.2) and economics consultant Sean Eslake (see Figure 18.8). We thank many other Australian academics for their advice and assistance on countless issues of detail and for helpful anonymous reviewer comments on the book.

Programs of research like this one are inevitably shaped by many different insightful conversations and productive collaborations with colleagues and friends. Especially influential on the ADA project's development were Stan Grant and Michelle Grattan, Gerry Stoker

(Southampton University) and other Democracy 2025 authors working with Mark Evans, plus staff at Canberra University in the period 2015–2020, especially David Marsh, Marian Simms (who very sadly died in 2023), Max Halupka, Brendan McCaffrie, Mick Chisnall, Paul Fawcett and John S. Dryzek. We also thank Alice Park, who helped develop the early format for this volume and generated materials and text included in our final chapter.

Any book of this scale takes a massive amount of time that eats into home life. Patrick Dunleavy thanks Sheila Dunleavy, without whose encouragement, ideas and forbearance the project could not have been sustained, let alone finished.

List of figures

Figure 1.1: A sample AV ballot paper for electing an MP to the House of Representatives 45
Figure 1.2: A simplified view of above the line voting (for six parties) or 'below the line' voting for 12 candidates in Senate STV elections 46
Figure 1.3: Voter turnout at federal elections 1901 to 1928, 2001 to 2023 47
Figure 4.1: The opinion polls during the campaign for a Voice to Parliament 85
Figure 4.2: The 2023 referendum outcome by seats 86
Figure 5.1: The proportion of first-preference votes won by the main parties at House of Representatives elections, 2001–2022 99
Figure 5.2: The Liberal-National Coalition share of the two-party preferred (TPP) vote, 2001–2022 99
Figure 5.3: The percentage of MPs won by parties at House of Representatives elections, 2001–2022 100
Figure 5.4: The Liberal-National Coalition's partisan advantage in terms of its percentage share of seats minus the two-party preferred vote; and the deviation from proportionality (DV) in the House of Representatives elections, 2001–2019 101
Figure 5.5: A simple example of how to calculate the deviation from proportionality (DV) score 102
Figure 5.6: The proportion of first-preference votes won by the main parties at Senate elections, 2001–2022 104
Figure 5.7: The percentage (%) of seats won by the main parties at Senate elections, 2001–2022 105
Figure 5.8: Deviation from proportionality and the levels of over-representation of the top three parties in Senate elections, 2001–2022 106
Figure 5.9: A 'crown diagram' view of the 2022 first-preference vote patterns across parties for the House of Representatives in the 138 districts where Labor and the Liberal-National Coalition were the top two parties 110
Figure 5.10: The patterning of seats in the 15 districts where one or both of the top two parties (either P1 or P2) in first-preference votes was *not* Labor or Liberal-National Coalition 111
Figure 5.11: Respondents' interest in elections and beliefs about political efficacy, in Australian Election Study surveys, 2001–2019 112
Figure 5.12: Among 2022 voters giving a first preference to the Teal Independents, which parties had they backed in the 2019 election? 113
Figure 5.13: The distribution of federal electoral district sizes in 2022 115
Figure 5.14: Experts' perceptions of electoral integrity in Australia as scores out of 100 (in 2017) 115
Figure 6.1: Illustrative picture of where Australian parties stood on two main ideological dimensions, and showing their primary vote support nationally, House of Representatives election, May 2022 129
Figure 6.2: Party memberships and representatives in state legislatures 131
Figure 6.3: How Australia's main party leaders are chosen 135

Figure 6.4: Average annual receipts for the top five Australian parties receiving donations from 2018 to 2021 136

Figure 6.5: Donations received by Australian political parties from 2018 to 2021 137

Figure 6.6: The proportion (%) of A$68.6 million federal election cost reimbursements provided to parties by the Australian Election Commission, following the 2019 election 138

Figure 7.1: Factors that make interest groups more or less politically influential 146

Figure 7.2: Australian interest groups reputedly with the largest number of members or supporters, 2023 148

Figure 7.3: Five disadvantaged groups and their interest group mobilisation, 2023 149

Figure 7.4: Who gave and who received major sums (of A$50,000 or more) as political donations in 2017–2018 154

Figure 7.5: Donations to parties by the Pharmacy Guild of Australia in 2017–2018 154

Figure 7.6: The decline of unionisation in Australia, 1986–2022 155

Figure 7.7: Changes in unionisation rates by industrial sector, 2016 to 2022 156

Figure 7.8: Percentage (%) of respondents in election surveys agreeing that 'unions have too much power', 1987 to 2019 157

Figure 7.9: The main sectors where critics argue that domestic big business is dominant 158

Figure 8.1: The main newspapers and press websites across Australia's states and major cities, and their usual political leanings, March 2020–March 2021 171

Figure 8.2: Usage of the Australian Broadcasting Commission's (ABC) broadcast news sources from 2020–2021 172

Figure 8.3: The comparative sizes of TV media outlets assessed by means of total visits 173

Figure 8.4: The percentage (%) of respondents answering 'Strongly agree' or 'Tend to agree' that media sources can be trusted to provide honest and objective information about COVID-19, by generation, in May 2021 183

Figure 9.1: The major social media apps in Australia in 2023 193

Figure 9.2: How Australians accessed online news content in 2016 and 2022 194

Figure 9.3: Generational differences in the main source of news among Australian respondents in 2021 196

Figure 9.4: How teenagers (aged 13–16) reported their main sources of information about politics in 2023 196

Figure 10.1: Women politicians at national level 212

Figure 10.2: Percentage (%) female members of Commonwealth House of Representatives and Senate, by party, May 2022 213

Figure 10.3: Percentage female representatives by party across all Australian parliaments: State, Territory and Commonwealth upper and lower houses, in 2023 and 2000 213

Figure 10.4: Proportion (%) of Australian Public Service (APS) employees by job classification and gender in December 2020 215

Figure 10.5: Female and male justices and judges, 30 June 2020 215

Figure 10.6: Proportions (%) of females and males, 20–74 years old, employed by different industries from 2019 to 2020 217

Figure 10.7: The gender pay gap in full-time adult weekly, ordinary time earnings, by state and territory, May 2021 218

Figure 11.1: Parties' seats in the House of Representatives, 2000–2022 233

Figure 11.2: Ministers as a share of all MPs in the House of Representatives, and of the governing party's MPs, 1951–2022 235

Figure 11.3: The top 10 topics asked of the PM and of other government ministers during the 2013 House sessions 241

Figure 11.4: The proportion of Acts considered in detail in the House of Representatives, and closure or guillotine curbs on debate, as a percentage (%) of all Acts passed (2000–2022) 243

Figure 12.1: The national first-preference vote shares of parties in Senate elections by party, 2000–2022 256

Figure 12.2: The number of senators by party, 2000–2022 256

Figure 12.3: The total number of reports issued in a year by Senate committees, from 1974–2022 262

Figure 12.4: The number of people represented by each senator across the states and territories in September 2022 264

Figure 12.5: Comparing the primary (first-preference) vote for the top two parties (Labor and the Liberal-National Coalition) in Senate and House of Representatives elections, from 1970–2022 265

Figure 12.6: The long-run trends in national vote share for the top two parties, versus the combined vote share for all other parties and independents in Senate elections, 1970–2022 265

Figure 12.7: Responses to survey questions about the Senate in the 2019 Australia Institute report 272

Figure 13.1: The cabinet committee structure in February 2021 (pre-COVID-19) 281

Figure 13.2: The system of COVID-19 governance during the pandemic 282

Figure 13.3: Public perceptions of the quality of COVID-19 leadership in Australia, Italy, the USA and the UK in May to June 2020 283

Figure 13.4: Four recent instances of leadership conflict 286

Figure 13.5: Underlying government cash balance as per cent of GDP (2000–2023/24, estimated) 292

Figure 13.6: Australian Government payments and receipts as a percentage (%) of GDP, 1970–2024 (estimated from 2021) 292

Figure 13.7: Estimates of expenses by function between 2015 and 2016 and 2022 and 2023 (as a percentage of spending) 293

Figure 13.8: The Australian budget timeline 294

Figure 14.1: COVID-19 management in the Anglophone liberal democracies from March 2020 to 3 October 2023 304

Figure 14.2: Ministers' and PMs' politically appointed office staffs in Australia and in Canada and the UK 313

Figure 14.3: How far Australian, New Zealand and UK public service participants in University of Canberra 2021 workshops agreed that potential features of the Westminster advisory system operated in their countries 315

Figure 14.4: The number of APS employees and proportions (%) of the total workforce working in the states and territories (in December 2023) 317

Figure 14.5: A snapshot view of the Australian Public Service in mid-2023 317

Figure 14.6: Barriers to improving service delivery recognised by senior APS officials in a 2019 study 319

Figure 14.7: Modern models of bureaucracy and how the APS use of digital technology has evolved in waves 320

Figure 16.1: Commonwealth and State governments' revenue and expenses, 2018–2019 (in A$ billions) 351

Figure 17.1: First-preference votes for parties in NSW Legislative Assembly elections, and Labor's two-party preferred (TPP) vote, 2002–2023 369

Figure 17.2: Seats won by parties in the NSW Legislative Assembly, 2002–2023 370

Figure 17.3: First-preference votes for parties in the NSW Legislative Council (upper house) elections under STV, 2002–2023 371

Figure 17.4: Seats held by parties in the NSW Legislative Council (upper house) following elections, 2002–2023 371

Figure 17.5: ICAC investigations into parliamentary and administrative misconduct in the period 2019–2021 373

Figure 17.6: The net approval rating in 2020 survey responses to the question, 'How well is your state government responding to the pandemic?' 375

Figure 17.7: Women members in the NSW Parliament in 2023 382

Figure 17.8: The activities of the NSW's Legislative Council committee system, 2015–2020 383

Figure 17.9: The 14 policy priorities of Gladys Berejiklian's premiership 385

Figure 18.1: The basic set up for Victoria's state elections 400

Figure 18.2: Victoria Legislative Assembly, first-preference vote shares, 2002–2022 401

Figure 18.3: Victorian Legislative Assembly, percentage of seats, 2002–2022 401

Figure 18.4: Victoria Legislative Council (upper house) elections, first-preference vote shares, 2002–2022 402

Figure 18.5: The percentage of seats in the Victoria Legislative Council (upper house) elections, 2002–2022 402

Figure 18.6: Women members in the 2018–2022 Parliament of Victoria 405

Figure 18.7: Premiers of Victoria by party, since the 1970s 407

Figure 18.8: Victoria's per capita gross state product (GSP) relative to the national average, and its goods and services tax (GST) relativity 409

Figure 19.1: Votes cast for parties in Queensland's state elections, 2009–2020 417

Figure 19.2: Seats won by political parties in the Legislative Assembly, 2009–2020 418

Figure 20.1: Party first-preference vote shares (and the two-party preferred vote for Labor), South Australia House of Assembly, 2002–2022 437

Figure 20.2: Party seats in the House of Assembly, 2006–2022 438

Figure 20.3: Party first-preference vote shares under STV in the South Australia Legislative Council (upper house) elections, 2002–2022 439

Figure 20.4: The balance of seats in the Legislative Council (upper house), 2002–2023 439

Figure 20.5: The effective number of electoral (ENEP) and parliamentary (ENPP) parties, House of Assembly and Legislative Council 440

Figure 20.6: Parties' seats in the Legislative Council and their index of voting power scores, since 2002 441

Figure 20.7: South Australian Parliament 2018–2022 – MPs with university degrees 443

Figure 20.8: South Australian Parliament 2018–2021 – MPs' and Legislative Councillors' employment backgrounds 444

Figure 21.1: The alternation of governments in Western Australia's Legislative Assembly (LA) from 1974–2024 465

Figure 21.2: Parties' first-preference vote shares in Western Australia's lower house AV elections (1971–2021) 466

Figure 21.3: The percentage of seats won by parties in Western Australia's Legislative Assembly, 1971–2021 466

Figure 21.4: Parties' seats numbers in Western Australia's Legislative Council (upper house), 1989–2021 467

Figure 21.5: Members of Western Australia's Legislative Assembly (lower house) and Legislative Council (upper house) by gender and party, 2017, 2021 and 2024 470

Figure 22.1: Party shares of first-preference votes in the Tasmania House of Assembly elections, 2002–2024 480

Figure 22.2: Party seats in the Tasmania House of Assembly elections, 2002–2021 481

Figure 23.1: Primary votes shares (%) won by parties in the Northern Territory Legislative Assembly, and the Labor TPP vote, 2001–2020 499

Figure 23.2: Seats won by parties in the Northern Territory Legislative Assembly, 2001–2020 500

Figure 23.3: Voter turnout in Northern Territory elections by region, 2012–2020 511

Figure 24.1: First-preference vote shares by party in ACT elections, 2001–2020 516

Figure 24.2: Seats won by parties in ACT elections, 2001–2020 517

Figure 25.1: Australia's 'big cities' in 2021 530

Figure 26.1: Australian elected representatives at all levels of government 546

Figure 26.2: The number of local councils in Australia, 1982–2012 555

Figure 28.1: Five overall quantitative index rankings of liberal democracies and how they rated Australia, 2017–2021 579

Figure 28.2: Some current quantitative index rankings of partial aspects of liberal democracy and how they rated Australia in 2020 580

Figure 28.3: Three current index rankings of the social outcomes or political equality aspects of liberal democracy, and how they rated Australia in 2020–2021 581

Figure 28.4: How citizens ranked their country in terms of how democratic it was, and how much freedom they had in 2017–2020 582

Figure 28.5: How Australian respondents compared with those in other established liberal democracies in terms of social and political trust, in 2017–2020 data 583

Figure 28.6: How Australian respondents compared with those in three other liberal democracies in their level of confidence in political parties, government and healthcare after the onset of the COVID-19 pandemic in May and June 2020 584

Figure 28.7: How Australia respondents rated the ease of finding government information and the quality of administrative services, compared with other countries in a cross-national OECD survey, 2022 585

Figure 28.8: Respondents' satisfaction with democracy in successive Australian Election Study samples, 2001–2022 586

Figure 28.9: Respondents' views about democracy in Lowry Institute surveys, 2012–2022 587

Figure 28.10: Australian respondents' trust in 'people in government', 2001 to 2022 588

Figure 28.11: 'Top 10' responses by citizens, elites and federal politicians to the survey question: 'What do you like about Australian democracy?' 588

Figure 28.12: 'Top 10' responses by citizens, elites and federal politicians to the survey question: 'What do you dislike about Australian democracy?' 589

Figure 28.13: How Lowry survey respondents' perceptions of Australia's 'best friend in Asia' changed between 2014 and 2022 594

Glossary

AAT	Administrative Appeals Tribunal
ABC	Australian Broadcasting Commission
ABS	Australian Bureau of Statistics
ACCC	Australian Competition and Consumer Commission
ACNC	Australian Charities and Not-for-Profits Commission
ACT	Australian Capital Territory, including Canberra
ADA	Australian Democratic Audit
AEC	Australian Electoral Commission
AFP	Australian Federal Police
AGO	Australian Geospatial-Intelligence Organisation
AHRC	Australian Human Rights Commission
AIDR	Australian Institute for Disaster Resilience
AIFS	Australian Institute of Family Studies
AIHW	Australian Institute of Health and Welfare
ALP	Australian Labor Party
ALGA	Australian Local Government Association
ALRC	Australian Law Reform Commission
ANAO	Australian National Audit Office
APS	Australian Public Service, the federal civil service
APSC	Australian Public Service Commission
At large elections	Elections that are held across a whole polity, as with state-wide elections for senators and some state's Legislative Council members. The whole area of the state or political unit is a single electoral district.
ASD	Australian Signals Directorate
ASIC	Australian Securities and Investments Commission
ASIO	Australian Security and Intelligence Organisation
ASIS	Australian Secret Intelligence Service
ASRA	Advanced Strategic Research Agency
ATO	Australian Tax Office
ATSIC	Aboriginal and Torres Strait Islander Commission
AUKUS	Australia–UK–USA defence agreement
AV	Alternative Vote – a system of preferential voting for parties or candidates in single member seats. Voters number their preferences from 1 (best) to N (worst). The smallest parties are eliminated from the count in sequence (and their voters' next preferences are transferred to those still in the race) until only two candidates remain (see TPP below), when the party with most votes wins.
BLM	Black Lives Matter
'bludger'	Australian term for 'scrounger', an undeserving (possibly fraudulent) recipient of welfare payments

'branch stacking'	An Australian version of entryism, where a potential candidate pays or persuades uncommitted people to join a local party branch in order to secure his or her nomination as the local candidate, or otherwise to control the branch
CDC	Community Development Councils
CFFR	Council on Federal Financial Relations
COAG	Council of Australian Governments, the top federal concertation body until 2020, when it was replaced by the National Cabinet
Coalition	The (permanent) coalition between the Liberal Party and the Nationals
Commonwealth	The national federal government in Australia
CPRS	Carbon Pollution Reduction Scheme
CRC	Convention of the Rights of the Child
CSIRO	Commonwealth Scientific and Industrial Research Organisation
DA	Democratic Audit, a systematic effort to assess how far major institutions in liberal democracies match up against the criteria set by democratic theory
DFAT	Department of Foreign Affairs and Trade
DHS	Department of Human Services
DIO	Defence Intelligence Organisation
dominant party system	A liberal democracy where the largest party is heavily advantaged vis-à-vis all other competitors. A characteristic (but not necessary) result is that the same incumbent party repeatedly wins successive elections over long periods.
double dissolution	A dissolution of Parliament called by the PM where all Senate seats are up for election as the same time as all House seats
DPM&C	Department of the Prime Minister and Cabinet
DV	The 'deviation from proportionality' score, measuring the difference between parties votes and seats shares (see Figure 5.5)
elders	The senior members of an Aboriginal community
Electoral district	A sub-area of the polity used to elect one or more members of a legislature – often called a 'constituency' outside Australia
ENPseats	Effective number of parties in seats Also sometimes called the 'effective number of parliamentary parties' (denoted ENPP)
ENPvotes	Effective number of parties in votes Also sometimes called the 'effective number of electoral parties' (denoted ENEP)
ERC	Expenditure Review Committee
First Nations	Indigenous people from Aboriginal or Torres Straits islander communities

FOI		Freedom of Information
FPTP		'First past the post' voting, the popularly used (but inaccurate) name for plurality voting (see below) where the party or candidate with the largest vote wins, irrespective of whether they have an overall majority of votes or not. There is no fixed 'winning post' here.
GBRMPA		Great Barrier Reef Marine Park Authority
GDP		gross domestic product
GFC		global financial crisis
GSP		gross state product, the state-level equivalent of GDP
House		House of Representatives, the lower chamber at federal level
House of Assembly		The name for the lower house in the South Australia and Tasmania Parliaments
HRLC		Human Rights Law Centre
IACL		International Association of Constitutional Law
ICAC		Independent Commission Against Corruption
ICCPR		International Covenant on Civil and Political Rights
IGIS		Inspector-General of Intelligence and Security
IPA		Institute of Public Affairs
IRAPS		Independent Review of the APS
ISP		Internet service providers
LA		Legislative Assembly – the name for the lower houses in the New South Wales, Victoria, and Western Australia Parliaments; and for the single legislatures in Queensland, Northern Territory and the Australian Capital Territory (ACT).
LC		Legislative Council – the name for the upper houses in the New South Wales, South Australia, Victoria, Tasmania, and Western Australia Parliaments.
LGBT+		Lesbian, gay, bi-sexual, trans-sexual+. This is the most commonly used acronym internationally
LGBTIQ+		Lesbian, gay, bi-sexual, trans-sexual, intersex, or queer+. This is the recommended official acronym in Australia.
MDBA		Murray-Darling Basin Authority
MFF		Minister for Finance at federal level
MOAD		Museum of Australian Democracy
MP		Member of Parliament, in the lower House of Representatives. Members of the upper house are senators.
MRRT		Minerals Resource Rent Tax
NDIA		National Disability Insurance Agency
NDIS		National Disability Insurance Scheme
NGOs		non-governmental organisations
NITV		National Indigenous Television
NMBC		News Media and Digital Platforms Bargaining Code

NPM	new public management	
NPP	new policy proposals	
NSW	New South Wales	
NT	Northern Territory	
NTPS	Northern Territory Public Service	
ONA	Office of National Assessments	
OPI	Office of Public Integrity	
PBO	Parliamentary Budget Office	
PEI	perceptions of electoral integrity	
PEO	Parliamentary Education Office	
PJCHR	Parliamentary Joint Committee on Human Rights	
Plurality voting	A system where the party or candidate in an election district with the largest vote wins, irrespective of whether they have an overall majority of votes or not. Also called 'first past the post' (FPTP).	
PM	prime minister	
PMB	Private Member Bills	
PMO	PM's office	
PNG	Papua New Guinea	
'Pork barrel' politics	An American metaphor for MPs or senators focusing on securing funds for specific local projects in their area (but funded nationally, so distributing the costs over other areas), so as to get themselves re-elected.	
PR	Proportional representation, any system of voting where seats are distributed in proportion to the votes won by parties or candidates	
Preferential voting	Any election system where voters can number their preferences from 1 (best) to N (worst). In Australian literature 'preferential voting' is often used (inaccurately) to mean just AV, whereas in fact STV (see below) and some other approaches are also preferential voting.	
Primary vote	A voter's first-preference vote for a party or candidate in a preference voting (preferential) voting system	
QLD	Queensland	
Quota	The proportion (%) of votes that a party or candidate must win in order to be absolutely certain of winning a seat in a PR voting system. It is given by 100% divided by the number of seats in the election district plus 1. For example, with 4 seats, it is 100%/5 = 20%.	
RBA	Reserve Bank of Australia	
RSPT	Resource Super Profits Tax	
SA	South Australia	

SBS	Special Broadcasting Service
SLO	Social Licence to Operate
STV	Single Transferable Vote, a proportional representation system using multi-seat elections and multi-preference voting. (See Chapter 5 for how it works.)
SWOT	strengths, weaknesses, opportunities and threats
TAS	Tasmania
Teal independents	Independent blue/green candidates (conservatives but environmentally concerned)
Torres Straits Islanders	Indigenous people living in the Islands of the Torres Straits, lying between Australia and Indonesia
TPP	Two-party preferred vote – the final stage of an STV election where only two candidates remain in the race, all others having been eliminated and their voters' preferences transferred in line with voters' numbering
UN	United Nations
UNFCCC	United Nations Framework Convention on Climate Change
VFI	Vertical financial imbalance – where the federal government collects far more taxes than it has service obligations, and makes transfers to states and territories, which have far more service obligations than tax resources
VIC	Victoria
yarns	Traditional stories told within Aboriginal communities
WA	Western Australia
WFH	working from home
WGEA	Workplace Gender Equality Agency

I

Foundations

1. Situating Australian democracy......... 33
   Patrick Dunleavy, Mark Evans, Harry Hobbs and Patrick Weller

2. Human rights and civil liberties 53
   Mark Evans and Stan Grant

3. The Constitution.................................. 70
   Harry Hobbs

4. The 2023 Voice to Parliament referendum 84
   Mark Evans and Michelle Grattan

1

Situating Australian democracy

Patrick Dunleavy, Mark Evans, Harry Hobbs and Patrick Weller

This book undertakes a democratic audit (DA) of Australia using the well-developed ethos of the wider DA workstream, about which the British philosopher David Beetham argued: 'Popular control and political equality comprise our two key democratic principles and provide the litmus test for how far a country's political life can be regarded as democratic' (1999, p.570). Following his lead (and that of Stuart Weir, another DA co-founder), our preferred way of administering this litmus test has been to undertake a detailed qualitative, text-based analysis of each aspect of Australian political life in the 28 chapters that follow. We also draw on lessons from an earlier application of DA principles to Australian federal institutions (Sawer, Aljorenson and Larkin, 2009) and extend the DA criteria here to also cover state politics and governance. An audit approach differs significantly from conventional (normatively detached) political science, which describes how politics works empirically in neutral, amoral terms (albeit with some distant resonances).[1] Our empirical analysis places an equal value on accurate evidence-based analysis, but we centre attention on how a political system's performance explicitly matches up directly against criteria that are normatively derived from liberal democratic theory and that pay attention to the importance of micro-institutions in sustaining democratic politics (Dunleavy, 2019). Of course, the two lenses often overlap in what they cover, but the audit approach is a distinctive one, relevant not just for political scientists and their students but also for citizens, politicians, administrators and media practitioners.

At a high level, being a liberal democracy means meeting (and balancing) five key goals:

What it takes to be a liberal democracy

- There must be (large) majority control of government via free and fair elections, genuine party competition, a vivid interest group process, and multiple other forms of political participation, operating in a diverse and free media and social media environment.
- Human rights and civil liberties must be developed and maintained for all citizens, ensuring equal treatment for all (even for unpopular minorities or people espousing disliked causes).

How to cite this chapter:

Dunleavy, Patrick; Evans, Mark; Hobbs, Harry; and Weller, Patrick (2024) 'Situating Australian democracy', in: Evans, Mark; Dunleavy, Patrick and Phillimore, John (eds) *Australia's Evolving Democracy: A New Democratic Audit*, London: LSE Press, pp.33–52. https://doi.org/10.31389/lsepress.ada.a Licence: CC-BY-NC 4.0

- Greater political and social equality must be consciously developed and pursued.
- Widespread political legitimacy must be achieved for the polity, marked by both popular consent and multiple (plural) centres of power, information and influence within the society.
- The polity must operate as an effective state – one with stable, unitary and consistently operating governance institutions (Dryzek and Dunleavy, 2009; Dunleavy, 1993). It must be able to carry out the key functions of all states, such as maintaining a legitimate monopoly of the use of force within its own secured territory, controlling borders, and protecting and advancing the welfare of its citizens.

In addition, all of these demanding objectives must be satisfactorily met *simultaneously*. For instance, if goals (i) and (iv) are met for most citizens, but the rights of minorities are trampled on (violating goal (ii) and likely also (iv)), then liberal democratic arrangements may still exist, but only in a badly flawed shape. And if an effective state cannot also be sustained, then the quality of democracy is greatly impaired, however 'perfect' or well-designed its institutions may seem, and the polity may collapse.

These are demanding criteria, and specifying what they imply for the component institutions and practices of a working political system needs to be done in a detailed way for each area, as the following chapters do. We seek to give a thorough-going, evidence-based review of how well the Australian government has performed against the criteria above, especially in terms of meeting them simultaneously while running an effective state. Needless to say, this has been difficult to do and improvement has taken decades to achieve. Every one of today's most advanced modern liberal democracies evolved from earlier non-democratic regimes, always carrying with them undemocratic historical legacies that took time to be corrected. Most contemporary liberal democracies still have substantial defects or limitations to address, as the Economist Intelligence Unit's (2022) category of 'flawed democracy' attests (see Chapter 28).

Australia's newly minted national polity was among the most democratically advanced in the world when it was established on 1 January 1901. Building on the good start made at state level (where secret ballots had long been used) and moving to compulsory voting in the 1920s, it evolved with a very stable constitution and polity. Yet its chequered colonial and post-colonial history (both pre- and post-foundation) has also contributed many enduring historical issues and current tensions, especially in terms of the rights of minorities. These include:

- how government by the majority of (historically 'white') citizens has related to the continent's First Nations peoples
- the wider operation of racist 'white Australia' policies over many decades from the 1920s to the 1990s
- decades of legal ill-treatment of gay citizens
- serious infringements of many other minority groups' rights over decades, not just by government but also by important civil society institutions such as churches and NGOs.

The first two of these four legacies are distinctively Australian issues, albeit in the context of the inheritances of colonialism and racism shared with other democracies. Australia's treatment of homosexual people was not particularly severe, but equal rights for LGBTIQ+ people were slow to be granted. The final legacy has also been one shared by many countries built up via colonisation and mass immigration processes.

However, in recent decades, many social policy improvements have been enacted in all these areas, and others are still in train. Taken alongside the establishment of free and fair elections, the peaceful and legitimate transfer of power between political parties, high levels of public satisfaction with liberal democratic values, and smoothly operating political processes have all contributed to making Australia a highly salient liberal democratic exemplar. In recent years, significant attention has also been paid to the 'balanced' character of the federal Constitution (which partitions power among the state and the federal governments), the legal system's stability and overall fairness, and the country's enviable economic record of avoiding recessions for three decades before the COVID-19 pandemic. Australia is also the world's only integrated, pan-continental governance system, with the federal and state authorities of a single nation state acting as stewards for a remarkable array of environmental settings, albeit with controversially laggard ecological policies in many areas (see Chapter 27).

Enumerating these distinctive points of interest is not meant to suggest that Australia's democratic arrangements are perfect. As in every liberal democracy, some substantial problems remain unresolved or only partly addressed in Australia, and they are reviewed in detail in the first section of Chapter 28, our concluding essay. In addition, the second part of that chapter situates Australia against other mature democratic countries, concluding that it has remained a stable but not outstanding polity among its near neighbours. Nonetheless, Australia provides some strong examples of innovative practices that other countries, especially in Anglosphere nations, may benefit from copying.

In this chapter, we begin by introducing for international readers (and recapping for Australian readers) two of the most distinctive features of Australia's political tradition. The first of these was the establishment of its hybrid Constitution and the subsequent development of its strong executive and party-run government. That impetus has sustained the country's historical political path, mostly for good but also with some drawbacks. Second, Australia follows 'strong democracy' principles not matched by any other major country – namely that everyone should vote and that every vote should count in choosing a government. This underpins some hallmarks of its politics – voting is compulsory; lower house elections use a majoritarian voting system, the Alternative Vote (AV); and upper houses use the Single Transferable Vote (STV). Because these topics are discrete ones, we review each of these aspects in a separate section, each followed by a short strengths, weaknesses, opportunities and threats (SWOT) analysis.

The historical development of Australian democracy

Australian government was the product of a convict and settler society, derived from British heritage, and imposed by colonial force on multiple First Nations communities who had lived on the continent and its neighbouring islands for over 60,000 years. Many excesses committed before democratisation and unification were nonetheless brushed over in the constitutional settlement and continued in more attenuated forms thereafter. And, as with any nation state, Australia has been a hostage of the traditions developed from its pre- and post-founding history and experiences. Some of its systems of government were adapted, with little questioning, from the British form of cabinet government and parliamentary conduct, with all its implicit presumptions about the nominal and actual distributions of power. But in the federal

Constitution of 1901, these arrangements were innovatively operationalised within an American federal structure of states (plus a Senate representing the states, superimposed on the parliamentary framework) and with a strong federal–state division of labour (see Chapter 3).

Over the 170 years since the six individual founding colonies gained forms of self-government, and in the 120 years since they federated, Australian political institutions have developed their own traditions, recognisably British or American in origin but decidedly different in practice. Many innovations – such as the secret ballot, compulsory voting, the central role of party caucus meetings, and the easy election and deselection of parliamentary party leaders – are distinctly Australian. Australian government is recognisably a parliamentary government, but one no longer identical to its Westminster predecessors. It bears a family resemblance, but is not in any way a clone.

The influence of the Constitution

In the middle and late 19th century, when the six separated British colonies spread across the vast Australian continent were given self-government of their domestic affairs, they copied British political institutions, with an elected lower house and an upper house either appointed or elected on a limited property franchise. The responsibility to develop the continent was the principal function of each colony's government, because only they had the ability to open up the vast territories. Governments were regarded as vast public utilities, providing roads, bridges and services, and (importantly) owning the mineral rights of all land below a depth of 10 metres.

Yet the political orientation focused solely on development was already changing. In 1891, following a long strike, the nascent trade unions formed the Labor Party as their political wing. Its organisational principles declared that Labor members were delegates, in contrast to the Burkean tradition of Members of Parliament (MPs) as representatives using their own judgement to further their constituents' (fundamental) interests. Labor MPs were responsible to the party and bound to vote in line with the decisions of the party conferences outside Parliament and the choices of the Labor parliamentary caucus party inside.

During the 1890s, delegates from the six colonies negotiated – in two constitutional conventions – the terms of a constitution that would create the Australian Commonwealth, operating in a remarkably democratic way for that period. In 1891, there were seven delegations, all nominated by their parliaments (including one from New Zealand). In 1897 to 1898, there were five state delegations (without Queensland or New Zealand), of which four were elected. Even if those elected (or appointed in Western Australia) were almost entirely colonial politicians, popular election facilitated considerable democratic engagement (Hirst, 2000, p.142). Of course, the franchise was still limited in important respects – to all white men, whether property owners or not. Yet this extension of those recognised as 'citizens' (all alike able to participate) was still noteworthy for its time. The process of enactment further burnished the Constitution's democratic credentials. In formal legal terms, the Constitution secured its force by an enactment of the imperial Parliament in Westminster. Yet in practice, the instrument was actually ratified in a referendum held in each colony. As Helen Irving has noted, its 'endorsement by the people and not the politicians' exemplified the 'democratic character' of the Constitution (1999, p.138).

Excluded from any participation in the constitutional conventions, however, and thereafter left unrecognised as full citizens and effectively unenfranchised, were the Aboriginal and Torres Strait Islander peoples. Although they were only expressly denied the vote in Queensland and Western Australia, elsewhere First Nations peoples faced numerous administrative barriers and many adverse micro-institutions (Dunleavy, 2019) that contributed to voter suppression and discouraged their individual or collective participation. Those events have haunted Australian politics for many decades. Without political participation rights, First Nations peoples were made subject to discriminatory and racist social policies enacted by majority rule and often partly carried out by white-dominated social institutions like churches, charities and so on. The abuses enacted at scale and targeted at First Nations peoples' communities included the compulsory sterilisation of women, the transfer of children into coercive institutions that systematically eliminated their ethnic identities, and the forced separation of children from parents. Policy towards First Nations peoples was often strongly influenced by overtly racist ideas and by aspects of the eugenics movement in the inter-war and early post-1945 periods. These oppressions endured until well into the 1960s.

Full political inclusion for First Nations peoples was only finally granted by a constitutional amendment approved by a national referendum in 1967. Two changes were made by this vote: the Commonwealth Parliament was empowered to pass laws for First Nations peoples, as it could for people of all other races; and section 127 of the Constitution, which did not count First Nations peoples for the purposes of electoral distribution and similar allocations, was repealed. But previous traditions of state 'tutelage' over Aboriginal bush communities remained in force, took years to liberalise, and have persisted in the face of severe social problems. Over time, a huge amount of damage was done to First Nations peoples, and the legacies of these protracted democratic failures have continued either unresolved or only partly addressed into modern-day politics.

By contrast, although women were at first allowed to vote and stand for election only in South Australia and in the Northern Territory (administered by the federal government from 1911 to 1978), they fared far better than First Nations peoples in quickly gaining the franchise and the right to stand for representative office. Long before almost all other (male-only) liberal democracies reluctantly followed suit, Australian women won these rights at the federal level in 1902 and in all the remaining Australian states in 1908. Some women's legal rights (for example, to own property and operate businesses) were well secured, but others took decades to be achieved – such as the right to be paid the same as men for equal work, gained only in 1969. Other key aspects of rights – such as effective protection for women against domestic violence or rape, or the actual realisation of equal representation in valued business and professional careers – remain works in progress (see Chapter 10).

Governance institutions

In many key aspects the Constitution document itself was an exercise in mythmaking about who does what, following UK practice. For instance, the prime minister (PM) and the Cabinet were not mentioned anywhere in its pages, and the executive power of the Commonwealth was and remains nominally vested in the Governor-General, the monarch's representative in Australia. Yet 'everyone always knew' that in practice the federal PM would be the head of the party or parties that could maintain a majority in the House of Representatives – the same thing had already applied at state level for four decades. Similarly, parties were not recognised in the Constitution (until 1977), yet from the outset Australian politics developed to give partisanship immense importance and a strong, at times almost vicious, character. Although the Constitution assigns power to MPs and senators (and state constitutions do likewise), it does not cover the operations of the political parties that in practice structure everything that happens within both chambers federally, and within state legislatures. Each party has set its own rulebook, subject to minimal regulation. Every MP has been open to challenge from party members in their district before every election. When it comes to internal party battles, numbers are all that matter.

In terms of style, Australian parliamentary politics has always been brutal, and still is. Politeness has been taken as a sign of weakness. Abusing opposing party members in derogatory terms has passed for debate. Even recently, question time battles turned Parliament into a coliseum, where opposition members sought to embarrass ministers, and ministers in turn launched tirades against the questioner, boosted by jeers and asides from their supporters behind them. Politics in Australia has never pretended to be a genteel profession. Four PMs have been deposed by their own party in the past decade – two from each side of politics (Tiffin, 2017).

However, in other respects, the Constitution has had immense influence. In order to reflect its federal nature, a great many extra provisions were carefully written down and their details fixed. The states retained all powers except those that they had explicitly granted to the federal government. The Australian Constitution and the state constitutions also followed the US template by more clearly dividing the government into three independent branches – the legislature (see Chapters 11 and 12), the executive (see Chapters 13 and 14) and the judiciary – who are clearly more separate than in some Westminster systems (see Chapter 3). In a 'pure' separation of powers, each branch has the authority to check or limit the other two, to prevent one arm of government from becoming supreme, so ensuring that the people remain free from government abuses. Because of the influence of 'responsible party government' ideas, however, Australia has not in fact operated under a strict separation of powers. For instance, the core executive of ministers and the premier must be drawn only from elected MPs and senators, and so government members have formed a substantial part of the relatively small legislatures at federal and state levels. In addition, critics argue that the Australian PM has had huge powers of patronage that can also undermine the independence of the three powers (see Chapter 13).

Nonetheless, the text and structure of the Constitution has underpinned a strict separation of powers between the judiciary and the executive/legislature. Reflecting this separation, and the need for federalism to be impartially regulated, the High Court of Australia has the power to review all legislative and executive acts. The High Court acts as the court of appeal for the Constitution and federal government actions and since the Constitution is a written one, it is justiciable. The court must decide whether a proposed act of the government or Parliament can be justified in terms of the powers enumerated within the Constitution. Australian judges have generally followed the common law tradition of mostly deferring to the practical needs of executive government. Yet the High Court can strike down laws as being inconsistent with the Constitution. Insulating judicial power from the political arms of government helps to safeguard the rule of law and ensures that cases are decided in a fair and impartial manner.

The written Constitution says little explicitly about citizen rights beyond the sphere of economics and trade. It spells out powers that are binding far more authoritatively than any convention or traditional practice. However, the Constitution was narrowly designed to describe the working of government and the enumeration of powers. Reflecting the time and the context when it was defined and entrenched, it does not incorporate any bill of rights (as the American template does, see Chapter 2), nor (as we have seen) does it give many details about how effective government should actually be run. Over time, the High Court has swung between a literal, 'black-letter' interpretation of the Constitution (which mostly implies 'nothing to be done' on civil liberties) and a position where it has found implied democratic rights and obligations within the document's wording.

The state delegates to the founding conventions also negotiated a permanent political defence of states' rights in the form of a Senate, based on the USA's upper house model, with an equal number of members (originally 6, now 12) from each state, regardless of their population sizes. The upper house members served for longer terms, and it was set up having equal powers with the lower house, with the exception that it could not initiate money bills. It can also reject any legislation, including the budget. From the outset, however, Australia's Senate was directly elected (before the USA, which only introduced votes in 1914). Since 1951, senators have been elected by proportional representation (PR). In the modern period, closer competition between the top two parties dominating the House of Representatives (the Liberal-National Coalition and Labor) plus increased public support for other parties in Senate elections, have meant that recent Australian governments have rarely had the numbers for an overall majority in the Senate (Browne and Oquist, 2021). Consequently, ministers have mostly needed to negotiate their legislative programmes through the upper house item by item, bill by bill, when they wished to pass new controversial laws. In 1975, in an incident that still casts a long shadow, a Senate majority hostile to the then Gough Whitlam Labor government, prevented approval of the federal budget, leading to the suddenly announced dismissal of the government by the Governor-General – perhaps acting legally but nevertheless improperly, as he did so without warning to the then PM. Since then, Senate politics has been more much consensual in its operations, and governor-generals have reverted to their proper (mostly honorary and non-political) functions.

Federalism has had another long-lasting implication. The Australian Parliament has sat for far fewer days than many of its Westminster counterparts. Since 2010, the fewest number of days the House of Representatives has sat in a year was 37 (in 2013, an election year); the most was 63 days (in 2014). (By contrast, the lower house in Canada sits for around 130 days a year and the UK's House of Commons for 140–160 days.) When Parliament is not sitting, there are fewer institutional mechanisms of federal government accountability operating in Canberra. With Parliament not being in session, the opposition has nowhere to grandstand in, and there are no regular meetings on which the media can report. And (as we will discuss) the Cabinet process has formally regarded secrecy as an essential component of governing.

The heart of federal government: the Cabinet and prime minister

The Australian Cabinet consists of around 20–23 ministers and constitutes the heart of government (Weller, 2007; Weller, 2009; Weller, 2021). In right-of-centre coalition governments, they have been members of the Liberal and rural National Parties, but the Labor Party has governed on its own (even in periods when it depended on support from the Greens or other MPs). One or the other of these top two parties has always been in power since 1910, albeit under different names. Cabinet ministers must be MPs; the majority sit in the House of Representatives, and around six are senators.

Cabinet is chaired by PMs and during much of the year it meets weekly. Each minister has their own sphere of functional responsibility, usually heading a government department. Outside Cabinet, there are another 8–10 junior ministers, appointed by the PM to assist Cabinet ministers. Attendance at Cabinet has been limited to Cabinet ministers, junior ministers with an item for discussion, the Cabinet secretary, the secretary of the prime minister and cabinet (PM and C) department, and two officials as note-takers. Although advisers and outsiders have played increasingly prominent roles in national politics and policy-making, it has been rare for any to attend Cabinet, and even rarer for them to speak.

Cabinet ministers are bound by collective responsibility to defend Cabinet decisions and those of its committees, whether or not they were in the room when the decision was made and whether they have argued for or against the eventual outcome. Discussions within the Cabinet room are meant to be confidential. The core proposition remains that ministers have their opportunity to put their case in Cabinet; if they are unsuccessful there, they accept their colleagues' decisions and support them in public and in the party room. In practice, dissatisfied ministers often engineer leaks in some deniable way, often designed to embarrass the PM or the winning Cabinet majority.

The Cabinet room is the PM's world and the working of Cabinet has remained their prerogative. It is the PM who decides what items will be on the agenda, in what terms they will be discussed, who will speak and in what order, when the discussion has gone on long enough to be closed down, and what the decision of Cabinet has been. Votes are not taken; rather, opinions are 'weighed'. Strategies can be used by PMs to delay proposals; sometimes they may sum up against the majority. Ministers have normally given PMs a degree of freedom. Whether or not they are calculating their leadership prospects all of the time, PMs are also aware of the potential tensions in their ministerial team, and they know that their likely successor is sitting around the table.

Ministers must be either MPs or senators, so the PM's choices are limited to parliamentarians. There has been no tradition of drawing in 'technical expertise' by appointing those who have skills but are not politicians. All Australian ministers have been political, not technical. The Attorney-General will usually be a lawyer, though not necessarily a distinguished one. There are no qualifications required for ministers. The route to office has been exclusively through the party and the backbench. The criteria for selection are more about having good political antennae than about any subject expertise.

In theory terms, all Westminster system PMs have the same key powers in managing Cabinet (the so-called three As): appointing people to Cabinet; allocating specific ministerial roles to each; and adjusting departmental missions, briefs and policy turfs (on occasion) (Dewan and Hortala-Vallve, 2009). On appointments, Liberal PMs normally choose their own party's ministers with a free hand. However, they are constrained by the key need to represent all states in the federal Cabinet, to include members from both the House of Representatives and Senate, to achieve a balance across party factions and, more recently, to improve the gender diversity of ministers. In coalition governments, a Liberal PM will generally negotiate with the National Party leader about how many ministers the party gets and what positions they hold. At federal level, the National Party leader has normally also been deputy PM in Liberal-National governments, although the salience of this role can vary with the incumbent PM.

From 1906 to 1993 the Australian Labor Party's parliamentary caucus elected the ministers, with internal party factions playing a key role. At times, ministers were imposed on a PM. In 2006, the leader of the opposition (Kevin Rudd) persuaded the caucus to allow him to select the ministers himself. In practice, when he became PM, he still negotiated with the faction and parliamentary leaders and the resulting Cabinet was probably little different from the one that the caucus might have elected.

On allocations, all PMs have retained the power to decide each Cabinet member's particular ministerial position, although they may negotiate with powerful players about accepting one of two alternatives. In general, PMs have tried to appoint ministers to ministerial briefs where their ideas about their department's issues agreed with those of the premier. And they have steered colleagues away from holding important roles in policy fields where the PM and minister had conflicting views. Since PMs know their colleagues' views in depth, this allocation problem has been much easier for them to handle than it might look at first sight (Dewan and Hortala-Vallve,

2009). Ministers in Australia also get a mandate letter, on appointment, telling them what the PM's priorities are. So, in Australia, whether ministers agree with the PM may not matter as much for policy outcomes as it does in the UK or other Westminster systems. The daily influence of the PM is more important than the initial appointment.

In terms of adjusting ministerial portfolios and roles, the PM has also retained quite a lot of freedom. Australian executive government departments have rarely been reorganised in wholesale ways. When needed, the federal PM can create a new department or agency in Canberra, or merge existing ones. However, portfolio boundaries have mattered a lot in the federal budgeting system, and they can be tweaked more often. Newly arising issues can be assigned across departments as the PM wishes, while issues that have increased in salience can be given to the departments of the PM's most trusted colleagues.

What are effectively 'inner cabinets' (that is, sub-groups of key Cabinet ministers deciding for the whole) can sometimes exist and they may masquerade as Cabinet committees. In 2008, Rudd, as PM, created a Strategic Priorities and Budget Committee to manage the impact of the global financial crisis (GFC) on Australia. It consisted of the four most senior ministers, who found the process useful and congenial, so that their agenda was extended to cover a whole range of items that were, in effect, pre-digested before they were presented to full Cabinet. The long-lasting Liberal-National ('Coalition') governments under John Howard (1996 to 2007) also held regular meetings of the parliamentary leaders of the two governing parties to pre-resolve issues. However, a closed process of decision-making can have severe consequences when Cabinet ministers object that they are being excluded from the key moments of debate.

Extensive advice has been available to all prime ministers in fulfilling their core role. The modern PM's Office (PMO) has had around 50 staff members, including several policy advisers, a powerful media office and advance planning teams. They are all partisan appointments in the sense that they serve the PM personally, not the government. The PM's chiefs of staff are likely to be key advisers, powerful players in government processes, sometimes acting as the PM's proxy. However, their power has not been personal but rather delegated. They have been influential only if they have the PM's confidence. The larger PM and C department is a civil service unit that provides the PM with not only the support required for the cabinet system but also a policy capacity to oversee and, if necessary, become deeply involved with proposals. It has never shrunk from providing alternative advice to that of departments, as one of its secretaries (the top official) noted. With a staff numbering in several hundreds, it serves the PM first and foremost, and thereafter the Cabinet through the PM.

When Parliament is sitting, weekly party caucus meetings provide a regular opportunity for objections and dissent to surface. Ministers and PMs attend party meetings and answer questions. House MPs and senators gain private 'voice' in exchange for their public support. If a government gets into difficulties then the caucus meetings play a critical role in deciding whether to call a leadership 'spill' (essentially a vote of no confidence) in the PM (or party leader in opposition). If that mechanism is triggered, then senators and MPs alone have always decided so far who the next leader should be. (Labor has a new leadership selection process that could also give party members votes, but it has never been activated yet – see Chapter 6.) As a result, the PM and leader of the opposition alike pay close and continuous attention to caucus sentiment, especially if their position in the opinion polls looks troubling.

Australian ministers have become used to working in their parliamentary offices, far removed from the heads of their departments housed elsewhere in Canberra. Ministers have operated at a distance from the public service officials, but supported by their partisan assistants and advisers, who have also been located in their parliamentary offices. Advisers have provided political and policy information, suggestions and strategies. They have often been seen as rivals to career public servants in steering ministers. The concentration of ministers, MPs, staff advisers, the press corps and the Cabinet room all within Parliament House has created a 'parliamentary bubble' that is physically cut off from the civil service departments placed around the city, and from the public beyond. Canberra is a government town; business works in Sydney and Melbourne. MPs interact all day in and out of the parliamentary chambers. That is, of course, while they are there (Chapter 13).

Putting the bits together

These features show how, while Australian federal government can in broad terms still be described as a Westminster system of parliamentary government, it has inevitably mutated into a unique form over the last century and more. Canberra governance remains Westminster in genus maybe – the DNA is clear – but Australia has many distinct practices.

Members in both houses of Parliament are elected by voting systems where voters indicate multiple preferences (see the next section). This means that most of the time, for the House of Representatives, voters are at some point required to choose between the top two major parties (the Liberal-National Coalition or Labor). The importance of the party label has helped Australian parties require absolute party discipline inside the federal legislature. Both have been key factors in ensuring that members of the House of Representatives have rarely exerted any independent or individual influence. It has been almost unknown for any of the top two parties' legislators to vote against their own government in either the House or the Senate. Yet, because party leaders, and thus PMs, are elected by their parliamentary party, they can be ejected by a sudden party room vote. A revolving door can create the impression of insecure premiers, constantly looking over their shoulders to ensure their support remains solid, but this has by no means always been true.

The government rarely has a majority in the Senate (elected by PR voting). Consequently, recent governments have had to negotiate almost everything through Parliament with the smaller parties and independents who hold the balance of power there. Hung parliaments can also occur in the House of Representatives. The Labor government depended on independent MPs from 2010 to 2013 for confidence issues.

For more traditional observers, Australia's long-established constitutional traditions – such as strong, single-party majority governments, a predominant focus on two-party politics, a reliance on 'common law' in the legal system, and links back to the UK (via the monarchy and common cultural assumptions and processes) – have been unquestionable sources of institutional strength. In this view, these institutions have helped create sustained success in handling the country's increased economic scale, major population growth and changing ethnic make-up over many recent decades.

Yet for other critics these and other features appear to be signs instead of Australia's only partial or stalled constitutional and political development, sitting uneasily alongside a still-delayed full transition to modernity in economic and cultural terms (see Chapters 3 and 28). In this view, much of Australia's political process has been too shallowly based, with equal citizenship rights still to be achieved in many dimensions. Some key constitutional elements (like the monarchy/Governor-General role as head of state and even the country's flag) have not been fully domesticated. And some central political processes in a liberal democracy (such as maintaining administrative impartiality or citizens' rights) remain vulnerable to failure under partisan pressure from electorally successful governing parties with significant power at their disposal.

Strengths, weaknesses, opportunities and threats (SWOT) analysis 1: governance

Current strengths	Current weaknesses
The 1901 Constitution was a forward-looking and remarkably democratic document in its day, for citizens. This ethos continued with the early emancipation of women.	The written Constitution was a colonial-era document and correcting for its omissions (such as civil rights for First Nations peoples) took decades, creating serious legacy issues that still resonated and remained unresolved at the time of writing. However, since 1924, compulsory voting has solved the problems of low turnouts that have sometimes affected other liberal democracies.
The 1901 written Constitution describes the form of government. The High Court can rule whether an act is within the Commonwealth's powers. The High Court has held that the Constitution assumes there will be collective Cabinet government.	The Constitution gives none of the details of how governing should operate and the document itself never actually mentions the Cabinet or the PM. That way executive government's work has been left to convention, tradition and convenience.
Weekly Cabinet meetings have retained their position within the core executive and federal government. Generally, PMs work through and with Cabinet and its committees. Maintaining Cabinet and party consensus has thus been a condition, not always achieved, for prime ministerial and governmental survival.	The PM may dominate Cabinet and will rarely be overruled, but they have to be careful not to make too many 'captain's choices' by announcing decisions without consulting Cabinet colleagues.
It was not until 1962 that all Aboriginal and Torres Strait Islander peoples became Australian citizens, and not until the 1967 referendum that they were granted the right to vote at the Commonwealth level. Election and parliamentary institutions have long been struggling to counteract this adverse legacy, most recently with renewed vigour since around 2015. At the time of writing, representation of First Nations peoples in the lower house had come into line with their presence in the population.	Historically, Aboriginal and Torres Strait Islander peoples have been badly under-represented as legislators in Australia's political institutions. However, in 2022 their numbers had grown to 11 (out of 227, just under 5 per cent) (Parliamentary Education Office, 2022). Other Australians of non-British and non-European origins and women have become better represented in the Senate, but they have remained under-represented in the House of Representatives (see Chapters 11 and 12).
The PM and cabinet system, allied with strong party discipline in the top two parties and their predominance in electoral politics and the legislature, is conducive to strong and effective government.	Without a human rights charter, executive government in Australia can appear dangerously unconstrained at times. Sometimes quite vicious partisanship on display in the House of Representatives has accentuated such misgivings.

Future opportunities	Future threats
The Voice for First Nations peoples was well worked out (Hobbs, 2018). The 2023 referendum proposal to establish a Voice to Parliament was backed by Labor, the Greens, some Liberal Party politicians and members and some other smaller parties. However, it was robustly opposed by the Liberal leader and his key colleagues and defeated resoundingly in the popular vote in October 2023 (see Chapter 4).	The 2017 Uluru Statement from the Heart, calling for a First Nations Voice enshrined in the Constitution, was rejected by the Liberal-National federal government (ABC News, 2017). The Albanese Labor government's proposed Voice for First Nations peoples to advise Parliament was a risky constitutional change. After it was decisively defeated in the referendum, the possibility of further advances on this issue remains unclear (see Chapter 4).
The failure of the 2023 Voice to Parliament referendum has not obviated the need for reform. Instead, it has pushed focus back on to informal constitutional and governance change. At the time of writing, relationships between the federal and state and territory governments appeared to provide the most likely source of change.	In Australia, surviving Westminster principles have come under challenge with mounting demands for better integrity safeguards, the increasing politicisation of the public service and gridlock between the political class and the bureaucratic class on the way forward (see Chapters 13 and 14).

Australia's distinctive voting arrangements

The heart of democracy is political equality – every vote (and voice) should count, and none should count for more than one. In all liberal democracies, the process of translating the votes cast by citizens into seats within the legislature has never been a straightforward one. Many countries have just one voting system that is used across almost all elections. The pioneers of democracy in Australia took political equality (for enfranchised citizens) perhaps more seriously than anywhere else in the world. They asked: 'If some citizens vote but others do not, how genuinely representative of their constituency majority can winning MPs be?' This logic underpinned the introduction of compulsory voting for both houses of the federal legislature in 1924.

Making every vote count also motivated the adoption of a voting system that is used almost nowhere else in the world – the Alternative Vote for lower house elections. (In Australia, this system is often called 'preferential voting', but for political scientists in general preferential voting is a larger category meaning voting by numbering multiple preferences in order, which includes other systems (such as STV) or rank order preferences for single office holders. Accordingly, to avoid confusion, we have used the unambiguous AV label here, which refers specifically and only to Australia's lower house system.) In AV, votes transfer between candidates, so that in the final run-off stage the person elected will be the one that has the most primary and transferred-in votes. In addition, some states introduced PR systems for their upper houses early on. In 1948, a PR system, STV, was adopted for future federal Senate elections, and it is now used to choose all state senators also (in the five states with upper houses – Queensland has no upper house).

Of course, these two systems were probably introduced originally for partisan self-interest reasons. AV was first used in 1918 when the incumbent government risked losing a key seat in a three-sided contest. And in 1948 some Labor senators thought they might lose all their upper house seats under the system then in use (called 'block voting'), so they looked to a proportional STV system to protect them against that. However, both AV and STV are now 'sanctified' by long use, and they have been retained because they aim to do different things. AV is a majoritarian system intended to ensure that the party with majority support in the most local electorates nationwide forms the government. Its rationale is that citizens as a whole can clearly signal either that they want the incumbent party of government to continue in office, or that it should be replaced by the opposition. By contrast, STV has been intended to match parties' votes with their Senate seats as closely as possible, but only within each of the country's six states and two territories. In modern times, the Senate has been seen as more of an amending chamber, acting as a check and balance on the House majority by representing the diversity of regional interests. In practice, it has also reflected partisan voting patterns nationwide fairly accurately, but this has been strictly a favourable by-product and not its rationale (Browne and Oquist, 2021; also see Chapter 12).

Lower house elections: the AV system

Elections to the lower House of Representatives take place in small single-member districts called 'electorates', averaging 110,000 adult citizens in each. The AV system demands a bit more of citizens than 'first-past-the-post' elections (still used in the USA, Canada, India and the UK). Voters mark the candidates for each local seat numerically (1, 2, 3, etc.). In federal elections, they must fill out all the available spaces, for instance marking 10 preferences if there are 10 candidates (although there are some variations from this requirement in the different states' lower house elections) – see Figure 1.1.

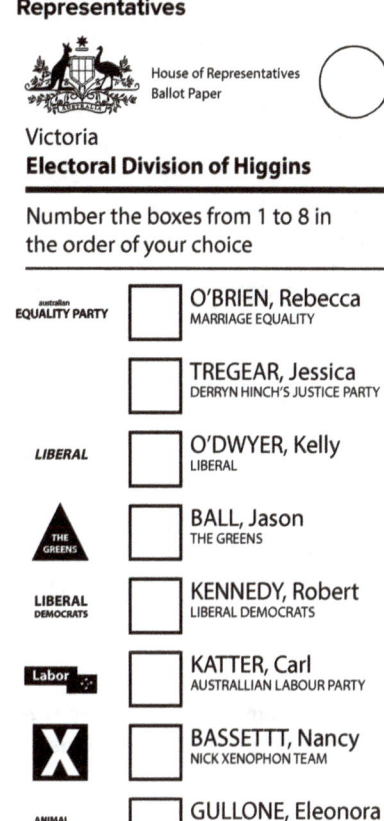

Figure 1.1: A sample AV ballot paper for electing an MP to the House of Representatives

Source: Wikipedia (2024).

First-preference votes are then counted and if one candidate has over 50 per cent support already, they are elected straightaway. However, if no candidate has yet passed this level, a process of eliminating the remaining candidate with the least votes starts, and the counters look at who voters backing this candidate put as their next (second) preference vote. These votes are then allocated to the respective candidates still in the race. This elimination of the bottom candidates goes on until either the leading candidate has majority support or only two candidates remain, when the one with most preferences by definition wins.

Upper house elections: the STV system

In the federal Senate, seats are assigned through PR at the level of whole states and territories. Whatever their population, each of the six states has 12 Senate seats and normally half of these are elected at each federal election, so that there are six seats up for election in each state. Because the constitutional purpose of the Senate is to represent every region of the country equally, from a national perspective its seats are technically malapportioned (when set against the number of citizens in each state). Tasmania has nearly 46,500 electors per senator, but for New South Wales this number is 675,000 people, over 14 times larger. For this reason, it makes little sense to compute the national proportionality score for Senate elections (but see Chapter 5).

Within each state, parties put up multiple candidates (up to six). Voters mark either their preferences for one party's whole list 'above the line' (from 1–6) or their preference order across twice as many individual candidates, spanning across different parties if they wish, 'below the line' (but 1–12). Figure 1.2 shows the two ways that a voter could complete their votes for a simplified STV ballot paper – the actual ones are bigger and more complex.

A complex counting process then allocates seats in order to the candidates that have the most votes, to achieve the best overall fit possible between party vote shares and their number of legislators. The total number of votes cast is divided by the number of seats being contested plus one. This gives a quota, or a vote share that guarantees a party one seat. In a six-seat state election, this is: 100 per cent of votes/(6 + 1) = 14 per cent. Any candidate with more than a quota

Figure 1.2: A simplified view of above-the-line voting (for six parties) or below-the-line voting for 12 candidates in Senate STV elections

A	B	C	D	E	F	
4	3	5	1	6	2	**Voter's Vote**
Party 1	Party 2	Party 3	Party 4	Party 5	Party 6	
Candidate Party 1	6 Candidate Party 2	Candidate Party 3	1 Candidate Party 4	Candidate Party 5	4 Candidate Party 6	
Candidate Party 1	10 Candidate Party 2	Candidate Party 3	2 Candidate Party 4	Candidate Party 5	7 Candidate Party 6	
Candidate Party 1	11 Candidate Party 2	Candidate Party 3	3 Candidate Party 4	Candidate Party 5	9 Candidate Party 6	
Candidate Party 1	12 Candidate Party 2		5 Candidate Party 4	Candidate Party 5	8 Candidate Party 6	
Candidate Party 1	Candidate Party 2			Candidate Party 5		**Preferences as Counted**

Source: Author's construction, drawing on Australian Electoral Commission (AEC, n.d.).

Note: In this example, either the voter must number at least six parties above the line (shown in blue), in which case candidates are allocated their vote during counting in the order each party has set (from the top of each party list to the bottom), or the voter could choose to mark their preferences across at least 12 individual candidates below the line (shown in red). For the latter the voter can decide to stick with a party's official ranking of its candidates, as with the top three red preferences within Party 4 in this example, or pick other candidates to prioritise – here the voter has up-rated the lower-placed candidates of Party 6 and Party 2.

gets a seat straightaway. Every time a seat is allocated to a party, one quota share of votes is deducted from its total remaining votes. Any surplus votes of an elected candidate are redistributed to their voters' second or next choices. Once this process has been done, there are usually one or two seats that are still unallocated. At this point, as in AV elections, STV switches over to knocking out the bottom candidate still in the race and redistributing their voters' preferences.

Compulsory voting and marking preferences

Around 21 liberal democracies across the world in theory require all citizens to vote, but the enforcement of this requirement (and hence the consequences of not voting) vary a great deal. Since 1924, Australia has taken a different, more committed stance at federal level, a lead that was copied at state level with some lags (up to the early 1940s). So not voting (without a legitimate excuse, such as illness) has incurred a noticeable fine. Alongside tiny Luxembourg, Australia has now become one of only two countries in the world where compulsory voting is enforced (International IDEA, 2023; Wikipedia, 2023). As a result, it has consistently had one of the highest validated voting rates of any liberal democracy (see Figure 1.3). Opinion poll evidence has also suggested that the proportion of people in favour of maintaining compulsory voting has been above 70 per cent (Bennett, 2005).

Preferential voting systems (like both AV and STV) are designed to make sure each vote counts. But what do people actually have to do in order to cast a ballot? Turning up to the polling station and then handing in a blank or defaced ballot paper has been accepted as voting (one type of informal voting), so does not attract a fine. But for the ballot paper to count as a formal vote it has to be filled in exactly as the rules say. Historically, in Australian elections, formal voting meant numbering *all* the candidates listed on the ballot paper in a single numerical sequence (1, 2, 3, etc.), increasing the risk of voters inadvertently casting invalid ballots (Hill and Young, 2007). Ballot papers for each AV election for the House list candidates by name, now arranged in a random sequence. Since the number of candidates used to be fairly small (for example three, four or

Figure 1.3: Voter turnout at federal elections, 1901 to 1928, 2001 to 2023

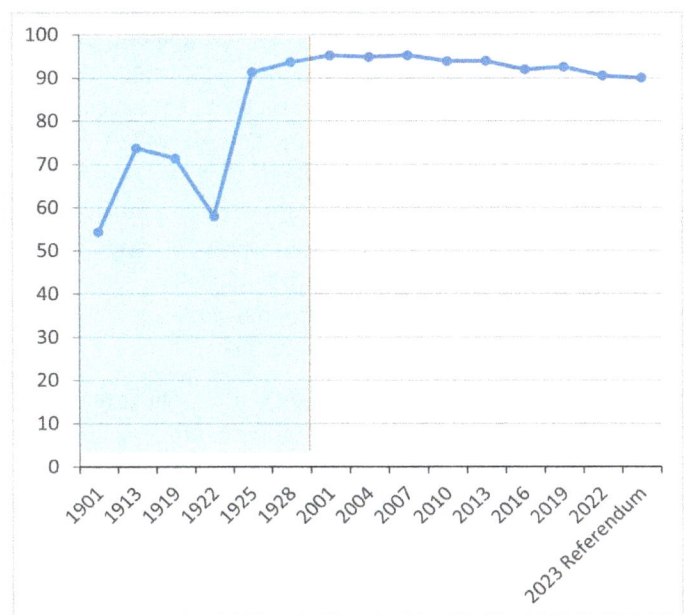

Source: Adapted from AEC, 2023.

Note: The figure shows voter turnout for the House of Representatives for elections from 1901 to 1928 (blue shaded area) and 2001 to 2023 (white area). Voter turnout is calculated as the number of votes cast divided by the number of enrolled voters.

five), numbering them in one strict sequence, with no duplicated or missed out numbers, was not too onerous a task. However, candidate numbers have increased over time so that in 2022 many districts had 10 or more candidates, and one even saw 16 candidates on the ballot paper (see Chapter 5). Where voters have clearly tried to meet the requirements, but have not in fact accurately done so, this too counts as informal voting (alongside blank or defaced ballots). The person has sincerely tried to discharge their duty to vote, but their ballot paper still cannot go into the count, even though officials make every effort to determine their intent (see Chapter 5). Across the three federal elections in 2016, 2019 and 2022, informal votes averaged 5.2 per cent of all ballots cast for the House and 3.7 per cent of those cast for the Senate (AEC, 2022).

In Senate STV elections, the number of candidates grew much larger much earlier on, and the design of the paper (with candidates arranged in party lists) meant that numbering everyone standing in a single order became more difficult. As a result, the rules were changed to allow voters to either cast a vote above the line, to endorse a party's whole list of candidates, or number all the candidates below the line on the ballot paper in sequence (which soon became a truly demanding task). In 2016, the below-the-line requirement was reduced so that voters choosing this option need only number 12 individual people (see Figure 1.2). In addition, an STV rule once allowed the leaders of small parties eliminated from the bottom during the STV counting process to specify how their bloc of above-the-line votes should be transferred to other parties. This created anomalies in the 2013 Senate election, where small-party candidates with very low levels of initial support could sometimes get elected with a coalition of other minor parties backing them; the rule was abolished in 2016.

Numbering a full slate of preferences (rather than casting a single ballot) allows voters to express their whole preference ordering and to know in a very reliable way that their view will at some stage determine the result if no candidate wins an outright majority on first preferences, which at the time of writing has only happened in a minority of seats (see Chapter 5). By contrast, the 'two party preferred' vote at the final AV run-off count stage ensures that every MP enjoys some form of majority endorsement (over all alternatives) in their area. As modern politics has become far more multidimensional and issue-based over time, and the Labor versus Liberal/National divide has no longer been as dominant as it once was, preference voting has also been a better fit, with most Australians having multiple parties that they could vote for and several others that they dislike. In first-past-the-post countries like the USA, Canada and the UK, the development of new or smaller parties has been inhibited because their supporters must choose between 'wasting their vote' (possibly year after year) or voting tactically for whichever of the larger parties in their area is their 'least bad' preference. By contrast, in Australia a Greens supporter, for example, can back their first preference but if the local winner will likely be either Labor or the Coalition the voter can still cast a second or later stage preference to effectively shape the outcome. This creates a far fairer playing field for new parties to enter competition (Farrell and McAllister, 2006). Cross-national evidence also suggests that multi-seat systems (which require preferential voting) help to achieve somewhat greater gender equality in legislatures, as has been true of the Senate versus the House (Hough, 2022).

Does preferential voting have any drawbacks? Critics argue that both AV and STV (if voting below the line) require that voters have a higher level of political knowledge in order to cast a vote. Some parties have handed out 'How to Vote' cards at polling places, which suggest that voters order the candidates on the ballot in a favourable order. In Queensland state elections, where it is acceptable to express only a single preference, some parties' cards have suggested that voters mark their local candidate and no others – which is ethically dubious as it potentially undermines the 'every vote counts' ethos. In the early 2000s, over half of voters told survey interviewers that they followed what the advice cards suggested, but the practice has declined and by 2019 less than 30 per cent of election survey respondents said they had done this (Cameron and McAllister, 2019, p.23).

Critics have also argued that by outlawing non-voting, the state and major parties have tried to compel engagement by citizens within their sphere. Parties and politicians have fewer incentives to go out and motivate voters or increase their interest in politics because voters have to show up at the polls anyway, however boring or remote politics has become for them. And parties have less need to recruit and engage party members, who are not needed to 'get out the vote' as much as if voting was voluntary. Others have argued, on freedom grounds, that citizens should have the right not to vote. And they see discarding informal votes before counting as devaluing the legitimate views of people who may want to register a protest vote (Sheppard, 2015). In more or less every decade, some of these arguments have resonated with Liberal-National politicians who saw a potential partisan advantage in voluntary voting, because they expected Labor voters to be less likely to turn out than Coalition supporters. But since other figures on the political right strongly dissented from changing the status quo, nothing has come of successive intra-party review initiatives.

Strengths, weaknesses, opportunities and threats (SWOT) 2: analysis – key election arrangements

Current strengths	Current weaknesses
Compulsory voting has meant that turnout in Australian federal elections has always been high (AEC, 2011). It has ensured that almost all Australians have had a say in elections and in policy-making (Evans, 2006). A majority of citizens support compulsory voting. In combination with preferential voting, it has also ensured that every vote counts and that (almost) every citizen votes (AEC, 2023).	Critics have argued that compulsory voting may tend to worsen a disconnect between parties and voters, because parties have fewer incentives to motivate voters or recruit and engage party members than they would in a voluntary voting system. Others have argued that citizens should have the right not to vote.
Preferential voting (numbering choices in order 1, 2, 3, etc.) reduces strategic voting. It provides a means for voters to sincerely express their full preference order, starting with their first choice of candidate or party, while also providing information on later preferences (especially as between the top two major parties) so that no votes are wasted.	Some critics have argued that the Australian electoral systems are made more complicated by preferential voting, which voters understand only imperfectly. This may increase the proportion of invalid votes.

Future opportunities	Future threats
Both AV and STV systems have now been pretty stable for many years and new generations of voters (including immigrants from elsewhere) have adapted easily to using them. This has boded well for their future stability.	Democratic backsliding by parties or self-interested strategies (like advising voters not to use their preferences beyond the top one) may undermine the efficacy of preferential voting.

Conclusion

Every political system in the world is *sui generis* in some ways. Just as with its flora and fauna, the Australian political system includes elements and mixes of elements found nowhere else in the world. Yet as a pioneer liberal democracy that has matured in a generally successful way, its unique system also holds out many potent lessons for other states and countries on how to balance different institutions – for example, combining a fixed constitution with evolving federal and state tiers of government, and using complementary types of voting system. We explore these lessons in detail in the remainder of this book and sum them up at the end (see Chapter 28).

Notes

1. Previously conducted 'democratic audit' applications in the UK and Australia in reverse chronological order include Dunleavy, Park and Taylor (2018); Wilks-Heeg, Blick and Crone (2012); Sawer, Aljorenson and Larkin (2009); Beetham, Ngan and Weir (2002); and Beetham and Weir (1999a). In addition, some DA methods issues are usefully addressed in Beetham (1999); Beetham and Weir (1999b); Beetham (1995); Jaensch, Brent and Bowden (2004); Uhr (2005); Maddox (2002; 2003); and Dunleavy and Margetts (1995).

References

ABC News (2017) 'Indigenous advisory body rejected by PM in 'kick in the guts' for advocates', *ABC News*, 26 October. https://perma.cc/V2YH-GJR5

AEC (Australian Electoral Commission) (2011) 'Compulsory voting in Australia'. https://www.aec.gov.au/about_aec/publications/voting/

AEC (2022) 'Informality (%) House of Representatives and Senate', 24 August. https://perma.cc/J5FL-2ADV

AEC (2023) 'Voter turnout – previous events'. 7 November. https://perma.cc/2UFC-8VBM

AEC (n.d.) 'Voting in the Senate'. https://perma.cc/Y3CM-RBQA

Beetham, David (ed) (1995) *Defining and Measuring Democracy*, London: Sage.

Beetham, David (1999) 'The idea of democratic audit in comparative perspective', *Parliamentary Affairs*, vol. 52, no. 4, pp.567–81. $ https://doi.org/10.1093/pa/52.4.567

Beetham, David and Weir, Stuart (1999a) *Political Power and Democratic Control in Britain*, London: Routledge. $ https://www.routledge.com/Political-Power-and-Democratic-Control-in-Britain/Beetham-Weir/p/book/9780415096447

Beetham, David and Weir, Stuart (1999b) 'Auditing democracy in Britain: Introducing the democratic criteria', *Political Power and Democratic Control in Britain*, London: Routledge. Ch.1, pp.3–21. $ https://perma.cc/FPR6-9NXG

Beetham, David; Ngan, Pauline; and Weir, Stuart (2002) *Democracy Under Blair: A Democratic Audit of the United Kingdom*, London: Politico's. $

Bennett, Scott (2005) 'Compulsory voting in Australian national elections', Australian Parliament, Department of Parliamentary Services. *Research Brief*. No. 6, 31 October. https://perma.cc/94DH-UKXA

Browne, Bill and Oquist, Ben (2021) *Representative, Still – The Role of the Senate in our Democracy*, Canberra: Australia Institute, Research Report. https://perma.cc/EE8D-B6MP

Cameron, Sarah and McAllister, Ian (2019) *Trends in Australian Political Opinion: Results from the Australian Election Study 1987–2019*, Canberra: The Australian National University. https://perma.cc/YP5F-S82A

Dewan, Torun and Hortala-Vallve, Rafael (2009) 'The three A's of government formation: Appointment, allocation, and assignment', *American Journal of Political Science*, vol. 55, no. 3, pp.610–27. $ https://doi.org/10.1111/j.1540-5907.2011.00519.x. OA at https://perma.cc/PLX3-KEYV

Dryzek, John and Dunleavy, Patrick (2009) *Theories of the Democratic State*, London: Palgrave. Now Bloomsbury Press. $ https://perma.cc/XP65-DUFP

Dunleavy, Patrick (1993) 'The state', in Goodin, Robert (ed) *A Companion to Contemporary Political Philosophy: Volume II*. Oxford: Blackwell, pp. 611–21. $ https://perma.cc/X45Y-4D3A

Dunleavy, Patrick (2019) 'Micro institutions and liberal democracy', *Political Insight*, vol. 10, no. 1, pp.35–39. https://doi.org/10.1177/2041905819838154

Dunleavy, Patrick; Park, Alice; and Taylor, Ros (eds) (2018) *The UK's Changing Democracy: The 2018 Democratic Audit,* London: LSE Press. OA at: https://doi.org/10.31389/book1

Dunleavy, Patrick and Margetts, Helen (1995) 'The experiential approach to auditing democracy' in Beetham, David, *Defining and Measuring Democracy*, London: Sage, pp. 155–72. $ https://perma.cc/V8KX-BMX8

Economist Intelligence Unit (EIU) (2022) *EUI Democracy Rankings, 2022*. https://perma.cc/F9WE-CE24

Evans, Tim (2006) 'Compulsory voting in Australia', Report on Australian Electoral Commission website, 16 January. https://www.aec.gov.au/About_AEC/Publications/voting/files/compulsory-voting.pdf

Farrell, David M and McAllister, Ian (2006) 'Voter satisfaction and electoral systems: Does preferential voting in candidate-centred systems make a difference?' *European Journal of Political Research*, vol. 45, no. 5, pp.723–49. $ https://doi.org/10.1111/j.1475-6765.2006.00633.x. OA at: https://perma.cc/4LQE-VJ43

Hill, Lisa and Young, Sally (2007) 'Protest or error? Informal voting and compulsory voting', *Australian Journal of Political Science*, vol. 42, no. 3, pp.515–21. $ https://doi.org/10.1080/10361140701513646

Hirst, John (2000) *The Sentimental Nation*, Sydney: Oxford University Press.

Hobbs, Harry (2018) 'Constitutional recognition and reform: Developing an inclusive Australian citizenship through treaty', *Australian Journal of Political Science,* vol. 53, no. 2, pp.176–94. OA at: https://perma.cc/T8KY-VWBA

Hough, Anna (2022) 'Trends in the gender composition of the Australian parliament', Parliament of Australia, Research Paper. https://perma.cc/S89C-9VYM

International IDEA (2023) 'Compulsory voting'. https://perma.cc/4NVK-2HKC

Irving, Helen (1999) *To Constitute a Nation,* Sydney: Cambridge University Press.

Jaensch, Dean; Brent, Peter; and Bowden, Brett (2004) *Australian Political Parties in the Spotlight, Report* (Research School of the Social Sciences, ANU), Report No.4, prepared for the Democratic Audit of Australia. OA at: https://perma.cc/5EY2-7GHF

Maddox, Graham (2002) *Federalism and Democracy,* Democratic Audit of Australia. Analysis and Policy Observatory, 1 September 2002, https://apo.org.au/sites/default/files/resource-files/2002-08/apo-nid8727.rtf

Maddox, Graham (2003) 'Federalism and democracy – a reply to Parkin', Online paper, University of New England. *ResearchGate.* https://perma.cc/YK3X-GGD4

Parliamentary Education Office (2022) 'How many Aboriginal or Torres Straits Islander MPs or senators are there and what are their names?', Response to a question, July. https://perma.cc/H5VQ-B75A

Sawer, Marian; Aljorenson, Norman; and Larkin, Phil (eds) (2009) *Australia – The State of Democracy*, Canberra: Federation Press.

Sheppard, Jill (2015) 'Compulsory voting and political knowledge: Testing a "compelled engagement" hypothesis'. *Electoral Studies,* vol. 40, pp. 300–07. OA at: https://perma.cc/FDK3-Z9PQ

Tiffin, Rodney (2017) *Disposable Leaders: Media and Leadership Coups from Menzies to Abbott*, Sydney: New South South Books.

Uhr, John (2005) 'How democratic is parliament? A case study in auditing the performance of Parliaments', Democratic Audit of Australia Discussion Paper, July. OA at: https://perma.cc/F8ZA-LCHF

Weller, Patrick (2007) *Cabinet Government in Australia, 1901–2006: Practice, Principles Performance,* Sydney: UNSW Press.

Weller, Patrick (2009) 'Cabinet government: Australian style', in John Wanna (ed) *Critical Reflections on Australian Public Policy: Selected Essays,* Canberra: ANU Press, pp. 73–84. https://perma.cc/B2UT-8F3W

Weller, Patrick (2021) 'Cabinet government: The least bad system of government?', in Podger, Andrew; de Percy, Michael; and Vincent, Sam (eds), *Politics, Policy and Public Administration In Theory And Practice,* Canberra: ANU Press, Ch.6, pp.139–54. http://press-files.anu.edu.au/downloads/press/n8214/pdf/ch06.pdf

Wikipedia (2023) 'Compulsory voting'. https://perma.cc/8GR7-MHSY

Wikipedia (2024) 'Electoral system of Australia'. https://perma.cc/BAW2-BDDW

Wilks-Heeg, Stuart; Blick, Andrew; and Crone, Stephen (2012) *How Democratic Is the UK? The 2012 Audit*, Liverpool: Democratic Audit. OA at: https://perma.cc/TQX2-B2XW

2

Human rights and civil liberties

Mark Evans and Stan Grant

A foundational principle of liberal democracy is that all citizens are equal and their fundamental human rights must be protected, including protection against the possible political actions of a majority who might seek to strip rights away from an unpopular or inconvenient minority group of people. In many countries, a statement of citizens' rights forms part of the constitution and is enshrined in law and enforced by the courts. This approach was not adopted at Australia's foundation in 1901, reflecting the influence of UK constitutional thinking at the time. Instead, the political system has relied on more diffuse and eclectic ways of protecting fundamental human rights – through common law, the courts and Parliament. At the time of writing Australia remains the only Western democratic nation without a bill or charter of rights, and where its democratic necessity is still questioned (Meagher, 2008).

The most conspicuous peoples to have borne the historic costs of this approach are Aboriginal and Torres Strait Islander peoples, who only gained full citizenship and civil rights in 1967, following a referendum that changed Australia's Constitution. However, this change rectified only one aspect of a history of oppression in the country's colonial period. Efforts to institutionalise more effective means of combatting the multiple disadvantages suffered by First Nations peoples and their communities continued, leading in October 2023 to the Labor government's attempt to create a special advisory chamber – the Voice to Parliament. If this had succeeded, it would have represented First Nations Australians' interests and monitored and scrutinised proposed legislation. However, it was turned down decisively by voters in a national referendum; currently, the next steps in Australia's reconciliation with its First Nations peoples remain unclear (see Chapter 4).

How to cite this chapter:

Evans, Mark and Grant, Stan (2024) 'Human rights and civil liberties', in: Evans, Mark; Dunleavy, Patrick and Phillimore, John (eds) *Australia's Evolving Democracy: A New Democratic Audit*, London: LSE Press, pp.53 -69. https://doi.org/10.31389/lsepress.ada.b Licence: CC-BY-NC 4.0

How must human rights and civil liberties be protected in a democracy?

- Liberal democratic states are now expected to respect a range of fundamental human rights set out in international human rights treaties such as the 1996 International Covenant on Civil and Political Rights ('the Covenant') (United Nations, 2023a). These extend from freedom from torture to the right to fair trial and freedom from discrimination.
- The functioning of any genuine democracy must be based on respect for these rights, without which individuals cannot participate freely or effectively in the political process.
- Human rights and civil liberties are intrinsic to every person. Respect for them cannot be overridden by electoral majorities, nor by the exigencies of government, without a state falling out of the ranks of liberal democracies.

Historically, human rights have not been given comprehensive and consistent legal protection in Australia, as shown by the recent developments highlighted in the following section. Thereafter, the strengths, weaknesses, opportunities and threats (SWOT) are summarised in an analysis of key issues in rights policies in Australia. Following the SWOT analysis, the chapter looks at three particular aspects of rights protection in more detail.

Recent developments

Many basic human and civil rights have remained unprotected in Australia for much of its recent history, and others have been only haphazardly covered by an assortment of laws. The nature of rights protection has remained precarious for many disadvantaged groups – including First Nations Australians, LGBTIQ+ people, the differently abled, and women exposed to domestic and sexual violence and sexism. Historically, non-white people also suffered major disadvantages – especially the hundreds of thousands of Chinese and Asian people in the north of the country who were forced to leave or denied property and voting rights and, later on, non-Anglophone and Asian people under the 'white Australia' policies from the 1900s to the 1960s.

In 2017, the Australian government was subject to a damning critique of its human rights record by the United Nations Human Rights Committee (UNHRC) with regard to the rights of children, the treatment of refugees, domestic violence, transgender rights, the sterilisation of intellectually disabled women and girls, and the impact of anti-terrorism laws on civil liberties (Guardian, 2017a). This assessment was given further validation by the Human Rights Measurement Initiative in 2021, which reported 'strikingly poor results' for Australia, 'particularly in terms of who is most at risk of rights abuses' – such as Aboriginal and Torres Strait Islander peoples, people that are differently abled, people with low socioeconomic status and refugees and asylum seekers (SBS News, 2021b).

Australia did consider the idea of introducing a Human Rights Act following an equally critical report from the UNHCR in 2009. In this it was reported that Australia had not:

- introduced legislation to give effect to the International Covenant on Civil and Political Rights (ICCPR)
- withdrawn its reservations to the ICCPR

- established appropriate procedures to implement the views of the Human Rights Committee
- amended counter-terrorism legislation to conform with ICCPR rights
- enacted a law to comprehensively protect the right to equality and non-discrimination
- enacted a law to protect against hate speech based on religion
- properly resourced the now defunct Indigenous representative body, the National Congress of Australia's First Peoples
- provided comprehensive reparations to members of the Stolen Generations – children forcibly removed from First Nations peoples' families and brought up in white households and communities (AHRC, 1997; Wikipedia, 2023a).

However, after a wide-ranging national consultation on the protection and promotion of human rights, the Australian government decided not to introduce a Human Rights Act. Ministers defended the decision by claiming that 'the enhancement of human rights should be done in a way that, as far as possible, unites rather than divides us' (Ball, 2013). During the consultation, the adoption of a Human Rights Act was supported by over 87 per cent of 35,000 public submissions and was a key recommendation of the National Human Rights Consultation Committee. In the states of Victoria and Queensland and in the Australian Capital Territory, Australia's international human rights obligations have been enshrined in domestic human rights legislation expressly protecting freedom of expression and assembly. But at the Commonwealth level, the Australian government instead adopted the Australian Human Rights Framework in April 2010. Subsequently, most of the key elements of the Framework at the federal level were terminated or suspended under Liberal-National Coalition governments. For example, in the period leading up to 2022 the federal government cut funding to the Human Rights Education Grants Scheme, backed away from its commitment to simplify and strengthen Commonwealth anti-discrimination laws and stalled implementation of Australia's National Action Plan on Human Rights.

One key Framework component was implemented: the strengthening of parliamentary scrutiny of human rights, through *The Human Rights (Parliamentary Scrutiny) Act 2011 (Cth)*, which came into operation in 2012. This legislation has:

- required that each new bill introduced into federal Parliament be accompanied by a Statement of Compatibility of the proposed law's compliance with Australia's international human rights obligations in seven different core international treaties
- established a new Parliamentary Joint Committee on Human Rights (PJCHR) to provide greater scrutiny of legislation for compliance with the human rights treaties to which Australia has become party.

Australia also has an independent Human Rights Commission, the AHRC, established by an act of federal Parliament in 1986 to 'protect and promote human rights in Australia and internationally' (AHRC, 2023a). The AHRC can conduct an inquiry into an act or practice which may be contrary to human rights and can attempt to resolve the issue through conciliation. The AHRC has been lauded internationally for its ability to investigate and uncover human rights abuses, but it has also been subject to federal government backlash on many of its reports. Legal critics argue:

> *If the AHRC is to act as a crusader for the victims of human rights abuses and enforce the law, the Commission's independence and special status should be recognised and protected. To perform its role most effectively, the AHRC cannot operate in fear of government reprisal. (Allen, 2010)*

Instead, the AHRC has faced the constant risk that the government of the day could punish it with funding cuts or by scaling back its powers for criticising executive actions or supporting litigation against the government. Ministers can also use their powers of appointment to pack the AHRC with political appointments due to the absence of a 'fair, open and merit-based selection process for commissioner positions' (Napier-Raman, 2021).

Australia did take several other steps towards the realisation of the ICCPR rights and the promotion of human rights more generally, including:

- acceding to the Optional Protocol to the Convention on the Rights of Persons with Disabilities in August 2009
- ensuring federal protection against discrimination on the new grounds of 'sexual orientation', 'gender identity', 'intersex status' and 'marital and relationship status' through the *Sex Discrimination (Sexual Orientation, Gender Identity, and Intersex Status) Amendment Act 2013 (Cth)*; this brought to an end most of the legal biases under which lesbian, gay, bisexual and transgender people suffered throughout the 20th century
- gradually working towards reform of the Constitution in consultation with First Nations peoples
- committing to ratify the Optional Protocol to the Convention against Torture in 2017.

In addition, a national advisory referendum to allow marriage equality for homosexual people was conducted by post (on a voluntary basis, without compulsory voting) between September and November 2016. After nearly 62 per cent of people voted in support of the proposal, in December 2017 the *Marriage Act 1961* was updated to define marriage as 'the union of two people to the exclusion of all others, voluntarily entered into for life' (see also Chapter 3). This step finally ended a key dimension of legal discrimination against homosexual people.

However, in some other areas, Australia clearly went backwards in the 21st century:

- The Rudd government established the National Congress of Australia's First Peoples as a First Nations representative body in 2010 (Wikipedia, 2023c). However, in 2013, the Abbott government withdrew its funding. In 2019, Ken Wyatt, the Minister for Indigenous Australians in the Morrison government, chose not to renew the organisation and instead developed a proposal for an alternative Indigenous Voice (Australian Government, 2021). This was supposed to involve 25–35 local and regional Voice bodies working with states and territories and local governments to form consultative groups that would input representatives on a national body. The proposal was criticised for failing to enact recommendations of the Uluru Statement from the Heart (2017), which was seen as a more representative view of First Nations Australians (Synot, 2019). Irrespective of one's views on the performance of the National Congress, critics argued that the rights of First Nations Australians should not have become a game of political football between governments.
- Australia continued to maintain a system of mandatory indefinite detention of asylum seekers in Nauru. Its facility on Manus Island, Papua New Guinea (PNG), was shut down after it was found to be unconstitutional by the PNG Supreme Court in 2016.
- The federal government instituted a policy of turning back boats at sea seeking to land visa-less migrants on Australian shores. This arguably violated its non-refoulement obligations under international law, whereby people who seek asylum may not be returned to a country in which there are reasonable grounds to believe they will be subjected to persecution (United Nations, 2023b).

- A Royal Commission established in 2016 investigated the protection and detention of children in the Northern Territory following reports of brutality against (mainly First Nations) children held in youth detention (Royal Commission, 2017). It found that the requirements of section 150 of the *Youth Justice Act 2005 (NT)* were not complied with. These sections embodied the principles contained in Rule 24 of the UN's 'Rules for the Protection of Juveniles Deprived of Their Liberty'.

- Australian police were given greater powers to lock up Aboriginal and Torres Strait Islander peoples without charge, despite previous scandals (SBS News, 2021a). Prisons in Australia are increasingly overcrowded, with the rate of imprisonment in 2021 double that of 1990. First Nations men are disproportionately affected (Guardian, 2017b). In these contexts, a report by Freedom House noted that:

    > *First Nations Australians continue to lag behind other groups in key social and economic indicators; suffer higher rates of incarceration; and report routine mistreatment by police and prison officials. Aboriginal and Torres Strait Islander children are placed in detention at a rate 22 times higher than that of non-Aboriginal children. Additionally, people with disabilities make up almost one-third of the prison population, and face harassment and violence in prisons.* (2022, section F4)

- Australia created more criminal offences under counter-terrorism legislation, which significantly restricted rights (AHRC, 2023b). And federal ministers also introduced the most extreme metadata retention laws among its allies, requiring all internet metadata to be kept by telecommunications service providers for two years. This can be accessed by law enforcement without a warrant or any independent authorisation (Gal, 2017).

Perhaps for these reasons, there was emphatic public support in 2019 to 2021 for creating a document that would set out the rights and responsibilities of Australia's citizens (83 per cent of respondents in one key survey, an increase from 66 per cent in 2019) (Deem, Brown and Bird, 2021). In 2021, three-quarters of respondents agreed that a Charter of Human Rights would 'help people and communities to make sure the government does the right thing', compared to 56 per cent two years earlier (Deem, Brown and Bird, 2021). The biggest increases in support were from young Australians, suggesting a generational attitudinal shift that promises reform in the long term. There was also increasing public support for a constitutional voice for First Nations Australians (61 per cent) (Deem, Brown and Bird, 2021).

The Voice to Parliament: origins

A year after its election in May 2022, the Albanese Labor government brought forward a proposal, developed over a long period in discussions between the centre-left parties and First Nations interest groups, to create a statutory advisory chamber for Parliament called the Indigenous Voice to Parliament. The initiative was a compromise proposal, falling well short of more radical demands, but as a constitutional amendment it would still have had to go through a rigorous progress, requiring approval in a nationwide referendum and passage through both houses of the federal Parliament and the parliaments of all six states. In fact, as Chapter 4 explains in detail, the referendum was lost decisively. In July 2023 the proposal still looked as if it might pass (Guardian, 2023). But the leader of the federal opposition (Peter Dutton) came out arguing for a 'No' vote in the Voice referendum – albeit with some controversy within his own party – and by October the proposal also came to grief on criticisms that the powers of the proposed Voice body were only vaguely formulated, creating a lack of clarity around what a 'Yes' vote would entail (so that 'Don't know' implied a 'No' vote).

This final-stage failure also partly reflected the force of the Australian political tradition in suppressing the case for a 'better' rather than a 'fair' go. As Stan Grant puts it:

> Australia simply does not accept that Aboriginal people are exceptional. Unlike every other nation with Indigenous peoples, we have no political standing as First Nations. Australia is an assimilationist project, a country without history and Australians want it that way. Migrants leave their histories behind. We don't mind ceremonial difference but not political difference. Put simply: the question of what constitutes Australia is settled. (in Grant and Jacobs, 2023)

Many activists had already turned their minds to the day after the referendum, when the next campaign would begin in earnest. At this stage, then, perhaps the most useful insight into the hopes that Aboriginal activists have vested in the Voice on behalf of their people and communities can be gleaned by a long quotation from a recent blog by Stan Grant and Jack Jacobs. The blog situates the Voice within the long historical perspective of decolonisation and the unique conditions of Grant's own people, the Wiradjuri nation:

> With liberal democracy struggling under the weight of its racist and violent history, now is a time for our voices to add more weight to the scales: to demand liberal democracy is responsible, accountable, and fit for the 21st century. Australian liberalism has passed from extermination to exclusion to assimilation but has stopped short of recognition. After two centuries of broken hearts and shattered dreams, it is little wonder hope can appear delusional.
>
> In Australia, Yorta Yorta man William Cooper sent a petition to King George VI to remind him of his moral duty to a people whose lands were 'expropriated' by the Crown and to whom the Crown denied legal status. He called for black seats in parliament to 'prevent the extinction of the Aboriginal race'.[1] And Pearl Gambayani Gibbs helped lead a day of mourning in 1938, proclaiming: 'I am more proud of my Aboriginal blood than of my white blood'. These figures implore us to remember that liberal democracy is but one way of living and being.
>
> Wiradjuri people have our own philosophy, 'yindyamarra'. It defies simple translation but it grounds respect in all we do. How do we bring respect – yindyamarra – to Australian democracy? Is our liberalism even capable of respecting the sovereignty never ceded of First Nations peoples? Yindyamarra is a Wiradjuri voice; a voice for justice. It calls us to build a world of respect grounded in our knowledge and being in a world worth living in. Yindyamarra is an antidote to Western nihilism and the worst of Western liberalism. Yindyamarra dares this nation to build a democracy worthy of that hope.
>
> A constitutionally enshrined First Nations Voice offers its own version of what Noel Pearson has spoken of as radical hope. Proponents of the Voice say it is a pathway to justice – to truth and treaty. Political philosopher Duncan Ivison says it 'prefigures a possible refounding of Australia'. But its modesty – a voice not a veto – risks losing faith with First Nations people. Prime Minister Anthony Albanese has already said it is a voice 'nothing more, nothing less'. He says the parliament will set the composition of the Voice. That begs the question: can

the parliament meet the urgency of the demands of Aboriginal and Torres Strait Islander peoples? The challenge of the Constitutional Voice is to honour the unending struggle of those Aboriginal and Torres Strait Islander champions who have sought to prise open the locked door of Australian democracy. (**Grant and Jacobs, 2022**; Note: the original text has been slightly re-ordered here to aid clarity.)

Strengths, weaknesses, opportunities and threats (SWOT) analysis

Current strengths	Current weaknesses
Australia signed the UN's Universal Declaration of Human Rights (UDHR) in 1972 and ratified it in 1980. In theory, therefore, the country has been bound by the UDHR's provisions and subject to cyclical evaluation of its human rights performance.	In practice, Australian governments have repeatedly been able to introduce legislation diluting international rights protection, especially in areas like national security and immigration. As a result, international human rights law has had a very limited impact on Australian public law or policy (**Human Rights Law Centre, 2023**).
A Parliamentary Joint Committee on Human Rights (PJCHR) was set up to scrutinise federal legislation for its compatibility with the seven core international human rights treaties. And the Australian Human Rights Commission (AHRC) was created to advocate for and investigate potential infringements of human rights.	Australia has never adopted the ICCPR into domestic law. Current legislation provides limited legal protection for core civil and political rights due to the absence of bills or charters of rights, or a human rights act. Human rights agencies rely on the executive and Parliament to implement their recommendations and are not genuinely independent from the executive, either financially nor politically.
Human rights agencies at the federal level have had strong investigative powers. Ministers have also had to respond to their reports (**Napier-Raman, 2021**).	In 2024 the PJCHR 'reported on its Inquiry into Australia's Human Rights Framework. By majority, it recommended the federal government introduce an Australian Human Rights Act' (**Chen, Debeljak and Tate, 2024**). Australia has been subject to ongoing international critique by the UNHCR for its human rights record (**Guardian, 2017a**) with regard to the rights of prisoners, First Nations children, the treatment of refugees, domestic violence, transgender rights, the sterilisation of intellectually differently abled women and girls, and the impact of anti-terrorism laws on civil liberties.

Human rights protection has been afforded at the state and territory level by the Australian Capital Territory's (ACT) *Human Rights Act 1998*, Victoria's *Civil Rights Act 2006* and Queensland's *Human Rights Act 2019*.	There has been little political consensus as to the actual substance of human rights guarantees across Commonwealth and state and territory government. The existing framework has been enmeshed in politics (especially between the top two parties) and has remained vulnerable to political manipulation.
Australia's laws require all telecommunications metadata to be kept by internet service providers (ISPs) for two years. This has provided some assurance to citizens or enterprises concerned about harmful social media content.	At the same time, Australia has introduced extreme arrangements for law enforcement agencies to gain access to all metadata kept by telecommunications service providers without a warrant or any independent authorisation.
Future opportunities	**Future threats**
As a signatory to the ICCPR, Australia has been an energetic advocate for extending and improving human rights protection internationally.	Management of the COVID-19 pandemic posed a considerable threat to civil liberties in Australia, one that needed to be carefully monitored and debated in an open and transparent way.
Human rights and civil liberties have enjoyed relatively strong domestic political support, particularly from younger age groups, and better legal protection in certain states (Victoria and Queensland) and territories (ACT). Similar laws might be passed by other states. There has been a strong commitment to rights values and activism in urban Australia.	Human rights have remained contested concepts in Australian political culture, and vulnerable to political attack especially when the rights are those of unpopular minorities such as terrorist suspects, migrants and other disfavoured social groupings. At the time of writing, the place of legal rights protection within Australia's constitutional culture remained uncertain.
With the Russian invasion of Ukraine in 2022, and apparent threats by China against Taiwan, international advocacy for rights protection has increased in salience. An upsurge in international concern at the erosion of civil liberties during the COVID-19 pandemic also created a space for the reassertion of the rights agenda. US President Joe Biden's Summit for Democracy in 2021, for example, identified three challenges for democracy – defending against authoritarianism, addressing and fighting corruption and advancing respect for human rights. If Australian ministers also seek to advance these aims, remedying domestic rights problems may also become more salient.	The mainstreaming of populist anti-immigration policies in electoral politics has created a political climate where rights have been placed at risk in order to placate a still-influential nativist sentiment among some voters.

The remainder of the chapter examines three other rights issues: the treatment of refugees, the rights issues raised by the COVID-19 pandemic experience, and some issues around social rights.

Detention of refugees

Australia has operated policies to process visa-less immigrants outside the country itself, in other Pacific island nations' lands, since 2001. Boats trying to reach Australia are intercepted by the Navy and escorted to offshore processing centres. This policy effectively prevents refugees from claiming asylum, which they would be able to do under international law if they had reached Australian territory. These policies and practices have been consistently criticised by the United Nations, by Australian human rights groups and by refugees themselves. In 2015, the United Nations adjudicated that Australia's system violated the convention against torture, a claim angrily rejected by PM Abbott (Guardian, 2015). The International Criminal Court's prosecutor said in 2020 that indefinite detention offshore was 'cruel, inhuman or degrading treatment' and unlawful under international law (Guardian, 2020). At least 12 people have died in the island camps (Guardian, 2018b), including one who was murdered by guards in a 2014 riot (Guardian, 2023). Others have died through medical neglect (Guardian, 2018c) and by suicide (Guardian, 2018a). Psychiatrists sent to work in the camps described the conditions as 'inherently toxic' (Guardian, 2014) and akin to 'torture'. The 'Nauru Files', published by *The Guardian* (2016), exposed the Nauru detention centre's own internal reports of systemic violence, rape, sexual abuse, self-harm and child abuse in offshore detention. However, the then long-serving Home Affairs Minister, Peter Dutton, on the right wing of the Liberal Party, strongly defended policies of punitive action towards refugees.

Following the closure of one of the offshore centres by the island government, in May 2021 the Morrison coalition government rushed through legislation that allowed it to lock up refugees in detention centres, potentiality for the rest of their lives. The legislation – one of the first laws passed by former Home Affairs Minister Karen Andrews – continued the legacy of Andrews' predecessor, Peter Dutton (Human Rights Law Centre, 2021). The *Migration Amendment (Clarifying International Obligations for Removal) Bill 2021* targeted refugees in immigration detention who cannot return to their home countries because of a risk of persecution or serious harm. While the new laws notionally provided protections against sending people to harm, the legislation actually gave the minister a new power to overturn refugee status (in breach of international law) and it contained no mechanism to prevent the indefinite detention of refugees who cannot be returned. The legislation was an attempt to shield the Morrison government from legal challenges in the courts against the lifetime detention of refugees. In April 2021, the JPCHR raised concerns that the legislation would result in fewer checks on indefinite detention and sought clarification from the minister. No response was published before the legislation was rushed through Parliament.

In January 2012, less than 3 per cent of people in Australian immigration detention had been detained for more than two years. Nine years later that number had grown to almost 30 per cent. The average period that a person was detained after being taken into immigration detention in Australia increased steadily, from less than 100 days in mid-2013 to more than 600 days at the end of 2020. This level has been vastly more than that of comparable liberal democratic jurisdictions, such as the UK and Canada, where people are more often detained for a period of days or weeks. In contrast, it has become common for people to be held in detention in Australia for five years or more. By mid-2023, Australia still had no legal framework for reviewing whether keeping someone in immigration detention is appropriate or necessary, and no limit has applied on how long they can be held. However, only the Greens have argued for a fundamental policy rethink, and the top two parties retain punitive policies on refugees as a disincentive against refugees seeking to reach the country, which they see as an electorally popular stance that cannot be touched.

Rights and the COVID-19 pandemic

The most difficult human rights issues arise where the rights of some groups in the nation can only be effectively maintained and defended by taking actions that restrict some rights of another group in society. Rights clashes of this kind especially occur around free speech, which cannot be an absolute – for example, most liberal democracies ban hate speech online and in public settings. Nonetheless, the ability of Australian citizens to come together and speak out on the issues they care about has been and remains fundamental to the health of democracy. Tireless, sustained protests were needed before Aboriginal and Torres Strait Islander peoples could change discriminatory laws so that they could gain the right to vote. Similarly, LGBTIQ+ people had to campaign ceaselessly to achieve marriage equality, and it took trade unions years to secure the eight-hour workday. People power also continues to play an invaluable role in protecting forests, important wetlands and natural areas of significance.

The right to public protests has long been crucial to people and communities building the public awareness and media visibility needed to secure policy changes, and it will likely always remain so. Peaceful protest has been protected under international human rights law in Australia (United Nations, 2023a). The High Court has also ruled that Australia's Constitution protects 'freedom of political communication', because the Constitution is premised on a democratic system of government. This means that laws and government decisions which unduly restrict political communication through limiting protest rights are constitutionally invalid.

The COVID-19 pandemic from 2020 to 2022 posed a serious threat to public health, and so some temporary and proportionate restrictions on gatherings and people's movement were necessary on public health grounds (and will remain so for similar future crises). However, democracy did not stop during the pandemic, and it was vital that crisis was not used as a gateway to impose lasting restrictions on protest rights. Proportionality and reasonableness had to underpin the application of any public health restrictions, which also had to be enforced in a fair way and without the use of excessive force or violence. In several recent cases, Australian courts confirmed that protest remained central to democracy even in a pandemic and that restrictions on protest action may be unlawful if they go beyond what is strictly necessary to protect public health.

For example, in the case of *Commissioner of Police v Gray (2020)*, the organisers of a Black Lives Matter (BLM) protest in Newcastle in July 2020 asked the Supreme Court of New South Wales to authorise the protest after police refused to do so. In deciding to authorise the protest, Justice Adamson said that social media was not an adequate replacement for traditional in-person protest, commenting that 'if this were the case, Ms Gray ... would not have gone to the trouble of organising the event'. Given that the protest was to take place at a time when many other activities involving the gathering of people had been allowed, and the first BLM protest was conducted in a peaceful manner with respect paid to social distancing, the judge went on to hold that 'to deprive such groups of the opportunity to demonstrate in an authorised public assembly would inevitably lead to resentment and alienation if the public risk concerns did not warrant it'.

In assessing the lawfulness of planned protest action, courts have also considered steps taken by protesters to comply with the latest public health guidelines. For example, in *Commissioner of Police (NSW) v Gibson* [7] (*Gibson*) in 2020, the NSW Supreme Court acknowledged that a previous BLM protest on 6 June 2020 (which was authorised on appeal in *Bassi v*

Commissioner of Police (NSW) had not led to any transmissions of COVID-19, despite there being at least 10,000 people in attendance. The Court also took into account the variety of safety measures that the organisers had proposed to reduce the risk to public health, even though the judges felt that the organisers lacked mechanisms to enforce them. Ultimately, in this case, the Court of Appeal refused authorisation on public health grounds, but the arguments made highlighted the legal relevance of steps taken by organisers to ensure protests were conducted responsibly in accordance with reasonable public health guidelines. In addition, Chapters 17–24 cover the experience of state and territory government policies responding to protests, including some colourful and at times turbulent demonstrations by anti-lockdown and anti-vaccination protestors. As Commonwealth, state and territory governments across Australia emerged from strict lockdowns and lifted restrictions, they also still had a responsibility to facilitate safe and peaceful protest as an essential component of a healthy democracy.

Issues for future legislation

Australia's COVID-19 pandemic experience of using emergency powers at state and federal levels strongly suggest that a new pandemic law needs to be developed to replace the existing emergency powers scheme to ensure adequate protection of human rights in times of crisis, guided by key human rights principles of necessity, proportionality and least restriction. In time of crisis, democratic transparency, oversight and accountability also need to step up, not shut down, to build and maintain public trust. Human rights obligations suggest that any new pandemic legislation should therefore incorporate nine key safeguards:

- Parliamentary scrutiny of the government's pandemic response: Dedicated cross-party parliamentary oversight committees, across Australia and internationally, have provided much-needed scrutiny and accountability of governments' pandemic responses and their use of emergency powers. Committee processes have given business, civil society and individuals a meaningful opportunity to provide information and feedback to help inform government decision-making. A dedicated parliamentary oversight committee should be established whenever pandemic powers are enlivened.

- Independent review of all public health directions: Extraordinary powers require commensurate oversight and accountability. An independent body or panel, with human rights and public health expertise, should be empowered to independently review and publicly report on the necessity and proportionality of all public health orders made during a pandemic.

- Transparency of human rights compatibility assessments: Timely transparency around the public health and human rights justification for pandemic measures will benefit public policy and public confidence.

- Detention review rights: Any person deprived of their liberty – in a pandemic or otherwise – should be able to seek review of their detention.

- Safe protests need to be allowed: A serious health crisis may also coincide with other profoundly important national and international events, where protests are vital for representing important viewpoints. COVID-19 restrictions in Australia were in force at the height of a global wave of BLM protests on systemic racism and state violence. It should not be an offence to leave home for the purpose of a protest that is otherwise compatible with public health directions. There should be a fair and accessible process for working with authorities to facilitate pandemic-safe protest actions.

- Stronger safeguards around police powers: The granting of discretionary powers to police under emergency response laws carries acute risks for over-policed groups, such as Aboriginal and Torres Strait Islander peoples and communities of colour. There must be transparency and accountability in the exercise of police powers, including the collection, reporting and independent analysis of enforcement data and independent investigation of police complaints. Any additional powers given to police must be removed once the pandemic is over.
- Punitive enforcement measures should be a last resort: Achieving compliance with pandemic rules should focus on community engagement and collaboration, addressing information barriers and providing support to vulnerable groups. The objects of the law should reflect this.
- Reducing the risks of super-spreading events among people held behind bars: Given the health vulnerabilities of children and adults detained behind bars and the super-spreading potential of those closed environments, pandemic legislation should include a trigger that requires steps to be taken to reduce the numbers of people in prisons. For example, making bail more available and granting leave, early release or parole to people whose health is most at risk and who are of low safety risk to the community.
- Protection of individuals' data: While the collection of check-in data through QR codes and other sources have assisted public health officials to improve the efficiency and effectiveness of contact tracing to manage COVID-19 outbreaks, it has long been recognised as important that check-in and contact tracing data is used for that purpose only and is accessible by public health officials only.

In all these respects, rights critics argued that the 2020–2022 period revealed many weaknesses and vulnerabilities. The eclectic arrangements presented potential threats where micro-institutions in spheres far removed from electoral politics might nonetheless stunt democratic processes (Dunleavy, 2019). By contrast, defenders of Australia's status quo argue that – with some exceptions – existing laws worked reasonably well, and citizens' trust in government improved despite lockdowns and compulsory vaccination mandates (see Chapter 28).

Social rights

Since 2021 when it began work, most observers have commended the PJCHR for its generally robust reviews of the human rights compatibility of proposed legislation. However, it has also generally been perceived to have had limited effectiveness and influence, because its recommendations are routinely ignored. For example, the PJCHR found that a proposed 'Foreign Fighters' law, which created an effective travel ban by introducing a new offence of entering or remaining in a declared foreign area, would effectively reverse the onus of proof and threaten the right to a fair trial and the presumption of innocence. The bill was passed anyway. Many ministerial responses to the PJCHR's recommendations essentially disagreed with its views, and some repudiated the PJCHR's warnings outright, even when the bills gave the minister extraordinary powers to revoke citizenship and authorise the use of force against detained asylum seekers. Even when bills were amended after a PJCHR report, there was usually no significant executive policy change by ministers and agencies. Government policy has typically been almost 'set in stone' by the time legislation has been tabled in Parliament, because of the number of approval processes required to reach that stage. And the PJCHR's low media profile, and its relatively weak influence with parliamentarians as a whole, has meant that ministers often feel confident in simply rebutting its arguments and ignoring recommendations wherever they can do so legally.

When the bill for the creation of the PJCHR went before Parliament in 2012, the Shadow Attorney-General at the time, George Brandis QC, called it 'the most important piece of human rights legislation in a quarter of a century' (Brennan, 2016). Its purpose was to

> *deliver improved policies and laws in the future by encouraging early and ongoing consideration of human rights issues in the policy and law-making process and informing parliamentary debate on human rights issues.*[2]

However, a recent review of its impact observed: 'These goals have not yet been realised. Indeed, the major achievements of the regime are difficult to identify' (Williams and Reynolds, 2015, p.506).

Although ministers in the Liberal-National governments from 2013 to 2022 started justifying their policies through a human rights lens, there has been no evidence that this 'culture of justification', as George Williams has termed it, has led to better laws (Williams, 2016). On the contrary, Williams argued that there was evidence of delay in the PJCHR reaching its conclusions, resulting in bills being passed prior to the PJCHR's final report being issued, and hence an extraordinarily high number of rights-infringing bills making it into law. Nor has the new rights regime's impact in the public sphere been strong, with the PJCHR receiving an average of just three mentions in the media per month.

The Religious Discrimination Bill 2021

A further human rights row flared up with the Morrison government's introduction of the *Religious Discrimination Bill 2021* (Wikipedia, 2023b). The bill sought to afford religious Australians greater freedom of speech than that allowed for non-religious expressions of conscience. In a submission to the human rights committee inquiry into the religious discrimination package, the leading academic expert George Williams argued that prioritising religious speech was 'deeply problematic in a secular nation' and had 'no basis' in the international law the bill purports to implement, which 'does not separate out religious speech for protection' (Williams, 2023). The Australian Lawyers Alliance also warned that the bill could be unconstitutional because it could curtail other rights, such as the rights of gay and lesbian staff and students to work and study in religious schools, and risked overriding state laws with more limited religious exemptions to discrimination law, such as Victoria's legislation (Beck, 2024). A grouping of moderate MPs within the Liberal Party secured an amendment to the bill that removed a previous protection for religious schools in a 1984 law, which had allowed these establishments to discriminate against LGTB+ people when hiring staff. Following that change, Christian groups influential on the right wing of the Liberal Party withdrew support for the bill and it was quickly dropped by ministers. Yet controversy over religious exemptions to legislation continued into the mid-2020s (Beck, 2024).

Labour rights

Trade union membership has been in general decline in Australia since 1986. This has been an important development for Australian democracy, since historically trade unions have formed the largest civil society movement. The proportion of employees who were trade union members fell from 43 per cent to 13 per cent for men and from 35 per cent to 16 per cent for women in 2020 (ABS, 2023; see Chapter 7 for a full discussion). There are many reasons for this declining membership, reviewed in Chapter 7, but one important factor has been the enactment of legislation by Liberal-National governments seeking both to 're-balance' industrial relations towards employers and to curtail union influence in Australian politics, which has predominantly been aligned with Labor.

Under the federal *Workplace Relations Act 1996*, passed by the Howard Liberal-National government, union preference and compulsory unionism were made illegal both for employees covered by the federal government system and for those outside but within reach of other Commonwealth powers. Similar legislative changes prohibiting compulsory unionisation at workplaces were enacted by Liberal-National Coalition state governments. The decline in trade union membership generally weakened the bargaining power of trade unions, certainly in the eyes of most Australians. However, the Australian Council of Trade Unions suggested in late 2021 that Australian workers had more bargaining power post lockdowns due to the limited availability of international labour during the pandemic (Guardian, 2021). And a careful 2019 analysis suggested that low wages growth was not caused by the declining bargaining power of trade unions (Bishop and Chan, 2019; also see Chapter 7).

Conclusion: the rights deficit

The protection of human rights has perhaps been the weakest component of Australia's representative democracy. The history of the Australian nation state since federation, along with its legacy of colonialism, has been a political tradition that emphasises the centrality of a strong executive (see Chapter 1). Australia has been governed through Parliament and not by Parliament, so that as long as the federal PM can secure a majority in the legislature and maintain party discipline, executive government can potentially remain a law unto itself. Historically, attempts to challenge or dilute the authority of the executive through human rights acts or bills and charters of rights have been given short shrift.

Does this record matter? Comparative evidence suggests that once parliamentary bills or charters of rights are established on the statute books, they have tended to become more and more embedded over time in the thinking and operations of the countries involved (Hiebert and Kelly, 2015). The longer they can endure, become known and begin to achieve effects, the more difficult it becomes for their critics or opponents to abolish or replace them. The experience in Britain provides evidence in support of this observation. Successive UK Conservative governments between 2010 and 2024 promised to replace the Labour government's *Human Rights Act* with a 'British Bill of Rights'. However, the complexity of this task, plus the bedrock of support for human rights among younger age groups, intellectual opinion-formers and swathes of civil society organisations meant that multiple replacement efforts foundered. A similar (if still contested and perilous) level of *de facto* 'weak entrenchment' might be feasible in Australia also.

It is also important to note that even in countries with bills of rights, the rights of minority groups remain vulnerable in times of crisis. Moreover, effective human rights protection also requires the equitable provision of legal aid to ensure that all citizens, irrespective of their social income, are able to practise those rights. These factors have undermined key premises underpinning the causal theory of human rights reform, namely that convention rights should be protected and enforced free from governmental constraints.

Judicial decisions

Commissioner of Police v Gray [2020] NSWSC 867, [39]-[40], [66].

Notes

1. For more on Cooper, see National Museum of Australia (2022).
2. Commonwealth, Parliamentary Debates, House of Representatives, 30 September 2010, 272 (Robert McClelland).

References

ABS (Australian Bureau of Statistics) (2023) 'Trade union membership', ABS. https://perma.cc/N83W-L97C

Allen, Dominique (2010) 'Voices in the human rights dialogue: The individual victim and the Australian Human Rights Commission', *Alternative Law Journal*, vol. 35, no. 3, p.159. $ https://doi.org/10.1177/1037969X1003500306

Australian Government (2021) 'Indigenous Voice co-design final report'. https://perma.cc/4BSN-D3M9

AHRC (Australian Human Rights Commission) (1997) *Bringing Them Home: The 'Stolen Children' report*. https://humanrights.gov.au/our-work/aboriginal-and-torres-strait-islander-social-justice/publications/bringing-them-home

AHRC (Australian Human Rights Commission) (2023a) 'About', AHRC webpage. https://perma.cc/K4CU-CAVA

AHRC (Australian Human Rights Commission) (2023b) 'Human rights and counter-terrorism laws'. https://perma.cc/SB26-NUW5

Ball, Rachel (2013) 'Human rights and religion – where does the balance lie?', *Right Now* blog, 25 February. https://perma.cc/J2JU-8FR7

Beck, Luke (2024) 'Why are religious discrimination laws back in the news? And where did they come from?', *LSJonline*, blogpost 25 March. https://perma.cc/Z7QA-VDJ6

Bishop, James and Chan, Iris (2019) 'Is declining union membership contributing to low wages growth?', Research Discussion Paper 2019 to 2002, Sydney: Reserve Bank of Australia. https://perma.cc/FD4G-9R3M

Brennan, Frank (2016) 'Seven warnings for Queensland as it considers a human rights act', *Eureka Street* blog, 31 October. https://perma.cc/3EHS-W7YB

Chen, Bruce; Debeljak, Julie; and Tate, Pamela (2024) 'Report finds "clear need" for an Australian Human Rights Act. What difference would it make?' *The Conversation*, 31 May. https://theconversation.com/report-finds-clear-need-for-an-australian-human-rights-act-what-difference-would-it-make-231376

Deem, Jacob; Brown, A. J; Bird, Susan (2021) 'Most Australians support First Nations Voice to Parliament: survey', *The Conversation*, 8 April. https://theconversation.com/most-australians-support-first-nations-voice-to-parliament-survey-157964

Dunleavy, Patrick (2019) 'Micro-institutions and liberal democracy', *Political Insight*, vol. 10, no.1. https://doi.org/10.1177/2041905819838154

Freedom House (2022) *Freedom in the World: Australia*. https://perma.cc/S66C-Z8QE

Gal, Uri (2017) 'The new data retention law seriously invades our privacy – and it's time we took action', *The Conversation*, 15 June. https://perma.cc/4BAY-XNXC

Grant, Stan; and Jacobs, Jack (2022) 'The power of yindyamarra: how we can bring respect to Australian democracy', *The Conversation*, 18 October. https://perma.cc/QE7J-5ZNP

Grant, Stan and Jacobs, Jack (2023) 'First Nations' sovereignty', podcast discussion by Grant, Jacobs and O'Sullivan, accessible from https://research.csu.edu.au/engage-with-us/yindyamarra-nguluway/podcasts/voice-to-parliament; https://open.spotify.com/episode/5P5gnZ0QgoCCOUCCcpZLnc?si=Xo6QGFw1RrqKdvRQ8wftZg

Guardian (2014) 'Australia's detention regime sets out to make asylum seekers suffer, says chief immigration psychiatrist' *The Guardian, Australia*, 5 August. https://perma.cc/QE5F-72RP

Guardian (2015) 'UN accuses Australia of systematically violating torture convention', *The Guardian, Australia*, 10 March. https://perma.cc/BRE7-YJMT

Guardian (2016) 'The Nauru files', *The Guardian, Australia*, Webpage. https://perma.cc/96XU-SV45

Guardian (2017a) '"Unacceptable": UN committee damns Australia's record on human rights', *The Guardian, Australia*, 19 October. https://perma.cc/QF2M-S3JY

Guardian (2017b) 'Prisons at breaking point but Australia is still addicted to incarceration', *The Guardian, Australia*, 29 December. https://perma.cc/W9ZX-YS27

Guardian (2018a) 'Iranian asylum seeker dies by suicide on Nauru', *The Guardian, Australia*, 15 June. https://perma.cc/7GVP-MLU5

Guardian (2018b) 'Deaths in offshore detention: the faces of the people who have died in Australia's care'. *The Guardian, Australia*, 20 June. https://perma.cc/S7K8-JGCT

Guardian (2018c) 'Hamid Kehazaei: Australia responsible for "preventable" death of asylum seeker', *The Guardian, Australia*, 30 July. https://perma.cc/5K2E-S573

Guardian (2020) 'Australia's offshore detention is unlawful, says international criminal court prosecutor', *The Guardian, Australia*, 15 February. https://perma.cc/J9UW-T2SC

Guardian (2021) 'Australian workers have more bargaining power post-lockdowns, ACTU says', *The Guardian, Australia*, 10 November. https://perma.cc/RSU5-WT2G

Guardian (2023) 'Voice to parliament polling tracker: how many people support or oppose the referendum', *The Guardian, Australia*, 26 July. https://perma.cc/JX7T-UCF3

Hiebert, Janet L and Kelly, James B (2015) *Parliamentary Bills of Rights*, Cambridge: Cambridge University Press.

Human Rights Law Centre (2021) 'Morrison government rushes through new laws that allow lifetime detention of refugees', 13 May. https://perma.cc/YGP3-67Y4

Human Rights Law Centre (2023) 'Ten Years Too Long', 30 June. https://perma.cc/M8B3-XVLV

Meagher, Dan (2008) 'The democratic credentials of statutory bills of rights (and those of a self-styled majoritarian democrat)', *King's Law Journal*, vol. 19, no. 1, pp.27–55, published online 29 April 2015. https://doi.org/10.1080/09615768.2008.11427687

Napier-Raman, Kishor (2021) 'AG bureaucrats feared backlash over Coalition's Human Rights Commission pick', *The Mandarin*, 16 November. https://perma.cc/P2TW-BZXY

National Museum of Australia (2022) 'Defining: William Cooper protests', 22 September. https://perma.cc/6KMM-N8B7

Royal Commission (2017) *The Protection and Detention of Children in the Northern Territory*, Report, 17 November. https://perma.cc/R3EL-3YSW

SBS News (2021a) 'Aboriginal people keep dying in police custody. More than half are accused of a minor crime', *SBS News*, 15 April. https://perma.cc/JBG7-TWX3

SBS News (2021b) 'Australia has delivered "strikingly poor" results on a new human rights scorecard', *SBS News*, 24 June. https://perma.cc/5GZ9-3J69

Synot, Eddie (2019) 'Ken Wyatt's proposed "voice to government" marks another failure to hear Indigenous voices', *The Conversation*, 30 October. https://perma.cc/GW3X-FRP4

Uluru Statement from the Heart (2017) 'Uluru Statement from the Heart'. https://perma.cc/NMA5-9P45

United Nations (2023a) 'International Covenant on Civil and Political Rights', adopted 1996. https://perma.cc/C7KF-55M2

United Nations (2023b) 'The principle of non-refoulement under international human rights law', Report section. https://perma.cc/6RDP-L5GT

Wikipedia (2023a) 'Stolen generations'. https://perma.cc/S8LP-MBWR

Wikipedia (2023b) 'Freedom of religion in Australia'. https://perma.cc/8FWB-XZTA

Wikipedia (2023c) 'National Congress of Australia's First Peoples, webpage. https://perma.cc/NJ2P-X5AG

Williams, George (2016) 'The legal assault on Australian democracy', *QUT Law Review*, vol. 16, no.2, pp.19–41. https://doi.org/10.5204/qutlr.v16i2.651

Williams, George (2023) 'Submission letter to the AHRC', 25 March. Online document on Australia Parliament site. https://perma.cc/56WZ-J75S

Williams, George and Reynolds, Daniel (2015) 'The operation and impact of Australia's parliamentary scrutiny regime for human rights', *Monash Law Review*, vol. 41, no. 2, pp.469–507. https://perma.cc/JX3K-FMMP

3

The Constitution

Harry Hobbs

Australia's system of government embodies a mixture of elements borrowed from the constitutional traditions of the UK and the USA. From the UK, the original architects of the Constitution adopted a Westminster system of representative and responsible government, set within the framework of a constitutional monarchy. From the USA, the drafters drew on strong concepts of the separation of powers, federalism and judicial review, though notably without an equivalent bill of rights.

What does democracy require of a constitution?

- A constitution should describe and establish the institutions of government and distribute and regulate power among and between them. Typically, powers are dispersed across multiple actors and institutions. While several models exist, the power to adjudicate should be insulated from the power to make and execute the laws to protect and promote individual liberty.
- A constitution should authorise and regulate the exercise of public power. Although this means institutions and branches of government should be limited by law, a constitution should also establish an effective and efficient system of government that can meet the needs of its citizens and respond to public demands.
- A constitution should empower all citizens with the capacity to participate in the processes of government on an equal basis. Distinct institutions and processes may need to be developed to promote the capacity of marginalised groups to participate in public decision-making.
- A constitution should recognise and respect the rights of marginalised groups that may otherwise find it difficult to have their interests protected in electoral competition.
- A constitution can identify the commitments, aspirations and values of the political community. The values identified should reflect a broad consensus of the community rather than be imposed by one group over another.

How to cite this chapter:

Hobbs, Harry (2024) 'The Constitution', in: Evans, Mark; Dunleavy, Patrick and Phillimore, John (eds) *Australia's Evolving Democracy: A New Democratic Audit*, London: LSE Press, pp.70–83. **https://doi.org/10.31389/lsepress.ada.c** Licence: CC-BY-NC 4.0

◆ A constitution should be capable of change. Although amendment of the constitution should be more difficult than amending ordinary legislation, the document should not be excessively difficult to modify in light of the changing needs and values of the citizenry.

The next section briefly covers some recent developments. The chapter then summarises the key strengths, weaknesses, opportunities and threats (SWOT) surrounding Australia's constitutional setup. After this analysis, three sections consider selected issues in more detail.

Recent developments

Australia's Constitution document was drafted at a series of constitutional conventions in the 1890s, using a process of drafting and ratification that was remarkably democratic for its time (Hirst, 2000; Irving, 1999). The resulting outcome has proven a durable document. Any proposed amendment to the Constitution must be approved by both houses of Parliament (or by one house of Parliament twice after a period of three months) and then submitted to the people of Australia in a referendum. It will only succeed if it obtains a majority of votes across Australia as a whole, plus a majority of votes in a majority of the states. The process is challenging. Some studies suggest Australia's Constitution is one of the most difficult to amend in the world (Hobbs and Trotter, 2017, p.59). Although 45 attempts at amendment have been made since 1901, the Constitution has been altered only eight times, and no amendments have been made since 1977.

The Australian Constitution established a federal system of government. In drawing on the USA model, the drafters sought to adopt a decentralised federation, whereby the states would retain significant responsibilities. In the years following federation, however, political authority in Australia has become increasingly centralised (Fenna, 2019). Two factors are often attributed to this trend: the open-textured nature of Commonwealth legislative power and the Commonwealth's fiscal dominance.

The growing strength of the federal government led to frequent claims that the states are obsolete and should be abolished (see, for example, Bob Hawke, quoted in Remeikis, 2016). The COVID-19 pandemic challenged this narrative, revealing the continuing vitality and political authority of the states (Browne, 2021). The pandemic did not change the text of the Constitution, but it strengthened the role of the states and led to a revamp of intergovernmental architecture (see Chapter 16). In part, the states' recent prominence owes much to the Commonwealth's initial reluctance to lead. The forceful intervention of state premiers was crucial to the Scott Morrison government introducing the JobKeeper and JobSeeker economic stimulus payments, while the initially disastrous COVID-19 vaccine rollout forced the states to maintain and extend extraordinary public health regulations. Nevertheless, the primary reason for the importance of the states in Australia's response to the pandemic is the allocation of legislative authority under the Constitution. Exercising their primary responsibility for health, education and law and order, the states managed the compulsory hotel quarantine process, imposed hard border closures and lockdowns to prevent the spread of the virus and administered the delivery of vaccines to residents.

These and other public health measures caused considerable tension. In 2020, businessman and former politician Clive Palmer challenged the Western Australia border ban under its COVID-19 policies, alleging that the law facilitating the closure violated the Constitution.

Section 92 of the Constitution provides that the movement of people among the states shall be 'absolutely free'. In *Palmer v Western Australia* 2021, the High Court dismissed Palmer's challenge, holding unanimously that the closure was valid because it was justified by the legitimate end of protecting the health of the community (2021 HCA [5]).

Recognising the need for a coordinated and flexible response to the COVID-19 pandemic, the prime minister (PM), state premiers and territory chief ministers created the National Cabinet in March 2020. In May that year, Morrison announced that the National Cabinet would replace the Council of Australian Governments (COAG). The National Cabinet met frequently and proved successful in providing a forum for governments to discuss and coordinate action across the federation. However, concerns around transparency have been raised (Saunders, 2020). Formally, it is a subcommittee of the federal Cabinet, and so the Commonwealth government asserted that Cabinet confidentiality applied to it. This makes little sense, as the National Cabinet is an intergovernmental forum composed of the leaders of nine separate governments accountable to nine separate parliaments. In August 2021, Senator Rex Patrick successfully challenged the assertion of Cabinet confidentiality (*Patrick v Secretary, Department of Prime Minister and Cabinet* 2021). The Commonwealth introduced legislation to overturn the ruling, but the bill lapsed at the dissolution of Parliament in April 2022. The new Labor federal government elected in 2022 continued the National Cabinet and maintained the fiction that its deliberations were protected by Cabinet confidentiality. By mid-2023, all but one state PM was Labor, but tensions around intergovernmental relations under the new body remain (see Chapter 16). The COVID-19 pandemic revealed the flexibility of Australia's governance arrangements.

Yet not everything is so malleable. The low success rate of efforts to change Australia's Constitution may have implications for the democratic authority of the Constitution document. One view is that the Constitution, like any law, derives authority from the ability of its subjects to reform it through legitimate means. To the extent that the Constitution may be perceived as unduly difficult to modify, that legitimacy is undermined (Hobbs and Trotter, 2017). In the past decades constitutional amendments – all of which have failed or not proceeded – have been proposed on the constitutional status of Aboriginal and Torres Strait Islander peoples, instituting human rights protections and replacing the monarch as head of state with a president (which would also mean 'repatriating' the Constitution by removing any reference to UK institutions). Most recently, the Labor government in March 2023 proposed a referendum on formally establishing a Voice for Aboriginal and Torres Strait Islander peoples that would be empowered to make representations to the Parliament and executive government, with a question phrased as follows: 'A Proposed Law: To alter the Constitution to recognise the First Peoples of Australia by establishing an Aboriginal and Torres Strait Islander Voice. Do you approve this proposed alteration?' Initial hopes for bipartisanship between the major parties on the proposal subsequently eroded, and the proposal was decisively rejected by voters in October 2023 (see Chapter 4). The pre-history of the Voice effort is also covered in this chapter.

Strengths, weaknesses, opportunities and threats (SWOT) analysis

Current strengths	Current weaknesses
The Australian Constitution has set the foundations for a stable and secure liberal democracy that has endured for over 120 years. This is a significant achievement, given that comparative studies show that, on average, constitutions last for around 17 years (Elkins, Ginsburg and Melton, 2009).	The absence of comprehensive human rights protections leaves many marginalised Australians vulnerable to legislative or executive action. Australia is the only democratic country in the world that does not have a constitutional or statutory bill of rights. In fact, the Australian Constitution still expressly empowers Parliament to pass laws that discriminate on the basis of race.
Australia's federal system of government enhances democratic participation by allowing citizens to engage with government more regionally and directly, as well as nationally. This arrangement is particularly valued in a country that (almost uniquely in the world) stretches across a whole continent.	The Australian Constitution no longer formally discriminates against Aboriginal and Torres Strait Islander peoples, but neither does it empower them with the capacity to have their unique interests and distinct voices heard in the processes of government. This democratic deficit challenges the capacity of First Nations peoples to participate. An initiative to create a Voice formally linked to Parliament for First Nations Australians was rejected in a national referendum in 2023.
Australia's relative success in dealing with the initial wave of the COVID-19 pandemic demonstrates that the country's flexible intergovernmental arrangements facilitate cooperation and coordination and are generally fit for purpose.	Australia's poor record of constitutional amendment has inhibited attempts to reform the instrument to bring it in line with the contemporary needs and values of its citizens. No formal change has been made since 1977, despite significant political, cultural and social changes within the Australian community.
Past efforts have been made to simplify some of the complex lines of accountability for public policy by transferring functions between the states and the federal government (with finance attached). Although proposals for large movements have failed to work, some small-scale adjustments have been made.	While federalism offers considerable advantages for Australia, the precise relationship between the federal government and the states causes complications. In particular, vertical fiscal imbalance clouds lines of accountability and responsibility (see Chapter 16).
Australian democracy is relatively stable. The balance provided by the existing constitutional set-up is credited by many observers with explaining the generally small scale of populist movements in Australia, and the absence of other changes that have potentially adverse implications for liberal democracy.	Australians appear to have little knowledge of their own Constitution. While survey data is dated, reports from the 1990s suggest that many Australians are unaware of the basic structure and institutions established under the Constitution.

Future opportunities	Future threats
By their nature, constitutions are designed to change slowly, especially written ones. Australia's arrangements combine both the secure foundations of a written constitution and a measure of the flexibility inherent in Westminster system arrangements.	As mentioned, the Australian Constitution has only been amended eight times since 1901 and has not been changed since 1977. There have been significant changes to Australian society since this date, but the Constitution itself has failed to keep up to date. This will continue to cause problems into the future.
The COVID-19 pandemic demonstrated the efficacy and accountability of federalism and Australia's intergovernmental architecture (see Chapter 16). This helped create a public mood more supportive of seeking consensus solutions, which lasted to the 2022 federal election and beyond.	Once the 'group jeopardy' posed by the initial stages of COVID-19 had passed, the National Cabinet's longer-term pattern of operations remained unclear. The Albanese government elected in 2022 has continued the system, albeit in a somewhat more consensual style, while some aspects remain in flux.
The rejection of the referendum proposal on constitutional recognition of First Nations peoples (and/or a republic) has provided an opportunity for a broader stocktake of the health of Australia's Constitution (see Chapter 4). This could be assessed via a new standing body that reports every 10 years on reform options.	The poor record of constitutional amendment is self-fulfilling. Parliamentarians have been unwilling to consider holding either a First Nations peoples or a republic referendum unless assured of the proposal's success in advance. This makes future reform harder to achieve. The Albanese government's 2023 proposal took a risk in an attempt to break this mould. However, it failed, despite being a very modest measure.

There are three dimensions of the Constitution that have occasioned a great deal of debate and where the issues involved are worth considering in detail. These are human rights and the role of the High Court, the position of First Nations peoples and issues around the country's continued links to the UK monarchy or possible transition to a republic.

Human rights protections and the High Court

Human rights protection is limited under the Australian Constitution. While the drafters borrowed heavily from the USA, they chose not to include comprehensive protections. Rather than a judicially enforced bill of rights, the drafters considered that 'the common law and political processes' (Williams and Hume, 2013, p.67) would prove the best guardian of individual liberty. As a result, the Constitution expressly protects only five individual rights:

- Section 41 guarantees the right to vote in federal elections to all persons who are enfranchised at the state level.
- Section 51(xxxi) provides that the Commonwealth government may acquire property on just terms only.
- Section 80 guarantees a right to trial by jury on all indictable offences.
- Section 116 provides for freedom of religion.
- Section 117 prohibits discrimination on the basis of state residency.

The list is small, but judicial interpretation has further narrowed the protection provided. For example, in *R v Pearson; Ex parte Sipka* the High Court held in 1983 that section 41 protected the voting rights of persons enfranchised prior to the adoption of the *Franchise Act 1902* and no longer has any effect. Similarly, although section 80 guarantees the right to jury trial for indictable offences, the High Court has maintained that Parliament can determine whether an offence is indictable or not, essentially allowing Parliament to bypass the protection (*Kingswell v The Queen* 1985). Finally, the High Court's formalistic reading of section 116 has meant that no law has ever been found to breach the protection of religious freedom (Beck, 2018).

Faith in Parliament was a key factor for the absence of a comprehensive bill of rights. Chief Justice Mason, for instance, has explained that this sentiment was 'one of the unexpressed assumptions on which the Constitution was drafted' (*Australian Capital Television v Commonwealth* 1992, p.136). This is true, but the absence of rights guarantees also reflects the racist attitudes of the day. As George Williams and David Hume have argued, the 'prevailing sentiment' that Chief Justice Mason identified 'was not [solely] due to a belief that rights across the whole community were generally well protected', but rather was 'driven by a desire to maintain race-based distinctions' (Williams and Hume, 2013, p.52). The drafters specifically empowered Parliament with plenary legislative authority to make laws that discriminate on the basis of 'race' and were careful to ensure that any legal constraints on this power were avoided.

Over the years, the absence of individual rights protections has prompted widespread calls for change. However, referendums to amend the Constitution to recognise certain human rights failed in both 1944 and 1988 and no legislated charter of rights has been enacted at the Commonwealth level. Nevertheless, three subnational jurisdictions – the Australian Capital Territory (ACT), Victoria and Queensland – have each enacted a statutory human rights act. Others may follow.

The Constitution contains few express protections, but the High Court has uncovered several rights implied by the text and structure of the instrument. For example, drawing on provisions that mandate that the legislative and executive branches of government are 'ultimately answerable to the Australian people' (*Nationwide News v Wills* 1992, p.47), the Court has held that the Constitution implicitly protects freedom of political communication as 'indispensable to that accountability' (*Australian Capital Television v Commonwealth* 1992, p.138). While the act of casting a ballot is the principal moment at which an elector holds their representative accountable, the Court has employed a broader notion of democratic accountability, declaring that the implied right operates across the electoral process and on all political matters (*Brown v Tasmania* 2017).

The High Court's capacity to ameliorate the absence of statutory or constitutional human rights protection through judicial creativity is significant but limited. In this case, the implied freedom of political communication is not strictly speaking a right, but rather an immunity from legislative and government action, meaning that legislation that infringes the implied freedom will be struck down. This can still promote democratic outcomes. In 2015, the Court upheld a law that imposed caps on political donations and banned property developers from making donations. Although holding that the law burdened the implied freedom, the High Court explained that the effect of the law was to promote rather than limit political communication. As Justice Gordon explained, the law ensures 'that *each* individual has an *equal* share, or at least a more equal share than they would otherwise have, in political power' (*McCloy v New South Wales* 2015, p.285).

The implied freedom enhances democratic values but the High Court's role in uncovering an implicit constitutional protection has attracted criticism. Judicial creativity is central to the common law, but constitutional reform should ideally be developed through the referendum procedure in section 128 rather than the judiciary. This ensures constitutional change has broad popular support across the community. It is also more comprehensive, as informal constitutional amendment is not available in all cases.

The position of First Nations peoples

The drafters noticeably did not draw on the law and governance traditions of the First Nations communities that had occupied and cared for the continent for some 60,000 years. While in several colonies Aboriginal and Torres Strait Islander peoples could vote for delegates to constitutional conventions, participation was not encouraged. In any event, no First Nations delegates attended the conventions, and their interests and aspirations were not considered in debate. The Constitution that was drafted simply ignored hundreds of existing Indigenous governing orders, blanketing multiple complex normative systems in a single legal framework that denied the reality and continuing vitality of those self-governing communities.

References to First Nations peoples in the final instrument were exclusionary. Three provisions stand out. Section 25 contemplated the disqualification of persons from voting on the basis of their race, section 51(xxvi) left responsibility for Indigenous affairs entirely in the hands of the states, while section 127 excluded 'Aboriginal natives' from the population count for the determination of electoral representation. Although it is not accurate to state that racial prejudice alone lay behind the drafting of each section, in combination these provisions contributed to symbolically, if not practically, exclude Aboriginal and Torres Strait Islander peoples from the new Australian nation (Arcioni, 2012).

Aboriginal and Torres Strait Islander peoples have long advocated for reform to the Australian Constitution to recognise their unique status and rights. In 1937, for instance, Yorta Yorta man William Cooper, Secretary of the Aboriginal Advancement League, gathered 1,814 signatures for a petition to King George V, calling for Indigenous representation in the federal Parliament. The petition was passed to PM Joseph Lyons, but Cabinet refused to forward it to the King (by then George VI). While racial prejudice undoubtedly contributed to Cabinet's decision, the federal government also pointed to section 51(xxvi) to note that it had no legislative authority in the field of Indigenous affairs (except for in the Commonwealth Territories). This changed in 1967. That year, a constitutional referendum repealed section 127 and amended section 51(xxvi) to provide the Commonwealth Parliament with a concurrent power to legislate with respect to Indigenous affairs. This was a momentous change that has facilitated significant beneficial legislation to protect and promote the rights of Aboriginal and Torres Strait Islander peoples, but the amendment fell far short of providing substantive equality and of meeting the aspirations of First Nations peoples (Hobbs, 2021).

The limits of the referendum were laid bare in a 1997 High Court decision. In *Kartinyeri v Commonwealth* 1998, the Court was asked whether section 51(xxvi) required the Parliament to enact laws for the benefit of Aboriginal and Torres Strait Islander peoples. Although the Court did not reach a definitive conclusion, the effect of the Court's decision is that the race power permits the federal Parliament to enact laws that impose a disadvantage on Aboriginal and

Torres Strait Islander peoples. This power has only ever been used in relation to Aboriginal and Torres Strait Islander peoples. The decision in *Kartinyeri* focused renewed attention on the need for substantive structural reform to the Australian Constitution to protect and promote the interests of First Nations peoples.

The 1967 amendments also had the effect of entirely removing any reference to Aboriginal and Torres Strait Islander peoples from the Constitution. This textual absence motivates a distinct project of symbolic, rather than substantive, constitutional reform. As then PM Tony Abbott explained, this project seeks constitutional recognition to 'complete our Constitution rather than change it' (ABC News, 2014). In 1999, a proposal that responded to the symbolic project of constitutional reform by proposing the insertion of a preamble 'honouring Aborigines and Torres Strait Islanders' but otherwise not making any structural amendments, was soundly defeated in a referendum. Nevertheless, calls for both symbolic and structural constitutional reform have increased over the last decade.

As Aboriginal and Torres Strait Islander peoples have highlighted, formal equality under the Australian Constitution fails to empower the unique voices and interests of First Nations peoples and communities in the processes of government. Australia's system of governance is 'built upon confidence in a system of parliamentary' representation (*McKinlay v Commonwealth* 1975, p.24), but the absence of comprehensive rights protection, together with the non-recognition of their distinctive status, leaves First Nations peoples vulnerable to the 'wavering sympathies of the Australian community' (Behrendt, 2003, p.8). Over the last decade, this vulnerability has motivated sustained focus on whether and how the Australian Constitution could be changed.

Contemporary debate on constitutional recognition commenced in 2007. In the lead-up to the federal election, PM John Howard revived the idea of a preambular statement of recognition that would be inserted in the Constitution. Howard was defeated at the 2007 election by Kevin Rudd, but the concept persisted. Constitutional recognition was raised by several groups at Rudd's 2020 Summit, though the government committed only to 'considering further' the idea of constitutional change (Commonwealth of Australia, 2009, p.187). As such, it was not until 2010, as part of PM Julia Gillard's negotiations to form a minority government, that the first major public process focusing exclusively on this issue commenced. Between 2010 and 2015, three public inquiries were conducted. These processes were the 2012 Expert Panel on Constitutional Recognition of Indigenous Australians, the 2014 Aboriginal and Torres Strait Islander Peoples Act of Recognition Review Panel and the 2015 Joint Select Committee on Constitutional Recognition of Aboriginal and Torres Strait Islander Peoples.

The final reports of these parliamentary and expert inquiries recommended a similar suite of constitutional reforms. However, they were beset by two major challenges. First, although the aspirations and views of First Nations peoples were given significant weight in these processes, this was only one element to consider in finalising a report that could obtain broad public support across the entire Australian community. For this reason, several potentially contentious proposals, such as sovereignty and treaty-making, were not included as part of the final package. Cobble Cobble woman and professor of law Megan Davis, a member of the Expert Panel, later revealed that 'resentment' over this decision percolated throughout the Indigenous community (Davis, 2017, p.136). Compounding frustrations further, no Commonwealth government ever publicly committed to a set of proposed reforms.

The reluctance of successive governments to engage meaningfully with the recommendations proposed by their own inquiries was an ongoing cause of concern for many Aboriginal and Torres Strait Islander peoples. So too was the fact that these processes seemed to foreclose discussion on matters of importance to Indigenous communities. As Aboriginal and Torres Strait Islander peoples consistently explained, the form of recognition eventually adopted must be suitable to those intended to be 'recognised'. A simpler and more appropriate process would engage first with Indigenous communities to ascertain their views on what 'constitutional recognition' means. The persistence and advocacy of Aboriginal and Torres Strait Islander leaders eventually forced the government's hand. In December 2015, PM Malcolm Turnbull established a Referendum Council that would specifically consult with Indigenous communities.

The Referendum Council held 12 dialogues across every state and territory. Meetings were capped at 100 participants to promote discussion. Attendance was by invitation, with the organisers seeking an inclusive mix of Traditional Owner groups, community organisations and key individuals in the region. A balance was sought between genders and across age groups, while Stolen Generations were also represented. The dialogues were conducted as a deliberative forum. Each took place over three days and included opportunities for large- and small-group discussions. The Referendum Council assisted delegates by providing information on the Constitution and the history of constitutional reform. This allowed delegates to discuss and assess different reform options in an informed manner, and to explain what recognition would mean for their communities. At the end of the three days, delegates confirmed a statement of their discussion and selected 10 representatives for a final convention at Uluru.

At Uluru, delegates issued the Uluru Statement from the Heart. Grounded in the delegates' inherent rights as the 'first sovereign Nations of the Australian continent', the Uluru Statement outlines three proposals to empower Indigenous peoples so that they can take 'a rightful place in our own country' (Uluru Statement from the Heart, 2017). Characterised as 'Voice, Treaty, Truth', the delegates called for a First Nations Voice to be put in the Constitution, with the power to advise the Australian Parliament on laws that affect Indigenous peoples, and a Makarrata Commission to oversee a process of treaty-making and truth-telling. The Uluru Statement was not unanimous. Seven delegates walked out in protest the day before the Uluru Statement was issued. Nonetheless, it reflects a formidable consensus among First Nations peoples, reached through a process of deliberation unmatched in Australian history.

It took five months for the Commonwealth government to officially respond to the Uluru Statement. When the government finally did respond, it rejected the Uluru Statement in its entirety, though its primary focus was on the First Nations Voice. In a press release, PM Malcolm Turnbull explained that the government 'does not believe such an addition to our national representative institutions is either desirable or capable of winning acceptance in a referendum'. He asserted further that the Voice was a 'radical change' that would undermine the 'fundamental principle' of 'all Australian citizens having equal civic rights' (Prime Minister, Attorney-General and Minister for Indigenous Affairs, 2017). However, this statement is not true. The First Nations Voice would have been advisory. It would not have had the capacity to veto, delay or vote on proposed legislation. A First Nations Voice would not have undermined equality but would have rectified a persistent democratic fault in Australian society. Although First Nations peoples have enjoyed equality in the electoral arena, their position as a demographic minority has made it difficult for them to be heard by government. A constitutionally enshrined First Nations Voice would have empowered First Nations peoples with the capacity to actively participate 'in the democratic life of the state' (Davis, 2017, p.131).

The government may have been eager to move away from the Voice. Given its origins in the deliberative process that led to the Uluru Statement from the Heart, however, it became clear that the Voice remained the only viable option for constitutional reform. This fact was recognised by another parliamentary committee in 2018 (Joint Select Committee, 2018, p.2). Initial public support for the Voice placed more pressure on government to reassess its approach. Replicating its roots in community deliberation, proponents of the Uluru Statement travelled widely across the country to educate the Australian public and build support for its recommendations. This strategy appeared to have been successful; a survey of poll data since 2017 conducted by the Centre for Aboriginal Economic Policy Research suggested that 70–75 per cent of voters with a committed position supported the Voice (Markham and Sanders, 2020, p.20).

The Commonwealth government under PM Morrison refused to engage fully with the Uluru Statement, but it did subtly reframe its position. Following his surprise re-election in 2019, Morrison initially called for 'more detail' to be provided on how the Voice could operate, but later forcefully ruled out holding a referendum on the body (Hobbs, 2020, p.631). Instead, the government sought to separate the idea of a First Nations Voice from its legal form. In late 2019 it established a National Co-Design Group, tasked with developing models for an Indigenous voice to government (not Parliament). The terms of reference specifically stated that constitutional change was 'out of scope' (NIAA, 2019, p.3). The Co-Design process nonetheless recommended that the government reconsider its position.

It took a federal election for that reconsideration to take place. In May 2022, the Labor Party formed a government. In his victory speech on election night, incoming PM Anthony Albanese affirmed that his government would hold a referendum to put a First Nations Voice in the Australian Constitution (Morse, 2022). Following on, the government moved slowly and deliberately. In July 2022, on the lands of the Yolngu nation at the Garma Festival, PM Albanese offered a starting point for discussion on the wording of the proposal. In September 2022, it set up two working groups to facilitate the involvement of Indigenous leaders in developing the referendum arrangements. These included the wording of the question (announced in March 2023), the timing of the poll and how to build community understanding, awareness and support for the referendum. In June 2023, following the release of a parliamentary committee report, the final wording of the proposed amendment was agreed:

> *In recognition of Aboriginal and Torres Strait Islander peoples as the First Peoples of Australia:*
>
> 1. *There shall be a body, to be called the Aboriginal and Torres Strait Islander Voice.*
>
> 2. *The Aboriginal and Torres Strait Islander Voice may make representations to the Parliament and the Executive Government of the Commonwealth on matters relating to Aboriginal and Torres Strait Islander peoples.*
>
> 3. *The Parliament shall, subject to this Constitution, have power to make laws with respect to matters relating to the Aboriginal and Torres Strait Islander Voice, including its composition, functions, powers and procedures.* (Reconciliation Australia, 2023)

A referendum was held in October 2023, but was decisively defeated (see Chapter 4).

Formal constitutional amendment is important, but it will not conclusively resolve issues arising from invasion and colonisation. The status and place of Aboriginal and Torres Strait Islander peoples within the Australian nation will continue to be the subject of debate. A recent High Court decision highlights this fact and places more pressure on Parliament and the government to engage meaningfully with First Nations peoples. In 2020, in *Love v Commonwealth; Thoms v Commonwealth*, the High Court was asked whether two First Nations people who were not citizens of Australia could be deported under the *Migration Act 1958 (Cth)* as 'aliens'. A four-member majority held that First Nations Australians, understood according to the test in *Mabo v Queensland (No 2)* 2020, 'are not within the reach of the "aliens" power' in the Constitution (2020: [81]). First Nations Australians therefore cannot be deported even if they are not citizens of Australia.

The decision caused immediate controversy, but it highlights the ongoing need to seriously engage with First Nations peoples and recognise their relationship to the Australian state. Two of the judges in the minority noted this in their dissent. Justices Gageler and Keane both expressly recognised that the plaintiffs' arguments were 'morally and emotionally engaging' and acknowledged that 'a strong moral case' (2020: [128] (Gageler J)) could be made for 'special recognition of Aboriginal people in the *Constitution*' (2020: [178] (Keane J)). In their Honours' view, these issues must 'be addressed by the Commonwealth Parliament in the outworking of those political processes' (2020: [130] (Gageler J)).

An Australian republic?

Australia is a constitutional monarchy whose head of state is King Charles III. Although the King also serves as head of state of the UK, along with several other Commonwealth countries, his role as head of state of Australia is separate. As a constitutional monarchy, the powers of the sovereign are limited by law and convention and exercised only on the advice of the elected government. The Constitution provides that the powers of the monarch have been delegated to the Governor-General, the King's representative in Australia. As such, the functions of the head of state are performed by Governor-General David Hurley.

Republicanism grew in prominence in the second half of the 20th century as sociocultural and legal changes helped to develop an independent sense of Australian nationhood. Some proponents argued that placing a hereditary monarch as Australia's head of state conflicted with Australian values, such as democracy and egalitarianism. Others wondered whether a British monarch could ever accurately represent Australia to the rest of the world (Jones, 2018). Drawing on this upsurge, in the early 1990s the Australian Labor Party endorsed a republic as its official policy and PM Paul Keating promised a constitutional referendum on the establishment of a republic. Despite polls suggesting a majority supported a republic, in 1999 Australians overwhelmingly rejected the proposed change. Several theories have been offered to explain this result, including division among its supporters over the model adopted.

The republican movement has struggled to attract attention following this defeat. Although successive polls have found that a slim majority of federal parliamentarians are in favour of a republic, no government has sought to expend political capital on the issue. Without effective leadership, support among ordinary Australians continues to slip. In January 2021, an online Ipsos poll found that only 34 per cent of Australians thought Australia should become a republic (Topsfield, 2021). The late-2023 defeat of the Voice referendum also damaged the prospects of any similar vote on the republic (Karp, 2023).

Two events may signal a shift:

- In May 2022, the Labor Party was victorious in the federal election. The new PM, Anthony Albanese, has long been a strong supporter of an Australian republic. In June 2022, Albanese appointed the country's first Assistant Minister for the Republic, demonstrating that it is on the government's radar.
- In view of the affection that many Australians held for Queen Elizabeth II, proponents of the Australian republic movement were resigned to wait until the end of her reign. The ascension of King Charles III, upon the death of his mother in September 2022, prompted renewed speculation and enthusiasm among republicans.

Several issues will need to be resolved before another referendum is held. These include technical questions relating to the model adopted, but also encompass broader foundational tensions. The most significant of these is Australia's relationship with First Nations peoples and communities. As Aboriginal and Torres Strait Islander peoples have long explained, 'a narrow debate over whether we should have an Australian or British head of state will not satisfy our expectations for change' (Gatjil Djerrkura, 1999, cited in Arvanitakis, 2011 and in McKenna, 2004, p.47). The question all proponents of a republic must ask is: 'What kind of republic do we want, a reconciled republic or a republic that repeats the injustices, errors and omissions of the constitutional monarchy?' (Gatjil Djerrkura, cited in Davis, 2018). An Australian republic will have to engage in the broader project of constitutional recognition of First Nations peoples. Following his election, PM Albanese confirmed that any move towards a republic would come after a referendum on a First Nations Voice. And following the Voice failure, Labor is likely to be wary of another referendum.

Conclusion

Constitutional issues and debates always matter for the quality of Australian democracy, but primarily in a background way. At times, one of the major two parties has had a consistent winning streak at the federal level, and sometimes its leaders seem to 'push the boundaries' of constitutional provisions and conventions (Forsey, 1984; Killey, 2014), limiting their use. Then their political opponents may voice fears that the constitutional set-up itself is proving unfair in preserving the political impartiality of the state, or unsafe in protecting the rights of particular groups in society. However, the Constitution is relatively complex and provides multiple balancing mechanisms – for instance, in general oppositions federally control some state governments (sometimes most of them). Majorities in the House of Representatives are often partly offset by a different balance of representation in the Senate. And the High Court has generally reined in abuses of ministerial power that raise democratic concerns. A longer-term concern may be that constitutional complexity and fixedness may in itself store up problems for a rapidly growing liberal democracy.

Judicial decisions

Australian Capital Television v Commonwealth. 1992. 177 CLR 106

Brown v Tasmania. 2017. 261 CLR 328

Kartinyeri v Commonwealth. 1998. 195 CLR 337

Kingswell v The Queen 1985. 159 CLR 264

Love v Commonwealth; Thoms v Commonwealth. 2020. 94 ALJR 1988

Mabo v Queensland (No 2) [1992] HCA 23, (1992) 175 CLR 1

McCloy v New South Wales. 2015. 257 CLR 178

McKinlay v Commonwealth. 1975. 135 CLR 1

Nationwide News v Wills. 1992. 177 CLR 1

Palmer v Western Australia. 2021. HCA [5]

Patrick v Secretary, Department of Prime Minister and Cabinet (2021) AAT 2020/5875

R v Pearson; Ex parte Sipka. 1983. 152 CLR 254

References

ABC News (2014) 'PM Tony Abbott to Start "Conversation" on Indigenous Recognition in 2014', *ABC News*, 1 January. https://perma.cc/4RWM-BWF3

Arcioni, Elisa (2012) 'Excluding Indigenous Australians from "The People": A Reconsideration of s 25 and 127 of the Constitution', *Federal Law Review*, vol. 40, no. 3, pp.287–315. https://perma.cc/X2ZZ-5UVL

Arvanitakis, James (2011) 'Is Crown Land Indigenous Land?', Institute for Culture and Society blog, 25 March. https://perma.cc/9Y8B-84NR

Beck, Luke (2018) *Religious Freedom and the Australian Constitution*, Abingdon: Routledge. $ https://perma.cc/8BSF-WHUZ

Behrendt, Larissa (2003) *Achieving Social Justice: Indigenous Rights and Australia's Future*, Annandale: Federation Press. $ https://perma.cc/8BSF-WHUZ

Browne, Bill (2021) 'State Revival: The Role of the States in Australia's COVID-19 Response and Beyond', The Australia Institute, Discussion Paper. https://perma.cc/6YAP-2X24 https://perma.cc/6YAP-2X24

Commonwealth of Australia (2009) *Responding to the Australia 2020 Summit*, Canberra: Australian Government Printing Service. https://perma.cc/W9C9-FZTL

Davis, Megan (2017) 'Self-Determination and the Right to be Heard' in Morris, Shireen (ed) *A Rightful Place: A Road Map to Recognition*, pp. 119–46. Carlton: Melbourne University Press.

Davis, Megan (2018) 'The Republic Is an Aboriginal Issue', *The Monthly*, April. https://perma.cc/6NYR-DNBA

Elkins, Zachary; Ginsberg, Tom; and Melton, James (2009) *The Endurance of National Constitutions*, London: Cambridge University Press. $ https://doi.org/10.1017/CBO9780511817595

Fenna, Alan (2019) 'The Centralization of Australian Federalism 1901 to 2010: Measurement and Interpretation', *Publius: The Journal of Federalism,* vol. 49, no. 1, pp.30–56. https://doi.org/10.1093/publius/pjy042

Forsey, Eugene (1984) 'The Courts and the Conventions of the Constitution', *University of New Brunswick Law Journal,* vol. 33, pp.11–42. https://perma.cc/EX8J-KRKA

Hirst, John (2000) *The Sentimental Nation*, Sydney: Oxford University Press.

Hobbs, Harry (2020) 'The Road to Uluru: Constitutional Recognition and the UN Declaration on the Rights of Indigenous Peoples', *Australian Journal of Politics and History,* vol. 66, no. 4, pp.613–32. $ https://doi.org/10.1111/ajph.12707

Hobbs, Harry (2021) *Indigenous Aspirations and Structural Reform in Australia*, London: Hart Publishing. $ https://perma.cc/38FJ-PQHC

Hobbs, Harry and Trotter, Andrew (2017) 'The Constitutional Conventions and Constitutional Change: Making Sense of Multiple Intentions', *Adelaide Law Review,* vol. 38, pp.49–84. https://perma.cc/E348-7RHW

Irving, Helen (1999) *To Constitute a Nation,* Sydney: Cambridge University Press.

Joint Select Committee on Constitutional Recognition relating to Aboriginal and Torres Strait Islander Peoples (2018) *Final Report*, Canberra: Australian Government Printing Service. https://perma.cc/YRR4-7BK4

Jones, Benjamin (2018) *This Time: Australia's Republican Past and Future*, Melbourne: Redback.

Karp, Paul (2023) 'Can Republicans Rally after Australia's Resounding No to Constitutional Reform on the Voice?', *The Guardian*, 22 October. https://perma.cc/59EF-AL89

Killey, Ian (2014) *Constitutional Conventions in Australia: An Introduction to the Unwritten Rules of Australia's Constitutions*, London: Anthem Press. $ https://perma.cc/SQ2V-58WW

Markham, Francis and Sanders, Will (2020) *Support for a Constitutionally Enshrined First Nations Voice to Parliament: Evidence from Opinion Research since 2017*, Centre for Aboriginal Economic Policy Research, Working Paper No. 138/2020. https://perma.cc/NU69-K5TV

McKenna, Mark (2004) *This Country: A Reconciled Republic?* Sydney: UNSW Press.

Morse, Dana (2022) 'Anthony Albanese Promised Action on the Uluru Statement from the Heart. So What is the Proposed Indigenous Voice to Parliament?', ABC News, 24 May. https://perma.cc/R2BX-2DR4

NIAA (National Indigenous Australians Agency) (2019) 'Terms of Reference National Co-Design Group'. https://perma.cc/4B9W-M24J

Prime Minister, Attorney-General, Minister for Indigenous Affairs (2017) 'Response to the Referendum Council's Report on Constitutional Recognition', Media Release, 26 October. https://perma.cc/96FM-KAAU

Reconciliation Australia (2023) 'Voice to Parliament', online webpage. https://perma.cc/R2M7-Q9L7

Remeikis, Amy (2016) 'Bob Hawke Says Abolish State Governments and Think Big to Fix the Nation'. *The Sydney Morning Herald*, 28 December. https://perma.cc/H7T8-TWUH

Saunders, Cheryl (2020) 'A New Federalism? The Role and Future of the National Cabinet', University of Melbourne School of Government, Policy Brief No. 2. https://perma.cc/JVA2-TRGT

Topsfield, Jewel (2021) '"No Sense of Momentum": Poll Finds Drop in Support for Australia Becoming a Republic', *Sydney Morning Herald*, 25 January. https://perma.cc/JC43-9F7J

Uluru Statement from the Heart (2017) 'Uluru Statement from the Heart', 26 May. https://perma.cc/3EXV-C52A

Williams, George and Hume, David (2013) *Human Rights Under the Australian Constitution* (2nd ed.), Sydney: Oxford University Press. $ https://global.oup.com/academic/product/human-rights-under-the-australian-constitution-9780195523119?cc=us&lang=en&#

4

The 2023 Voice to Parliament referendum

Mark Evans and Michelle Grattan

In October 2023, the Labor government called a nationwide referendum on its Voice to Parliament proposal. This continued a longstanding effort to pursue reconciliation with First Nations peoples at the federal level by establishing a special representative chamber, called the Voice to Parliament, that would be consulted on legislation and other matters. The proposal needed to secure majority support in at least four of the six states and be endorsed by a majority of voters nationally. After a vigorous campaign, however, the Voice vote resulted in the proposal's convincing rejection by a margin of 60 per cent to 40 per cent nationally, with majorities against it in every state and territory except the small Australian Capital Territory.

After outlining the criteria that applies to holding national referenda in liberal democracies, this chapter looks at the background to the Voice to Parliament proposal and the national campaign around it, explaining the resounding 'No' vote and why First Nations peoples themselves were divided on the issue. A short section then provides a strengths, weakness, opportunities and threats (SWOT) analysis of the process. The concluding section explores some potential prospects for rebuilding trust between the Commonwealth government and First Nations peoples.

How should referenda be conducted in a liberal democracy?

- Since the heart of liberal democracy is representative government, and this involves using a legislature and executive to settle policy after elections and consultations, national referenda should only be used carefully, and in contexts where the civil rights of all citizens and the rule of law are protected.
- National referenda are most suitable for considering major constitutional changes and, perhaps, other alterations of longstanding legal or policy arrangements, after the issues involved have been extensively debated.
- A dichotomous (Yes versus No) referendum question should be defined only after a long process of public consultation and preparation, and sustained search for consensual agreement on the precise wording of the question choices to be put to voters. Ideally, there will be a neutral public campaign of clarification of the exact implications of the choice for voters.

How to cite this chapter:

Evans, Mark and Grattan, Michelle (2024) 'The 2023 Voice to Parliament referendum', in: Evans, Mark; Dunleavy, Patrick and Phillimore, John (eds) *Australia's Evolving Democracy: A New Democratic Audit*, London: LSE Press, pp.84–94 **https://doi.org/10.31389/lsepress.ada.d** Licence: CC-BY-NC 4.0

- The final campaign arrangements and implementation of the referendum should be regulated impartially by the normal election integrity agency in a non-partisan and neutral way.
- Ideally, the two 'sides' in the campaign will not be political parties directly, but special campaign committees/organisations spanning across multiple parties and operating inclusively to showcase diverse opinions or rationale for Yes or No voting.
- For a referendum outcome to be binding, the requirements must be constitutionally specified in a clearcut way.

Recent developments: the lead-up and the campaign

The Voice to Parliament referendum was always a gamble against the odds of history. Only 8 of the previous 44 referendum questions had been passed. None had succeeded where there was a split between the major parties, and it was always likely that the right-wing leader of the Liberal-National opposition, Peter Dutton, would make a fight of the issue. For Prime Minister (PM) Anthony Albanese, on many fronts a cautious leader, this was a major roll of the political dice. And for First Nations peoples, too, the referendum was yet another test of their faith in the ability of Australia's democratic settlement to right historic wrongs.

Figure 4.1: The opinion polls during the campaign for a Voice to Parliament

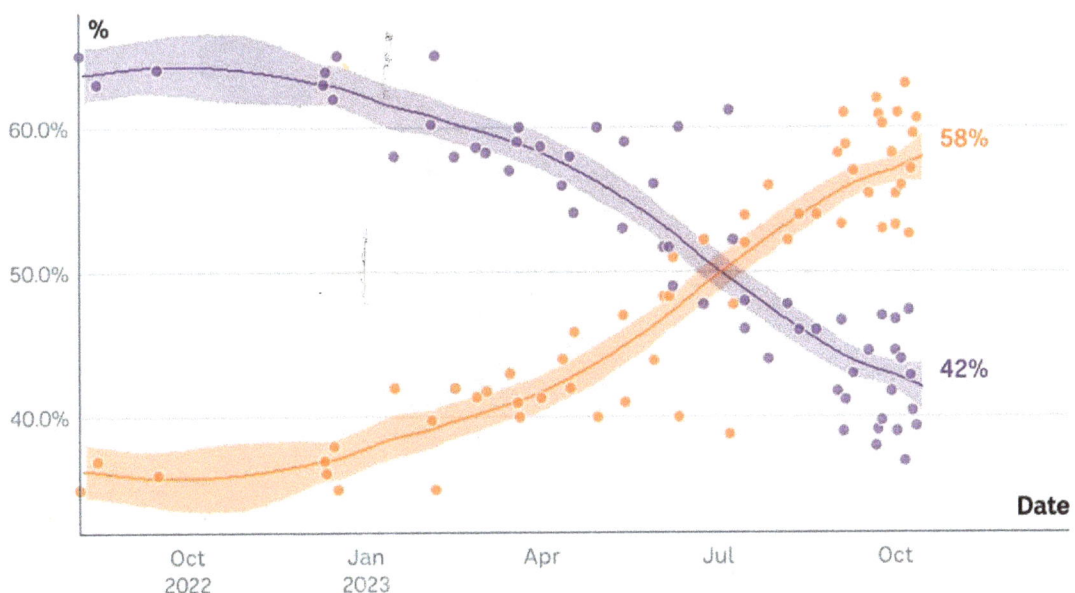

Source: Professor Simon Jackman and ABC News.

Notes: The solid purple line shows the estimated mean % support for 'Yes' at each date, and the solid orange line shows that for 'No'. The lighter shaded areas along each line show the 95 per cent credible intervals for these estimates. The dots show the results for individual polls. The last polls were on 15 October.

On federal election night in May 2022, Albanese recommitted himself to the 2017 Uluru Statement from the Heart, which called for a Voice to be embedded in the Constitution, as well as 'a Makarrata Commission to supervise a process of agreement-making between governments and First Nations and truth-telling about our history' (Uluru Statement, 2017). Prime Minister Albanese hoped that the Voice would be the big social reform of his first term in government. For a time in 2022, polling suggested that his optimism might be vindicated (see Figure 4.1). However, the Australian electorate's long-standing conservatism about constitutional change was increased by Liberal-National opposition raising concerns about the nature and consequences of the proposed body, fanned by a populist scare campaign. As 2023 progressed, these changes decisively sank the Voice.

On 14 October 2023, six out of every 10 Australians voted 'No'. The campaign was notable for being led by First Nations peoples on both sides. Particularly effective on the 'No' side was Northern Territory Senator Jacinta Nampijinpa Price, who entered the Senate only at the 2022 election. Ironically, she was catapulted into the post of Shadow Minister for Indigenous

Figure 4.2: The 2023 referendum outcome by seats

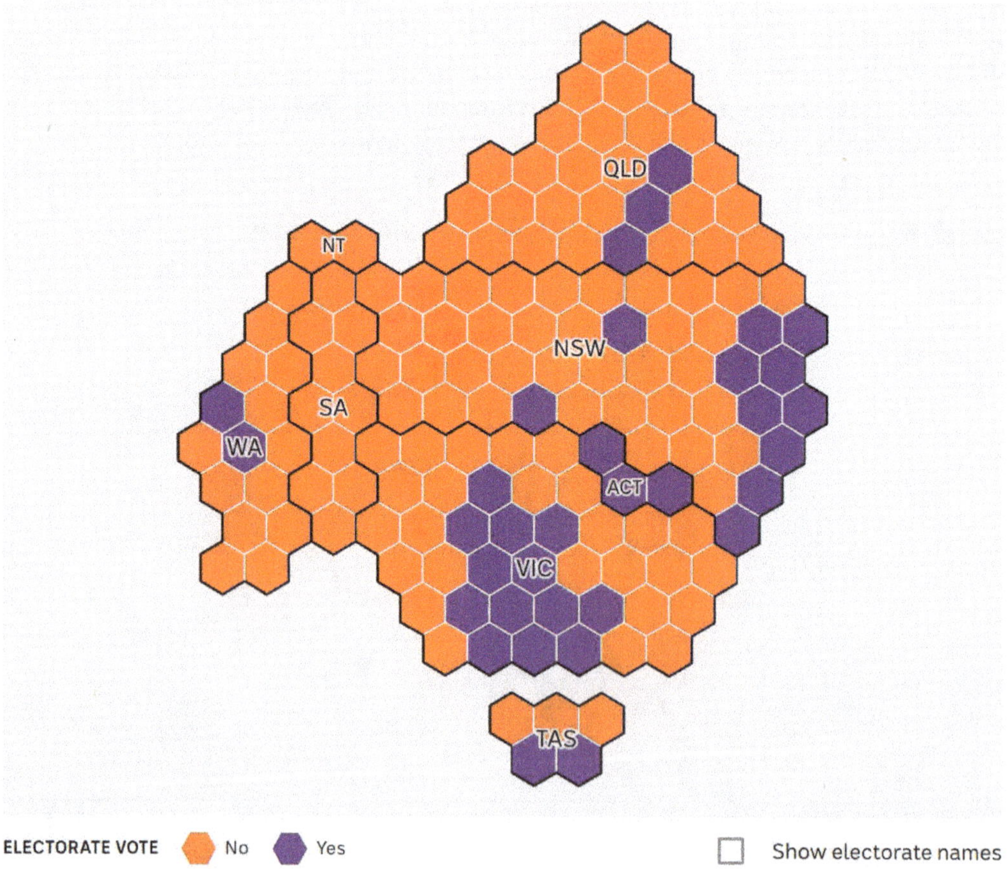

Source: ABC Election Analyst, Antony Green.

Note: Figure 4.2 uses one dot for each House of Representatives seat, placed in the approximate geographic position of that district. It aims to produce a 'map' of Australia that avoids obscuring the densely populated east coast and main cities, and seeming to overweight the least populated (often desert) regions, as orthodox maps often do.

Australians because its previously occupant, Julian Leeser, quit the frontbench to campaign for the 'Yes' side. Having Price and another First Nations leader, Warren Mundine, front the 'No' campaign further polarised debate.

A striking feature of the result was how the 'Yes' attitudinal pattern broadly resembled that of the (unsuccessful) 1999 referendum for a republic. Both proposals had the strongest support among better educated, prosperous progressive voters, attracted to social change issues (see Figure 4.2). The ABC's election analyst Antony Green noted

> how much lower the Yes percentage vote was in many traditional Labor seats. The seats where the Yes percentage was higher are clustered in seats won by Greens and 'teal' independents at the 2022 election, and also several Liberal seats gained by Labor. (2023)

The results do not tell us anything about how people are likely to vote at the next general election, due by May 2025 (just as the 1999 referendum voting pattern was not a predictor of the 2001 election). However, they do suggest that if a Labor government was to be re-elected, its chances of going ahead with another referendum for a republic have been greatly reduced.

The steps leading up to a voice

Multiple attempts were made to build up national-level representative and advisory bodies for First Nations peoples before the Voice proposal. (Chapters 16–24 on the individual states cover the state-level reconciliation processes.) The most important of these was the Aboriginal and Torres Strait Islander Commission (ATSIC), instituted in 1999 by the Hawke Labor government. It had a much more ambitious remit than the Voice, because it had both representative and executive functions (Wikipedia, 2023). It was abolished by the Howard government in 2004, despite calls for it to be reformed rather than scrapped. Before the 2007 election, the Liberal leader, John Howard, promised that if re-elected he would hold a referendum 'to formally recognise Indigenous Australians in our Constitution' (Bragg, n.d.). There was no suggestion of a Voice.

Over the subsequent decade, an enormous amount of work went into the question of how to achieve appropriate constitutional recognition. The work proceeded along several separate but interconnected tracks, including through parliamentary inquiries, by conservatives who favoured constitutional recognition and through a process of First Nations consultations. Ultimately the most important, the latter route resulted in the Uluru Statement from the Heart, issued at what its First Nations authors described as 'the 2017 National Constitution Convention' (Uluru Statement, 2017). Calling for a Constitutional Voice, the statement referred back to the landmark successful referendum of half a century before: 'In 1967 we were counted, in 2017 we seek to be heard.' The statement, however, received a cold reception from the Turnbull Cabinet, which rejected the Voice as a 'third chamber' of Parliament. The Morrison government commissioned an inquiry by First Nations leaders Marcia Langton and Tom Calma on the Voice, but opposed putting it in the Constitution and preferred local and regional voices to a national one. In the end, nothing was achieved.

The campaign

On 30 July, at the 2022 Garma Festival in the Northern Territory, the new Labor PM Albanese proposed draft wording for the Voice, which stated that the Voice 'may make representations to Parliament and the Executive Government on matters relating to Aboriginal and Torres Strait Islander Peoples' (NIAA, 2023). Parliament would have power to make laws on the 'composition, functions, powers and procedures' of the Voice. Over the year that followed, the argument about the Voice would involve many issues, including:

- the right of one group to have a special place in the Constitution
- the Voice's potential for dividing, or conversely uniting, the country
- the likely effectiveness of the Voice in helping to 'close the gap' of First Nations disadvantage
- whether the Voice would disrupt government and trigger legal challenges.

Legal experts Frank Brennan and Greg Craven, long-time participants in working for a Voice, were among those who warned of potential unintended legal consequences of the wording, although many other experts, including former Chief Justice Robert French, dismissed potential legal concerns. Attorney-General Mark Dreyfus did try to secure some recalibration; a minor wording change was made, but PM Albanese's advisory referendum working group would not go as far as Dreyfus had proposed. The government bolstered its argument against legal critics with advice from the Solicitor-General.

When public support seemed high, the government had considerable faith in a positive 'vibe' helping to carry the Voice through. They felt that people were recognising the justice of what PM Albanese referred to as First Nations peoples' 'generous invitation' and responding positively to it (Albanese, 2023). The government did not want to allow the debate to get bogged down in detail. But, especially after Peter Dutton, in April, joined the Nationals in declaring the Liberal Party's opposition to the Voice (Guardian, 2023a), it became clear that a lack of detail was a serious handicap for the 'Yes' campaigners. Even if it had wanted to, the government could not have provided full detail, because that was to be settled later in consultation with First Nations peoples, and only after a successful referendum.

The campaign presented a dilemma for the Labor government. It was not directly running or controlling the 'Yes' campaign, although this was its referendum and it was obviously campaigning hard for a 'Yes' vote. Another problem was that PM Albanese's messaging suffered from a lack of clarity. On the one hand, he presented the Voice as simply an opportunity for First Nations peoples to be heard; on the other, he suggested it would be a very powerful instrument in closing the disdvantagement gap. His opponents took advantage of this ambiguity by adopting the high-impact campaign slogan 'If you don't know, vote no'. This simple bumper sticker made it easier for Australians to vote 'No'.

The 'No' side always had the easier task. It simply had to fan voters' doubts, and ask questions to which there were no answers. As the months dragged on, the campaign became nastier, bringing some evidence of racism to the surface. This was Australia's first referendum in the era of social media, and debate raged about 'misinformation' and 'disinformation'. Much information was hotly contested.

The Edelman Trust Barometer 2023 also suggested that Australia was already on a path to increased polarisation, driven by a series of macro forces (distrust in key societal institutions such as government and media, a lack of shared identity, systemic unfairness, heightened societal fears and economic pessimism) that had weakened the country's social fabric and created increasing division in society. The report found almost half of Australians (45 per cent) agreeing that the nation was more divided than before. Major dividing forces were identified as 'the rich and powerful' (72 per cent), followed by hostile foreign governments (69 per cent), journalists (51 per cent) and government leaders (49 per cent) (Edelman Trust, 2023). Only just over two-fifths of Australians said that they trusted their government leaders – not a strong context for enacting a history-making reform.

The trust of First Nations peoples – hard to build, easy to lose

The Yindyamarra Nguluway research program at Charles Sturt University, led by Stan Grant Jnr, involved yarns with 24 Wiradjuri Elders before, during and after the referendum campaign.[1] The findings were worth noting, because they showed that despite the national polls reporting clear majority First Nations support for a 'Yes' vote (Sydney Morning Herald, 2023), some Elders were in fact initially divided on voting 'Yes', fatalistic about the prospects of change and distrusting of the process. Their comments included: 'We've been here before countless times. Promises, promises but little has changed for my family and community.' There was also deep disdain for the fact that the change process was couched in the context of giving a Voice to Parliament to nations that have never ceded sovereignty. 'We have been nations for thousands of years. We don't need to be granted a Voice to Parliament to be a nation. It has such a colonial feel to it.' Although the Uluru Statement from the Heart was seen as an important step forward, many Elders viewed it as an elite invention: 'As beautiful as it is, it didn't involve us. It was designed by self-appointed leaders who don't live on country. At the very least a grassroots process of reconciliation across all of our nations should have come first.'

Nonetheless, the general view that emerged by the end of the yarns was that the Voice was an imperfect but necessary gateway to a more detailed conversation about the future of Australian democracy. 'I couldn't look my Grandmother in the face if I didn't vote Yes. All she's struggled for lost in the stroke of a pencil' [Quotes from yarns]. Across the yarning it became evident that despite misgivings, Wiradjuri Elders had become marginally more trusting, confident and future-focused. As one Elder put it: 'We started to believe.' Ultimately, local areas with the largest proportion of First Nations peoples in Australia heavily backed a 'Yes' vote (ABC, 2023).

Understanding 'No'

Some commentators have argued that the 'No' vote was simply a matter of poor timing, with the referendum perceived by the 'silent majority' of voters as a tiresome distraction from cost-of-living problems. Certainly, zero-sum ultimatums do not tend to go well for governments calling them in times of economic uncertainty (as the case of Brexit in the UK shows). Others have pointed to a poor process, arguing that if the referendum question had been confined to constitutional recognition for Australia's First Nations peoples it would have won. This claim is in keeping with the argument that Australians would have been more comfortable with a constitutional statement that recognised the historic claim of right of First Nations peoples and the need for them to have a 'fair go', rather than the 'better go' that may or may not have been delivered through a Voice. Of course, even consultative mechanisms with constitutional force can still be ignored by stealthy governments. Some critics on the left have argued that something more deep rooted was at play: continued commitment to assimilation and a latent discomfort with multiculturalism. As former PM John Howard said in a speech delivered in 2023: 'I think one of the problems with multiculturalism is we try too hard to institutionalise differences, rather than celebrate what we have in [common].' Hence, for Howard, the 'No' vote was a vote for 'unity' (Guardian, 2023b).

In addition, the rights tradition in Australia has historically been good at protecting mainstream individual rights (especially perhaps those of the wealthy), but the state of human rights for many disadvantaged groups, particularly First Nations peoples, has long remained precarious. In 2017, the Australian government was subject to a damning critique of its human rights record by the United Nations Human Rights Committee (Guardian, 2017; UNHCR, 2017) with regard to the rights of children, the treatment of refugees, domestic violence, transgender rights, the sterilisation of intellectually disabled women and girls and the impact of anti-terrorism laws on civil liberties (see Chapter 3). The Human Rights Measurement Initiative, in 2021, reported multiple issues for Australia (SBS News, 2021), 'particularly in terms of who is most at risk of rights abuses', such as Aboriginal and Torres Strait Islander peoples, people with disabilities, people with low socioeconomic status and refugees and asylum seekers (Human Rights Watch, 2021).

Strengths, weaknesses, opportunities and threats (SWOT) analysis

Current strengths	Current weaknesses
Australia's Constitution provides for amendments to be made to it via a referendum so long as (1) a national majority of voters vote 'Yes' and (2) the state parliaments of four of the six states also vote 'Yes'. This double-majority criterion is clear and long established. There was a good chance that had condition (1) been obtained, condition (2) would have followed. But the 'Yes' vote could not muster a national majority of support.	Critics argue that the double-majority criterion is so hard to overcome that the Constitution is becoming immoveable (see Chapter 3).
The referendum question was clear cut and agreed consensually. The Labor government saw their proposal as coming after a long process of previous consultation and action at state and federal levels. They sought an approval in principle for a national Voice, to be followed by detailed consultation on the precise arrangements involved.	Critics of the Voice proposal argued strongly that the actual make-up and powers of the consultative assembly proposed and how it would be integrated with legislative and government decision-making were still obscure, and that a 'Yes' vote would give the government too much of a blank cheque on the final set-up and powers of the proposed body.
The referendum was well conducted by the Australian Electoral Commission and most campaigning on both sides was conducted in considerate ways.	Critics from the 'Yes' campaign argue that the 'No' campaign was a 'scare' campaign, featuring disinformation and heavily funded by wealthy interests. Some social media messaging at times evoked past racist attitudes towards First Nations peoples and allowed the expression of threatening or discriminatory opinions.
Future opportunities	**Future threats**
The processes by which Australia reconciles past colonisation hurts suffered by First Nations peoples and seeks to remedy their current disadvantagements will likely continue at state and local levels.	Efforts at reconciliation with First Nations peoples may become stalled or lose impetus, and their disadvantage even more entrenched.

After the Voice's failure, what next?

Many First Nations peoples and others on the centre or left blamed the strong opposition of Liberal leader Peter Dutton for the referendum's defeat. While the Liberals' dissent was undoubtedly the nail in the Voice's coffin, it seems very doubtful that the 'Yes' case would have prevailed even if Dutton had taken a more benign attitude. The most that he could have delivered would have been a free vote for Liberal MPs; regardless of what he did, many Liberal MPs and others on the right would have run a fierce campaign against the Voice.

When the polling showed the Voice was heading for defeat, there were calls for PM Albanese to scrap or delay the referendum. This was never realistic, because the PM had by then gone too far. Indigenous peoples would have seen such a step as a betrayal. But more reasonable questions might be asked about whether PM Albanese should have promised a constitutional Voice in the first place, when it was obviously going to be extraordinarily difficult to deliver. The alternative would have been to create a Voice by ordinary legislation that could then be put into the Constitution at a later date, if and when there was a strong prospect of such an initiative succeeding. That approach would not have satisfied those driving and supporting the Uluru Statement. But other critics argue that achieving this much would have been better than nothing.

As it turned out, the referendum not only ended with no Voice being established, but also had other negative consequences for First Nations peoples. In particular, it opened the way for an unravelling of the bipartisan support for the treaty process that had been under way in Queensland. It has also led to some questioning of welcome-to-country ceremonies. On social media a great many disinformation messages were aired about the treatment of First Nations peoples, and overtly racist views multiplied during the campaign period. Hence a process designed to address racial bigotry and promote reconciliation actually unleashed racism and appeared to have set back reconciliation.

What can be done?

We held a panel discussion in Canberra a few days before the referendum. Our last question to a Wiradjuri emerging leader was about what would happen if the referendum did not succeed. She answered, 'Then Wiradjuri nation building goes on, as it has for thousands of years.' So how might the spirit of the 40 per cent nationwide 'Yes' vote be used positively to support the needs and future aspirations of First Nations communities?

First, as Stan Grant Jnr put it with his final words on ABC's Q+A program early on in 2023, we need a commitment to *Yindyamarra Winhanganha*:

> This phrase, which is sacred to the Wiradjuri people, means 'the wisdom of respectfully knowing how to live well in a world worth living in'. People of goodwill on both sides of the vote will want to recognise that all Australians became responsible for closing the gap opened up in the campaign through strengths-based interventions.

Second, at a high politics level, the Voice would have been of symbolic significance as an act of restorative justice. But, in more practical ways, its failure mattered most at the local scale in affecting (or not) the lives of First Nations peoples. International evidence suggests that the best way of achieving improvements for disadvantaged minorities has been through community development councils (CDCs). These are designed to reduce poverty by empowering communities through improved governance and social, human and economic capital. They develop their own community plans, prioritise initiatives through whole-of-community direct decision-making, make bids for development funding and manage and deliver their own development projects. The establishment of directly elected CDCs lies at the heart of this strategy – putting communities in charge of their own development process and providing them with technical support and resources to deliver co-designed projects that matter to them.

Third, co-design by default, supporting the expectations of First Nations communities, inevitably requires both a better understanding of their service needs and aspirations and a service culture that attempts to 'see' like First Nations peoples. This is why co-design has moved to centre stage in public sector production around the world, for both online and offline citizen interactions. It places the selected members of society, in this case the First Nations community or citizen, at the centre of a planned process of collaborative learning. The process of learning focuses on the achievement of very specific outcomes, such as a fit-for-purpose nation-building plan. It draws on ways of working that are commonplace in product design and formulates interventions through understanding the lives of others and walking in their shoes. Co-design has been widely used in the development of interventions to combat various forms of marginalisation and carry out new governance practices or service innovation. In sum, design thinking has become a fundamental tool of public policy design and analysis, and it should be mandatory for all services, programs or projects aimed at supporting First Nations peoples.

Of course, there is also a chance that the next generation of Australian voters will take the initiative and right historic wrongs. According to a suggestive survey of next-generation students visiting the Museum of Australia Democracy (Evans, Stoker and Halupka, 2019), young Australians want to see a more participatory and representative democracy with the capacity to address long-term policy problems and bring in a fairer, tolerant and egalitarian democracy. 'Indigenous constitutional recognition' was their third priority issue, above gender equality and climate change. Given that young Australians are now among our most active and engaged citizens, the promise of change remains (Guardian, 2023c).

Conclusion

The Voice referendum produced a clear verdict in an appropriate and legitimate way that has been widely accepted as clearly expressing the views of Australians. Key lessons will no doubt be learnt for any future referendum (for example, on Australia's links with the UK monarchy), especially regarding the need for the precise implications of a 'Yes' vote to be fully specified.

Note

1   We acknowledge the traditional owners of the lands on which we developed this article – the Wiradjuri, Ngunnawal and Ngambri people. The yarns, led by Stan Grant Jnr and observed by Professor Evans, were held on three occasions: at the Warangesda Festival in Darlington Point (Canberra), Bathurst and Wagga Wagga. The interpretation of the data from the yarns rests with us.

References

ABC (2023) 'Anthony Albanese says surveys show between 80 and 90 per cent of Indigenous Australians support the Voice. Is that correct?', *ABC News*, 1 August. https://perma.cc/5L94-666V

Albanese, Anthony (2023) 'Aboriginal and Torres Strait Islander Voice referendum question', Press Conference, 23 March. https://perma.cc/LZ9E-YGZ2

Bragg, Andrew (n.d.) '2007 – John Howard's commitment', Australian Dictionary of National Biography, https://perma.cc/3ZGQ-5YSQ

Edelman Trust (2023) 'Australia on a path to polarisation: Edelman Trust Barometer 2023', Edelman's 2023 Trust Barometer, 8 February. https://perma.cc/8BM2-3XK8

Evans, Mark; Stoker, Gerry; and Halupka, Max (2019) 'Don't believe the stereotype: these 5 charts show our democracy is safe in the hands of future voters', *The Conversation*, 12 December. https://perma.cc/B3UE-FT4L

Green, Antony (2023) 'The Voice referendum results by vote type and electoral division', *Antony Green's Election Blog*, 24 October. https://perma.cc/2ETX-Q9D7

Guardian (2017) '"Unacceptable": UN committee damns Australia's record on human rights', *The Guardian, Australia*, 19 October. https://perma.cc/QF2M-S3JY

Guardian (2023a) 'Peter Dutton confirms Liberals will oppose Indigenous voice to parliament', *The Guardian, Australia*, 5 April. https://perma.cc/BG9Q-G6P5

Guardian (2023b) 'John Howard says he "always had trouble" with the concept of multiculturalism', *The Guardian, Australia*, 2 November. https://perma.cc/988R-T9WC

Guardian (2023c) 'Australians aren't joining in any more – and it appears to be having big political consequences', *The Guardian, Australia*, 11 November. https://perma.cc/YY4B-4HZ7

Human Rights Watch (2021) 'Australia: Address abuses raised at UN review – countries criticize failures on refugees, children, Indigenous rights', Human Rights Watch, 21 January. https://perma.cc/894B-WCA4

National Indigenous Australians Agency (2023) 'Culture and empowering communities', Webpage. https://perma.cc/KTR6-B6NY

SBS News (2021) 'Australia has delivered "strikingly poor" results on a new human rights scorecard', SBS News, 24 June. https://perma.cc/5GZ9-3J69

Sydney Morning Herald (2023) 'Indigenous support for Voice falls, but keeps majority', *Sydney Morning Herald*, 11 October. $ https://perma.cc/5Y24-6VS9

Uluru Statement (2017) 'The Uluru Statement from the Heart'. https://perma.cc/3EXV-C52A

UNHRC (United Nations Human Rights Committee) (2017) 'Report of the Special Rapporteur on the rights of Indigenous peoples on her visit to Australia: note / by the Secretariat'. https://perma.cc/4J5Z-EYZK

Wikipedia (2023) 'Aboriginal and Torres Strait Islander Commission', Wikipedia. https://perma.cc/GM3H-ZSU6

National Politics

5. Elections and voting 97
   Patrick Dunleavy and Mark Evans

6. Political parties 120
   Patrick Dunleavy and Mark Evans

7. Interest groups and corporate power
   143
   Patrick Dunleavy

8. Mainstream media 166
   Patrick Dunleavy

9. Social media 191
   Max Halupka

10. Gender equality and rights 206
    Pia Rowe

5

Elections and voting

Patrick Dunleavy and Mark Evans

The Alternative Vote (AV) system used to elect the federal House of Representatives (and the lower houses of the state and territory legislatures) is almost unique in the world, as is Australia's demanding form of compulsory voting, which requires voters to mark multiple preferences (see Chapter 1). The three-year cycle for House federal contests is also the joint shortest term for a parliamentary government in the world, along with New Zealand. (The USA has two-yearly congressional elections, but a four-year presidential executive term.) Australia also has an upper house at the federal tier (and in five of the six state parliaments) elected by a well-regarded proportional representation system, the Single Transferable Vote (STV). The integrity of elections was once poor in some Australian states (in some cases lasting for decades). But in modern times these problems have been rectified and Australian elections (federal and state) have long met the highest international standards.

What does democracy require for all the voting systems that elect the legislature?

- Votes should be translated into seats in a way that is recognised as legitimate by most citizens (ideally almost all of them).
- No substantial part of the population should regard the result as illegitimate, nor suffer a consistent bias of the system 'working against them'.
- If possible, the system should have beneficial effects for the good governance of the country.
- If possible, the voting system should enhance the social representativeness of the legislature and encourage high levels of voting across all types of citizens' criteria for elections.

How to cite this chapter:

Dunleavy, Patrick and Evans, Mark (2024) 'Elections and voting', in: Evans, Mark; Dunleavy, Patrick and Phillimore, John (eds) *Australia's Evolving Democracy: A New Democratic Audit*, London: LSE Press, pp.97–119. **https://doi.org/10.31389/lsepress.ada.e** Licence: CC-BY-NC 4.0

What does democracy require for the electoral system for the lower house of the federal legislature – the Alternative Vote?

- It should accurately translate parties' votes *nationally* into seats in the legislature.
- If possible, it should foster close links between MPs and voters in their local areas.
- If possible, the system should give clear signals of the overall government direction wanted by a majority of voters.

What does democracy require for the electoral system for the upper house of the federal legislature – the Single Transferable Vote?

- It should accurately translate parties' votes *within each state or territory* into seats in the legislature.
- It should foster the national representation of overall state interests.
- If possible, the system should have beneficial effects in correcting any biases in the representation of parties nationally arising from the lower house elections, especially in giving seats to otherwise-excluded parties – a 'balancing' effect.

The chapter begins by reviewing recent changes in Australia's elections and party competition features. Next, a strengths, weaknesses, threats and opportunities (SWOT) analysis summarises the key democratic achievements and limitations of voting and elections. Following that, three sections consider more specific aspects of Australian elections operations relevant for democratic auditing.

Recent developments

The 2022 federal elections produced important developments in patterns of voting and partisan success in both the House of Representatives and the Senate, pluralising the representation of parties in both houses, but without denting the governing predominance of the top two parties, Labor and the (permanent) Liberal-National Coalition. After presenting recent election outcomes for each house, the final sections of the chapter explores how fairly their respective electoral systems worked.

House elections

Historically, Labor and the Liberal-National Coalition have dominated the lower house elections for decades, winning far more first-preference votes than any competitors. However, this pattern has tended to erode in recent years, as Figure 5.1 below shows. The top two parties' share of first-preference votes was three-quarters in 2019, but only two-thirds in 2022, and it has broadly trended down over time, from 84 per cent in 2004. Green voting has wobbled but gradually grown larger in this century, reaching one in eight votes in 2022. In general, the 'left' side of the political spectrum has been more fragmented between Labor and the Greens than has been

Figure 5.1: The proportion of first-preference votes won by the main parties at House of Representatives elections, 2001–2022

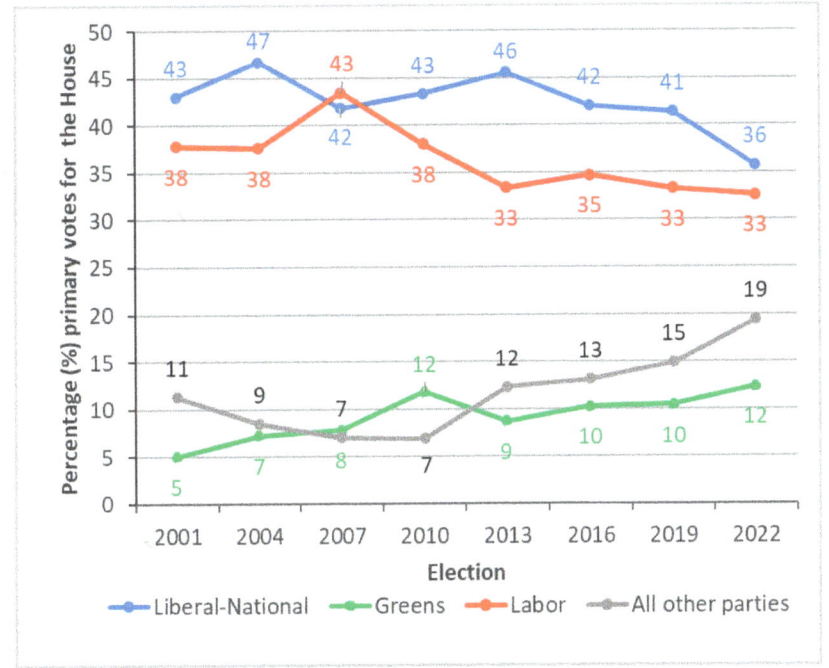

Source: Compiled by the author from AEC (2023a).

Notes: Results for 2022 and earlier years can be accessed from the AEC's webpage. 'All other parties' includes Katter, Pauline Hanson's One Nation, Family First, Xenophon, Democrats, Center, United Australia and all smaller micro parties at different times.

Figure 5.2: The Liberal-National Coalition share of the two-party preferred (TPP) vote, 2001–2022

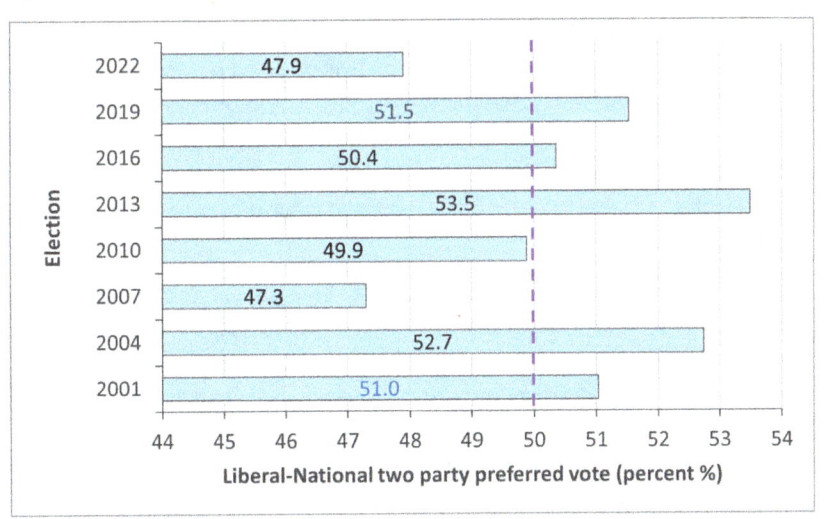

Source: Compiled by the author from AEC (2023a).

Note: The zero on the horizontal axis is not shown here; the scaling starts at 44 per cent.

true on the right, although at times parties to the right of the Liberal-Nationals have won small chunks of support (as with the 5 per cent for the Palmer party in 2022). In 2007, Labor beat the Liberal-National Coalition in primary votes, but in 2010, when it just clung on to power, it was 5 per cent behind. In 2022 Labor won convincingly overall at later stages of the AV count (the two-party preferred vote, or TPP vote), but still got 3 per cent less in primary votes than the Liberal-National Coalition.

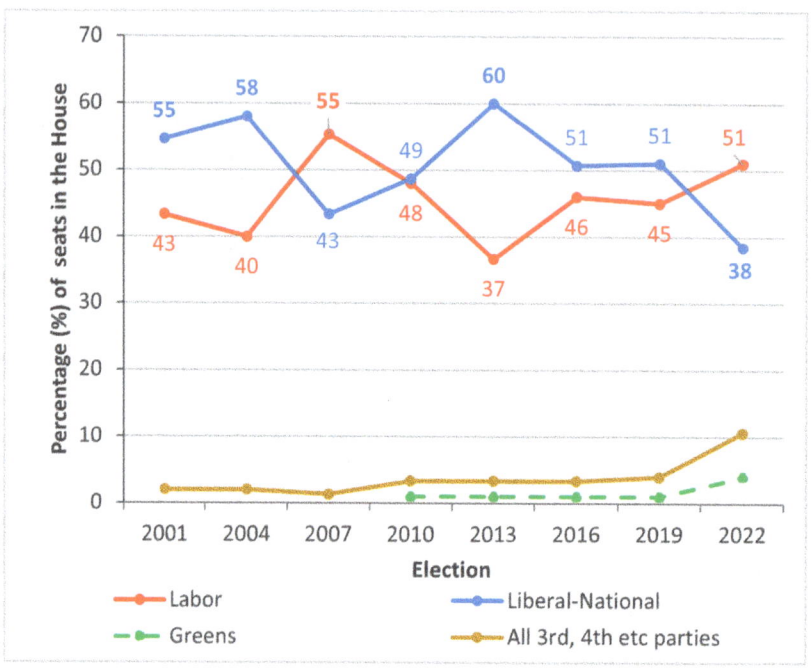

Figure 5.3: The percentage of MPs won by parties at House of Representatives elections, 2001–2022

Source: Compiled by the author from AEC (2023a).

Notes: The House had 150 seats from 2001 to 2016, and 151 thereafter, so a majority always required 76 seats. The Greens won a seat from 2010 to 2019 and four seats in 2022. In 2022, the Independents included seven Teal Independents. Smaller party seats are hard to show here, but Katter won a seat from 2013 to 2022, Centre from 2019 to 2022, Xenephon in 2016 and Palmer in 2013.

In order to understand seats outcomes we need to look at the TPP vote stage. This is the last stage in AV counting, where other candidates have been eliminated from the count and it has come down to the last two largest parties. In 138 out of 153 House contests the top two parties were the Liberal-Nationals and Labor; Figure 5.2 shows that the contest for TPP between them has often been very tight indeed. Historically, most Greens voters have used their later preferences votes to back Labor, as they clearly did in 2007 and 2022, and mostly in 2010 – the three occasions in Figure 5.2 where there was also a centre-left majority in primary vote shares. On the other five occasions the Liberal-National Coalition has received the TPP majority, drawing support from a range of other smaller parties and also the backing of some Greens voters.

Because the TPP numbers have hovered very close to the majority level (50.1 per cent), the differences in the percentages of lower house seats won by the top two parties, shown in Figure 5.3, have diverged sharply in some elections (notably 2013) and Labor has done better in terms of seats percentages than the vote share might suggest (even in its big 2013 defeat). In 2022, it gained over half the seats although its primary vote was only a third of the total. The representation of third and fourth parties lagged behind their vote share until 2022 when it picked up appreciably.

How fair are the lower house elections?

One of the most basic tests of the democratic performance of a country's electoral system asks: What is the difference between the proportion of votes cast for a particular party and that party's representation in parliament? In AV the key voting indicator for determining winning seats is the TPP vote, shown in Figure 5.2. The Liberal-National Coalition's net TPP lead over Labor is tracked in Figure 5.4. In every election since 2001, the party with the most TPP votes has always formed the government in a very reliable manner, even in 2010 when the incumbent

Figure 5.4: The Liberal-National Coalition's partisan advantage in terms of its percentage share of seats minus the two-party preferred vote, and the deviation from proportionality (DV) in the House of Representatives elections, 2001–2019

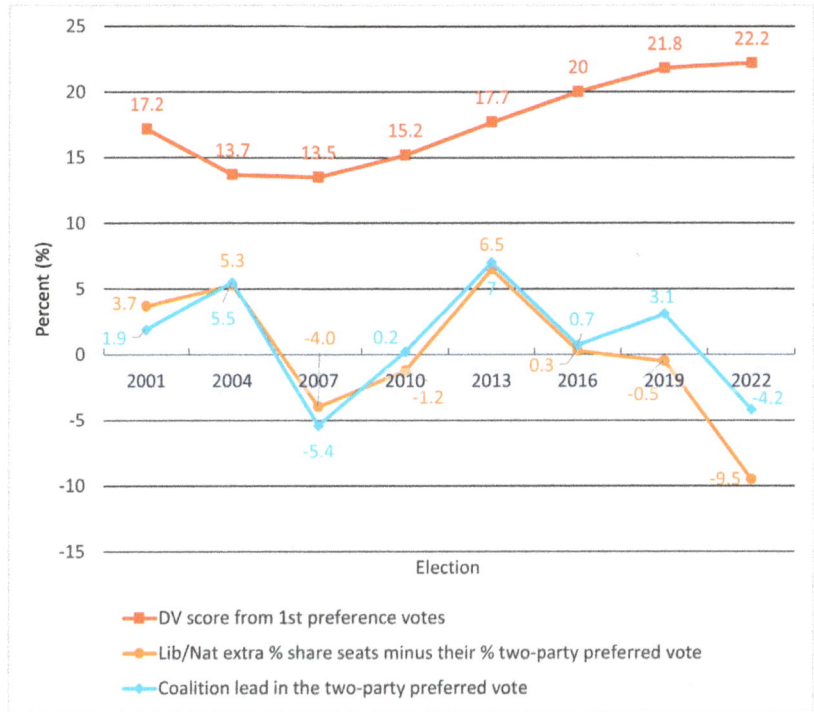

Source: Compiled by the author from AEC (2023a).

Notes: The blue line, the Liberal-National Coalition lead in the TPP vote, shows the Coalition percentage vote share minus the Labor vote share. The orange line, showing the Coalition's advantage, indicates how far the Liberal/National parties were over-represented against their parties' TPP vote preferences at the end of the AV counting process. The DV score shows the percentage of MPs winning seats in the House of Representatives that was not justified in terms of their first party vote shares.

Labor government won a tiny lead (just 0.2 per cent) but the same seats as the opposition Liberal-National Coalition. Labor nonetheless secured enough additional support from smaller parties to stay in office until 2013. Thus, the AV voting system has reliably delivered the 'right' winner (which occasionally has not happened in state elections, notably in South Australia – see Chapter 20).

Many democratic voting systems give a 'winner's bonus' to the largest party in the form of a bigger lead in seats than their lead in terms of votes, as happens in Australia. To track this over time compared with the TPP votes, the orange line at the bottom of Figure 5.4 shows the Liberal-Nationals' share of House seats minus their TPP percentage. This measure shows their advantagement in representation when they won most votes, and how far they were disadvantaged in terms of seats when they lost. In the main this index has moved remarkably closely together with the Liberal-National Coalition's lead in TPP terms. The seats percentage advantage for the Liberal-Nationals is generally a little bit higher than its TPP advantage, but by tiny amounts in elections up to 2016. In 2019, however, the Liberal-National Coalition gained more of an advantage than its TPP lead, but was then more substantially under-represented in 2022 than before. This seems to have been chiefly due to the rise of the Teal Independents, discussed in detail later in this chapter. In this way, the AV system's operations clearly determine why the top two parties have so far won almost all the House seats, and monopolised government between them.

Comparing other parties' seats shares with their primary votes, it is important to bear in mind that even in democracies with proportional representation (PR) election systems, small parties

Figure 5.5: A simple example of how to calculate the deviation from proportionality (DV) score

Party	% votes	% seats	Deviations
A	45	65	+20
B	30	22	-8
C	20	12	-8
D	5	1	-4
Total	100	100	

Next add up the positive and negative numbers in the Deviations column, ignoring their signs, to get a number called the 'modulus' = 40.

To eliminate the double-counting involved in the modulus, divide by two, so DV score = 20.

Source: (Dunleavy, 2018, Figure 2).

may often be denied seats, as happens in Australia. The Greens (Australia's third largest party) particularly suffered before 2022 because they got a tenth of votes nationwide but rarely enough in any given electoral district to make it past the AV first-votes stage. In 2019, for example, they received 10 per cent of first-preference votes but won just one seat in Parliament (Melbourne). In 2022, their one-eighth (12.5 per cent) national support won them only four seats (2.6 per cent, thanks to three new ones in central Brisbane). Other minor parties on the far right, the United Australia Party and Pauline Hanson's One Nation, each received over 4 per cent of first-preference votes in 2019, although neither won a seat in Parliament. However, in 2022, the Independents on 5 per cent nationally did unusually well by winning 10 seats (6.7 per cent), thanks to some Liberal-National voters defecting to the Teal Independents over policies for the environment and women's issues, plus some of their candidates attaining concentrated support in specific local areas.

A second key test of an election system is how far parties' seats shares compare with their first-preference support (their 'primary vote') – the political alignments that arguably matter most to voters. Here the achievements of AV clearly do come at some cost to the proportionality of elections. The top line in Figure 5.4 shows a key indicator of democratic responsiveness, known as the deviation from proportionality (DV) score, which is widely used in political science to compare liberal democracies. Figure 5.5 shows how to calculate the DV score in the most straightforward way. The deviations between each party's vote share and its seat share are added up (ignoring the + or – signs) and then divided by two to eliminate double-counting. The larger the DV score is, the greater the proportion of seats that have been 'misallocated' to parties that do not 'deserve' them in terms of their first-preference vote shares. Because very small parties with dispersed votes across districts almost always cannot win any seats, the minimum achievable DV score in any country is not really zero, but approximately 4–5 per cent (or more if lots of tiny, 'no hope' parties or one-off candidates contest elections in many districts).

Looking back to Figure 5.4, the DV line (at the top) shows a quite different patterning from the other lines. The DV score has risen significantly in each of the last four elections, mainly because of the rise in votes for the Greens and other smaller parties. In every election the parties over-represented in terms of winning seats compared with their first-preference votes are the Liberal-National Coalition and Labor. In 2004 and 2007, just over one in eight seats were being 'misallocated' to the big two parties, out of line with voters' first preferences. But in the 2016–2022 period this proportion reached over a fifth. All the top line numbers in Figure 5.4 are high for a liberal democracy – for example, in the USA, which has first-past-the-post (FPTP) voting, the DV score is under 10 per cent. Recent DV scores of over 20 per cent are on a par with other Westminster FPTP countries (like the UK, Canada or India) and more than twice the DV values in most European liberal democracies.

How much does this matter? Advocates for a majoritarian system like AV argue that it is more likely to produce parliamentary majorities where the responsibility for government decisions is clear, enhancing satisfaction with democracy (**Blais and Gélineau, 2007; Foa et al., 2020**). Voters can reward or punish the incumbent party at the next election according to its performance, with a clear replacement government also known well in advance of people voting (Norris 2004). On the other hand, minority governments formed only after elections by ad hoc coalitions (not the regular Liberal-National concertation which persists across many elections) can blur responsibility and, therefore, accountability for government performance. Some analysts also claim that majoritarian systems lead to more effective opposition parties and more rigorous parliamentary debate, while others argue that governments in FPTP and AV systems do more economic regulation, helping consumers by creating lower price levels (**Rogowski and Kayser, 2002**).

The potential downsides of majoritarian electoral systems include an adversarial dynamic between parties, centred more on competition than on collaboration to produce long-run national interest policies. Voters for election-winning parties are less satisfied than voters backing election losers, with a greater gap in in majoritarian systems than in PR systems (**Foa et al., 2020**). This may even open the way for election 'bad losers' to query the legitimacy of election results, as Donald Trump did in the USA after his 2020 defeat. For voters who support small parties, the experience of them being denied effective representation despite winning hundreds of thousands of votes is a bruising one and may damage trust in democracy. Advantaged parties may also use their cushioning against new competitors entering and winning seats so as to support joint 'cartel' arrangements with other advantaged parties, keeping in place election, campaigning or party funding arrangements from which they benefit. Lastly, single-member districts in many countries have been shown to damage the numbers of women in parliament compared to multi-seat systems. These strengths and weaknesses of majoritarian systems are evident in the House of Representatives elections.

Looking beyond the federal level at the five other Australian lower houses in states, and the unicameral legislatures in Queensland and the two territories, all their legislators serve fixed four-year terms. They use AV voting in single-member districts (albeit with some small variations) and in single-member constituencies, with the notable exception of Tasmania (which uses STV in multi-member districts – see Chapter 22). Labor and Liberal-National predominance is a feature of all eight polities. The largest states (NSW and Victora) have large lower houses, while states with small populations have fewer members (as in Tasmania). All state and territory electoral districts have quite small populations and local areas, so that elected members can become well known locally. Since states and territories handle most of the public services and regulation issues most likely to engage voters' attention, localism has good aspects (high levels of voter information) and potential drawbacks (sectional pressures on representatives).

Senate elections

The Senate is elected using STV with 12 seats for each state and 2 for each territory (see Chapter 1). Senate seats are usually held for six-year terms, with half of senators being elected every three years. (If a rare 'double dissolution' of the Senate occurs, then the number of seats contested is 12 per state. It is also possible in this conjuncture that an incumbent senator may lose their seat after serving only three years.) Since 1959, the Senate has used a PR electoral system. Internationally, these systems have produced very different voting behaviours among citizens (backing a greater variety of parties) and seats outcomes (producing more multi-party results) when compared with majoritarian systems such as AV or plurality rule (FPTP).

In fact, voters in Australia's upper house elections only rather slowly changed their behaviour to more multi-party voting, even in this century. Before 2010, the Liberal-National Coalition got above two-fifths first-preference support, and before 2022 it stayed not far below that (Figure 5.6). Labor reached this level only once, in 2007, and subsequently dropped to gain less than a third of first-preference support for the last four elections. In 2001, one in six people were choosing to give their first-preference backing to one of the third, fourth or lower-placed parties, with less than a third of this share going to the Greens (Figure 5.6). By 2010, the non-top-two share of votes topped a quarter, and within that share the Greens were backed by one in eight voters. Greens support subsequently fell back for three elections, before returning to its 2010 level in 2022. The share of primary votes going to fourth, fifth and other smaller parties has kept growing since 2010, however, and the votes share for all parties outside the top two (including the Greens) has been a third of the total since 2016. Who these other smaller parties have been is discussed in detail in Chapter 12 on the Senate. Voting patterns for these groupings are hard to analyse over time because some have been episodic or discontinuous competitors (standing only in years when their chances looked better or in individual states where they had

Figure 5.6: The proportion of first-preference votes won by the main parties at Senate elections, 2001–2022

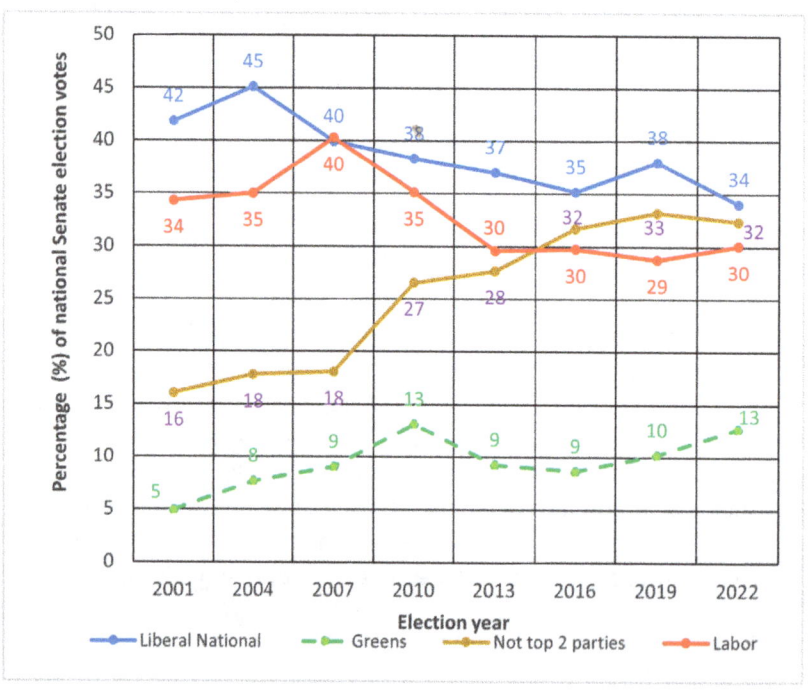

Source: Compiled by the author from AEC (2023a).

Note: The line for all parties below the top two includes the Greens votes shown.

Figure 5.7: The percentage (%) of seats won by the main parties at Senate elections, 2001–2022

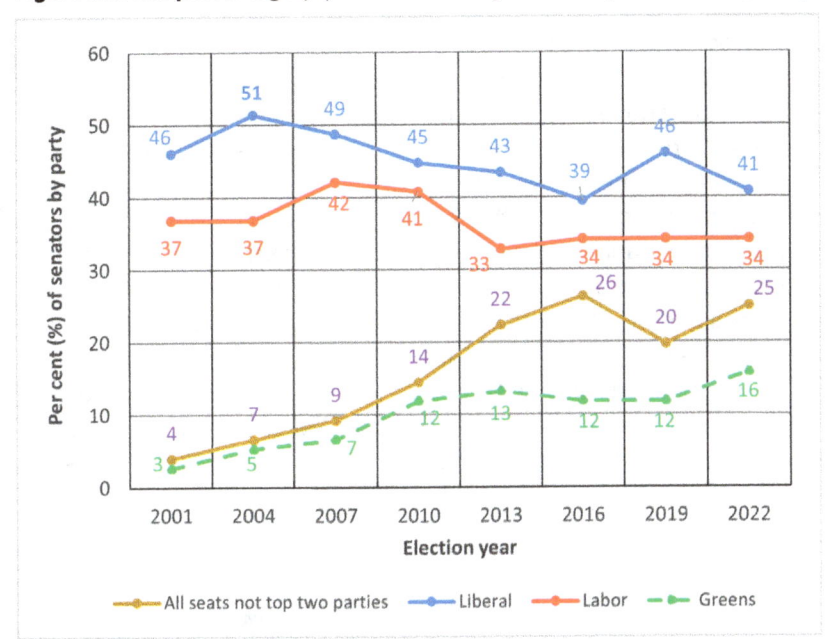

Source: Compiled by the author from AEC (2023a).

Note: The line for all parties below the top two includes the Greens seats shown.

surged for some reason, and then taking a break). Some 'surges' of support in a particular state were produced by a well-known legislator leaving one of the top two parties to stand under a new party label, or as a 'disguised' independent relying on their past partisan reputation, without starting a distinct party of their own. Other parties have been single-issue cause groups. Genuine independents have also been elected in particular states, and in 2022 the Teal Independents, which are discussed later in this chapter, swelled this vote share.

Turning to seats outcomes (Figure 5.7), they have clearly followed the over-time pattern of voters' behaviours (in Figure 5.6), as we would expect with a PR system. However, in six member STV seats, the formal 'quota' of votes that a party must achieve in order to secure a seat is still 1/(6 + 1), which is 14 per cent. This relatively high level has helped the largest parties at the expense of the smallest ones (who are eliminated early on from the STV counting process). In fact, senators can be elected with much lower levels of initial support than the formal quota, especially where they attract a lot of second or third preferences from voters for other parties.

Of the top two parties, the Liberal-National Coalition have enjoyed the most 'bonus seats' success (Figure 5.7). However, they only gained one (narrow) single-party majority (in 2004) and a close miss (in 2019) – on both occasions they needed senators from smaller parties on the centre right to back them to pass new laws. Since 2000 Labor has never got a Senate majority on its own, and most recently has flatlined on a third of the seats for four elections. However, with Greens support it won in 2010, was almost there in 2007 and controlled exactly half the chamber (without a majority) in 2022. The top two parties' share of Senate seats declined somewhat, from 88 per cent in 2004 to 75 per cent by 2022. The Greens regularly won an eighth of seats from 2010 to 2019, enjoying a slight seats bonus, which persisted in 2022. By contrast, all other, smaller parties have tended to be under-represented in terms of senators compared to their national vote share – piling up votes across the states, but not winning seats. One exception was the double dissolution election of 2016, when the larger numbers of 12 seats being contested per state lowered the formal quota needed for parties to win seats under STV to a 13th of the vote (under 8 per cent) and less than that in practice.

How fair are the upper house elections?

Knowing that the Senate is elected by a PR system in multi-seat state-wide elections, we might expect that the deviation from proportionality score would be much lower than it is in the House elections. However, Figure 5.8 shows that this is only partially the case. The Senate's DV score has been 14 per cent or more for the last four elections. This is less than the recent House numbers (above 20 per cent), but it is still a relatively high score in international terms and well above those in most European countries with PR systems. There are several reasons for this. First, a larger number of voters fragment their Senate first-preference votes across smaller parties with little chance of winning seats – creating gains that can be mopped up in bonus seats by the top two parties and the Greens, as Figure 5.8 shows. For any electoral system in the world the level of votes for tiny parties defines the lowest level that the DV score can go to. Second, the six-seat competitions at state level cannot easily be accurate because the number of seats available is limited. Indeed, in most states, if you were to calculate a DV score for the state only, it would have been above 20 per cent in 2022. Third, the same biases in representation in Figure 5.8 apply in almost all of Australia, so that there is little scope for patterns in different state results to offset each other.

In some other countries (like Spain) high DV scores can be created in PR systems by malapportionment – that is, seats themselves being distributed unfairly between areas. And of course, in Australia the upper house seats are very unfairly distributed, with large and tiny states each getting the same 12 senators. However, in recent history, this malapportionment has actually mitigated and not accentuated the quite high Senate DV scores – for example, the Greens' under-representation in senators for large population states like NSW and Victoria has been offset by their winning more seats in smaller states like Tasmania. Of course, this is only true in terms of party labels, since a party's presence in one state may not compensate their voters who go unrepresented in other states, and state parties themselves differ somewhat in their policy priorities.

Figure 5.8: Deviation from proportionality and the levels of over-representation of the top three parties in Senate elections, 2001–2022

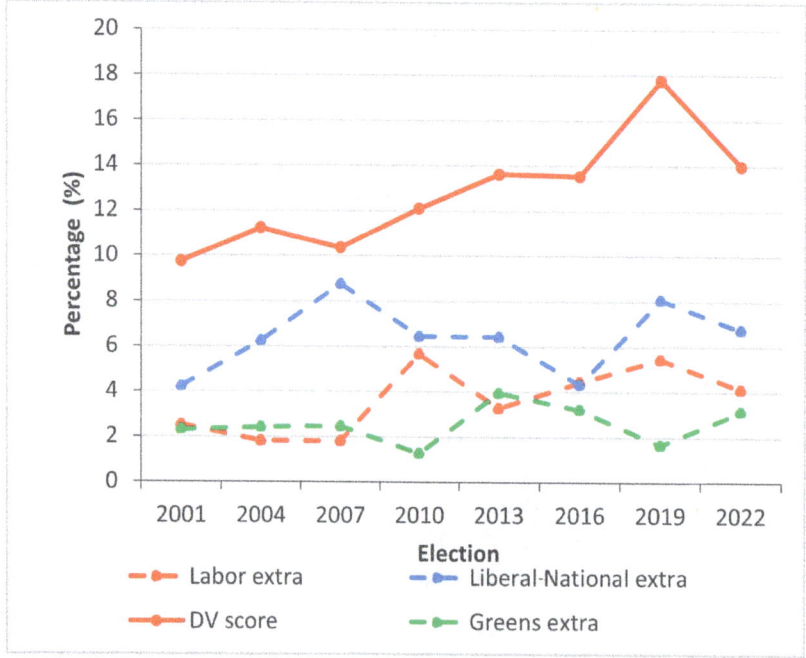

Source: Computed by authors from AEC (2023a).

Note: The top line shows the DV score. The dashed line second from the top shows Liberal-National over-representation in terms of seats percentage compared to its primary votes percentage; the bottom two dashed lines show this for Labor and the Greens. Taken together these 'seats bonuses' account for the DV scores, with all seats deficits accruing to third or lower-ranked parties.

Nonetheless some recent commentators have suggested that Senate elections are 'fairer' than those for the House:

> In the most recent House of Representatives election [2019 then], the Coalition and Labor together received 75 per cent of the vote but 96 per cent of the seats. The Greens received 10 per cent of the vote but 1 per cent of the seats, and independents and minor parties received 15 per cent of the vote and 3 per cent of the seats. By contrast, the Coalition and Labor received 67 per cent of the vote in the last two Senate elections but hold 80 per cent of the seats in the Senate. The Greens received 10 per cent of the vote but hold 15 per cent of the seats, and other minor parties and independents received 23 per cent of the vote but hold 5 per cent of the seats. (Browne and Oquist, 2021, p.32)

Looking beyond the federal level, four other Australian state upper houses, called Legislative Councils (LCs), are smaller bodies than the Senate, ranging in size from 15 members in Tasmania to 42 members in NSW. Four states also use STV voting (albeit with some small variations), either with all members elected every four years (in Victoria and from 2025 in Western Australia) or with half of members elected at a time and serving for eight years. Tasmania elects LC members by halves, but using the AV system in single-member districts. In NSW and Western Australia (from 2025) whole-state elections are for very large districts (22 and 37 seats respectively) – ones where almost any party (no matter how small) will win representation under STV. In South Australia, 11 members at a time are chosen (implying a formal quota of 8 per cent), but Victoria uses 5 member seats with a high quota of 17 per cent (favoring the two largest parties).

Strengths, weaknesses, opportunities and threats (SWOT) analysis

Current strengths	Current weaknesses
Australia's electoral arrangements are balanced and allow for the expression of different benefits. Having a majoritarian electoral system in the House of Representatives and PR in the Senate (using STV) has combined the strengths of both types of electoral system in one design. AV (mostly) produces clear majorities in the House that help simplify and increase government accountability to voters. PR for the Senate means a lower overall likelihood of the government having a majority in the review chamber – thereby putting in place valuable extra checks and balances on government policy-making.	The majoritarian AV system design in the House of Representatives leads to markedly disproportional electoral outcomes, advantaging the top two parties at the expense of all other parties and independents. It also serves to discourage new entrants, even with multiple preferences that avoid 'wasted votes' from people backing them. Critics also argue that by making Senate majorities elusive or narrow, STV makes it harder for the government to pass controversial legislation, even when changes are evidently needed or demanded by the public.

The electoral importance of voters' and MPs' party loyalties, especially for politicians in the top two parties, has helped governments in the lower house to limit the extent of any 'pork barrel' politics to meet the demands of individual MPs. However, critics argue that it has allowed overly strong executive actions to develop unpunished, as with the 'sports rort' and 'robodebt' controversies at the time of the 2019 elections (see Chapters 13 and 14).	Critics argue that the small party senators have often become the marginal 'veto players' who are crucial for many controversial legislation votes. Ministers have regularly had to buy off the agreement of these individuals or small or regionally specific parties, by making 'pork barrel' concessions to specific state interests.
Australia has a short electoral cycle of three years (see later in this chapter). Therefore, citizens have more frequent opportunities to have their say in elections and they can more quickly vote out governments they are unhappy with.	Short election cycles mean a government has a very limited window of perhaps two years in which to tackle 'hard' policy choices before campaigning in earnest resumes. Critics argue that semi-permanent campaigning makes it more difficult to do long-term policy-making. It also makes it harder for citizens to evaluate the performance of governments.
The prime minister (PM) can call the election at an exact time of their choosing. But in practice this is limited by the short election term (plus factors like holiday periods). This power nonetheless provides a valuable if limited counter-vailing influence to some of the inherent difficulties for incumbents of governing in a public-interested way.	Giving PMs discretion on the precise election data has advantaged incumbents, while also creating uncertainty for opposition parties about the timing of elections. The power may accentuate the political-business cycle temptation to 'rig' policies to work at their best in a planned election window in short-term ways that boost the governing party's chances but may be sub-optimal for the national interest.
A key role of parties is to recruit new talent for political life. The local scale of campaigning for House elections (and their frequency) has both reduced the barriers to new people gaining political experience and cut the costs of getting involved.	Near-continuous campaigning for elections means that the most common pathway into a parliamentary career is to begin by working as a political staffer for a major party, and then to transition to standing as a candidate to be an MP (see Chapter 6). This professionalisation of politics has made MPs less diverse and created more of a disconnect between legislators and their communities.
Cross-national evidence shows that single-member electoral districts inhibit the chances of women being selected as parties' candidates in winnable seats. In recent decades there has been some increase in women's representation in the House, notably at the 2022 election with the impact of the Teal Independents (see later in this chapter). By contrast, competing for votes in multi-member seats has fostered women's representation. In 2022 the Senate became more than 50 per cent female for the first time. Labor's voluntary party quotas have been a key factor in increasing women's representation both there and in the House of Representatives.	Single-member districts for electing MPs, plus party selectorates' pro-male biases, have meant that women's representation was still only 31 per cent in the House of Representatives in 2022, and has lagged far behind parity for decades. In international rankings, Australia slipped to 58th in terms of the share of women parliamentarians (Hough, 2022; Inter-Parliamentary Union, 2021).

Australian elections are conducted with high integrity overall (Karp et al., 2017; Mackerras, 2022), thanks to the professional and non-partisan management of elections by the Australian Electoral Commission (AEC) and state equivalents. The public largely trust public services to deliver free and fair elections.	Two key weaknesses for electoral integrity in Australia include biased press media coverage (Finkelstein, 2012; Young, 2011) (see Chapter 8) and only partly regulated campaign finance (Cameron and Wynter, 2018; Centre for Public Integrity, 2020) (and see Chapter 7). Occasionally serious wobbles occur in bipartisanship over how elections are conducted (Ransley, 2021). Polls show that citizens are concerned about possible hidden or disproportionate influence arising from large-sum money and political finance donations by firms involved with politics – such as property companies (Karp, Knaus and Evershed, 2020).
Most of the Australian population have cared who wins elections and have believed that who people vote for can make a big difference to their lives.	Despite overall high confidence in the electoral process itself, long-term data shows that many citizens have become more distrustful of politicians and more dissatisfied over time with the performance of democracy in Australia.
Future opportunities	**Future threats**
Following increased immigration to Australia from Asian countries, increasing ethnic diversity is likely to be better recognised in future election candidates and successes, especially in urban House seats.	The momentum for representation of First Nations peoples has remained contested between the top two parties. Since the 2023 referendum for the Voice failed to pass (see Chapter 4), their isolation from most electoral politics will likely not decrease.
The period of greater partisan convergence in policy stances during the COVID-19 pandemic increased public trust in government (Bennett Institute for Public Policy, 2022). 'Fringe' candidates and movements have failed to win seats, showing that Australia has relatively few problems of increasing polarisation of 'mainstream' party voters, such as that found in the USA.	

The rest of this chapter looks at three issues with federal elections in more detail: the quality of representation and citizens' political engagement, the overall integrity of election processes, and the effects of Australia's rapid (federal) electoral cycle.

The quality of representation and citizen's political engagement

So far, the analysis in this chapter has only focused on national data, which inherently averages across the electoral results of the electoral districts for House elections (or states for the Senate). How people see their party doing nationally matters a lot to voters, in particular whether it is apparently treated fairly or not in terms of seats for votes. But so does what happens in their own local area.

One way to capture the variations across districts is shown in Figure 5.9, called a 'crown diagram'. In this case, the blue outline shows the competition space for eight parties because the average number of parties per seat in the 2022 election was 7.6. With eight parties competing, the result must lie within this space – in fact, the smallest number of parties contesting a district in 2022 was 4 and the largest number was 16, but we cannot draw all these competition spaces here, and so the blue triangle is the best we can do. On the horizontal axis, we chart the percentage vote for the first-preference vote of the largest party nationally (Labor) at district level, minus the percentage first-preference vote for the Liberal-National Coalition (the second ranked party). The diagram covers all the seats (138 out of 153) where these were the

Figure 5.9: A 'crown diagram' view of the 2022 first-preference vote patterns across parties for the House of Representatives in the 138 districts where Labor and the Liberal-National Coalition were the top two parties

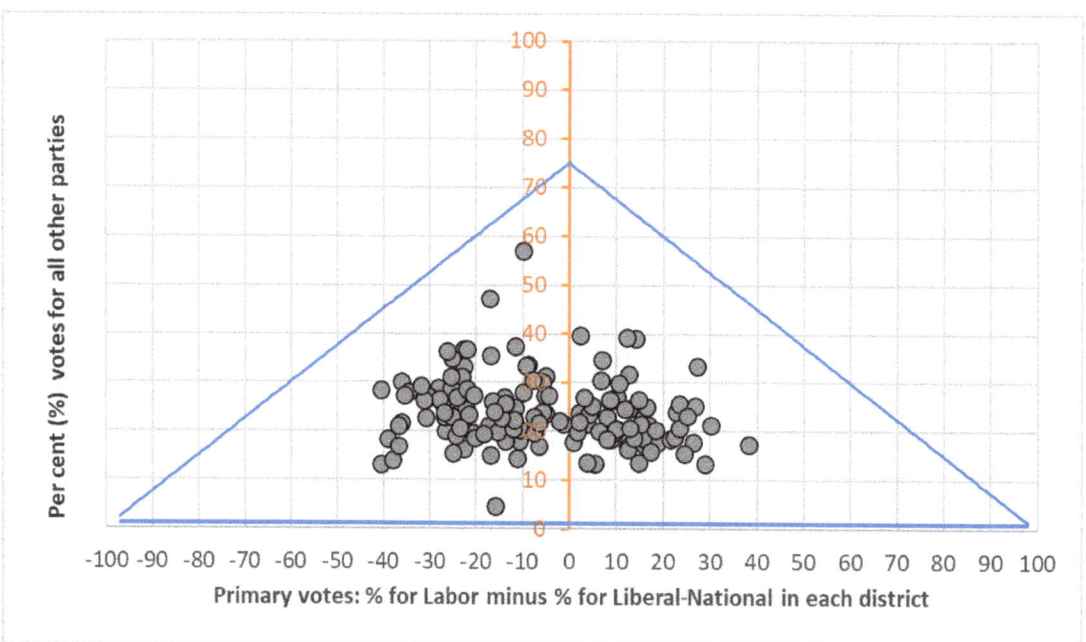

Source: Computed by the author using data from division results at AEC (2022).

Notes: The horizontal axis shows the Labor lead (in per cent) over the Liberal-National Coalition at district level, with Labor ahead for positive results and behind for negative results. The vertical axis shows the percentage total vote for all third or lower-ranked parties. The circles show the outcomes for individual districts. The triangular outline shows the feasible competition space for eight-party competition – all possible results must lie within this area.

Figure 5.10: The patterning of seats in the 15 districts where one or both of the top two parties (either P1 or P2) in first-preference votes was not Labor or Liberal-National Coalition

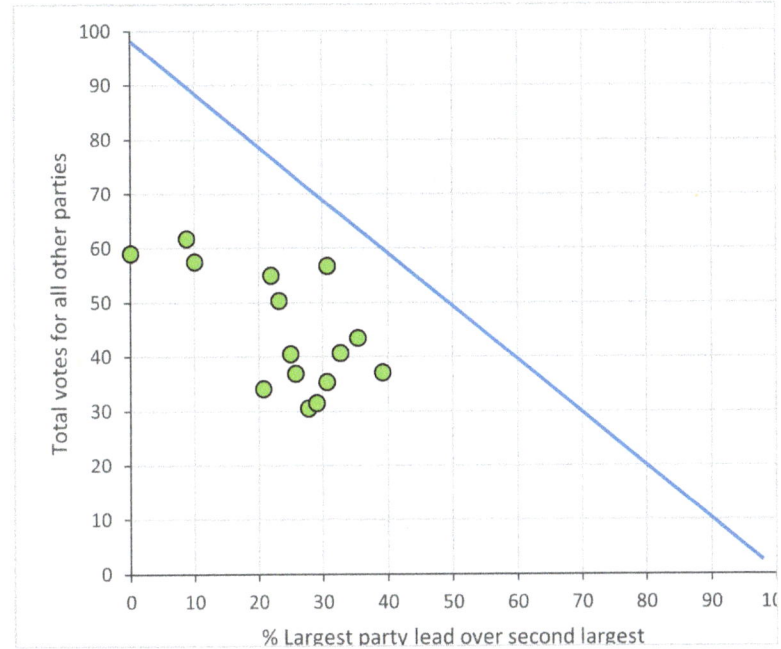

Source: Compiled by the author using data from division results at AEC (2022).

Notes: The horizontal axis here shows the percentage lead of the largest party (P1) in first-preference votes over those for the second-ranked party (P2). The vertical axis shows the percentage total vote for all third or lower-ranked parties. The circles show the outcomes for individual districts. The space below the diagonal line shows the feasible competition space for eight-party competition in this representation – all possible results must lie within this area.

top two parties. On the right-hand side of the diagram, with positive scores, Labor was ahead in a district; on the left, with negative scores, the Liberal-National Coalition was beating it locally. But the 2022 contest was emphatically a multi-party one, and so the vertical axis in Figure 5.9 shows the combined votes for all other parties in each district – the higher up the score from bottom to top that a district's circle is situated, the more third, fourth and other parties won votes there.

The pattern in Figure 5.9 shows that the large majority of local results in 2022 fell in the middle of the diagram, the zone where no single party wins an overall majority of the votes. There were considerably more seats where the Liberal-National Coalition came top on first preferences, on the right of the diagram, with some seats having large gaps (over 30 percentage points) between the Liberal-National Coalition and Labor. In some seats the Coalition candidate actually won a majority of first-preference votes and so was elected straightaway, without any further need to redistribute votes between parties. By contrast, Labor had very few safe seats where it was well ahead of the Liberal-National Coalition by 30 points or more, and no seats where it won a majority of the first-preference votes. This situation reflects Labor's dependence on transfers of voters' second or subsequent preferences to it in order to achieve a narrow majority of seats. The district outcomes are also well inside the competition space for eight-party contests, and relatively far from the top boundaries shown.

Figure 5.9 also shows that in 2022 the total votes for the non-top-two parties (those that were ranked third, fourth, etc.) averaged 20 per cent. In those seats where Labor and the Liberal-National Coalition formed one of the top two parties, the smaller parties' primary votes were never lower than 12 per cent; they ranged up over 30 per cent in a few Labor seats and far more in some districts that the Liberal-National Coalition held. The five uppermost circles in Figure 5.9 show seats where more voters backed the ensemble of smaller parties competing than

Figure 5.11: Respondents' interest in elections and beliefs about political efficacy, in Australian Election Study surveys, 2001–2019

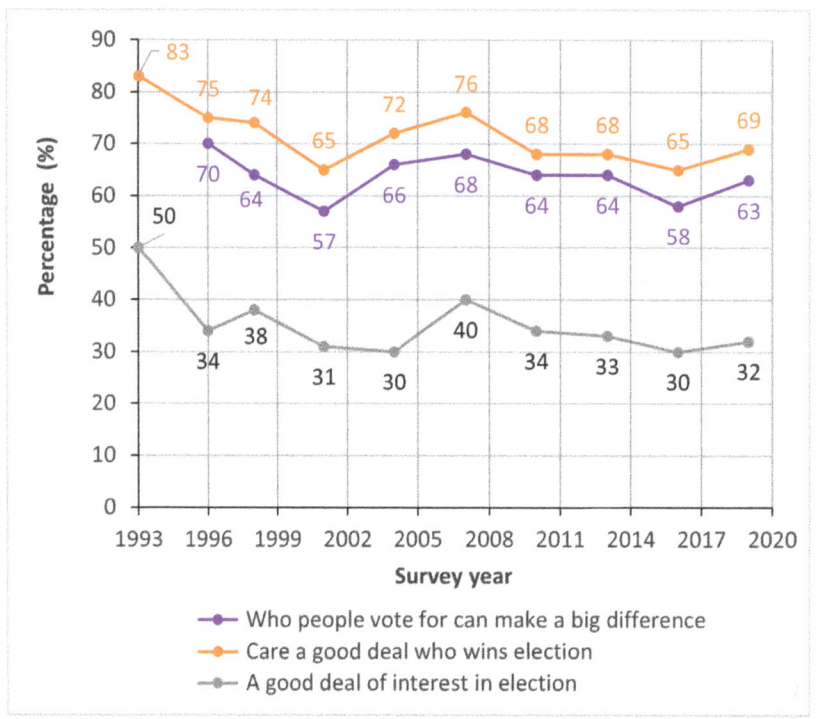

Source: Compiled by author using data from Cameron and McAllister (2019).

Note: 'Who people vote for can make a big difference' shows the percentage of respondents that selected 1 or 2 on a scale of 1–5, where 1 is 'Who people vote for can make a big difference' and 5 is 'Who people vote for won't make any difference'. Unfortunately, these questions were not asked at the 2022 federal election – see Cameron et al. (2022).

the top two parties. So multi-party competition was clearly an important feature of the 2022 election. These local outcomes (and especially Labor's apparently weaker position here in first-preference votes than the Liberal-National Coalition) also illustrate the importance of AV's two-party preferred vote, which Labor went on to win nationally and in half of all seats in 2022.

In addition, however, there were 15 seats in 2022 where an independent, the Greens or another smaller party (like Katter and Xenophon in their 'home' districts), succeeded in becoming either the first-ranked party (P1) or the second-ranked party (P2) locally in terms of their first-preference votes. In Figure 5.10, the horizontal axis shows the percentage of P1 votes minus those for P2 – and again all the results come from areas where the largest P1 party's lead was less than 40 per cent. As was to be expected, given how these cases came to be charted separately, the total vote for smaller parties shown on the vertical axis is higher here, never less than 30 per cent and in some cases near to or above 60 per cent.

Voters whose party 'loses' the election nationally may often be disappointed, but if their vote contributed to a local win for either their first-preference party or a party they supported in the TPP vote, this might compensate a good deal for an adverse national result. AV ensures that a maximum number of Australian voters can be assured that their preferences shaped their local outcome, either by forming part of the winning TPP majority or by providing the TPP runner-up with a vote.

How strongly felt are later preferences in voters' utility functions? Is a late-preference choice as important to them as a first-preference vote? There is not much data on this, and historically political scientists have relied on asking voters if they 'identify' with a party – a rather controversial and disputed notion (Bergman, Tran and Yates, 2019) – or, more recently, just whether in general they 'prefer' one party. In 2022 the Australian Election Study found that 30 per cent of their survey respondents preferred the Liberal-National Coalition, 28 per cent Labor, 10 per cent the Greens and fully 24 per cent no party (Cameron et al., 2022, Figure 3.1). This might suggest that some later vote transfers are not necessarily deeply felt or thought through.

A final battery of questions in the Australian Election Study surveys asked in a consistent way over decades whether their respondents thought that voting makes a 'big difference', or whether respondents 'cared a good deal' about election results or had a 'a good deal of interest' in the election outcome. These are rather vague questions and so people could perhaps answer them in lots of different ways, but the questions have been consistently worded and administered. Figure 5.11 shows that in this century the patterns of responses have been pretty stable over time, with over two-thirds of respondents saying that they cared about the election outcome, and fluctuations in this measure tracking closely the somewhat lower level of respondents endorsing the statement that 'who people vote for can make a difference'. The proportion of survey respondents who said they had 'a good deal of interest' in the elections has been much lower, and has been just a third for the last decade. In Figure 5.11 a few pre-21st century results for these questions are also included, to show that current levels on all three indices are appreciably lower than those reached in the 1990s, something of a golden era for democratic satisfaction in Australia.

The Teal Independents

The change of government after almost nine years of conservative rule and three Liberal PMs was the big story of the 2022 election. But the second key development was that 16 'crossbench' MPs were elected to the House of Representatives in 2022: 6 women independents dubbed 'Teal' to signify their blue-green credentials, 4 Greens, and a handful of candidates winning on their local reputations as small-party MPs or other independents. The Teal wins were part of a well-organised campaign, contesting a wider range of seats and with funding support secured by the Climate 200 campaigns guru Simon Holmes à Court. All of them occurred in 'blue-ribbon' Liberal seats and reflected the apparent public indifference of the Liberals and successive PMs (Tony Abbott and Scott Morrison in particular) to a range of women's issues that soared in prominence after the 'Me Too' movement and allegations of misogynistic behaviour by (mainly Liberal) politicians. One consequence was that '[a] gap between men and women backing the coalition [that had] opened up in 2019 ... was reduced but still there in 2022, with 39 per cent of men backing them but only 32 per cent of women' (Cameron et al., 2022, Figure 5.2).

The Teal candidates were generally centre-right Liberal women (although there were some men also) who left their party to campaign on greater and quicker response to environmental issues and climate change and on taking women's issues seriously. By standing in apparently very secure Liberal seats, they aimed both to detach some moderate Liberal voters to back them and to convince centre and left voters that a broader coalition could win in right-of-centre seats, because

Figure 5.12: Among 2022 voters giving a first preference to the Teal Independents, which parties had they backed in the 2019 election?

2019 vote	Per cent
Labor	31
Greens	24
Other	23
Coalition	18
Too young, not eligible	4
Total	100

Source: Cameron et al. (2022, Figure 3.2).

otherwise even dissatisfied moderate Liberal voters would stay party-loyal and not back Labor or the Greens in such seats.

A good deal of media commentary after the election focused on the Teals' successes in attracting former Liberal voters. But in fact, such people were always likely to form only a minority of the Teal voters. Figure 5.12 shows that less than one in five Teal 2022 voters came from 2019 Liberal voters, and well over half from Labor and the Greens. There are some difficulties here, because the Australian Election Study sample of Teal supporters was not a large one and the analysis relies on recalled votes (which voters may 'reconstruct' or mis-remember). Yet the close match of Figure 5.12 with the Teals' intelligent campaign strategies and the targeted areas where they succeeded both suggest that this data should be taken seriously (Cameron et al., 2022, p.18).

How far the Teal phenomenon is indicative of a new ratcheting up of what Cameron et al. (2022) term 'partisan dealignment' remains to be seen, especially as in other 2022–2023 state elections held in Victoria and NWS similar Teal campaigns did not produce wins, despite taking place in smaller seats. In NSW, the Teals were perhaps disadvantaged by the state's different variant of AV, which allows voters to indicate some preferences only, rather than requiring voters to number all candidates (as federal AV does). In Victoria, they were at a funding disadvantage and were competing against an incumbent Labor government, not Liberal ministers (see Chapter 18). It may be that the Teal moment will turn out to be another 'surge' quasi-party that has problems sustaining itself between elections or carrying over victory in one political conjuncture into different future situations, for example with growing Liberal votes. Alternatively, given the Liberals' move to the right under the leadership of Peter Dutton, the Teals may be able to consolidate their local electoral support and extend their appeal to new areas, in the process achieving a lasting diversification of party competition (see Chapter 6).

Electoral integrity

One of the most disturbing trends in 'backsliding' democracies like the USA and Hungary has been a shift by many politicians (especially on the right) to voter suppression tactics against their opponents' voter groups or areas, using a series of micro-institution changes to restrict who can vote and how much difficulty they face in doing so (Dunleavy, 2021). If all else fails, the areas in which elections can take place can also be 'gerrymandered' to create artificial malapportionment between opposition parties' votes and seats. Sustained action on these lines in the USA has been missed by political scientists placing too much trust in a few objective indices of election performance (for example, Little and Meng, 2023). However, rigging elections in these ways has become impossible in Australia, because non-partisan electoral commissions control elections districting and voting processes at the federal and state levels. A proposal by PM Morrison and Liberal ministers to increase the requirements for voters to identify themselves raised some suspicions of potential partisan voter suppression tactics, but it was abandoned in 2021 (Miller, 2021). However, in the past severe malapportionment to favor the Liberal-National Coalition by over-representing rural areas persisted in some state elections, like Queensland and South Australia, into the 1970s (see chapters 19 and 20).

At federal level the AEC (2021) has operated on the primary requirement that federal House districts should be equalised as far as possible. This has meant that the middle majority of seats (those falling between the upper and lower quartiles) had electorates from just below 110,000 to just above 120,000 in 2022 (see the middle column in Figure 5.13), with the result that the majority of MPs in 2022 were chosen by 96,000 to 106,000 voters each (the last column). Votes cast in the largest seats were only 10,000 above the upper quartile number. However, the AEC recognised a need for a few large and very scantily populated or inaccessible areas to be much smaller than average seat sizes, with four seats in the Northern Territory and Tasmania having electorates of below 80,000, well below the lower quartile level.

These variations have been accepted by all parties as legitimate, however, and all the other operations of the AEC have been well regarded and attracted consensus agreement. A study using a large international group of expert political scientists has also rated the integrity of most aspects of Australia's elections process very highly and mostly on a par with the best international comparator democracies, as Figure 5.14 shows. However, the following three aspects were scored poorly by experts:

Figure 5.13: The distribution of federal electoral district sizes in 2022

Indicator	In districts	
	Size of electorates	Votes cast in 2022
Maximum	133,500	116,220
Upper quartile	121,360	105,640
Median size	114,390	100,910
Mean size	*114,100*	*99,950*
Lower quartile	109,140	96,140
Minimum	71,890	51,010

Source: Computed from AEC (2023b).

Notes: A quarter of all seats lie above the upper quartile, between the upper quartile and the median, between the median and the lower quartile, and below the lower quartile. The median is the district that is exactly halfway down the size list. The mean is given by: total population divided by number of seats. All numbers are rounded to the nearest 10.

- Voter registration, where processes are relatively unmodernised and run by the states.
- Campaign finance, where at both federal and state levels incumbent politicians from the top two parties have been reluctant to restrict the maximum sizes of donations and keen to raise the minimum sizes at which declaring donations becomes compulsory (Centre for Public Integrity, 2020; and see Chapters 6 and 7).

Figure 5.14: Experts' perceptions of electoral integrity in Australia as scores out of 100 (in 2017)

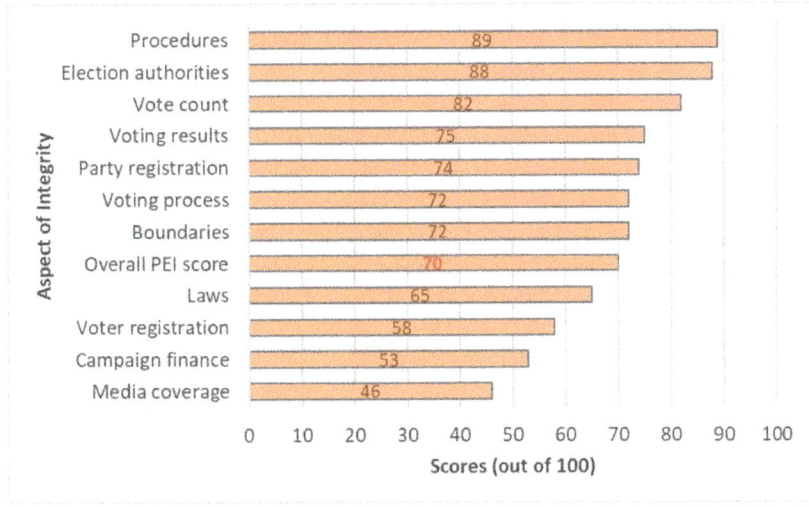

Source: Compiled by the authors from data in Norris, Wynter and Cameron (2018).

Notes: Figure 5.14 shows the Perceptions of Electoral Integrity (PEI) expert survey scores across 11 dimensions of electoral integrity. Estimates are on a scale from 0–100, where higher scores indicate higher levels of integrity. Very high: 70+; high: 60–69; moderate: 50–59; low: 40–49; very low: <40.

- Worst of all, as shown in Figure 5.14, is the rating of the role of the media in Australian elections – mainly due to the heavy partisan imbalance in the press favouring the Liberal-National Coalition and the virulence and directness of right-wing press campaigns.

Additionally, in 2019 the incumbent federal ministers 'played' government advertising on Liberal-National Coalition talking points right down to the wire, before the PM finally announced the election date (and the purdah on public advertising came into force) at short notice. This experience was not repeated in 2022.

The federal electoral cycle

In the history of democratic reforms, shortening the term of elected representatives has been a characteristic demand of the most radical reformers, but one rather rarely implemented, albeit with some exceptions. In 1789 the USA constitutional founding fathers set up Congressional elections for their entire lower house every two years (reflecting their strong anti-monarchism). The English Chartist mass movement in the early 19th century demanded annual parliamentary elections, but UK political elites retained the country's familiar five-year maximum parliamentary terms. In all the Australian states and territories, elections for the lower house must now occur every four years. Around the world, 90 per cent of countries hold elections every four or five years (Pickering, 2016). Thus, three-year federal elections are short terms for a parliament and an executive dependent on it.

In addition, the federal PM can pick the precise date for an election, and premiers regularly go to the polls before 36 months have passed if there seems to be a partisan advantage in doing so. From 1990 to 2013, the average House term was actually 32 months (Pickering, 2016). Half-Senate elections normally coincide with every election for the House of Representatives, but a PM can also choose to precipitate a double-dissolution election for all Senate seats at once, as Abbot did in 2016. Senators normally serve up to six-year terms.

Critics of three-year House terms argue that they induce election fatigue and create unnecessary expense (Rhodes, 2017). Perhaps more serious criticisms claim that they add to government costs and accentuate chronic political short-termism in Australia. Governing elites repeatedly 'kick into the long grass' troublesome or potentially unpopular decisions that nonetheless may have to be made at some point in the national interest (see Chapter 15). Especially if the partisan control of government or the PM changes at an election, then no sooner has a new set of ministers come to power and put through perhaps a year's or 18 months' worth of new legislation than they must start scanning the polls and anticipating the next election as the 'long campaign period' begins. And six months before the likely next election date (that is, no more than 26 to 30 months into a term), a blanket disinclination to push through deeply contested or difficult laws or executive actions may set in. In the formal election period itself, the rules around civil service purdah mean no new policy announcements are made.

Since three-year terms are specifically included in the Australian Constitution, however, they are very hard to change. It would require a referendum to do so, and probably bipartisan support for a change, which has never been forthcoming. In 1988 the Hawke Labor government proposed fixed four-year terms for both the House and the Senate in a national referendum held without bipartisan support from the Liberal-National Coalition. Only a third of electors backed it

(Galligan, 1990, p.498), adding to three previous referendum rejections by voters since 1970 (in 1974, 1977 and 1984). Perhaps more voters might have backed the House proposal in 1988 had it not been linked to changes also for the Senate (Bennett, 2000). Because Senate and House elections have been held on the same day, a four-year House term (as in the states) would also imply either lengthening senators' terms to eight years or perhaps reviving the 1988 proposal of four-year terms for the upper house as well.

Moving to fixed election times, removing the PM's ability to select the date has also been advocated as a way of stamping out the potential for months of games-playing by opportunistic PMs – who sometimes seek to mislead their rivals that they might go very early if the opinion polls look favourable. But defenders of the status quo suggest that in Westminster systems it helps PMs to combat the inherent difficulties of being an incumbent at elections if they can seek a new mandate to govern at a time of their choosing (Bennett, 2000). Some Australian states have settled on a mixed approach. Victoria and South Australia have maximum four-year parliaments, but also require a minimum of three years between elections, which eliminates premiers calling an election too early or too opportunistically (Bennett, 2000).

Conclusion

Compared with other liberal democracies (and especially Westminster system countries), Australia's unique electoral systems perform very well in getting citizens to communicate a great deal of information about their preferences in elections, and then counting these in sophisticated ways that ensure every vote can help shape the outcome, in both House and Senate elections, in different ways. Preferential (AV) systems have normally privileged the main parties, however, and national DV scores are high in the House and relatively high in the Senate – mainly because many voters disperse their support across multiple tiny parties or candidates. However, the success of the Teals in 2021 shows that past patterns can change, confirming the growth of 'party dealignment' detected by many observers since 2000. STV in the Senate helps independents and has been a major check on the legislative program of the federal government. Australian voters also get plenty of choice among three main established parties (Labor, the Liberal-National Coalition and the Greens) plus independents and smaller parties. Populist politics by new parties has remained a small phenomenon, before and after the COVID-19 pandemic, which some analysts argue has reduced populist policies' appeal crossnationally (Bennett Institute for Public Policy, 2022), for a while.

Surprisingly, the past links between federal MPs and their constituents have not been all that strong (certainly far less than has been true of representatives in state lower houses). However, constituency linkages may well become more important because of the rise of independents and partisan dealignment, meaning that MPs will not be able to rely as much on long-run party loyalties and polarisations among their electors. In terms of social diversity, the representation of women and First Nations peoples improved significantly at the 2022 election. However, the Australian Parliament remains unrepresentative for Chinese Australians, Indian Australians (the fastest growing groups in the population) and in terms of age.

Note

1. We are most grateful to Professor Sarah Cameron of Griffith University for her advice on many election aspects. The analysis and opinions here are our responsibility alone.

References

Australian Electoral Commission (2021) 'The AEC's role,' AEC. https://perma.cc/J8VA-ZHLD

Australian Electoral Commission (2022) 'Tally room, divisional results', 2022 Federal Election', AEC. https://perma.cc/DXC8-4DCU

Australian Electoral Commission (2023a) 'Federal elections', AEC. https://perma.cc/9PRW-GUZH

Australian Electoral Commission (2023b) 'Elector count by division, age group and gender', AEC. https://perma.cc/ZF3V-DWND

Bennett, Scott (2000) 'Four-year Terms for the House of Representatives'. Parliament of Australia, 29 August, Research Paper. https://perma.cc/9AW8-YQ6D

Bennett Institute for Public Policy (2022) 'The Great Reset: Public Opinion, Populism, and the Pandemic', Bennett Institute for Public Policy, University of Cambridge, 14 January. https://perma.cc/PZ62-C3R3

Bergman, Elizabeth; Tran, Dari Sylvester; and Yates, Philip (2019) 'Voter Identification,' in Norris, Pippa; Cameron, Sarah and Wynter, Thomas (eds) *Electoral Integrity in America: Securing Democracy*, pp.102–13, New York: Oxford University Press. $ https://perma.cc/BC8X-TQAE

Blais, André and Gélineau, François (2007) 'Winning, Losing and Satisfaction with Democracy', *Political Studies*, vol. 55, pp.425–44. https://perma.cc/T3GK-7ZP8

Browne, Bill and Oquist, Ben (2021) *Representative, still – The role of the Senate in our democracy*, Canberra: Australia Institute. https://perma.cc/P5VF-ZGQ3

Cameron, Sarah and McAllister, Ian (2019) Trends in Australian Political Opinion: Results from the Australian Election Study 1987–2019, Canberra: The Australian National University. https://perma.cc/URM9-847Y

Cameron, Sarah and Thomas Wynter (2018) 'Campaign finance and perceptions of interest group influence in Australia', *Political Science*, vol. 70, no. 2, pp.169–88. $ https://doi.org/10.1080/00323187.2018.1562307

Cameron, Sarah; McAllister, Ian; Jackman, Simon; and Sheppard, Jill (2022) *The 2022 Australian Federal Election – Results from the Australian Election Study*, Australian Election Study Web Report, Griffith University. https://perma.cc/URM9-847Y

Centre for Public Integrity (2020) 'Hidden money in politics: What the AEC disclosures don't tell us', Briefing Paper, Centre for Public Integrity, February 2020. https://perma.cc/9VJR-WWHP

Dunleavy, Patrick (2018) 'The Westminster "plurality rule" electoral system', Chapter 2.1 in Dunleavy, Patrick; Park, Alice; and Taylor, Ros (eds) *The UK's Changing Democracy: The 2018 Democratic Audit*, pp. 45–55. London: LSE Press. https://doi.org/10.31389/book1.b

Dunleavy, Patrick (2021) 'Micro-institutions and democracy, *Political Insight*, vol. 10, no. 1. https://doi.org/10.1177/2041905819838154

Finkelstein, Raymond (2012) Report of the independent inquiry into the media and media regulation. https://perma.cc/YN75-YHRB

Foa, R.S.; Klassen, A.; Slade, M.; Rand, A.; and Williams, R (2020) 'Global Satisfaction with Democracy Report 2020', Cambridge, UK: Centre for the Future of Democracy. https://perma.cc/F9SW-7B9A

Galligan, Brian (1990) 'The 1988 Referendums and Australia's Record on Constitutional Change,' *Parliamentary Affairs,* vol. 43, no. 4, pp.497–506. $ https://doi.org/10.1093/oxfordjournals.pa.a052271

Hough, Anna (2022) 'Trends in the gender composition of state and territory parliaments', Parliament of Australia, 27 May. https://perma.cc/2S9R-YRZ9

Inter-Parliamentary Union (2021) 'Women in Politics: new data shows growth but also setbacks'. https://perma.cc/2S9R-YRZ9

Karp, Jeffrey; Alessandro, Nai; Ferran, Martinez i Coma; Grömping, Max; and Norris, Pippa (2017) *The Australian Voter Experience: Trust and confidence in the 2016 federal election*, Sydney: The Electoral Integrity Project. https://perma.cc/SL3B-JSGL

Karp, Paul; Knaus, Christopher; and Evershed, Nick (2020) 'Liberal party received $4.1m in donations from property tycoon's company,' *The Guardian*, 3 February. https://perma.cc/4GP2-2E48

Little, Andrew and Meng, Anne (2023) 'Measuring Democratic Backsliding', *PS: Political Science and Politics*. Revised 2024. $ http://dx.doi.org/10.1017/S104909652300063X or OA at: 10.2139/ssrn.4327307

Mackerras, Malcom (2022) 'How Does Australia's Voting System Work?', Electoral Integrity project, blogpost, 7 September. https://perma.cc/KHM4-C4D5

Miller, Paul (2021) 'Good riddance: the costs of Morrison's voter ID plan outweighed any benefit', *The Conversation*, 1 December. https://perma.cc/CG8R-76DA

Norris, Pippa (2004) *Electoral Engineering: Voting Rules and Political Behavior*, Cambridge: Cambridge University Press.

Norris, Pippa; Wynter, Thomas; and Cameron, Sarah (2018) 'Perceptions of Electoral Integrity (PEI 6.0)', Electoral Integrity Project (EIP), Harvard Dataverse. https://perma.cc/KF75-YY9F

Pickering, Heath (2016) 'Three-year parliamentary terms are too short', *Huffpost* website, 16 May. https://perma.cc/H6E4-GV7G

Ransley, Ellen (2021) 'Opposition slams Morrison government for 'discriminatory' voter integrity bill,' *The Australian (Weekend)*, 28 October. https://perma.cc/72UG-Z6MQ

Rhodes, Campbell (2017) 'How often should we have an election – every three years or every four?', Museum of Australian Democracy at Old Parliament House, blogpost, 25 July. https://perma.cc/BQA2-WHMR

Rogowski, Ronald and Kayser, Mark Andreas (2002) 'Majoritarian Electoral Systems and Consumer Power: Price-Level Evidence from the OECD Countries', *American Journal of Political Science*, vol. 46, no. 3, pp.526–39. OA: https://mark-kayser.com/wp-content/uploads/2021/01/RogoKayserAJPS2002_Majoritarian-Electoral-Systems.pdf

Young, Sally (2011) *How Australia Decides: Election Reporting and the Media*, Cambridge: Cambridge University Press. $ https://doi.org/10.1017/CBO9780511984778

Political parties

Patrick Dunleavy and Mark Evans

In Australia, as in other 'Anglosphere' liberal democracies (like the USA, UK or Canada), political parties have moved in the last three decades from being widely trusted and relatively uncontroversial parts of the political system, to being criticised as increasingly unrepresentative of society and blamed for an erosion of liberal democratic integrity and quality. Yet political parties have multiple, complex roles to play in liberal democracies, especially in federations (Ghazarian, 2024; Jackson et al., 2022; Marsh, 2006). Thanks to its electoral systems, Australia has not suffered from partisan over-polarisation, nor any major slide towards populism. However, the party system has some significant weaknesses, for which some reforms have been advocated.

What does democracy require for political parties and a party system?

Parties (and now other forms of election-fighting organisations, like referendum campaigns) are diverse, so four kinds of democratic evaluation criteria are needed:

(i) Structuring competition and engagement

- The party system should provide citizens with a framework for simplifying and organising political ideas and discourses, providing coherent packages of policy proposals, so as to sustain vigorous and effective electoral competition between rival teams. In a federal system, this role needs to work both nationally and in (most) component states.

- Parties should provide enduring brands, able to sustain the engagement and trust of most citizens over long periods. Because they endure through time, parties should behave responsibly, knowing that citizens can effectively hold them to account in future. In a federation, some brand differentiation will occur across states, but national coherence is still needed.

- Main parties should help to recruit, socialise, select and promote talented individuals into elected public office, at state and national government levels. In cities and local areas, the major parties can often play a key role in organising political space.

How to cite this chapter:

Dunleavy, Patrick and Evans, Mark (2024) 'Political parties' in: Evans, Mark; Dunleavy, Patrick and Phillimore, John (eds) *Australia's Evolving Democracy: A New Democratic Audit*, London: LSE Press, pp.120–142. https://doi.org/10.31389/lsepress.ada.f Licence: CC-BY-NC 4.0

- Party groups inside elected legislatures (such as MPs and senators federally and in state legislatures), plus associated elites and members in the party's extra-parliamentary organisations at state and federal levels, should help to sustain viable and accountable leadership teams. They should also be important channels for the scrutiny of public policies and the elected leadership's conduct in office and behaviour in the public interest.

(ii) Representing civil society

- The party system should be reasonably inclusive nationally and at state level, covering a broad range of interests and views in civil society. Parties should not exclude or discriminate against people on the basis of gender, ethnicity or other characteristics.
- Citizens should be able to form and grow new political parties easily at state and federal levels, without encountering onerous or artificial official barriers privileging existing, established or incumbent parties.
- Party activities should be regulated independently at both state and federal levels by impartial officials and agencies, so as to maximise electoral integrity and prevent self-serving protection of existing incumbents.

(iii) Internal party democracy and transparency

- Long-established parties inevitably accumulate discretionary political power in the exercise of their functions. This creates some citizen dependencies upon them and always has oligopolistic effects in restricting political competition (for example, concentrating funding and advertising/campaign capabilities in main parties). To compensate, the internal leadership of parties and their processes for setting policies should be responsive to a wide membership, one that is open and easy to join.
- Leadership selection and the setting of main policies should operate democratically and transparently to members and other groupings inside the party (such as party MPs or members of legislatures) (Jaensch, Brent and Bowden, 2004). Independent regulation should ensure that parties stick both to their own rule books and to public interest practices.

(iv) Political finance

- Parties should be able to raise substantial political funding of their own, but subject to independent regulation to ensure that effective electoral competition is not undermined by inequities of funding.
- Individuals, organisations or interests providing large donations to parties or other election-fighting organisations (such as referendum campaigns) must not gain enhanced or differential influence over public policies, or the allocation of social prestige (such as honours).
- All donations must be fully transparent, with no payments made from front organisations or foreign sources. The size of individual contributions should be capped where they could raise doubts of undue influence over parties or individual legislators.

The traditional view of parties was captured by Ian McAllister:

> *The hallmark of Australian politics is the dominance of party. The vast majority of voters identify with and vote for one of the major political parties: gaining election at federal level is next to impossible without the benefit of one of the three party labels – Liberal, National or Labor; and minor parties [sic] have played little part in shaping the development of the party system. (2002, p.379)*

This has also been a long-settled pattern. Historically the top two parties became the dominant foci of political activity almost from the outset of the Australian federation (see Chapter 1). The unbroken duopolistic control of government ministries by either the Liberal-National Coalition or the Australia Labor Party (ALP) has continued. But their complete control of policy has been qualified by hung Senates and narrowing House of Representatives majorities. And their combined share of primary votes has fallen fairly consistently over the five elections from 2010 to 2022 (see Chapter 5), reaching just 68 per cent of the total in the last of these. Almost as many 2022 voters chose another party to support as backed Labor – which nonetheless went from second place in the primary vote to an overall win, largely thanks to getting second-preference support from Green voters.

Recent developments

In theory, Australians can change their party of government every three years at federal elections, but this has rarely happened in modern times. Instead, when voters have shifted allegiances, they have tended to give a new party of government two or three terms, giving them the benefit of the doubt, partly sustained by the country's continuous economic growth over three decades. Even when a switch of party of government occurs, the changes of seats involved can be fairly small and the new government may have a narrow majority. This was the case in 2019 when Scott Morrison, a relatively new prime minister (PM) who had toppled his predecessor as Liberal leader only less than a year beforehand, unexpectedly won a small but stable majority (Gauja, Sawer and Simms, 2020). He went on to prove himself a determined but perhaps overly combative PM, with a robust alpha-male style that ultimately proved inappropriate to the times.

PM Morrison's apparent laggard reactions in combatting global warming, despite the devastating bush fires of 2019 to 2020, and various lurches away from bipartisanship into criticisms of Labor state governments during the COVID-19 pandemic of 2020–2022, diminished the government's popular appeal. Criticisms of the misogynistic or alleged bullying conduct of some Liberal and National politicians also went largely unaddressed. After the 2019 election campaign, it also later emerged that the Liberal-National government had practised partisan tailoring of government programs to focus spending on target seats important for it to win. Following later scandals in the Liberal Party in New South Wales (NSW), PM Morrison also went back on his December 2018 promise to create a federal anti-corruption agency that would be a 'serious new commission with teeth … to protect the integrity of Australia's Commonwealth public administration' (Gordon, 2022).

Labor recovered relatively quickly from its 2019 election defeat. Its Members of Parliament (MPs) and senators elected Anthony Albanese unopposed after his predecessor resigned. In May 2022, the incumbent Coalition lost support and fell behind Labor in the crucial two-party preferred (TPP) vote, and additionally lost some seats to disillusioned former Liberals standing as independents. A reconstructed and now relatively consensual leader, Albanese steered Labor successfully to lead a narrowly victorious election strategy, winning Green voters' support in the 2022 election. This was despite Labor garnering less of the primary vote than the Coalition and suffering some unexpected defeats in Queensland's coal-mining and primary industry seats.

On election night, Scott Morrison conceded defeat and resigned as Liberal party leader. Normally the Liberal deputy leader, Josh Frydenberg (who had been Treasurer), would have been expected to succeed Morrison, but he lost his Kooyong seat. The Liberal MPs and senators went on to elect unopposed the experienced but controversial 'hard man' MP Peter Dutton as their leader. Initially, at least, this did little to stem a substantial post-election decline in the party's fortunes, with Dutton at first lagging well behind PM Albanese's initial soaraway evaluations. However, the 2023 loss of the Voice referendum and 'cost of living' worries brought this period to a close.

More than one in seven of 2022 MPs in the House of Representatives were elected to the crossbench, with the Teal Independents (all women) winning a handful of previous Liberal-National seats on fairly conservative policies but linked to faster action on global warming and taking women's issues seriously (see later in this chapter). Green voters' support was critical in securing the overall Labor victory, although the smaller party also unexpectedly won three inner-city Brisbane seats by defeating Labor candidates. On the political right, over 12 per cent of the primary vote went to small parties, damaging Coalition chances in some seats – even though most of this voter base backed Liberals or National in the TPP vote. The political prominence of anti-vaccination movements during the COVID-19 lockdowns did not trigger any effective revival in terms of far-right parties winning seats, but more than 1 in 12 voters backed one or another of various small parties in this space.

Clearly, then, the rise of new parties, movements and issue orientations has changed a great deal over the last two decades of Australian politics. At the time of writing the new parties were still small, and the shifting start-ups on the far right have faced problems in building permanent support bases, given the high threshold needed to win seats in the single-member House constituencies under the Alternative Vote (AV) (see Chapter 5). But Australia's third, fourth and other parties have ceased to be minor in their impacts or significance (Gauja and Gromping, 2020).

Strengths, weaknesses, opportunities and threats (SWOT) analysis

Current strengths	Current weaknesses
At the time of writing, some political scientists had recently characterised Australia's party system as highly stable. However, the rise of the Greens at Labor's expense, changes in the relative partisan strength of the Liberals and Nationals, and the successes of independents at the federal level have all created significant dynamism, especially in the 2022 national election. Teal Independents and Greens especially were able to reach the final stage in important local AV seats, due to voters' disaffection with the main two parties.	Thanks to the operations of AV, the long-established Liberal-National Coalition and Labor parties have been in a privileged position in dominating second-preference votes for lower houses at both the federal and state levels. This privileged hegemony has long made it harder for newer or alternative parties to win MPs and to attract and retain activists and financial support.
The use of proportional representation (PR) elections has allowed parties outside the top two to win representation in the federal Senate at Canberra and in some state upper houses (Ghazarian, 2024). The Greens have increased their capabilities as a party (Jackson, 2016). But various small right-wing parties have proved evanescent and dependent on one leading figure for their representation in the legislature or funding.	Under AV, new or smaller parties cannot win seats unless they can make it into the TPP vote final stage of the counts. Hence, parties running third or fourth can accumulate substantial votes across many seats without winning any MPs. Historically, local independents have been the key exceptions to two-party dominance, and usually not for very long periods.
In terms of structuring the political/ideological space for voters, the Labor versus Liberal-National divide has generally captured a (moderate) left-wing to (robust) right-wing politics that has been well understood by voters. This ideological dimension centres around societal equality and welfare state provision versus low taxation/private enterprise. It also links to major social interests – the Liberals with business (Brett, 2006) and the conservative middle class (Brett, 2003), the Nationals with rural areas (Cockfield, 2020) and Labor with trade unions and urban liberals.	The two main parties have been conspicuously poor in handling the issues that do not fit neatly into left- versus right-wing politics, especially around climate change and global warming (see Chapter 27). Labor's position has been fractured between trade unions representing carbon industries (like Queensland coal mining) and urban middle-class supporters pressing for faster climate policy changes (Crowe, 2018). Up to the 2022 election, the Liberal-National Coalition was dominated by factions minimising the scale of climate change challenges – contributing to the Teal Independent phenomenon in 2022.

Political polarisation between the top two parties has generally been relatively restrained, despite periodic rhetorical excesses or blunt speaking. In modern times, abuses by incumbents to boost their tenure in office have still occurred, but in small ways only. Attempts by populist politicians (mainly of the right) have created occasional surges of support, without creating any lasting or cumulative election-fighting capacity (C. Johnson, 2020).	Critics argue that the top two parties have responded to populist issue surges by incorporating into their programs some semi-populist policies that inhibit civil rights (for example draconian restrictions on illegal immigrants) or that postpone action on threatening issues (like climate change or Australia's relations with China).
Public trust in Australia's political parties re-grew in encouraging ways during the COVID-19 pandemic from 2020 to 2022, partly because the parties (most of the time, and in their official discourses) stressed bipartisan cooperation and joint working. Occasional lapses from this stance occurred but were generally quickly retreated from.	In some repeated lapses away from bipartisanship, at times mainstream Liberal or National politicians at federal and state levels made efforts to blame COVID-19 restrictions on Labor state governments. However, populist right parties and anti-mask movements, together with significant numbers of the Coalition parties' state and local activists and smaller office-holders, ensured that the myths and other unfounded positions involved were widely repeated and their impacts considerably magnified.
The main two parties have consistently shown an ability to attract serious leaders to become lower house politicians at the state level and as federal MPs.	The normal longer term for senators (six years instead of three) was supposed to diversify the type of people in federal politics. However, the dominance of the established party machines has meant that differences in age and experience between MPs and senators have not been large.
The gender diversity within the top two parties has improved considerably in terms of more women entering federal politics in winnable seats and reaching ministerial ranks. A record 102 women were elected to the 47th Parliament. However, recent sexual misconduct scandals (a particular problem for the Liberals and Nationals) have highlighted deeper issues of misogyny. They also partly contributed to the success of Teal Independents women candidates. The ethnic diversity of parties has continued to be dominated by politicians of white, Anglo, Irish or European origins. Nonetheless, in 2022 Ed Husic and Anne Aly became the first two Muslim federal ministers.	First Nations representation improved in the 47th Parliament, with a record 11 parliamentarians elected – 5 per cent of the total number of federal politicians, representing 3.8 per cent of the population. The Australian Bureau of Statistics (2023) has shown that appreciable percentages of Australian citizens were born overseas in India (2.8), China (2.3), the Philippines (1.2), Vietnam (1) and other Asian countries – and they continue to face barriers to entering Australian parties (Wikipedia, 2023e).

The federal legislature sits for relatively short sessions, and MPs and senators get to spend much of their year in their home areas (see Chapter 5). So, running for legislative office has been feasible for a wider range of politically interested people. State legislatures sit for even shorter time periods, and across much of the country they are far closer and more geographically accessible than Canberra.	Despite their formal openness to the public and internal democracy, the increased professionalisation of politics has radically narrowed the recruitment avenues followed by most MPs and senators at the federal level, with paid advisors, journalists and party/union officials progressing most up the political ladder. In the late 2010s and the 2020s, signs of the professionalisation of party roles have multiplied also in the states, especially the three biggest states (NSW, Victoria and Queensland).
The process of joining an Australian party has generally been open and straightforward. Many internal events are open to any member to attend, internal voting and decision opportunities are well advertised to members, and membership fees are low. Forming a new party involves registering with the Australian Electoral Commission (AEC), but has been relatively straightforward.	Although most party members are also more active on social media than politically uninvolved citizens, party campaigning on the internet tends to be dominated by 'loyalist' or repeated official messages by the parties' legislators, party communications offices and professionals, paid party staffers and the most strongly involved party activists (**Humphrys, Copland and Mansillo, 2020**).
The regulation of federal elections by the AEC has been impartial and independent of the parties. And all Australia's states and territories now have parallel bodies that administer state elections professionally. Australia scores highly on international studies of political integrity at both federal and state levels (**Norris, Wynter and Cameron, 2018**). This change has been a radical improvement on the historical record of partisan malapportionment and election 'fixes' by dominant parties at state level (in South Australia and Queensland, which lasted into the 1970s and 1980s).	Micro-institutions – very tiny rules or practices apparently far removed from the direct administration of elections themselves – can nonetheless often have a significant bearing on their democratic fairness (Dunleavy, 2021). The Labor–Liberal/National duopoly of power, and restricted constraints on ministerial powers, has resulted in Australia being chronically vulnerable to over-use of public resources by incumbents for partisan ends. Recent examples include the Morrison government's partisan concentration ('rorting') of federal funding onto coalition marginal constituencies in the run-up to the 2019 federal elections (**Martin, 2023**). The Morrison government ministers also injected more clearly partisan themes favouring the incumbent government into government-paid advertising right up until the last possible date before the 2019 election was formally called. However, both these aspects improved in 2022.

Political finance in Australia has been fairly 'clean', with strong rules against political corruption and considerable transparency around parties' spending and receipts of large donations. Smaller parties like the Greens and Independents generally rely more on individual supporters' donations (Gauja and Jackson, 2016; Jackson, 2015). Attempts by wealthy individuals to 'buy' their way into a political presence with heavy funding have generally failed, as with Clive Palmer's $100 million intervention in the 2022 federal election, where his 'party' won no seats.	Australia's top two parties depend heavily on large financial contributions from business (both parties) and trade unions (for Labor). Business funding rules are open-ended and powerful vested interests can spread smaller donations across many successful MP candidates so as to maximise their access (for example, see Chapter 7 on the Pharmacy Guild of Australia). Large corporation donations and active media campaigning have achieved some major political effects, notably the scrapping of Labor's carbon taxes in 2012. In an era of politically active billionaires achieving huge influence across the world, the Palmer case highlights that there has been a huge gap in Australia regulation, namely the absence of a cap on any one individual's funding of political activity.
The strong Liberal-National dominance in terms of press media support at elections has been partly offset by the non-political character of the Australian Broadcasting Commission (ABC), and bipartisan coverage rules for most TV news outputs. Having one dominant newspaper per state may also encourage some editorial efforts at inclusiveness in political coverage.	Strong press and even some TV media biases, combined with acute imbalances in press coverage of issues and leaders on partisan lines, remain the key area where party competition at and between elections has always been seriously unbalanced – see Chapter 8.
Parties' campaign activities have increasingly moved online, using social media to disseminate information and memes to supporters and floating voters.	However, studies suggest that digital campaigning largely replicates more traditional patterns of activity, with most social media use being by strongly involved party members and exactly mirroring party lines on issues (Chen, 2013; Kefford, 2018). Moderately involved party members show more independence in their choices of content but are less active.
Future opportunities	**Future threats**
Recent elections show that Australia's party system has diversified, with, at the time of writing, a Labor/Green coalition on the left and greater Liberal-National differentiation on the right, plus the Teal Independents, if they survive. If smaller parties can succeed in building out bastions of strong local party support, they may be able to reach the TPP stage in AV across more areas, creating more of a multi-party system in the House of Representatives, which might match the more diverse party mix produced by PR systems in the federal Senate and some other state upper houses.	Alternatively, the top two parties may retain their privileged hegemony at the TPP stage of AV counts even though their core (first-preference) support falls and gets smaller, even in areas where they win seats. Such a pattern may lengthen lags in the top parties adjusting their policies to movements of public opinion. For example, a Labor MP dependent on Green voters' support to win, or a Liberal candidate who needs Teal Independent votes, may be influenced to be more active on green issues. But in each case, they would still be constrained by strong party discipline to stick to national policies.

Greater diversity in the parties that Australian voters support has tended to 'coalitionalise' both left-wing and right-wing politics, as the top two parties may need to attract support from outside their ranks. An optimistic analysis argues that this increases the need for ministers to consult broadly to pass legislation and favours the development of more balanced and deliberative policies.	Some critics, especially on the political right, argue that the weakening position of the top two parties increases the likelihood of hung legislatures (or small majorities at best), extending from the Senate to the House of Representatives. They worry that the strength of government may decline, with greater difficulties in ministers legislating or tackling difficult or 'wicked' issues (Marsh, 1995).
Citizen vigilance about ministerial and party behaviours has continued to increase on social media, shortening reaction times in Australian politics and increasing the capacity of public opinion to scrutinise detailed issues (see Chapter 9).	Critics argue that social media have limited length and content, and so tend to open up internal party debates to populist opinion surges or tendencies.
Scandals around misogynistic behaviour by federal legislators and party officials led to electoral damage for both the Liberal and National Coalition parties in 2022. This may accelerate changes in the gender mix of Liberal candidates in future. Improved rules of behaviour for party machines and elected politicians around gender and diversity issues are also likely.	

The remaining sections of this chapter consider how political parties structure political competition, the democracy and transparency of intra-party decision-making and, lastly, political finance issues.

How parties structure political competition

Since the earliest elections in the late 19th century, the dominant ideological dimension in Australian politics – the central set of issues around which the top two parties have differentiated their appeal – has been a left versus right one, focusing on socioeconomic equality and distribution versus growth debates. On the left side, from its outset the Australian Labor Party was based in the trade union movement and organised around ideas like 'a fair go' to secure decent wages and conditions for working people. In the modern period, the party has defended unions in regulating industrial bargaining and focused on providing key welfare state services like social security, Medicare, public education and housing assistance to medium- and low-income groups. On the right side, the Liberals stress enterprise and supporting business to deliver economic growth (Barry, 2020). They accept the welfare state yet are critical of high taxation and alleged welfare abuses, and generally condemn strikes, especially in public services. The Nationals share these stances, but from a distinctive perspective rooted in rural and regional Australia and especially supporting agriculture, mining and other outback primary industries and 'country' ways of life.

Historically, both parties have been relatively centrist, as they were again in 2022, with their positioning illustrated in Figure 6.1. Unfortunately this diagram cannot be based on the systematic mapping of party stances in voters' ideology space that is feasible in some countries. Instead,

Figure 6.1: Illustrative picture of where Australian parties stood on two main ideological dimensions and their primary vote support nationally, House of Representatives election, May 2022

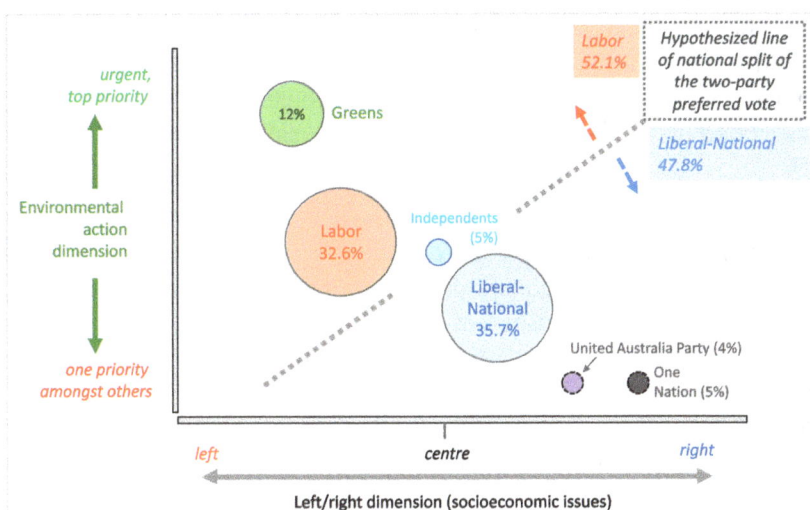

Source: Designed by the authors.

Notes: This figure is diagrammatic only. It shows all parties receiving at least 3 per cent of the national vote in the House of Representatives election. The size of each circle approximately reflects the size of each party's primary vote. Parties with dashed borders failed to win any seats.

it reflects only the authors' impressionistic summary of how most political scientists and expert commentators picture the main dimensions of political competition. The top parties' generally centrist convergence has been partly because they need to attract two-party preferred votes from people who are not their primary supporters. Yet in a characteristically Australian way the rhetoric of leading politicians has also often been robust and frank about their opponents, and in the past periods of greater polarisation did occur, especially when an incumbent party apparently on a 'winning streak' felt itself secure from effective opposition challenges.

Since the 2010–2016 travails of the Labor party in introducing and then withdrawing a carbon tax, a second key dimension of Australian party competition has been the environmental issues around climate change and global warming. Labor was historically pulled between two poles: on the one hand, the shrinking but heavily unionised workforces involved in Australian coal mining and fossil fuel exploitation (especially in Queensland) and, on the other hand, the liberal/progressive and often green-orientated middle and working classes of Australia's big cities (including Brisbane). Fighting on two fronts (especially since 2019), Labor was keen to stem its losses of support to the Greens by more vigorously criticising Liberal-National governments for their lagging and luke-warm responses to tackling environmental issues.

The Coalition's positioning on the environmental dimension has changed over time, as evidence of environmental damage from global warming mounted and public alarm swelled during the unprecedented bushfires of 2019 to 2020. In 2013 both wings of the Liberal-National opposition fully backed the fossil fuel corporations' intensive public and media campaigns against the carbon tax. By 2019 only a few, isolated voices on the centrist wing of the Liberals (like the deposed former party leader John Hewson) were calling for more full-hearted adoption of 'green economy' measures. The Liberal stance later evolved to rhetorically endorse the needs for some environmental policy changes, but only those that were 'affordable' and that could be implemented gradually so as to avoid economic damage to the fossil fuel industry and employment. Some National politicians were franker in downplaying the need for policy reforms and wanting them to be extended over decades. In 2017 Scott Morrison, when he was the Treasurer, took a large lump of coal into the House of Representatives, brandishing it at his Labor opponents from the front bench during his speech and urging them not be scared of it (Guardian, 2017). Allied with both the Coalition parties' substantial funding from fossil fuel industries, this incident and other events in Morrison's time as PM (such as going on holiday with his family during the height of the bushfire crisis) cemented a public view of Morrison and the Liberals as pro-carbon and complacent about climate change, even though the Turnbull government had previously signed up to the Paris Agreement on reducing carbon emissions by 25 to 30 per cent by 2030.

The Greens' placement on Figure 6.1 has been clear on the vertical dimensions, with the party advocating the fastest, most concerted and far-reaching programme for reducing Australia's carbon emissions and moving towards a green economy based around solar and wind power, ending the burning of fossil fuels for power or transport as soon as feasible (S. Johnson, 2020). There has been more controversy about where the Greens should be placed on left/right socioeconomic issues, with trade unions and left-wing critics arguing that the party's politicians do not support organised Labor nor the welfare of workers and the poorest in society as consistently as Labor does. However, the issue mix involved in contemporary left/right politics has evolved from its earlier 'legacy' configuration. The Greens may have reservations about trade union power (often mobilised against carbon reductions), but they have consistently been more progressive than Labor on issues like the taxation of corporations, the treatment of immigrants, the importance of local democracy and public involvement, fostering a many-sided equality of rights amongst diverse groups, and peace-based international relations. So, it seems safest to picture the Greens as somewhat to the left of Labor on these newer urban or 'lifestyle' aspects of left/right politics.

On the far right of Figure 6.1, a succession of smaller parties has organised around 'freedom' issues like protecting hunting and fishing, bikers and rural areas from government 'interference', plus some disguised hostility to ethnic minorities, some conspiracy theories, and anti-vaccination mobilisations during the different state COVID-19 lockdowns. Their importance rests heavily on their ability to win seats at federal Senate elections (Ghazarian, 2015) and in state upper houses under the Single Transferable Vote (STV).

The Teal independents at federal and state level

The rise of the Teals was part of a long-term trend, reflecting substantial shifts in the electoral landscape and in voters' values, which created the space for populist movements to challenge the established two-party system. The Liberal-National Coalition's perceived foot-dragging on acting on climate change and the establishment of a federal anti-corruption commission, plus the perceived insensitivity of its PM and other leaders to women's issues, triggered some prominent defections by Liberals to stand as independents in safe seats (Guardian, 2022). They attracted about a fifth of their support from former Liberal voters, but the rest mainly from Labor and Green voters seeing them as more viable anti-government candidates. Greatly helped by the funding guru Simon Holmes à Court and Climate 200 (a grassroots crowdfunded outfit trying to compensate for a 'lost decade' of climate policy stasis), Teal candidates emerged in numerous electorates, and six Teal MPs were elected (Holmes à Court, 2022). They have gone on to meet regularly as a group in the House of Representatives and developed a well-worked-out strategic position and issue orientation. However, in subsequent state elections in Victoria, NSW and Queensland, Teal candidates narrowly missed winning seats – so that their ability to entrench at the state as well as federal levels and have some hope of 'breaking the mould' of two-party dominance remains uncertain at the time of writing (Colebatch, Evans and Grattan, 2023).

Internal party democracy and governance

Political parties in liberal democracies are complex organisations. Despite the growth in salience first of mass media campaigning and then social media coverage of political events, the top national parties still have (and need to retain) substantial memberships to populate a network of local branches covering all Australia's states and territories, constituencies and electoral districts. A key to retaining members' involvement has long been a substantial measure of internal party democracy and transparency, initially over local candidate selection, more sporadically over shaping party policy and, most recently, a possible membership role in the choice of national party leaders.

Party members and social representativeness

Political parties' declining ability to recruit members and represent significant sections of citizens has been a major point of criticism, especially when contrasted with Australia's constantly increasing population size throughout the modern period. However, Figure 6.2 shows that in fact the modern picture has not solely been one of decline. The Liberal Party's membership has more or less halved in the last four decades and shows little sign of stabilising – especially after the Teal Independents' success in the 2021 federal election. Their key coalition partner, the National Party, grew its membership in rural and regional Australia in the 1990s, but that subsequently declined by around a third. The party has still retained almost twice as many members as the Liberals. Turning to Labor membership, it has fluctuated quite markedly, falling by half in the 1980s and 1990s, but then re-doubling in the last two decades. The Greens have grown their member numbers fairly consistently since their founding in 2002, as well as building an effective election-fighting organisation in some specific constituencies. Yet even after acknowledging fluctuations in party memberships rather than any invariable decline, involvement with parties has clearly remained a minority pastime amongst Australian citizens.

Figure 6.2: Party memberships and representatives in state legislatures

Aspect	Liberal Party	National Party	Labor Party	The Greens
Approximate number of members in 2020	50,000 to 60,000	100,000	60,100	15,000
Modern movements in membership	Higher point 75,000 (in 1990)	High point 130,000 (in 1990)	Low point 26,000 (in 2002)	Low point 2,000 (in 2002)
Membership in 1980	110,000	75,000	55,000	0
% share of all state lower house members (2023)	37% (includes LNP Queensland)	not applicable	57%	3.5%
% share of all state upper house members (excludes Queensland) (2023)	27%	not applicable	42%	6.5%

Source: Compiled by the authors from Humphrys, Copland and Mansillo (2020); Wikipedia (2023a, 2023b, 2023c, 2023d).

Do the party members of the major parties in Figure 6.2 represent Australian society? This would be a difficult task with such small membership numbers and given that we might ask for social representativeness at three different levels – local, state and national. Recent available data on party memberships has been largely limited to the national level (Gauja and Gromping, 2020). It shows that party members are generally considerably more male, elderly, and Anglo-Irish than are Australia's population as whole. However, this pattern has been more moderately present in Australia than in some other liberal democracies (like the USA and UK, where elderly members strongly predominate). The presence of women has increased in both local branches and higher-tier party committees, and there are some signs that more recently growing ethnic groups (of south Asian origin) are also participating more in major cities.

We do not have much information on state parties' representativeness, but their territorial success within state legislatures across Australia provides some relevant evidence. Figure 6.2 shows that in 2020 the top two parties still largely monopolised representation in state legislatures. Labor and the Liberal-National Coalition were dominant in lower houses, holding 94 per cent of seats between them. But in five states with upper houses (four elected by STV proportional representation) this share drops to below 70 per cent. The Greens are more present in states' upper than lower houses, but even there they usually only hold one or two seats in each state.

The key power of party branches: shaping who joins the governing elites

Critics also argue that the parties have long since ceased to be mass organisations, and so their ability to represent ordinary citizens has consistently fallen. Local party organisations remain varied because they are grounded in their communities, but politics has come to be seen by most citizens as a minority interest or specialist activity. This social marginalisation has been strengthened by a trend towards the greater professionalisation of even local party office-holding or campaigning in both federal and state elections. In the Labor Party, this might take the form of a politically ambitious official in a local trade union branch seeking to make their mark as a local political activist, as a prelude to securing a paid role as an aide to a Labor member of the federal Parliament or a senior Labor figure in a state government or state legislature. From there a promotion pathway for this person might lead to an appointment as an aide to a federal minister, providing valuable experience to draw on when they then look for their own nomination to contest a seat in the House of Representatives. On the Liberal-National side, someone from a 'political' profession (a journalist, social media expert, or possibly a lawyer or an executive in a regulated industry) might work as a local activist and campaigner, using that as a gateway to a similar upward path as a political advisor to Liberal-National legislators and so forth, perhaps assisted by the greater availability of business and donor funding for political aides on the political right.

The crucial activity that local party members have always controlled is to vote on who their local candidate for lower house elections should be. Incumbent MPs and state legislators have most often been reselected, but alternative local challengers have sometimes emerged when an MP has been touched by scandal or falls out of sympathy with their constituency party. Occasionally an MP or even minister may be targeted by a well-funded alternative candidate willing to commit the time and resources to trying to win the local nomination. Competition to represent the opposition party has generally been more intense in winnable seats.

The restricted size, diversity and social representativeness of the main parties' memberships has sometimes meant that local 'selectorates' can be influenced by branch stacking, where one candidate for the party's nomination seeks to radically enlarge the local membership (for example, by paying supporters to join *en masse* as members) in ways that favour them (Gauja, 2020). In close-fought races for party nominations, relatively small numbers of votes have tipped the outcomes between candidates one way or another. One particular area of branch stacking was historically important in the Labor Party, where far-left or communist activists sought to become members in local parties or trade union branches with a view to shifting opinion to the left and securing the candidacy of strongly left-wing people. Countering such 'entryism' efforts also led some local Labor parties and trade union branches to effectively close their membership in restrictive ways, so as to perpetuate the grip on control of the more centre-right Labor factions. In the 2010s, some Australian movements on the right began to follow branch-stacking tactics similar to those used by polarising American Republican movements. This created problems for the Liberals, especially with religious and anti-abortion groups seeking influence in seats with small local memberships, aiming to secure candidates congenial to their views.

The selection of candidates for the federal Senate or state upper houses are made by state committees within the party apparatuses, which are generally controlled by the state party leadership. In the Labor Party and the Liberal-National Coalition, the position in which candidates are listed on each party's STV list or ticket makes the key difference to which people get elected, with only those in the first four slots having any realistic chance of winning a seat. The party leaderships (or other influential figures, like some state trade union leaders in Labor) have generally been able to assign their list's top slots to the most loyal or most ideologically congenial candidates – although popular politicians may also win places, because having them head up the party's list will attract more votes. For smaller parties (like the Greens) only the top one or maybe two candidates per state have regularly won seats under STV.

Local deliberation and influence in higher-tier party policy commitments

The other local party role, historically assigned importance as the 'nursery of democracy' and a key foundation for a 'civic culture', has been the quality of deliberative discussions within local party branches and its influence on local MPs and state senators. In the heyday of mass parties – particularly in the Labor Party, with its formally affiliated unions – the grassroots participation of members was seen as a critical source of inputs from significant social groups. As this role has withered, party members' involvement with branches has tended to revolve more around helping with campaigns, fund-raising, social events and social media activity online. The most serious debates occur only periodically, when a branch has considered changing its candidate or has needed to choose a new candidate – at these junctures, local party discussions have often come alive, with a wide range of issues being canvassed. Otherwise, 'hard core' members have increasingly seemed to take their cues from their party's senior politician via social media, which they largely seek to amplify (Humphrys, Copland and Mansillo 2020). Moderately involved members have picked up and repeated party messages much more selectively, and fringe members or non-joining supporters even less. Nonetheless, overall social media reactions have generated valuable instant feedback for MPs and party communication professionals about which of their messages have resonated with members and reached the wider public.

In addition, local branches contribute to higher-level policy debates by electing delegates to state and federal conferences, and state councils or executive committees are chosen to run business between conferences. Each state party committee chooses top officials to run its apparatus and control donations and funding, and they discuss policy issues regularly with the party's state legislators. However, committee decision-making has typically been slow-moving, with preparatory work on drafting resolutions and manifestoes taking months – a time scale that matches poorly with the modern pace of political, media and social media changes.

Political scientists have long debated the bureaucratisation of party politics, first analysed by Robert Michels (1915), with each party's permanent staff and senior elected officials (rather than members) essentially controlling all processes above the local selectorate level. More recently, the professionalisation of a wide range of campaigning roles ('policy wonks' and think tanks, speech writers, communications experts, pollsters, political advertisers, finance raisers, and social media strategists) has increased. The 'permanent campaign' at federal level (Van Onselen and Errington, 2007) has increased the premium on professional expertise. Communications factors especially have supplemented the dominant judgement on policy and organisational issues previously made by elected representatives and party elites (Mills, 2020). Increasingly, campaigning has also become data-driven and dependent on sophisticated IT-driven targeting strategies (Dommett, Kefford and Kruschinski, 2023). Formally, all these developments have (in theory) been melded into the pre-existing channels of party policy-making, but in practice they have tended to supplant them.

The Labor Party historically took most seriously the principles of internal party democracy pyramiding up to match government levels (Manwaring, 2020). A National Conference convenes every three years to define the party's overall electoral commitments in broad terms, usually in close conjunction with the national party leadership and its key trade union backers. There has been a long history of occasional clashes at state or federal level, with the extra-parliamentary party sometimes demanding that the Labor Party champion more left-wing or 'socialist' policies than the parties' MPs and senators are prepared to endorse. For example, from 2017 to 2019 the West Australia Labor party (influenced by a trade union leader) voted through a set of program commitments that the successful West Australian leader Mark McGowan then conspicuously ignored (see Chapter 21).

The Liberal Party's founding leader, Robert Menzies, initially created party structures in the 1920s that made each state party autonomous and set up only weak machinery at the federal level. Under the Howard governments (1996 to 2007), however, federal influence over state parties considerably increased. Yet, in practice both the Liberal and National parties defer to their elected MPs and senators to set party policy commitments, although they must take account of grassroots members' opinions. In the National Party, the ideology of 'countrymindedness' has especially assigned importance to the views of 'deep rural' party branches.

The Greens are also structured as a confederation of eight state and territory parties, plus a network of local branches and a separate mode of joining for First Nations people. They stress local democracy in many aspects, including the choosing of candidates and the setting of policies by extra-parliamentary party conferences at the state and federal levels. The Greens choose two co-convenors to be the federal party's public media face, one a woman and one a man.

Choosing a party leader

Until very recently, no Australian party involved their members in the country at large directly in the choice of party leaders. Figure 6.3 shows that has remained the firm position of the Liberals and Nationals for choosing their national party leader, who must sit in the House of Representatives. The Greens have co-convenors outside Parliament, but their legislators also choose a leader from amongst their own ranks. All three parties can 'spill' (that is, eject from office) their leader in a confidence vote confined to members of the party room in Canberra, including both MPs in the House and senators. It is only when an incumbent leader has actually been voted out that rival alternative leaders need to declare their candidacy for the leadership. Where two or more rival candidates emerge, additional party room votes decide which candidates go forward to the last two and contest for election.

However, following the Rudd–Gillard clashes in the Labor Party from 2011 to 2013, the then PM, Kevin Rudd, introduced new arrangements where the final choice of party leader (in a two-horse race) would be made by what would normally be called an 'electoral college', giving 50 per cent weight to the party room caucus members and the other half of the total weight to the votes of the national membership. However, member votes can only be activated if two or more Labor members of the federal Parliament stand against each other. In 2019, Bill Shorten resigned as Labor leader following the party's disappointing election performance, but no contested election followed. Instead, Anthony Albanese announced that he would stand; a few

Figure 6.3: How Australia's main party leaders are chosen

Aspect	Liberal Party	National Party	Labor Party	The Greens
Who can trigger and decide a 'spill' vote to potentially remove an incumbent PM or leader of the opposition?	A simple majority (50%+1) of party MPs and senators voting in the party caucus			Simple majority of Green MPs and senators
If a leader loses the 'spill vote', who determines who can stand for leadership?	Nominations by party MPs and senators (usually two, sometimes one or three candidates)			Unclear, given the party's usually small numbers of legislators
Voting system used to get to last two candidates	Run-off ballots amongst party MPs and senators, eliminating the bottom candidate in each round until only two candidates are left			
Time allowed before last vote	One or two days	One or two days	Six weeks, for party members to vote	
Voting system used to decide between the final two candidates	Simple majority of Liberal MPs and senators	Simple majority of National MPs and senators	Simple majority of weighted votes of (i) MPs and senators (50%); and (ii) party members (50%)	Simple majority of Green MPs and senators (since 2005)

Source: Compiled by authors from multiple party websites.

days later another candidate (Chris Bowen) emerged, but then withdrew. Two other Labor MPs considered standing but, in the end, following discussions with Albanese, they did not, so that Albanese ended up being elected unopposed by the MPs and senators in the party room and Labor members never got to vote. Albanese's position was protected for his first year as leader, and after that his poll ratings increased while those for the Morrison government declined. In the 2022 election, Albanese's win cemented his position as both PM and Labor leader and gave him mass democratic legitimacy for the first time.

Financing campaigns and publicity

Modern political campaigning has become an expensive activity, raising important questions for all political parties that have transitioned away from a mass membership basis to contemporary small numbers. In the mass party model, most financing was provided by local membership dues paid to branches, plus donations by members, with standard portions remitted to the state or federal parties to cover their organisational expenses and activities. In the Labor Party, this was supplemented by local trade union bloc donations to branches, to cover affiliated memberships, and to state and federal parties for their campaigns and activities. For the Liberals and Nationals, individual donations by business corporations (often at higher-tier party levels) predominate, along with donations by wealthy individuals or smaller businesses, sometimes at local and sometimes at state/federal levels.

All donations to federal parties over a lower limit of $16,300 in 2023–2024 (AEC, 2024a) have to be publicly declared by law to the Australian Electoral Commission (AEC), which publishes (around a year late) an annual transparency list of which parties have received funding from which donors. Because campaigning costs in state and territories are much less, disclosure limits were much lower there in 2022, at or near $1,000 in NSW, Victoria, Queensland and the Australian Capital Territory (ACT), and at between $2,600 and $5,00 in the remaining states (Muller, 2022). These limits create an important democratic safeguard, since they ensure that larger gifts made to parties can be tracked, sometimes with embarrassing results. For example, it emerged that one of the largest personal donors to the Liberal Party from 2017 to 2018 was in fact the PM of the time, Malcom Turnbull. In a more systematic way, the register also shows how the Labor/Liberal-National duopoly translates into much larger donor receipts than those for any other party, as figures 6.4 and 6.5 demonstrate. The Liberals' and Nationals' average annual receipts for 2018–2021, at $111 million when added together, was substantially more than gifts to Labor,

Figure 6.4: Average annual receipts for the top five Australian parties receiving donations from 2018 to 2021

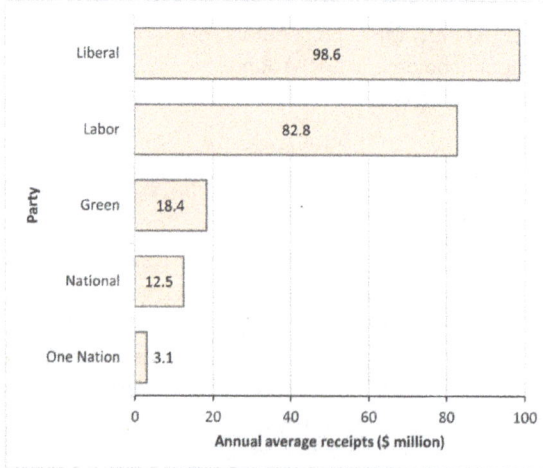

Source: Compiled by authors from data in AEC (2022).

Figure 6.5: Donations received by all Australian political parties from 2018 to 2021

Party	2018–21 receipts (3 years) $ million	% of major party receipts	% of all party receipts
Liberal	295.9	45.8	38.0
Labor	248.5	38.5	31.9
Green	55.2	8.5	7.1
National	37.5	5.8	4.8
One Nation	9.2	1.4	1.2
Total major party receipts	646.3	100.0	83.0
All other parties	132.6		17.0
Total receipts, all parties	**778.9**		**100.0**

Source: Compiled by authors from data in AEC (2022).

chiefly reflecting the greater donor power of big business and trade associations donating to the Liberals. The Greens (who rely on their membership plus philanthropic foundations for mostly small donations) were well behind, but also have a smaller membership.

Figure 6.5 shows that the top two parties (Liberal-National and Labor) received three-quarters of all political donations, although it is also notable that over $44 million a year, or a sixth of all monies donated, went to very small parties with no seats and relatively few chances of winning representation.

Major donors to state parties have often been companies with important interests that are regulated by that tier of government. The importance of continuous economic growth in financing regular urban expansion has meant that donations from property companies have come under ever more critical scrutiny and occasioned several corruption scandals. Similarly, fossil fuel and mining company donations to state parties or politicians have attracted increasingly critical public attention to the power of big business (see Chapter 7).

At federal party level, some large companies either split their donations across the top two parties or donate only via cut-outs (for example, channelling donations below the minimum registration limit via business executives or their wives) to avoid negative publicity or problems from consumers if they back one party. Quite a range of trade associations follow similar strategies by breaking up very substantial political donations into smaller packets given directly to party candidates of the top two parties. Yet critics argue that the interests involved often have strong reasons for getting politicians to lobby for detailed rule changes favouring them. An example is the retail pharmaceuticals industry, which funds dozens of local campaigns in federal seats while its members' turnovers and profits are shaped directly by Medicare regulations.

However, even with growing donations by business and wealthy people, the membership stagnation in Australian parties (plus declining trade union memberships supporting Labor) might spell increasing difficulties for the political parties were it not for the federal government since 1984 providing public funding of political party expenses in running federal election campaigns. Each party receives an 'as-of-right' payment immediately after an election (in 2019 set at $11,000 per seat). If the party gets more than 4 per cent of the vote in any contest, then

Figure 6.6: The proportion (%) of A$68.6 million federal election cost reimbursements provided to parties by the Australian Electoral Commission following the 2019 election

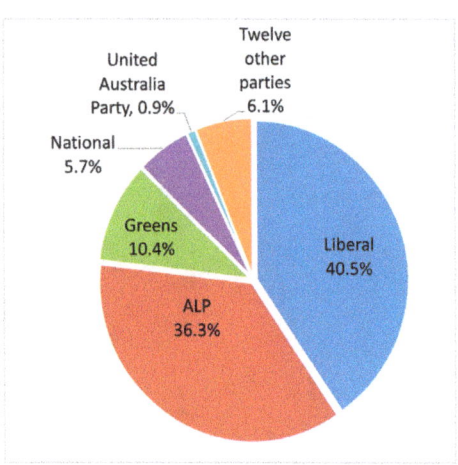

Source: Chart created by authors from data in AEC (2020, Table 1).

Notes: The final slice (6.1 per cent) covers payments to 12 smaller registered political parties. In addition, just over A$1 million was paid to independent or non-party candidates.

it can also submit a claim to the AEC for a variable reimbursement of its expenses, depending on how many primary votes it gets in such contests (set at just over $3 per vote in 2019). This system means that the top two parties plus the Greens regularly do well in terms of federal funding. In 2019, over three-quarters of the funding paid went to the top two parties and a tenth to the Greens (Figure 6.6). However, more than one in eight dollars paid out by the AEC also went to 13 other smaller parties – though only the United Australia Party met the 4 per cent cut-off criterion and gained more substantial funding.

Public money subsidies to political parties (even based on primary AV votes) remain controversial. Some political scientists argue that the state underpinning especially the most important governing and opposition parties reflects a 'cartel party' system (Ward, 2006). Here the key parties are co-opted by official subsidies into acting as agents for the state apparatus to explain itself and public policies to voters, instead of being a genuinely independent political input mechanism – a role that parties can no longer fulfil because of their small minority status in the population. The importance of public funding reimbursements places a premium on parties accurately documenting the costs of their activities. It also meshes with the more onerous requirements on political parties to track and declare to the AEC all major donations to promote the greater bureaucratisation and professionalisation of politics, with local party branches delegating most finance-related issues to higher-tier party officials (Gauja et al., 2022).

The cartel party analysis also chimes with the shrinking away of any clearly separate intra-party discussion and deliberation spaces under the impact of continuous media coverage and ever more intrusive social media coverage of previously semi-private spaces where party members and elites could interact behind some kind of veil of secrecy. With all intra-party debates open, and members taking their cues from media, social media or elite politicians anyway, public funding has added an extra layer of protection for established governing elites against losing their positions to newer rivals. Counter-critics have argued that the 'cartel' image greatly underplays the ever-changing character of major party organisations and their relative autonomy (still) in shaping their own distinctive and robust internal political debates, from which public funding in no way detracts.

Conclusion

Australia's party system has evolved slowly, but the accumulation of changes evident in the 2020 federal elections, and in state politics also, has been considerable (Kefford et al., 2018). The majoritarian AV system for lower house elections (and to some extent public funding subsidies) continue to protect the Labor Party and Liberals and Nationals from party diversification processes, but the Senate elections nationally and in most states show that their appeal remains dominant, even with STV elections. Some critics argue that their dominance is artificially maintained by compulsory voting (see Chapter 5), which has kept turnout levels very high (AEC, 2024b)

Only the Greens have so far shown in a consistent way that they can organise around new issues, gain continuous representation in Parliament beyond winning for a time in isolated constituencies, and build a national profile and organisation. Many small parties have started out on the right organising around populist, 'freedom' or covert ethnic resentment issues, but they have failed to match any of these three achievements. For example, Pauline Hansen's One Nation has not sought to develop into a national party organisation. Moreover, the emergence of successful community-based centrist movements, such as the 'Voice for Indi', led first by Cathy McGowan and now by Helen Haines, has remained localised. And the Teal Independents cannot be viewed as a political party because, at the time of writing, they do not yet match AEC requirements for a political party, namely a constitution specifying an intention to endorse candidates and at least 1,500 members.

Defenders of Australia's party system have argued that it has adapted (albeit gradually and in a laggard way) to accommodate the growth of environmental and climate change issues, and to handle what public choice political science acknowledges as some of the unavoidable difficulties involved in moving from a one-dimensional to a two-dimensional ideological space. They have also argued that its nationwide resilience to populist movements and to short-term 'surge' movements has proved a valuable asset for an enduring and stable liberal democracy, demonstrated especially in the bipartisan consensus on anti-COVID-19 measures which managed to marginalise strident anti-vaccination voices and some quite large demonstrations.

However, critics have argued that the far right has only remained small because the established centre-right Liberal or National parties shifted their policy agendas to accommodate and legitimate right-wing movements of public opinion (for example by holding would-be asylum seekers in tough conditions on islands overseas and by Liberal leader Pete Dutton opposing the Voice for Indigenous Australians in 2023). They have also argued that the top two parties are a legacy oligopoly protected – by AV voting and public funding – from the consequences of their own stagnant memberships, their increasing dependence on corporation or pressure group funding, and their shrinking autonomy versus the media or social media influences. The legitimacy of Australian political parties has been falling among the wider public (Jennings et al., 2020), but also among civil society organisations and even the many non-political business sectors.

References

Australian Bureau of Statistics (2023) 'Australia's population by country of birth', ABS webpage. https://www.abs.gov.au/statistics/people/population/australias-population-country-birth/latest-release#key-statistics

AEC (Australian Electoral Commission) (2020) *Election Funding and Disclosure Report: Federal Election 2019,* AEC. https://perma.cc/5S46-LUES

AEC (2022) 'Transparency register', AEC. https://perma.cc/4H2X-W47J

AEC (2024a) 'Disclosure threshold', webpage. https://aec.gov.au/Parties_and_Representatives/public_funding/threshold.htm

AEC (2024b) 'Voter turnout, previous events'. https://perma.cc/2UFC-8VBM

Barry, Nicholas (2020) 'The Liberal Party', in Guaja Anika; Sawer, Marian and Simms, Marian (eds), *Morrison's Miracle: The 2019 Australian Federal Election.* Canberra: ANU Press, Ch. 14, pp. 295–312. https://doi.org/10.22459/MM.2020

Brett, Judith (2003) *Australian Liberals and the Moral Middle Class: From Alfred Deakin to John Howard*, Cambridge: Cambridge University Press.

Brett, Judith (2006) 'The Liberal party' in *Government, Politics, Power and Policy in Australia*, (ed) Summer, J. ; Woodward, D. and Parkin, NSW: Pearson Education, pp. 206–25.

Chen, Peter (2013) *Australian Politics in a Digital Age.* Canberra: ANU Press. https://perma.cc/49NU-Y2HY

Cockfield, Geoff (2020) 'The National Party of Australia', in Guaja, Anika; Sawer, Marian and Simms, Marian (eds), *Morrison's Miracle: The 2019 Australian Federal Election.* Canberra: ANU Press, Ch. 15, pp.313–28. https://doi.org/10.22459/MM.2020

Colebatch, Tim; Evans, Mark and Grattan, Michelle. (2023) 'New populisms and party crashers: Are the teals breaking the mould of Australian politics?', *AQ-Australian Quarterly,* vol. 94, no.3, pp. 14–23. $ https://perma.cc/8FLG-4HAR

Crowe, Shaun (2018) *Whitlam's Children: Labor and the Greens in Australia 2007–13,* Melbourne: Melbourne University Publishing. PhD thesis version. https://perma.cc/U835-BUCF

Dommett, Katharine; Kefford, Glenn; and Kruschinski, Simon (2023) 'Introduction', in *Data-Driven Campaigning and Political Parties: Five Advanced Democracies Compared.* Oxford: Oxford University Press, pp.1–16. $ https://perma.cc/GU8D-3V6B

Dunleavy, Patrick (2021) 'Micro-institutions and liberal democracy', *Political Insight*, vol. 10, no. 1. $ https://doi.org/10.1177/2041905819838154 OA at https://blogs.lse.ac.uk/politicsandpolicy/micro-institutions-in-liberal-democracies/

Gauja, Anika (2020) 'Explainer: What is branch stacking, and why has neither major party been able to stamp it out?', *The Conversation,* 15 June. https://perma.cc/795R-JX25

Gauja, Anika and Gromping, Max (2020) 'The expanding party universe: Patterns of partisan engagement in Australia and the United Kingdom', *Party Politics*, vol. 26, no. 6, pp.822–33. $ https://doi.org/10.1177/1354068818822251

Gauja, Anika and Jackson, Stewart (2016) 'Australian Greens party members and supporters: Their profiles and activities', *Environmental Politics,* vol. 25, no. 2, pp.359–79. $ https://doi.org/10.1080/09644016.2015.1104803

Gauja, Anika; Sawer, Marian; and Simms, Marian (2020) *Morrison' Miracle: The 2019 Australian Federal Election,* Canberra: ANU Press. https://doi.org/10.22459/MM.2020

Gauja, Anika; Mills, Stephen; Miragliotta, Narelle; Tham, Joo-Cheong; Nwokora, Zim; and Anderson, Malcolm (2022) 'The impact of political finance regulation on party organisation', *Parliamentary Affairs*, vol. 73, no. 1, pp.1–21. $ https://doi.org/10.1093/pa/gsy028

Ghazarian, Zareh (2015) *The Making of a Party System: Minor Parties in the Australian Senate*, Melbourne: Monash University Publishing.

Ghazarian, Zareh (2024) 'The Australian party system', in Diana Perche; Nicholas Barry; Alan Fenna; Zareh Ghazarian; and Yvonne Haigh (eds) *Australian Politics and Policy*. Sydney: OER Collective. https://oercollective.caul.edu.au/aust-politics-policy/chapter/the-australian-party-system/

Gordon, Josh (2022) 'Fact check: What did Morrison say about a federal ICAC?', *Sydney Morning Herald*, 15 April. https://perma.cc/XA46-8S59

Guardian (2017) 'Scott Morrison brings coal to question time: what fresh idiocy is this?' *The Guardian, Australia*, 9 February. https://perma.cc/M8EP-AAXR

Guardian (2022) 'Teal independents: Who are they and how did they upend Australia's election?', *The Guardian, Australia*, 23 May. https://perma.cc/CZ6W-NN44

Holmes à Court, Simon (2022) *The Big Teal*, Melbourne: Monash University Publishing.

Humphrys, Elizabeth; Copland, Simon; and Mansillo, Luke (2020) 'Anti-Politics In Australia: Hypotheses, Evidence And Trends'. *Journal of Australian Political Economy*, No. 86, pp.122–56. OA whole issue: https://www.ppesydney.net/content/uploads/2021/01/JAPE-86.pdf#page=122 OA article only at: https://perma.cc/ZPT6-SLFX

Jackson, Stewart (2015) 'The Australian Greens', in Miragliotta, Narelle; Gauja, Anika and Smith, Rodney (eds) *Contemporary Australian Political Party Organisations*, Clayton, VIC: Monash University Press, pp.37–49. $ https://perma.cc/5YVK-3TJQ

Jackson, Stewart (2016) *The Australian Greens: From Activism to Australia's Third Party*, Melbourne: Melbourne University Press. $ https://perma.cc/UDW7-58Q4

Jackson, Stewart; Lelliott, Joff; Brincat, Shannon; Bourne, Josephine; and Economou, Nick (2022) 'The origins and evolution of the major parties', in *Australian Politics in the Twenty-First Century: Old Institutions, New Challenges*, Cambridge: Cambridge University Press, Chapter 8, pp.184–210. $ https://doi.org/10.1017/9781009103701

Jaensch, Dean; Brent, Peter and Bowden, Brett (2004) *Australian Political Parties in the Spotlight*. Report. (Research School of the Social Sciences, ANU), Report No.4, prepared for the Democratic Audit of Australia. https://perma.cc/5EY2-7GHF

Jennings, Will; Valgarðsson, Viktor; Stoker, Gerry; Devine, Dan; Gaskell, Jen; and Evans, Mark (2020). Report No 8: 'Political trust and the COVID-19 crisis: Pushing populism to the backburner? A Study of Public Opinion in Australia, Italy, the UK and the USA', *Australia: Democracy 2025*, p.22. https://perma.cc/R5XU-PGR2

Johnson, Carol (2020) 'Ideology and Populism', in Gauja, Anika; Sawer, Marian; and Simms, Marian (eds) *Morrison's Miracle: The 2019 Australian Federal Election*, Canberra: ANU Press, Ch. 5, pp.91–106. https://doi.org/10.22459/MM.2020

Johnson, Samuel (2020) 'The Australian Greens', in Guaja, Anika; Sawer, Marian; and Simms, Marian (eds), *Morrison's Miracle: The 2019 Australian Federal Election*, Canberra: ANU Press, Ch. 16, pp. 329–42. https://doi.org/10.22459/MM.2020

Kefford, Glenn (2018) 'Digital media, ground wars and party organisation: Does stratarchy explain how parties organise election campaigns?' *Parliamentary Affairs*, vol. 71, no. 3, pp.656–73. $ https://doi.org/10.1093/pa/gsx084

Kefford, Glenn, Murphy-Gregory, Hannah; Ward, Ian; Jackson, Stewart; Cox, Lloyd; and Carson, Andrea (2018) *Australian Politics in the Twenty-first Century: Old Institutions, New Challenges*, Melbourne: Cambridge University Press.

McAllister, Ian (2002) 'Political Parties in Australia: Party Stability in a Utilitarian Society', Chapter 13 in Farrel, David; Webb, Paul and Holliday, Ian (eds) *Political Parties in Advanced Industrial Democracies*, Oxford: Oxford University Press, pp.379–408. $ https://doi.org/10.1093/0199240566.003.0013

Manwaring, Rob (2020) 'The Australian Labor Party', in Guaja, Anika; Sawer, Marian and Simms, Marian (eds), *Morrison's Miracle: The 2019 Australian Federal Election,* Canberra: ANU Press, Ch. 13, pp. 277–94. https://doi.org/10.22459/MM.2020

Marsh, Ian (1995) *Beyond the Two Party System*, Cambridge: Cambridge University Press.

Marsh, Ian (2006) *Political Parties in Transition?* Sydney: Federation Press.

Martin, Sarah (2023) 'The sports rorts saga and a "stench" that clung to the Coalition', *Guardian*, 18 May. https://perma.cc/K7CK-SRX8

Michels, Robert (1915) *Political Parties: A Sociological Study of the Oligarchical Tendencies of Modern Democracy*, Library of Congress. OA at: https://perma.cc/YVN3-877N

Mills, Stephen (2020) 'Party campaign communications', in Guaja, Anika; Sawer, Marian and Simms, Marian (eds), *Morrison's Miracle: The 2019 Australian Federal Election.* Canberra: ANU Press, Ch. 23, pp. 455–72. https://doi.org/10.22459/MM.2020

Muller, Damon (2022) 'Election funding and disclosure in Australian jurisdictions: A quick guide', Parliament of Australia, Report, 16 February. https://perma.cc/54GX-CBKY

Norris, Pippa, Thomas Wynter, and Sarah Cameron (2018) *Perceptions of Electoral Integrity Dataverse* (PEI 6.0), edited by The Electoral Integrity Project, Harvard Dataverse. https://dataverse.harvard.edu/dataverse/PEI

Van Onselen, Peter, and Wayne Errington (2007) 'The democratic state as a marketing tool: The permanent campaign in Australia', *Commonwealth and Comparative Politics,* vol. 45, no. 1, pp.78–94.

Ward, Ian (2006) 'Cartel parties and election campaigning in Australia', in Marsh, Ian (ed) *Political Parties in Transition*, Sydney: Federation Press, pp.70–93.

Wikipedia (2023a) 'Australian Labor Party'. https://perma.cc/G3DR-EAQ5

Wikipedia (2023b) 'Liberal Party of Australia'. https://perma.cc/9M25-GU47

Wikipedia (2023c) 'National Party of Australia'. https://perma.cc/7VBR-XKL8

Wikipedia (2023d) 'Australian Greens'. https://perma.cc/KUM9-JM99

Wikipedia (2023e) 'List of Asian Australian politicians'. https://perma.cc/69LZ-Y2WU

7

Interest groups and corporate power

Patrick Dunleavy

Like other Anglosphere liberal democracies, Australia has very little formal regulation of the interest group process, although by the time of writing a few practices (such as lobby donations to parties and politicians) were closely regulated. A great deal of democratic practice in this area still relies on unwritten political norms and conventions, and on politicians and officials acting in public-interested ways because they believe in democratic norms. The latter may be subverted if business corporations or wealthy individuals can coerce or influence governments into favouring their interests over others – the problem of 'corporate power'.

How should the interest group process operate in a liberal democracy?

- Politicians should recognise a need to supplement electoral and public opinion influences via continuously being open to dialogue with different sectional interests among citizens and firms about detailed policy design and who bears the costs of policy changes. Decision-makers should recognise the legitimacy of autonomous collective actions and mobilisations by different groups of citizens, and value the transparent consideration of diverse points of view.
- All stakeholders should have an ability to freely form interest groups and to lobby elected representatives and government officials on decisions affecting them, operating within the law and common ethical norms.
- In a democratic society the resources for organising collective 'voice' and political action in pressure groups, trade unions, trade associations, NGOs, charities, community groups and other forms should be readily available, along with opportunities for securing media coverage and explaining their case to citizens at large.
- The costs of organising effectively should be low and within reach of any social group or interest. Ideally, resources for different interests should be reasonably equitably distributed. Where a balanced representation of all affected interests is conspicuously hard to achieve, then philanthropic or even state assistance should be available to ensure that the policy process does not systematically disadvantage particular groups. This imperative is especially strong where historically the civil rights and legitimate needs of a given group or set of communities has been disregarded.

How to cite this chapter:

Dunleavy, Patrick (2024) 'Interest groups and corporate power', in: Evans, Mark; Dunleavy, Patrick and Phillimore, John (eds) *Australia's Evolving Democracy: A New Democratic Audit*, London: LSE Press, pp.143–165. **https://doi.org/10.31389/lsepress.ada.g** Licence: CC-BY-NC 4.0

- Because of inequalities in resources across interest groups, decision-makers should discount the input they receive to take into account which lobbies are easier or more difficult to organise.
- Policy-makers should also re-weight the inputs they receive so as to distinguish between shallow or even 'fake' harms being claimed by well-organised groups and deeper harms potentially being suffered by hard-to-organise groups.
- Where a policy change means that new costs or risks must be imposed on some groups in a policy area, decision-makers should seek to allocate the costs involved to those groups best able to insure against them.
- Because of the 'privileged position of business' in terms of controlling discretionary resources critical for overall social welfare and shaping political debate, liberal democracies confront particular difficulties in ensuring that the power of major corporations, private business more generally and wealthy individuals is controlled and regulated so as to maintain a relatively equitable interest group process. This is likely to involve controlling business's capacity to shape public opinion, dominate policy analysis and relevant information, and withhold resources vital for state policy.

The chapter begins by briefly reviewing the recent empirical experience of group politics in Australia, set against the background expectations of the pluralist theory central to modern democracies. A strengths, weaknesses, opportunities and threats (SWOT) analysis then summarises key points of debate around interest group politics and corporate power. After the SWOT analysis, three sections consider further group inequalities, donations and corporate power.

Recent developments

Modern pluralist theories of the democratic process do not claim that interest groups have 'equal' power in any sense. Instead they argue that multiple different centres of power in society should be acknowledged and welcomed as legitimate in the political process. And there should be no guaranteed ability for the electoral wishes of an 'apathetic' majority to over-ride the legitimate intense preferences of minorities relating to their own welfare and concerns within civil society. Easy mobilisation by interest groups and their ability to access politicians and officials are also key safeguards against abuses of civil rights and essential human liberties (see Chapter 3). The following subsections review key expectations in pluralist theory and then consider how far Australian group politics matches that model.

Group pluralism

Any group in Australian society with shared interests should be able to easily put together an organisation and engage in the political process, confident that its legitimacy will be recognised both by elected politicians and by public service officials, so long as it acts in in legal and ethically appropriate ways. Consultation processes should be equitably organised and take account of the full diversity of public views about policy options. This does not mean that politicians can or should 'equally accommodate' every interest (even if that were feasible, which it is not). Nor does it mean letting every group have a veto power to block any policy changes adversely affecting them – for this would be a recipe for complete social gridlock (see Chapter 15). Resolving policy issues where there are sharp conflicts of interest between different social and economic groups often entails making a choice where someone must incur a loss – because any option will carry costs for some group. However, in democratic theory, politicians and public administration officials are obligated:

- to always register different groups' costs from alternative policy proposals accurately and appreciate them in detail
- to modify policy designs as far as possible so as to minimise the overall social costs (which is often feasible)
- to mitigate the burden falling on any one group as far as possible
- perhaps to compensate a group for a change that affects them adversely
- to allocate costs, where they have to be incurred, efficiently across social interests to those groups that can most cheaply and easily insure or protect themselves against such costs (Horn, 1995, Ch. 2).

For instance, on the last point, collecting income taxes from workers in firms inevitably creates transaction costs for someone. Getting employers to bear most costs by collecting pay-as-you-go taxes for their employees is the cheapest way to do it, and firms can employ dedicated staff to handle tax business and offset these costs against their profits.

How are politicians and officials made accessible in liberal democracies? A 'ladder' of freely available participation opportunities should exist. Low-cost options on the ladder include writing emails, letters and social media messages to MPs or departments; sending back public feedback forms; signing online petitions; or people showing up at MPs' local offices or 'surgeries' to explain in detail how policy problems have affected them. Medium-cost activities include people joining and paying membership subscriptions to fund a pressure or other collective group to represent their case to politicians and the media; supporting lobbying activities with funding or time; making formal complaints through public administration channels; and taking part in official consultation exercises, like public meetings.

High-cost activities might include people taking part in public protests, demonstrations, strikes or peaceful civil disobedience – activities that more forcefully communicate to policy-makers how strongly they feel about an issue. If people are willing to incur such high costs, they demonstrate to politicians that persisting with contested proposals will likely cause voters to change allegiance or back opposition parties, and create possible reputational damage for particular unpopular politicians. Well-organised groups pursue many low- and medium-cost options simultaneously, reserving high-cost options more for 'last ditch' mobilisations if previous lobbying activities have not succeeded.

The group process is important for government and opposition, because how far a given group climbs up the 'ladder' of organising and mobilising costs provides politicians with high-quality and reliable information about its members' preference intensities. While an email or letter campaign to MPs might be ignored or assigned little salience, and a professionally run media advertising campaign discounted, evidence of people incurring real costs to get their point across will count far more. What then determines differences in the influence or power of different groups? Pluralist theory recognises that a diverse set of nine main factors will determine a group's relative influence in a relatively complex overall way. These factors are summarised in Figure 7.1.

Figure 7.1: Factors that make interest groups more or less politically influential

Factor	Expected to be influential, and why	Expected not to be influential, and why
1. Potential size of group (if everyone supported it)	Large groups may shape more voters' views and influence election outcomes.	Small minority groups are trivial for election outcomes.
2. Actual membership size		
3. Group's mobilisation rate (i.e. actual members/ potential members)	Well-mobilised, active groups can better sway their members' actions and bear organising/campaign costs.	Passive and poorly mobilised groups.
4. Can groups easily organise private benefits (selective incentives) for their members?	Usually, smaller groups can do this best, because non-joining is visible and affects outcomes. A few larger groups may just be 'lucky' in this aspect.	Usually, larger groups cannot do this, because individual non-joiners are invisible. And in large groups any one person not joining will not worsen the group's outcomes in a noticeable way.
5. Access to resources	Wealthy groups can fund campaigns and use skilled professionals for lobbying.	Groups with weak funding rely on amateur lobbying and philanthropy to get heard (Madden, Scaife and McGregor-Lowndes, 2005).
6. Pivotality within major social or partisan cleavages or conflicts	Non-aligned or 'swing' groups are able to swing their support behind different political or societal coalitions and extract a price for it from political leaders.	Groups already firmly aligned in social or political conflicts (e.g. trade unions supporting Labor, or business backing Liberals); their support may be taken for granted by political leaders, since they are committed already.
7. Legitimacy	Well-established, 'respectable' and moderate groups that play by the rules of parliamentary politics and represent non-controversial causes.	'Extreme' groups, those that reject parliamentary politics or have relied on 'direct action', and new groups, especially those representing controversial viewpoints.
8. Reputation for success	Groups that have previously fought and won fiercely contested issues and demonstrated political and campaign skills, strong membership backing and access to big resources.	New groups and those who have previously lost out in contested issues or whose campaigns visibly failed.
9. 'Coalitionality', i.e. ease of joining coalitions with other interests	Non-ideological groups, those most controlled by their leaderships, and groups able to build 'coalitions of minorities' with different and non-clashing interests. For example, libertarian groups opposing 'nanny state' restrictions might ally with interests seeking to stop vaccines, curb anti-smoking measures or ease firearm controls on guns.	Groups that are ideologically 'locked-in', especially if group policy is controlled by grassroots members.

Source: Derived from (Dunleavy, 1991, Ch. 4).

So, overall, the pluralist prediction is that:

Group influence *is some weighted function of*	P (its potential size)	+ A (its actual size)	+ M (its mobilisation rate)	+ S (access to selective Incentives)
	+ T (its total resources)	+ V (its pivotality)	+ L (its legitimacy)	+ R (its reputation)	+ C (its coalitionality)

Australia: empirics

Political scientists have not been able to determine how these different factors are weighted, but the majority pluralist view among them insists that within liberal democracies no group ranks high on all these factors at once. For instance, Australian trade unions have 1.5 million members and some occupations and industries are well mobilised (especially the public services). Unions are able to mass together annual union membership fees and so run effective organisations. They can also offer selective incentives, for example by providing legal protection to members. These bases sustain unions' ability to undertake collective industrial bargaining with employers and to periodically mount costly effective strikes or other actions when needed. Yet unions have also faced sharply declining memberships in many industries (see Figure 7.6 later in this chapter) and must constantly battle with powerful business corporations, and often environmental lobbies. Unions have also been thoroughly aligned with the Labor Party (and so rarely pivotal). Indeed, unions regularly confront threats to their bargaining capabilities and effectiveness for members from restrictive government policies, especially under Liberal-National governments (who may believe they have few union voters to lose).

Many groups may also be well situated on most of the factors in Figure 7.1 in one narrow area of policy-making, but still be relatively uninfluential in others. So pluralists argue that that there is no overall, fixed power structure, but instead a multiplicity of different and shifting power centres. Previously long-established patterns of influence can also be changed if public and political opinion shifts against them. For instance, rural and shooting interests were long seen as powerful in maintaining relatively lax gun laws in Australia's states, and strongly linked to the Coalition parties on the right. But after a mass shooter killed 20 people in 1996, Howard's Liberal-National government and all the states pushed through a National Firearms Agreement that imposed stricter gun controls nationwide (Guardian, 2016). No other mass shootings have recurred (up to late 2023), a very different picture from the complete stalemate on gun controls in the USA.

Looking more systematically at how many interest groups operate in Australia, and how they are endowed with the resources listed above, is tricky, because recent data is lacking. Many major business, professional and well-established civil society associations are organised primarily in branches at the state/territory level (and sometimes in larger cities too). Additionally, they come together at federal level via annual conferences and meetings and operate national executive committees. However, some trade associations and trade unions are strongly organised at both levels, but may focus most intensively on federal lobbying. Long-established issue advocacy groups, plus organisations like unions strongly linked to major political parties, also permanently operate branch networks spanning across both levels. Their balance of activity reflects who does what in the overall allocation of Australian governance functions across tiers (see Chapter 16).

Figure 7.2 shows a selection of some of the interest groups that were reputedly amongst the largest in modern Australia in 2023. The trade union movement was still perhaps the largest overall in terms of the total union members, brought together within the Australian Council of Trade Unions (ACTU). However, many of the component unions have different policy lines on key issues and controversies, for example over climate change mitigation measures needed. Two large business associations and the farmers' federation also feature in the list, and two health professional bodies (for nurses and doctors). The largest civil society and non-economic groups are the Red Cross, the Australian Conservation Foundation (ACF) and the pressure group for older citizens.

Figure 7.2: Australian interest groups reputedly with the largest number of members or supporters, 2023

Group	Type	Members or 'supporters'	Type	Political alignment
Australian Council of Trade Unions (ACTU) – representing 1,500,000 union members	Peak association	46 unions	Trade union	ACTU itself is neutral, but many unions are Labor aligned
Australian Conservation Foundation (ACF)	Environmental/ interest group	700,000	Interested citizens	Neutral
Australian Chamber of Commerce and Industry (ACCI)	Peak association	300,000	Business owners	Neutral
Australian Nursing and Midwifery Federation (ANMF)	Peak body for profession	300,000	Nurses/midwives	Neutral
National Seniors Australia	Social interest group	200,000	Interested citizens	Neutral
Australian Red Cross (with 700,000 supporters)	Philanthropic group	90,000	Interested citizens	Neutral
Australian Medical Association (AMA)	Peak body for profession	90,000	Doctors	Neutral
National Farmers' Federation	Peak association	80,000	Farmers	Liberal/National
Australian Industry Group (Ai Group)	Peak assocation	60,000	Business owners	Liberal/National

Source: Compiled by author using data from the 2023 Wikipedia pages, checked against the organisation home pages for each of these groups.

Environmental groups and those representing the interests of women, LGBTIQ+ communities, ethnic/language identities, First Nations peoples and other demographic groupings tend to be more locally or community based. They mostly have less well developed or more episodic/ fluctuating levels of state or federal organisational 'pyramiding', depending on the issues being addressed at different times or in particular campaigns. With the expansion of social media and the ready availability of apps and other aids for lowering organisations' communication and administration costs, many smaller cause groups and special interest associations (for example, resident associations) are essentially federations of home-based organisers who may now be able to match many of the activities previously requiring office-based staff financed from membership dues. Internet-based funding and means of engaging supporters who are not members are also increasingly critical and to some extent can substitute for obtaining large donations and contracting a media/PR agency to run campaigns.

The other side of the coin involves considering the most disadvantaged groups in Australian society and their capacity to organise and secure political attention to their needs and concerns. Figure 7.3 shows the five groups that in the still-recent past (around the turn of the century) suffered from what most observers would regard as serious, policy-induced disadvantages, and compares that with more recent experience in terms of policy attention and patterns of group mobilisation. In all these cases, previously very bad situations for these groups have greatly improved in recent decades. However, among a minority of Australians, there are still some continuing strong mobilisations around contemporary issues that sustain prejudicial or discriminatory public attitudes that are hard to eradicate completely.

Figure 7.3: Five disadvantaged social groups and their interest group mobilisation, 2023

Social group	Situation at the start of the 21st century	Public policy situation, 2023	Pattern of group mobilisation, 2023
Women	Despite equal pay legislation, women were still discriminated against in pay levels and woefully under-represented at the top of corporations and within the political system. Levels of both reported and unreported abuse and violence against women were high.	Gender-based pay gaps have reduced (see Chapter 10) and women's representation in politics has improved towards parity with men. Company boards and top private sector positions show less equal progress. The 'Me Too' movement and scandals in Parliament, plus the political success of Teal Independents, have broadened the range of discriminatory sexism being criticised and acted against.	Highly decentralised, multiple-state and big-city groups, with vocal political and public campaigning on 'Me Too' issues, pay and promotion, and reproductive issues.
People with disabilities	Welfare provision for disabled people was partial and under-funded.	The National Disability Insurance Scheme (NDIS) has improved access to services and benefits (DSS, 2017), but discrimination in public transport access remains considerable. Public attitudes have improved, but people with disabilities still suffer labour market exclusion and ageism in their senior years.	Seven main disability organisations (some individual associations, a consortium of associations and others in company form) receive government funding (DSS, 2017) and must be consulted by public policy-makers on relevant changes.

Social group	Situation at the start of the 21st century	Public policy situation, 2023	Pattern of group mobilisation, 2023
LGBTIQ+ communities	Prejudice against homosexuals and lesbians was substantial and people could routinely expect some public hostility, reflecting quite recent decriminalisation. Legal discrimination continued.	Transgender groups continue to experience public hostility from a substantial minority of peoples. Gay people have greater but not yet complete public acceptance and can still be targeted by homophobes. Gay marriages have finally been accepted and legal disadvantages have gone.	Well-developed state and conurbation groups, with a focus on annual city Pride marches, vocal political and public campaigning.
Refugees and asylum seekers	Some 900,000 refugees have been re-settled in Australia since 1945. But since 2010 only people with valid visas have been allowed, and those without (often 'boat people') have been housed offshore under poor conditions (e.g. on access to healthcare).	Visa-less refugees and asylum seekers face long periods of detention and limited access to public services. Pathways to resettlement are restrictive. Public hostility to refugees and asylum seekers' interests on the political right and as a component in public opinion remains prominent.	A range of small philanthropic cause groups campaign on behalf of refugees and asylum seekers, who are unable to organise themselves politically.
First Nations Australians	Aboriginal and Torres Strait Islander peoples have faced long-run historical mistreatment by government, gaining full civil rights only in 1967.	Indigenous Australian communities in 'bush' areas of the Northern Territory and Queensland still face intractable social problems of joblessness, substance abuse and household violence. Elsewhere, First Nations people confront less acute but still serious disadvantages.	A slow-burn civil and political rights and cultural movement most recently focused at national level on the First Nations Voice to Parliament referendum. But this was lost decisively in October 2023 (see Chapter 4). Future progress is hard to foresee.

Source: Compiled by author using information from the 2023 home pages for each organisation and also any relevant Wikipedia pages.

In terms of securing access to political power centres and attention from public service officials, some civil society groups and mobilisations were largely excluded from direct influence during the COVID-19 pandemic – notably a wide range of anti-lockdown and anti-quarantine protestors and later on the many vocal anti-vaccination groups, plus groups promoting health disinformation and a wide range of often bizarre conspiracy theories. In many cases, legal compulsion was used to coerce dissenters from many of these groups into meeting public health regulations, and major party politicians often united to condemn especially 'extreme' demonstrations or propaganda, which was also generally excluded from broadcast news and discussions. Did this dismissive treatment infringe democratic norms? Pluralists would argue that it does not, since the COVID-19 sceptics and anti-vaxxers were allowed to demonstrate, mobilise and communicate their messages online and via print, lobby public authorities and dispute their policies, and probe the public health evidence. In addition, there were two strong and over-riding reasons why these movements were handled by government in a generally unresponsive way. Decision-makers wanted to maximise the welfare of the vast majority of citizens in the face of a very serious threat to health. And most politicians were concerned to combat any degradation of the public realm by giving credence to completely unevidenced and irrational disinformation. Yet politicians' and public service concerns to minimise any 'extreme' reactions and public resistance (however badly founded) did also clearly influence lockdown policy in most states, which ended restrictions as soon as possible (see Chapters 17 to 22).

Strengths, weaknesses, opportunities and threats (SWOT) analysis

Current strengths	Current weaknesses
The importance of interest group politics has been fully acknowledged by politicians and officials at federal, state and local levels and recognised in the country's 'civic culture'. The resources needed to form effective interest groups are widely available, and internet mobilisation tools have even further lowered the information and organisation cost barriers to forming associations.	Critics have pointed out that in the recent past many minority groups in Australia suffered from legal oppressions and policy-induced harms because majority-seeking politicians were unable or unwilling to take unpopular actions needed to defend their civil liberties and human rights. Some minorities, like asylum seekers and refugees not using official routes, and transgender people, still suffer from similar mistreatment or prejudices from some other citizens.
Group influence depends on multiple different factors (see earlier in this chapter), and pluralist authors argue that no interest groups score well on all factors at once. In general, large groups can potentially shape substantial votes on their own, while minority groups with small memberships have to rely on joining a 'coalition of minorities' – that is, pooling their influence to promote their interests shared with other favourable minority groups (ones whose interests do not clash with theirs).	In recent years, many Australian voluntary institutions (like churches, charities and some NGOs) have been indicted for their past treatment of disadvantaged people in their care, with adverse impacts on social trust. A recent analysis estimated the percentages of Australians in four groups (Kamp et al., 2023) – the very distrusting (15 per cent), those that are largely unsure about how much they can trust various groups and institutions (17 per cent), those that are somewhat trusting (42 per cent) and those that are largely trusting (26 per cent). Not all associations have acted in socially positive ways, as some social movement mobilisations around bizarre conspiracy theories continue to demonstrate.
Some previously large and apparently dominant groups, notably the trade unions and established Christian churches, have declined in size and salience so that they operate as more 'normal' interests than in the past. Overall, the pluralism of interest group politics has greatly increased in recent decades.	Trade union decline has been accompanied by an increasing imbalance of economic power in the workplace between employers and workers, and the growth of major social inequalities. Before 2022, Liberal-National governments' restrictions on unions' ability to organise effectively often made this worse, for ideological reasons.

Corporations and wealthy individuals can influence politics via party donations, which are strictly controlled, but they control few votes directly. Major corporations tend not to make spectacularly large or one-sided donations or political interventions, which are far more the behaviour of somewhat 'rogue' business executives, like Clive Palmer. Most major Australian companies 'hedge' against political risks by making only medium-sized donations relatively equally across the top two parties.	Business has become more concentrated in Australia over time (Sims, 2016). It now occupies a clearly privileged position within the interest group universe, and by expanding its ideological, informational and media power it has more than compensated for having only a minority of votes that are directly controlled. Business interests have increasingly set a dominant neo-liberal framework for all policy debates. Australian voters worry more about the power of big business than about trade union power, and this effect was most marked under Coalition governments (Cameron and Wynter, 2018).
The development of corporate social responsibility (CSR) and big firms' action on environmental and social governance (ESG) both demonstrate that business interests themselves must pay close attention to their public reputations, the views of their increasingly active and articulate customers, their workforce, and political and policy measures. Old-fashioned, 'hard threat' measures (like the Google and Facebook showdowns with the federal government in 2021 on the mandatory media code, see Chapter 9) are no longer sustainable for business.	Corporations have repeatedly and systematically intervened in the political process to mobilise resources in defence of their sectional economic interests. Strikingly successful media and ideational campaigns have frustrated any action on corporate taxation, drastically slowed efforts to mitigate climate change, and biased economic policy-making consistently to major corporation interests (see below in this chapter).
Future opportunities	**Future threats**
The expansion of social media has increased the scope, immediacy and appeal of citizen activism in ways that now fundamentally constrain large or institutionally dominant groups' ability to get away with scandals or inaction on inequalities – witness the change in corporate behaviours about bringing women onto boards and acting against sex discrimination within their firms.	The development of artificial intelligence (AI) will almost certainly expand the ability of corporations and wealthy interests to flood social media with disinformation campaigns and materials designed to demotivate opponents. Australian regulators are poorly placed to take any effective countervailing measures.
	Only constant vigilance by unions, anti-corporate interest groups and citizens, plus some centre-left politicians can prevent the further continuous accretion of corporate power at the expense of all other social interests.

The remainder of the chapter considers how the interest group funding of political parties shapes unequal group influence; to what extent trends in group mobilisation have been adverse for the largest civil society groups, especially the trade unions; and if business and corporate power has become dominant in Australian politics.

Interest groups and party funding

One of the most direct and controversial linkages between interest groups and policy-making concerns the existence of large donations by groups or companies and individuals linked to major groups (like business or the unions). Of course, donations are closely regulated and any gift to political parties over a threshold of A$16,900 must be declared to the Australian Electoral Commission (AEC), which publishes an annual list of donations. However, there has been no upper limit on how large gifts can be. Critics argue that business influence in particular can be disguised by corporate executives making large individual gifts that are well understood to be for a specific interest. Sceptics argue about the legitimacy of large donations, querying whether they might lead to creating dependency or expectations about policy stances from the recipient parties. On a pessimistic view:

> *Even with reform of the system of funding political parties, the wealthy will find a way to buy political power – whether through the direct sponsorship of politicians and parties, or through the acquisition of media businesses, or through the financing of think tanks. To put it another way, the voices of the super-wealthy are heard by politicians well above the babble of the crowd ... It means that we are more vulnerable than perhaps we have been since the 19th century to the advent of rule by an unelected oligarchy. (Peston, 2008, p.346)*

By contrast, pluralist defenders of the status quo argue that in fact donations are quite diverse, and that no flow-back of benefits for publicised donations can be organised without running foul of strong anti-corruption laws at state level and legislation, recently strengthened at federal level.

Figure 7.4 shows what types of donors gave the largest gifts of A$50,000 or more in 2017–18 – an off-year for elections except in Queensland and Western Australia. These large gifts to parties totalled just under A$9.3 million then. Over a third were company donations to the Liberals, followed by individual donations, again to the Liberals, and then trade union donations to Labor (mainly in the two election states). Trade associations also gave extensively to Labor and less so to the Liberals, and a few companies supported the Nationals. Overall, nearly half of the big donations (48 per cent) went to the Liberals and 36 per cent to Labor. However, in 2017–18 the single largest donation made was of A$600,000 to the Greens, from a retired professor in her will. Elsewhere in the listing it was apparent that companies and unions preferred to fragment their donations across state and federal parties, perhaps to avoid attracting attention. Some large companies also followed 'balanced' funding strategies, giving approximately the same funding to the top two parties. Trade associations also often split their funding in this way. Trade unions divided their funding across state and local units, making gifts chiefly to their relevant part of the Australia Labor Party (ALP). Labor attracted few large individual donors in this year, but did somewhat better with smaller donations. The Greens relied almost wholly on individual donors, some of whom gave medium-sized sums, reflecting the party's appeal based on its espousing a 'cause' and not merely being a standard election-fighting organisation.

Figure 7.4: Who gave and who received major sums (of A$50,000 or more) as political donations in 2017–18

Thousands of Australian dollars (A$)

Party	Type of donor				Total received
	Companies	Individuals	Trade associations	Unions	
Liberal	3,032	1,500	270		4,802
Labor	1,009	92	637	1,580	3,318
Greens		750			750
National	264				264
Australian Conservatives	100				100
Katter	50				50
Total given	4,455	2,342	907	1,580	9,284

Source: Compiled by author using data from the AEC (2020).
Note: There were 85 donations above A$50,000 in this year.

However, just looking at donations by size, or focusing attention (as most critics do) on large companies alone, may not capture the ability of interest groups to make multiple small donations in ways that cumulatively have a great effect, especially in the case of companies or trade associations transacting with the government for contracts, or where business fortunes are closely bound up with government regulation or subsidy schemes. A case in point involves community pharmacists whose peak national professional body is the Pharmaceutical Society of Australia, which makes no donations and remains resolutely non-political. In addition, however, an association called the Pharmacy Guild of Australia has represented the specific interests of 5,700 community pharmacists, including large chains and small businesses. They are heavily dependent on regulations about what Medicare's Pharmaceutical Benefits Scheme (PBS) pays for drugs – expected to total A$4 billion a year in 2020 to 2025 (Russell, 2019). These firms have also wanted to prevent too much competition arising in many community settings and in the use of online prescribing. The guild has been extremely active politically, both in federal politics and at state level. Figure 7.5 shows that in 2017–18 they made nearly a hundred donations, split into many small amounts, across the top two parties, with more going to Labor (historically a staunch defender of community pharmacies' role and of Medicare generally).

Figure 7.5: Donations to parties by the Pharmacy Guild of Australia in 2017–2018

Party	Total (A$)	Number of donations	Average donation amount (A$)
Labor (ALP and four state parties)	139,540	29	4,810
Liberal (two state parties)	43,280	23	1,880
National	37,620	41	920
Total	220,440	93	2,370

Source: Computed by the author using data from the AEC, reproduced at ABC News (2019).
Note: Numbers in columns 1 and 3 are rounded to the nearest 10.

The end result has been an intensely active and vigilant group exercising a lot of influence, and apparently getting a lot of direct return for its members in terms of beneficial changes strongly affecting these firms, who typically get 40 to 46 per cent of their annual incomes from public funds:

> *The lobbying capabilities of the Pharmacy Guild executive and its members, the reach into every community, and the substantial political donations they make, mean politicians are always nervous about treading on community pharmacies' toes.*
>
> *Community pharmacies have a unique ability to garner public support for their causes from loyal customers. This can be a potent deterrent for any politician proposing changes the Pharmacy Guild views as adverse* (Russell, 2019).

The decline of large groups?

The dominant large-membership interest group for much of Australia's history has been the trade union movement, which in the mid-1980s accounted for almost half the working population. However, a series of trends, plus the vigorous anti-union laws of the Howard government in the 1990s, helped to produce a big decline in membership, and by 2022 the trade union movement stood at just one in eight workers (Figure 7.6). The development of part-time working and later the gig economy, plus the deindustrialisation of large manufacturing plants with many (mostly male) workers and the globalisation of production functions to China and elsewhere, explain much of the early spectacular declines in this chart. For instance, in 1993 the unionisation rate for part-time workers was fully 19 percentage points less than for full-time workers. Improvements in union appeals to women and part-time workers began to stabilise the situation from 2016 onwards, but the COVID-19 pandemic and working from home did not help there.

Figure 7.6: The decline of unionisation in Australia, 1986 to 2022

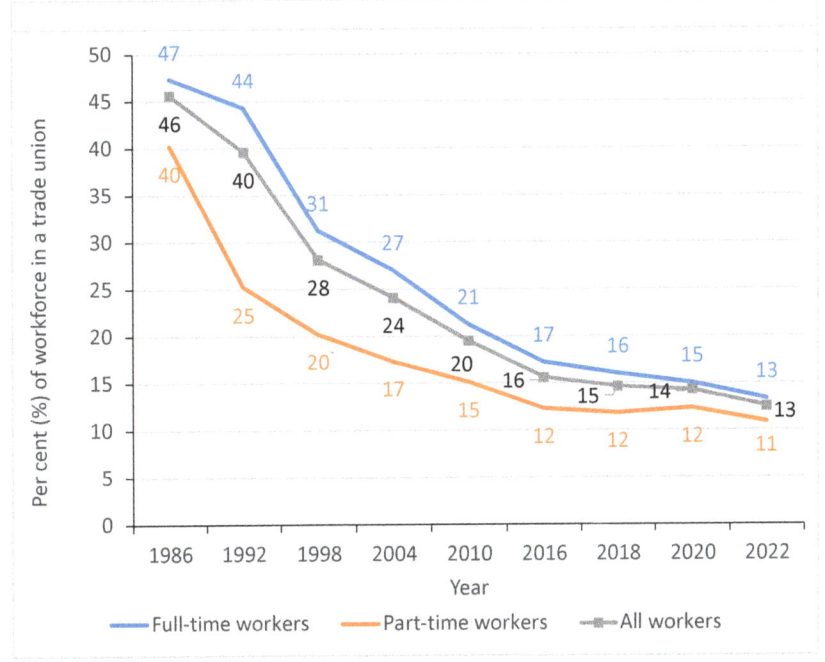

Source: Compiled by the author using data from the Australian Bureau of Statistics (2023).

Note: Numbers rounded to nearest digit.

Given the decline of manufacturing, much of modern trade unions' membership is concentrated in professional occupations, chiefly inside the public services (and mostly at state level). Thus, Figure 7.7 shows that public administration, healthcare and education are among the most unionised industrial sectors, with over a fifth of workers being members in 2022. Two other top five areas (shaded in Figure 7.7) are infrastructure and transport. The order of sectors in Figure 7.7 is set by the extent of declines in membership from 2016 to 2022 (in the rightmost column). Here the top sectors were public administration, mining and financial services – the first and third possibly reflecting the effects of working from home. Elsewhere decline was less steep, but still apparently hard for the unions to stem. Only one small sector – arts services – saw any unionisation increase.

Figure 7.7: Changes in unionisation rates by industrial sector, 2016 to 2022

Industrial sector	Unionisation rate (%) 2022	Decline (% points) since 2016
Public administration and safety	22.5	−8.3
Mining	10.2	−6.3
Financial and insurance services	6	−5.0
Electricity, gas, water and waste services	21.6	−4.4
Manufacturing	9.9	−4.2
Construction	9.7	−3.9
Retail trade	8.1	−3.8
Transport, postal and warehousing	19.8	−3.7
Healthcare and social assistance	20.2	−3.3
Wholesale trade	2.4	−3.3
Education and training	30.1	−3.0
Agriculture, forestry and fishing	1.3	−2.4
Other services	3.7	−2.4
Administrative support services	3.4	−2.3
Information, media and telecommunications	7.2	−1.0
Accommodation and food services	1.6	−0.7
Professional, scientific and technical services	2.1	−0.6
Rental, hiring and real estate services	2.4	−0.2
Arts and recreation services	9.5	0.3

Source: Compiled by author using data from the Australian Bureau of Statistics (2023).

Falling union memberships have also been very visible for the Australian public. Figure 7.8 shows that the share of respondents to the Australian Election Study endorsing the view that unions are too powerful fell considerably in recent decades, stabilising above 40 per cent since 2010.

Figure 7.8: Percentage (%) of respondents in election surveys agreeing that 'unions have too much power', 1987 to 2019

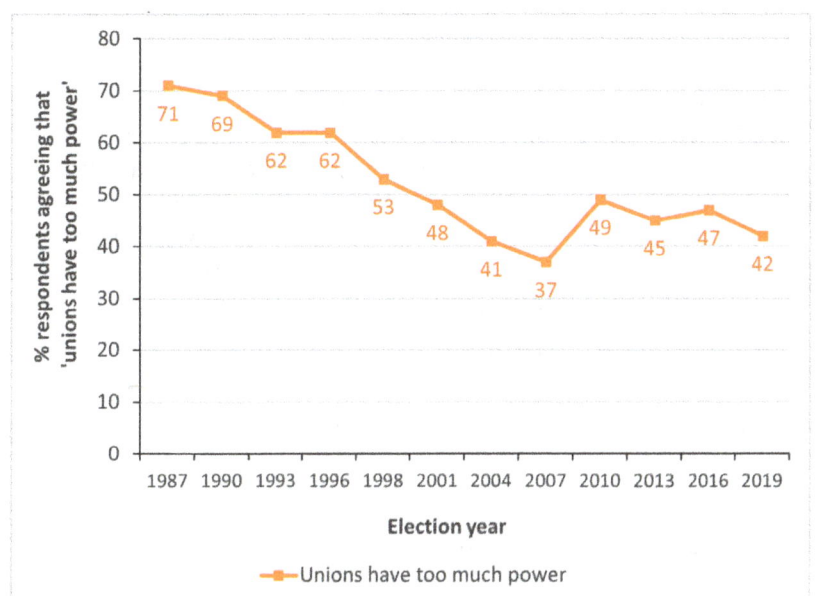

Source: Adapted from Cameron and McAllister (2019, p.108).

The outcomes of industrial disputes themselves have also showed some declining union efficacy over time. A third shaper of trade unions' legitimacy were the interactions with Liberal–National Coalition and Labor federal governments over industrial relations policies in three main periods, namely:

- from 1996 to 2007, when the Howard Coalition government systematically attacked unions' legitimacy, seeking to reduce their policy influence
- from 2007 to 2013, when unions once again became 'insider' groups under the Rudd–Gillard Labor governments (albeit with policy differences among them)
- from 2013 to 2022, when the unions again moved to being 'outsider' groups under the Coalition governments (Wright and McLaughlin, 2021).

Some manual worker unions recovered some bargaining power thanks to labour shortages during and after the COVID-19 pandemic, and the labour movement as a whole returned to insider group status with ministers after the narrow Labor victory in the 2022 federal election.

The problems of corporate power and wealth distortions

As the case of the community pharmacies illustrates, businesses very often have a direct interest in shaping public policies, and attention has focused especially on the political power of big corporations. Lenin famously claimed that the democratic states were 'tied by a thousand threads' to the interests of capitalists, a position that liberal authors have always rejected. Yet a range of pluralist theorists have argued that we should be concerned about 'the privileged position of business', which makes corporations' influence completely non-comparable to that of normal interest groups (Dryzek and Dunleavy, 2009, pp.132–34; Head, 1993):

> The system works that way not because business people conspire or plan to punish us, but simply because many kinds of institutional changes are of a character they do not like and consequently reduce the inducements we count on to motivate them to provide jobs and perform their other functions [within their discretion]. (Lindblom, 1982, p.327)

And 'even in the democracies, masses are persuaded to ask from elites only what elites wish to give them' (Lindblom, 1977, p.136).

In Australia, around two-thirds to three-quarters of respondents in major election surveys have consistently endorsed the claim that 'business has too much power' across the last two decades, up around 10 per cent on previous eras (Cameron and McAllister, 2019, p.108). Lindy Edwards has argued that:

> Australia's 10 largest and most powerful corporates … all operated in industry sectors dominated by one to four businesses. Each of these companies tower over long production and supply chains, and a significant element of their corporate strategy centres on scraping the wealth out of those chains and concentrating it in their own hands … Australia is teetering on the edge of a 'Medici Cycle' where economic and political power has become mutually reinforcing, and the largest companies use their political power to secure laws to further entrench their economic dominance. (2022, pp.95 and 97)

Figure 7.9 shows the industrial sectors that are most cited by critics as showing evidence of overwhelming corporate power (Denniss and Richardson, 2013; Edwards, 2018, 2020).

Figure 7.9: The main sectors where critics argue that domestic big business is dominant

Sector	Main evidence cited	Additional sources
Mining giants	Strong industry campaign to defeat mining levies and carbon taxes under the Rudd–Gillard governments; subsequent climate change denialism over coal and oil mining; heavy government subsidies given to fossil fuel projects. State and federal government dependency on mining tax revenues has been high, while mining provides scarce, well-paid jobs in sparsely populated regional areas. In more populated areas local residents' resistance to exploitative mining has sometimes been greater (Christie, 2019).	Maher, 2022; Gilding, Merlot and Leitch, 2016; Mikler, Elbra and Murphy-Gregory, 2019; Grudnoff, 2013; Marsh, Lewis and Chesters, 2014; Buckley, 2019; Eccleston, and Hortle, 2016; Bell and Hindmoor, 2013.

Fossil fuel industries more generally	Climate change denialism was also sponsored by oil and gas interests and powerful media interests.	Lucas, 2021; Goods, 2022; Wilson, 2016
Big four banks	Very strong oligopoly. Widespread banking malpractices before the Royal Commission into Misconduct in the Banking, Superannuation and Financial Services Industry (2019) and its reform proposals were subsequently greatly watered down.	Richardson, 2012; Johnson, 2013
Superannuation funds	Government mandates all employees to invest 12 per cent of salary in funds and regulations which restricts levels of market competition and consumer access to funds.	Denniss and Richardson, 2013
Retail giants, Coles and Woolworths, and food manufacturing peak associations	Top two firms dominate the industry and act to maintain minimal regulation of obesogenic marketing and food/alcohol threats to public health.	Needham et al., 2019; O'Keeffe, 2019
Gambling industry	Widespread evidence of adverse effects especially in poor neighbourhoods; weak regulation of debt-inducing behaviours, especially in terms of 'pokies' (slot machines) operated also by many social clubs.	Ting et al., 2021
Telstra	Privatised former state telecoms operator that has retained a market-dominant position in broadband and mobiles sector, inhibiting competition. Strong political connections.	
Management consultants	A handful of large (international) firms have received very large government contracts over decades as public services staffing thinned out, plus a 'revolving door' of senior staff acting as political advisors to politicians. In 2022 to 2023 a scandal broke over PriceWaterhouseCoopers (PwC) apparently using inside government information to advise its private industry clients.	Josserand, 2023; Podger, 2023; Anaf and Baum, 2023
Media (press and private sector TV giants)	High level of media oligopoly nationally and regional dominance at state level. Politicians directly depend on proprietors and journalists for coverage, especially in the highly partisan press. See Chapter 8.	Boulus and Dowding, 2014
Australian branches of internet platform companies	Google, Facebook, Apple, X (formerly Twitter) and other global firms have increasingly dominated political news dissemination within Australia. Government intervention on behalf of media companies to mandate GAFAM (Google (Alphabet); Apple; Facebook (Meta); Amazon; and Microsoft) firms paying for news content showed Liberal-National ministers acting at the behest of media corporations. However, the global platform companies still internally regulate most aspects of internet safety, competition and innovation (as with AI), while government regulation lags years behind. See Chapters 8 and 9.	See Chapter 8

Source: Author-created table from sources listed in the table.

The case most commented on in the corporate power literature concerns the mining industry and especially its highly effective campaign against the Labor government's 2010 resources super-tax (see references in Figure 7.9). The big two firms rounded up many smaller companies to seriously threaten an investment strike, and spent A$25 million on an advertising campaign targeting government changes. The firms successfully built a broader coalition with the Business Council of Australia and with some trade unions. In Queensland and West Australia, the two states most affected, the industry increased political funding support of the Liberals by a factor of 10. A subsequent disastrous drop in Labor support in the polls lead to intra-party dissent and the withdrawal of the policy.

Subsequently, the mining firms and oil and gas industry substantially exploited their victory to campaign vociferously against the regulation of carbon emissions, supporting climate denialism and making effective donations. One indicator of this recent influence was given by the extent of state and federal government subsidies for mining projects:

> *A 2013 estimate by the Australian Institute found that the federal government provided the mining industry with over $4.5 billion per year in subsidies (Grudnoff, 2013). A more recent IMF report, which estimated global fossil fuel subsidies, found that in 2015 the Australian government provided US $29 billion in post-tax subsidies, a figure amounting to 2.3 per cent of GDP (Coady et al., 2019, p.35). In addition to direct subsidies, the federal government has also heavily funded rail and port infrastructure required by the mining industry. For example, the controversial Adani Coal mine in Southern Queensland will receive $4.4 billion in subsidies over the next 30 years, without which it would not be commercially viable. (Maher, 2022, p.70)* [URL links here are our additions]

Observers have drawn an acute contrast between how Australia and Norway regulate the whole resources sector (Cleary, 2016).

Of course, big business companies directly control few votes – although their employee numbers can be significant overall (as with the retail giants) or be concentrated in states where they can have a lot of regional and local influence (as with the mining giants, headquartered in Western Australia). So how does business influence operate so much more effectively than the kinds of campaigning that other groups can do? David Beetham (2011, pp.7–8) and many other writers point out that business imposes seven systemic constraints on government capacity:

- *Economic globalisation* has been a potent disincentive to governments trying to regulate key industries, as the fear of domestic industries being undercut by overseas competitors worsened. Many more sectors of the economy have become 'financialised' via privatisation and deregulation of state enterprises and via the growth of para-state contracting by big corporations taking over more services and controlling key assets. These changes have greatly speeded up the government's weakening grip on domestic capital. Occasionally the Australian government has shown itself able to face down investment strike threats, as with the collapse of the resistance by Google and Facebook/Meta to the 2022 media code (see Chapter 9). However, ministers here only acted on behalf of domestic Australian capital (the news media) with significant political clout.
- *Corporate fiscal strategies* have greatly undermined Australian government revenues through the tax avoidance industry – depriving government of corporation taxes especially, which almost no major Australian companies are still paying. For fear that firms would exit the country, the Canberra government has perforce had to wait for an OECD initiative to standardise a minimum corporation tax of 15 per cent across industrial nations, but this has been hung up for years.

- *Complex corporate architectures* of inter-firm transfers and holdings of assets have accelerated this problem. International companies can transfer-price assets and shift their tax domiciles in ways that are hard to control. Privatised utilities and public service suppliers can create large debt burdens and remortgage assets so as to extract 'shareholder value' at taxpayers' expense, often selling on debt-laden companies to hedge funds and less scrupulous or influenceable companies overseas.

- *Top pay levels* for corporate executives and other wealthy individuals have boosted their combined income pay and share options and other benefits to unprecedented levels, with a huge range of justifications being used (Pepper, 2022). 'Tax efficient' structures have been created that the Australian Tax Office has struggled to keep up with, and there has also been extensive evidence of tax avoidance.

- *Operational issues* inside the public sector have accelerated a steep decline in government expertise and organisational capacity. In every sector, public authorities must compete for expert professional staff with a private sector that can cream off their best public service staff with higher salaries and more innovative (less regulatory or procurement-only) work. The result has been the extensive inter-penetration of regulators and industry bodies. The supposedly independent chairs of regulators can often only come from the industry that they will regulate and to which they will return after a relatively brief time in government. Mainstream economic theory suggests that they will rationally act in ways that maximise their future job prospects when they return to the industry, pursuing only minimal interventions that safeguard corporate interests. Major companies maintain governmental relations units that also forecast and seek to mitigate adverse political developments via direct contacts with officials, special advisors and politicians (Bell, 2023). They particularly offer public service officials access to key relevant private information to aid policy-making, but in return for influence over legislative and regulatory drafting. Similarly, in public administration, the hollowing out of the public service (especially at federal level) leads to a high reliance on management consultants and other industry executives by major firms straddling the public/private sector divide. The 2022–23 controversy over PwC giving information from secret Treasury briefings to private industry clients demonstrated the many problems in maintaining essential barriers ('Chinese walls') between corporate dealings and public clients' information (Anaf and Baum, 2023; Josserand, 2023; Podger, 2023).

- *Ideological influence via think tanks and media operations* has been a massive area where corporations, trade associations and business professional groups have expanded their influence, often using anonymous donations to pro-business or sector-defense 'think tanks' (or even more beholden 'junk tanks' and 'front organisations'). These maintain a steady flow of informational and influence pressures for the adoption of neo-liberal policies.

- *Post-service compensation for political leaders* has increasingly opened up a path that has led retired top politicians to move into very lucrative occupations advising major corporations, who alone can afford their spiralling consultation or even dinner-speaking fees.

> Compensation for politicians should be seen as income over a lifetime. In many developed democracies, politicians in retirement can make huge incomes. With an eye to post service retirement, politicians may adopt positions on policies that are not in the public interest – in effect selling public policy. (Peters and Burns, 2023, p.590)

Just as former UK premiers and USA politicians quickly became multi-millionaires in their own right as a result of their corporate power linkages after leaving office, so Scott Morrison (for instance) will likely soon join their ranks.

Conclusion

Systematic academic studies of Australia's interest group processes at federal and state levels have been strikingly lacking in recent decades. Perhaps this reflects a professional consensus among most political scientists that pluralist accounts of diverse power centres, multiple key factors that no group monopolises, and easy mobilisation into politics are somehow 'obviously' or manifestly accurate? However, the sub-literature on corporate power takes a different line, one based more on structural analyses and case studies, while the recent history of many minorities leaves little room for complacency that the hidden injustices of past eras have no or few modern parallels. Beyond any room for doubt, Australian civic culture now supports a very vigorous and strongly contested group process. It also seems that philanthropic support and cause groups, plus perhaps the impact of social media in lowering the costs of organising politically (see Chapter 9), have meant that the scope of involvement with governments by many previously excluded and disadvantaged minorities has become greater than in earlier decades.

References

ABC News (2019) 'Australia's largest donors revealed: Discover the millions funding politicians', 31 January. https://perma.cc/N8S8-N28M

Anaf, Julia and Baum, Fran (2023) 'It's not just tax. How PwC, KPMG and other consultants risk influencing public health too', *The Conversation*, 24 July. https://perma.cc/3BGX-HC4A

AEC (Australian Electoral Commission) (2020) 'Election Funding and Disclosure Report: Federal Election 2019', AEC. https://perma.cc/5S46-LUES

Australian Bureau of Statistics (2023) 'Trade union membership', ABS. https://perma.cc/N83W-L97C

Bell, Stephen (2023) 'Large firms in Australian politics: The institutional dynamics of the government relations function', *Australian Journal of Political Science*, vol. 58, no. 1, pp.124–40. $ https://doi.org/10.1080/10361146.2022.2142517

Bell, Stephen and Hindmoor, Andrew (2013) 'The structural power of business and the power of ideas: The strange case of the Australian mining tax', *New Political Economy*, vol. 19, no.3, pp.470–86. $ https://doi.org/10.1080/13563467.2013.796452

Beetham, David (2011) *Unelected Oligarchy: Corporate and Financial Dominance in Britain's Democracy*, Briefing paper, 26 July, London: Democratic Audit. https://perma.cc/M7GK-5NWU

Boulus, Paul and Dowding, Keith (2014) 'The press and issue framing in the Australian mining tax debate', *Australian Journal of Political Science,* vol. 49, no. 4, pp. 694–710. $ https://doi.org/10.1080/10361146.2014.948378

Buckley, Tim (2019) 'Billionaire Adani being subsidised for Carmichael thermal coal mine: Adani's thermal coal mine in Queensland will never stand on its own two feet', Institute for Energy Economics and Financial Analysis (IEEFA) Discussion Paper, 29 August. https://perma.cc/H2Q9-A4U8

Cameron, Sarah and McAllister, Ian (2019) *Trends in Australian Political Opinion: Results from the Australian Electoral Study 1987–2019*, Canberra: Australian National University. https://perma.cc/URM9-847Y

Cameron, Sarah and Wynter, Thomas (2018) 'Campaign finance and perceptions of interest group influence in Australia', *Political Science*, vol. 80, no. 1, pp. 169–88. $ https://doi.org/10.1080/00323187.2018.1562307

Christie, Katie (2019) 'The limitations of business power in Australia: A case study of coal seam gas in Gloucester'. PhD Thesis, University of Canberra. https://doi.org/10.26191/qdrf-w642

Cleary, Paul (2016) 'Poles apart: Comparative resource sector governance in Australia and Norway', *Australian Journal of Political Science,* Vol. 51, no. 1, pp.150–62. $ https://doi.org/10.1080/10361146.2015.1126041

Coady, David; Parry, Ian; Nghia-Piotr Le; and Shang, Baoping (2019) 'Global Fossil Fuel Subsidies Remain Large: An update based on country-level estimates'. International Monetary Fund (IMF), Working Paper, no. 89. https://perma.cc/4ASE-SASX

Denniss, Richard and Richardson, David (2013) *Corporate Power in Australia,* Canberra: The Australia Institute, Policy Brief No. 45, February 2013. https://perma.cc/AK9C-K9GN

Department of Social Services (2017) 'National disability representative organisations', DSS. https://perma.cc/7Q39-VQMA

Dryzek, John and Dunleavy, Patrick (2009) *Theories of the Liberal Democratic State*, London: Palgrave. Now Bloomsbury Press. $ https://perma.cc/XP65-DUFP

Dunleavy, Patrick (1991) *Democracy, Bureaucracy and Public Choice – Economic Explanations in Political Science*, London: Routledge 2014 reissue. $ https://doi.org/10.4324/9781315835228

Eccleston, Richard and Hortle, Robert (2016) 'The Australian mining tax debate: Political legacies and comparative perspectives', *Australian Journal of Political Science,* vol. 51, no. 1, pp.102–09. $ https://doi.org/10.1080/10361146.2015.1126042

Edwards, Lindy (2018) 'Corporate power in Australian policy making: The case of unfair contract laws', *Australian Journal of Public Administration*, vol. 78, no. 4, pp. 516-29. https://doi.org/10.1111/1467-8500.12350

Edwards, Lindy (2020) *Corporate Power in Australia: Do the 1% Rule?* Melbourne: Monash University Publishing. $ https://perma.cc/Y6WP-9YQZ

Edwards, Lindy (2022) 'The core of corporate power in Australia', *Journal of Australian Political Economy*, No. 90, Summer 2020/23, pp.92–104. https://perma.cc/5JKS-RWVG

Gilding, Michael; Merlot, Elizabeth; and Leitch, Shirley (2016) 'The power of hope: The mobilisation of small and mid-tier companies in the mining industry's campaign against the Resources Super Profits Tax', *Australian Journal of Political Science,* vol. 51, no. 1, pp.122–33. $ https://doi.org/10.1080/10361146.2015.1126043

Goods, Caleb (2022) 'How business challenges climate transformation: An exploration of just transition and industry associations in Australia', *Review of International Political Economy,* vol. 29, no. 6, pp.2112–34. $ https://www.tandfonline.com/doi/full/10.1080/09692290.2021.1956994#:~:text=Embracing%20the%20language%20of%20transition,economy%2C%20rather%20than%20simply%20a

Grudnoff, Matt (2013) 'Pouring more fuel on the fire: The nature and extent of federal government subsidies to the mining industry', The Australia Institute, Policy Brief, no. 52, June. https://perma.cc/F459-LQSE

Guardian (2016) 'It took one massacre: How Australia embraced gun control after Port Arthur', *The Guardian*, Australia, 14 March. https://perma.cc/6CL2-LRAA

Head, Brian (1993) 'Lindblom on business power and public policy', in Redner, Harry (ed), *An Heretical Heir of the Enlightenment: Politics, Policy, and Science in the Work of Charles E. Lindblom*, Boulder: Westview Press, Ch. 11. $ https://doi.org/10.4324/9780429038495-12

Horn, Murray (1995) *The Political Economy of Public Administration*, Cambridge: Cambridge University Press. $ https://doi.org/10.1017/CBO9780511528163

Johnson, M (2013) *Corporate Power in Australia,* The Australia Institute, Policy Brief, no. 45, February. https://perma.cc/2LUT-9JXT

Josserand, Emmanuel (2023) 'Who needs PwC when consultancy work could be done more efficiently in-house?', *The Conversation*, 14 June. https://perma.cc/T4XQ-UXJ9

Kamp, Allana; Dunn, Kevin; Sharples, Rachel; Denson, Nida; and Diallo, Thierno (2023) 'Understanding trust in contemporary Australia using latent class analysis', *Cosmopolitan Civil Societies*, vol. 15, no. 2. $ https://doi.org/10.5130/ccs.v15.i2.8595 OA at: https://eprints.qut.edu.au/61389/1/61389.pdf

Lindblom, Charles E (1977) *Politics and Markets: The World's Political Economic Systems*, New York: Basic Books. $

Lindblom, Charles E (1982) 'The market as prison', *Journal of Politics*, vol. 44, no. 2, pp.324–36. $ https://doi.org/10.2307/2130588

Lucas, Adam (2021) 'Investigating networks of corporate influence on government decision-making: The case of Australia's climate change and energy policies', *Energy Research and Social Science*, vol. 81, no. 102271. https://doi.org/10.1016/j.erss.2021.102271

Madden, Kym; Scaife, Wendy; and McGregor-Lowndes, Myles (2005) *Giving Australia: Research on Philanthropy in Australia: Summary of Findings*, Canberra: Commonwealth of Australia. https://eprints.qut.edu.au/61389/1/61389.pdf

Maher, Henry (2022) 'The relationship between neoliberal ideology and state practice: Corporate power in the Australian mining industry', *Australian Journal of Political Science.*, vol. 57, no.1, pp.59–74. $ https://doi.org/10.1080/10361146.2021.2014397

Marsh, David; Lewis, Chris; and Chesters, Jenny (2014) 'The Australian mining tax and the political power of business', *Australian Journal of Political Science,* vol. 49, no. 4, pp.711–25. $ https://doi.org/10.1080/10361146.2014.954985

Mikler, John; Elbra, Ainsley; and Murphy-Gregory, Hannah (2019) 'Defending harmful tax practices: Mining companies' responses to the Australian Senate Inquiry into tax avoidance', *Australian Journal of Political Science*, vol. 54, no. 2, pp.238–54. $ https://doi.org/10.1080/10361146.2019.1601682

Needham, Cindy; Sacks, Gary; Orellana, Liliana; Robinson, Ella; Allender Steven; and Strugnell, Claudia (2019) 'A systematic review of the Australian food retail environment: Characteristics, variation by geographic area, socio-economic position and associations with diet and obesity', *Obesity Reviews*, vol. 21, no. 2, 4 December. https://doi.org/10.1111/obr.12941

O'Keeffe, Patrick (2019) *Making Markets in Australian Agriculture: Shifting Knowledge, Identities, Values, and the Emergence of Corporate Power.* London: Palgrave Macmillan. $ https://doi.org/10.1007/978-981-13-3519-8

Pepper, Alexander (2022) *If You're so Ethical, Why Are You so Highly Paid? Ethics, Inequality and Executive Pay,* London: LSE Press. OA at: https://doi.org/10.31389/lsepress/eth

Peston, Robert (2008) *Who Runs Britain?* London: Hodder and Stoughton. $ https://perma.cc/FE5B-N8VH

Peters, B. Guy and Burns, John P (2023) 'Debate: Politicians and their vast post-service wealth', *Public Money and Management*, vol. 43, no. 6, pp. 590–91. $ https://doi.org/10.1080/09540962.2023.2198907

Podger, Andrew (2023) 'Consultants like PwC are loyal to profit, not the public. Governments should cut back on using them', *The Conversation*, 19 May. https://perma.cc/RGQ3-TKCV

Richardson, David (2012) 'The rise and rise of the big banks: Concentration of ownership'. The Australia Institute, Technical Brief No. 15, December. https://perma.cc/5TNQ-8PQZ

Royal Commission into Misconduct in the Banking, Superannuation and Financial Services Industry (2019) Final Report, Volume 1, 4 February. https://perma.cc/ZPF8-8X4A

Russell, Lesley (2019) 'What is the Pharmacy Guild of Australia and why does it wield so much power?', *The Conversation*, 27 November. https://perma.cc/LBV2-JHUY

Sims, R (2016), 'Is Australia's economy getting more concentrated and does this matter?', Australian Competition and Consumer Commission Address to RBB Economics Conference 2016, Sydney, pp. 1–12. https://perma.cc/42ES-4ES2

Ting, Inga; Shatoba, Katia; Workman, Michael; Scott, Nathanael; and Palmer, Alex (2021) 'Under the influence', ABC News, 24 March. https://perma.cc/Y48E-AK4F

Wilson, Jeffrey D (2016) 'Killing the goose that laid the golden egg? Australia's resource policy regime in comparative perspective', *Australian Journal of Political Science,* vol. 51, no. 1, pp.110–21. $ https://doi.org/10.1080/10361146.2015.1126045

Wright, Chris F and McLaughlin, Colm (2021) 'Trade union legitimacy and legitimation politics in Australia and New Zealand', *Industrial Relations*, vol. 60, no. 3 pp.338–69. https://doi.org/10.1111/irel.12285

8

Mainstream media

Patrick Dunleavy

The recent history of 'democratic backsliding' in countries like Hungary, or the modern rise of authoritarian systems that maintain façade elections (like Putin's Russia), both demonstrate that elections are worthless if they are not conducted within rules that guarantee media diversity and at least a rough balance in the partisanship of news sources available to citizens. Australia retains a longstanding conventional media system of a mixed privately and publicly owned kind, with a particular version adapted to its federal structure and politics (Griffiths, 2021; Tiffen, 1994).

What does liberal democracy require of a media system?

- The media system should be diverse and pluralistic, including different media types, operating under varied systems of regulation, designed to foster free competition for audiences and attention, and a strong accountability of media producers to citizens and public opinion.
- Taken as a whole, media regulations should guard against the distortions of competition introduced by media monopolies or oligopolies (dominance of information/content 'markets' by two or three owners or firms), and against any state direction of or dominance over the media.
- A key part of media pluralism is a 'free press', that is, newspapers that are privately owned, where new entrants can enter competition freely and media-specific forms of regulation are avoided or minimised. Only normal forms of legal supervision and business regulation (those common to any industry) should apply to the press, so that a full range of (legitimate, non-violent) political opinions can be expressed.
- In broadcasting, on the other hand, free competition has been restricted in the past by network effects, state control of limited bandwidth, and the continuing salience and immediacy of TV/radio for citizens' political information. So here all liberal democracies have judged that a degree of 'special' regulation of broadcasters is needed to ensure balanced or bipartisan or neutral coverage of politics, especially in election campaign periods. However, regulation of broadcasters must always be handled at arm's length from control by politicians or state officials, by an impartial quasi-non-governmental organisation (quango) with a diverse board and professional staff.

How to cite this chapter:

Dunleavy, Patrick (2024) 'Mainstream media', in: Evans, Mark; Dunleavy, Patrick and Phillimore, John (eds) *Australia's Evolving Democracy: A New Democratic Audit,* London: LSE Press, pp.166–190. https://doi.org/10.31389/lsepress.ada.h Licence: CC-BY-NC 4.0

- Where government funds a state broadcaster (like the Australian Broadcasting Corporation or the SBS channel), this should also be set up 'at arm's length', and with a quango governance structure. Government ministers and top civil servants should avoid forms of intervention that might seem to compromise the state broadcaster's independence in generating political, public policy or other news and commentary.
- The professionalism of journalists, broadcasters and commentators is an important component of a healthy media system. Professional training, employment incentives and the 'reputational economy' in media organisations should all encourage these groups to internalise respect for the public interest. The self-regulation of media professions' value systems should provide important safeguards against excesses or irresponsible behaviours, while maintaining competition and incentives for innovation.
- The overall media system should provide citizens with reliable and diverse political information, and muster evidence and commentary about public policy choices, in ways that are easy to access, at very low cost. The system should operate as transparently as possible, so that truthful/factual content predominates, and mistakes or 'fake news' are both quickly uncovered and counteracted.
- Where any media reporting is unfair, incorrect or invades personal and family privacy then ordinary people should be able to secure practical redress. Citizens are entitled to expect that media organisations will respect all laws applying to them, and will not be able to exploit their power so as to deter investigations of media misbehaviour or prosecutions by the police or prosecutors.
- Journalists investigating or commenting on possible wrongdoing by politicians, state agencies, corporations or other powerful interests should be able to cite a public interest motivation as a sufficient defence against legal actions to suppress coverage. Media organisations should enjoy some legal and judicial protection against attempts to harass, intimidate or penalise them by state agencies, large and powerful corporations, other organised interests, or very wealthy people.
- At election times especially, the press and broadcasters should inform the electorate accurately about the competing party manifestos and campaigns, and use their coverage to encourage citizens' democratic participation.

Along with most liberal democracies, Australia has well developed and long-established systems for guaranteeing media pluralism, which includes six main components:

- A *free press*, one that is privately owned and regulated chiefly by normal business regulations and civil and criminal law provisions, is one key centrepiece. All the major newspapers (except *The Australian* which is truly national) are based in different state capitals, and their relative sizes reflect the scale of their state's population. They normally adopt either a strong political alignment to one party (usually the Liberal-National Coalition) – or a more bi-partisan or variable stance towards the top two parties (Liberal-National Coalition or Labor), especially in state politics. A voluntary self-regulation scheme has provided limited redress in the event of material inaccuracies or journalistic misbehaviours (Finkelstein and Tiffin, 2015).

- A *publicly owned national broadcaster* – the Australian Broadcasting Commission (ABC) – is the second most long-established component of the Australian media system (Inglis, 1983). It is operated by a quango, the ABC Board, with most members and the chair appointed by the federal government. Without its own advertising revenues the ABC has been almost wholly funded by budgets agreed with the Treasury and Canberra ministers. However, the ABC is supposed to operate at arm's length from any political control at the Commonwealth and state levels. In practice, since the ABC changed from being a commission to a government corporation in 1983, Coalition governments have consistently cut its funding overall and Labor governments have increased it (Ricketson and Mullens, 2022).

- In addition, there is a publicly subsidised *hybrid (public broadcaster) company*, the Special Broadcasting Service (SBS), that seeks to cater for ethnic minorities and non-English language groups (like Italian, Greek, French, etc.) that might otherwise be neglected by commercial ('mainstream') private TV and radio companies. A special channel of SBS is the NITV (National Indigenous Television), a channel that provides coverage largely produced by and relevant to aboriginal communities and people.

- The final component of the broadcasting system has been a small set of *commercial TV and radio companies* (again based in state capitals) with political coverage regulated by the same requirement to be politically impartial (especially at election time). An industry self-regulation body also adjudicates public complaints insulated from control by politicians, the state and from the broadcasters themselves.

- A lot of reliance has also been placed on *journalistic professionalism*, with graduate staff following common standards of reporting and editorial accuracy (Joseph and Richards, 2014). Breaches of these norms may fall foul of self-regulation bodies, but they are chiefly enforced informally by weak and inconsistently applied social sanctions, such as reputational damage or career disadvantages for people within the profession who breach good journalism norms.

- *Social media* has become an increasingly salient component of the Australian media system, and like the free press remains largely unregulated, beyond normal legal provisions such as action against 'hate speech' or defamation. The biggest online sites and associated social media are journalistically produced by newspapers, and generally operate on the same lines, although with less political agenda-setting of news priorities. However, much politically relevant content has also been generated by a wide range of non-government organisations (NGOs), pressure groups and individual citizens, many of whom are strongly politically aligned and may not feel bound by journalistic standards, such that unchecked 'disinformation' on non-mainstream media social sites has been an escalating problem (see Chapter 9).

How far does this 'ideal type' pluralist media model stand up as a foundation for Australian political democracy? I begin by looking at how the recent movement of both press and broadcast outlets online has created a single, strongly convergent media system (more than ever before), potentially undermining diversity of sources for citizens in securing political information. Next, I consider in summary form the current strengths and weaknesses of Australia's conventional media system from a democracy perspective, and assess emerging future opportunities and threats in a SWOT analysis. The sections following that evaluate issues of particular concern in more detail.

Recent developments

The dominant media trend of modern times has been that both print and broadcast sources have converged towards having online content and users have shifted online, moving away from legacy print and broadcast formats. The 2012 Finkelstein Inquiry already raised the issues for both the press and broadcast media (Pearson, 2012; Finkelstein and Ricketson, 2012; Fernandez, 2012), but little happened after it, especially on press self-regulation (Finkelstein and Tiffen, 2015). Subsequently, previous trends accelerated with potentially averse implications for citizens' political knowledge because it may erode a previous diversity of political news outlets driven by differently weighted and autonomous journalistic imperatives – the search for a good story and defence of the public interest (Tiffen, Rowe and Curran, 2017). These foundations have been important for maintaining an overall media system where political information has been checked for accuracy and some measure of overall impartiality and equal access to political news has been maintained by media counter-vailing forces (Joseph and Richards, 2014; Weaver and Willnat, 2014).

Of course, the twin poles of a free press and impartial broadcast news cannot remain fully separate, and some measure of story-pooling is inevitable. Press journalism can often 'set the tone' for overall coverage across all channels, and titles may sometimes launch concerted campaigns on issues that they sustain over many rounds of the news cycle, sometimes reflecting a clear partisan imperative. But operating on different dynamics means that the press and broadcast media can in principle serve as checks and balances on each other. A newspaper lead story or partisanly driven campaign that draws on inaccurate data or lacks substance will wither if TV and radio give it no airtime, and gaining a reputation for inaccuracy might damage its readership numbers. By contrast, suppose that the publicly funded ABC or regulated private broadcasters should fear the consequences of running stories critical of the incumbent government or public agencies (because ministers worsen their funding or regulatory regimes) – here newspapers' freedom to set their own agenda and pursue good stories should ideally ensure that important issues are covered and not suppressed or marginalised.

In the internet and digital news age, Australians especially have dramatically shifted their news-following behaviours and habits to respond to the immediacy and convenience of news coverage on the web. Both the press and broadcasters have developed their online offerings in very effective ways, despite much of their content having been historically appropriated and rerun free on the social media sites of the giant platform companies, especially Google, Facebook, X (formerly Twitter) and Apple. While Apple News created relationships with content providers for some time, the other firms resisted paying anything for media content. Both the newspapers and private TV firms complained loudly about the damage they suffered in developing paying online readerships because of the platforms making their news available free of charge, while the Silicon Valley giants countered that the reproduction of news on their channels secured massive free publicity for the papers and private TV channels. In 2021, an important intervention by the federal government radically changed this situation and platform providers began paying something to news content generators.

In fact, the growth of paying online audiences in Australia was very rapid and successful by comparison with other media markets in mature liberal democracies. Press sites financed by subscriptions and advertising have increasingly hosted video materials as well. Meanwhile free-to-view sites run by the ABC and other TV channels have also grown very fast, focusing on their own video content but also encompassing many text-based stories. The primary consequence has been a massive *convergence* of the press and broadcasters, with both sets of companies becoming large-scale online news operators of video/audio and text stories, and attracting similar kinds of audiences and modes of consumption. Online news competition has become the most intense sphere of interactions, especially around political news. Many more stories are now covered and multiple sites give real-time updates to an audience that has become news-hungry and adept at accessing and comparing sources. In addition, all the press and broadcast sites have developed strong social media operations to connect with their audiences (see Chapter 9).

In short, the growth of conventional media online and in digital forms has proved a dramatic challenge to the pluralist logic for separating out the press and the broadcast realms into distinct spheres with their own characteristic mode of operating. For journalists, managers and corporations in both spheres there remain some particularities and differences. Important aspects of press operations in political news and commentary have created some content that broadcasters never normally handle, like hosting individual commentators expressing strongly held opinion-based perspectives such as Andrew Boult on Sky News. Similarly, press outlets have shown a greater capacity to initiate and pursue stories over a long time, providing in-depth coverage and sustaining concerted 'campaigns' on certain issues or scandals (see below), or targeting individual politicians caught up in scandals. Broadcasters have mostly handled commentary more in bi-partisan formats like the ABC's flagship discussion programme, Q + A, where (rough) balance between the top two parties' interests and perspectives has been sought and mostly achieved. However, some late-night 'current affairs' programmes on Sky News have hosted commentary that has proved very similar to the Liberal-national papers or even the far right (Guardian, 2023). Broadcast news has sometime joined in 'wolf-pack' episodes where all journalists have scented a major scandal or revelation and run similar negative, personality-driven stories But broadcasters have only really launched major initiatives of their own via a handful of TV investigative programmes, operating in circumscribed ways (for example, Ting et al., 2022). Despite these differences, for both sides of the supposed conventional media divide, maximising their digital audiences and binding them closer via social media have become key additional organisational and journalistic devices, essential for their survival and flourishing.

The development of online press news has centred on the state capitals across Australia, where covering both federal and state politics has helped the newspaper industry maintain a vigorous presence in political debate. Recent estimates suggest that in an average seven-day period, over 94 per cent of citizens over 14 years old (nearly 20 million people) either read a print title or accessed news from a press-run website or application (see Figure 8.1). Around three-quarters of Australians read or accessed news via metropolitan titles located in state capital cities, with the top three papers racking up cross-platform audiences of more than five million each (and the *Sydney Morning Herald* topping 8.5 million). The top eight sources reached close to or above three million readers each, and included just two 'national-alone' titles – *The Australian*, and the business-orientated *Financial Review*. In 2022, nearly one in five (18 per cent) of respondents to the Reuters Institute (2022) survey reported paying for an online subscription, with a third of these also paying for local news (p.27). Over half of subscribers paid for two or more, national and regional titles. One in eleven paid a subscription to a foreign press title, perhaps reflecting strong 'country of origin' interests among new Australian citizens, or the restricted coverage of international news in many domestic papers.

The turn to digital news largely kept the pre-existing (legacy) architecture of the newspaper industry intact. The right-hand columns of Figure 8.1 show that just two companies have long dominated the press universe, Rupert Murdoch's News Corporation with five key titles reaching in all a total audience of 20.1 million Australians in 2020–21, and Nine Media reaching

Figure 8.1: The main newspapers and press websites across Australia's states and major cities, and their usual political leanings, March 2020–March 2021

Newspaper	Thousands (000s)				Per cent audience (%) both modes	Core state and city	Online access	Owner	Politics
	Print readers	Digital readers	Total cross-platform audience	Both modes readers					
Sydney Morning Herald	2,012	7,683	8,519	1,176	13.8	NSW, Sydney metro	Free	Nine Media/Fairfax	Centrist, mixed, critical
The Age	1,585	5,186	5,990	781	13.0	Victoria, Melbourne metro	Free	Nine Media/Fairfax	Mixed, critical
The Australian	3,047	2,632	5,092	587	11.5		Paywall	Murdoch	Pro Liberal/National Coalition
Daily Telegraph	2,485	3,027	4,879	633	13.0	NSW, Sydney metro	Paywall	Murdoch	Anti-Labor, pro Coalition
Herald Sun	2,571	2,838	4,562	847	18.6	Victoria, Melbourne metro	Paywall	Murdoch	Anti-Labor, pro Coalition
Financial Review	1,212	2,298	3,295	215	6.5	Business remit	Paywall	Nine Media	Pro business
Courier-Mail	1,564	1,768	2,913	419	14.4	Queensland, Brisbane metro	Paywall	Murdoch	Right wing, pro Coalition
West Australian	1,203	842	1,764	281	15.9	West Australia, Perth	Paywall	Seven West Media	Leans right, but has endorsed Labor
Adelaide Advertiser	894	1,160	1,725	329	19.1	South Australia, Adelaide	Paywall	Murdoch	Anti-Labor, pro Coalition
Canberra Times	205	735	908	32	3.5	ACT & Queenbeyan NSW	Free		Centrist & Labor
The Saturday Paper	511	359	846	24	2.8	Weekly, long-form journalism			Mixed
Newcastle Herald	235	320	542	13	2.4	NSW, Newcastle, Hunter region and Central Coast		Australian Community Media	Mixed
Mercury	160	299	432	27	6.3	Tasmania, Hobart		Murdoch	Anti-Labor, pro Coalition

Sources: Compiled by author from data on Roy Morgan Single Source (2023). 'Newspaper Cross-Platform Audience, 12 months to March 2023', webpage: https://www.roymorgan.com/readerships/newspaper-cross-platform-audience. See also Alpha Beta Australia (2020). Digital data include Apple News subscribers.

Note: Percentages sum to more than 100 per cent because people use multiple media sources.

17.8 million. Of course, these numbers include a substantial overlap in the two major firms' readerships and online audiences, which is hard to track. In most states only a small proportion of Australians remain outside this reach.

Does ownership matter for political news diversity? Australia's highly oligopolistic market has always shown strong partisanship of the press, demonstrated in the last column of Figure 8.1. This longstanding pattern is strongly entrenched even among Anglosphere democracies (Noam and the International Media Concentration Collaboration, 2016). With a few occasional departures (and unusual exceptions at state level) all the Murdoch titles are normally in favour of the Liberal-National Coalition, strongly critical of Labor and virulently hostile to the Greens and green issue coverage, a stance largely shared by the business-orientated *Financial Review* owned by Nine Media. In Melbourne Nine's *The Age* has been more balanced in its coverage, but in New South Wales its dominant *Sydney Morning Herald* has normally been conservative and anti-Labor, albeit behind more of a veil of even-handedness. Only a few genuinely different and digital-only 'press' sources have broken through to a mass audience, notably the centre-left Australian *Guardian* (an offshoot of the British paper) and *The Conversation,* which tends to reflect the centre-left position of most Australian universities faculty, albeit in a serious and evidence-based manner.

Turning to the broadcasters, the ABC has long maintained an impressive reach in terms of its political news on TV and on national and local radio, as Figure 8.2 shows. Despite pressures from the press and commercial TV for the corporation to restrict its online activity, the ABC has also been able to develop strong online offers, including many text-based news items. These have been restricted far less than in the UK, for instance (where the regulator forced the BBC's

Figure 8.2: Usage of the Australian Broadcasting Commission's (ABC) broadcast news sources from 2020–2021

Type of news accessing	Platform	Thousands
ABC News on TV	News and current affairs (main channel and ABC NEWS weekly reach)	6,595
	ABC NEWS channel weekly reach	3,912
ABC News Digital	ABC news and current affairs weekly users	12,190
ABC news social	YouTube monthly unique users	12,272
	Facebook monthly unique users	815
	News and current affairs category iview – monthly plays	3,085
	News livestreams on iview – monthly plays	2,702
	YouTube news on-demand – monthly plays	22,809
	YouTube livestream – monthly views	3,593

Source: Compiled by author using data from Australian Government Transparency Portal (2022) Australian Broadcasting Corporation Annual Report 2021. Webpage on 'Audience Reach', News. https://www.transparency.gov.au/publications/infrastructure-transport-regional-development-and-communications/australian-broadcasting-corporation/australian-broadcasting-corporation-annual-report-2020-21

Note: The orange rows here show the average number of people reached weekly on average. The white rows show unique users per month. The green rows show individual download/access totals per month, many of which may be repeated accesses from the same people. The ABC app for viewing past ABC programmes is 'iview'.

website to host only text stories that have aired on TV or radio). In line with international trends, ABC audience numbers grew appreciably during the COVID-19 pandemic. However, by 2022, the proportion of survey respondents saying that they trusted the ABC fell to 66 per cent, down from 78 per cent in 2018 (Reuters Institute, 2022).

For the commercial terrestrial TV channels (which also operate commercial state and local radio stations), it is unfortunately not feasible to get clear news-only numbers for audience reach, and so we need to use web visits as an acceptable proxy of the relative size of audiences. Figure 8.3 shows total visits in a month in mid-2023 (including many repeat visits, so different from previous unique visitors data) for three main news-specific commercial TV web domains (shown shaded), and for other (more general) whole-channel domains where news-only data has not been available. For comparison, the top row shows the ABC News channel number, which was more than double the reach for Nine News, three times that for 7News, and nearly eight times that for Sky News, the 24-hour news channel.

Figure 8.3: The comparative sizes of TV media website outlets assessed by means of total visits

Rank	Outlet	Total monthly visits (000s)	Location	Type of web domain
1	ABC News (Australia)	70,312	Sydney, Australia	Public corporation news website
2	Nine News Australia	30,820	Sydney, Australia	Private TV channel national news
3	7News	20,601	Sydney, Australia	Private TV channel national news website
4	NITV	12,947	Crows Nest, Australia	Semi-private corporation web domain
5	SBS	12,947	New South Wales, Australia	Semi-private corporation web domain
6	Sky News Australia	8,832	New South Wales, Australia	24 hours news channel website
7	Foxtel	5,978	New South Wales, Australia	Private digital TV channel web domain
8	Channel 9	4,985	Australia Willoughby	Private TV channel national web domain
9	The Seven Network	3,968	Sydney, Australia	Private TV channel national web domain
10	Seven Network	3,968	Australia	Private TV channel national web domain

Source: Compiled by the author from data on Muck Rack (2023) 'Top 10 TV Stations in Australia', 17 June, webpage (no longer available); similarweb (2023); and Wikipedia; (2024).

Note: The third column shows all monthly visits to each Web domain (including many repeat visits to a site by the same people or organisations), as measured by SimilarWeb in mid-June 2023. In the final column on the right, yellow shading indicates news-specific sites, while white shading indicates a broader website including cultural or entertainment materials as well as news.

The entries in white rows are for whole channel sites (and so not directly comparable) but news accesses were likely a substantial share of the SBS total (partly for its overseas news coverage). Overall, commercial TV has continued to add to the diversity of the media system in ways that have been comparable in scale to the role of the ABC.

For all terrestrial and free-to-air TV services, both private and public, media digitalisation has had a further significant impact on how the public access news. While 36 per cent of people regularly access free-to-air TV, 40 per cent of Australians have increasingly watched TV dramas, films and specialist documentaries (for example, for gardening, cooking or housing improvements) in separate internet subscription channels (like Netflix, Binge, Disney, etc.) or used ABC's free digital platform (Stock, 2023; Lotz and McCutcheon, 2023a and 2023b). Subscribers to pay-TV have dramatically reduced their use of terrestrial TV. This shift has been particularly rapid because of the commercial channels' heavy reliance for revenues on advertising breaks that lengthen the time needed to watch a film or drama far more than in other liberal democracies (like the UK or France), and also limited public take-up of commercial TV's digital services to one in seven people. The increasing specialisation of viewing habits has especially affected young people, with only a quarter of those under 34 regularly accessing terrestrial TV. The primary consequence for political news has been a large reduction in people serendipitously acquiring news by seeing or hearing it on a general purpose, free-to-air channel (whether ABC or commercial) before or after a drama/film or documentary. It seems likely then that people are increasingly accessing only searched-for news online. And critics argue that in future there is a risk that a substantial section of citizens may stop watching news altogether as they shift only to internet TV. However, compulsory voting has perhaps meant that this danger has been least likely to occur in Australia, and as yet there are few signs of this potential problem taking off.

When asked in the Reuters Institute (2022) survey whether they mostly read news or watched it, over three-fifths of Australians surveyed (61 per cent) said that they mainly read about it and only one in eight (12 per cent) that they chiefly watched. Eleven per cent thought it was about the same and 16 per cent did not know (pp.13, 15). This suggests the primacy of newspaper sites plus broadcasters' text webpages. Yet there has also been plenty of evidence of people using diverse news sources in the paragraphs above – for instance, a third of people claimed to have listened to a podcast in the last month, and 18 per cent said that they had accessed news by email.

Overall, the evidence has suggested so far that Australian citizens cultivate a healthy scepticism about what they read, see or hear from conventional media. In the Reuters Institute (2022) survey, the proportion saying that they 'trust most news most of the time' was 41 per cent. Yet only 29 per cent thought that news organisations in their market were politically far apart (compared with 41 per cent in the USA and 37 per cent in the UK). Perhaps linked to the COVID-19 pandemic, the proportion of people who said that they sometimes or often avoided the news reached 41 per cent in 2022 (up from 29 per cent in 2019). Only 4 per cent of these 'avoider' respondents older than 35 said that they sometimes struggled to understand the news, but this proportion was four times larger among people under 35.

Strengths, weaknesses, opportunities and threats (SWOT) analysis

Current strengths	Current weaknesses
Australia has retained a conventional media system that has remained pluralistic, thanks to reforms in the late 1980s that separated out the ownership of print media and broadcasting channels; plus the continued bi-partisan regulation of broadcast news, and public funding for the ABC and SBS channels news operations. The partisan allegiances of most newspapers are strong and heavily favour the Liberal-National Coalition at most elections. But state-level partisanship by titles sometimes differs from their federal political allegiance, and even nationally newspaper partisanship may vary over time.	Australia's press and private TV and radio industries are heavily concentrated in the hands of just a few corporations and individuals (see Figures 8.1 and 8.3). Media ownership has been among the most concentrated in any liberal democracy, for decades. However, there has been some evidence that News Corp no longer has the influence on public opinion that it may once have enjoyed (Tiffen, 2022).
Earlier pluralistic expectations looked to professionalisation of the media increasing journalistic independence and thus tending to reduce or marginalise the political influence of media owners. Before 2010, there were signs that Australian journalists moved somewhat left, while press outlets stayed mainly right wing (Joseph and Richards, 2014: Table 10.4). Similarly, anonymous corporation ownership was at one time expected to displace the personal influence of owners and billionaires.	In practice, Australia has been the archetypal case of repeated (if changing) 'buccaneering' press and media tycoons with strong political views, who have actively sought to shape political and policy coverage to boost parties or causes that they favour. Among many striking examples, Rupert Murdoch was for long the leading case. His influence lasted for decades (Sabbagh, 2023) and was strongly attacked by former PM Kevin Rudd and many on Australia's centre-left (see below).
The importance of state politics in Australian federalism, especially for 'bread and butter' issues (like healthcare, education, transport and the environment) has sustained relatively strong regional newspaper media and broadcast news at state level.	A relatively weak 'self-governing' system for the free press has operated to regulate its coverage via the Australian Press Council. The regulation of public and private broadcasters' news at election time has been relatively strict. The ABC board regulates its coverage, and the Australian Communications and Media Authority oversees private broadcasters. Broadcast rules have secured more equal coverage for all parties, albeit often with a bias to the top two parties. However, outside campaign periods, broadcast regulation has tended to weaken. Notably some highly partisan current affairs late-night programmes evading regulation have been hosted by Sky News and others.

As in the USA, a single dominant newspaper has emerged in the very large capital cities of each state, where most people live. However, state-based papers have had some incentives to moderate or sometimes vary their partisan approaches to politics at the state and federal levels, in order to maximise their regional readership and avoid creating an opening for potential rivals in their state.	Major newspapers have developed critically important news websites as reading online has become the dominant form in which people acquire political and policy news. With greater 'real time' immediacy and the ability to generate many versions and variants of stories online, the level of self-policing of their content by newspapers has declined and a greater potential for salient disinformation with partisan and policy consequences has opened up (see Chapter 9 on social media). The online presence of press baron corporations and private broadcasters have been greatly extended in convergent ways, undermining the 1987 rule change supposedly keeping these channels separate.
A world-leading policy intervention by coalition ministers in 2021 was the News Media and Digital Platforms Bargaining Code (see below). It responded to media companies' complaints that they were threatened by the social media platform firms' coverage of news occurring without any payment for the content. The Code targeted the big internet platform companies (like Facebook, Google and X (formerly Twitter)), requiring them to reach an agreement and make some payment to news outlet whose content they ran. After an initial standoff when the companies threatened to withdraw services from Australia, the platform companies agreed to make substantial (but undisclosed) payments to support reporting and revenues in the main Australian newspapers and even news broadcasters.	The payments that platform giants have made under the Code to conventional media outlets were individually negotiated, and the amounts involved in each deal were not made public. It seems likely that smaller, independent media outlets have more difficulty in securing a deal or receiving substantial compensation amounts. By contrast, the existing financial and public dominance of major players have been reinforced.
Australia has no Bill of Rights (among other devices) to safeguard media independence. However, from the early 1990s, the High Court introduced and developed an 'implied freedom to communicate on matters of politics and government' that has provided some protection for the media. In general, however, Australia judges tend to find for the executive whenever conflicts of interest arise with the media, and so the alleged 'freedom' above has not been consistently developed.	Barriers to media fairness and respect for the rights of ordinary citizens have been created by the media corporations' financial ability to initiate and defend legal challenges more easily than ordinary citizens. Large corporations, wealthy individuals and government agencies are the only actors who can realistically use the legal system and courts to secure redress for misreporting or quasi-defamation.
Peer group surveillance of journalism, plus citizen vigilance, have both been extended by the growth of social media (see Chapter 9). In the digital era, misconduct or mis-reporting are both more likely to be quickly identified and called out, with reputational damage for 'serious' journalists. But this does not apply to columnists or journalists working for populist titles.	Instances of journalistic unprofessionalism and harassment of non-public figures in the news recur regularly. Expectations in earlier decades that a generally greater and more specialised professionalism would develop among press journalists over time have not been met.

Future opportunities	Future threats
The ability of Australia's media to surface and run major stories independently of government and corporate power centres has been demonstrated by a range of successful legal defences against efforts to 'chill' investigative journalism. For instance, in June 2023, three newspapers that had run well-evidenced stories accusing a much-honoured army SAS veteran of killing prisoners in Afghanistan years before were vindicated by a judgement in a defamation civil case brought by the soldier but funded by the billionaire chief executive of Nine media. The Albanese government's 2023 launch of the Independent Commission Against Corruption (ICAC) at the federal level may boost the media's ability to hold politicians and agencies to account for wrongdoing.	Without well-established media rights there always remains potential for the strong executive (in Australian federal government especially) to 'over-react' to media stories critical of government policy in ways that 'chill' journalistic freedom. In 2019, the Australian Federal Police raided and seized papers from the offices of broadcaster ABC and the home of a Sunday paper journalist. Both had published leaked official files on military misconduct and espionage issues. After a ding-dong legal battle in court, the seized files were never returned, but the police did not pursue any prosecutions (see below).
As free-to-air channels' dominance over key programme types (such as drama, film and documentaries) reduces, so the evidence shows that Australians are increasingly seeking out news actively online, rather than relying on channels to structure their access. Compulsory voting may work against any tendency for increased numbers of citizens to avoid political news altogether.	The growth of subscription channels and broadcast media specialisation may reduce citizens' 'synergistic' exposure to political news on terrestrial channels, a trend especially likely among younger people.
There are some signs in the Australian media system of 'shock jocks' or media stars with strong polarising politics. But most broadcast media coverage still counter-balances the fairly conventional partisanship of the major newspapers.	More polarised broadcast media on the USA Fox News model might develop in future as broadcasting and video-casting/podcasting blur together, as with Sky News late night comment shows, which some Liberal politicians have decried as leading their party towards extremist positions (Guardian, 2023).

From a democratic point of view most of the key issues around the media's role in politics revolve around the link between key media and corporate centres of power, the media's independence from government interferences, and the apparently ever-closer symbiotic relationships between the media and politicians and parties. I examine each in turn in the sections below.

Media independence and corporate control

Defenders of the free press as critical for maintaining the public accountability of government and the public services received an important boost in June 2023 when a judge dismissed the defamation civil law case brought by former SAS officer Ben Roberts-Smith against two journalists (Nick McKenzie and Chris Masters) and the *Sydney Morning Herald*, *The Age* and *Canberra Times*. In a 2018 story, the journalists claimed that Roberts-Smith had shot dead several Taliban prisoners in Afghanistan during the deployment of Australian troops there in 2003 and 2014, and quoted several eye-witnesses in each case. After a trial lasting 110 days and costing $15.6 million, when SAS members broke their unit's normal vow of silence to testify against Roberts-Smith, the judge found that on the balance of probabilities the allegations were true – that Roberts-Smith was a war criminal, and had in addition bullied troops under his command and lied in court (**Doherty and Visontay, 2023**). The case was a *cause celebre* because Roberts-Smith was undoubtedly a brave soldier who was awarded the VC in 2011, and his medals were displayed at the official Canberra War Memorial (**Drennan, 2023**). He was also the son of an eminent judge, held a key job with Seven Network, and had his case funded in full by Seven Network's billionaire owner Kerry Stokes (as a philanthropic act).

This then was a classic instance where a powerful government official – in this case a much-honoured soldier who was initially defended by the armed forces and even honoured as Australia's 'Father of the Year' in a public poll (**Drennan, 2023**) – was held to account in the public interest by the operations of independent journalists building a story (over several years) and the editors of a free press deciding to run huge risks to publish it, despite the involvement of a powerful media corporation and its billionaire owner. Only diverse private ownership of the media can guarantee this level of autonomy, say defenders of the press. And the involvement of major corporations also ensured that the defending journalists and papers could draw on sufficient resources to contest the substantial costs of the defamation case, let alone damages had any been awarded.

The activities of independent media plus more questioning attitudes by journalists have also played a key role in triggering more diffuse issues, as with a discernible polarisation in government–media relations over gender equality issues in 2021–22. The catalyst was PM Scott Morrison's initially dismissive response to a report by Samantha Maiden (the political editor of News.com.au) about serious allegations of sexual misconduct brought by a former Liberal Party woman staffer (Brittany Higgins) against a colleague. In what proved to be Australia's #MeToo event, Morrison's insensitive remarks were seen by the Canberra lobby journalists as epitomising the Coalition's longstanding propensity for misogyny, which dated back to the poor treatment of former Labor PM Julia Gillard. Later on Morrison also intervened in Liberal candidate pre-selection processes in Sydney's leafy suburbs in ways that alienated the more progressive liberal voters there and further reinforced the misogyny narrative. As Chapter 5 shows, gender equality issues thereafter become one key mobilising theme and source of success for the Teal movement and likely contributed to Morrison's downfall in the 2022 federal election (**Media Watch, 2022a**).

Concentrated media ownership and political influence

However, the wider picture of a few exceptionally wealthy individuals owning virtually all salient press corporations (outlined above and in Figure 8.1) has given rise to a great many democracy-related issues and concerns. Australia has a long and chequered history of tycoons with right-wing, pro-business political views using press outlets to grow their political influence aggressively and shape public opinion, especially at election times (Papandrea and Tiffen, 2016). Key figures have included Kerry Packer, the press tycoon who built the Channel Nine Network and to retain his press titles sold it to Alan Bond (involved in corruption in Queensland and Western Australia (Barry, 2001)) in 1987. However, by far the most interventionist owner over decades has been Rupert Murdoch via his company News Corporation Australia (hereafter News Corp), which started out from a small Adelaide newspaper. Initially backing the Liberal-National Coalition, he temporarily threw his greatly enlarged media's weight behind Gough Whitlam as Labor leader, but only for a short while before reverting to the right. From the 1970s on Murdoch expanded into the UK and USA but retained strong interests in Australian politics and public affairs.

In 2009, the Labor PM Kevin Rudd accused News Corp and Murdoch of running a 'vendetta' against him. Murdoch (by then a US citizen and so unable to own Australian broadcasters, only newspapers) countered that he was 'over-sensitive'. When the Liberal-National Coalition fared well in the 2013 federal election Murdoch tweeted: 'Aust. election public sick of public sector workers and phony welfare scroungers sucking life out of economy. Other nations to follow in time' (Guardian, 2013). Tony Abbott later declared that 'Rupert Murdoch has more impact than any living Australian' (Chalmers, 2015). After News Corp was investigated in the UK for hacking celebrities' and politicians' phones and Murdoch had to close the *News of the World* title and sell his UK Sky TV and Sky News channels, criticism of the Murdoch titles mounted on the Australian centre-left, with Rudd again prominent (Mayne, 2013). For many it became a fact widely accepted across the Australian political system that News Corp always acted as an arm of the Liberal-National Coalition, especially when they were in government, and as a propaganda machine during elections (Media Watch, 2022b).

During the 2019 to 2022 period, the general stance of the Murdoch press of denying climate change, or minimising its extent or impacts, together with columnists giving credence to disinformation about it, sparked renewed controversy over the alleged 'culture of fear' that Murdoch's operations created for opponents. Rudd again claimed: 'We don't have press freedom. Murdoch's journalists are not free journalistic agents. They are tools and a political operation with a fixed ideological and in some cases commercial agenda' (Simons, 2020). News Corp's own publicists and other defenders deny that company or Murdoch involvement alters their journalists' stories or editorial lines, and argue that readers can always leave for other sources in the free press market if they are unhappy. But the selection of journalists and columnists has clearly been one that sustains a particular political agenda.

However, News Corp may no longer have the influence on public opinion that it once did, with critics arguing that the company has increasingly produced niche products for niche audiences of 'alienated, older whites, mobilising their resentments over status anxiety' (Tiffen, 2022). News Corp's diminishing market power was reflected in its declining share of advertising revenue as a consequence of the increase in the share of online advertising, which grew from 25 to 53 per cent of revenues between 2012 and 2019 (Alpha Beta Australia, 2020; and see Chapter 9). Google and Meta received two-thirds of the income (ACCC, 2019). This change impacted on News Corp's and other content providers' ability to generate public interest journalism, and potentially challenged the media's ability to hold the powerful to account. However, the Liberal government mounted something of a rescue effort for the press, as the next paragraphs discuss.

The 2021 News Media and Digital Platforms Bargaining Code

In many countries the media industry has complained for years that their expensively produced content has been appropriated and relayed free of charge by four of the GAFAM (Google, Apple, Facebook, Amazon and Microsoft) internet platform companies (the exception being Amazon). Apple negotiated payments to media companies in the late 2010s when it launched Apple News, but the other three firms (plus X [formerly Twitter], TikTok and other smaller social media platforms) held out against contributing. They argued that media outlets gained immeasurably from the free publicity they got from content being reproduced online where millions of readers and viewers could reach it.

Following a long-lasting Australia Competition and Consumer Commission investigation which broadly supported the media outlets' case (ACCC, 2019), in 2020 Liberal-National Coalition ministers decided to end the stalemate in negotiations. A bill was introduced to Parliament to make mandatory the application of a News Media and Digital Platforms Bargaining Code (NMBC) that the government had painstakingly negotiated with both sides of the dispute over the previous year. The NMBC required the big internet platform companies (like Facebook, Google and X [formerly Twitter]) to voluntarily negotiate a (non-public) agreement with each of the news outlets whose content they reproduced. If the companies refused to comply then the department would intervene to itself conduct a mandatory arbitration process between the platform companies and media outlets, and to compel payments. This was the first time such a scheme had ever been implemented in any liberal democracy, and the platform companies initially reacted adversely to it, threatening not to comply and instead to withdraw all news services from their Australian sites and customers. In the submission phase for the new legislation 'Google Australia director Mel Silva said the bill was "untenable" and that the company would discontinue access to its search engine within Australia if the NMBC was enacted without changes' (Wikipedia, 2023a). As the legislation progressed through Parliament in February 2021, Google changed its mind and negotiated lump sum deals with Seven West Media, Nine Entertainment Co., and News Corp to provide content for the company's new 'News Showcase' feature.

On 17 February 2021, Facebook implemented its threat, cutting out all Australia news from its Facebook sites. Its action triggered widespread domestic and international condemnation of its 'blackmail' stance. The PM, Scott Morrison, declared that: 'Facebook's actions to unfriend Australia, cutting off essential information services on health and emergency services, were as arrogant as they were disappointing' (Meade, 2021). The adverse publicity, plus the potential regulatory costs for other Silicon Valley companies if multiple countries turned to direct government regulation to compel payments, led to a speedy reappraisal. The blocking action was called off, and Facebook negotiated voluntary (and undisclosed) private payment agreements with Australian outlets as the NMBC required and resumed news coverage on its sites.

The NMBC's implementation attracted political support across the spectrum and was generally welcomed by companies and journalists, although they argued that the NMBC's funding remained far smaller than the value that platform companies gained from press and broadcast stories (Treasury, 2022):

> More than 30 deals have been reached after the first year of operation, with the number of media companies much higher: NMBC allows collective bargaining for the companies with revenues below 10 million Australian dollars; one of the agreements involved 84 smaller companies, another 24. The total value of the

> deals was 200 million Australian dollars. Notable failures include the inability of the Special Broadcasting Service and The Conversation to reach an agreement with Facebook. (Wikipedia, 2023a)

However, critics argue that the scheme effectively reinforces the already strong positions of the established press and TV corporation giants, while smaller, independent media outlets have not secured deals or useful funding. In addition, 'Google and Meta remain highly critical of Australia's NMBC and what they see as an arbitrary requirement to pay well-established commercial news businesses under threat of government designation' (Flew, 2023a; Flew, 2023b).

The societal roles of mainstream media

The media's influence relevant for democracy has sometimes been too narrowly construed, as just about holding government officials and politicians to account or raising and explaining policy issues. However, there is a vital and wider 'fourth estate' role in holding *all other major institutions* in civil society to account for their actions and policies. And in Australia (as in other liberal democracies like the USA and Britain), there have been numerous, apparently pretty well-founded accusations of past collusion by the press and broadcasters with other social and organisational elites to marginalise or suppress coverage of historic scandals. Cases uncovered only after years of silence include the long history of sexual assaults carried out by clergymen within both the Catholic and Anglican churches, and the 'forced adoption' of many children of unmarried mothers:

> *It seems that religious and welfare bodies agreed that the solution to illegitimate babies was adoption by a married woman who was 'fit' to mother. From the 1950s to the 1970s, these organisations established homes across Australia 'to support and protect young, single pregnant women' where mothers later alleged coercion and mistreatment to get them to surrender their children.* (Gair, 2012)

Historic investigations also revealed numerous scandals around Australia's treatment of First Nations peoples well into the 20th century, including the removal of 10 to 33 per cent of Indigenous and mixed-race children from parents for fostering with white families. The number of children involved here possibly reached 70,000. Many of the 500,000 children imported from the UK without their parents and then fostered to Australian families under the 'Home Children' scheme also experienced ill-treatment. This scheme operated throughout most of the first three decades after 1945, and was another example where no media dogs barked for years before the official Australia Senate reports on 'Forgotten Australians' of 2001 and 2004.

Both across several states and at national level also, the available evidence in all of these instances suggests that journalists and editors either avoided investigating or covering potential scandal stories of which they were made aware, in some cases for decades, or backed off from pursuing initial investigations after elite lobbying. Partly also this stance stemmed from fear of costly defamation and libel cases against them (such as the Roberts-Smith example above). But undoubtedly media owners and editors were susceptible to informal coercion from powerful economic or social actors in national or state circles and influenced by an 'elite consensus' that dismissed victims' allegations as unfounded.

However, as the Roberts-Smith defamation case above also illustrates, the current media dynamic has developed towards greater independence and more relatively autonomous journalistic judgement about what stories about other institutions were worth pursuing in the public interest. In this respect, Australian public law has not always been helpful, as the sensational trial of the Melbourne Catholic Cardinal George Pell on historical sexual assault charges in 2018 illustrated. In 2018, a Victoria state judge issued a suppression order to limit reporting of the case, and in 2019 state prosecutors sent a letter to just short of 100 journalists threatening contempt of court charges. They later filed charges against 36 individual journalists and organisations. A trial in the Victoria Supreme Court started in later 2020 and ended four months later when all the charges against individual journalists were dropped and the outlets involved paid a fine of $1.1 million. Every liberal democracy needs some media controls to safeguard court cases against 'trial by media', since sensationalist reporting can potentially distort the legal process, especially in jury trials. But given the past history of media non-coverage of sexual misbehaviours by Catholic priests and other clergy, the Victoria law officers' reactions seemed heavy-handed.

From a different perspective, the widespread willingness of powerful and activist media to breach the restrictive court order in the Pell case also raises issues around the risks to ordinary citizens and organisations that can arise. Few Australians can confidently afford to risk high legal costs by suing outlets where they are misreported or defamed, and two self-regulation mechanisms are supposed to fill this gap by providing for low-costs complaints to be impartially assessed and outlets forced to justify their reporting and issue retractions for errors. Yet critics argue that both these mechanisms are weak and ineffective, with approaches and attitudes skewed towards the owners and corporate editors of the outlets involved:

> *The Australian Press Council is the accountability body for the newspaper publishers and their online platforms – though not individual journalists. The accountability body for commercial radio and television and their online platforms is the Australian Communications and Media Authority, though once again not for individual journalists or broadcasters.*
>
> *Neither of these bodies has any credibility among journalists. As* [the journalist union] *MEEA said* [in announcing its 2021 withdrawal from both bodies]*, its members are more concerned about getting a going-over on ABC TV's 'Media Watch' program than about anything the formal regulators do.* (Mueller, 2021)

Academic critics also argue that as elsewhere, self-regulation efforts run by media organisations themselves have proved remarkably inept and achieved very low public credibility in Australia (Gaber and Tiffin, 2018).

Perhaps surprisingly though, the Australian public's trust in newspapers has not been particularly lower than it has been for broadcast media. Between 2016 and 2018 trust in the different media sectors declined very slightly across the board, for all sources – for radio (from 41 to 38 per cent), TV (from 36 to 32 per cent), print media (from 31 to 29 per cent), and for web-based media (from 26 to 20 per cent) (Stoker, Evans and Halupka, 2018, p.40). Yet during the COVID-19 pandemic public trust in the mainstream media improved to the levels shown in Figure 8.4. Overall, two in five Australian respondents said that they trusted the media on COVID-19 information, far below the four-fifths who trusted 'scientists and experts'. Responses were relatively consistent across different generation groups, with younger people trusting mainstream media only a little less than older generations. A noticeable exception to the increase in trust during the pandemic was social media, where trust levels showed continued decline, attributed to controversies over 'fake news' (abundant around COVID-19's origins, treatment and vaccinations) and to data and privacy scandals (see Chapter 9).

Figure 8.4: The percentage (%) of respondents answering 'Strongly agree' or 'Tend to agree' that media sources can be trusted to provide honest and objective information about COVID-19, by generation, in May 2021

Column	Total	Builders	Baby Boomers	Generation X	Millennials	Generation Z
Years born range		1925–45	1945–65	1965–79	1980–94	1995–2203
Television media	40	45	45	39	36	36
Radio media	39	41	44	41	34	37
Newspaper media	38	40	41	39	36	34
Social media	15	14	11	15	19	14
No. of respondents	1,184	282	284	303	210	105

Source: Re-presented from Stoker, Evans and Halupka, 2018 *Democracy 2025 Report No. 1: Trust and Democracy in Australia – Democratic Decline and Renewal*, Canberra: Democracy 2025/Museum of Australian Democracy. See also (Evans, Halupka and Stoker, 2018).

Note: the question asked was: 'To what extent do you agree or disagree with the following statements?' 'I trust [source] to provide honest and objective information about COVID-19.'

Sample: n=1184, Weighted by age, gender, location.

For comparison: Asked about their trust in 'Scientists and experts', between 78 and 80 per cent in every generation group responded 'Strongly Agree' or 'Tend to Agree'.

In other surveys, public trust in journalists has consistently been low, averaging around 30 per cent of Australians who trust journalists. However, different question wordings can produce different responses. In the World Values Survey, only 18 per cent of Australia respondents said that they had 'a great deal ' or 'quite a lot of confidence in the press', above the UK (on 13), but far below the levels in the USA, France and Italy (all on 30), Sweden (40) or Canada (43) (Sheppard, McAllister and Makkai, 2018; World Values Survey, 2018). Gender differences have important effects also, with the majority of female respondents believing sexism to be widespread in the media, an increase attributed to broader cultural awareness of sexism and gender issues.

An alternative insight on how citizens and elites see the media and democracy is covered in our concluding Chapter 28. We show there that surveys of what citizens and political elites liked or disliked about Australian democracy saw the media's roles very differently (see Figures 28.11 and 28.12). Political elite respondents rated a free press as their 4th ranked 'like' in 2016 and as their 10th ranked like in 2019. But in 2019 the elites' top dislike was 'Media misrepresentation (misinformation, pressure)'. By contrast, citizens did not mention a free press in their likes, while their 3rd ranked dislike was that 'The media has too much power'. However, in one area citizens and elites' dislikes did seem to show some concurrence. Elites included as their 3rd ranked dislike in 2019 'The personalisation of politics by the media and decline in media standards', while in 2018 for citizens their 10th ranked dislike was that 'The media focuses too much on personalities and not enough on policy'.

Media freedom and government intervention

In April 2018, Annika Smethurst, a journalist with a strong record of investigative reporting at both the state and federal levels, was working as the political editor of the News Corp title *Sunday Telegraph*, and published 'top secret' emails between the civil service heads of the Department of Home Affairs and the Department of Defence concerning an alleged plan to allow greater surveillance of Australian citizens by the security services. In mid-2019, the Australian Federal Police (AFP) raided Smethurst's home and the Sydney offices of ABC looking for classified intelligence documents and seized files and papers. The action triggered a storm of criticism from the media with News Corp calling it 'a dangerous act of intimidation'. By contrast, the then-PM Scott Morrison made only a weak defence of the need for the police action.

That same week the AFP also raided the offices of ABC News and took away dozens of files relating to a 2017 story that the network had run (and was continuing to work on) about misconduct by the Australian military in Afghanistan (see above), as well as intelligence service spying powers. A second storm around media freedom followed and the ABC's managing director stated that: 'The ABC stands by its journalists, will protect its sources and continue to report without fear or favour on national security and intelligence issues when there is a clear public interest' (Elfrink, 2019). Both the warrants used in the raids cited a 1914 law and were fiercely disputed by the media organisations involved. The ABC sued the police to secure the return of the seized documents but their case was dismissed in February 2020. However, two months later the High Court ruled that warrants relied upon by the AFP were invalid and the cases were later dropped by the AFP. Both these cases illustrate that there have been some relatively frequent conflicts of interest between government agencies and politicians and media organisations, with the media normally now taking a pretty robust line to defend their journalists and their ability to protect sources and operate in an independent fashion.

The relationship between the commercial media and politicians and officials was also affected by the fact that the government itself has been one of the biggest sources of advertising revenue (especially in the COVID-19 pandemic). Normally most publicly funded advertising is about matters of public information that are politically neutral and without any salience for partisan politics. A very notable exception occurred in the run up to the May 2019 election when PM Scott Morrison was gearing up to call an election despite his poll ratings lagging slightly behind the Labor party. In addition to 'rorting' (illegitimately channelling) money differentially to key constituencies (see Chapter 13), ministers also spent a great deal of money on government advertising in the newspapers and on commercial terrestrial TV right up to the PM's final announcement of the election date. Ministers claimed nothing untoward here, arguing that the advertisements were just 'neutral' messages about government policies. In fact, they bore an almost uncanny resemblance to the Liberal-National government's 'talking points' and later campaign slogans, and in other liberal democracies (such as the UK) would have been banned accordingly. Critics argued that the heavy flow of money to the media organisations was bound to have dulled the running of critical stories on the topics of the advertisements, contributing to the sports rorts and other scandals only surfacing *after* the election had safely delivered an unexpected win for the Coalition. This problem of public money being spent in ways favouring the incumbent party were not repeated in the run-up to the 2022 federal election, when perhaps civil servants were more careful to insist on the need for impartiality.

The symbiosis between the media and political elite

Scholars of media have long studied a process known as 'mediatisation' by which the press, TV and now online media have 'colonised' or come to dominate a whole range of other social systems, from financial and economic markets, through cultural activities and political processes – imposing on them an increasingly strong 'discipline' about how issues and decisions can be communicated, in what tempos and discourses (Kissas, 2019). Some observers argue that the media system has inter-locked with political and governmental processes, undermining their ability to operate as separate domains. A second symbiosis explanation stresses a continuing separation of the political and journalistic institutionalist logics, but also their growing together from both ends due to the interdependence of politicians and journalists on each other. The final view instead stresses the 'omni-presence' of the media as a factor causing all social actors to adjust how they behave, not least in political life where the central questions are 'How will this play with the media? And with voters?'

When the new Parliament House in Canberra opened in 1988 (replacing the small and cramped older building from the 1920s in the capital's Parliamentary Triangle) it was designed from the outset to co-house multiple functions – the debating chambers; the PM's office, cabinet room and ministers and their office teams in a ministerial wing; party rooms and MPs' and senators' offices; and in a separate section, the offices of the news media – all co-existing within the same mega-building. So, perhaps even more than in other countries, political journalists operate in exceptionally close day-to-day proximity with senior politicians and their staff when Parliament is sitting, and they develop very close relationships and knowledge of each other (van Dalen and van Aelst, 2014). Consequently, in Australian federal politics, and to a lesser degree in state governments and parliaments, there are exceptionally close exchanges – politicians seeking to place or leak information or commentary, and journalists hunting for news angles and story lines ahead of competitors. By contrast, the main federal departments and agencies are located mainly across downtown Canberra and some in Sydney, so that journalist-administration links are much less close. These features of the Canberra village have undoubtedly contributed to the strong general media representation of Australian policy-making in terms that habitually stress the short-term dominance of politicians and partisan interests over the rational analysis of options and administrative feasibility. Because ministers and their private offices mostly live isolated from their departmental offices but cheek by jowl with media reporters the mediatisation of federal politics has been particularly cohesive. Of course, in specialist areas of journalistic expertise, like economics, finance or science reporting, journalistic scrutiny remains tougher and better informed. But within newspapers and TV channels, specialist staff also face strong competition from general or political journalists with their own systems of networks with politicians seeking to 'place' stories.

Many features of how Parliament itself operates reflect this strong influence (see Chapters 11 and 12) – such as the salience of question time in the House of Representatives, prime ministerial dominance and 'gladiatorial' clashes with the opposition leader, or the all-pervasive backdrop image of the Parliament building in many thousands of political press conferences or journalists giving 'packages' of news updates to camera. Media intensity has heightened through the 24-hour news cycle, driven by the ABC and Sky's specialist news channels, bolstered by the development of social media briefings by politicians and staffers and media commentary. It is argued that 'mediatisation' has contributed to who gets to be selected as an MP or senator, to how politicians interact with all other political players (including government departments and agencies when they are in office), and to the dominance of media management roles in political staffing. The characteristic results alleged are the creation of a shallow, personality-focused political news where the independence of the media has been blurred in a symbiotic political-media system.

In contrast, supporters of the media's current role argue that journalistic professionalism incorporating strong public interest elements has increasingly become well developed, strengthening arguments that the media are well able to defend their autonomy, especially against the classic 'hard' control means of ownership, government legal restrictions and politicians seeking to manipulate coverage – all of which are relatively crude and ineffective in the social media age. Unfortunately recent data on Australian journalists as a profession has been scarce, but they were already 80 per cent graduates in a 2013 study. It also found that 90 per cent of journalists rated a role 'to be a watchdog of government' as 'extremely important', while 80 per cent wanted to report news as fast as possible, and 72 per cent to 'provide analysis of events' (Joseph and Richards, 2014). These were far higher levels than those among journalists in almost all other liberal democracies. Yet in 2019 Australia dropped out of the top 20 of the *World Press Freedom Index* compiled by Reporters without Borders, and fell even further to rank 27th by 2023 (Wikipedia, 2023b; Reporters without Borders, 2019). Of course, rankings and scores of this kind are eminently contestable, but among Anglosphere countries only the USA scored lower.

Conclusion

Conventional news media occupy a critical role in ensuring the vitality of liberal democratic politics, both by generating citizens' interest and involvement in politics and by helping to ensure that politicians and governments act in ways that respect rights, operate fully within the law and sustain democratic principles and citizens' rights. In recent decades, the Australian media has demonstrated a strongly independent capacity to scrutinise not only the political realm but also other important institutions across civil society. However, this has not always been the case with many historical scandals surfacing through serendipity rather than due process. Significant concerns also persist around the domination of the media system by just a few media corporations run by activist tycoons, the political imbalance of press coverage against Labor and the Greens, the aggressive support of climate change denialism in the Murdoch media, and the increasingly symbiotic relationship between politicians and media outlets. The disturbing combination of news by algorithm, declining civic discourse and information being used as a weapon in a hyper-partisan war of ideas have had serious implications for the quality of democratic practice.

In any liberal democracy a delicate balance has to be struck between affording the media the freedoms it requires to perform its civil watchdog role and guaranteeing the public's right to know, and ensuring that it performs its democratic role responsibly. On the government side this requires less 'spin' in political communication and the development of respectful working relationships with the media industry. On the media system side, this requires commitment to the democratic value of a free and responsible media, balancing the concentration of media ownership through funding public interest journalism with professional ethical requirements of accuracy, fairness, truth-telling, impartiality, and respect for persons. Above all it requires building citizen capacity to address 'truth decay'.

Increasing criticism of media power is especially worrisome given the media's traditional fourth estate role as a check on the power of executive government. Key modern problems revolve around what the Rand Corporation calls 'truth decay', the loss of trust in data, analysis and objective facts in political life (**Kavanagh and Rich, 2018**). As mainstream media have increasingly been read online so many problems of the online environment may transfer to them – including increasing disagreement about evidence and analytical interpretations of facts and data; the blurring of the line between opinion and fact; the burgeoning volume, and resulting influence, of opinion and personal experience over fact; and declining trust in formerly respected sources of factual information. Ideological polarisation and media fragmentation accentuate these risks and may further channel political discourse into separate partisan ghettoes, creating a risk that 'Echo chambers ringing with false news make democracies ungovernable' (**Benkler, Faris and Roberts, 2018**, p.5). External cyber-interference by non-democratic countries could compound this problem. Recent Chinese, Iranian and Russian interference in democratic elections was apparently intended not just to favour one candidate over another, but to disseminate mistrust and confusion where voters lose faith in democracy itself (**Guardian, 2019**).

References

Alpha Beta Australia (2020) *Australian Media Landscape Trends – September 2020*. Sydney: Alpha Beta. Online report. https://accesspartnership.com/wp-content/uploads/2023/03/australian-media-landscape-report.pdf

Australian Competition and Consumer Commission (ACCC) (2019) 'Digital platforms inquiry preliminary report 2017–19'. https://perma.cc/XA3E-WU57

Australian Government Transparency Portal (2022) *Australian Broadcasting Corporation Annual Report 2021*, webpage and report. https://perma.cc/VJ4A-3DRM

Barry, Paul (2001) *Going for Broke*, Sydney: Bantam.

Benkler, Yochai; Faris, Robert; and Roberts, Hal (2018) *Network Propaganda: Manipulation, Disinformation, and Radicalization in American Politics*. New York: Oxford University Press. https://perma.cc/B33B-V67B

Chalmers, Max (2015) 'Rupert Murdoch has "more impact than any living Australian" says Tony Abbott', *New Matilda*, blogpost, 13 November. https://perma.cc/XK83-9YA7

Doherty, Ben and Visontay, Elias (2023) 'Australian SAS veteran colluded with and threatened witnesses in defamation trial, judge finds', *Irish Times*, 6 June. https://perma.cc/HH3X-VMP3

Drennan, Jonathan (2023) 'War hero defamation verdict a vital victory for the press – and for the pursuit of truth in war', *Irish Times*, 12 June. https://perma.cc/8PGU-YEES

Elfrink, Tim (2019) '"A bad, sad and dangerous day": Australian police raid public broadcaster, seize emails and documents', *Washington Post*, 5 June. https://perma.cc/U7DD-9V2C

Evans, Mark; Halupka, Max and Stoker, Gerry (2018) *How Australians Imagine Their Democracy: The 'Power of Us'*, Canberra: Democracy 2025/Museum of Australian Democracy. https://perma.cc/ALG8-WK95

Fernandez, Joseph (2012) 'Finkelstein inquiry too flawed to lead to real reform', *The Conversation*, 14 March. https://perma.cc/E799-U4RJ

Finkelstein, Roy and Ricketson, Matthew (2012) *Report of the Independent Inquiry into the Media and Media Regulation: Report to the Minister for Broadband, Communications and the Digital Economy*, 28 February 2012. Available from the Analysis and Policy Observatory. https://perma.cc/T5BY-3K2Q

Finkelstein, Roy and Tiffen, Rodney (2015) 'When does press self-regulation work?' *Melbourne University Law Review*, vol. 38, no. 3, pp.944–67.

Flew, Terry (2023a) 'Australia's news media bargaining code: A new institutional perspective', *American Affairs Journal*, webpage April. https://perma.cc/BLU7-3GRQ

Flew, Terry (2023b) 'The turn to regulation in digital communication: The ACCC's digital platforms inquiry and Australian media policy', *Media, Culture and Society*, vol. 43, no.1, pp.48–65. https://doi.org/10.1177/0163443720926044

Gaber, Ivor and Tiffen, Rodney (2018) 'Politics and the media in Australia and the United Kingdom: parallels and contrasts', *Media International Australia*, vol. 167, no. 1, pp.27–40. $ https://doi.org/10.1177/1329878X18766721

Gair, Susan. (2012) 'Re-writing Australia's history of forced adoption', *The Conversation*, blogpost, 28 February. https://perma.cc/MX3N-3WUB

Griffiths, Mary (2021) 'Media and democracy', in Barry, Nick; Chen, Peter; Haigh, Yvonne; Motta, Sara C; and Perche, Diana (eds) *Australian Politics and Policy*, Senior Edition, Sydney: University Sydney Press, pp.141–68. https://perma.cc/2J76-RKNG

Guardian (2013) 'Murdoch celebrates conservative victory in Australia with Twitter tirade', *Guardian, Australia*, 9 September. https://www.theguardian.com/media/2013/sep/07/murdoch-cheers-tony-abbott-victory

Guardian (2019) 'Not just Russia: China and Iran may target US elections, experts say', *Guardian, Australia*, 30 October. https://perma.cc/6YQH-DWYP

Guardian (2023) 'Matthew Guy says some "dangerously politically stupid" Sky News hosts are damaging the Liberal party', *Guardian, Australia*, webpage, 2 May. https://perma.cc/8KED-YG4J

Inglis, KS (1983) *This Is the ABC: The Australian Broadcasting Commission 1932–1983*, Melbourne: Melbourne University Press. Second edition, 2006 Melbourne: Black Inc. $ Some snippets on https://books.google.co.uk/books?id=a4dux2ITWjcC&source=gbs_navlinks_s

Joseph, Beate and Richards, Ian (2014) 'The Australian journalist in the 21st century', in Weaver, David H and Willnat, Lars (eds) *The Global Journalist in the 21st Century*, New York: Routledge, Ch. 10, pp.115–26. https://perma.cc/L99C-8TJC

Kavanagh, J and Rich, Michael D (2018) *Truth Decay: An Initial Exploration of the Diminishing Role of Facts and Analysis in American Public Life*. Santa Monica, CA: RAND Corporation. https://perma.cc/CDK6-8RCD

Kissas, Angelos (2019) 'Three theses on the mediatization of politics: Evolutionist, intended, or imagined transformation?', *The Communication Review*, vol. 22, no. 3, pp.222–42. $ https://doi.org/10.1080/10714421.2019.1647726

Lotz, Amanda; and McCutcheon, Marion (2023a) *Australian Screen Stories Viewing Report: Part 1: Watching Series and Movies in the 21st Century*. Working Paper. Queensland University. https://eprints.qut.edu.au/238930/

Lotz, Amanda; and McCutcheon, Marion (2023b) *Australian Screen Stories Viewing Report: Part 2: Streaming Behaviour and Content Discovery*. Working Paper. Queensland University. https://eprints.qut.edu.au/239388/

Mayne, Stephen (2013) 'Kevin Rudd and Rupert Murdoch: A brief history', *Guardian, Australia,* 2 September. https://perma.cc/4HDJ-9YL4

Meade, Amanda (2021) 'Prime minister Scott Morrison attacks Facebook for "arrogant" move to "unfriend Australia"'. *Guardian, Australia,* 18 February. https://perma.cc/DUB8-E48D

Media Watch (2022a) ABC TV, 'Teal threat'. Episode 14, 16 May 2022. https://perma.cc/E8HM-CRNM

Media Watch (2022b) ABC TV, 'Election 22'. Episode 15, 23 May 2022. https://www.abc.net.au/mediawatch/episodes/ep-15/13894998

Muck Rack (2023) 'Top 10 TV stations in Australia', 17 June, webpage.

Mueller, Dennis (2021) '10 years after Finkelstein, media accountability has gone backwards', *The Conversation,* 25 April. https://perma.cc/D6RB-7PR6

Noam, Eli and the International Media Concentration Collaboration (2016) *Who Owns the World's Media? Media Concentration and Ownership around the World.* Oxford: Oxford University Press. https://doi.org/10.1093/acprof:oso/9780199987238.003.0001

Papandrea, Franco and Tiffen, Rodney (2016) 'Australia', in Noam, Eli and the International Media Concentration Collaboration, *Who Owns the World's Media? Media Concentration and Ownership around the World,* Oxford: Oxford University Press.$ https://doi.org/10.1093/acprof:oso/9780199987238.003.0001

Pearson, Mark (2012) 'The media regulation debate in a democracy lacking a free expression guarantee', *Pacific Journalism Review,* vol. 18, no. 2, pp.89–101. https://doi.org/10.24135/pjr.v18i2.266

Reporters without Borders (2019) *2019 World Press Freedom Index.* https://perma.cc/J2RF-9GDX

Reuters Institute (2022) *Digital News Report 2022,* Newman, Nic; Fletcher, Richard; Robertson, Craig T.; Eddy, Kirsten; and Rasmus Kleis Nielsen. Oxford University: Reuters Institute for the Study of Journalism. https://perma.cc/CT6F-LSJX

Ricketson, Matthew and Mullins, Patrick (2022) *Who Needs the ABC?* Scribe. $ https://perma.cc/3MPE-FWR4

Roy Morgan Single Source (2023) 'Newspaper cross-platform audience, 12 months to March 2023', webpage. https://perma.cc/4AVX-3MJK

Sabbagh, Dan (2023) 'Power and scandal: How Murdoch drove the UK, US and Australia to the right', *Guardian, Australia,* 21 September. https://perma.cc/265Z-GV5D

Sheppard, Jill; McAllister, Ian and Makkai, Toni (2018) 'World Values Survey, Australia, Online panel survey, 2018', https://doi.org/10.26193/ZXF0SQ , ADA Dataverse, V1. Also https://dataverse.ada.edu.au/dataset.xhtml?persistentId=doi:10.26193/ZXF0SQ

similarweb (2023) 'Top websites ranking', webpage. https://perma.cc/58D9-C2MD

Simons, Margaret (2020) '"Culture of fear": Why Kevin Rudd is determined to see an end to Murdoch's media dominance', *Guardian, Australia,* webpage. 16 October. https://perma.cc/3VA7-9XSH

Stock, Petra (2023) 'Australians switching on streaming, turning off free-to-air TV', *Cosmos* magazine, 3 April. https://perma.cc/SWL7-NC5J

Stoker, Gerry, Evans, Mark and Halupka, Max (2018) *Democracy 2025 Report No. 1: Trust and Democracy in Australia – Democratic Decline and Renewal,* Canberra: Democracy 2025/ Museum of Australian Democracy. https://perma.cc/T3YH-YRTZ

Tiffen, Rodney (1994) 'Media policy' in Brett, J; Gillespie, J; and Goot, M (eds) *Developments in Australian Politics,* Melbourne: Palgrave Macmillan, pp.322–47.

Tiffen, R (2022) 'Will News Corp change its position after Labor's election win? Not if the US example is anything to go by'. *The Conversation,* 30 May 2022. https://perma.cc/9KVZ-WE5D

Tiffen, R; Rowe, D; and Curran, J (2017) 'News consumption, political knowledge and political efficacy', in Griffen-Foley, B and Scalmer, S (eds) *Public Opinion, Campaign Politics and Media Audiences: New Australian Perspectives*. Melbourne: Melbourne University Press, pp.208–42.

Ting, Inga; Shatoba, Katia; Workman, Michael; Scott, Nathanael; and Palmer, Alex (2022) 'Under the influence', ABC News webpage, 24 March. https://perma.cc/P8XC-QD7Z

Treasury (2022) *News Media and Digital Platforms Mandatory Bargaining Code – The Code's First Year of Operation*, Canberra: Australian Government. https://perma.cc/2J76-HTMV

van Dalen, Arjen; Peter Van Aelst, Peter (2014) 'Political journalists: Covering politics in the democratic-corporatist media system', in Weaver, David H and Willnat, Lars (eds) (2014) *The Global Journalist in the 21st Century*. New York: Routledge. https://perma.cc/L99C-8TJC

Weaver, David H and Willnat, Lars (eds) (2014) *The Global Journalist in the 21st Century*, New York: Routledge. https://perma.cc/L99C-8TJC

Wikipedia (2023a) 'News Media bargaining code', Encyclopaedia entry. https://perma.cc/T7HS-WYN2

Wikipedia (2023b) 'World press freedom index', Encyclopaedia entry, https://perma.cc/48AC-JXR8

Wikipedia (2024) 'Television ratings in Australia', webpage. https://perma.cc/562P-2D5C

Willnat, Lars; Weaver, David H; and Choi, Jihyang (2013) 'The global journalist in the twenty-first century', *Journalism Practice*, vol. 7, no.2. World Values Survey/ Policy Institute, Kings College London https://doi.org/10.1080/17512786.2012.753210

World Values Survey (2018) *World Values Survey, Wave 7*, World Values Survey/ Policy Institute, Kings College London. 'WVS-Australia team presents wave 7 findings and methodology at the 6th Biennial ACSPRI Social Science Methodology Conference in Sydney'. https://www.worldvaluessurvey.org/WVSNewsShow.jsp?ID=396 Click link to presentation at the end.

9

Social media

Max Halupka

Digital technology and online services now influence most corners of Australian society, from the way that government and businesses operate and influence lives, through to the everyday actions of citizens – the things people do, and how they do them. They have also come to form part of the communicative core of Australia's democracy. The COVID-19 pandemic for a time forced through a series of related changes, as social distancing became a public health necessity for the common good, and traditional means of socialising were strained, especially in Australia's dominant big city urban areas. Citizens, enterprises and agencies all embraced new digital technology practices as the principal way to maintain community and stay 'informed' on current events, with lasting implications for working patterns (WGEA, 2021; AIHW, 2023), retailing, private and government services, and political life.

How should the social media system operate in a liberal democracy?

- Social media should enhance the pluralism and diversity of the overall media system, lowering the costs for citizens in securing political information, commentary and evidence, and improving their opportunities to understand how democracy works.
- Social media should be easily accessible for ordinary citizens, encouraging them to become politically involved by taking individual actions to express their views in responsible ways, and enabling them to take collective actions to promote a shared viewpoint.
- The overall media system should operate as transparently as possible, so that truthful/factual content predominates, it quickly drives out misinformation, and 'fake news', 'passing off' and other lapses are minimised and rapidly counteracted.
- The growth of social media should contribute to greater political equality by re-weighting communication towards members of the public and non-government organisations, reducing the communication and organisational advantages of corporate actors, professional lobbyists or 'industrialised' content promoters.

How to cite this chapter:

Halupka, Max (2024) 'Social media', in: Evans, Mark; Dunleavy, Patrick and Phillimore, John (eds) *Australia's Evolving Democracy: A New Democratic Audit,* London: LSE Press, pp.191–205. **https://doi.org/10.31389/lsepress.ada.h** Licence: CC-BY-NC 4.0

- By providing more direct, less 'mediated' communications with large publics, social media should enhance the capacity of politicians and parties to create and maintain direct links with citizens, enhancing their understanding of public opinion and responsiveness to it.

- Social media technologies (such as Facebook, X (formerly Twitter), Google, YouTube, Snapchat and Instagram) have brought about radical changes in how the media systems of liberal democracies operate. Social media should unambiguously enhance citizen vigilance over state policies and public choices, increasing the 'granularity' of public scrutiny, speeding up the recognition of policy problems or scandals, and reaching the widest relevant audiences for critiques and commentary of government actions.

- Platform providers argue that they do not generate the content posted on millions of X (formerly Twitter) sites or Facebook pages, but only provide an online facility that allows citizens, NGOs and enterprises to build their own content. However, these large companies also reap important network and oligopoly effects that increase their discretionary power, and their platforms have become increasingly salient factors in democratic politics. Therefore, regulation of their activities should be considered if they create monopolies or oligopolies, suppress rival competitors, unfairly undermine the viability of established media, fail to deal with extremism and hate speech, or damage the integrity of elections or other political participation processes.

- Platform providers must take their legal responsibilities to 'do no harm' seriously and respond quickly to mitigate new social problems enabled by social media that are identified by public opinion or elected politicians, such as fake news and online harassment of minorities.

- The development of regulations and law around fast-changing 'new goods' like social media often lags behind social practice. Legislators and government need to be agile in responding to emergent problems created by social media, or to existing problems that are re-scaled or change character because of them. Where existing controls or actions to mitigate effects are already feasible in law, their implementation needs to be prioritised and taken seriously by police forces and regulators.

- As with conventional media, citizens should be able to gain published corrections and other effective forms of redress (including appropriate damages) against reporting or commentary that is illegal, unfair, incorrect or invades personal and family privacy. Citizens are entitled to expect that platform companies will respect all laws applying to them in speedily taking down offensive content, and that the firms will not be able to exploit their power to deter investigations or prosecutions by the police or prosecutors.

How users behave online, and the internal regulation of these key sites by providers, now occupy a central place in debates about how Australian democracy and society operate. The chapter reviews recent developments and then considers overall strengths, weaknesses, opportunities, and threats (SWOT analysis). After this SWOT analysis, the remaining sections explore three topics in more detail.

Recent developments

All the main social media channels in Australia are controlled by globally owned internet platform companies, with Facebook and other apps owned by Meta dominating national user tables, as Figure 9.1 shows. While Facebook has been in decline in many other advanced countries, its Australian market share has fallen only gradually and in 2023 it still remained the top app used both for all purposes, and for getting news. Facebook Messenger also ranked third for all purposes, but only sixth for news. The only non-Meta programmes in the Figure were Google's YouTube video app and X (formerly Twitter), which has not been particularly successful in Australia. Other smaller but recently growing apps have included WeChat, and TikTok. Competition in the market between the global players has been intense and now defunct platforms include Myspace, Vine and Google Plus.

The platform companies offer people, other enterprises, state agencies and civil society organisations a space where they can:

- consume information on a variety of topics from a diverse range of sources
- create information in the form of content, such as text, images, or videos
- aggregate content which is relevant to their interests
- distribute any created and/or aggregated content, such as news-media
- and connect with others in commonly accessible spaces.

The giant corporations involved have all claimed that content-users are responsible for any harms or inaccuracies they create, and that they can only regulate what gets put up by setting general (impartial) rules. They have also strongly argued that specific social media regulations are a job that governments should steer clear of, especially in liberal democracies. Critics argue that the companies have done and still do far too little to root out hate speech and other evils – because their algorithms used to generate traffic (and attract online advertising) are deliberately designed to be addictive. They show viewers content that they find interesting, and in particular seek to prioritise 'clickbait', 'disinformation', sensational content and extreme opinions over more accurate, serious or considered materials. Over time too, the ways in which users access social media apps and news content have also shifted increasingly towards using mobile phones, rather than PCs or tablets (Figure 9.2), which may cut the times and reduce the focus that users give to news. In 2022, nearly two-thirds (61 per cent) of Australian survey respondents said that they got news from their mobile phones, while 44 per cent of consumers highlighted that it was their main device for doing so, a notable increase over time.

Figure 9.1: The major social apps in Australia in 2023

App used (company)	For all (%)	For news (%)
Facebook (Meta)	64	32
YouTube (Google)	57	23
Instagram (Meta)	42	14
X (Twitter)	20	12
WhatsApp (Meta)	29	10
Facebook Messenger (Meta)	48	9

Source: Reuters Institute (2023) Reuters Institute Digital News Report 2023, written by Newman, Nic; Fletcher, Richard; Robertson, Craig T; Eddy, Kirsten; and Nielsen, Rasmus Kleis. https://reutersinstitute.politics.ox.ac.uk/sites/default/files/2023-06/Digital_News_Report_2023.pdf

Figure 9.2: How Australians accessed online news content in 2016 and 2022

	2016	2022
Phone	51	61
Computer, PC	60	40
Tablet	27	22

Source: Reuters Institute (2022) *Reuters Institute Digital News Report 2022*, Newman, Nic; Fletcher, Richard;. Robertson, Craig T; Eddy, Kirsten; and Nielsen, Rasmus Kleis. https://reutersinstitute.politics.ox.ac.uk/sites/default/files/2022-06/Digital_News-Report_2022.pdf

As Australians have increasingly used the internet and social media to supplement everyday communication and actions, they have moved away from relying on more traditional forms of media, including for political information. The *Digital Platforms Inquiry Report* by the Australian Competition and Consumer Commission demonstrated that social-media platforms were now salient and completely unavoidable partners for many Australian businesses, including the news-media (ACCC, 2019). This report set off a two-year process where the federal government (partly acting at the behest of the conventional media corporations) sought to force the platform companies to pay media firms for reusing their news content – a saga covered in detail in Chapter 8. Platforms such as Google and Facebook initially threatened to withdraw services from the country, but eventually caved-in to the government pressure and began paying for reusing Australian news content under private arrangements to avoid a mandatory media code.

A second area of acute concern with social media is that it allows users (individuals or organisations) to create and disseminate content at whim. So, while news media and journalism, and the content they create, has traditionally been the home of professionals, social media has allowed individuals with no prior expertise to fill the role of information provider. This information can be reconstituted into 'news', regardless of its factuality. Of course, this is not to ignore or marginalise the significant contribution that governments make to the propagation of misinformation. However, at the individual level, misinformation plays havoc on the everyday citizen's capacity to discern truthful news from propaganda. In a time where we rely increasingly on the connective capacity of social media, we are faced with the challenge of reflecting, understanding and integrating 'good' information from 'bad'. While social media has made it much easier to be connected and to socialise, it has also made it increasingly difficult to ascertain factual commentary from fanatical.

Australia's systems of governance, representation and policy have found it difficult to maximise social media spaces within the scope of healthy democratic action. Social media's greatest promise was its capacity to connect everyone to everyone else. This was also a promise of greater connection between citizens and political or state authority, resulting in better representation, accountability and more direct citizen involvement in decisions that influence their lives. Social media and the internet created a means of direct, public communication to political representatives – who traditionally may have been outside the reach or influence of everyday citizens. Social media can contribute the citizen 'vigilance' vital to liberal democracy.

However, as social media usage developed it became increasingly apparent that the new apps do not necessarily or just facilitate authentic and autonomous connections between isolated or dissociated groups. Rather social media algorithms determining what content people see can solidify personal interests within narrow networks, so that individuals live more in social media structures of already curated and like-minded content – potentially polarising differences between political groups and ideas. The connective capacity of online organisations has been shown to be effective in replicating or supplementing the traditional structures of collective action (Bennett and Segerberg, 2013). Yet the way in which these platforms have been structured continues to distance aspects of Australian community from one another.

There has also been an increased dialogue around the censorship or regulation of online and social media content. The federal government has a long history of trying to censor the internet and restrict the flow of content that it deems inappropriate. And during the COVID-19 pandemic all governments became strongly concerned with protecting public health by maximising accurate information and minimising the visibility of diverse sources of misinformation, such as conspiracy theories linking the pandemic to bizarre causes (for example, 5G phone masts) or seeking to inhibit people taking vaccines. These concerns increased the salience of questions around what content is healthy for Australian democracy and society. Prime Minister (PM) Scott Morrison criticised social media as an environment which lacked the accountability needed for a functioning democratic society. Influential calls have been made to censor or criminalise individuals who use social media platforms for disruptive or abusive behaviour (such as doxing) yet raising acute concerns over the censorship or control of the means of information flows counter to the founding ideals of a liberal democracy.

Both the bushfires in 2019–20 and the COVID-19 pandemic showed that social media now comprises an embedded feature of Australia's critical information network. To this end, it goes without saying that these spaces become principal targets for external influence and manipulation. Recent work has found that certain social media platforms are facilitating the erosion of Australia's national liberal-democratic identity (Jensen and Chen, 2021). Advances in social media technology and usage have consistently outpaced the design of government media regulations, and the understanding and resulting policy of representatives, creating increasingly large cracks in Australia's public safeguarding, and even its national defence network. Approaches to social media policy have been haphazard, sporadic and uneven at the same time as these innovative apps have become an unavoidable partner for most Australians in their daily lives.

How Australians use social media

As more Australians have used social media as their primary source of news there has been a gradual decrease in the proportion of consumers relying on traditional news sources for their information, like TV, radio and print, although Chapter 8 shows how conventional mass media have also built up their online offerings to dominant positions within the news media landscape. However, there have been some important and long-lasting generational differences in preferred news sources (Figure 9.3). For a majority of the youngest group in 2021 (Generation Z), social media was their largest source of news, followed by online news sites, while less than a fifth relied on TV news. Also for this group, YouTube (35 per cent) had overtaken Facebook (34 per cent) as the most popular social media platform for news. There has been an acute contrast here with the older groups for whom TV and radio remain the overwhelmingly dominant news sources. In between these poles, the Generation Y group resembled Generation Z in relying heavily on social media and online sources, with only a quarter mainly dependent on TV and radio. The Generation X group were more balanced in their use of different sources, with most people using TV considered as a single medium (and almost half broadcast news), but online news plus social media combined are slightly more important (Park et al., 2021, p.53).

Figure 9.3: Generational differences in the main source of news among Australian respondents in 2021

Age group	Social media	Online news	TV	Radio	Print
Generation Z (born after mid 1990s)	54	21	19	2	3
Generation Y (born 1980s to late 1990s)	37	32	23	3	5
Generation X (1965–1981)	17	33	40	7	3
Baby Boomers (1946–65)	8	22	56	10	5
Aged over 75	10	7	60	13	10

Source: Compiled from Park et al., 2021, *Digital News Report: Australia 2021*, News and Media Research Centre, University of Canberra, p.53. https://apo.org.au/node/312650

The continued role of social media in Australian life, coupled with a decline in intentional or purposive news consumption, calls into question the perceptiveness of the everyday Australian citizen in what constitutes news. News may not be flagged as explicitly as in conventional media, but this does not mean that the content does not have significant shaping capacity on the individual's understanding of any given topic. *The Digital News Report: Australia 2021* (Park et al., 2021, p.12) found that Australians consumed news on Facebook incidentally rather than intentionally, with almost half of those who used Facebook for news (46 per cent) viewing news while they are on the platform for other reasons. However, the report suggested that when users did see news, it was most likely to come from mainstream news outlets or recognised journalists. As Chapter 8 discusses, while using platforms for news most users said that they pay attention to mainstream news outlets and journalists.

If we were to extrapolate from the results above to guess where teenagers get their information about politics, and bearing in mind that people in this age group are heavy online users, we

Figure 9.4: How teenagers (aged 13 to 16) reported their main sources of information about politics in 2023

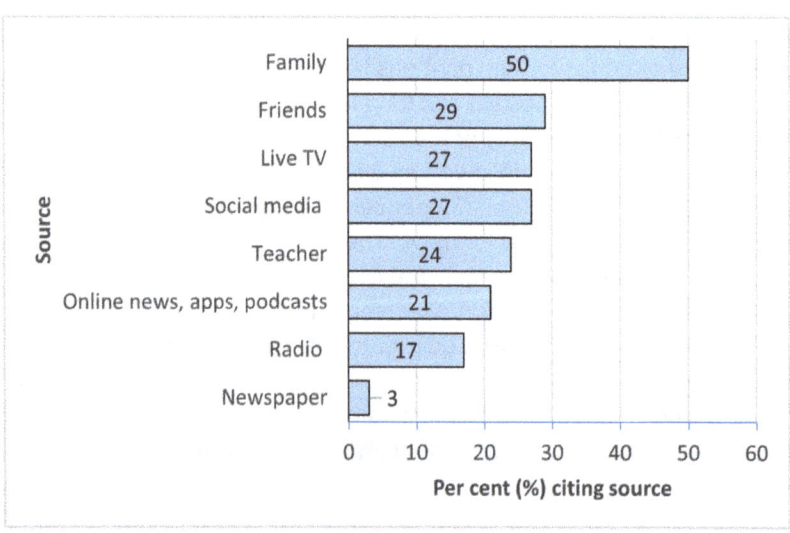

Source: Figure designed by author using data from Notley et al., 2023, *News and Young Australians in 2023: 'How Children and Teens Access, Perceive and are Affected by News Media'*. Report Western Sydney University, University of Canberra, QUIT Digital Media Research Centre, p.6.

might expect that internet or social media sources would predominate. However, in fact, Figure 9.4 shows that the traditional sources stressed in political socialisation literature predominate, with school, family and friends important (Notley et al., 2023). Live TV and social media tied as media sources, but teenagers also read news online and used apps. This fits with a narrative of a lot of indirect news consumption in earlier work (Evans, Stoker and Halupka, 2019), but suggests some substantial online news engagement. Perhaps this finding is part of the standard story of socialisation, where political understanding has mostly been taken from sources closer at hand (as with face-to-face contacts)? The importance of young people's understanding of politics as related to social media is unpacked a bit more later in the chapter.

Strengths, weaknesses, opportunities and threats (SWOT) analysis

Current strengths	Current weaknesses
Social media has great potential to close the gap between citizens and political representatives, allowing for more direct lines of communication and engagement. For instance, they allow political parties to connect in real time with wide audiences, facilitating the coordination of new networks. By replying and commenting, people have low-cost opportunities to contact and influence decision-makers at a national or local level.	It is important to make new connections from citizens to political authorities in ways that increase the representativeness of democracy, the quality of public debate and the accountability of actions. Critics argue that platform company algorithms create pockets of special interests, where the lines of communication are centred on insider/outsider status. In politics, this could result in different groups becoming isolated from contacts with others along party or ideological lines, with a risk of increasing political or ideological polarisation among voters. Social media reinforces political attitudes, rather than challenging them.
Social media allows politicians to express their views and reactions to events in real time, facilitating the free flow of ideas between representative and citizen (Taylor, 2018).	Some politicians use social media as a platform for angry and often inaccurate polemic. Corrections are rare and often go unnoticed (Taylor, 2018).
Social media provides free and open spaces where content can be created and shared with a wider community. The growth of social media expands the potential public foundations for a pluralistic and diverse media system.	The primary cost of apparently 'free' social media has been that users 'become the product' themselves. Social media platforms have made money by selling the user's online behavioural data profiles and preferences to advertisers and other vested interests.
Social media platforms such as Google and Facebook act as convenient gateways to digital-based services. Australia's social media environments function as 'one-stop-shops', centralising a range of differentiated services into a single platform.	Most social media users have no choice but to accept the complex 'terms of service' that companies enforce, or else lose the functionality, services, and networks that the major platforms provide.

Adverse by-product effects of social media use on established or paid-for journalism and media diversity need to be taken into account. Social media companies argue that their activities are similar to 'disintermediation' ('cutting out the middleman') processes in other industries, allowing citizens more choice in how they gain information or services. Yet losses of advertising revenue to platform corporations that critically threaten the viability of existing media (like broadcasting and print/paid for newspapers) may have net negative effects on the overall media system.	Facebook and Google provide a cheap way for any political campaigner with money or large numbers of supporters to reach voters, often in a highly targeted way. Policy-makers need to consider how the new capabilities here affect the autonomy of citizens' voting decisions, and whether electoral law – which imposes obligations and restrictions on broadcasters – should be extended and adapted to encompass political advertising on social media platforms.
Social media enables rapid and unprecedented scrutiny of policy-making and politicians' pronouncements, with stakeholders' and experts' opinions freely available on X (formerly Twitter). Some liveblogs have tried to curate them, but this body of knowledge and inputs remains diffuse (Taylor, 2018).	Armed with huge cash reserves (often gained from setting up complex tax-avoidance schemes), the giant platform corporations have diversified into social media conglomerates. Facebook (which owns Instagram and WhatsApp), Google (which owns YouTube) and to a lesser extent X (formerly Twitter), now dominate social media platforms. These corporations' power to shape how democratic discourse happens online has been and remains considerable, and almost unregulated at nation state level (Taylor, 2018).
Social media has been used successfully by some politicians in Australia to connect and organise with their followers. In some cases, social media functions as envisioned, and politicians use these platforms to engage a range of topics and ideas.	The capacity for parties and politicians to create greater engagement exists, yet in the main they continue to employ social media as a platform to circumvent accountability, and disseminating misleading information, that does little to enhance the standard of public debate.
Unaffiliated citizens, who are not part of a given political party, interest group of civil society body can nonetheless comment on these organisations' and politicians' behaviour at very low cost. They can quickly disseminate their message to a wide audience via social media and have some chance of evoking wider agreement or informative responses from other like-minded people (Taylor, 2018).	Most 'retweeters' and 'likers' are not professional journalists writing for fact-checked publications, but ordinary citizens with lower levels of information. So, critics argue that inaccurate and misleading information ('fake news') can spread more quickly (Taylor, 2018). Indeed, platform companies may have an interest in more sensational and irresponsible content continuing to circulate, since it may generate more interest and click-throughs than more prosaic but accurate information.

Digital-only publication and dissemination via social media have lowered the start-up costs for many alternative media outlets, broadening the range of professionally produced news and commentary available to citizens (Taylor, 2018). Videoblogs and podcasts have increasingly blurred the boundaries between conventional (high cost) media and low cost social media.	Digital-only publishing by highly committed or partisan publishers or web-broadcasters has also enabled some operators to flood online platform systems with multiple biased or untrue messages in ways that are completely non-transparent and ever-changing (Taylor, 2018). Disinformation and evils such as hate-speech are very hard to regulate either by governments or even by the platform companies themselves – although critics argue that they spend far too little on monitoring and are slow to ban even conspicuous offenders.
Future opportunities	**Future threats**
Social media, as a relatively new aspect of society, provides us a rare opportunity to structure something 'right', from the beginning. The regulation and structuring of social media platforms should be geared towards social good, maximising the avenues of citizen politics and engagement, while also serving as means to connect political parties. When structured with citizen interests at heart, social media can create new networks and structures to engage in the political process more broadly.	Stakeholders and experts were not given a sufficient consultation period to properly assess the Online Safety Bill 2021 and its potential impacts. The Bill was introduced only 10 days after submissions in response to the draft exposure bill closed, and the Committee accepted submissions in response to the Bill for only seven days. Given the extent of the changes introduced by the Bill, this was not a sufficient consultation period. Critics argue that the law leaves Australia significantly vulnerable on multiple fronts, including risks to national security, business innovation and growth, political participation, and governance (Suzor et al., 2021).
Social media has given 'new Australians' (those who form part of a diaspora from another country) with a means to connect with others regionally and nationally, strengthening domestic community ties and aiding cultural integration. Yet they also have helped communication to family and communities overseas. Foreign language social media platforms have provided a vital service for new Australians, as they have often been the first and lasting source of news information. For Australians with English as a second language, social media has provided information in an accessible format.	Social media has been used by extraterritorial entities and some other states in ways designed to undermine Australia's social cohesion, national identity, and liberal democratic ideals. Australians have been participants in an ongoing cyber-war that they were largely unaware of.

For the development of Australian society and democracy, three key remaining issues remain fiercely debated – about the maintenance of trust and impartiality, demands for the censorship of the internet and online social media content, and impacts on young people. The remaining sections cover each in turn.

Impartiality

The conversation around trust and impartiality relates to broader concerns around misinformation, national security and propaganda. Of principal concern here is the extent to which citizens now trust the multitude of news sources by which they find themselves bombarded every day. And does how citizens trust their news sources influence the formation of their political views? For instance, as innovative forms of news generation and consumption have come to predominate, how far has the capacity of everyday citizens to navigate a liberal democracy successfully, and formulate their own political interests, increased? Social media has given individuals a place of public debate where facts sometimes appear to be optional and opinions have dominated discussion.

Notions of impartiality and trust have varied significantly across generations according to the survey for *Digital News Report* (Park et al., 2021). Respondents who were Baby Boomers, or older people 75+ , were the most likely to support the notion that news should provide and question a variety of points of view in a news story, so that consumers can make up their own minds. Four-fifths (82 per cent) of Baby Boomers and 88 per cent of the 75+ group supported this notion of journalism, while only 68 per cent of Generation Z respondents supported the same ideal. On the issue of neutrality, 72 per cent of those aged 75+ felt that news should remain neutral on all issues, whereas only 42 per cent of Generation Z supported this position. There may be policy experience or media use factors involved here. The younger generation's view may reflect their experience with wicked problems, like climate change, where a prolonged and 'neutral' approach has hindered affirmative action. Alternatively, or as well, the younger generation's increased use of the internet and social media to search for critical information may have exposed them to the subjectivity of digital content creation more frequently, and lowered their expectations that impartiality is achievable.

The same survey's Australian respondents were overall less supportive of each of the propositions related to the impartiality of news when they got their news predominantly from social media. Just over two-thirds (69 per cent) of people relying on social media as their main source of news saw outlets as institutions that should reflect a range of views, by comparison with four-fifths of those who got their news predominantly from radio. Half of Australian respondents who used social media as their main source of news consumption agreed that content outlets should try to be neutral on all issues, compared with 69 per cent of those who mainly use print news sources. Substantial majorities of Australian respondents supported the proposition of giving equal time to all sides of the story, but the number was lower for people whose main source was social media, at 65 per cent, than for print news readers (79 per cent) or those who listen to radio news (83 per cent).

Looking more specifically at variations between social media platforms, the same survey found that Instagram users were the least supportive of the ideals of impartiality, neutrality and equal time (Park et al., 2021, p.34), while X (formerly Twitter) users at 77 per cent were most likely to agree that outlets should present a range of views. Among Facebook and YouTube users, 58 per cent supported the proposition that news outlets should be neutral on all issues, and that all sides should receive equal time – the highest levels for these items. Overall, of those who accessed news via Facebook or YouTube, only three-tenths of respondents supported the idea that some issues should not be reported in a neutral manner, the lowest levels for this item. X (formerly Twitter) news consumers were the most likely to support news outlets giving equal time to views the media operators deemed weak.

Censorship

In October 2021, asked about the potential censorship of Australia's social media, PM Scott Morrison claimed that 'social media has become a coward's palace where people can go on there, not say who they are, and destroy people's lives' (Attwood and Williams, 2021). His critical statement was indicative of the Liberal-National government's wider position on social media – which were seen not as a means of enriching liberal democracy, but rather as a source of disturbing personal and social issues. Australian politicians in general have also not focused much on the social goods arising from social media (such as the potential for democratic strengthening), but rather on their role as avenues of political criticism that should be limited more. Coalition ministers especially saw a lot of content as adversarial, and thus running counter to their capacity to govern effectively.

This logic has ignored the lines of accountability that social media has provided in better connecting representative and citizen, allowing voters to hold politicians more continuously accountable, in more detail and in real time for any actions taken which undermine democracy. For example, the 'robodebt' crisis over the government illegally trying to reclaim welfare funding from 'overpaid' families (discussed in Chapter 13) was given a limited amount of coverage on conventional news media and professional journalists. But it was overwhelmingly on social media and via the online criticisms of academics and lawyers involved with protest groups that the scandal was kept alive and continuously in focus before it eventually crumbled in the courts and under criticism from integrity agencies. Social media agitation also kept the issue going until a change of government in 2022 allowed the forensic examination of the 'robodebt' policy disaster by a Royal Commission.

However, a different view of social media has been most widely adopted by Australian politicians, one which assumes that social media is a public space where individuals can, and will, propagate harm. In particular, both Liberal and National ministers framed social media as primarily a social harm, a problematic viewpoint that led past rhetorical denunciation to a legislative attempt to control social media, and what citizens do in these spaces. The Online Safety Bill 2021 was introduced in Australia during the COVID-19 pandemic to update national guidelines for online safety. The bill looked to replicate and build upon the enhancing Online Safety Act of 2015, contributing to the ongoing regulation and control of social media in Australia. A new agency was tasked to police the new powers, eSafety Commissioner (2023) and the new Act:

> ... retains and replicates certain provisions in the Enhancing Online Safety Act 2015, including the non-consensual sharing of intimate images scheme; specifies basic online safety expectations; establishes an online content scheme for the removal of certain material; creates a complaints-based removal notice scheme for cyber-abuse being perpetrated against an Australian adult; broadens the cyber-bullying scheme to capture harms occurring on services other than social media; reduces the timeframe for service providers to respond to a removal notice from the eSafety Commissioner; brings providers of app distribution services and internet search engine services into the remit of the new online content scheme; and establishes a power for the eSafety Commissioner to request or require internet service providers to disable access to material depicting, promoting, inciting or instructing in abhorrent violent conduct for time-limited periods in crisis situations. (Parliament of Australia, 2021)

The bill was immediately criticised on the grounds that it did more damage to Australia's approach to social media as a democratic nation, than any good it did in strengthening protections for citizens. Critics argued that the legislation was rushed and not based on a sound understanding of the way in which social media, and the internet more broadly, operates in contemporary society. A team of academic law researchers compiled a response to the bill that outlined a long series of recommendations to sharpen up and narrow much of the regulation (Suzor et al., 2021, p.2) including, but not limited to these points:

> - remove intent from the definition of 'cyber-abuse material targeted at an Australian adult' to enable takedown powers to function effectively.
>
> - remove 'offensive' from the definition of 'cyber-abuse material targeted at an Australian adult' in order to avoid an overly-broad definition.
>
> - extend the cyber-abuse scheme to 'conduct', in addition to 'material', empowering the Commissioner to deal with abuse that is perpetrated through repeated harassing posts that may not be viewed as harmful in isolation.
>
> - extend the cyber-abuse scheme to 'identifiable groups of Australian people', in addition to 'a particular Australian adult', in order to ensure that threats and harassment against multiple people (or classes of people) are within scope.

Few of these points were accepted or embodied in the legislation finally passed.

Some politicians in Australia have chiefly framed social media as a realm not only needing to be censored, but for its content providers to be punished for their criticisms of politics. In 2021 the then New South Wales Deputy Premier, John Barilaro, pressed a defamation legal action against a YouTuber and political satirist, Jordan Shanks, better known as 'friendlyjordies'. The case ended in an apology but cost the satirist $100,000 in legal costs (Douglas, 2021; Glitsos, 2021; Guardian, 2021). Here, a sitting member of state government employed state resources to limit the distribution of political content on a citizen's social media channel. Critics argue that there is a critical difference between some necessary regulation of harmful content, and the targeted censorship, and use of state force, to silence political commentary. That risk seems to be ignored if politicians only show a disregard for social media avenues of civic engagement, and could end up eroding citizens' ability to freely criticise their government in online spaces.

Young Australians and social media

Social media means that the politicisation of people's views may occur at a far younger age. Australian teenagers are not that different from adults in political attitudes (Chowdhury, 2021) but are becoming more 'political' at a younger age. Yet structures of democracy have been slow to recognise this. To effectively engage this evolving demographic, governments must reconsider the role that young people play in shaping politics in the future through the education and socialisation that they receive in early formative years.

In 1990, Australia ratified the 'Convention of the Rights of the Child' (CRC), agreeing to take action to make sure that all children in Australia can enjoy key rights: 'The CRC sets out all the basic rights that children need to do well: like having a home and a family, getting a good education, being able to access quality health care, being safe from harm, and having a voice' (Australian Human Rights Commission, 2019, p.3). Article 12 of the Convention requires governments to ensure that children and young people can participate in decisions that affect them. Accessing the views of young Australians, a Whitlam Institute report ('What matters to young Australians') presented the most comprehensive contemporary study of young Australians available (Collin and Hugman, 2020). Exploring 30,000 essay entries, collected over a 10-year period, it found that young people have an articulated interest and personal stake in Australian democracy. Although they remain a largely marginalised group in politics, young Australians express complex and sophisticated understandings of the representativeness of governments. The report found that young people both write and think about actions on specific issues, such as climate change, homelessness and bullying, and it demonstrated their participatory capacity, challenging narratives that see young people as politically apathetic or disinterested in democracy.

Yet a systematic review of Australian and international research on young people, democracy, citizenship and participation in the period 2009 to 2019 argued that the political views and practices of young people have been under-researched, particularly for those aged under 18 (Collin and McCormack, 2020). More evidence has been needed on how young people understand issues, and conceptualise different agents, structures and responsibilities within the Australian democratic system – and social media is critical here. Focusing on the 'changing and persistent forces that shape experiences of youth, politics, democracies and societies' (Collin and McCormack, 2020, p.9) contrasts with the more traditional approaches asking whether younger demographics satisfy or 'fall short' of meaningful democratic engagement and civic participation. Recent publications present evidence of the relationship between the perception of systems of democracy, and early education, in shaping the political behaviour and views of future citizens (Ghazarian et al., 2020; (for USA) Oxley et al., 2020). If the system of governance is delegitimised for people at a young age, they may be set for a path of long-term political disengagement. The democratic health of a nation likely depends on that nation's investment in the political education of its youth.

I noted earlier that young people (aged 18–34) are increasingly using social media as their preferred means of communication, entertainment and news, but children still at school (aged 12–18) are more dependent on traditional means of political socialisation (and see Ghazarian et al., 2020). Yet this situation may transition fast on their leaving home or starting work. If Australian government and political elites view social media platforms only in restrictive and hostile terms, focusing on their control and censorship alone, they risk not engaging with the scope of young people's developing political attitudes.

Conclusion

Citizens and their political leaders still need to decide where the public good rests with social media, and how the democratically helpful or harmful aspects of the shift to less controlled communication can be assessed or balanced constructively. For instance, social media undoubtedly helped bring Australians together in the acute pandemic times, when social distance became a necessity. More broadly, many aspects of social media have facilitated social progress, from boosting and pluralising citizens' access to societal information and improving business innovation, through to improving entertainment and the general quality of life. Yet conservative critics and others are also right to draw attention to the new kinds of social harm that unregulated or weakly regulated social media may facilitate, such as hate speech, cyber-bullying, or disinformation. But making censorship and control the main discussed response to digital challenges may impoverish democratic debate and mean that the restrictive actions and views of elected representatives seem to speak more to a narrative unconcerned with (or even antipathetic to) the people's participatory aspirations.

References

ACCC (Australian Competition and Consumer Commission) (2019) 'Digital platforms inquiry – final report', ACCC Report, June. https://perma.cc/T5ZK-TSTF

AHRC (Australian Human Rights Commission) (2019). *Children's Rights in Australia: A Scorecard*, Report, 20 November. https://perma.cc/MDP2-JD8S

AIHW (Australian Institute of Health and Welfare) (2023) 'Changing patterns of work', Webpage 7 September. https://perma.cc/TYT9-NX5R

Attwood, Alexia and Williams, Carly (2021) 'Deputy Prime Minister Barnaby Joyce says the government is not joking over plans to regulate social media.' *ABC News*, 9 October. https://perma.cc/5TPV-U2VU

Bennett, W Lance and Segerberg, Alexandra (2013). *The Logic of Connective Action: Digital Media and the Personalization of Contentious Politics*, Cambridge: Cambridge University Press. $ https://perma.cc/RSU4-Q3BF

Chowdhury, Intifa (2021) 'Young Australians are supposedly "turning their backs" on democracy, but are they any different from older voters?', *The Conversation*, 3 August. https://perma.cc/ER43-6GZG

Collin, Phillippa and Hugman, Sky (2020) *What Matters to Young Australians? Exploring Young People's Perspectives from 2010–2018*, Whitlam Institute Report, 24 November. https://perma.cc/JN4P-63ZH

Collin, Phillippa and McCormack, Jane (2020) *Young People and Democracy: A Review*, Whitlam Institute Report, August. https://perma.cc/K722-A5JA

Douglas, M (2021) 'Defamation actions and Australian politics', *UNSW Law Journal Forum*, 2021, forthcoming. Preprint SSRN 3857025. https://perma.cc/XVG4-2UXT

eSafety Commissioner (2023) eSafety Commission website homepage. https://www.esafety.gov.au/

Evans, Mark; Stoker, Gerry; and Halupka, Max (2019) 'Don't believe the stereotype: These 5 charts show our democracy is safe in the hands of future voters', *The Conversation*, 19 December. https://perma.cc/B3UE-FT4L

Ghazarian, Zareh; Laughland-Booy, Jacqueline; De Lazzari, Chiara; and Skrbis, Zlatko (2020) 'How are young Australians learning about politics at school? The student perspective', *Journal of Applied Youth Studies*, vol. 3, 13 July, pp.193–208. $ https://doi.org/10.1007/s43151-020-00011-7

Glitsos, Laura (2021) 'NSW deputy premier threatens to sue FriendlyJordies, reminding us that parody hits in a way traditional media can't,' *The Conversation*, 5 May. https://perma.cc/6H6Z-CKMJ

Guardian (2021) 'Friendlyjordies defamation case: Jordan Shanks apologises to John Barilaro to settle claim', *Guardian, Australia,* 4 November, webpage. https://perma.cc/T6WG-PFZJ

Jensen, Michael J. and Chen, Titus C (2021) 'Illiberal media in a liberal democracy: Examining identity in Australia's Mandarin language news', *Issues and Studies*, vol. 57, no.2. $ https://doi.org/10.1142/S1013251121500053

Notley, Tanya; Chambers, Simon; Zhong, Hua (Flora); Park, Sora; Lee, Jee Young; and Dezuanni, Michael (2023) *News and Young Australians in 2023: How Children and Teens Access, Perceive and are Affected by News Media*, Report, Western Sydney University, University of Canberra, QUIT Digital Media Research Centre. https://perma.cc/2X4H-SBAC

Oxley, Zoe M; Holman, Mirya R; Greenlee, Jill S; Bos, Angela L; and Lay, J Celeste (2020) 'Children's views of the American presidency', *Public Opinion Quarterly*, vol. 84, no. 1, pp.141–57. $ https://doi.org/10.1093/poq/nfaa007

Park, Sora; Fisher, Caroline; McGuinness, Kieran; Lee, Jee Young; and McCallum, Kerry (2021) *Digital News Report: Australia 2021*, News and Media Research Centre, University of Canberra. https://perma.cc/B8SV-96PP

Parliament of Australia (2021) 'Online Safety Bill 2021'. https://perma.cc/YDC8-MWE8

Reuters Institute (2022) *Reuters Institute Digital News Report 2022,* Newman, Nic; Fletcher, Richard;. Robertson, Craig T; Eddy, Kirsten; and Nielsen, Rasmus Kleis. https://perma.cc/6SA4-TNCM

Reuters Institute (2023) *Reuters Institute Digital News Report 2023,* Newman, Nic; Fletcher, Richard; Robertson, Craig T; Eddy, Kirsten; and Nielsen, Rasmus Kleis. https://perma.cc/98YV-8MG5

Suzor, Nicolas; Nelson, Lucinda; Gillett, Rosalie; and Burgess, Jean (2021) *QUT Digital Media Research Centre submission in response to the Online Safety Bill 2021*, Office of the Australian Information Commissioner (OAIC), Australian Government, QUT Report. https://eprints.qut.edu.au/208582/

Taylor, R (2018) 'Social media and democratic vigilance', in Dunleavy, Patrick; Park, Alice; and Taylor, Ros (eds) (2018) *The UK's Changing Democracy: The 2018 Democratic Audit*. London: LSE Press, Chapter 3.4. https://doi.org/10.31389/book1.i

Workplace Gender Equality Agency (WGEA) (2021) 'Flexible work post-COVID', WGEA Publications, 8 December. https://perma.cc/JV3A-A6CY

10

Gender equality and rights

Pia Rowe

Are historical inequalities and discrimination based on gender being rectified in Australia, and is the pace of recent change fast enough? The World Economic Forum's (2021) annual global comparisons showed Australia's progress towards gender equality coming to a halt, with the country dropping six places in the Global Gender Gap Report's overall rankings, moving down to 50th (out of 156 countries), and placed 70th for women's 'economic participation and opportunity', and 54th in terms of 'political empowerment'. However, these slumps were soon ameliorated and by 2023 Australia ranked 26th in the WEF Global Gender Gap overall ranking, 38th for economic participation and opportunity, and 29th for political empowerment. These previously lacklustre and recently improved indicators tell a vivid story of a country where past positive narratives of progress towards gender equality often contrasted with the stark realities of a culture where traditionally masculine leadership norms permeated every facet of the society (especially for lesbian and transgender women in the past (AHRC, 2014)) hampering efforts to effect lasting change, especially via the political process. Yet recent positive movements, and changes in the tenor of policy debates under the Labor government, also demonstrated that raising the political salience of gender issues can have considerable effects.

What does democracy require in terms of gender equality?

- People of all genders must enjoy genuine equality in terms of civil rights (covering equal pay, employment rights, property rights, access to legal services and protections, access to care services spanning all facets of the whole human lifecycle, and marriage and partnership laws).
- Political and public life should be organised to maximise the equal chances of all people regardless of their gender identity or biological sex to be involved in democratic politics – to vote and stand for election, to take part in party and political processes, to contribute to public debate and discussion, and to stand for public office and rise to the top in political life.
- Employment in the public service sector (and in firms working on public sector contracts) should serve as exemplars of good practice in improving gender equality more broadly.

How to cite this chapter:

Rowe, Pia (2024) 'Gender equality and rights', in: Evans, Mark; Dunleavy, Patrick and Phillimore, John (eds) *Australia's Evolving Democracy: A New Democratic Audit,* London: LSE Press, pp.206–228. https://doi.org/10.31389/lsepress.ada.j Licence: CC-BY-NC 4.0

- No one should be subject to differential discrimination in political, public or private life, nor to demeaning discourses in terms of public and media discourses based on their individual social attributes such as gender, race, ability, religion, sexual orientation and age. There should also be equal visibility in the media.
- Where barriers to gender equality are proven to exist, it is desirable for public regulations or interventions to at least temporarily be undertaken to secure appropriate and feasible ameliorative actions (consistent with maintaining the civil rights of all citizens).
- The fundamental human right to feel safe and secure is realised for all through the elimination of gender-based violence.

Recent developments

Gender equality in Australia has been at a crossroads in recent years. On the one hand, there has been a significant increase in the public's interest in gender equality and growing political salience for gender issues. From online activism (#MeToo, #EnoughIsEnough, #LetHerSpeak), to national protest movements (Nally, 2021) and mainstream TV shows (*Ms Represented* on ABC Television), gender equality has shifted from a niche scholarly topic into a mainstream issue of interest. The success of the Teal Independents in the May 2022 federal election 'cashed in' many of these previously diffuse gains in salience, with (mainly) women candidates mobilising strongly around women's issues and successfully displacing Liberal MPs in one of the election's most important developments (see Chapter 5). The new Labor administration (with Greens support) also took a much more activist position on remedying gender inequality than had its Coalition predecessor and gave increased priority to the care economy.

In the public sphere there have been several positive developments. For the first time there is an equal representation between men and women parliamentarians in the Senate. In another Australian first, after Victoria's Gender Equality Act was passed in February 2020 (Victoria Parliament, 2020), Dr Niki Vincent was appointed the state's first Public Sector Gender Equality Commissioner in September 2020, signalling the state government's commitment to gender equality in practice (Victoria Public Sector Gender Equality Commissioner, 2021). Under that Act, public sector entities must report on their progress on workplace gender equality. At federal level, following the Sex Discrimination Commissioner Kate Jenkins' *Respect@Work* report submission to the government (AHRC, 2020), the Senate passed the Sex Discrimination and Fair Work (Respect at Work) Amendment Bill 2021 in September 2021. The legislation will bring into law some of the recommendations from the landmark report.

However, despite increasing awareness and support for gender equality – at least in principle – numerous policies already in place, and women faring well in some areas, such as education, where they are more likely than men to have attained a bachelor's degree (35 per cent female to 29 per cent male) or above, in other areas progress has been either extremely slow, completely stalled, or worse yet, gone backwards (ABS, 2023a).

The treatment of women in politics featured prominently in much of the media headlines in recent years. Sadly, for a long time it appeared that not much had changed since Julia Gillard's 'misogyny speech' went viral around the world in 2012 (Gillard, 2012), with increasing reports of discrimination, sexism and abuse surfacing in the media. As late as 2021, some female

MPs argued that the abuse 'is so normalised as to be expected in public office', and they experience it both online and in real life, and from both the public and their colleagues alike (Majumdar, 2021). Perhaps predictably, many women at all levels of government reported that the widespread bullying and harassment impacted their aspirations for political leadership, or a career in politics entirely. These complaints proved fertile grounds for women Teal Independents in competing against Coalition MPs at the 2022 election.

Politics and leadership aside, the harrowing statistics of gender-based violence remain a dark spot in Australian society, spanning from home and school to work and the media. As Natasha Stott Despoja argued: 'The figures in Australia belie the fact that we consider ourselves an equal, fair, safe nation because clearly, while women and children are living in fear and losing their lives, we're not a safe nation in that respect, and we've got a lot of work to do' (Despoja, 2019). The uncomfortable truth that women in Australia are not safe at work was also publicly acknowledged by the Prime Minister (PM) Scott Morrison at the Women's Safety Summit in September 2021 (ABC News, 2021c; Morrison, 2021). Unfortunately, the situation is not any better in the private sphere. As noted by the PM, every nine days a woman is murdered by a current or former intimate partner, and one in four women experience physical or sexual violence by a current or former intimate partner in Australia. This is, he aptly noted, 'our national shame'.

Equally concerning is the fact that, despite years of research and evidence, far too often structural change still hinges on individuals' willingness and ability to share their trauma with the media and public. Grace Tame, Australian of the Year 2021, is one such example (Burnside, 2021). Ms Tame, a sexual assault survivor, fought to overturn the gag laws preventing victims speaking out in public. When aged 15, she was groomed and raped by her teacher at a private girls' school in Tasmania. Her abuser and the media were able to speak about the event publicly, while Ms Tame herself was silenced by the law. Similarly, while the *Respect@Work* report was released to the public in March 2020, it was Brittany Higgins going public with the allegation she had been raped by a colleague in Parliament House (Wikipedia, 2023; and see Chapter 13) that prompted the national reckoning into the issues it detailed, more than a year later (ABC News, 2021a). Given the extent of data and statistics already available, ministers relying on individuals reliving their trauma in public forums before acting seemed inexcusable.

Finally, the full impacts of the COVID-19 pandemic on gender equality in Australia have continued to work through, and from very early on it was clear that it had differential impacts on men and women. A 2021 Grattan Institute report laid bare the myriad ways in which the COVID-19 pandemic recession created a 'triple-whammy' for women, who were more likely to lose their jobs, more likely to do additional unpaid labour, and less likely to get government support. Mothers in couples and single parents (80 per cent of whom are women) were more likely to leave the paid workforce, further magnifying the long-term economic impacts on women. Curiously however, the federal government's direct financial support and recovery focused on male-dominated construction and energy sectors, while the childcare sector (which is 95 per cent women) was the first one to be taken off the JobKeeper scheme. In addition, Australian federal government decided to discontinue the free childcare arrangement in place during the first set of lockdowns in 2020, despite all the evidence of its crucial role in the economic recovery post-COVID-19 (ABC News, 2020).

Strengths, weaknesses, opportunities and threats (SWOT) analysis

Current strengths	Current weaknesses
Under the Workplace Gender Equality Act 2012 all private sector organisations with more than 100 employees are required to report annually to the Workplace Gender Equality Agency (WGEA) on progress against defined gender equality indicators. Labor ministers have fully implemented the Respect@Work report's recommendations, in particular, the so-called 'positive duty' on companies and organisations to take steps to prevent harassment and discrimination (ABC News, 2021b), and subsequently to shift their culture from punishment to prevention	The gender pay gap has hovered between 14 per cent and 19 per cent for 20 years.
The Australian Public Service (APS) has been an exemplar of good practice, and it managed to close several gender gaps in the workforce, excluding the most senior SES levels. The APS Commission in partnership with the Office for Women conducted a refresh of the APS Gender Equality Strategy, launched in 2021 (APSC, 2021a and 2021b) and expanded in 2023. The federal government agreed in 2021 to Respect@Work's recommendation to amend the 2012 WGEA to cover public sector agencies (they were previously exempt) (Williamson and Colley, 2021).	The WGEA's Public Administration and Safety Industry Snapshot (WGEA, 2023) shows that gender pay gaps remained high in the public services administration and that women's representation ranged from 66 per cent in clerical ranks, to below 30 per cent in manager positions.
The overall figures for women in politics have improved, reaching parity in the federal Senate. Parties that have adopted quotas have witnessed faster improvements in female representations than those that rely on the concept of 'merit'.	The number of women in the House of Representatives improved in 2022 but has long lagged behind changes in the Senate. Significant discrepancies exist between political parties, with those on the centre-right reluctant to adopt quotas.
In recent years, the women's movement has been strongly reinvigorated, as the Teal Independents' progress in 2022 illustrated (see Chapter 5). There has been increased mainstream interest and activism in securing meaningful (50/50) gender equality in professional and senior roles.	Yet the culture of politics remains male-oriented, and benchmarks of success do not reflect the diversity of the Australian population. Due to the negative reputation of politics, young women in Australia are reluctant to pursue a career there, and thus future progress in gender equal representation is not guaranteed.
The women's movement is well represented and very active on social media, and women's prominence on ABC, in other broadcast media and the press has increased (see below).	Polarisation of social media audiences and the increased radicalisation of men's right activists have contributed to a society that is less tolerant of diversity.

Action to reduce violence against women is a prominent area of Labor's Gender Equality Action Plan in 2023, and its salience was dramatised by controversies over abuse of women in Parliament itself, where new codes of practice were needed. Some states (such as Victoria) have longstanding programmes (see Chapter 18) and more are launching initiatives.	Among liberal democracies Australia still has high levels of violence against women. Instances of domestic and gendered violence against women and girls increased in Australia during COVID-19 lockdowns, in line with the Executive Director of UN Women, Phumzile Mlambo-Ngcuke labelling of its global impacts as a 'shadow pandemic' (Mlambo-Ngcuke, 2020).
The United Nations recommended that Australia develop a specific national action plan on violence against Indigenous women (Carlson, 2021), which began to happen in the 2023 National Strategy for Gender Equality (PM&C, 2023a)	While the government's fourth action plan to reduce violence against women and their children (Department of Social Services, 2019) named support for Aboriginal and Torres Strait Islander women and their children as a priority, no real change was evident (Carlson, 2021). Hopes for improvement rest on the strengthened 2023 National Strategy (Prime Minister's and Cabinet Office, 2023a).
Australia has consistently ranked #1 on the women's education indicator in the World Economic Forum's Global Gender Gap Report (2021).	Despite women's workforce participation increasing, they are still more likely to work reduced or part-time hours and take time off from work. The workforce also remains heavily gender segregated, and leadership in the private sector remains male-dominated.
The APS employment database acknowledges gender diversity beyond binaries and classifies data into three categories of gender: Male, Female, and X (with X representing individuals who are indeterminate, unspecified, or intersex). Numerous global and national indices already exist to map out the state of gender equality in Australia in detail. In addition, a wealth of tools and procedures – partly due to learnings from other countries – are now available online through governmental bodies such as the Workplace Gender Equality Agency.	Failure to collect data on sex, sexual orientation and gender identity is likely to result in a service gap to already vulnerable populations (Stephenson and Hayes, 2021). In addition, there is a lack of comprehensive population-wide statistics on violence experienced by LGBTIQ+ people in Australia.
Future opportunities	**Future threats**
Historically, quotas and affirmative measures are divisive in Australia, but where quotas have been implemented, they have been shown to improve gender equality. To help increase both the diversity and the social acceptance of such measures, instead of 'quotas for women' the rhetoric and tools should focus on implementing 40:40:20 gender quotas.	Many Australians still believe in traditional gender norms, and due to structural constraints, unpaid labour in the private sphere is still predominantly done by women. The unequal division of care labour combined with inadequate care infrastructure and high cost of childcare further hamper their paid work prospects. Experience of gender-based violence are high in Australia (see below) and increasing for women.

While COVID-19 was economically disruptive, the experiences of lockdowns also demonstrated that flexible working from home (WFH) practices are possible and may also boost productivity in some settings and roles. Post-COVID-19, flexible WFH practices across different sectors saw some rollback, but left some positive effects on equality, diversity and women's morale more broadly – often creating one or two extra days a week at home for women and many men. In 2023, 37 per cent of employees still regularly worked from home, compared to 40 per cent in 2021 (ABS, 2023b).	The Federal Government's recovery package inadequately addressed the differential impacts of the COVID-19 pandemic on women (Grattan Institute, 2021). For instance, 23 per cent of women reported experiencing high or very high levels of psychological distress, compared with 17 per cent of men (ABS, 2021c). Recovery from the COVID-19 pandemic set back some gender equality developments.
Affordable and/or universal childcare is the single most important factor in determining women's workforce participation. Shared parental leave has been shown to improve engagement, morale and productivity at work. Yet women continue to be the primary carers, and even when offered, men have not used paid parental leave provisions. Critics argue that abolishing the 'primary' and 'secondary' carer labels, along with gender-neutral parental leave provisions, would help change the situation.	When care norms are being discussed, the focus is often solely on children. However, caring duties include people of all ages and abilities. Without adequate care infrastructure in place, an ageing population will put more pressure on women to do unpaid care labour. There has been some progress on incentivising parental leave for men and reducing the stigma associated with taking time off work for care duties.
	Mature aged women are the fastest growing demographic facing homelessness (see later in this chapter).

The rest of the chapter discusses four key aspects of gender equality in detail – political leadership, employment and money, gender and violence, and the media and culture.

Political leadership

Media headlines about the treatment of women in Australian politics highlighted a past culture that was in many ways toxic and hostile to those who do not adhere to traditional male leadership norms. The numbers of prominent women at high levels in political life have been abysmal. Since federation in 1901, there has been only one female Governor-General (Dame Quentin Bryce, from 2008 to 2014), and one female PM (Julia Gillard, from 2010 to 2013). However, there has been some progress in terms of MPs and senators, as Figures 10.1a and 10.1b show. The number of MPs oscillated around 40 (out of 173, below three-tenths) with little definite signs of improvement until 2019 and 2022 due to the Teal Independents' success, and Liberal losses helping parties with more women in winnable (single member) seats. This still meant that there were only 20 more women in the House of Representatives than in 2001 (Figure 10.1a). By contrast, the number of women senators (elected by Single Transferable Vote (STV) in multi-seat competitions) grew more consistently in recent decades, moving from three-tenths in 2001 to over half by 2022 (Figure 10.1b). At the party level, significant differences persisted in 2022, with Labor reaching parity in the lower house, while in the upper house Labor (plus the Greens and the Nationals) had majority female representation (Figure 10.2). By contrast, fewer than one in five Liberal plus National MPs was a woman in 2022, following their losses, although these parties had more women senators.

Figure 10.1: Women politicians at national level

(a) Women in the House of Representatives

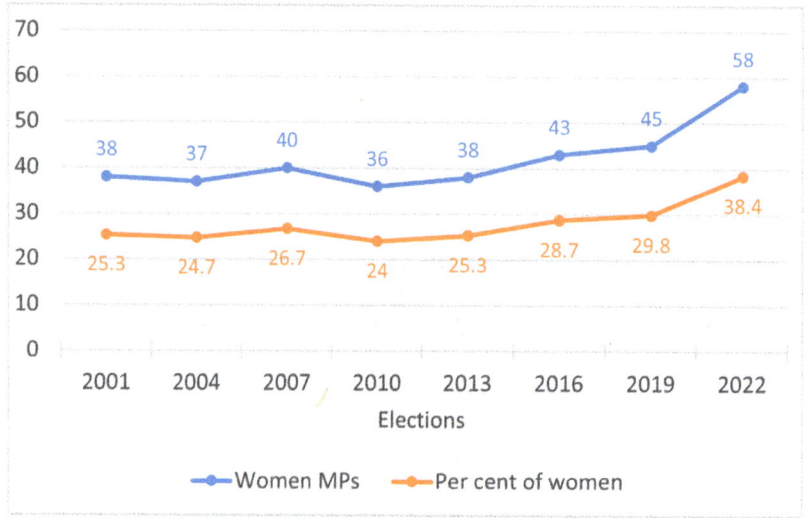

(b) Women in the Senate

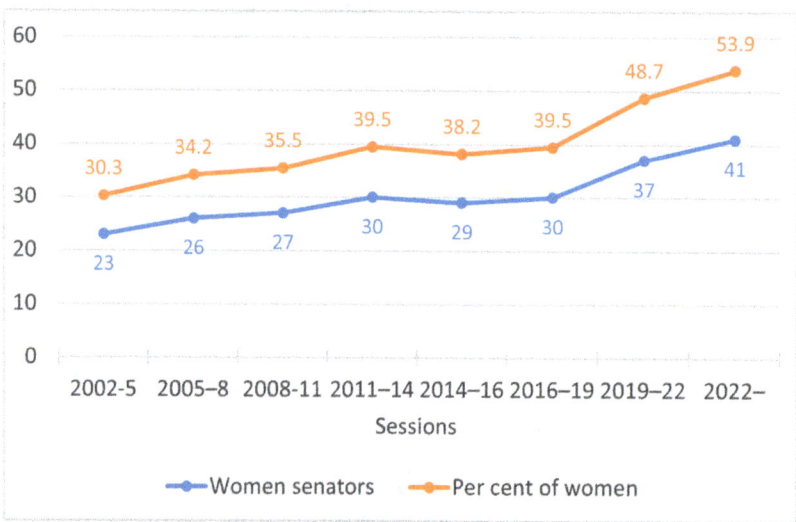

Source: Parliament of Australia (2024); Hough, 2022: Table 2.

Note: In Figures 10.1a and 10.1b the blue lines show the actual number of women legislators, and the orange lines show what percentage of all legislators in the chamber were women.

Gender equality and rights

Figure 10.2: Percentage (%) members who were women, in the Commonwealth House of Representatives and Senate, by party, May 2022

Party	Per cent (%) of House MPs who are women	Per cent (%) of senators who are women	Per cent (%) of each party's Parliamentarians who are women
Labor	47	62	51
Liberal	21	39	28
National	13		27
All other parties		46	55
Total	38	54	44

Source: Computed from Parliament of Australia (2023). Hough, 2022.
Note: General election outcomes. Liberal Party data include Country Liberal Party. Shaded cells indicate N base was too small to calculate percentages.

Figure 10.3: Percentage female representatives by party across all Australian parliaments: State, Territory and Commonwealth upper and lower houses, in 2023 and 2000

Legislature	Per cent (%) women in December 2023	Per cent (%) women in February 2000	Per cent point increase
ACT Legislative Assembly	60	12	48
Commonwealth: Senate	**57**	**29**	**28**
Tasmania Legislative Council	53	27	26
South Australia Legislative Council	50	23	27
Western Australia Legislative Assembly	49	23	26
Northern Territory Legislative Assembly	48	12	36
Tasmania House of Assembly	48	28	20
Victoria Legislative Assembly	46	24	22
NSW Legislative Council	45	21	24
Victoria Legislative Council	45	27	18
NSW Legislative Assembly	41	18	23
Commonwealth: House of Representatives	**39**	**22**	**17**
Western Australia Legislative Council	39	21	18
South Australia House of Assembly	34	30	4
Queensland Legislative Assembly	31	19	12

Source: Parliament of Australia (2020); Hough (2023): Table 1.
Note: As Figure 10.1, per cent numbers here include changes from by-election outcomes up to December 2020. NSW = New South Wales. Numbers in the last column are rounded up or down as appropriate.

In state legislatures much the same patterns occurred as well from 2000 up to 2023 (see Figure 10.3). At this time, Australian Capital Territory (ACT) (at 56 per cent) and Tasmania's upper house (53 per cent) had the highest total level of female representation. In nine other state legislatures, the percentage of women also showed some notable increases (of 20 percentage points or more, from low bases). Queensland's single house and South Australia's lower house showed the lowest levels, with only around a third of their legislators being women (see Figure 10.3).

The key improvements achieved after previous stagnation can be attributed to parties using three main types of quotas: reserved seats; legal candidate quotas; and political party quotas (for a full description on how these function, see Hough, 2021). The Labor Party adopted a mandatory 35 per cent pre-selection quota for women in winnable seats in 1994, which was replaced by the 40:40:20 system (40 per cent men, 40 per cent women, 20 per cent any gender) in 2012, and in 2015 the party adopted targets of securing 45 per cent female representation by 2022 and 50 per cent by 2025. By contrast, the Liberal party in the recent period resisted implementing any form of gender quotas to improve the party's female and gender diverse representation. Internationally, over 100 countries have implemented political gender quotas with clear effects in improving women's representation.

In some parliaments, seats are also reserved for other diversity categories, such as the seven Māori electorates in New Zealand's Parliament (2022). Similar measures could also be considered in Australia, where the lack of diversity in politics has been apparent for years. For example, a report from the Australian Human Rights Commission (2018) showed that only 4 per cent of federal MPs had non-European ancestry, compared to 19 per cent of the Australian population. The underrepresentation of cultural and linguistic diversity is particularly stark for Asian Australians, even though an estimated 15 per cent of the adult population are of Asian heritage (Chiu, 2021).

However, the issue of gender diversity and representation of other diversity attributes cannot be considered in isolation from the direct impact on the decision-making process, including issues that are deemed important and necessary for inclusion in the first place. How Australian politics lags behind becomes apparent when we investigate the structural reforms – or lack thereof – to make the parliament a family-friendly workplace. In recent years there has been a concerted effort for politics to be more inclusive of those with childcaring duties, and in the Australian context where women continue to do most of the care labour, such support is crucial. However, such improvements have sometimes been decades in the making: 'The new Australian Parliament building opened in 1988 with squash courts, a swimming pool, a meditation room but no childcare centre. It took years of campaigning to win one [for children under three] – from 1983 to 2009' (Sawer, no date). The number of politicians who have resigned citing 'family reasons' indicated that past measures are clearly inadequate in meeting the needs of modern parents, although some more family-friendly timings and rules were brought in in July 2022 (McLeod, 2022).

Public sector

The Australian Public Service (APS) put a concerted effort into improving gender equality and diversity in its workforce, with tangible results. As of December 2020, women made up 60 per cent of the whole APS. According to APSC data (see Figure 10.4), women have reached, and in many cases exceeded, parity with men at every level up to and including executive level 1 (EL1). Women also achieved parity at the senior executive service Band 1 classification (SES1), with SES

Figure 10.4: Proportion (%) of Australian Public Service (APS) employees by job classification and gender in December 2020

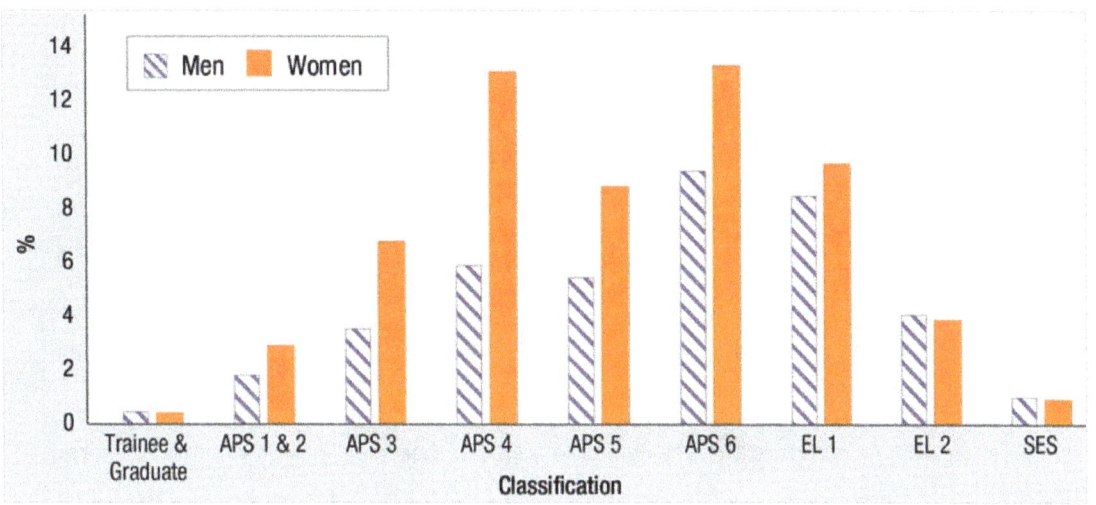

Source: APSC (2020) 'Diversity' in 'APS Employment Data 31 December 2020 release', https://www.apsc.gov.au/employment-data/aps-employment-data-31-december-2020-release/diversity and see also APSC (2021a) and APSC (2021b); Coade (2023).

Note: The grades here run from APS1 and APS2 (the lowest) on the left, in progression up to the SES (Senior Executive Service, the top grade) on the right.

Figure 10.5: Female and male justices and judges, 30 June 2020

	Female justices/judges	Male justices/judges	Per cent (%) female
High Court Justices	3	4	
Federal Court	14	38	27
Family Court	18	20	47
Federal Circuit Court	26	42	38
State Supreme Courts/ Courts of Appeal	49	128	28

Source: Compiled from Australian Bureau of Statistics (ABS) (2020a) 'Gender Indicators, Australia, December 2020'.

Note: Percentages shown for all types of judges where N > 20.

Band 2 and in the SES Band 3 were not far behind, at 44 and 46 per cent respectively. By 2020 the proportion of women joining the SES was also the highest ever recorded (APSC, 2020). In 2020 the government had also reached gender parity on government boards, and women held 52 per cent of positions by July 2023 (PM&C, 2023b).

The judiciary also showed improvements in gender balance, albeit more slowly. As Figure 10.5 shows, women have long been outnumbered by men in all categories, with the widest gap in senior courts. By mid-2020, 37 per cent of Commonwealth justices and judges were women (61 women versus 201 men) – the highest proportion in the past decade. Across all courts the share of women increased to reach 45 per cent of all judges by mid-2023 (AIJA, 2023).

Employment sectors and money

Despite concerted efforts to increase women's workforce participation, significant gender inequalities persist. Women in 2022 comprised 47 per cent of all employed people, but only 38 per cent of all full-time employees; they made up 68 per cent of all part-time employees (WGEA, 2022). In 2023, 71 per cent of men and 62 per cent of women were in work (ABS, 2023a). The labour force participation rate for women is lower than that of men in all age groups, except 15–19 years. Furthermore, while unemployment rates are similar for women and men aged 20–74 (just under 5 per cent), parental status has differential gendered impacts. The unemployment rate for mothers with a dependent child under six years is almost double that of fathers (5.3 per cent and 2.8 per cent). Similarly, the underemployment rate – that is, people in the workforce who want to work more hours and are available – was 10 per cent for women, and 7 per cent for men (ABS, 2023a).

In 2019–20, nearly a third of women (32 per cent) and over one in five men (22 per cent) aged 20–74 years were not in the labour force. The largest gender difference was in the 30–39 age group, where women were around three times more likely than men to be out of the labour force. As the ABS suggests, this may be because women in this age group were more likely to take the major role in childcare. For parents whose youngest child is six years or younger, only around two-thirds (65.5 per cent) of women compared to nine-tenths of men (94.4 per cent) participated in the workforce. While these numbers improved significantly when the youngest child is aged 6–14 years, the rates remained lower for women than men (80.2 per cent and 92.4 per cent respectively), and women worked fewer hours per week than men (ABS, 2023a).

Gender diversity and caring roles cannot be considered in isolation from cultural diversity. Aboriginal and Torres Strait Islander women continue to be under-represented in the workforce. Research indicates that Indigenous women who are also carers face 'triple jeopardy' at work (WGEA, 2021a). In essence, they are more likely to feel unsafe at work, more likely to carry extra expectations to make their workplace culturally sensitive and engaged, and less supported when they encounter racism and unfair treatment.

Australia's workforce has also remained gender-segregated for the past 20 years (WGEA, 2019). In some cases, the proportion of women in traditionally female-dominated industries such as healthcare has increased, while some male-dominated industries (construction and transport) have reported a decline in female representation (see Figure 10.6).

Figure 10.6: Proportions (%) of females and males, 20–74 years old, employed by different industries from 2019 to 2020

Industrial sector	Males (%)	Females (%)	Difference	Comment
Healthcare and social assistance, *mostly government*	22	78	-56	Mostly women
Education and training, *mostly government*	28	72	-43	
Retail trade	45	55	-10	Relatively balanced
Accommodation and food services	46	55	-9	
Administrative and support services [*many in government*]	47	53	-6	
Financial and insurance services	50	50	0	
Arts and recreation services	50	50	0	
Public administration and safety [*mostly government*]	51	49	2	
Rental, hiring and real estate services	52	49	3	
Other services	54	46	9	
Professional, scientific and technical services [*many in government*]	57	43	13	
Information media and telecommunications	61	39	22	Mostly men
Agriculture, forestry and fishing	67	33	33	
Wholesale trade	67	33	34	
Manufacturing	73	28	45	
Electricity, gas, water and waste services	76	24	52	
Transport, postal and warehousing	80	20	60	
Mining	83	17	66	
Construction	87	13	75	

Source: ABS (2023a) 'Gender Indicators: Key economic and social indicators comparing males and females including gender pay gap and life expectancy'.

Note: Sectors with strong government sector employment are noted in italics comment in column 1. Numbers are rounded in all columns.

In the private sector, female representation at leadership levels continued to lag. In 2020, women filled under 33 per cent of key management positions, and were 28 per cent of directors, 18 per cent of CEOs, and under 15 per cent of board chairs (WGEA, 2021b). What's more, 30 per cent of company boards and governing bodies had no female directors (compared with under

1 per cent for boards with no men). However, in public companies, the rates were somewhat better – for example, just over a third of directors in the ASX 200 were women by 2021. Women also progressed into management roles at a faster rate than men, but if the early 2020s rate of progress continue, it would take two decades to reach gender parity in full-time management positions, while for CEOs the WGEA in 2021 estimated that gender equality was still 80 years away.

The COVID-19 pandemic adversely impacted women's paid labour – women were more likely than men to lose jobs and hours during the recession because they were more likely to work in the hardest hit industries and occupations, work part-time (part-timers were more likely to lose jobs) and work in short-term casual jobs which were ineligible for government support such as the JobKeeper scheme (see Grattan Institute, 2021, Figure 2.1). Of course, women's employment improved as the first large-scale lockdowns in 2020 ended, but the Australian Reserve Bank expected unemployment to remain above 5 per cent into 2023.

Gender pay gap

Australia's full-time gender pay gap – calculated by the WGEA using data from the ABS – has barely shifted in the past two decades, and as of May 2021 was 14 per cent, so women's full-time average weekly ordinary time earnings were 86 per cent of men's (WGEA, 2021c) (see Figure 10.7). There were also significant differences between states and territories, which can be partly explained by their different industry profiles. For example, the high gap in Western Australia reflects its concentrated mining and construction sectors, while the majority of the ACT workforce is employed in the public administration and safety sector (see Figure 10.7).

On average, women's weekly earnings across all industries stood at $1,580 compared to men's $1,840, or $261 less than men. If you include overtime payments, the full-time total earnings gender pay gap rose to nearly 17 per cent. Adding in the part-time workforce widened the gap to 31 per cent. In real terms, this means that on average women earned $486 less than men per week. In mid-2023, the ABS found gender pay gaps of 9 to 28 per cent on six different measures (ABS, 2023a).

Figure 10.7: The gender pay gap in full-time adult weekly, ordinary time earnings, by state and territory, May 2021

State/territory	Gender gap
Western Australia	21.9
Queensland	15.8
New South Wales	14.5
Northern Territory	12.7
Victoria	12.2
Tasmania	8.4
Australian Capital Territory	7.9
South Australia	7.0

Source: WGEA (2021c) See Australia's Gender Pay Gap Statistics, 27 August. See also (WGEA 2021d).

In female-dominated organisations the average remuneration has remained lower than in male-dominated ones, and performance pay has played a greater role in male-dominated occupations. Across Australia, the gender pay gap in 2021 was highest in professional, scientific and technical services at 25 per cent, followed by financial and insurance services at 24 per cent and healthcare and social assistance at 21 per cent, and lowest in other services, under 1 per cent, and in public administration and safety at 7.3 per cent (WGEA, 2021c).

The gender pay gap has obvious implications on superannuation as well, with Australian women retiring with 25 per cent less superannuation than men (Australian Super, 2023), although this has improved a lot since 2017. However, the pay gap is not the only reason for this inequality. Women are more likely to take time off paid work for caring duties, more likely to work part-time, more likely to do unpaid labour, and on average still lived four years longer than men by 2023. Women are also more likely to be affected by the 'double penalty effect', where time out from work (or reduced hours) not only reduce their superannuation balance, but also slow down their career progression and future earning potential.

In addition, 2020, some 240,000 women aged 55 or older and another 165,000 women aged 45–54 were at risk of homelessness. Those most at risk were people who:

- had been at risk before
- were not employed full-time
- were an immigrant from a non-English-speaking country
- were in private rental housing
- would have difficulty raising emergency funds
- were Indigenous
- were a one-person household
- were now a lone parent after being married (Faulkner and Lester, 2020).

These risk factors compound each other, and a person's propensity to be at risk of homelessness is cumulative over time.

Parental leave

In Australia, women continue to be more likely to assume the primary care role for the children. In 2019, over 93 per cent of primary parental leave in the non-public sector (paid or unpaid) was taken by women. Just 1 in 20 Australian fathers took primary parental leave, which is low by global standards, and it is influenced by a number of social and economic challenges, including the gender pay gap, the lack of legislated 'shared parental leave' and the labels 'primary' and 'secondary' carer, with limited support available for secondary carers, if at all, and the social norms which reinforce the traditional male/breadwinner, women/carer roles (AIFS, 2019). The high cost of childcare has played a significant role in maintaining these gender roles, since the full-time net childcare fees absorb a quarter of household income for an average earning couple with two children compared to the OECD average of 11 per cent (Wood, Griffiths and Emslie, 2020), and many Australian parents with children under five report that they struggle with the costs (Phillips, 2023).

The 'workforce disincentive rate' is a measure of the financial deterrent facing secondary earners wanting to work more hours. The present disincentive rate has been shown to have a deeply gendered labour market impact since a family's secondary earner is typically female (David, 2020). If both parents earn $60,000 a year and the secondary earner works more than three days a week, the secondary earner loses 90 per cent of the income on the fourth day, and all of it on the fifth day.

Unpaid labour and care

Unpaid labour in the private sphere refers to the cooking, cleaning, household management, caring and family logistics. It is pivotal to the functioning of families and our society more broadly, but its full impacts are often unacknowledged. WGEA estimated that the monetary value of unpaid care work in Australia in 2016 was around $650.1 billion, the equivalent of 50.6 per cent of GDP (WGEA, no date). And Australian women did *311 minutes* of unpaid domestic work and care per day, compared to the OECD female average of 262 minutes (Craig, 2020). On average, women spent 64 per cent of their weekly working time on unpaid care labour, *compared to 36 per cent for men* (WGEA, no date). In real terms, for every hour Australian men committed to unpaid care work, women performed 1 hour and 48 minutes.

It is important to note that caring duties go far beyond dependent children, and rapidly changing demographics will necessitate different types of support infrastructure. In Australia, the prevalence of disability is similar in men (17.6 per cent) and women (17.7 per cent). Around 10.8 per cent of Australians provide unpaid care to people with disability and older Australians, while 3.5 per cent of the population aged 15 and over (861,600 people) are primary carers. Women provide the bulk of this care, representing 7 in every 10 primary carers (ABS, 2019). The ageing population has also generated a phenomenon colloquially referred to as the 'sandwich generation' – that is, people who are in the workforce, while simultaneously caring for their children and their ageing parents. In some scenarios, the women carers may even be helping out with their grandchildren simultaneously, and go through this phase of life while also going through the menopause (Australian Seniors, 2020).

The Albanese government from 2022 onwards signalled that public policies would place more emphasis on upgrading Australia's care economy. Early measures included reforms to sole parent and parental leave policies, equal remuneration initiatives and the enactment of the positive duty of employers to prevent sexual harassment in the workplace.

Gender-based violence

Gender-based violence refers to any act 'that causes or could cause physical, sexual or psychological harm or suffering to women, including threats of harm or coercion, in public or in private life' (OurWatch, no date). In 2015, then Minister for Employment and Minister for Women, Michaelia Cash, proclaimed that violence against women had become a 'national crisis' in Australia – a claim that is still backed up by the current statistics (Cash, 2015). According to OurWatch, 1 in 3 Australian women has experienced physical violence since the age of 15; 1 in 5 has experienced sexual violence; 1 in 3 has experienced physical and/or sexual violence perpetrated by a man since the age of 15 (OurWatch, no date). From 2020–21, the ABS reported that while 6 per cent of males 'experienced sexual violence since the age of 15', that number was over 22 per cent for females (ABS, 2021a). According to the ABS, 2.2 million women and 718,000 men aged 28 and over have experienced sexual violence in their lifetime. Despite policy measures supposedly challenging sexual violence, the prevalence of sexual assault has increased at times for women (notably 2012 to 2016), but not for men (ABS, 2021a). Disconcertingly, in some surveys about sexual violence by a male perpetrator experienced by women, only 26 per cent perceived the incident as a crime at the time.

In general, Australian women have been three times more likely than men to experience violence from an intimate partner – echoing the UN's statement that 'home' is the most dangerous place for women and children worldwide. Family violence can happen to anyone, but some communities have been more vulnerable than others. Women with disabilities have been two times more likely than women without disabilities to have experienced sexual violence and intimate partner violence (ABS, 2021b). The statistics regarding Indigenous women experiencing violence at higher rates than other women in Australia are well documented (Carlson, 2021; AIHW, 2019). For example, Indigenous women are 32 times more likely to be hospitalised as a result of family violence, and five times more likely to die from homicide than non-Indigenous women. In Western Australia, First Nations mothers were 17.5 times more likely to be killed than other mothers.

Aboriginal and Torres Strait Islander peoples are also subject to disproportionate incarceration rates. While they make up around 2 per cent of the national population, they constitute 27 per cent of the prison population, and Aboriginal and Torres Strait Islander women have long constituted over a third (37 per cent in 2021) of the female prison population (ALRC, 2017; Howard-Wagner and Brown, 2021). To put this in context, the rate of Indigenous women's imprisonment is 465 per 100,000, compared to 22 per 100,000 for non-Indigenous women, and 29 per 100,000 for non-Indigenous men. Violence against Indigenous women also extends to government-mandated acts, such as the high rates of removal of children from their families (Family Matters, 2020).

Media coverage of police brutality is less in the Australian media than some countries (such as the USA). But numerous examples show that the authorities often fail to respond accurately (Guardian, 2021), or in the worst case scenario, sometimes further subject Indigenous peoples to violence (SBS, 2020). In addition, the media often frames Indigenous women as 'deserving' of violence rather than condemning the perpetrator (Carlson, 2021). The Queensland Government established a specific Women's Safety and Justice Taskforce, which aims to examine coercive control and review the need for a specific offence of domestic violence, as well as the experience of women across the criminal justice system (Queensland Government, no date). Solutions such as 'women's police stations' have also featured in some debates, but a group of Australian researchers have argued that there is not sufficient evidence of their efficacy (Porter et al., 2021).

Despite the existence of in-depth data and legislative action to address the problem (such as making child sexual abuse a specific criminal offense), resolving high levels of sexual violence does not seem any closer in Australia. In the case of sexual abuse, for example, an estimated 87 per cent of victim-survivors do not report the experience to police, and in the recent past less than 10 per cent of reported cases ended in conviction (ABC News, 2021b). One of the reasons suggested for this has been linked to persistent community attitudes. A historical culture of violence has persisted, which demands that Australian men should be physically and mentally tough (Piper and Stevenson, 2019). And in the case of Indigenous populations, some deeply ingrained assumptions in Australia's colonial history effectively condoned the abuse and murder of women by partners or relatives within Indigenous communities (Carlson, 2021).

Gender, the media and culture

A snapshot of Australia's most influential news sites found that women accounted for only 34 per cent of direct sources quoted in the media, and 24 per cent of indirect sources (that is, sources named but not directly quoted) (Price and Payne, 2019). Men constituted 95 per cent of direct sources in sports-related stories, 82 per cent in business and finance stories, 79 per cent in law, crime and justice stories, and 41 per cent in stories relating to celebrities/

royals. The largest single category of news stories in the dataset related to government and politics (23 per cent), and that category was dominated by male writers, both direct and indirect sources, photographers, and subjects in the photos. The media also portrayed men and women politicians in the past in ways that were starkly different and gendered (Williams, 2017). Comparing the treatment of former PMs, Julia Gillard's and Malcom Turnbull's respective ascensions to leadership, one article found that Gillard was portrayed as the 'backstabbing murderer', while Turnbull was simply 'taking back the reins'.

However, there is hope that change is possible. The Australian national broadcaster ABC News established its 50/50 Project to commission and deliver more content that prioritises diverse women's experiences and perspectives, and to increase the contribution of women as expert talent or commentators and contributors across its programming (ABC News, 2019a). At its founding, men's voices dominated ABC News' coverage, with the male/female split around 70/30; by March 2021, the split was 49/51 in favour of women (Gorman, 2021).

Cultural barriers to gender equality

As the evidence on the many gender gaps shows, despite being seen as a modern democracy, Australia is still in many ways conflicted when it comes to gender equality. On the surface, the vast majority of Australians express egalitarian values, but surveys have shown that people still hold multiple, and often contradictory, value systems when it comes to gender equality in practice (Ghazarian and Lee-Koo, 2021). For example, more than one in three men, and one in four of all Australians still believed that 'it is important to maintain traditional gender roles so that families function well and children are properly supported'. Surprisingly, young men often expressed traditional views, with 35 per cent of Generation Z males (aged 18–23) believing that caring for children is best done by women, and 32 per cent of millennial males believing that men are better suited to leadership roles. In addition, one in three Australians agreed or strongly agreed with the statement: 'Most women do not aspire to leadership positions because they have family responsibilities'. And while two-thirds of Australian women believe that gender equality should be a policy priority in Australia, 35 per cent of men thought that the government is already doing enough to promote equal opportunities for women (Ghazarian and Lee-Koo, 2021).

Perhaps unsurprisingly, given the nature of media coverage of politics and politicians, 63 per cent of women and 53 per cent of men believe that sexism in Australia is most widespread in politics (Ghazarian and Lee-Koo, 2021). Annabel Crabb's TV documentary *Ms Represented* also showed that female politicians across the spectrum report similar experiences when it comes to being heard at work among their colleagues (Crabb, 2021). Terming it 'gender deafness', the former Foreign Minister Julie Bishop (the only female in Tony Abbott's first cabinet) described the way in which ideas by women were often ignored until appropriated by a male colleague. Crabb found evidence this was an enduring phenomenon: South Australia's Dame Nancy Buttfield (Liberal, elected to the Senate in 1955) described this particular experience in exactly the same terms as Greens Senator Sarah Hanson-Young, elected more than half a century later and for a much more progressive party (ABC News, 2017).

In terms of workplace diversity and inclusion, progress has been patchy at best and cultural barriers continue to impact people differently based on their identity markers such as ethnicity, sexuality or gender identity. For example, recent research showed that Indigenous women 'in culturally unsafe workplaces were over 10 times more likely to be often or very often treated unfairly at work than Indigenous women who work in culturally safe businesses, and around 20 times more likely to hear racial or ethnic slurs' (WGEA, 2021a). Same-sex marriage was legalised in 2017, but LGBTIQ+ people continue to experience harassment and hostility in their everyday lives (Powell, Scott and Henry, 2020). And although the Australian Public Service generally appears to perform well on many traditional gender equality markers, some media incidents suggested that discrimination and exclusion takes place within the centre of government. In 2019 PM Scott Morrison 'vowed to "sort out" a gender-inclusive toilet sign posted at his department' (ABC News, 2019b). In 2021 Peter Dutton banned events celebrating the International Day Against Homophobia, Biphobia, Intersexism and Transphobia (IDAHOBIT) in the Department of Defence, noting that while discrimination was not tolerated, he also did not want to pursue the 'woke agenda' (Sydney Morning Herald, 2021). However, the incoming Labor government in 2022 outlined a far-reaching National Strategy to Achieve Gender Equality setting out an ambitious and wide-ranging remit for action (PM&C, 2023a) on many fronts.

Conclusion

Despite many positive developments in the Australian public sector in general, Australia still has a long way to go to reach gender equality in practice. From cultural norms to structural barriers, the myriad ways in which women continue to be marginalised have a profound impact on the validity of our democracy as a whole. As Drude Dahlerup argued: 'Can one honestly speak of democracy if women and minorities are excluded, even if the procedures followed among privileged men in the polity fulfil all the noble criteria of fair elections, deliberation and rotation of positions?' (Dahlerup, 2018). Nor is it simply a matter of legislative change alone, since cultural norms continue to impact people's behaviour long after the structural barriers have been removed, as we have seen with the slow uptake on parental leave among fathers. It is also important to note the difference between formal equality and substantive equality: '[Institutional] practices may not directly discriminate against women, but they can effectively inhibit women's participation by relying on norms reflecting male life patterns as benchmarks of eligibility or success' (Charlesworth, 1995). The positive news is that in the 2020s there seems to have been a greater willingness from our current leaders across the political spectrum to implement and drive this action in many facets of society.

References

ABC News (2017) 'Making *Ms Represented* revealed Australian women in Parliament have one shocking experience in common', *ABC News*, 19 July. https://perma.cc/FF2X-8NRK

ABC News (2019a) 'How our 50:50 Project aims to increase the representation of women on ABC News', *ABC News*, 22 August. https://perma.cc/U6T7-KF5X

ABC News (2019b) 'Scott Morrison vows to "sort out" gender-inclusive toilet sign posted at his department', *ABC News*, 29 August. https://perma.cc/U9YQ-SDDG

ABC News (2020) 'Free child care to end in July after Minister says it did its job during coronavirus', *ABC News*, 8 June. https://perma.cc/VJ7Z-ZFS9

ABC News (2021a) 'Keely has helped thousands of sexual assault survivors, but only knows two who've seen their abuser jailed', *ABC News*, 13 March. https://perma.cc/P4DY-CGAP

ABC News (2021b) 'What were the Respect@Work women's safety recommendations, and how is the government finally acting on them?', *ABC News*, 6 September. https://perma.cc/8MBN-XUMC

ABC News (2021c) 'PM opens women's safety summit with call to change way "some men think they own women"', *ABC News*, 6 September. https://www.abc.net.au/news/2021-09-06/womens-safety-summit-domestic-violence-scott-morrison/100436862

ABS (Australian Bureau of Statistics) (2019) 'Disability, Ageing and Carers, Australia: Summary of Findings'. https://perma.cc/SK5F-CFQU

ABS (Australian Bureau of Statistics) (2020a) 'Gender Indicators, Australia, December 2020' webpage. https://perma.cc/FFM5-4WUH

ABS (Australian Bureau of Statistics) (2021a) 'Sexual Violence – Victimisation', 24 August. https://perma.cc/LFG2-XB2V

ABS (Australian Bureau of Statistics) (2021b) 'Disability and Violence – In Focus: Crime and Justice Statistics', 13 April. https://perma.cc/2TB5-JFQV

ABS (Australian Bureau of Statistics) (2021c) 'Household impacts of COVID-19 survey: Insights into the prevalence and nature of impacts from COVID-19 on households in Australia', 14 July. https://perma.cc/UCE9-3GBC

ABS (Australian Bureau of Statistics) (2023a) 'Gender indicators: Key economic and social indicators comparing males and females including gender pay gap and life expectancy – education' https://perma.cc/WZG9-DDC2

ABS (Australian Bureau of Statistics) (2023b) 'Working arrangements: Working arrangements and forms of employment, such as casual work, fixed-term, independent contractors, shift work, job flexibility and job security', August. https://perma.cc/EE8G-JHXX

AHRC (Australian Human Rights Commission) (2014) 'Face the facts: Lesbian, Gay, Bisexual, Trans and Intersex People'. https://perma.cc/ZYY8-S5UG

AHRC (Australian Human Rights Commission) (2018) *Leading for Change: A Blueprint for Cultural Diversity and Inclusive Leadership Revisited (2018),* Report, 11 April. https://perma.cc/79EX-ZA4X

AHRC (Australian Human Rights Commission) (2020) Respect@Work: Sexual Harassment National Inquiry Report. https://perma.cc/LY7D-H84N

AIHW (Australian Institute of Health and Welfare) (2019) *Family, Domestic and Sexual Violence in Australia: Continuing the National Story*, Cat. no. FDV 3, Canberra: AIHW. https://perma.cc/PCQ4-K9BR

AIFS (Australian Institute of Family Studies) (2019) 'Fathers and parental leave', Emma Walsh, Conference report. https://perma.cc/3WPH-T76S

AIJA (Australian Institute of Judicial Administration) (2023) 'AIJA Judicial Gender Statistics', webpage, June. https://perma.cc/W8HR-2SRN

ALRC (Australian Law Reform Commission) (2017) *Pathways to Justice: An Inquiry into the Incarceration Rate of Aboriginal and Torres Strait Islander Peoples*. Final Report No 133, December. https://perma.cc/9JM7-3377

APSC (Australian Public Services Commission) (2020) 'APS Employment Data – Diversity', APSC webpage. 31 December. https://perma.cc/8MRN-HEDP

APSC (Australian Public Service Commission) (2021a) 'Diversity' in 'APS Employment Data 31 December 2020 release', APSC webpage. https://perma.cc/8MRN-HEDP

APSC (Australian Public Services Commission) (2021b) 'Australian Public Service Gender Equality Strategy refresh', 6 July. https://perma.cc/7H6W-H8G6

Australian Seniors (2020) 'The sandwich generation phenomenon is taking its toll', 12 November. https://perma.cc/3S8L-WM3L

Australian Super (2023) 'Superannuation delivering for Australians, but challenges remain', Blogpost, 29 November. https://perma.cc/D8ZD-PRQT

Burnside, Niki (2021) 'Sexual assault survivor and advocate Grace Tame named 2021 Australian of the Year', *ABC News*. 25 January. https://perma.cc/A5PV-2SLF

Carlson, Bronwyn (2021) 'No public outrage, no vigils: Australia's silence at violence against Indigenous women', *The Conversation*, 16 April. https://perma.cc/5WN2-4C2T

Cash, Michaelia (2015) 'We Have a National Crisis When It Comes to Violence Against Women in Australia', Huffington Post, 11 November. https://perma.cc/WBW7-EGMK

Charlesworth, Hilary (1995) in Slaughter, Anne-Marie, and Hilary Charlesworth. 'The Gender of International Institutions.' Proceedings of the Annual Meeting (American Society of International Law), vol. 89, 1995, pp. 79–85. $ http://www.jstor.org/stable/25658893

Chiu, Osmond (2021) 'Australian politics should be as diverse as its people', *The Interpreter*, Lowry Institute, 23 March. https://perma.cc/W5EN-4BTJ

Coade, Melissa (2023) 'Minister celebrates APS gender parity milestone in latest employment data', *The Mandarin*, 15 September. https://www.themandarin.com.au/230304-minister-celebrates-aps-gender-parity-milestone-in-latest-employment-data/

Crabb, Annabel (2021) 'Making Ms Represented revealed Australian women in Parliament have one shocking experience in common', ABC News, 19 July. https://perma.cc/FF2X-8NRK

Craig, Lyn (2020) 'COVID-19 has laid bare how much we value women's work, and how little we pay for it', *The Conversation*, *Australia*, 21 April. https://perma.cc/2B8N-3943

Dahlerup, Drude (2018) *Has Democracy Failed Women?* Democratic Futures series, Cambridge: Polity Press. $ https://www.wiley.com/en-us/Has+Democracy+Failed+Women%3F-p-9781509516360

David, Fiona (2020) 'We need a new childcare system that encourages women to work, not punishes them for it', *The Conversation*, 13 July https://perma.cc/DLL4-4LAW

Department of Social Services (2019) 'Fourth Action Plan of the National Plan to Reduce Violence against Women and Their Children 2010–2022', Commonwealth of Australia. https://perma.cc/43RH-PPJZ

Despoja, Natasha Stott (2019) '"On Violence" – Interview with Natasha Stott Despoja AM', 50/50 by 2030 Foundation, University of Canberra, 14 April. https://perma.cc/DET7-AK9D

Family Matters (2020) *The Family Matters Report 2020: Measuring trends to turn the tide on the over-representation of Aboriginal AND Torres Strait Islander children in out-of-home care in Australia.* https://apo.org.au/node/309453

Faulkner, Debbie and Lester, Laurence (2020) '400,000 women over 45 are at risk of homelessness in Australia', *The Conversation*, 3 August. https://perma.cc/7LJV-95UD

Ghazarian, Zareh and Lee-Koo, Katrina (eds) (2021) *Gender Politics: Navigating Political Leadership in Australia*, Sydney: New South. Some information about the book here.

Gillard, Julia (2012) 'Julia Gillard's "misogyny speech" in full', ABC News, https://www.abc.net.au/news/2022-12-13/act-national-film-and-sound-archive-2022-sounds-of-australia/101761872 Also available at: https://perma.cc/R93Q-2QS3

Gorman, Ginger (2021) 'How the ABC is smashing the glass ceiling', 50/50 by 2030 Foundation, University of Canberra, 8 July. https://perma.cc/5EN2-ETYQ

Grattan Institute (2021) *Women's work: The impact of the COVID crisis on Australian women*, Wood, Danielle; Griffiths, Kate; and Crowley, Tom, Grattan Institute Report No. 2021-01, March. https://perma.cc/CVH5-9DUZ

Guardian (2021) 'Calls for inquiry after Sydney police arrest Indigenous woman having a panic attack', *Guardian, Australia,* 1 April. https://perma.cc/4G5W-846J

Hamann, Katie (2021) 'What were the Respect@Work women's safety recommendations, and how is the government finally acting on them?', 6 September.

Hough, Anna (2021) 'Quotas for women in parliament', Parliament of Australia, Parliamentary Library, 19 April. https://perma.cc/ZS67-2DXV

Hough, Anna (2022) 'Trends in the gender composition of the Australian parliament', web report, 20 April. https://perma.cc/S89C-9VYM

Hough, Anna (2023) 'Gender composition in Australian parliaments by party: A quick guide', Parliament of Australia, updated 31 May. https://www.aph.gov.au/-/media/05_About_Parliament/54_Parliamentary_Depts/544_Parliamentary_Library/Research_Papers/2022-23/QuickGuide/QC-GenderCompositionAustralianParliamentsMay23.xlsx?la=en&hash=268CACEAF8228CE57B50E51A87F46C84A10AB18A

Howard-Wagner, Deirdre and Brown, Chay (2021) 'Increased incarceration of First Nations women is interwoven with the experience of violence and trauma', *The Conversation*, 6 August. https://perma.cc/4J86-LEAB

Jenkins, Keira (2020) 'NT police officer fined for assaulting two Aboriginal women and a man', NITV News, 25 March. https://perma.cc/TM2G-5PGL

McLeod, Catie (2022) 'Federal parliament to become more family friendly after changes to rules for MPs', news.com.au, 27 July. https://perma.cc/G49U-MYGD

Majumdar, Medha (2021) 'The missing women of Australian politics – research shows the toll of harassment, abuse and stalking'. *The Conversation*, 28 September. https://perma.cc/H4Q6-M37P

Mlambo-Ngcuke, Phumzile (2020) 'Violence against women and girls: The shadow pandemic', UN Womens Organization, 6 April. https://perma.cc/3S5P-L7ES

Morrison, Scott (2021) 'Prime Minister Scott Morrison Women's Safety Speech LIVE | 10 News First', 6 September. On YouTube https://www.youtube.com/watch?v=8ZkyAeOoV0k

Nally, Alicia (2021) 'Women's March 4 Justice: Thousands march at rallies around Australia to protest against gendered violence', *ABC News*, 15 March. https://perma.cc/Z3LG-TE53

New Zealand Parliament (2022) 'MPs and electorates'. https://perma.cc/XXC7-S398

OurWatch (no date) 'Quick facts about violence against women'. https://perma.cc/RGA4-457X

Parliament of Australia (2020) *Women parliamentarians in Australia 1921–2020*, Hough, Anna; Wilson, Janet; and Black, David, Parliamentary Library Research Paper Series, 2020–21, updated 9 December. https://perma.cc/X3CF-MR9Z

Parliament of Australia (2023) 'The gender composition of the 45th Parliament', webpage. https://perma.cc/6VTZ-89YC

Parliament of Australia (2024) 'Gender composition in each Parliament', Parliament webpage, https://perma.cc/AN5D-6H96

Phillips, Ben (2023) 'Yes, childcare is costly, but nowhere near as costly as recent reports suggest – here's why', *The Conversation, Australia.* 30 October. https://perma.cc/96AA-A3ST

Piper, Alan and Stevenson, Ana (2019) 'The long history of gender violence in Australia, and why it matters today', *The Conversation*, 14 July. https://perma.cc/E8KZ-JF6P

Porter, Amanda; Deslandes, Ann Louise; McKinnon, Crystal; and Longbottom, Marlene (2021) 'Women's police stations in Australia: Would they work for "all" women?'. *The Conversation*, 17 September. https://perma.cc/89V5-DJE8

Powell, Anastasia; Scott, Adrian J; and Henry, Nicola (2020) 'Digital harassment and abuse: Experiences of sexuality and gender minority adults', *European Journal of Criminology*, vol. 17, no. 2, pp.199–223. https://doi.org/10.1177/1477370818788006

Price, Jenna and Payne, Anne Maree (2019) *2019 Women for Media Report: You Can't Be What You Can't See*. Women's Leadership Institute Australia. https://perma.cc/KK6Q-8WUA

Prime Minister and Cabinet Office (PM&C) (2023a) 'National Strategy to Achieve Gender Equality, Discussion Paper, National Strategy to Achieve Gender Equality Consultations'. https://perma.cc/5VYM-E3CG

Prime Minister and Cabinet Office (PM&C) (2023b) 'Gender balance on Australian government boards', webpage July. https://perma.cc/7A43-MWPG

Queensland Government (no date) 'About the Women's Safety and Justice Taskforce', webpage. https://perma.cc/4AHU-JF7B

Sawer, Marian (no date) 'Australian parliaments – still not family friendly', *ANU Reporter*, vol 48, no. 2.

SBS (2020) 'NT police officer fined for assaulting two Aboriginal women and a man', SBS, 25 March. https://perma.cc/TM2G-5PGL

Stephenson, Elise and Hayes, Jack (2021) 'LGBTIQ+ people are being ignored in the census again. Not only is this discriminatory, it's bad public policy', *The Conversation*, 10 August. https://perma.cc/Y6FN-PBPH

Sydney Morning Herald (2021) 'Defence emails reveal staff shame at Dutton's "tone-deaf" IDAHOBIT morning tea ban', *Sydney Morning Herald*, 14 October. https://perma.cc/SU48-5Y8B

Victoria Parliament (2020) 'Gender Equality Act 2020'. https://perma.cc/SH68-CDL2

Victoria Public Sector Gender Equality Commissioner (2021) website: https://perma.cc/U3JB-6KTR

WGEA (Workplace Gender Equality Agency) (no date) 'Unpaid care work and the labour market', Insight Paper. https://perma.cc/6WAX-Q5EX

WGEA (Workplace Gender Equality Agency) (2019) 'Gender segregation in Australia's workforce'. 17 April. https://perma.cc/R39V-JQB8

WGEA (Workplace Gender Equality Agency) (2021a) 'Australian-first research on Indigenous women's working lives reveals Aboriginal and Torres Strait Islander mums and carers most at risk at work', 26 October. https://perma.cc/Q32K-YRVA

WGEA (Workplace Gender Equality Agency) (2021b) 'Gender workplace statistics at a glance 2021', 19 August. https://perma.cc/PP9V-FXKM

WGEA Workplace Gender Equality Agency (2021c) 'Gender workplace statistics at a glance 2021', 24 February. https://perma.cc/N6ZW-7JMM

WGEA Workplace Gender Equality Agency (2021d) 'Gender pay gap data', Webpage https://www.wgea.gov.au/pay-and-gender/gender-pay-gap-data

WGEA Workplace Gender Equality Agency (2022) 'Gender equality workplace statistics at a glance 2022', WGEA webpage, 24 February 2022. https://perma.cc/N6ZW-7JMM

WGEA (Workplace Gender Equality Agency) (2023) 'Public Administration and Safety Industry Snapshot', Webpage. https://perma.cc/BZG5-YLGA

Wikipedia (2023) '2021 Australian Parliament House sexual misconduct allegations', webpage. https://perma.cc/AHR9-5MVE

Williams, Blair (2017) 'A gendered media analysis of the prime ministerial ascension of Gillard and Turnbull: he's "taken back the reins" and she's "a backstabbing' murderer". *Australian Journal of Political Science,* vol. 52, no. 4, pp.550–64. $ https://doi.org/10.1080/10361146.2017.1374347

Williamson, Sue and Colley, Linda (2021) 'The public sector to report on gender equality', *The Mandarin*, 9 April. https://perma.cc/Z4SM-RVT4

Wood, Danielle; Griffiths, Kate; and Emslie, Owain (2020) 'Permanently raising the Child Care Subsidy is an economic opportunity too good to miss', *The Conversation*, 26 April. https://perma.cc/63FM-6F6C

World Economic Forum (2021) 'Global Gender Gap Report 2021', March. https://perma.cc/YC5Q-FY5A

III

Federal Government

11. Parliament – the House of Representatives 231
    Sarah Moulds

12. Parliament – the Senate 253
    Brenton Prosser, Mary Walsh and John Hawkins

13. Prime Minister, Cabinet and government 275
    Mark Evans and Patrick Dunleavy

14. The Australian Public Service 301
    John Halligan and Mark Evans

15. Government policy-making 326
    John Butcher

16. How democratic is Australian federalism? 346
    John Phillimore and Alan Fenna

11

Parliament – the House of Representatives

Sarah Moulds

The House of Representatives forms one half of Australia's bicameral (two-chamber) national Parliament. To exercise its important representative and law-making functions, its members (MPs) meet in Canberra for an average of only 67 days (20 sitting weeks) of the year. Often described as the 'lower chamber' or the 'People's House', the eucalypt-green hues of its décor provide the critical backdrop for Australian government. The Prime Minister (PM) must be an MP, and the majority of government ministers in practice also. The House of Representatives shares many of the same law-making powers as the Senate, but is pre-eminent in budget roles. (Australia's Constitution limits the Senate's ability to introduce 'money bills' or laws that seek to appropriate funds for government expenditure).

In order to form a stable government, the PM must be able to survive a no confidence vote in the House, and normally control a majority of MPs to pass legislation. The Alternative Vote (AV) system used to elect MPs (see Chapter 5) has almost always delivered a clear majority for either the Liberal-National Coalition or the Australian Labor Party (ALP) in modern times – with the significant exception of 2010 to 2013 when a Labor government relied on support from a handful of Independent MPs to survive in a 'hung parliament'.

What does democracy require for the federal legislature?

(i) Focusing national debate, and scrutinising and controlling major decisions by the executive

- Elected representatives should normally maintain full public control of federal government services and state operations, ensuring public and parliamentary accountability through conditionally supporting the government, and articulating reasoned opposition, via its proceedings.
- The House of Representatives' floor debates and question times should be a critically important focus of national political debate, articulating 'public opinion' in ways that provide useful guidance to the government in making complex policy choices.

How to cite this chapter:

Moulds, Sarah (2024) 'Parliament – the House of Representatives', in: Evans, Mark; Dunleavy, Patrick and Phillimore, John (eds) *Australia's Evolving Democracy: A New Democratic Audit,* London: LSE Press, pp.231–251. **https://doi.org/10.31389/lsepress.ada.k** Licence: CC-BY-NC 4.0

- Federal legislators should regularly and influentially scrutinise the current implementation of policies, and the efficiency and effectiveness of federal government services and policy delivery.
- Individually and collectively, federal legislators should seek to uncover and publicise issues of public concern and citizens' grievances, giving effective representation both to majority and minority views, and showing a consensus regard for serving the public interest.

(ii) *Passing laws and controlling the executive's detailed policies*

- In the preparation of new laws, the federal legislature should supervise federal government consultations and help ensure effective pre-legislative scrutiny.
- In considering legislation, the federal parliament should undertake close scrutiny in a climate of effective deliberation, seeking to identify and maximise a national consensus where feasible.
- Ideally, pre-legislative scrutiny will ensure that the consequences of new laws are fully anticipated, changes are made to avert 'policy disasters' and risks are assigned to those societal interests which can most easily insure against them.

The chapter begins by surveying recent changes in the lower house and then moves on to summarise the key strengths, weaknesses, opportunities and threats surrounding its operations from a democratic point of view.

Recent developments

In recent years, two key aspects of the House of Representatives' operations have dominated public attention – the long-run two-party and executive dominance over MPs, and the shorter term proliferation of delegated executive law-making during the COVID-19 period 2020 to 2022 – which for a time reduced the legislature's ability to control government and ministerial behaviour. The chapter considers each in turn, before moving to a summary of the strengths and weaknesses of the House of Representatives mapped against the criteria above. After this SWOT analysis, three sections explore key aspects of the House of Representatives' operations in more detail – daily Question Time; how the House scrutinises legislation; and how it seeks to engage with Australian citizens.

Executive and two-party dominance in the House of Representatives

The Australian Constitution provides for the separation of different branches of government (the legislature, the executive and the judiciary) and puts in place some strong legal safeguards against unbridled executive power, including the doctrine of responsible government within the federal parliament (Hamer, B, 2004; Hamer, D, 2004; Kerr, 2009). However, (following British practice at the time of founding) the text of the Australian Constitution does not provide any explicit description of the relationship between ministers and the Parliament. As in the UK, disciplined political parties have thrived and become the key vehicles facilitating executive dominance of the House of Representatives (Prasser, 2012).

Debates within the House of Representatives often appear to be locked into binary political positions, with MPs generally voting on 'whipped', partisan lines, creating a ritualistic series of exchanges whose outcomes are almost always predictable in advance. The long-term predominance of the top two parties (Labor and the Liberal-National Coalition) has accentuated this pattern, with the Nationals the smaller component in the Coalition holding around 15–16 seats in recent elections (Figure 11.1). All other representatives were in single figures until 2022 (Figure 11.1). However, the Greens, Katter and Xenophon/Centre Alliance at least established a continuous presence across multiple recent elections. And in 2022, the electoral arrival of the Teal Independents boosted the independent total to 10 seats, and with the Greens winning four seats too, this meant that MPs outside the top two parties made up more than one-tenth of the House for the first time.

Robust exchanges between MPs also occur behind the scenes, including in cabinet and within the party room of the majority ruling political party, mostly outside of the parliamentary or public gaze. Individual MPs may be subject to formal or informal party disciplinary action for dissent seen as lack of loyalty or other indiscretions. The powerful influence exerted by the party room of the governing political party, and in particular by the cabinet, has dominated much political discourse in recent years (Parliament of Australia, no date, a). During the COVID-19 period, executive dominance modes of decision-making were also extended within the Australian federal system in the form of the 'National Cabinet', providing a ministerial-level forum for state, territory and federal governments around Australia to respond to the pandemic (see Chapter 13).

Figure 11.1: Parties' seats in the House of Representatives, 2000 to 2022

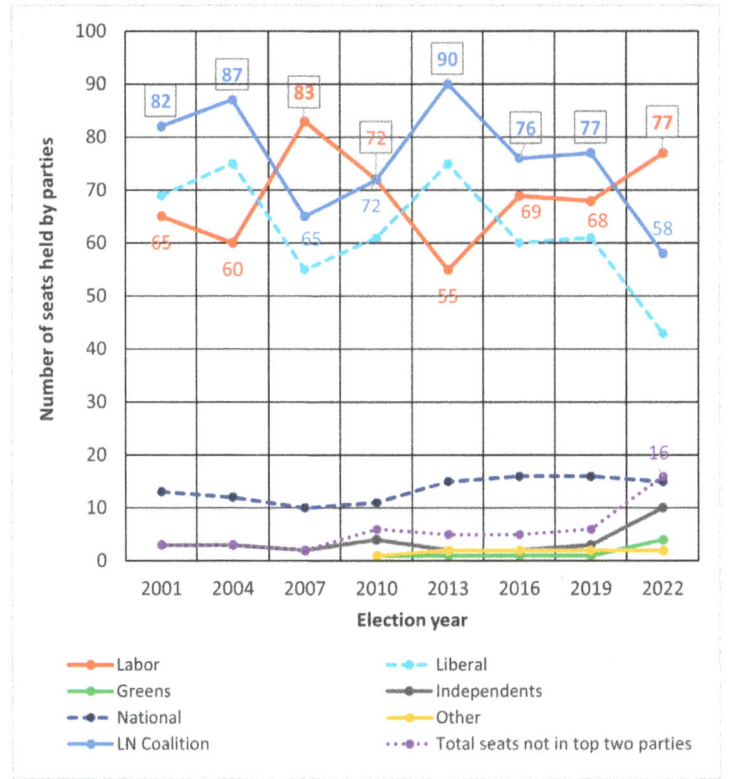

Source: Parliament of Australia (no date, b), 'Political Parties in the House of Representatives', Info sheet no. 22 'Political Parties'.

Note: There were 150 Members in the House of Representatives until 2016, and 151 since 2019. A majority needed 76 votes throughout the period and parties above this level are shown in bold. For the party forming the ministry, numbers are shown boxed. There was a minority Labor ministry 2010 to 2013, with backing from other MPs.

In their day-to-day behaviours in the House of Representatives, MPs from the Liberal-National Coalition and the Australian Labor Party have almost always supported the official party 'line' even on controversial moral or ethical issues. However, there have been examples of weakened party cohesion, particularly when party leaders (both PMs or Leaders of the Opposition) were showing signs of declining popularity or support, or had just lost a general election. Government 'backbenchers' (MPs from the ruling government party not holding ministerial posts) have on occasion 'broken the party line', rebelling in order to attract attention to a particular issue of key interest to their electorate (7 News, 2021). At other times, a dissident vote may form part of a political manoeuvre to exercise influence over their political colleagues (Sloane, 2022).

The parliamentary branch of the ALP has been dominated for decades by strongly developed 'factions' associated with different state groupings of MPs and left/right ideological positions (Leigh, 2000). In the 2010 to 2013 Labor Government, intra-party faction fights among MPs and senators produced rapid changes of leaders in the 'Rudd-Gillard-Rudd' period (Gauja et al., 2012). New party rules subsequently required the federal ALP leader to be chosen by a vote of grass-roots party members, and not just the 'party room' in Parliament (as was the case 2010 to 2016). But Anthony Albanese was elected unopposed as leader following Labor's 2019 defeat (see Chapter 6). Following his party's 2022 return to power, he promised to pursue a consensual style of governance, not least because of Labor's knife-edge majority in the House.

Party caucus control has generally remained the order of the day for the Liberal and National parties (Kam, 2009). When the Coalition is in power, two different 'party rooms' support different leaders – the Liberals choosing the PM (who picks most ministers from Liberal ranks), and the Nationals choosing the Deputy PM (who picks a sub-set of ministers) (PEO, no date). Out of power, the party rooms also choose the leader and deputy leader of opposition. Outside Queensland, relatively few MPs are elected as National Party members. National Party members seek to emphasise rural Australian interests and some have strong opposition to green environmental issues.

While the Liberal-National Coalition historically strove to create an appearance of unity, more recently deepening divides on policy issues, including on the issue of climate change (ABC News, 2021a), led to increasing instability, sometimes with dramatic consequences (Cockfield, 2021). Two Liberal PMs in turn lost the confidence of the Liberal Party room and were replaced after 'spill' votes to eject them from leadership, Abbot in 2015 (Hurst, 2015; and see Tiffen, 2017) and Turnbull in 2018 (Beaumont, 2018). The Nationals have also seen ministers and leaders resign over scandals and policy divisions that threatened to disrupt relations between the coalition parties (Guardian, 2020).

Internal party politics, and personality-based disagreements and scandals, have sometimes hampered MPs from the more urgent tasks of policy development and community engagement (Australian Financial Review, 2021b). The hegemony of party-political interests associated with the Liberal-National Coalition and the ALP can work to dilute the effectiveness of scrutiny of legislation and other accountability mechanisms, including Question Time (see later in this chapter). Critics have also suggested that these factional tensions in both major parties have undermined the ability of the House of Representatives to effectively articulate 'public opinion' in ways that provide useful guidance to the federal government in making complex policy choices and to identify and maximise a national consensus where feasible (O'Brien, 1986). This has been especially apparent when it comes to complex policy challenges such as climate policies (Hanna, no date) or transitioning Australia's economy – a challenge that has plagued both Labor and Liberal governments in recent years, despite polls indicating strong public

Figure 11.2: Ministers as a share of all MPs in the House of Representatives, and of the governing party's MPs, 1951 to 2022

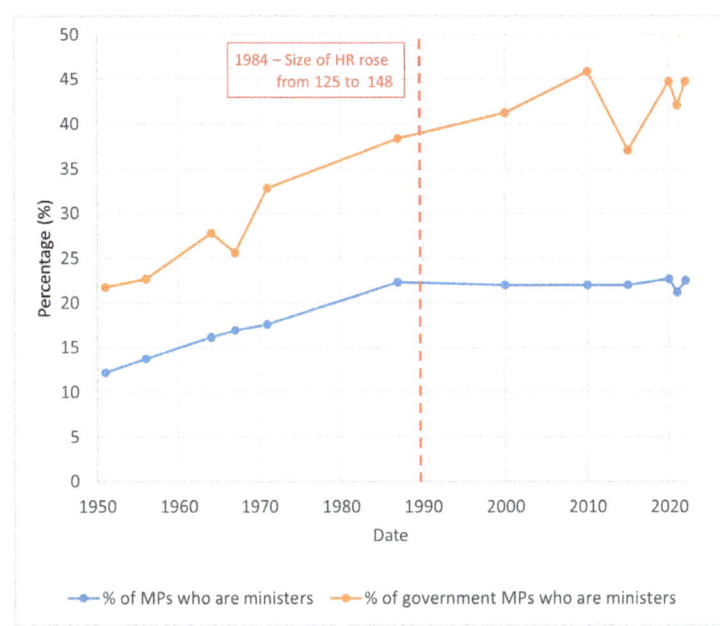

Source: Compiled from Parliament of Australia (2021a), 'Appendix 10 – Party affiliations in the House of Representatives' and Wikipedia (2024), 'Albanese ministry'.

Note: The size of the House increased from 125 to 148 seats in 1984, as shown by the red dotted vertical line.

support for achieving net zero carbon emissions by 2050 (Lowy Institute, 2021; Hanna, no date). Yet the 2022 elections marked some change from the previously stark top-two party character of the House of Representatives, with new MPs for the Teal Independents securing election and increased conservative prominence for global warming, integrity in politics, and women's issues, previously seen as neglected by the coalition parties (see Chapter 5).

The small size of the House of Representatives has always accentuated the ease of party control over its operations. With just 151 MPs (far smaller than the 650 lower house members in the UK or the 450 in the USA), any grouping of 76 or more MPs commands a majority. In recent times, closer party competition has meant that few governments have had more than 85 MPs backing them. Under the 'Westminster system' all ministerial positions have to be filled by MPs or senators, covering 23 cabinet ministers, plus an 'outer ministry' of 7, and 12 Parliamentary secretaries – 42 positions in all. Two-thirds of ministers are MPs, so taking these 28 ministers out means that a government may have just 48 backbench MPs, and rarely more than 57. Any government will account for a fifth of all MPs, and after close-run elections for over two-fifths of the majority party's MPs (Figure 11.2). Put another way, a PM who can keep their ministers loyal (admittedly a hard thing to do at some key points), plus retain support from 12–20 more backbench MPs (depending on the majority party's size), can in theory retain control within their parliamentary party and thus the House. They have a well-developed system of party discipline enforced by whips to help them do that.

This system of 'whipping votes' and strong party discipline has recently been associated with bullying behaviour within the parliament (Lambert, 2021), particularly when used against female MPs by male colleagues in powerful ministerial positions (see Chapter 13). It remains to be seen whether the tight control historically exercised by Australian PMs over their parliamentary colleagues continues to characterise future House of Representatives.

Some commentators have argued that Australian voters are tired of the spectacle and drama of in-fighting within and between the major political parties, and have seen this mood as underlying a turn to non-party candidates to represent their interests – perhaps even an 'age of Independence' (Rodrigues and Brenton, 2010). Following the 2022 elections, the top party balance in the House was close. And the presence of Greens, Teal Independents and other independents contributed to the development of a more consensual style by the new Labor PM, Anthony Albanese, which seemed successful in securing him strong opinion poll support for his first year in office, but may be challenging to sustain over the full parliamentary term.

COVID-19 and House operations

Members of the House of Representatives represent electoral divisions with an average of just under 109,000 voters, but they span across a whole continent. The largest area represented by one MP has been Durack in Western Australia spanning across approximately 1.6 million sq. km, while the smallest has been Grayndler in New South Wales with an area of 32 sq. km. Many MPs come from areas of NSW and Victoria quite close to Canberra, but most still have to fly in for the three bursts of sitting weeks each year. Parliamentary arrangements have always had to meet the travel needs of the farthest flung MPs, but they have always focused on face-to-face interactions in the main chamber and in committee sessions.

The COVID-19 pandemic had a profound impact on both the policy and law-making focus of the House of Representatives and how it conducted parliamentary business (Grattan, 2020). In August 2020, for the first time, the Australian Parliament fully embraced a 'hybrid model' of parliamentary sittings (Moulds, 2020a), because some MPs were unable to travel to Canberra for health reasons or due to COVID-19 border restrictions imposed by states on travellers from other states (ABC News, 2020). The hybrid model involved some in-person attendance by MPs in the chamber (with social distance protocols observed) and other MPs participating via secure video link. This way of working became an ongoing feature within the House as the pandemic progressed, with the inclusion of perspex screens at the dispatch box and other protective measures including masks being used during sittings in 2021.

The remote access features employed in the Chamber sessions of the whole House drew from the more familiar practice of remote sittings employed by parliamentary committees. For some time prior to the pandemic, committees had experimented with the use of video and telephone links to enable witnesses and MPs to contribute to committee discussions from remote locations. However, even with these new arrangements, House sitting days were reduced during the early stages of the pandemic, leaving some to raise questions about the extent to which a partially constituted House could continue to perform its important democratic functions and uphold the traditionally claimed virtues of the Westminster model of responsible government. And while the parliamentary committees in the Senate experimented with digital communication technologies and social media as they set about scrutinising ministers' pandemic responses, the House committees were far less active or experimental in their approach to scrutiny of government action.

Strengths, weaknesses, opportunities and threats (SWOT) analysis

Current strengths	Current weaknesses
Historically the House of Representatives followed many of the adversarial traditions of the UK's House of Commons, but evolved its own distinctive practices – which aim to promote orderly parliamentary business and debate (organised on party lines) and direct ministerial accountability. They are premised on the assumption that the best outcomes will emerge through a robust contest of opposing ideas. However, within these traditions bi-partisan cooperation has often emerged on less controversial legislation.	Historically, much of the House of Representatives' time and energy have been consumed in strongly partisan behaviours that critics saw as often ritualistic, point-scoring or unproductive in terms of developing and enacting legislation (Williams, 2020) and that were found to be unacceptable and contributing to an unsafe working environment for women (Jenkins, 2021). Deliberative debate and efforts to achieve policy objectives in line with community needs and interests have often seemed to take second place to electioneering and maximising party interests.
Government legislation takes up half of the House's annual 670 hours of sessions, and other routine House business and processes absorb another 20 per cent. Yet there has generally been a high level of collaboration of government and opposition and cross-bench to manage legislation and other business of the House. And a large number of Bills introduced by the government receive opposition or cross-party support (Parliament of Australia, no date, c). While government MPs have the power to apply guillotine motions to curtail debate, such measures are relatively rarely used, although government management of the House business can be used to stymie debate at times.	No MPs except ministers (notionally acting with the Governor-General's approval) can propose legislation that increases government appropriations in any way, severely limiting individual MPs' abilities to influence the implementation of public policy without first garnishing ministerial support. This means that although approximately 30 per cent of the business conducted in the House of Representatives has been allocated to private member business, few laws or policy changes result from proposals introduced by non-government members or backbenchers without ministerial support, except on some conscience issues (Warhurst, 2008).
The Speaker has an important role, enshrined in section 35 of the Constitution, and chairs the meetings of the House in line with that and the Standing Orders. Although regarded as a political appointment, successive Speakers have endeavoured to act with impartiality and have generally engendered respect from MPs regardless of their party.	The Speaker has been an MP drawn from the majority party, and so rarely acts strongly against its interests. As in the UK, almost all the key rules governing MPs' behaviour are embodied in Standing Orders, which can be altered by a simple majority vote of MPs. So the government party has normally been able to construe or alter them in ways it prefers.
A key role of the Speaker has been to moderate oral Question Time in the House, where ministers must give immediate answers to queries without notice. A highly dramatic setting, Question Time offers citizens an important opportunity to judge whether their performance entitles the government to re-election (Parliament of Australia, 2021b).	Critics argue that Question Time proceedings can be shouty, combative and highly adversarial in nature, with many examples of condescending, irrelevant speech and disrespectful behaviours being displayed by members from the full spectrum of political parties (Melleuish, 2021). Historically, the Speaker has not usually been able to constrain the PM or other ministers to answer the specific question asked, rather than government responses making more general political points.

Legislative scrutiny, including through parliamentary committees and the bicameral system, has remained an important constraint on governments' behaviour. It has caused the inclusion of safeguards in new laws that promote parliamentary oversight and set limits on the use of executive power. Legislation has often been passed following amendments moved in response to House or Senate Committees and with cross-party agreement. The House has 17 committees that consider legislation and scrutinise departmental activities and spending.	Party dominance of the committee stage of legislation can mean that poorly drafted laws reach the statute book unchanged. Although MPs accept many Senate amendments to bills that have previously been passed by the House, most of these changes usually come in the form of amendments proposed by government ministers (Moulds, 2020b). Minsters may be unwilling to adopt even sensible legislative amendments if the government of the day 'has the numbers' to pass the legislation in its original form. So, the interactions between the two chambers of parliament can – but do not always – result in constraining executive dominance.
Committee hearings in public allow a wide range of groups in society to give evidence and put their case directly to legislators, in a high-profile public setting. Committee chairs and secretariat staff are increasingly embracing innovative ways of reaching out to seldom-heard communities for their views.	Government MPs have normally formed the majority in all House committees, giving the government effective control over their activities and recommendations. Party discipline has often worked to limit these committees from achieving an independent voice, applying robust scrutiny to government policy or representing a more impartial position in response to the evidence received.
The budget process makes up a large and important part of House proceedings and MPs have much more collective influence on government spending than the Senate can have. Budget reports to parliament are detailed and form an important part of federal administration accountability.	Budget debates in the House often descend into party-political battles, with little detailed focus on budget performance, or the policy objectives justifying specific expenditure.
Future opportunities	**Future threats**
The COVID-19 pandemic saw the House of Representatives experiment with the use of digital technologies to facilitate remote participation in sittings and debates, and to connect with community members and experts engaging with House Committees (Mills, 2020). The experience demonstrated the potential to use digital technology to diversify the range of people engaging with the House and its processes. If developed further there could be a potential for MPs to reach younger people and groups previously disconnected from House affairs, as well as adding extra channels for the already well-informed.	As the COVID-19 pandemic fades into the past, so too have hopes that the experience would provide a catalyst for the House of Representatives to embrace digital technologies to help Australians understand the business of the House. Many Australians remain disillusioned with and disconnected to their national parliament and their state counterparts.

The pandemic also provided new opportunities for Australia to rethink its federal structure, including the way the House of Representatives engages with state premiers and Chief Ministers from the territories. (Many Australians were also forced to pay much closer attention to the announcements from the state's premiers and parliament than they were accustomed to, sparking some voter frustration – see Chapter 13). However, this also fostered an important 'liaison role' for members of the House. Some House MPs were able to act as important conduits between their constituents and federal ministers and cabinet during the pandemic – for example, by raising the interests of individuals particularly harshly impacted by decisions at both the state and federal level. Combined with the growth of more independent MPs, a renewed focus on 'local' issues (and on a more bi-partisan issue) by members of the House of Representatives could provide some counter-weight to overly strong party-political dominance and encourage more active community engagement.	During the COVID-19 pandemic, state premiers and parliaments exercised their constitutional authority to make laws in response to emergencies and to insulate their populations from others. Apart from issues around controlling entry to Australia, some commentators argued that this left the federal parliament wondering what its job was. This was perhaps particularly problematic for the House of Representatives, where MPs are obliged to rather 'artificially' express the interests of their electorates at the 'national level', despite their constituents' immediate focus being on the delivery of services and decisions being made at the state and territory level.
A growing trend towards independent candidates winning House seats might also increase the diversity of parliament, raise the profile of new policy issues and public interests and temper the influence of the major parties.	Traditional party-structured parliamentary processes in the House of Representatives may not adapt very well to the presence of MPs who 'blur' the party divide after a close election outcome, as with the new group of Teal Independents elected in 2022 (Nikkei-Asia, 2022).
In the Uluru Statement from the Heart (2017) First Nations peoples called for a constitutionally enshrined First Nations Voice to Parliament and a Makarrata Commission to supervise a process of agreement-making and truth-telling. If implemented, these measures could begin to chart a pathway towards genuine reconciliation between First Nations Australians and the broader community.	The Australian Parliament historically excluded Indigenous Peoples' voices (Maddison, 2010). However, recent elections have seen some modest increases in Aboriginal representation in the federal parliament. By July 2022, three MPs (and eight senators) were First Nations peoples (PEO, 2022; Larkin and Galloway, 2021). Despite this, progress on realising the constructive dialogue and historical redress-making called for in the Uluru Statement (2017) remains slow and partial. In early 2023, the federal parliament enacted legislation that triggered a constitutional referendum on the proposal to establish a First Nations Voice. In October 2023, under the constitutionally prescribed referendum procedure, the people of Australia voted to oppose the First Nations Voice proposal (see Chapter 4). This outcome has created uncertainty about the future implementation of other aspects of the Uluru Statement from the Heart (2017), particularly at the federal level.

Legislatures are complex institutions and their detailed processes carry out a range of functions. The chapter next considers three key operations of the House – daily Question Time; the way that the House scrutinises legislation including through the committee system and budgetary control processes; and how the House goes about representing and engaging with Australian citizens.

Question Time

When the House of Representatives is sitting – that is, from February to April (the Autumn sittings), May to June (the Budget sittings) and August to December (the Spring sittings) – the first hour of every day has been reserved for Question Time when MPs can put oral questions without notice to the PM or ministers, who are all expected to attend. The Leader of the Opposition has been guaranteed three questions to the PM, and other slots are allocated by the Speaker to MPs in strict party alternation. Whereas the British PM must attend the House of Commons for questions only for one half an hour per week, Question Time in the Australian House has historically provided a more important and intensive level of parliamentary oversight and accountability. However, the informational quality of the exchanges often leaves observers frustrated and disappointed (Turpin, 2012).

Question Time in the House has often descended into a type of 'gladiatorial combat', where the two party leaders battle for the attention of their parliamentary colleagues and attending journalists, lying in wait to capture the best 'one liners' for the evening news (Allington, no date). Question-and-response exchanges have almost always been lively, and sometimes raucous, with government and opposition MPs using a wide range of theatrical techniques to 'drown out' or intimidate their political opponents. Unsurprisingly, clips from Question Time have formed a key part of the Australian broadcast media's staple diet. They have powerfully shaped and coloured most voters' views of what federal parliamentary proceedings are like.

Both government and opposition front-benchers must carefully prepare their strategies for Question Time. The PM and ministers have relied for some relief on the rule that the Speaker must take questions from government and opposition MPs' in strict alternation. Empirical studies have shown that 97 per cent of questions from government party MPs are 'Dorothy Dixer' or bogus questions (named after a historical past master of the art, American journalist Elizabeth Meriwether Gilmer, alias 'Dorothy Dix'). They have typically invited premiers or ministers to commend the efficacy of one or another aspect of government policy, the alleged success of a government initiative, or the great benefits bestowed on that MP's own electoral division by government budget largesse (Serban, 2019, pp.156–59, 206–09). Both ministers and the opposition front bench strategise at length in the morning before Question Time, with the opposition choosing attack lines for the day (especially for their leader) and the PM and colleagues anticipating questions and devising rebuttals. As a result, many of the most memorable exchanges in the House have been highly scripted. Every now and then, however, a more spontaneous response has emerged, as in the case of the now-famous 'misogyny speech' delivered in 2012 by former PM Julia Gillard in response to a motion moved by the then Leader of the Opposition Tony Abbott (Gillard 2012; Wikipedia, 2023a).

During Question Time in the House, most attention has always focused on the questions put by the leader of the opposition, their front benchers and backbench MPs to the PM, although

Figure 11.3: The top ten topics asked of the PM and of other government ministers during the 2013 House sessions

(a) Asked of PM

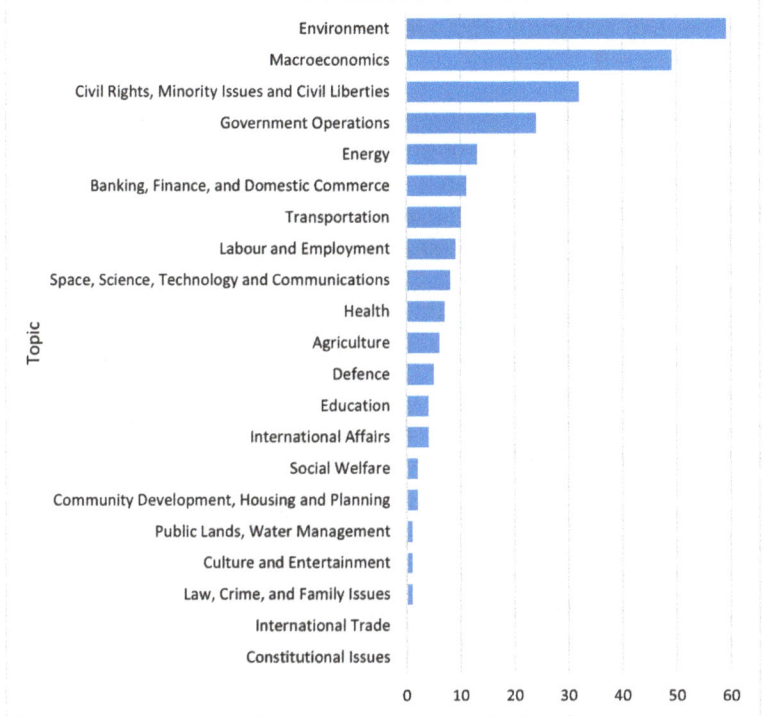

(b) Asked of other ministers

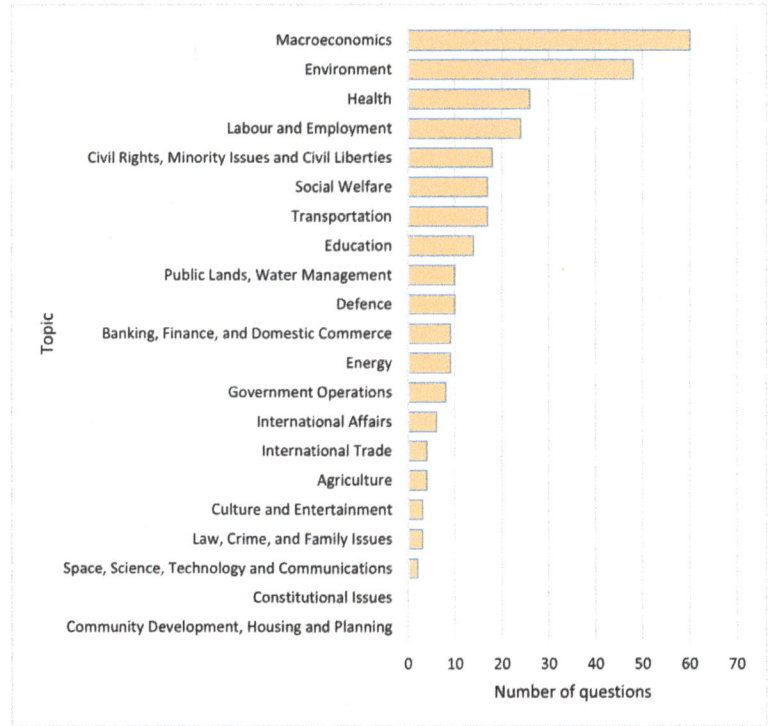

Source: Compiled from Serban (2021) 'The practice of accountability in questioning prime ministers: Comparative evidence from Australia, Canada, Ireland, and the United Kingdom', British Journal of Politics and International Relations, vol. 25, no. 1, pp.1–22, Figure 3.

Note: We are most grateful to Ruxandra Serban for permission to reproduce a redrawn version of her data. Data are drawn from 540 questions asked in the 2013 sessions of parliament, under the Julia Gillard government.

questions to other ministers have also sometimes been critical, especially if a mistake has been made or a scandal has occurred. The most recent detailed study (Serban, 2019, 2021) covered the 2013 sessions under the Gillard Labor government. Figure 11.3 shows that the focus was overwhelmingly on topical issues of the day, with the PM alone answering almost half of the questions put in that year (46 per cent, or just under 250 over the year) and ministers the rest (just over 290 questions).

Figure 11.3 also shows the numbers of questions asked across the top 10 topics covered in the study period. That year was dominated by the then Labor government's withdrawal of its carbon tax proposals under acute pressure from major Australian business interests, creating perhaps an unusual prominence for environmental matters. Second in the ranking were macroeconomics concerns. Although other ministers were responsible for different aspects of the national economy, including the Treasurer, often these questions were still directed towards the PM as head of government. Questions raised on matters relating to civil rights and minority issues and economic-related questions have often dominated the questions directed at the PM. By contrast, Figure 11.3 shows that while the top two topics also concentrated on the environment and macroeconomics, there was a second marked clustering around employment, health and social welfare issues, shown in the bottom part of the Figure.

While the Serban study provides an important glimpse into the flavour of Question Time during a single House session, the nature and focus of questions directed at PMs and ministers has also varied over time in response to the dynamic political issues of the day. For example, in late 2019 and early 2020, PM Morrison was asked many questions about his response to the bush fires. In 2021–22, there was a strong emphasis on questions to the PM about COVID-19 and later many related to the allegations of sexual harassment and gender discrimination within the parliament.

Chamber debates and scrutinising legislation

In the last 20 years, the House of Representatives passed an average of 159 new Acts per year, with the number range of such new laws as low as 102 (in the 2016 election year) and as high as 206 (in 2012). Given that the House sits for an average of only around 630 hours a year, and that only half this time has been allotted to government legislation, this throughput has always implied relatively brief consideration time for most prospective laws. In fact, only around a third of these pieces of legislation were 'considered in detail', which normally indicates a more controversial or complex piece of law-making.

Government whips can use 'closure' motions to shut down debates so that the ministry can maintain its legislative timetable, and their use has risen to average 32 motions a year in the decade since 2013. A more drastic measure is the guillotine – a procedure that allows a majority of MPs (and hence the government) to stop debate on a bill automatically at a pre-determined time, however, many of its clauses have been considered or not considered. On average in the last decades this procedure was used fewer than 10 times. However, Figure 11.4 shows that there was a good deal of variation from year to year, with extended debates, closure motions and guillotine motions normally related to the volume of legislation. Some peak years for all these indices of more intense partisan conflict occurred in 2016, 2014 and 2011. The number of formal votes (divisions) was also high in these years (at somewhat above or below 190 votes).

Figure 11.4: The proportion of Acts considered in detail in the House of Representatives, and closure or guillotine curbs on debate, as a percentage (%) of all Acts passed (2000–2022)

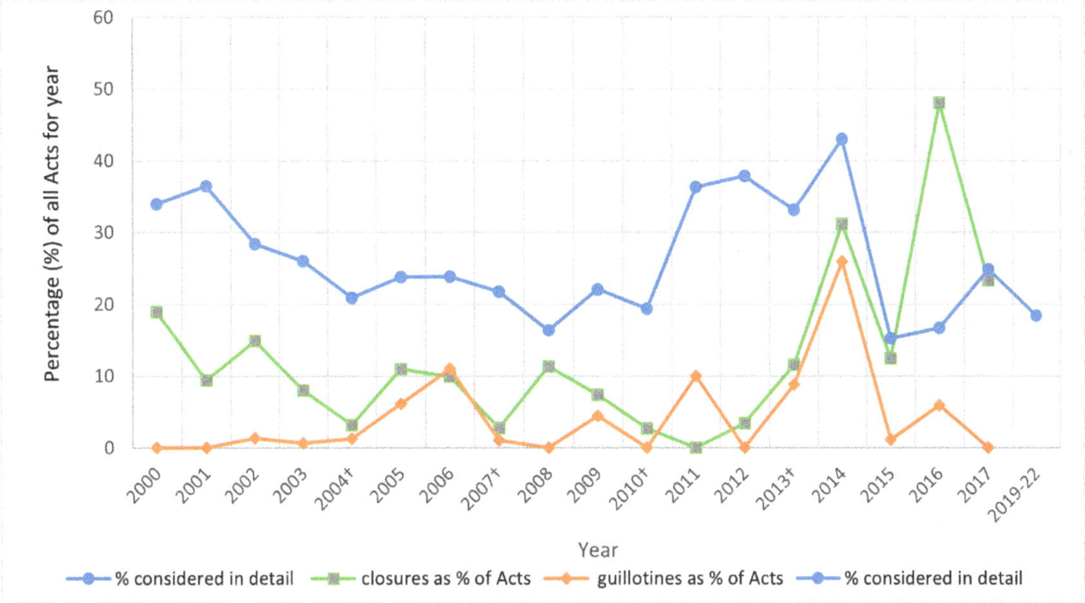

Source: Compiled by ADA team from Parliament of Australia (no date, d) 'Appendix 17 – Consideration of legislation by the House' and (2022) 'Bills considered in detail 46th Parliament'.

Committee scrutiny

The House of Representatives has a system of committees made up of members from across different political parties and organised around 17 thematic or ministerial portfolio areas, such as Agriculture and Water Resources, Health, Aged Care, Social Policy and Legal Affairs. In theory, House committees have provided forums for more detailed consideration of proposed legislation and policy issues and an opportunity for scrutiny of proposed laws or expenditure priorities. The parliamentary committee system also has had the potential to play an important role in undertaking scrutiny of executive action and to identify impacts on and breaches of individual rights (Grenfell and Moulds, 2018).

However, in practice, the House committee system suffered from a number of weaknesses, many of which related to executive dominance and the party political allegiances of committee members overriding other considerations. Even when a parliamentary committee has been able to identify specific legislative amendments or draw attention to the misuse or overuse of executive power, the impact of such recommendations has been muted if the government chose to ignore its report or had 'the numbers' in the House of Representatives and the Senate to continue to pursue its legislative and policy agenda. These weaknesses were particularly pronounced with House committees chaired by government members, and where government members hold the majority. While some House committees may appear to consider proposed government bills closely, they have rarely questioned major government policies or objectives. For example, no House committees undertook detailed scrutiny of the government's pandemic response in 2020–21.

Special select committees can achieve stronger results, particularly when established to inquire into specific issues or proposed legislation or they offer an alternative source of information to government, as on counter-terrorism (Moulds, 2020b). For example, in December 2020, a House select committee was set up to look into mental health and suicide prevention. Through its public hearings, this committee provided opportunities for the community to interact with parliament, and offered new information on a challenging policy issue. Sometimes such activity led to 'behind the scenes' negotiations on policy between government backbenchers and ministers that has led to policy or legislative changes. However, even when a House committee has been able to conduct a meaningful public hearing and generate a detailed written report, MPs may be limited by party allegiances in their ability to give effect to such recommendations.

The relatively muted scrutiny activity of the House committees can be contrasted with the work of Senate committees, which have sometimes had majorities of non-government members – making them more likely to be able to apply rigorous scrutiny and oversight of executive action, and to hold government to account for its expenditure and policy implementation. A good example was the Senate Committee on COVID-19 which actively scrutinised government policy responses (see Chapter 12). However, House MPs have also been involved in 21 Joint Committees (involving members of both the House and the Senate), including the Parliamentary Joint Committee on Human Rights. It has a legislated mandate to consider all proposed new laws (and some delegated legislation) against human rights standards. That committee has been invested with the power to conduct public inquiries into legislation giving rise to significant human rights concerns, including laws proposing to limit freedom of speech or promote freedom of religion

Budget processes and scrutiny

Constitutionally, the budget procedures of the House of Representatives offer an important opportunity for the parliament to exercise oversight over federal government expenditure, ensuring public and parliamentary accountability. A key constitutional provision makes clear that proposed laws appropriating money may not be initiated in the Senate and must only be introduced with the consent of the Governor General (which effectively means by a minister). This means that proposals to spend public money have always started their journey in the House of Representatives, but their implications are regularly scrutinised by the Senate, including through the Senate Estimates process (see Chapter 12). Traditionally, each May, the Treasurer outlines the government's planned and projected expenditure in his or her second reading speech for the Federal Budget appropriation bill, commonly known as the Budget Speech. This traditional Budget Speech timing has been disrupted considerably in recent times in response, at least in part, to the COVID-19 pandemic.

The federal parliament has also been supported by the Parliamentary Budget Office (PBO) which improves transparency around fiscal and budget policy issues by providing confidential costing services to all parliamentarians (Stewart, 2013; Stewart and Jager, 2013). It publishes a report after every election that shows the fiscal implications of major parties' election commitments. The PBO also conducts and publishes research that enhances the public understanding of the budget and fiscal policy settings.

Although the parliament has the ultimate control of government expenditure should it veto appropriation bills, in practice, the government has what is known as the 'financial initiative'

(Department of Finance, no date). Only the government can request that an appropriation be made, or increased, or propose to impose or increase taxation. As in the UK (from which this rule historically derives), legislation proposed by MPs outside government cannot increase public spending.

In a number of instances the government has been accused of misusing this 'financial initiative' capability, for example, by building-in broad discretionary funds that can be distributed by ministers potentially on the basis of party-political interests rather than community needs (sometimes described as 'pork barrelling' (Connolly, 2020). Controversies in 2018 to 2019 over the 'sports rort' allegations and roads funding focused on marginal electorates to benefit the coalition parties (see Chapter 13) highlighted a looseness and apparent lack of legal force attaching to conventions for ensuring non-political administration and accountability around some discretionary expenditures.

Representing a diverse society

The demographic characteristics of MPs never reflected the diversity of Australia's population in earlier periods, and they have only partially improved in recent times. A majority of House members have continued to be white, middle-class, middle-aged males. First Nations peoples were historically excluded, and even in 2024 there are only three First Nations MPs. More recently, the under-representation of Chinese-Australians and Indian-Australians was particularly pronounced. In the 2019 to 2021 Parliament, only 47 MPs were female compared to 104 males, just 31 per cent, despite women constituting just over half of the Australian population. In 2022, women MPs increased to 58 (38 per cent of the House), making up nearly half of Labor MPs (36 out of 77), and 11 out of 17 Independent and others (Wikipedia, 2023b). However, only just over one in five Liberal MPs was a woman, and only one in eight National MPs.

Academic studies have documented that an unequal political community reflects and reproduces social inequality, and can entrench and exacerbate structural disadvantages limiting the full engagement of many Australians, including those living in regional and remote areas, those from culturally and linguistically diverse backgrounds and First Nations peoples. There have been some examples of successful efforts by House of Representatives' members to counteract these imbalances by reaching out to a more diverse cross-section of their constituents (see Hendriks and Kay, 2019). Yet, for many people within the Australian community, the official rhetoric that emphasises the importance of citizen participation has rarely been realised in practice (Hendriks, Dryzek and Hunold, 2007).

The practical implications of a lack of diversity can be very serious for the working culture of the House of Representatives. Since 2019, there has been a sharp focus on the workplace culture within the Australian Parliament, and in particular, the high incidence of sexual harassment and gender-based discrimination experienced by female members of parliament and their staff. This impacted directly on sitting ministers and senior government figures, as well as prompting renewed discussions about past incidences and practices. Grave allegations were made by Brittany Higgins and others about their experiences of gender-based violence and discrimination while working within the federal parliament (ABC News, 2021b). They led to a series of marches across the country where Australian women demanded that their government and their elected representatives listened to their calls for gender equality. An independent inquiry into Parliament House culture was established by the Australian Human Rights Commission (Jenkins, 2021) and a National Summit on Women's Safety took place in September 2021.

In 2021, the parliament enacted the Respect at Work Bill 2021, designed to respond to some of the findings of the Australian Human Rights Commission's 2020 national inquiry report on sexual harassment *Respect@Work* (AHRC, 2020). Members of the House of Representatives have also reflected on their cultural practices and offered practical changes to procedures like Question Time designed to be more inclusive of a broader range of members (Parliament of Australia, 2021b). However, some advocates considered these changes before the 2022 federal election to have been inadequate to address the structural and cultural shortcomings that have given rise to gender-based discrimination in the past (Australian Financial Review, 2021b; Guardian, 2021).

The growing public demand for a more diverse and inclusive Parliament follows previous debates around the eligibility of MPs who held 'allegiances' to countries other than Australia. In *Re Canavan* and *Re Gallagher* the courts were asked to rule on the 'foreign allegiance prohibition' contained in section 44 of the Constitution (Nikias, 2019). Previously this had been seen as relatively benign. However, it was interpreted by the High Court in 2017 as rendering ineligible any person who held citizenship from a foreign country, even in circumstances where a law of a foreign power dictates that the person is a citizen, and even if they had done no positive act to confirm that foreign allegiance (Twomey, 2018). As a result, eight sitting federal legislators became ineligible to sit in the parliament, triggering a series of by-elections across the country. There remains ongoing debate as to whether and how this interpretation of constitutional eligibility to run for the Canberra Parliament should be changed in the future, and what it might mean in a diverse multicultural nation like Australia – where a significant proportion of citizens were born overseas or have strong family connections to other countries (Morgan, 2018).

New ways of communicating with the public

The COVID-19 pandemic in 2020 to 2022 led to an increase in political engagement among Australians and increased use of digital tools for communication (Evans et al., 2020). The Parliament's 2019 Digital Strategy provided a statement of intent for the future delivery of digital services for the legislature and has since been updated (Parliament of Australia, 2019). It was based around the need to ensure that the parliament remains a safe and accessible workplace, and an institution with which the Australian community can engage. The Strategy recognised that digital technology has been and remains a 'critical enabler for parliamentary business', and that Australian citizens legitimately expect to be able to engage with Parliament's work through digital as well as older processes.

As Evans et al. (2020, p.24) note, digital media has been deployed successfully by citizen-led initiatives and new digital parties as a mobilisation tool for enhancing community engagement with parliaments around the world. They offer new opportunities for 'eParticipation' with the Australian House of Representatives. For example, the e-petition system employed in Australia since 2016 has resulted in an exponential increase in petitions being considered by the House Petitions' Committee and referred to ministers each year (Parliament of Australia, no date, e). This system has generated over 2,000 exchanges between community members and parliamentarians since being digitalised in 2016.

However, as the digital infrastructure of the federal parliament has expanded, so too have the potential risks associated with cyber-attacks and foreign influence. In February 2019, and again in March 2021, federal parliament computer networks were compromised in what the media reported were likely the result of a foreign government attack. In its 2020 to 2021 Annual Report, the Australian Security and Intelligence Organisation (2023) reported eight major attacks from 2014 to 2022 and numerous disruptions, echoing its comments in 2019 that the growth in the number of Australians working from home during the global COVID-19 pandemic has increased Australia's exposure to a range of hostile actors in cyberspace. They warned that state and non-state malicious cyber actors may attempt to take advantage.

Conclusion

Public confidence in the House of Representatives perhaps began to recover after the 2022 election, but it has remained fragile. Longstanding issues associated with lack of diversity and a white, middle-class, male-oriented culture in the legislature have continued to undermine efforts by some MPs to improve connections between the people and the 'People's House'. As in many democracies (Belin and de Maio, 2020), this fragile trust was tested during the COVID-19 pandemic, where emergency executive law-making and state/federal tensions characterised much of Australia's pandemic response. Explosive revelations about sexual harassment within parliament, and gender-based discrimination have also had a negative impact on public perceptions of parliamentary culture and practice. Expense scandals relating to the allocation of funds by minsters to projects in marginal seats also raised questions about the effectiveness of existing accountability and oversight structures, and led to calls for additional statutory safeguards, including establishing a federal Independent Commission Against Corruption, resisted by Liberal/National ministers but enacted by Labor ministers after 2022. The Labor government under Albanese also promised changes, including a more consensus style of working and rigorous standards of behaviour, yet such good intentions are often hard to sustain amidst the cut and thrust of partisan politics.

Some digital experiments and experiences have offered new opportunities to explore how to improve the visibility of House proceedings among everyday Australians and might provide pathways for more meaningful interaction between the community and members of parliament. However, the ongoing dominance of party-politics, potently expressed through highly adversarial House debates and Question Time proceedings, remains a barrier to ensuring that the House of Representatives provides a forum for national policy debate and generates useful guidance to the government in making complex policy choices. For many young Australians contemplating a career in parliament or looking to identify solutions to complex social problems such as climate change and intergenerational equality, the House of Representatives retains an image of a hostile and unproductive space.

Judicial decisions

Re Canavan [2017] HCA 45

Re Gallagher [2018] HCA 17

Notes

We are most grateful to Dr Ruxandra Serban for permission to reproduce a redrawn version of her data from her 2020 'How are prime ministers held to account? Exploring procedures and practices in 31 parliamentary democracies' and 2021 'The practice of accountability in questioning prime ministers: Comparative evidence from Australia, Canada, Ireland, and the United Kingdom', papers, and for discussing her findings with the editors.

References

7 News, Australia (2021) 'Morrison government in damage control as Liberal MP votes against the government', 25 November. https://perma.cc/27QB-MR4R

ABC News (2020) 'Victorian politicians wanting to travel to Canberra for parliamentary sittings face two weeks in quarantine', *ABC News*, 6 August. https://perma.cc/R4XD-3CSJ

ABC News (2021a) 'Nationals' demands for Liberals over climate change policy finalised, taken to Prime Minister Scott Morrison', *ABC News*, 21 October. https://perma.cc/42GG-HGJ4

ABC News (2021b) 'Read what Brittany Higgins had to say when she spoke at the women's march', 15 March. https://perma.cc/23F7-TXBM

Allington, Patrick (no date) 'On the abolition of Question Time', *Griffith Review*, no. 51, https://perma.cc/TPT5-PLPH

AHRC (Australian Human Rights Commission) (2020) *Respect@Work: Sexual Harassment National Inquiry Report*. https://perma.cc/LY7D-H84N

AHRC (Australian Human Rights Commission) (2021) *Independent Review into Commonwealth Parliamentary Workplaces – Progress Update*, July. https://perma.cc/9TVF-KJGL

ASIO (Australian Security and Intelligence Organisation) (2023) *Australian Security and Intelligence Organisation, Annual Report 2022–23*, Canberra: ASIO. https://perma.cc/8L9W-H769

Australian Financial Review (2021a) 'Australia must have a new macroeconomic framework', *Australian Financial Review*, 3 February. https://perma.cc/RH74-PC3A

Australian Financial Review (2021b) 'Government shies away from major sex harassment fixes', *Australian Financial Review*, 8 April. https://perma.cc/T7V9-3EW8

Beaumont, Adrian (2018) 'How the hard right terminated Turnbull only to see Scott Morrison become PM', *The Conversation*, 24 August. https://perma.cc/MQM3-RLWF

Belin, Célia and de Maio, Giovanna (2020) *Democracy After Coronavirus: Five Challenges for the 2020s*, Foreign Policy, Report. August. https://perma.cc/2QKV-78SZ

Cockfield, Michael (2021) 'The National Party used to be known for its leadership stability – what happened?', *The Conversation*, 21 June. https://perma.cc/4G8P-8X7E

Connolly, Susanna (2020) 'The regulation of pork barrelling in Australia', *Parliament of Australasian Parliamentary Review*, vol. 35, no.1, pp.25–53. https://perma.cc/9EJF-5HUN

Department of Finance (no date) 'The budget process'. https://perma.cc/R79E-USWE

Evans, Mark; Valgarðsson, Viktor; Jennings, Will; and Stoker, Gerry (2020) *Political Trust and Democracy in Times of Coronavirus – Is Australia Still the Lucky Country? A Snapshot of the Findings From a National Survey*, Canberra: Democracy 2025. https://perma.cc/YCN4-HR6Z

Gauja, Anika; Styles, Chris; Lowe, David; Robinson, Geoffrey; Fuller, Glen; Mahoney, James; Abjorensen, Norman; and Robin Tennant-Wood (2012) 'Gillard vs Rudd: The best of *The Conversation's* coverage', *The Conversation*, 27 February. Written by https://perma.cc/39D8-59GM

Gillard, Julia (2012) 'Transcript of Julia Gillard's speech', *The Sydney Morning Herald*, 10 October. https://perma.cc/D7FG-PXRY

Grattan, Michelle (2020) 'View from the hill: "Virtual" participants and border restrictions will make for a bespoke parliamentary sitting', *The Conversation*, 17 August. https://perma.cc/2Z6A-WU93

Grenfell, Laura and Moulds, Sarah (2018) 'The role of committees in rights protection in federal and state parliaments in Australia' *University of New South Wales Law Journal*, vol. 41, no. 1, pp.40–79. https://perma.cc/BDB7-6H4M

Guardian (2020) 'From novelty cheque to full-blown scandal: A timeline of the sports rorts saga', *Guardian*, Australia, 12 March. https://perma.cc/5C4L-8LVE

Guardian (2021) 'Australian women are in a state of rage. They have to be taken seriously', *Guardian*, Australia, 7 February. https://perma.cc/PR2Y-EDJQ

Hamer, Barbara (2004) 'Chapter 1: The origins of responsible government', Parliament of Australia. https://perma.cc/U74S-4R6H

Hamer, David (2004) *Can Responsible Government Survive In Australia?* Second edition of 1994 book, on the Parliament of Australia website at: https://perma.cc/M7B5-HVCK

Hanna, Emily (no date) 'Climate change – reducing Australia's emissions', Parliament of Australia briefings webpage. https://perma.cc/33XQ-N4Y9

Hendriks, Carolyn M and Kay, Adrian (2019) 'From "opening up" to democratic renewal: Deepening public engagement in legislative committees', *Government and Opposition*, vol. 54, no. 1, pp.25–51. $ https://doi.org/10.1017/gov.2017.20

Hendriks, Carolyn; Dryzek, John; and Hunold, Christian (2007) 'Turning up the heat: Partisanship in deliberative innovation', *Political Studies*, vol. 55, no. 2, pp.362–83. $ https://doi.org/10.1111/j.1467-9248.2007.00667.x

Hurst, Daniel (2015) 'Australian leader Tony Abbott ousted by Malcolm Turnbull after party vote', *Guardian*, Australia, 14 September. https://perma.cc/42HH-SE82

Jenkins, Kate (2021) 'Set the Standard: Report of the Independent Review into Commonwealth Parliament Workplaces'. Canberra: Australian Human Rights Commission. https://perma.cc/HAS6-5YEH

Kam, Christopher J (2009) *Party Discipline and Parliamentary Politics*. Cambridge: Cambridge University Press. $ https://doi.org/10.1017/CBO9780511576614

Kerr, Duncan (2009) 'The High Court and the Executive: Emerging challenges to the underlying doctrines of responsible government and the Rule of Law', *University of Tasmania Law Review*, vol. 28, no. 2, pp.145–181. https://www.austlii.edu.au/au/journals/UTasLawRw/2009/8.pdf

Lambert, Tarla (2021) 'Bully-boy tactics used against Bridget Archer show Morrison's learnt nothing where respect of women is concerned', *Womens' Agenda* blog, 28 November. https://perma.cc/VH9F-4YJ5

Larkin, Dani and Galloway, Kate (2021) 'Constitutionally entrenched voice to parliament: Representation and good governance', *Alternative Law Journal*, vol. 46, no. 3, pp.193–98. $ https://doi.org/10.1177/1037969X211019807

Leigh, Andrew (2000) 'Factions and fractions: A case study of power politics in the Australian Labor Party', *Australian Journal of Political Science*, vol. 35, no.3, pp. 427–48. https://perma.cc/2BJV-EYWQ

Lowy Institute (2021) 'Paying the price: Australians want action on climate change', by Hannah Lesor, 26 May. https://perma.cc/E8LN-9BQD

Maddison, Sarah (2010) 'White parliament, black politics: The dilemmas of Indigenous parliamentary representation' *Australian Journal of Political Science*, vol. 45, no. 4, pp.663–80. $ https://doi.org/10.1080/10361146.2010.517180

Melleuish, Gregory (2021) 'Question Time reforms are worthy but won't solve the problem of a broken political culture', *The Conversation*, 18 May. https://perma.cc/86L4-EF9R

Mills, Stephen (2020) 'Parliament in a time of virus: Representative democracy as a "non-essential service", *Australasian Parliamentary Review*, vol. 34, no. 2. https://perma.cc/36W7-Q8P4

Morgan, James (2018) 'Dual citizenship and Australian parliamentary eligibility: A time for reflection or referendum?' *Adelaide Law Review*, vol. 39, no. 2, pp.439–51. https://perma.cc/TT48-8FA4

Moulds, Sarah (2020a) 'As the first "remote" sitting starts in Canberra, virtual parliaments should be the new norm, not a COVID bandaid', *The Conversation*, 23 August. https://perma.cc/V8GH-KLMT

Moulds, Sarah (2020b) *Committees of Influence: Parliamentary Rights Scrutiny and Counter-Terrorism Lawmaking in Australia*, Singapore: Springer Singapore. $ https://doi.org/10.1007/978-981-15-4350-0

Nikias, Kyriaco (2019) 'Dual citizens in the federal parliament: *Re Canavan, Re Ludlam, Re Waters, Re Roberts [No 2], Re Joyce, Re Nash, Re* Xenophon (2017) 349 Alr 534', *Adelaide Law Review*, no.3, pp.479–91. https://perma.cc/H3SV-6TRG

Nikkei-Asia (2022) Australia's Labor, 'Teal Independents' tap female voter frustration', Nikkei, 20 May. Written by Rurika Imahashi. https://perma.cc/53A2-6TA5

O'Brien, Patrick (1986) *The Liberals: Factions, Feuds and Fancies,* Sydney: Penguin Books Australia.

Parliament of Australia (no date, a) 'The Cabinet'. https://bit.ly/3M9Uzx9

Parliament of Australia (no date, b) 'Political Parties in the House of Representatives', Info sheet no. 22 'Political Parties'. https://perma.cc/L2V9-ZPVW

Parliament of Australia (no date, c) House of Representatives 'Bills considered in detail – 46th Parliament'. https://bit.ly/3m2gMCz

Parliament of Australia (no date, d) 'House of Representatives Practice (17th edition), Appendix 17 – Consideration of legislation by the House'. https://perma.cc/VQS3-M85S

Parliament of Australia (no date e) 'House of Representatives – petitions', webpage. https://perma.cc/X5FL-QVJK

Parliament of Australia (2019) 'Parliament of Australia Digital Strategy 2019–22', webpage. https://perma.cc/FBU2-BWV2

Parliament of Australia (2021a) 'House of Representatives Practice, Appendix 10 – Party affiliations in the House of Representatives', Webpage. https://perma.cc/6BV2-NWHC

Parliament of Australia (2021b) *A Window on the House: Practices and Procedures Relating to Question Time*, March. https://perma.cc/A53V-7FD2

Parliament of Australia (2022) 'Bills considered in detail 46th Parliament'. https://perma.cc/4MB9-Z6MG

PEO (Parliamentary Education Office) (no date) 'Why do the Nationals and Liberals work together while the other parties (Labor, Greens, etc) are by themselves?' https://bit.ly/3ZwycFj

PEO (Parliamentary Education Office) (2022) 'How many Aboriginal or Torres Straits Islander MPs or senators are there and what are their names? https://perma.cc/T5QM-X25R

Prasser, Scott (2012) 'Executive growth and the takeover of Parliament of Australias', *Australasian Parliamentary Review*, vol. 27, no. 1, pp. 48–61. https://perma.cc/WV8H-6LMK

Rodrigues, Mark and Brenton, Scott (2010) 'The Age of Independence? Independents in Parliament of Australias', *Australasian Parliamentary Review*, vol. 25, no. 1, pp.109–35. https://www.aspg.org.au/wp-content/uploads/2017/09/10_Rodriques-IndependentA.pdf

Serban, Ruxandra (2019) *Questioning Prime Ministers: Procedures, Practices and Functions in Parliamentary Democracies*. London School of Economics, PhD Thesis.

Serban, Ruxandra (2020) 'How are prime ministers held to account? Exploring procedures and practices in 31 parliamentary democracies', *Journal of Legislative Studies*, vol. 28, no. 2, pp.155–78. https://doi.org/10.1080/13572334.2020.1853944

Serban, Ruxandra (2021) 'The practice of accountability in questioning prime ministers: Comparative evidence from Australia, Canada, Ireland, and the United Kingdom', *British Journal of Politics and International Relations*, vol. 25, no. 1, pp.1–22. https://doi.org/10.1177/13691481211058584

Sloane, Michael (2022) 'Floor crossings in the House of Representatives on the morning of 10 February 2022', *FlagPost blog,* Parliament of Australia. https://perma.cc/2TG4-JT24

Stewart, Miranda (2013) 'The Australian Parliamentary Budget Office: A Sustainable Innovation in Fiscal Decision-Making?', University of Melbourne Legal Studies Research Paper No. 628, 27 February. https://perma.cc/7AC6-6324

Stewart, Miranda and Jager, Holly (2013) 'The Australian Parliamentary Budget Office: Shedding light on the dark arts of budgeting', *Public Law Review*, vol. 24, no. 4, pp.267–88.

Tiffen, Rodney (2017) *Disposable Leaders: Media and Leadership Coups from Menzies to Abbott*. Sydney: New South Wales Publishing.

Turpin, Andrew (2012) 'An attempt to measure the quality of questions in Question Time of the Australian Federal Parliament', in ADCS '12: Proceedings of the Seventeenth Australasian Document Computing Symposium, December 2012', pp. 96–103. $ https://doi.org/10.1145/2407085.2407098

Twomey, Anne (2018) 'Re Gallagher: Inconsistency, imperatives and irremediable impediments', *Australian Public Law,* blog, 28 May. https://perma.cc/F9UQ-4KCS

Uluru Statement (2017) The Uluru Statement from the Heart. https://perma.cc/3EXV-C52A

Warhurst, John (2008) 'Conscience voting in the Australian Federal Parliament', *Australian Journal of Politics and History*, vol. 54, no. 4, pp.579–96. https://doi.org/10.1111/j.1467-8497.2008.00517.x

Wikipedia (2023a) 'Julia Gillard's misogyny speech' given 9 October 2012. https://perma.cc/W3EP-8J3H

Wikipedia (2023b) 'Women in the Australian House of Representatives'. https://perma.cc/FC2K-LGQK

Wikipedia (2024) 'Albanese ministry'. https://perma.cc/C2UN-WNJ4

Williams, Blair (2020) 'Inside the toxic sexist culture of Australia's political bubble', Australian Institute for International Affairs blogpost, 20 November. https://perma.cc/D37T-AQW9

12

Parliament – the Senate

Brenton Prosser, Mary Walsh and John Hawkins

The Australian Senate has often been described as unique in both its structures and powers (Bach, 2003; Taflaga, 2021, p.55). Despite some historical Westminster roots in the UK's (still completely unelected) House of Lords (Kippin and Campion, 2018), Australia's directly elected upper house has strong similarities to the powerful Senate in the USA. For instance, it was designed as a chamber to protect the interests of the states against a potentially over-powerful federal government. It also sought to protect the smaller states and territories from the influence of more populous states. However, as party discipline has strengthened in the Senate, its members have increasingly become nationally-orientated party politicians.

The design of the Senate was intended as a check and balance. Twelve senators are (re)elected from each state to serve for a six-year term. To provide extra stability, they have normally been replaced half at a time (along with two senators from each of the territories every three years when House of Representatives elections occur). A proportional election system (the Single Transferable Vote (STV)) is used to choose members. Since the 1950s, no major party has won an outright majority of seats (although the Liberal Party secured a majority in 2004 in coalition with the National Party). As a result, Labor and conservative dominance has been constrained for six decades. Internationally, the powers of the Australian Senate are second only to that of the USA (Parliament of Australia, 2023a).

In a bicameral legislature, what does democracy require from the second or upper chamber?

- If an elected upper chamber has *fully equal powers* to the lower house, it should act to represent voters in much the same way as the lower house, broadening the range of interests that have to be considered before policy is finalised. It may revise, delay, decide or even initiate legislation in its own right.

How to cite this chapter:

Prosser, Brenton; Walsh, Mary and Hawkins, John (2024) 'Parliament – the Senate', in: Evans, Mark; Dunleavy, Patrick and Phillimore, John (eds) *Australia's Evolving Democracy: A New Democratic Audit*, London: LSE Press, pp.253–274. https://doi.org/10.31389/lsepress.ada.l Licence: CC-BY-NC 4.0

- If instead an elected upper house has *lesser powers* than the lower house, it is mainly seen as a check and balance constraining the majority in the lower house, and enhancing public and parliamentary accountability through conditionally supporting the government, and articulating reasoned opposition. Scrutiny by the upper house should offer a safeguard against ill-advised legislative changes. This is especially the case where new legislation could breach liberal democratic principles, impair civil rights, change the nature of the federation, or make long-run alterations in how the political process operates that favour the lower house majority party.

Australia's Senate lies somewhere between these two models.

- An elected Senate where the election districts are states within a federation (as in Australia) should re-balance the geographical representation of different parts of the country compared with the lower house – to secure more equal influence for all states (and to provide some additional representation for territories).
- Any upper house should improve the accountability of the executive to the legislature and to public opinion, as well as facilitate and improve the technical operation of legislative drafting, scrutiny and amendment. Upper house proceedings should provide an important focus of national political debate and articulate 'public opinion' in ways that provide useful guidance to the government in making complex policy choices.
- Having a bicameral legislature should increase access channels from civil society to the executive, in equitable and accountable ways. Individually and collectively, senators (like MPs) should seek to uncover and publicise issues of public concern and citizens' grievances, giving effective representation both to majority and minority views, and showing a consensus regard for serving the public interest.
- An upper house elected in a different way from the lower house should broaden the representation of different social groups in the legislature.
- Where elected senators have longer terms of office, this is often intended to increase the range of expertise available among legislators and within the pool of potential ministers, by attracting different kinds of people to stand from those contesting the shorter-cycle lower house elections. Senators' roles should foster a degree of greater policy continuity, especially on issues where civil society actors must make decisions with some long-run predictability (for example, investing in pensions).
- Any elected Senate should be able to scrutinise and maintain full public control of government services and state operations as much as the lower house, assessing the current implementation of policies, and the efficiency and effectiveness of government services and policy delivery.

In theory and design, Australia's Senate meets all the above requirements.

Recent developments

The founders of the Australian Federation examined the nature of upper houses in other countries in the 1890s and then selected features for their Senate. Such is its unique blend of qualities, that the commentator Stanley Bach (2003) likened it to a platypus (a unique Australian mammal that Europeans first thought must be a hoax combination of features from multiple species). European and American political scientists are often surprised by descriptions of the Australian parliament as a 'Westminster system', given its many exceptions to the rule – the Senate being among the most notable. On his retirement in 2021, the then Senate President, Scott Ryan, described the Australian Senate as 'one of the most powerful upper houses in the democratic world' (Murphy, 2017). It is distinctive in both its parliamentary structures and legislative strength.

The Senate was deliberately designed to have almost equal powers to the House of Representatives. It has been a house that both introduces and reviews legislation. By convention, the Prime Minister (PM) and most ministers come from the House of Representatives, but senators do provide (a minority of) Cabinet ministers. Another key feature of the modern Senate has been the prolonged presence of third or fourth party, micro party and independent senators. These parliamentarians make up the 'crossbench', which apart from one period of three years, have held or shared the deciding vote ('balance of power') in the Senate since 1981. The Senate also has a robust committee system outside of the legislative process, which provides scrutiny to bills, examines issues of public interest and holds the public/civil service to account. These factors explain why Australia's upper house has been an important check on the government's executive, legislative powers and (via its committees) on wider public administration.

This chapter begins by discussing two key factors affecting how the Senate now works – changes in party fortunes and voting patterns in Senate elections to May 2022, and the Senate's role during the COVID-19 pandemic. Next, the Senate's strengths, weaknesses, opportunities and threats are summarised from a democratic point of view. Following this SWOT analysis, the remainder of the chapter delves deeper into three selected aspects of the Senate's operations.

Senate elections

Using the STV system to elect multiple senators in each state encourages Australian voters to behave differently in upper house elections. A wide range of parties and candidates have stood for the Senate and won voters' support. First-preference votes for the top two 'major' parties (the conservative Liberal-National Coalition, and the progressive Labor Party) has been less. Many voters choose to support upper house candidates from third parties, but also a range of single-issue micro-parties or independents. In terms of democratic fairness, the Senate election is best analysed at the individual state and territory level since the results reflect only the pattern of votes in each sub-national area (see Chapter 5). Yet it remains interesting to consider the national vote shares of the major parties in upper house elections, which differ from the House of Representatives pattern. They show a clear trend away from the major parties (Figure 12.1). Notably, the first-preference vote for non-major party senators exceeded the Labor Party's votes for the upper house over the last decade.

Figure 12.1: The national first-preference vote shares of parties in Senate elections by party, 2000–2022

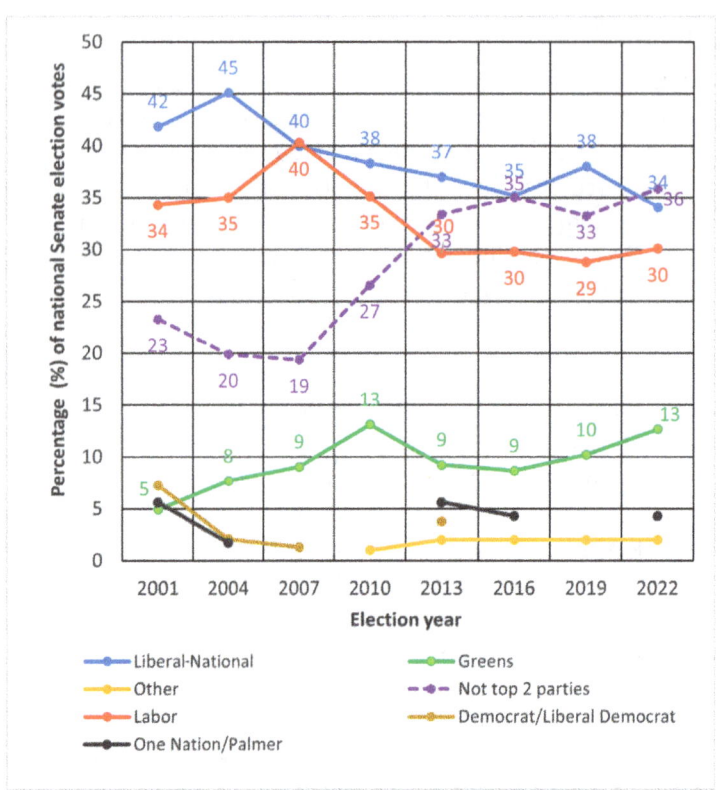

Source: Compiled from summary data in Parliament of Australia (2017) 'Federal election results 1901–2016' and Australian Electoral Commission (2023). https://www.aec.gov.au/elections/federal_elections/

Figure 12.2: The number of senators by party, 2000–2022

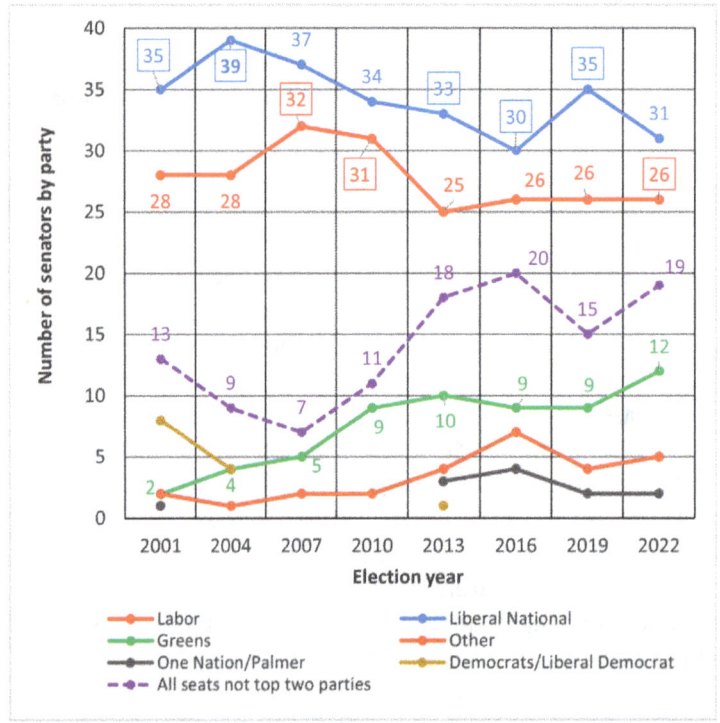

Source: Compiled from summary data in Parliament of Australia (2017) 'Federal election results 1901–2016'; Parliament of Australia (2020) 'Parliamentary Handbook for the 46th Parliament, p.465; and Senate of Australia (2023) 'The Parliament of the Commonwealth of Australia: The Senate – List of Senators, 47th Parliament as at 30 May 2024'.

Note: There are 76 seats, so a majority requires 39 senators, obtained only once in this chart, by the Liberal-National Coalition in 2004. The party holding the ministry is shown boxed. The 2016 election was an unusual 'double dissolution' of the whole Senate, when all 12 seats in each state were contested at the same time.

The story for most of the last 40 years of the Senate has been that of a third minor party (early on the Australian Democrats and then later the Australian Greens) having enough numbers to hold (or share) the 'balance of power' in the Senate. The exception to this was in 2004, where only four senators (5 per cent) were elected from outside the two major parties. This was due in no small part to the electoral demise of the Australian Democrats third party after supporting the Howard Government to introduce a controversial goods and service tax. That said, over a sixth of the votes still went to third parties, small parties or independent candidates at that election.

This high vote across non-major party groups has not always translated directly into more seats. It should be noted that in six member, state-wide contests, the formal quota needed to win a seat is the total votes divided by the number of seats plus one, which equals 14.3 per cent (or 33.3 per cent in the two-seat territories). These levels have been a tall order for small parties or independents to reach, even if they attract considerable preferences via the STV system. But it is not unprecedented. South Australian Independent Senator, Nick Xenophon, alone won almost 25 per cent support in 2013, while Independent Senator, David Pocock, won the second Australian Capital Territory (ACT) seat ahead of the Liberals in 2022.

That said, Figure 12.2 shows that the Liberal-National Coalition has had the largest representation in the Senate this century, followed by Labor. The Greens have been continuously represented in the chamber over the last 20 years, growing from 2 to 12 senators. The number of seats for non-major parties has also trended upwards, peaking at 20 out of 76 senators in 2016, and 19 senators in 2022. Other parties winning seats across the period have included the Australian Democrats (early on) and Liberal Democrats, centrist micro parties like Family First and Xenophon team, and right-wing groupings like One Nation and Palmer United. All have experienced difficulties in building a stable party organisation to support sustained electoral performance. All the trends covered here have longer term roots that we analyse after the SWOT analysis below.

Post 2022 developments

Labor returned to power at the May 2022 Federal Election, with a very slim majority in the House of Representatives and a minority share in the Senate. The strong performance of the Greens meant that with their backing the government only needed the vote of one additional senator to pass 'progressive' legislation (although this number increased with a Labor senator leaving the party in mid 2024). Early post-election commentary identified a more participatory and democratic orientation by the new Albanese Labor Government than under his Coalition predecessors, Morrison and Abbott (Dennett, 2022). As noted above, a Labor and Independent senator were elected for the first time to the ACT's two seats at the 2022 election. This contributed to removing a long-held inconsistency in the legislative powers between states and territories, a move that the ACT government had long campaigned for (Evans and Jervis-Bardy, 2022; Neale, 2022). This was one example of the changing composition of the Senate contributing to more democratic practices.

Another issue after the 2022 election revolved around a national referendum to include an Indigenous Voice to Parliament in the Constitution. Set for late 2023, it was a key commitment made by the Albanese Government. In early 2023, tensions over the issue changed the composition in the Senate with one Greens member splitting from the party, requiring the government to then secure two votes in addition to the Greens. Hopes were raised that, if successful, this constitutional change, along with the emergence of community-based 'Teal' conservative-environmental (blue-green) Independents with grassroots mandates (Wallace, 2022; Wahlquist, 2022), could contribute to new demands for culturally appropriate and diverse public engagement by government and public administrators. However, the Voice proposal was convincingly defeated in October 2023 (see Chapter 4). For the moment then, the Senate's role in shaping the renewal of Australia's democratic foundations has remained unchanged.

The Senate and the COVID-19 pandemic

During the 2020 to 2022 COVID-19 pandemic period, the Senate provided significant questioning of ministers' performance in a relatively independent manner. A powerful Senate committee was set up to monitor how the Coalition government was performing. In April 2002, its extensively critical final report called for a Royal Commission to examine federal policy-making during the period (Senate Select Committee on COVID-19, 2022a). However, the Liberal-National Coalition senators on the committee issued their own dissenting report, arguing both that the government's performance was appropriate and that a further investigation was not needed (Senate Select Committee on COVID-19, 2022b). At the time of writing, the Albanese Government has rejected a recommendation made for a Royal Commission (Hevesi, 2023), but this example illustrates the potential national influence of the Senate committee system (see also Senate of Australia, 2024).

Strengths, weaknesses, opportunities and threats (SWOT) analysis

Current strengths	**Current weaknesses**
The Senate's STV electoral process is a proportional one, which responds to the public's state-wide votes and counts multiple preferences, creating a reasonable match of votes cast and seats won.	Voting at Senate elections is usually mostly driven by national party positions and issues, rather than by distinctive state or regional interests. The formal quota of votes needed to win a seat is quite high (over 14 per cent), which favours the larger parties. They are often somewhat over-represented at the expense of seats for fragmented micro- or very small parties.
The overall make-up of the Senate state and territory vote often matches the national breakdown of votes cast (Trudgian, 2016). Such results have been happy accidents (rather than predictable or justified outcomes of state-wide contests). But they have tended nonetheless to enhance the upper house's legitimacy with the public.	Senate seats are not distributed according to population size, and the number of constituents per senator varies very markedly across the most and least populous states, contributing to very different work demands and practices for senators.
There is evidence that substantial numbers of citizens are content to see no overall party majority in the Senate, viewing it as a check on the power of an executive with a House majority. Some voters may actively adjust their Senate preferences to help achieve this outcome.	Crossbench (or potentially backbench) senators hold the balance of power in passing new legislation between the Liberal-National Coalition and Labor, which leaves the Senate open to (often unfounded) claims that these senators are able to exploit their pivotality to 'pork barrel' for their state or territory.

Senate procedures and conventions protect against partisan and populist extremes, both from major parties' over-reach and unreasonable crossbench demands.	Strongly observed major party discipline can result in the deciding vote on amendments or passage of a bill being held by one unaffiliated senator. This may seem to make them excessively powerful, but only if their demands have been more reasonable than the opposition's position, and so long as major party discipline has been maintained.
Senators have genuine powers to hold ministers and the executive to account, and have utilised them in independent and critical ways (especially when in opposition).	The staffing quota for advisers to assist senators were originally based on backbencher workloads, but this has improved as governments have recognised the legislative workload of crossbenchers and potential delays. However, understaffing can constrain the capacity of senators to hold the executive to account, as does the limited formal induction and training for senators and their staff on these genuine powers.
The Senate committee systems have considerably developed in activity levels and salience and in recent decades have contributed in important ways to improve policy scrutiny, public accountability and national debate.	Senate committees cannot direct the activities of the executive. Committee reports (and dissenting reports) often emerge along party lines, which can dilute the power of committee findings back in the chambers. Increasingly, committees investigate matters prior to parties stating their formal position at second reading, which encourages partisan committee behaviour and inhibits debate.
Future opportunities	**Future threats**
The Senate and its committees have embraced extensive evidence-gathering (for example, for its 2022 COVID-19 report) and new ways of working with citizens. Embracing more deliberative processes through new technologies or citizens' assemblies could enhance this innovativeness.	The emergence of a National Cabinet involving the PM and state and territory premiers in high-level discussions occurred in response to COVID-19 but has continued under both the major parties. Its role raises acute questions about whether the historic role of Senate (as the primary representative of the states and territories) will continue or decline in significance (see below).
There has been a growing diversity in social representation in the Senate, which could be further encouraged in dimensions beyond gender balance.	Presidential-style politics, declining major party membership and traditional party conventions all present a challenge to more socially diverse contributions by major party senators, as well as encouraging diversity and balance across the Senate.
As more parties establish an enduring Senate presence, share the deciding vote and dissolve major party dominance, conventions around party discipline, executive direction and public administration may need to loosen to win Senate support, potentially opening the door to more deliberative and inclusive community approaches to public engagement.	Intense media coverage and/or the 24-hours news cycle places pressure on crossbench senators to take up positions on legislation early, often prior to full examination of evidence, public engagement or the parliamentary process being enacted. For a senator to subsequently be seen to change their public position ('back-flip') has been considered a significant risk for senators whose election was not protected by a major party label.

The remainder of the chapter looks in more detail at four aspects of the Senate's operations – its purposes, powers and processes, including committee activity; the electoral and party influences on its composition, and effects on governance; the Senate's role on 'democracy' issues; and some tensions around and possible reforms to the upper house's operations.

Purposes, powers and processes

One key purpose of the Senate has been to act as a safeguard against dramatic or undemocratic legislative changes. As a distinctively constituted elected chamber that produces its own legislation, it acts as an influential check and balance. Because Australian governments generally have had a majority in the House, but not the Senate, the latter became a key locus for parliament to fulfil its role of holding the executive to account. The Senate can also facilitate the technical operation of legislation, through independent drafting, review, amendment and passage of laws. The Senate's committee system has been particularly important here. It can provide a wider range of social perspectives among upper house legislators due to the presence of members from smaller parties, particularly those holding the balance.

The powers of the Senate to introduce, amend or block legislation have made it central in ensuring public and parliamentary accountability. Although there are no specific procedures that prevent the Senate rejecting Budget supply bills, the convention since the 1975 dismissal of Labor PM Whitlam by the Governor-General has been that the Senate cannot hold the government 'to ransom'. Should resistance still occur, a government with a majority has the strategic option of calling a 'double dissolution' of all members and a combined vote across both houses should any bill be blocked twice (with double the number of MPs meaning that they are likely to be able to override a Senate deadlock). These factors restrict the use of Senate powers in ways that might obstruct governments.

An important power to scrutinise the implementation of policies and the actions of governments has been the Senate's ability to order ministers to provide information on issues of public concern. This can be through formal orders to produce documents or amending legislation to include provisions for appropriate disclosure. In practical terms, these powers by far exceed those within Freedom of Information laws and are so broad that they can require documents to be created. These powers include a further measure under a standing order that requires governments to make public all provisions of any Act that have been proclaimed each year. Failure to comply can come with sanctions on ministerial powers (effectively to 'bench' ministers). The Senate also has the power to censure ministers, an important integrity measure that has resulted in ministerial resignation. That said, these measures have rarely been applied. A more frequently applied sanction has been delaying legislative activity and the government's progress on its agenda until relevant information is produced. Time has always been a vital and finite resource for governments on a three-year electoral cycle.

The legislative process

Despite the Senate's formal powers to hold up government activity, the vast majority of legislation passes with the support of both major parties and/or the crossbench members. However, the extent that this occurs in a climate of fruitful deliberation that seeks to maximise a national consensus has been less clear. There has been a growing partisan and populist element within the Senate in recent years, while contributions within the chamber (even after second reading stage) have become more partisan. For instance, a new convention to refer legislation to Senate committees immediately on entering the upper house (rather than after second reading) has reduced constructive deliberation. This change has resulted in senators remaining silent on proposals in committee until the official party position has been made public at second reading. This misses the opportunity to link chamber and Senate committee deliberation and amendment prior to the third reading. Such trends towards partisanship in Australian politics have presented a threat to the Senate's democratic contribution.

The chamber also plays an important role in shaping national political debate through floor proceedings and questions. Members have introduced measures to encourage the democratic use of time for chamber business, such as placing time limits on answers at question time and publishing a roster of numbers of questions per party. The chamber also produces reports on speaking time by party per session to demonstrate relative parity across all parties. It has established set time limits for government to respond to parliamentary reports. Another procedural contribution was the establishment of deadlines for introducing legislation in each session (the 'cut off'). This procedure has prevented the introduction of a large numbers of bills at the end of a sitting period with a demand for immediate passage and addressed concerns about lack of proper scrutiny due to an 'end-of-session rush'.

Senate committees

While both houses in parliament have committees, the Senate committees have secured more prominence and influence. Committees date from the first year there was a Senate, and a system of permanent ('standing') committees was introduced in 1970. These standing committees complement an earlier 'scrutiny' committee process and take two forms, 'legislation' and 'references'. The 'legislation' committees, with chairs from the government, inquire into bills before the Senate and are often mini-partisan forums. In the 20 years from 1970 to 1989, only 55 bills were referred to committees, but in the next 30 years (1990 to 2019) this number passed 2,400 (Browne, and Oquist, 2021, p.26). The 'references' and select committees, with non-government chairs, look into specific topics referred to them by the Senate. These inquiries are typically conducted over a period of months and depending on the subject matter tend not to be partisan (or not *as* partisan). In the modern period many more committee reports have been issued, typically now between 150 and 230 a year (Figure 12.3).

Conventions play a big role in determining how committees operate as John Uhr (2005, p.20) noted:

> *Conventions are fragile things but the Senate conventions seem to imply that whenever there is not a government majority, then the preferred practice is to share power among all represented political groupings: including a share of the power to control Senate committees. Since 1994 the Senate standing committees have been divided into references committees, with non-government chairs and non-government majorities, and legislation committees where the government retains control.*

The Scrutiny of Delegated Legislation Committee (which was originally established in 1932) allows the parliament to review regulations that are not made by the parliament but by a minister acting under authority granted to them by existing laws. These 'legislative instruments' may not attract much attention in the full chamber or with the public, but they can generally be disallowed by parliament. A recent example of the Committee's work was a September 2021 report on regulations governing the Australian Charities and Not-for-Profits Commission (ACNC). Notwithstanding assurances from the Assistant Treasurer, the Committee felt that the regulations unduly limited the ability of charities' staff to engage in political advocacy. The Committee recommended that the Senate disallow the instrument. This was a good example of how the committee's work in examining and drawing attention to regulations has made an important democratic contribution.

Figure 12.3: The total number of reports issued in a year by Senate committees, from 1974–2022

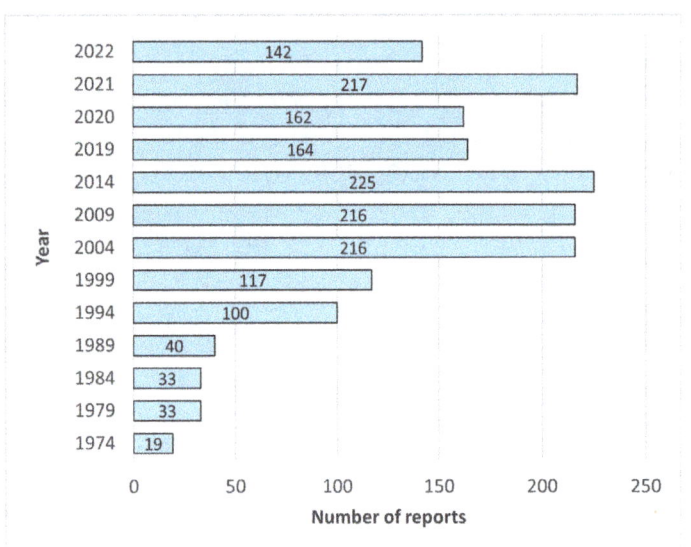

Source: Chart from data in Browne and Oquist, 2021, *Representative, Still – The role of the Senate in our Democracy, Research report, Canberra: The Australia Institute, March, p.26; and* Senate of Australia, 2024.

Senate committees also meet for 'estimates' hearings where the senators have the chance to question senior public servants directly about programs, activities and spending within their departments. Often feared by senior public/civil servants for their depth of information and quality of questioning, these committees have played an important democratic role in extending national political debate and the accountability of federal public administration.

The emergence of National Cabinet

Prime Minister Scott Morrison's creation of a new National Cabinet in April 2020 included himself, State Premiers and Territory Chief Ministers, and was a major change in federal-state government relations (covered elsewhere in Chapters 13 and 16), superseding the Council of Australian Governments (COAG). The stated aim of this change was so that National Cabinet would meet more regularly, avoid excessive bureaucracy and make national decisions more rapidly (particularly in response to the global pandemic). However, a less evident aim could be to sideline an increasingly complex Senate that has not been controlled by major party partisanism, with more non-major party senators representing distinctive regional interests in Canberra.

The 'National Cabinet' has no constitutional basis. At its formation, it was characterised by PM Morrison as effectively a sub-committee of the PM and federal cabinet, and thus not subject to direct scrutiny by parliament. The National Cabinet members are not part of the federal parliament. Yet, given its composition, the new body may present a threat to the Senate and suggest a further diminishing of its role as the key representative of state and territory interests, which had already occurred under the weakened COAG arrangements that the National Cabinet replaced (see Chapter 16). Of particular concern has been that its deliberations have been secret and not subject to the level of democratic scrutiny provided by Senate procedures and provisions.

However, the Senate used its powers to push back. In August 2021, Senate crossbencher, Rex Patrick, brought a case before the Administrative Appeals Tribunal (AAT) that the PM had been incorrect to suggest that federal cabinet confidentiality could be extended to National Cabinet meetings. Subsequently, Coalition ministers introduced legislation into the parliament that would extend secrecy provisions in the Freedom of Information (FOI) Act to extend the secrecy provisions of Federal Cabinet to the 'National Cabinet'. Senators were critical of this move, accusing the PM of attempting to block public scrutiny of deliberation and decisions affecting federal, state and territory governments. This provides a clear example of the way in which the Senate's presence, powers and ongoing demands for transparency and accountability can challenge executive power. In July 2022, the Albanese Labor government indicated that it would continue to use the vehicle of a 'National Cabinet' and these debates remain ongoing.

Senate elections, party competition and 'hung' politics

As the voice of the states, the Senate was intentionally designed to provide a different style of geographical representation from the lower house. Seats in the House of Representatives are allocated in a strict, population-proportional way, and constituency sizes are regularly adjusted to maintain the (broadly) equal influence of citizens' votes across the country. As noted earlier, Senate seat numbers are permanently fixed and 'malapportioned' in population terms as a deliberate constitutional decision. The ratio of senators to state populations shows a strong variation with NSW having over 680,000 people per senator, and Tasmania fewer than 144,000 (Figure 12.4). If citizens want to take an issue only to senators from the same political party, then even for the top two parties the Figure shows that the number of people per senator are higher still. The democratic implications of this design have often been hotly contested, not least from Labor and left-wing perspectives that have at times seen the upper house as a conservative force thwarting the popular will for progressive change policies. For instance, in 1992, former Labor PM Paul Keating proclaimed in the lower house (with characteristic hyperbole) that he 'would forbid [the Treasurer] going to the Senate to account to [those] unrepresentative swill' (Ricketts, 2013).

The allocation of seats is invariant and not reviewed. The only change in the Senate electorate's sizes occurs with population growth, and the only variation in seat numbers contested at once occurs when a federal PM uses their rarely used power to precipitate a 'double dissolution' of both the House and the Senate (reducing the quota for election). This has only happened once this century, in 2016, when the PM Turnbull called a double dissolution, but failed to get a stronger number of major party senators as he had hoped.

In a perceptive analysis, Willumsen, Stecker and Goetz (2019) showed that voters in different states formed different expectations of their senators. Tasmanians expect to interact personally with their senators, while in the biggest states: '[Overload] makes those activities which allow representatives to be responsive to a large number of people at one time more attractive' (p.3). The study also found two effects in behaviour of senators. As the size of their states increased, senators asked more questions of ministers, perhaps anxious to demonstrate activity on voters' behalf. But at the same time, as diversity of their state's population and economy rose, senators also moved fewer amendments and bills in the chamber, perhaps because the collective interests of the state were more complex. Further, the study found that the more senators their party had in a given state, the less that senators tended to be active in the chamber (Willumsen, Stecker and Goetz, 2019).

Figure 12.4: The number of people represented by each senator across the states and territories in September 2022

State/territory	Population (in 000s)			Liberal-National senators	Labor senators
	per senator	per Coalition senator	per Labor senator		
New South Wales	682	1,366	2,048	6	4
Victoria	554	1,331	1,664	5	4
Queensland	446	1,071	1,785	5	3
All Australia	*344*	*843*	*1,005*	*32*	*26*
Western Australia	234	561	561	5	5
Australian Capital Territory	230	na	459	0	1
South Australia	152	305	457	6	4
Northern Territory	125	251	251	1	1
Tasmania	47	143	143	4	4

Source: Computed using data in Australian Bureau of Statistics (2023) 'National, state and territory population'.

Note: All population per senator numbers are shown in thousands, and are also rounded to the nearest 10,000 people. States have 12 senators each, and territories two each.

In this analysis, opposition senators asked more questions and moved more amendments than those on the government side, as did senators with more education or previous occupations of higher or professional status (Willumsen, Stecker and Goetz, 2019). When there was a hung parliament overall, or an evenly split Senate, legislators as a whole also asked more questions to the government. Ministers in the Senate were generally the least active members, presumably because they had additional executive roles and could not ask questions outside their briefs. However, they were very active in the chamber in managing government business and moving amendments. Although only one study, this work points to important ways that Senate composition contributes to forms of democratic activity by senators.

Political development and the Senate's character

Over and above the impact of constitutionally fixed features, the long-run development of the Senate's operations has been affected by some slower, 'glacial' changes in Senate politics (since proportional representation for its elections was first introduced in 1951). The chamber has slowly come to better reflect the diversity of political views within the Australian community. We noted above a strengthening tendency for Australian voters to choose different parties in the two houses in recent years, resulting in a lower major party first-preference vote in the Senate elections (see Figure 12.1). This pattern has longer term roots. Figure 12.5 shows that since the 1980s there have generally been fewer major party primary votes for the Senate than for the House of Representatives and with a more consistent recent decline in this trend line. In the past many smaller or even micro parties historically did not run in the House of Representatives districts where they stood little chance of winning the single seat. However,

Parliament – the Senate   265

Figure 12.5: Comparing the primary (first-preference) vote for the top two parties (Labor and the Liberal-National Coalition) in Senate and House of Representatives elections, from 1970–2022

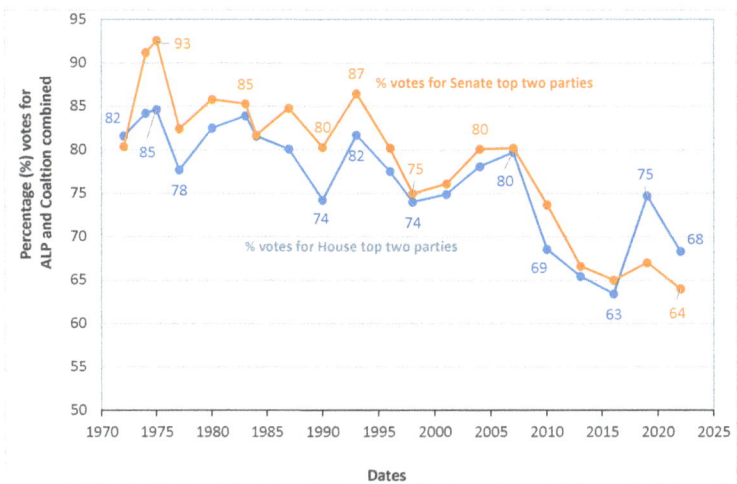

Source: Compiled from summary data in Parliament of Australia (2017) 'Federal election results 1901–2016'; and Figures 12.1 and 12.3 above.

Note: The dates on the horizontal axis show five-year intervals, not the dates of elections. The vertical axis starts at 50 per cent here, to show over-time changes more clearly. Only select vote share numbers are given for the two lines to show variations.

Figure 12.6: The long-run trends in national vote share for the top two parties, versus the combined vote share for all other parties and independents in Senate elections, 1970–2022

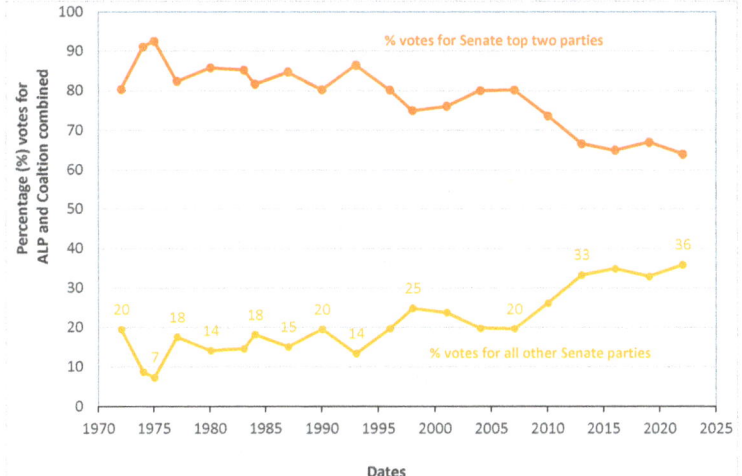

Source: Compiled from summary data in Parliament of Australia (2017) 'Federal election results 1901–2016'; Parliament of Australia (2023b) 'The representation of small parties and independents'; and Figure 12.3 above. See also Ghazarian (2017).

Note: The dates on the horizontal axis show five-year intervals, not the dates of elections. Only select numbers are given for the two vote share lines to show variations.

even this pattern of candidacies has also changed markedly in recent years, especially with the rise of Teal and other independents in the 2022 Federal Election (see Chapters 5 and 11).

The growing support for a third or minor party and independent candidates in Senate elections has also seemed to be a strategic decision by the electorate (Ghazarian, 2017). Some voters have wanted the Senate to provide an accountability and legislative check on the government. For many years, one minor party successfully ran in the Senate on a slogan of 'keeping the bastards honest'. This sentiment has continued to resonate in the attitudes of many Australians to the role of the Senate. Figure 12.6 demonstrates that the trend for more pluralised Senate election voting also goes back a long way (although with some bobbing up and down) and has created a long-run decline of the two major parties' combined vote share. However, these voters' preferences were previously fragmented rather ineffectually between small parties or independents championing particular state issues.

The accountability of crossbenchers

Some observers have criticised the shift toward micro-party or 'single-issue' senators and argued that it has been an unwelcome change when considered in combination with the major parties increasingly needing crossbench support to pass new laws. In addition, the smaller micro party that won Senate seats in a given state has sometimes generated surprises, especially because they can have significant influence if the two major parties are closely tied, or if either has needed a few votes to secure a majority.

For the most part, the party that has held a majority in the House of Representatives has not also held a majority in the Senate. Until 1972, this was not a major problem for the Government as the party holding the 'balance of power' in the Senate generally supported policies similar to those of the Government. The election of the Rudd Labor Government in 2007 represented a further tipping point for the Australian Senate when it formed in 2008. Previously, the deciding vote had resided with a single established minor party (the Democratic Labor Party (DLP), or Australian Democrats or Australian Greens). Labor's task in managing legislation through the Senate became more challenging as there was now more than one party with whom to negotiate. From 2008, the Senate's 'balance of power' was shared by a mix of the Greens small party, the Family First micro party and Independent Senator Nick Xenophon. The period from 2011 saw further growth in micro parties and independent senators, while the number of crossbenchers peaked at 20 senators in the 2016 double dissolution, and Labor returned to government in 2022 needing not only the Greens but one or two more senators in order to pass contested laws.

These trends have not been welcomed by the major parties, as the Keating comment quoted above demonstrated. Some public leaders and commentators have described the fragmentation trend as undemocratic because of the potential for one or a small number of senators to 'hold the nation to ransom' in 'balance of power' situations. In fact, such situations are solely produced by strict voting whips operating in the major party vote blocs. That is, minor parties only have the 'balance of power' when it has been given to them by the disciplines of the major parties. This nuance has often been lost in public commentary.

The most often cited cause for concern has been that independent senators can receive disproportionate concessions (pork-barrelling) for their states in return for giving support on critical votes – a factor alleged to have applied in the cases of Tasmania Senator Brian Harradine with the sale of public communications company (Telstra) under the Howard government (Grattan, 2014) and Senator Nick Xenophon with economic concessions in response to the global financial crisis of 2008 to 2010 (Siegall, 2016). In practice, however, the potential for 'balance of power' situations to produce undemocratic results has been overstated. When the demands of single senators exceed what has been deemed reasonable by the government, the multi-party nature of the 'balance of power' typically has resulted in unreasonable demands being rejected. In short, the crossbench only has power as long as its demands are more palatable than the Opposition.

Meanwhile, the practical politics of the 'balance of power' can also result in expanded (and arguably more representative) legislative activity. Vital to this contribution have been the parliament-funded Office of the Clerk Assistant (Procedure) and the Parliamentary Library (and more recently the Parliamentary Budget Office) – which all provide expert advice and rigorous research to non-government senators that can support them in exercising their legislative responsibilities. There have been notable examples where Private Member Bills (PMBs), instigated by senators outside of the government, have won the support of opposition parties to move to the House of Representatives, and a handful of Senate-initiated PMBs have even passed successfully through both houses. However, far more commonly, non-government senators have introduced PMBs to draw attention to a national issue, following which the government has introduced its own comparable bill. Another possible channel of influence has occurred when a PMB moved by an opposition gets converted into government policy on their return to majority in the House.

The Senate's role on 'democracy' issues

To explore how Senate operations have fostered the democratic quality of Australian democracy in positive ways, three case studies are illuminating. The first is historical and illustrates the role of senators from outside the two major parties. The second demonstrates the unique role and operation of Senate committees. The third case is a recent example where the Senate was instrumental in holding the executive to account.

Government in minority and the Fair Work Act

As noted earlier, the government in the House of Representatives has usually been in the minority in the Senate. However, there was one notable exception with one-party majorities in both Houses, namely the Coalition government under PM John Howard between 2004 and 2007. This was a period where the government sought to make significant changes to industrial relations, including exemptions to unfair dismissal, through its *Work Choices* legislation, which used national corporation powers to shift responsibility for industrial relations away from the states and territories and to the Commonwealth. The bill passed the Senate by 35 votes to 33 (with even some coalition members not voting for it) (Parliament of Australia, 2005). The Act was deeply unpopular with the trade unions, and many commentators believed that the controversy around it contributed to the government's subsequent electoral defeat.

The incoming Rudd Labor Government promised to use the same powers to reverse these changes through its *Fair Work* laws. *Fair Work* sought to introduce 'modern awards' around national standards for federal employees and in doing so drive change with other employees and at other levels. Particularly, it sought to 'harmonise' awards by shifting jurisdictional awards to national level, introducing a 'no disadvantage' transition test and reining in unfair dismissal arrangements (Stewart and Forsyth, 2009). However, the government had only a minority of seats in the Senate and needed the support of the Australian Greens and one of two crossbenchers for the passage of these bills. Two controversial issues emerged that left Senators Xenophon and Fielding with the decisive vote.

The first issue related to inclusions and transitions within the 10 new modern awards. The government, along with peak bodies, lobbied the senators strongly around the national support for these changes. However, Senator Xenophon claimed that through consultation with members of these peak bodies and citizens from his state of South Australia he had identified unfair conditions – centring around too large a shift in too short a time from state to modern awards in some states. He also argued that this was a national rather than state-specific challenge. Xenophon raised these issues with the government in early 2009.

Ministers signalled that they would proceed as intended. Senator Xenophon then drew on his party colleagues in the South Australia's upper house (the Legislative Council) to threaten to block the enabling legislation. This was important because each jurisdiction had to vote to refer their provisions to the Commonwealth. The move resulted in strong consultations, with the outcome being that retail, café and catering were removed from the hospitality sector and put into their own award category (with specific transitions). The horticulture award was also varied around flexible hours, casual rates and transition provisions. The referral legislation subsequently passed both houses of the South Australian Parliament. This example shows senators' powers in a government minority setting being used to address the needs of citizens that would otherwise have been excluded by legislation, and to impress distinctive state needs on ministers.

However, a second issue highlights the limits on these powers. Earlier, there had been strong disagreement about the number of employees to be used to designate a small business, one that would be exempt from the full laws on unfair dismissal. The Liberal-National's previous *Work Choices Act* provisions set this at 100 employees, while Labor sought to reduce this to 15 employees. Senator Xenophon believed that this number was too low and moved an amendment for the threshold to be set at 20 full-time equivalent employees that passed the Senate in early March 2009. In response, ministers made the counter-vailing case that this new limit was unworkable. After negotiations with Senator Fielding, the government passed additional legislation to set a transition limit at 15 full-time equivalent employees for 18 months, before returning to the intended 20 people after that. Both examples demonstrate the powers of non-government members in the Senate to create important detailed wins for their states and more granular representation of state-specific interests, while also demonstrating the constraints applying if a government deems an individual specific demand too extreme.

The establishment of the Banking Royal Commission

The powers of Senate committees can also result in greater scrutiny and policy change, as the case of the Banking Royal Commission (2019) shows. For several years before 2017, there had been public criticism of the treatment of customers by the four major banks (ANZ, Commonwealth Bank, National Australia Bank and Westpac). This attracted more attention when, in May 2014, the Australian Broadcasting Commission's *Four Corners* program broadcast an investigation of the sales-driven culture within the Commonwealth Bank's financial planning division. The Senate Economics Committee had been conducting an inquiry into the performance of the Australian Securities and Investments Commission (ASIC) since June 2013. They used ASIC's responses, which they described as complacent, to highlight misconduct within the Commonwealth Bank's financial planning division. One of the recommendations of the Committee's report was the establishment of an independent inquiry, such as a Royal Commission, to review the actions of the Commonwealth Bank. The Liberal-National government's response in October 2014 rejected this recommendation.

In subsequent months, more evidence emerged of improper conduct at other major banks. In April 2016, the then Treasurer Scott Morrison described the proposed commission as 'a reckless distraction that puts at risk confidence in the banking system' (Coorey and Frost, 2017). However, from the government ranks, Senator John Williams dissociated himself from the Treasurer's remarks. A member of the Economics Committee, he was a longstanding critic of the banks (and of ASIC) and believed consumers and small business were not adequately protected. He supported the call for a Royal Commission.

While the Coalition Government was returned at the 2016 Federal Election, pressure for an inquiry into the banks continued to mount. In March 2017, a private member's bill was introduced by the Australian Greens, and supported by a number of crossbench senators, to establish an inquiry. The Labor Opposition said it would vote in favour and Senator Williams announced he would 'cross the floor' to support it, meaning that it would pass the Senate. Opposition to a Royal Commission was also wavering among government backbencher MPs, which meant that it could have passed in the House of Representatives as well. Faced with the prospect of an inquiry whose terms of reference would be set by the crossbench and opposition, the four major banks reversed their position opposing a Royal Commission and instead wrote to the PM saying they would now support one appointed by the government. The government then announced a Royal Commission, which reported in February 2019 (Banking Royal Commission, 2019), recommending a whole raft of changes to secure greater responsibility, regulation, scrutiny and accountability on the part of banking directors and the banking industry. Opinions differed on how many of the 76 Commission-proposed changes were implemented by the early 2020s (Butler, 2021; Ziffer, 2022). Significant changes had nonetheless been precipitated.

Holding ministers to account for wrongful dismissal

In October 2020, Christine Holgate, the Chief Executive of Australia Post, appeared before a Senate Estimates Committee. The extraordinary events that followed provide a way of understanding the importance of the committee system in the Senate, its powers to uncover issues of public concern and hold the Executive to account. She had been accused of inappropriately awarding four Australia Post executives with Cartier watches as a reward for brokering a multi-million-dollar deal for major banks to continue to allow banking through post offices. She told the Senate that she could have awarded the four executives bonuses of $150,000 each, but chose not to. Up until this point, there had been no suggestion that her actions were in any way controversial.

Later that day in Parliament, the then Communications Minister, Paul Fletcher, asked Holgate to 'stand aside' claiming he was 'shocked and concerned' at what had been revealed in the Senate Estimates Committee that morning. Prime Minister Morrison subsequently said to Parliament, that if the chief executive did not wish to stand aside, she has been instructed to and 'if she doesn't wish to do that, Mr Speaker, she can go!' (Atkins, 2021). Holgate subsequently stood down. She denied voluntarily standing down. She claimed she was bullied and that the decision was made by the Australia Post Board Chairman, because (she believed) the PM had instructed it.

Five months later in April 2021, Holgate appeared in front of the Senate Environment and Communications References Committee. They were told the findings of a review by the law firm Maddocks into her dismissal found no deliberate dishonesty or fraud on Holgate's part and that it was within her rights as chief executive to make such gifts. Holgate suggested to the Committee that she was stood down not because of the gifts, but because she disagreed with many of the findings of the secret report by Boston Consulting Group to privatise parts of Australia Post. The Committee shared the Maddocks inquiry's concerns about disturbing direct government interference in an independent statutory authority. This occurred at the time, unbeknown to the Committee, when the PM had also had himself secretly sworn in as the Finance Minister. Ultimately, partly due to the interventions by Senate committees, Holgate received a $1 million dollar compensation payoff for wrongful dismissal in 2021.

Tensions and possible reforms affecting the Senate

Of course, the Australian Senate has not realised some form of democratic utopia. It has also been a legislature with inherent internal tensions. The first, and perhaps most enduring, tension within the Senate occurs between senators representing the citizens within their state or territory and the party position. This revolves around the democratic requirement on elected officials to try to represent all members of the community, including minority groups or those silenced in debates between majority groups. Although parties take state differences into account, it cannot be reasonably expected that the national position of the big parties especially will align with the interests of individual states or territories (and regions within them) on every issue.

A second tension revolves around the role of the Senate in controlling the actions of the executive. Parliamentarians are expected to regularly scrutinise the design, implementation, efficiency and effectiveness of government policy. For much of its history, this requirement was met by the Senate operating primarily as a house of review. However, as prominent third parties have grown and increasingly held the balance between government and the main opposition with deciding votes, some of the upper house parliamentarians have viewed themselves as equal legislators. Expressed in the 'oppose or amend' dilemma, should these legislators decide to appeal to an anti-government electoral base (oppose), they lose the opportunity to mitigate the harder elements of potentially successful legislation for those same groups (amend). At its most potent, this dilemma can split minor parties or damage their electoral survival (as noted previously with the Australian Democrats).

While presidential-style PMs were far from unprecedented in Australian political history, the consistent presence of presidential-style PMs since 2007 has created other issues for accountability. These developments have constrained the prominence, independence and influence previously available to portfolio ministers, while increasing pressure on ministers in both houses to toe the line set by the PM. These potential barriers to ministerial scrutiny in the legislature highlight the importance of Senate powers of ministerial censure and ordering of documents.

A prominent change in recent times has been the rise of the populist senators (Marks, 2017). A further shift away from the 'reviewer' and 'legislator' roles, these senators have argued that their popular appeal provides them with an independent 'mandate' to that of the executive. On this basis, they have sought to introduce legislation and engage less constructively with ministers or government policy. Increasingly, this has resulted in negotiations played out through the media, with questions raised about the extent that this has been driven by politics and enhancing a senator's public profile, rather than seeking genuine policy improvements. Such developments have potentially presented a challenge to the past conventions and operations in the Senate and mean that its democratic foundations cannot be taken for granted.

Reforms to reset Senate elections

An ongoing issue surrounding the Australian Senate has been the representation secured by micro parties and independent senators since 1984. Changes made to the STV voting system for the Senate in 1984 allowed for voters to select a single party preference 'above the line' on their ballot papers, rather than having to number every preferred candidate individually – although this remains an option for voters who use the 'below the line' part of the ballot paper (see Chapter 5). This change facilitated the election of more minor and micro party candidates. It was also increasingly subject to a process labelled 'preference harvesting' where the leaders of micro parties agree to swap their voters' second or later preferences with other parties, notifying the Australian Electoral Commission on how such transfers should take place. This can occur when the major parties support smaller parties in return for their voters' later preferences, or when micro parties swap preferences between each other. In some cases, new micro parties with names designed to appeal to certain elements in the community were established just to feed later preferences to existing parties.

A prominent example occurred prior to the 2013 Federal Election. Several deals were negotiated by the 'preference whisperer' consultant, Glenn Druery, who worked as an adviser to some of the micro parties. The result of this collaboration was the election in Victoria of Senator Ricky Muir of the new Australian Motoring Enthusiasts Party. Muir's party won only 0.5 per cent of the first-preference votes in the state, but he received later preferences from 22 other parties (nine of which started the count with more primary votes than Muir). The accumulated votes saw Muir win the last Senate seat in Victoria.

Following the 2013 election, the Joint Standing Committee on Electoral Matters (JSCEM) investigated these matters. Its chair, Tony Smith, concluded that the Senate voting system had delivered some 'outcomes that distorted the will of the voter' (Parliament of Australia, 2018). The Committee unanimously recommended the introduction of optional preferential voting for the 'above the line' party votes (i.e., numbering parties with their 1,2, 3 if votes wished) and only requiring voters to fill in a limited number of preferences for individual candidates 'below the line'. In effect, this recommendation would reduce the ability of parties' leaders (rather than their voters) to control how their later preferences were allocated.

In February 2016, PM Malcolm Turnbull announced that his government would attempt to implement the JSCEM recommendations. The measures received the support of the major and third parties and were applied from the 2016 Federal Election. However, that election was a 'double dissolution' with every Senate place vacant. This reduced the formal quotas for winning a seat (from over 14 to under 8 per cent). The Coalition's senate members fell to a 20 year low, while the reduction in quota also helped the Greens and smaller parties to win more seats (see Figure 12.2). In effect, this dissolution dissolved the intended potential positive impact for larger parties.

At the 2019 Federal Election, where half the Senate was up for election, the changes to the voting system seemed to have more of their intended effect (see Figure 12.2). There was a marked decline in the number of parties contesting the election, while only two micro parties and no independent senators were elected. Broadly, this was seen as an electoral improvement as it still enables independent or micro party members to be elected to the Senate, but in a way that was shaped more directly by voter intention. It also demonstrated the role of the Senate and its committees in renewing its democratic basis. In the 2022 Senate elections One Nation, United Australia and the Jacqui Lambie Network, plus one independent, won seats.

Public understanding of the Senate and its elections

A 2021 survey report of Australia citizens' views of the Senate by the Australia Institute found that the public had a fairly accurate view of the chamber's powers, with most people ascribing it more functions than it actually has exercised (see Figure 12.7; and Browne and Oquist, 2021). In addition, voters seemed to be broadly knowledgeable about how the Senate elections worked and were content with using a different system of voting (see Uhr, 2005).

Figure 12.7: Responses to survey questions about the Senate in the 2019 Australia Institute report

Question asked	Per cent (%) of respondents			
Which system of election is fairer?	19 *House*	10 *Senate*	37 *Equally fair*	34 *DK/No view*
2019: Better for Australia if the Government does or does not have a Senate majority	42 *Does*	31 *Does not*	27 *DK/No view*	
2021: Better for Australia if the Government does or does not have a Senate majority	36 *Does*	35 *Does not*	29 *DK/No view*	

Source: Browne and Oquist, 2021, *Representative, Still – The role of the Senate in our Democracy, Research report*, Canberra: The Australia Institute, March, p.26. Note: DK indicates 'don't know'

In addition, Browne and Oquist argue that in terms of the national match between votes cast for the Senate and members elected, the chamber has been less disproportional than the House of Representatives – which may bolster the public's positive view of it. Finally, by 2021, respondents were rather evenly divided on whether it was a good thing to have a Senate majority for the government or not, with government supporters more critical and those backing opposition parties more content. However, Browne and Oquist's (2021) key conclusion is that the Senate remains 'democratic still'.

In terms of representing the diversity of Australia's population, the Senate has also performed better than the House. It achieved a gender-balance with 51 per cent of members being women in 2019. The first two Indigenous parliamentarians were both senators and there continues to be more First Nations senators than MPs. Senators with Asian ancestry, women, Muslim and openly gay senators were also elected before their counterparts in the lower house. The first female party leaders were also in the Senate. There are grounds for the conclusion that the Senate is an avenue to present and represent more diverse perspectives within the parliament.

Conclusion

To be useful, the Senate needs to be neither a 'rubber stamp' nor an 'unrepresentative' obstruction. Walking this middle path requires it not to be dominated by the executive, the most vigorous members of the opposition, or an over-confident crossbench (or backbench). A key challenge that underlies each of these scenarios is the ongoing strictness of party discipline. Labor, with its tradition of caucus solidarity, has never been comfortable to release this bind. The Liberal-National Coalition parties pay lip service to the idea of state-specific voting, but in practice crossing the floor has become very rare. Meanwhile, the challenge of partisanship is exacerbated by periods of presidential-style politics and the influence of 'balance of power' populists. An obvious enhancement to the Senate's influence would be for backbenchers from both sides to feel free to vote in the interests of their states and territories, rather than adhering to party discipline. Greater diversity in intra-party voting would reduce the likelihood of the final vote being in the hands of a few pivotal crossbenchers and might even enhance the quality of regional, socially diverse and more deliberative representation. That said, the long-established and deliberately designed representation, structures, processes and conventions of the Senate continue to be its greatest protection against such threats. In summary, it is our contention that the origins and operations of the Australian Senate have historically been among the most democratic in Commonwealth nations. Our judgement of the current state of the Senate is that, although faced with both opportunities and threats, it has remained a resilient institution supporting Australia's democracy.

Note

The authors would like to acknowledge the support of Clerk of Senate, Richard Pye, with this chapter.

References

Atkins, Dennis (2021) 'PM's bullying of Christine Holgate shows his true colours', *The New Daily*, 9 April. https://www.thenewdaily.com.au/opinion/2021/04/09/dennis-atkins-holgate-morrison

Australian Bureau of Statistics (2023) 'National, state and territory population', 21 March. https://perma.cc/K9JP-DVNN

Australian Electoral Commission (2023) 'Federal elections'. https://perma.cc/2UFC-8VBM

Bach, S (2003) *Platypus and Parliament: The Australian Senate in Theory and Practice*, Australian Senate, Canberra. Available open access at https://perma.cc/UY5R-GUPT

Banking Royal Commission (2019) *Final Report: The Royal Commission into Misconduct in the Banking, Superannuation and Financial Services Industry*. February. https://perma.cc/X9C2-XLTJ

Browne, Bill and Oquist, Ben (2021) *Representative, Still – The Role of the Senate in our Democracy*, Research report, Canberra: The Australia Institute, March. https://perma.cc/P5VF-ZGQ3

Butler, Ben (2021) 'Banking royal commission: Most recommendations have been abandoned or delayed', *Guardian*, Australia, 18 January. https://perma.cc/HE8K-CPDU

Coorey, Phillip and Frost, James (2017) 'Cranky banks urge Scott Morrison to drop aggressive tactics', *Australian Financial Review*, 1 June. https://perma.cc/SSD4-GYQ4

Dennett, H (2022) 'Jobs and skills white paper: Anthony Albanese gives Treasury an invitation for frank and fearless advice', *Canberra Times*, 11 July. https://perma.cc/FJ73-LDKC

Evans, Steve and Jervis-Bardy, Dan (2022) 'Territory rights bill passes Senate, ACT and NT able to consider voluntary assisted dying laws', *Canberra Times*, 2 December. https://perma.cc/8QSD-85B4

Ghazarian, Zareh (2017) 'Small parties, big changes: The evolution of minor parties elected to the Australian Senate', Lecture in the Senate Occasional Lecture Series at Parliament House, Canberra, 17 March. https://perma.cc/HPY8-RYDC

Grattan, Michelle (2014) 'Brian Harradine – a one-off who played the power of one to the max', *The Conversation*, 14 April. https://perma.cc/79Q6-JV4Q

Hevesi, Bryant (2023) 'Albanese government "still seeking advice" on probe into Australia's response to COVID-19 pandemic seven months after PM's call', Sky News Australia, 29 March. https://perma.cc/5F74-WY7W

Kippin, Sean and Campion, Sonali (2018) 'How undemocratic is the House of Lords?', https://doi.org/10.31389/book1.m Chapter 4.4, in Dunleavy, Patrick; Park, Alice; and Taylor, Ros (2018) *The UK's Changing Democracy: The 2018 Democratic Audit*, London: LSE Press. https://doi.org/10.31389/book1

Marks, Kathy (2017) 'The rise of populist politics in Australia', Webpage, *BBC News* 1 March. https://perma.cc/L2AH-GCP6

Murphy, Katherine (2017) 'Scott Ryan on trust, partisanship and why he left Turnbull's frontbench', *Guardian, Australia*, 23 November. https://perma.cc/T9ZW-PUE5

Neale, Hannah (2022) 'Federal election 2022: A look back at the promises made to Canberrans', *Canberra Times*, 28 May. https://perma.cc/54RR-MYWM

Parliament of Australia (2005) Workplace Relations Amendment (Work Choices) Bill 2005, 14 December. https://perma.cc/U9HK-RZBP

Parliament of Australia (2017) 'Federal election results 1901–2016'. https://perma.cc/R2G9-QSM9

Parliament of Australia (2018) 'The new Senate voting system and the 2016 election', webpage, 25 January. https://www.aph.gov.au/About_Parliament/Parliamentary_Departments/Parliamentary_Library/pubs/rp/rp1718/SenateVotingSystem

Parliament of Australia (2020) Parliamentary Handbook for the 46th Parliament. https://perma.cc/J8S8-JH2Z

Parliament of Australia (2023a) 'Senate powers, practices and procedures'. https://perma.cc/YL6L-EH7Q

Parliament of Australia (2023b) 'Electing Australia's Senators' – Parliament of Australia. https://perma.cc/YL6L-EH7Q

Ricketts, Kieran (2013) 'The collected insults of former PM Paul Keating', *ABC News*, 11 November. https://perma.cc/7ZH9-N7SQ

Senate of Australia (2023) 'The Parliament of the Commonwealth of Australia: The Senate, List of Senators, 47th Parliament as at December 2023'. https://perma.cc/KP7C-GH5Q

Senate of Australia (2024) 'Register of Select Committee reports: Commencing 1970–30 April 2024'. https://perma.cc/TN4F-9V2G

Senate Select Committee on COVID-19 (2022a) *Final Report*, April. https://perma.cc/RFB6-YAZJ and in PDF form: https://perma.cc/GXA3-3T5C

Senate Select Committee on COVID-19 (2002b) *Coalition Senators' Dissenting Report*, webpage, April. https://perma.cc/BQ8A-96XE

Siegall, Matt (2016) 'Australian senator Xenophon emerging as kingmaker in tight election', *Reuters*, 2 July. https://perma.cc/6DMB-JQHF

Stewart, Andrew and Forsyth, Anthony (2009) *Fair Work: The New Workplace Laws and the Work Choices Legacy*, Sydney: The Federation Press.

Taflaga, Marija (2021) 'Executive government', in Barry, Nick; Chen, Peter; Haigh, Yvonne; Motta, Sara C; and Perche, Diana (eds) *Australian Politics and Policy* Senior Edition *2021*, Sydney: University Sydney Press, pp.51–67. https://perma.cc/3CXG-BTDF

Trudgian, Tim (2016) 'Just how representative are the houses of parliament of how Australians vote?', *The Conversation*, 12 July. https://perma.cc/SM5W-CRFQ

Uhr, John (2005) 'How democratic is parliament? A case study in auditing the performance of Parliaments', Democratic Audit of Australia Discussion Paper, June. https://perma.cc/2TL3-S2AU

Wahlquist, Calla (2022) 'Teal independents: Who are they and how did they upend Australia's election?' *Guardian, Australia*, 23 May. https://perma.cc/28NN-UBZM

Wallace, Chris (2022) 'Rise of teal independents upsets Australian political orthodoxy'. *Nikkei Asia*, 9 May. https://perma.cc/P6L4-9L7W

Willumsen, David M; Stecker, Christian; and Goetz, Klaus H (2019) 'Do electoral district size and diversity affect legislative behaviour?', *Australian Journal of Political Science*, vol. 54, no. 1, pp.37–64. https://doi.org/10.1080/10361146.2018.1537390

Ziffer, Daniel (2022) 'Did the Royal Commission fix banking or are banks back to behaving badly?', *ABC News*, 25 November. https://perma.cc/J8VW-NSW5

13

Prime Minister, Cabinet and government

Mark Evans and Patrick Dunleavy

How well does the dominant centre of power in the Australian Commonwealth operate – spanning the Prime Minister (PM), cabinet, cabinet committees, ministers and critical Commonwealth departments? How accountable and responsive to parliament and the public is the 'core executive'? And how effective are these key centres of decision-making in making policy? Do they consistently serve the interests of Australian citizens?

What does democracy require of the core executive, along with wider federal government?

- The central institutions at the heart of government – PM, cabinet, ministers, cabinet committees, top officials and central departments – should provide clear unification of public policies across the federal government, and coordination with state governments, so that the Australian state operates as an effective whole, and citizens and civil society organisations can better understand decision-making.

- The core executive especially, and federal government more widely, should continuously protect the welfare and security of Australian citizens and organisations. Government should provide a stable and predictable context in which citizens can plan their lives, and enterprises and civil society can conduct their activities with reasonable assurance about future government policies.

- Both strategic decision-making within the federal core executive, and more routine policy-making across Commonwealth departments, should foster careful deliberation to establish the most inclusive possible view of the 'public interest'. Effective policy should maximise benefits and minimise costs and risks for Australian citizens and stakeholders.

- Checks and balances are needed within the core executive to guard against the formulation of ill-advised policies through 'groupthink' or the abuse of power by one or a few powerful decision-makers. Where 'policy fiascos' occur, the core executive must demonstrate a concern for lesson-drawing and future improvement.

How to cite this chapter:

Evans, Mark and Dunleavy, Patrick (2024) 'Prime Minister, Cabinet and government', in: Evans, Mark; Dunleavy, Patrick and Phillimore, John (eds) *Australia's Evolving Democracy: A New Democratic Audit*, London: LSE Press, pp.275–300. **https://doi.org/10.31389/lsepress.ada.l** Licence: CC-BY-NC 4.0

- The core executive and government should operate fully within the law, and ministers should be effectively scrutinised by and be politically accountable to parliament. Ministers and departments/agencies must also be legally accountable to the courts for their conduct and policy decisions.
- Policy-making and implementation should be as transparent as possible, while recognising that some special core executive matters may need to be kept secret, for a time. Parliament should always be truthfully informed of decisions and policy plans as early as possible, and both House of Representatives and Senate debates and scrutiny processes should influence what gets done.
- Policy development should ideally distribute risks to those social interests best able to insure against them (that is, at lowest cost). Consultation arrangements should ensure that a full range of stakeholders can be and are easily and effectively involved. Freedom of information provisions should be extensive and implemented in committed ways.

In any political system the executive is the part that makes policies and gets things done. At the national level, the Australian executive consists of the Commonwealth government – the PM and all ministers, plus the Australian Public Service (APS) departments and large agencies headquartered in Canberra (see Chapter 14), each making policy predominantly in a single area. This centre also funds and guides all other federal agencies staffed by the APS. The most critically important of these bodies – often called the 'core executive' in comparative political science – is a smaller, inner set of institutions, especially the PM and cabinet, on which the Australian Constitution (following the Westminster system pattern) remains largely silent (see Chapter 1). It merely refers to the appointment of ministers by the Governor-General to administer Departments of State.

As in most other Western democracies the 'core executive' actors in Canberra are the PM, the cabinet that they appoint, cabinet committees, and senior ministers and officials in a few really key Commonwealth 'central' departments. The list here includes the PM's Office (PMO), the Department of the PM and Cabinet (DPM&C), the Treasurer and Treasury, the Minister of Foreign Affairs and the Department of Foreign Affairs and Trade (DFAT), the Department of Finance and its minister, the intelligence services, and the independent Reserve Bank of Australia (RBA). (The RBA separately sets interest rates, raises national debt and is a powerful independent central bank, whose role has nonetheless been key for government economic policy-making.) The central agencies – DPM&C, Treasury and Finance – are those that coordinate government as a whole. The Department of the PM and Cabinet supports the PM, cabinet, portfolio ministers and assistant ministers to achieve the government's policy agenda in a coordinated way. Treasury manages macro-economic and financial policy (including setting total state spending) and federal financial relations with the state governments. The Department of Finance distributes and manages the budget and controls public expenditure through the government's fiscal strategy. The Australian Public Service Commission (APSC) is also a central agency within the PM and cabinet portfolio, with a focus on managing the whole of the government's workforce strategy, building workforce capability and promoting integrity.

Line departments and agencies and their ministers run all the remaining functions of government, with each having one or more portfolios. To some extent, each cabinet minister has been a 'baron' in their own department, with the closest access to its information, systems and permanent staffs. Each minister maintains their own ministerial office, next to Parliament's debating chambers and just a floor below the one that is occupied by the press and broadcast media. Ministerial offices are run by a powerful chief of staff and mainly staffed by politically appointed advisors and assistants, plus liaison officials from the main department. Each department also supervises a wide range of other agencies charged with implementing different discrete services and regulatory arrangements within the portfolio. Major line agencies at department level and below also play significant roles (APSC, 2023).

Recent developments

In the last decade, one of the most distinctive aspects of the Australia core executive has been the rapid rotation of PMs, sometimes characterised as part of a wider 'disposable leaders' tradition that has also seen many state premiers toppled (Tiffen, 2017). From 2010 to 2019, four consecutive PMs in office (Rudd, Gillard, Abbott and Turnbull) were challenged by a rival in their own party, and overthrown in a 'leadership spill' or vote of the parliamentary caucus (see below). This is not a new practice. Prime ministers such as John Gorton (1969 to 1971) and Bob Hawke (1983 to 1991) were removed by their party rooms, while Malcolm Fraser (1975 to 1983) survived party room challenges. Yet the frequency of caucus and party room challenges to incumbent PMs has undoubtedly increased in the past decade.

After his surprise election victory in 2019, PM Scott Morrison's authority within his government appeared supreme. However, the bushfire crisis of 2019 to 2020 quickly diminished his standing. The PM took too much time to acknowledge the scale of the crisis, eschewed the opportunity to play a coordinating role with the affected state leaders as they managed the emergency response, and went on a poorly timed holiday in Hawaii with his family. For many months he also seemed to deny the role of climate change and his own government's pro-carbon policies in contributing to the climate emergency. By January 2020, public fears of smoke pollution across Australia's biggest cities grew and fires raged out of control in regional areas, particularly in New South Wales. Morrison belatedly recognised the need for decisive action. He apologised for his holiday escape, committed more Commonwealth aid, sent troops to help the state governments worst affected and visited fire sites to express sympathy and support for victims and firefighters. As the crisis receded from late February, Morrison announced generous promises of fast economic support although, over a year later, research funded by activist group GetUp! shows that less than half of that funding had been allocated (Lloyd-Cape, Jackson and Lewis, 2021).

Strengths, weaknesses, opportunities and threats (SWOT) analysis

Current strengths	Current weaknesses
With voting for the House of Representative elections every three years (or sooner if the PM wants to call an early election) Australian PMs always closely watch their popularity in the opinion polls, enhancing their responsiveness to voters' views.	Policy short-termism has been built into the thinking of most governments, unless the governing party is well ahead of the opposition in opinion poll ratings and so can envisage a longer tenure in power.
In 'normal' times, Australian government can be strongly unified, with clear PM and cabinet control, strong ministers supervising the Commonwealth departments, single-party governments and relatively clear policy stances. This was the case even during the Labor minority government from 2010 to 2013. Arguably though this continued PM and cabinet control hinged on the relationship management and negotiation skills of then-PM Julia Gillard, in dealing with independents who held the balance of power.	Four of the last five PMs have lost office through leadership 'spill' elections or internal machinations in their party's parliamentary caucus in 'exceptional' times – those where the PM seemed to be performing below expectations in the polls against the opposition, and a rival potential leader organised a party coup against them. This trend to 'disposable leaders' can contribute to policy short-termism.
The PM's 'three As' powers over their own party's ministers are extensive. They appoint people to cabinet, allocate their portfolios and assign policy issues across departments. Typically, in Labor governments, ministers have been elected by caucus through a process heavily managed by party factions, with the PM then assigning portfolios and retaining the ability to fire ministers.	Theoretically the PM's powers are so great that they can *over*-homogenise their governments, so arranging the policy trade-offs of ministers from their own party that they will perfectly implement just the premier's preferences. In 'normal' times, most ministers are highly dependent on the PM's patronage and access for influence.
Frequent reshuffles allow the PM to monitor ministers' performance and fine-tune overall government performance.	With Liberal-National governments, the National party leader has always been the deputy PM, and co-controlled what roles the smaller party's ministers get to play. With Labor governments, a less clear-cut balancing of strong factional groupings constrains PM's choices. Both effects may protect failing or misbehaving ministers from being easily disciplined by the PM, as shown by the 2019–20 'sports rorts' affair (also known as the McKenzie scandal).

Current strengths	Current weaknesses
The PM's powers should help ensure coherence across government policies, and the maintenance of an effective structure of departments.	In pursuit of purely political advantages, PMs have often re-jigged ministerial portfolios. They have also sometimes pushed through more expensive reorganisations of Commonwealth departments and agencies to emphasise political priorities. This administrative churning can be costly and may disrupt policy-making.
Collegial discussion in cabinet and the cabinet committee system provides key checks on the power of PMs and their political office. They are supposed to foster greater deliberation before policy commitments are made, and provide a balanced approach, with ministers representing the interests of their portfolios' stakeholders, and also diverse public reactions.	Australia has only a small system of top cabinet committees, which the PM (with the help of the Cabinet Secretary) can relatively easily control. Morrison was even accused of running a 'one-man committee' where he was the only permanent member (Karp, 2020).
Decisions within cabinet and the core executive are normally made on far more than a simple majority rule (51 per cent agreement). Instead, an initial search looks for a high level of consensus across ministers/departments. This may give way to deciding on a smaller but still 'large majority' basis (for example, 60 per cent agreement), especially in crises or situations where the status quo is worsening over time.	Collegial cabinet decision-making has been limited because a PM can control the routeing of issues through committees and can bypass them via discussion just with a relevant minister. In 'normal times', strong integration of government communications also enforces complete solidarity across all ministers, without any guarantee of participation in decisions. Two cabinet committees (on national security and parliamentary business) make binding decisions that cabinet cannot then overturn. Ministers may fight back against losing out by 'adversarial leaking', which is in turn routinely denied.
Because of these processes, the principle of 'collective responsibility' binds cabinet ministers to publicly back every agreed government policy, and not to talk 'off their brief'. Wider ministerial solidarity also requires all ministers to follow the government line and always vote in line with party policy. Instances of any MPs voting against the party line in the Liberal-National Coalition are almost unheard of, and in the Labor Party are grounds for expulsion.	Compared with non-'Westminster system' democracies Australia still has relatively few checks and balances on the PM or the core executive. In the House of Representatives, ministers in governments with secure majorities have mostly escaped any unfavourable consequences of bad policies.
Policy-making can take place swiftly when needed, as Australia's decisive response to the COVID-19 pandemic demonstrated. The resilience in crisis-handling and capacity to respond to demanding contingencies are generally high.	Some 'groupthink' episodes have occurred, as in the delayed response to 2019–20 fires. In areas like immigration a pursuit of 'strong' policy has sometimes meant Australia acting in breach of international law.

Current strengths	Current weaknesses
Australia's institutions are strongly rooted in a tradition of relatively effective government, confident and immediate administrative implementation of ministerial decisions (when they are clear), and (normally) high levels of public acceptance and legitimacy. Some long-running core executive policy ambiguities were resolved in 2020 to 2023 (see Chapter 28)	Because of short periods of PMs in office and frequent elections, there has been limited evidence of much substantial policy-learning capacity within the core executive. This has been reinforced in recent years by the lack of adequate record keeping to underpin institutional memory in Australian PMOs (Rhodes and Tiernan, 2014).
Governments are expected to consult (most) affected interests on major policy changes (see also Chapters 7 and 8). Because governments seldom control the Senate with majorities, independent and opposition senators have often been able to 'moderate' government legislation changes, and block potentially extreme legislation.	Even on relatively mundane legislation, ministers and departments often choose to ignore or override politically inconvenient feedback received. They can push ahead with harsh policies that then backfire, as with the 'robodebt' policies in 2017 to 2019, later ruled illegal in the courts. The Senate has rarely been able to moderate or constrain ministers' executive actions. Where Senates are likely to oppose actions, governments often seek non-legislative avenues to achieve their ends.
All ministers sit in parliament and are directly and individually accountable there for their actions. The Freedom of Information (FOI) Act secures public transparency. Modern media, interest groups and social media scrutiny has been intense, rapid and fine-grained.	Ministerial decision-making operates in a climate of pervasive secrecy (still enforced by the Official Secrets Act). Ministers often withhold information from parliament, reject FOI requests on questionable grounds, and manipulate the flows of information to their own advantage. They incur only small costs when found out, unless a scandal takes root.
	Long-running power conflicts occur between leadership rivals. A powerful, up-and-coming minister (often the Treasurer, or deputy PM under Labor) can amass enough influence with parliamentary and cabinet colleagues to exercise a 'blocking veto' on the PM in their portfolio. Such stand-offs may either result in policy inaction, or lead to extra time spent to achieve a bargained compromise between the PM and the vetoing minister.
Future opportunities	**Future threats**
Australia managed to avoid the worst impacts of the 2008 to 2011 global financial crisis, and was 'lucky' again in its experience with the COVID-19 pandemic. Relatively continuous economic growth could provide a basis for strong core executive governance performance (under either major party). However, conflicts with China and adverse climate change events – floods, fires and drought – could occur.	Even longer-lasting PMs have conspicuously avoided addressing Australia's long-running policy problems – such as adjusting to climate change; managing the tension between being economically dependent on China but allying militarily and diplomatically with the USA; or finding policies to better combat the poor social and economic conditions in many Indigenous communities.

Figure 13.1: The cabinet committee structure in February 2021 (pre-COVID-19)

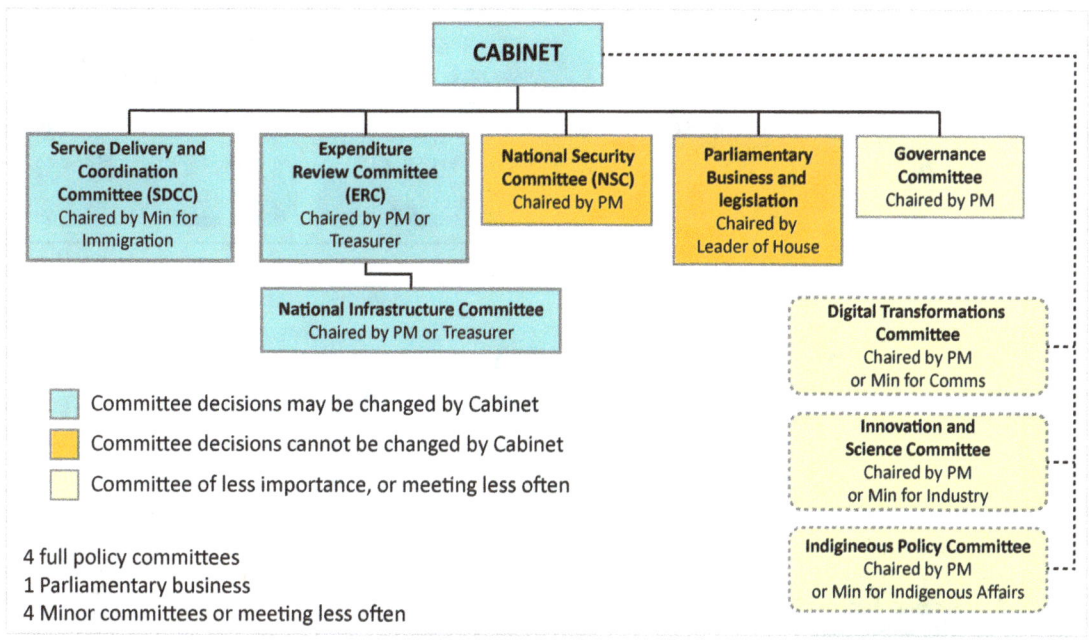

Source: Australian Government (2021a), Cabinet Committees.

The onset of the COVID-19 crisis in March 2021 saw considerable change in the previously operating cabinet committee system. In non-COVID-19 times, Australia has only a small set of cabinet committees, whose configuration under the Morrison government in early 2021 is shown in Figure 13.1. Of the top six committees that meet regularly, two make decisions that bind the rest of the cabinet without a possibility of being overturned, one being in the area of national security where the PM and their National Security Advisor dominate, and the other being for parliamentary and legislative business, which has been a largely technical issue, albeit of great importance for ministers promoting legislation. Of the four committees, the Expenditure Review Committee has been seen as most influential. Some others involve some junior ministers, have larger memberships and may not in fact meet often, making their influence hard to gauge.

With 23 ministers holding portfolios, cabinet committees are an important way of securing integration and most are, in principle, chaired by the PM (except the Service Delivery and Coordination Committee), with the PM's close advisor the Cabinet Secretary a member of all of them. In the 'named' permanent members of the committees, only the Deputy PM, Treasurer and Minister for Finance have three or four positions – most ministers have only two or even just one.

During COVID-19, new structures were established and have endured, especially the National Cabinet (see Figure 13.2). The National Cabinet is comprised of the PM and all state and territory chief ministers. It was technically set up as an intergovernmental forum to play a crisis leadership role in combating COVID-19. Westminster conventions of cabinet (such as collective responsibility) did not apply to the National Cabinet. Most observers at the time believed that 'it is COAG by another name' (Menzies, 2021), referring to the Council of Australian Governments (COAG), the primary intergovernmental forum in Australia from 1992 to 2020 (see Chapter 16). Emergency coordination mechanisms were also established in specific Commonwealth departments, such as the Emergency Relief National Coordination Group in the Department of Social Services.

Figure 13.2: The system of COVID-19 governance during the pandemic

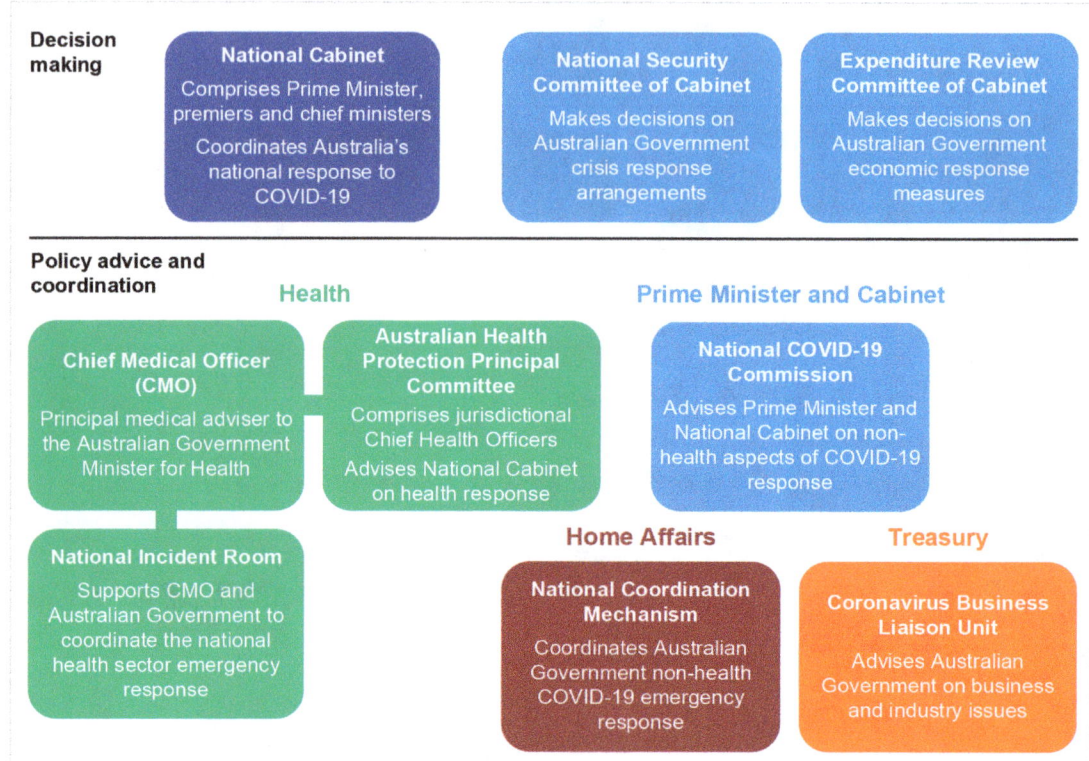

Source: ANAO (2020a), *Management of the Australian Public Service's Workforce Response to COVID-19, December, Figure 2.5, p.31*, CC-BY-NC-ND licence.

During the initial onset of the COVID-19 pandemic (in the first quarter of 2020), the Commonwealth government acted far more decisively than during the bushfires. Ministers and senior officials carefully evaluated competing international and national advice at the pandemic's beginning, which informed the decision for a quick closure of Australia's border with China. The World Health Organization (WHO) at first recommended against shutting borders (2020) but the then Chief Medical Officer Brendan Murphy pressed for closure on 1 February 2020, based on studying the epidemiological evidence from China, from where Australia's cases were originating. It was a bold step by the Morrison government, given the importance to the economy of Chinese students and tourists, and Morrison put the decision squarely on the health advice (Prime Minister's Office, 2020). 'Up until today it has not been the advice of the Chief Health Officer, and our medical experts that this has been necessary,' Morrison said. 'But now the advice had changed' (Evans and Grattan, 2021, p.24).

Morrison was far more willing to adopt the national coordination role that he had neglected in the bushfire crisis, frequently bringing the state and territory first ministers together, initially through COAG and then in what became the National Cabinet. National Cabinet ensured frequent discussions and sharing of information, but Morrison and the state premiers disagreed publicly, particularly about state border closures and hard lockdown decisions taken by state governments to suppress COVID-19 outbreaks (again because he deplored their economic costs).

Figure 13.3: Public perceptions of the quality of COVID-19 leadership in Australia, Italy, the USA and the UK in May to June 2020

(Percentage of country's respondents saying 'Strongly agree' or 'Agree' to statements)

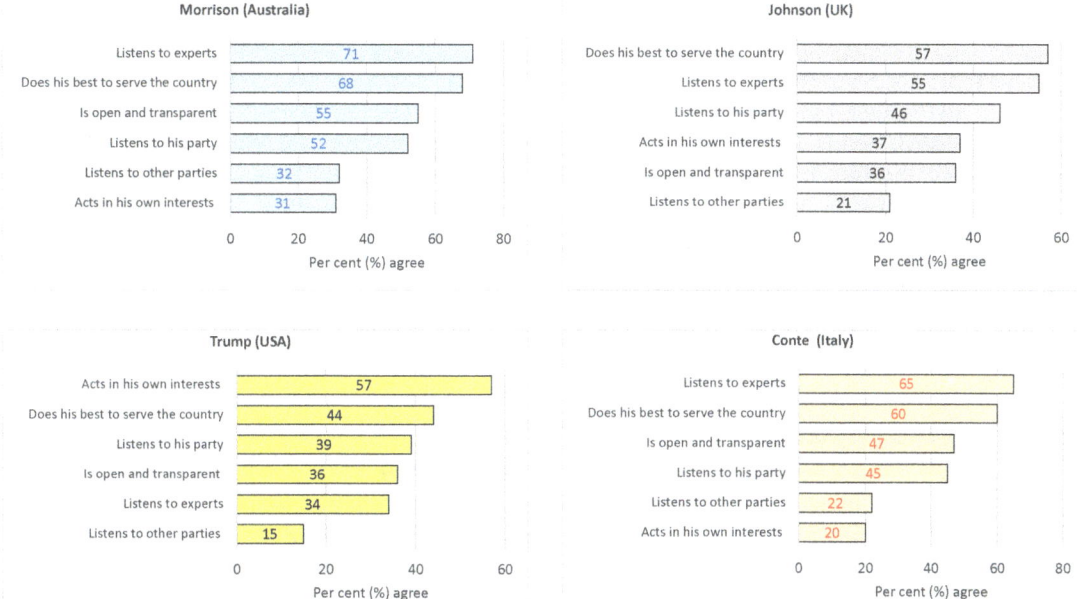

Source: Compiled from Jennings et al. (2021a), *Political Trust and the COVID-19 Crisis – Pushing Populism to the Backburner? A study of public opinion in Australia, Italy, the UK and the USA*, IGPA/ MoAD/Trustgov, Democracy 2025 Report No 8, Figure 15.

Note: Base: All respondents were adults. N = 1,061 in Australia, 28 May–15 June; N = 1,167 in the UK, 18–19 May; N = 1,150 in the USA, 19–23 May; and N = 1,134 in Italy, 21–22 May 2020.

In mid-2020, Australia was widely viewed by the public as having successfully managed the pandemic, especially compared to the USA, UK and other European countries. Australians' trust in their government almost doubled in a year from 29 per cent to 54 per cent (Evans et al., 2020). Figure 13.3 shows that PM Scott Morrison was at this period more favourably seen than his counterparts in the UK and Italy. For both Morrison and Conte, acting in their own self-interest was perceived by only a fifth of respondents, whereas 37 per cent agreed with this for Johnson in the UK and 57 per cent for President Trump in the USA. Morrison fared much better than Trump in the USA, who was also seen as more partisan and not listening to experts.

In the initial stages of the pandemic in early 2020, other surveys showed that leaders in a large number of countries enjoyed an increase in public confidence (Evans et al., 2020). The approval rating of Italian PM Giuseppe Conte hit 71 per cent in March 2020 – 27 points higher than the previous month – despite the fact his country was in the throes of a deadly first wave of the pandemic (De Feo, 2020). German Chancellor Angela Merkel saw her approval rise to 79 per cent (Henley, 2020), while the PMs of Canada and Australia, Justin Trudeau and Scott Morrison, saw similar surges in popularity during the early months of the pandemic.

That picture had changed by mid-2021. Australia remained locked down with a stalled vaccine rollout, while the USA, UK and other countries were opening-up. And public trust in the government soon eroded again. A July 2021 Essential poll showed people's support of the government's handling of the pandemic sliding nine points from 53 per cent to 44 per cent (Murphy, 2021). In addition, 30 per cent of respondents described the government's COVID-19 strategy as poor, compared to 24 per cent a month earlier.

The upsurge of support was partly explained by a 'rally-round-the-flag' effect often seen in crises (Hetherington and Nelson, 2003). In Australia, Morrison's approval rating soared on the back of his effective handling of the initial threat, judicious decision-making on early closure of international borders and an atypical coordination of state and federal governments via the National Cabinet. Moreover, a severe threat like a pandemic can make people more information-hungry, anxious and fearful. COVID-19 became a powerful shared experience for people. It touched most households through people's connections with health and social care workers and their communication with relatives, co-workers or friends who were in lockdown or unfortunate enough to get sick.

Yet, research also suggests many people do not lose their capacity for reason or critical judgement in a crisis (Jennings et al., 2021b). For example, people can oppose wars or other heavy-handed responses to terrorist attacks even if such attacks make them more anxious or fearful. Above all, the competence and outcomes of the government's actions matter. If the government was to be perceived as not able or willing to adequately respond to a threat, then public support will certainly fade. As a case in point, for a short period of time the Australian public was disenchanted with the slow rollout of the vaccine program and mixed government messaging over the relative risks of the AstraZeneca vaccine. In response, Morrison brought in Lieutenant General John Frewen and his team from the army to coordinate Operation COVID Shield in collaboration with the Department of Health. Yet despite the operation's outstanding performance (73.4 per cent of the population fully vaccinated by 3 December 2021) public trust declined 12 points from 54 per cent to 42 per cent in just two months (Evans, 2021). Despite these considerable achievements, the Morrison government lost power in the 2022 election – and so the COVID-19 experience did not lead to Australia bucking the previous trend for short-term federal PMs.

One contributing factor in the Liberal-National Coalition's defeat was the emergence of several scandals in the 2019 to 2021 period that created later problems for the government – such as uncontrolled government advertising in the run-up to the 2019 election breaching partisanship rules, using public funds in the 'sports rorts' and 'car parks' programs for partisan ends, and ministers endorsing harsh and ultimately illegal actions against welfare recipients in the 'robodebt' affair (see below, and Chapter 14). These reflected some enduring problems of executive predominance, weak controls on a majority government's power, and the lack of accountability of ministers and particularly of their advisors, as well as the debasing of standards in public life that have continued to stir controversy. This is discussed in sections below. Many of the deeper roots of accountability problems can be traced to how the portfolios for ministers relate to the public service departments they are responsible for, with the rise of political ministerial advisors and staffs 'politicising' many new areas of policy-making, again in polarising, non-deliberative ways, and the lack of any strong measures of accountability or oversight governing their actions and behaviour. The sparsity of checks and balances on senior politicians' behaviour was also highlighted during 2020–21 by a series of allegations of sexual misconduct and abuse by ministerial staffers, including serious allegations against the Attorney-General, albeit from a time long before he entered parliament (see below).

Like its predecessors from both parties, the Morrison government's most serious problems concerned the Australian core executive's strong pre-disposition towards short-term policy-making produced by three-year elections and frequent leadership challenges. Prime ministers and cabinets have long tended to pick 'quick fixes' that kick major problems into the long grass, rather than tackling them in good time. The threat that climate change poses to Australia, the driest inhabited continent in the world, has long been one such area – especially after Labor's attempt to introduce a 'carbon tax' during 2008 to 2009 backfired electorally and was reversed (ABC News, 2014). After the 2019–20 bushfires, it also proved a key factor undermining the Morrison government electorally (see Chapter 5). A second, pressing issue was the tension between Australia's trade dependence on China but its strong defence and diplomatic alliance with the USA and Western nations, which was decisively resolved in 2021 by the Morrison government's commitment to building nuclear submarines with the USA and UK, the AUKUS deal (discussed in Chapter 28). The core executive's record of tackling these policy dilemmas is briefly discussed at the end of the chapter.

The Labor government which took office in May 2022 followed conventional government patterns, with 22 cabinet ministers representing a broadly equal balancing of 'left' and 'right' factional politicians in Labor's senior ranks, plus seven 'outer ministry' appointments and 12 people in the 'assistant ministry', and with four 'special envoys' also – an overall total of 45 executive members. With a tiny majority in the House of Representatives and none in the Senate, the PM Anthony Albanese cultivated a very different, consensual policy style compared with his predecessor, with more of an emphasis on consultation, and quite a degree of policy continuity (for example, on the AUKUS deal, see Chapter 28).

The 'disposable leaders' controversy

From 2010 to 2019, there were repeated instances of conflicts at the very top of Australian government, between the PM and other senior ministers in their government (see Figure 13.4). This reflects a wider pattern in Australian state government for sitting PMs (and party leaders more widely) to be challenged and often deposed by rivals (Tiffen, 2017).

Leaders have been vulnerable because of the following:

- Australia has federal elections every three years (in contrast to the four or five years in most liberal democracies). Australian major party leaders have typically been elected and de-selected by the parliamentary caucus, that is all the party's members of the House of Representatives and Senate meeting in the party room (see Chapter 11). Because this is a relatively small group of professional politicians, they can be organised at short notice to hold a vote. So Australian PMs have had none of the protection afforded to party leaders in other liberal democracies (where long-winded leader elections by party mass membership have to be triggered, often with uncertain results).

- The 'spill' vote has been a uniquely Australian institution, allowing party representatives to express no confidence in a current leader and vote them out, without them at this stage having to be challenged explicitly or publicly by a declared rival candidate – with all the risks of failure, party unpopularity and apparent disloyalty that a 'stab in the back' entails. The rival will of course be publicly named and attacked, but they can profess their loyalty to the premier, while carefully calibrating a plot against them in secret.

- Only if the incumbent leader loses the spill, does a second stage leadership election open up. Rival candidates can now freely stand for the vacant post, with little stigma from having brought about the previous leader's downfall, and a spill vote can be requested by a rival candidate's supporter as a means of testing the level of dissatisfaction with the PM, without necessarily getting the rival's hands dirty.

- The Liberals and Nationals (in coalition in government) have both retained this long-established set up. Turnbull and Morrison each displaced their predecessors by a vote in the Liberal party room alone. In late 2019 a challenge to the National leader (and Deputy PM) in the National party room was for a time trailed as a possible consequence of the 'sports rorts' controversy, but it failed to materialise (see next section).

- However, Labor at the federal level has reformed its procedures, so that a spill motion now requires a higher threshold to unseat a Labor leader (75 per cent for an incumbent PM and 60 per cent for an opposition leader). If there is more than one candidate for the leadership position, the leader would be chosen by a weighted vote, where 50 per cent of the total votes consists of a party membership vote, and the other 50 per cent consists of the party caucus vote in parliament (and see Chapter 6). This mechanism has proved cumbersome to activate and seems to more or less rule out challenges to any future sitting Labor PM (although this has not been tested in practice yet). It confines the party to removing a losing leader after an election, essentially choosing a new one for the whole of the next three-year term, although in practice Albanese became leader unopposed in 2019.

Figure 13.4: Four recent instances of leadership conflict

Case 1: Kevin Rudd became Labor leader by challenging the incumbent in December 2006. Shortly afterwards, Labor won the 2007 election and Rudd appointed Julia Gillard first as a super-ministry head with welfare responsibilities, and later as a formally recognised Deputy PM. After a short period of rivalry, Gillard announced before the 2010 election that she would challenge Rudd for the leadership. Knowing that he could not win, Rudd did not contest a leadership 'spill'.
Case 2: Gillard led Labor into the 2010 election and emerged as the largest party, but could only form a minority government with some independent MPs' support after a hung parliament outcome. After a few months' absence from the cabinet, Rudd became Foreign Minister, a post he held until 2012 when rumours of tensions with the PM lead to him resigning. Gillard herself called a pre-emptive leadership spill and won. But a year later Rudd challenged formally for the Labor leadership and, this time, Gillard was unseated. After a few months of Rudd in office as PM for a second term, Labor lost the ensuing general election.
Case 3: Tony Abbott challenged incumbent Liberal leader Malcolm Turnbull in a leadership spill while the party was in opposition in 2009, beating him by one vote. After first not winning the 2010 election, Abbott later went on to clearly win the 2013 general election. He brought Turnbull into his cabinet as Minister for Communications, a relatively small portfolio, but one that aligned with Turnbull's policy interests. There were repeated rumours that Turnbull would challenge for the leadership, always denied. But as the government's troubles continued, Abbott survived a vote for a spill motion moved by backbenchers Luke Simpkin and Don Randall in February 2015. Then, in September 2015, Turnbull challenged and overturned Abbott in a leadership spill by 54 votes to 44 to become PM.
Case 4: Turnbull's performance in office was poor and his right-wingers hampered his efforts to move Australia towards green policies. As his opinion poll ratings lagged behind the opposition in the run-up to the National Energy Guarantee policy announcement in mid-2018, right-wingers (covertly assisted by his Finance Minister, Morrison and Immigration Minister, Peter Dutton) precipitated a leadership spill and Turnbull was ejected. In the subsequent leadership election, Morrison became PM, later leading the Liberal-National Coalition to a narrow victory over Labor at the May 2019 election.

Source: Compiled by the authors from a wide literature, and Tiffen (2017) Disposable Leaders: Media and Leadership Coups from Menzies to Abbott, New South Publishing.

'Governance' scandals and standards of conduct

Many of the most serious governance issues in the Australian core executive have been raised by government or ministerial misconduct that breached (or has been alleged to breach) the norms and conventions of 'collective and ministerial responsibility' on which any 'Westminster system' of party-dominated politics depends. These informal but morally salient rules have traditionally been seen as 'tripwires' that prevent two-party politics becoming over-polarised in nakedly partisan ways, or dissuade powerful ministers from abusing their position for party advantage or penalising social groups who support the opposition. Four recent cases have given grave cause for concern, according to critics of the Morrison government.

Politicising government advertising. In early 2019, it was common knowledge in the political world that the PM would soon call an election. One of the first principles of rule-of-law government is that the incumbent party should not be able to exploit state resources for its own partisan ends. But Morrison's administration made a series of ostensibly 'government information' adverts extolling the spending carried out under federal programmes for roads, schools and the way that taxes had been minimised, all of which were run incessantly on every commercial TV channel in the run-up to the election. The announcement of polling was delayed to the last possible minute to 'milk' every possible advantage from the adverts. Ministers claimed that the whole exercise had been approved by the Secretary of DPM&C and Secretary to the Cabinet, Phil Gaetjens, Scott Morrison's former Chief of Staff. In other 'Westminster' systems, like the UK, these adverts would never have been permitted.

'Rorting' and the role of political advisors. Concern over hyper-partisanship in Australian politics has focused on whether advisors now give ministers the potential to run their own 'mini-department' and interfere far more in the allocation of funds. In the run-up to the election, Sports Minister and Deputy Leader of the Nationals, Bridget McKenzie, had her staff draw up an elaborate spreadsheet of local schemes eligible for funding under a program to improve local sports facilities, organised by the type of parliamentary constituency they were in. The minister's staff prioritised funding for the government-held marginal seats and areas where they hoped to capture the seat from Labor, plus awarding large improvement funds to Coalition ministers' seats even where they already had elite-level facilities (ANAO, 2020b). Eminently deserving schemes in safe Labor areas were rejected, as were some in safe Liberal-National Coalition areas. When the spreadsheet was revealed in a Senate hearing, the minister brazenly refused to resign, claiming to have done nothing wrong, while Morrison tried to take the heat out of what became known as the 'sports rorts' case by promising a second round of funding for deserving projects passed over as electorally unimportant. Eventually it emerged that McKenzie had approved a facilities grant to a gun club of which she was herself a member, and on this ethical issue she had to resign (Murphy, 2020). But other critics alleged a far wider political favouritism in much larger programs, notably in urban roads improvements.

Allegations of sexual assault within government. In 2021, ministers' offices were drawn into an acute controversy after Brittany Higgins, a former staffer to then-Defence Industry Minister, Linda Reynolds, alleged that she had been raped by another ministerial advisor in Reynolds' office in 2019, and that she felt she was put under political and career pressure not to report it at the time. Less than two weeks later, allegations emerged that a current minister, later revealed to be Attorney-General Christian Porter, had in 1988, at the age of 18, raped a 16-year-old girl.

The alleged victim died by suicide in 2020 and Porter launched a defamation claim against the ABC and reporter Louise Milligan for publishing the allegation, even though the story did not name him. A series of other examples of sexual misconduct and sexist behaviour by staffers and politicians within parliamentary offices emerged over the weeks after Higgins' allegations were made public, confirming a deeply entrenched culture of inappropriate and allegedly abusive behaviour in parliamentary offices, particularly towards women. It further raised issues of an accountability deficit concerning the personal conduct of Australian ministers and advisors. When important office-holders can 'mark their own homework' with few effective checks and balances, as still largely happens with ministers in 'Westminster systems', there is a danger that they or their powerful lieutenants may overstep the boundaries of acceptable behaviour. Critics argue that the 'pressure cooker' atmosphere and relative isolation of the Parliament building add other risks of poor, club-like organisational cultures developing.

The 'robodebt' policy fiasco. This concerned a policy that operated from 2016 to 2020, which started when the welfare agency Centrelink linked up records of welfare payments and taxable income declared by households using an automated algorithm (Commonwealth Ombudsman, 2017). At the insistence of an ambitious minister, Christian Porter, who promised hundreds of millions of dollars could be saved by cracking down on 'welfare fraud', the agency began issuing thousands of automated claims for alleged over-payments of welfare benefits, which placed the onus of proof on individuals to demonstrate they did not owe the amounts generated by automated debt calculations (Senate Community Affairs References Committee, 2020). Thousands of people received large demands for payment based on faulty calculations, creating demands for wrong or grossly exaggerated amounts. The agency's phone lines immediately collapsed under the weight of queries and complaints, but ministers kept on insisting everything was all right well into 2017. Eventually, the scale of problems with the program emerged and it was suspended, after which a long-running legal challenge made its way through the courts, culminating in a declaration that the program was illegal in 2020 and instructing the government to pay back the money collected. A total of 470,000 incorrect debt demands were issued, resulting in an estimated $721 million of wrongful payments to be returned (with some claims that repayments will reach $1bn (Henriques-Gomes, 2020). No compensation was paid to the families involved for the trouble, extreme anxiety and anguish caused.

The new Labor government in May 2022 appointed a QC (Catherine Homes) to undertake a Royal Commission to investigate the 'robodebt' episode, fulfilling the party's call (backed by the Greens) for a full investigation. In summer 2023, she reported, and her findings were devastating, concluding not only that the scheme was inherently administratively flawed in perfectly predictable ways but that it was in some key respects illegal (Royal Commission into the Robodebt Scheme, 2023, p.iii):

> *What has been startling in the Commission's investigation of the Robodebt scheme has been the myriad of other ways in which it failed the public interest. It is remarkable how little interest there seems to have been in ensuring the Scheme's legality, how rushed its implementation was, how little thought was given to how it would affect welfare recipients and the lengths to which public servants were prepared to go to oblige ministers on a quest for savings.*
>
> *Truly dismaying was the revelation of dishonesty and collusion to prevent the Scheme's lack of legal foundation coming to light. Equally disheartening was the ineffectiveness of what one might consider institutional checks and*

> balances – the Commonwealth Ombudsman's Office, the Office of Legal Services Coordination, the Office of the Australian Information Commissioner and the Administrative Appeals Tribunal – in presenting any hindrance to the Scheme's continuance.

A closed section of the report referred a number of individuals to the Australian Federal Police, the Public Services Commission and other regulatory bodies. It was unclear at the time of writing if any of these referrals concerned former ministers, but a range of very senior APS officials and advisors to government were clearly involved.

In the aftermath of the final report, Kathryn Campbell, secretary of the Department of Human Services from 2011 to 2017, was suspended without pay from her position as a special advisor on the AUKUS nuclear submarine project, a position with a $900,000 salary (ABC News, 2023). Additionally, a PwC consultant who testified to the Royal Commission was dismissed in the hours after the final report was released (Mandarin, 2023; Wikipedia, 2023).

Commonwealth departments and ministers

In the Australian version of the 'Westminster system', relations between ministers and public servants have some significant differences from the UK source model. In particular, there has been a wider separation between politicians and administrators in Canberra than anywhere in Europe. Large ministerial offices have helped ministers run their portfolio(s). They each include numerous staff drawn from the 415 government 'political advisors' (Finance and Public Administration Committee, 2020). Most are party aides or activists used to working with each minister, plus ex-journalists, think-tankers or policy experts, several of whom are drawn from the Australian Public Service but not acting as public servants. Junior ministers are normally found in the same portfolio, supported by small offices. Junior ministers plus the minister's chief of staff and their chief communications advisor are typically salient figures who carry a lot of weight in policy-making alongside the minister themselves. Each office also includes public servants seconded from the relevant department to facilitate close liaison. The ministerial offices are all located together in Parliament buildings at the heart of Canberra's Parliamentary Triangle, with the media housed just upstairs from them in the same building. Critics argue that this has tended to increase ministers' and advisors' obsession with continuous news management and short-term political objectives, rather than fostering long-run policy-making, and that it contributes to misunderstandings between ministers' offices and their departments.

Meanwhile, the main public service department for the minister's portfolio will be located elsewhere – sometimes adjacent to the Parliamentary Triangle, or at a distance in the civic centre or even a Canberra suburb. Each department is headed and run by a Secretary and a Deputy Secretary, and includes numerous divisions headed by policy-level staff, the most senior of whom form a management board. Some observers see a trend towards 'mega-departments' with more integrated functions (see Halligan, 2019) and larger executive management teams. The department communications and media staff work closely and continuously with the powerful political staff members of the minister's office. And, at any given time, the heads of particular divisions in the department will be working closely with the ministers' political advisors on new legislation or executive actions to implement the minister's priorities. On many more routine and short-term matters a wide range of department staff will liaise with their colleagues seconded to the minister's office, such as answering parliamentary questions or enquiries from the minister.

This leaves long-range management of the department resting with the secretaries, who have typically been appointed for a five-year term, which must then be renewed or the secretary then moves elsewhere (including into retirement). Their time is often taken up with assisting ministers whom they see regularly, attending important policy meetings, including preparing for cabinet committees and inter-departmental meetings, plus trouble-shooting myriad operational matters that arise. In many departments, deputy secretaries manage long-range planning, budgeting and strategic initiatives. Critics argue that secretaries and their deputies have progressively retreated from their previous policy roles as fearless and dispassionate advisors, into becoming mere managerialists within their department and facilitators of ministerial political imperatives, however short-termist or ill-advised they may be (Weller, Scott and Stevens, 2011). A link has often been drawn between the heightened risk of termination of secretaries in recent decades, and this change in the frankness and fearlessness of their advice and conduct. The integration between Australian ministers and their departments has consequently been far less than in any European liberal democracy or the UK (where the ministers are expected to mainly sit in offices within the departmental headquarters, liaising with their civil service chief every day and divisional heads regularly, and operating with only a small staff of advisors).

Depending on the structure of their portfolios (settled by the PM and reflected in budgetary structures), Australian ministers may have a range of secondary agencies whose activities they supervise – many agency HQ buildings may be located in other parts of the country. However, the Canberra offices (averaging just under 5,200 staff) are clearly the politically dominant bodies, while most agencies are smaller in size (under 300 staff on average) and have a semi-autonomous character, albeit that they are governed by boards with chairs and members appointed by the host minister. Although a few regulatory agencies are set up to be independent, most are not in practice. So, Australia remains very distinct from the New Zealand model, where all ministers have multiple portfolios, each run by small policy-only ministries dealing with much-larger arms-length agencies. In Australia, the minister's writ clearly runs throughout all the administrative bodies in their portfolio.

Ministerial effectiveness and portfolio reorganisations

One of a PM's most potent uses of executive powers involves their unilateral control over the structure of government departments. The machinery of Commonwealth government is determined by the PM and reflects the political priorities of the government of the day. As in other 'Westminster systems', Australian PMs can abolish, merge, de-merge and reorganise ministerial portfolios and even their underlying departments at will. Prime ministers have scrapped or merged departments at times, and created new ones to reflect their political priorities, to respond to external changes, or to reflect the portfolios of particular ministers. All the main policy departments – plus a few major agencies running core state services (such as the large National Disability Insurance Service with over 4,500 staff) – covering 60 per cent of the Commonwealth workforce, work in administrative organisations whose structure can be changed by the PM. Machinery of government changes only require the Governor-General's approval, which is a formality and always given. There has been no parliamentary approval or scrutiny of this process – unlike in Canada, where parliament must vote to approve any reorganisation of departments within a year of them coming into effect, or the previous status quo is restored. By contrast, almost all the executive agencies within the APS are set up by legislation, and so they can only be reorganised by enacting new laws, and thus gaining the approval of parliament.

In practice, despite this significant capability and the constraints of a three-year electoral cycle, on average Australian Commonwealth ministers have stayed in a given post for an average of 20 months in recent times (Sasse et al., 2023, Figure 6). This tenure has been very similar to that in other 'Westminster system' countries. Australian ministers also stay in their posts twice as long as those in Japan, much the same time as cabinet members in the USA, and more than those in France or Italy. However, their time in office is around half that of ministers in Germany, and substantially less than in most other European major countries.

During 2019–20, a particularly large-scale change was made to the structure of Commonwealth departments when the Department of Human Services (DHS) was formally transformed into a new mega-agency, Services Australia (Morrison, 2019), set up on the same model as a similar body developed some years earlier by the Liberal-National Coalition government in New South Wales. The agency aimed to handle in a more integrated, efficient and customer-responsive manner all the main transfer and welfare services previously run by DHS in departmental form. Although SA has an agency structure – with its own chief executive and more freedom to shape its own internal affairs, like other agencies – it was also set up with its own minister. In practice, it somewhat resembles the Australian Taxation Office, a kind of super-agency or sub-department run by public servants but politically controlled in many key aspects rather than being an executive agency proper.

Budgetary control within government

Australian fiscal policy has long been orchestrated through a medium-term framework that includes:

- maintaining federal public debt at 'prudent' levels, very low before 2008 but considerably higher since then
- a stable and predictable tax system, well-enforced
- not loading future generations with debt
- intervening to moderate cyclical economic fluctuations.

Across the Turnbull-Morrison administrations, this has required managing slower growth – globally and domestically; fluctuations in commodity prices and terms of trade; low inflation and income growth; and guiding Australia's economy in transition.

Following its election on 2 July 2016, the Turnbull government aimed to achieve budget surpluses over the course of the economic cycle (see Figure 13.5). A 'budget repair' strategy was designed to 'deliver budget surpluses building to at least 1 per cent of GDP consistent with the medium-term fiscal strategy' (Morrison and Cormann, 2018). In 2019, it was on course to achieve some success and the Commonwealth government was projected to generate its first budget surplus in a decade, when these ambitions (always subject to political vagaries) were blown badly off course by the fiscal impact of COVID-19 (see Figures 13.5 and 13.6). Apart from this period, the key feature of Figure 13.6 has been how little planned changes occurred in any indices. Similarly, Figure 13.7 shows that the allocation of budgets across portfolios and functions has remained pretty stable over time, with most reduction occurring in 'general public

Figure 13.5: Underlying cash balance as a percentage of GDP (2000 to 2023/24, estimated)

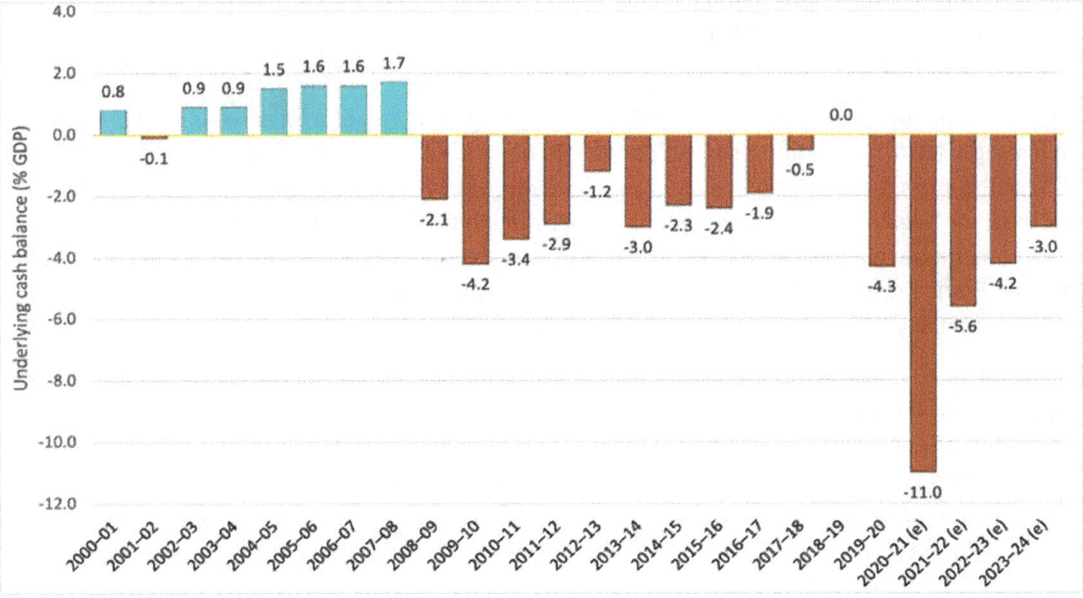

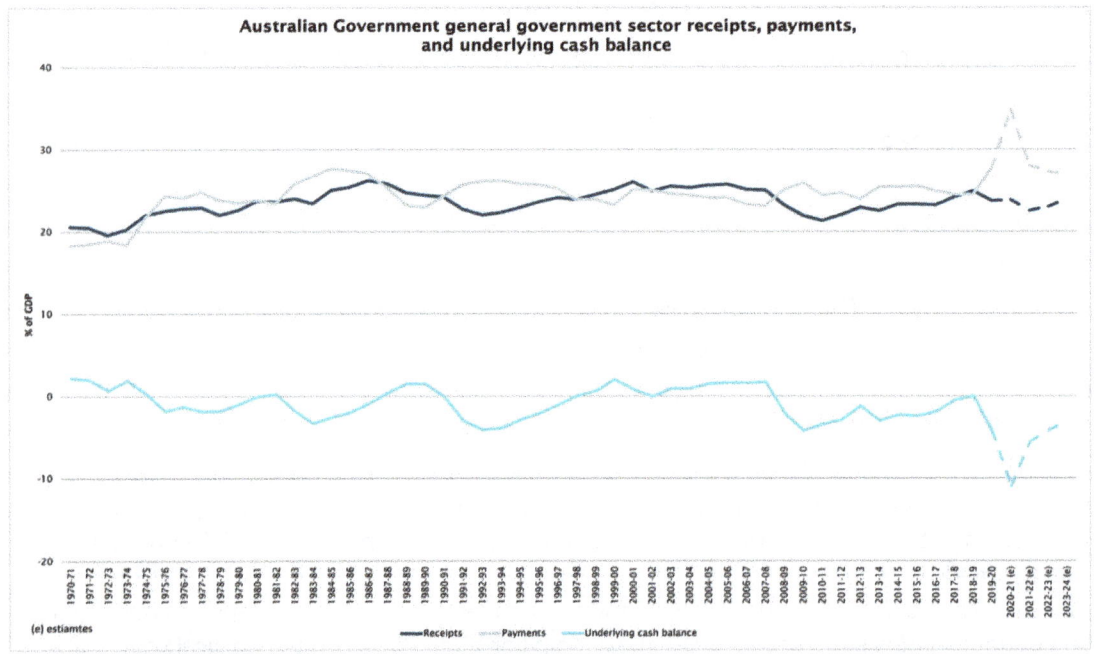

Source: Taken from Australian Government (2021b) Budget Archive 2020–21, Budget Paper 1 – Budget Strategy and Outlook, Budget 2020–21, Paper No. 1, Statement 11: Historical Australian Government Data', Table 1. Web Report.

Note: Estimated 2021 onwards.

Figure 13.6: Australian government payments and receipts as a percentage (%) of GDP 1970–2024 (estimated from 2021)

Source: Australian Government (2021b) Budget Archive 2020–21, Budget Paper 1 – Budget Strategy and Outlook, Budget Strategy and Outlook 2020–21, Paper No. 1, Statement 11: Historical Australian Government Data', p.11.6. Web Report. And Australian Government, Budget strategy and outlook: budget paper no. 1: 2020–21, statement 5: Revenue – online supplementary tables.

Note: Estimated 2021 onwards.

services' and the largest increase in defence. The Coalition government strategy's budget rules required any new spending measures to be offset by reductions in spending elsewhere, with the Treasury banking budget surpluses in good times. In power since May 2022, Labor ministers broadly maintained this regime.

The Treasurer runs all economic policy-making and has normally been the number two minister in any Australian government. The Treasury has also played the dominant role in setting the overall budget within which the APS must operate. However, the detailed management of budgets across departments, and the expenditure review processes by which departments secure finance for their programs, rests with the separate Minister for Finance (MFF) and the cabinet's Expenditure Review Committee (ERC). The ERC has examined all proposals in the context of the government's overall fiscal strategy, and run reviews of individual ongoing programmes. Figure 13.8 shows the timeline normally followed for budget-setting.

New policy proposals (NPPs) have historically come from several sources: the PM/cabinet decisions; portfolio ministers' priorities; responses to reviews/reports; and election commitments. The Treasury and the Department of Finance provide policy advice on the NPPs from portfolios submitted with estimates in the cabinet/ERC briefing process. Treasury also put up their own NPPs, reflecting their privileged role in the Commonwealth government advisory system.

The portfolio distribution of the budget across services is as shown in Figure 13.7 and again has been generally stable over time. The big three spending areas are on welfare payments (paid directly to citizens), other miscellaneous spending and healthcare, where the federal government runs Medicare and provides grants to the states and territories who run hospitals and other services. Five other services account for over 5 per cent of the budget, including education support, defences, general public services and transport. A further six services account for less than 2 per cent of the budget each.

Figure 13.7: Estimates of expenses by function between 2015 and 2016 and 2022 and 2023 (as a percentage of spending)

Per cent (%) spending on	2015–16	2022–23 projection
Social security and welfare	35.4	35.8
Other purposes	19.1	21.1
Health	16	16
Education	7.5	7.3
Defence	6.0	6.7
General public services	5.6	4.3
Other economic affairs	2.2	1.6
Transport and communication	2	2
Fuel and energy	1.5	1.7
Public order and safety	1.1	1
Housing and community amenities	1.1	0.9
Recreation and culture	0.8	0.7
Mining, manufacturing and construction	0.8	0.5
Agriculture, forestry and fishing	0.6	0.5
Total expenses	100	100

Source: Compiled by authors from Australian Government (2021b) Budget Paper No.1 2019–20.

Note: Numbers are rounded to nearest 0.1 of total.

Figure 13.8: The Australian budget timeline

Overall budget process	Planning and prioritising	Government priority setting	September to May, Year 1
		Cabinet submission	
		ERC decision-making	
		Budget Cabinet	
		Budget delivered to Parliament	
	Spending and monitoring	Mid-year economic fiscal outlook	October/November/December, Year 1
	Reporting and reviewing	Final budget outcome	30 September, Year 2

Source: Compiled from Department of Finance (no date).

The PM, Treasurer and MFF establish policy priorities at the start of the budget process. The MFF then negotiates bi-laterally with each of the other 13 main departments on their portfolio totals and breakdowns within them, seeking to reach agreement within the Treasurer's limits (Figure 13.8). The ERC of cabinet acts as referee for this process where agreement proves hard to reach, and ultimately the PM may intervene. Australia's apparatus of Treasury and Department of Finance control make it one of the world's most well-run state budget systems, with little over-spending and normal, moderate under-spending.

Although senior public servants frequently complain that ministers keep them on short rations and under-staffed, Australian federal government has never really faced the kind of drastic austerity programs enacted in the UK, USA and many European countries between 2008 and 2010. Australia not only survived this global economic crisis almost unharmed, but has been able to draw on 30 years of continuous growth without recessions (before the COVID-19 pandemic). While APS staff numbers have stayed static for decades now, overall federal spending has progressively increased. Real cuts in programmes, and crude 'do less for less' strategies are relatively rare.

Australian government IT has also improved in the last decade, placing it regularly in the top five countries for UN and other rankings. Australian administrative elites have generally accepted that digital government has become a priority for effective policy-making now (Dunleavy and Evans, 2019a; Dunleavy and Margetts, 2023). However, an ambitious program of 'cultural change' around IT launched by former PM Malcolm Turnbull in 2016 with the creation of the Digital Transformation Office was reined back to a more conventional effort under Morrison (Dunleavy and Evans, 2019b). Several different but not completely adequate major project evaluation systems operate to ensure that IT disasters are restricted – so most areas except defence (and in recent times the national broadband program) have delivered IT systems fairly reliably. However, the Commonwealth government has never yet had any coherent program for improving government sector productivity – the Productivity Commission has mainly concentrated its reports on the private sector.

Australia's 'secret state'

Although Australia is only a medium-sized country, and has no nearby 'enemy states' (at least formally), it has maintained a substantial 'secret state' including:

- the Australian Security and Intelligence Organisation (ASIO, the internal security service)
- the Australian Secret Intelligence Service (ASIS, overseas intelligence)
- the Australian Signals Directorate (ASD, electronic and other tech surveillance)
- the Defence Intelligence Organisation (DIO, military intelligence)
- the Australian Geospatial-Intelligence Organisation (AGO, a small body that does satellite intelligence mainly).

Their activities have been supervised by the Office of National Assessments (ONA), which coordinates information, reporting to the DPM&C or its key committees. The PM sanctions major decisions and reporting runs from the agency to ONA and the PM&C department, with the PM's top political staffs sometimes involved. Australia has a developed inter-departmental national security apparatus, which focuses on the National Security Advisor to the PM, who can convene a National Crisis Committee in a crisis to discuss policy. A lot of its focus has been on the prevention of terrorist attacks.

Australia has close working relationships with the US intelligence organisations, with ASIS linked to the CIA and ASD working with the USA National Security Agency. Less important strong links are to agencies in three other 'Anglosphere' countries (the UK, New Zealand and Canada) in the 'Five Eyes' network, and on a lower level to some Asian closely allied countries (like Japan and Singapore). These overseas ties, plus a long British imperial history of running intelligence and now national security in very tightly constrained subgroups of ministers, explain why the cabinet's small National Security Committee makes decisions that cannot be reviewed or overturned in main cabinet.

Of Australia's five intelligence agencies, only ASIO makes an annual report to parliament. All sensitive information in it has been redacted, but it is known that ASIO had 1,930 staff and an annual budget of AU $591 million in 2020. The budgets and staffing of the other four agencies have not been disclosed. Since 1986, a supposedly independent Inspector-General of Intelligence and Security (IGIS) has had powers to investigate if agencies have misused their powers and inform parliament, but this has been a low-profile body with few staff or powers.

These highly non-transparent arrangements have fuelled persistent controversy about the existence of an 'inner state', one that controls the drone killings of terror suspects in military action zones overseas, and some extra-legal actions of national security or army special forces. ASIS has been accused of colluding in the renditions and torture of terror suspects implemented by USA agencies in Iraq and Afghanistan from 2002 to 2008, and of using information gained from a program where prisoners were sent for interrogation to US-allied states where torture was still in use. Other allegations of malpractice in a 'deep state' have frequently surfaced, especially given Australian armed forces involvement in the two Iraq wars and Afghanistan, where Australian Defence Force inquiry reports have suggested serious misbehaviours by Australian elite soldiers (see Chapter 8; BBC, 2020).

Policy failures and failures to act

Most criticisms of the Australian core executive as a policy-making apparatus focus on ministerial elites being too short-termist and powerful vis-à-vis their 'generalist' public servants, able to instruct the implementation of ill-advised policy or stifle change completely. Both the leading politicians and the special advisors who ride into office on their coat-tails are generalists who have honed their skills in adversarial politics over many years. They may tend to view policy issues principally (perhaps almost solely) in terms of partisan and career advantages and risks. This has led critics to suggest that Australian Commonwealth government over the past two decades has been plagued by policy stagnation, with limited progress in addressing long-term challenges associated with demographic change, income inequality, productivity growth, energy policy and climate change.

Climate change inaction

As the driest inhabited continent in the world, with huge solar potential, and a country exposed to regular spectacular heatwaves and associated bushfire outbreaks, Australia might be expected to be a leading advocate for rapid climate change counter-measures and a speedy end to the burning of fossil fuels (see Chapter 27). However, the giant mining companies have played a significant role in fuelling the economy's growth and providing exports of cheap coal to China and other markets, and have a lot of political clout. They have contributed significant funds to the Liberal-Nationals and some Labor politicians (see Chapter 7), and governments of both parties kept Australian policy changing at a glacial pace before 2022 (Clean Energy Council, 2021). Solar power previously fell behind but since 2019 subsidies at the state government level and big cost cuts for panels have stimulated a rapid growth of solar power, reversing Australia's previous laggard position.

However, phasing out of fossil fuel vehicles has only recently started to be discussed, with no federal government commitment on a date – compared with (say) Victoria, where a phase-out by 2035 has been proposed (Australian Financial Review, 2023) or the UK where new fossil-fuel vehicles cannot be sold after 2035, and where all such vehicles must be phased out by 2040. And along with President Trump's USA, Australia under Liberal-National Coalition governments was long a prominent recalcitrant in efforts to combat climate change, and an advocate of the 'least progressive option' on almost every occasion. Only in 2021 did Morrison accept the need for a transition to a net-zero emissions economy by 2050, long after every Australian state and territory had officially set this target.

The summer of 2019 to 2020 dramatically highlighted the vulnerability of Australia's big cities to global warming, with bushfires entirely engulfing huge areas of Australia, the deaths of an estimated half a billion wild animals and a loss to the economy equivalent to A$100 billion (although rebuilding with state aid also created a later spring-back stimulus). From 2019 to 2020, the damage covered all the main populated areas of the south and east of the continent (whereas the 2018 to 2019 fire season principally affected the less populated north and west of the country). Cities like Melbourne, Sydney and Canberra suffered weeks of intense smoke pollution penetrating every building, with a huge cost in adverse health effects.

The Morrison government reacted very late to the fire threat, and some Liberal-National Coalition MPs continued to deny any link between the 'black summer' disaster and global warming. Ministers intervened to mitigate immediate short-term damage, but made only incremental changes in Australia's wider climate change policies. It was only when President Trump's defeat in November 2020 heralded a renewal of American commitment to combatting the climate emergency that Australia belatedly took hesitant steps to avoid seeming too isolated from the international consensus on urgent action to stem the adverse effects of fossil-fuel burning.

Foreign policy

A second area of acute core executive failure to define workable long-run policies has been Australia's increasingly fraught position as a close ally of the USA, and a country heavily dependent on the USA's military and diplomatic protection, while its major exports of iron ore, coal and agricultural products go to China. From 2016 to 2021, as former President Trump dragged Morrison's government with it into an escalating series of conflicts with Beijing, while Xi Jinping's regime increasingly cultivated a brusque and hectoring diplomatic style, Australian foreign policy increasingly seemed to be hypnotised in the lights of an oncoming car crash. There seemed no easy way out of the dilemma, dramatising the argument of critics that Australia (despite years of effort) remained a 'stranded' white nation in an Asian setting (Walker, 2019). Albanese's government continued past Liberal-National Coalition policies of rapidly increasing the small defence budget in the next decade, hoping that a Biden presidency would dial-down the conflict with China, and as China's stance softened this seemed to work (see Chapter 28). However, ministers have seemed to have few viable alternative strategies in view.

Yet, in 2021 the Morrison government was galvanised into action and implemented a sweeping and decisive change in Australia's defence posture by suddenly cancelling a contract for conventional submarines with a French contractor (and paying hefty compensation), and setting in place a new AUKUS arrangement for Australia to gain new nuclear-powered submarines of far greater capability (in time). Accepted by the Albanese shadow cabinet (after just 24 hours' notice of the changes), the AUKUS arrangements initially prompted a harsh Chinese counter-response. Yet Chapter 28 shows that Australia actually proved able to sidestep much of the anticipated damage. The Albanese Labor government also back-peddled on Morrison's harsh policy rhetoric, recreating links to Beijing while also reaffirming its AUKUS commitment. Thus, Canberra seemingly has (partly) resolved its previous dilemma.

Conclusion – the 'clammy hands of centralism'

The 'Corona crisis' period had both positive and negative impacts on executive governance in Australia. In domestic policy terms, Australia's core executive worked smoothly and (apart from some spotty over-reach of executive powers) it has clearly not degenerated in the 21st century, unlike (for instance) its UK counterpart (Dunleavy, 2018; Bevan, 2023). Australia's governance retains core strengths, especially a weight of tradition that regularly produces better performance under pressure, reasonably integrated action on national security for citizens, and the ability to securely ride out crises. Moreover, while public trust in the political class has faded on the path to recovery (Evans, 2021), the APS has largely remained one of Australia's most trusted institutions.

Significant problems remain, including the dominance of the Commonwealth executive within the federation amply demonstrated in this audit (see Chapter 16). Within the federal tiers, Westminster principles of parliamentary democracy came under challenge from 2016 to 2022 with mounting integrity problems, the increasing politicisation of the APS (demonstrated in acute form by the robodebt fiasco) and gridlock between the last Liberal-National Coalition government and the APS on the way forward reflected in the abortive 2019 APS Review. Labor ministers have promised greater consensualism in policy-making and put forward a new public service bill. But it has exceptionally modest provisions and critics argue it does little to strengthen any future APS capability to constrain ministers on integrity or egality grounds (see Chapter 14). In short, the executive wields disproportionate power in Australia's democratic settlement which undermines the effectiveness of traditional checks and balances through the separation of powers. Moreover, recurring 'policy short-termism' and inaction on issues like climate change decision-making at the heart of government gives further cause for concern. The Commonwealth government's successful management of fiscal policy, maintenance of long-run economic growth and largely effective response on COVID-19 are offset by policy inertia in other key areas, the short-term reactionary nature of much policy development in Canberra and the limited impact of evidence-based policy-making beyond the public health and economic spheres.

References

ABC News (2014) 'Carbon tax: A timeline of its tortuous history in Australia', 10 July. https://perma.cc/JQ5Q-MCPC

ABC News (2023) 'Kathryn Campbell first senior bureaucrat suspended after robodebt royal commission', ABC News, 20 July. https://perma.cc/6TXS-U8UE

ANAO (Australian National Audit Office) (2020a) *Management of the Australian Public Service's Workforce Response to COVID-19*, 1 December, Figure 2.5, p.31. https://perma.cc/W567-J5VZ

ANAO (Australian National Audit Office) (2020b) *Award of Funding under the Community Sport Infrastructure Program: Australian Sports Commission*, Auditor-General Report No. 23, ANAO. https://perma.cc/2XW4-CSYQ

APSC (Australian Public Services Commission) (2023) 'APS agencies – size and function'. Webpage, 10 February. https://web.archive.org/web/20220323031432/https://legacy.apsc.gov.au/aps-agencies-size-and-function

Australian Financial Review (2023) 'Ban petrol car sales, phase out gas by 2035: Andrews' expert panel', *Australian Financial Review*, 17 May. https://perma.cc/A7NF-RZGK

Australian Government (2021a) 'Cabinet committees', 19 November. https://perma.cc/S8CK-ZGVD

Australian Government (2021b) *Budget Archive 2020–21, Budget Paper 1 – Budget Strategy and Outlook*, Budget 2020–21, Paper No. 1, Statement 11: Historical Australian Government Data', Web Report. https://perma.cc/7NK3-3WDE

BBC News (2020) 'Australian "war crimes": Elite troops killed Afghan civilians, report finds', 19 November. https://perma.cc/FG2B-UJJ3

Bevan, Gwyn (2023) *How Did Britain Come to This? A Century of Systemic Failures of Government*, London: LSE Press. https://doi.org/10.31389/lsepress.hdb

Clean Energy Council (2021) *Clean Energy Australia*, Report. https://perma.cc/H86V-4NE6

Commonwealth Ombudsman (2017) *Centrelink's Automated Debt Raising and Recovery System: A Report About the Department of Human Services' Online Compliance Intervention System for Debt Raising and Recovery*, April. https://perma.cc/GTQ2-MXC6

De Feo, Gianluca (2020) 'Coronavirus: perché cresce la popolarità dei leader?', *You Trend*, 8 April. https://perma.cc/Z6WN-CKY7

Department of Finance (no date) The Budget Process: Overview ' https://perma.cc/X96V-TVHU

Dunleavy, Patrick (2018) Chapter 5.2 'The core executive and government', in Dunleavy, Patrick; Park, Alice; and Taylor, Ros (eds), *The UK's Changing Democracy: The 2018 Democratic Audit*, LSE Press. https://doi.org/10.31389/book1.o

Dunleavy, Patrick and Evans, Mark (2019a) 'Digital transformation', in Evans, Mark; Grattan, Michelle; and McCaffrie, Brendan (eds) *From Turnbull to Morrison: Understanding the Trust Divide*, Melbourne University Press. $ https://perma.cc/LPL4-Z6DK

Dunleavy, Patrick and Evans, Mark (2019b) 'Australian administrative elites and the challenges of digital-era change', *Journal of Chinese Governance*, vol. 4, no. 2, pp.181–200. $ https://doi.org/10.1080/23812346.2019.1596544 or OA at: https://perma.cc/7XDB-K2NG

Dunleavy, Patrick and Margetts, Helen (2023) 'Data science, artificial intelligence and the third wave of digital era governance', *Public Policy and Administration*, 25 September online. https://doi.org/10.1177/09520767231119873

Evans, Mark (2021) 'Scott Morrison's pandemic popularity boost has vanished, along with public trust in our politicians', *The Guardian*, Australia, 15 November 2021. https://perma.cc/TC8T-5JAM

Evans, Mark and Grattan, Michelle (2021) 'Health expertise and Covid-19 – managing the fear factor', *Australian Quarterly*, vol. 92, no. 2, pp.20–28. https://www.jstor.org/stable/26999989

Evans, Mark; Valgarðsson, Viktor; Jennings, Will; and Stoker, Gerry (2020) 'Political trust and democracy in times of coronavirus: Is Australia still the lucky country?'. Democracy 2025. https://perma.cc/JC5Q-QFLY

Finance and Public Administration Committee (2020) 'Personal employee positions as at 1 october 2020, budget estimates 2020–21, tabled document 12', Parliament of Australia, 21 October. https://perma.cc/LMK4-2EM8

Halligan, John (2019) 'Nadir or resistance for the Australian Public Service', in Evans, Mark; Grattan, Michelle; and McCaffrie, Brendan (eds) *From Turnbull to Morrison. Trust Divide*, Melbourne University Press, pp.144–162. $ https://perma.cc/LPL4-Z6DK

Henley, Joe (2020) 'Democratic leaders win surge of approval during Covid-19 crisis', *Guardian*, Australia, 2 April. https://perma.cc/G5T5-YDMU

Henriques-Gomes, Luke (2020) 'Robodebt: Total value of unlawful debts issued under Centrelink scheme to exceed $1bn', *The Guardian,* Australia, 10 June. https://perma.cc/Z648-ZQ2G

Hetherington, Marc J and Nelson, Michael. (2003) 'Anatomy of a Rally Effect: George W. Bush and the War on Terrorism' *PS: Political Science and Politics*, vol. 36, no. 1. (Jan), pp.37–42. https://www.uvm.edu/~dguber/POLS234/articles/hetherington2.pdf

Jennings, Will; Valgarðsson, Viktor; Stoker, Gerry; Devine, Dan; Gaskell, Jen; and Evans, Mark (2021a) *Political Trust and the COVID-19 Crisis – Pushing Populism to the Backburner? A Study of Public Opinion in Australia, Italy, the UK and the USA*, IGPA/ MoAD/Trustgov. Democracy 2025 Report No 8. https://perma.cc/GS6X-T7Y5

Jennings, Will; Stoker, Gerry; Bunting, Hannah; Valgarðsson, Viktor; Gaskell, Jennifer; Devine, Daniel; McKay, Lawrence; and Mills, Melinda C (2021b) 'Lack of trust, conspiracy beliefs, and social media use predict COVID-19 vaccine hesitancy', *Vaccines*, vol. 9, no. 6, p.593. https://doi.org/10.3390/vaccines9060593

Karp, Paul (2020) 'Scott Morrison's one-man cabinet committee an "abuse of process", Labor says', *Guardian,* Australia, 2 March. https://perma.cc/4G37-46AU

Lloyd-Cape, Matt; Jackson, Shirley; and Lewis, Abigail (2021) *Smokescreen: The Rhetoric and Reality of Federal Bushfire Recovery Funding,* GetUp! Percapita, February. https://perma.cc/X8NJ-8UVB

Mandarin (2023) 'First robodebt royal commission scalp confirmed at Pwc', *The Mandarin*, 7 July. By Julian Bajkowski and Tom Ravlic. https://perma.cc/26AZ-B6CB

Menzies, Jennifer (2021) 'Explainer: What is the national cabinet and is it democratic?' *The Conversation*, 31 March. https://perma.cc/H5B5-TGXH

Morrison, Scott (2019) 'Structure of government', Media Release, New Press Office of the PM, 5 December.

Morrison, Scott (Treasurer) and Cormann, Mathias (Minister for Finance) (2018) 'Budget 2018–19: Budget strategy and outlook, budget paper No,1, 2018–2019', The Commonwealth of Australia, 8 May. https://perma.cc/EV83-A5WK

Murphy, Katharine (2020) 'Bridget McKenzie resigns following sports rorts affair'. *Guardian*, Australia, 2 February. https://perma.cc/2BAW-4FRU

Murphy, Katharine (2021) 'Guardian Essential poll: Scott Morrison approval drops six points during latest Covid lockdowns', *The Guardian, Australia,* 5 July. https://perma.cc/G5E5-WAF8

Prime Minister's Office (2020) Press Conference Transcript, 18 March. https://pmtranscripts.pmc.gov.au/release/transcript-42738

Rhodes, RAW; and Tiernan, Anne (2014) *The Gatekeepers: Lessons from Prime Ministers' Chiefs of Staff,* Melbourne University Press. $ https://www.mup.com.au/books/the-gatekeepers-paperback-softback#sthash.jz7KiWhN.dpuf

Royal Commission into the Robodebt Scheme (2023) *Report: Royal Commisssion into the Robodebt Scheme*, Canberra: Commonwealth of Australia Report, 7 July. https://robodebt.royalcommission.gov.au/system/files/2023-09/rrc-accessible-full-report.PDF

Sasse, Tom; Durrant, Tim; Norris, Emma; and Zodgekar, Ketaki (2020) 'Government reshuffles: The Case for Keeping Ministers in Post Longer', Institute for Government, London, UK. https://perma.cc/G7XW-89CX

Senate Community Affairs References Committee (2020) *Centrelink's Compliance Program: Second Interim Report.* Commonwealth of Australia, September. https://perma.cc/5ZWZ-HJRY

Tiffen, Rodney (2017) *Disposable Leaders: Media and Leadership Coups from Menzies to Abbott,* NewSouth Publishing.

Walker, David (2019) *Stranded Nation: White Australia in an Asian Region.* University of Western Australia. https://perma.cc/WM96-ZMZB

Weller, Patrick; Scott, Joanne; and Stevens, Bronwyn (2011) *From Postbox to Powerhouse: A Centenary History of the Department of the Prime Minister and Cabinet 1911–2010*, Allen and Unwin. $ https://perma.cc/8VQA-ZUFE

Wikipedia (2023) 'Royal Commission into the Robodebt Scheme'. Webpage. https://perma.cc/RL8H-WEPC

World Health Organization (WHO) (2020) *Report of the Director-General 146th Meeting of the Executive Board*, 3 February. https://perma.cc/Q7U5-5TXF

14

The Australian Public Service

John Halligan and Mark Evans

The civil services of nation states are long-lived, perhaps even 'immortal' organisations. The Australian Public Service (APS) has existed in some form for over 120 years (since the 1901 Constitution), although it has changed hugely across this period. It helps ministers shape and deliver Commonwealth policies from its headquarter departments in Canberra and administers federal programs across all the states and territories. Liberal democracies rely on political processes to constantly energise bureaucracies with new ideas, and to closely supervise how public administrators implement decisions. Yet citizens' rights and the operations of civil society are also premised on the impartial and equal administration of laws, regulations and services delivery, without any political favouritism and based on dispassionate (rational) advice – both factors requiring a delicate balance in how the APS operates.

What does democracy require for how the APS operates, and wider public service delivery systems?

- Services provision and implementation, and the regulation of social and economic activities, should be controlled by democratically elected officials. Decisions should be deliberative, carefully considering the interests of all relevant actors.
- Before significant policy or implementation changes are made, fair and equal engagement arrangements should allow service recipients and other stakeholders to be consulted in meaningful ways.
- The management of Commonwealth programs and services should be impartially conducted within administrators' legally available powers.
- All citizens should have full and equal access to government and the services and goods to which they are entitled. Their rights should be protected in decision-making and 'due process' rules followed.
- Wherever 'para-state' organisations (NGOs or private contractors) deliver services, public value standards (action within the law, equal treatment and access, respect for human rights, and freedom from corruption) should apply.

How to cite this chapter:

Halligan, John and Evans, Mark (2024) 'The Australian Public Service', in: Evans, Mark; Dunleavy, Patrick and Phillimore, John (eds) *Australia's Evolving Democracy: A New Democratic Audit,* London: LSE Press, pp.301–325 https://doi.org/10.31389/lsepress.ada.n. Licence: CC-BY-NC 4.0

- Public services, contracting and regulation should be free from corruption, with swift action taken against evidence of possible offences.
- The public service should recruit and promote staff on merit, having due regard to combatting wider societal discrimination that may exist. Its social make-up should reflect the population being served, with recruitment biases addressed on the basis of race, ethnicity, gender, disability, historic under-representation or other factors.
- The public service should ideally be a 'representative bureaucracy', whose social make-up closely reflects that of the population being served – although this has often been hard to achieve.
- Government services should be efficient, effective and deliver 'value for money', with agency performance appropriately documented in timely public documents.
- The efficacy of government interventions and regulations should be assessed in a balanced and evidence-based way, allowing for consultation with both organised stakeholders and unorganised sets of people.
- Procedures for complaints and citizen redress should be easy to access and use, and agencies should operate them in transparent and responsive ways, fulfilling 'freedom of information' requirements.
- In a liberal democracy, the public service and the political executive have complementary roles. The public service should provide the impartial and non-partisan component and institutional memory and expertise, while politicians contribute the dynamic and voter-responsive political element. The mutual check-and-balance functions between the two should foster balanced and improved decision-making.

The Australian Public Service (APS) is responsible for designing and implementing federal policy and regulation (as specified by ministers and Parliament), identifying and diffusing standards, and delivering certain services directly to citizens. For example, Services Australia is the welfare/Medicare arm of government, while Business.gov.au hosts a wide range of programs designed to help enterprises and business. The Canberra federal departments provide funding to states and territories for national infrastructure (such as roads, schools, and hospitals), administer defence and national security arrangements, and supervise many APS agencies and some government enterprises, such as Australia Post and Snowy Hydro.

Line agencies at department level and below are grouped into five categories or 'functional clusters' (APSC, 2023a) to allow comparisons to be made between agencies with similar primary functions, as follows:

- Policy: organisations involved in the development of public policy (for example, Education, Foreign Affairs, Social Services or Health).
- Smaller operational: organisations with fewer than 1,000 employees involved in the implementation of public policy (for example, the Australian Digital Health Agency, Digital Transformation Agency, or Fair Work Commission).
- Larger operational: organisations with 1,000 employees or more involved in the implementation of public policy (for example, Defence, Home Affairs, Australian Tax Office, or Services Australia).
- Regulatory: organisations involved in regulation and inspection (for example, AUSTRAC, Australian Competition and Consumer Commission, or the Office of the Fair Work Ombudsman).

- Specialist: organisations providing specialist support to government (for example, Australian Trade and Investment Commission, Royal Australian Mint, or Commonwealth Ombudsman).

In December 2023, these tasks needed a staff of just over 170,000 in the APS (see Figure 14.4 below), plus just under 60,000 people in the Australian Defence Force (APSC, 2022a). This number was up from 154,000 in 2021, and from 120,000 in the mid-1990s (when Australia's population was around 18 million people, compared to just under 26 million now). Private contracting for federal government has increased markedly in this period, and estimates of the size of the 'para-state' of consultants, contractors and NGOs working for the Commonwealth under the Morrison Coalition government was 54,000 full-time equivalent staff in 2020–21 (37 per cent of the APS number that year), at an annual cost of just under A$21 billion (Guardian, 2023).

The official values embodied in the APS from the outset, and codified in the constantly updated APS Code of Conduct (APSC, 2022b), have aimed at ensuring the highest standards of conduct in public office by maintaining:

- impartial administration, serving all citizens and enterprises equally
- non-partisan and apolitical advice, providing governments of whatever political persuasion with advice that is frank, honest, timely and based on the best available evidence
- staff who are committed to service and can sustain an 'institutional memory' of how to get things done
- administrative processes that are open and accountable to the community
- respect for different peoples and traditions
- strong ethical behaviours, with the APS acting with integrity, in all that it does.

These values all imply some considerable areas of autonomous action by APS staff – for example, in avoiding any suggestion of political favouritism, or preventing the use of state power and public monies for partisan purposes.

Criticisms of the APS have mainly come from the political right, who doubt that political controls are enough to ensure that staff with 'jobs for life' are working as efficiently and innovatively as businesses, and therefore seek to minimise the scale of direct government administration and employ private contractors instead. Others argue that by operating in a 'Canberra bubble' most APS staff lack immediate contact with everyday life across Australia. Some critics from the political left argue that the APS has 'sold out' on political impartiality, with Canberra's elite administrators aligning themselves all too easily with 'neo-liberal' values and viewpoints up to 2022, a view that has also been contested (Shergold and Podger, 2021).

Recent developments

Three recent developments illustrate some achievements that the APS can lay claim to, while also highlighting some evolving problems that the service still faces. The COVID-19 pandemic triggered a rapid and distinctively Australian style of administrative response at the federal level, and some interesting conflicts around federal and state policy-making as well. Prior to this, an Independent Review of the APS (IRAPS, 2019a) made some substantial recommendations for changes, some of which have been acted upon. Two of the key players in IRAPS also moved to top positions in the APS with reform responsibilities (see next section). Lastly, in 2023, a Royal

Commission on the Robodebt Scheme (Royal Commission, 2023) very strongly criticised the roles of senior federal officials and private sector consultants working for departments in a 2016 to 2018 welfare benefits policy fiasco, with some strong implications for how the APS in future gives policy advice, ensures that policies are legal, and operates department accountability to parliament.

Managing the COVID-19 crisis

Arguably Australia was a 'lucky country' throughout the international peak of the pandemic in 2020–21, because of its relative isolation from international air traffic and its effective governance of international borders. Advice by the APS strongly pushed PM Scott Morrison to ban tourists and other arrivals early on (in late March 2020). Like New Zealand, Australia's response started early and evolved, drawing on strong, historical experience of how to combat threats of international disease. The robust enforcement of quarantine procedures (returning residents were required to spend 14 days in strict quarantine hotels) and the slow/careful process of shipping back citizens stranded overseas (in line with quarantine capacities), were also reflective of past APS approaches.

Of course, the key national political decisions around pandemic policy were made by Morrison and Liberal-National ministers, but the influence of the APS has been traced by many commentators in aspects of the effective handling of the threat in 2020–21, facilitated by political bipartisanship from Labor, and by coordination of policies with state governments across the federation via the National Cabinet (Menzies, 2020; and see Chapter 16).

Australia's record in the management of COVID-19 was a highly creditable one up to summer 2021, with just under 11.5 million COVID-19-related cases, just 19,600 deaths and a rate of COVID-19 deaths per million population that was less than a quarter of those in countries like the USA or UK, and the lowest of the Anglosphere liberal democracies (Figure 14.1). Even given Australia's initial advantages from its relative isolation, federal policy implementation on overseas travel and state governments' actions on lockdowns were both swift and effective, with additional economic help from the Commonwealth government to counteract the effects of lockdowns and the impact on the travel industry. The APS was also perceived domestically and internationally to have managed COVID-19 effectively (ANAO, 2020b; Craft and Halligan, 2020a; Haseltine, 2021). Certain federal policy initiatives worked relatively poorly, including a COVID-19 notification app using the Bluetooth capability of Apple and Android smartphones. It was downloaded by only a small minority of the population – largely because state government requirements varied, and use of their tools took off much faster than the federal app.

Figure 14.1: COVID-19 management in the Anglophone liberal democracies from March 2020 to 3 October 2023

Country	Cases (in 000s)	COVID-19 deaths (in 000s)	COVID-19 deaths per million population
USA	103,804	1,124	3.4
UK	24,659	221	3.3
Canada	4,617	51.7	1.4
Australia	**11,402**	**19.6**	**0.8**
New Zealand	2,236	12.6	2.5
Ireland	1,704	8.7	1.7

Source: Computed from data at John Hopkins Coronavirus Resource Center (2023) 'COVID-19 management in the Anglophone democracies, 31 August.

However, later policy controversy focused on the slow vaccine rollout and mixed messaging from federal ministers that appeared to criticise policies in Labor-controlled states – a lapse from bipartisanship that created significant public dissatisfaction. Although some vaccine supplies were received earlier, a comprehensive national vaccination plan agreed with the states and territories was only finally announced in late July 2021, and by early October 2021 the proportion of the population vaccinated was 62 per cent, placing Australia well down the lists of developed, wealthy countries internationally. However, thereafter the pace of vaccination picked up and reduced the pandemic's later-stage intensity.

Overall, though, senior APS staff felt that COVID-19 demonstrated their ability to cut through red tape and decision-making silos and engage in fast policy-making, budgeting and service delivery, moving from idea quickly to action. The experience also highlighted the importance of collaborative governance, defined as a 'cross-sector governance arrangement between government and non-government stakeholders to carry out a public purpose, designed to approach complex social problems with diverse stakeholders' (Butcher and Gilchrist, 2020). The use of collaborative instruments was already a feature of Commonwealth governance, but became more politically salient due to the imperative for whole of government responses to the dislocation caused by the bushfire crisis and then by the pandemic. The opposition of a minority of Australians to lockdowns and even vaccinations also called for careful behavioural management of policy measures that were always controversial for some.

Collaborative governance was also an approach that had been promoted in the IRAPS Review (IRAPS, 2019a and IRAPS, 2019b; see the next sub-section) as a key mechanism for building a 'flexible APS operating model that makes collaboration the norm'. In practical terms this meant:

- an approach that was task-driven, using horizontal teams to create a 'marble cake' apparatus that could span across sectors and focus tightly on policy problems
- getting the right people, with the right expertise, around the table at the right time
- cutting through policy and tier-of-government silos and spans of control to maximise effective action
- better management of stakeholders by leveraging off the wider administrative footprint of states and territories, cities and local governments
- focusing on outcomes-driven performance measurement, undertaken during the crisis in near-real time (Althaus and McGregor, 2019).

Specific examples established during COVID-19 included the Emergency Relief National Coordination Group, established in 2020 to ensure effective national distribution of emergency relief and identify opportunities for coordination. In addition, the National COVID Vaccine Taskforce was created in 2021 under Coordinator-General John Frewen with the mission of ensuring that 'every eligible and willing Australian will be vaccinated by the end of 2021' (Yousef et al., 2022). The Taskforce was a response to public dissatisfaction with the slow vaccine rollout, and the need to improve coordination and planning and increase public confidence through clear messaging

Other types of evidence also suggest that COVID-19 stimulated innovative approaches. In workshops with 80 senior APS officials in August 2021, we asked them to nominate examples of innovation. The most mentioned responses were IT-led innovation in communication, capability and collaboration, flexible working, and faster policy-making. Using collaborative delivery networks and adopting 'agile' methods of developing new IT were also mentioned as improving the quality of cross jurisdictional communication, enhanced the quality of collaboration and enabled flexible work (see below).

The 2019 Review of the Australian Public Service

The promising APS response to COVID-19 came just a few months after the 2019 publication of the 'Independent Review of the Australian Public Service' (IRAPS, 2019a), an important exercise based on an inclusive engagement process that aimed to be far more representative of views across the APS, a striking difference from previous attempts (Evans, 2018). The Review's 'priorities for change' aimed to bolster the APS's independence within Australia's 'Westminster system' tradition, upgrade institutional capacity, reduce hierarchy, and build a flatter, integrated and agile collaborative problem-solving capability around a 'One APS' culture (IRAPS, 2019b). Of the 40 recommendations, the government agreed to implement 15, and accepted aspects of a further 20 (PM Morrison, 2019). Two were noted, and three were rejected. The government did embrace recommendations for reinstituting regular capability reviews of agencies (Podger and Halligan, 2023). It agreed to establish separate professional streams for digital, data and human resources, and to build capability and support career paths in these critical areas.

The Morrison government repeatedly stressed that they would not amend the legislation in force, the Public Service Act 1999. And any recommendation that might potentially undermine the power of ministers and the government was rejected. Among these were some of the most important – covering a legal code and more APS experience for ministerial advisors, greater cooperation (in normal times) with state and territories, and giving the APS commissioner powers to initiate investigations and reviews. The PM also dismissed the idea that the APS should move to common core conditions and pay scales over time to enable it to become a united high-performing organisation, arguing that current policies around APS pay and conditions were working effectively. The Review's claim that too much reliance was being placed on external consultants was also dismissed. Critics argued that any proposals threatening ministers' control, or running counter to the government's agenda, were removed. Thus, systemic or long-run APS reform was again side-tracked, prompting calls for a parliamentary inquiry (Podger, 2019).

The 2023 Royal Commission on the Robodebt Scheme

As in most advanced industrial states, the Australian Commonwealth government makes key transactions with most citizens in two roles – first, as taxpayers via annual income tax declarations, run by the Australian Tax Office (ATO); second, as recipients of welfare benefits, many of which are income-contingent and run month by month by Services Australia, part of its Centrelink operation, and formerly under the Department for Human Services (DHS). The Robodebt Scheme began life in 2014 as an effort to check whether some people or households were being paid more in income-contingent benefits than they were perhaps entitled to, given the income they had declared to the ATO (Wikipedia, 2023). Liberal-National Coalition ministers in the governments of Tony Abbott, Malcolm Turnbull and Scott Morrison were determined to compare between ATO and DHS datasets and to seek repayments from anyone found to have been 'overpaid', even though the two datasets were not easily (some might say legitimately) comparable. The Scheme pushed ahead in 2015 with a manual checking process, and was then launched as an automatic, IT-driven process in 2016 with a big fanfare about eliminating welfare 'fraud' estimated by ministers to be in the hundreds of millions of dollars (Royal Commission, 2023; Podger and Kettl, 2023).

Households affected by the Scheme received strongly worded letters requiring them to immediately repay sums, based on the data calculations made without any appeal process or legal recourse to query the edict. In many cases, the sums involved were large and related to payments from years beforehand, so that many households could not afford to pay back money that had already been spent. Large numbers of citizens jammed DHS helplines without securing any answers, and these promptly collapsed under the load so that people could not make contact at all with Centrelink or the DHS (Royal Commission, 2023; Podger and Kettl, 2023). Debt recovery agencies were quickly activated to secure the return of 'overdue' allegedly overpaid sums. Households or individuals with debts were cut off from other benefits until the debts were cleared, in a very coercive manner. Media and civil rights and pro-welfare groups quickly dubbed the project 'robodebt' and complaints and revelations about the Scheme sustained what a later Royal Commission into the affair termed a 'crescendo of criticism' through most of 2017 (Royal Commission, 2023, p.153).

From 2017, several inquiries and investigations were made by integrity bodies (the Ombudsman and the Australian National Audit Office) and a Senate committee investigated the Scheme. They criticised aspects of its implementation but were assured by ministers and officials that it was well thought through, rested on solid legal basis and that they were confident in its soundness. The 2023 Royal Commission raised serious questions about the possibility that officials and advisors gave inaccurate answers at this stage, effectively undertaking a 'cover-up' of the Scheme's serious legal and administrative flaws. As a result, the Scheme 'rolled on' through 2018 and it was eventually terminated only in 2019. Following legal action, the government was required to repay some 'overpayments' collected back to the households involved. In May 2020, in the face of a class-action lawsuit, the Morrison government announced that it would scrap the debt recovery scheme, with 470,000 wrongly issued debts to be repaid in full, totalling A$1.2 billion in all (Henriques-Gomes, 2020). Following the report, some senior civil servants' careers were brought into disrepute (Bajkowski and Ravlic, 2023; ABC News, 2023).

The Royal Commission (2023) also found that a considerable number of senior APS officials and advisors from the private sector went along with ministerial imperatives when they should not have done so, and then covered up the always shaky and perhaps illegal nature of the powers used to implement the Scheme from the outset. For many commentators, these were clear-cut and severely adverse consequences of the over-politicisation of the public services (Podger and Kettl, 2023). The Royal Commission report's Chapter 23 on 'Improving the Australian Public Service' opened with a quote from Gordon de Brouwer (the Australian Public Services Commissioner in 2023):

> I think what we can see [in the robodebt episode] is that to some degree, the service, parts of the service, at times have lost its soul, lost its focus on people, its empathy for people. We'll need to reflect on how we discharged our legal and ethical responsibilities under law, including in our leadership, and we'll need to examine and act to strengthen our systems, including training and performance management across the service, to ensure that what we've seen so far isn't repeated. (Royal Commission, 2023, Report, p.637)

The Royal Commission also concluded that:

Many of the failures of public administration that led to the creation and maintenance of the Scheme can be traced to features of the APS structure. These features included:

- the separation of responsibilities between agencies in relation to the development and maintenance of government programs and the lack of clear definition of those responsibilities
- a lack of independence on the part of [*department*] secretaries
- woefully inadequate recordkeeping practices
- a lack of understanding on the part of some of those involved of the APS' role, principles and values (Royal Commission, 2023, Report p.637).

But of course, it lay outside the Royal Commission's terms of reference to make concrete proposals for what detailed changes were needed. Instead, commentators noted a twin-track Commission approach (Podger, 2023):

- to clarify the role of the APS and to strengthen its independence particularly by addressing the processes for appointment, termination and performance management of secretaries, which would greatly dilute incentives for excessive responsiveness to ministers
- the 'naming and shaming' of individual public servants, including the referral of some for further investigation and possible sanctions, thus highlighting the potential consequences of excessive political responsiveness.

The Albanese government's reform agenda

Mounting concerns with post-COVID-19 governance under the Morrison government eventually contributed to it losing the 2022 election (see Chapter 5). Post-election, the Labor government paid greater attention to integrity and the mitigation of corrupt practices including:

- the establishment of a National Anti-Corruption Commission in 2023 comparable to ones already well-established at the state level
- securing a speedy Royal Commission into Robodebt (see above)
- reviews were conducted of grants administration and processes, along with issues with responsible government.

A more balanced executive branch with firmer checks and balances, and improved transparency and accountability became apparent.

The Labor government's program was partly an extension of the Independent Review process because of the continuity of key participants, but this was under a new agenda that addressed both the consequences of neo-liberal 'new public management' (NPM), and institutional strengthening (Halligan, 2023). The need to 'reshape traditions that fall on hard times' (Davis, 2021) and the craft of public administration (Shearer, 2022) came to the fore. The head of the Australian National Audit Office (Grant Hehir) publicly 'called out' the APS on the need for more integrity and criticised the failure of departments to follow the intentions of the Performance Governance and Accountability Act on applying performance management (Hehir, 2023; and see Macdonald, 2023).

So, principles, integrity and values were now a priority. An overdue rebalancing of the system (Halligan, 2020) was now explicit in official statements about rebuilding capability through 'increasing the number of direct, permanent public sector jobs, reducing the use of consultants and outsourcing, abolishing the average staffing level cap, and restoring the independence of vital public sector institutions' (APSC, 2022a). The government's APS priorities covered improving integrity (with the National Anti-Corruption Commission foremost here), enhancing capability, acting as a model employer and recognising the centrality of people and businesses to policy and services (Gallagher, 2022, 2023; Halligan, 2024).

By 2023, the Labor government seemed less keen to formally address the tricky issues of restricting ministers' powers in relation to the APS. However, a 'Public Service Amendment Bill 2023' proceeded to implement some of the 2019 APS Review findings, so as to:

- create a new Australian Public Service (APS) Value of 'Stewardship'
- require the Secretaries Board to prepare an APS Purpose Statement
- require agency heads to uphold and promote the APS Purpose Statement
- provide that ministers must not direct agency heads on individual employment matters
- require agency heads to put in place measures to enable decision-making to occur at the lowest appropriate classification
- require regular capability reviews [of departments]
- require the Secretaries Board to request and publish regular long-term insights report
- require agencies to publish annual APS Employee Census results and respond to relevant findings through an action plan (Parliament of Australia, 2023).

By 2023, the APS reform program was also defined around four pillars – integrity, placing people and business first, model employer, and capability – each with associated outcomes. Three phases of progress were envisaged: establishing the foundations, embedding and continuous improvement. The first phase entails developing the program logic, designing delivery and implementation architecture, launching initiatives, and developing a transformation strategy. Twelve departments and agencies are leading on 44 initiatives. Several are complete, for example, the National Anti-Corruption Commission, an employment audit, an in-house consulting service, and annual reporting on APS reform (APS Reform, 2023a). It is too early to tell what difference this ambitious program will make, or whether it will be sustained if there should be a change of government.

Strengths, weaknesses, opportunities and threats (SWOT) analysis

Current strengths	Current weaknesses
The APS has a long tradition of political accountability. The APS culture has been non-partisan, able to work with governments of different political complexions and tackle new issues with competence.	In recent times, the APS's claim to political independence was undermined by an increasingly interventionist political executive. Under Liberal-National Coalition governments, the PM and ministers increasingly sought to control who got top civil service jobs and to reduce the role that permanent public servants played in policy-making. The APS capability overall has been sapped by 20 years of restrictive staffing ceilings, tight limits on administrative spending, and the externalisation of public service work to contractors. Deficits in specific capabilities have been ignored.
Australian public administration has been generally effective and reasonably up to date in its organisational practices. The APS has had a well-developed pattern of continuous improvement and searching for best practices.	The dominant public management organisational culture became largely short-termist and risk-averse, since secretaries and deputy secretaries have short-run contracts only. This reflects the environment of political management.
The APS has performed well in comparative terms. It has been viewed as an international pioneer in the diffusion of best practice regulation, data management, digital tax governance, 'one-stop shop' service delivery, social inclusion, policy programming and the design of income contingent loans in higher education financing.	The extensive use of external consultants both in normal times and during the pandemic exposed a significant capability deficit in the APS (Jenkins, 2020). The former head of the Service, Martin Parkinson, castigated departments that 'abrogated their core responsibility and have become over-reliant on consultants' (quoted in Easton, 2018). In 2023, controversy swelled up over PwC (PricewaterhouseCoopers) briefing industry clients with information obtained working on government contracts leading to one survey showing that half of Australians wanted government to rely less on consultancies (Australian Financial Review, 2023).
Australia's record in digitally transforming public services has been a strong one, particularly in areas with large-scale citizen interactions (for example, tax and human services (OECD, 2024)).	Attracting and retaining skilled IT staff and changing APS culture to be fully digital have both been difficult. After 2016, the Digital Transformation Agency became more regulatory and less culture-changing in its mission. The robodebt fiasco was also an early effort to implement 'big data/artificial intelligence' (BDAI) methods that failed spectacularly.

Australia's cyber-security performance has been around average for liberal democracies, thanks to strong international cooperation.	As in all liberal democracies, the cyber-security threats to the security of APS departments' and agencies' information management systems have grown over time. Government's dependence on online services and cloud provision has also greatly increased.
The APS has had a strong tradition of contingency planning and resilience in crises, and effective front-line agencies. The government learned lessons from the bushfire crisis and put them to good effect in managing COVID-19. The establishment of the National Cabinet as the epicentre of COVID-19 governance, and the effective use of experts, both proved invaluable to the government's effective response.	Evidence-based policy-making tended to be the exception rather than the rule in the more ideologically-driven Morrison and Abbot governments. Since 2022, Labor ministers (with a far smaller majority) claim to have changed their approach.
Women are well represented in the APS workforce as a whole and are more present at the senior staff (SES) level than the average picture for OECD countries (see Chapter 10).	The APS has an ageing workforce that has remained unrepresentative of the community in terms of other diversity measures (see below).
The reporting of policy and administration has been improved through the Performance Framework, meeting the obligations of the Public Governance, Performance and Accountability Act, passed in 2013.	Most APS reporting still focuses on output measurement, rather than outcome-based measurement. Productivity data for government services are not systematically collected or published, with most measures covering 'value for money' in ways that are hard to compare over time.
COVID-19 demonstrated the adaptive capacity of the Commonwealth departments and agencies to redesign and deliver government services under pressure. The APS's own surveys (APS Reform, 2023b) showed that 72 per cent of respondents were satisfied with public services.	The delivery of services has been hampered by siloed delivery systems, poor information and communication systems, unnecessary complexity, and poor delivery culture. Levels of public trust were lower in the APS survey (APS Reform, 2023b) at 61 per cent than levels of satisfaction.
Corruption and fraud by individual APS staff members in federal government have been rare, especially compared with the state administrations in Australia.	The previously long-entrenched ability of the APS to prevent political favouritism or ministerially mandated maladministration has clearly been eroded. The 'sports rorts' and car parks controversies (Karp, 2020; and see Chapter 13), the robodebt debacle (see above), and government advertising sailing close to the wind of being partisan propaganda in the run-up to the 2019 federal election (Lewis, 2019), all suggest that politically appointed secretaries at the DPM&C and in departments had little interest in or capacity for curbing excesses of ministerial power.

Future opportunities	Future threats
The renewed importance of state intervention and good governance during the COVID-19 pandemic boosted pressures to secure the independence and authority of the APS within the federal system under the Albanese government (see below).	If the past erosion of the APS's independence and authority resumes in the 'new normal', critics argue that the APS may be completely politicised, which the outsourcing of its functions to private sector consultants accentuates. In addition, government ministers (of any party) tend to want to avoid close scrutiny, creating continuing pressures on transparency, oversight, integrity and accountability (Podger and Kettl, 2023).
Outcome-driven policy, better program and service management and measurement, under 'new public management' (NPM) have long been expected to lead to better outcomes for citizens and increased public sector productivity.	Evidence of either productivity advances or of NPM practices improving government costs has remained elusive. Critics argued that in Australia, NPM tended to work against effective digital government by increasing the 'separatism' of management in departments and agencies, and under-emphasising the need to shift to a more joined-up 'digital-era' organisational culture (Podger and Kettl, 2023; Dunleavy et al., 2008).
After the 2019 Review (IRAPS, 2019a), the APS may be able to put more emphasis on building up staff's professional skills and digital literacy, and recruiting a more diverse and socially inclusive workforce.	Government faces heightened competition for high-skilled knowledge workers, and hence tends to be driven back towards relying on external consultants, who contribute less to modernising organisational cultures and accumulating 'collective institutional memory'. Three-quarters of agencies reported shortages of digitally skilled and technically qualified staff (Bajkowski, 2023).
The 'footprint' of APS staff in cities, regional towns and shires spread across the country could be used to promote more localism in federal policy implementation.	The continued relative isolation of many APS staff in the 'Canberra village' and nearby NSW fuels some distance from everyday Australians (see Figure 14.4). Citizen distrust can increase the costs of delivery – as with vaccine denial or hesitancy during the COVID-19 crisis.

The remainder of this chapter considers how the politicisation of the executive, policy-making and policy development has affected the APS. Next, the chapter considers the more enduring character of the APS as a whole and recent efforts to sustain its reputation as a modernising and efficient service.

The APS and the politicisation of the executive branch

Under Australia's 'Westminster system' of government, the PM can extensively reshape the machinery of Commonwealth government and the operations of the APS to reflect their government's political priorities, and their style of leadership. Relations between politicians and bureaucrats traditionally centred on the co-existence of the neutral public service and a politically accountable but 'responsible' government. Tensions between them were kept in balance by applying well-established conventions. However, this 'balancing' act has become increasingly dependent on the overarching role acquired by departmental secretaries and the willingness of the political class to stay in its lane.

The three most recent Liberal-National Coalition PMs took different approaches to this aspect of their role. Tony Abbott (2013–2015) demonstrated a 'hard', rather conflictual stance with public servants that focused firmly on budgeting constraints (Donnison, 2014). He appointed private sector business executives to undertake a 'Commission of Audit' (Guardian, 2014; Senate, 2021), which was sharply critical of the APS's capabilities and performance: its report was seen as biased (Senate, 2021) and demanding 'cradle to the grave' spending cutbacks (ABC, 2014). During his time in office, APS advice was often treated as contestable, and cutbacks to achieve smaller government programs conditioned how the public service operated (Halligan, 2016). During his premiership, Malcolm Turnbull (2015–2018) offered more of an olive branch to the APS elite, and a more 'liberal' approach to modernising public service development (Easton, 2016), but this approach did not last. From 2018 to 2022, Scott Morrison's style emphasised a reassertion of political authority and the importance of delivery on his political priorities – although this focus was then overshadowed and knocked off course by COVID-19. The introduction of the second largest fiscal stimulus package in the world, and the return of 'big government' to combat COVID-19, fundamentally changed his government's fiscal strategy and heightened the role of the public service (Cranston, 2020).

However, across all three Liberal-National Coalition administrations, a dominant theme remained: the politicisation of the executive level and the expansion of the power of ministerial offices relative to the permanent administration of departments and agencies. In recent years, cabinet and other ministers have hired substantial numbers of political appointees to assist them with policy development and monitoring, as the 'Anglosphere' 'Westminster system' comparisons in Figure 14.2 show. Australia and Canada have been furthest along this road, with many more ministerial advisors, while the PM's offices there have accounted for less than one in six of all advisors, falling to one in eight under Albanese. The UK has been more restrictive, closely rationing advisors to ministers so that the PM's office there has been dominant. Yet similar complaints of the politicisation of policy-making have been voiced by critics in all three countries.

Figure 14.2: Ministers' and PMs' politically appointed office staffs in Australia and in Canada and the UK

Country	Politically appointed staff in			
	All ministers' offices	PMs' office	Total	Per cent (%) in PMs' offices
Canada	490	91	581	16
Australia	**416**	**56**	**472**	**12**
UK	70	43	113	61

Sources: for Canada, Craft and Halligan (2020b); Cabinet Office UK (2021); Finance Department, 2023, numbers as at 1 May.

Particular concerns have been raised when ministers intervene to force out the top officials (secretaries) for undisclosed reasons – with departures mostly occurring in three situations. The first has been when a secretary insists on providing professional advice to a mission-committed minister who both resists and resents it. Critics argue that: 'Telling a minister what he or she does not want to hear will certainly result in being sacked – or not having the appointment renewed' (Burgess, 2017). The second has happened when a secretary strongly supports the policy of the government of the day but becomes vulnerable with a change in the PM and a new allocation of government roles. The third situation has occurred when 'machinery of government change' needed for wider reasons has been used to dispose of dissenting voices. Morrison dismissed secretaries identified with the policy hub and who were advocates of an APS role in policy development, when he was initially fixated on reducing the APS role to one of just delivery.

Other prominent victims included Andrew Metcalfe, a supporter of a contested program and one of three secretaries sacked by Abbott's government. He was later reappointed in 2019. Martin Parkinson 'retired' from the position of Secretary of the Department of Treasury when Tony Abbott became PM, then became Secretary of the Department of Prime Minister and Cabinet under Malcolm Turnbull, but was later replaced by PM Scott Morrison. The Turnbull years (2015 to 2018) were notable for a movement away from the more confrontational aspects of Abbott's central control and a more tactful handling of secretaries' appointments/displacements. Turnbull recognised the need to review the state of the public service with the APS Review. The Morrison government then reverted to type with the removal of five department heads in 2019, when the number of federal departments was reduced from 18 to 14. This machinery of government change was also made with little apparent APS advice or input (Bartos, 2019).

The Albanese government has made commitments that marked a redefinition of ministers' relations with the APS. In particular, the Labor government will differ from the Coalition government on key aspects of public sector management. For example, Labor has promised to:

- abolish the Average Staffing Level (ASL) cap
- reduce 'waste' and 'excessive reliance' on contractors, consultants and labour-hire companies
- invest nearly A$500 million in 'rebuilding capability', particularly in service delivery roles at Services Australia, Veterans' Affairs, and the National Disability Insurance Agency (NDIA)
- establish an Advanced Strategic Research Agency (ASRA) in the Defence Portfolio (Hamilton, 2022).

It remains to be seen how significant these changes and other commitments will turn out to be, but the changes are grounds for optimism.

Capability deficit

Policy advice and development capability is an integral component of the civil service in the 'Westminster system', but it has been identified as an ailing traditional skill that has been difficult for the current APS to revive. The strong managerialism of the era of new public management (NPM) pushed running departments and agencies to the forefront as the core APS activity and made it the primary responsibility of senior public servants. Policy advice was instead increasingly provided by the entourages of staffers that ministers brought in with them (see above). But it was also attributable to the outsourcing of policy activity to consultants and to politicisation. Among the Anglophone countries, Australia has the heaviest reliance on consultants and outsourcing, which has undermined public service capability. The value of consultancy services increased from under A$400 million to over A$1.1 billion in the decade up to 2018–19 (ANAO, 2020a).

The APS's policy role changed under NPM, because senior executives were now expected to mainly manage policy delivery. The centrality of the APS's policy role within the advisory system was already downgraded by 2010 as political executives became more assertive. More recent analysis of departmental capability reviews (submission 26) presented to a Senate committee indicates that departments varied widely in terms of the quality and extent of their policy capability, ranging from well-developed to laissez faire (Halligan, 2021). They were generally weak on six dimensions: policy development, setting strategy, research and analysis, policy implementation, stakeholder engagement and evaluation.

Figure 14.3: How far Australian, New Zealand and UK public service participants in University of Canberra 2021 workshops agreed that potential features of the Westminster advisory system operated in their countries

Country	Percent (per cent) agreeing that:	
	Male participants	Female participants
'Evidence is a condition of better policy-making'		
Australia	94	97
New Zealand	97	97
UK	93	95
'There is an ongoing tension between short-term imperatives and evidence-based policy-making'		
Australia	84	85
New Zealand	85	87
UK	82	84
'Work time is spent on retrofitting evidence to decisions that have already been taken'		
Australia	76	80
New Zealand	73	78
UK	82	83
'There is ministerial indifference over the facts'		
Australia	64	62
New Zealand	59	63
UK	61	64
'Work time is spent on developing evidence-based policy, programs or interventions'		
Australia	24	20
New Zealand	27	22
UK	18	17

Source: Evans and Stoker (2022) Saving Democracy, London: Bloomsbury, p.114. Reproduced with permission.
Note: Numbers are the percentages of respondents agreeing with each statement.

The emergence of advisory capacity outside the public sector has created a more contested marketplace for policy advice (Tiernan, 2011) and greater 'competition for the ministerial ear'. (MacDermott, 2008). Ministers have wanted to increase the range of inputs, and this may have improved decision-making. However, APS staff and external critics have claimed that before the COVID-19 crisis there was a fashion for deciding policy first and developing evidence to justify it later on – with so called 'policy-based evidence' entering the 'Westminster-system' lexicon (Varghese, 2016).

In workshops held between 2016 and 2020, we asked groups of senior policy officers in Australia, New Zealand and the UK what were the main barriers to evidence-based policy-making. The findings suggest that civil service elites in all three countries were champions of evidence-based policy-making but their political masters were generally not (Figure 14.3). Moreover, due to a combination of a short-termist pathology and the 24/7 media cycle, some staff said they spent much of their time engaged in 'policy-based evidence-making', retrofitting evidence to support decisions already made. They identified three key barriers: disconnection, mistrust and poor understanding between the worlds of ideas/research and action/practice; a static view of academic research that needed to be linked to ongoing exchanges; and the perception that there was limited capability or incentives in the system to use genuine research.

Policy scientists report that the best practice principles of policy-making are often overlooked. The Institute of Public Affairs analysed 20 public policies using the 10 criteria of the 'Wiltshire test for good policy-making' (Breheny and Lesh, 2018). The project was commissioned 'to coax more evidence-based policy decisions ... by reviewing and rating high profile government decisions'. They found that only seven met these criteria, suggesting that more policy has been made on the basis of partisan convictions or ideology, rather than 'what works'. The parlous position of the system was described by the former head of the public service, Dr Martin Parkinson, as the 'degradation of policy expertise'. However, the COVID-19 crisis brought scientific and research expertise back into focus as key elements in policy decisions, for a time at least.

The character of the Australian Public Service

Looking comparatively, the APS has long been rated as effective by international observers, who see it as a an active and reform-minded civil service. Australia ranked third in the International Civil Service Effectiveness Index (Blavatnik School of Government, 2019) – although that was influenced by 'new public management' factors and placed all the Anglosphere democracies highly, with the UK at no.1 (see Chapter 28). The World Bank placed the quality of Australia's overall governance in its top 10 countries overall in 2021 (World Bank, 2021). The OECD (2024) ranked Australia fourth among its member countries in 2023 in terms of its development of digital services.

With just over 170,000 staff the APS has long been one of Australia's largest employers, and so its staffing numbers and trends have been closely watched. Staff numbers grew by 3 per cent in both 2019–20, and then again in 2020–21, largely because of the need to respond to first the bushfire crisis and then COVID-19. Although the APS is routinely presented in the media as centred only in Canberra, in fact just under two in every five staff (around 65,000 staff) were based there at the end of 2023 (see Figure 14.4). The remainder were distributed across the states and territories as shown. In line with the Australian population as a whole, additional analysis shows that around half of the APS staff worked in the large capital cities that account for the bulk of the populations of each state (and of the Northern Territory). So only about 1 in 10 APS staff worked in areas of 'regional Australia' more rural or remote than the state capital cities.

Women have been well represented in the APS compared to the civil service in other OECD countries, accounting for three in five staff in 2020, compared to just over half in the OECD average (see Figure 14.5). Women also made up 37 per cent of senior executive staff, above the OECD average (which was 32 per cent). However, the APS workforce was relatively older than Australia's (admittedly young) population, with only one in eight employees aged under 30, and a third aged over 50 (APSC, 2020) In 2020, 22 per cent of the APS workforce were born outside of Australia, with England the most common overseas country of birth, though

Figure 14.4: The number of APS employees and proportions (%) of the total workforce working in the states and territories (in December 2023)

State	2023	Per cent
ACT Canberra	64,940	38.1
New South Wales	28,290	16.6
Victoria	28,540	16.8
Queensland	21,560	12.7
South Australia	11,260	6.6
Western Australia	8,140	4.8
Tasmania	4,190	2.5
Northern Territory	2,010	1.2
Overseas	1,410	0.8
Total	170,330	100

Source: APSC (2023a) *Trust in the Australian Public Services – 2023 Annual Report*, online report.

Note: Numbers of staff in column 2 are rounded to the nearest 10, and percentages in column 3 are rounded to nearest 0.1%.

Figure 14.5: A snapshot view of the Australian Public Service in mid-2023

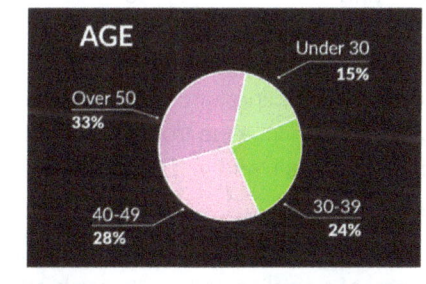
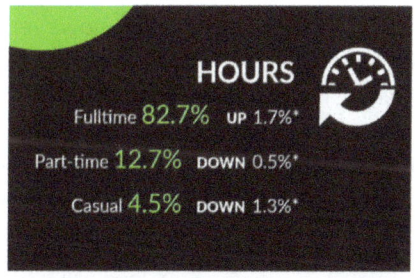
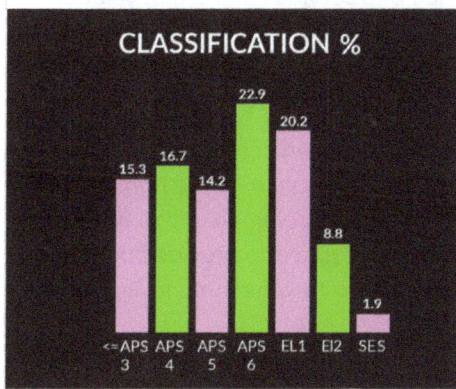
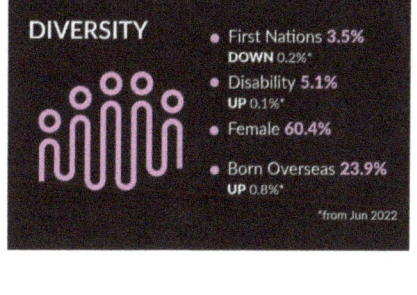

Source: APSC, 2023b. Reproduced with permission. See also APSC, 2023c.

the proportion from England has been falling. In 2001, nearly a quarter of those APS employees born overseas were born in England (24.3 per cent), but by the end of 2020 this number had fallen to 13.6 per cent. Seven of the remaining top 10 countries of birth were Asian. The proportion of staff born in India and China has been increasing with the general population. None-the-less critics argue that:

> *More than half of Australians are either first- or second-generation immigrants. However, our public servants [do] not reflect this diversity. The problem becomes acute at the senior executive level. Only 7 per cent of senior executives in the APS identify as being from a non-English speaking background.* (Lin, 2024)

Aboriginal and Torres Strait Islander peoples constituted 2.2 per cent of the APS workforce in 2015 and grew to 2.9 per cent by 2019 and 3.5 per cent in 2022, but mainly in the lowest ranks. Improving their representation has been an APS priority for 2020 to 2024 (APSC, 2022c; Australian Government, 2020). Compared to many other occupational groups, the APS has maintained a strong emphasis on full-time working and makes only a small use of casual staff.

Enhancing service delivery and digital modernisation

Beginning in 2019, the Morrison Coalition government showed renewed interest in the quality of service delivery, demonstrated by the launch of Services Australia as a giant executive agency (not an orthodox government department) to 'drive greater efficiencies and integration of Government service delivery' (Gourley, 2019). The PM avowedly sought by this change: 'some congestion-busting ... so Australians can get access to those services in a more timely and efficient way for them, making better use of technology and better integrating service delivery across different portfolio' (Gourley, 2019).

The level of public trust in the APS initially increased significantly during the early COVID-19 period, rising from 38 to 54 per cent between 2019 and 2020 for the reasons discussed above (Evans et al., 2020). Subsequently, however, the slow vaccine roll-out and mixed government messaging over the risks of the AstraZeneca vaccine punctured public trust in government again within a short period (Evans, 2021). The 2023 Citizen Experience Survey showed four-fifths of respondents satisfied or very satisfied with APS services (up from pre-COVID-19), with three-fifths of respondents seeing services positively in detail, and half finding the time involved to settle issues acceptable (APSC Reform, 2023b).

Yet the APS also identified sources of public dissatisfaction with the delivery of public services, and in particular service complexity and the absence of a service culture that valued the time of citizens (APS Reform, 2022). Figure 14.6 shows the key types of barriers to improving regional (grass roots) service delivery that senior officials in a University of Canberra workshop said that APS senior officials have recognised and sought to tackle, including:

> *siloed systems that are not conducive to service delivery; complexity in service design and access; difficulty in finding the right information, at the right time, in the right context; reactive service management; poor communication with users about entitlements and obligations; users being required to provide information multiple times; and the complexity of tools provided by government.* (Evans et al., 2019, p.88)

Figure 14.6: Barriers to improving service delivery recognised by senior APS officials in a 2019 study

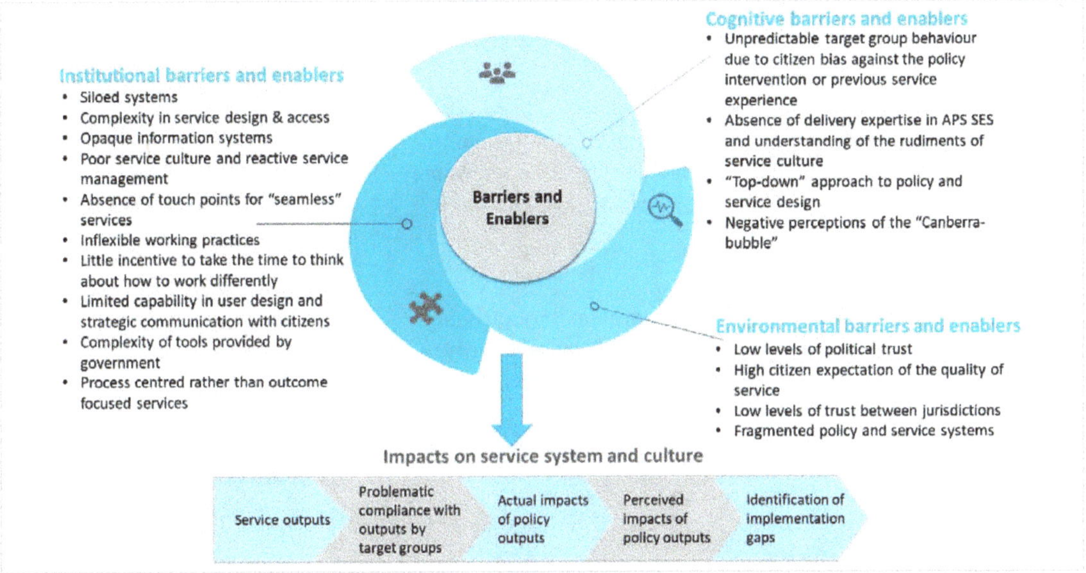

Institutional barriers and enablers
- Siloed systems
- Complexity in service design & access
- Opaque information systems
- Poor service culture and reactive service management
- Absence of touch points for "seamless" services
- Inflexible working practices
- Little incentive to take the time to think about how to work differently
- Limited capability in user design and strategic communication with citizens
- Complexity of tools provided by government
- Process centred rather than outcome focused services

Cognitive barriers and enablers
- Unpredictable target group behaviour due to citizen bias against the policy intervention or previous service experience
- Absence of delivery expertise in APS SES and understanding of the rudiments of service culture
- "Top-down" approach to policy and service design
- Negative perceptions of the "Canberra-bubble"

Environmental barriers and enablers
- Low levels of political trust
- High citizen expectation of the quality of service
- Low levels of trust between jurisdictions
- Fragmented policy and service systems

Impacts on service system and culture

Service outputs → Problematic compliance with outputs by target groups → Actual impacts of policy outputs → Perceived impacts of policy outputs → Identification of implementation gaps

Source: Evans et al. 2019. *Trust In Australian Regional Public Services: 'Citizens Not Customers – Keep It Simple, Say What You Do And Do What You Say'*, Report to the APS, Institute for Governance and Policy Analysis, University of Canberra, Figure 7, p.89.

A fundamentally important way of enhancing the quality-of-service delivery in modern public administration (as in business) has been through the development of better digital and online services. This was a key contribution of the Turnbull government, and Morrison also sought to build on it in establishing Services Australia to make 'best use of technology and digital applications' (Gourley, 2019). In 2020, Australia was listed among the top five performing countries with very high E-Government Development Index scores (UN, 2022), based on its online service, telecommunication infrastructure and human capital. These performance indicators largely correspond with the implementation of 'digital era governance 1' (DEG1) interventions (Dunleavy and Evans, 2019a), which used technology to 'join up' activity across departments or tiers of government, creating client-focused agencies driven by 'end to end', user-focused redesign of services or the development of digital platforms for service delivery (Figure 14.7). The highest performing countries showed high investment in online technologies, followed 'digital first' targets for the delivery of core transactional public services and followed a whole-of-government approach – which has often been harder to do in federal countries.

Conclusion: A public service renaissance?

The APS has a strong record of achievement in providing the executive with high quality advice, maintaining the stability of the policy and service system over time, meeting the government's fiscal strategy, and delivering effective Commonwealth governance. Its ability to adapt and respond to crisis has been impressive and departments and agencies have made significant strides in digital service transformation. However, the formal responsibility of the

Figure 14.7: Modern models of bureaucracy and how the APS use of digital technology has evolved in waves

Model	Main focus	Examples of the role of IT/digital technology
New Public Management (implemented 1990–2010) focuses on managerial control and assumes a world with most data held as closed.	Managerial modernisation emphasizing disaggregation, competition, incentivisation.	Tokenistic adoption of IT for better service delivery, but undermined by oligopolistic IT markets, weak e-Gov, no citizen role.
Digital Era Governance 1 (started 1995–2010) deploys new technology to enhance government's nodality obligation at the epicentre of society's information networks	Reintegration through shared services; digitalisation of paper/phone-based systems; system integration through new governance instruments; focus on user design.	Creation of major online transactional services and contact centres: Australian Tax Office's My Tax; Services Australia integration across Medicare and social security/welfare; myGov portal site for 15 departments' services.
Digital Era Governance 2 (beginning 2005–2020) embracing the 'internet of things' to enhance nodality and the social web and developing capability in big data analytics and artificial intelligence.	Acceptance of the mantra that digital services reduce or contain costs. Radical online modernisation of transactional agencies and older regulatory agencies (e.g., immigration). Strengthening the reintegration of services; proactive systems integration; more nodality; service design with the user experience centre-stage.	Improving call centres with AI systems; personalising services delivery more; using social media. Active accounts on MyGov increased to 26 million in 2023 (from under 12 million in 2017), and accesses to 350 million annually (Australian Government, 2023). Efforts to transform APS culture on digital change with the Digital Transformation Agency, reflected in high international rankings (OECD, 2024).
A third wave of DEG changes (starting 2022 onwards) focusing on big data/artificial intelligence approaches, algorithmic governance and cloud computing, allied with a strong focus on changing the whole organisational culture of civil services (Dunleavy and Margetts, 2023).	Exploiting 'big data' insights (Dunleavy, 2016), developing machine learning and other AI approaches. Speeding up new policy development via agile and cloud computing solutions. Diversifying IT suppliers. Absorbing Silicon Valley and tech industry working practices and consumer responsiveness into public administration and regulation (Dunleavy and Evans, 2019a and 2019b).	Development of fully robotic services (like e-passport gates, drones in defence and civilian uses etc); AI-driven policy initiatives (but unlike the premature robodebt effort). Digital estate treated as critical national infrastructure (Australian Government, 2023).

Source: Dunleavy and Margetts (2023), 'Data science, artificial intelligence and the third wave of digital era governance', Public Policy and Administration, Online First, Table 1.

APS under the Public Service Act 1999 to provide apolitical advice for 'the Government, the Parliament and the Australian public' has experienced historic challenges. The erosion of the Service's independence and authority by ministers and advisors under Coalition governments in particular diminished its policy advisory role and capability, and accentuated the perceived remoteness of Canberra policy-makers from the citizens it serves. The Albanese government has sought to both address these problems and achieved some changes. However, Labor would need to secure a second term for ministers to succeed in embedding the long-term improvements in how public services operate envisaged by the APS reform agenda. In the past, the main causes of the failure of reform implementation were changes of government – and a future Liberal-National government would undoubtedly do things differently.

References

ABC News (2014) 'Commission of Audit recommends cradle-to-grave cuts in report released by Federal Government', ABC News, 1 May. https://perma.cc/R7GH-2H6E

ABC News (2023) 'Kathryn Campbell first senior bureaucrat suspended after robodebt royal commission', ABC News webpage, 20 July. https://perma.cc/W7LR-85BY

Althaus, Catherine and McGregor, Carmel (2019) *Ensuring a World-class Australian Public Service: Delivering Local Solutions,* ANZOG research paper for the Australian Public Service Review Panel, March. https://perma.cc/SPZ7-ZNLH

ANAO (Australian National Audit Office) (2020a) *Australian Government Procurement Contract Reporting Update, Auditor-General Report No. 27 2019–20*, Commonwealth of Australia, p.45. https://perma.cc/CQ6E-XYE4

ANAO (Australian National Audit Office) (2020b) 'Management of the Australian public service workforce response to Covid19', Webpage. https://perma.cc/PD8Q-XHR6

APSC (Australian Public Service Commission) (2020) 'Chapter 3: Diversity', *APS Employment Data 31 December 2020 release*. https://perma.cc/M2HC-YD62

APSC (Australian Public Service Commission (2022a) 'Size and shape of the APS', APSC webpage. https://perma.cc/MTR2-JBBY

APSC (Australian Public Service Commission) (2022b) 'APS Code of Conduct'. https://perma.cc/CD65-E8QF

APSC (Australia Public Service Commission) (2022c) '2.2 First Nations peoples', Webpage. https://www.apsc.gov.au/working-aps/state-of-service/2022/report/culture/state-service-report-2021-22-chapter-2-diverse-and-inclusive-workplaces/22-first-nations-peoples

APSC (Australian Public Service Commission) (2023a) 'APS Agencies – size and function', 10 February. Webpage. https://www.apsc.gov.au/aps-agencies-size-and-function

APSC (Australian Public Service Commission) (2023b) 'APS Employment Data 30 June 2023 Interactive database'. https://perma.cc/DR5U-MXCJ

APSC (Australian Public Services Commission) (2023c) 'The Australian Public Service at a glance 30 June 23', APS Employment Data, 30 June, webpage. https://perma.cc/3DRN-BKPN

APS Reform (2022) '2020–2021 Citizen Experience Results Summary', APS Reform webpage. https://perma.cc/G5BD-4X8P

APS Reform (2023a) 'Section One: Overview of APS Reform', Webpage. https://perma.cc/X423-E5G5

APS Reform (2023b) 'Trust in Australian public services: 2023 annual report'. https://perma.cc/43TV-97NC

Australian Financial Review (2023) 'One in two want government to cut use of big four firms: Survey', *Australian Financial Review*, 20 December. https://perma.cc/QS5A-C9BC

Australian Government (2020) *Commonwealth Aboriginal and Torres Strait Islander: Workplace Strategy 2020–2024*. https://perma.cc/8ZCS-X9FV

Australian Government (2023) 'Critical National Infrastructure – the MyGov User Audit Volume I Findings and recommendations. https://perma.cc/EU58-8EQ4 and Vol 2 Detailed Analysis. https://perma.cc/MHN9-MH4Q

Bajkowski, Julian (2023) 'State of the service? Yet again, tech and digital top APS declared critical skills shortages', *The Mandarin*, 30 November. https://perma.cc/5UJA-GABP

Bajkowski, Julian; and Ravlic, Tom (2023) 'First robodebt royal commission scalp confirmed at PwC', The Mandarin, 7 July. https://perma.cc/CJE8-Q2AH

Bartos, Stephen (2019) 'Scott Morrison's department shake-up is just the beginning', *Canberra Times*, 5 December. https://perma.cc/T42H-RRGE

Blavatnik School of Government (2019) The International Civil Service Effectiveness (InCiSE) Index, Oxford University. https://perma.cc/2HZJ-69AN

Breheny, Simon and Lesh, Matthew (2018) *Evidence Based Policy Research Project*. Melbourne, Institute for Public Affairs/Per Capita. https://perma.cc/J7VJ-RPLL

Burgess, Verona (2017) 'APS leadership turnover set for another jolt – for better or for worse', *The Mandarin*, 12 July. https://perma.cc/ZD5L-HVM9

Butcher, John and Gilchrist, David (2020) *Collaboration for Impact: Lessons from the Field*, Canberra: ANZSOG/ANU Press. https://perma.cc/7LSK-LZTA

Cabinet Office (UK) (2021) *Annual Report on Special Advisers 2021*, 15 July. https://perma.cc/769X-EZBD

Craft, Jonathan and Halligan, John (2020a) 'Executive governance and policy advisory systems in a time of crisis', in Boin, Arjen; Brock, Kathy; Craft, Jonathan; Halligan, John; 't Hart, Paul; Roy, Jeffrey; Tellier, Geneviève; Turnbull, Lori (eds) 'Beyond COVID-19: Five commentaries on expert knowledge, executive action, and accountability in governance and public administration', *Canadian Public Administration*, vol. 63, no. 3, pp.344–50. $ https://doi.org/10.1111/capa.12386

Craft, Jonathan and Halligan, John (2020b) *Advising Governments in the Westminster Tradition: Policy Advisory Systems in Australia, Britain, Canada and New Zealand*. Cambridge: Cambridge University Press. $ https://doi.org/10.1017/9781108377133

Cranston, Matthew (2020) 'Australia's rescue package the world's biggest, bar one', *Financial Review*, 6 May. https://perma.cc/WJP8-4QR8

Davis, Glen (2021) 'The first task is to find the right answer ... Public service and the decline of capability', Jim Carlton Annual Integrity Lecture, Melbourne Law School, Melbourne University, 7 May. https://perma.cc/F7R2-8YUN

Donnison, Jon (2014) 'Tony Abbott's Australian budget: Brave or foolhardy?' *BBC News*, 13 May. https://perma.cc/22JG-F3LJ

Dunleavy, Patrick (2016) '"Big data" and policy learning', in Stoker, Gerry and Evans, Mark (eds) *Methods that Matter: Social Science and Evidence-Based Policymaking*, Bristol: The Policy Press. http://eprints.lse.ac.uk/66131/1/Dunleavy per cent20_Big per cent20Data per cent20and per cent20policy per cent20learning_Author_2016.pdf

Dunleavy, Patrick and Evans, Mark (2019a) 'Digital transformation', in Mark Evans, Michelle Grattan, and Brendan McCaffrie (eds) *From Turnbull to Morrison, Trust Divide*, Melbourne University Press, pp.242–55.$ https://perma.cc/7Y8A-EL27

Dunleavy, Patrick and Evans, Mark (2019b) 'Australian administrative elites and the challenges of digital-era change', *Journal of Chinese Governance,* vol. 4, no. 2, pp. 181–200. $ https://doi.org/10.1080/23812346.2019.1596544 OA at: https://perma.cc/X6FN-H54N

Dunleavy, Patrick and Margetts, Helen (2023) 'Data science, artificial intelligence and the third wave of digital era governance', *Public Policy and Administration*, 25 September. Online First. https://doi.org/10.1177/09520767231198737

Dunleavy, Patrick; Margetts, Helen; Bastow, Helen; and Tinkler, Jane (2008) 'Australian e-Government in comparative perspective', *Australian Journal of Political Science*, vol. 43, no.1, pp.13–26. $ https://doi.org/10.1080/10361140701842540

Easton, Stephen (2016) 'Turnbull: "Look to other jurisdictions" and plagiarise the best ideas', *The Mandarin,* 20 April. https://perma.cc/S9HZ-554T

Easton, Stephen (2018). 'Australian Public Service to start running citizen-satisfaction surveys', *The Mandarin,* 4 July. www.themandarin.com.au/95214-australian-public-service-to-start-running-citizen-satisfaction-surveys/

Evans, Mark (2018) *Australian Public Service Reform: Learning from the Past and Building for the Future*, Canberra: IPAA. https://perma.cc/4EVB-JPZ5

Evans, Mark (2021) 'Public trust in the government's COVID response is slowly eroding. Here's how to get it back on track', *The Conversation*, 11 July. https://theconversation.com/public-trust-in-the-governments-covid-response-is-slowly-eroding-heres-how-to-get-it-back-on-track-163722

Evans, Mark and Stoker, Gerry (2022) *Saving Democracy,* London: Bloomsbury. https://perma.cc/3DXQ-Y82N

Evans, Mark; Dare, Lain; Tanton, R; Vidyattama, Y; and Seaborn, J (2019) *Trust in Australian Regional Public Services: 'Citizens Not Customers – Keep It Simple, Say What You Do and Do What You Say'*, Report to the APS. Institute for Governance and Policy Analysis, University of Canberra. https://perma.cc/V8GH-9UBH

Evans, Mark; Valgarðsson, Viktor; Jennings, Will; and Stoker, Gerry (2020) *Democracy 2025 Report No 7: Political Trust in Times of Coronavirus: Is Australia Still the Lucky Country?* July, Canberra, Democracy 2025/Trustgov. https://perma.cc/C8E4-YDTA

Finance Department (2023) Response to Freedom of Information request about Personal employee Positions, as at 31 May. https://perma.cc/8SFQ-GCLX

Gallagher, Katy (2022) 'Albanese Government's APS Reform agenda'. Speech to the Institute of Public Administration Australia, 13 October. https://perma.cc/EV8U-EZ2F

Gallagher, Katy (2023) 'Annual statement on APS Reform', Speech, 2 November. https://perma.cc/9BRH-2BRC

Gourley, Paddy (2019) 'Public sector informant: Finding meaning in Scott Morrison's public service: "pep talk"', *Canberra Times*, 4 June. $ https://perma.cc/A8LB-CRSH

Guardian, Australia (2014) 'Commission of Audit report in full – Towards responsible government', *Guardian, Australia*, 1 May. https://perma.cc/4YRS-NM9Z

Guardian, Australia (2023) 'Morrison government spent $20.8bn on consultants and outsourcing public service in final year, audit finds', *Guardian, Australia,* 5 May. https://perma.cc/K4F4-2U8C

Halligan, John (2016) 'Mapping the Central State in Australia', Conference Paper: IPSA 2016 World Congress. https://perma.cc/6CZU-JCLW

Halligan, John (2020) *Reforming Public Management and Governance: Impacts and Lessons from Anglophone Countries*, Cheltenham: Edward Elgar. $ https://perma.cc/D6WD-JLAQ

Halligan, John (2021) 'Submission 26: Senate Finance and Public Administration References Committee Inquiry into the Current Capability of the Australian Public Service, 2021'. Submission No. 26. https://perma.cc/CS9C-2D62

Halligan, John (2023) 'Public administrative reform in Australia', in Massey, Andrew (ed), *International Handbook of Public Administration Reform,* Cheltenham: Edward Elgar, Chapter 21, pp.390–410. $ https://perma.cc/AP3K-37C3

Halligan, John (2024) 'Corruption and accountability in Australian Government'. In Ali Farazmand and C. Atkinson (eds), *Corruption and Accountability Problems in Modern Government: A Comparative Analysis*, Routledge, forthcoming.

Hamilton, Peter (2022) 'The Australian Government public sector', Parliamentary Library Briefing book, Australian Parliament website page. https://perma.cc/H976-2EQT

Haseltine, William (2021) 'What can we learn from Australia's Covid-19 response?', *Forbes Magazine*, 24 March. https://perma.cc/53R3-SVYF

Hehir, Grant (2023) Keynote, Institute of Public Administration Secretary Series, National Gallery of Australia, Canberra, Transcript, 12 September. https://perma.cc/XA45-H6KR

Henriques-Gomes, Luke (2020) 'Robodebt: Total value of unlawful debts issued under Centrelink scheme to exceed $1bn', *The Guardian*, Australia, 10 June. https://perma.cc/Z648-ZQ2G

Independent Review of the Australian Public Service (IRAPS) (2019a) *Our Public Service, Our Future: Independent Review of the Australian Public Service.* https://perma.cc/2KQV-NQKA

Independent Review of the Australian Public Service (IRAPS) (2019b) 'Priorities for change', 19 March. https://perma.cc/52D9-UAZJ

Jenkins, Shannon (2020) 'Big Four consultancy firms receive $640 million a year to perform "day to day" public service jobs', *The Mandarin*, 17 June. https://perma.cc/768T-ZEGC

John Hopkins Coronavirus Resource Center (2023) 'COVID-19 management in the Anglophone democracies', 31 August. https://perma.cc/46BH-M624

Karp, Paul (2020) 'Sports rorts: Coalition approved at least six grants without an application form, documents reveal', *The Guardian, Australia,* 21 July. https://perma.cc/Y5WH-6Q6F

Lewis, Peter (2019) 'The escalation in dirt and "gotcha" moments in the election campaign drags focus off actual policy', *Guardian, Australia,* 7 May. https://perma.cc/BTU2-6X4Z

Lin, Jin (2024) 'Our public service needs cultural diversity targets', *Blavatnik Institute blog,* 27 January. https://perma.cc/A3PX-99WH

MacDermott, Kathy (2008) *Whatever Happened to 'Frank' and 'Fearless'? The Impact of New Public Management on the Public Service*, Canberra: ANU Press. https://perma.cc/JZ4T-BH59

Macdonald, Anna (2023) 'ANAO calls out public sector integrity', *The Mandarin*, 5 September. https://perma.cc/7VLB-PZTE

Menzies, Jennifer (2020) 'Explainer: What is the national cabinet and is it democratic?' *The Conversation*, 31 March. https://perma.cc/LXU7-455T

OECD (2024) *2023 OECD Digital Government Index: Results and Key Findings,* Paris: OECD. https://perma.cc/3YSV-N8KV

Parliament of Australia (2023) 'Public Service Amendment Bill 2023', Webpage. https://perma.cc/UQ5S-56E6

PM Scott Morrison (2019) 'Delivering for Australians – a world class Australian Public Service'. Media Release. https://perma.cc/76N5-5ZHG

Podger, Andrew (2019) 'Report on public service overhaul a good start, but parliamentary inquiry is needed', *The Conversation,* 18 December. https://perma.cc/67EG-6XLH

Podger, Andrew (2023) 'Accountability of the public service: Robodebt royal commission highlights personal responsibilities', *Canberra Times,* 14 July. $ https://perma.cc/HRD7-YPV5

Podger, Andrew and Halligan, John (2023) 'Australian Public Service Capability', in Podger, Andrew; Chan, Hon. S; Su, Tsai-tsu; and Wanna, John (eds) *Dilemmas in Public Management in Greater China and Australia,* ANU Press. https://perma.cc/2S54-ZPUQ

Podger, Andrew and Kettl, Donald F (2023) 'How much damage can a politicized public service do? Lessons from Australia', *Public Administration Review,* 12 December, vol. 84, no. 1, pp.160–72. https://doi.org/10.1111/puar.13789

Royal Commission into the Robodebt Scheme (2023) *Final Report,* Canberra: Commonwealth of Australia report, 7 July. https://perma.cc/V5AB-U4ZG

Senate (2021) 'Abbott Government's Commission of Audit', Senate committee report. https://perma.cc/4ZMM-QL4T

Shearer, Christine (2022) *Constructing the Craft of Public Administration: Perspectives from Australia*, Sydney: Palgrave Macmillan. $ https://doi.org/10.1007/978-3-030-81896-8

Shergold, Peter and Podger, Andrew (2021) 'Neoliberalism? That's not how practitioners view public sector reform', in Podger, Andres and Vincent, Sam (eds) *Politics, Policy and Public Administration in Theory and Practice*, Canberra: ANU Press, Chapter 14, pp.335–72. $ https://perma.cc/Z6WJ-V6H2 Also OA at: https://doi.org/10.22459/PPPATP.2021.14

Tiernan, Anne (2011) 'Advising Australian Federal Governments: Assessing the evolving capacity and role of the Australian Public Service', *Australian Journal of Public Administration,* vol. 70, no. 4, pp.335–46. $ https://doi.org/10.1111/j.1467-8500.2011.00742.x

UN (United Nations, Department of Social and Economic Affairs) (2022) *E-Government Survey 2022: The Future of Digital Government.* https://www.un-ilibrary.org/content/books/9789210019446/read

Varghese, Peter (2016) 'Parting reflections: Secretary's speech to IPAA', Department of Foreign Affairs and trade, webpage. 9 June. https://perma.cc/282E-U55Z

Wikipedia (2023) 'Royal Commission into the Robodebt Scheme', Webpage. https://perma.cc/P4PU-TTK8

World Bank (2021) 'Worldwide governance indicators'. https://perma.cc/A2KB-4FPP

Yousef, Muroj; Dietrich, Tim; and Rundle-Thiele, Shary (2022) 'Actions speak louder than words: Sentiment and topic analysis of COVID-19 vaccination on Twitter and vaccine uptake', *JMIR Formative Research,* 15 September, vol. 6, issue. 9, no. e37775. https://doi.org/10.2196/37775

15

Government policy-making

John Butcher

The processes underpinning the conceptualisation, design and implementation of public policy can either serve democratic values, or they can embody democratic deficits. A good policy process asks whether appropriate authorisation exists for a proposed policy; asks what the policy is intended to achieve; questions the assumptions underpinning the proposal; stress-tests the feasibility of implementation; considers the strengths and weaknesses of alternative options; and asks whether a 'licence' exists to enact the policy.

What criteria for a democratic policy process should government and public sector bodies meet in a liberal democracy?

- Is there an electoral mandate for the policy? Do policy proposals logically flow from the platform set out by the governing party in an election campaign? Or, in the absence of an electoral mandate, has the government made the case for policy responses to problems that emerge under circumstances where it is not possible for government to seek approval from the electorate?

- Is the policy consistent with an election promise and/or party values and priorities? In general, the electorate expects governments to keep their promises. And, in general, governments intend to keep their promises, although circumstances (such as the make-up of the parliament, and their consequent ability to pass legislation) might curtail their aspirations.

- Whose interests are served by the policy? It might be popularly supposed that policy settings are responsive to, and guided by, the preferences of electors as interpreted and mediated by political actors. It is more realistic, however, to suppose that voter preferences are of lesser importance than those of 'interests' with the influence and means to donate money (and to openly back) political parties.

- Has the need for the policy been established? In an ideal world, policy is proposed to address problems about which there is a shared concern and understanding. Some policy proposals, however, might best be described as 'solutions looking for problems'.

How to cite this chapter:

Butcher, John (2024) 'Government policy-making', in: Evans, Mark; Dunleavy, Patrick and Phillimore, John (eds) *Australia's Evolving Democracy: A New Democratic Audit,* London: LSE Press, pp.326–345. **https://doi.org/10.31389/lsepress.ada.o**. Licence: CC-BY-NC 4.0

- Is there a legal basis for the policy? Public policy derives legal authority from the Constitution, supporting legislation and delegated (or subordinate) legislation. A fundamental democratic obligation of government is to ensure – and provide assurance – that public policy is 'legal'.
- Is the policy process transparent and accountable? Not infrequently the implementation of public policy occurs in ways that deviate from the normative expectations of good public administration. This might include deficiencies in transparency, accountability, governance and process.
- Does the policy require a social licence and does a social licence exist? Social Licence to Operate (SLO) is fundamentally concerned with issues of transparency, accountability, legitimacy and, most importantly, trust, particularly in circumstances in which stakeholder communities have not, historically, enjoyed input into, or influence on, decisions that affect their lives – especially decisions made by big business and/or by government.

Recent developments

Over the past two decades Australian governments – federal, state and territory – committed to policy-making frameworks that were citizen-centred and evidence-based. Lip service was also given to policy-making that offered voice and agency to those affected by policy and encouraged collaboration across organisational, domain and sector boundaries. While there was scant evidence of success against these aspirations, evidence of practice that fell short of government aspirations was abundant. Path dependence, organisational and programmatic silos, the influence of powerful interests, and political expediency all acted to preserve the status quo and allowed democratic deficits to persist.

This chapter begins with a SWOT (strengths, weaknesses, opportunities and threats) analysis that gives a granulated answer to the criteria questions posed above. After the SWOT analysis, three sections consider: how policy happens; democracy, policy and civic engagement; and the fit between each of the audit criteria above (in that order) and the modern policy process.

Strengths, weaknesses, opportunities and threats (SWOT) analysis

Current strengths	Current weaknesses
Opportunities have long existed for ordinary members of Australian political parties[1] to influence policy priorities and election platforms. This can occur at the party branch level and cascade upwards to party conferences where members may be able to formally ratify or amend party positions on a range of matters (see Chapter 6).	The rules governing member input into policy priorities vary between the major parties. The two biggest parties, Labor and Liberal, have seen their member base decline over the years and, in reality, party decisions tend to be influenced by factional blocks, often with institutional backing (for example, trade unions or business lobbies). This means that many policy domains are susceptible to 'capture' by sectional interests.
In the absence of consistent, formalised and institutionally sanctioned avenues for voter input into policy priorities, formulation or design, the Australian media has long played an important role in facilitating disclosure and providing forums within which the political and practical merits of government policy can be debated (Chapter 8).	The continuing decline of traditional news media in the face of digital transformation poses challenges for in-depth investigative reporting and analysis, meaning that the existence of an informed policy-literate public cannot be taken for granted (see Chapter 8). Moreover, the influx of diverse non-traditional media means that the provenance and reliability of reporting is unreliable, and often takes the form of echo-chambers that might reinforce and amplify uninformed opinion (see Chapter 9).
Non-aligned social movements have emerged as a counter to the transformation of the major political parties from social and political movements into political 'machines'. As the influence of ordinary party members has reduced, and the power of career party officials has increased, emerging social movement organisations have been able to take advantage of new forms of digital outreach to curate alternative spaces in which policy discourse can occur (see Chapter 7).	The new digital media is an unruly space occupied by a bewildering array of voices that reflect a broad spectrum of political opinion. These digital spaces are frequently characterised by hyper-partisanism and polarised viewpoints, so policy-makers face major challenges when attempting to engage with such diverse audiences (Chapter 9). As a result, policy-makers sometimes find themselves reacting to developments on social media platforms, such as Facebook and X (formerly Twitter), whose capacity to accurately represent public sentiment is difficult to gauge.

Civil society is an important institutional pillar of Australian democracy. Civil society organisations have long sought to represent the voice of marginalised communities through policy advocacy. Australia's is not a polity in which ordinary citizens' and voters' engagement with public policy ends at the ballot box (Chapter 7). Civil society organisations often act as trusted intermediaries between communities of interest and the government and public service.	Civil society is sometimes regarded by government as an irritant, or as an impediment to policy implementation. Civil society organisations (not-for-profits) engaged in contracted service delivery are sometimes discouraged from engaging in policy advocacy or commentary. Also, because civil society comprises a broad spectrum of organisations and viewpoints, it is sometimes possible for government to privilege the voice of organisations whose positions align with their preferred policy, over those that are critical of government.
The past two decades have seen the emergence of important discourses in the fields of public administration and governance. Academically driven for the most part, these conversations have also been taken up by executive government. Today the underpinning concepts of multi-party collaboration, deliberative democracy, network governance, co-production and co-design, evidence-based policy, and citizen-centred policy are well understood and have become embedded in policy parlance.	Unfortunately, theoretical and conceptual understandings have not translated well into practice. The problem of achieving more inclusive policy styles lies with factors such as path dependence, institutional rigidity, risk aversion, organisational and programmatic silos, and systems of public sector governance that reinforce fidelity to the government's agenda, even at the cost of sound policy or the public good.
Dedicated and independent anti-corruption agencies exist in most Australian states, and their investigatory powers help curb malfeasance in public office. On occasion they may probe the behavior of even the most senior politicians.	Until recently Australia has lacked a federal anti-corruption body. At the 2022 federal election, Labor pledged to establish 'a powerful, transparent and independent National Anti-Corruption Commission' (Gallagher, 2022 and 2023; Halligan, 2024). After the election, ministers subsequently pushed the proposal through parliament, proclaiming it 'the single biggest integrity reform this parliament has seen in decades'. An effective anti-corruption body would help to reduce the influence on the federal policy process of powerful interests and reinforce the primacy of the public good in policy-making.
Australia's Freedom of Information regime is similar to those of other G7 liberal democratic countries and allows considerable media and citizen access to non-confidential government information.	Ministers and officials often use the shield of 'privacy' or commercial confidentiality to avoid providing information. Australian governments have also used draconian security legislation to pursue whistle-blowers and to silence critics, including journalists, suggesting a worrying anti-democratic impulse. In addition, lobbyists and powerful interests are sometimes able to leverage undue influence on the policy process in ways that are arguably contrary to the public interest. Unchecked, this poses a threat to democratic purpose.

Future opportunities	Future threats
Digital platforms, including social media, provide new opportunities for engagement (see Chapter 9). Policy-makers can curate virtual spaces in which stakeholders can join discussions about policy priorities, options and preferences, thereby democratising the policy process. The COVID-19 pandemic, for example, helped to demonstrate the convening power and reach of digital platforms.	Policy-makers will need to be astute in their attempts to leverage the convening power of digital platforms. The digital world is fragmented, and likely to fragment even further, accentuating the challenges of curating spaces in which diverse voices can be heard. The democratic potential of digital convening cannot be fully realised without systemic and institutional change in other aspects of the polity.
Policy-makers can already take advantage of unprecedented flows of data to devise policy options that are localised (or even personalised), responsive and adaptive. When coupled with the right analysis and engagement strategies, policies driven by 'big data' potentially allow government impacts on stakeholders' lives to be anticipated and fine-tuned to minimise harms and maximise benefits. Increasing access to real-time data has greatly extended the scope of economic, social and scientific policy interventions, as in the COVID-19 pandemic.	Big-data flows and real-time data have also enabled extensive covert surveillance of the population by security and other state agencies. Critics argue that the potential to misuse these technologies in ways inimical to democratic purposes cannot be under-estimated and has been only weakly controlled.
A growing body of research and practice on participatory approaches to policy-making focuses on the application of systems thinking in a design-led approach (Blomkamp, 2021). These citizen-centred approaches are participatory in nature and utilise collaboration and co-design principles to improve public policy (see Chapter 14).	Participatory approaches to policy design have been debated for over a decade. Although the use of systems-thinking and design-led approaches has been trialled in some locations, and has shown promise in addressing complex societal problems 'in place', the methods required are difficult to embed in 'hierarchical and bureaucratic' public sector organisations where the requisite skills are often in 'short supply' (Blomkamp, 2021, p.17). Moreover, our systems and practices of policy governance – including ministerial oversight – and a tendency to emphasise control over accountability and transparency, might militate against their widespread adoption. Brenton Holmes observed: 'The APS [Australian Public Service] will take its cue from government, and the challenges of its becoming truly collaborative and citizen-centric will be augmented or diminished in line with ministers' willingness or reluctance to allow genuine devolution of decision-making to frontline professionals and the citizens with whom they engage' (Holmes, 2011).

How does policy happen?

In order to reflect on the nexus between democracy and public policy, it is important to contemplate the nature of public policy and the policy process, given that:

> [P]olicy affects our birth, the manner in which we are raised and educated, our access to health care, the quality of our physical environment, how we conduct ourselves, whom we might marry, our access to employment, our rights at work, our access to housing, how we raise our children and even the quality of our deaths and what we are able to pass on to the generations succeeding us ... Policy provides a framework for what can and ought to occur in prescribed situations. However, policy is also malleable and is subject to interpretation and adjustment as circumstances change. Changing expectations, attitudes, beliefs, values and behaviours often lead, eventually, to changes in government policy. (Butcher and Mercer, 2024)

Governments and decision-makers take their policy cues from various quarters: from key institutions (including religious institutions and the press); 'interests' (including industry sectors, professional associations, lobby groups and lobbyists); experts (think-tanks, academics); and from the public (often as mediated by the press and political actors). Encouragingly, Carson, Ratcliff and Dufresne (2018, p.17) conclude that 'Australian MPs, notwithstanding strong party discipline, seek to respond to constituent preferences.' However, they do so 'imperfectly, and with caveats', noting that 'under certain circumstances parties ignore public opinion on matters that are important to party goals' (Carson, Ratcliff and Dufresne, 2018, p.16) – like winning elections.

There are many highly contested issues where one might expect to observe a lack of congruence between public opinion and policy responsiveness such as voluntary assisted dying, or the decriminalisation of cannabis. Whether or not legislators take heed of public opinion on these matters might depend on whether the public considers them to be important or not (relative to other policy areas, such as the economy, jobs or education). If parties calculate that the electoral cost of supporting a particular policy option exceeds the cost of rejecting change, then the status quo will likely prevail.

Democracy, policy and civic engagement

We might say that democracy is best served when the public – including those who vote and those who do not – are engaged, civically aware and informed. Indeed, the official view (as expressed by the Australian Bureau of Statistics (ABS)) is that when citizens participate in civil society their concerns, needs and values can be incorporated into government decision-making and, thereby, 'arrive at better collective decisions that are supported by the population' (ABS, 2010).

Yet, in 2006, the ABS found that the rate of participation in one or more civic or political groups was only 19 per cent of all persons aged 18 years and over:

> This level of involvement varied with age. It was 23 per cent for those aged 45 to 64 years, with lower levels of involvement from younger and older persons. The civic or political groups that people were most likely to be active in were

> trade union, professional and technical associations (7 per cent), environmental or animal welfare groups (5 per cent), followed by body corporate or tenants' associations (4 per cent). (ABS, 2007)

Scroll forward 15 years and the situation had not much improved. The ABS (2020) found only 14 per cent of employees (1.4 million) were trade union members, down from 40 per cent in 1992 (see Chapter 7 for a fuller analysis). Similarly, membership in the major political parties had plunged since the 1960s, accompanied in recent years by an upsurge of engagement in social movements such as GetUp and interest in independents and minor parties (Davies, 2020). The reason would appear to be, in part, that for people to be engaged, and stay engaged, they need some assurance that they can influence outcomes and that their engagement 'matters'.

In a 2021 parliamentary report, former Labor Senator Kim Carr observed that 'the level of civic engagement and debate in this country is disturbingly low' (Legal and Constitutional Affairs References Committee, 2021a). Even the dissenting report issued by Liberal senators lent support to the proposition that despite voters' enduring belief in democracy, 'a lack of knowledge among Australians of Australia's democratic history, and the significance and rarity of our institutions' leave many people (especially the young) 'ill equipped to engage as civic citizens' (Legal and Constitutional Affairs References Committee, 2021b).

Audit criteria for a democratic policy process

The remainder of the chapter focuses on the audit criteria for a democratic policy process set out at the start of the chapter.

Is the policy consistent with an election promise or mandate or with political values?

Policy platforms at elections are usually expressed as broad expressions of intent. They rarely go much beyond generalities, and while they might foreshadow specific measures to give effect to policy intent, the detail of those measures and their implementation is often not revealed until after an election. In general, voters expect governments to implement the policies set out as part of a party election platform or, at the very least, policies consistent with the parties' values and philosophy. Similarly, voters might reasonably expect the opposition, crossbench parties and independents to advocate for alternative policy options; seek to represent the views and concerns of the broader community; and hold governments to account.

Policy consistency is a virtue in a representative democracy and governments have often felt the wrath of voters when they have failed to keep their promises or have acted in a manner inconsistent with their undertakings (Sydney Morning Herald, 2004). Electors sometimes take a dim view of governments introducing policies for which they have not previously obtained a mandate from voters and might be inclined to punish ministers who fail to implement policies for which an electoral mandate had been given. Two examples from the Howard Coalition and Rudd Labor governments come to mind.

In the lead-up to the 1996 election, John Howard invented a category of 'core' promises, which would be kept, leaving the public to infer that everything else was 'non-core' (Quiggin, 2013).

Although this distinction created a political space in which a failure to keep non-core promises might be justified, it did not give the government licence to implement policies for which it did not have a political mandate.

Kevin Rudd's first Labor government suffered a major loss of political capital in 2009 when it walked away from an emissions trading scheme after Rudd himself had declared climate change to be the greatest moral, economic and social challenge of our time (Chubb, 2014). It did not matter to the public that the composition of the parliament at the time was not conducive to legislating such a policy: the fact that the government walked back on a signature policy seriously undermined the standing of the Prime Minister (PM) and his government and led, ultimately, to Rudd's replacement by his deputy, Julia Gillard. Conversely, the Gillard Labor government experienced enormous backlash when it implemented a carbon pricing mechanism after the PM had announced prior to the federal election that, 'there will be no carbon tax under the government I lead' (Marks, 2013).

When Malcolm Turnbull replaced Tony Abbott as PM in a leadership ballot on 14 September 2015, he said he had no plan to change the government's policies, but he would do so 'if they don't work as well as we think, or we think others can work better'. A few days later he added: 'When governments change policies, it's often seen as a backflip, or a backtrack, or an admission of error. That is rubbish. We've got to be agile all the time' (2021 statement, archived at ABC, 2024a). During the 2022 federal election campaign, Labor Opposition Leader Anthony Albanese promised to fully implement tax cuts legislated in 2019 by the Morrison Coalition government (Remeikis, 2022). According to diverse commentators, these cuts would disproportionately benefit persons on higher incomes at an enormous cost to the Treasury. On numerous occasions, however, PM Albanese reiterated Labor's intention to keep that promise, despite unease within the party and on the crossbenches. But in January 2024, the government, citing advice from Treasury officials, announced that it was obliged by current economic circumstances to revise its position to offer tax relief instead to people on low and medium incomes. Although the opposition parties decried the 'broken promise' and labelled the PM and the Liberal-National government as untrustworthy (ABC News, 2024b), the Coalition later voted for the proposed change in February 2024. For its part, the government seems to have hoped that offering tax relief to millions more citizens would negate voter unease about a broken promise (Probyn, 2024).

Policy reversals – or 'back-flips', as they are charmingly called in Australia – are seen by some observers as the 'irritating accoutrements of contemporary politics' (van Onselen and Errington, 2007). Politicians need to be alive to the electoral consequences of such irritations. In general, governments intend to keep their promises, although circumstances might curtail their aspirations. Governments will be criticised by the opposition, the crossbench, interest groups and the media for any failure to give effect to their election commitments, regardless of the reasons. They will also be criticised for persevering with policy promises in the face of evidence that the policy is ill-founded – climate change policy offers examples of both tendencies.

Policy over-reach?

Governments might occasionally be called upon to design and implement policies for which no electoral mandate has been sought or secured, notable examples being the Howard Coalition government's gun buy-back scheme formulated in response to the 1996 Port Arthur massacre; the Rudd Labor government's economic stimulus package, which sought to cushion the

Australian economy from the worst effects of the 2007 to 2009 Global Financial Crisis (GFC); and the Commonwealth, state and territory governments' (quite bipartisan) responses to the global COVID-19 pandemic (Quiggins, 2020).

Where policy responses are made to existential threats to the community, governments will seek retrospective authorisation by voters when they eventually go to the polls. If the public perception of threat is still on-going then governments might be rewarded for their actions. For example, state elections held at the height of the COVID-19 pandemic saw incumbent governments returned with increased majorities in Western Australia and Victoria – jurisdictions with the toughest COVID-19 regimes in the country (see Chapters 18 and 21). However, if government action results in a threat being averted – as might be argued in the case of the Rudd government's fiscal stimulus package of 2008/09 – voters may not perceive a direct link between the action taken and the risk avoided, and political 'rewards' for those actions might be denied. Conversely, where public perception of an existential threat is on-going – as was the case of the global pandemic – governments might reap political dividends even when their policy actions represent a sharp pivot away from the platform upon which they were elected. This was the case for the Morrison Coalition government, which was obliged to massively increase spending (and incur debt) to sustain the economy through the worst of the pandemic despite setting the achievement of budget surpluses as a core priority in pre-pandemic times (Kenny, 2020).

Voters understand that circumstances may arise between elections that demand an urgent policy response where governments are unable to seek electoral approval. Indeed, the public expects government to respond to emerging challenges and to govern in the public interest. But that does not mean that governments have a *carte blanche* to indulge in policy adventurism, and voters have a limited tolerance for government overreach. For instance, consider the Howard Liberal-National Coalition government's *Workplace Relations Amendment (Work Choices) Act* 2005; it entailed significant changes to Australia's workplace relations system that ministers said would make it more flexible, simple and fair (Parliament of Australia, 2005; Wikipedia, 2024; see also Chapter 12). The Coalition had long sought to re-regulate workplace relations, and from the 2004 election Howard's government enjoyed a majority in both the House of Representatives and the Senate – a rarely granted mandate in Australia. Despite this, the policy met with strong opposition from trade unions and the public and had mixed support from factions within the government itself, and several states raised High Court challenges to the new legislation (Centre for Public Impact, 2017). Work Choices was widely seen as a case of radical reform that exceeded public expectations and the coordinated campaign against the policy was a factor in the government's defeat at the 2007 election (Woodward, 2010).

Of grand visions and small targets

If policy consistency can sometimes be construed as a virtue, 'visionary' or reformist policy can become a 'pariah', according to Errington and van Onselen (2021). They examined cycles of policy daring and timidity in Australian politics, noting that reformist policy propositions can easily be demonised, especially during election campaigns. This is the work of many hands: a hyper-partisan media focused on headlines and lacking the will or capacity for cogent analysis; an uninterested and unengaged electorate; and a combative political arena in which political actors are more interested in published political polls than they are in engaging in rational discourse about policy futures. The authors conclude that: 'We shouldn't expect political leaders to show courage – to use a term currently in fashion – when the electorate and the media reward a more conservative approach' (Errington and van Onselen, 2021, p.2).

It is particularly difficult for opposition parties to bring bold policy to the table because they lack the resources of government to comprehensively test and present their ideas. Political commentators often hearken back to 1993 when Liberal Opposition leader John Hewson went into a federal election with a complex and ambitious policy agenda called 'Fightback' that became the subject of a massive scare campaign mounted by Labor. An election that some considered 'unlosable' by the opposition instead saw the return of the Keating Labor government. Fast forward to 2019 when Labor Opposition leader Bill Shorten took a far more modest set of tax reform proposals to an election; they were also subject to a 'scare campaign' that contributed to the unexpected return of incumbent PM Scott Morrison (SBS News, 2019).

A retrospective analysis of missed opportunities for 'worthwhile' policy reform published by The Grattan Institute (Daley, 2021) suggested that Australia's governance had weakened since the 1990s, resulting in a 'gridlock' of policy reform. Many factors were implicated in this decline, including changes in our media landscape; a weakened and pliant public service; the influence of unaccountable ministerial advisers; opaque decision-making; complex processes for appointing and dismissing senior public servants; ministerial influence over government contracts and grants; political patronage; and the corrosive effects of political donations, campaign finance and lobbying. Unfortunately, there appears to be little appetite in the major parties for the kinds of institutional reforms required to address these sources of democratic deficit.

Party values and policy design

In an ideal world, policy proposals, policy design and supporting legislation are consistent with the stated values, ideals and priorities of the governing party, and so keep faith with the party membership and their voter base and the expectations of voters at large. And in general, we have seen a high degree of fidelity between party ideals and the actions of government. Sometimes, however, the link between ideals and actions has been tested and stretched by political pragmatism and can lead to internal tensions or rifts between elected representatives and the party membership. An obvious example has been the treatment of asylum seekers by both Labor and Liberal governments – in particular, mandatory detention and off-shore detention of so-called 'irregular arrivals'. Government actions here have been portrayed by critics as either an abrogation of classical liberal values (in the case of the Liberal Party of Australia) or humanist traditions (in the case of the Labor Party).

In general, governments and ministers intend to keep their promises, but circumstances can curtail their aspirations. A detailed analysis of 232 election promises made in six policy areas by the Gillard Labor government during the 43rd Parliament (2010 to 2013) was undertaken by Carson, Martin and Gibbons (2019). Working from sources such as *Hansard*, official political communications, budget papers and media reports, the researchers found that five out of every six promises (87 per cent) were kept, although some 'needed to be altered in some way and were only partially kept', reflecting 'the compromise required to get bills through the two Houses, neither controlled by the Labor party'. In spite of this, the Gillard government ended up being 'tarred with perceptions of deception'.

Whose interests are served by the policy?

It might be popularly supposed that policy settings are responsive to, and guided by, the preferences of electors, as interpreted and mediated by political actors. However, it is more realistic to suppose that voter preferences are of lesser importance than those of interest groups with the influence and means to donate money (and to openly back) political parties. This is consistent with the 'investment theory' of political influence first outlined by Thomas Ferguson (1983); he further expanded upon this in *Golden Rule: The Investment Theory of Party Competition and the Logic of Money-driven Political Systems* (1995). Ferguson argued that when political parties are reliant on donors to raise campaign funds, they are also highly susceptible to the influence of wealthy donors seeking to shape policy settings to suit their interests (see also Chapter 7 on the political power of business). Moreover, where information flows can be shaped by wealthy 'investors', electors might be persuaded to vote *against* their own interests.

Between elections, wealthy interests can exert considerable influence on Australian policy in ways that might be inimical to the public interest and trust in government. In 2010, for example, the Rudd Labor government capitulated to an overwhelming media and political campaign mounted by the mining industry against its proposed Resource Super Profits Tax (RSPT) (Sanyal and Darby, 2011). The RSPT was based on a recommendation included in the Henry Tax Review (Henry, 2010) to tax mining profits flowing from the 2010 commodity boom. Yet the Rudd government was castigated by the conservative press as 'anti-business' and 'out-of-touch' (Manne, 2011). In the end, the government introduced only a watered-down Minerals Resource Rent Tax (MRRT), which was itself later repealed by the Abbott Coalition government in 2014 (Murray, 2015).

Sometimes, however, lobbying by civil society organisations has encouraged governments to change course by mobilising public opinion against policy proposals. For instance, in 2021 the Morrison Liberal-National Coalition government announced plans to implement 'independent' reviews for clients of the National Disability Insurance Scheme (NDIS) to determine claimants' eligibility (Jervis-Bardy, 2021). The reviews would thenceforward be carried out by NDIS-appointed healthcare professionals using standardised tools that replaced the existing system in which prospective participants chose their own doctors and health professionals to conduct the assessments (Michael, 2021). The government contended that the new system would be 'fairer' and result in more consistent assessments. The opposition, cross bench MPs and disability advocates, however, portrayed the move as a 'cost cutting exercise' and lacking in empathy (SBS News, 2021). Following an 'enormous backlash' by people with a disability and their advocates, and resistance from State and Territory disability ministers, the Commonwealth relented (Guardian, 2021), and placed the implementation of standardised assessments on indefinite hold (SBS News, 2021).

It could be argued that policy investors tend to exacerbate the democratic deficits associated with the policy process whereas civil society generally seeks to remedy democratic deficits. However, civil society and big business do not occupy a level playing field. In general, registered not-for-profit organisations in Australia are not especially wealthy and refrain from participating in partisan political activities as this might disqualify them from charitable status. In addition, many not-for-profits also provide services under government contracts containing clauses that constrain their ability to engage in policy advocacy. Business interests are not similarly constrained, and do not operate under the same pressures for transparency or public scrutiny.

Has the need for the policy been established?

Theories of policy-making generally assume that action is taken only when a significant problem emerges and there is a widespread or shared concern about it. Some policy proposals, however, might best be described as 'solutions looking for problems.' Occasionally, politicians come under the sway of some interest group or think-tank that is promoting a policy solution to some purported problem. And they may become so enamoured with the elegance of the solution on offer that they neglect to establish that a problem exists – or, if it does exist, that the 'problem' warrants the cost and effort required to implement the solution. In some instances, this has involved the problematisation of particular societal groups – for example, First Nations peoples, unemployed young people, or asylum-seekers. In others it has involved problematising public institutions – for example, the public service, statutory or regulatory bodies, or even government itself. Some might argue that the waves of structural reforms implemented under the banner of New Public Management – downsizing, privatisation, deregulation, commercialisation, outsourcing – were offered as solutions to the problem of big, inflexible, unresponsive, inefficient and expensive government. Debate continues about which was worse, the cure or the disease?

One clear example of a 'solution looking for a problem' from the last term of the Morrison Coalition government (2019 to 2022) was a proposal to require Australian voters to produce identification at the polling booth (Karp, 2021). The Electoral Legislation Amendment (Voter Identification) Bill 2022 represented a significant departure from historical practise wherein Australian voters are only required to have their names crossed off a list of eligible voters (Parliament of Australia, 2022). Compulsory voter ID was championed by the One Nation Party and reflected tropes then prevalent in American political discourse concerning unfounded allegations of widespread voting irregularities in the 2020 USA election (UNSW Newsroom, 2021). Indeed, the RMIT Factlab reviewed claims of multiple voting and found that voter fraud in Australia was 'negligible' (2022). This finding was supported by evidence given in 2019 to the Joint Standing Committee on Electoral Matters by the Australian Electoral Commissioner, who emphasised that multiple voting is 'by and large a very small problem' (Parliament of Australia, 2019). Barely two months after it was announced the government withdrew the Bill in the face of a widespread backlash and uncertainty around support by a key crossbench senator (Quiggin, 2021).

Even where there is broad agreement about the existence of a problem, whether the proposed solution is the 'right' one may still be debated. For example, on the question of climate change and other environmental problems such as pollution, deforestation, threatened species, et cetera, the policy preferences of the major parties are often at odds, and the policy preferences of governments are often at odds with public opinion (see Chapter 27). Even when a policy solution has gained broad acceptance, the public and other communities of interest might feel that it is compromised by ideological rigidity, capture by special interests, or political expediency.

Is the policy 'legal'?

In Australia public policy derives legal authority from the Constitution, supporting legislation passed by Parliament (see Chapter 2), and delegated (or *subordinate*) legislation made by ministers and officials with powers specifically conferred on them (O'Sullivan, 2011). A fundamental democratic obligation on ministers (and the APS) is to consistently ensure that public policy is always lawful. On occasion, however, already enacted government policies have been overturned because subsequent legal challenges revealed that they lacked a sound constitutional or legal basis.

In 2011, for instance, the full bench of the High Court found unlawful the Gillard Labor government's plan to implement an agreement that involved transferring from Malaysia 4,000 persons certified as refugees, in exchange for the Malaysian government accepting 800 asylum seekers from Australia (O'Sullivan, 2011). In another example, in 2014 the High Court unanimously ruled as unconstitutional a Howard-era policy, the National School Chaplaincy Program, implemented eight years earlier to enable the Commonwealth to fund schools to employ chaplains to provide counselling support for students (ABC News, 2014). And in 2021, the Federal Court of Australia ruled illegal the Morrison Coalition government's so-called 'Robodebt Scheme', a scheme through which Australia's welfare payments agency Centrelink sought to recover alleged over-payments to pensioners. The Court described it as a 'very sorry chapter in Australian public administration' (Henriques-Gomes, 2021). (See Chapters 13 and 14)

In each of these cases the courts did not find that the government *knowingly* implemented unlawful policy. Nevertheless, were it not for the legal action taken by the plaintiffs, the unlawful nature of the policies would not have come to light. While these cases demonstrate that public policy must be lawful, and that on occasion policy can be overturned via recourse to the courts, legal action is costly and is not an option for ordinary citizens. Were it not for the financial backing of civil society organisations (CSOs) or (in the robodebt case) a class action led by a major law firm, these policies might have remained unchallenged.

Is the policy process transparent and accountable?

Not infrequently, the implementation of public policy occurs in ways that deviate from the normative expectations of good public administration, owing to deficiencies in transparency, accountability, governance and/or process (Commonwealth Ombudsman, 2007). Often such deficiencies reflect shortcomings in organisational culture, or capacity and capability deficits (for example, insufficient resources or relevant experts) (Katsonis, 2019). In some cases, the spirit of a policy that could have public benefits can be corrupted when implementation is distorted by political interference.

In 2020 the Australian National Audit Office (ANAO, 2020) found that $100 million in grant funding awarded by the Minister for Sport under the Community Sport Infrastructure Program 'was not informed by an appropriate assessment process and sound advice' and showed 'evidence of distribution bias'. Their report concluded:

> *The award of funding reflected the approach documented by the Minister's Office of focusing on 'marginal' electorates held by the Coalition as well as those electorates held by other parties or independent members that were to be 'targeted' by the Coalition at the 2019 Election.* (ANAO, 2020)

In a later audit of the administration of grants under the larger, $660 million National Commuter Car Park Fund, ANAO (2021) found that: 'Departmental advice did not contain an assessment against the investment principles or policy objectives and it was not demonstrated that projects were selected on merit.' A large majority of the sites selected for funding (77 per cent) were located in electorates held by Liberal or National (that is, government) MPs. A majority of projects (64 per cent) were located in Victoria where:

> *Coalition-held electorates [constituencies] were twice as successful in attracting funding as those held by the ALP at the time of selection. Further in this respect, all seven 'successful' Coalition-held electorates attracted multiple projects – ranging from two to six projects.* (Ng, 2021)

Both these cases were labelled as exercises in 'pork-barrelling' by the opposition and crossbenches, and by the political commentariat (Podger, 2021). One observer commented:

> *Australia has a single member electorate parliamentary system, which makes it more susceptible to pork-barrelling than multi-member electorates like Norway or Spain. The belief is that politicians who 'bring home the bacon' for their constituents are electorally rewarded for doing so.*
>
> *This means there are incentives for the central cabinet to strategically apportion benefits to marginal electorates to increase prospects of electoral success. There is also an incentive to bias the apportionment of funds towards the party in power ... In short, rorts scandals keep happening because governments believe that channelling money to marginal and government electorates will win them elections.* (Ng, 2021)

The sport clubs and car parks programs both failed the standards of transparency, accountability or administrative effectiveness most electors would hope to see. Instead, both confirmed the low expectations that many Australians hold for the political class. When elected representatives make decisions about the use of public funds based primarily on narrow political considerations – whether or not they have legal authority to do so – they contribute to the democratic deficit that many Australians believe afflicts our democracy.

Does the policy have (or need) a Social Licence to Operate?

The concept of a Social Licence to Operate (SLO) originated in, and is usually associated with resource extraction industries (CSIRO, 2020). However, it is increasingly being applied in other domains, and is an emergent organising concept in the delivery of human services (Butcher, 2019). Social Licence to Operate is fundamentally concerned with issues of transparency, accountability, legitimacy and, most importantly, trust, particularly where groups have had little or no input into or influence on decisions affecting their lives – especially those made by big business or by government. SLO seeks to give voice and agency to stakeholder communities that not only stand to be affected by policy decisions, but also have historically been marginalised by, or had impaired access to, conventional avenues for political engagement.

Although SLO has crept into the language of Australian politics and the bureaucracy, as yet there is no consistent operational framework that allows policy-makers to determine whether an SLO exists. Governments might claim that seeking an SLO is redundant because of an implicit 'electoral licence to operate'. Yet, given the scale of the trust deficit, it might be wise to treat such claims cautiously or sceptically. A democratic audit can ask questions along the following lines to help establish whether an implicit or explicit SLO exists:

- Is there reason to suppose that an SLO may be relevant to a given policy proposal? For example:
    - Does the policy domain have a history of democratic and/or trust deficits?
    - Could social harms arise as a result of poor implementation?
    - Is there a legacy of affected stakeholders being politically or economically marginalised?
- Have the costs and benefits, or disbenefits, of policy proposals been clearly communicated to affected stakeholders?
- Were there meaningful avenues for the public and/or affected stakeholders to make inputs into policy design and implementation?
- Were the communication or consultation approaches utilised with the public or affected stakeholders inclusive and accessible? For example, was the language appropriate for the target audiences? And were appropriate avenues utilised, especially for marginalised or hard-to-reach communities?
- Did affected stakeholders show confidence and *trust* in the process underpinning the development and implementation of the policy?

Consider a recent policy case for which it might be argued that a social licence either did not exist or existed imperfectly. In November 2019, PM Scott Morrison announced plans for a A$499 million project to re-develop the Australian War Memorial (AWM) in Canberra (Australian War Memorial, 2019; 2021). The nine-year scheme entailed major refurbishments to the AWM precinct and a near doubling of its exhibition space. It also required the demolition of Anzac Hall, an award-winning building completed in 2001 at a cost of $17 million (Australian Institute of Architects, 2021; Stead, 2021). The proposed re-development was widely criticised by heritage specialists (Cheng, 2019), the Australian Institute of Architects, and even former directors of the Memorial (Australian Institute of Architects, 2021; Stead, 2021). Concerns focused on the high costs and the demolition of the existing exhibition hall. An inquiry by a parliamentary committee in 2020 supported the re-development proposal, but noted criticisms of the AWM's consultation process and acknowledged divergent views held by members of the public and relevant stakeholders (Parliamentary Standing Committee on Public Works, 2021). A majority of people making public submissions did not support the re-development overall (Stewart, 2021). Yet in June 2021 the National Capital Authority (NCA) (2021) cleared the way for early works to proceed (Parliamentary Standing Committee on Public Works, 2021). Although there was a consultation process overseen by the AWM, and a process of regulatory review by the NCA as well as an inquiry by a parliamentary committee, the result of those processes was, in the minds of many, a foregone conclusion. Neither the AWM, the NCA, nor the joint committee had any incentive to overrule the government's decision, regardless of public opinion. As one AWM employee observed, the consultation process 'wasn't a poll on whether the project was supported' (Parliamentary Standing Committee on Public Works, 2021). This statement underlines a problem that commonly afflicts public consultation processes: they are about *telling* the public about policy, rather than *listening* (see also, Stewart, 2009).

It is understandable that changes affecting a cherished national institution like the Australian War Memorial – which commemorates (and some say glorifies) Australian martial history – will elicit strong public opinions. That diverse stakeholders held diametrically opposing opinions about the appropriateness of the AWM re-development proposal was not unexpected. Although there was some public support for the re-development – including key stakeholders representing the interests of Australian veterans – it could not safely be concluded that this amounted to a social licence.

Conclusion

Public policy is an artefact of political contest, a contest governed by the democratic norms prevailing in any given polity. Moreover, public policy is the ultimate formal output arising from political contest. One might expect, therefore, that policy – and policy outcomes – will reflect and embody the democratic virtues and deficits endemic within a political system. This chapter has explored some important sources of democratic deficit in Australian policy-making from the federal sphere. Similar deficits no doubt operate at the state and territory levels. Although these examples generally concern instances of democratic deficit, this is partly a function of the extent to which the cases engendered heated public debate: by contrast, democratic 'enhancements' appear to be less 'newsworthy').

Much of the literature dealing with participatory approaches to policy design and implementation concerns policy-making in the human services space. Participatory approaches can best be applied in policy spaces where there is a clear line of sight between the application of policy and its impact on the community. There are other policy spheres, however, where the line of sight is opaque, or where ordinary citizens cannot be expected to possess the detailed specialist knowledge required. National security, defence, trade and foreign affairs, for example, are policy fields that are generally the domain of subject area specialists. In this regard intermediary organisations, academic researchers, think-tanks and civil society organisations can act as important vanguards against executive overreach.

Former British PM Winston Churchill famously said in 1947:

> Many forms of Government have been tried, and will be tried in this world of sin and woe. No one pretends that democracy is perfect or all-wise. Indeed it has been said that democracy is the worst form of Government except for all those other forms that have been tried from time to time ... (Churchill, 1947; see also Quinault, 2001, p. 218)

Often cited in broad defence of democratic principles, this famous passage may seem to suggest that democracy is only the 'least worst' form of government yet devised. The democratic model to which Churchill alluded was, and remains, an imperfect vehicle for the expression of the popular will and the balancing of competing and sometimes conflicting interests: and it is almost certain that Churchill could not have envisioned many of the modern adaptations to contemporary democratic practice in Australia. Of course, no model of policy-making is perfect and Australia's is no exception. But perhaps we can go so far as to say that for all its imperfections Australian policy-making, like Australian democracy itself, might be the 'least worst' alternative.

Note

1   Here 'parties' are referred to in the plural because in Australia governments often comprise at least two parties and, sometimes, independents. In the case of Liberal-National Coalition governments, for example, the electorate would reasonably expect each party to advocate within government for policy positions and formulations consistent with their core values and priorities. Similarly, in Labor-Green governing coalitions at the state and territory level (such as have occurred in the Australian Capital Territory and Tasmania) one would expect the minor partner (the Greens) to advocate for their preferred policy positions within the bounds of any coalition agreement.

References

ABC News (2014) 'Commonwealth funding of school chaplaincy program struck down in High Court', Australian Broadcasting Corporation, 19 June. https://perma.cc/EN97-BER6

ABC News (2024a) 'Promise tracker: The Coalition Government's 2013 election commitments', Australian Broadcasting Corporation/ RMIT University/ Monash University. https://perma.cc/7KF8-ZH58

ABC News (2024b)' Peter Dutton says government's stage 3 tax cut change is purely political move from Anthony Albanese'. Australian Broadcasting Corporation, 7 February, webpage. https://perma.cc/R8FX-B794

ABS (Australian Bureau of Statistics) (2007) '4159.0 – General social survey: Summary Results, Australia', 2006. https://perma.cc/B7BD-4AP5

ABS (Australian Bureau of Statistics) (2010) 'Democracy, governance and citizenship, 1370.0 – Measures of Australia's progress', 2010, Archived Issue. https://perma.cc/YE67-QPCE

ABS (Australian Bureau of Statistics) (2017) '1800.0 – Australian marriage law postal survey, 2017: National results'. https://perma.cc/6D4U-RJBJ

ABS (Australian Bureau of Statistics) (2020) 'Trade union membership by employment and socio-demographic characteristics such as full-time/part-time, age, industry, occupation, education, earnings'. Reference period August 2020. https://perma.cc/N83W-L97C

ANAO (Australian National Audit Office) (2020) *Award of Funding under the Community Sport Infrastructure Program.* Performance Audit Report; Auditor-General Report No.23 of 2019–20. Published Wednesday 15 January. https://perma.cc/RDJ9-HMUZ

ANAO (Australian National Audit Office) (2021) *Administration of Commuter Car Park Projects within the Urban Congestion Fund.* Performance Audit Report: Auditor-General Report No.47 of 2020–21. Published Monday 28 June. https://perma.cc/4RP7-6WE7

Australian Institute of Architects (2021) 'Submission, Block 3 Section 39, Campbell Australian War Memorial'. https://perma.cc/5X7D-EPGL

Australian War Memorial (2019) 'Prime Minister announces Memorial Development Project plans'. https://perma.cc/5YKU-H69U

Australian War Memorial (2021) 'Public Consultations'. https://perma.cc/3G87-JRYV

Blomkamp, Emma (2021) 'Systemic design practice for participatory policymaking'. *Policy Design and Practice*, vol. 5, no. 1, pp.12–31. DOI: 10.1080/25741292.2021.1887576. https://doi.org/10.1080/25741292.2021.1887576

Butcher, John R (2019) '"Social licence to operate" and the human services: A pathway to smarter commissioning?' *Australian Journal of Public Administration*, vol. 78, no. 1, pp.113–22. https://perma.cc/M65N-6MJP

Butcher, John R and Trish Mercer (2024) 'Making public policy' in Diana Perche; Nicholas Barry; Alan Fenna; Zareh Ghazarian; and Yvonne Haigh (eds) *Australian Politics and Policy: Senior Edition*, Sydney University Press, Chapter 11, p.505. https://perma.cc/FS78-BPCU

Carson, Andrea; Martin Aaron; and Gibbons, Andrew (2019) 'And now for a newsflash: politicians actually do keep their promises', *The Conversation*, 15 April. https://perma.cc/V3N8-CTAW

Carson, Andrea; Ratcliff, Shaun; and Dufresne, Yannick (2018) 'Public opinion and policy responsiveness: The case of same-sex marriage in Australia', *Australian Journal of Political Science*, vol. 53, no. 1, pp.3–23. https://doi.org/10.1080/10361146.2017.1381944

Centre for Public Impact (2017) 'Work Choices Legislation in Australia'. https://perma.cc/E26K-4WFD

Cheng, Linda (2019) 'Australian War Memorial approval derided as a "disgraceful decision"'. Industry News, *ArchitectureAu*. https://perma.cc/APA5-BNVW

Chubb, Philip (2014) 'The day the Rudd government lost its way on climate change', *Sydney Morning Herald*, May 9, 2014. https://perma.cc/SAC6-SBRR

Churchill, W (1947) Speech in the House of Commons, published in 206–07 *The Official Report, House of Commons* (5th Series), 11 November 1947, vol. 444, cc.

Commonwealth Ombudsman (2007) Fact Sheet, 'Ten principles for good administration'. https://perma.cc/A6GU-DKR3

CSIRO (2020) *Social Licence to Operate*. https://perma.cc/D22V-UMYW

Daley, John (2021) *Gridlock: Removing Barriers to Policy Reform*, Report, The Grattan Institute. https://perma.cc/C527-MCJD

Davies, Anne (2020) 'Party hardly: Why Australia's big political parties are struggling to compete with grassroots campaigns', *The Guardian*, Australia, 12 December. https://perma.cc/3539-JVBP

Errington, Wayne, D and van Onselen, D.P (2021) *Who Dares Loses: Pariah Policies,* Monash University Publishing. https://perma.cc/9MVP-DJ5Q

Ferguson, T (1983) 'Party realignment and American industrial structure: The investment theory of political parties in historical perspective', *Research in Political Economy*, vol. 6, pp.1–82.

Ferguson, T (1995) *Golden Rule: The Investment Theory of Party Competition and the Logic of Money-driven Political Systems*, University of Chicago Press.

Gallagher, Katy (2022) 'Albanese Government's APS Reform agenda'. Speech to the Institute of Public Administration Australia, 13 October. https://perma.cc/EV8U-EZ2F

Gallagher, Katy (2023) 'Annual statement on APS Reform', Speech, 2 November. https://perma.cc/9BRH-2BRC

Guardian (2021) 'Linda Reynolds says Coalition will keep "some form" of independent NDIS assessments', *Guardian, Australia*, 3 May. https://perma.cc/ZBS6-8JZS

Halligan, John (2024) 'Corruption and accountability in Australian Government' in Ali Farazmand and C. Atkinson (eds), *Corruption and Accountability Problems in Modern Government: A Comparative Analysis*, Routledge, forthcoming.

Henriques-Gomes, Luke (2021) 'Robodebt responsible for $1.5bn unlawful debts in "very sorry chapter", court hears', *Guardian, Australia,* 7 May. https://perma.cc/D2R5-N7QL

Henry, Ken (2010) *Australia's Future Tax System Review Final Report*, Australian Government, The Treasury. https://perma.cc/TGD7-TDFN

Holmes, Brenton (2011) 'Citizens' engagement in policymaking and the design of public services', Research Paper no. 1, 2011–12. Politics and Public Administration Section, 22 July 2011. https://perma.cc/SK3Y-7M3N

Jervis-Bardy, Dan (2021) 'David Tune NDIS review "tampered" to justify independent assessments: ALP', *The Canberra Times*, 6 April. https://perma.cc/9D6N-C4L7

Karp, Paul (2021) 'Voters will be asked to show identification to vote under Morrison government proposal', *The Guardian*, Australia, 26 October. https://perma.cc/KD58-KYT6

Katsonis, Maria (2019) 'Rethinking policy capacity, competencies and capabilities', *The Mandarin*, 10 June. https://perma.cc/LH8F-E6JM

Kenny, Mark (2020) 'Despite huge coronavirus stimulus package, the government might still need to pay more', *The Conversation*. 22 April 2020. https://perma.cc/66V3-2DZ4

Legal and Constitutional Affairs References Committee (2021a) *Nationhood, National Identity and Democracy: Australia in the wider world*, Commonwealth of Australia. https://perma.cc/NLX5-JN4M

Legal and Constitutional Affairs References Committee (2021b) 'Dissenting report by government senators: Senator the Hon Sarah Henderson and Senator Paul Scarr'. *Nationhood, National Identity and Democracy: Australia in the wider world*, Commonwealth of Australia. https://perma.cc/WF5R-LHT8

Manne, Robert (2011) 'Rudd's downfall: Written in The Australian', Australian Broadcasting Corporation: ABC News, 4 September. https://perma.cc/NX3J-BCQ5

Marks, Russell (2013) 'Redefining the lie: Politics and porkies', *The Conversation*, 6 August. https://perma.cc/3LZ5-3B26

Michael, Luke (2021) 'We know it's bullsh*t': Advocates say independent assessments will be a disaster for NDIS participants', *Pro Bono News*, 2 March 2021. https://perma.cc/56JV-LP2V

Murray, Ian (2015) 'The Minerals Resource Rent Tax is Dead, Long Live Resource Rent Taxes?' *The University of Western Australia Law Review*, vol. 40, pp.111–37. https://perma.cc/6GDG-RAKWf

NCA (National Capital Authority) (2021) 'Block 3 Section 39 Campbell– Australian War Memorial Early Works', Government of Australia. https://perma.cc/83K6-XAG9

Ng, Yee-Fui (2021) 'The "car park rorts" story is scandalous. But it will keep happening unless we close grant loopholes', *The Conversation*, 20 July. https://perma.cc/6RTH-VAF5

O'Sullivan, Maria (2011) 'Malaysia solution: High Court ruling explained', *The Conversation*, 31 August. https://perma.cc/8XD6-R4AX

Parliament of Australia (2005) Workplace Relations Amendment (Work Choices) Bill 2005, 14 December. https://perma.cc/SK3Y-7M3N

Parliament of Australia (2018) *House of Representatives Practice, Seventh Edition*: Chapter 10, Delegated Legislation. https://perma.cc/XT5F-CXCD

Parliament of Australia (2019) *Official Committee Hansard, Joint Standing Committee on Electoral Matters, Conduct of the 2019 federal election and matters related thereto*, Friday, 6 December 2019. https://perma.cc/66MR-3S4C

Parliament of Australia (2022) Electoral Legislation Amendment (Voter Identification) Bill 2022, February 2022. https://perma.cc/7H5U-3DTY

Parliamentary Standing Committee on Public Works (2021) *Report 1/2021*, Parliament of the Commonwealth of Australia, February 2020, p.39. https://perma.cc/JY9Q-3CP4

Podger, Andrew (2021) 'Sports rorts shows the government misunderstands the public service', *The Conversation*, 30 January. https://perma.cc/RN42-NX9W

Probyn, Andrew (2024) 'When does a broken promise turn into a forgivable flip? Albanese is about to find out', *9 News*, 24 January. https://perma.cc/D2UA-S92N

Quiggin, John (2013) 'Hidden in plain sight: commission cuts and non-core promises', *The Conversation*, 5 September. https://perma.cc/V42M-XSA2

Quiggin, John (2020) 'The coronavirus stimulus program is Labor's in disguise, as it should be', *The Conversation*, 12 March. https://perma.cc/U8HU-ME5D

Quiggin, John (2021) 'Good riddance: The costs of Morrison's voter ID plan outweighed any benefit', *The Conversation*, 1 December. https://perma.cc/Q3CE-YZDV

Quinault, John (2001) 'Churchill's view of democracy', *Transactions of the Royal Historical Society*, vol. 11, pp. 201-220. https://www.jstor.org/stable/3679421

Remeikis, Amy (2022) 'Stage-three tax cuts: What are they, how do they work and why do they exist?' *The Guardian*, Australia, 9 October. https://perma.cc/Q83W-CY97

RMIT Factlab (2022) 'Actually, voter fraud is negligible in Australian elections', 10 May. Written by Ellen Blake. https://perma.cc/4BNV-5TU4

Sanyal, Kali and Darby, Paige (2011) 'Budget Review 2010–11 Index, Budget 2010–11: Taxation, Resource super profits tax', Parliamentary Library. https://perma.cc/3ZFK-BKDU

SBS News (2019) 'Is it 1993 and Fightback all over again?', SBS News, Published online 19 May. https://perma.cc/TES8-FNPJ

SBS News (2021) 'Amid "enormous backlash", the government hits pause on NDIS independent assessments', SBS News, 15 April 2021. https://perma.cc/4ENQ-NQJA

Stead, Naomi (2021) The Australian War Memorial, *The Saturday Paper*, Architecture. https://perma.cc/5JEH-WP95

Stewart, Jenny (2009) *The Dilemmas of Engagement: The Role of Consultation in Governance*, Australia and New Zealand School of Government (ANZSOG), Canberra: ANU Press. DOI: http://doi.org/10.22459/DE.06.2009

Stewart, Selby (2021) 'Australian War Memorial's $500m redevelopment clears final hurdle despite wave of public opposition', *ABC News*, 7 June. https://perma.cc/C8ZE-VRZP

Sydney Morning Herald (2004) 'Let's have the honest truth, once and for all', *Sydney Morning Herald*, National, Opinion, 18 August. https://perma.cc/MVT2-GFUU

UNSW Newsroom (2021) 'Voter ID laws: An imported solution to a problem Australia doesn't have', 21 October. https://perma.cc/DR7S-FAE3

van Onselen, Peter and Errington, Wayne (2007) 'From vitriolic criticism to ungainly praise: Locating John Howard's political success', *AQ: Australian Quarterly*, vol. 79, no. 2 (March–April), pp.4–11. https://www.jstor.org/stable/20638458

Wikipedia (2024) 'WorkChoices'. Online encyclopaedia webpage. https://perma.cc/WFQ6-6NU4

Woodward, Dennis (2010) 'WorkChoices and Howard's defeat', *Australian Journal of Public Administration*, vol. 69, no. 3, pp.274–88. https://doi.org/10.1111/j.1467-8500.2010.00690.x

16

How democratic is Australian federalism?

John Phillimore and Alan Fenna

Federalism is a central feature of the Australian constitution and system of government. While often seen in principle as a way of promoting greater democracy by bringing government closer to the people, federalism has also been accused of obstructing elected governments and creating closed processes of intergovernmental decision-making. In Australia, the financial dominance of the Commonwealth (federal) government has led to the centralisation of power away from the states and blurring of the lines of responsibility for government policy and performance. An earlier democratic audit (DA) argued that 'the question of how to make intergovernmental decision-making democratic, transparent and accountable remains one of the most intractable problems of Australian democracy' (Sawer, Abjorensen and Larkin, 2009, p.310). This chapter critically examines this claim, noting some important recent developments in the position of the states and peak level intergovernmental relations.

What does democracy require of Australia's federal system?

- Federalism should operate under a clear and well-adjudicated set of rules that can be changed democratically, but only via a process ensuring that the perspectives of both the national community and the constituent units are respected.
- The resulting structure should be intelligible to the people it serves. In particular, it should be reasonably apparent which level of government holds primary responsibility for any given policy responsibility or role.
- The division of tasks between tiers of government should respect the principle of subsidiarity, namely, that decisions be made at the lowest tier of government practicable for the matter in question.
- Each tier of government should have an appropriate degree of fiscal, policy and administrative autonomy and assured capacity to perform their functions adequately.
- There should be effective mechanisms and arrangements for communication, negotiation, cooperation, coordination, and collaboration between the tiers of government. Those mechanisms should embody principles of mutual respect and be as consistent as feasible with the standard democratic principles of transparency, accountability and representativeness.

How to cite this chapter:

Phillimore, John and Fenna, Alan (2024) 'How democratic is Australian federalism?', in: Evans, Mark; Dunleavy, Patrick and Phillimore, John (eds) *Australia's Evolving Democracy: A New Democratic Audit*, London: LSE Press, pp.346–364. https://doi.org/10.31389/lsepress.ada.p. Licence: CC-BY-NC 4.0

The Australian federal system, launched in 1901, was brought about by the individual colonies agreeing to unite while relinquishing only a minimum of their powers and responsibilities. Since then, though, the federal government has exerted a strong centralising influence, taking control of the key tax-raising powers, and leaving the states heavily dependent on Commonwealth transfers to fund their service provision (Fenna, 2019). That, in turn, has given rise to structures of intergovernmental relations that raise issues of accountability and transparency. However, in recent years, two important developments have run counter to these trends – a resurgence of the states' roles on salient or decisive issues; and adjusted structures of intergovernmental relations.

Recent developments – the resurgence of state governments

The apparently ineluctable process of centralisation within Australian federalism has continued in a variety of ways. Yet a recent twofold reassertion of the policy roles of the states has cut across that long-term trend. A first key area was climate change politics, where the dominance of the Liberal-National Coalition in Canberra (2013–2022) created a policy vacuum into which the states moved energetically (Fenna, 2023). The most efficient policy instrument for reducing greenhouse gas (GHG) emissions is a carbon tax of some form, and constitutionally this is only available to the Commonwealth government. However, there are numerous other mechanisms available to state and territory governments that might achieve the same goal. This is particularly the case since the leading source of GHG emissions in Australia is electricity generation, which is entirely within state jurisdiction. Particularly but not exclusively under Labor governments, the states have played an active role in promoting the switch to renewables in electricity generation, and that long-run transition is well underway. While the Commonwealth ministers resisted any commitment to net-zero-by-2050 until the very eve of COP26 in 2021, almost all states had already legislated this target.

A second key area is that the states have maintained responsibility not only for the vast bulk of service delivery to citizens, but also for most of the regulation of everyday life within their jurisdictions. Their dominant role was demonstrated very clearly when the COVID-19 pandemic reached Australia's shores in early 2020 (Fenna, 2021). The state governments led the way with pandemic control measures, with Victoria's prolonged lockdowns being the clearest example. The states run the health systems, and under their public health Acts, the states also regulate the operation of businesses and public space. It was the states who organised quarantine for arriving travellers (by agreement with the Commonwealth, who have authority to legislate for quarantine in the Constitution). Additionally, the states run the public-school systems and thus were the ones deciding whether it was safe for in-class teaching to continue. And if there was any remaining doubt about the states' central role in management of the pandemic, their decisions to close their respective borders to travellers from other states provided an unambiguous answer.

Throughout the crisis, Commonwealth ministers regularly objected to the enthusiasm with which states exercised their control powers, most strenuously in respect of border closures. Yet, in a notable departure from normal practice in Australian federalism, those objections carried little weight, and the states prevailed. The rediscovery of state power led to a heightened prominence for state premiers and territory chief ministers within their own jurisdictions and on the national political stage.

COVID-19 and the National Cabinet system

Immediately the COVID-19 pandemic began in March 2020, Prime Minister (PM) Scott Morrison suspended the existing mechanism for peak Commonwealth–state coordination, the Council of Australian Governments (COAG). In its place he convened National Cabinet, a more informal and collegial (and much more frequent) meeting of the heads of government, aimed at addressing the country's response to the pandemic. National Cabinet was advised from the outset on COVID-19 by the Australian Health Protection Principal Committee (AHPPC), consisting of the chief medical or health officers of the Commonwealth, states and territories), and by the National Coordination Mechanism (convened by the federal Department of Home Affairs), which worked across all jurisdictions (including also private industry and other stakeholders), to advise on non-health issues.

This more collegial approach was welcomed by the states because it introduced a measure of more consensual or collective decision-making – characterised approvingly as 'co-design' by the Victorian government (Victoria Government, 2020). Within two months, PM Morrison announced that the change was permanent (Karp, 2020; PM, 2020). The earlier COAG model would cease. In its place, National Cabinet would continue to meet regularly (at least every two weeks during COVID-19 and monthly after that) and be advised by experts such as the AHPPC.

In addition, the PM announced that a new National Federation Reform Council would meet annually, consisting of the National Cabinet, the Council on Federal Financial Relations (CFFR), comprising the Treasurers of all Australian governments, and the Australian Local Government Association (ALGA), to focus on priority issues. The Council met twice (in December 2020 and 2021).

National Cabinet met (virtually, in almost all instances) on 32 occasions in 2020 and a further 28 times in 2021, creating an unprecedented degree of personal interaction and engagement between the nation's heads of government. Post-pandemic the tempo decreased: in 2022, the incoming Labor government committed to four meetings a year, and held five in 2023 (federation.gov.au, no date). Despite occasional public differences over lockdowns and borders in particular, the establishment and operation of National Cabinet was generally welcomed and was regarded as an important element in Australia's comparatively successful handling of the pandemic (for example, Lecours et al., 2021; Downey and Myers, 2020). Yet Liberal-National Party ministers always sought to minimise the transparency of National Cabinet proceedings up to the government's defeat in May 2022. Subsequently, issues around its hybrid nature (not part of the rest of the cabinet system but similar in being a solely executive body) have been 'fudged' to some extent by Labor ministers also (see below).

At more detailed policy levels, National Cabinet established five Reform Committees (in the areas of Health, Energy, Infrastructure and Transport, Skills, and Rural and Regional) reporting to it. Composed of Commonwealth, state and territory portfolio ministers they were charged with supporting the National Cabinet's 'job creation agenda'. In October 2020, National Cabinet also accepted the recommendations of a review to rationalise and streamline the system of Ministerial Councils (Conran, 2020). These meetings of portfolio ministers had a historical tendency to grow in number and were a regular target of criticism from leaders and business for being ineffective and obstructionist. Following the review, councils were re-badged as 'Ministers' Meetings', with around 10 being ongoing, regular meetings and another 10 time-limited to a maximum of 12 months, only meeting when needed. Another 20 or so ministerial forums or councils were disbanded, although they could meet to consider one-off issues.

The incoming federal Labor government of Anthony Albanese, elected in May 2022, essentially retained these arrangements, albeit with some modifications and simplification following a review by the First Secretaries Group, the heads of the PM/premier's department in each jurisdiction (FSG, 2022). The term 'Ministerial Council' was reinstated; 20 such councils were mandated to report annually to National Cabinet on their work plans. Ten of these Ministerial Councils were also to report regularly on priorities tasked to them by National Cabinet. Another change was a decision to invite a representative of the ALGA to one meeting of National Cabinet per year. This partially compensated for former PM Morrison's decision to abolish COAG, of which ALGA was a member. It also meant that Morrison's National Federation Reform Council (which included ALGA) was no longer needed.

Strengths, weaknesses, opportunities, and threats (SWOT) analysis

Current strengths	Current weaknesses
The system of intergovernmental relations (embodied in National Cabinet and before that COAG) has proved to be a reasonably well-developed and flexible instrument for managing the practical policy and administration relationship between the Commonwealth and the states.	The system has lacked institutionalisation through intergovernmental agreement, legislation or constitutional provision. Critics argue that such formalisation would provide a procedural framework more conducive to genuine discussion and compromise between the two levels of government and be more democratic in nature.
Deploying the tax-raising finance capabilities of the federal government to address 'welfare state' and macro-economic issues has been a key foundation of socioeconomic progress in the post-1945 period, and it remains crucial today. The intergovernmental machinery has been a minimalist solution for ensuring that federal transfer monies are well spent and has also assisted in developing national markets in economically beneficial ways.	The extensive overlap of federal and state responsibilities, and some duplication of monitoring and policy-making capabilities, have reduced effectiveness and efficiency in a number of high-budget policy areas, such as education and healthcare. The states, meanwhile, have been made excessively dependent on Commonwealth transfers.
Heads of government have been prepared and able to work together productively in times of emergency. The apparently cooperative, serious and productive nature of National Cabinet meetings to deal with COVID-19 provided a stark contrast with previous experience.	The complexity of intergovernmental relations often resulted in opportunistic behaviour, mistrust and conflict between politicians at different tiers – often along party lines. It enabled 'blame-shifting', along with opportunistic forms of politics such as 'grandstanding' for a home audience rather than negotiating constructively. Before COVID-19, Australians (and their leaders) had come to expect this pattern from federalism and intergovernmental relations.

National Cabinet has recently adopted – and published – Terms of Reference, thereby introducing an element of formality to its proceedings that was formerly lacking in meetings of first ministers.	The 'National Cabinet' terminology is misleading; it is not a 'cabinet'. The PM solely controls its institutional set-up and that of its committees. And the premiers and other participants from state and territory governments are accountable only to their own parliaments and voters.
Future opportunities	**Future threats**
National Cabinet's favourable reputation in the 2020–2022 period showed that productive intergovernmental relations are possible. In an optimistic scenario, that momentum towards more constructive engagement would be maintained,	A more realistic view is that 'business as usual' federalism will progressively resume over time, with governments at both tiers seeking to maximise short-run partisan goals.
Labor has held power federally, and in all states and territories except Tasmania, since March 2023. This may offer greater opportunities for federalism and intergovernmental relations to operate in a more concerted and effective manner.	While the Morrison government's proposed Commonwealth legislation on National Cabinet lapsed in 2021–2022, the failure of both the new Labor government and of state and territory leaders to rule it out shows that efforts to give the National Cabinet's proceedings privileged status could well recur. This could unnecessarily diminish transparency and democratic accountability to citizens.

The remainder of this chapter looks in more detail at three main areas of debate around intergovernmental relations: the extent to which executive federalism has warped the constitution or made policy-making less effective; the implications of executive federalism for Australia's democracy, transparency and public trust; and proposals for reform, many of them longstanding.

Constitutional provisions and executive federalism

Australia's federal system has been operating now for over 120 years, following the decision of Britain's previously separated self-governing Australian colonies to join together in a federal union through the then-unusually democratic procedure of colony-by-colony referendums. The new constitution recognised two tiers of government, dividing powers (and thus responsibilities) between them. The states were to continue as the primary agents of governance in most domestic matters while the Commonwealth was assigned a limited list of powers, concerned in the most part with maintaining the economic union and managing the country's external relations. On that basis, the two orders of government were to operate each in their own spheres and thus no provision was made for mechanisms of cooperation between them other than the Inter-State Commission (sections 101–104), which rarely operated and is now effectively defunct. Moreover, while the Senate was designed to give states equal representation, as a popularly elected body it was not designed in a way that would provide the state governments with any direct input into national decision-making.

Figure 16.1: Commonwealth and State governments' revenue and expenses, 2018–2019 (in A$ billions)

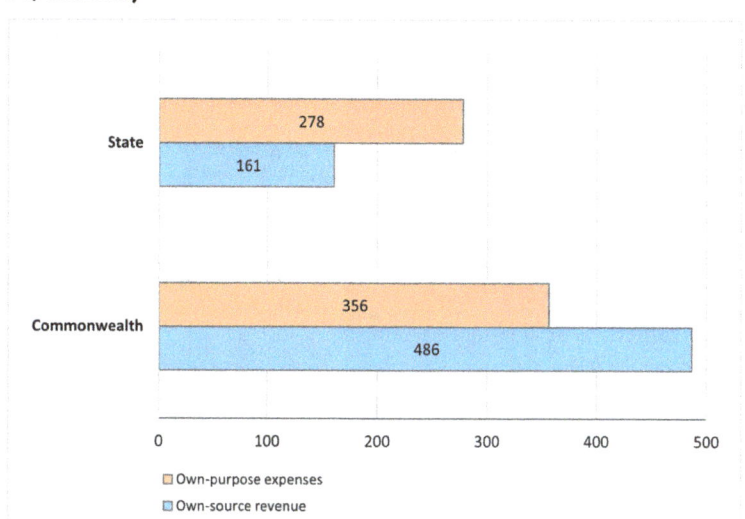

Source: Redrawn chart from data in Australian Bureau of Statistics (2019) Government Finance Statistics, Australia, 2018–19.

Note: 'Own-source revenue' is defined as total revenue minus grant revenue. 'Own-purpose expenses' are defined as total expenses minus grants to other levels of government.

In a number of respects, Australia remains very much the federation it was originally. In others, however, it has changed greatly, evolving to adapt and respond to the enormous economic, social and political changes of the 20th and 21st centuries. It did not take long for the notion of separate spheres to give way to a reality of increasing overlap as economic and social modernisation occurred. The Commonwealth expanded its role in the federation as broad interpretations of its enumerated powers were made by the High Court, and the states were excluded from the main revenue sources, sales tax and income tax in 1942. This left the states with access to only a motley collection of minor taxes, such as stamp duty on transactions, or buying a house or car and highly dependent on transfers from the Commonwealth. A high degree of Vertical Fiscal Imbalance (VFI) resulted whereby the Commonwealth raised considerably more revenue than it required for its own functions, while the states are dependent on the Commonwealth for a substantial part of their revenue base (on average, up to half), of which half in turn comes with strings attached (see Figure 16.1). Further High Court decisions continued to whittle down what little taxing power remained with the states, notably *Ha* in 1997 and *Vanderstock* in 2023.[1] Over the decades, the Commonwealth has been able to use its fiscal dominance to make conditional, or 'tied', grants to the states under section 96 of the Constitution, underpinning a long-running process of centralisation (Fenna, 2008; Fenna, 2019). That expanded role has introduced a steadily greater degree of de facto *concurrency* into the division of powers, with both levels of government playing important roles in many policy areas that were once predominantly or exclusively the domain of state governments. It also promoted a division of labour whereby the Commonwealth imposed particular policy directions while the states continued to manage the actual service provision. Reform is periodically mooted but rarely implemented (Fenna, 2017).

As the two levels of government became increasingly intertwined, a greater premium was placed on ways of negotiating their relationship and coordinating their actions. As in other parliamentary federations, intergovernmental relations became centred on meetings between portfolio ministers and, at the peak of the system, meetings of the 'first ministers' or heads of government (Phillimore and Fenna, 2017). In 1992, the latter were formalised as COAG, comprising the PM, premiers, the chief ministers of the two self-governing territories, and the president of the ALGA. Over the years, various Ministerial Councils were established to bring together portfolio ministers from the country's governments to deliberate on matters of shared concern. These were made officially subordinate to COAG.

COAG was not placed on any kind of constitutional or legislative basis or even modestly institutionalised through a formal agreement between Australia's governments. Thus, the extent to which it operated, and the way in which it operated, was almost entirely at the PM's discretion. COAG decisions were not in themselves binding on the various governments. Sometimes those decisions were formalised as intergovernmental agreements, which, although having a contractual or legalistic character, are not legally enforceable and are not laws. Their bindingness is political in character and their force comes from any actions taken, particularly legislative action, by the various governments pursuant to those agreements.

For example, in 1999, the Commonwealth and the states signed the *Intergovernmental Agreement on the Reform of Commonwealth–State Financial Relations* that committed the Commonwealth to distributing all the net proceeds of the new Goods and Services Tax (GST) to the states and giving the states a right of veto over changes to the new tax (federation.gov.au, 1999). However, this agreement in itself had no legal force, which only came when the Commonwealth Parliament passed legislation giving effect to that agreement, the *A New Tax System (Commonwealth–state Financial Arrangements) Act 1999*. Similarly, in the years leading up to the start of the COVID-19 pandemic in March 2020, the Commonwealth and the states signed a number of intergovernmental agreements outlining how responsibilities would be divided and cooperation maintained in just such an event. Again, those provided working protocols, but not enforceable rules.

Critics have argued that the linking of Commonwealth and state governments' policy-making and its management through the closed COAG process of executive federalism had important implications for policy-making:

- Commonwealth tied grants have skewed state priorities and reduced their policy autonomy.
- Commonwealth intrusion into policy areas that were traditionally state responsibilities has led to inefficiencies and duplication.
- Fiscal dependence of the states on the Commonwealth, combined with overlapping roles and responsibilities, often led to 'blame-shifting', where politicians at one tier of government ascribed responsibility for poor policy outcomes to politicians or agencies at the other tier. This pattern is common in health, aged care and childcare. During COVID-19, the failures of the hotel quarantine system led to criticism of state governments, who in turn were critical of the Commonwealth, since quarantining of outsider arrivals is a federal enumerated power under the constitution. Similarly, both levels of government were critical of each other at various stages of the pandemic over who was responsible for the initial slow rollout of vaccines, with the Commonwealth relying on GPs and pharmacies (for which it is responsible) and the states using clinics run by their health services and hospitals.
- Fiscal imbalance can also lend itself to political opportunism that generates a lack of trust in relations between governments. While in the federations of Germany and South Africa there is an obligation for 'good faith' behaviour in the conduct of intergovernmental relations, no such requirement exists in Australia. Relations between the Commonwealth and the states have often been marked by adversarial (artificially over-polarised) politics; grandstanding (with politicians orating for their home constituents rather than negotiating effectively); last minute ultimatums setting out 'take it or leave it' policy proposals; and breaches of previously agreed fiscal and policy positions (Rimmer, Saunders and Crommelin, 2019, pp.15–16).

Performance accountability

The formal accountability arrangements around intergovernmental relations, policies and institutions have not been extensive. The overlap of roles and responsibilities means that traditional accountability agencies, such as auditors-general, are limited in the extent to which they can question and make recommendations to their own governments for the performance of programs that may, for example, be funded by the Commonwealth but implemented by the states.

A less commonly considered aspect is *performance* accountability. Australia pioneered the use of performance and benchmarking processes in federations (Fenna and Knüpling, 2012). This began in the mid-1990s with the creation of the National Competition Council and its assessments of state and territory government reform under the National Competition Policy, in return for payments from the Commonwealth. Benchmarking of state and territory service provision was also instituted by COAG in 1994 through a joint Commonwealth–state exercise, which is published annually by the Productivity Commission as the *Report on Government Services* (Banks and McDonald, 2012). This report provides comparative information on the efficiency and effectiveness of a range of state government services, such as housing, childcare, hospitals, prisons and schools, although its effectiveness is often questioned.

These two types of accountability were combined in the COAG Reform Council, which was established in 2006 and which under reforms introduced in 2008–2009 reported to COAG on the progress that states and territories were making toward agreed benchmark outcomes in areas covered by Specific Purpose Payment and National Partnership agreements (Fenna, 2014; Fenna and Anderson, 2012; O'Loughlin, 2012). However, following a change of government, in 2014 the Commonwealth abruptly terminated the Reform Council without any protest from the states and territories.

Independent agencies

In one important area, however, consensual policy-making has emerged and been consistent over time, operating insulated from partisan politics. Australia has a long tradition of establishing independent agencies for a host of public policy issues, many of which involve shared governance between the states and the Commonwealth (Phillimore and Harwood, 2015, p.59). The bulk of these are what Poirier and Saunders (2015, p.467) call 'joint institutions' – designed to achieve shared goals in specific policy areas and responsible to jointly established and governed bodies.

Such joint institutions have covered a multitude of roles, including evaluation (the former COAG Reform Council and National Water Commission); research and analysis (Australian Bureau of Statistics; Institute for Health and Welfare); policy advice (Food Standards Australia and New Zealand; National Transport Commission); regulation (Australian Competition and Consumer Commission; Office of the Gene Technology Regulator; Great Barrier Reef Park Authority; Australian Energy Regulator, Australian Health Practitioner Regulation Agency); or a combination of these (Australian Curriculum, Assessment and Reporting Authority). For most of these bodies, membership and operational rules were established through intergovernmental agreement (and associated Commonwealth legislation). In many cases, membership of boards was jointly (or separately) decided by the Commonwealth and the states and territories, or the states and territories may have the ability to veto Commonwealth-proposed members. Depending on whether the agency was established by Commonwealth legislation, or mirror legislation, or by intergovernmental agreement alone, they report either to a Commonwealth minister or to a Ministerial Council (Phillimore and Fenna, 2017, pp.611–13).

Independent agencies are formally accountable to their Ministerial Council. In most cases, the board members and sometimes even the chief executive has been appointed by the Commonwealth in consultation with the states. Yet these agencies also tend to develop their own independence, expertise and authority. Thus, while the extent of direct Commonwealth dominance and control may be reduced, it is not necessarily replaced by increased state influence; instead, it leeches away to bodies that are effectively 'quasi-governmental'. Critics argue that democratic accountability is thereby diluted, with both Commonwealth and state ministers effectively abdicating responsibility for how these agencies operate in normal conditions, despite having established them in the first place.

Federalism, transparency and democratic accountability

Blame shifting and avoiding responsibility are always temptations for politicians dealing with difficult and often complex policy realities. Where such tactics appear to succeed, leaders have stronger incentives to adopt them. Yet blame shifting and opportunistic populism are also unambiguously bad for democracy, because they make it more difficult for voters to allocate responsibility or hold decision-makers to account when things go wrong. Over the long term, these evasive reductions in transparency also reduce public trust in government. In response, proposals or initiatives for reform and a recalibration of roles and responsibilities are periodically put forward, but almost always come to nought (for example, PM&C, 2015; NCA, 2014; Senate, 2021).

For most federalism scholars, democracy is almost an essential prerequisite of federalism (for example, Burgess and Gagnon, 2010). However, while one may not be able to have real federalism without liberal democracy, one can certainly have democracy without federalism. There have always been voices on the left raising an alarm that the restrictions imposed by federalism can compromise the democratic nature of Australia's system of government. This is primarily because of the way the division of powers can – or, at least, historically could – obstruct a party elected to office at the national level from fulfilling some of its policy goals. In a background paper for the original Democratic Audit of Australia, Graham Maddox (2002) argued precisely this – that federalism is undemocratic because at times it has presented an obstacle to the policy ambitions of the Labor Party at the national level. Similarly, the authors of *Australia: The State of Democracy* claimed that 'the federal division of powers, set out in rigid constitutions overseen by constitutional courts, may present ... obstacles to democracy' (Sawer, Abjorensen and Larkin, 2009, p.295).

Others pointed out, though, that such claims confuse the possibility of presenting obstacles to the ambitions of some political parties with the idea of presenting obstacles to democracy itself. Andrew Parkin (2003) argued that while federalism might be at odds with one particular type of democracy, namely, 'winner-take all majoritarianism within a unitary state', it also enhances democracy in several ways. In particular:

- federalism necessitates a more consensual approach to national decision-making
- it allows regional and local communities their own democratic self-government

it provides citizens with more, and more accessible, avenues for political access and influence. Underpinning this is the normative principle of *subsidiarity*, which holds that decisions should be taken at the lowest level of government, as close to the people as is practicable.

A more widespread concern is not that federalism in general compromises democracy, but that *one particular aspect* of modern federalism has an undemocratic character. This is the way that an increasing amount of governing is done in closed processes of executive negotiation and decision-making between the PM or ministers and the premiers and chief ministers. Geoffrey Sawer (1970, pp.7–8) warned a half century ago, this 'tends to erode responsible government'. Specifically, he meant that it eroded the accountability of the executive to parliament, and thereby to the people. Executive federalism does this primarily because it leads to arrangements 'so divided between the respective governments that no one Government ... can be held responsible for the whole of the activity in any one parliament'.

Federalism scholars in Canada identified the same problem, adding that executive federalism 'contributes to undue secrecy' and further reduces the level of 'citizen participation in public affairs', partly because of the increased complexity of multi-tier policy-making (Smiley, 1979, p.105). However, from the Canadian francophone and Québec perspective, executive federalism is seen as actually *more* democratic since it gives the francophone community a stronger voice in the federation than it would otherwise have (for example, Gagnon, 2010; Hueglin, 2013).

Lacking a Québec, the more likely view in Australia is that 'the question of how to make intergovernmental decision-making democratic, transparent and accountable remains one of the most intractable problems of Australian democracy' (Sawer, Abjorensen and Larkin, 2009). The grounds on which the authors of the original Democratic Audit of Australia came to this conclusion were:

> *(a)* the division of powers may be 'impeding the evolving will of the people expressed through electoral majorities'
>
> *(b)* the division of responsibilities obscures lines of accountability and allows blame shifting
>
> *(c)* the tendency towards opacity in intergovernmental relations (Sawer, Abjorensen and Larkin, 2009, pp.295–96).

Subsequently, Kildea (2012) argued along similar lines that Australian intergovernmental relations are deficient in transparency, accountability and participation – problems that he suggests could be ameliorated somewhat by a few 'achievable reforms'. We return to these towards the end of this chapter.

Transparency issues around National Cabinet

An interesting recent illustration of the problems associated with executive-controlled federal politics arose out of the claim that National Cabinet is a cabinet as normally understood in terms of responsible cabinet government. In 2020, under federal Freedom of Information (FOI) law, independent Senator Rex Patrick asked for minutes and other documents concerning the formation and functioning of National Cabinet. Disclosure was refused by the Department of the Prime Minister and Cabinet (PM&C) on the grounds that National Cabinet was a sub-committee of federal Cabinet and hence exempt from disclosure under FOI. Senator Patrick challenged this refusal in the Administrative Appeals Tribunal (AAT) and in August 2021, Justice White found quite emphatically that National Cabinet did not fall within the meaning of a committee of the Commonwealth cabinet and ordered that the documents be provided to Senator Patrick.[2]

On the same day that the Commonwealth government indicated that they would not appeal that decision, the Morrison government introduced the COAG Legislation Amendment Bill into the federal parliament, which declared that National Cabinet was established as a committee of the Commonwealth Cabinet. Had this law been passed, National Cabinet proceedings, documentation and decisions (and those of its committees) would have remained confidential and exempt from disclosure under FOI and the operation of other legislation. The Bill's Explanatory Memorandum argued that confidentiality was 'critical to the effective operations of the National Cabinet, enabling issues to be dealt with quickly, based on advice from experts'. The Morrison government's legislation was roundly criticised by academics, expert bodies such as the Law Council and the Australian Human Rights Commission, as well as non-government senators. Senator Patrick (2021a, p.53) argued that it 'would be a severe blow against transparency and accountability'. The only submission in support of the legislation to the Senate Committee investigating it was the one made by the Department of the Prime Minister and Cabinet (PM&C) itself. Many other submissions were forceful, even excoriating, in their criticisms (for example, Twomey, 2021).

At the heart of the AAT decision was the observation that National Cabinet cannot be regarded as a committee of the federal Cabinet. Apart from the PM, none of its members are members of the federal Cabinet; they are not appointed by the PM; and they are not members of, or responsible to, the federal Parliament. Indeed, the terms of reference of National Cabinet (disclosed to Senator Patrick after his AAT victory) note that the Commonwealth, states and territories retain their 'sovereign authority and powers' and their individual responsibility for implementing decisions of National Cabinet. There is no formal obligation of collective ministerial responsibility: if a state premier chooses to criticise or even act in defiance of a decision of National Cabinet, they are not bound to resign, as might be expected (or required) in a system of responsible cabinet government. Instead, they are each responsible to their own parliament. As Anne Twomey (2021) pointed out, such meetings of first ministers are designed 'to be a body of equals that makes collective decisions, with each being responsible to their own legislature and people for any action taken in implementing those decisions'. If National Cabinet was 'treated as nothing more than a committee of the Commonwealth Cabinet ... this would traduce their [that is, the premiers and chief ministers] power and role in the federation ... and subjugate [them] to the Commonwealth's will and power'.

Concerning confidentiality and other safeguards for executive action, critics argued that provisions already existed in FOI laws to grant exemption to disclosing documents that could cause damage to relations between the Commonwealth and a state, or which could divulge communications made in confidence on behalf of a state or the Commonwealth, if disclosure is deemed to be contrary to the public interest. However, under the proposed legislation, all material from its key committees (such as minutes of the Australian Health Protection Principal Committee) that had previously been accessible under FOI would no longer be.

The legislation stalled after the Senate committee reported (split along party lines) in October 2021. Subsequently, federal Coalition ministers still acted as if National Cabinet was indeed a committee of Cabinet, and the PM&C refused further access to documents under FOI on Cabinet exemption grounds, arguing that since the AAT decision in August 2021, other evidence needed to be taken into account (Patrick, 2021b). In particular, a joint statement was released on 17 September 2021 by the PM, premiers and chief ministers regarding the importance of confidentiality to relationships between them (PM and Premiers and Chief Ministers, 2021). This included the statement that 'meetings and operations of National Cabinet have been conducted in line with the process outlined in the Commonwealth Government's Cabinet Handbook'. Nevertheless, as Twomey (2021) argued, the joint statement 'does *not* assert that the National Cabinet is a committee of the Commonwealth Cabinet' – unlike the legislation tabled in the Commonwealth Parliament. Given the Senate's opposition, the legislation was not brought to a vote and lapsed when the parliament was prorogued in advance of the 2022 election.

Under the new federal Labor government, National Cabinet has provided more clarification regarding its operations including, for the first time, publishing comprehensive terms of reference (PM, 2022; NC, no date). These include a section on 'National Cabinet confidentiality and handling of National Cabinet documents'. The continuing need for confidentiality regarding discussions and documents is maintained; however, it is conceded that 'National Cabinet documents will be subject to different information management laws in each jurisdiction'. Furthermore, the Commonwealth agrees to consult with the states and territories regarding any requests for National Cabinet documents made to it under Commonwealth FOI laws, and states and territories agree to consult with each other and the Commonwealth regarding any requests they receive. If another FOI test arises, it is very likely that only a court ruling will resolve matters.

Legislative federalism

Australia's intergovernmental relations are predominantly executive-led, consisting largely of meetings between ministers and/or officials from the different jurisdictions. Parliamentary involvement is normally limited except for those cases where government requires legislative approval for particular initiatives, programs or funding. A range of legislative techniques are used across the federation to give effect to intergovernmental agreements (Phillimore and Harwood, 2015, pp.51–52; Twomey, 2007). The technique that provides the least amount of ongoing autonomy and capacity to states and territories is a *referral of powers*. Section 51(xxxvii) of the Constitution permits the Commonwealth to legislate in regard to matters referred to it by any state or states. States may refer matters individually or collectively, and non-referring states may subsequently join the referral or adopt the Commonwealth law. The referral option 'represents a mechanism whereby, through cooperation, complete uniformity of legislation, administration and adjudication can be achieved in areas not otherwise within Commonwealth power' (Saunders, 2002, p.71). The referral route has been used sparingly since Federation but a little more actively in recent years (Lynch, 2012). Examples include mutual recognition of certain skilled occupations; the regulation of corporations and securities; and criminal code powers concerning terrorism.

Another legislative technique is so-called *uniform legislation*, which involves one jurisdiction enacting a law that is then adopted by other parliaments. While this restricts the autonomy and capacity of individual states and territories, it lessens the risk of the Commonwealth exceeding or extending its powers beyond the legislation. It also normally involved states and territories working together to achieve harmonisation, thus enabling them to be active policy players. The technique is often associated with the establishment of a policy-making or regulatory body on which states and territories are represented directly or have a say over key appointments.

A related legislative technique involves a *model law* being developed (often by a Ministerial Council), with each state parliament then enacting it in an agreed form. States can sometimes make variations to the model to meet local circumstances. This technique provides for a degree of harmonisation, while still allowing jurisdictions to implement their own versions and retain some ownership over implementation. Commonwealth legislation that has been mirrored in the states and territories include consumer protection; offshore minerals and petroleum; censorship; and financial transactions reporting. This legislative technique has also been used by states and territories to cover areas where the Commonwealth has no direct involvement (for example, child protection and interstate transfer of prisoners).

Close parliamentary oversight of these legislative options is relatively rare. As governments generally have a clear majority in their lower Houses, the limited scrutiny that does take place (for example, through committees) generally occurs where the governing party lacks a majority in the upper house of parliaments. Indeed, some state upper houses have been critical of uniform and mirror legislation placed before them by their governments. There is, though, little organised or regular scrutiny.

One exception is Western Australia, whose upper house has a Standing Committee on Uniform Legislation and Statutes Review. That committee has a standing order requiring it to consider and report on any proposed legislation that 'ratifies or gives effect to a bilateral or multilateral intergovernmental agreement to which the government of the state is a party; or ... introduces a uniform scheme or uniform laws throughout the Commonwealth' (Legislative Council, no date, pp.71–72). This can lead to delays in the passage of uniform legislation, which can provoke criticism by business groups for undermining the harmonisation of regulations and therefore increasing business costs.

Reform proposals

Various proposals have been put forward to address perceived deficiencies in the operation of Australian federalism, particularly in respect of the chronic overlap and duplication and the resulting problem that citizens cannot necessarily know which government to hold accountable in a number of policy fields. The most sustained effort in recent years to rethink the respective roles and responsibilities of the two levels of governments was the Reform of the Federation White Paper process launched by the Commonwealth in 2014. That enquiry engaged with stakeholders and the broader public, produced discussion papers and even a Green Paper, but (like the COAG Reform Council) was unceremoniously terminated following a change of prime minister (PM&C, 2015).

The entrenched level of VFI, the complexity of modern governance and the pragmatic nature of most Australians' attitudes toward federalism make it highly unlikely that reform of the basic structures of Australian federalism towards a 'clean lines' division of roles and responsibilities is possible. Indeed, an ANZSOG paper deems them to be 'false hopes' (Rimmer, Saunders and Crommelin 2019, p.13). The authors of that paper argue that proposals for reform need to be directed instead towards better interjurisdictional engagement – in other words, the nuts and bolts of intergovernmental relations.

Improving intergovernmental relations has both an efficiency and a democratic element – but the two may not always be compatible. As noted above, much of intergovernmental relations in

Australia is marked by a lack of trust and respect and an absence of formalisation of the basic institutions and rules of the game. On occasions, this informality and flexibility can be useful, as COAG's swift and complete replacement with National Cabinet might suggest. However, it can also be a danger – in particular, the Commonwealth does not need to abide by the 'rules' of intergovernmental relations, because there are none. In 2014, for example, PM Abbott simply refused to convene a COAG meeting, despite being asked to by seven (out of eight) premiers and chief ministers. Similarly, the Commonwealth abolished the COAG Reform Council that same year, without any reference to the states and territories. Some form of 'rules-based order' would assist with promoting more effective, equitable and efficient intergovernmental relations. In particular, it would help to protect the states against Commonwealth unilateralism and dominance, and force the Commonwealth to justify and defend its actions more than it does currently. However, there is no inherent reason why even a reformed system of intergovernmental relations would be more democratic, transparent or accountable (as experience with another executive-run area – international relations – suggests). Parliaments and accountability agencies seem destined to play a decidedly secondary role.

Improvements have been suggested by parliamentary inquiries (SCRAF, 2011) and others. Paul Kildea (2012, pp.85–90) suggested four key areas of institutional reform:

- *Improving information flows*, through having a central register of intergovernmental agreements, and advance publication of COAG and Ministerial Council meeting agendas.
- *Formalising* the status and operations of intergovernmental bodies (then COAG), through complementary legislation in the Commonwealth and state parliaments.
- *Expanding the role of federal and state parliaments* by obliging premiers and ministers to report on the outcome of meetings and table their minutes; as well as increasing parliamentary scrutiny of legislation and intergovernmental agreements (not just those requiring legislative implementation), including scrutinising draft agreements on occasion.
- *Expanding opportunities for public participation* and consultation in intergovernmental relations.

Since then, there have been some improvements in transparency relating to information provision. There is now a central website repository of intergovernmental agreements, and the outcomes of National Cabinet and Ministerial Council meetings are routinely published via media statements from the ministers chairing those meetings. But these are after-the-event exercises in information provision. There is still no real involvement of parliaments or the public (for example, through interest group consultation and participation) in influencing the agenda or the deliberations of these meetings. As Kildea (2012, p.87) himself acknowledged, though, in intergovernmental relations there is almost unavoidably a trade-off between transparency and accountability, on the one hand, and flexibility, efficiency and workability on the other. So far, the demands of the executive at both Commonwealth and state levels have trumped those of the legislature – which may be for perfectly good reasons.

There has been less justification, however, for the historical lack of formalisation of the meetings of first ministers (first COAG, now National Cabinet), or Ministerial Councils. While National Cabinet functioned well during the pandemic, there was initially no particular reason to believe that collegiality would continue in normal times, and observers have long argued that it is desirable to 'lock in' some key operational features in order to provide more predictability and stability to intergovernmental relations. This would offer some protection to states and territories and add a level of accountability and democratic legitimacy (Kildea, 2012, p.86; Wanna et al.,

2009, p.16). On this front, some progress has been made. As noted above, at its meeting on 9 December 2022, National Cabinet agreed to (and published) Terms of Reference (NC, no date). At four pages in length, these cover core issues such as membership, minimum frequency of meetings (four per year), agendas (including a standing item for discussion of state and territory priorities), priorities, decisions and record of meetings, out-of-session processes, confidentiality, and caretaker provisions. While still short of either a formal Intergovernmental Agreement or legislation, this is still a notable improvement on more than 30 years of informality and *de facto* Commonwealth dominance.

Conclusion

The COVID-19 crisis was a shot in the arm for Australian federalism and reminded the wider public of some of federalism's democratic virtues. It demonstrated subsidiarity at work, with state governments and leaders being able to respond to local needs and preferences on a range of issues, be they lockdowns, school closures or border restrictions. The crisis also promoted a productive case of competitive, if not quite laboratory, federalism. Citizens, media and parliaments could look across borders and compare policy settings and outcomes in other states with those of their own jurisdiction and ask questions of their leaders accordingly.

At the same time governments were able to cooperate and act together nimbly and effectively in National Cabinet, supporting each other where needed – for example, with the Commonwealth financially supporting the states with their health response, while the states helped the Commonwealth meet its quarantine responsibilities. National Cabinet also enabled leaders to challenge each other's positions, rather than the traditional pattern of the Commonwealth invariably getting its way due to its fiscal dominance. This led to better policy-making and outcomes.

Yet the pandemic also confirmed that intergovernmental relations is by its nature a relatively closed process. Executives (first ministers, ministers and their bureaucrats) met to discuss and negotiate policies and programs, with little if any involvement at any stage from the main institutions of representative democracy, such as parliaments or oversight agencies. This seems to be a reasonable price to pay to achieve rapid, effective and agile intergovernmental decision-making between democratic governments. The original democratic audit's assertion that 'the question of how to make intergovernmental decision-making democratic, transparent and accountable remains one of the most intractable problems of Australian democracy' is quite misleading in this respect (Sawer, Abjorensen, and Larkin, 2009). Executives remain accountable to their respective parliaments, and it is not clear how transparent these exercises in Commonwealth–state diplomacy need to be.[3] Some institutions and practices function best when they are indirectly rather than directly democratic.

Notes

1. *Ha v New South Wales*, 189 CLR 465; *Vanderstock and Anor v State of Victoria*, HCA 30. For a scathing critique of the majority ruling in the latter, see the dissenting opinions.
2. *Patrick and Secretary, Department of Prime Minister and Cabinet (Freedom of Information)*, AATA 2719 (August 2021).
3. The phrase adverts to Richard Simeon's classic work *Federal–Provincial Diplomacy: The Making of Recent Policy in Canada*, Toronto: University of Toronto Press, 1972.

References

Australian Bureau of Statistics (2019) *Government Finance Statistics, Australia, 2018–19,* Annual webpage. https://perma.cc/RNK3-S47P

Banks, Gary and McDonald, Lawrence (2012) 'Benchmarking and Australia's report on government services', in Fenna, Alan and Knüpling, Felix (eds) *Benchmarking in Federal Systems*, Melbourne: Productivity Commission, pp.199–226. https://perma.cc/QV8R-GG58

Burgess, Michael and Gagnon, Alain-G (2010) 'Introduction: Federalism and democracy,' in Burges, Michael and Gagnon, Alain-G (eds) *Federal Democracies*, Abingdon: Routledge, pp.1–25. https://www.routledge.com/Federal-Democracies/Burgess-Gagnon/p/book/9781138969643

Conran, Peter (2020) *Review of COAG Councils and Ministerial Forums: Report to National Cabinet*, Commonwealth of Australia (Canberra). https://perma.cc/Q6W3-CAJ8

Downey, Davia Cox and William M. Myers (2020) 'Federalism, intergovernmental relationships, and emergency response: A comparison of Australia and the United States', *American Review of Public Administration,* vol. 50, no. 6–7, pp.526–35. https://doi.org/10.1177/0275074020941696

federation.gov.au (no date) 'National Cabinet Terms of Reference', webpage. https://perma.cc/45VJ-7HC6

federation.gov.au (1999) 'Intergovernmental Agreement on the Reform of Commonwealth-State Financial Relations', webpage, 25 July. https://perma.cc/YM2F-YY2B

Fenna, Alan (2008) 'Commonwealth fiscal power and Australian federalism', *University of New South Wales Law Journal,* vol. 31, no. 2, pp.509–29. https://perma.cc/NDW2-K2PF

Fenna, Alan (2014) 'Performance comparison in Australian federalism', in CEDA, *A Federation for the 21st Century*, Melbourne: The Committee for Economic Development of Australia, pp.94–100. https://perma.cc/Y2BG-N38N

Fenna, Alan (2017) 'The fiscal predicament of Australian federalism,' in Bruerton, Mark; Arklay, Tracey; Hollander, Robyn; and Levy, Ron (eds) *A People's Federation*, Leichhardt NSW: Federation Press, pp.134–46.

Fenna, Alan (2019) 'The centralization of Australian federalism 1901–2010: Measurement and interpretation', *Publius,* vol. 49, no. 1, pp.30–56. https://doi.org/10.1093/publius/pjy042

Fenna, Alan (2021) 'Australian federalism and the COVID-19 crisis,' in Chattopadhyay, Rupak; Knüpling, Felix; Chebenova, Diana; Whittington, Liam; and Gonzalez, Phillip (eds) *Federalism and the Response to COVID-19: A Comparative Analysis*, Abingdon: Routledge, pp.17–29. https://www.taylorfrancis.com/books/mono/10.4324/9781003251217/federalism-response-covid-19?refId=1eb115ee-6378-467b-a70f-fb6bfd2ba1db&context=ubx

Fenna, Alan (2023) 'Climate governance and federalism in Australia,' in Fenna, Alan; Jodoin, Sébastien; and Setzer, Joanan (eds) *Climate Governance and Federalism: A Forum of Federations Comparative Policy Analysis*, Cambridge: Cambridge University Press, pp.14–40. $ https://doi.org/10.1017/9781009249676.002

Fenna, Alan and Anderson, Geoff (2012) 'The Rudd reforms and the future of Australian federalism,' in Appleby, Gabrielle; Aroney, Nicholas and John, Thomas (eds) *The Future of Australian Federalism: Comparative and Interdisciplinary Perspectives*, Cambridge: Cambridge University Press, pp.393–413.

Fenna, Alan and Knüpling, Felix (eds) (2012) *Benchmarking in Federal Systems,* Melbourne: Productivity Commission. https://perma.cc/QV8R-GG58

FSG (First Secretaries Group) (2022) *A Culture of Cooperation: First Secretaries Group's Review of Ministerial Councils, Final Report to National Cabinet*, Canberra: Commonwealth of Australia. https://perma.cc/P3SJ-VZD5

Gagnon, Alain-G (2010) 'Executive federalism and the exercise of democracy in Canada', in Burgess, Michael and Gagnon, Alain-G (eds) *Federal Democracies*, Abingdon: Routledge, pp.232–50. https://www.routledge.com/Federal-Democracies/Burgess-Gagnon/p/book/9781138969643

Hueglin, Thomas (2013) 'Federalism and democracy: A critical reassessment', in Skogstad, Grace; Cameron, David; Papillon, Martin and Banting, Keith (eds) *The Global Promise of Federalism*, Toronto: University of Toronto Press, pp.17–42. https://www.degruyter.com/document/doi/10.3138/9781442619197-003/html

Karp, Paul (2020) '"Coag is no more": National Cabinet here to stay with focus on post-Covid job creation', Guardian Australia, 29 May. https://perma.cc/BHG5-KAXM

Kildea, Paul (2012) 'Making room for democracy in intergovernmental relations', in Kildea, Paul; Lynch, Andrew and Williams, George (eds) *Tomorrow's Federation: Reforming Australian Government*, Leichhardt NSW: Federation Press, pp.73–91.

Lecours, André, Béland, Daniel; Fenna, Alan; Fenwick Beck, Tracy; Paquet, Mireille; Rocco, Philip; and Waddan, Alex (2021) 'Explaining intergovernmental conflict in the COVID-19 crisis: The United States, Canada, and Australia,' *Publius* vol. 51, no. 4, pp.513–36. https://doi.org/10.1093/publius/pjab010

Legislative Council (no date) *Standing Orders*, West Perth, WA: Parliament of Western Australia.

Lynch, Andrew (2012) 'The reference power: The rise and rise of a placitum?' Kildea, Paul; Lynch, Andrew; and Williams, George (eds) in *Tomorrow's Federation: Reforming Australian Government*, Leichhardt NSW: Federation Press, pp.193–209.

Maddox, Graham (2002) *Federalism and Democracy,* Democratic Audit of Australia.

NCA (National Commission of Audit) (2014) *Towards Responsible Government,* Canberra: Australian Government.

NC (National Cabinet) (no date) 'National Cabinet Terms of Reference' https://perma.cc/45VJ-7HC6 Accessed 10 January 2023.

O'Loughlin, Mary Ann (2012) 'Benchmarking and accountability: The role of the COAG Reform Council,' in Fenna, Alan and Knüpling, Felix (eds) *Benchmarking in Federal Systems*, Melbourne: Productivity Commission, pp.247–66. https://perma.cc/QV8R-GG58

Parkin, Andrew (2003) *Federalists Can Be Democrats – and Democrats Ought to Be Federalists: A Response to Maddox.* Democratic Audit of Australia.

Patrick, Senator Rex (2021a) *Dissenting Report: An Arrogant and Foolish Endeavour,* Finance and Public Administration Legislation Committee (Canberra). https://perma.cc/ZD3B-XJT6

Patrick, Senator Rex (2021b) 'PM in disgraceful defiance of Justice White's National Cabinet decisions: Further legal proceedings pending', webpage, 5 November.

Phillimore, John and Alan Fenna (2017) 'Intergovernmental councils and centralization in Australian federalism,' *Regional and Federal Studies,* vol. 27, no. 5, pp.597–621. $ https://doi.org/10.1080/13597566.2017.1389723

Phillimore, John and Harwood, Jeffrey (2015) 'Intergovernmental relations in Australia: Increasing engagement within a centralizing dynamic', in Chattopadhyay, R and Nerenberg, K (eds) *A Global Dialogue on Federalism Booklet Series, volume 8: Intergovernmental Relations in Federal Systems*, pp. 12-15. Canada: Forum of Federations and IACFS. https://perma.cc/WZ7Z-4CFB

Prime Minister, and Premiers and Chief Ministers (2021) 'The importance of confidentiality to relationships between the Commonwealth and the states and territories', https://pmtranscripts.pmc.gov.au/sites/default/files/2022-06/national-cabinet-statement-the-importance-of-confidentiality-to-relationships.pdf

PM (Prime Minister) (2020) 'Scott Morrison MP, Prime Minister, Press Conference,' Transcript, 26 March 2020. https://perma.cc/KHF5-TW43

PM (Prime Minister) (2022) Media Statement, 'Meeting of National Cabinet'. 9 December. https://www.pm.gov.au/media/meeting-national-cabinet-4

PM&C (Department of the Prime Minister and Cabinet) (2015) *Reform of the Federation: Green Paper,* Commonwealth of Australia (Canberra), 23 June. https://perma.cc/EA2C-5J2K

Poirier, Johanne and Saunders, Cheryl (2015) 'Conclusion: Comparative experiences of intergovernmental relations in federal systems', in Poirier, Johanne; Saunders, Cheryl; and Kincaid, John (eds) *Intergovernmental Relations in Federal Systems: Comparative Structures and Dynamics*, Don Mills ON: Oxford University Press, pp.440–98.

Rimmer, Ben; Saunders, Cheryl and Crommelin, Michael (2019) *Working Better with Other Jurisdictions,* Carlton, Victoria: Australia and New Zealand School of Government. https://perma.cc/5YAB-PNJV

Saunders, Cheryl (2002) 'Collaborative federalism', *Australian Journal of Public Administration,* vol. 61, no. 2, pp.69–77. $ https://doi.org/10.1111/1467-8500.00274

Sawer, Geoffrey (1970) *Cooperative Federalism and Responsible Government in Australia*, Alfred Deakin Lecture Trust.

Sawer, Marian; Norman Abjorensen, Norman; and Larkin, Phil (2009) *Australia: The State of Democracy*, Leichhardt NSW: Federation Press.

SCRAF (Select Committee on the Reform of the Australian Federation) (2011) *Australia's Federation: An Agenda for Reform,* The Senate (Canberra). https://perma.cc/J9C6-ZEA5

Senate (2021) 'Abbott Government's Commission of Audit', Senate committee report. https://perma.cc/4ZMM-QL4T

Smiley, Donald V (1979) 'An outsider's observations of federal–provincial relations among consenting adults', in Simeon, Richard (ed) *Confrontation and Collaboration: Intergovernmental Relations in Canada Today*, Toronto: Institute of Public Administration of Canada, pp.105–113.

Twomey, Anne (2007) 'Federalism and the use of cooperative mechanisms to improve infrastructure provision in Australia', *Public Policy,* vol. 2, no. 3, pp.211–26. Open access at https://papers.ssrn.com/sol3/papers.cfm?abstract_id=1370701

Twomey, Anne (2021) 'Submission' to the *COAG Legislation Amendment Bill 2021 [Provisions], Submission 8,* Canberra: The Senate. https://perma.cc/QK3V-MT8B

Victoria, Government of (2020) *Victorian Government Submission to the Senate Select Committee on COVID-19,* Melbourne: Government of Victoria. https://perma.cc/NW8W-AGZA

Wanna, John; Phillimore, John; Fenna, Alan; and Harwood, Jeffrey (2009) *Common Cause: Strengthening Australia's Cooperative Federalism,* Brisbane: Council for the Australian Federation. https://perma.cc/N6LE-MKFH

IV

State and Local Politics

17. New South Wales 367
    Mark Evans

18. Victoria 392
    Tom Daly and James Murphy

19. Queensland 415
    Cosmo Howard and Pandanus Petter

20. South Australia 432
    Rob Manwaring, Josh Holloway and Andrew Parkin

21. Western Australia 453
    John Phillimore, Martin Drum, Sarah Murray, Peter Wilkins, Narelle Miragliotta and Benjamin Reilly

22. Tasmania 478
    Lachlan Johnson, Richard Eccleston and Mike Lester

23. Northern Territory 497
Rolf Gerritsen

24. Australian Capital Territory 514
Brendan McCaffrie

25. Local democracy in metropolitan regions and big cities.................. 529
Graham Sansom and Su Fei Tan

26. Systems of local government..... 544
Su Fei Tan and Graham Sansom

17

New South Wales

Mark Evans

New South Wales (NSW), Australia's most affluent and densely populated state, includes the Sydney metropolitan area and has a population of close to 7.5 million people. As a result, it accounts for 47 seats in the federal House of Representatives (nearly a third of the total). Its powerful state government has often accentuated that political importance, with the largest lower house of any state (93 seats) elected by the Alternative Vote (AV) and often showing strong 'pendulum' swings between the top two parties (the Australian Labor Party and Liberal-National Coalition). The upper chamber, the Legislative Council (LC), is chosen using the single transferable vote (STV) proportional voting system. It has rarely had single-party majorities, fostering greater political stability.

What does a democratic state government require?

Key elements include:

- An effective state constitution that provides an anatomy of legitimate public power to: define the limits of state governmental powers; make government accountable to the people by providing for checks and balances; promote long-term structures. A constitution typically (1) lasts for an indefinite term; (2) is difficult to change; and (3) reflects a consensus among those who are subject to its limits and afforded its protections. It condenses the preferences, values and views of the state's people; provides legal authority for the exercise of governmental powers; specifies the civil and human rights of all citizens; and creates (or clarifies) any (legal) duties/obligations that the government must observe or satisfy. The state's relationship with the Commonwealth government is governed by the federal constitution.

- Rights for Aboriginal and Torres Strait Islander peoples should be fully recognised and implemented as for all citizens. The histories, languages, cultures, rights and needs of Aboriginal and Torres Strait Islander communities and peoples should be addressed, so as to remedy historical injustices.

How to cite this chapter:

Evans, Mark (2024) 'New South Wales', in: Evans, Mark; Dunleavy, Patrick and Phillimore, John (eds) *Australia's Evolving Democracy: A New Democratic Audit,* London: LSE Press, pp.367–391. **https://doi.org/10.31389/lsepress.ada.q**. Licence: CC-BY-NC 4.0

- Electoral systems for the state's Legislative Assembly (LA) and LC should accurately translate parties' votes into seats, in different ways that are recognised as legitimate by most citizens. Ideally the voting systems should foster the overall social representativeness of the two houses of the legislature. Elections and the regulation of political parties should be impartially conducted, with integrity.
- Political parties at state level should sustain vigorous and effective electoral competition and citizen participation. They should enable the recruitment, selection and development of political leaders for state government; formulate viable policy agendas and frame political choices for state functions; and form governments or, when not in power, hold governments accountable. Political parties should uphold the highest standards of conduct in public life.
- The core executive and government should operate fully within the law, and ministers should be effectively scrutinised by and politically accountable to parliament. Ministers and departments/agencies must also be legally accountable to independent courts for their conduct and policy decisions. Responsive government should prioritise the public interest and reflecting state public opinion. Its core executive (premier, cabinet, ministers and key central departments) should provide clear unification of public policies across government, so that the state operates as an effective whole. Both strategic decision-making within the core executive, and more routine policy-making, should foster careful deliberation to establish an inclusive view of the 'public interest'.
- The administration of public services should be controlled by democratically elected officials so far as possible. Officials in state public services should act with integrity, in accordance with well-enforced codes of conduct, and within the rule of law. The rights of all citizens should be carefully protected in policy-making, and 'due process' rules followed, with fair and equal public consultation on public service changes. Public services, contracting, regulation and planning/zoning decisions should be completely free from corruption.

Recent developments

Three recent developments have dominated democratic politics within NSW – electoral competition in the state since 2000; the re-emergence of corruption problems within NSW politics; and the handling of two major crises – the bushfires that raged across the state (2019–2020), and the COVID-19 pandemic (2020–2022). After considering these developments, a SWOT analysis summarises the overall main strengths and weaknesses of NSW's democracy. The later sections of this chapter then examine four features of state politics in more detail.

Electoral politics

New South Wales politics in the last two decades has been dominated by the top two parties (the Liberal-National Coalition and Labor), as they were in the previous century. Between them they have always commanded four-fifths of the votes in the Alternative Vote (AV) and single-member constituency elections for the NSW lower house, each seat having 53,000 to 65,000 electors. The Liberal-Nationals enjoyed a period of hegemony from 2011 to 2023, but that was preceded and followed by periods when Labor was the largest party (Figure 17.1). Although the Greens have regularly scored a tenth of first-preference votes, and independents have

Figure 17.1: First-preference votes for parties in NSW Legislative Assembly elections, and Labor's two-party preferred (TPP) vote, 2002–2023

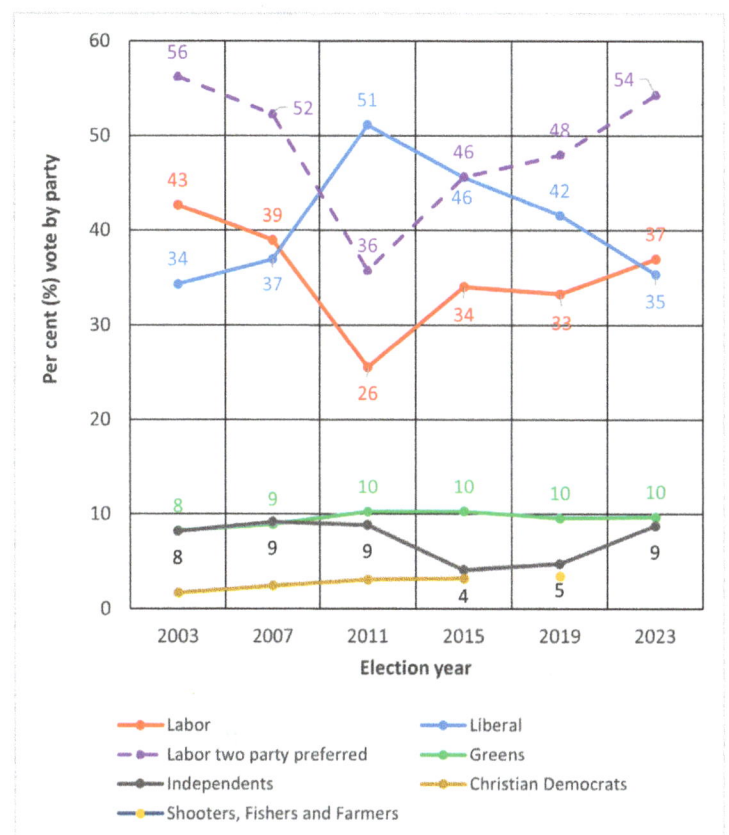

Source: Created from data in NSW Electoral Commission (2023a) 'State election results', various dates.

achieved some success, these smaller vote shares have been flat rather than growing over time. The dashed purple line in Figure 17.1 shows Labor's 'two party preferred vote' at the end stage of the AV counting process. Even though Labor has attracted most Greens voters' later preferences, when Michael Baird and then Gladys Berejiklian were the Liberal leader, this was not enough to give Labor a majority. Labor recovered from its disastrous 2011 performance, but its level of support remained depressed for two further elections. In 2023 Labor relied on getting 17 per cent of votes from other parties' supporters to narrowly win the 'two-party preferred' (TPP) vote. (This is the final count stage of the AV system, with only two parties remaining – see Chapter 5.)

As a 'majoritarian' voting system, a key test for AV is whether elections actually give most seats to the 'correct' party, the one winning most of the TPP. Figure 17.2 shows that in NSW it did. There has been a characteristic AV tendency to somewhat over-reward the largest party with seats at the two-party preferred stage of vote. In 2011 the Liberal-National Coalition won nearly three-quarters of all seats after winning 51 per cent of first-preference votes, but it received 64 per cent of the TPP that year (Figure 17.1). In 2015 the Liberal-National coalition won 58 per cent of seats on 46 per cent of first-preference votes, but it also got 54 per cent of TPP that year. These clear outcomes have helped create legitimacy for incoming governments, with ministers able to use their mandates to push through manifesto policies. Critics argue that allied with strong party discipline they have contributed to perhaps overly strong governments, with the

Figure 17.2: Seats won by parties in the NSW Legislative Assembly, 2002–2023

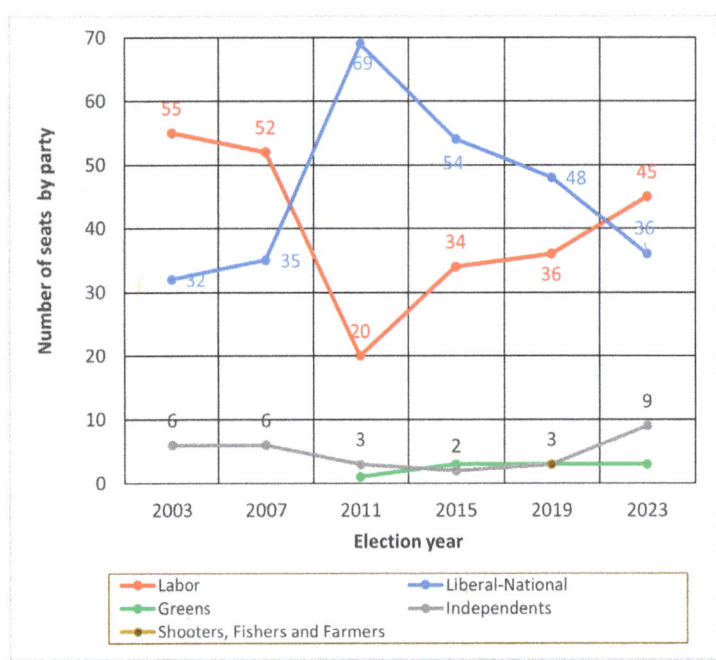

Source: Created from data in NSW Electoral Commission (2023a) 'State election results', various dates.

Note: The Legislative Assembly has 93 seats, so a majority requires 47 seats.

executive occupying a dominant position vis-à-vis Parliament (as elsewhere in Australia's states).

Turning to the NSW upper house, this is the Legislative Council (LC), with 42 seats. Members serve for eight years, with half elected at each state election, using STV in multi-member constituencies. This is a proportional representation (PR) system designed to ensure that parties' seats shares are closely matched with their vote shares. The single transferable vote also transfers voters' preferences between parties and candidates if they would otherwise be 'wasted'. Figure 17.3 shows that the same voting trends that occurred in the lower house elections also broadly prevailed in upper house voting patterns. However, the top two parties between them have commanded a far smaller share of first-preference votes – initially three-quarters of votes, falling somewhat to around two-thirds in 2019 and 2023. However, the Greens' support has again been around a tenth of primary votes, no higher than in the AV elections. Instead, a wide and shifting range of other small parties (some single-issue causes) have commanded the remaining 15–20 per cent of votes, as Figure 17.3 shows.

When it comes to gaining Council seats, the Greens have been somewhat more successful, winning one in nine seats, as Figure 17.4 shows. Other smaller or more episodic parties have generally won at least as many or more seats in total, with the result in any given year shaped by current events and the vote transfers between minor parties agreed by their leadership. With between 8 and 12 seats going to the Greens and smaller parties, neither the Liberal-National Coalition nor Labor has commanded a majority in the upper chamber this century. However, Labor has generally been able to rely on the Greens when in office. And the Liberal-National Coalition got close to a majority in 2015 and could generally appeal to Council members from parties like the Christian Democrats or 'Shooters, Fishers and Farmers' for support, often by tailoring policies elsewhere to 'fit' with a particular member's strong policy commitments or constituency interests. Nonetheless, the Council has been an effective 'House of Review', and its slower-changing composition has increased continuity in state policy-making.

Figure 17.3: First-preference votes for parties in the NSW Legislative Council (upper house) elections under STV, 2002–2023

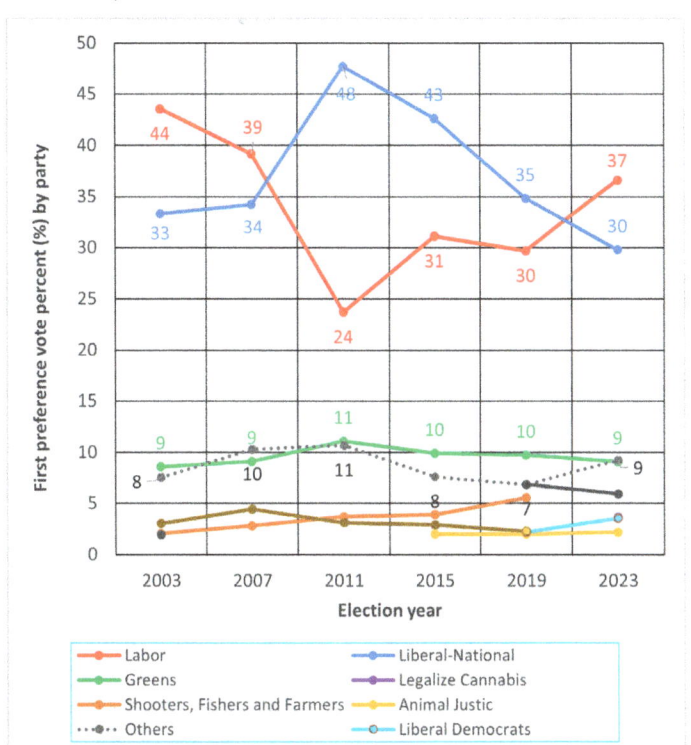

Source: Created from data in NSW Electoral Commission (2023a) 'State election results', various dates.

Figure 17.4: Seats held by parties in the NSW Legislative Council (upper house) following elections, 2002–2023

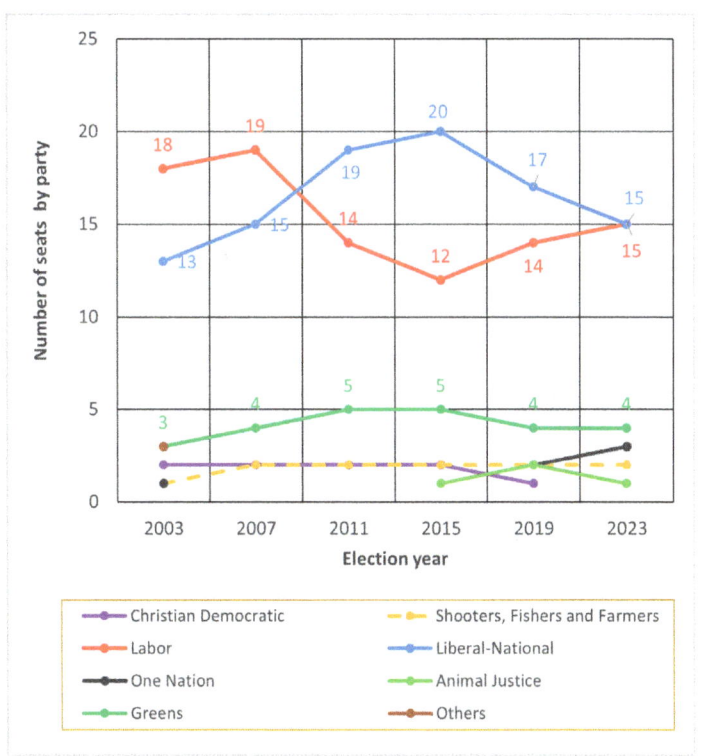

Source: Created from data in NSW Electoral Commission (2023) 'State election results', various dates.

Notes: The LC has 42 seats, so a majority requires 22 seats.

Preventing corruption and malfeasance

New South Wales has long had one of the most rigorous anti-corruption systems in the country, and for good historical reasons. State politics has struggled to escape a traditional association with criminality ('big city' criminal gangs), cronyism and corruption, reflecting problems of urban growth, soaring property markets and mega public finance projects weakly supervised by NSW regulations and controls (Wikipedia, 2023a):

> *Politics then (and now) was a honey pot for some: needy, greedy ministers and MPs were looking to benefit from public works, jobs, development and government contracts, as well as through the manipulation of the criminal justice system ... NSW has also always had a sleazy subterranean network of fixers and door-openers who could influence decisions for the right price ... Sydney has traditionally been thought of as a corrupt old town. Whether this was because of its buccaneering origins in the convict era or because it was where all the action took place has long been an open question.* (Clune, 2020)

In the mid-1980s, incoming Liberal Premier Nick Greiner created the Independent Commission Against Corruption (ICAC) (ICAC, no date) to clean up state governance once and for all. This was in response to a perfect storm of corruption allegations against members of the preceding Labor government (led by Neville Wran between 1976 and 1986 (Tiffen, 2021), when the corrective services minister and chief magistrate were both tried and subsequently imprisoned for corruption. The ICAC was given significant investigative powers, a broad anti-corruption brief and genuine independence from ministers and the legislature. In the late 1990s, the importance of ICAC independence was underlined when the Wood Royal Commission found entrenched and systemic corruption due to contacts with criminals in the NSW state police (Wood, 1997).

In recent years, the ICAC has been very active in identifying and investigating potential breaches of parliamentary and administrative standards, demonstrating the capacity of NSW integrity agencies to shore up the protective powers of democracy (see Figure 17.5). Although it should be noted that several of these investigations are yet to be concluded, their frequency raises the suspicion that corrupt practices have become culturally embedded in NSW government. The period under study will be remembered as one of ICAC assertiveness culminating in the 2021 resignation of former Premier Gladys Berejiklian.

By any standards this was a disappointing track record with serious breaches of integrity happening in both the political and public service realms. A wider report (ICAC, 2018) on trends and events in corruption made for gloomy reading, and a 2020 report on corruption in water management (a critical area of infrastructure development in Australia) 'made 15 recommendations to the NSW Government to improve the management of the state's water resources, after the undermining of the governing legislation's priorities over the past decade by the responsible department's repeated tendency to adopt an approach that was unduly focused on the interests of the irrigation industry' (ICAC, 2020a). More optimistically, two high-level reviews sought to safeguard the independence of the ICAC by drawing attention to the role of ministers and the government in deciding annual funding for integrity agencies and the provision of additional funding to address unforeseen integrity problems. One 2020 study by the state Audit Office examined financial management, and another by the Public Accountability Committee of the upper house in early 2021 examined the budget process for independent oversight bodies and the administration of Parliament itself.

Figure 17.5: ICAC investigations into parliamentary and administrative misconduct in the period 2019–2021

Type of investigation	Incident
Parliamentary misconduct	In 2021 Premier Gladys Berejiklian resigned in the wake of the ICAC launching an investigation into whether she broke the law by failing to report the conduct of her ex-lover, the former Wagga Wagga MP Daryl Maguire.
	The ICAC investigated the following cases of misconduct by two MPs – one who resigned as a minister and one who resigned as a parliamentary secretary (ICAC, 2022).
	In May 2021, Gareth Ward stepped down from his role as the minister for families and from the Liberal party room after revealing he was the subject of a police investigation (Guardian, 2021a).
	In September 2019, Premier Berejiklian announced that she had accepted John Sidoti's offer to stand aside from Cabinet where he had served as minister for sport, multiculturalism, seniors and veterans while the ICAC undertook an investigation into him (ICAC, 2022).
	Premier Berejiklian announced in July 2018 that Daryl Maguire had resigned from his position as parliamentary secretary after evidence of telephone recordings involving Mr Maguire was heard by ICAC staff (ICAC, 2020b).
Administrative misconduct	Cases here included a Service NSW officer allowing improper access to restricted database information (ICAC, 2021a); a FACS official who corruptly obtained nearly A$1.7 million for his own company (ICAC, 2020c); and an ICT manager in DFSI who 'hijacked' a business name to obtain A$0.5 million (ICAC, 2019). The ICAC also launched several institutional investigations of maladministration during this period.

Sources: As referenced in Figure 17.5.

In June 2021, the ICAC published a report (Operation Eclipse) into the Regulation of Lobbying, Access, and Influence in NSW (ICAC, 2020b). The ICAC found that new legislation, or significant reform of the current *Lobbying of Government Officials Act 2011* (the *LOGO Act*), was required to safeguard the public interest against the inherent lobbying risks of corruption and undue influence. While interest group lobbying contributed to positive outcomes in the public interest when conducted ethically and honestly, Operation Eclipse and other ICAC investigations had shown that lobbying, access and influence can result in favouritism, or even corrupt conduct. The prevailing regulation was deficient:

> 'The LOGO Act, while a step in the right direction, falls short of implementing all of the 17 recommendations made by the Commission more than 10 years ago in its previous lobbying investigation, Operation Halifax,' [ICAC] Chief Commissioner [Peter] Hall said. 'In Operation Eclipse, the ICAC has made a further 29 recommendations to address this shortfall and to better regulate lobbying practices in NSW.' (ICAC, 2020b)

In June 2023, the ICAC issued a 688 page report which found that former Premier Berejiklian had engaged in 'serious corrupt conduct' and breached the public's trust, by intervening to allocate state contracts to a former MP with whom she was having a relationship (Graycar, 2023). This brought to a climax a period of ICAC assertiveness that attracted some criticism.

Critics on the right claimed that ICAC activism was driving talented business people away from entering politics, as well as bringing an untimely end to Berejiklian's otherwise very successful political career. The former Liberal NSW Health Minister Brad Hazzard (one of the former premier's closest allies and confidantes during the COVID-19 pandemic) challenged whether the state's corruption watchdog should conduct inquiries in public. He had 'strong views about the model and how it could be fixed' insisting on an integrity review (Guardian, 2021b; Sydney Morning Herald, 2021a). Members of the general public also questioned the timing of Berejiklian's (forced) resignation given that the pandemic was still continuing at the time (October 2021). However, Berejiklian's Liberal successor as state Premier, Dominic Perrottet made it clear that he had no intention in interfering with or repealing the ICAC's powers (Guardian, 2021c), and neither did his Labor successor following the 2023 election. In that campaign period it was also clear that integrity in public office had again become an issue of significant political salience in NSW. Given the Coalition defeat amid corruption concerns, it seems likely that the integrity challenge will warrant and receive close attention, with future ministers motivated to ensure that elected and non-elected officials act with integrity, in accordance with well-enforced codes of conduct, and within the rule of law.

Crisis politics – bushfires and the COVID-19 pandemic

New South Wales is the most densely populated state, and most of its population is concentrated in and around Sydney and a few other cities and towns. In terms of area, it is only the fifth largest state in Australia, but it still has an extensive landmass (just under 801,000 sq kms). Much of it consists of bush forest and pasturelands, where summer wildfires regularly occur, usually on a manageable scale. However, the 2019–2020 bushfire season proved to be devastating, with unprecedented large, intense and uncontrollable fires that claimed 25 human lives, burnt over 2,000 homes and killed an estimated one billion animals (not counting invertebrates) (Pickrell, 2020). At the height of the crisis acrid smoke from the NSW fires blanketed the Sydney conurbation for days on end. In contrast to the apparently slow-to-react federal PM Scott Morrison, the Liberal state Premier Gladys Berejiklian emerged from the bushfire crisis with an enhanced reputation (Clune, 2021). As Niki Savva (2020) put it:

> When the fires hit NSW, she made a point of being there, every day, standing next to the fire chief, Shane Fitzsimmons, supporting him and allowing him to do his job. She visited affected communities. Her embraces were accepted. No one refused to shake her hand [which happened to PM Scott Morrison].

The government was also transparent about its performance, commissioning an independent expert inquiry into the 2019 to 2020 bushfire season. Its final Report in July 2020 concluded:

> This season also challenged assumptions about how we fight fires ... despite the bravery and ingenuity of our firefighters in the face of enormous risk, capable Incident Management Teams coordinating the responses to the various big fires, and the huge expenditure on firefighting. We need to know much more about bush fire suppression methods and how effective they are, especially in the face of megafires like these. Techniques and strategies that worked in previous seasons often did not work as well in the 2019–20 season ...There are important firefighting enhancements needed – more emphasis on getting fires out early; improved backburning protocols; training and information around heavy plant use; the right mix of aerial firefighting assets; and increased aerial night firefighting. There is

Figure 17.6: The net approval rating in 2020 survey responses to the question, 'How well is your state government responding to the pandemic?'

Date in 2020	Victoria	New South Wales	Queensland	Southern Australia	Western Australia
Per cent saying 'very well' or 'fairly well' minus per cent saying 'very badly' or 'fairly badly'					
July	30	62	84	88	98
November	56	78	70	87	96
Change	26	16	-14	-1	-2
Per cent saying 'very well' minus per cent saying 'very badly'					
July	8	22	2	60	82
November	30	41	44	60	75
Change	22	19	42	0	-7

Source: Scanlon Foundation (November 2021), 'Mapping Social Cohesion 2020 Report', computed by the author from Table 25.

> also a need for improved telecommunications, both to ensure the community can access the information it needs to make timely and appropriate decisions, and to enhance firefighting capability. (NSW Bushfire Inquiry, 2020)

Berejiklian responded in much the same way to the COVID-19 outbreak in the state from 2020 to 2022, although this time with the Chief Medical Officer (Kerry Chant) by her side (NSW Parliamentary Research Service, 2021). Although the second wave of the outbreak proved to be more difficult and unpredictable to manage, by the time of the premier's resignation in October 2021 (following corruption or 'sleaze' allegations), the spread of the disease was coming under control. Berejiklian's calm, competent and transparent approach in daily press conferences held in the worst times resonated with the electorate. Public trust increased. As noted earlier, until COVID-19, Australians' trust in 'people in government', 'legislative assemblies' (28 per cent), and 'political parties' (11 per cent) were at their lowest on record. The effective management of COVID-19 shifted public opinion at both the Commonwealth (up to the vaccine rollout) and state levels. In mid-year 2020, public confidence in the NSW government's tackling of the disease was well below levels in three smaller and less affected states (the right most columns in Figure 17.6), but clearly above the very low levels in Victoria. Over the next six months, confidence in the Liberal-National state government increased, especially looking at the net strong approval rows ('very well' minus 'very badly') where net approval doubled.

As well as building public support despite long periods of lockdown and an upsurge in social protest, and later some political uncertainty over the premiership change, NSW ministers also proved transparent in terms of their willingness to reflect on the government's performance in managing the pandemic crisis. Relatively few major outbreaks of the disease happened, but in all over 2.2 million cases of COVID-19 occurred by June 2022, as measured by an extensive testing programme (NSW Health, 2022). Over the pandemic period (2020–mid-2022) 7,300 deaths were attributed to COVID-19. NSW was also relatively quick to get going with vaccinations against COVID-19. By March 2022, more than 17 million shots had been administered, despite some anti-vaccine protests and conspiracy theories circulating on social media. The LC's Public

Accountability Committee launched a long-running inquiry into a wide range of public issues and complaints over incidents throughout the period, but it was generally supportive of the government's efforts.

Strengths, weaknesses, opportunities, and threats (SWOT) analysis

Current strengths	Current weaknesses
AV elections for the lower house LA have regularly awarded majorities of seats to whichever of the top two parties is ahead in the two-party preferred vote, fulfilling their majoritarian rationale.	AV tends to slightly over-reward the largest party in primary votes with LA seats, at the expense of the Greens and smaller parties.
STV elections for the LC clearly follow much the same trends as in the lower house, but match the seats shares of the Greens and smaller parties to their vote shares.	Which of the 'Other' parties wins LC seats is something of a lottery, shaped by close-to-election events and how minor party leaders agree that their unused votes should transfer from one to another candidate.
The majoritarian lower house LA and the proportionally representative upper house LC balance each other in realising different kinds of political benefits. The LA's clear alternation of state premiers and ministers in office prevent democratic sclerosis, while the greater continuity in Council elections and the fact that no one party commands an LC majority helps to foster more consensual legislation.	Bargaining between ministers and smaller parties to secure a LC majority for their legislation can lead to 'trades' that look like 'pork barrel' politics (see Chapter 15) directing benefits to particular members' areas.
Elections in NSW are free and fair, with strong quality assurance underpinning its electoral process through the independent Electoral Commission.	There have been no recent reviews of the NSW Constitution despite evidence of strong public support for constitutional change in two areas: protecting and advancing the rights of Aboriginal and Torres Strait Islander Peoples and support for a Bill or Charter of Human Rights (perhaps similar to that in neighbouring Australian Capital Territory (ACT).
The NSW executive has mostly operated in ways that have been responsive and effective. The Liberal-National Coalition governments before 2022 effectively handled two of the most dramatic crises in recent Australian history. The NSW State Government has demonstrated significant transparency in articulating its governing vision, priorities and outcomes. Sporadically arising integrity issues have not yet had adverse impacts on public trust.	State governments have continued to suffer from integrity problems, most notably the resignation of the state Premier Berejiklian (in October 2021) over failing to act impartially in the award of publicly funded contracts.

The state parliament has been effective in holding the executive to account. The committee system is working well and generally meeting its objectives. The parliament responded well to the challenges of COVID-19. The committee system has discharged its functions effectively in terms of executive scrutiny.	Despite the development of a new ePetition platform, the state parliament still has a very traditional approach to connecting with NSW citizens and the quality of parliamentary debate is not measured in both Houses.
Political parties play an important role in promoting electoral competition and citizen participation.	Before 2023, NSW political parties performed badly in ensuring gender equality and First Nations representation in the membership of the parliament, but recent improvements have occurred (Gobbett, 2017).
NSW has a strong ICAC, which has repeatedly acted firmly against some significant problems of continuing corruption in state politics and public services, including investigating the state premier (Berejiklian) while she was in office (see above).	The independence of the ICAC could be threatened by the fact that ministers determine its finances, and by some party-politicised questioning of its powers and activities.
The NSW public service is leading the way in organising public service production around publicly valued outcomes and using digital technology and user-centred design to enhance the quality of delivery.	It is evident that integrity in public office in both the public sector and politics has become an issue of significant political salience.
	The capacity of the NSW State Government to respond to the challenges of recovery is undermined by the size of its tax revenue base. The gap between NSW's share of expenditure and share of tax revenue has widened more than any other advanced economy in the federation, and more than most unitary states tracked by the OECD.
In policy terms, the NSW State Government has performed relatively strongly in measures of urban economic development as measured by gross state income (GSI) per capita and employment. Other indices (such as Year 9 education outcomes, health costs, homelessness, and energy efficiency) have also fared well. NSW also has generally strong results on good governance (transparency and accountability), electoral integrity and public finance measures.	Compared to other states, the NSW State Government has performed relatively poorly in measures of regional development and employment, regional health outcomes, and urban housing stock and rental stress.

Future opportunities	Future threats
NSW is uniquely placed to benefit economically from the global move towards carbon neutrality due to a large (and windy) land mass, high solar radiation, plentiful ocean access and strong human capital to form the basis of innovation in carbon abatement technologies and regenerative agriculture.	A coherent and coordinated strategy that defines clear goals and corresponding policy settings for the path to achieving net zero emissions is needed as soon as possible and preferably by 2050.
Outcome-driven policy, program and service management and measurement will lead to better outcomes for citizens and increased public sector productivity.	Policy-program-service fragmentation will continue to increase the costs of delivery and fail to deliver good outcomes for citizens.
Legislative and resource support for oversight and integrity agencies will enable the suppression of administrative and political misconduct.	Continuing pressure on transparency, oversight, integrity and accountability mechanisms might lead to a slump in or the collapse of public trust.
Regional growth in Sydney regional and coastal corridors provides an opportunity for attracting skilled migrants.	Lack of investment in regional infrastructure may undermine growth opportunities.
Bridging the capability deficits in the NSW Public Service is needed to build professional skills and a diverse and inclusive, digitally literate workforce, which is led with integrity and *communicates* with influence.	The state public service has sometimes failed to compete for highly skilled knowledge workers. A failure to address the issue of increasing wage inequality may also exacerbate the size of the urban and regional poor and undermine social cohesion.
There is potential to leverage off the NSW public service footprint to promote localism.	Continued disconnection of the 'Sydney village' from regional Australia leads to increased public distrust and escalating costs of delivery.
Building on successful COVID-19 experimentation may help establish new productive ways of working.	The escalation of the cyber-security threat to the security of the NSW government information management systems is worrying.
Exploiting the opportunities afforded by advances in digital technology could enhance real-time decision-making and improve the 'end-to-end' quality of the service experience.	The persistence of the US–China–Australia trade war meant that two-way trade with China declined 3 per cent in 2020, totalling A$245 billion (Australia's global two-way trade declined 13 per cent during this period).

The chapter will now consider four more detailed aspects of democracy in NSW – the state's (static) constitution, how well parties have represented citizens and communities, the role of parliament in holding ministers to account, and the operations of the core executive and public services.

Constitutional containment

Normally written constitutions are made deliberately hard to change as a means of stabilising fundamental political arrangements against poorly considered or ill-advised changes. However, the NSW Constitution is relatively easy to change as the *Constitution Act 1902* can be modified by simple majorities of both Houses. Since 2019, two such changes have been made to the *Constitution Act 1902* by an ordinary amendment Act in Parliament, both of them responding to issues around the management of the COVID-19 pandemic (NSW Legislation, no date). One change in 2020 enabled persons previously required to be physically present under the *Constitution Act 1902* to be present in other ways (allowing MPs to attend digitally) and it also enabled Bills to pass without actually being physically presented in person to the Governor. After 18 months, these provisions were repealed and then extended via a new constitution amendment act (NSW Government, 2021).

With these minor exceptions, however, there have been no recent reviews of the NSW Constitution despite evidence of strong public support for constitutional change in two areas – protecting and advancing the rights of Aboriginal and Torres Strait Islander Peoples; and the idea of a state-level Bill or Charter of Human Rights, perhaps on the lines of those already on the statue book in Victoria, Queensland and the ACT (see Chapter 3).

Aboriginal and Torres Strait Islander Peoples

In 2023, there were 255,000 First Nations citizens in NSW, more than any other state by a long way, and five times the number in neighbouring Victoria (Australian Bureau of Statistics, 2023). First Nations Peoples formed 4.1 per cent of the state population, slightly higher than the national average. Some fairly recent NSW legislation promoted the rights of First Nations Australians, such as the *Aboriginal Languages Act 2017* (NSW Government, 2017). It provided for the establishment of an Aboriginal Languages Trust to facilitate and support Aboriginal language activities to reawaken, protect and grow them. It also mandated the development of a strategic plan for the further nurturing of these languages. This is an important issue for First Nations Peoples, since there are a great many Aboriginal languages (between 250 and 363), each freighted with distinctive cultural heritage and associated with a distinct community and area of the country. Historically many languages have been lost or are now spoken by very few people. In NSW there are three 'living languages' spoken by more than 100 people (Wikipedia, 2023b).

On the idea of a state treaty with First Nations Peoples, up to 2023 Liberal-National Coalition ministers had not commenced any process to negotiate such a treaty, in contrast to some other states and territories (for example, Victoria, Queensland and the ACT). However, the Labor opposition's 2019 election manifesto included a commitment to begin a treaty process (Guardian, 2018). In March 2021, 63 per cent of NSW survey respondents supported a constitutional voice for Australia's First Nations Peoples (Deem, Brown and Bird, 2021). In early 2023, the Coalition ruled out any state treaty with First Nations people (Guardian, 2023a). The state Australian Labor Party (ALP) manifesto included a plan for 'a pathway to a treaty' once in government (O'Neill, 2023), promising a year-long consultation process, set back by the loss of the national Voice referendum in 2023 (see Chapters 3 and 4).

Charter/Bill of Rights debate

Australia remains one of the few common law countries without a Bill of Rights, although Victoria, Queensland and the ACT have human rights acts (see Chapter 3). Surveys of Australian people have shown increasing majorities of respondents endorsing the idea of a Bill of Rights, with support growing especially among younger age groups (Human Rights Law Centre, 2021). However, the tradition of strong executive government in NSW has generally militated against either of the top two parties being keen to progress the issue at state level. A Standing Committee on Law and Justice was established in early 2001 to explore the case for a NSW Bill of Rights. In October the same year its report asserted that:

> ... it is not in the public interest to enact a statutory Bill of Rights. Its finding is based upon the undesirability of handing over primary responsibility for the protection of human rights to an unelected judiciary who are not directly accountable to the community for the consequences of their decisions. The Committee believes an increased politicisation of the Judiciary, and particularly the judicial appointment process, is a likely and detrimental consequence of a Bill of Rights. The independence of the Judiciary and the supremacy of a democratically elected Parliament are the foundations of the current system. The Committee believes both could be undermined by a Bill of Rights. (Standing Committee on Law and Justice, 2001)

Thrust into renewed prominence by the COVID-19 experience, the rights landscape in NSW remains a complex and fragmented one to describe, but seems to work reasonably well in protecting mainstream rights (Cho, 2022) rather than the rights of minorities (see Chapter 2).

Political parties and community representation

Comparative evidence suggests that (in theory) parties and the politicians who represent them perform three sets of *overlapping* and *reinforcing* functions in a democratic political system – governance, community linkage and integrity roles. In terms of their governance role: they support the recruitment, selection and development of political leaders for government; formulate viable policy agendas and frame political choices; and form governments, or, when not in power, hold governments accountable. The community linkage role involves expressing broad values and ideological positions to capture the wider concerns of citizens and educating citizens about political issues. Traditionally this role would also include supporting the recruitment, selection and development of local political leaders. And, perhaps most significantly, political parties are supposed to be guardians of liberal democratic norms and values, organisations that uphold the highest standards of conduct in public life. This is termed the 'integrity' role, and it plays a crucial role in linking state and local politics and maintaining trust between government and citizen.

The evidence from NSW outlined above suggests it is the integrity role of parties that has been most in decline in state parties, below the level of legislators or ministers. Critics allege that the 'New South Wales Labor Party is wildly corrupt' and that 'Thanks to gerrymandered and malapportioned [internal] party elections, the New South Wales branch is dominated by factional power brokers and bureaucrats' (Chiu, 2022). In 2021, the ICAC investigated whether state branch officials of the ALP, members of the Chinese Friends of Labor, political donors and others had entered into, or carried out, a scheme to circumvent prohibitions or requirements of the legislation relating to political donations. Other local-level scandals have related to Labor 'branch stacking' (artificially enlarging the membership to win a seat nomination) and allegations of Liberal Party members on a local council receiving funds to be friendly to a Sydney developer (Australian Financial Review, 2023). At the senior party levels, on the Liberal side several ministers were investigated by the ICAC during the 2019–2023 government and in 2021 the state premier resigned over misconduct. The ICAC later declared the misbehaviour involved as corruption after its investigation, a verdict that the new Labor premier refused to endorse to the media.

Integrity problems inside the top two parties have not translated into problems with elections themselves, however. The state's independent Electoral Commission is responsible for conducting, regulating and reporting on general elections and by-elections for the NSW Parliament (NSW Electoral Commission, 2023b). Its brief includes:

- running independent, fair and accessible elections
- providing transparent processes and guidance to assist political participants (including candidates, parties, elected members, donors, third-party campaigners and lobbyists) to comply with their legal obligations
- publishing political donation and expenditure disclosures and registers of political parties, candidates, agents, third-party campaigners and political lobbyists
- engaging with the public to make it easier for people to understand and participate in the democratic process
- investigating possible offences and enforcing breaches of electoral, funding and disclosure, and lobbying laws
- maintaining the electoral roll.

The Electoral Commission compiles reports for parliament and maintains a register of political donations and electoral expenditure disclosures demonstrating that elections and the regulation of political parties are impartially conducted, with integrity (NSW Electoral Commission, 2023c).

As in other Australian states, the NSW political parties have played a critically important role in promoting electoral competition and citizen participation but have performed poorly on some 'shaping' aspects. For instance, in terms of ensuring gender equality in the legislature, Figure 17.7 illustrates the scope of the continuing under-representation of women in parliament, with a 59/41 per cent male/female ratio in the LA, and a 71/29 per cent ratio in the LC (Parliament of NSW, 2023). Helped by setting a quota for women, Labor has been further ahead in ensuring equality in the LA, with the Liberals previously lagging. But the former Premier Gladys Berejiklian said that she was now open-minded on introducing quotas in the Liberal Party, because party targets to increase the number of women candidates had failed (Sydney Morning Herald, 2021b). In 2019, Berejiklian became the first female NSW premier to win a general election, a major milestone both for her personally and for NSW women in politics.

The representation of First Nations peoples, and those of Australian Chinese or Australian Indian identity, has historically been scarce in the membership of both chambers (Parliament of Australia, 2017). There were only two First Nations members of the NSW LA up to 2023, despite having the largest and fastest growing Aboriginal and Torres Strait Islander population in the country as a whole. There were no Australian Chinese or Australian Indian members, despite these groups being the fastest growing populations in NSW (and indeed across Australia).

Figure 17.7: Women members in the NSW Parliament in 2023

Party	Legislative Assembly (LA) (93 members)		Legislative Council (LC) (42 members)	
	2019–2022	2023 on	2019–2022	2023 on
Labor	17	22	4	6
Liberal	10	9	2	6
National	3	2	2	2
Greens	2	3	5	4
Others	1	2	1	2
All women	**33** 35 per cent	**38** 41 per cent	**14** 33 per cent	**20** 48 per cent

Source: Parliament of NSW (2023) 'Women members in the NSW Parliament: statistics, as at 9 May'.

Parliament and the executive

As in other states, the LA is where the state premier and ministers sit and where the government party has normally had a majority, as it did this century up to 2019. Strong party whipping in the house means that executive decisions can be scrutinised by the main opposition at question time and in debates, but ministers are normally protected from any censure or criticism, unless on matters attracting bi-partisan dissent. Legislation also generally goes through the LA with only government-side amendments, but since bills also have to pass the LC, ministers may make more concessions with this in mind. This pattern changes somewhat when the governing party has no LA majority on its own, as is the case following the 2023 election, where Labor and Greens had to negotiate a coalition agreement. From 2019, the Liberal-National Coalition government previously had a majority of just one, but negotiated extra support from among the 'other' MPs to cushion this margin.

Debates in the LA pretty much follow the Australian norm of vigorous argument and language deployed in an adversarial manner, but rarely shedding much additional illumination on policy issues. There are exceptions to this pattern, often occurring where ministers introduce a bill 'nailing their colours to the mast' in the usual manner, but then run into difficulties with a powerful interest group linked to the governing party or crossbenchers. Blunt cites the example of the NSW Government's Police Death and Disability Bill 2011, which saw a two-week period between the Bill being introduced and debate resuming. He writes:

> *During the intervening period there was clearly a great deal of activity, lobbying and negotiations, particularly involving the Police Association. Indeed throughout the final sitting week of the year, a negotiating team from the Police Association were frequently seen in the parliamentary cafeteria between meetings with cross bench members and government officials.* (Blunt, 2014)

In May 2023, the new Assembly speaker, Independent MP Greg Piper, declared his intention to 'bring the "bear pit" out of the gutter', promising to 'prioritise improving parliamentary workplace safety and removing the "venom" from debate' (Guardian, 2023b). He also pledged action on issues about improper conduct towards women MPs and parliamentary employees raised in the previous period.

The full house LA debates are also underpinned by a well-developed and active committee system. In the 2015–2020 period, Figure 17.8 shows that there were on average over 20 hearings, spanning nearly 80 hours and covering hundreds of submissions and witnesses. While the 2020–2022 pandemic had a significant impact on how the Committee system operated, activity levels stayed high, thanks to video-conferencing.

Full house debates are more restrained in the LC, as befits a house of review, and policy issues are sometimes better explored during the passage of legislation. The upper house also has a committee system that was very active in a scrutiny role over the COVID-19 period. The Select Committee on the LC Committee system reported in November 2016 that:

Figure 17.8: The activities of the NSW's Legislative Assembly committee system, 2015–2020

Activity	Five years, 2015–20	
	Total	Annual average
Submissions	3,178	636
Witnesses	1,145	229
Meetings	511	102
Hearing hours	391	78
Reports	147	29
Hearings	102	20

Source: Parliament of NSW (2016) Select Committee on the Legislative Council Committee System.

> ... the Legislative Council committee system is working well and generally meeting its objectives. Nevertheless, a small number of issues emerged during the inquiry requiring further attention. These include the perceived need for the Legislative Council to play a more significant role in legislative scrutiny, the framework for committee powers, the duration of Budget Estimates hearings and the efficacy of the government response process. (Parliament of NSW, 2016)

The Select Committee also noted that the quality of parliamentary debate is still to be measured in both houses with any degree of sophistication – an issue that all parliaments struggle with – which means that we do not have a complete data set on the quality of executive scrutiny (see also Blunt, 2014).

COVID-19 changes and connecting with citizens

Generally acting in a bi-partisan manner parliament responded effectively to the challenges posed by COVID-19. The lower house Speaker noted in his 2019–2020 Annual Report that '... the LA did far more than simply manage during the pandemic. Rather, the staff and Members of the Assembly used the opportunities of 2020 to innovate ...' (Parliament of NSW, 2020a). This included using the change imperative of social distancing to modernise working practices through pairing arrangements, the development of a new e-Divisions app to support 'walk-through' divisions and reliable digital record-keeping, including a new Running Record. When the public galleries closed, the LA was also able to pivot live-streaming via social media and digitised video tours of the Chamber and hearings and meetings were transitioned to virtual platforms.

Possibly the most innovative response to COVID-19 by Parliament was the development of a new e-petitions platform described as a 'Covid-safe opportunity for citizens to collect signatures digitally instead of in-person and on paper'. This engagement instrument will also help parliament to connect better with NSW citizens in remote and regional areas. However, despite this recent advance Parliament still has a very traditional approach to connecting with NSW citizens. In 2020, the Parliament of NSW (2020b) published a Communications, Engagement and Education Strategy. However, there was general agreement that the state parliament had to improve its work in this area. The 2019–2020 Annual Report of the LA noted:

> We have both a duty and a desire to engage with the public we represent and to ensure that they are aware of and understand the Assembly's role and work; and just as importantly that they are encouraged to get involved and participate in that work if they wish. It is only through promoting the work of the Assembly, building awareness of the benefits of a successful democracy, and providing real opportunities for engagement that trust and confidence in processes and the Parliament of NSW is maintained. Specific initiatives for 2020/21 reporting year will include developing a range of outreach activities in metropolitan and regional areas that connect people of all backgrounds with the Assembly, its Committees and our elected representatives. (Parliament of NSW, 2020a)

The core executive, premier and government

After the long-running, four-term Labor premiership of Bob Carr (1995–2005) subsequent premiers have served for shorter periods of three to four years at most, but the top two parties have alternated in power in longer blocks of time, each with several changes of premier along the way, Labor from 1995–2012, and then the Liberal-National Coalition from 2012–2023. Since the state government controls a broad range of services that matter a great deal to NSW citizens, running the government involves keeping track of multiple policy areas simultaneously.

The 14 top policy priorities of Gladys Berejiklian's premiership are shown in Figure 17.9 to demonstrate that every state government sets out highly specific policy pledges, focusing on precise deliverables and on a quantitatively specified level of improvement promised. This approach reflected her Liberal-National Coalition government's public face commitments to being transparent and 'business-like' in improving government efficiency. The new Labor government from 2023 is likely to follow a similar stance on both fronts, reflecting an NSW state tradition of ministers embracing specific targets that are publicised to voters.

In addition, in September 2021, the Liberal-National Coalition government also committed to its 'Net Zero Plan Stage 1: 2020–2030' as the foundation for NSW's action on climate change. It seeks to deliver a 50 per cent cut in emissions by 2030 compared to 2005 levels (up from a previous emissions reduction target from 35 per cent. This ambitious move came at a time when the Liberal-National federal government remained publicly split on the issue, reflecting Australian states' ability to 'nudge' Commonwealth policy along, and the 'competition by comparison' that goes on among states.

In part, this approach reflects the confidence that single party governments with strong majorities can have that their measures will pass parliament. Ministers are accountable via Question Time and Assembly debates, but unless there are internal differences within the governing party, they are safe in office and rarely need to backtrack on their announced policies. Ministerial turnover is also moderate, although changes of state premier normally trigger some other consequential movements of portfolios. However, the structure of departments has been relatively stable, with one major exception, the creation of Services NSW,

Figure 17.9: The 14 policy priorities of Gladys Berejiklian's premiership

Lifting education standards

1. Increase the proportion of public school students in the top two NAPLAN [school assessment] bands (or equivalent) for literacy and numeracy by 15 per cent by 2023, including through statewide rollout of 'Bump It Up'.

2. Increase the proportion of Aboriginal students attaining year 12 by 50 per cent by 2023, while maintaining their cultural identity.

Keeping children safe

3. Decrease the proportion of children and young people re-reported at risk of significant harm by 20 per cent by 2023.

4. Double the number of children in safe and permanent homes by 2023 for children in, or at risk of entering, out-of-home care.

Breaking the cycle

5. Reduce the number of domestic violence reoffenders by 25 per cent by 2023.

6. Reduce adult reoffending following release from prison by 5 per cent by 2023.

7. Reduce street homelessness across NSW by 50 per cent by 2025.

Improving the health system

8. Improve service levels in hospitals: 100 per cent of all triage category 1, 95 per cent of triage category 2 and 85 per cent of triage category 3 patients commencing treatment on time by 2023.

9. Improve outpatient and community care: reduce preventable visits to hospital by 5 per cent through to 2023 by caring for people in the community.

10. Reduce the rate of suicide deaths in NSW by 20 per cent by 2023.

Better environment

11. Increase the proportion of homes in urban areas within 10 minutes' walk of quality green, open and public space by 10 per cent by 2023.

12. Increase the tree canopy and green cover across Greater Sydney by planting one million trees by 2022.

Better customer service

13. Increase the number of government services where citizens of NSW only need to 'Tell Us Once' by 2023.

14. Implement best-practice productivity and digital capability in the NSW public sector. Drive public sector diversity by 2025 through:

- having 50 per cent of senior leadership roles held by women
- increasing the number of Aboriginal Peoples in senior leadership roles
- ensuring 5.6 per cent of government sector roles are held by people with a disability.

discussed later in this chapter. Apart from the considerable integrity issues affecting ministers and politicians discussed earlier, the executive and public services operate within the law. In fact, recent executive decision-making has only been legally contested once. In 2017, some councils successfully challenged in the courts the executive's policy of pushing ahead council mergers, an embarrassing defeat (Sydney Morning Herald, 2017). No proceedings against ministerial actions were initiated by the Law Enforcement Conduct Commission, the NSW Ombudsman, or the Electoral Commission.

The Grattan Institute's (2018) State Orange Book provided a comparative assessment of the policy performance of Australia's states and territories. As one of the largest and richest states NSW might be expected to have performed well, as indeed it did on measures of urban economic development (as measured by GSI per capita and employment), improving Year 9 education outcomes, keeping down health costs, combatting homelessness, and promoting energy efficiency. However, the state did poorly in measures of regional development and employment (in more rural areas away from the Sydney conurbation) and regional health outcomes, and while urban housing stock grew insufficiently the levels of 'rental stress' increased. NSW also had the strongest results on good governance (transparency and accountability), electoral integrity and public finance measures.

NSW is statistically the most affluent state in Australia with balanced income (12 per cent) and wealth (13 per cent) and contributes over 50 per cent of Australia's gross domestic product (GDP) (McCrindle, 2023). It has 7 out of 10 of the richest suburbs, the largest infrastructure investments in the nation and a broad base of industries (Canstar, 2024). However, the same ranking shows that it also suffers from significant urban and regional poverty with 8 out of 10 of the poorest suburbs in Australia. Sydney dropped from third to eleventh in the 2021, *Economist's* 2021 Global Liveability Survey (Sydney Morning Herald, 2021c), but soon returned to fourth in 2023.

Outcomes-driven public service production

In 2013, the NSW public services began an evolution of the previous administrative model, a change that reflected the improvements made in digital and online services delivery. In a large state with huge regional areas far from the nearest state offices it made sense to enhance online services. The state also created in-person 'one-stop shops' and smaller part-time hubs in more accessible towns. Key to these changes was the creation of a single agency, called Services NSW. It specialised in services delivery across multiple portfolios or conventionally separate policy departments, and its service remit and website always sought to avoid being 'siloed'. Over time, a larger share of state services moved over to delivery via Services NSW. The service reported high levels of customer satisfaction for consumers (82 per cent) and businesses (81 per cent) in 2020, up slightly from 2016 (NSW Public Services Commission, 2021). But it also reported that more could be done to improve interactions between government and consumers and businesses. Six years after its start the same core ideas were also picked up by the Liberal-National Coalition government at federal level:

> *Services Australia will pick up its lead from a similar organisation established by the New South Wales Government called Services New South Wales, which I think has been a very important reform in New South Wales and made dealing with government much easier,' Morrison said. 'That's what we want government to be for Australians, we just want it to be much easier.* (Canberra Times, 2019)

The NSW public service is also committed to continuous improvement, periodically reflected in a range of commissioned reviews leading to tangible reforms in public service management and delivery, such as those on recruitment in 2018 and on state employment in 2020.

Australia has experienced over a decade of experimentation in outcomes performance management since the introduction of the Intergovernmental Agreement on Federal Financial Relations in 2008 heralded a new approach to negotiating, managing and monitoring the transfer of funds from the Commonwealth to the states and territories. In terms of better practice in Australia – the NSW government (working closely with Social Ventures Australia), has led the way in the transition to outcomes-driven performance management. Up to 2023, the NSW government had the most ambitious reform agenda, and had started reorganising its whole governance system around the achievement of politically mandated outcomes through clusters of agencies with shared outcomes and accountabilities underpinned by outcomes budgeting (for example, the 'stronger communities' cluster (Audit Office of NSW, 2019). In 2020–2021, the NSW government also introduced outcome budgeting (NSW Budget, 2022). There were 37 agreed outcomes, which covered the totality of all government activity, and had embedded in them the premier's 14 Priorities (see earlier, Figure 17.9).

Two senior NSW state government executives interviewed by the author in 2021 observed:

> This has been the biggest reform of NSW government since Federation but has largely gone on under the radar. (Executive 1)

> We feel empowered and liberated. We can focus on those things that matter most. It's very motivating. (Executive 2)

In addition, all the state executives interviewed for this chapter viewed high-quality collaboration between government and the community of practice as the key to achieving good program outcomes. One commented: 'It can only work through a co-governance approach.' They also observed that the same trust systems need to be built between Commonwealth and state governments to join up information management systems to enable a whole-system approach to outcomes measurement: 'This will allow us to target need and shift resources to where they can have best value' (*Executive 3*). Public service officials argue that it is the performance (supply) of government that matters most in orienting the outlooks of citizens and building trust, together with commitment to procedural fairness and equality.

Vertical fiscal imbalance

Although NSW is the largest economic actor in the federation, like all other states (except West Australia) it is acutely dependent on Commonwealth government transfers, since the federal government collects most of the largest and most buoyant taxes (see Chapter 16). An increased vertical fiscal imbalance within the federation has been caused by the Commonwealth incrementally accreting economic power, by engaging in policy domains not conferred upon it by the Constitution and using funding agreements to control policy systems and indicative programs. OECD data shows that from 1995–2017, the state and local share of expenditure by all Australian governments increased by 4.7 percentage points, but their share of national tax revenues fell by 3.1 percentage points. The gap between NSW's share of expenditure and share of tax revenue has widened more than any other advanced economy federation, and more than most unitary states tracked by the OECD.

In the aftermath of bushfires and COVID-19, the capacity of the NSW state government to meet the economic and social challenges of recovery was undermined by the restricted size of its tax revenue base. In August 2020, a Review Panel completed the *NSW Review of Federal Financial Relations*. It concluded that:

> … state and territory governments (collectively, 'the states') confront a significant decline in their tax revenues at the same time as they inject all of their fiscal firepower into the economy to avoid serious economic collapse. They now face an era of higher debt, challenging their ability to sustainably deliver essential services and infrastructure. With economic recovery now a priority, the question facing the Review is how state governments can provide taxpayers with reliable, quality government services, while keeping the taxes they pay as low as possible. (Thodey, 2021)

Conclusion

The evidence presented here suggests that the NSW Government appears Janus-faced, like its former premier, Gladys Berejiklian. She will be remembered as an intelligent, resilient, calm and highly effective politician caught up in a tissue of minor lies against her better judgement. The democratic system will of course survive, but this and other scandals have done nothing to quell the view that NSW politics continues to be a 'honey pot for the needy and greedy' at a time when it needs the moral authority to rise to the great challenges, from climate change to inequality, that they must confront. It is evident that a lack of integrity in public office in both the public sector and politics has become culturally embedded and is an issue of significant political salience. Nor is the composition of the NSW government and parliament yet representative of the community it serves either in gender or ethnic terms.

However, the state election of 2023 showed that voters were aware of problems and were prepared to take enough action to ensure that course corrections occurred. And perhaps change may also happen in the newly 'hung' legislature. In many other respects, NSW democratic institutions are in good shape with free and fair elections, close legislative, media and social media scrutiny of ministers, and an executive that has publicly committed to being accountable, transparent, responsive and effective. The NSW system of justice and integrity agencies has proved robust, independent and fair, and the public services have generally been run professionally and with some innovation and creativity.

Note

The author acknowledges the generous support of the NSW Parliamentary Research Service. However, responsibility for the interpretation of the evidence and data lies with him alone and is not the official position of the NSW Parliamentary Library.

References

Audit Office of NSW (2019) 'Stronger communities 2019', NSW Auditor-General's Report, 5 December. https://perma.cc/X6L6-9EZ5

Australian Bureau of Statistics (2023) 'Estimates of Aboriginal and Torres Strait Islander Australians', webpage, 21 September. https://perma.cc/7MB2-HCZH

Australian Financial Review (2023) 'ICAC raids homes of NSW Liberal members', *Australian Financial Review*, webpage, 16 April. https://perma.cc/WLD2-GCEG

Blunt, David (2014) 'Parliamentary speech and the locations of decision making'. Paper presented at the Australasian Study of Parliament Group, 2014 National Conference, Sydney, 2 October. Available at: https://perma.cc/53V2-4UVW

Canberra Times (2019) 'Public sector informant: Finding meaning in Scott Morrison's public service "pep talk"', *Canberra Times*, webpage, 3 June. https://perma.cc/9QN5-HK6M

Canstar (2024) 'Top 10 richest and poorest suburbs in Australia', webpage, 11 August. https://perma.cc/XL5Y-LMX8

Chiu, Osmond (2022) 'The New South Wales Labor Party is wildly corrupt. It needs democratic reform', *Jacobin*, webpage, 20 September. https://perma.cc/X8UE-NDKP

Cho, Josephy (2022) 'NSW parliament's oversight of human rights in the first year of the COVID-19 pandemic', *Alternative Law Journal*, March, vol. 47, no. 1, pp.67–73. https://doi.org/10.1177%2F1037969X211054574

Clune, David (2020) 'The long history of political corruption in NSW – and the downfall of MPs, ministers and premiers', *The Conversation*, 15 October. ABC News site. https://perma.cc/A8DM-WTSN

Clune, David (2021) 'Stadiums, bushfires and a pandemic: How will Gladys Berejiklian be remembered as premier?', *The Conversation*, 1 October. https://perma.cc/CGV8-N6AR

Deem, Jacob; Brown, AJ; and Bird, Susan (2021) 'Most Australians support First Nations Voice to parliament: Survey', *The Conversation, Australia,* 9 April. https://perma.cc/DQR4-XZ4Y

Gobbett, Hannah (2017) 'Indigenous parliamentarians, federal and state: A quick guide', Parliament of Australia webpage. https://perma.cc/S3YD-KEBX

Grattan Institute (2018) *State Orange Book 2018: Policy Priorities for States and Territories.* Institute Report. https://perma.cc/LHA3-2JQB

Graycar, Adam (2023) '"Grave misconduct": Gladys Berejiklian corruption report should put all public officials on notice', *The Conversation*, 29 June. https://perma.cc/R87Z-NS33

Guardian (2018) 'NSW Labor plans to sign treaty recognising Indigenous ownership', *Guardian*, Australia, webpage, 25 January. https://perma.cc/V68B-HFK3

Guardian (2021a) 'NSW MP Gareth Ward steps down as minister over sexual violence allegations which he denies', *Guardian, Australia,* 13 May. https://perma.cc/X9ZF-C43A

Guardian (2021c) 'Conservative warrior, economic reformer, premier? Meet Dominic Perrottet, NSW's likely next leader', *Guardian, Australia,* 4 October. https://perma.cc/BJ5U-4XJZ

Guardian (2021b) 'A person of high integrity': Hazzard praises Berejiklian and raises questions about Icac', *Guardian, Australia,* 3 October. https://perma.cc/AT8B-5U8N

Guardian (2023a) '"Not on the agenda": NSW minister rules out state treaty with First Nations people', *Guardian*, Australia, webpage, 9 March. https://perma.cc/QQG4-TNGP

Guardian (2023b) 'Likely NSW speaker Greg Piper wants to bring "bear pit" out of the gutter', *Guardian*, Australia, webpage,16 April. https://perma.cc/HL4M-279C

Human Rights Law Centre (2021) 'COVID-19 sees huge increase in support for a Charter of Human Rights: poll', Webpage. https://perma.cc/SD6Q-ZZAY

ICAC (Independent Commission Against Corruption) (No date) 'History and development of the ICAC Act', webpage. https://perma.cc/VT8X-5HGM

ICAC (Independent Commission Against Corruption) (2018) *Corruption and Integrity in the NSW Public Sector – An Assessment of Current Trends and Events.* Report of Independent Commission Against Corruption (NSW). https://perma.cc/J6T8-TGLM

ICAC (Independent Commission Against Corruption) (2019) 'ICAC finds DFSI ICT project manager corrupt after "hijacking" business name to obtain half-million dollar benefit', webpage. https://perma.cc/4F3X-2XJ8

ICAC (Independent Commission Against Corruption) (2020a) 'ICAC recommends changes to government water management in NSW after years of focus on irrigation industry interests', webpage, 27 November. https://perma.cc/673M-A8UD

ICAC (Independent Commission Against Corruption) (2020b) 'Former NSW MP for Wagga Wagga – allegations concerning breach of public trust and dishonest or partial exercise of official functions (Operation Keppel), completed investigation', webpage. https://perma.cc/ZMT9-ANYX

ICAC (Independent Commission Against Corruption) (2020c) 'ICAC finds former FACS officer corruptly obtained over $1.67 million for own company', webpage, 27 August. https://perma.cc/TKZ3-B7CE

ICAC (Independent Commission Against Corruption) (2021a) 'ICAC finds Service NSW officer corrupt over improper access of restricted database information and other conduct', webpage, 11 May. https://perma.cc/K4QX-4AFK

ICAC (Independent Commission Against Corruption) (2021b) 'Lobbying and the NSW public sector – the regulation of lobbying, access and influence in NSW (Operation Eclipse)', webpage. https://perma.cc/49WS-RLLL

ICAC (Independent Commission Against Corruption) (2022) 'NSW State Member for Drummoyne – allegations concerning improper influence and breach of public trust', webpage. https://perma.cc/RZW4-AMLK

McCrindle (2023) 'Income and wealth distribution by state', webpage. https://perma.cc/9NSN-AAEH

NSW Budget (2022) *NSW Budget 2022–23 No.02 Outcomes Statement Budget Paper,* NSW government report. https://perma.cc/EHR6-VYJQ

NSW Bushfire Inquiry (2020) *Final Report of the NSW Bushfire Inquiry,* 25 August, Department of Premier and Cabinet (NSW) Report. https://perma.cc/X5SL-P3LF Also at: https://perma.cc/2SYF-LFPL

NSW Electoral Commission (2023a) 'State election results', webpage. https://perma.cc/P8JU-KF5Q

NSW Electoral Commission (2023b) 'What we do', 23 August. webpage. https://perma.cc/AD3A-MBGC

NSW Electoral Commission (2023c) 'View disclosures', webpage. https://perma.cc/P8JU-KF5Q

NSW Government (2017) 'NSW legislation: Aboriginal Languages Act 2017 No 51', webpage. https://perma.cc/R9WG-HYDA

NSW Government (2021) 'Constitution Amendment (Virtual Attendance) Bill 2021', Webpage. https://perma.cc/32K6-MSNW

NSW Health (2022) 'Covid 19 in NSW', webpage, June. https://perma.cc/Q5HX-5LM7

NSW Legislation (no date) 'Constitution Act 1902 No 32', webpage. https://perma.cc/UCG9-JDL3

NSW Parliamentary Research Service (2021) 'The impact of the COVID-19 pandemic on parliament', ebrief no.1, webpage, July. https://perma.cc/DRL8-MCCT

NSW Public Services Commission (2020) *State of the NSW Public Sector Report 2020.* https://perma.cc/8WMS-QTN7

O'Neill, Marjorie (2023) 'NSW, pathway to treaty', ALP (Australian Labor Party) NSW webpage. https://perma.cc/RGD7-66CF

Parliament of Australia (2017) 'Indigenous parliamentarians, federal and state: A quick guide', webpage, 11 July. https://perma.cc/S3YD-KEBX

Parliament of NSW (2001) Inquiries 'A NSW Bill of Rights', 17 October, PDF report. https://perma.cc/J36P-AFAA

Parliament of NSW (2016) 'Select Committee on the Legislative Council Committee System report, *The Legislative Council committee system*'. 28 November. https://perma.cc/DU9G-4NYL

Parliament of NSW (2020a) *Annual Report for the Department of the Legislative Assembly 2019–2020.* https://perma.cc/Y7UA-MMPU

Parliament of NSW (2020b) *Communications, Engagement and Education Strategy,* webpage. https://perma.cc/U3KA-XJRS

Parliament of NSW (2021) 'Women in Parliament', Briefing Paper by Laura Ismay. https://perma.cc/EAZ3-RUQ3

Parliament of NSW (2023) 'Women members in the NSW Parliament - statistics', 9 May, Webpage. https://perma.cc/K3MW-BXW7

Pickrell, John (2020) 'Australian fires have incinerated the habitats of up to 100 threatened species', *Science News*, 13 January. https://perma.cc/338V-PC34

Savva, Niki (2020) 'Scott Morrison should follow Gladys Berejiklian's lead', *The Australian*, webpage, 12 March.

Scanlon Foundation (2021) *Mapping Social Cohesion – The Scanlon Foundation Surveys*, November. Commentary Andrew Markus, Melbourne, Monash University. https://perma.cc/MY4K-CQQ6

Standing Committee on Law and Justice (2001) 'A NSW Bill of Rights', NSW Parliament webpage, 3 October. https://perma.cc/J36P-AFAA

Sydney Morning Herald (2017) 'Council victories in final embarrassing merger defeat for government', 1 August, webpage. https://perma.cc/5F9X-H6WV

Sydney Morning Herald (2021a) 'Hazzard has 'strong views' of how ICAC should work', Sydney Morning Herald, webpage, 3 October. https://perma.cc/PES8-5YKG

Sydney Morning Herald (2021b) 'Premier says she is open to quotas because targets to increase women have failed', 24 March webpage. https://perma.cc/FLS8-L9NR

Sydney Morning Herald (2021c) 'Premier says she is open to quotas because targets to increase women have failed', 24 March webpage. https://perma.cc/F8LZ-3TV7

Thodey, David (2021) *NSW Review of Federal Financial Relations – Supporting the Road to Recovery*, Report to NSW Treasury. https://perma.cc/5VKF-U5QF

Tiffen, Rodney (2021) 'Was Neville Wran corrupt?', *Inside Story*, webpage, 31 August. https://perma.cc/H77A-L9RT

Wikipedia (2023a) 'Corruption in Australia', webpage. https://perma.cc/3HV8-U74B

Wikipedia (2023b) 'Australian Aboriginal languages', webpage. https://perma.cc/PJQ8-LTLP

Wood, Justice James Roland (1997) *Royal Commission into The New South Wales Police Service: Final Report*, May 1997, Australian Police. https://perma.cc/LL28-F2EG

18

Victoria

Tom Daly and James Murphy

Victoria is one of the two largest, earliest developed and economically richest Australian states (generating a quarter of national gross domestic product (GDP)). With a population of 6.6 million people, heavily concentrated in the Melbourne conurbation, the state nonetheless has a land area exceeding 227,000 sq kms, much of it bush. Though its party system took longer to settle than other Australian jurisdictions, its political control has swung between the top two political parties, with Labor dominant in recent times and the state government taking a robust and distinctive line during the COVID-19 pandemic. With a bicameral parliament (comprising the Legislative Assembly (LA) and the Legislative Council (LC)) and a mature public service, the state has played an important role in shaping overall Australian political trends, partly because its Constitution is relatively easily amended by a simple majority vote in both houses.

What does a democratic state government require?

Key elements include:

- An effective state constitution that provides an anatomy of legitimate public power to: define the limits of state governmental powers; make government accountable to the people by providing for checks and balances; promote long-term structures. A constitution typically (i) lasts for an indefinite term; (ii) is difficult to change; and (iii) reflects a consensus among those who are subject to its limits and afforded its protections. It condenses the preferences, values and views of the state's people; provides legal authority for the exercise of governmental powers; specifies the civil and human rights of all citizens; and, creates (or clarifies) any (legal) duties/obligations that the government must observe or satisfy. The state's relationship with the Commonwealth government is governed by the federal constitution.

- Rights for Aboriginal and Torres Strait Islander Peoples should be fully recognised and implemented as for all citizens. The histories, languages, cultures, rights and needs of Aboriginal and Torres Strait Islander communities and peoples should be addressed, so as to remedy historical injustices and establish a meaningful degree of self-government.

How to cite this chapter:

Daly, Tom and Murphy, James (2024) 'Victoria', in: Evans, Mark; Dunleavy, Patrick and Phillimore, John (eds) *Australia's Evolving Democracy: A New Democratic Audit*, London: LSE Press, pp.392–414. **https://doi.org/10.31389/lsepress.ada.r**. Licence: CC-BY-NC 4.0

- Electoral systems for the state's LA and LC should accurately translate parties' votes into seats, in different ways that are recognised as legitimate by most citizens. Ideally the voting systems should foster the overall social representativeness of the two houses of the legislature. Elections and the regulation of political parties should be impartially conducted, with integrity.
- Political parties at state level should sustain vigorous and effective electoral competition and citizen participation. They should enable the recruitment, selection and development of political leaders for state government; formulate viable policy agendas and frame political choices for state functions; and form governments or, when not in power, hold governments accountable. Political parties should uphold the highest standards of conduct in public life.
- The core executive and government should operate fully within the law, and ministers should be effectively scrutinised by and politically accountable to Parliament. Ministers and departments/agencies must also be legally accountable to independent courts for their conduct and policy decisions. Responsive government should prioritise the public interest and reflect state public opinion. Its core executive (premier, cabinet, ministers and key central departments) should provide clear unification of public policies across government, so that the state operates as an effective whole. Both strategic decision-making within the core executive, and more routine policy-making, should foster careful deliberation to establish an inclusive view of the 'public interest'.
- The administration of public services should be subject to appropriate control by democratically elected officials as far as possible. Officials in state public services should act with integrity, impartiality, in accordance with well-enforced codes of conduct and within the rule of law. The rights of all citizens should be carefully protected in policy-making, and 'due process' rules followed, with fair and equal public consultation on public service changes. Public services, contracting, regulation and planning/zoning decisions should be completely free from corruption.

State governments have considerable (but not total) control over major services like education, healthcare, transport and emergency services that matter greatly to citizens, and they make regulations on key economic areas of great significance for enterprises and civil society. These roles were especially emphasised by developments in crisis management and issues relating to constitutional change. We begin with these recent events, before moving to a more systematic (SWOT) analysis of strengths and weaknesses of democratic control. The last part of the chapter looks at some key long-term issues in more detail.

Recent developments

The state governments bear the primary responsibility for responding to severe domestic crises, most commonly environmental developments like fires and flooding, which regularly threaten life and limb across Australia, but also encompassing public health emergencies. These roles were especially and almost continuously salient for the Victorian government from 2019 to early 2023, first with bushfires and later with the COVID-19 pandemic. We also briefly consider issues around constitutional changes.

The 2019 to 2020 bushfire emergency

Bushfires have been highly salient in Victorian politics, particularly since the catastrophe of 'Black Saturday' in February 2009, when 117 people died in more than 400 fires across the state within a couple of days, Australia's highest-ever direct loss of life from bushfires (Ambrey, Fleming and Manning, 2017). Following a major Royal Commission many changes were implemented in state response systems (Victoria Bushfire Royal Commission, 2010). The improved systems generally worked well from November 2019 to February 2020, when fires in eastern Victoria as well as neighbouring New South Wales burnt over 1.5 million hectares. An estimated 60,000 people were evacuated from East Gippsland, an extensive diversity of wildlife perished, and the bushfires affected 1,000 registered Aboriginal heritage sites (Victoria Government, 2023a). This time only five people died directly in fire, but 300 homes were destroyed, insurance costs ran to A$18.6 million, and another 120 people were estimated to have died later from conditions worsened by bushfire smoke effects (AIDR, 2023).

The response of the state premier, Labor's Daniel Andrews, was deemed by some observers to be 'professional, calm, empathetic and commanding' and 'competent' (ABC, 2020a), based on a decade of preparations and institutional reforms in Victoria for large-scale fires (Towell, 2020). That said, the final report of an independent inquiry into the 2019–2020 bushfires, completed by the Inspector-General for Emergency Management in July 2021, indicated a need to strengthen resilience before, during and after emergencies (IGEM, 2021). The Victorian government accepted all 15 recommendations in the report and committed to a further reform program for the state's emergency management sector.

The COVID-19 pandemic

While the bushfires were generally handled in a consensual manner, the COVID-19 pandemic generated much greater controversy around the core executive's emergency response (Melbourne Law School, 2021). In mid-March 2020, ministers declared a 'State of Emergency' and imposed a succession of emergency measures, including mask and social distancing mandates, lockdowns and curfews (Big Australia, 2021). These measures were in place intermittently from March 2020 to late October 2021, restricting public gatherings and barring individuals from leaving their homes except under a strict set of limits. During this time, Melbourne endured 'the world's longest COVID-19 lockdown', a total of 262 days or almost nine months (Reuters, 2021). Although not subjected to the same level of restrictions, regional Victoria was also subject to social distancing and mask mandates, and occasional lockdowns (ABC, 2021a).

Opponents of these measures quickly mounted intense criticisms of them, frequently focused personally on the state Premier Andrews. Critics developed a 'Dictator Dan' narrative in which he and the Labor government were portrayed as following an authoritarian agenda (Washington Post, 2020). More measured criticism focused on a number of policy failures, such as ineffective privatised hotel quarantine (Rundle, 2020), the premier's personal dominance of the emergency response (Pesutto, 2020), and the disproportionate impact of an excessive focus on policing on First Nations and other minority communities during lockdowns (Liberty Victoria, 2021). An indication of the stringency of state actions was a rapid 'hard lockdown' imposed on 3,000 residents of public housing towers in Melbourne in July 2020 to suppress the spread of COVID-19. This last measure was deemed by the state ombudsman to be contrary to rights protected by Victoria's Charter of Human Rights and Responsibilities (VEOHRC,

2023), such as the freedom of movement and right to liberty (Victoria Ombudsman, 2020). A December 2020 report concluded:

> Despite the best efforts of those on the ground, the early days of the lockdown were chaotic: people found themselves without food, medication and other essential supports. Information was confused, incomprehensible, or simply lacking. On the ground few seemed to know who was in charge. No access to fresh air and outdoor exercise was provided for over a week. In a particularly unfortunate act, temporary fencing for an exercise area was erected one night, surrounded by police, and although quickly taken down, reinforced the residents' sense of being imprisoned. (Victoria Ombudsman, 2020)

Despite broad early acquiescence to the lockdowns (Guardian, 2020a), public protests grew from small gatherings in September 2020 (Guardian, 2020b) to thousands in October and November 2021 (ABC News, 2021b). Later protests were ostensibly objecting to vaccine mandates and proposed legislation to overhaul the framework for pandemic responses (the 'Pandemic Bill' (Victorian Legislation, 2021) discussed later in this chapter). However, they were also fuelled by a mixture of conspiracy theories and misinformation concerning lockdown, vaccines and the nature of the proposed laws (Thomas, 2021). Observers noted an intensifying rhetoric of retribution against the executive, with small groups of protesters displaying violent imagery and chanting death threats against the premier and government, and clashing with police, with little appeal to reason or meaningful alternative proposals (The Age 2021b).

However, Victoria's experience with COVID-19 rates was also seen as a strong policy success internationally, with only 143,000 cases occurring from March 2020 to December 2021, resulting in 1,443 lives lost (or 217 cases per million people). In the same period, nearly 129,000 people recovered. The state also administered 16.3 million COVID-19 tests. Polling evidence found that when samples of Victoria adults were asked 'How well is your state government responding to the pandemic?' in July 2020, 62 per cent said, 'very well' or 'fairly well'. This clear majority view nonetheless compared poorly to levels of 80–95 per cent in other Australian states.

The later vaccination push (which mandated vaccination for visitors to many health, social care and governmental office settings) was met with virulent opposition by the state's numerous but minority anti-vaccine campaigners. Yet the overwhelming majority of people agreed with the vaccination push and by November 2021 over 88 per cent of Victoria's adult population had received two vaccine doses, among the highest rates achieved either in Australia or internationally (Department of Health, 2021). Following the rollout of the vaccine, by November 2021 polling respondents rating the state government response as 'very' or 'fairly good' rose to 80 per cent (although this was still below rates of 88 per cent to 97 per cent in other states). The government was also viewed as having shown transparency in its pandemic response, including establishing an official inquiry into the hotel quarantine system, which reported in December 2020 (Quarantine Inquiry, 2020). Ministers also made amendments to legislation proposed in late 2021 in response to criticisms.

Victoria also kept in place many COVID-19 restrictions longer than other jurisdictions, easing most lockdown restrictions (for example, to allow recreational visits between families or neighbours) only in May 2022, and ending the declaration of a pandemic in September that year – while still requiring vaccination in state government settings. As in other places where severe restrictions were eased, 2022 saw a growth of infections (often among unvaccinated or only partly vaccinated people), eventually pushing Victoria's COVID-19 death toll above 6,600 people by January 2023 (Victoria Department of Health, 2024).

The Pandemic Bill

Although it was not itself a constitutional amendment, significant controversy surrounded the government proposal in late October 2021 of new legislation, the Public Health and Wellbeing Amendment (Pandemic Management) Bill 2021 ('the Pandemic Bill'). It significantly changed the legal framework governing health emergencies and the powers of the executive. The power to declare a pandemic was transferred from the chief health officer to the premier; permitted the state's pandemic status to be declared for up to three months at a time with no outer limit; provided wide powers to a health minister to make public health orders; expanded detention powers; and created an independent Pandemic Management Advisory Committee, with members including public health, human rights and community representatives.

Non-partisan analysts and public law academics recognised the Victorian government's claims that the Pandemic Bill initially presented had significantly improved the current pandemic law by clarifying the legal authority for the exercise of governmental powers and safeguarding democracy and human rights, including greater considerations for transparency around key decision-making, personal information protection, better oversight and scrutiny processes, and a fairer approach to sanctions for health order breaches (Melbourne Law School, 2021). However, they also strongly urged further amendments, particularly more parliamentary oversight, strengthening protections for the right to protest, and appeal of detention orders.

In the conventional political arena, the Liberal-National opposition decried the Pandemic Bill as a 'draconian' measure (The Age 2021a; The Age, 2021b). One MP, David Davis, even tabled a constitutional amendment Bill in the LA to require a 60 per cent special majority approval in both houses of parliament before a state of emergency (or a disaster) could be declared or renewed, which inevitably failed (Australasian Lawyer, 2021). However, in response to opposition, media and public criticisms, the government announced a range of proposed amendments in November 2021 (HRLC, 2021). These included a legal requirement that the premier must be satisfied on 'reasonable grounds' that a serious risk to public health exists before declaring any pandemic. There was also express recognition that the Charter of Human Rights and Responsibilities applies to pandemic restrictions.

We discuss in the section on elections (after the SWOT) how the trials and controversies over COVID-19 policies affected the Andrews government. Labor suffered a 6 per cent loss of primary AV votes support in the November 2022 state elections, chiefly to the Greens and the Liberal opposition. But at the second preferred vote stage, Labor managed to contain this loss with transferred votes from the Greens and others, so that it retained largest party status and hence ministerial office in the lower house of the state legislature.

Constitutional and legal changes

As in some other Australian states (like New South Wales) the COVID-19 pandemic raised issues about how the Constitution of Victoria can generally be amended by a simple majority passing a Bill in both houses of Parliament to change aspects of the *Constitution Act 1975*. There are some exceptions, including provisions requiring a more stringent procedure such as a public referendum (for example, for altering the number of MPs in the LA). A special majority of three-fifths of members in both houses is needed for the third reading of some specific bills (for example, amending provisions on eligibility to vote).

In fact the one amendment to the Constitution passed by parliament in 2021–2023 (Victorian Legislation, 2023) concerned a different issue, placing a permanent ban on unconventional gas extraction through hydraulic fracturing – 'fracking' – on grounds of environmental protection (Premier, Victoria, 2021). The ban met the Andrews Labor government's 2018 election pledge to entrench a legislative ban on fracking in the state constitution. It followed a long-term campaign that included 26 local councils expressing concerns over fracking, and 75 regional communities declaring themselves gas field and coal free (Melbourne FOE, 2021). There was also a government 'Inquiry into Unconventional Gas in Victoria' in (Parliament of Victoria, 2015). The costitutional ban was condemned by the Institute of Public Affairs (IPA) think-tank as an unprecedented 'autocratic, illiberal and undemocratic' policy restriction on future governments' freedom of manoeuvre (IPA, 2021). However, it was a manifesto pledge and enjoyed significant support among environmental campaigners, farmers, and the public (ABC, 2017).

Strengths, weaknesses, opportunities, and threats (SWOT) analysis

Current strengths	Current weaknesses
Elections in Victoria are free and fair, and their conduct has strong quality assurance underpinning its electoral process through an independent Electoral Commission.	Turnout among some groups, especially First Nations citizens and those from non-English-speaking backgrounds, is lower, even with compulsory voting. This feeds through into reduced participation by such groups in wider political life.
Party competition in Victoria is vigorous and transfers of government occur periodically between the top parties, Labor and the Liberal-National Coalition. The main parties are effective in recruiting people to run for political office and structuring elections so that voters have clear choices.	Issues such as 'branch stacking' within parties present a weakness in standards. Evidence suggests that they have the potential to seriously damage trust in parties, parliament and government (see below).
The AV system for Victoria's lower house almost always awards most seats and majority control of government to the party winning most (TPP stage) votes, in line with majoritarian principles.	Under AV smaller parties find it hard to win lower house seats. The disproportionality of the voting system grows when they win more support.
The balance of press alignments at elections in Victoria are more even than elsewhere since *The Age* in Melbourne is Australia's most important national paper taking an independent line.	Media partisanship at election time in Victoria is strong, with the Murdoch press and to a lesser degree Sky News, always strongly aligned behind the Liberal-National Coalition parties.

The proportional representation, single transferable vote (PR–STV) system for upper house (LC) elections gives smaller parties a better chance of winning seats, and they quite often hold the balance of power.	LC elections tend to create 'safe' seats for major parties, limiting accountability. They also use the group voting ticket (GVT) system, abolished in much of Australia due to its vulnerability to 'preference harvesting', and subsequent election of members off minuscule primary votes (for example, the Democratic Labour Party in 2022).
The state parliament (and particularly the upper house) is broadly effective in holding the executive to account and has taken significant operational measures to continue functioning during crisis.	The pandemic demonstrated that to keep parliament fully running during emergencies it needed new solutions, including the use of hybrid models, mixing in-person and remote attendance.
The LA's committee system has generally met its scrutiny objectives, for example, in conducting timely inquiries into the executive's COVID-19 response.	Public participation in the state parliament's deliberations remains under-developed.
The state government has shown an effective core executive under alternative parties and sets of ministers. The government showed creativity in adapting its operations to address crisis challenges in 2019–2022, including managing sometimes tense relations with federal government ministers.	Concerns were raised regarding the centralisation of executive power during the COVID-19 pandemic, including through proposed legislation to reform the legal framework for emergencies.
The state government has performed well on some measures, such as economic development (for example, youth unemployment), education (for example, Year 9 education outcomes), health (for example, mortality rates), and transparency and accountability.	Ministers and state agencies have performed less well or poorly on some issues, such as regional incomes, government funding to state schools and rental stress in housing.
The public service met crisis challenges successfully through embracing a flexible and data-driven approach, by adapting its structures and lines of accountability, and investing in digital transformation.	Ombudsman's reports have suggested that public agencies still had much to do to understand the basic human rights guaranteed by the Victorian Charter of Rights and Responsibilities, especially in improving training. They have also criticised creeping politicisation of public sector appointments over recent years.
Concrete steps taken toward the negotiation of a treaty with the state's First Nation peoples present a positive development.	Indigenous communities have suffered inequities in outcomes across a range of wellbeing indicators.
Local government benefited from new laws promoting public participation and gender equality.	City and local governments depend on the state for their powers and much of their finance, and their effectiveness varies a good deal from place to place.

Future opportunities	Future threats
Resolution of a Treaty with First Nations peoples – which could include significant constitutional, institutional and electoral reforms – will be a major opportunity for enhancing the democratic credentials of the state.	Political extremism and violence are growing problems, evident during and after Victoria's COVID-19 lockdowns. Though small in scale, violent rhetoric and actual violence between protesters and police or counter-protesters has become an increasing issue. The threat has been acknowledged by law enforcement agencies as a serious one, and counter-extremist measures – including Victoria's distinctive ban on Nazi symbols – have become an area of legislative action.
Reform to the controversial GVT system for upper house elections should be a priority. Other jurisdictions around Australia have largely abolished GVT already and Victoria is overdue reform to this system.	The growing support for small and even fringe political parties – parties that often fail to get elected, or if they do, are often sidelined by major parties in the governing process – equates to an increasing share of the electorate functionally unrepresented and disenfranchised.

The remainder of the chapter focuses on three main areas – state politics and elections; the operations of parliament and diversity issues around state politics; and the role of the government and wider public services.

Elections and party politics

All the members of the state parliament's two houses are chosen at Victoria's four-yearly elections, using the combination of AV lower house and STV upper house elections found elsewhere in Australia (see Figure 18.1). At the LA level, the top two parties (the Liberal-National Coalition and Labor) dominated state politics from the 1950s until the late 1990s, when the Greens became established, consistently recording a vote share around 10–11 per cent since (Figure 18.2). Since 2000, the top parties have recorded somewhat smaller shares of the primary vote, but this has been masked by their continuing domination of the two-party-preferred vote. For example, in 2018, Labor won 62.5 per cent of the seats (55) on the basis of just under 43 per cent of the first-preference vote, due to receiving overall 57 per cent support at the 'two-party preferred vote' stage, boosted by Greens voters (Figure 18.2). Disproportionality at this stage was thus a modest 5 per cent. Most of the remaining seats (27, or 31 per cent) went to the Liberal-National Coalition, while the Greens (on 11 per cent) and independents (with 6 per cent support) each won 3 seats. (Twelve minor parties won nearly 5 per cent of votes between them but no seats.)

In 2022, the turmoil in Victorian politics surrounding COVID-19 produced a strong uptick in votes for smaller parties in the LA elections, with Labor losing some support and a record 28 per cent of votes going to third, fourth and small parties combined. However, Labor managed to retain 55 per cent of the two-party preferred vote (and 56 out of 88 seats), despite falling to 37 per cent in its primary vote share, again due to Green voters' support.

Figure 18.1: The basic set up for Victoria's state elections

	Legislative Assembly (LA) (lower house)	**Legislative Council (LC) (upper house)**
Voting system	Alternative Vote (AV)	PR–STV (Single Transferable Vote)
Main outcome sought	Majoritarian – the largest party forms a government	Parties' seats share is proportional to their votes share
Districts used	88	40
Seats per district	One	Eight regions, each with five seats and around 0.5 million voters
Preferences expressed by	Numbering local candidate in order. Victoria's voters need to mark all candidates standing in a complete preference order	Option A: choosing a party's GVT which allocates preferences to all candidates on the ballot Or Option B: numbering a minimum of five candidates in order
Choice of candidates within each party	None – each party nominates one candidate per seat	Voters taking Option B on the ballot paper must choose at least five people to support, either within each party's list of candidates, or picked across parties, or a mix of both.
Limits on proportionality	A district magnitude of one seat means that only a party that can come first in primary and secondary AV votes can win	With 5 seats per region, to win a seat a candidate must normally get a 'quota' approximating 17 per cent of all votes. (However, candidates with far fewer votes may occasionally be elected, depending on competition circumstances in each region.)

Source: Designed for this Audit.

In terms of seats, Figure 18.3 shows that, due to AV, the top two parties have continuously dominated the lower house, often with exaggerated or 'reinforced' majorities won by the largest party, interspersed with an occasional near-balance in party representation. The historic pattern has been for single-party (Labor or Liberal-National Coalition) government and the recent LA elections suggest no change in this is likely.

Turning to the upper house, the LC is elected in eight large five-seat constituencies using the proportional STV system. In the past, voting was effectively dominated by the top two parties until the end of the 1990s, and a majority party sometimes controlled the upper house for long periods. However, since 2002 the Greens became established with over a tenth of votes, and support for other small parties (and independents) has grown fast, so that the governing party must negotiate its legislation more with other parties (Figure 18.4). In the 2018 Legislative Council elections, Labor won 39 per cent of the vote, gaining 18 seats overall, two in every region, and three seats in three areas – sufficient to maintain effective control of the Legislative Council with three other Council members' votes. With 29 per cent support the

Figure 18.2: Victoria Legislative Assembly, first-preference vote shares, 2002–2022

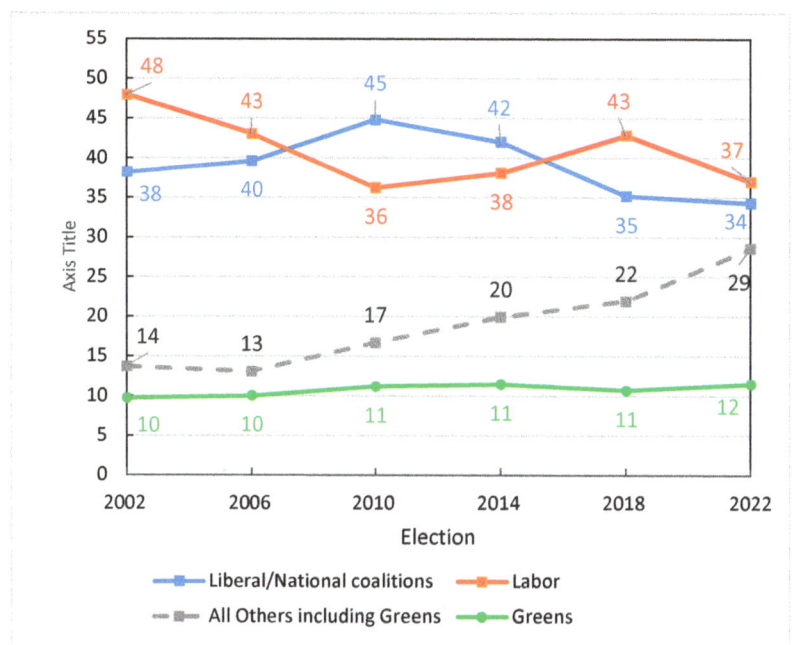

Source: Compiled from data in Victorian Electoral Commission, 2023a.

Figure 18.3: Victorian Legislative Assembly, percentage of seats, 2002–2022

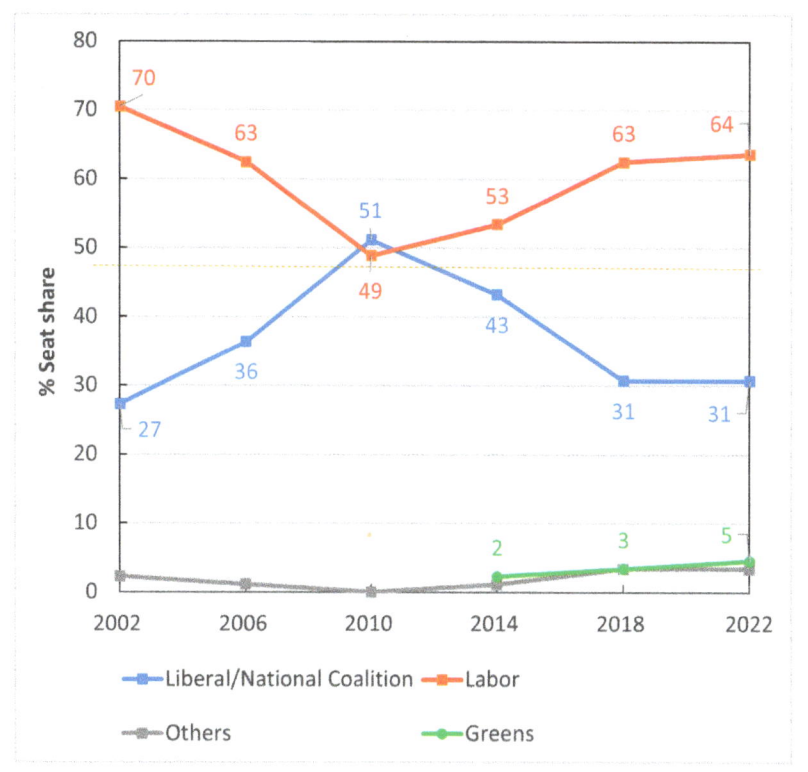

Source: Compiled from data in Victorian Electoral Commission, 2023a.

Figure 18.4: Victoria Legislative Council (upper house) elections, first-preference vote shares, 2002–2022

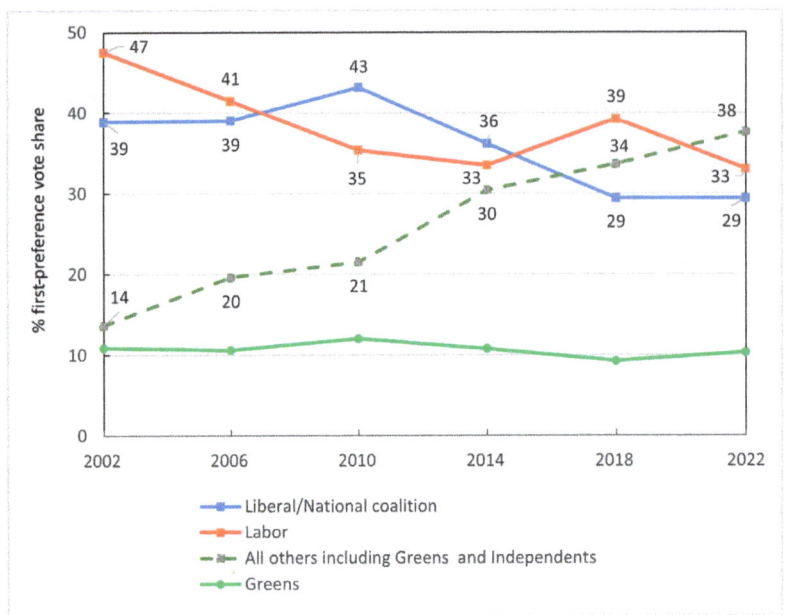

Source: Compiled from data in Victorian Electoral Commission, 2023a.

Figure 18.5: The percentage of seats won in the Victoria Legislative Council (upper house) elections, 2002–2022

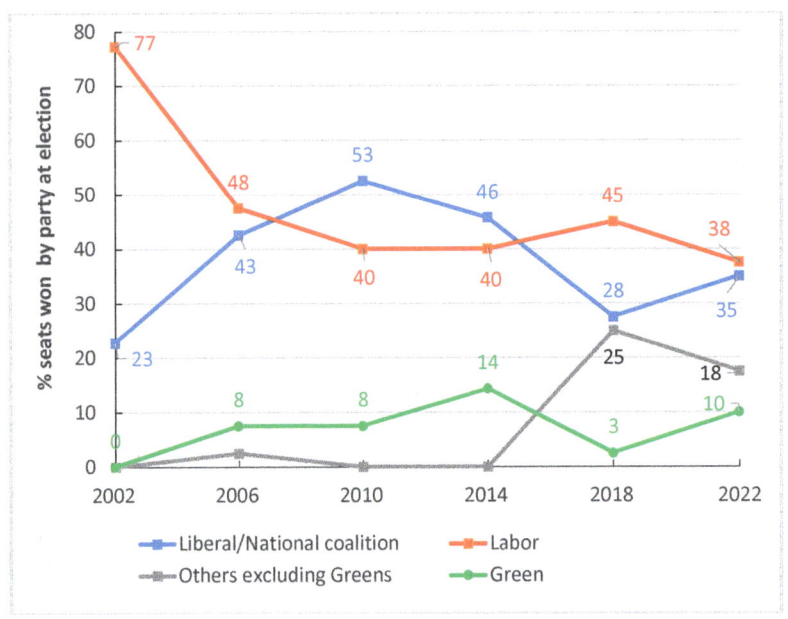

Source: Compiled from data in Victorian Electoral Commission, 2023a.

Liberal-National Coalition lost five seats that they had previously held and fell back to 11 seats, one in each of six regions, and two in the remainder. Five smaller parties also won seats, with three for the Justice Party and two for the Liberal Democrats. The Greens won only a single seat at this stage.

Post-COVID-19, the 2022 Legislative Council elections saw support for all other parties combined at just under 38 per cent of votes beating vote shares for both Labor (33 per cent) and Liberal-National Coalition (29.4 per cent). Labor support fell to a third of first votes, losing three seats. The Greens picked up four seats with later Labor votes transfers to them, and the opposition made no progress. Other parties won seven of the 40 Legislative Council seats (Figure 18.5). The Legislative Council thus remained 'hung', as it has been since 2006, but in practice controlled by a 'progressive' bloc of Labor, Greens, Legalise Cannabis and Animal Justice.

Only half the Legislative Council seats were elected at a time until 2002 and Figure 18.5 shows that this often resulted in sharply varying seats outcomes at these elections. Since 2006 all Legislative Council seats are elected at the same time, which has made the system more proportional and resulted in less variations in the proportion of seats won by the top two parties. The smaller parties did not benefit much at first, but since 2014 their seats have increased, and they have held the balance of power in the house.

The integrity of elections in the state has been high, owing in large part to the work of the Victorian Electoral Commission (2023b), an independent and impartial agency established in 2002. Its responsibilities have spanned conducting, regulating and reporting to parliament on State and local council elections, as well as certain statutory elections and polls. It also maintains the electoral roll, promoting public understanding and awareness of electoral issues; and supports the work of the Electoral Boundaries Commission. In 2018 legislative changes strengthened the funding and political donation disclosure regime in Victoria, and the Victorian Electoral Commission maintains a register of political donations and electoral expenditure disclosures (Victorian Electoral Commission, 2023c).

Parliament, parties and reconciliation

The State Parliament of Victoria was challenged by the COVID-19 crisis. Measures, such as adjournment, social distancing mandates and limits on the number of members allowed at sittings, resulted in fewer sittings (Centre for Public Integrity, 2020). For instance, in 2020 the LA sat for 38 days, compared to 44 days in 2019, and the LC sat for 42 days, compared to 51 in 2019. From April to August 2020, Parliament sat for just seven days, including a long period of lockdown during which a raft of executive measures was taken, with significant impacts on individuals' lives across Victoria. The Parliament's failure to take fuller adaptation measures to ensure that it could continue to carry out its functions was criticised – for instance, because other parliaments in the UK and Canada amended standing orders and parliamentary regulations to permit 'hybrid' sittings with members attending in person and remotely. A policy brief by the Centre for Public Integrity (2020) argued that:

- the Victorian Constitution appeared not to pose an obstacle to parliament functioning remotely and the parliament's standing orders could be amended as required to facilitate remote sitting and voting

- the introduction of hybrid and virtual sittings as adopted by the UK should be considered in Victoria, and, if these formats were determined to be appropriate, they should be made available for implementation on an as-needs basis
- should the switch to online proceedings need to be staggered, priority should be given to Question Time to enable the parliament to resume its scrutiny function as soon as possible.

That said, parliamentary committees continued to meet and conduct business, converting committee rooms to permit video conferencing, and more broadly accelerating rollout of new technologies, enabling members and parliamentary staff to make a rapid transition to work-from-home arrangements (Victoria Parliament, 2021a).

The Parliament of Victoria was recognised as having among the more sophisticated committee systems for rights scrutiny in Australia (Moulds, 2020). In the COVID-19 period, scrutiny achievements included the February 2021 Inquiry into the Victorian government's response to the COVID-19 pandemic conducted by the joint Public Accounts and Estimates Committee (Victoria Public Accounts and Estimates Committee (2021)), charged with reviewing the measures taken by the Victorian government to manage the pandemic (including as part of the intergovernmental National Cabinet), and any other matter related to the pandemic. The committee made a range of recommendations, including greater transparency on the roles and responsibilities of officials during any future state of emergency or state of disaster, and reviewing the effectiveness of the state Department of Health's pandemic communications to multicultural communities.

Other influential scrutiny of executive action since 2019 also included independent inquiries into the state's bushfire response and the hotel quarantine system, as well as Ombudsman investigations into the government's handling of the rapid 'hard lockdown' of public housing towers in July 2020. These all demonstrated a diverse ecosystem of oversight bodies capable of assessing government action, identifying problems and proposing solutions. Some analysts have suggested that greater attention should be paid to maintaining a higher level of functioning in future crises.

Political parties

Research suggests that political parties perform three sets of overlapping and reinforcing functions in a democratic system: *governance* (especially fostering government leadership and acting as a vehicle for rational policy formulation); *community linkage* (fostering local leaders, as well as reflecting the policy preferences and priorities of citizens and helping to inform citizens about political issues); and *integrity* (upholding standards of conduct in public life and the political arena). As regards the first two dimensions, in Victoria an enduring weak link is the under-representation of women, young people, minorities and Indigenous communities in political parties, and by extension, political institutions. Figure 18.6 shows the numbers of women representatives in the state parliament. In terms of ethnicity, approximately 10 per cent of Victorian MPs have non-European (and non-Indigenous) ancestry (Guardian, 2021), which may be as little as half of the percentage in the total state population (Victoria Government, 2016). Civil society initiatives have sought to address this gap: for example, the Pathways to Politics Program for Women, based in Melbourne and in operation since 2016, seeks to increase diverse female participation in politics by providing women with the knowledge and skills to run for political office (Melbourne University, 2023). Similarly, the organisation Not Too Young To Run (2024) has been established to encourage young people to campaign for political

Figure 18.6: Women members in the 2018–2022 Parliament of Victoria

Legislative Council (LC)	Legislative Assembly (LA)
18 out of 40 members	34 out of 88 Members
10 Australian Labor Party	25 Australian Labor Party
3 Liberal Party	4 Liberal Party
1 Derryn Hinch's Justice Party	2 Nationals
1 Fiona Patten's Reason Party	2 Independent
1 Nationals	1 Victorian Greens
1 Victorian Greens	
1 Independent	

Source: Compiled from information in Parliament of Victoria, 2024.

Note: To find exactly the data used here, go to the linked page, specify year as 2022 in left hand margin search box, and search separately for LA and LC members. The page is continuously updated, so to find current information, specify the most recent year.

office in all levels of Australian politics, noting statistics such as the majority of councillors in Victorian local councils are still men aged over 46, an increase in councillors aged over 76, and a decrease in those aged under 25 (3AW, 2021).

At local government level, the *Local Government Act 2020* was described as 'the most ambitious reform to the local government sector in over 30 years' (Arndt, 2020). It included mandatory training for electoral candidates and requirements to involve the public in decision-making, and it has prompted a proliferation of citizen engagement initiatives, such as consultative citizens' panels and specific guidance on citizen engagement in rural and regional areas (Victoria Government, 2023b). In addition, the *Gender Equality Act 2020* required all councils across Victoria's 79 local government areas (as well as other public sector agencies such as universities) to assess, report on and formulate plans to progress gender equality in their organisations. Voter turnout at local council elections in October 2020 reached a record high point of over 81 per cent (ALGA, 2020), and resulted in Victoria's local government achieving the closest to gender parity of local governments nationwide, with 44 per cent of councillors being women, and an express aim of achieving 50 per cent by 2025 (ABC News, 2020b). This compares to 40 per cent of female MPs in Victoria's parliament, and 38 per cent in the federal parliament.

As regards standards of integrity in the party-political system, deficiencies in Victoria have included allegations of 'branch stacking' within both the Labor Party and Liberal Party (ABC News, 2021c). An investigation by the Independent Broad-based Anti-corruption Commission into 'branch stacking' in Labor's Heidelberg branch focused on allegations that the membership fees of hundreds of disinterested people were covered by specific individuals in order to artificially enhance their influence within the party by directing the new members on how to vote (IBAC, 2022). The issue led to the resignation of four state government ministers and also revealed breaches of the *Members of Parliament (Standards) Act 1978*, such as employing staff for party-political purposes using public funds.

Reconciliation with Aboriginal and Torres Strait Islander Peoples

Two significant developments concerning the state's recognition of, and relations with, its nearly 58,000 Traditional Owners and First Peoples (ABS, 2023) got under way from 2017 onwards, not via a constitutional amendment but using a separate, long-run, consensus-building exercise. First, following similar processes in the Australian Capital Territory, Queensland and Western Australia, the state government commenced a process to negotiate a treaty with Victoria's First Nations peoples (Victoria Government, 2023c). Phase 1 began with two new bodies established in 2017: a representative Aboriginal Community Assembly (since renamed the First Peoples' Assembly of Victoria (FPAV)) comprising 32 representatives; and an independent body, the Victorian Treaty Advancement Commission. Phase 1 ended in December 2019 when the State Minister for Aboriginal Affairs made a step required by the 2018 law and declared the FPAV to be the Aboriginal Representative Body for the purposes of treaty negotiations (after the outcome of Aboriginal community elections and on the recommendation of the of the Victorian Treaty Advancement Commissioner). Phase 2, extending into 2022, involved the establishment of an independent Treaty Authority, setting rules to govern the process, creating a self-determination fund to support the equal standing of Aboriginal representatives, and devising a dispute-resolution mechanism (O'Sullivan, 2021). Phase 3 (expected to happen in 2022–2024) will centre on the treaty negotiations: there is no fixed deadline for concluding the treaty process. The loss of the federal referendum on the Voice to Parliament (see Chapter 4) included a majority of Victoria's voters supporting 'No', and its implications remain to unfold, but the treaty negotiation process was ongoing, at time of writing.

Second, the Victorian government provided funding to establish the Yoorrook Justice Commission in May 2021 whose work continued (Yoorrook Justice Commission, 2023). It has drawn inspiration from truth-telling processes in South Africa and Canada to shine a light on past and ongoing injustices experienced by Traditional Owners and First Peoples since colonisation (Walsh, 2021). It will establish an official record and shared understanding of its impact, and the resilience and diversity of First Peoples' cultures, as well as making recommendations for healing, systemic reform, and legal, policy and educational change. The Commission is scheduled to provide its final report in June 2025. These processes are viewed by many as just one step in a broader long-term process aimed at enhancing cross-community understanding and centralising the experiences of First Peoples in Victoria's democratic society:

> As [leading scholar] Marcia Langton puts it, the Yoorrook commission will be 'a significant step forward in educating the wider community about Indigenous history.' One hopes [it will mean] getting Victorian non-Indigenous communities to listen closely in the spirit of dadirri, advocated by Senior Australian of the Year Miriam-Rose Ungunmerr, which will be a demanding task in its own right, time-consuming, even inter-generational. (Walsh, 2021)

The state's core executive and wider public services

Historically Victoria's core executive has seen some extended periods with the same premier in office, notably Liberal leaders such as Henry Bolte (premier 1955–1972) and Rupert Hamer (1972–1981). More recently, Labor Premier Daniel Andrews – premier for nearly nine years, was considered a dominant figure on the state's political landscape (Figure 18.7). Victorian ministers have been drawn from only the party of government and the tradition has been for tight control by premiers, governments and parties over their legislators.

Critics have long expressed concerns about over-centralisation of power in the office of the Victorian premier, but such concerns were heightened during the leadership of Daniel Andrews, and particularly during the pandemic. During that crisis, the Victorian Government established a Crisis Council of Cabinet (Victoria Public Accounts and Estimates Committee, 2021). The Crisis Council of Cabinet operated until November 2020 as the core decision-making body for all matters related to the pandemic, including responsibility 'for implementing the decisions of the National Cabinet'. It temporarily replaced the functions of existing cabinet committees, with ministers assigned portfolios dedicated to the COVID-19 response. Mirroring the restructuring of cabinet, senior tiers of the Victoria public service were restructured into a number of 'missions' to support the Crisis Council of Cabinet and COVID-19 response activities (Victoria Public Accounts and Estimates Committee, 2021). These included managing the public health emergency, delivering essential services and managing the economic emergency. Departmental secretaries acted as mission-leads, reporting not to their portfolio ministers but directly to the premier on the delivery of their missions (Quarantine Inquiry, 2020). This innovation raised concerns regarding excessive centralisation of the public service's work and practical concerns about lines of accountability.

As the COVID-19 emergency waned, previous patterns of government organisation and accountability have been largely restored, but Andrews remained an interventionist premier through to his retirement in September 2023.

Figure 18.7: Premiers of Victoria by party, since the 1970s

	Year 0	Year 1	Year 2	Year 3	Year 4	Year 5	Year 6	Year 7	Year 8	Year 9
2020s	Andrews									
2010s	Baillieu		Napthine		Andrews (2014 to present (2024))					
2000s								Brumby (2007–2010)		
1990s	Kirner	Kennett (1992–1999)								Bracks
1980s	Thompson	Cain Jr (1982–1990)								Kirner
1970s	Bolte	Hammer (1972–1981)								

Source: Parliament of Victoria (2024).

Note: Labor premiers are shown in two shades of pink, and Liberal-National premiers in two shades of blue to help show boundaries where the same party retained the premiership. Start and end dates are in brackets for long-stay premiers (including part years).

An over-centralised premiership notwithstanding, observers have concluded that the Victorian executive is generally responsive and effective. The Grattan Institute's *State Orange Book 2018* provided a comparative assessment of the policy performance of all Australia's states and territories (Grattan, 2018). The Victorian government performed well on measures, such as economic development (for example, youth unemployment), education (for example, Year 9 education outcomes), health (for example, mortality rates), and transparency and accountability. However, it was seen as performing poorly on issues such as regional incomes, government funding to state schools and rental stress.

Transparency has been a more mixed area. Transparency about policy-making in the Victorian government has included a reasonably detailed articulation of top governing priorities, such as that set out in successive state budgets (Victoria Government, 2024). They focused on state-specific issues, such as improving mental health care, improving job creation, investing in education, transport infrastructure and gender equality. The Victorian Aboriginal Affairs Framework 2018–2023 set out a framework and policy direction for government planning and action to address inequities and improve outcomes for Aboriginal Victorians (Victoria Government, 2023d). The executive also produced a Climate Change Strategy, which set out a roadmap to net-zero emissions by 2050 and interim targets of reducing the state's greenhouse gas emissions by 28 to 33 per cent by 2025 and 45 to 50 per cent by 2030, compared to their 2005 levels (Victoria Government, 2022). The state targets were both more ambitious and more detailed than the targets in the federal net-zero plan under the Morrison government (Department of Climate Change etc, 2021). In broader terms of open government, however, the Andrews government, and several state governments before it, have been lambasted by journalists and civil society groups for their culture of secrecy, particularly in regard to Freedom of Information (FOI) requests. Citizens and journalists seeking information about policy decision-making processes have been routinely frustrated by prohibitive fees, massive delays, and restrictive censoring.

Like other states across Australia, a significant challenge for Victoria is its weak revenue-raising power, and the vertical fiscal imbalance with the Commonwealth (see Chapter 16). Victoria's per capita gross state product has trended downwards in recent years and its revenue-raising capacity for goods and services tax (GST) (which are returned to states by the Commonwealth) has decreased over time, to a level now almost 10 per cent lower than the national average in the period 2019–20, as Figure 18.8 demonstrates. Its dependence on Commonwealth grants to finance services has thus increased. Although it is not possible to convey the complexity of this challenge here, the existing structural arrangements are viewed as having a significant impact on the state's ability to invest in vital services for their citizens now, such as education, health and mental health, as well as planning for the future.

Restructuring, digital transformation and rights in the public service

From 2019 onwards, the Victorian public service faced demanding challenges, especially due to the COVID-19 crisis, including: rapid policy change and redeployment of resources; enhancing mobility between departments; and accelerating expansion of digital public services provision. To progress the digital transformation of the public service's work the government committed almost A$196 million to establish Digital Victoria in 2020, with the aim of simplifying and centralising IT services across the state (Victoria Government, 2023d). In

Figure 18.8: Victoria's per capita gross state product (GSP) relative to the national average, and its goods and services tax (GST) relativity

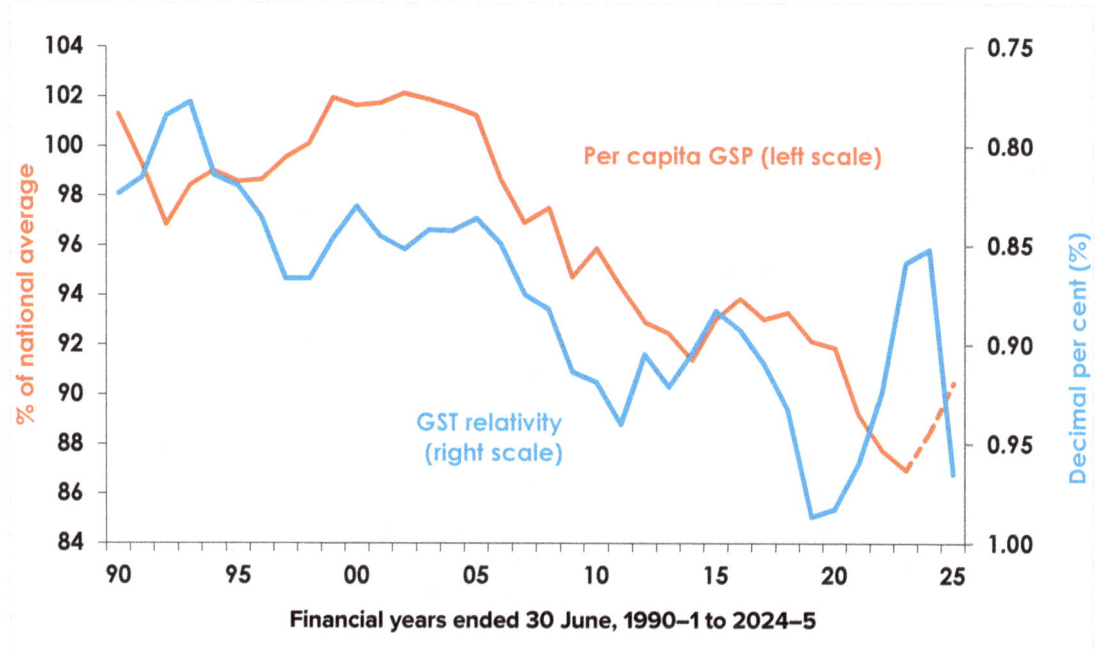

Source: Eslake (2021), Victoria's share of revenue from the GST', Submission to the Victorian Legislative Assembly Economy and Infrastructure Committee's Inquiry into Commonwealth support for Victoria, Chart 4.

Note: The zero is suppressed here. Per capita GSP (= 'gross state product') means the percentage share of the national average per capita GSP level in the state of Victoria; GST relativity shows how the rate of 'goods and services' tax in Victoria as a decimal percentage compared to the national average rate.

July 2021 the government announced investment of A$35.2 million in digital twin technology, which presents vast sets of data on a single platform to create a digital simulation of the real world, with the aim of helping to inform policy formulation and implementation (Victoria Government, 2021).

Concerns were also raised about gaps in the protection of human rights across the Victorian public service. In August 2021, the Victorian Ombudsman announced that her office had received over 3,000 complaints in the previous 12 months, indicating that a range of public agencies had taken actions demonstrating a failure to understand, and protect, fundamental human rights guaranteed by the Victorian Charter of Rights and Responsibilities (Victorian Ombudsman, 2021). While the Ombudsman's response prompted reversal of many decisions, improved policies, and other actions by agencies to better respect individuals' rights, these failures suggest that both fuller training and transformation of organisational culture may be needed to ensure that individuals' basic rights are protected in the delivery of public services.

Conclusion – rebuilding public life and public trust

Liberal democracy in Victoria is broadly well-functioning. Democratic institutions met the challenges posed by the bushfire and COVID-19 emergencies in an effective and adaptive manner. The regulation of voting and party competition supports the conduct of free and fair elections, notwithstanding problems with GVTs and internal party governance. Levels of competition in state elections are strong. In both national and international terms, the executive can be characterised as accountable, responsive and effective. The Victorian parliament plays an enduringly significant role in holding the executive to account. The state court system, and integrity and oversight agencies have discharged their duties effectively. The public service has carried out its governance role with professionalism and adaptability, even if creeping politicisation raises doubts about how long that will last. Advances in gender equality and representation, and steps toward treaty negotiation processes with Victoria's First Nation peoples, have also indicated trends toward a more inclusive political system.

However, key deficiencies in Victoria's democratic system include the tendency toward excessive centralisation of power in the executive; a certain executive disregard for parliament as demonstrated during the pandemic; under-representation of many demographics in parliament; and a lack of rights consciousness in the public service. The state, and particularly the capital Melbourne, faced significant challenges in rebuilding after pandemic lockdowns, including not only economic recovery, but reanimating public spaces and public life, and addressing the breakdowns in public trust that sparked growing anti-lockdown and later anti-vaccination protests against the government. Some of these challenges, such as the impact of some bizarre misinformation on public discourse, cannot be fully addressed at the state or even national level. However, others, such as integrity issues, are entirely within state institutions' power to address robustly.

Despite the many challenges faced since 2019, and enduring political controversy surrounding the government's response to these challenges, democracy in Victoria appears resilient. Public compliance with emergency measures and the success of the vaccination drive reflected a strong sense of solidarity across Victorian society, which is at the core of any democratic system. That solidarity is based, at least partly, on trust in representative government and state institutions. The challenge for the future is for state leaders and institutions to act in a way that preserves, and even enhances, that trust.

Note

This chapter was written by Tom Daly and James Murphy, who also interpreted all the data. It also draws, in a number of places, on unpublished research compiled by Paul Scarmozzino at the Melbourne School of Government.

1   See Centre for Public Integrity (2020); HRLC (Human Rights Law Centre) (2021); the Law Institute of Victoria (2020); and Liberty Victoria (2021).

References

3aw.com (2024) Australian NGO website. https://perma.cc/EHM8-BSLN

ABC News (2017) 'Fracking ban to be introduced in Victoria after Coalition backs Government legislation', ABC News, webpage, 7 February. https://perma.cc/W3CC-JF2V

ABC News (2020a) 'Daniel Andrews's bushfire response draws praise, but bigger tests may be to come', ABC News, 14 January 2020. https://perma.cc/KU65-MTWE

ABC News (2020b) 'Record number of women elected in Victorian local council elections', ABC News, webpage, 17 November. https://perma.cc/GP7P-3BCF

ABC News (2021a) 'All of Victoria now in lockdown after more than 61 new COVID-19 cases, Shepparton outbreak grows', ABC News, 20 August. https://perma.cc/2TGT-MUKP

ABC News (2021b) 'Thousands protest in Melbourne CBD as Victoria records 1,221 new local COVID-19 cases, four deaths', ABC News, webpage, 12 November. https://perma.cc/3XYZ-E3S4

ABC News (2021c) 'What is branch stacking? Inside the political issue driving Victoria's anti-corruption hearings', ABC News, webpage, 12 October. https://perma.cc/2WV2-DM5K

ABS (Australian Bureau of Statistics) (2023) 'Estimates of Aboriginal and Torres Strait Islander Australians', Agency, webpage, 30 June. https://perma.cc/7MB2-HCZH

AIDR (Australian Institute for Disaster Resilience) (2023) 'Victoria, November 2019–February 2020, Bushfires – Black Summer', Knowledge Hub webpage. https://perma.cc/KPF2-H7S9

ALGA (Australian Local Government Association) (2020) 'Voters flock to Victorian local government elections', Press release, 20 November. https://perma.cc/A365-TZU2

Ambrey, Christopher L; Fleming, Christopher M; and Manning, Matthew (2017) 'The social cost of the Black Saturday bushfires', *Australian Journal of Social Issues,* vol. 52, no. 4, pp.298–312. https://doi.org/10.1002/ajs4.21

Arndt, Kathryn (2020) 'Closest to the people: Local government democracy and decision-making in disaster', Policy Brief No 6, Melbourne School of Government. https://perma.cc/4EDA-82GG

Australasian Lawyer (2021) 'New state of emergency bill seeks to amend Victorian Constitution', *The Australasian Lawyer*. Written by Paulinet Tamaray, 18 November. https://perma.cc/4JEX-UY9V

Big Australia Bucket List (2021) 'Timeline of every Victoria lockdown (dates and restrictions)', 10 August. https://perma.cc/8MJS-VKYV

Centre for Public Integrity (2020) 'Where there's a will there's a way: How to keep the Victorian Parliament running during the COVID-19 crisis', Briefing Paper, August. https://perma.cc/FNT5-BVT8

Department of Climate Change, Energy, the Environment and Water (2021) 'Australia's long-term emissions reduction plan', Commonwealth Department webpage, https://perma.cc/K4F9-GQ6W

Department of Health and Aged Care (2021) 'COVID-19 vaccine rollout update – 17 November 2021', Commonwealth Department webpage. https://perma.cc/4LHC-QF3P

Eslake, Saul (2021) 'Victoria's share of revenue from the GST', Submission to the Victorian Legislative Assembly Economy and Infrastructure Committee's Inquiry into Commonwealth support for Victoria, online document, 20 September. https://perma.cc/S773-TQ93

Grattan Institute (2018) *State Orange Book 2018: Policy Priorities for States and Territories,* Institute Report. https://perma.cc/H5GU-M7AN

Guardian (2020a) '"It's got to be a big stick": Melburnians, perhaps surprisingly, are all for lockdown', *Guardian*, Australia, 28 August. https://perma.cc/T8GB-KNRU

Guardian (2020b) 'Melbourne anti-lockdown protests: At least 15 arrested in violent clashes with police', *Guardian*, Australia, 5 September. https://perma.cc/GA3P-M28M

Guardian (2021) 'Australia's state parliaments lagging on racial and cultural diversity, report finds', *Guardian*, Australia, 6 August. https://perma.cc/VX7D-KH7U

HRLC (Human Rights Law Centre) (2021) 'Victoria's pandemic law: New human rights and accountability safeguards welcomed', Human Rights Law Centre, 16 November, webpage. https://perma.cc/RKD4-TMH4

IBAC (Independent Board-based Anti-corruption Commission) (2022) 'Investigation: Operation Watts', Agency website, November. https://perma.cc/3TTG-MWMT

IGEM (Inspector General for Emergency Management) (2021) 'Implementation monitoring of "Review of 10 years of reform in Victoria's emergency management sector" and "Inquiry into the 2019-20 Victorian Fire Season – Phase 1" - Progress Report – 2021', https://web.archive.org/web/20230303112406/https://www.igem.vic.gov.au/fire-season-inquiry/inquiry-reports/inquiry-into-the-2019-20-victorian-fire-season-phase-1-report

IPA (Institute of Public Affairs) (2021) 'Constitutional ban on fracking autocratic, illiberal and undemocratic', Institute of Public Affairs Blogpost, 4 March. https://perma.cc/FT6F-AHP2

Law Institute of Victoria (2020) 'Government accountability vital during COVID-19', by Karen Derkely, blogpost, 10 June. https://www.liv.asn.au/Web/Law_Institute_Journal_and_News/Web/LIJ/Year/2020/06June/Government_accountability_vital_during_COVID-19.aspx

Liberty Victoria (2021) 'Liberty Victoria response to pandemic specific legislation', Liberty Victoria, webpage, 3 November. https://perma.cc/L3XC-J2XH

Melbourne FOE (Friends of the Earth) (2021) 'Community win: Victoria's fracking ban enshrined in constitution', Friends of the Earth, webpage, 4 March. https://perma.cc/YXN6-UL9H

Melbourne Law School (2021) 'A discussion of Victoria's pandemic bill', webinar, University of Melbourne. https://www.youtube.com/watch?v=eHmwdoN2Pq0

Melbourne University (2023) 'Pathways to politics for women: Changing the face of politics', Melbourne University, online details. https://perma.cc/M97Q-9QG6

Moulds, Sarah (2020) 'Scrutinising COVID-19 laws: An early glimpse into the scrutiny work of federal parliamentary committees', *Alternative Law Journal*, vol. 45, no. 3, pp.180–87. https://journals.sagepub.com/doi/pdf/10.1177/1037969X20946990

Not Too Young to Run (2024) Australian NGO website. https://perma.cc/6K7P-Q658

O'Sullivan, D (2021) 'Treaties and re-setting the colonial relationship: Lessons for Australia from the Treaty of Waitangi', *Ethnicities*, vol. 21, no. 6, pp.1070–92. $ https://doi.org/10.1177/1468796821999863

Parliament of Victoria (2015) 'Inquiry into unconventional gas in Victoria', PP No 116, Session 2014-15. https://web.archive.org/web/20210408170711/https://www.parliament.vic.gov.au/406-epc-lc/inquiry-into-unconventional-gas-in-victoria

Parliament of Victoria (2020) 'DPS Annual Report 2020'. https://perma.cc/M4MZ-4AWZ

Parliament of Victoria (2024) 'Former Members Database'. https://web.archive.org/web/20240801003321/ https://www.parliament.vic.gov.au/about/history-and-heritage/people-who-shaped-parliament/former-members/

Pesutto, John (2020) 'New strategy, new voices: Time to change Victoria's crisis approach?' Melbourne School of Government, Governing During Crises: Policy Brief No. 7, 10 August. https://perma.cc/EQ2A-W5WV

Premier, Victoria (2021) 'Enshrining Victoria's ban on fracking forever', webpage, 4 March. https://perma.cc/E5D8-WHV7

Quarantine Inquiry (2020) 'COVID-19 hotel quarantine inquiry'. https://perma.cc/BBR8-KLG4

Reuters (2021) 'Melbourne readies to exit world's longest COVID-19 lockdown', *Reuters*, 21 October. https://perma.cc/HYV4-RDB3

Rundle, Kristen (2020) 'Reassessing contracting-out: Lessons from the Victorian hotel quarantine inquiry', Melbourne School of Government, Governing during crises: Policy Brief No. 7, 21 September. https://perma.cc/EBF3-RTDT

The Age (2021a) '"Draconian": Government introduces new pandemic laws into Parliament', *The Age*, 26 October. https://perma.cc/QDW6-VZCB

The Age (2021b) '"Coercive powers": Former minister Adem Somyurek threatens to scupper pandemic bill', *The Age*, 17 November. https://perma.cc/L9NM-EJYQ

Thomas, Elise (2021) 'The threat of conspiratorial COVID-sceptic extremism', Institute for Strategic Dialogue, 16 November. https://perma.cc/7AT6-SL55

Towell, Noel (2020) 'Andrews has spent years preparing for this crisis. And it shows', *The Age*, 3 January. https://perma.cc/J3NM-BDGJ

VEOHRC (Victorian Equal Opportunity and Human Rights Commission) (2023) 'About the Charter', webpage. https://perma.cc/2J5M-B53H

Victoria Bushfire Royal Commission (2010) *Final Report*, Melbourne: Government Printer for the State of Victoria. https://web.archive.org.au/awa/20100927012935mp_/http://pandora.nla.gov.au/pan/96781/20100923-0223/www.royalcommission.vic.gov.au/finaldocuments/summary/PF/VBRC_Summary_PF.pdf

Victoria Department of Health (2024) 'Victorian Covid 19 surveillance report', 9 August. https://perma.cc/NF4T-K29G

Victoria Government (2016) 'Victoria's diverse population, 2016 Census', Department of Premier and Cabinet, Brochure online. https://nla.gov.au/nla.obj-607568299/view

Victoria Government (2021) 'Landmark investment to create state-wide digital twin', Department of Transport and Planning Press release, 12 July. https://perma.cc/VXY6-KSSL

Victoria Government (2022) 'Victoria's climate change strategy', Webpage, 7 May. https://perma.cc/G5GS-UM9L

Victoria Government (2023a) '2019–20 Eastern Victorian bushfires'. https://perma.cc/S5BW-GG49

Victoria Government (2023b) 'Engage Victoria', Online Consultation website, https://perma.cc/PPP6-GVNU

Victoria Government (2023c) 'Pathway to treaty', Agency webpage, updated 17 May. https://perma.cc/4UXR-LRW4

Victoria Government (2023d) 'Victorian Aboriginal affairs framework 2018–2023', Agency webpage. https://perma.cc/QRY9-KVYD

Victoria Government (2023e) 'The digital strategy 2021–2026', Agency webpage and report, https://perma.cc/ZFJ6-6TXA

Victoria Government (2024) 'Budget priorities – Explore the Victorian budget 2024/25 priorities' https://perma.cc/MW43-NVS8

Victoria Parliament (2021a) *Annual report 2020–21*, Department of Parliamentary Services. https://perma.cc/9BDE-GPM7

Victoria Public Accounts and Estimates Committee (2021) 'Inquiry into the Victorian Government's response to the COVID-19 pandemic', Parliament webpage, 2 February. https://perma.cc/F8VS-9UZ9

Victorian Electoral Commission (2023a) 'State election results', Agency webpage. https://perma.cc/7Y2Z-V5R3

Victorian Electoral Commission (2023b) Agency webpage. https://perma.cc/65NM-E7RQ

Victorian Electoral Commission (2023c) 'Political donations', Agency webpage. https://perma.cc/9E7H-2UBR

Victorian Legislation (2021) 'Public Health and Wellbeing Amendment (Pandemic Management) Bill 2021', webpage. https://perma.cc/AR5L-ST3Y

Victorian Legislation (2023) 'Constitution Amendment (SEC) Bill 2023'. https://perma.cc/ZUE5-XC3J

Victorian Ombudsman (2020) 'Investigation into the detention and treatment of public housing residents arising from a COVID-19 "hard lockdown" in July 2020', Ombudsman, webpage, 17 December. https://perma.cc/V3XW-Z5SA

Victorian Ombudsman (2021) 'Victorian Ombudsman receives over 3000 human rights complaints', Agency webpage, 4 August. https://perma.cc/2YXK-TE77

Walsh, Pat (2021) 'Learning from Timor-Leste's experience for Victoria's Yoo-rrook commission', Blogpost, Eureka Street, 23 March. $ https://perma.cc/N9EZ-TJ2A

Washington Post (2020) 'Australia's coronavirus "dictator" enforces a drastic lockdown. He's still popular,' *Washington Post*, 15 September. https://perma.cc/PP6G-MKEW

Yoorrook Justice Commission (2023) 'Latest news', Agency webpage, 6 December. https://perma.cc/2LPB-J6FJ

# 19

Queensland

Cosmo Howard and Pandanus Petter

Queensland is Australia's second largest state by area and third largest by population. Among the states it stands out in constitutional terms in having only a single legislative chamber, and politically in having a sharp mismatch between balanced major party fortunes at state level but Liberal-National dominance at federal elections. The state includes significant mining and tourism industry interests and a relatively large Aboriginal and Torres Strait Islander population. From the late 1950s state politics was dominated by the Liberal-National Coalition party until electoral reforms in the late 1980s ushered in fairer election competition, contributing to Labor predominance in recent times.

What does democracy require of Queensland's political system?

- An effective state constitution that provides an anatomy of legitimate public power to: define the limits of state governmental powers; make government accountable to the people by providing for checks and balances; and promote long-term structures.
- Aboriginal and Torres Strait Islander peoples should be afforded full individual civil and human rights. The histories, languages, cultures, rights and needs of Aboriginal and Torres Strait Islander communities and peoples should be addressed.
- The electoral system for the Legislative Assembly (LA) should accurately translate parties' votes into seats in the state legislature, in a way that is recognised as legitimate by most citizens. Ideally the voting system should foster the overall social representativeness of the legislature. Elections and the regulation of political parties should be impartially conducted, with integrity.
- The political parties should sustain vigorous and effective electoral competition and citizen participation. They should enable the recruitment, selection and development of political leaders for state government; formulate viable policy agendas and frame political choices for state functions; and form governments or, when not in power, hold governments accountable. Political parties should uphold the highest standards of conduct in public life.

How to cite this chapter:

Howard, Cosmo and Petter, Pandanus (2024) 'Queensland', in: Evans, Mark; Dunleavy, Patrick and Phillimore, John (eds) *Australia's Evolving Democracy: A New Democratic Audit*, London: LSE Press, pp.415–431. https://doi.org/10.31389/lsepress.ada.s. Licence: CC-BY-NC 4.0

- The state legislature should normally maintain full public control of government services and state operations, ensuring public and parliamentary accountability through conditionally supporting the government, and articulating reasoned opposition, via its proceedings. It should be a critically important focus of Queensland's political debate. With no upper house, the legislature in a unicameral state must have processes that incorporate a plurality of viewpoints and subject a majority government to some effective checks on its power.
- The Queensland government should govern responsively, prioritising the public interest and reflecting state public opinion. Its core executive (premier, cabinet, ministers and key central departments) should provide clear unification of public policies across government, so that the state operates as an effective whole. Both strategic decision-making within the core executive, and more routine policy-making, should foster careful deliberation to establish an inclusive view of the 'public interest'.
- The core executive and government should operate fully within the law, and ministers should be effectively scrutinised by and politically accountable to Parliament. Ministers and departments/agencies must also be legally accountable to independent courts for their conduct and policy decisions.
- In the wider state, public service officials should act with integrity, in accordance with well-enforced codes of conduct, and within the rule of law. The administration of public services should be controlled by democratically elected officials so far as possible. The rights of all citizens should be carefully protected in policy-making, and 'due process' rules followed, with fair and equal public consultation on public service changes. Public services, contracting, regulation and planning/zoning decisions should be completely free from corruption.
- At the federal level, the Queensland government should effectively and transparently represent its citizens' interests to the Commonwealth government and Parliament.

Recent developments

The top two factors affecting the practice and quality of democracy in Queensland have been improvements in accountability and representation, and the government's responses to the COVID-19 pandemic. Some long-running aspects of state policy-making are considered after the SWOT analysis below.

Elections, accountability and representation

Queensland returned to a 'normal' single party majority in 2017, after the 2009–2015 period of a dramatic landslide, seat swings and minority government. In 2020, the Labor government strengthened its primary vote a little and its two-party preferred support, making Anastacia Palaszczuk the first female premier to win three elections in a row, and the leader of the first state government in Australian history to increase its vote share across three elections (Figure 19.1). After the election, the leader of the state opposition resigned amid public infighting in the Liberal National Party of Queensland (LNP). The Greens picked up an important political scalp: the former Labor stronghold of South Brisbane, once held by Premier Anna Bligh and more recently by Deputy Premier and Treasurer Jackie Trad. In December 2023, after leading the state during the

Figure 19.1: Votes cast for parties in Queensland's state elections, 2009–2020

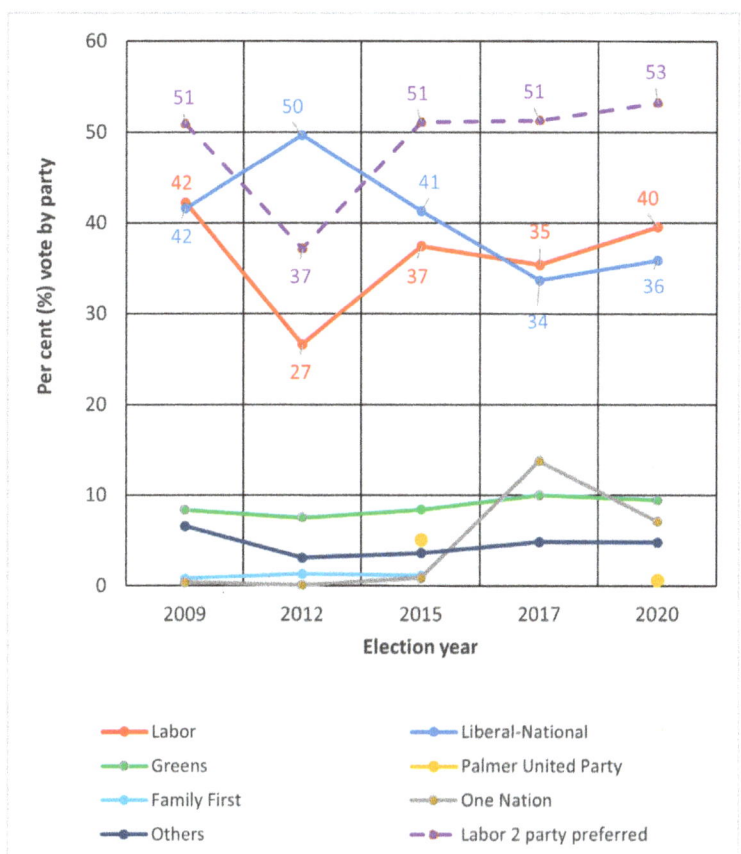

Source: Compiled from data in Queensland Electoral Commission (2023) 'Election results and statistics'.

Note: The Palmer United Party did not stand candidates in years not shown.

pandemic period, Anastacia Palaszczuk resigned as premier, with her former deputy Steven Miles taking over in the lead up to the 2024 election (Petter 2023).

In terms of seats the top two parties still dominated representation in the LA, maintaining a historically entrenched pattern (Figure 19.2). However, this apparent 'business as usual' picture coincided with some ongoing changes in the running of elections, as well as the composition of the Parliament. Along with a move to more stable fixed four-year terms from then on, the Parliament also included a diverse crossbench of minor party MPs: two Queensland Greens, three Katter's Australian Party (a socially conservative and economically protectionist party with support in North Queensland), a single One Nation member (representing Australia's main right-wing populist party) and one independent. Given the lack of an upper house with multiple-member constituencies in Queensland, this represented an unusual level of diversity of opinion in Parliament. The parliamentary crossbench was also granted extra resources for parliamentary staff by the Queensland Independent Remuneration Tribunal (2021) with the aim of improving their ability to scrutinise legislation and conduct research. Despite this, the government's majority and unicameralism have meant these voices have limited structural power to influence legislation and hold the government to account.

In the federal Parliament, Queensland accounts for 30 seats, with the vast majority (two-thirds) held by the Liberal-National Party in 2022 and 2019, and the Coalition gaining over half of the 'two party preferred vote'. Labor won only a handful of seats at federal level, a historical weakness considerably worsened in 2022 when the Greens won three of the Brisbane federal seats.

Figure 19.2: Seats won by political parties in the Legislative Assembly, 2009–2020

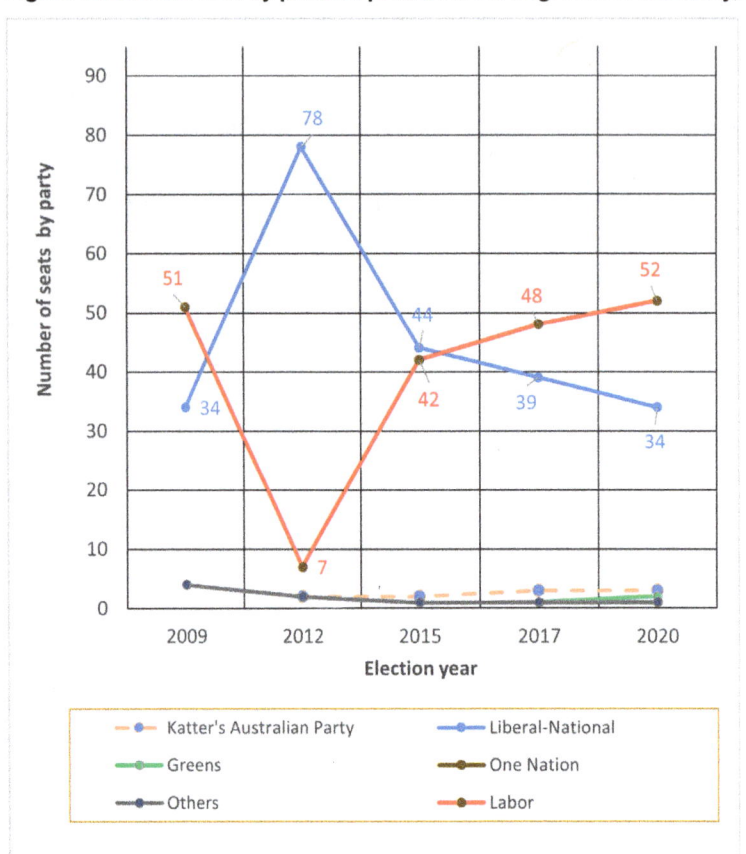

Source: Compiled from data in Queensland Electoral Commission (2023) 'Election results and statistics'.

Note: The number of LA seats was 89 up to 2015 (majority = 45), and 93 from 2017 on (majority = 47).

Concerns around integrity dogged the Parliament and political system in recent years. The state government faced an integrity scandal when Deputy Premier Jackie Trad stepped down from her cabinet positions over allegations of impropriety in property dealings and interference in the process to appoint a school principal in her electorate. Although cleared of wrongdoing, the controversy contributed to the loss of her seat in the 2020 election (Pollard, 2020). In response to a climate of perceived corruption, laws and regulations designed to cap political campaign spending, improve the accountability of ministers and ban donations from property developers were introduced in 2020 and took effect in 2022 (Palaszczuk, 2022). However, opposition members argued that these laws were skewed to benefit the Labor government, because they limited donations to candidates by individuals and organisations without preventing multiple unions making separate donations to the same campaign (McCutcheon and Hartley, 2020).

In terms of the political representation of historically excluded groups, recent parliaments have produced mixed results. The assembly still under-represented women (with the second lowest women members among the states), a deficit exacerbated by the lack of an upper house (Laing and Madde, 2024). The legislature included three Indigenous MPs at the election, second only to the Northern Territory's five (Richards, 2021). These included the first Aboriginal and first Torres Strait Islander women elected to the state's parliament. One of these, Leeanne Enoch, a Quandamooka woman, also became a cabinet minister. In substantive terms, legislation was introduced that sought to recognise traditional Torres Strait Islander cultural practices of customary adoption within family law (Palaszczuk, 2020a). The Palaszczuk government also continued work on a formal treaty with Aboriginal and Torres Strait Islander peoples as part of ongoing reconciliation reforms, where state-level progress may be impaired by the 2023 federal referendum results rejecting a First Nations Voice to Parliament (see later and Chapter 4).

The COVID-19 pandemic

Queensland largely escaped significant direct health impacts from COVID-19 in 2020 and 2021, yet the pandemic had a powerful effect on politics in the state. In the context of Australia's federally fragmented response to COVID-19 – where states and territories went their separate ways in handling the pandemic – Queensland's Labor government took a consistently hardline approach to suppressing the virus (Salisbury, 2020a). The state's border to Australia's other populous states remained closed for much of 2020, and border restrictions were imposed again in August 2021 due to the surge of cases in the 'Delta' variant, with police and military maintaining roadblocks along the border with New South Wales (NSW) and searching all vehicles attempting to enter the state.

Queensland's aggressive suppression policy generated some conflict along party lines. Both the federal conservative government, NSW and some state Liberal-National opposition politicians criticised the border closures during 2020, citing negative impacts on personal freedoms and economic activity, including Queensland's tourism industry (Guardian, 2020). However, the Queensland government effectively controlled the political debate within the state surrounding COVID-19, fending off criticism by comparing the state's experience to its southern neighbours, where COVID-19 outbreaks led to extended lockdowns. Meanwhile, political pressure from the economic stresses of the pandemic was blunted by state and federal pandemic payments. Increasing activity in the state's two largest employment sectors (healthcare and construction) also muted pressure for the reopening of borders. Finally, intra-state tourism partly offset the collapse that quarantines caused in international and interstate visitors. The government also enjoyed a prestige gain from the temporary relocation of clubs and the finals matches of the two major football codes from NSW and Victoria to Queensland (ABC News, 2021). The October 2020 state election was the first in Australian history to be contested by the top two major parties both led by women (Salisbury, 2020b). It also provided many insights into Queensland voters' reactions to COVID-19 decision-making, with results somewhat less clear cut than some observers expected (see below). There were swings to incumbents of both major parties in individual seats, along with some wins for minor parties (see Figure 19.1).

Despite dominating the politics of COVID-19, the Queensland government did not escape controversy over its handling of the pandemic. Its choice to defer to the advice of the Chief Health Officer (CHO) Dr Jeanette Young was partly credited with the state's successful suppression of the virus. Dr Young also became the public face of the government's media messaging surrounding the pandemic response. She was made the next Governor of Queensland in a further symbolic nod to the government's deference to expertise. At the same time, Dr Young's dramatic public condemnation of the AstraZeneca vaccine (Zillman, 2021) was criticised for stoking vaccine hesitancy and contributing to Queensland long having the second lowest vaccination rate of the Australian states (McKenna, 2021). The arrival of the Delta COVID-19 variant and the implementation of the vaccination program created new challenges for a government committed to virus suppression. However, the Palaszczuk government was able to navigate the challenges of engaging in a meaningful public conversation about opening borders, and balancing civil and economic freedoms with an inevitable rise in cases and deaths (Wordsworth, 2021).

Strengths, weaknesses, opportunities and threats (SWOT) analysis

Current strengths	Current weaknesses
Queensland managed to avoid significant outbreaks of COVID-19 during 2020–2021, in part due to the government's proactive use of short, sharp lockdowns. As a result, the state became for a time a magnet for individuals and families seeking new opportunities, as well as public events that could not run in southern states. This helped attract and retain human capital in the public and private sectors.	Having consistently 'gone hard and early' on COVID-19, and coming near last in the vaccination coverage, the state had to struggle to create a dialogue about opening up its borders later on. The dominance of the pandemic on the political and policy agenda also sidelined other urgent problems, such as environmental protection and socioeconomic inequality. This suited the government in the short term, but it may have created serious problems for long-term structural adaptation.
The Queensland government relied on clear communication, consistency and expert advice to build widespread support for its pandemic responses. Trust in the government and institutions has been high, and public cooperation generally forthcoming.	Democratic representation is skewed along several dimensions in Queensland. Labor dominates state politics while the Liberal-National Coalition hold more than two-thirds of the seats at federal level. Meanwhile, the urban-regional/rural divide has grown in recent elections. This makes compromise and structural reform on critical 'wedge issues' like climate and conservation difficult.
The opposition in the LA was unable to attain much traction during COVID-19. A larger number of crossbench MPs secured voice within Parliament on issues, such as human rights, renters' rights and the environment.	Queensland's unicameral Parliament continued to provide a weak forum for scrutiny and accountability of the government's COVID-19 agenda and performance. The lack of an upper house means that committees are consistently controlled by the government.
On issues of 'morality policy', such as the decriminalisation of abortion and assisted dying, Queensland has largely managed to avoid fractious public debates and political polarisation found in other jurisdictions. At the same time, MPs had the opportunity to raise constituents' views and representatives of religious groups have had their voices heard.	Public corruption remained a serious problem in Queensland. There was considerable debate about the appropriate roles of the various institutional actors involved in anti-corruption work. Both major parties stand accused of undermining the reforms implemented after the Fitzgerald Inquiry (1989) and a political consensus on corruption mitigation remains elusive.
Political support for and appreciation of the public service has rebounded since the turbulence of the Newman government (2012–2015). Greater attention has been paid to ensuring that state staff are supported through permanent employment and managed so that they succeed in their roles (Queensland Government, no date).	Local government democracy was to some extent marginalised in the COVID-19 period's consolidation of the state government's authority. This effect was compounded by corruption scandals in local governments. This produced worrying examples of non-consultation with local communities over developments that impacted them, such as the location of government-run quarantine facilities in the pandemic period.

Future opportunities	Future threats
The state's capacity to attract major national sporting and cultural fixtures, and international mega events such as the 2032 Olympics, suggest the potential for further diversification of the economy, opening up opportunities for traditionally disadvantaged groups to participate more fully in social and political life.	The survival of education and tourism industries at their current scale depended on the full return of interstate and international travel. The potential for conflict between the state and federal governments' other important intergovernmental issues, such as the protection of the Great Barrier Reef, lessened after Labor's 2022 return to power federally.
Population growth in Queensland, especially in the regions, provided a chance to reduce gaps between wealthy south-east Queensland and the rest of the state. This may potentially mitigate the urban–rural polarisation that has existed in Queensland and limited the state's capacity to address major policy challenges. Current expansion of infrastructure in south-east Queensland, including school expansion and new mass transit systems, could potentially foster inclusion and participation and reduce regional disconnection.	Economic development, interstate migration and mega events have rapidly changed the socioeconomic complexion of many areas of Queensland, including inner-city Brisbane and large regional centres. There is a danger that growing inequality will reduce relative opportunities for the least well off.
In 2020, there was an outpouring of support for the Black Lives Matter movement, creating a window of opportunity to address the colonial legacy of First Nations peoples' ongoing disadvantage, over-policing and misalignment in bureaucratic relationships with communities.	Law and order has remained a hot button issue in Queensland politics. The Labor government has been determined not to be politically outgunned on the issue. The Liberal-National Coalition rhetoric often suggests they favour extending policies that are known to disproportionately affect First Nations peoples and their communities, including youth.
Current debates about the appropriate framework of corruption prevention in Queensland offer an opportunity to rethink the existing model, introduce greater parliamentary oversight and build community awareness and consensus.	Corruption prevention remains a polarised issue. While the political disagreement has faded somewhat from the Newman days, this has been achieved through a watering down of corruption provisions. There is a danger that the cultural and systemic problems identified by the Fitzgerald Inquiry (1989) could re-emerge.
After the Liberal-National 2020 election defeat, party polarisation on public services somewhat reduced. The new opposition leader called for a different approach to public services (Lynch, 2020).	Support for the public service became a sharply political issue from 2012–2015 and subsequently continued to be salient, with both the Labor government and the Liberal-National opposition keen to signal loyalty to public servants. Reforms to employment conditions and performance management processes have enhanced job security but may make it harder to address underperformance at individual and organisational levels.

Queensland democracy faces some long-run tensions, and three of these are explored in more detail in the rest of this chapter. The state's strong government/unicameral legislature tradition has softened a little and some key legislative reforms have somewhat redressed the balance in favour of rights. Changes to public administration continue to create some issues. And finally, examples of increasing social disadvantage raise new issues for governance.

Reconciling strong government with democratic accountability

Although its popularity had begun to wane at the end of 2023, the state's strong government was widely perceived as 'getting the job done' and was credited by voters with keeping Queenslanders safe during the COVID-19 crisis. However, some of this came at the expense of holding government accountable, creating a vibrant representative political community and instituting necessary structural reforms to address problems like inequality and climate change. Queensland has tended to produce long periods of one-party dominance in government – Labor was in power 1932–1957, followed by the Liberal Nationals in 1957–1989. Labor has occupied the Treasury benches for all but six of the last 32 years. The electoral successes of the Queensland Australian Labor Party (ALP) under Premier Palaszczuk, and the popularity of her hardline response to COVID-19, seemed to signal a continuation of a tradition of executive-dominated majoritarian government, even after her resignation.

Queensland's history has shown that executive dominance carried a risk of reduced accountability (Coaldrake, 1989), which may adversely affect the quality of democratic deliberation and lead to poorer outcomes for citizens. The Palaszczuk government's approach to addressing these concerns showed that they were sensitive to political pressure, and keen to be seen as fighting corruption and improving the accountability of elected representatives. Despite legislative action designed to improve the standards of ministerial accountability, curb political donations by property developers at both state and local level, and enforce higher standards of conduct in local government, substantial concerns have remained. They centre on the proper use and operation of statutory oversight bodies and on the use of Parliament as an effective means of keeping the executive accountable. The Crime and Corruption Commission had some recent success in bringing cases of political and police misconduct to trial and proved instrumental in the investigation and dismissal of corrupt local governments. However, it has been criticised for focusing on these high-profile cases at the local level, while many other complaints are sent back to referring agencies to investigate in-house after routine assessments.

On the other hand, the Office of the Independent Assessor, which investigates routine misconduct by local councillors, was sometimes overwhelmed by the volume of often spurious complaints referred to it (State Development and Regional Industries Committee, 2022). Its officers also faced criticism for undermining the independence and democratic legitimacy of elected local government officials. Councillors faced complicated new codes of conduct and were intimidated by the broadly defined terms of reference and investigative powers of the body (Stone, 2021). It was also not matched by any equivalent body focusing purely on state government. So, while the Labor government made moves in the right direction on corruption and accountability, more resources were needed to tackle the problem, but ministers had little political incentive to do so.

Enhancing scrutiny and diversity

Some steps have enhanced the Queensland Parliament's suitability as a platform for meaningful legislative debate and the representation of historically excluded groups. Extra resources for crossbench MPs became independent of the premier's discretion and gave minor parties and independents greater adequacy and certainty of funding support. This has reduced the ability of the executive to bargain with or punish these representatives based on political or electoral calculations, a pattern that occurred a good deal in the past (Bavas, 2019). It also enhanced the capacity of non-traditional parliamentarians to produce independent research and use Parliament as a platform to give voice to their constituents or debate the government more effectively. However, ongoing concerns have remained about how much meaningful input the opposition and crossbench can contribute to legislative debates and consultation, not least since the actual number of sitting days in Parliament (36 in 2023) remains comparatively low. This amplified the COVID-19-period effect of regular manipulation of standing orders in Parliament to 'gag' or curtail debate on important legislation, or force votes when the opposition had not had a chance to read amendments (McCutcheon, 2020a).

The parliamentary committee system and yearly budget estimate sittings are intended to act as a means of scrutinising government, reviewing legislation and consulting with important stakeholders before it is drafted. Both aspects were reformed in 2011, yet since the operation and timeframes of these systems were often dominated by the governing party they have not always allowed proper scrutiny and opposition input (Pretty, 2020).

Turning to the diversity of representatives, the 2020 Parliament and executive (Cabinet) now included more women and Aboriginal and Torres Strait Islander MPs than in the past (Harris Rimmer and Stephenson, 2020). However, like other Australian jurisdictions there are no reserved seats in Parliament or legislated quotas designed to improve the representation of women or ethnic minorities. The ALP has operated candidate selection policies that set aspirational targets, and has had some success in advancing female candidates, yet Labor has shown no inclination for legislated quotas. The Liberal-National Coalition at state level has also remained ideologically resistant to any such measures.

Structural reform to the constitutional and administrative relationship between the Queensland government and Aboriginal and Torres Strait Islander peoples was another ongoing concern. Premier Palaszczuk publicly endorsed an Indigenous Voice to Parliament at the Commonwealth level without committing her government to a solid model of how to incorporate one at the state level (Queensland Government, 2020a and 2020b). The Queensland Labor government also initiated a process of consultation with the eventual aim of an official treaty supported by a commitment to truth-telling and education about the colonial past. A bill was introduced into Parliament to establish a First Nations Treaty Institute and a formal Truth Telling and Healing Inquiry, and amend existing legislation that reflects discriminatory policies of the past with bipartisan support. The Bill followed the signing of the Path to Treaty Commitment on 16 August 2022, which ministers saw as 'historic' (Palaszczuk and Crawford, 2023). However, many observers suggested that Aboriginal and Torres Strait Islander peoples will not be granted meaningful political autonomy or influence in Parliament soon. Instead, developments will reflect a tendency toward incremental progressivism used by the government of Queensland to manage challenges across several policy areas.

After the defeat of the Labor government's Voice to Parliament national referendum in October 2023, fears were raised that social media disinformation and polarisation generated in parts of the No campaign might set back the prospects for further progress in Queensland (see Chapter 4). Indeed, in response to the result the Liberal-National opposition abandoned their previous support for the process (Gillespie and Smee, 2023). Given the inequalities faced by Aboriginal and Torres Strait Islander peoples and the failure of successive governments to address these through meaningful, consultative action, the need for urgent reforms seems plain. However, in current conditions Queensland's present incremental approach looks unlikely to produce such a change soon.

Funding and legislative protections designed to reduce First Nation peoples' dependence on the continued political will of the sitting government have not yet fully materialised (see below). Although the government appointed an independent Treaty Advancement Committee to continue consultation and report next steps to Parliament (Palaszczuk and Crawford, 2021), the opposition's commitment to any process was far from guaranteed even before their change of heart in 2023 (Hobbs, Whittaker and Coombes, 2019). Therefore, as occurred in South Australia, when a treaty process was abandoned with a change of government, any tangible outcomes of recognition and self-determination might still be lost to the vicissitudes of politics (Hobbs, 2019). Further constitutional innovations of the kind seen elsewhere (like Victoria's elected First Peoples' Assembly (2021) or reserved seats in Parliament like those for the Māori in New Zealand (Taonui, 2017)) are definitely not on the current political agenda.

In terms of other reconciliation policies, recent funding announcements and legislative activities (like the provision of grants to teach and preserve Indigenous languages (Queensland Government, 2023a) and acknowledgement of Torres Strait Islander practices in family law) have formed part of the current government's Path to Treaty policy (Queensland Government, 2023b). This initiative was designed to give due recognition to the peoples displaced by European colonisation, and to redress past wrongs committed against them. However, while the government set up a panel of eminent experts to conduct community consultation and produced a report about next steps in 2020, actions to give effect to their recommendations took time to materialise. Labor ministers' response to the Path to Treaty process indicated in principle agreement with many of the suggestions, but did not commit them to concrete timelines – and also included caveats regarding spending on items such as a Treaty development institute and future fund to ensure continuity of the process, justified in terms of the uncertainties of COVID-19 (QDATSIP, 2020).

In more substantive policy areas, Aboriginal and Torres Strait Islander Queenslanders have continued to face disproportionate challenges. For instance, in recent years they made up 20 per cent of the homeless population but were only 5 per cent of the total population. Indigenous incarceration has been 10 times the rate of non-Indigenous people in Queensland, and only grew further between 2020 and 2021 (Australian Bureau of Statistics, 2021). Indigenous and youth crime featured heavily in political campaigning in recent years, particularly in relation to marginal electorates in the state's north. The issue came to political prominence during the 2020 election when the opposition proposed a controversial youth curfew, sparking civil liberties groups to characterise the election as a 'law and order auction' (Queensland Council for Civil Liberties, 2020). This campaign was politically unsuccessful, in part because the Labor government also promised tough law-and-order measures (Sarre, 2020) that have been criticised by community groups and youth advocates. State Labor also declined to support reforms to increase the age of criminal responsibility from 10 to 14 years, against the advice of experts on crime and human rights and in contrast to the position of the federal Labor party (Hall, 2021).

For some other minority groups, however, the Labor government tried to extend human rights. The state delivered several legislative and policy outputs in recent years that reflected majority public positions on controversial and historically vexed issues, while minimising partisan conflict over these matters. The government pursued a broadly consensual agenda of legal rights reforms, including the formal decriminalisation of abortion in 2019; the introduction of a human rights Act to expand the scope of the existing anti-discrimination framework; and legislation on Voluntary Assisted Dying in 2021.

Public services and policy challenges

Queensland's public services were a key source of political controversy in the recent past. Some of this residue reflects the legacy of the radical Newman years (2012–2015), when the Liberal-National government cut public service positions (Hawthorne, 2012), and appointed senior officials seen to be personally loyal to Newman and other Liberal-National figures. The then premier also used disparaging rhetoric to criticise the inefficiency and ineffectiveness of the Queensland public service (Australian Associated Press, 2012). Newman's loss of a massive parliamentary majority within the space of a single term has been partly attributed to a backlash from public sector workers, who have long made up a significant proportion of the Queensland workforce (QGSO, 2021). Health and social service delivery has been the largest employer in the state, while core public administration and public safety sectors employ more Queenslanders than all the primary industries. The Labor government subsequently reinstated more than twice the number of public servants cut by Newman, and Labor ran a campaign during the 2020 election warning Queensland voters not to 'risk cuts' by returning to a Liberal-National government (Palaszczuk, 2020b). Following the 2020 election, the new Liberal-National opposition leader publicly pledged not to cut the public service and made such promises a core component of the 2024 campaign (Riga and Pollard, 2023).

Despite the expansion of public service positions under the Palaszczuk government, the sector also attracted continued critical attention in relation to integrity and corruption. Public agencies were implicated in the controversy surrounding Deputy Premier Jackie Trad's involvement with the selection of the principal for the new Brisbane South State Secondary College. It was determined that the public service had inappropriately involved her in the appointment process in order to anticipate the Deputy Premier's wishes (McCutcheon, 2020b). A Crime and Corruption Commission (2020) report found evidence that the Education Department falsified documents and misled the media and public about the process, and a senior official was stood down pending investigation. Earlier on in 2016, at the local government level, the Crime and Corruption Commission's (2017) Operation Belcarra found problems with corruption and political donations, which led to the mass sacking of the city councils in Ipswich and Logan (ABC News, 2019) – two major satellite cities of the state's capital – and a subsequent series of regulatory reforms (QCC, 2018). Concerns were also raised about policy shifts that have resulted in more matters of public service misconduct being handled in-house, with suggestions that the government bowed to pressure from the police union to weaken the system of independent scrutiny of police set up in the wake of the landmark 1989 Fitzgerald Inquiry (Smee, 2019).

While Queensland retained a capable public service, it faced a series of structural challenges in adapting to the post-COVID-19 environment. Some of the underlying challenges were addressed in a series of earlier reviews by Peter Coaldrake (Jenkins, 2019) and Peter Bridgman (2019). These addressed the Labor Government's pledge to restore permanent employment as the default arrangement in the Queensland Public Service (QPS), which sought to make the QPS an 'employer of choice'. Reforms to the legislative framework for the QPS in 2020 created a stronger environment for worker rights, including new provisions for transforming casual roles into ongoing positions. In addition, there were new steps and principles to guide performance management in a more 'positive' direction, separating it from disciplinary procedures and placing a greater onus on organisations and managers to demonstrate they have worked to engage and support staff before initiating action for underperformance (Queensland Government, no date). These developments aimed to reduce job insecurity in the QPS, but the changes 'will also likely see an increase in the complexity of and challenges to performance management processes' (Tobin, 2020). If the state service's recurrent shortage of skilled labour continues, this could lead to a significant structural shift in the power relationship between agencies and their employees, with implications for the future capacity of the public service to implement change and manage performance.

From crisis management to structural adaptation

Queensland's response to COVID-19 reminded voters of the advantages of strong, stable executive government in tackling emergency management issues. Other responses to recent natural disasters (especially recurring severe flooding and coastal typhoons in the 2020s) also showed that the Queensland government has a well-developed capacity for crisis management, both at the political level and within the public service. Yet governments should not just respond to crises; they also need to consider how to adapt to them to reduce future costs, and they should explore how public policy settings might be changed to reduce the likelihood of future crises. Some of the biggest policy challenges in Queensland fall under this category – they can be made better or worse by government action and inaction. However, Queensland's democratic institutions and processes have not been optimised for the structural adaption required to address these challenges.

Environmental protection and adaptation to the impacts of climate change have remained serious and highly contentious issues in Queensland (and see Chapter 27). The state spans subtropical, tropical and arid regions, making it prone to a wide range of severe weather events, which are predicted to worsen in frequency and severity with climate change, producing social, economic and environmental costs that are not evenly distributed across the state (Queensland Department of Environment and Science, 2019). With strong inter-regional differences in the state's economic and employment base, no easy compromise between economic development and environmental sustainability has been able to be reached, to date.

Primary industries are concentrated in central and western Queensland in the form of agriculture and mining, and they make up an important share of the state's GDP, revenue and total land use. While tourism experienced a downturn due to COVID-19, it has remained a key component of the economy in the north and south-east coasts of the state. Meanwhile, the majority of the populated areas in the south-east corner have formed a mainly service-based economy built on retail, human/professional services and construction. Politically, state and federal Labor have struggled to manage tensions between the different industrial sectors and concerns about the changing face of employment and the need to transition to a greener economy. Controversy around the Adani Coal Mine was a totemic issue for pro-mining and pro-environmental movements, playing a key role in successful Green campaigns in inner-city Brisbane seats, and in Liberal-National campaigns in the central and northern districts. This was a wedge issue for Labor, as highlighted by the party's poor showing at federal elections in 2019 (when the Australian Greens' 'Adani caravan' drew the attention of both left-leaning and pro-coal communities to Labor's ambivalent stance on the issue) and again in 2022, when the party lost seats to the Greens in Brisbane (Horn, 2019).

The profile of social inequality has also changed rapidly in Queensland, with particularly dramatic effects in the area of housing affordability, requiring a rethink of Queensland's historically limited investment in social housing during an earlier era of cheap and plentiful private housing stock (Australian Institute for Health and Welfare, 2023). While Queensland increased its investment in social housing in recent years, it also remained second to the bottom of Australian states for per capita net recurrent social housing expenditure – that would have to increase by 27 per cent to reach the national average (AGPC, 2021). Queensland has long prided itself as a region of opportunity, prosperity and equality. While there have always been groups that were left out of this 'fair go' ideal, critics argue that the state risks entrenching and expanding an underclass that has been economically excluded and politically marginalised, unless structural reforms to social services and housing are implemented. Dramatic increases in housing insecurity and shortages during the pandemic period meant that housing affordability for people on average incomes came to be among the worst in the country (Australian Institute for Health and Welfare, 2023). The government responded with an allocation of A$2 billion over four years for social housing (Riga and Gramenz, 2021), as well as large-scale land releases for suburban development of private housing in south-east Queensland. It also sought to reform rental laws to provide additional certainty of tenure to tenants. However, critics in the housing sector and parliamentary crossbench argued that these reforms did not go far enough to prevent social marginalisation (Gramenz, 2021).

Conclusion

The COVID-19 pandemic reinforced a long-standing Queensland political tendency for voters to reward strong and decisive executive government, further entrenching the dominance of the executive over political and policy processes in the state. Despite this, the Labor government sponsored initiatives that built the capacity of opposition voices to challenge government policy. It successfully managed controversial legislative processes in the area of morality policy, and at least made a start on Aboriginal and Torres Strait Islander peoples' issues. While voters rewarded the Labor government of Anastacia Palaszczuk with a third term and an increased parliamentary majority, critics have argued that all is not well for democracy in the 'Sunshine State'. Regional polarisation, a politically weak opposition for much of the pandemic period, and an institutional framework that has allowed the government to truncate debate in pandemic times have added to longer term difficulties in response to politically divisive structural problems, including climate change and worsening social inequalities. Queensland has also continued to struggle to undertake the structural reforms required for the expansion of democratic representation, maintenance of economic prosperity and preservation of environmental values. Reforms to parliamentary procedures and greater resourcing for the crossbench cannot overcome the serious representative and deliberative deficiencies and risks produced by unicameralism, while the changes made to integrity institutions seem to be producing too much and too little accountability at the same time. Therefore, questions remain about whether Queensland can build on its success in short-term crisis management during 2020–2022 to confront the 'slow crises' of social inequality and climate change.

References

Australian Associated Press (2012) 'Bureaucrats "drunk" on power: Newman', *Brisbane Times*, 16 February. https://perma.cc/P59N-4RUP

Australian Institute for Health and Welfare (2023) 'Housing affordability', web article, 7 September. https://perma.cc/5XLR-57P9

ABC News (2019) 'Logan City Council sacked by the Queensland Government', *ABC News Online*, 1 May https://perma.cc/Q4QA-VYMS

ABC News (2021) 'Twelve NRL clubs to move into Queensland hubs amid NSW COVID-19 outbreak', *ABC News Online*, 11 July. https://perma.cc/YWM2-E9LD

AGPC (Australian Government Productivity Commission) (2021) 'Report on Government Services 2021 PART G, SECTION 18: Housing', *Productivity Commission*. https://perma.cc/458M-YK3Q

Australian Bureau of Statistics (2021) 'Corrective Services, Australia, June Quarter', 16 September. https://perma.cc/EF2F-68QG

Bavas, Josh (2019) 'Queensland Premier forced to apologise after threatening Katter MPs over Fraser Anning speech', *ABC News Online*, 22 October. https://perma.cc/MA6Q-DFGR

Bridgman, Peter (2019) 'A fair and responsive public service for all: Independent review of Queensland's state employment laws', *State of Queensland Department of Premier and Cabinet*. https://perma.cc/94MC-PVFS

Coaldrake, Peter (1989) *Working the System: Government in Queensland*, University of Queensland Press, Australia. https://perma.cc/2CA7-DHRX

First Peoples' Assembly of Victoria (2022) 'Annual report, 2021'. Web document. https://www.firstpeoplesvic.org/wp-content/uploads/2022/06/FPAV_AnnualReport2021_A4_FINAL_Digital_V8-1.pdf

Fitzgerald Inquiry (1989) *Report of the Commission of Inquiry into Possible Illegal Activities and Associated Police Misconduct*. https://perma.cc/J9L5-DKB9

Gillespie, Eden and Smee, Ben (2023) 'Queensland LNP abandons support for treaty with First Nations people', *The Guardian, Australia*, 18 October. https://perma.cc/Y6FL-KJ4E

Gramenz, Emilie (2021) 'Proposed changes to leasing and tenancy agreements for renters met with mixed reactions', *ABC News Online*, 19 June. https://perma.cc/75TY-XN4H

Guardian (2020) 'NSW ramps up criticism of Queensland border closure', 9 September. https://perma.cc/E7R6-XJKY

Hall, James (2021) 'New bill in Queensland parliament to lift the age of criminal responsibility', *NCA Newswire*, 15 September. https://perma.cc/BQ29-8ZYX

Harris Rimmer, Susan and Stephenson, Elise (2020) 'Queensland is making election history with two women leaders, so why is the campaign focused on men?' *The Conversation*, 25 October. https://perma.cc/ABH6-MRXF

Hawthorne, Maree (2012) '14,000 jobs to go but no sackings: Newman'. *ABC News Online*, 14 September. https://perma.cc/3L7V-UEC3

Hobbs, Harry (2019) 'A Queensland treaty: Current steps and potential challenges', *Alternative Law Journal*, vol. 45, no 1, pp.25–30. https://doi.org/10.1177%2F1037969X19891709

Hobbs, Harry; Whittaker Alison and Coombes, Lindon (2019) 'As the federal government debates an Indigenous Voice, state and territories are pressing ahead', *The Conversation*, 16 July. https://perma.cc/J6PL-VDWG

Horn, Allyson (2019) 'Election 2019: Why Queensland turned its back on Labor and helped Scott Morrison to victory', *ABC News Online*, 19 May. https://perma.cc/5Z5S-H59L

Jenkins, Shannon (2019) 'Queensland public sector needs "talent"', *The Mandarin*, 11 June. https://perma.cc/69R4-NA65

Laing, Kate and Madden, Cathy (2024) 'Gender composition of Australian parliaments by party: A quick guide', *Australian Government Department of Parliamentary Services*, 8 June. https://perma.cc/5Z7S-B6ZT

Lynch, Lydia (2020) 'LNP leader wants "new approach" for Queensland's public service', *Brisbane Times*, 3 December. https://perma.cc/AY3R-8D2A

McCutcheon, Peter (2020a) 'Why the Palaszczuk Government is accused of exploiting coronavirus to avoid parliamentary scrutiny', *ABC Online*. 31 July. https://perma.cc/D7FD-XV5N

McCutcheon, Peter (2020b) 'Jackie Trad school appointment fiasco poses serious questions about the independence of Queensland's public service', *ABC News Online*, 2 July. https://perma.cc/M5C4-QDPK

McCutcheon, Peter and Hartley Anna (2020) 'Political donations and election spending capped in Queensland as "historic" laws pass Parliament', *ABC News Online*, 18 June. https://perma.cc/L27T-62SP

McKenna, Kate (2021) 'Queensland has some of the lowest full COVID-19 vaccination rates in the country, and experts say there are a few reasons why', *ABC News Online*, 7 September. https://perma.cc/3PBU-YKZD

Palaszczuk, Annastacia (2020a) 'Torres Strait Islander families a step closer to legal recognition', *Media Statement*, 16 July. https://perma.cc/78F2-WJN4

Palaszczuk, Annastacia (2020b) '2020 Palaszczuk Labor campaign launch', *annastaciapalaszczuk.com*, 18 October. https://web.archive.org/web/20220309234009/https://www.annastaciapalaszczuk.com.au/media-releases/2020-palaszczuk-labor-campaign-launch/

Palaszczuk, Annastacia (2022) 'Nation leading electoral reforms commence today', *Media statement*, 1 July. https://perma.cc/G9TY-R4A3

Palaszczuk, Annastacia and Crawford, Craig (2021) 'Queensland Treaty Advancement Committee members announced', Media Statement, 14 February. https://perma.cc/8N37-ZLSF

Palaszczuk, Annastacia and Crawford, Craig (2023) 'Treaty and truth-telling in new legislation', Media Statement, 22 February. https://perma.cc/7RUR-NZND

Petter, Pandanus (2023) 'Who is Queensland's next premier, Steven Miles?', *The Conversation*, 12 December. https://perma.cc/6ZYU-F8VS

Pollard, Emma (2020) 'Jackie Trad unseated in South Brisbane – a bruising election loss for a party high-flyer', *ABC News Online*, 31 October. https://perma.cc/6SMC-MRZE

Pretty, Lynda (2020) 'Queensland's scrutiny of proposed legislation by parliamentary committees: Do they make for more considered, rights-compatible law?' *Australasian Parliamentary Review*, vol.35, no.1, Winter/Spring, pp.54–76. https://perma.cc/9NAV-RHFB

QCC (Queensland Crime and Corruption Commission) (CCC) (2017) 'Operation Belcarra a blueprint for integrity and addressing corruption risk in local government', *The Crime and Corruption Commission*, 1 October. https://perma.cc/S3E4-KZG5

QCC (Queensland Crime and Corruption Commission) (CCC) (2018) 'Culture and corruption risks in local government: Lessons from an investigation into Ipswich City Council (Operation Windage)', August. https://perma.cc/3E97-MCM7

QCC (Queensland Crime and Corruption Commission) (CCC) (2020) 'An investigation into allegations relating to the appointment of a school principal', 20 July. https://perma.cc/E43N-E4XW

QDATSIP (Queensland Department of Aboriginal and Torres Strait Islander Partnerships) (2020) 'Queensland Government Treaty Statement of Commitment and response to recommendations of the Eminent Panel'. *Tabled Papers Parliament of Queensland 5620T1358,* August. https://perma.cc/JR9L-7QV7

QGSO (Queensland Government Statistician's Office (2021) 'Labour and employment - State'. *Queensland Treasury*, 16 September. https://perma.cc/FYS2-ZBZF

Queensland Council for Civil Liberties (2020) 'LNP Townsville curfew proposal', media release, 22 November. https://perma.cc/W863-KHBJ

Queensland Department of Environment and Science (2019) 'Climate change in Queensland', webpage. https://perma.cc/4YEP-L4GM

Queensland Electoral Commission (2023) 'Election results and statistics – State election results', webpage. https://perma.cc/4JKW-UTRN

Queensland Government (no date) 'Public Service Employment Framework: Understand changes to the public service employment framework', Queensland Government Website. https://perma.cc/PVH6-HPTL

Queensland Government (2020a) 'Treaty Statement of Commitment and response to recommendations of the Eminent Panel', Brisbane: State of Queensland, August, https://perma.cc/JR9L-7QV7

Queensland Government (2020b) 'Report from the Treaty Working Group on Queensland's Path to Treaty February 2020, *Department of Seniors, Disability Services and Aboriginal and Torres Strait Islander Partnerships,*10 February. https://perma.cc/E62Y-SWGH

Queensland Government (2023a) 'Indigenous languages grants', 1 September. https://perma.cc/AD4R-8BJG

Queensland Government (2023b) 'Queensland's Path to Treaty'. 30 November. Queensland Government. https://perma.cc/A7YE-59K6

Queensland Independent Remuneration Tribunal (2021) 'Determination 23/2021 additional staff member and remuneration determination: 2021 Review of the additional staffing levels for cross bench members of the 57th Parliament', 24 February. https://perma.cc/9LDF-VPHX

Richards, Lisa (2021) 'Indigenous Australian parliamentarians in federal and state/territory parliaments: A quick guide', *Australian Parliamentary Library.* 15 June. https://perma.cc/5PTR-QWAN

Riga, Rachel; Gramenz, Emilie (2021) 'Social housing advocates label Queensland's 2021 budget spending a "band aid" that won't solve crisis', *ABC News Online,* 15 June. https://perma.cc/92CG-688F

Riga, Rachel and Pollard, Emma (2023) 'This week in Queensland politics saw the ghost of Campbell Newman past haunt Labor and the LNP', *ABC News Online*, 24 November. https://perma.cc/9HDD-YAH2

Salisbury, Chris (2020a) 'Did someone say "election"?: How politics met pandemic to create "fortress Queensland"', *The Conversation,* August 12. https://perma.cc/9XWE-W57L

Salisbury, Chris (2020b) '"Three-peat Palaszczuk": Why Queenslanders swung behind Labor in historic election', *The Conversation*, 1 November. https://perma.cc/54PX-N6F2

Sarre, Rick (2020) 'Queensland's LNP wants a curfew for kids, but evidence suggests this won't reduce crime', *The Conversation*, 22 October. https://perma.cc/89HU-UK7E

Smee, Ben (2019) 'Queensland to repeal police discipline system set up after Fitzgerald inquiry', *The Guardian, Australia,* 12 March. https://perma.cc/SE9G-EEQV

State Development and Regional Industries Committee (2022) *Inquiry into the Independent Assessor and Councillor Conduct Complaints System*. October. Report No. 28, 57th Parliament, Queensland. https://documents.parliament.qld.gov.au/tp/2022/5722T1670-4778.pdf

Stone, Lucy (2021) '41 misconduct complaints against Brisbane councillor Jonathan Sri dismissed', *ABC Radio Brisbane*, 18 August. https://perma.cc/3ZCN-GMJZ

Taonui, Rawiri (2017) 'New Zealand elections: Māori seats once again focus of debate', *The Conversation*, 8 September. https://perma.cc/8H2V-SUD5

Tobin, Andrew (2020) 'Stage 1 reforms for Queensland public sector encourage job security and positive performance management', *Hobgood Ganim Lawyers*, 4 September. https://perma.cc/A4FT-VGAX

Wordsworth, Matt (2021) 'Premier Annastacia Palaszczuk will soon need to have an awkward conversation with Queensland about opening up to COVID-19', *ABC News Online*, 4 September. https://perma.cc/E23U-S22Z

Zillman, Stephanie (2021) 'Queensland's Chief Health Officer rejects Prime Minister's comments on AstraZeneca's COVID-19 vaccine for under-40s'. *ABC News Online*, 30 June. https://perma.cc/97GA-BC7Q

20

South Australia

Rob Manwaring, Josh Holloway and Andrew Parkin

South Australia (SA) is one of the country's oldest states, having been proclaimed as a freely settled colony in 1836 and assuming self-governing status in 1856. Much of its area remains sparsely inhabited, with Adelaide as the dominant population centre on the south coast. With 1.8 million people the state ranks fifth in size. Until the mid-1970s elections in the state were shaped by a significant malapportionment of its electoral boundaries, which over-allocated seats to rural and regional areas, with voters in Adelaide and its surrounds badly under-represented – a gerrymander nicknamed the 'Playmander' (after former Premier Playford). However, following electoral reforms in 1974 the state has been a more even battleground, although the Australian Labor Party (ALP) has tended to dominate the winning of elections.

What does democracy require of South Australia's political system?

- *An effective state constitution* to secure and underpin liberal democracy in the state.
- *Aboriginal and Torres Strait Islander peoples* should be afforded full individual civil and human rights.
- *Electoral systems* for the state's lower and upper houses should accurately translate parties' share of votes into seats in the state legislature, in different ways that are recognised as legitimate by most citizens. Ideally, the voting systems should foster the overall social representativeness of the two houses of the legislature. Elections and the regulation of political parties should be impartially conducted, with integrity.
- The *political parties* should sustain vigorous and effective electoral competition and citizen participation. Political parties should uphold the highest standards of conduct in public life.
- The *Parliament* should normally maintain full public oversight of government services and state operations, ensuring public and parliamentary accountability.
- An *effective bicameral system* (two chamber) to ensure that the legislative branch meets its representative and accountability functions.

How to cite this chapter:

Manwaring, Rob; Holloway, Josh; and Parkin, Andrew (2024) 'South Australia', in: Evans, Mark; Dunleavy, Patrick and Phillimore, John (eds) *Australia's Evolving Democracy: A New Democratic Audit*, London: LSE Press, pp.432-452. https://doi.org/10.31389/lsepress.ada.t. Licence: CC-BY-NC 4.0

- *The South Australian government* should govern responsively, prioritising the public interest and broadly reflecting state public opinion. Its core executive (premier, Cabinet, ministers and key central departments) should oversee a coherent and well-coordinated implementation of public policies and management of public services across government.
- The *core executive* and government should operate fully within the law, and ministers should be effectively scrutinised by and politically accountable to Parliament. The administration of public services should be controlled by democratically elected officials as far as possible.
- In the wider *state public service* officials should act with integrity, in accordance with well-enforced codes of conduct, and within the rule of law.
- The South Australian government should effectively and transparently represent its citizens' interests at *the Commonwealth level*.

The chapter begins by covering some recent developments, then the strengths and weaknesses of South Australia's democratic processes is summarised in a SWOT analysis. Following that, the state's electoral processes, constitutional and human rights issues, and relations between the executive and Parliament are considered in more detail.

Recent developments

The political management of the COVID-19 pandemic in South Australia in the early 2020s provided an interesting insight into the operation of executive government and on the degree to which it can be held to account via the parliamentary process. Important statutory powers were exercised by two non-elected public officials, the Police Commissioner in his capacity as State Coordinator (under the Emergency Management Act) and the Chief Public Health Officer (under the Public Health Act). Partly in recognition of these statutory powers, and partly as a matter of political judgement, the minority Liberal-National government under Premier Steven Marshall created a COVID-19 Transition Committee, including these two officers as key members, to advise on the imposition of border-closure and lockdown measures.

The Transition Committee decisions had significant impacts on South Australians (and indeed on anybody wanting to enter South Australia). They were largely exercised by public officials within the executive branch, albeit with the consent and collaboration of the premier and the Minister of Health. Parliamentary approval was required in April 2020 for the new *Covid Emergency Response Act 2020* to enable various policy and executive actions, such as protecting residential and commercial renters affected by the pandemic. Important concessions were forced on the government by virtue of its minority status in the House of Assembly. In September 2021, Labor and the crossbenchers succeeded in adding a regional representative to the Transition Committee while also limiting the extension period for special measures.

At the 2022 state elections, the incumbent Liberal government (which had been there only for a single term) fared badly and Labor under Peter Manlinauskas swept to power with a comfortable majority (27 of the 47 seats in the House of Assembly). However, as in 2018 the Legislative Council (LC) (with 22 seats) remained evenly divided between the top two parties, with two Greens and a One Nation member holding the balance.

Strengths, weaknesses, opportunities and threats (SWOT) analysis

Current strengths	Current weaknesses
The state's constitution has provided for the stable and effective operation of liberal democracy and has been adjusted in a flexible manner. Government through the COVID-19 pandemic was effective, parliamentary consensus was maintained in support and policies did not create as much controversy or minority opposition as in some other states.	There is some lack of clarity about when a referendum should be used to amend the *Constitution Act 1934* (South Australia Parliament, no date a). As a result, Parliament can potentially change aspects of the Constitution without due deliberation. Some provisions included in the *Constitution Act 1934* have not operated as intended, for example, the state-wide winner of the two-party preferred vote was supposed to form the government under a 1997 'fairness' rule. This was removed in 2017.
The position of the Aboriginal and Torres Strait Islander peoples has been constitutionally recognised, and a state apology given in 1997 about past practices ignoring their rights. Several government activities and strategies have sought to redress the historical disadvantage that Indigenous people have suffered, with some recent progress. Longstanding legislation has secured key civil rights (for example, against sex discrimination, and equal opportunity for women (South Australia Parliament, no date b). In 2023, South Australia became the first Australian state to have a constitutionally enshrined Indigenous Voice to Parliament.	To date, there has been no substantial progress in negotiating a Treaty with Aboriginal and Torres Strait Islander peoples, as advocates demand. Few Indigenous Australians have ever been elected to Parliament. There have been governance issues with some Aboriginal-controlled bodies, and progress on remedying past inequalities has been slow. The state has no comprehensive human rights charter.
The state's Alternative Vote (AV) electoral system, applied in the House of Assembly, and proportional representation (PR), used in the LC, balance majoritarian and proportional elements. Elections have been conducted with a high level of integrity and have produced relatively stable periods of governments by one or other of the top two parties. Beyond the two-party axis some new dynamics in electoral competition have been growing, perhaps more slowly than in some other states.	There is a lack of clarity about whether the electoral system should facilitate two-party preferred majorities at the state-wide level producing House of Assembly majorities. In the recent past, long periods of single-party incumbency reflected a lack of competitiveness between the top two parties. The erratic votes for small parties in the LC elections also reflect their weakness as party organisations and difficulties in becoming established competitors.
A cap on party political donations has been in place since 2013, with relatively high levels of compliance. There has been little evidence of significant 'dark money' influence in state politics. South Australia has a well-established, albeit narrow, mainstream media landscape.	The compliance regime for political donations has been complex and the South Australian Electoral Commissioner has lacked the resources to investigate in penetrating ways. South Australia has the highest candidate deposit fees in the nation, which may somewhat inhibit new parties or independent candidates. As in other states, media diversity has been limited.

Within Parliament, many MPs have had key skills and professional backgrounds suited for law-making roles.	There has been significant under-representation in Parliament of women (ECSA, 2023a), people from non-European ethnic minority backgrounds, working class backgrounds and people with disabilities.
South Australia saw a strong executive and public sector response to COVID-19. In the official view the ministerial code of conduct and the component of ministerial responsibility requiring acting with integrity both remained effective (South Australia Government, 2021). Parliament scrutiny provides stable and generally effective democratic accountability.	As in other states, there has been a tendency for the executive to dominate the relatively small Parliament, especially if a government has a comfortable majority of MPs in the House of Assembly. The component of ministerial responsibility where politicians answer for mistakes made by departments and agencies in their brief has weakened over time (Selway, 2003). In addition, a code of conduct for MPs has been lacking for many years, and parliamentarians voted unanimously in 2021 to reduce the scope of the Corruption Commission.
In the Weatherill Labor era (2011–2018) there was a focus on deliberative democracy and consultation arrangements remain active. Online consultation opportunities in relation to draft policy initiatives are now mostly routine.	There was a shift away from supplementing democracy with citizen juries and other deliberative processes since 2018, and no new initiatives have occurred since.
Future opportunities	**Future threats**
The *Constitution Act* has arguably become due for some 'housekeeping' reforms. Rights legislation can be enhanced and reformed. There could also be scope to find new mechanisms for citizen voice and input.	Parliamentary sovereignty may impede or veto any wider amendments to the Constitution. There has been only a limited appetite for more significant constitutional reform. The top two parties have been reluctant or unwilling to introduce reforms of citizen rights or democratic improvements.
Political parties could prioritise recruitment of Aboriginal and Torres Strait islander Peoples. The Voice to the South Australian Parliament, established in 2023, has the potential to improve Indigenous representation and promotion of key issues.	Political parties have been reluctant to pre-select candidates from Aboriginal peoples, and slow to commit to combatting systemic racism and disadvantage compared with other priorities (like seeking the 'law and order' vote).
A review of the effectiveness of regulation of parties and political donations has become overdue (for example, to introduce 'real-time' disclosure of donations). The continued role of smaller parties and independents may improve competition in the House of Assembly. Scope also exists to innovate around electoral law and modernise to reflect digital technologies.	There remains a risk of 'cartel' behaviour by the two major parties to restrict competition where their interests are congruent. On the other hand, greater party fragmentation across the two houses could make the 'balance of power' dynamics in legislating more complex. In terms of diversity, some parties are reluctant to introduce mechanisms to improve representation such as quotas. Key demographic groups lack a direct voice in Parliament.
New developments in inter-governmental relations, such as the National Cabinet, strengthened the negotiating role of the state premier and ministers, especially since South Australia has been a strong financial beneficiary of arrangements.	Ministerial accountability on inter-governmental matters has been weaker at state level, with less parliamentary scrutiny.

As in other Australian states, the separate electoral and party politics dynamics of South Australia have thrown up some distinctive democratic issues, especially around the party winning the House of Assembly state-wide two-party preference vote not necessarily forming government. The constitutional set-up in the state and the picture on human rights and diversity also merit a closer look. Finally, we explore how the executive and legislature have operated and some issues around public services.

Elections and electoral systems

South Australia has the same system mix as most other states, with the majoritarian Alternative Vote (AV) electoral system used for the lower house (the House of Assembly) and proportional representation (the Single Transferable Vote (STV)) for the upper house (the LC) (Gallagher and Mitchell, 2018). The differing electoral systems shape voting behaviour and the wider party system. Since 1970, the House of Assembly has had 47 members, and hence 24 votes are required to gain a majority there. All MPs in the lower house serve four-year terms. The LC has 22 members (MLCs), each serving eight-year terms, with half the upper house facing election on alternate cycles.

Lower house

The House of Assembly is elected via 47 single member seats using AV. This system favours the top two parties who almost alone can win the required majority (whether on primary votes or redistributed preference votes) in local seats, although there can also be a handful of independents. Figure 20.1 charts the first-preference votes received by the Liberal-Liberal Country League and Labor parties this century in the lower house elections using AV. It also shows the support for independents and small parties – which here includes the Greens. Despite regularly receiving 8 or 9 per cent of votes across the state this century, the Greens have yet to win a seat, which in practice would require getting into the top two in the AV primary vote and then, if necessary, winning a majority via the distributed preferences of the eliminated major-party candidate. A similar fate has befallen Family First with around 4 per cent support. Another feature of the state has been the absence of the Nationals as a separate party (except in one seat): their rural supporters at national level need to vote Liberal in state elections (a situation explained historically by the Liberal Party having evolved from the Liberal and Country League label).

The lower house is a relatively small body, with 47 seats and hence a majority line of 24. It is elected every four years and in terms of parties winning seats it has always been dominated by the Liberals and Labor; recent elections have proved no exception (Figure 20.2). At each recent election three or sometimes four independents have been elected, in seats where their local reputation was strong. Unusually, they held the balance in the house from 2014–2018, and one member gained a ministerial post in the Labor government. The Nationals have not won any seats across the three elections since 2010.

Figure 20.1: Party first-preference vote shares (and the two-party preferred vote for Labor), South Australia House of Assembly, 2002–2022

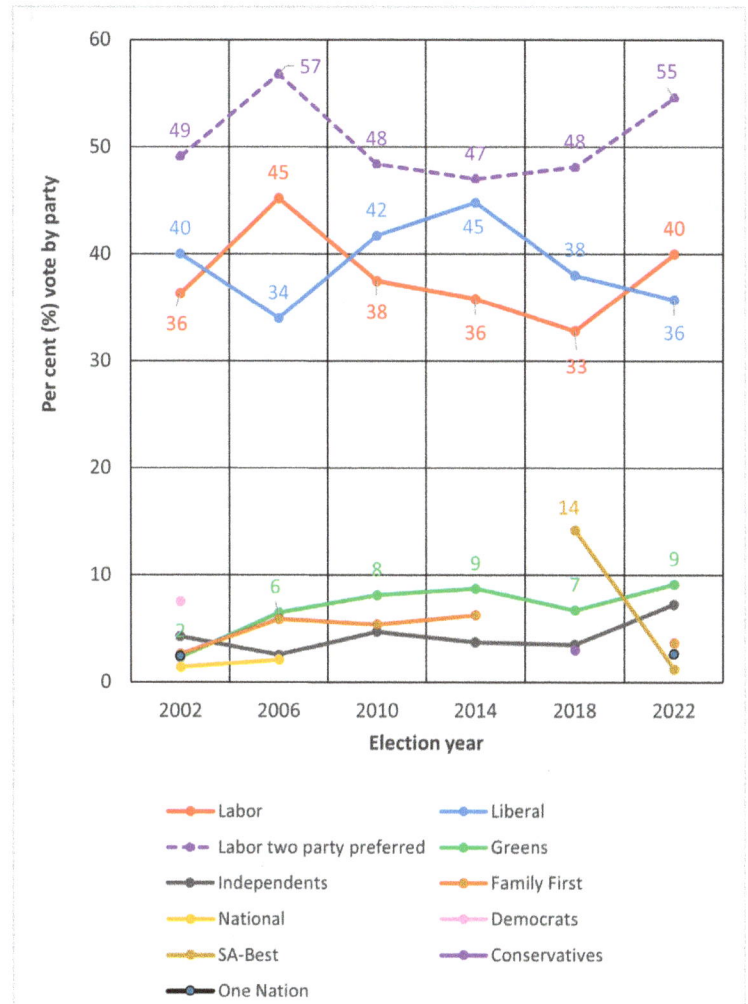

Source: Compiled from data in Electoral Commission of South Australia (ECSA) (2023a).

How accurately does the AV electoral system translate movements in public opinion between elections into changes of seats? The pre-1974 history of gross malapportionment being maintained for decades in South Australia (when Labor was disproportionately disadvantaged, and metropolitan Adelaide badly under-represented) gives some insight into more recent concerns with the 'fairness' of electoral boundaries. Ideally, on democratic grounds the party winning the state-wide two-party preferred vote for the House of Assembly would also be the party gaining most seats, and thus form the government. Until recently a boundary fairness provision was included in the *Constitution Act*. Introduced by Labor in 1991 (magnanimously, after it had been returned to government with a minority of the two-party preferred vote), the provision mandated a post-election redrawing of electoral boundaries to ensure 'as far as practicable' that the party securing 50 per cent or more of the two-party-preferred vote should be able to be 'elected in sufficient numbers to enable a government to be formed' at the next election (Lynch, 2016, 7). Yet in December 2017, the 'fairness' provision for AV elections was removed from the *Constitution Act*, following a successful bill proposed by the Greens in the Legislative Council.

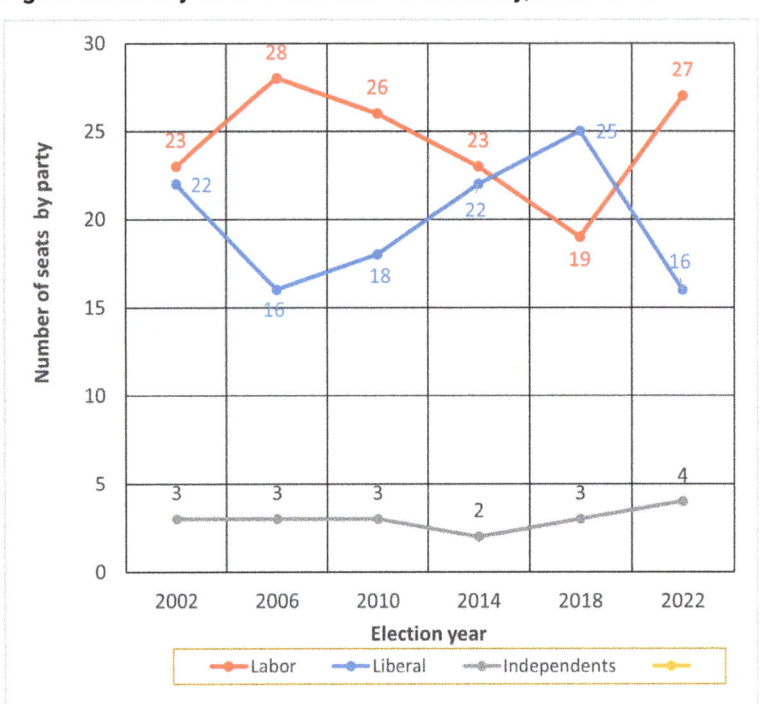

Figure 20.2: Party seats in the House of Assembly, 2006–2022

Source: Compiled from data in Electoral Commission of South Australia (ECSA) (2023a).

The story here has been that the electoral pursuit of this aspect of 'fairness' proved problematic and difficult to achieve. Despite the fairness provision, the Liberal Party narrowly won the two-party-preferred vote in the 2002, 2010 and 2014 elections with 51–52 per cent state-wide, yet the party did not form the government because it lagged Labor in terms of House of Assembly seats won (see Figures 20.1 and 20.2). By contrast, in 2006 and 2022, Labor won the 'Two party preferred' (TPP) vote state-wide, and both times formed majority governments. There was no deliberate design behind these apparent 'wrong winner' anomalies; rather the results demonstrated the limits of the 'as far as practicable' aspiration embedded in the provision. South Australia and its electorate have a distinct geography, with a highly concentrated urban population (particularly in and surrounding Adelaide). The formation of government therefore tends to be determined by a handful of marginal seats in metropolitan areas. This poses an ongoing challenge for the Liberal Party in particular, as its voters over recent elections disproportionately reside in rural and regional areas, piling up large majority wins in safe seats, while Labor's vote is more 'efficiently' spread across the seats it needs to win. Despite conscientious efforts by the Electoral District Boundaries Commissioners to redraw boundaries in a way that could accommodate this geographic pattern at the next election, this was not consistently achieved.

Upper house

Turning to the upper house, the LC is much smaller in size at 22 seats and is elected in halves every four years, in one state-wide constituency with 11 seats. Following significant electoral reforms by the Dunstan Labor government in the 1970s, both voting behaviour for the LC and its composition shifted dramatically. There has been a noteworthy shift in first-preference votes

South Australia 439

Figure 20.3: Party first-preference vote shares under STV in the South Australia Legislative Council (upper house) elections, 2002–2022

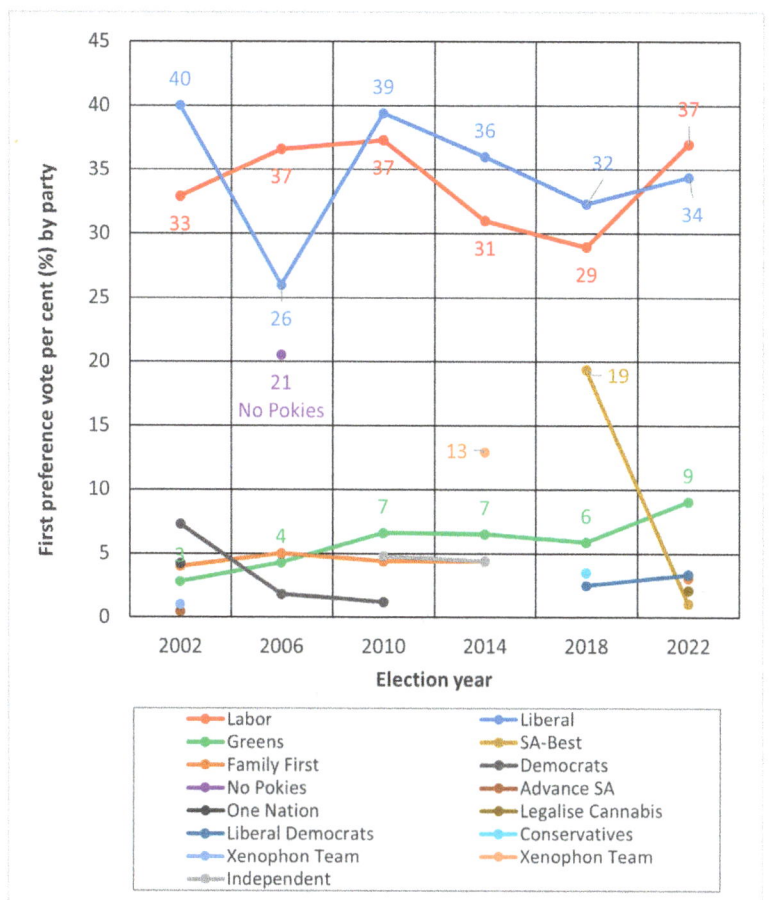

Source: Compiled from data in ECSA (Electoral Commission of South Australia) (2023a).

Figure 20.4: The balance of seats in the Legislative Council (upper house) 2002–2023

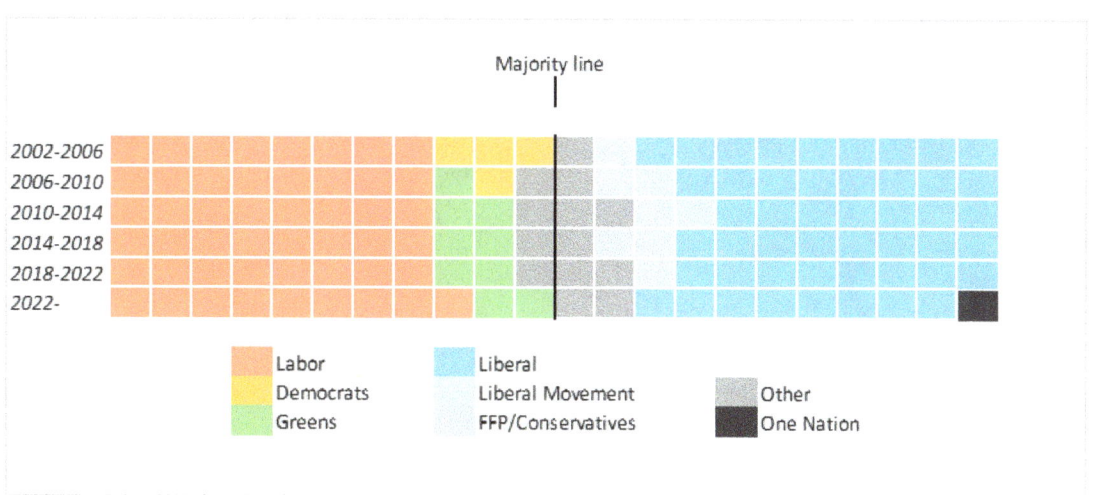

Source: Compiled from data in Electoral Commission of South Australia (ECSA) (2023a).

Note: Each square represents a seat: 12 are required for a majority in a chamber with 22 seats.

for the upper house towards smaller parties and independents, as Figure 20.3 shows. The top two parties continued to dominate in most years, but there were blip results too for parties that appear and then vanish – like 21 per cent for the 'No Pokies' party in 2006, and 19 per cent for SA Best in 2018. Initially, the Democrats and later the Greens helped to deny any clear majority to either major party, and small-party elected members have almost always held the 'balance of power', as the seats map in Figure 20.4 shows. Therefore, South Australians have demonstrated a strong tendency to vote for a more diverse LC, creating an upper chamber where neither major party holds a majority of seats and new legislation must be negotiated through. The breakthrough of Pauline Hanson's One Nation at the 2022 state election was notable, given that South Australia, and the country more widely, have not experienced the electoral growth of radical-right populist parties to the same extent as countries, such as the UK and Sweden.

Parties and the party system

As explained in Chapter 5, political scientists have developed ways of counting parties for party system analysis, and not merely tallying them, but weighting them since not all parties are equally significant (Laakso and Taagepera, 1979). To examine party dynamics, in Figure 20.5, we apply the 'effective number of parties' measure to the party vote shares, and to resulting seats won, at elections from 2002 to 2022. There was far greater fragmentation in votes (measured in the electoral index) than in terms of seats (measured by the parliamentary index), pointing to the lack of proportionality in translating votes into seats – particularly in 2018 in the House of Assembly. While expected in a majoritarian setting like the House, the 'proportional' electoral system used for the LC has still not resulted in a chamber as diverse in party profile as voters' aggregated preferences. The difference in fragmentation between the lower and upper houses highlights the differing representative configurations of the two chambers. However, in 2022 the number of parties (ENEP) also dropped back considerably for both chambers.

Figure 20.5: The effective number of electoral parties (ENEP) and parliamentary parties (ENPP), in the House of Assembly and the Legislative Council

Election year	House of Assembly		Legislative Council	
	Electoral ENEP score	Parliamentary ENPP score	Electoral ENEP score	Parliamentary ENPP score
2002	3.3	2.4	3.5	2.8
2006	3	2.2	4	3.9
2010	3.1	2.2	3.2	3.5
2014	2.9	2.2	4.2	3.5
2018	3.6	2.2	4.3	3.3
2022	2.2	2.2	3.1	3.3

Source: Author's calculation from data in Figures 20.1 to 20.4.

Note: The effective number of electoral parties (ENEP) is another name for ENP votes, and the effective number of parliamentary parties (ENPP) is another name for ENP seats.

Figure 20.6: Parties' seats in the Legislative Council and their index of voting power scores, since 2002

Party	Seats held [and per cent (%) of all voting power]				
	2002–2006	2006–2010	2010–2014	2014–2018	2018–2022
Labor	8 [28]	8 [28.6]	8 [33.9]	8 [28.6]	8 [28.6]
Liberal	9 [36]	8 [28.6]	7 [23.2]	8 [28.6]	8 [28.6]
Democrats	3 [28]	1 [7.1]			
Xenophon/ SABest	1 [4]	2 [14.3]	2 [12.5]	1 [7.1]	2 [14.3]
FFP/ Conservative	1 [4]	2 [14.3]	2 [12.5]	2 [14.3]	1 [7.1]
Greens		1 [7.1]	2 [12.5]	2 [14.3]	2 [14.3]
Other			1 [5.4]	1 [7.1]	1 [7.1]
Effective number of relevant parties (ENRP)	3.5	4.7	4.6	4.7	4.7

Source: Author's calculation from seats data in Figures 20.2 and 20.4.

Note: Table cells show the number of LC seats held by each party, with the resulting per cent of voting power shown by the standardised Banzhaf index (shown in brackets). The effective number of relevant parties (ENRP) in the bottom row counts all parties able to change vote outcomes and is calculated for each LC term.

Modern South Australia electoral competition has been quite different from a 'two-party system', with the decisions by smaller parties on whether to stand and their success in winning votes having significant effects. However, control of state ministries and government formation has remained with the two major parties. Historically, political stability was one of South Australia's defining features, with often long periods of rule by one party (especially in the period before 1968). Since then, there have also been long periods of rule for the Liberals (under three premiers Brown, Olsen and Kerin) from 1994–2002, and Labor (under Dunstan and Corcoran) from 1970–1979, (under Bannon and Arnold) from 1982–1994 and (under Rann and Weatherill) from 2002–2018. The single Liberal term from 2018–2022 was thus unusual.

Focusing on the Labor versus Liberal contest alone could obscure the enduring impact of independent Members of Parliament (MPs), whose presence contributed to several minority governments – including the 2021–2022 Marshall Liberal government. Significant, too, has been the expansion of small party and independent influence in the passage of legislation through the LC. We can gain some insight by calculating the relative legislative 'bargaining power' of parties and independents (see Figure 20.6). Bargaining power here is determined not only by the number of seats, but also the broader configuration of seats across all parties in the chamber. (We use the best-known voting power measure the normalised Banzhaf (1965) index.)

The 'voting power' index shows the top two parties as well ahead of other actors, but as rarely having more than around 30 per cent of the voting power each. And (looking back also to Figure 20.4) we can see that in 2002–2006, for instance, the three Democrats in the LC held as much influence as the eight Labor Councillors on this measure, due to the Democrats' crucial 'balance of power' role. What these calculations make clear, across each parliamentary term, was the relatively limited capacity of government or opposition alone to determine LC outcomes.

Finally, we can also use these bargaining power figures as bases for an alternative measure of party system fragmentation, weighting them as in the 'effective number of parties' index used above to create the 'effective number of relevant parties' (ENRP), devised by Dumont and Caulier (2005). Shown in the bottom row of Figure 20.6, this is a weighted estimate of how many parties matter in determining overall outcomes: it suggests that a truly multi-party legislative environment has emerged, and arguably consolidated, in the state's powerful upper chamber.

Regulating political parties

The regulation of political parties is vexed and complex. A range of issues applicable to Australia as a whole were set out in Gauja and Sawer (2016). While some of the more serious concerns were directed at the more populous Australian states and at the national-level situation (see Chapter 1), concerns have remained about the potential role and influence of 'dark money' influencing parties and candidates. The regulation of political parties in South Australia is governed by the *Electoral Act* 1985, administered by the Electoral Commission of South Australia (ECSA, 2023b). The entry barriers for registering a political party are comparatively low. Within the state, parties must pay an annual fee of A$500, have a constitution and have 200 registered members – or a parliamentarian (by contrast, federal parties require 1,500 members, while Victoria and Western Australia require 500 members). It is notable, too that South Australia has the highest candidate deposit fees of any state and territory (in South Australia, candidates must pay A$1,000, whereas the costs elsewhere range from A$250 to A$500). The deposit is returned if the candidate wins more than 4 per cent of the total number of formal first-preference votes.

The same legislation also governs campaign finance and donation regulations in South Australia. All parties, candidates and third parties must create a designated account. All donations, gifts and loans to state parties over the indexed threshold (A$5,310 in 2023) must be declared, along with gifts of A$200 or more, or loans in excess of A$1,000. Donors must also declare gifts over the threshold limit. Political gifts are broadly defined, and political event tickets are capped at A$500 per person. South Australia's disclosure scheme involves two reporting cycles. In an election year, returns are required by 5 February, and then on a weekly basis until 30 days after the election. These regulations are relatively recent, and transparency around donations was only introduced in 2013. There remain some concerns about the complexity of the requirements, which has led to some double-reporting (ABC, 2018). In June 2021, the Marshall Liberal government introduced new legislation to tighten up aspects of the regime, including enhancing the powers of the Electoral Commissioner to oversee the system. The Malinauskas government has indicated, in 2024, that it seeks to ban all political donations to political parties in the state.

Media diversity

A healthy and vibrant media system is increasingly seen as an essential aspect of a strong democracy. While much of the regulation around the media and press freedoms are federal government issues, along with some key media protections, there are still issues at the state level. A key area of concern in South Australia has been the issue of media diversity and ownership. In effect, South Australia has only one daily newspaper – the *Adelaide Advertiser* and its sister paper *The Sunday Mail*, both owned by News Corp, the company in which the Rupert Murdoch family has a controlling interest. Their only real competition has been the online news source *InDaily*, which reports on state politics and related matters. However, its scope and reach are much more limited. There are also ongoing concerns about the changing media environment of the digital era, where local newspapers have been closed in South Australia (InDaily, 2020a), as across the nation. While ABC News and the commercial TV channels run dedicated South Australian news-desks, there have been ongoing concerns about jobs cuts to the sector (InDaily, 2020b), centralisation of editorial decision-making to the eastern states, and potentially negative impacts on news coverage of political events.

Assessing the significance of this pattern of ownership and control among the mainstream media outlets is, in South Australia as elsewhere, now complicated by the advent of well-patronised social-media platforms providing alternative channels for the promulgation and communication of political information and comment.

Diversity in political representation

The principle of political equality is strongly linked to the value of representation. In a modern democracy, the elected representatives should broadly reflect the communities they seek to speak for. On a number of demographic characteristics, the South Australian Parliament has under-represented key groups. In 2020, the Electoral Commission for SA research found that only 29 per cent of parliamentarians were women, the lowest rate across *all* Australian parliaments, and below the national average at 37 per cent (Marx, 2020). Critically, the report found that overall female representation had declined since 2006, and that South Australia also had one of the lowest rates of female representation in its Cabinet. In 2022, Labor increased its number of female MPs, but the Liberals did not, with signs of long-run difficulty for the party in addressing this matter (ABC, 2023).

MPs from culturally and ethnically diverse communities have also been under-represented in the current South Australian Parliament. According to the 2021 Census, about 24 per cent of South Australians were not born in Australia, with the percentages for the most common other countries of birth being England 5.3, India 2.5, China 1.4 and Vietnam 1.0 (Australian Bureau of Statistics, 2022 and no date). While MPs with Greek and Italian heritage have been elected over time, there were only two members in the 54th Parliament from non-European backgrounds, Jing Lee (Liberal) and Tung Ngo (ALP), both in the LC.

In other characteristics, most MPs now have a university undergraduate degree (Figure 20.7), a considerably higher proportion than for South Australians as a whole. Similarly, certain professions and employment backgrounds have been over-represented compared with the wider South Australian population. Some backgrounds were clearly linked to partisanship.

Figure 20.7: South Australian Parliament 2018–2022 – MPs with university degrees

Chamber	Total number	Number with university degrees	Degree per cent (%)
House of Assembly	47	35	75
Legislative Council	22	15	68
Total	69	50	72

Source: Compiled by the authors from 54th Parliamentary directory for South Australia.

Note: Based on MPs stating they have a university undergraduate degree.

Figure 20.8: South Australian Parliament 2018–2022 – MPs' and Legislative Councillors' employment backgrounds

Background	Number with university degrees	Per cent (%)
Business	19	28
Law	12	17
Unions	9	13
Public Sector	9	13
Other/unclassified	5	7.2
Farming/Primary Industries	4	5.8
Media/Journalism	4	5.8
Local Government	4	5.8
Staffer	3	4.3
Total (both houses)	**69**	**100**

Source: Compiled by the authors from 54th Parliamentary directory for South Australia.

Eighteen of the 19 MPs from the business/private sector were either Liberals (or former Liberals), and all nine MPs from a trade-union background were from the ALP. In sum, using education and employment backgrounds as proxy indicators for class, these data suggest a strong over-representation of MPs coming from middle and high socioeconomic backgrounds.

While data on some other demographic groups has been lacking, there are signs of under-representation among MPs of other vulnerable groups, such as people with disabilities. A notable exception was Kelly Vincent, who has cerebral palsy, was elected to the upper house in 2010 and served until 2018. Her term as an MP saw Parliament install ramps and adapt equipment to meet her needs as a wheel-chair user. In common with other parliaments, young people also tend to be under-represented (Kelly Vincent was also the youngest ever South Australian MP at 21 years old). And we note below that only one MP has identified as having an Aboriginal heritage.

Constitutional issues and human rights

The Constitution Act 1934 is the foundation of South Australia's political system, and it sets out the main framework of South Australia's political system. The doctrine of responsible government entails that the executive branch (the premier and their government) is held accountable to the legislative branch (the Parliament), and in turn, through free and fair regular elections, to the voters of South Australia. In South Australia's bicameral system where there is a breakdown between the two houses, section 41 of the *Constitution Act* provides for a 'deadlock' provision. In effect, if a government bill was to be consistently blocked in the Legislative Council then it can trigger the government to seek permission to dissolve Parliament and cause new elections. From time to time, there have been calls to abolish the upper house in South Australia, and in 2015 the then Labor Premier Mike Rann considered but backed away from holding a referendum on the issue. However, there has been very limited elite or public demand for a unicameral system, such as that in Queensland.

Section 8 empowers the South Australian Parliament to vary the *Constitution Act*. There are a few limits to this, for example, Parliament cannot abolish the upper house without approval by a referendum. Otherwise, the effect has been that Parliament has shown a willingness to change the constitution via legislation, on a regular basis (no less than 14 times since 2000). Most recently, there was a push to introduce a new provision to ensure that the Speaker of the House must be independent of any political party. There have been concerns that while there are benefits to a parliamentary capability, which allows the constitution to be amended on a regular basis, key reforms can take place without due consideration. In addition, a case could be made that the Constitution is due some 'tidying up' or housekeeping reforms (for example, around section 48, which guarantees the franchise for women, a legacy of the suffragette struggle to ensure constitutional protections for women). The last time a Constitution Convention was held in South Australia was in 2003, following the unexpected win of the Rann Labor government. The proposed reforms that came out of this occasion, including greater use of Citizen Initiated Referenda, failed – in part, because there was not significant 'widespread desire' for constitutional change (Bastoni, 2007).

First Nations peoples

Unlike the Australian federal constitution, the South Australian Constitution recognises its First Nations peoples (Part 1), and explicitly notes that the establishment of South Australia 'occurred without proper and effective recognition, consultation or authorisation of Aboriginal Peoples of South Australia'. An Apology was delivered on 28 May 1997 to the First Nations peoples, which acknowledged 'past injustice and dispossession'. However, this section of the *Constitution Act* does not have legal force. In some respects, South Australia has been a state that has taken a lead in securing Aboriginal rights. For example, in 1966 the South Australian government was the first in the country to introduce path-breaking land rights legislation for First Nations peoples (MOAD, no date). In 2023, South Australia was the first state government to constitutionally enshrine a Voice to Parliament.

A wide range of public institutions and activities have sought (and still seek) to address Aboriginal disadvantage and give voice to First Nations people in South Australia. The 2018–2022 Premier Steven Marshall held the portfolio for (South Australia Government, 2023), and was supported by, the South Australian Aboriginal Advisory Council (SAAAC). Efforts were also got under way, for the first time, to enable Aboriginal people to directly elect representatives to SAAAC (InDaily, 2020c). The South Australian government produced an Aboriginal Affairs Action Plan, and in 2021 refreshed its implementation strategy, as part of the relaunched 'closing the gap' agenda. Yet, an ongoing area of concern are issues relating to the governance of Aboriginal-controlled bodies. In the face of some criticism, the government approved a Parliamentary Inquiry into the governance issues of Aboriginal-controlled organisations (NITV News, 2021).

Until the 2023 Voice to Parliament, South Australia has lagged some other states and territories. Under the Weatherill Labor government, there was a push to establish a Treaty with South Australia's Aboriginal People. However, the election of the Liberal government in 2018 'paused' and brought an end to this process (Guardian, 2018). In other areas, South Australia has made little progress, and counted only one among Australia's Indigenous parliamentarians (Gobbett, 2017) – Kyam Maher (Wikipedia, 2023), appointed to fill a casual vacancy in the Legislative Council in 2012, making South Australia the last state and territory in the country to select an Indigenous MP. Maher became Leader of the Government in the LC and Attorney-General following the March 2022 election.

Human rights

The protection of civic rights and key freedoms are key defining characteristics of a strong liberal democracy. Traditionally, in Westminster-inspired political systems, rights protections have been within the prerogative of Parliament rather than constitutionally based, with legislation introduced to protect citizens from discrimination on the grounds of sex, race and ethnicity. Australia remains one of the few advanced industrial nations without a codified Bill of Rights or Human Rights Charter at the national level. In recent times, there has been a push for state governments to introduce human rights charters (Staub, 2019), and the Australian Capital Territory (ACT), Victoria and Queensland have adopted various human rights charters. In South Australia, an attempt to introduce a bill of rights on similar lines was made in a 2004 private members bill, but this failed, and civil rights advocates would argue that South Australia lags in this respect.

Consultation and deliberative democracy

Much modern democratic theory has emphasised the importance of consultation and deliberation as valued components of democratic decision-making. Since the Rann era (2002–2011), there has been a dedicated focus on improving consultation, and the South Australia government's 'YourSay' website has been a key portal for citizen input (South Australia, 2023). In recent years, there has also been a strong focus on 'deliberative' democracy. The main ideas here have been that voters should have more influence between elections, and that the quality of government decisions can be enhanced by better deliberation, or discussion. Labor Premier Jay Weatherill was a noted fan of this movement, and under his government instigated a range of 'new' deliberative techniques, including citizens' juries in 2015 (South Australia Government, 2015). The effect of this was mixed, with criticism particularly directed at the process relating to a citizen jury on the nuclear fuel cycle (Donaldson, 2016). Yet, it showed a rare willingness to enhance South Australia's core democratic institutions. The Marshall government elected in 2018 showed little to no enthusiasm for these kinds of 'new' deliberative and democratic techniques, and the post-2022 Labor government has yet to signal much change.

The executive and Parliament

The executive branch of the South Australian government features familiar Westminster-style institutions. In formal constitutional terms, the executive branch is headed by the State Governor, representing the Crown, and executive power is technically exercised by an Executive Council over which the Governor presides. However, as is true nationally (see Chapter 1) and in other Australian jurisdictions this formal constitutional description is misleading and anachronistic. The political and administrative control of the South Australian executive branch has lain in the hands of the premier and the ministers who comprise the state Cabinet (even though the Cabinet is not mentioned in South Australia's *Constitution Act*). The Cabinet members have generally been drawn from the elected parliamentary members of the party or coalition that controls the House of Assembly. However several times over the past twenty years Labor Cabinets have also included Independent members, either to support a minority Labor government (2002–2006) or later simply to bolster Labor's majority. These Independent members of Cabinet have been conceded the in-principle capacity to vote against the government (of which they have formally become a member) in the House of Assembly, a practice in serious tension with Westminster-derived norms of responsible government. Cabinet can exercise a range of executive powers. These include prerogative powers arising from its embodiment of the authority of 'the Crown' as well as statutory powers arising from authority explicitly delegated or entrusted to the executive through past legislation (Selway, 1997, p.104). This all adds up to a considerable scope for the exercise of executive decision-making. The position of premier has always been especially significant and sits at the apex of executive power.

The primary mechanism for executive accountability is through the state Parliament, and ongoing concerns have remained about the extent to which such potentially dominant executive power can be held to proper account through parliamentary scrutiny. Yet, some political factors have provided a level of constraint and democratic accountability. Parliament can constrain the operations of the executive branch in some enduring ways. The maximum size of the Cabinet is not in the gift of the premier but is explicitly limited to 15 members by section 65(1) of the *Constitution Act*, which is essentially a piece of legislation passed by, and subject to amendment by, the Parliament. Increasing from the previous size of 13 required both houses of the state Parliament to approve the necessary amendment in December 1997. However, as in other Westminster systems, unwritten conventions of collective and individual ministerial responsibility have remained vital. The doctrine of collective ministerial responsibility for government actions (and associated ministerial solidarity in public) has worked reasonably well in South Australia.

However, greater concerns have focused on the effectiveness of the doctrine of individual ministerial responsibility for matters within their departmental brief. In the traditional conception each minister ought to be considered responsible not only for the appropriateness and integrity of their own individual actions but also for any mistakes or maladministration made by the departments and agencies for which they are responsible. In the case of serious mistakes, ministers were expected to resign from Cabinet. This aspect of the doctrine has undoubtedly weakened over recent decades. For example, the ministers with responsibility for child protection in successive recent South Australian governments have sadly had to deal with well-documented cases of child neglect or abuse (for example, ABC, 2022), to which serious administrative errors or oversights made in their periods of office have arguably contributed. None of these ministers resigned.

On the other hand, the expectation has remained strong that ministers should act with integrity as individuals, as embodied in a Ministerial Code of Conduct under which 'Ministers are expected to behave according to the highest standards of constitutional and personal conduct in the performance of their duties' (South Australia Government, 2021). And resignations from the South Australia Cabinet on matters relating to personal integrity are not uncommon. Three ministers resigned from the Marshall Cabinet in July 2020 over matters relating to their entitlement to accommodation allowances payable to non-metropolitan MPs (Slessor, 2020).

The collective and individual dimensions of ministerial responsibility come together to afford some protection to ministers when implementing Cabinet-endorsed decisions. Premier Stephen Marshall was particularly mindful of this important principle. After the Murray Darling Basin Royal Commission report in early 2019 made critical remarks about actions taken by his Minister for the Environment, Marshall was quick to defend the minister: 'David Speirs [had] the support of Cabinet. ... It was a position supported by Cabinet and it was the right decision' (Siebert, 2019). Later he remarked: 'We don't leave ministers hung out to dry. If there are issues, we work on how to collectively solve the problem' (Richardson, 2019).

Ultimately, the continuation of a government in office depends on the continuing support of that government by a majority of members of the House of Assembly. A vote of no confidence by a House majority would mean that the government would need to resign. This can be an important constraint on the work of the premier and ministers. While usually the premier and ministers can count on the support of other parliamentary members of their own political party, this cannot be taken for granted. For example, the Marshall government lost its majority in the House of Assembly as a result of various events where several members left the Liberal Party and moved to the crossbenches. Even though these crossbench members could probably have been relied upon to support the Marshall government on any confidence vote, they were also in a position to demand policy concessions or otherwise constrain governmental decision-making. For example, in March 2021, the crossbenchers with the support of the Labor opposition were able to win a House of Assembly vote setting up a parliamentary inquiry into the land access granted to mining companies for mining and exploration (Harmsen, 2021). South Australia has become accustomed to periods in which the government has not enjoyed a party majority in the House of Assembly (notably the Rann Labor government from 2002–2006). In all these cases, the scope of Cabinet decision-making was being constrained by the balance of power within the House of Assembly. Irrespective of their House of Assembly support, it has also been common for South Australian governments to not control a majority in the Legislative Council (see earlier).

The Ombudsman and the Independent Commissioner Against Corruption

In South Australia's parliamentary democracy, there are two other lesser but still key sources of executive accountability – the Ombudsman and the Independent Commissioner Against Corruption (ICAC). The State Ombudsman is an independent agency established to investigate complaints about administrative decisions of the South Australian government departments and authorities (Ombudsman SA, 2021). During 2021–22, the office managed more than 5,000 complaints (OmbudsmanSA, 2022, p.10).

Problems of corruption have historically tended to be more severe at the state government level than federally. In South Australia, the office of the ICAC and the Office of Public Integrity (OPI) were established in September 2013. Their motivating purpose was to take a proactive role in building integrity and tackling corruption and maladministration. The OPI supports the Commissioner by receiving and processing complaints or allegations for investigation by the Commissioner. The *ICAC Act 2012* mandated that public officials must refer to ICAC any suspected cases falling within ICAC's purview. During the 2019–2020 financial year, ICAC initiated 25 new corruption investigations, referred a further 44 matters to the SA Police, and referred six cases to the Office of the Director of Public Prosecutions (ICAC and OPI, 2020, p.6).

In principle, ICAC and OPI should be important bodies in ensuring integrity in government and politics and, in this way, contributing to democratic accountability. The work of the ICAC has led to some prominent prosecutions of not only senior public servants but also several MPs. However, the role of ICAC in South Australia has been controversial. In late 2021, in a rare display of unanimity among all members of the SA Parliament in both Houses of Parliament, the scope of the ICAC's role was significantly reduced. Its critics argued that the powers entrusted to the ICAC were too broad ranging, leading it to focus on relatively unimportant matters better left to the normal justice system. Several high-profile prosecutions collapsed in court due to insufficient evidence. ICAC's powers were said to be too wide-ranging. Some of its investigations had caused significant reputational damage and did not afford individuals due procedural fairness (Fewster and Henson, 2021). Consequently, the amendments to the *ICAC Act 2012* unanimously approved by Parliament in September 2021 limited ICAC's jurisdiction to matters of corruption. Matters of maladministration and misconduct in public office were henceforth confined entirely to the State Ombudsman.

This stripping away of some ICAC powers was controversial, with the serving ICAC Commissioner arguing that it put 'politicians out of reach' (Vanstone, 2021). She pointed out that, because there was no 'code of conduct' applicable to MPs, politicians appeared to have removed themselves from the Ombudsman's jurisdiction (Lee, 2021). The development of a code of conduct for MPs had been under active consideration by a parliamentary committee since the early 2000s, although a draft was published in October 2021 (Lee, 2021).

Commonwealth-State relations

Commonwealth-State relations also raise interesting questions about democratic accountability. Much of the intergovernmental negotiation happens within the realms of executive government through meetings of ministers and/or public officials, rather than through more transparent parliamentary processes. Intergovernmental agreements can be reached by the executive branch without requiring parliamentary debate or parliamentary assent to legislation. Relatively low-population states like South Australia arguably benefit disproportionately (relative to their population) from intergovernmental transfers and relations. In intergovernmental forums, each state more-or-less counts equally, and in this way South Australia gets a strong say in the adoption of new regulatory regimes, policy reforms or funding arrangements. South Australia can also benefit from national governments seeking to shore up their local electoral popularity in federal seats that matter to them, a common explanation for why so much national defence spending (such as submarine construction and maintenance) has been directed to Adelaide.

Ministers involved in intergovernmental meetings or inquiries that involve 'significant policy or program issues, or issues that have a cross portfolio impact' are expected to inform the state Cabinet via a note or submission seeking Cabinet approval (DPC, 2021). This mechanism was intended to ensure that a coherent SA whole-of-government position was maintained with Cabinet authorisation, without which norms of responsible government – and, in turn, democratic accountability – might be weakened. South Australian premiers have also been long accustomed to meeting with the federal PM and other state premiers in occasional meetings to discuss matters of mutual concern, typically on issues where a coordinated national approach is sought. In a notable development during the COVID-19 pandemic, the National Cabinet was established in March 2021 and consolidated in 2022 (see Chapters 13 and 16), with the SA premier as an automatic member. It has become a permanent feature of Australian governance, and yet has no clear accountability relationship to any particular representative or legislative body, although the SA premier reports briefly on its deliberations to Parliament (with five meetings in 2023).

Conclusion

South Australia has clearly operated as a stable and largely effective democratic state, without major problems and using processes to ensure a good deal of integrity. Recent global trends have arguably seen democracy in retreat across the globe (see Chapter 28), although this claim of an overall 'democratic backsliding' trend is disputed by other political scientists (for example, Little and Meng, 2023). The South Australian political system has not experienced any broader challenges associated with democratic backsliding or political over-polarisation , even during the intensified debates and strong government interventions of the COVID-19 pandemic. Political partisanship has remained relatively constrained. The political succession of premiers and governments occurred in uncontroversial ways in 2018 and 2022. And corruption and maladministration problems in the public service have broadly been controlled, if not eliminated. However, there is still clear scope to improve democratic practice, especially in the realm of greater government accountability, protecting civic and human rights, regulating the conduct of elected politicians themselves, diversifying political representation, and extending consultation and deliberation processes.

References

ABC (2018) 'Curious Campaign: Who are the big donors at the SA election?', ABC website page, 16 March. https://perma.cc/YAH5-MQSE

ABC (2020) 'Three SA ministers step down amid state expenses scandal', ABC website page, 26 July. https://perma.cc/5968-8F8F

ABC (2022) 'Death of six-year-old Munno Para girl Charlie renews scrutiny of South Australia's child protection system', ABC website page, 23 July. https://perma.cc/2R27-X5GQ

ABC (2023) 'Female representation in South Australia's parliament is a challenge for the political right', ABC website, 6 March. https://perma.cc/J4TN-GD8F

Australian Bureau of Statistics (no date) ABS webpage, 'South Australia – 2016 Census All persons QuickStats'. https://perma.cc/FHU5-QXNP

Australian Bureau of Statistics (2022) 'Snapshot of South Australia', ABS webpage, released 28 June, https://perma.cc/24FZ-PYUY

Banzhaf, J (1965) 'Weighted voting doesn't work: A mathematical analysis.' *Rutgers Law Review* vol. 19, pp. 317–43.

Bastoni, Jordan (2007) 'The South Australian Constitutional Convention: Why did it fail?', *Flinders Journal of History and Politics,* January, vol. 24, pp. 46–67. https://search.informit.org/doi/pdf/10.3316/ielapa.201203323

Constitution Act 1934 (1934) https://perma.cc/9KET-R686

DPC (Department of the Premier and Cabinet, South Australia) (2015) 'Reforming democracy: Deciding, designing and delivering together', Department of Premier and lCabinet (SA) website page, 13 August. https://apo.org.au/node/121691

Donaldson. David (2016) 'Going nuclear: Inside SA's deliberative policymaking citizens' juries', *The Mandarin,* 27 October. https://perma.cc/JR5E-ZS6U

DPC (Department of the Premier and Cabinet, South Australia) (2021) 'Intergovernmental matters', Adelaide, https://web.archive.org/web/20211227171103/https://www.dpc.sa.gov.au/responsibilities/cabinet-and-executive-council/cabinet/what-goes-to-cabinet/intergovernmental-matters

Dumont, Patrick and Caulier, Jean-Francois (2005) 'The "effective number of relevant parties": How voting power improves Laakso-Taagepera's Index', MPRA paper no. 17846, University Library of Munich, Germany, pp. 1-28. https://perma.cc/7ANK-LUNY and published version $ https://perma.cc/WK86-BCWA

ECSA (Electoral Commission of South Australia) (2023a) 'The under-representation of women in South Australia's Parliament', Research Report, August 2020. https://perma.cc/ZX2R-TDDA

ECSA (Electoral Commission of South Australia) (2023b) 'State and by-election reports', Agency website. https://perma.cc/36HT-FEBR

ECSA (Electoral Commission of South Australia) (2023c)' About ECSA', webpage. https://perma.cc/AW4F-B82B

Electoral Act (1985) PDF copy of legislation on the South Australia Parliament website. https://perma.cc/6LAE-MJA2

Fewster, S and Henson, E (2021) '"ICAC only has itself to blame" as controversial reforms sail through parliament', *The Advertiser*, 24 September. https://perma.cc/B494-7FTD

Gallagher, Michael and Mitchell, Paul (2018) 'Dimensions of variation in electoral systems' in Herron, Erik S; Pekkanen, Robert J, and Shugart, Matthew S (eds) *The Oxford Handbook of Electoral Systems,* Oxford: Oxford University Press.

Gauja, Anika and Sawer, Marian (eds) (2016) *Party Rules? Dilemmas of political party regulation in Australia*, Canberra: Australian National University Press.

Gobbett, Hannah (2017) 'Indigenous parliamentarians, federal and state: A quick guide', Briefing by Australian Parliament Library Service, 11 July. https://perma.cc/U5WZ-SKGX

Guardian (2018) 'South Australia halts Indigenous treaty talks as premier says he has "other priorities", *Guardian, Australia*, 30 April. https://perma.cc/RMR9-RM57

Harmsen, Nick (2021) 'Crossbench exposes Marshall Liberal Government's minority status', *ABC News*, 2 March. https://perma.cc/296V-U92J

ICAC and OPI (Independent Commissioner Against Corruption and the Office of Public Integrity) 2020, 2019–20 Annual Report, Adelaide. https://perma.cc/VB2D-PV56

InDaily (2020a) 'SA country newspaper closes "indefinitely" and Messenger stops printing', *InDaily* website, 1 April. https://perma.cc/KH8G-JF8B

InDaily (2020b) 'More job cuts for News Corp and ABC in South Australia', *InDaily* website, 10 June. https://perma.cc/5PXJ-56RW

InDaily (2020c) 'Parliament warned of "institutional racism" within SA Govt', *InDaily* website, 11 December. https://perma.cc/BT3H-7NU3

Laakso, Markku and Taagepera, Rein (1979) '"Effective" number of parties: A measure with application to West Europe', *Comparative Political Studies*, vol. 12, no. 1, pp.3–27. OA at: https://www.researchgate.net/profile/Markku_Laakso/publication/241645380_The_Effective_number_of_parties_a_measure_with_application_to_West_Europe/links/0deec538c60cf997cc000000/The-Effective-number-of-parties-a-measure-with-application-to-West-Europe.pdf

Lee, S (2021) 'With no code of conduct, SA politicians can't be investigated for misconduct, ICAC says', *ABC News*, 1 October, https://perma.cc/YE6D-A6CP

Little, Andrew and Meng, Anne (2023) 'Subjective and objective measurement of democratic backsliding', Paper to 2022 APSA Conference posted on Social Science Research Network (SSRN), https://perma.cc/AM5K-QP6Y

Lynch, Sasha (2016) *Electoral Fairness in South Australia*, Working Paper 38. Melbourne: Electoral Regulation Research Network/Democratic Audit of Australia Joint Working Paper Series. https://perma.cc/XFP7-ECSR

Marx, Daniel (2020) 'The under-representation of women in South Australia's Parliament', Briefing Paper 3, August. https://perma.cc/Y22B-9L3L

MOAD (Museum of Australian Democracy) (no date) 'Aboriginal Lands Trust Act 1966 (SA)', Webpage https://perma.cc/YNR7-9MNH

NITV News (2021) 'SA inquiry into governance of Aboriginal organisations attracts criticism', NITV station website, 27 February. https://perma.cc/99XP-Y2WE

OmbudsmanSA (2021) 'History of the office', Adelaide, https://perma.cc/E4R5-R8S6

OmbudsmanSA (2022) *2021–2022 Annual Report*, Adelaide, https://perma.cc/3BAH-8P4V

Richardson, Tom (2019) '"We don't hang ministers out to dry": Marshall rules out 2019 reshuffle', *InDaily*, 15 March. https://perma.cc/6ADC-XJ93

Selway, Bradley (1997) *The Constitution of South Australia*, Federation Press, Leichhardt NSW.

Selway, Bradley (2003) 'The "vision splendid" of ministerial responsibility versus the "round eternal" of government administration' in Macintyre, Clement and Williams, John (eds) *Peace, Order and Good Government: State Constitutional and Parliamentary Reform*, Wakefield Press, Kent Town, pp.164–77.

Siebert, Bension (2019), 'Cabinet backed decision slammed by River Murray inquiry', *InDaily*, 1 February, https://perma.cc/48NY-7FKD

Slessor, Camron (2020) 'Three ministers resign amid expenses scandal as SA Premier announces Cabinet reshuffle', ABC News, 26 July. https://perma.cc/5968-8F8F

South Australia (2023) 'Your say', government website. https://perma.cc/FQH7-LAUG

South Australia Government (2015) *Reforming Democracy: Deciding, Designing and Delivering Together Reforming*, Official Report, 13 August. https://perma.cc/EPD7-QL4U

South Australia Government (2021) *Ministerial Code of Conduct*, Department of the Premier and Cabinet, Adelaide, https://perma.cc/V6CR-SZUD

South Australia Government (2023) 'Aboriginal affairs and reconciliation', webpage. https://perma.cc/YW8L-7ASS

South Australia Parliament (no date) 'The Constitution Act 1934'. https://perma.cc/B543-VRCC

South Australia Parliament (no date) 'Equal Opportunity Act 1984'. https://perma.cc/4XL5-9CTT

Staub, Zak Victor (2019) 'Human Rights Acts around Australia', UNSW Human Rights Institute web page, https://perma.cc/Z3UG-STCV

Vanstone, A (2021) 'ICAC's ability to hold politicians to account is under threat', *InDaily*, 23 September, https://perma.cc/9WTG-8DGY

Wikipedia (2023) 'Kyam Maher', https://perma.cc/4JLH-3VYS

21

Western Australia

John Phillimore, Martin Drum, Sarah Murray, Peter Wilkins, Narelle Miragliotta and Benjamin Reilly

Western Australia (WA) is huge, rich, sparsely populated – and different. Occupying one-third of Australia's landmass, but with just 10 per cent of its population, and geographically distant from the eastern seaboard, the state has always had a distinctive identity, partly due to the prominence of primary industries. Although much of WA's area is desert, there are massive mineral resources, notably iron ore, petroleum and natural gas, but also including gold, diamonds, nickel and rare metals like lithium. Agriculture is important too, especially wheat and premium wines. With around 10 per cent of the national population, WA is responsible for over half of Australia's goods exports.

The state was the last Australian colony to achieve self-government and the last to join the federation. To this day, WA often retains a separate, sometimes antagonistic, attitude towards the Commonwealth government and even to the rest of the country. State leaders and voters have long criticised the Commonwealth over a lack of federal funding, including in the past 20 years when WA's massive mineral wealth provided it with hefty royalties, and it received less federal tax income under a programme to equalise state resources. Eventually, WA secured a deal on receiving more Goods and Services Tax (GST) revenues in 2018. During the COVID-19 crisis, the state also adopted stricter border controls on incomers than other states, and kept them in place for longer, with high levels of support for the Labor government's stance from its population.

WA's politics and governance have also been quite distinctive. Historically, the state's rural areas were heavily over-represented, and full electoral equality was only finally achieved in late 2021, following a massive election win by Labor that gave them majority control of both houses of the state parliament for the first time.

What does democracy require of Western Australia's political system?

- An effective State constitution to secure and underpin liberal democracy in the State.
- Aboriginal and Torres Strait Islander peoples should be afforded full individual civil and human rights.

How to cite this chapter:

Phillimore, John; Drum, Martin; Murray, Sarah; Wilkins, Peter; Miragliotta, Narelle; and Reilly, Benjamin (2024) 'Western Australia', in: Evans, Mark; Dunleavy, Patrick and Phillimore, John (eds) *Australia's Evolving Democracy: A New Democratic Audit,* London: LSE Press, pp.453–477. **https://doi.org/10.31389/lsepress.ada.u**. Licence: CC-BY-NC 4.0

- Electoral systems for the state's lower and upper houses should accurately translate parties' votes into seats in the state legislature, in different ways that are recognised as legitimate by most citizens. Ideally, the voting systems should foster the overall social representativeness of the two houses of the legislature. Elections and the regulation of political parties should be impartially conducted, with integrity.
- The political parties should sustain vigorous and effective electoral competition and citizen participation. Political parties should uphold the highest standards of conduct in public life.
- The parliament should normally maintain full public control of government services and state operations, ensuring public and parliamentary accountability.
- An effective bicameral (two chamber) system should ensure the legislative branch meets its representative and accountability functions.
- The WA government should govern responsively, prioritising the public interest and reflecting state public opinion. Its core executive (premier, cabinet, ministers and key central departments) should provide clear unification of public policies across government.
- The core executive and government should operate fully within the law, and ministers should be effectively scrutinised by and politically accountable to parliament.
- In the wider state public service officials should act with integrity, in accordance with well-enforced codes of conduct, and within the rule of law.
- The administration of public services should be controlled by democratically elected officials so far as possible.
- The WA government should effectively and transparently represent its citizens' interests at the Commonwealth level.

Recent developments

The key recent developments affecting democratic processes in WA focused on the state's firm response to the COVID-19 pandemic. The political fall-out from this stance strengthened Labor's recent grip on power, which may be reinforced in future by the final completion of electoral reforms made in 2021.

COVID-19 policy: 'An island within an island'

Politics and government in WA from March 2020 to mid-late 2022 were dominated by the COVID-19 pandemic. WA largely adopted an 'elimination' (as opposed to a minimisation) stance to the virus (Government of Western Australia, 2023, p.8). Using the state's physical isolation to its advantage, Labor Premier Mark McGowan enforced a 'hard border' with the rest of the country. At the start of April 2020, he declared that 'we will be turning Western Australia into its own island within an island – our own country' (West Australian, 2020). Although the state's border controls came down at times, for much of the pandemic (697 days) they stayed in place, with travellers to WA needing pre-approval to come and then being required to quarantine for 14 days (Guardian, 2022). Initially, there were even intra-state restrictions on travel within WA.

Over time, the state government gradually opened up travel internally, with more generous arrangements than in other states for group gatherings and few requirements to wear masks (Government of Western Australia, 2023). The mining industry was strongly encouraged to domicile fly-in fly-out workers in WA (Winter, 2020), as well as instituting a tough testing regime for its workforce. These policies enabled the industry to continue operating throughout the pandemic, helping WA to take advantage of the high prices for iron ore.

Health-wise, the policy was effective, with barely any community transmission of the virus (Government of Western Australia, 2023). During 2020 and 2021, the few deaths that did occur were people either from passing cruise ships or freighters. The tough policy on interstate arrivals was extremely popular. The premier's approval rating rose astronomically, reaching 91 per cent (Law and Ison, 2020) by September 2020. For most of 2020 and 2021, WA had a very limited number of days in lockdown, and life was lived virtually 'as normal' for most of the period. For businesses not dependent on international travel, economic activity was strong and unemployment in WA went from being above the national average pre-pandemic to the lowest of all the states by December 2021 (3.4 per cent).

The tight borders were not universally popular. Protests occurred at various intervals. National media and senior federal ministers complained about the state's isolationism (Ison, 2021), while other commentators likened the state to North Korea's 'hermit kingdom' (Loiacono, 2021). Queensland businessman Clive Palmer mounted a legal challenge (Karp, 2020) to the WA government after being denied entry into the state, citing section 92 of the Constitution ('trade, commerce, and intercourse among the States ... shall be absolutely free'). Some factual questions in the case were addressed in the Federal Court in August 2020 and it was resolved in the High Court in November 2020, with the state winning. The Commonwealth Attorney-General, the WA politician Christian Porter, initially formally intervened on Palmer's side and called witnesses to support his case. But following outrage from the WA state government, public criticism, and opposition from *The West Australian* newspaper, the federal government withdrew from the case (Carmody, 2020).

For the Liberal Party in WA, this misjudgement by Commonwealth Liberal ministers compounded problems it was already experiencing after its state leader, Liza Harvey, called for the state's borders to be opened in May and June 2020 (Zimmerman and Kruijff, 2020), just before the number of cases exploded in Victoria. In November 2020, Liza Harvey resigned as Leader of the Opposition. Her successor was a first-time MP, Zac Kirkup, who took on the role very late in the electoral cycle and lost badly in March 2021.

WA's success in keeping COVID-19 out meant that it was slower in getting vaccination rates up to desired levels, because it was difficult to stress the urgency for high vaccination rates to enable a return to 'normal life', when life within the state's borders already appeared to be that way. After the more infectious Omicron variant gained hold elsewhere in the country, Premier McGowan made a 'backflip' announcement (Carmody, 2022) in January 2022 when he postponed the border opening from the previously announced 5 February. While still broadly supported by the community, the decision was strongly criticised by *The West Australian*, other media, and high-profile business leaders, who urged certainty to assist in planning and for the government to acknowledge there would never be a perfect time for WA to reopen (Bennet, 2022). *The West Australian*'s position was influential because it has been the state's only newspaper, and its owners (Seven West Media) also own Channel 7, WA's most popular television network.

In terms of parliamentary processes, COVID-19 presented a number of challenges for maintaining parliamentary accountability. Under emergency legislative provisions, some delegated executive orders, such as directions (see, for example, *Emergency Management Act 2005* (WA), section 77(2A)) were not subject to standard scrutiny processes. Further, parliamentary participation was at times rendered difficult by lockdowns and social distancing requirements. One recommendation of a committee report into parliament's pandemic response was that the 1899 Constitution should be amended to ensure that, by parliamentary standing orders, remote participation and voting could be assured. The state's Auditor-General also played an important role in providing a series of reports that assessed the government's response to the pandemic, including the vaccine roll-out (OAG, 2021a), economic stimulus initiatives (OAG, 2021b), and hardship support provided to local governments (OAG, 2021c).

There were also significant developments in the public services during the pandemic. A State of Emergency and a Public Health Emergency were declared, and other aspects of the state bureaucracy were directed to act in support of the state's efforts to control the pandemic and guide the government's broader response. The Police Commissioner became the State Emergency Coordinator while the Chief Health Officer also played a crucial role. The premier appointed the Public Sector Commissioner as State Recovery Controller, and that officer advised the premier during National Cabinet meetings in the pandemic period. Interestingly, the Director-General of the Department of the Premier and Cabinet (DP&C) – nominally the head of the central 'core executive' agency – did not undertake this role. This follows WA's tradition of not having a particularly strong DP&C within the core executive, unlike in other states or the Commonwealth. In September 2022, the premier announced that the state of emergency was finally to end (Spagnolo, 2022).

Political dominance by Labor under Mark McGowan

For almost 50 years, political power at the state level in WA alternated regularly between the Labor and Liberal parties, with each holding government for multiple terms. The most recent change of government occurred in March 2017, when the Labor Party led by Mark McGowan won a convincing victory (Wahlquist, 2017), ending Liberal Party Premier Colin Barnett's eight years in office. Labor won nearly 70 per cent of seats (41 out of 59) in the Legislative Assembly (LA), a record for it at the time and a highly unusual outcome under the Alternative Vote (AV). Given WA's previous history, it was widely expected that the 2021 election might see a tighter contest, before a tougher fight (and possible change in government) in 2025.

Instead, the onset of COVID-19 gave McGowan an opportunity to demonstrate the politics of 'them and us', isolating WA from the rest of the country. Helped by missteps from both the state Liberal Party and the federal Coalition government (see earlier), McGowan dominated the state political landscape and achieved the largest victory in Australian electoral history at the March 2021 state election (Green, 2021). This time Labor won nearly 90 per cent of seats (53 out of 59), with a first-preference vote of almost 60 per cent (a swing towards it of 18 per cent) and almost 70 per cent of the two-party preferred vote. The Liberals were reduced to a humiliating two seats in the LA. The National Party leader, whose party won just four seats, became the Leader of the Opposition, the first time the role fell to a National Party leader in WA since 1947.

Labor's political dominance was also replicated in the 2021 Legislative Council (LC) elections for WA's upper house. It won a majority there for the first time ever, with 22 of the 36 seats (61 per cent). This result gave the party an opportunity, which it quickly grasped, to change the electoral system for the LC by removing regional vote weighting favouring rural areas, along with other reforms (see later). Labor's overwhelming numbers in both houses of the parliament, combined with McGowan's personal dominance of the political scene, raised fears for some observers (Drum, 2021) about the prospects of Labor wielding 'total control', with few checks and balances to prevent government ministers doing as they wish. Were the imbalance of representation to continue, the state could become a 'dominant party system', where the same party wins power continuously, and alternation with the opposition parties ceases to operate (Dunleavy, 2010).

These concerns were reinforced in 2022 when the Liberals lost five WA seats at the federal election, and WA recorded the strongest Labor vote of all the states, helping deliver federal government to Anthony Albanese. However, McGowan's cautious and conservative manner and approach, and the operations of the WA parliament, suggest that lack of accountability concerns have so far been unfounded (Phillimore, 2022a). Still, there are undoubtedly challenges to be faced in terms of ensuring a proper level of accountability and scrutiny of government actions. If a 'dominant party system' does develop, then democratic responsiveness will depend on the media, integrity institutions and civil society more generally being vigilant, as well as the non-Labor parties in parliament.

Post-McGowan: politics as usual?

The shock retirement of Premier Mark McGowan in May 2023 (Ho and Sturmer, 2023), arguably the most popular political figure in WA history, opened the possibility of politics returning to a more traditional, competitive environment. His successor, Premier Roger Cook, while serving as Deputy Premier to McGowan for the duration of his government, has not commanded the same authority or popularity as his predecessor. Furthermore, the new premier had to face the usual array of government challenges, decisions and performance emanating from a government six years old, with controversies in health, housing, juvenile justice and cultural heritage among others (Drum, 2023).

In 2023 there also were significant changes to the leadership of the opposition parties. Mia Davies, the first Nationals leader of the opposition in WA since 1947, resigned as leader to make way for Shane Love. Of greater consequence for the 2025 election, Libby Mettam replaced David Honey as Liberal Party leader. As health spokesperson, Mettam was a visible figure in the WA media, and promised a stronger critique of government performance. In 2024 new figures also emerged, seeking to stand for the Liberals and take back their traditional strongholds in Perth, which had been won by Labor in 2021. The most notable of these was Basil Zempilas, the Lord Mayor of Perth, who announced his intention to run for the seat of Churchlands. With the departure of McGowan and the spectre of COVID-19 removed from the political scene, the next state election (in 2025) may prove to be a much closer affair than 2021.

Electoral reform for the upper house

Like most Australian states Western Australia has a bicameral legislature. For many decades both the lower house (the LA elected in 59 single member districts using AV), and the upper house (the LC elected via the Single Transferable Vote (STV)) were 'malapportioned', with rural and regional districts being dramatically over-represented in terms of seats compared with the dominant population centres around the Perth metropolitan area. In 2006 this problem was changed for the LA, with a broadly proportional allocation of seats according to population, but with some considerable advantage for the largest single member (rural) districts (see later).

However, the 2006 reforms retained WA's long-standing division of the Council seats between six districts (each with six seats) of widely varying numbers of voters, with members elected using STV. Some were very large geographically but had relatively small numbers of voters compared to the Perth metropolitan regions. Demographic trends made it ever more apparent that without reform, the already excessive 'malapportionment' of seats in the LC would only increase in future. By 2021, voters in the Mining and Pastoral Region had six times, and those in the Agricultural Region four times, the LC representation of voters in metropolitan Perth.

During the 2021 state election campaign, the Labor leader Mark McGowan repeatedly asserted that reform of the upper house was 'not on the agenda'. However, Labor's unprecedented victory at that election meant that the party could finally address what it saw as its long-running disadvantage in the districting system for the LC. (Regional vote weighting had a long history in WA and because of it, Labor had never previously won a majority of seats in the LC.) In addition, a number of anomalous results occurred in the allocation of seats to so-called 'micro parties' under the proportional representation STV system.

Labor thus quickly pursued the party's long-heralded reforms to bring about 'one vote, one value' in LC elections. In September 2021, a Ministerial Expert Committee on Electoral Reform (McCusker et al., 2021) headed by an eminent former WA governor Malcolm McCusker (and including three authors of this chapter) tabled a proposal for achieving 'electoral equality' in the LC. The resulting *Constitutional and Electoral Legislation Amendment (Electoral Equality) Act 2021* scrapped the system of electoral districts for the upper house and replaced them with a 'whole-of-state' electorate (also called 'at large' elections) (LAWA, 2021). The number of LC members also rose from 36 to 37. These changes mirrored electoral reforms adopted previously by New South Wales (NSW) and South Australia (SA), although those states elect only half their upper house members every four years, whereas WA chooses all 37 at the same time.

To tackle the micro-parties' problem, the reform followed moves already made in NSW, SA and federally, by abolishing Group Voting Tickets (GVT). This move aimed to prevent complex 'preference harvesting' deals between political parties that had sometimes enabled micro-parties to win representation via the vagaries of STV's ticket voting preference flows, despite the candidates eventually elected having almost no voter support on first preferences. WA voters will now be able to vote preferentially 'above the line', rather than having to accept the whole of their favoured party's preference list (usually set only by party leadership – see Chapter 5).

However, by electing so many members at large, a much lower threshold for winning upper house seats now applies, meaning that smaller parties of both the left and the right will have an increased potential to win seats regularly. Mathematically, 2.6 per cent of the vote will now *guarantee* that a party will win a seat under STV, compared with a notional 16 per cent under the old districts system. (In practice, under the previous system the vote share needed to win a seat in a region was often far less than 16 per cent. For example, in 2021 the Daylight Saving Party secured a seat with just 0.2 per cent of the first-preference vote in one region.) So, the Greens, One Nation and other small parties were potential beneficiaries of the change, and most of them supported the committee's proposal, while only the Liberals and Nationals publicly opposed it. The legislation also introduced new thresholds for parties to receive group recognition on the ballot paper, thereby preferencing those parties who could demonstrate significant public support. The system will have its first test in the 2025 state election and will likely deliver seats more directly in proportion with the statewide primary votes received by the different political parties. By 2024, early indications were that there would not be a proliferation of new parties contesting the WA ballot in 2025 (WAEC, 2024).

The longer-term effects of WA's shift away from 'malapportioning' seats that favour its 'hinterland' areas may also be significant. Past over-representation of agriculture and mining both reflected and helped shape the regional dominance of those interests. Over time, more equitable representation of citizens may help to rebalance and diversify WA's economic, social and cultural profile.

Strengths, weaknesses, opportunities and threats (SWOT) analysis

Current strengths	Current weaknesses
Historically there has been regular alternation of the top two parties (Liberal-National and Labor) in power in WA's state government (see below). Close competition between them (and to attract smaller parties' votes via preference transfers) tends to encourage responsiveness to voters' concerns.	Labor's overwhelming 2021 support (building on its 2017 victory), together with the striking weakness of the Liberal Party, raised fears that the accountability of the Labor state premier and ministers might weaken, especially with ALP majorities in both houses of parliament in place until 2025 at least. Especially in the LA, very few opposition or non-Labor MPs remain to maintain committees and other scrutiny processes.
The LC reform to remove rural seats' advantages has been defended in terms of ensuring electoral equality. The diversity of representation in the LC has remained greater (until 2021) and will certainly be reinforced by newly state-wide elections under STV in 2025.	Labor has taken the opportunity to rectify previous disadvantages imposed on it by the LC's malapportioned electoral system. Minor parties and independents are more likely to hold the balance of power in the LC in future as a result of the changes, thereby increasing the potential for them to 'hold the government hostage' on legislation, despite representing a small share of the electorate as a whole.
The final scrapping of WA's historic malapportionment of seats to rural areas and against urban population centres made a major improvement in the integrity of WA's previously defective election systems. The LA's districting system still incorporates a moderate advantage for voters in rural areas, on a par with that found in other liberal democracies and federally.	Government, politicians and their advisors in both major parties often have close connections to business, and in particular to the resources sector, which can cast doubt on the ability of government to act in the public interest.
Legislation passed in late 2023 strengthens election donation laws and improves transparency and accountability. The laws moved WA from being one of the weakest to one of the strongest jurisdictions in terms of real-time disclosure of donations, expenditure caps, and banning foreign donations, and it removes parties from direct involvement in postal voting.	

McGowan was an unusual Labor leader nationally in not being formally aligned with any particular faction in the party room or state organisation. McGowan's successor Roger Cook was selected as leader by the WA Labor caucus despite not getting endorsement from his own faction. The Nationals in WA largely pursue their own agenda, separate to the Liberal party.	Major party factional politics created some turbulence and adverse publicity for the top three parties. Labor faction fights in 2017 and 2019 went public. An internal Liberal party report found evidence of 'entryism' by groups with relatively extreme religious views. The Nationals' detachment from the Liberal Party since 2006 has made conservative politics somewhat fractious.
Gender equality in both the lower and upper houses has improved considerably in the last decade.	Most improvement in gender diversity in 2021 was due to changes made by Labor to get more women candidates in winnable seats. The Liberal and National parties have not matched such measures.
WA has had its share of political scandals in the past, most notably a series of dubious business–government relations that resulted in massive financial losses for the state in the late 1980s and early 1990s — an episode commonly referred to as 'WA Inc' (Wikipedia, 2023a). Since 2006, however, WA has strengthened anti-corruption and transparency institutions, mostly with bipartisan agreement. Integrity agencies and wider internal public service safeguards against wrongdoing have also been strengthened.	Clean state governance still suffers from occasional but important relapses – well demonstrated by the 2019–2021 conflicts between the Corruption and Crime Commission and majorities in the LC, along with isolated new corruption cases inside public service agencies.
The state has a well-developed media system, with a single major newspaper *The West Australian* (Wikipedia, 2024) enjoying large majority readership, and the most popular TV channel (Seven), both being owned by a locally based business (Seven West Media). Both outlets give a great deal of coverage to state politics and regional or local developments. Regionally dominant media have some incentives to be inclusive in their political coverage.	The lack of media diversity creates something of a local media monopoly for Seven West Media corporation. *The West Australian*'s strongly set-out political and editorial stances hence have enjoyed an exaggerated and unhealthy political importance. A strong bonding of a successful political leader and party with state-dominant media may accentuate the risks of a dominant party system becoming established.

Future opportunities	Future threats
The 'effective number of parties' in WA in terms of votes has remained stable for both the LA and LC until very recently. In terms of seats, it fell sharply in the LA in 2021 (which became almost a one-party chamber) and somewhat in the LC. This remained a single anomalous election outcome, and one that reflected the unusual political conditions in the COVID-19 pandemic. Most political scientists argue that dominance requires continuous electoral victories over a long period (Bogaards and Boucek, 2010). Fears of a Labor 'dominant party system' becoming established are hence premature. Labor ministers have also taken pains to bring other parties along with their electoral reforms (although not the main opposition), and to act moderately in other constitutional legislation.	Some political scientists argue that a 'dominant party system' can be recognised after just one or two election victories where a single party is so advantaged over competitors in terms of leadership or ideological position that they cannot credibly compete with it (Dunleavy, 2010). What matters is whether its opponents are fragmented ideologically into small groupings that cannot cooperate, and if the top party can change political institutions in its own long-run favour. Free and fair elections still occur, but the same party 'always' wins; or wins for many elections in a row; or if it loses temporarily, it is quickly restored to power (as in modern Japan). Unless the WA Labor government suffers a very dramatic loss of support by the next state-wide elections in 2025, it could hold power for at least 12 years continuously through to a 2029 election, and possibly longer.
In the LC a more pluralistic party system is likely to result when the first state-wide STV elections are held in 2025.	The infiltration of religious groups into the Liberal party, and their increased salience in its internal politics, may both work to increase political polarisation. So too may a potential reinvigoration of far-right populist parties, because LC voting reforms will improve their chances of representation.
The state's strong economy and favourable budget position provides the state government with potential scope for undertaking policies to improve economic diversity.	WA's economy has been heavily reliant on exports to China, which may lead to a potential for foreign interference, or alternatively expose the state to external political shocks.

Several aspects of WA's state politics and governance raise issues that need exploring in detail. This chapter considers first long-run issues around the Constitution, Aboriginal people and relations with the Commonwealth. Then the dramatic recent changes in elections and party competition are considered, set against the longer history of state politics. Finally, the chapter examines the accountability of government, especially in the light of persistent corruption problems in state public services.

The state constitution and its lasting effects

After British settlement began in 1829, WA achieved self-government relatively late, in 1890. While the rest of the continent was abandoning its convict foundations, WA still encouraged convict transportation from 1850–1868, to assist in building its population. However, substantive economic development was only really achieved with the gold rush based around Kalgoorlie in the late 1880s and 1890s. The massive influx of people from the eastern colonies in turn was a key factor in WA finally voting for federation, although this occurred so late (in July 1900) that Western Australia was not even mentioned in the preamble to the *Commonwealth of Australia Constitution Act*, where the five other colonies 'agreed to unite in one indissoluble Federal Commonwealth'. The sense of being distinctive and different to other places has proved enduring in WA. In 1933, two-thirds of WA electors voted at a referendum to secede from the Commonwealth, although this never eventuated. WA's more isolationist attitude toward border protections during the COVID-19 pandemic have reinforced this sense of 'them and us'.

Government structures and institutions in WA are similar to those in most mainland States, with a bicameral parliamentary government, two-party politics and a strong executive based on the British model (see Miragliotta, Murray and Harbord, 2024). Despite using AV elections in line with the rest of Australia, for decades the electoral system in WA was distinctively weighted towards rural interests, which was only fully removed in late 2021.

In terms of its founding documents, Western Australia maintains a twin constitutional structure. The *Constitution Act 1889* (WA) (sometimes termed the '1889 Constitution'), which was based on imperial legislation first enacted in the UK House of Commons, established responsible government in the then-colony of WA. The *Constitution Acts Amendment Act 1899* (WA) (the '1899 Constitution'), contains many of the amendments subsequently made to the original constitution. Provisions in section 73 of the 1889 Constitution have meant that making any further constitutional consolidation has often been seen as being in 'the too hard basket'. The constitutional provisions relating to the core governmental branches (the legislature, the executive and the judiciary) are thus still spread across both Acts.

In 1978, amendments were made by the then Liberal-National government (led by Sir Charles Court). They specified that a successful referendum would now be needed to amend certain provisions of the Constitution, as well as absolute majorities in both houses of parliament. These changes related to attempts to abolish the position of Governor, to remove the LC, to reduce the number of MPs in either house of parliament, or to move away from the 'direct election' of members of parliament. (This likely referred to the then prospect of WA moving to a party list voting system.) In effect, these so-called 'entrenchment provisions' targeted Labor Party policies of the time. Notably, the 1978 provisions insisting upon future referenda, were themselves passed without a referendum. However, not all constitutional change activates these procedural provisions. As noted above, the *Constitutional and Electoral Legislation Amendment (Electoral Equality) Act 2021* (Western Australia Legislation, 2021), passed in late 2021, changed both the 1889 Constitution and 1899 Constitution so as to introduce a 'whole of state' electorate for the now 37 members of the LC. But because this involved an increase in the number of MPs (not a decrease), it was not covered by the entrenchment provisions and hence did not require a referendum.

The position of Aboriginal peoples

As a result of its colonialist record, WA has had, and indeed continues to have, a difficult and sometimes fraught history of relationships between Aboriginal peoples and the state government and other interests (Curthoys and Martens, 2013; Curthoys and Lydon, 2016; Kwaymullina, 2020). According to the 2021 census, Aboriginal peoples in WA comprise 3.3 per cent of the population. They have faced many years of struggle, displacement, racist policies and ongoing intergenerational trauma – manifesting in their radical over-representation in the criminal justice system, as well as disproportionate levels of homelessness and poor health. In 1995 the Liberal-National WA government of the time opposed the Commonwealth Native Title laws in the wake of the *Mabo* decision but lost in the High Court.

Historically, relations between the state's economically dominant mining sector and Aboriginal peoples have often been antagonistic, although there had been improvements in the years since the *Native Title Act* was passed. In 2015 the state's 1889 Constitution was amended to provide in its preamble that:

> *And whereas the Parliament resolves to acknowledge the Aboriginal people as the First People of Western Australia and traditional custodians of the land, the said Parliament seeks to effect a reconciliation with the Aboriginal people of Western Australia.* (Western Australia Legislation, 2015)

Unlike most other state constitutional equivalents this wording did not contain a clause providing that the acknowledgement was to have 'no legal effect'. However, it has seemed unlikely that such a preambular statement would have such an effect in any event. As Josie Farrer MLA stated in the 2015 Bill's Second Reading speech, (LAWA, 2015) '[r]ecognition, acknowledgement and acceptance are necessary steps to true and lasting reconciliation, and this bill is just one of those steps'.

Another notable positive development was the South West Native Title Settlement (DP&C, 2022). Originally legislated for in 2016 by the Liberal government, the Settlement commenced in February 2021. It was then the most comprehensive native title agreement negotiated in Australia, involving around 30,000 Noongar people and covers approximately 200,000 square kilometres of the south-west region of the state. Six Indigenous land use agreements were negotiated between the Noongar people and the WA government, the Noongar Land Estate has been established, and annual payments of A$50 million and A$10 million are being made into a Future Fund and Operation Fund respectively.

However, improvements in relations were fundamentally shaken in 2020 by mining giant Rio Tinto's complete destruction of the supposedly protected 46,000 year old caves at Juukan Gorge (Wikipedia, 2023b) belonging to the Puutu Kunti Kurrama and Pinikura people (PKKP People). The company acted under the terms of a ministerial permission given in 2013, creating a huge controversy that later led to the resignation of Rio's chief executive and two other board members. A subsequent Commonwealth parliamentary inquiry (JSCNA, 2020) by a joint standing committee of both houses made a number of recommendations calling for restitution by Rio Tinto and several legislative and policy reforms. The PKKP Aboriginal Corporation's submission (2020, p.7, [2]) to the Inquiry Stated:

> *The PKKP People are deeply hurt and traumatised by the desecration of a site which is profoundly significant to us and future generations. The Juukan Gorge disaster is a tragedy not only for the PKKP People. It is also a tragedy for the*

> *heritage of all Australians and indeed humanity as a whole. The rarity of this site demonstrates its value as a record of human development through massive environmental change which has also been recorded over a period of at least 46,000 years – a record which has now been put at grave risk.*

The Juukan Gorge calamity also highlighted the inadequacies of WA's Aboriginal cultural heritage legislation, which allowed the destruction to take place. New legislation (McGowan and Dawson, 2021) was passed in late 2021 to increase the protections for Aboriginal cultural heritage. However, many Aboriginal groups and other observers were critical (Knowles, 2021), arguing that it did not go far enough. The minister retained the ultimate decision-making power, rather than allowing relevant Aboriginal owners a right of veto over proposed developments affecting Aboriginal heritage.

When the new Act finally came into effect in July 2023, it was subject to further fierce criticism, especially from agricultural groups and landowners, supported by local media. The new rules required anyone with property bigger than 1,100 square metres to perform potentially costly cultural heritage checks with local Aboriginal groups and apply for permits before development. After just five weeks, the new Premier, Roger Cook, abruptly announced the government would repeal the Act, leaving the discredited 1972 legislation (under which the Juukan Gorge destruction had occurred) in place, albeit with some amendments. Many of the flaws in the new Act were blamed on the haste with which they were introduced into parliament and the lack of considered debate there, which was made possible by the Labor government's large majority in both houses (Towie, 2023).

Commonwealth–State relations

Playing the WA card, and hitting back at 'eastern states' critics along the way, has been a tried and tested tactic of successive WA governments, as Labor and McGowan's successful and popular handling of the COVID-19 demonstrated. In adopting this stance, the government was greatly assisted by its strong fiscal position. This has in turn been helped by the outcome of a previous clash with the Commonwealth and the other states over the distribution of receipts from the GST paid within WA. The distribution of GST revenues to the states and territories is determined by a formula overseen by the Commonwealth Grants Commission designed to achieve 'fiscal equalisation' between jurisdictions. Because of its strong state finances, for many years WA received well under 50 per cent of the GST revenues generated in WA under this formula. Many years of bipartisan complaints from WA eventually resulted in the Commonwealth in late 2018 passing legislation that ensured that its GST revenues would be 'topped up' to reach a floor of 70 per cent of the GST generated in the state (increasing to 75 per cent from 2024–2025). This equated to a top-up of A$1.5 billion in 2020–2021. By 2023–2024, the 'top up' to 70 per cent increased WA's GST receipts by A$5.6 billion compared to what it would have received under the old formula – helping to underwrite the state's strong financial position.

The changed GST formula has come in for severe criticism from other states, in particular NSW (Scarr, Law and Zimmerman, 2021), who are unimpressed at WA's massive budget surpluses (A$5.6 billion in 2020–2021; A$3.3 billion in 2023–2024) while all other governments have gone heavily into deficit. However, in the lead up to the 2022 federal election, both the then prime minister (PM) and federal leader of the opposition ruled out any change to the formula. This approach was surely influenced by the fact that WA had several marginal seats in the federal parliament. The new Labor PM, Anthony Albanese, has said he will wait for a planned review of the new system by the Productivity Commission (not due until 2026) before considering any changes. The 'McGowan factor' was assumed to have contributed to Labor's success by winning four additional federal seats in WA in 2022 (Parker, 2022), thereby making WA an important state politically for the Albanese Government.

Party competition, elections and representation

Like most states in Australia, Western Australians elect representatives to two chambers. The LA is the lower house and the chamber where government is formed, with most ministers and the premier drawn from its ranks. Members are elected from 59 single seat electorates. Currently (in 2024), almost three quarters (73 per cent) of these districts are located within the Perth Metropolitan Region, and the remaining 16 outside. Voting for members uses full preferential voting under AV: each elector must number all boxes on the ballot in order to lodge a formal vote. Under the *WA Electoral Act*, there must be a redistribution of the 59 LA districts every four years, which ensures that the boundaries of electorates always vary between each electoral cycle.

After over a century during which regional vote weighting was maintained for the LA, in 2005 a system of 'one vote one value' was finally achieved for the lower house. Most of the LA's districts now contain relatively even numbers of electors, under the Act's requirement that the districts must be no more than 10 per cent above or below the Average District Enrolment (ADE). However, there was still an exception made for very large districts. Here alone 'notional' electors are added at a rate of 1.5 per cent of the overall geographic size. In addition to this, the redistribution commissioners are permitted a tolerance of 20 per cent below the ADE in these districts, after the notional electors are added. This has had a marked impact on a small number of remote electorates, most notably North West Central, which is extremely large geographically (almost 820,600 square kilometres): in 2021 this district had just 10,990 electors, when the average district enrolment for the state as a whole was 29,100. The latest redistribution in 2023 abolished this seat and replaced it with an extra Perth-based electorate, reflecting population trends.

The Labor and Liberal parties have been the dominant actors in the Western Australian party system. Since 1974, they have largely alternated in office, with each occupying office on a total of seven occasions (Figure 21.1).

Figure 21.1: The alternation of governments in Western Australia's Legislative Assembly (LA) from 1974–2024

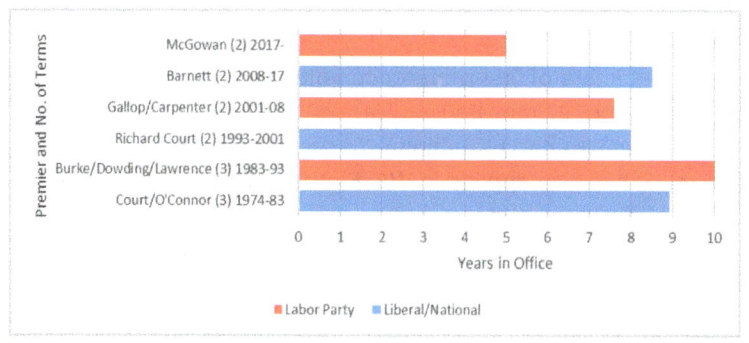

Source: Compiled from data in Western Australian Electoral Commission (2023).

Figure 21.2: Parties' first-preference vote shares in Western Australia's lower house AV elections (1971–2021)

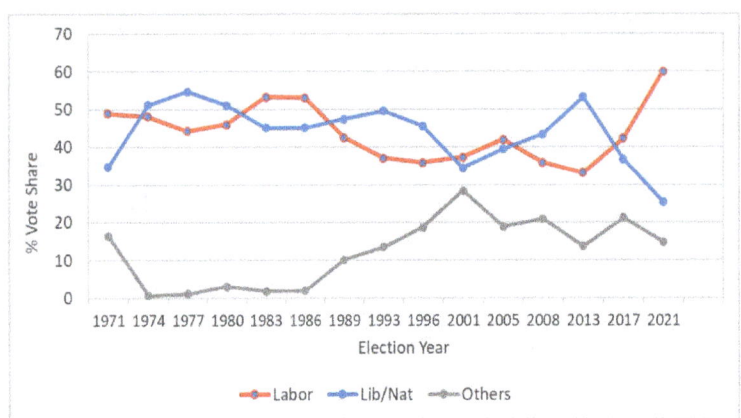

Source: Compiled from data in Western Australian Electoral Commission (2023).

Figure 21.3: The percentage of seats won by parties in the Western Australia's Legislative Assembly, 1971–2021

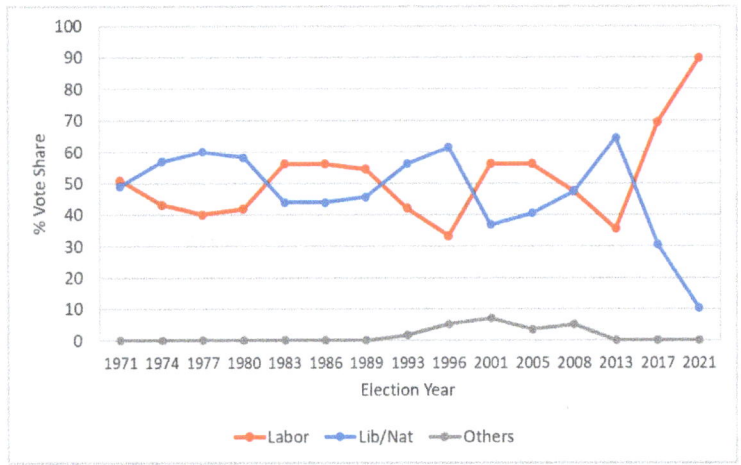

Source: Compiled from data in Western Australian Electoral Commission (2023).

These regular changes in government reflect quite large swings in the share of LA first-preference votes secured by the major parties (Figure 21.2). In terms of LA seats, AV has tended to deliver 'reinforced' majorities of seats to the largest party, giving the Liberal-National Coalition clear mandates to govern in six elections since 1971, and Labor in seven cases, compared with only two cases of minority government (2008 and 1971) when the top two parties won similar seat numbers (Figure 21.3).

Since the mid-1990s though, a significant share of first-preference votes has also been won by smaller parties, especially the Greens and at times Pauline Hanson's populist One Nation party, and independents. However, the top two parties' nationwide dominance of the two-party preferred vote under AV (see Chapter 5) has also applied in WA. Figure 21.3 shows that smaller parties have found it very hard to win seats in the state lower house, with no representation before 1989, a peak of just 8 per cent of seats in 2001, and no representation again since 2013.

Upper house elections

Turning to the LC, electoral reforms passed in 1986 abolished the former system of single member seats and instead introduced STV in six regions, beginning with the 1989 election. However, rural malapportionment remained. Figure 21.4 shows that ever since STV was adopted, the Liberal-National Coalition most often controlled the upper house – except in 2001–2005, and since 2017. Until the 2021 election, Labor had never held a majority in the upper chamber since self-government was achieved in 1890. Under STV, the number of members of the Council (MLCs) from non-major parties generally increased. But while several smaller parties have gained election to the LC, only the Greens have held a consistent presence in the chamber since 1993. In 2021 Labor's historic strong dominance squeezed all other parties' ability to win seats.

The Liberal-National Coalition held a Council majority in 1989–2001, there was a hung LC from 2001–2008, and the Coalition held a majority again in 2008–2017. From 2001–2008, the LC was 'hung', with Labor and Greens members effectively controlling it, but not having an absolute majority required to pass constitutional amendments (the presiding officer does not have a substantive vote). This configuration recurred in 2017–2021. The first Labor-only majority was from 2021 onwards.

Another factor involved in LC elections was exactly how electors had to vote on the STV ballot papers. From 2006–2021 it was the only upper house in the Australian states to retain full preferential voting. In order to lodge a 'formal vote' people either had to (i) cast their ballots 'below the line' (that is, numbering absolutely all the candidates in order, usually more than 40 per district); or more simply (ii) vote 'above the line' by numbering 1 in just one box for their preferred party or group.

Most voters opted for the simpler second option, which meant that votes for eliminated candidates and the surplus preferences of elected candidates could be re-allocated in accordance with GVT lodged by political parties – rather than following the voters' own choices. As a result, various small or micro-parties were able to work together to exchange between them the preferences of those voters who initially supported them in complex sequences.

Figure 21.4: Parties' seats numbers in Western Australia's Legislative Council (upper house), 1989–2021

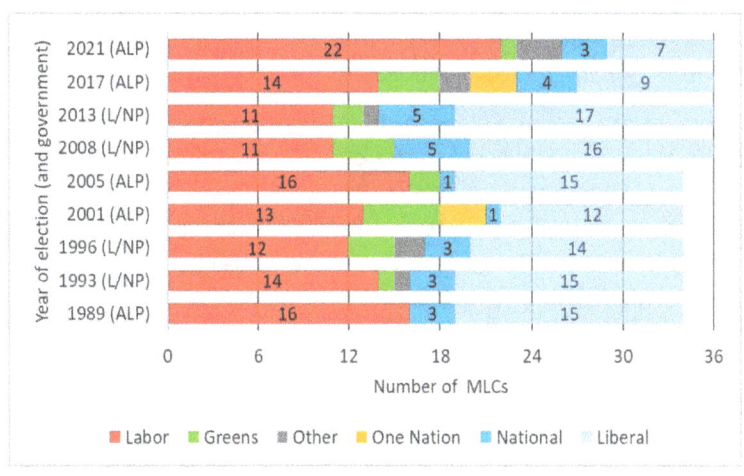

Source: Compiled from data in Western Australian Electoral Commission (2023).

Note: A majority required 18 seats from 1989 to 2005 (when there were 34 members), and 19 from 2008 (36 members in total). From 2025 there will be 37 members, and the majority will remain 19 seats.

The 2021 election of a candidate from the Daylight Saving Party in the Mining and Pastoral Region on just 98 first-preference votes (or 0.2 per cent of all formal votes in that region), was an extreme example of this 'preference harvesting' at work. The 2021 electoral reform should prevent similar events in future and give voters' own choices more weight. State-wide elections may increase the numbers of candidates on voters' ballot papers, although other changes to the legislation have been made to reduce this risk.

A final dimension of electoral competition has been the WA organisations' roles in supporting their party's national performance in the federal elections. While Labor regularly performed strongly at state elections, it tended to under-perform federally. Since the early 1990s, Labor's share of the vote in WA at federal elections was consistently below 40 per cent, and it sank below 29 per cent in 2013. However, this pattern reversed spectacularly (Phillimore, 2022b) at the 2022 federal election. In WA federal seats, Labor secured 37 per cent of the primary vote and 55 per cent of the two-party preferred (TPP) vote, with a swing towards it on TPP of 10.5 per cent, three times the national average. Labor won nine of the 15 federal seats in WA, compared to just five out of 16 seats in 2019.

Party organisations

In terms of internal organisation, Labor's policy positions and leadership personnel have long been shaped by a faction system, similar to that operating at federal level (see Chapter 6). In 2017 a realignment of Labor's faction system created internal discord, culminating in a public dispute between Mark McGowan (the 'centrist' Parliamentary leader since 2012, and one of only six Labor MPs unaligned with any of the factions) and a leading union boss, and the re-statement of the 'democratic socialisation of industry' in the party's platform in 2019 (Hondros, 2019). In the same year, an acrimonious conference of the state Labor Party (Guardian, 2019) led to a 'walk-out'. Subsequent election victories strengthened the premier's authority within the party. Concerns about a toxic work culture within the party organisation (Hastie, 2021) also persist.

Much more dramatic organisational and electoral challenges have confronted the Liberal Party. An internal party review (Bourke, 2021) commissioned following the 2021 state election debacle documented the growing influence of evangelical groups, factional manipulation of local branches, membership decline, falling financial receipts and a fracture between the party's organisational and parliamentary wings. The review found 'corruption of the essential mechanisms that guide and are intended to preserve the integrity of the Party' and warned that without significant reform the party's future was 'bleak'. The Liberals' poor showing in WA at the 2022 federal election reinforced the severity of its internal problems.

Rural demographic changes continue to threaten the National Party's electoral survival. In 2006, the Nationals sought to improve their electoral prospects by terminating their coalition arrangement with the Liberals in favour of a looser post-election 'alliance' that traded legislative support for ministries and funding commitments (Phillimore and McMahon, 2015). Although the Nationals emerged as the official opposition party in the LA following the 2021 State election, the end of advantageous electoral malapportionment for LC elections might induce a further reconsideration of its relationship with the Liberals if the Nationals' seat share in that chamber declines.

Regulating political parties

Political parties are regulated by the *Electoral Act 1907*, administered by the Western Australian Electoral Commission. To be eligible for registration (essential for contesting elections) a party must have a party secretary, a constitution and at least 500 members who are electors at the time that the party applied for registration. In 2021, a new law created a A$2,000 non-refundable fee to register and a requirement to produce a declaration signed by party members in support of the party's application for registration.

WA has until recently been a laggard on election campaign finance matters. Before new legislation was passed in November 2023, there were no expenditure caps, party disclosures of gifts and income were delayed by up to 15 months, and parties registered to contest federal elections benefited from a loophole that allowed them to disclose gifts at the much higher federally mandated threshold (currently A$14,300, compared to A$2,500 at state level). There were also no bans on foreign donations.

WA provides for some election expenditure to be reimbursed for candidates or parties that receive more than 4 per cent of the first-preference vote. At A$2.26 per valid first-preference vote (in 2023), up to the amount of the election expenditure, this funding has been lower than most other Australian jurisdictions, and is not automatic. Parties must provide evidence of having incurred legitimate electoral expenditure. Administrative funding has not been available for parties (or candidates).

In 2020, Labor introduced legislation proposing changes to disclosure, the reporting of donations and the imposition of expenditure caps, which would have improved openness and transparency (although still not to the same extent as in Queensland or NSW). However, the bill lapsed when Parliament was dissolved for the 2021 election.

In 2023, Labor introduced much more ambitious legislation, which passed in November that year and will apply to the 2025 state election (Cook and Quigley, 2023). This legislation imposes expenditure caps on political parties, candidates and third-party campaigners in an effort to 'level the playing field' on campaign spending. The new legislation requires any donation to a political party or candidate over A$2,600 to be disclosed by the end of the next business day during the official election campaign period (and within seven days outside the election period). The legislation also bans all foreign donations, increases penalties for non-compliance and largely removes parties from involvement in postal voting. In recognition of the increased obligations on parties, the rate of public reimbursement will increase from A$2.26 to A$4.40 per primary vote, although WA's rate remains the lowest of any Australian state or territory with public funding.

The social representativeness of legislators

How far parliament represents the broader population has been an important democratic consideration. The parties' selection processes are key here. Important segments of society under-represented in WA's parliament have included women, migrants, and Aboriginal peoples. As in many jurisdictions, using STV for the LC has been accompanied by greater representation of women and minorities. However, this still depends on political party pre-selection processes, especially in the two major parties. WA's Labor has for many years instituted a policy that required virtually equal representation of women in 'winnable' seats. The Liberal Party has not gone down the same path. It continues to rely on an ostensibly merit-based system to influence the gender composition of its parliamentary membership.

Figure 21.5: Members of Western Australia's Legislative Assembly (lower house) and Legislative Council (upper house) by gender and party, 2017, 2021 and 2024

Legislative Assembly	2017		2021		2024	
	Men	Women	Men	Women	Men	Women
Labor	26	15	27	26	26	27
Liberal	11	2	1	1	1	2
National	4	1	3	1	2	1
Total	41	18	31	28	29	30

Legislative Council	2017		2021		2024	
	Men	Women	Men	Women	Men	Women
Labor	7	7	9	13	9	12
Liberal	8	1	6	1	6	1
National	3	1	3	0	2	1
Other	7	2	3	1	4	1
Total	25	11	21	15	21	15

Source: Compiled from data in Western Australian Government (2022) and author's calculations.

Note: The 2024 figures reflect the outcome of two by-elections in the LA, both of which saw retiring male MPs replaced by women. One of these, a female National MLA, later defected to the Liberal Party. The LC figures reflect a resignation by a National MLC (male) and replacement by a woman, and an ALP female MLC resigning whose male replacement now sits as an independent.

Labor's advances in the last two elections meant that overall gender equity in representation has now been achieved in the LA (an extra 11 Labor women MLAs were elected in the 2021 landslide), but not in the LC (Figure 21.5). However, Labor moved to near gender-equity in LC representation in 2017, and by 2021 had more women MLCs than men.

Liberal representation in the legislature has fallen so much that trends for the party are now hard to assess, but they do not yet seem to have redressed their historic gender imbalance. In 2017, female representation in the Liberal party room (both LA and LC) was very low, with 19 men and only three women, or less than 10 per cent. After 2021 there was still only one female Liberal MLC, compared to 6 men. The Nationals were not much better. In 2017 their party room had 7 men and two women, and in 2021, 6 men and one woman. In the Council, the Greens had two men and two women in 2017, but smaller parties have generally had too few seats to discern any trend in this respect.

In terms of ethnic group diversity, Labor's 2021 victory brought an Aboriginal MP into the LA, and three members that were born in India. In the LC, there was an Aboriginal member, as well as MLCs born in China, Ethiopia (a Sudanese refugee) and Serbia. Official profiles for the other parties do not indicate any notably non-Anglo/Celtic members.

Reducing the previous over-representation of regional interests might be thought to reduce the diversity of area interests represented in parliament. However, MPs representing regional seats do not actually need to be from regional WA. Traditionally, several members – including those representing rural regions in the Council – have lived in the metropolitan area, while others have had their electorate offices in Perth.

Government accountability and public sector corruption issues

State governments were historically far more prone to corruption problems among politicians and top officials than was true of the federal administration, partly because state politicians exercise direct control over mineral exploration activities, and regulate property development and substantial public sector contracting. Western Australia had a massive political/corporate scandal in the 1980s known as WA Inc, as previously mentioned (Wikipedia, 2023a). Subsequently, the public service in the state established a strong focus on integrity as an integral component of sound public management and leadership. A multi-faceted approach to oversight also resulted in far more public reporting.

The Public Sector Commission (PSC) has a leadership role including promoting and maintaining integrity, conduct and ethics across the whole WA government sector (WAPSC, 2022a). The PSC integrity strategy (WAPSC, 2021) has four key improvement areas: planning and acting; modelling and embodying a culture of integrity; learning and developing knowledge and skills; and being accountable – with extensive actions listed for public authorities and for individuals, along with measures of success for public authorities. In 2022 the PSC launched a capability review framework (WAPSC, 2022b) to address 21 capabilities to ensure that integrity and risk related to resources were 'embedded in all aspects of the agency including governance and administration; systems and controls; culture and attitude; and accountabilities and responses'. Eight reviews are being trialled over two years and it will then be evaluated to determine if it has met its objectives.

In addition, oversight has been provided by a web of integrity agencies including the powerful Corruption and Crime Commission set up in 2004, the Auditor-General and the Ombudsman with reports provided to parliament and available to the public and the media. Notwithstanding these arrangements, the WA public sector has experienced several integrity failures that have posed questions about the efficacy of the current arrangements and whether the state has in fact been on a pathway to the highest standards of integrity. Three aspects are of note – some recent corruption cases in the administration; conflicts between ministers, the LC and the Corruption and Crime Commission; and court cases against WA brought by businessman Clive Palmer.

Public services corruption cases

In 2019 and 2020 a number of cases of public sector corruption came to light. One involved three executives and several contractors for a large health service agency (Clarke, 2020) who were charged with corruption and fraud following many years of investigation by the Corruption and Crime Commission into the payment of kickbacks to the health officers in return for the awarding of contracts.

Most shocking was the case of Paul Whyte, former acting CEO of the Housing Authority who then became Assistant Director-General in the Department of Communities when the two agencies later merged. He was found to have stolen A$27 million over 11 years through an elaborate system of fake invoicing by shell companies that he controlled, for housing work that was never undertaken. While the cases eventually came to light, the scale and nature of the corruption has raised questions about systemic public administration problems and the effectiveness of WA's integrity agencies. Whyte's extravagant lifestyle (including spending on racehorses and gambling) eventually helped to bring him down and in 2021 he was sentenced to 12 years jail (Menagh, 2021). Several alleged accomplices from outside the public sector were also charged. As a result of these and other cases, ensuring the integrity of public sector procurement processes became an urgent issue, highlighting the central role of the Corruption and Crime Commission (Corruption and Crime Commission, 2021a) at the same time as it has been in the parliamentary spotlight.

The Corruption and Crime Commission case

The Corruption and Crime Commission was established in 2004 (replacing an earlier anti-corruption agency) and has been a strong but controversial body. Since 2019 two related contests between the parliament and the WA government around the Corruption and Crime Commission's powers took place around parliamentary privilege and the appointment of the Corruption and Crime Commission's Commissioner.

In mid-2019 it was revealed that the Corruption and Crime Commission was investigating potential misuse of parliamentary electoral allowances, notably by three former Liberal members of the LC. The Corruption and Crime Commission issued notices to secure the LC members' emails from the state's DP&C, but the LC objected (Department of Justice WA, 2021) that the Corruption and Crime Commission was interfering with parliamentary privilege, an important constitutional provision that protects legislators from being intimidated by law cases or having their speech in the chambers curtailed. Eventually, the Corruption and Crime Commission seized the laptop and two hard drives of former MLC Phil Edman. Subsequently, an interim report from the Corruption and Crime Commission revealed that he had spent A$78,000 of his electoral allowance on speeding fines, visits to a strip club, travel to meet women for sex, and other illegitimate purposes. It also apparently contained potentially politically explosive communications between Edman and colleagues.

Labor ministers complained that the LC was attempting to protect its members (and former members) from scrutiny. In turn, the LC argued that it was protecting the freedom of speech and proceedings of parliament and its members. Citing the UK's historic 1688 Bill of Rights, the LC passed a motion ordering its chief officer (the Clerk) not to follow the directive from the Corruption and Crime Commission, because the two bodies had not reached agreement on the appropriate procedure for determining which emails were subject to parliamentary privilege. The Corruption and Crime Commission returned the laptop and hard drives while the LC President (a Labor member) defended the LC's actions and took legal action in the Supreme Court against the Labor government and the Corruption and Crime Commission to clarify the matter.

The Supreme Court decision (Department of Justice WA, 2021) provided support for both sides. The vast majority of documents sought by the Corruption and Crime Commission could not reasonably be blocked by a claim of parliamentary privilege and the laptop and hard drives were ordered to be released to the Corruption and Crime Commission for its investigation. However, the Court also decided that genuinely privileged material must remain with the parliament. The judgement noted that the absence of a protocol between parliament and the Corruption and Crime Commission for dealing with Corruption and Crime Commission investigations was a key source of the problem. In December 2021 such a protocol was signed (Corruption and Crime Commission, 2021b) which should avoid issues in future.

Another important clash between the parliament and the executive over the Corruption and Crime Commission (Jenkins, 2020) followed in 2020 when the government attempted to re-appoint John McKechnie QC as Commissioner of the Corruption and Crime Commission. As required by law the premier made a recommendation to parliament's Joint Standing Committee on the Corruption and Crime Commission. Its four members (two Labor, one Green and one Liberal) needed to provide bipartisan support for the recommendation if it was to go ahead. But they did not do so, nor did they disclose their reasoning. There was much conjecture about which members had refused to support the appointment. The Liberal Party leader and most MPs publicly supported the re-appointment, but the Committee stood firm in its view, with even its Labor chair defending the integrity of its processes and members. A standoff ensued.

Labor ministers publicly suspected some Committee members of wishing to prevent or obstruct Mr McKechnie and the Corruption and Crime Commission's investigation into possible misuse of taxpayer allowances by LC members (as discussed). Accordingly, in 2020 they introduced legislation to enable the Commissioner to be re-appointed as a one-off, with majority and bipartisan support of the whole parliament. This legislation was rejected by the opposition-dominated LC in 2020. At the 2021 election, Labor promised to reintroduce the law and it eventually passed (McGowan and Quigley, 2021) after the party won an LC majority.

Clive Palmer legislation

The McGowan government's battles with the Queensland businessman and would-be populist politician Clive Palmer were not confined to the issue of the state's hard borders during the pandemic. In August 2020 ministers took an unprecedented step by having the parliament pass legislation that sought to block a legal action brought by Palmer that reportedly could have cost the state up to A$28 billion (Perpitch and Laschon, 2020). Mr Palmer challenged the legislation on constitutional grounds, claiming that legislation targeted at him alone breached the 'rule of law' requirement that laws be general in their effects. However, in October 2021 the High Court dismissed his case.

Palmer's original claim was for compensation that he said he was owed over a stalled iron ore project in the Pilbara region. The dispute stemmed from former WA Premier Colin Barnett's refusal in 2012 to formally assess a mine proposed by Palmer's company Mineralogy, which the businessman claims breached a state agreement inked in 2002. The state chose not to go to arbitration, a process provided for in the agreement, fearing the potential cost of losing the arbitration case would be too high. There is no constitutional provision at state level comparable to the 'on just terms' compensation section (section 51) included in the Commonwealth Constitution. With the rejection of several bases of challenge, WA was able to have the legislation upheld in the High Court.

While generally popular, there was unease in some quarters at the state's targeting of a particular company via legislation, and at the potential 'sovereign risk' it might present to current and prospective investors, which Palmer claimed could deter companies from investing in WA in the future. To date, this wider issue of loss of confidence in the state does not appear to have materialised. The uniquely conflictual nature of the relations between Palmer and the WA government has not apparently shaped investors' views and similar state interventions to block claims for compensation have been viewed as extremely unlikely.

In addition, Palmer took defamation action (Raphael, 2022) against Premier Mark McGowan (who in turn counter-sued Palmer) in the Federal Court of Australia. Very minor damages (Clarke, 2022) were awarded to both men, with strong criticisms from the judge that the case had ever come to court in the first place. In 2022–2023, Palmer's company, Zeph Investments, which is the parent company of Mineralogy and registered in Singapore, commenced an action via Australia's free trade agreement with Singapore (Weber and Perpitch, 2023).

Conclusion

Once the COVID-19 pandemic eventually receded, WA's democratic politics faced several challenges, including how to handle pressures on its health system. Social issues, including housing shortages, high rents and homelessness, major problems in the youth justice system, and violence against women also increased in prominence. The cost of living rose sharply from 2022, increasing pressure on governments to provide relief. Longer-term economic issues included creating and sustaining a more diversified economy less dependent on mining, dealing with the energy transition away from fossil fuels in a state with abundant natural gas and prominent and powerful resource companies, and competing with other states for skilled labour. However, with buoyant public finances the WA state government had been in a position to do more than other states to combat these issues.

Politically, the WA Labor government has been contending with high expectations borne out of its landslide electoral victory in 2021, which included winning seats in areas that were traditionally conservative leaning. The end of emergency conditions plus dealing with the normal pressures of government were always likely to produce some political re-balancing in the run-up to the next state election. However, the resignation of popular Premier Mark McGowan in May 2023, and the announcement in February 2024 that media personality and Lord Mayor of Perth, Basil Zempilas, would be seeking Liberal Party preselection for a lower house seat, makes the 2025 election potentially much more competitive than the lopsided party numbers in the current parliament might suggest. In democratic terms, Labor's legislative hegemony might be regarded as a threat if the party were to be tempted to exploit its majority further to buttress its future electoral chances. But there are few signs of this and, if anything, caution continues to be the government's hallmark.

References

Bennet, Michael (2022) 'If not now, when, Mr McGowan? It's a fair question', *Australian Financial Review*, 21 January. https://perma.cc/AL8T-Y5XD

Bogaards, Matthijs and Boucek, Francoise (2010) *Dominant Political Parties and Democracy: Concepts, Measures, Cases and Comparisons*, Routledge/ECPR Studies in European Political Science, Abingdon, Oxon, England: Routledge.

Bourke, Keane (2021) 'WA Liberal Party review finds "unethical and underhand" conduct in March election lead-up', *ABC News*, 28 August. https://perma.cc/R2YV-CEBR

Carmody, James (2020) 'Commonwealth withdraws from Clive Palmer border case, Prime Minister's letter to WA Premier reveals', *ABC News*, 2 August. https://perma.cc/XT9R-DC54

Carmody, James (2022) 'Mark McGowan announces delay to WA border opening amid fears Omicron will "cripple" state', *The West Australian*, 20 January. https://perma.cc/LUV8-XG4Y

Clarke, Tim (2020) 'How WA's shocking North Metropolitan Health Service corruption scandal played', *The West Australian*, 7 June. https://perma.cc/4TAA-9P5T

Clarke, Tim (2022) 'Mark McGowan v Clive Palmer trial judgement finds both guilty of defamation', *The West Australian*, 2 August. https://perma.cc/B99N-FE27

Cook, Roger and Quigley, John (2023) 'Cook Government delivers fair and transparent electoral system', Government media statements, 28 November. https://perma.cc/7CKS-JP32

Corruption and Crime Commission (2021a) 'Exposing corruption in Department of Communities. Government of Western Australia.' https://perma.cc/E934-FDDU

Corruption and Crime Commission (2021b) 'Presiding officers of the Legislative Council and the Legislative Assembly, and the Commissioner of the Corruption and Crime Commission sign historic Protocol', Government of Western Australia. https://perma.cc/9P55-4UYV

Curthoys, Ann and Lydon, Jane (2016) *Governing Western Australian Aboriginal people: Section 70 of WA's 1889 Constitution* / edited by Ann Curthoys and Jane Lydon. *Studies in Western Australian History,* vol. 30, Western Australia: Centre for Western Australian History, The University of Western Australia. https://perma.cc/YD9B-A6SW

Curthoys, Ann and Martens, Jeremy (2013) 'Serious collisions: Settlers, indigenous people, and imperial policy in Western Australia and Natal', *Journal of Australian Colonial History,* vol. 15, pp.121–144.

Department of Justice WA (2021) *The President of the Legislative Council of Western Australia -v- Corruption and Crime Commission,* Department of Justice WA (Perth). https://ecourts.justice.wa.gov.au/eCourtsPortal/Decisions/ViewDecision?returnUrl=%2feCourtsPortal%2fDecisions%2fFilter%2fSC%2fRecentDecisions&id=4e527584-1667-4c82-a795-68dcff3d3b9b&AspxAutoDetectCookieSupport=1

DP&C (Department of the Premier and Cabinet) (2022) 'South West Native Title Settlement'. https://perma.cc/4DNP-AJBF

Drum, Martin (2021) 'Labor's thumping win in Western Australia carries risks for both sides', *The Conversation,* 14 March. https://perma.cc/J7ZH-AGN2

Drum, Martin (2023) 'After 24 hours of drama, Roger Cook becomes the next premier of Western Australia', *The Conversation,* 31 May. https://perma.cc/MJ7J-5NNM

Dunleavy, Patrick (2010) 'Dominant political parties and democracy: Concepts, measures, cases and comparisons', in Bogaards, Matthijs and Boucek, Francoise (eds) *Rethinking Dominant Party Systems*, London UK: Routledge, pp.23–44. Open access at https://eprints.lse.ac.uk/28132/

Government of Western Australia (2023) 'Review of Western Australia's COVID-19 Management and Response', Report July. https://perma.cc/HE62-2RDB

Green, Antony (2021) 'Western Australian state election 2021: Analysis of results', blogpost on antonygreen.com.au, 16 August. https://perma.cc/NNK6-GJA7

Guardian (2019) 'WA Labor conference: Chaos after walkout during Welcome to Country', *The Guardian, Australia,* 24 August. https://perma.cc/5JDD-X4BG

Guardian (2022) 'Western Australia border reopens after 697 days as the "hermit state"', *The Guardian, Australia*, 2 March. https://perma.cc/4S64-8BW4

Hastie, Hamish (2021) '"We need cultural change": Women formerly employed by WA Labor mull legal challenge after workplace bullying claims', *WA Today,* 8 April. https://perma.cc/C6QE-UFN4

Ho, Cason and Sturmer Jason (2023) 'Mark McGowan stands down as WA Premier in shock announcement, citing exhaustion', *ABC News,* 29 May. https://perma.cc/76PV-NHKA

Hondros, Nathan (2019) 'Party bosses apologise for conference chaos as former minister calls WA Labor "barking mad"',*WA Today*, 27 August. https://perma.cc/HT6A-2Q5S

Ison, Sarah (2021) 'Prime Minister Scott Morrison calls WA's lockdown approach "absurd" in latest COVID plan swipe', *The West Australian,* 24 August. https://perma.cc/VHN5-NX8H

Jenkins, Shannon (2020) 'Political stoush ends McKechnie's time as WA corruption watchdog, despite premier's backing', *The Mandarin,* 28 April. https://perma.cc/8LG3-DKY3

JSCNA (Joint Standing Committee on Northern Australia) (2020) 'Never again', Report, Canberra: Parliament of Australia. https://perma.cc/4C5Z-DMPD

Karp, Paul (2020) 'Clive Palmer's challenge against Western Australia's border ban rejected by high court', *The Guardian, Australia,* 6 November. https://perma.cc/EF62-UPJ9

Knowles, Rachael (2021) 'WA Government cops backlash after passing of Cultural Heritage Bill', *National Indigenous Times,* 16 December, https://perma.cc/AC8Q-E6MH

Kwaymullina, Ambelin (2020) *Living on Stolen Land*, Broome, Australia: Magabala Books.

Law, Peter and Ison Sarah (2020) 'Coronavirus: Mark McGowan now boasts 91 per cent approval rating as support for WA's hard border grows', *The West Australian,* 2 September. https://perma.cc/5W2N-ATJM

LAWA (Legislative Assembly of Western Australia) (2015) Parliamentary Debates (Hansard), 17 June. https://www.parliament.wa.gov.au/Hansard/Hansard.nsf/0/FDAAF3135457A3FC48257F4D000EA4E6/$file/A39%20S1%2020150617%20All.pdf (Ms Josie Farrer MLA)

LAWA (Legislative Assembly of Western Australia) (2021) 'Constitutional and Electoral Legislation Amendment (Electoral Equality) Act 2021'. https://perma.cc/F7KZ-7LGH

Loiacono, Rocco (2021) 'How long can Marshal McGowan and his hermit kingdom stand?' *Spectator,* 8 November. https://perma.cc/G9PM-7L6X

McCusker, Malcolm; Phillimore, John; Murray, Sarah; and Drum, Martin (2021) 'Ministerial Expert Committee on Electoral Reform', Government of Western Australia (Perth). https://perma.cc/H7F5-KJKW

McGowan, Mark and Dawson, Stephen (2021) 'Historic laws passed to protect WA's Aboriginal cultural heritage', government media statements, 15 December. https://perma.cc/L5K6-WEDQ

McGowan, Mark and Quigley, John (2021) 'John McKechnie QC reappointed Corruption and Crime Commission Commissioner', government media statements, 25 June. https://perma.cc/MMA7-5KEB

Menagh, Joanna (2021) 'Former WA public servant Paul Whyte sentenced to 12 years in jail for stealing taxpayer millions', *ABC News,* 19 November. https://perma.cc/9WFZ-9BKD

Miragliotta, Narelle; Murray, Sarah; and Harbord, Justin (2021) 'Western Australia', in Perche, Diana; Barry, Nicholas; Fenna, Alan; Ghazarian, Zareh; and Haigh, Yvonne (eds) *Australian Politics and Policy: Senior Edition*, Sydney: Sydney University Press, pp.318–34. https://open.sydneyuniversitypress.com.au/9781743328415/9781743328415-western-australia.html#Chapter17

OAG (Office of the Auditor-General) (2021a) 'WA's COVID-19 vaccine roll-out', Government of Western Australia. https://perma.cc/DM3F-F8PT

OAG (Office of the Auditor-General) (2021b) 'Roll-out of State COVID-19 stimulus initiatives: July 2020 – March 2021', Government of Western Australia. https://perma.cc/WYH5-ZT8M

OAG (Office of the Auditor-General) (2021c) 'Local Government COVID-19 financial hardship support', Government of Western Australia. https://perma.cc/L454-7GUK

Parker, Gareth (2022) 'Albanese's road to the Lodge was paved by Mark McGowan', *Sydney Morning Herald*, 22 May. $ https://perma.cc/U73K-89E9

Perpitch, Nicolas and Laschon, Eliza (2020) 'Clive Palmer's WA damages claim blocked as bid to delay urgent legislation fails', *ABC News,* 13 August. https://perma.cc/PXZ9-QW5P

Phillimore, John (2022a) 'Does Labor have "total control" in Western Australia?', *The Conversation,* 29 June. https://perma.cc/N3DY-X35D

Phillimore, John (2022b) 'Swing when you're winning: How Labor won big in Western Australia', 22 May. https://perma.cc/LJX3-V7VT

Phillimore, John and McMahon, Lance (2015) 'Moving beyond 100 years: The "WA approach" to National Party survival', *Australian Journal of Politics and History,* vol. 61, no. 1, pp.37–52. https://doi.org/10.1111/ajph.12085

PKKP (Puutu Kunti Kurrama People and Pinikura People) (2020) 'Submission to the Joint Standing Committee on Northern Australia inquiry into the destruction of 46,000-year-old caves at the Juukan Gorge in the Pilbara Region of Western Australia', Parliamentary Inquiry submission. https://perma.cc/6P7L-NY9Q

Raphael, Angie (2022) 'Mark McGowan v Clive Palmer: Defamation trial between pair delayed', *Perth Now*, 25 January. https://perma.cc/CVR3-5R2A

Scarr, Lanai, Law, Peter; and Zimmerman, Josh (2021) 'NSW Treasurer lashes Mark McGowan, calling WA Premier "Gollum of Australian politics"', *The West Australian*, 10 September. https://perma.cc/JY6J-YYW4

Spagnolo, Joe (2022) 'WA to end State of Emergency ending Mark McGowan's border closure powers after COVID-19 pandemic', *Perth Now*, 4 September. https://perma.cc/7E3K-AEB6

Towie, Narelle (2023) 'Divisive, confusing and stressful: Western Australia's Aboriginal cultural heritage laws in a mess', *The Guardian, Australia*, 13 August. https://perma.cc/XUP4-YRBV

WAEC (Western Australian Electoral Commission) (2023) Webpage on elections/past elections. https://perma.cc/L7CJ-7SD3

WAEC (Western Australian Electoral Commission) (2024) Registered political parties in WA. https://perma.cc/V5C2-8MRQ (Accessed 3 February 2024)

Wahlquist, Calla (2017) 'Western Australian election: Mark McGowan declares victory for Labor after record-breaking swings', *The Guardian, Australia*, 11 March. https://perma.cc/F6FH-4CTW

WAPSC (WA Public Sector Commission) (2021) *Integrity Strategy for WA Public Authorities 2020–2023*, Government of Western Australia (Perth). https://perma.cc/C4KA-P62Z

WAPSC (WA Public Sector Commission) (2022a) *Conduct and Integrity in the WA Government Sector*, Government of Western Australia (Perth). https://perma.cc/BU58-K9JW

WAPSC (WA Public Sector Commission) (2022b) *Framework for Reviewing Agency Performance*, Government of Western Australia (Perth). https://perma.cc/7KJV-7PZE

Weber, David and Perpitch, Nicolas (2023) 'Clive Palmer to sue Australia for $300 billion over iron ore project in WA's Pilbara region', *ABC News*, 30 March. https://perma.cc/7N7N-D58F (Accessed 5 February 2024)

West Australian (2020) 'Coronavirus crisis: WA Premier Mark McGowan declares State as its "own country" with borders to close Sunday', *The West Australian*, 2 April. $ https://perma.cc/M9NF-DPSA

Western Australia Legislation (2015) 'Constitution Amendment (Recognition of Aboriginal People) Act', 2015, webpage. https://perma.cc/K9VH-J5PP

Western Australia Legislation (2021) 'Constitutional and Electoral Legislation Amendment (Electoral Equality) Act', webpage. https://perma.cc/K29J-54QZ

Western Australian Government (2022) '2022 women's report card an indicator report of Western Australian women's progress'. https://perma.cc/AU25-M29L

Wikipedia (2023a) 'WA Inc', online encyclopaedia page. https://perma.cc/A7T4-9U4R

Wikipedia (2023b) 'Juukan Gorge', online encyclopaedia page. https://perma.cc/GH6Z-RSPC

Wikipedia (2024) 'The West Australian', online encyclopaedia page. https://perma.cc/HAB3-PJQ7

Winter, Caroline (2020) 'Western Australia encourages FIFO workers to settle there permanently after COVID-19 pandemic', *ABC News* 18 May, https://perma.cc/C56X-SG24

Zimmerman, Josh and Kruijff, Peter de (2020) 'Coronavirus crisis: Liza Harvey says "it's time to open up WA border"', *The West Australian*, 19 May. https://perma.cc/L73U-K8H9

22

Tasmania

Lachlan Johnson, Richard Eccleston and Mike Lester

Tasmania is Australia's most southerly state, an island separated from the main continent, and the smallest of the six full states in the Commonwealth in terms of its population, area and economy. Yet politically it pulls above its weight, electing 12 senators (compared with two for the Canberra territory), and at times leading the national political debate on some issues. The state is also unique in using the standard two Australian voting systems, but the 'wrong' way around (Tasmanian Electoral Commission, 2023a). Proportional representation (PR) has been used to elect its 25-member *lower* chamber (the House of Assembly) in five member seats for terms of up to four years. However, under recently passed legislation, the Assembly will be 'restored' to its former size of 35 members effective from the March 2024 election (TDPC, 2022). The Alternative Vote (AV) is used to elect Tasmania's 15-member *upper* chamber (the Legislative Council (LC)) annually, in a rolling program of elections for two or three single member seats each year, with members serving fixed six-year terms. Having multi-member seats for lower house elections and single-member seats for the upper house is the inverse of all other states with bicameral (two chambers) legislatures. Tasmania's political system has several distinctive features, which have evolved over time, contributing to a unique political culture, and providing key points of difference from the other Australian states.

What does a democratic state government require?

Key elements include:

✦ An effective state constitution that provides an anatomy of legitimate public power to: define the limits of state governmental powers; make government accountable to the people by providing for checks and balances; and promote long-term structures.

✦ Aboriginal and Torres Strait Islander peoples should be afforded full individual civil and human rights. The histories, languages, cultures, rights and needs of Aboriginal and Torres Strait Islander communities and peoples should be addressed.

How to cite this chapter:

Johnson, Lachlan; Eccleston, Richard; and Lester Mike (2024) 'Tasmania', in: Evans, Mark; Dunleavy, Patrick and Phillimore, John (eds) *Australia's Evolving Democracy: A New Democratic Audit,* London: LSE Press, pp.478–496. https://doi.org/10.31389/lsepress.ada.v. Licence: CC-BY-NC 4.0

- Electoral systems for the state's lower and upper houses should accurately translate parties' votes into seats in the state legislature, in different ways that are recognised as legitimate by most citizens. Ideally, the voting systems should foster the overall social representativeness of the two houses of the legislature. Elections and the regulation of political parties should be impartially conducted, with integrity.
- The political parties should sustain vigorous and effective electoral competition and citizen participation. They should enable the recruitment, selection and development of political leaders for state government; formulate viable policy agendas and frame political choices for state functions; and form governments or, when not in power, hold governments accountable. Political parties should uphold the highest standards of conduct in public life.
- The parliament should normally maintain full public control of government services and state operations, ensuring public and parliamentary accountability through conditionally supporting the government, and articulating reasoned opposition, via its proceedings. It should be a critically important focus of Tasmania's political debate.
- The two houses should have different roles and functions, with the House of Assembly providing the premier and most of the cabinet, and much of the political impetus. The LC should operate in ways that further incorporate a plurality of viewpoints and subject a majority government to some effective checks on its power.
- The Tasmanian government should govern responsively, prioritising the public interest and reflecting state public opinion. Its core executive (premier, cabinet, ministers and key central departments) should provide clear unification of public policies across government, so that the state operates as an effective whole. Both strategic decision-making within the core executive, and more routine policy-making, should foster careful deliberation to establish an inclusive view of the 'public interest'.
- The core executive and government should operate fully within the law, and ministers should be effectively scrutinised by and politically accountable to parliament. Ministers and departments/agencies must also be legally accountable to independent courts for their conduct and policy decisions. In the wider state public service officials should act with integrity, in accordance with well-enforced codes of conduct, and within the rule of law.
- The administration of public services should be controlled by democratically elected officials so far as possible. The rights of all citizens should be carefully protected in policy-making, and 'due process' rules followed, with fair and equal public consultation on public service changes. Public services, contracting, regulation and planning/zoning decisions should be completely free from corruption.
- At the Commonwealth level the Tasmanian government should effectively and transparently represent its citizens' interests.

The chapter considers two recent developments, Tasmania's changing political scene, and how the state coped with the COVID-19 pandemic, before a SWOT analysis that surveys the overall strengths and weaknesses of Tasmanian democracy. The later sections cover several aspects of elections and party politics, how government and parliament operate, and some potential deficiencies in the state's unique constitutional set up.

Tasmania's changing electoral politics

In 2022, the ABC's veteran political commentator Antony Green remarked:

> Tasmania has been a Labor stronghold for most of the post-war period. Labor governed the state for 44 of the 47 years between 1935 to 1982, had a controversial reprise as a minority government between 1989 and 1992, and won four elections in a row for 16 years in office between 1998 and 2014.
>
> At state level, the tide seems to have turned against Labor since Will Hodgman led the Liberal Party to victory in 2014. Hodgman became only the second Liberal Leader to win re-election as premier in 2018, and Hodgman's successor Peter Gutwein led the Liberal Party to a third victory in May 2021. It was the first time the Tasmanian Liberal Party had achieved a third term in office. The Labor Party was split by internal divisions before Premier Gutwein called the May 2021 state election. (Green, 2022)

A glance at the parties' shares of first-preference votes, shown in Figure 22.1, could be interpreted as supporting this narrative. Labor support fell dramatically from over half in 2002 to just above a quarter in 2014 and 2021, albeit with a small uplift in between. Votes for the Greens, who have been active in Tasmanian politics in various guises since the 1970s, also fell from nearly a fifth in the first elections this century to around a tenth of voters in the past two. By

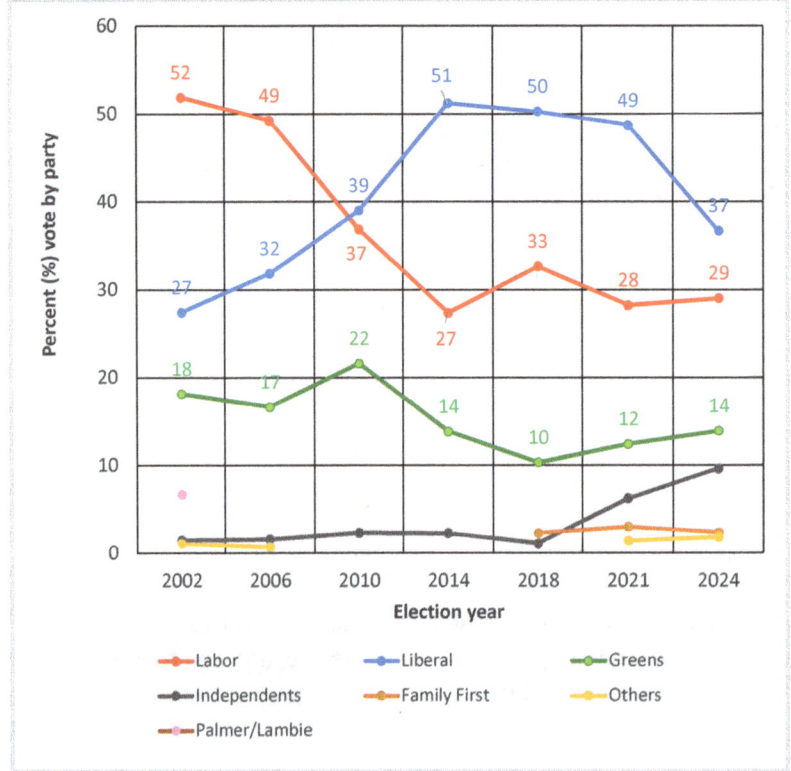

Figure 22.1: Party shares of first-preference votes in the Tasmania House of Assembly elections, 2002–2024

Source: Compiled from data in Tasmanian Electoral Commission (2023b) and Wikipedia (2024a).

contrast, the state-wide Liberal party soared from a quarter of voters in 2002 to run consistently at around a half since 2014. However, at the 2024 state election, called early by the Liberal premier Jeremy Rockliff after two of his MPs defected to the crossbench, the top two parties' support somewhat converged and Green and other voting increased (9News, 2024).

In terms of Assembly seats, the Single Transferable Vote (STV) PR system – in a variant called Hare-Clark in Tasmania – has reliably rendered votes cast into seats. There have been some occasional wobbles arising from Tasmania using the five federal election districts as five-member seats for the Assembly elections. Seats of this size imply that no party or candidate can win representation unless they formally receive around 16 per cent of the final vote count, or somewhat less (depending on the specific ways that votes are cast). Even with transfers this has been a tall order for Tasmania's smaller parties, and even independents are rarely elected (Figure 22.2). The Greens have managed to win and retain seats, and they supported the Labor government from 2010 to 2014 in office when they held the balance of power. However, the main trend has been that the change in voting patterns in Figure 22.1 has translated into a reversal of Labor and Liberal fortunes from 2014 onwards (Figure 22.2). In 2024, the number of seats in the Assembly was increased (from 25 to 35), so that although the Liberal seats total increased, their share of seats fell (from over half to two fifths). Yet, as at previous elections, Labor conceded that the Liberals should reform a minority government, since they retained the largest number of seats (9News, 2024).

Figure 22.2: Party seats in the Tasmania House of Assembly elections, 2002–2021

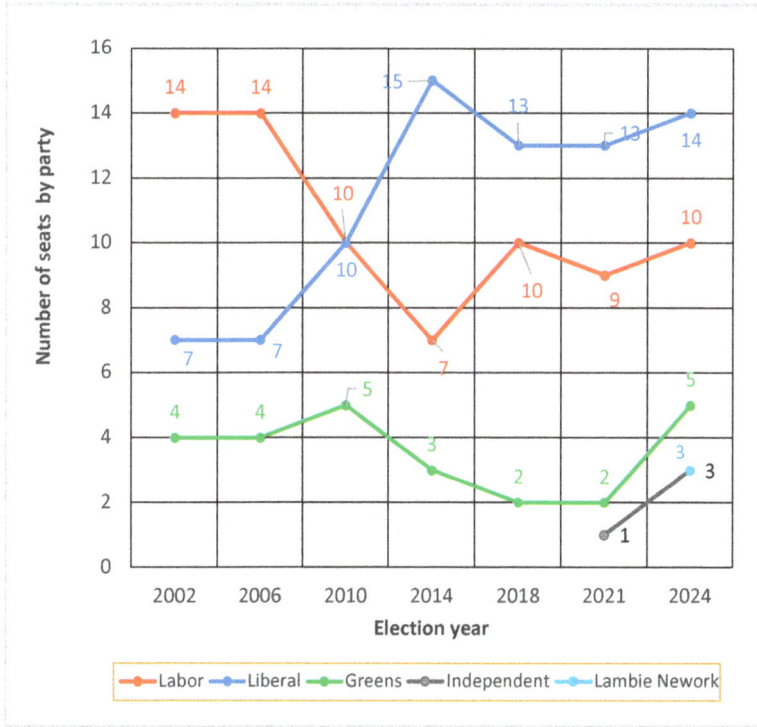

Source: Compiled from data in Tasmanian Electoral Commission (2023b) and Wikipedia (2024a).

Note: There were 25 members up to 2021, so a majority required 13 MPs. In 2024, the number of seats increased to 35, so a majority requires 18 MPs.

In the past, political scientists argued that minority governments are 'much more frequent in the PR electoral systems' (Powell, 2014, p.4), while, in contrast to 'first past the post' and AV voting systems, PR creates a challenge to the traditional Westminster two-party model (Bogdanor, 1984, p.121). Arguably, PR helps minorities and coalitions to endure by supplying small parties as 'contract partners' whose main aim has been to exist to negotiate post-election agreements to secure policy outcomes rather than necessarily to win government themselves (Cody, 2008, pp.27–29).

Historically, Tasmania has had a high count of minority governments, given its adoption of the Hare-Clark PR voting system in 1907 (Moon, 1995, p.147). This 'pure' version of STV allows independents and minor parties to more easily secure representation in the House of Assembly. In the 34 elections since it was introduced, independents or third parties have won seats in all but nine. In two of those nine where no independent was elected, Labor and the Liberal Party each won 15 seats. From 1989, when five Greens were elected to the House of Assembly, until 2021 Tasmania had three 'hung' parliaments which resulted in minority governments. All Tasmanian elections have been close and there has been a long-running argument about the prospects and benefits – or otherwise – of single-party majority governments. However, five out of the past six elections delivered exactly that (under the old seats total), the STV system notwithstanding. With the change to 35 seats in 2024, another minority government was formed.

Turning to the LC (the upper house), its 15 seats are elected using the AV system in sub-divisions of the state's five federal districts small enough for a single seat, but whose somewhat artificial boundaries are not necessarily well known to Tasmanians. Voters need to number all candidates in order of preference. Historically, the upper house was dominated by independents with local reputations able to garner majorities at the two-party preferred vote final stage of AV. For a long time, it was the only parliamentary chamber in Australia where most members were independents, not subject to party control, and thus able to provide more autonomous scrutiny of government proposals. However, in recent years both Labor and the Liberals have fielded candidates who have proved able to win seats. The LC membership in spring 2023 showed Labor and the Liberals holding four seats each and the crossbench independents seven seats. In general, governments have had to negotiate legislation through the LC, rather than being able to rely on a single-party majority there.

Elections for the LC's single-member electorates are conducted in a fairly unusual way. Members are elected for six-year terms with elections alternating between three divisions in one year and two divisions the next. This cycle repeats ad infinitum. Another atypical feature is that the state's government has no power to ask the governor to dissolve the upper house in the event that it ever used its theoretical power to vote down the annual budget and block supply. As a result, and unlike other state upper houses and the federal Senate, the LC never has to face either a full or half-house general election. With only a third or less of seats contested each year, and with many independents also winning seats, tracking voting behaviours for upper house elections has been difficult. The make-up of the chamber is discussed in the next section.

The COVID-19 pandemic

Throughout the 2020–2022 pandemic crisis period, Tasmania as an island state was in the unique position of having no land borders with other Australian states. Instead, it could rely on the far more easily implemented checks on people arriving at seaports and airports. From March to December 2020, travellers deemed to be 'non-essential', including returning residents, were subject to a mandatory 14-day quarantine, with fines for breaches implemented. Within the island, the Liberal state government's response was also relatively relaxed, with the few lockdowns imposed only where large outbreaks of the virus occurred early on, or in responses to surges in other Australian cities leading to temporary bans on entry from badly affected areas (Wikipedia, 2023a). More or less bipartisan support for this approach also meant that the 2021 elections did not prompt any major changes in the policy. The vaccination rollout was comprehensive and by 2023, aided by the state mandating it for non-essential retail and some workforces, with three-quarters of adults having three injections and almost all aged citizens four. A few isolated protests against this alleged 'medical apartheid' resulted, but nothing like the movements elsewhere in the country (Washington Post, 2021). Mandatory vaccination was scrapped in March 2022 (Constitution Watch, 2022). In all, fewer than 270 deaths from COVID-19 were recorded in Tasmania by spring 2023 (Tasmanian Department of Health, 2023). However, just under 290,000 COVID-19 cases were monitored after mid-December 2021 from a population of 570,000 (when systematic tests in the state were first put in place). Political disruption was minimal, although LC elections in three seats in 2020 were postponed for a fairly short time (from May to August) (Wikipedia, 2023b).

Strengths, weaknesses, opportunities and threats (SWOT) analysis

Current strengths	Current weaknesses
The state's electoral systems operate with high integrity. Tasmania's particular version of the STV electoral system used for House of Assembly elections – Hare-Clark voting – is somewhat complex for voters. But it closely translates aggregate voter preferences across parties into well-matched parliamentary representation, especially in the enlarged Assembly with 35 seats from 2024 onwards. At its best, the system also encourages compromise and collaboration among elected members in representing their constituency.	The five-member seats for elections to a smaller lower house were deliberately introduced by the top two parties with a view to curtailing the ability of the Greens and other small parties to win seats. They were used up to the 2021 election. The formal quota of support (the threshold needed to win a seat) was one-sixth of the total vote, although particular configurations of the vote may mean that the last seat in a constituency goes to a party with somewhat less than this level. From 2024 on seven-seat elections in the five electoral districts should give greater proportionality, and the formal quota drops a little to an eighth of votes.
Tasmania's uniquely constituted upper house changes incrementally each year with annual elections and has been relatively influential because of the dominance of independent members there. Its distance and independence from the lower house have been a valuable asset for Tasmanian democracy. Maintaining the independence of the state's upper house prevents its devolution into a 'rubber stamp' and encourages effective, rigorous review, ultimately helping to produce better and more considered policy.	Party politicisation of the LC has increased in recent years, with a majority of members now from the top two parties, reducing its distinctiveness somewhat.

Tasmania has not experienced difficulty in forming governments, even when no party has an overall majority. Either formal coalition agreements have been reached or parties holding the balance of power have agreed to vote supply and support confidence in government motions. Most recent governments have had majority support. The premier can also call an election within the four-year maximum limit, benefiting the incumbent party by ensuring that voting takes place at the most advantageous time, as occurred in 2021. However, this has not been common.	Tasmania's small parliament has been a major source of weakness. With a typical ministry of nine, a party needs just four more MPs to form a government. The talent pool from which to draw a cabinet and ministry has simply been too shallow. And ministers will typically have to cover several crucial portfolio areas (numbering 40 in all), limiting their ability to give each policy area the time and attention it deserves. Accountability to parliament likewise suffers given the scarcity of government backbenchers and the increased responsibility that naturally falls to unelected ministerial staff under this arrangement. In August 2022, however, the Liberal state government committed to restoring parliament to its former size (35 members) at the 2024 state election (**TDPC, 2022**).
Corruption linked to elected politicians has been rare. However, some internal party battles between factions can become intense, as with Labor before the 2021 election. And donations can influence elections as in the 2018 election, 'which turned largely on Labor's promises of gambling and pokies reform' (**Guardian, 2021**). The Liberal party received huge donations from vested gambling interests, but the public were left oblivious to the fact until well after the election' (**Guardian, 2021**).	Tasmania still relies on weak federal legislation spending limits to regulate donations to political parties, but these have been far too high to be effective within the smaller cockpit of state politics. Tasmania's Integrity Commission has some restrictions on investigating party finances while elections are under way. State election disclosure legislation being debated in the Tasmanian Parliament in 2023 was not as comprehensive as that in other Australian states.
Tasmanian public service has been generally effective and public administration has for the most part been well regarded by citizens. The state's Integrity Commission has powers to investigate the administration of public services in most circumstances.	There are some limits on the Integrity Commission's ability to follow through investigations of public service agencies and no statutory requirement for public officials to report suspected or potential corrupt conduct.
In theory, there is a right to information process for citizens. The broader transparency of state government has generally been high, with vigilant MPs and active mainstream and social media coverage of issues.	The under-resourcing of Tasmania's Right to Information system has led to the creation of a huge backlog of requests and unacceptable delays accessing public documents. Average delays in responses are now so long as to render the general 'right' largely ineffective.
Tasmania has a dynamic civil society, a wide range of engaged interest groups, and vigorous public debates about state policy-making. There are few signs of over-polarisation in partisan debates, nor of recent 'democratic backsliding.'	Some conspiracy theories and uglier mobilisations against vaccines and supposedly 'woke' issues (such as the rights of transgender or Aboriginal Tasmanians) have occasionally arisen.

Future opportunities	Future threats
The Tasmanian government has recently completed a review of the *Electoral Act 2004* and in 2021 Liberal Premier Peter Gutwein pledged a new donations limit of A$5,000.	Critics argue that the donations limit for a small state like Tasmania should be no more than A$1,000. At the time of writing, Tasmania's upper house was in the process of debating the government's proposed A$5,000 limit, which would be (with SA) the equal highest threshold in the country (Australia Institute, 2023; Eccleston and Jay, 2019).
Constitutional issues have been handled flexibly by altering the *Constitution Act 1934*, using normal parliamentary processes only.	Critics argue that Tasmania's Constitution has become outdated and riddled with blank, repealed, obsolete or irrelevant sections. It provides little or no guidance on a wide range of important matters, is arcane and inaccessible, and lacks the authority of a supreme or fundamental law. Since it has never been put to a referendum it is hard to see that it represents the settled will and values of Tasmanians.
The Tasmanian government has committed to a timeline for historical truth-telling and treaty discussions with the state's Indigenous peoples. The process will be led by senior constitutional law experts – including a former Tasmanian Governor (Kate Warner) – alongside Indigenous elders and community leaders.	Notwithstanding the important commitment to the truth-telling and treaty process, historically, treaty discussions with Tasmanian First Nations peoples have occurred only slowly and made little progress. The preamble of the *Constitution Act* referring to Indigenous peoples is largely symbolic and confers no specific, actionable rights.

The rest of the chapter explores three key issues with clear implications for effective democratic governance in Tasmania– the roles of parliament, the executive and public service; the operations of the electoral systems and party competition; and some constitutional and human rights issues.

Parliament and the executive

Like most states, Tasmania has a bicameral parliament. However, the state's Constitution does not fully specify the relationship between the two houses or their roles in several key areas beyond any doubt and some uncertainties remain (Gogarty et al., 2016). The appointment of the ministry for instance was not fully specified. In practice, whichever party and leader commands a majority in the House of Assembly forms the government, and most of the ministers come from there. In theory, the Tasmanian LC retained the power to reject money Bills (budgets), and thus send the lower house to an election without its own members having to face the polls – making it an unusually powerful upper house in comparison to other Westminster systems. Yet, since a famous stand-off in the 1880s, the LC has not exercised this power. One further issue has been that there is no longer a formal mechanism to resolve deadlocks between the House of Assembly and the LC, which must instead be negotiated case by case. In addition, Tasmania's Constitution does not clearly articulate the relationship of the ministry to parliament. This has left the authority and responsibilities of Parliament vis-à-vis the government and core executive somewhat unclear, and possibly creates a theoretical lack of accountability or even a risk of a constitutional crisis.

The small size of both chambers in parliament accentuated these problems. The issue of parliamentary reform has never been too far from the forefront of political debate in Tasmania. Throughout the early 1990s, calls to reduce the number of MPs in the state parliament culminated in a 1998 decision to cut the House of Assembly from 35 to 25 members and the upper house from 19 to 15. The change arose ostensibly as a 'productivity offset' to justify a controversial 40 per cent pay rise for MPs, after trade union and public opinion demands that MPs should be treated the same as other workers following a previous period of public sector wage restraint and austerity. However, cutting the House's size also suited the political agenda of the two major parties, who saw it as a chance to make it harder for the Greens to win seats by lifting the formal quota required to win a seat from one-eighth (12.5 per cent) of the total votes cast with seven-member seats to one-sixth (17 per cent) with five-member seats (Crowley, 1999).

Political commentators argued that the decision to cut seats reduced parliamentary accountability, made it difficult to fill ministerial positions (leading to a growing number of ministerial appointments from the upper house) and disadvantaged small parties by raising the formal quota needed to elect a House of Assembly member under the Hare-Clark proportional electoral system. In 2010, the leaders of the three parties represented in Tasmania's parliament, Labor, the Liberals and the Greens, signed a pact to restore the House of Assembly to its pre-1998 size. The agreement for parliamentary reform of September 2010 also committed the parties to: examine reforms to laws relating to electoral donations; set limits on electoral spending; introduce fixed terms of parliament; introduce a code of conduct for members; tighten rules about conflicts of interest; and provide more parliamentary resources for MPs. At first, little meaningful change came of this pact.

However, in February 2021 a joint party select committee handed down a report recommending that the lower house be increased by 10 members (Whiteley, 2021). The committee found that the 1998 decision to cut MP numbers was harmful because:

- It eroded the underpinning purpose of the Hare-Clark system (to achieve PR). Restoring 35 members to the House of Assembly to (giving five seven-seat constituencies) would more accurately reflect the original representative purpose of the Hare-Clark system and voters' preferences.

- There was compelling evidence that the reduction in MPs undermined the democratic accountability of the House of Assembly, as there are now too few members who were not part of the executive to effectively represent their constituencies. The reduction reduced the capacity of the lower house to undertake its parliamentary functions, particularly its role in robustly debating legislation, undertaking inquiries, policy development and achieving timely quorums for parliamentary committees. A much smaller government backbench also resulted in limited competition for ministerial positions and challenges filling ministerial vacancies. This has negatively affected governance in Tasmania. The 7 to 10 (maximum) ministers in the Tasmanian government also hold more portfolio responsibilities and thus shoulder a greater workload than their interstate counterparts, which has impacted on good governance. Yet if the capacity of the House of Assembly to be an effective forum for scrutiny of the executive was to be retained, the committee recommended keeping a maximum of 10 ministers even in a 35-seat House.

The committee's proposal to restore the Assembly to 35 seats was finally acted on, and the early March 2024 election was the first under the new system (see Figures 22.1 and 22.2 earlier).

Under STV, by-elections for the lower house are rare because vacancies that arise between elections (through an MP resigning, for example) are filled by recounting the votes of the retiring member in that division from the preceding election. In July 2020, the resignation from parliament of a government Braddon backbencher (Joan Rylah) highlighted another weakness of the 25-seat House: a shortage of replacement candidates for casual vacancies. Rylah had been elected on a countback following the earlier resignation of her Braddon colleague and former minister Adam Brooks. Following her resignation, Rylah was in turn replaced by Felix Ellis. Under Tasmanian electoral laws, recounts of the votes that elected the retiring member are used to fill casual vacancies. As normal, under STV, the major parties usually nominate five candidates for the full slate of seats in each division and technically any of the unsuccessful candidates in the electorate may be nominated as a replacement. In practice, voters' preference flows have always meant that after recounting the seat has always gone to a candidate lower down the list put forward by the same party. However, in this case the resignation left the government with just a one-seat majority. After Ellis, there were no remaining unsuccessful Liberals who had stood in the Braddon election. If another government member resigned or could not remain a member, there would be no automatic replacement. Thus, instead of a recount, the government would be forced to take the extraordinary step of advising the governor of a need for a by-election (which electoral law allows if needed), because the loss of one seat would cause it to lose its majority.

Responsible government and the core executive

Tasmania's core executive has been constrained by many of the same structural and institutional barriers. The state's cabinet typically consists of nine members, some of whom hold up to six different portfolios. This situation limits the talent pool from which ministers can be drawn and inevitably results in some ministers presiding over a wide range of disparate portfolio areas. In addition, agency structures in the state and ministerial portfolios have not been aligned. For example, the Tasmanian Department of State Growth (2021) reported to seven of the nine cabinet ministers in the 2021 parliament. The core executive also has increasingly relied on majority party members of the LC to serve as ministers. However, while there has been a clear convention that the state premiers should always sit in the lower house, it has become increasingly common for ministers (including Treasurers, second after the premier) to sit in the upper houses of other Australian parliaments, suggesting that the Tasmanian experience has neither been uncommon nor necessarily problematic (Young, 2014). The Tasmanian premier has one power not found elsewhere. While all other states and territories have fixed four-year terms for their house of government, Tasmania alone currently has a maximum four-year term. Therefore, the premier may call an election sooner than the limit if they choose, as happened in 2021, when the Liberals won (for them) an unprecedented third term of office by going to the polls 12 months early.

Despite the small size of the Tasmanian parliament and the associated machinery of government, there remains a lack of general coordination across government, with fragmented organisational structures complicating the flow of information while creating high barriers to effective collaboration and resource sharing. A recent Independent Review of the Tasmanian State Service (TSS) conducted by Ian Watt found that:

> *antiquated, outdated, and inappropriate structural, legal, and administrative arrangements ... make it harder to focus on whole-of-government issues; make it more difficult to lead and manage appropriately; impede the ability to respond in a timely way to changes in the needs of community and business; and supress the quality of services delivered.'* (2020, p.11)

For these reasons, organisational problems in areas requiring agencies to collaborate – or indeed where whole-of-government coordination is needed – have led to suboptimal outcomes and exacerbated existing resource constraints through duplication (see also Watt, 2021, p.22). There are legislative instruments (such as the *State Policies and Projects Act 1993*) (Tasmanian Legislation, 2023) that are designed to ensure a whole-of-government approach to complex issues such as planning, public health or climate change. But they have not been used for this purpose in recent years.

Intergovernmental relations

Dealings between the federal government and the states cover key resources (see Chapter 16) and are critically important for a small jurisdiction like Tasmania, due to its relatively high dependence on Commonwealth funding and revenue. With its lower economic gross state product (GSP), Tasmania has benefited substantially from horizontal fiscal equalisation across the states but has been vulnerable to changing external economic conditions and sometimes arbitrary or political decisions at the federal government level. All states benefit from the federal revenue via various grants and equalisation payments (due to vertical fiscal imbalance) but have no constitutional assurance that their fiscal needs will be met. States without large natural resource bases to exploit (or whose natural resource exploitation potential has been disproportionately impacted by federal treaties or agreements) have had a weaker position in intergovernmental negotiations compared to their larger or richer counterparts. For instance, recent changes to the formula for distributing Goods and Service Tax (GST) receipts across the states moved towards 'reasonable equalisation' from 'full equalisation', which disproportionately impacted smaller jurisdictions like Tasmania (TDTF, 2021). The distribution of equalisation funding was also made more difficult still by the COVID-19 pandemic and associated debates about movement, borders and travel restrictions.

On the other hand, Tasmania's equal representation with 12 members in the federal Senate arguably presents a clear opportunity to advocate for Tasmanian interests at the Commonwealth level. In federal House of Representatives elections, the state has only five MPs, usually split between the top two parties and with an occasional independent. However, at Senate elections the state's voters are uniquely privileged by having one senator per 21,000 Tasmanians. In addition, the state's voters have consistently used 'below-the-line' senate voting to pick candidates across party lists, and this has delivered several independent representatives to the Senate crossbench. Some (such as former Senator Brian Harradine and current Senator Jacquie Lambie) have used the balance of power in Canberra's upper house to extract valuable concessions and benefits for the state over a number of years.

Public administration and public services

The TSS is small in absolute terms compared with most other state public services, employing just under 32,000 people (or 25,000 full-time equivalent posts). There are nine state departments and eight other agencies or statutory authorities. As in many other jurisdictions, public services have in recent years been grappling with ever-increasing service delivery expectations among citizens despite tight funding constraints. Demographic challenges associated with an ageing and highly decentralised population add further complexity to these issues in Tasmania. The operating environment for public servants underwent some unprecedented changes during the COVID-19 pandemic, requiring a far more agile and unconventional approach across almost all areas of public administration.

According to the independent review of the state service mentioned (Watt, 2021), the most important issues for public services have been twofold: diseconomies of small scale, due to weak structures and whole-of-government coordination; and technological readiness. Providing a full range of services in a small regional or remote jurisdiction will always be more challenging due to the small absolute size of the public sector, but this issue is exacerbated in the TSS by duplication, resource-sharing constraints, 'silos', and fragmentation. The Watt Review noted that while 'siloing' occurs widely across public agencies, the impact has been 'disproportionately high in a small state service', so that the TSS 'is likely to be missing out on the benefits of building and leveraging economies of scale, while exacerbating single person or system dependencies' (Watt 2020, p.60).

Second, a lack of technological readiness and preparedness for digitisation have also hindered service provision, increased the cost of public interactions, and potentially even compromised the security of sensitive public data in Tasmania. In 2021, the TSS was rated the least prepared public service in the country in terms of 'digital readiness' (Intermedium, 2021). The Watt Review (2020, p.71) reported that:

> digital infrastructure is outdated; platforms and software are being band-aided, with obsolescence not far off; and there is no whole-of-Government roadmap for bringing the TSS up to date. Moreover, cybersecurity is not highly-prioritised and data is not being used effectively to improve the quality of services.

Community confidence in the administration of public services could also benefit from addressing a handful of key systemic or legal weaknesses around the resourcing and management of the freedom of information process. The first of these issues, the FoI process (or 'Right to Information' (RTI) in Tasmania), has been an issue for some years. A combination of unnecessarily onerous requirements, a worrying trend toward default resistance to disclosure, and under-resourcing of the state's RTI office resulted in average wait times for RTI requests reaching as high as 881 days (or 2.4 years) in recent times (Compton, 2018).

Voting, elections and party competition

Data on the Tasmanian public's understanding of and opinion regarding the STV/Hare-Clark voting system used in its lower house elections are scarce. However, analysis of voting patterns in elections for the state's federal senators does suggest a higher level of familiarity with PR systems in Tasmania than in most other states and territories. In 2016, nearly two-thirds of

Tasmanians voted ('below the line') for individual candidates rather than numbering the box for their preferred political party 'above the line', thereby allowing that party to allocate their preferences (although there were other factors that year, including changes to the minimum number of preferences and a highly publicised personal campaign for one Labor senator). Tasmania and the ACT consistently post the highest number of 'below-the-line' ballots in national Senate elections, suggesting that Tasmanian voters are more comfortable with PR and quota preferential voting than counterparts in other jurisdictions.

But do outcomes meet most voters' hopes or expectations of choosing a government able to enact the agendas on which it campaigned? This question is a difficult one to answer. In recent state elections, both of the top two parties have insisted they will not govern in a minority, which could create a constitutional crisis if neither has a majority of MPs, and it might seem to ignore the electorate's potential choice of a hung parliament. It is normal for political parties to campaign for majority government (Strom, 1990) and to rule out making minority government agreements with those parties whose ideologies or policies they vehemently oppose. Opposition parties may also pledge not to form a minority government after one election as part of a longer-term strategy to win an overall majority at the following election. In the Tasmanian context, the Greens consistently reserve the right not to support any government they believe to be guilty of corruption or maladministration. For example, they brought down the Field Labor government in 1992 because of its decision to pursue an increase in woodchip exports, defining this as maladministration. However, it is vastly different for a party to campaign against minority government than to refuse to form a government, a strategy that cannot usually work for incumbent governments.

The political parties

In the post-war period, there was a noticeable fall in combined voter support for the top two parties Labor and the Liberal-National Coalition in both Commonwealth and state elections, from a total of 96 per cent support in 1949 to 80 per cent in 1998 (Bennett, 1999). For example, in his thesis on the impact of post materialism on the Tasmanian Labor Party, Patmore (2000) argued that the Labor Party's history, Tasmania's Hare-Clark electoral system, and the existence and persistence of post materialism in the community contributed to the emergence of environmental parties and a consequential decline in the Australian Labour Party's (ALP) vote share. For the 13 elections in the 46-year period from 1946 to 1986, the average vote share for the ALP in Tasmania was 48.4 per cent. This compares with an average of 38.5 per cent for the nine elections between 1989 and 2018 (see Wikipedia, 2024b).

Yet in the 21st century, no further real decline in two-party dominance has occurred and state politics has remained centred on their adversarial competition. Each party has enjoyed long periods of majority government in the modern era. For example, long-lasting Liberal governments under Hodgman, Gutwein and Rockliff were in power from 2014 to the present. (The Rockliff minority Liberal government's four-year term also could last to 2028.) Successive four-term Labor governments also occurred under Bacon, Lennon, Bartlett and Giddings from 1998–2014. Though generally robust, Tasmania's party system does demonstrate a number of potential vulnerabilities, including dwindling membership, dealignment with communities, thinning links to civil society and less loyal constituencies. Intra-party battles have sometimes been intense, such as those that plagued Labor before the 2021 election and led to the national ALP seeking to reassert internal party discipline (Green, 2022).

Yet the Greens have also become established as the third party in Tasmania over the last three decades. Although their vote dropped below their 2014 peak in the last decade or so, they have proved persistently able to compete (unlike various short-lived micro-parties and 'surge' parties) and to shape state policies, and they won more seats in 2024. They have also provided senior personnel with political clout, twice serving as partners in minority governments. The most recent case was a coalition with two ministers in the Bartlett/Giddings Labor government from 2010–2014. Earlier on, the Greens also held the balance of power and afforded supply and confidence to the Rundle Liberal government between 1996–1998, which governed in minority with no arrangement with the Greens. Before that, the party also reached the Accord agreement with the Field Labor government in 1989–1992.

A major source of vulnerability has remained the state's outdated and inadequate *Electoral Act 2004*. Tasmania's donations disclosure regime is currently the weakest of any state in Australia. As the law stood until recently:

> *Tasmania is the only Australian state that does not have state-based legislation regulating the disclosure of gifts and donations to political parties, politicians or election candidates and the only jurisdiction not to regulate 'third parties' in elections.* (Tasmanian Department of Justice, 2021, p.14)

The nationwide Commonwealth disclosure threshold for donations (at time of writing A$14,300) is far too high to be effective in state politics. It did not curtail opportunities for undue influence exerted by third parties or via political donations in Tasmanian elections, nor reassure the public that politics were 'clean'. This issue came to a head at the 2018 state election, in which reform of the licensing, regulation, and taxation of poker machine operators ('pokies') was a dominant issue. While the state government has accepted the recommendations of the review in principle, the revised threshold currently under discussion (up to A$5,000) would still be very high for a small polity (Guardian, 2021). A threshold of A$1,000 would bring Tasmania into line with most other Australian states and critics argue that it is the maximum that should be considered, given the historically corrosive influence of political donations on voters' confidence in the Tasmanian democratic process. As this volume goes to press, Tasmania's upper house was still debating a A$5,000 limit proposed by ministers that would put Tasmania (along with SA) onto the highest level of any state (Eccleston and Jay, 2019).

The powers of the Tasmanian Integrity Commission (TIC) are a second important area of vulnerability. Critics of the TIC have identified areas of weakness, including the lack of a specific campaign finance disclosure regime and the Commission's inability to investigate potentially corrupt or inappropriate conduct during election campaigns due to the dissolution of Parliament (Brown et al., 2019; Minshull, 2020). In addition, there is no statutory requirement for public officials to report suspected or potential corrupt conduct.

Constitutional issues and human rights

Tasmania's constitution has very deep historical roots, which has some implications for how it operates today. Following the creation of a new 'blended' LC in 1851, and the end of convict transportation in 1853, an act to establish a parliament and responsible government in 'Van Diemen's Land' (as the state had been known until that time) was drafted, passed and enacted after Crown approval in 1855, creating a 15-member upper house (to replace the pre-existing

LC) which was able to grant or deny assent to bills debated and passed by a 30-member lower house, the House of Assembly. This act has been amended and updated numerous times throughout its long history (notably including its amendment to recognise Tasmanian Aboriginal people in 2016) but it remains substantively similar to its original form in most major respects.

The Tasmanian Constitution's lack of clarity on the functioning of parliament has in the past led to conflict and even the risk of major constitutional crisis. For instance, in 1879, the LC invented a novel and unintended role for itself in the amendment of money bills, which led to a standoff culminating in the upper house adjourning indefinitely. Constitutionally precluded from dissolution by the Governor, this situation essentially held the House of Assembly to ransom, hamstringing government business for three months (Museum of Australian Democracy, 2021). Notwithstanding these early tussles over the LC's role in amending money bills and ability to hinder government business, for the most part Tasmania has avoided major constitutional crises since. However, there is no lack of potential for problems to arise.

The Constitution provides no guidance on the relationship between the two houses of Parliament, stating only that 'the Governor and the Legislative Council and the House of Assembly shall together constitute the Parliament of Tasmania'. A second oversight is that despite an inferred power that was read in to the *Enabling Act 1850* (Lumb, 1991), the Tasmanian Constitution provides no explicit general law-making powers to parliament (Museum of Australian Democracy, 2021). As yet, however, parliament has faced no constitutional challenge to general law-making and has also amended the *Constitution Act* itself frequently over some 170 years, so it is probably safe to assume that this latter issue is an unlikely ground for crisis.

The *Tasmanian Constitution Act* also makes no assertion of the supremacy of parliament that would make clear that the state government is subordinate to parliament, although such a provision is a feature of most other post-colonial Westminster constitutions. Consequently, there is no explicit or general constitutional requirement that the ministry collectively, or ministers individually, report to parliament (although many individual acts obviously place reporting requirements on the relevant ministers, once in office). This oversight at the general level creates a very real risk of constitutional crisis at every election, because all ministerial positions are vacated seven days after the return of the writs, regardless of whether parliament has met or whether any party or group can guarantee to the Governor that they have the confidence of parliament or supply for government.

In addition to these meaningful potential vulnerabilities for effective, accountable and transparent government (Gogarty, 2016), the constitution also contains several repealed or blank sections and references to obsolete colonial-era legislation despite its silence on other crucially important matters. The *Consensus Statement on the Reform of the Tasmanian Constitution*, drafted by a panel of legal and constitutional experts in 2016, mirrors and expands upon these concerns, noting that the *Constitution Act 1934*:

- is a consolidation of imperial and colonial legislation and other instruments that has never been put to the Tasmanian people for consultation or consent
- does not contain any statement as to the social, legal, or constitutional values upon which Tasmanians declare their government rests
- provides no express power for the parliament to legislate for the people of Tasmania or the basis upon which it should make such laws
- contains a large number of blank, repealed, redundant or irrelevant provisions
- does not properly describe many of the organs of the state, their powers, or duties

- is not clear, readily accessible, transparent, or reflective of the actual conduct of government and the affairs of state
- is not legally a fundamental or superior law in any way, but one that can be modified in the normal way by any parliament
- is the least reviewed, reformed, or entrenched State Constitution in Australia (Gogarty et al., 2016).

These findings clearly demonstrate that clarification and protection of constitutional governance in Tasmania need to be addressed. Changing the constitutional order is too easy and relies too much on respect for Westminster conventions, which neither MPs nor the public understand. This was clearly demonstrated in 1998 when the viability of parliament as an institution was compromised for partisan advantage by reducing its size in order to limit the power of the Tasmanian Greens (Crowley, 1999). However, in some cases, this problematic situation has enabled a complementary and effective legislative role for the upper house. The recent process of developing and eventually legislating a Voluntary Assisted Dying bill is a good example of this role.

Aboriginal and Torres Strait Islander peoples

While real progress has been made in recent years, the legacies of historical abuse, racism, violence and dispossession of lands continue to cast a long shadow over relations between Indigenous and non-Indigenous Tasmanians. Aboriginal people continue to bear a considerable burden of disadvantage in many of the state's social and economic systems. However, recent efforts are slowly beginning to recognise their First Nations peoples status and to consider and address their systematic under-representation in Tasmania's democracy and government. Following a Committee report (Tasmania Parliament, 2015), in 2016, the *Tasmanian Constitution Act* was amended to include official recognition of Aboriginal Tasmanians and their constitutions in the state's founding document. Flawed as that document is (see earlier) this recognition is a welcome and long overdue update. The Constitution's preamble now includes the following text:

> And whereas the Parliament, on behalf of all the people of Tasmania, acknowledges the Aboriginal people as Tasmania's First People and the traditional and original owners of Tasmanian lands and waters; recognises the enduring spiritual, social, cultural and economic importance of traditional lands and waters to Tasmanian Aboriginal people; and recognises the unique and lasting contributions that Tasmanian Aboriginal people have made and continue to make to Tasmania ... (TDPC, 2023)

In addition, the lower house Select Committee on the *House of Assembly Restoration Bill 2020* (which recommended increasing the size of Parliament to its former size) found that the under-representation of Tasmanian Aboriginal people in parliament was an historical and contemporary failing that required remedy. The committee acknowledged that, while there had been members elected to the Tasmanian parliament who were Aboriginal, there was no formal Aboriginal representation there. The committee found this lack of formal representation for First Nations peoples negatively impacted on the communities' capacity to advocate for, and progress, reforms. It thus recommended the establishment of dedicated parliamentary representation for the Tasmanian Aboriginal community. However, it also noted there were a number of issues that needed to be resolved before legislation could be enacted to bring this about, including: ensuring that all Aboriginal Tasmanians are represented; how eligibility would be determined and by whom; whether dedicated seats should be in the House of Assembly or the LC; and how the election of Aboriginal members would work within the Tasmanian electoral framework. To achieve this outcome, the committee recommended that the matter should be further examined by a joint parliamentary inquiry.

Perhaps most importantly, at the opening of the new parliament on 22 June 2021, the government announced through new governor Barbara Baker that there would be a fresh attempt to reconcile with Tasmania's First People, the Palawa, including the possibility of a treaty. The government appointed outgoing governor and University of Tasmania law Professor Kate Warner and her UTAS colleague Professor Tim McCormack to consult with Aboriginal people on a pathway to reconciliation. A government commissioned report in 2021 also recommended the establishment of a Truth Telling Commission to pursue deliberative reconciliation with Aboriginal peoples (TDPC, 2021).

Conclusion

Tasmania's vigorous democracy, high participation rates in STV/Hare-Clark voting, and unique electoral processes have attracted some admirers from other states and internationally, reflecting some of the advantages of having a 'micro-state' population with the full status of a state. In part thanks to intergovernmental transfers, state government has generally been responsive to citizens' wishes. The competition of the top two parties, the presence of the Greens in the legislature and the LC's lack of a government majority have all helped ensure that scrutiny on most salient issues has been effective. Flaws remain, however, especially the over-reduction in the size of the state parliament's lower house (impairing its scrutiny capacities), plus the significant barriers that five-member seats pose for new parties' ability to get established in the House of Assembly. A final challenge confronting both Tasmanian and Australian democracy is how to best recognise and represent First Nations peoples as a key pillar of the broader and long overdue reconciliation process.

References

9News (2024) 'Tasmanian Labor concedes defeat in state election', 9News Australia, 24 March webpage. https://perma.cc/T9AB-GDS7

Australia Institute (2023) 'New political donations laws will help level the playing field and afford fairer elections to all Tasmanians', original article by Eloise Carr, 15 August, in *The Mercury*. https://perma.cc/LSG5-SNSD

Bennett, S (1999) 'The decline in support for the major parties and prospect for minority government', *Politics and Public Administration*, vol. February, 1999, pp.1–16. https://perma.cc/7RJ4-E2V5

Bogdanor, Vernon (ed) (1984) *Parties and Democracy in Britain and America*, New York: Praeger.

Brown, AJ; Ankamah, Samuel; Coghill, Ken; Graycar, Adam; Kelly, Kym; Prenzler, Tim; and Ransley, Janet (2019) 'Governing for integrity: a blueprint for reform', Transparency International Australia. https://perma.cc/V3PX-TL4V

Cody, Howard (2008) 'Minority government in Canada: The Stephen Harper experience', *American Review of Canadian Studies*, vol. 38, no. 1, pp.27–42. https://doi.org/10.1080/02722010809481819

Compton, Leon (2018) 'Right to Information backlog blows out, reviews taking over two years', *Australian Broadcasting Corporation*, webpage, 21 November. https://perma.cc/UY3Q-QVED

Constitution Watch (2022) 'Australian state Tasmania drops vax mandates', 9 March, website page. https://perma.cc/JS73-NZAK

Crowley, Kate (1999) 'A failed greening? The electoral routing of the Tasmanian Greens', *Environmental Politics*, vol. 8, no. 4, pp.186–93. $ https://doi.org/10.1080/09644019908414502

Eccleston, Richard and Jay, Zoe (2019) *Insight Ten: Campaign Finance Reform for Tasmania: Issues and Options*, Hobart: Institute for the Study of Social Change. https://perma.cc/MTD6-V24Z

Gogarty, Brendan (2016) 'State constitutional reform: The Tasmanian experience', *Australian Public Law*, blogpost 11 May. https://perma.cc/K36V-WQD5

Gogarty, Brendan; Williams, George; Tate, Michael; Sealy, Leigh; Clark, David; Henning, Terese; Hilkemeijer, Anja; Stokes, Michael; Herr, Richard; Patmore, Peter; Verney, Matthew; Bartl, Ben; and Gates, Simon (2016) 'Australian Association of Constitutional Law Working Group on Tasmanian Constitutional Reform: Consensus statement on the reform of the Tasmanian constitution', *The University of Tasmania Law Review*, vol. 35, no. 1. https://perma.cc/6LYY-YA2A

Green, Anthony (2022) 'Federal election preview: Tasmania', *ABC* Webpage, 31 January. https://perma.cc/C4L4-QVCN

Guardian (2021) 'Tasmania's vow to reform political donation laws shines spotlight on federal inaction', *Guardian, Australia*, website, 16 February. https://perma.cc/CZ6A-H2L6

Intermedium (2021) 'Digital government readiness indicator 2021', Intermedium. https://perma.cc/AJ47-SHZA

Lumb, Richard Darrell (1991) *The Constitutions of the Australian States*, St Lucia: University of Queensland Press, Original edition, 1977.

Minshull, Leanne (2020) 'Good government in Tasmania'. The Australia Institute. https://perma.cc/4FB6-AKRS

Moon, J (1995) 'Minority government in the Australian States: From ersatz majoritarianism to minoritariasm?', *Australian Journal of Political Science*, vol. 30, no. special issue, pp.142–63.

Museum of Australian Democracy (2021) 'Founding documents: Constitution Act 1855 (Tasmania)'. https://perma.cc/4DRT-G4YX

Patmore, P (2000) 'Structure and ideology in the Tasmanian Labor Party: Postmaterialism and party change', Phd thesis, University of Tasmania. https://doi.org/10.25959/23207342.v1

Powell, G B (2014) 'Minority governments, election rules and ideological congruence', *American Political Science Association (APSA) 2014 Annual Meeting Paper*, pp.1–35. SSRN Open access version https://perma.cc/E9DJ-V4XV

Strom, K (1990) *Minority Government and Majority Rule*, Studies in rationality and social change, Cambridge, UK; New York: Cambridge University Press.

Tasmanian Department of Health (2023) 'Covid 19 – Weekly statistics', Department website 17 March. https://perma.cc/6FH2-J8AM

Tasmanian Department of Justice (2021) 'Electoral Act Review, Final Report', Hobart: Tasmanian Government, February. https://perma.cc/8F3K-FGS9

Tasmanian Department of State Growth (2021) 'Department of State Growth: Our ministers', Tasmanian Government. https://perma.cc/8WCZ-HCSH

Tasmanian Electoral Commission (2023a) 'Voting systems in Tasmania – A summary', Agency webpage. https://perma.cc/26BD-YSRY

Tasmanian Electoral Commission (2023b) 'Election snapshots', Agency webpage. https://perma.cc/CD2X-N7B6

Tasmanian Legislation (2023) 'State Policies and Projects Act 1993', webpage, August. https://perma.cc/2MLT-TPYX

Tasmanian Parliament (2015) 'Inquiry into the constitutional recognition of Aboriginal people as Tasmania's First People', House of Assembly Standing Committee on Community Development, No. 35. https://perma.cc/KE5Q-TUEZ

TDPC (Tasmanian Department of Premier and Cabinet) (2021) *Pathway to Truth-Telling and Treaty*, Report to Premier Peter Gutwein, Tasmanian State Government. Report Prepared by Professor Kate Warner, Professor Tim McCormack and Ms Fauve Kurnadi, November. https://perma.cc/FKP2-WDWA

TDPC (Tasmanian Department of Premier and Cabinet) (2022) 'Expansion of Parliament Bill: Public submissions', Government webpage, October. https://perma.cc/MR6X-KPTK

TDPC (Tasmanian Department of Premier and Cabinet) (2023) 'Constitutional recognition of Tasmanian Aboriginal people', Agency webpage. https://perma.cc/JD9A-WAFR

TDTF (Tasmanian Department of Treasury and Finance) (2021) 'Occasional paper: New GST distribution arrangements'. Hobart: Tasmanian Government. https://perma.cc/8RGL-MWHT

Washington Post (2021) 'Death threats, mock hangings and a used condom: Anti-vaxxers target Australian politicians', *Washington Post*, website, 1 December. https://perma.cc/5UE6-TB3U

Watt, Ian (2020) 'Independent review of the Tasmanian State Service: Interim report', Tasmanian Government Department of Premier and Cabinet. https://perma.cc/G7LU-67TD

Watt, Ian (2021) 'Independent review of the Tasmanian State Service: Final report'. Tasmanian Government Department of Premier and Cabinet. https://perma.cc/HXS6-MESG

Whiteley, Cameron (2021) 'Petition launched for Tasmanian parliament's lower house to be increased to 35 members', *The Mercury*, 12 August, webpage. $ https://perma.cc/RT2W-96ZU

Wikipedia (2023a) 'The Covid-19 pandemic in Tasmania'. Online encyclopaedia webpage. https://perma.cc/4PWL-YUC9

Wikipedia (2023b) 'Tasmanian Legislative Council periodic election. Online encyclopaedia webpage. https://perma.cc/RJ79-U8T2

Wikipedia (2024a) '2024 Tasmanian state election'. Online encyclopaedia webpage. https://perma.cc/KKM8-EXET

Wikipedia (2024b) 'Category: Results of Tasmanian elections', Online encyclopaedia webpage. https://perma.cc/WLN4-JL3J

Young, John (2014) 'Should Upper Houses have Ministers?', *Australasian Parliamentary Review*, vol. 29, no. 1, pp.87–101. https://perma.cc/GR5W-SW9H

23

Northern Territory

Rolf Gerritsen

Occupying a sixth of Australia's landmass, stretching down in a huge rectangle from Darwin at the continent's northern tip across mainly desert terrain past Alice Springs and Uluru, the Northern Territory (NT) is nonetheless a politically small jurisdiction. With only around 1 per cent of the national population (about 244,000 people) it also includes the highest proportion of Aboriginal citizens (approximately 65,000) who make up 28 per cent of the NT's population. Two-thirds of these (in the 'bush' communities) live outside the major urban centres, in small remote settlements, often in poor conditions. With a large urban population in Darwin and surrounds, and often subject to emergencies like floods and drought, the public service delivery demands in the NT are complex and unique. The NT has a substantial public sector – currently around 24,000 full-time equivalent (FTE) employees, about a quarter of the total workforce.

Historically ruled first by a Commonwealth-appointed administrator, then later by an Executive Council, in 1978 the NT obtained self-government with its own directly elected Legislative Assembly (LA) and responsible government (Heatley, 1979) and has developed its own style of politics (Carment, 2007). By 1982 it assumed the last of its service delivery responsibilities from the Commonwealth (Smith, 2021). The NT budget is buoyed by federal transfers, but the territory has a small and narrowly based economy – essentially resource extraction, government and tourism, with some cattle and fisheries. Government assistance to industry has tended to favour tourism and resource extraction. 'Boom and bust' cycles can occur, as recently happened while the gigantic Ichthys LNG (liquid natural gas) project was constructed. The COVID-19 pandemic also substantially affected the economy through adverse impacts on the important tourism industry.

What does democracy require of the Northern Territory's political system?

- An effective constitution that provides an anatomy of legitimate public power to: define the limits of territory governmental powers; make government accountable to the people by providing for checks and balances; and promote long-term structures.

How to cite this chapter:

Gerritson, Rolf (2024) 'Northern Territory', in: Evans, Mark; Dunleavy, Patrick and Phillimore, John (eds) *Australia's Evolving Democracy: A New Democratic Audit,* London: LSE Press, pp.497–513. https://doi.org/10.31389/lsepress.ada.w. Licence: CC-BY-NC 4.0

- Aboriginal and Torres Strait Islander peoples should be afforded full individual civil and human rights. The histories, languages, cultures, rights, and needs of Aboriginal and Torres Strait Islander communities and peoples should be addressed.
- The electoral system for the single house, the LA, should accurately translate parties' votes into seats in ways that are recognised as legitimate by most citizens. Ideally, the voting system should foster the overall social representativeness of the legislature. Elections and the regulation of political parties should be impartially conducted, with integrity.
- The political parties should sustain vigorous and effective electoral competition and citizen participation. They should enable the recruitment, selection and development of political leaders for territory government; formulate viable policy agendas and frame political choices for NT functions; and form governments or, when not in power, hold governments accountable. Political parties should uphold the highest standards of conduct in public life.
- The LA should normally maintain full public control of government services and territory operations, ensuring public and parliamentary accountability through conditionally supporting the government, and articulating reasoned opposition, via its proceedings. It should be a critically important focus of NT's political debate, operating to include a plurality of viewpoints and subject a government to effective checks on its power.
- The NT government should govern responsively, prioritising the public interest and reflecting territory public opinion. Its core executive (the chief minister, ministers and key central departments) should provide clear unification of public policies across government, so that the territory government operates as an effective whole. Both strategic decision-making within the core executive, and more routine policy-making, should foster careful deliberation to establish an inclusive view of the 'public interest'.
- The core executive and government should operate fully within the law, and the chief minister and other ministers should be effectively scrutinised by and politically accountable to parliament. Ministers and departments/agencies must also be legally accountable to independent courts for their conduct and policy decisions. In the wider NT public service officials should act with integrity, in accordance with well-enforced codes of conduct, and within the rule of law.
- The administration of public services should be controlled by democratically elected officials so far as possible. The rights of all citizens should be carefully protected in policy-making, and 'due process' rules followed, with fair and equal public consultation on public service changes. By uniting what are normally state and local government functions, NT governance should be holistic. Public services, contracting, regulation and planning/zoning decisions should be completely free from corruption.
- At the Commonwealth level the NT government should effectively and transparently represent its citizens' interests to federal government.

The chapter begins by covering some recent developments in the NT's electoral and party politics and looking at its COVID-19 experience. A SWOT analysis (covering strengths, weaknesses, opportunities and threats) then considers the main aspects of governance that bear on the quality of democracy within the NT. After the SWOT, three enduring aspects of NT governance are considered in greater depth – strong government, relations with the federal government, and lastly some chronic defects in NT's democratic operations.

Recent developments

Subnational governance in Australia is shaped mainly by political and government practices in states. But in territories there is also vigorous party competition at elections (covered first here) and substantial policy responsibilities for governments, as the COVID-19 episode demonstrated.

Elections and party politics

The LA is a unicameral (one chamber) legislature elected every four years in single seat districts allocated in a population-proportional way (with around 5,000 voters in each area). Voting uses the Alternative Vote (AV) system with full preference numbering across all candidates. If no one wins outright majority support, the votes for the least popular candidates are redistributed in accordance with second or third preferences, with a two-party preferred vote (TPP) at the final counting stage. As elsewhere, this system favours the top two parties, Labor and the Country

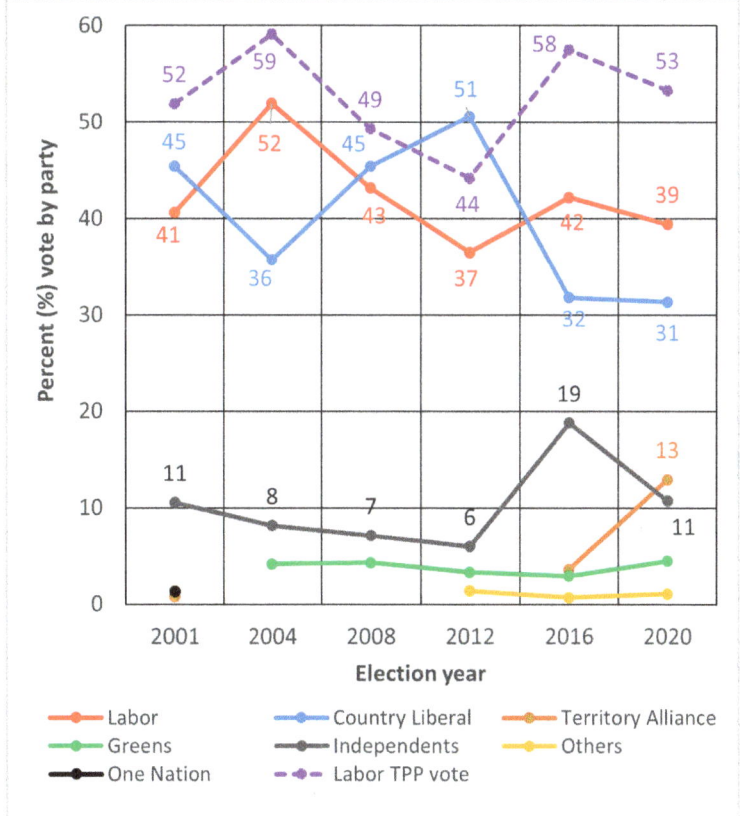

Figure 23.1: Primary votes shares (%) won by parties in the Northern Territory Legislative Assembly, and the Labor TPP vote, 2001–2020

Source: Compiled from data in Northern Territory Electoral Commission (2023) 'Past Legislative Assembly elections', (NTEC, 2023).

Note: TPP = two-party preferred vote, at the final stage of the AV system's vote-counting.

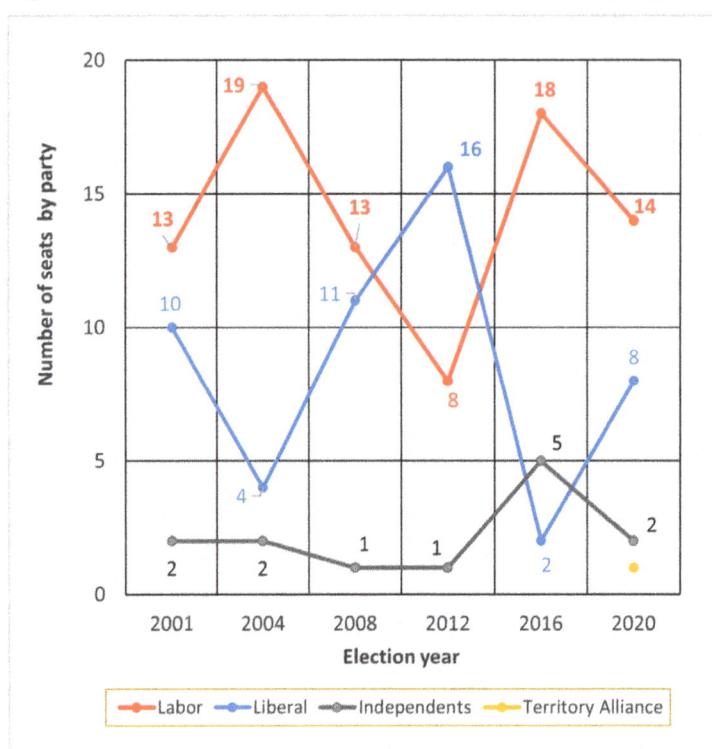

Figure 23.2: Seats won by parties in the Northern Territory Legislative Assembly, 2001–2020

Source: Compiled from data in Northern Territory Electoral Commission, (2023) 'Past Legislative Assembly elections', (NTEC, 2023).

Note: The Legislative Assembly has 25 members, so a party with 13 or more seats has a majority.

Liberal Party (CLP) (as they are termed in the NT – see Smith (2011 and 2021)). Electoral contests are relatively stable, featuring vigorous contests for votes dominated by these two parties through this century (Figure 23.1) After each election, one of the two formed a government in their own right, with no coalitions (Figure 23.2).

How democratically have elections operated? Normally, the AV election has allocated most seats to the same party that wins the TPP vote, but in 2008 Labor won a narrow majority of one seat despite being slightly below the CLP in the TPP at the last stage of the AV counting process (see Chapter 5). Far more serious, however, is the capacity of the system to exaggerate the largest party's seats total (and under-represent the opposition) where one party wins the TPP contest decisively. For instance, after the 2016 election, the CLP was reduced to just two members in the LA, despite having won over one-third of the primary (first-preference) votes. Independents have been a feature in the LA since strong local reputations can attract enough voters to win. The current LA has two independents, one an Aboriginal Member of the Legislative Assembly (MLA) for Mulka in north-eastern Arnhem Land. The persistence of independents is long-term. Most parliaments since self-government have had at least one independent (most often a CLP defector).

The AV system has prevented third or fourth parties with more evenly spread support winning any seats. The Greens have recently achieved a consistent but non-growing third-party status, while a series of micro-parties have risen and fallen, often within one electoral cycle. In the 1980s, there was a National Party attempt (led by former CLP Chief Minister, Tuxworth) to penetrate the Labor-CLP duopoly – but it failed to make an impact. However, Sanders (2020, p.596) argues that the relative success of independents in winning seats:

> has reflected a continuing strong two-party system, not a weakening one. Six

> of ten successful independents in NTLA elections have been 'splitters' from the Country Liberal Party in times of intra-party turmoil. Their subsequent electoral success as independents in divisions previously very safe for the CLP leads to the hypothesis ... that independents succeed in electoral divisions where one major party attracted twice the votes of the other or more.

Other political scientists agree on such effects under first past the post (FPTP) voting (as in the USA, UK and India) if one party has more than 68 per cent support – here, even when the top group A splits evenly in two, the top faction A1 would still defeat the opposition group B (Dickson and Sheve, 2007). In Australia's AV system this kind of split is feasible at much lower levels of support (for example, 58 or 60 per cent), since the largest faction of the dominant grouping A1 can expect to pick up most second preferences from the smaller faction A2 after any split. Partly because of such 'safety valves' for two-party dominance, the current system seems to have had the support of the voting public. Only isolated voices have called for creating multi-member electorates or for introducing proportional voting.

The NT selection system ensures that the biggest population centre, the greater Darwin-Palmerston area, provides 15 of the 25 members of the LA. Trends in public opinion there have usually decided the election. In only one election since 1978 has the party with the most Darwin area seats failed to form/retain government. That was in 2012, when the 'bush' (Aboriginal) seats temporarily swung to the CLP. This urban preponderance (when we include the two seats in Alice Springs and the seat in Katherine) has some potentially undemocratic implications (explored shortly).

Concerns have also been raised that the small scale of single member seats contributes to the 'capture' of MLAs by civil society interests in their area. In the 1980s, the CLP government began subsidising sports and ethnic groups. This led to a plethora of ethnic community halls that has remained a feature of Darwin. At that stage, there was little difference between policies in the NT and the other states (except, perhaps, for the funding of community halls). In addition, some social welfare advocacy groups received establishment grants, basically so they could more effectively compete for Commonwealth program grants.

In the 21st century, this system expanded to include a wide range of pressure groups. It began with the Martin Labor Government providing an administrative grant to the Amateur Fishermen's Association. Administration grants to civil society groups are now common. Consequently, subsequent NT governments have spent over A$80 million on constructing boat ramps for amateur weekend fishermen in the last decade, as well as instituting the closure of several river estuaries to professional fishermen – two examples of 'Darwin-centric' policies.

Most NT citizens seem to have decided that this kind of 'civic capture' has not been a serious rein on NT democracy. Like the Vicar of Bray, the leaders/managers of all the beneficiary associations cheerfully refrain from criticising whatever government is in power, and so the chief consequence of the phenomenon may be widespread cynicism and some impoverishment of public debate. However, some adverse democratic implications of this system were exposed in 2020, when a vice president of the Chamber of Commerce was obliged to resign because of his hostile attitude to the Gunner Labor government. It was revealed that the Chamber also received an administration grant from the government.

Policies in the COVID-19 pandemic

The NTs relative isolation makes it difficult to reach except by air or sea, and this proved to be an advantage during the COVID-19 pandemic. Tourism was badly hit in 2020–2022 by visitor restrictions but other industries were not. Cases reached nearly 106,000 by April 2023, but with only 91 deaths (NT Health Department, 2023). The Labor government was re-elected in 2020 partly on its early record of handling the pandemic onset. Subsequently, vaccination campaigns proved successful, reaching 95 per cent for the first two doses, and 76 per cent for three. Rates in remote communities were significantly lower but still reached above 80 per cent. The NT was relatively quick to reopen to tourists and visitors in 2022.

Strengths, weaknesses, opportunities and threats (SWOT) analysis

Current strengths	Current weaknesses
The LA is elected by the AV system in single member seats, with voters having to number all candidates in preference order. At most elections, the largest number of seats went to whichever of the top two parties won the TPP vote.	The AV system has tended to accentuate (rather than mitigate) the seats advantage of the largest party – on occasion making an effective opposition difficult and sometimes almost impossible (for example, in 2016–2020).
In any liberal democracy, effective government requires the aggregation of and choice between interests and policies. Therefore, strong governing party cohesion in the Labor Party and the CLP has generally been accepted by NT public opinion as a necessary democratic price to pay for effective government.	As in other Australian jurisdictions, the operations of the LA have been limited by the robust use of their majorities by governments to secure their policy and political agendas. Outright majority control is the norm in NT politics, with only a few independents supplementing the top two parties' MLAs (see Figure 23.2). Therefore, modern, disciplined party systems have sometimes circumscribed parliamentary debate.
NT politicians are closely responsive to constituents' needs, thanks to the small size of electorates (around 5,000 voters each). Close contacts between MLAs and their constituents have accentuated MLA's incentives to deliver on seat-specific gains in their area.	The attractions of 'local pork' benefits have created many grants or infrastructure given to sporting clubs. Conventional party politics exhibits an 'urban bias', partly because of the major electoral predominance of Darwin and a few other towns in deciding election outcomes, given the broadly population-proportional distribution of MLA seats. Higher turnouts by urban citizens and party organisations and media coverage focused in the same areas accentuate this effect.

Aboriginal people have won some representation in the LA under the single member contests with AV. The NT government has made some steps to better integrate its many Aboriginal citizens within policy-making.	Aboriginal involvement in conventional politics has historically been low, with much diminished turnout at elections and little presence in party organisations, as candidates or as elected MLAs.
	Conditions in some bush communities are poor and chronic problems with high unemployment, alcohol abuse, male violence and high incarceration rates for Aboriginal men have not ameliorated, despite extensive federal government involvement.
Most party campaigning has been 'responsible' in its handling of ethnic tensions between Aboriginal people and others, with the major parties competing to offer viable alternative visions of NT governance priorities.	Some electioneering around youth and crime issues and about how Aboriginal communities have been run has exacerbated ethnic tensions at times.
The NT public service is competently run and has not faced significant corruption problems.	Attracting talent to the NT public service has been difficult, and its operations are mostly located in major urban areas. Some administrative processes may cause unspent funding intended for bush areas to be 'clawed back' and spent in more populated places.
	The centralisation of functions within NT public services has eroded the capability of local governments (especially 'bush' local governments) to carry out significant functions.
Future opportunities	**Future threats**
Had the 2023 Voice referendum not failed, the renewed national impetus towards recognition of an enhanced voice for Aboriginal peoples under the Albanese Labor government at federal level might have helped renew the impetus for change in NT, which has far and away the largest proportion of Aboriginal citizens.	Partisan divisions on ways to progress Aboriginal people's involvement nationally may acquire adverse extra salience in the NT context, increasing social tensions.
Even an upper house in the NT would be unlikely to change the fact of strong governing party control of the legislature or to foster more genuine processes of legislative review – unless its electoral system was likely to produce minor parties or independents holding the balance of power in the upper house.	

The chapter now examines executive-legislature relations in the NT in more detail, then its relations with the federal government, and lastly four main defects in the democratic quality of the NT's governance arrangements.

The executive, Legislative Assembly and policy-making

A key requirement of an effective democracy is a responsive and responsible executive arm with an effective bureaucracy, and machinery for converting political inputs from voters and interest groups into effective policy. As elsewhere in Australia, policy is made by ministers deciding in cabinet and affirmed or legislated for in the LA. Parliamentary debate has been vigorous and well-reported in the still reasonably strong NT media. Therefore – if they wish to be – citizens can be well-informed about both state and local issues.

The NT's legislature is as effective as any other in Australia, although it is dominated by the executive, which maintains formal control over government services and operations. The LA began its life with the expectation that its practices and procedures would be 'Westminster system' in tone, in effect operating in the same way as the older Australian subnational legislatures. The CLP easily won the first self-government election in 1978, and its MLAs appointed the chief minister and supported their government so that a majoritarian parliamentary orderliness became the norm. The new legislature also copied other states' practices by establishing a standard array of legislative committees – for example, a Standing Orders Committee and a Legal and Constitutional Committee. Opposition MLAs complained of what they saw as scandals – such as the misuse by government members and senior civil servants of official credit cards, and ministers' executive actions being overturned in the courts. But these complaints were defended as unexceptional by the government majority in the LA. Over time, some additions were made to the oversight by the legislature, including a procedure requiring MLAs to register interests, again following other states' initiatives. The NT has not had any register of lobbyists, making it the only Australian jurisdiction without one. In 1992, the Perron Government was grappling with a growing budget deficit and introduced an Estimates Committee, though this eventually languished.

Oppositions in the LA have usually decried the government's lack of transparency and accountability and sometimes when they come to occupy the Treasury benches the new ministers may introduce corrective measures. Two periods of consequential institutional reform of this kind occurred in recent years. The Martin-led Australian Labor Party (ALP) government was elected in 2001 (after they spent 23 years in opposition). The new majority quickly introduced an Expenditure Review Committee and passed both a *Freedom of Information Act* and a *Fiscal Integrity and Transparency Act* – which required the publication of the up-to-date financial state of the NT government 10 days before any LA election. The Martin Government also pioneered the idea of 'Community Cabinets', where cabinet meetings were held in remote communities in an attempt to engage local (mostly Aboriginal) communities. Subsequently, this mechanism atrophied.

A second initially reforming Labor government under Michael Gunner was elected in a landslide (with an artificially boosted majority) in 2016, following the spectacularly colourful period of the Giles CLP government (Smee and Walsh, 2016). Strong Labor party discipline was maintained during parliament and Labor expelled three of its MLAs from the party caucus for criticising government policy. However, following other jurisdictions, ministers did create an Independent Commission Against Corruption (ICAC). In practice, this body proved to be under-resourced, and it was criticised after revelations about illegal recording of conversations. In recent years, the government's enthusiasm for the ICAC waned as the body made damaging findings against Labor ministers. The ICAC process is currently in disarray, as whistle-blowers are reluctant to come forward.

At the 2020 election, Labor was returned to office after a successful plebiscitary style campaign, based on Chief Minister Gunner's competent management of the NT's borders during the early stages of the COVID-19 pandemic. Subsequently, the government become more majoritarian in its dealings with the LA. In its first term, it allowed an independent speaker, but she was replaced by a Labor MLA after the election. In 2021, the government majority abolished the Legislative Scrutiny Committee, which gave the opposition MLAs access to impending legislation. The sitting time for the Expenditure Review Committee was also reduced. The government also used its numbers in the LA to protect one of its MLAs (the member for Blain) from facing possible adverse findings by the Privileges Committee.

Policy-making in the NT has often been criticised for alleged favouritism in the way that it awards beneficial goods like public service appointments or contracts, and some people equate favouritism with 'corruption'. However, there have not in fact been any scandals akin to (say) Queensland in the 1980s, or to a jurisdiction like NSW, where former ministers have been jailed. In the first two decades of self-government, the courts occasionally came into conflict with the government as some ministers overstepped their legislative powers (Heatley, 1990; Smith, 2011). Particularly in the 1980s, some ministers were 'colourful' characters and were forced to introduce supplementary legislation when the courts overturned their regulations. But this phenomenon has decreased.

Given the NT's small scale, some perceptions of favouritism may be almost inevitable, since a minister or public servant allocating a contract possibly knows all the local applicants from their electoral district of just 5,000 voters. Another insight into the inevitable limits of scale is suggested by the fact that recently two government departments had CEOs who are siblings. And when the CLP opposition accused the chief minister of using parliamentary entitlements to fund some travel during the 2020 election campaign, in breach of conventions covering the 'caretaker' pre-election period, the officer who signed off the chief minister's travel turned out to be his brother-in-law.

In terms of its legal system and courts the NT has a similar but smaller system of courts as the other states, including a Supreme Court and lesser courts equivalent to the magistrates' courts in the states. Appointments to these courts are formally made by the NT's administrator (the title for its Crown representative) upon the recommendation of the first law officer, the Attorney-General. In the late 1990s, some (most?) jurists were unhappy about the 'mandatory sentencing' policy of the NT's CLP government, which limited judicial discretion in sentencing. This policy was abolished by the incoming Labor government in 2001. More recently, there has been no observable tension between the courts and the ministry. Legislators sometimes complain about lenient sentencing by the courts in criminal matters, but no more so than in Australia's other jurisdictions. Arguably, the judicial system is the most efficient of the three elements of the NT state structure.

Local government

Given its huge area and the wide dispersion of the population in smaller communities the NT has a system of local governments that depend on NT legislation for how they are set up. For over 20 years after self-government some of these 'bush' local governments were incorporated under Commonwealth legislation, although they were treated administratively and financially as part of NT's local government system. A complete NT takeover of legislative responsibility was formalised in 2007 after the NT government unilaterally amalgamated 65 bush local governments into seven large regional bodies, initially Shires and now called Regional Councils. Unlike other states, the NT government retains control of local planning and purpose zoning powers for areas, but in other respects NT's local government system is broadly similar to local governments in other states. The Minister or the Department of Local Government sometimes imposes duties and restrictions on these local democracies, which some critics claim are arbitrary or deny local democracy.

Interactions with the Commonwealth

In constitutional terms the NT's self-government is a creature of the *Commonwealth Act 1977* that established it. Some implications of this dependence on the Commonwealth have adversely affected the democratic workings of the NT polity. NT ministers have operated a system circumscribed by Commonwealth authority, formal and informal or implied, which limits how far NT voters can control their representatives.

Because of various political controversies, NT's policy sovereignty was circumscribed in some respects in that legislation. The Commonwealth retained its pre-self-government control over national parks, uranium mining and Aboriginal land rights. Canberra ministers' control over the Kakadu and Uluru national parks irked subsequent NT governments, who saw this as an infringement of the NT government's authority. The Fraser federal government also controlled uranium mining in the NT up to 1983, presumably because it was politically contentious.

The Commonwealth also refused to repatriate its *Aboriginal Land Rights Act (1976)* to the NT Assembly's control. Under that legislation, 50 per cent of the NT's land area and 70 per cent of its coastal waters still implicitly come under this national Act. This has been an important diminution of the powers over land (and development) of the NT government. In the first two decades of self-government, CLP governments frequently challenged or opposed Aboriginal land claims made under that Act (Smith, 2011). Opposition to the Act also pervaded the successful electoral strategies of the CLP for this period.

Some other retentions of powers have been altered or made less impactful. The federal government initially retained industrial relations in NT as its responsibility, in order to allow former Commonwealth public servants to maintain their superannuation (CSS) rights after they joined the NT Public Service. In 1988, the Commonwealth unilaterally handed these financial obligations over to the NT, as part of Hawke government decisions to 'normalise' its fiscal relations with the NT. In addition, in 1978 the Commonwealth left intact its tax regime for the Jabiru uranium mine and the Gove alumina operation under their pre-existing arrangements. This latter measure had little practical effect since the Commonwealth simply transferred these revenues to the NT government.

The situation remains, however, that the *Northern Territory (Self Government) Act (1978)* is a Commonwealth instrument, which the federal parliament can amend when it chooses. In 1996, the Commonwealth amended the Act to override voluntary euthanasia legislation that the Northern Territory Assembly had enacted. The Commonwealth shows no inclination to reverse that decision even now, despite the fact that the majority of states have enacted similar legislation. In 2007, during the NT Emergency Response (the 'Intervention' as it is known), the Howard government overrode or suspended NT legislation passed by Labor that blocked its purpose. The NT government was not even told of the 'Intervention' before it occurred. For four years, 2008–2012, in response to allegations of the widespread sexual abuse of Aboriginal children and violence inflicted against Aboriginal women, special measures were applied by the federal Parliament to Aboriginal communities in NT. These included bans or constraints on access to alcohol or pornography, alterations in how education and health services were operated and changes in how welfare payments were made (Wikipedia, 2023). The measures were eased by later federal legislation, but not completely removed.

Financially also, Northern Territory governments are beholden to the Commonwealth. The large majority (four-fifths) of NT governmental revenues derives from Canberra. This has included a general-purpose grant derived from the disbursement of the Commonwealth's Goods and Services tax (GST) revenue, covering around 60 per cent of NT revenues. A further 20–25 per cent of NT revenues have come as specific-purpose grants from the Commonwealth. In addition, the NT government has faced some large budget deficits, which ultimately seem likely to involve or require Commonwealth solutions. Thus, the Northern Territory's fiscal dependence on federal government is comprehensive. The relationship between the NT and Commonwealth governments resembles that of mendicant and master. Yet, because the NT has normally been so insignificant in Canberra politics, it has mostly evaded close Commonwealth attention.

Four key defects of NT governance and democracy

Territory governments of both persuasions govern responsively, as well as attempting to prioritise the public interest and reflect public opinion. However, there are four serious defects in the democratic arrangements for the NT. First, responsiveness and the incorporation of public opinion and interests is largely focused upon Darwin and to a lesser extent the other urban centres. State policies have thus been configured chiefly to the advantage of urban NT residents. Second, some monies intended for bush communities have instead landed back in urban areas. Third, some Aboriginal communities remain under different legal and rights regimes than those applying to other NT citizens, and progress towards 'normalisation' has been slow. Fourth, the electoral system and party competition have not successfully involved or incorporated Aboriginal interests at the same level as other citizens. Any definition of democratic government should include governments taking an inclusive view of the 'public interest', providing equitable access to rights and public services, and taking measures to involve those citizens most reticent about democratic engagement. Critics argue that, manifestly, the NT polity has performed poorly on these counts (Gerritsen, 2010a).

The urban 'bias' of public policies

NT elections are almost always decided in Darwin and its surrounds, so it is perhaps to be expected that the incorporation of public opinion and interests by ministers and MLAs is also focused upon Darwin and to a lesser extent the other urban centres, while remote Aboriginal communities are neglected. Because of the area's scale and character, urban bias has become the central organising principle of the NT.

Budgets and fiscal management strategies are adapted to ensure that the lion's share of expenditure goes to Darwin. Critics argue that there has been over-expenditure on services demanded by urban citizens – like wave pools and NT-subsidised sporting events (such as the V8 Super Cars and AFL matches) to say nothing of the ubiquitous boat ramps for weekend amateur fishers. These components have been embedded in NT government outlays and strategic spending priorities reflect an implicit assumption that 'economic development' primarily occurs in Darwin. For example, the NT spends only around 2 per cent of its budget on roads, as against 5 per cent in South Australia, a jurisdiction of about the same area and with a similar geography. Urban bias is also indicated by other areas of public services, such as culture and recreation services, on which the NT spends much more than the Commonwealth Grants Commission's needs assessment indicates.

Critics also argue that in this century the NT public service (NTPS) has burgeoned from 14,000 FTE staff to 24,000 FTE staff, most of whom are based in Darwin or other towns. The NT public service is larger than that in the Australian Capital Territory (ACT), a jurisdiction with almost twice the population. According to the Grants Commission's estimates, the NTPS is 50 per cent bigger than required for the NT's unique circumstances. Critics allege that it has become overloaded with managers and administrators, while service delivery officer numbers have stagnated. As the numerical significance of government employees has grown in the influential greater Darwin electorates, it seems probable that these voters are unlikely to support cutbacks (potentially perhaps their own loss of a job).

As a consequence, the NT's net debt has been projected to reach at least A$30 billion by 2030, or about six times the level of NT government's own current annual revenues. Controlling the growth of NT debt, is difficult for several reasons. Many incomer residents within NT later retire 'down south' to other parts of Australia. Since they will not be around when the debt crisis peaks, there has been no political constituency willing to make serious sacrifices to reduce the NT's long-term indebtedness. Any party that proposed cutbacks as necessary to reduce the fiscal imbalance could risk losing the subsequent election.

Fiscal laxness may have other potential democratic implications if a future Commonwealth government eventually comes to believe that it must take action to curb the growth of NT's debt. One option might be for federal ministers to take back administration of the NT finances for some period, or for Canberra to assume the direct responsibility for providing services to the Aboriginal communities. Both options would significantly reduce the power of NT citizens to control their own affairs – although neither is foreseeable at the time of writing under the Albanese Labor government.

The diversion of resources from Aboriginal communities

This brings us to the NT's unique position with regard to its Aboriginal citizens. Over and above the strong urban priorities outlined above, critics argue that part of the urban benefits distributed by NT governments have apparently been financed by the *de facto* appropriation of money 'earned' by Aboriginal communities' disadvantagement. This can be shown in how the NT government deals with its general-purpose revenue grant from the Commonwealth GST collections. The Commonwealth Grants Commission allocates the GST revenue between the states and territories on the basis of relative disadvantage (although this element has declined with the recent Commonwealth changes to the GST distribution formula). Because the NT's non-urban Aborigines are among the most disadvantaged communities in Australia, the NT's share of the disbursement is inflated to meet these challenges to service delivery. The NT normally gets about four times more per capita than does the average state. Yet, about one-third of this additional money has been spent on purposes other than remediating Aboriginal disadvantage (Gerritsen, 2010b). Effectively, the NT's underprivileged Aboriginal population has cross-subsidised services to the relatively privileged people of Darwin (and to a lesser extent the other larger urban centres).

In addition, fiscal management strategies have systematically distributed budgeted regional expenditure back to the centre. Budgeted expenditure for Aboriginal services has instead been 'clawed back' to pay for an excessively large bureaucracy in Darwin. A good example concerns the Indigenous housing budget. From 2019 both the NT government and the Commonwealth each committed A$110 million annually to Aboriginal housing in the territory (DLGHCD, 2019). However, by 2023, NT ministers and officials had not spent more than A$68 million of its A$110 million budget allocation, so that in effect unspent funding of over A$30 million was returned to consolidated revenue. Meanwhile the Aboriginal housing crisis has continued, and COVID-19 rates in Aboriginal communities were exacerbated because of overcrowding. Administrative charges by the administrative centre on specific purpose programs, both those that NT-funded and NT-delivered on behalf of the Commonwealth, are also routinely between 30 and 40 per cent of the budgeted outlays, much of which is not spent in the communities affected and so 'leaks' elsewhere. This fiscal-cum-political nexus has ensured that the Aboriginal people living in non-urban areas have not achieved their fair or intended share of overall fiscal resources.

The disadvantagement of Aboriginal communities

For the NT to be a full democracy, its Aboriginal peoples should be afforded full individual civil and human rights. This is formally the case. However, as elsewhere in the world, research has shown that Indigenous peoples suffered serious social and cultural dislocations during the 'colonisation' period (Grant, 2022). These deep-lasting harms have contributed to many different contemporary disadvantages of Aboriginal communities that may at seem only distantly connected – including differentially high rates of male criminal offending, high incarceration rates especially for young men, and community distancing from law and order and court institutions (where adverse stereotypes by police, courts and juries long contributed to differential treatment). Blighted chances of gaining employment and lack of job opportunities in bush communities have in turn contributed to long-running problems with alcohol and drugs abuse, and unusually high patterns of violence against women and children. Routing funding through aboriginal community networks ran into problems by the 2000s with opaque financial flows and allegations of elders diverting public monies to unintended uses.

The 2008–2012 'Intervention' strategies of implementing intense restrictions on bush communities' access to alcohol, drugs, pornography and other products, restrictions that have never been applied elsewhere in Australia, were justified in the name of protecting the rights of women, young people and children from male abuse. Some substantial long-term improvements in protecting the most vulnerable groups have been achieved. But increasingly federalised efforts (managed from within the Department of Prime Ministers and Cabinet (DP &C) in Canberra) have also encountered substantial difficulties in achieving progress within bush communities towards more normal forms of social control and social life, better housing conditions, or access to meaningful employment. The 'urban bias' of the NT's political economy and the apparent diversion of some resources to meeting the demands of more politically influential NT citizens are both especially serious in this context.

The electoral deficit in representing Indigenous people's interests

The electoral disengagement of Aboriginal people has also made the four problems addressed worse. Without necessarily meaning to do so, the electoral system has tended to disaffiliate and disengage Aboriginal interests. That was not initially the case at self-government, but it has become an increasing problem with the passage of time. The Northern Territory Electoral Commission (NTEC) (2023) was established in 2004 to provide a fair, impartial and professional electoral service. It conducts elections for the LA, local government and other organisations upon request. In practice, the NTEC has always been dependent upon Commonwealth support, especially for voter enrolment, which has always been carried out by the Australian Electoral Commission (AEC). This has meant that the NTEC is susceptible to both NT government funding shortfalls and an ongoing decline in Commonwealth electoral effort in the NT. The NTEC is too poorly resourced and staffed to effectively carry out its functions of electorally including the non-metropolitan Aboriginal population.

The actual conduct of elections in the NT is free, impartial and professional. Voting and counting are conducted ethically, relatively efficiently and in accord with the letter of the law. Yet a large proportion of the electorate has been excluded, or has excluded itself, from the electoral process. Aboriginal people have represented the majority of these people, and given their salience within the NT population numbers, it is unsurprising that electoral enrolment and voting participation rates in the NT are the lowest in the nation.

This deficit in participation is made worse by the fact that the demography of the NT has contributed to relative under-enrolment anyway, because of great population 'churn'. Each year many people, mostly young, come to the NT for seasonal employment and they have rarely enrolled. Other inhabitants view their stays in the NT as being just for a few years and also do not bother to enrol or change their previous enrolment elsewhere. Lower enrolment has also gone along with more non-voting, across all types of voters. These factors help explain why the turnout in Darwin's NT elections has usually been about 80 per cent of the enrolled voters (see Figure 23.3), fully 10 percentage points lower than the national average.

In the early years of self-government, there was a serious effort to maximise the Aboriginal vote and federal AEC enrolment teams visited bush communities to recruit voters. On election days, both federal and NT, static polling booths were established in the larger communities and mobile polling teams visited smaller communities. Yet this initial effort substantially eroded over time, initially because of CLP hostility to the fact that Aborigines overwhelmingly voted Labor. The process started during the 1983 election, when the Education Department banned bush community teachers (supposedly overwhelmingly Labor supporters) from manning static polling booths. In more recent elections, mobile polling teams have visited large communities for only a few hours on election day, and voter turnout can be inhibited by unanticipated clashes with funerals or ceremonial 'business'.

Worse effects came from the NT's dependence upon Commonwealth electoral authorities for voter enrolment. The Liberal-National federal government in power until 2022 used the postal service and cross-tabulations of changes in or establishment of residence for the enrolment of new voters. For example, if a voter changes their Medicare or driver's licence address, they will be contacted by post by the AEC about changing their place of enrolment. Yet young Aboriginal men (in particular) have tended not to have a Medicare card or a residential address, or even an inclination to register to vote. So, for this and other reasons relying upon the postal system has been an entirely inappropriate mechanism for Aboriginal voters. The ineluctable consequence

Figure 23.3: Voter turnout in Northern Territory elections by region, 2012–2020

Region	2012 Votes	2012 Turnout %	2016 Votes	2016 Turnout %	2020 Votes	2020 Turnout %
Darwin	58,080	84	64,380	79	68,340	81
Remote	21,960	62	21,990	59	24,400	62
Alice Springs	10,970	78	9,800	83	9,050	78
Katherine	4,210	81	4,140	78	4,040	70
Total outside Darwin	37,130	68	35,920	66	37,490	66
Total NT	**123,904**	**77**	**100,300**	**74**	**105,830**	**75**

Source: Compiled from data in NTEC, 2023, 'Past Legislative Assembly elections' (NTEC, 2023).
Note: Vote numbers are rounded to the nearest 10 for easier reading.

has been that a large number – official estimates suppose about 27,000, or about one-third – of Aboriginal people are disenfranchised. In effect, the current enrolment system verges on undemocratic Aboriginal voter suppression. Its adverse effects are clearly shown by record low voter turnouts in elections for Australia (Figure 23.3), with all urban areas achieving four-fifths turnout thanks to compulsory voting, but levels in remote communities fully 20 percentage points lower, and running at two-thirds of the rate in all other Australian jurisdictions.

In the 2012 NT election, the bush Aboriginal vote surprisingly turned against Labor, delivering government to the CLP. This shift was driven by Aboriginal hostility to the 2007 'Intervention' (implemented by Canberra but with Labor in power in Darwin), as well as the earlier forcible amalgamation of Aboriginal local governments (an NT Labor policy). The subsequent CLP government was characterised by exceptional leadership infighting and turbulence, with 13 different reshuffles of the ministry, the loss of the initial leader (Mills) and challenges to his successor (Giles) (Smee and Walsh, 2016). At the 2016 federal election Aboriginal voters reversed their dalliance with CLP and returned to backing Labor. Interestingly, federal elections for the seat of Lingiari (which covers most of the NT) showed higher proportions of Aboriginal voter turnout. This was partly because of an active MP there, but also revealed Aboriginal people's support of the Commonwealth's *Land Rights Act 1976*. By contrast, remote Aboriginal communities have little attachment to the NT government.

Conclusion

In essence, the governance of the NT is institutionally an isomorphic mirror of the Westminster traditions of political jurisdictions across Australia. Its judiciary, executive arm, legislature and public service operate in a familiar manner. Having a single-house legislature elected using AV voting has contributed to major party dominance and some severely disproportional election outcomes that have crippled opposition scrutiny. Micro-politics in local districts has also contributed to a trend for both Labor and CLP ministries to 'capture' civil society in ways that effectively mute criticism of the incumbent government. These patterns have also contributed to four other distortions or problems for NT democracy – an 'urban bias' towards Darwin and other city voters' concerns, some divergence of funding from Aboriginal communities, long-standing patterns of Aboriginal communities' disadvantagement, and low levels of participation in state elections by Aboriginal voters. Beyond Darwin and the main urban centres, there is a still different and less complete kind of democracy.

References

Carment, David (2007) *Territorianism: Politics and Identity in Australia's Northern Territory, 1978–2001*, North Melbourne: Australian Scholarly Publishing.

Dickson, Eric S and Sheve, Kenneth (2007) 'Social identity, electoral institutions, and the number of candidates', *British Journal of Political Science,* vol. 40, no. 02. https://doi.org/10.1017/S0007123409990354 Open access at: https://perma.cc/3LFT-LELW

DLGHCD (Department of Local Government, Housing and Community Development, NT) (2019) Northern Territory Housing Strategy 2020-2025. https://tfhc.nt.gov.au/__data/assets/pdf_file/0010/765433/nt-housing-strategy-2020-2025.pdf

Gerritsen, Rolf (2010a) 'The post-colonial state as an impediment to Aboriginal development: an Arnhem Land example', in Gerritsen, Rolf; Larson, Silva; Griffith, Dennis A; Welters, Riccardo; McRae-Williams, Eva; Stoeckl, Natalie; Stanley, Owen; Schlesinger, Christine and Greiner, Romy (2010) *North Australian Political Economy: Issues and Agendas.* Darwin: Charles Darwin University Press (CDU Press). Chapter 5, pp. 70–85. https://hdl.handle.net/10070/799305

Gerritsen, Rolf (2010b) 'A post-colonial model for north Australian political economy? The case of the Northern Territory' in in Gerritsen, Rolf; Larson, Silva; Griffith, Dennis A; Welters, Riccardo; McRae-Williams, Eva; Stoeckl, Natalie; Stanley, Owen; Schlesinger, Christine and Greiner, Romy (2010) *North Australian Political Economy: Issues and Agendas.* Darwin: Charles Darwin University Press (CDU Press). Chapter 2, pp. 18–40. https://hdl.handle.net/10070/799305

Grant, Stan (2022) 'The power of yindyamarra: How we can bring respect to Australian democracy', *The Conversation*, 18 October. https://perma.cc/QE7J-5ZNP

Heatley, Alistair (1979) *The Government of the Northern Territory*, Brisbane: University of Queensland Press.

Heatley, Alistair (1990) *Almost Australians: The Politics of Northern Territory Self-Government*, Darwin: ANU North Australia Research Unit monograph.

NT Health Department (2023) 'COVID-19 data', webpage, 14 April. https://web.archive.org/web/20230322190429/https://health.nt.gov.au/covid-19/data

NTEC (Northern Territory Electoral Commission) (2023) 'Past Legislative Assembly elections', Agency webpage. https://perma.cc/M6AY-63FY

Sanders, Will (2020) 'Comparing Northern Territory elections, 1974–2016: Independent success in a strong two-party system', *Australian Journal of Politics and History*, 21 December, vol. 66, no. 4, pp.596–612. $ https://doi.org/10.1111/ajph.12706

Smee, Ben and Walsh, Christopher (2016) *Crocs in the Cabinet. Northern Territory Politics: An Instruction Manual On How Not To Run A Government*, Sydney: Hachette Australia.

Smith, Robyn (2011) *Arcadian Populism: The Country Liberal Party and Self-Government in the Northern Territory*, Darwin: Charles Darwin University PhD thesis.

Smith, Robyn (2021) 'Northern Territory', Chapter 14 https://oercollective.caul.edu.au/aust-politics-policy/chapter/northern-territory/ in Perche, Diana; Barry, Nicholas; Fenna, Alan; Ghazarian, Zareh; and Haigh, Yvonne (eds) (2024) *Australian Politics and Policy: Senior Edition*, Sydney: Sydney University Press. https://doi.org/10.30722/sup.9781743329542

Wikipedia (2023) 'Northern Territory national emergency response', Online encyclopaedia page. https://perma.cc/DP96-XCPS

24

Australian Capital Territory

Brendan McCaffrie

Many federal systems have 'designed capitals', new cities built and planned from the outset as federal government areas and not controlled by any of the federated states, and in this respect the Australian Capital Territory (ACT) – including Canberra and surrounds – is similar to Washington DC or Brasilia. Initially directly administered by the federal government, in 1989 the ACT was granted self-governing territory status, despite its population voting against that in a 1978 plebiscite (ACT Legislative Assembly, no date, a). Subsequently, the city and environs have grown in population terms but the ACT is the second smallest Australian state or territory by population (with 454,000 people), although an affluent one (with a gross state product (GSP) larger than Tasmania's). As a 'government town' (where over 29 per cent of the workforce are public servants), the city population is relatively wealthy and highly educated, with 37 per cent of residents holding university degrees, compared with 22 per cent nationally.

What does democracy require of the ACT's political system?

A territory should maintain its own democratic institutions including:

- An effective territory constitution that provides an anatomy of legitimate public power to: define the limits of ACT governmental powers; make government accountable to the people by providing for checks and balances; and promote long-term structures.
- Aboriginal and Torres Strait Islander peoples should be afforded full individual civil and human rights. The histories, languages, cultures, rights and needs of Aboriginal and Torres Strait Islander communities and peoples should be addressed.
- The electoral system for the single house, the Legislative Assembly (LA), should accurately translate parties' votes into seats in ways that are recognised as legitimate by most citizens. Ideally, the voting system should foster the overall social representativeness of the legislature. Elections and the regulation of political parties should be impartially conducted, with integrity.

How to cite this chapter:

McCaffrie, Brendan (2024) 'Australian Capital Territory', in: Evans, Mark; Dunleavy, Patrick and Phillimore, John (eds) *Australia's Evolving Democracy: A New Democratic Audit,* London: LSE Press, pp.514–-528. https://doi.org/10.31389/lsepress.ada.x. Licence: CC-BY-NC 4.0

- The political parties should sustain vigorous and effective electoral competition and citizen participation. They should enable the recruitment, selection and development of political leaders for territory government; formulate viable policy agendas and frame political choices for territory functions; and form governments or, when not in power, hold governments accountable. Political parties should uphold the highest standards of conduct in public life.
- The LA should normally maintain full public control of government services and ACT operations, ensuring public and parliamentary accountability through conditionally supporting the government, and articulating reasoned opposition, via its proceedings. It should be a critically important focus of ACT's political debate. It should operate in ways that incorporate a plurality of viewpoints and subject a government to effective checks on its power.
- The ACT government should govern responsively, prioritising the public interest and reflecting ACT public opinion. Its core executive (the chief minister, ministers and key central departments) should provide clear unification of public policies across government, so that the territory operates as an effective whole (spanning both territory and local government functions). Both strategic decision-making within the core executive, and more routine policy-making, should foster careful deliberation to establish an inclusive view of the 'public interest'.
- The core executive and government should operate fully within the law, and the chief minister and other ministers should be effectively scrutinised by and politically accountable to parliament. Ministers and departments/agencies must also be legally accountable to independent courts for their conduct and policy decisions. In the wider ACT public service officials should act with integrity, in accordance with well-enforced codes of conduct, and within the rule of law.
- The administration of public services should be controlled by democratically elected officials so far as possible. The rights of all citizens should be carefully protected in policy-making, and 'due process' rules followed, with fair and equal public consultation on public service changes. By uniting what are normally state and local government functions, ACT governance should be holistic. Public services, contracting, regulation and planning/zoning decisions should be completely free from corruption.
- At the Commonwealth level the ACT government should effectively and transparently represent its citizens' interests to federal government.

The chapter begins with two recent developments. Next a SWOT analysis summarises some strengths of democracy in the ACT, plus some weaknesses. The later sections cover how the LA and ACT government operate, and the ACT's specific constitutional arrangements.

Recent developments

The territory has a distinctive system of government, with the ACT also being the local government throughout its area. Politics in Canberra has generally been left-leaning, and its proportionally elected legislature rarely produces single-party majority governments, recently requiring a series of governing agreements between Labor and the Greens. As elsewhere in Australia, key recent changes have been the evolution of the ACT's fairly stable political scene, and how the territory coped with the COVID-19 pandemic.

Elections and party competition

The ACT has a unicameral (one chamber) legislature, the Legislative Assembly (LA), with 25 members since 2016 (previously it had only 17 seats). The LA is the key focus of representative politics in the ACT, since the territory runs all the functions normally handled by state and local governments, giving the government significant policy and service delivery breadth. Members of the LA (MLAs) are elected under the Hare-Clark version of the single transferrable vote (STV), which is a proportional representation system (ACT Legislative Assembly, no date, b). There are five election districts with five seats in each. The formal quota of preferences needed to win a seat is a sixth [100/(the number of seats +1)] or 16.7 per cent, which is a relatively high level (see Chapter 5).

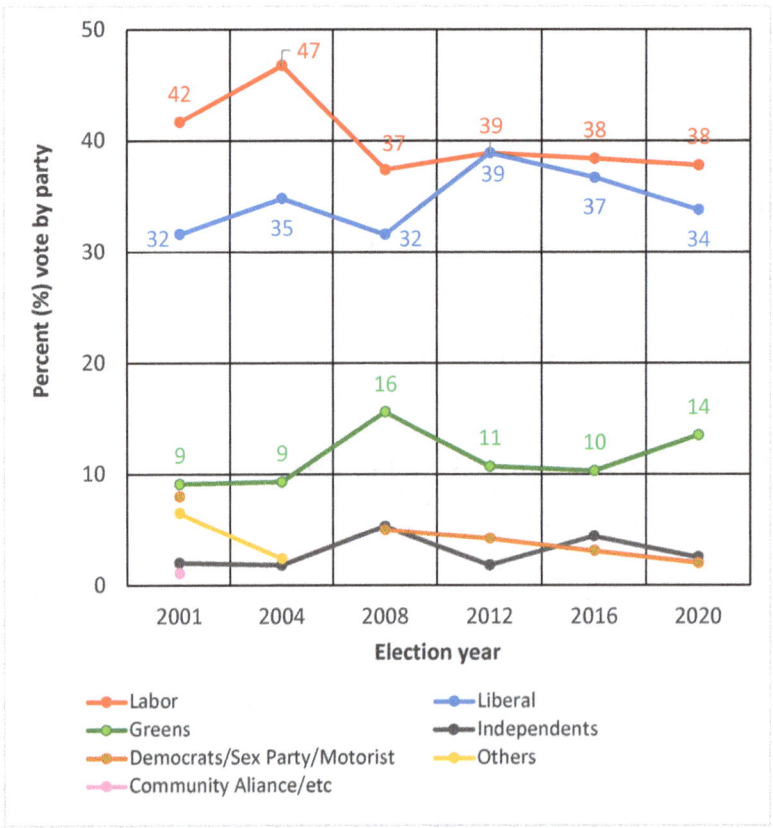

Figure 24.1: First-preference vote shares by party in ACT elections, 2001–2020

Source: Compiled from data in ACT Electoral Commission (2023) 'Past ACT Legislative Assembly elections'.

Figure 24.2: Seats won by parties in ACT elections, 2001–2020

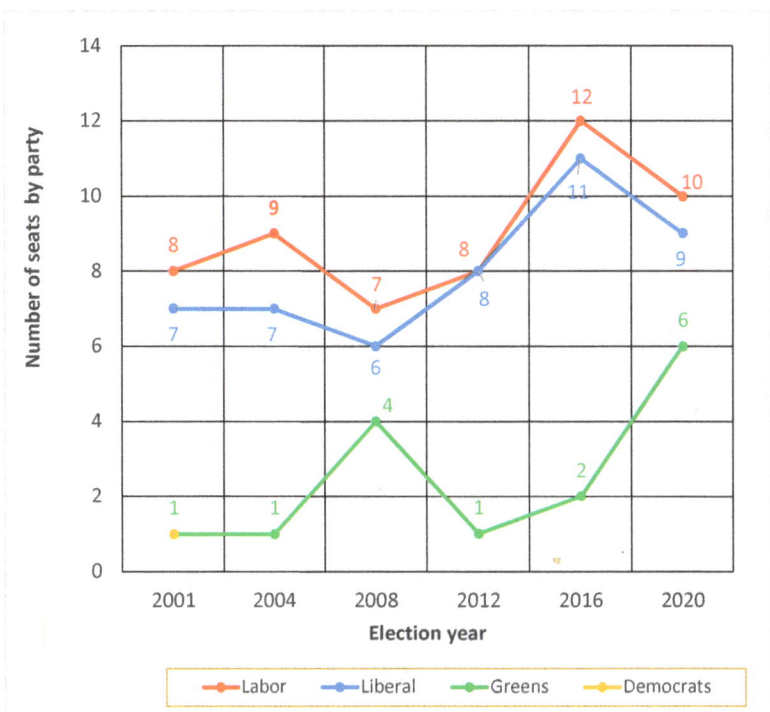

Source: Compiled from data in ACT Electoral Commission (2023) 'Past ACT Legislative Assembly elections'.

Note: Nine seats were needed for a majority from 2001–2012, and 13 seats since 2016.

Labor and the Liberals have been the top two parties, generally accounting for about three-quarters of all first-preference support, and ultimately receiving preferences from those who vote for other parties. Labor has received the most votes in all 21st century elections, except 2012 when Labor received 41 fewer votes than the Liberals, the two parties effectively tying on 38.9 per cent of the vote (Figure 24.1). The Greens have generally gained around 10 per cent of the vote but did a little better in 2008 and 2020. At most elections this century around 15–20 per cent of voters overall have supported a changing mix of smaller parties who have not gained seats. However, in early ACT elections some smaller parties did win representation.

The top two parties and the Greens have thus been the only ones to win seats recently, because of the relatively high quota needed in five seat districts. The proportional STV system requires voters to number at least as many preferences on their ballot paper as there are candidates. A comparison of Figures 24.1 and 24.2 shows that it has been very accurate in awarding proportionate seats between the top two parties, which have been the main beneficiaries of small parties not winning representation. The Greens also gained significantly more seats than their first-preference vote share in 2008 and 2020 (winning nearly a quarter of seats both times).

The three main ACT political parties compete vigorously at election time as well as throughout their terms, especially in promising improved levels of services, and in the Liberal's case lower taxes. One area of more adversarial controversy was the long-running plan for a big capital project to develop a light rail or tram system for Canberra, which Labor and the Greens supported after it was one of the Greens' key conditions for backing a Labor government after the very tight 2012 election. At the 2016 election, the Liberals vehemently opposed completing the first northern stage. Following their defeat, even the Liberals accepted that the project should go ahead (despite some cost inflation), and the first phase successfully opened in 2019. After the

2020 Labor-Green victory local media reported that all parties had come to love light rail, and it attracted considerable federal government subsidies from Liberal-National ministers (ABC News, 2021a). But within a year the new Liberal ACT leader, Elizabeth Lee, was again promising to scrap the southern extension of the project if her party was elected in 2024 (ABC News, 2022).

As with other proportional representation systems, majority governments are rare in the ACT, and either coalition or minority governments have formed after nine of the ten ACT elections. Coalition governments between Labor and the Greens have operated for the whole of this century except 2004–2008, when Labor had a slender overall majority of one (Figure 24.2). By the end of the current LA term (in 2024), Labor will have been the main party of government for 23 consecutive years. At the same date the Canberra Liberals will have been in opposition for all but six of the ACT's 35 years of self-government, having won just two of the ten ACT elections. As a result of Labor's dominance, the ACT has not benefited from the democratic renewal and publicly visible accountability that can come from regular changes of government. The increasing influence of the ACT Greens within the government as a junior coalition partner in recent years has provided a greater variety of ideas within the government, and helped ensure that the main governing party cannot take the electorate for granted. Policy divergences between Labor and the Greens are often significant and meant that the increased number of Greens MLAs after the 2020 election had policy effects.

As with other jurisdictions it has been difficult to assess the strength of party membership and party democracy, because of the secrecy with which parties conduct many of their internal affairs. However, it is safe to assume that membership numbers have been small, and that this has consequent effects on the quality of internal party democracy. The Labor and Liberal parties have been subject to vigorous contests internally to win pre-selection for candidacy, but normally with trade unions and other consolidated interests being expected to have a substantial effect on the outcomes. The lack of transparency of party organisations has been a problem for ACT democracy (as elsewhere). That said, there has not been evidence of wrongdoing within the main ACT parties.

The small number of MLAs for each party can mean that ACT parties have few options for leadership positions, creating less pressure on leaders from within the party than in some other Australian jurisdictions. The threat of leadership spills has thereby diminished, and until 2016 almost all government MLAs were ministers, often holding a very large number of portfolios. The expanded LA of 25 now allows for a government backbench, and the ministerial load has become better spread than it used to be (Halligan and Sheehy, no date). Yet in early 2023, the nine government ministers each held several portfolios, including six held by Deputy Chief Minister Yvette Berry. The challenges of having single ministers responsible for multiple portfolio areas are common across Australia's states and territories. Arguably, this can lead to a democratic deficit if certain portfolios receive less attention than they require.

The COVID-19 pandemic

Early in the pandemic period, COVID-19 affected the ACT less than most jurisdictions. The ACT avoided any community transmission of the disease for over a year before the mid-2021 New South Wales delta variant outbreak reached the ACT in August, sparking a snap lockdown. Although the lockdown lasted for more than two months, it did not create large protest events seen in other capital cities. The 'compliant' population of the ACT rapidly became one of the most vaccinated jurisdictions in the world. At the end of March 2022, 98 per cent of the eligible

ACT population (aged 5 and over) had received at least two COVID-19 vaccine doses. While no recent statistically robust data from the ACT has confirmed this, the correlation between compliance with COVID-19 restrictions and trust in government has been observed in other jurisdictions (Denemark, Harper and Attwell, 2022; Sarracino et al., 2022), and it seems likely that the ACT population was more trusting of government than other Australian jurisdictions. Similarly, across many liberal democracies complaints about government measures being too stringent were more common among groups with the least education who make up a smaller fraction of the population in the ACT than elsewhere in Australia (Rieger and Wang, 2022).

The ACT government responded quickly to the COVID-19 outbreak in 2020, locking down early when few active cases were in the community and spending A$23 million to purchase a deployable field hospital to increase the capacity of the ACT health system to care for COVID-infected patients. When the ACT suppressed the early 2020 COVID-19 outbreak, the field hospital was repurposed as a COVID-19 vaccination centre, and later as a COVID-19 testing facility. As the ACT area is small and entirely surrounded by New South Wales, with many Canberra workers living in towns outside its borders, they could not easily close borders like many other states (ABC News, 2020). About 25,000 people normally commute into the ACT every day and rely on it for crucial health and education services. In addition, although only nine major roads traverse the border, a total of around 70 roads could be used as entrance and exit points. Consequently, the ACT government's ability to act to prevent COVID-19 entering the territory was limited by the actions of the neighbouring New South Wales Government.

Strengths, weaknesses, opportunities and threats (SWOT) analysis

Current strengths	Current weaknesses
ACT has conducted free and fair elections and has strong quality assurance underpinning its electoral process through its independent Electoral Commission.	The ACT Constitution is not under the control of the ACT itself and can be altered at the whim of the Commonwealth Parliament. The ACT does not have proper legislative independence from the Commonwealth.
The ACT government has shown strong commitment to the principle of inclusion of First Nations ACT citizens.	Institutions designed to include First Nations citizens have not been highly representative of the ACT First Nations population. First Nations peoples have not yet established a Treaty with the ACT government. There are significant welfare outcome gaps for ACT First Nations peoples compared with other ACT citizens, in many economic and social policy areas.
The ACT Government handled the COVID-19 pandemic well and has shown a capacity to develop and manage long-run projects like the light rail network (despite cost increases).	The legislature has been limited in its capacity to hold a majority executive to account. Government MLAs are bound to vote with the executive whenever a unanimous cabinet decision has been reached. Debate has usually been brief, and committee inquiries into bills have been relatively infrequent.

The executive has been clear about the nature and content of the agreements that hold the Labor-Green coalition together and the nature of decision-making within the executive.	It has been a long time since the last non-Labor government. The generally progressive ideology of the ACT population has meant that alternations of power are rare.
The executive has generally been transparent, responsive and effective, but has at times had its integrity questioned.	The recently established ACT Integrity Commission is in its infancy and still has work to do to demonstrate its effectiveness in undertaking anti-corruption inquiries.
People in the ACT appear to have had strong trust in government – for example, as evidenced by high COVID-19 vaccination take-up – but direct data on this has been lacking.	The ACT Government has a small tax base, and it has faced challenges in the past in responding to emergencies, like bushfires.
The ACT public service (ACTPS) has been professional, relatively effective and officials have generally performed with integrity.	There has long been room for the ACTPS to be more transparently outcomes-focused, particularly in its service delivery.
The LA has done a good job of equalising gender make-up and representing women's issues. It has generally represented minority groups within the ACT population well.	Canberra has a small media, so the resources to provide public oversight of ACT democratic practice have been slender. As in other small jurisdictions, should a main local news provider collapse financially or cut back its services, then public engagement with democracy and oversight of ACT democracy could be strongly affected.
Future opportunities	**Future threats**
As the larger 25-member LA matures, the LA's committee system may become more active and effective, which would help the legislature to play a larger role in holding the executive to account.	The ACT budget position has had its difficulties, with debt forecast to increase over the coming years, and with significant budget deficits forecast throughout the forward estimate years. The ACT has limited avenues to raise revenue given the small size of its economy, and lack of major industries beyond government employment.
There are opportunities for the ACT Integrity Commission to become a valued part of the ACT democratic system.	Failures to improve transparency, oversight, integrity and accountability mechanisms might damage the ACT's public trust.
The move towards remote working means that the ACT stands to gain in population from 'tree changers' seeking to escape larger cities, such as Sydney and Melbourne.	The ACT's quality of democracy may continue to be eroded by future Commonwealth Government incursions into ACT policy. This could have a negative effect on public satisfaction with ACT democracy.
Given high levels of trust in ACT government, and of citizens' understanding of government operations, there are opportunities to further experiment with public engagement mechanisms and to be a world leader of democratic practice.	If First Nations outcomes in the ACT are not improved, this quite disaffected group within the ACT will incur further disadvantages.
	An underfunded health system may come under increasing pressure as the population ages, with potential negative consequences for public perceptions of ACT government and democracy.

The remainder of the chapter explores the role of the executive and LA, and some constitutional and rights issues that are salient in the ACT.

The executive and Legislative Assembly

In many respects the LA has been well placed to maintain a strong check on executive power, as the central institution within the ACT's democracy. Despite being a unicameral assembly, the Hare-Clark electoral system means that there are few majority governments in the ACT, allowing the LA to consistently perform its review function. But executive control has also been strong. Cabinet has provided a well-articulated mechanism for policy deliberation, because an incentive towards unanimity in decision-making was contained in the Labor-Green parliamentary agreement. This has meant that ministers have needed to ensure they have persuaded colleagues on initiatives and decisions – helping a strongly executive-led government to stay reasonably responsive.

The LA has a somewhat effective committee system (Halligan and Sheehy, no date), with cross-party membership of standing committees and a history of frequent opposition to party committee chairs (ACT Legislative Assembly, 2023). Historically, however, relatively few bills have been referred to committees for inquiry (below 10 per cent in 2012–2017 and 11 per cent in 2018). Under the committee rules for the current term, bills have been referred to the relevant standing committee by default, but in most cases the committees have resolved not to undertake an inquiry into them. Of 48 bills introduced from November 2020–December 2021, 12 resulted in inquiries (including one by a select committee). At 25 per cent, this is a greater proportion than in recent years, but it is unclear whether this change has made a practical difference to the oversight of bills. It remains the case that for most bills, formal legislative oversight has been confined to relatively brief debate in the chamber, with the LA typically debating bills for 40–50 minutes each. (Note: the average length of debate fell between 40–50 minutes for each of the years 2012–2018, more recent data are not available.)

A reasonable number of private members' bills are introduced to the LA. According to the 2020–2021 Business of the Assembly Report, the first 13-months of the current legislative term saw nine introduced (ACT Legislative Assembly, 2022), of which two passed, while over the same period 31 of 38 government bills passed.

Executive control relies on a strong working relationship between the two governing parties, Labor and Greens, with three Greens counted among the current nine ministers. The formal agreement between the two parties provides for guaranteed support on votes of supply (budget) and confidence, as well as establishing the key legislative priorities of the government (Labor-Greens, 2022). It also guarantees that all Labor and Greens MLAs will vote in support of the Labor-Green government whenever cabinet decisions are unanimous. This has been a significant limitation on the capacity of the LA to maintain a check on executive power.

Of the 25 current MLAs 14 are women, a clear indication that parties and voters in the ACT have had less trouble supporting female politicians than many other Australian parliaments. In addition, Andrew Barr, Chief Minister since 2014 (to date of writing) was the first head of an Australian state or territory government to openly identify as LGBTI+. The LA has typically reflected the ACT's ethnic and cultural diversity relatively well – however, Canberra has long been less ethnically diverse than larger Australian cities, such as Sydney and Melbourne.

Transparency and accountability

The ACT has a mixed record in terms of accountability and transparency. It was among the first jurisdictions to adopt the practice of publishing all ministers' appointment diaries, which has been recognised as good democratic practice (see ACT Government, 2024). However, the ACT government was recently subject to a range of Auditor-General's investigations particularly over the sale of, and acquisition of, land for questionable prices. (Large tracts of land across the new city are publicly owned and released periodically at commercial prices to developers, when the ACT government has finalised plans for areas and installed the infrastructure needed.) These inquiries typically stopped well short of accusing the executive of impropriety, but they also consistently identified questionable practices particularly in land sales and fuelled public demand for an Integrity Commission.

Several ACT government land purchases and sales came under scrutiny and criticism from the ACT Auditor-General, after appearing to have resulted in the ACT government losing out financially either with land sold under its value or purchased over value. For instance, one land swap arrangement in the Canberra suburb of Dickson, involved the Construction, Forestry, Mining and Energy Union-linked Tradies Club selling two blocks of land to the ACT government, while the government sold the Tradies Club a nearby carpark, at an apparent net cost to the government of around A$2.5 million (ACT Auditor-General, 2018). Criticism of a lack of transparency arose during another land purchase as part of the Government's City to the Lake project (ABC News, 2016). These deals raised questions over the probity of ACT land development processes but were thoroughly investigated by an independent auditor and have since also been investigated by the new ACT Integrity Commission.

The ACT was the last Australian state/territory to establish an Integrity Commission, which commenced operations in July 2019. Over the next two years it completed and published no investigatory reports, attracting media criticism (CityNews, 2021) – finally finishing its first Special Report in March 2022, and two others later that year. The ACT Integrity Commission was additionally constrained by having no jurisdiction over ACT policing functions, which are provided by the Australian Federal Police. Overall, it has not yet become clear that the ACT has an effective accountability agency, although the new Commission may yet become an effective instrument for investigating and preventing corrupt practices and may improve perceptions of ACT government accountability. Appearances are that as staffing levels in the Commission have grown, activity has also increased.

Another factor in assessing the transparency and accountability of ACT government has been the relatively small local news media. The lack of news media resources is a serious problem for most small jurisdictions. Local ABC radio programs have covered ACT politics, and the *Canberra Times* has provided detailed coverage of city developments. Yet, journalists' jobs have been cut back, leaving media capacity to hold ACT governments to account stretched.

Responsive government

Given its wide range of state and local government functions, the geographical closeness of ACT government to its population, and the ideologies of its long-time governing coalition parties, executive decisions have generally appeared to be responsive to community attitudes. There are challenges in providing evidence, however, because the ACT has not been included in many attitudinal surveys conducted in larger jurisdictions. The Barr government (in power since 2014) has at times been criticised for apparent arrogance or failure to listen to the community, particularly on new urban development issues that affect nearby residents and formerly open spaces. This criticism led to a range of measures aimed to improve connection between government and citizens, including the 'YourSay' online feedback portal (YourSay, 2023). A citizens' jury was used to inform the territory's compulsory third-party injury vehicle insurance scheme, but such juries have not been used widely. The ACT has a strong history of utilising a range of other citizen engagement mechanisms, such as deliberative forums, co-design and other traditional means of gathering citizens' opinions. As with other jurisdictions, the use of more citizen-led processes has been patchy, and more likely in situations where there has not been a strong political desire that a policy be determined or implemented a particular way.

Criticism of the ACT government somewhat abated following some of these moves, but this had less to do with these measures, and was more about general improvement in perceptions of the government's performance, particularly during the COVID-19 pandemic. At the time of writing (late 2023), the Labor-Greens government can claim to be the most progressive government in Australia, reflecting the 'natural' bias in the ACT's population. It has been a national leader in renewable energy policy, with the ACT producing 100 per cent of its energy needs from renewable sources. It has also been a leader in equality for minorities, legalising cannabis and a range of other progressive policies.

The Labor-Green parliamentary agreement for 2020–2024 included a number of measurable outputs and outcomes, such as the provision of A$15,000 interest free loans for installing household and business rooftop solar power systems and other zero emissions technologies, and the delivery of at least 250MW of new 'large-scale' battery storage distributed across the ACT area (to guard against power losses) (Labor-Greens, 2022). Other portfolio level documents have outlined vaguer strategic priorities such as the *Economic Development Priorities 2022–25* (ACT Government, 2022) and the *Canberra Health Services Strategic Plan 2020–23* (ACT Government, 2020). Similarly, while the Labor-Green coalition agreement contained measurable indicators, there was little opportunity for citizens to observe updates on the progress towards goals. Budget papers have provided measures of success on strategic indicators for each portfolio – for example, on health (ACT Treasury, 2021). But these were published in a format difficult for the general public to read and were not so clearly outcomes-focused as in other states (such as New South Wales). The ACTPS has not had the same strong focus on outcomes measures recognised as best practice elsewhere, for example, in state administration in New South Wales and South Australia. An output-focus in reporting has remained, so that the quantity of government activity (for example, number of forms processed, or patients receiving treatment) has been recorded more readily than the effectiveness of those activities in achieving ACT government goals.

The generally positive assessment of the responsiveness of ACT government comes with a caveat, that there are significant marginalised and disaffected groups within its population. Indigenous people's outcomes have trailed behind those of non-Indigenous residents (see shortly). And social and economic disadvantage throughout the ACT population has long been more prevalent than many casual observers of the apparently affluent ACT realise. In 2020, about 38,000 of the ACT's 431,800 residents (8.8 per cent) lived in poverty, meaning the ACT has been far from immune to the inequality challenges faced by most other jurisdictions (ACTCOSS, 2020).

Public services administration

Since 2011, the ACTPS has been organised into eight directorates covering health and hospitals, community services, education, environment and sustainable development, justice, and community safety (but not policing), transport and city services, and the Chief Minister, Treasury and Economic Development Directorate (CMTEDD). There are also a range of public sector bodies outside of the public service itself, such as the Electoral Commission, Integrity Commission, and Auditor-General among many others. Following the 2011 Hawke Review into the ACTPS, CMTEDD has led a coordinated whole-of-government approach to policy-making and implementation (Halligan, 2015). Past debate in the ACT context often revolved around the challenges of ministers holding multiple portfolios, but the increase in the number of ministers has helped here, at least somewhat. Structurally and culturally, the ACTPS has a similar relationship with its ministers as most other Australian jurisdictions – that is, one of considerable political control, particularly on policy matters.

The ACTPS delivers an amalgam of services that other jurisdictions deliver at state level (for example, education, health, etc.) and municipal services (waste collection and management, maintenance of paths and street trees, etc.) typically performed by local governments throughout Australia. As a result, services have been provided with a greater uniformity than in most states, since the ACT does not have a range of local governments pushing different approaches in different parts of the territory. This has been both positive and negative in democratic terms. The territory does not suffer from the sharp geographical inequalities in service provision that can be an issue in large states. However, the relatively large, multi-member electorates have meant a somewhat greater disconnect between MLAs and micro-local issues in specific areas than normally applies in the wider local government model (Halligan, 2015).

Like other Public Services, ACTPS has made active efforts to preserve the integrity of public administration and to enforce compliance with its codes of conduct. In 2016, responsibility for investigating alleged misconduct within the ACTPS passed to the Public Service Standards Commissioner. The *2020–21 State of the Service Report* noted 98 misconduct proceedings, a 27 per cent increase in reports from the previous year (CMTEDD, 2021). The cause of this trend was unclear, although issues in handling the pandemic may have played a part. Most misconduct was not suspected illegality but lack of courtesy and respect, a failure to perform duties, and bullying and harassment. In 2021, 11 possible instances of fraud involving ACT officials were referred to the ACT Integrity Commission (Canberra Times, 2022). Examples of proven illegal conduct are rare, and the ACTPS has generally been considered to be an effective and ethical service, which operates within the law.

The ACT constitution and rights

A key feature of the ACT system of government, as in the Northern Territory, has been that it has limited power and independence, with self-government conferred by an Act of the Commonwealth Parliament (the *Australian Capital Territory (Self-Government) Act 1988*. The Commonwealth has retained the power to amend the terms of ACT self-government, as well as to overrule specific Acts brought about by the ACT LA. This Commonwealth power has been used infrequently, usually to prevent the ACT from acting in ways that diverge strongly from the ideological approaches of the Commonwealth government of the day. In 2006 the Liberal-National government under John Howard overturned the ACT's laws allowing same-sex marriage. Similarly, Liberal-National Commonwealth ministers repeatedly refused to allow the ACT (or the Northern Territory) to enact laws on voluntary assisted dying, including an October 2021 instance, where the Attorney-General Michaelia Cash denied a request by both the ACT and Northern Territory governments on this issue (ABC News, 2021b). Given its demographic characteristics and voters' behaviours, arguably the ACT has suffered significant democratic limitations.

Another constitutional weakness of the ACT has been that (unlike the states) ACT government could (in theory) be effectively amended or abolished by the Commonwealth parliament. Yet there has been and remains no way for the ACT alone to change the document that acts as its constitution. There may have been little risk of the Commonwealth parliament acting maliciously or unfairly to alter the ACT's fundamental governing arrangements. Yet the fact that the status quo is not constitutionally entrenched and that the ACT can make no constitutional changes are both significant democratic limitations. Recent developments have somewhat diminished the Commonwealth's position relative to the ACT. Before 2011 Commonwealth ministers alone could exercise the power to overrule territory legislation, but that provision was changed so that the right was retained only by the federal parliament as a whole (Halligan, 2019). In 2013, the ACT also gained the ability to determine the size of its Legislative Assembly.

Aboriginal and Torres Strait Islander peoples

At the 2021 Census the ACT had the second smallest per capita First Nations population (2.2 per cent) of any state or territory (ABS, 2023a). The ACT government has made efforts to include First Nations peoples in government, but like other Australian jurisdictions, much work remains to be done to achieve equality of outcomes for First Nations and non-Indigenous peoples. The government has not yet established a treaty with the traditional owners of ACT lands, though as part of the governing coalition's parliamentary agreement after the 2020 election, it committed to commencing Treaty discussions (Labor-Greens, 2022). Relatedly, the parliamentary agreement included a commitment to repealing the 2001 Namadgi Agreement, which gave a 99 year Special Aboriginal Lease over the famous Namadgi National Park south of Canberra only on the exclusionary condition that all existing native title claims were dropped and that no new applications were submitted (Wensing, 2021).

In 2008, the ACT created a seven-member body, the Aboriginal and Torres Strait Islander Elected Body to act as an elected voice for Indigenous people to the ACT LA (ATSIEB, 2023). While there has been evidence of good levels of engagement between ATSIEB and the ACT Government and LA, an independent 2015 review of the ACT Aboriginal and Torres Strait Islander Elected Body (ATSIEB) legislation found that there was a need for more engagement between the Body and the First Nations community (Janke, 2015). The turnout for ATSIEB elections has been persistently low, with only 269 votes cast in 2021 despite an estimated 4,567 enrolled First Nations voters in the ACT (ACT Electoral Commission, 2021; Australian Electoral Commission, 2023).

In terms of outcomes, the ACT government has shown strong commitment to efforts to close the socioeconomic gaps between First Nations and non-Indigenous Australians. The ACT Aboriginal and Torres Strait Islander Agreement 2019–2028 intends to achieve this through self-determination, and Indigenous-led solutions to current causes of the gap in outcomes (ACT

Community Services, 2019). However, in several respects the ACT cannot yet be considered successful. Data for December 2021 showed that 26 per cent of prisoners in ACT were First Nations peoples, a vast overrepresentation given that First Nations peoples are 2 per cent of the ACT population (ABS, 2023b). There was also a steady increase in the proportion of First Nations prisoners over the past decade, up from 13.4 per cent in 2011. Similarly, a quarter of children in care within the ACT in 2021 came from Aboriginal and Torres Strait Islander households, a rate more than 12 times that of other households (Family Matters, 2023, Figure 2).

Conclusion

The ACT has been home to a thriving democracy, though not one without its challenges and areas for improvement. The institutional structure of the ACT government and its politics are well designed, and though there are some limitations in the constitutional independence of the ACT, the three branches of government and the public service and various independent and statutory bodies have been well placed to fulfil key functions of ACT democracy. In terms of possible reforms, the legislative branch could begin to play a greater role in keeping the executive in check, and there are signs that this may be beginning to happen. And more remains to be done to ensure that the accountability and integrity mechanisms of the ACT are operating to the level required of a mature democracy.

The long-running stranglehold on power of Labor-led governments contains a risk – for if power does not alternate, conditions that support poor political and government practices (termed 'scelerosis' by some commentators) could develop. This risk may be heightened if the already small ACT media landscape suffers from the collapse of any of its main contributors. The view of Canberra as a quiet, quaint and organised city, with high median incomes and education levels can also easily obscure weaknesses and failings in the ACT's democratic practice, such as rising social inequality in the city.

The educated, trusting and fairly progressive population has largely been reflected in the membership of the LA and in the government and its direction. Canberrans are knowledgeable about politics and value democracy. These traits will surely safeguard ACT democracy for many decades to come, but some of the ACT's young institutions of self-government need to mature, and opportunities to experiment and innovate will need to be taken further, if the ACT is to become the shining beacon of democratic practice to which its politicians and citizens aspire.

References

ABC News (2016) 'ACT auditor-general criticises lack of transparency in Government land acquisitions', webpage, 30 September. https://perma.cc/3DTW-JCF4

ABC News (2020) 'Closing ACT border is so difficult, and provides so few benefits, authorities say it's not worthwhile', ABC Webpage, 15 August. https://perma.cc/V3QD-3QTA

ABC News (2021a) 'End of the line: How Canberra's political parties learned to love the ACT's light rail network', webpage, 24 February. https://perma.cc/B5HE-X6TY

ABC News (2021b) 'Request to allow for voluntary assisted dying laws in ACT and NT denied by Attorney-General Michaelia Cash', ABC webpage, 8 October. https://perma.cc/6ZHX-EFPY

ABC News (2022) 'Canberra Liberals promise to dump light rail to Woden if elected in 2024', webpage, 4 December. https://perma.cc/4E3F-ACA7

ACT Auditor-General (2018) 'Tender for the sale of block 30 (formerly block 20) section 34 Dickson', ACTAG Report No. 3. https://perma.cc/4VH6-KPNT

ACT Community Services (2019) ACT *Aboriginal And Torres Strait Islander Agreement 2019–2028*, web document. https://perma.cc/YA77-STSX

ACTCOSS (ACT Council of Social Service) (2020) 'Factsheet: Poverty and inequality in the ACT', Factsheet, 15 October. https://perma.cc/E5DF-G6AR

ACT Electoral Commission (2021) 'ACT Aboriginal and Torres Strait Islander Elected Body – 2021 Election Report', Web document, July. https://perma.cc/7RUE-T8QP

ACT Electoral Commission (2023) 'Past ACT Legislative Assembly elections', Agency webpage. https://perma.cc/YZP7-HTQZ

ACT Government (2020) 'Canberra health services strategic plan 2020–2023', PDF report.

ACT Government (2022) 'ACT's economic development priorities 2022–25', Web document. https://perma.cc/5DN9-38CH

ACT Government (2024) 'Ministerial diaries disclosure', ACT Open Information webpage. https://perma.cc/5KYG-GYMX

ACT Legislative Assembly (no date, a) 'The road to self-government', webpage factsheet. https://perma.cc/Y73C-N2R8

ACT Legislative Assembly (no date, b) 'How members are elected', webpage factsheet. https://perma.cc/839D-CSNG

ACT Legislative Assembly (2022) '2020–21 Business of the Assembly Report', January. https://perma.cc/52CW-GSXK

ACT Legislative Assembly (2023) 'Committees', webpage. https://perma.cc/2MV2-RM2M

ACT Treasury (2021) 'Budget 2021–22, Budget Statements C – ACT Health Directorate, Canberra Health Services, ACT Local Hospital Network', Web document. https://perma.cc/3KCC-3G7W

ATSIEB ACT Aboriginal and Torres Strait Islander Elected Body (ATSIEB) (2023) Institution website. https://perma.cc/44DK-FGYM

Australian Bureau of Statistics (ABS) (2023a) 'Estimates of Aboriginal and Torres Strait Islander Australians', webpage. https://perma.cc/8EHU-XPKS

Australian Bureau of Statistics (ABS) (2023b) 'Aboriginal and Torres Strait Islander prisoners', webpage. https://perma.cc/LYJ6-3MXQ

Australian Electoral Commission (2023) 'Indigenous enrolment rate', webpage, 6 February. https://perma.cc/7UT3-T8LS

CMTEDD (Chief Minister, Treasury and Economic Development Directorate) (2021) 'State of the Service 2021-22 Annual Report' https://perma.cc/S46R-ZPDP

Canberra Times (2022) 'ACT public servants caught committing fraud with 11 referrals to integrity commission in 2020–21', *Canberra Times*, 2 January. $ https://perma.cc/47T6-JWVH

CityNews (2021) 'Two years on and not a peep from the ACT anti-corruption commission', Webpage, 22 September. https://perma.cc/X9WE-Y74J

Denemark, David; Harper, Tauel; and Attwell, Katie (2022) 'Vaccine hesitancy and trust in government: A cross-national analysis', *Australian Journal of Political Science*, vol. 57, no. 2, pp.145–63. $ https://www.tandfonline.com/doi/full/10.1080/10361146.2022.2037511

Family Matters (2023) *The Family Matters Report 2023 – Measuring Trends To Turn The Tide On The Over-Representation Of Aboriginal And Torres Strait Islander Children In Out-Of-Home Care In Australia.* https://perma.cc/8DPH-UQXC

Halligan, John (2015) 'Governance in a hybrid system: Designing and institutionalising the Australian Capital Territory', *Policy Studies*, vol. 36, no. 1, pp.4–17. https://doi.org/10.1080/01442872.2014.981054 (paywall)

Halligan, John (2019) '"Established as a body politic"…: Thirty years of self-government in the ACT – Chief Minister's Governance Lecture for 2019', Canberra: Institute for Governance and Policy Analysis, University of Canberra, ACT Government, Archives webpage. https://perma.cc/XK9H-UEXY

Halligan, John and Sheehy, Benedict (no date) *Review of the Performance of the Three Branches of Government in the Australian Capital Territory against Latimer House Principles*, Report to the ACT Government. https://perma.cc/VBF7-XMYJ

Janke, Terri (2015) *Review of the Aboriginal and Torres Strait Islander Elected Body Act 2008,* Consultant's Report to the ACT Government. Not online. https://perma.cc/9K5R-4B8Q

Labor-Greens (2022) *Parliamentary and Governing Agreement – 10th Legislative Assembly for the Australian Capital Territory,* Joint webpage document, Australian Labor Party and the Greens. https://perma.cc/4WU3-6EYC

Rieger, Marc Oliver and Wang, Mei (2022) 'Trust in government actions during the COVID-19 Crisis', *Social Indicators Research,* vol. 159, pp. 967–89. https://doi.org/10.1007/s11205-021-02772-x

Sarracino, Francesco; Greyling, Talita; O'Connor, Kelsey; Peroni, Chiara; and Rossouw, Stephanié (2022) 'Trust predicts compliance with Covid-19 containment policies: Evidence from ten countries using big data', *IZA Discussion Paper No. 15171.* https://perma.cc/2S9M-M5NN

Wensing, Ed (2021) 'Unfinished business – Truth-telling about Aboriginal land rights and native title in the ACT', Discussion Paper, March on the webpage of The Australia Institute (Canberra). https://perma.cc/RN3Q-LDUZ

YourSay (2023) ACT Government web program – 'List of ACT engagement projects'. [Updates] https://perma.cc/N2NK-WFC3

25

Local democracy in metropolitan regions and big cities

Graham Sansom and Su Fei Tan

Two-thirds of Australians live in the seven metropolitan regions surrounding the national and state capitals, which include 10 individual cities (local government areas) with populations of more than 250,000 – our criterion here for 'big city' status. A further 9 per cent live in other 'big cities', making 19.3 million people in all (three-quarters of Australia's total). So, what is the character and quality of their local democracy?

What does democracy require of metropolitan and big city governance?

- Inclusive, equitable and purposeful elected representation of local and (sub)regional communities at all levels of government.
- Appropriate democratic oversight of planning, environmental management, infrastructure provision and service delivery at both local- and metro-scale.
- Forums for informed public debate on metropolitan and big city management.
- Meaningful devolution of authority for local and sub-regional planning, infrastructure and service delivery to local governments, along with necessary funding and/or powers to raise revenue.
- Respect for and responsiveness to local communities' identity, sense of place, needs and aspirations, including arrangements for ongoing engagement and 'neighbourhood' democracy.
- An absence of unwarranted interventions by state governments into the processes of local democracy and decision-making.
- Effective mechanisms for inter-government cooperation, both vertical and horizontal.

How to cite this chapter:

Sansom, Graham and Tan, Su Fei (2024) 'Local democracy in metropolitan regions and big cities', in: Evans, Mark; Dunleavy, Patrick and Phillimore, John (eds) *Australia's Evolving Democracy: A New Democratic Audit,* London: LSE Press, pp.529–543. https://doi.org/10.31389/lsepress.ada.y. Licence: CC-BY-NC 4.0

The chapter begins by covering some recent developments and then considers the strengths, weaknesses, opportunities and threats (SWOT) in Australia's metropolitan regions and big city governance. After the SWOT analysis we review four areas of concern in more detail.

Recent developments

The urban governance of Australia's metropolitan regions has been heavily dominated by the states, with local government and, in different ways, the Commonwealth playing essentially supporting roles (Sansom and Dawkins, 2013). Figure 25.1 shows that Australia's capital-city metropolitan regions account for between 42 and 79 per cent of their respective state's populations. Because they have constitutional authority for local government, and the populations of capital-city regions are so salient in state politics, state ministers and agencies typically control all the key elements of metropolitan management and planning – including urban transport, main roads, water, sewerage and drainage, pollution control, major open spaces, cultural and sporting facilities, and the approval of most major development proposals. Elsewhere in the world several or all of these key functions for managing city development would be the responsibility of local government.

Figure 25.1: Australia's 'big cities' in 2021

Metro-regions and larger cities (State: % of state population)	Local areas included	Population (000s)	Component areas with over 250,000 people
Greater Sydney (NSW: 66%)	34	5,367	Canterbury-Bankstown, Blacktown, Central Coast, Northern Beaches, Parramatta
Greater Melbourne (VIC: 79%)	31	5,159	Casey, Wyndham
Greater Brisbane (QLD: 49%)	9	2,561	Brisbane (1.2 million), Moreton Bay, Logan
Greater Perth (WA: 77%)	31	2,125	
Greater Adelaide (SA: 76%)	19	1,377	
Gold Coast (QLD: 12%)	1	606	
Lower Hunter (NSW: 6%)	4	515	
Australian Capital Territory (ACT)	1	431	
Sunshine Coast (QLD: 6%)	1	320	
Wollongong-Shellharbour (NSW: 4%)	2	288	
Geelong (VIC: 4%)	1	252	
Greater Hobart (TAS: 42%)	4	239	

Source: Compiled from data in Australian Bureau of Statistics (2023) 'Latest release – Regional population'.

Note: State capitals = green rows. Populations in 2021. City of Sydney population 214,800. City of Melbourne population 169,000. The Australian Capital Territory (ACT/Canberra) is effectively a city-state (see Chapter 24).

The picture has been somewhat different in South East Queensland (Greater Brisbane plus the Sunshine and Gold Coasts), where 95 per cent of the metropolitan region's 3.5 million people live in just seven municipalities, including five with populations in excess of 300,000. The City of Brisbane alone houses 46 per cent of the metro-region's population: it has an annual budget of around A$4 billion and is a key provider of metropolitan infrastructure and services, including some highways and parts of the public transport system. Also, the conurbation has an influential, region-wide Council of Mayors. Even there, however, the last two decades have witnessed a marked shift towards state control. Outside the state capital regions, local government has been able to play a more prominent role in big cities, although in most cases its functions remain limited to 'lower order' municipal services and infrastructure.

Potentially, the Commonwealth (federal) government is also a significant player by virtue of its constitutional powers over immigration (a major driver of city growth), transport and communications, and some aspects of environmental management. Federal financial strength has been a key factor, given the needs of both state and local governments for funding support – especially for major infrastructure projects. For the most part, however, federal involvement in big city governance has been cautious, patchy and arms-length. Even when there has been the political will to do more, the federal bureaucracy may have lacked the skills for effective, closer engagement.

Strengths, weaknesses, opportunities and threats (SWOT) analysis

Current strengths	Current weaknesses
All metropolitan/big-city local governments have had a power of general competence or its equivalent (to work for the good of their population). They have been required to undertake increasingly sophisticated strategic planning in consultation with their communities.	Local governments have suffered from a persistent compliance and 'poor cousin' culture, due to the unfettered powers of states, a heavy regulatory burden and constraints on their own-source revenues. Community consultation, especially by state agencies, has often appeared tokenistic or ultimately ineffectual.
There are guarantees of democratic local government in some state constitutions, and in several jurisdictions voting is compulsory in local government elections. State-level independent electoral commissions monitor the integrity of local elections (see Chapter 26).	There is no constitutional protection for local democracy in New South Wales (NSW), nor nationally. State governments can intervene in local affairs as they see fit and may shape or 'engineer' local elections. Voting for local government remains voluntary in some states, with lower turnouts despite the growth of mail-in voting in some areas (see Chapter 26).
Mayors have a substantial presence in all the capital city regions. They are popularly elected in all South East Queensland, Adelaide and Tasmanian councils, plus Newcastle, Wollongong and some large metropolitan councils in Sydney and Perth.	Other big city councils in Greater Sydney and Melbourne, as well as Geelong, have had only weaker, indirectly elected mayors.

The Australia-wide Council of Capital City Lord Mayors (CCCLM) has advocated on some big city issues, and the Council of Mayors for South East Queensland (COMSEQ) has played a regional leadership role (for example, over the 2032 Olympics and City Deal negotiations with the federal government).	No body similar to COMSEQ has existed in other metropolitan regions. The governance of connected metro-regions has been constrained by widespread resistance to creating upper-tier municipalities and statutory sub-regional groupings, other than for specific functions (for example, waste management) or for 'special projects'.
Some big-city councils have demonstrated excellence in neighbourhood planning, place-based management and community engagement. Some have used deliberative democracy techniques (for example, citizen juries and online panels).	There has been no legislative provision for elected sub-municipal councils (akin to the community boards in New Zealand) even in very large and populous local government areas. The concept has been explicitly rejected on several occasions by both state and local governments, and partly as a result the quality of community engagement has remained patchy.
Very large municipalities have shown a potential to expand services to meet their community's needs, to protect their sense of place and to advocate forcefully to state and federal governments.	States can and have used their constitutional powers to override local preferences as they see fit. Municipalities' authority to plan and control has been progressively reduced in most states. States have often outsourced major service/infrastructure provision to private companies. Alternatively, they have established commercialised entities with minimal democratic oversight. Big municipalities have lacked any additional status or powers compared to smaller towns or shires. The high fragmentation of local government areas in most of the country has fostered a 'lowest common denominator' approach to local policy and relationships.
There has been longstanding federal government support for local government in terms of both policy and financial assistance.	The Local Government Ministers Council was abolished in 2011. And after almost 30 years as a member of the Council of Australian Governments (COAG) the Australian Local Government Association was largely excluded from the 'National Cabinet' that replaced COAG in 2020. It has been assured of participation in only one out of four or five meetings annually that were continued by the Labor federal government from 2022.
There have been some positive examples of inter-government partnerships (for example, in South East Queensland and Greater Hobart). Local government has also been included to varying degrees in federal-state 'City Deals' launched in 2016.	The prevailing pattern of increasing state domination of big-city governance, planning and service delivery has not changed. Thus far, City Deals have simply funded projects and failed to advance devolution. (The federal Labor government elected in May 2022 promised 'genuine partnerships' but in practice the City Deals have largely lapsed.)
Melbourne's Metropolitan Partnerships have brought together appointed members from communities and business with municipal CEOs to advise the state government on key issues.	No similar arrangement has existed elsewhere, except to some extent Hobart. The Melbourne Partnerships have been purely advisory and often lacked close links with key state agencies and decision-making processes.

Compulsory voting and high turnout in all state and federal elections have meant that popular preferences in big cities and metropolitan regions strongly affected election outcomes and have been closely monitored. These areas are typically represented by multiple state and federal parliamentarians, providing varied channels of influence. Local party members and MPs could potentially exercise effective democratic oversight of metropolitan and local governance and decision-making by state authorities and councils.	At both the state and federal levels the dominance of executive governments over parliaments has meant that individual MPs tend to focus on defined constituencies and interest groups, rather than the identity of localities. Parliamentary oversight committees deal primarily with functions, ministries, or ad hoc issues, rather than 'whole-of-government' or regional coordination.
Future opportunities	**Future threats**
The return of an Australian Labor Party (ALP) government in 2022 might bring renewed federal interest in cities and support for local government and civil society to play a stronger role (see ALP, 2019). However, this is yet to materialise.	There has been a trend towards increasing state dominance during the COVID-19 epidemic that may well continue. Municipalities' role could potentially be reduced to that of a 'line manager' for state agencies. Revenue constraints (for example, rate-capping) and competition with state taxes and charges (for example, stamp duty/land tax/special levies) may intensify as states struggle to balance budgets.
There may be scope to promote the democratisation of metropolitan planning and development agencies by including local government and community representatives on their boards. Enhanced democratic oversight of metro regions by state parliaments could also be possible.	Democratic oversight could be further reduced as more state-controlled functions and key assets are outsourced or privatised (for example, private certification of development approvals, toll roads and parts of the public transport network).
Local government could enhance its status and influence by collectively pursuing a broad-based localism agenda for big cities that combines four elements – a focus on place management; closer community engagement (with a view to strengthening local support); expanded inter-municipal cooperation at sub-regional and metropolitan levels; and effective policy development and advocacy nationally.	The local government voice has been at risk because of ongoing divisions within local government itself – a plethora of different associations, alliances and professional institutes. Cooperation has often been resisted due to local political or place rivalries and fears of 'amalgamation by stealth'. The national association has been weak, and state associations have tended to focus heavily on local-state tensions rather than federal opportunities. The policy space has also been dominated by urban growth pressures and the development lobby at the expense of local interests and democracy.
More popularly elected and/or authoritative mayors could give local government greater political clout, a clearer mandate to pursue policy agendas, and boost local willingness to collaborate (sub) regionally and nationally.	Local government may well continue down the recent path of neoliberal managerialism with weak mayors and insufficient numbers of councillors to provide effective community representation.

The rest of the chapter focuses on a number of significant concerns about the quality of big-city democracy and urban planning and management, including the weak structural position of municipalities within federalism. Some recent proposals for reform are considered.

Deficiencies in elected representation

A strong argument has been made that Australia's big cities have suffered from a significant democratic deficit (Nicholls and Spiller, 2020), and seem fated to continue to do so, because:

- there are no elected (directly or indirectly) multi-functional metropolitan authorities, and special-purpose agencies rarely have formal local government and/or community representation on their boards. Nor are there any upper-tier, sub-metropolitan local governments (as will be seen shortly)
- by international standards, Australian municipalities have very small numbers of councillors, and most have 'weak' mayors without the authority or mandate to provide necessary political leadership and advocate effectively on behalf of their communities
- due to their broader responsibilities and associated political demands, state and federal governments typically lack a consistent focus on metropolitan and big-city issues, and their major ministries are defined by function, not place
- the effectiveness of state and federal MPs representing big-city electorates has been constrained by broader policy and party-political considerations, and by limited opportunities for parliamentary oversight (particularly at state level) of the key ministries and agencies that manage metropolitan and regional planning and infrastructure.

The City of Brisbane has 27 councillors, but all the other big-city municipalities across Australia are limited to no more than 15 – and most have fewer than that. The ratio of councillors to population in big cities can be 1:20,000 or more. Even with 26 councillors (plus the popularly elected Lord Mayor), Brisbane's ratio has risen to about 1:46,000 people; and with only 15 councillors Gold Coast's ratio has become 1:40,000. Moreover, in all jurisdictions except Queensland councillors and mayors are nominally part-time and lack adequate, dedicated staff support (often they have none).

The small numbers of councillors have made it difficult for urban councils to reflect the demographic, cultural and socioeconomic diversity of big-city society. Moreover, diverse place-based representation may suffer from an evident trend away from multi-councillor wards and towards holding local elections 'at large'. This has been linked to the 'board of directors' concept and a view (associated with new public management thinking) that ward councillors' interests get in the way of strategic management. In large cities this stance runs the risk of sidelining truly local democracy along with place-based planning and governance.

Councils are elected by a universal residential franchise, but in addition all the states except Queensland have retained some form of property based voting rights for non-resident owners. This appears to have at most a marginal impact on the outcome of elections, but it does flag the importance that state governments have historically attached to property and business interests in terms of the economic base of big cities – and hence of the state. In the central city councils of Melbourne and Sydney this perspective led to businesses being given two votes each as a means of strengthening recognition of their interests in central business districts, although in the case of Sydney that provision was recently repealed.

Local government Acts describe mayors as civic leaders and may assign them significant additional responsibilities compared to other councillors. Yet in most cases their ability to 'steer the ship' has been tightly constrained. The City of Brisbane, Queensland municipalities in general and, to a lesser extent, other central capital city councils, are exceptions to this rule.

Other metropolitan regions and big cities have been characterised by 'weak' mayors with limited statutory authority and few if any personal staff. Often, they are elected indirectly by their fellow councillors (rather than by the populace) and must be re-elected every one or two years. Unless they enjoy the support of a united and consistent majority on the floor of council, are trusted by their colleagues to provide strong leadership, and are perhaps given significant delegated powers, mayors usually find it difficult to achieve the stature and community support required to deal effectively with state ministers and agencies and in inter-government forums.

In 2013, the NSW Independent Local Government Review Panel (2013) proposed that all mayors of larger municipalities should be popularly elected, but that proposal was rejected following strong opposition from local government itself. However, in Western Australia a similar proposal was implemented through an amendment to the local government Act in 2023 (Wikipedia, 2023).

Municipal structures and roles

The quality of local democracy in metropolitan regions and big cities depends heavily on the ability of municipalities to advance and advocate community interests. Local government Acts now grant municipalities a 'power of general competence' or its equivalent – the authority to take whatever lawful action may be necessary to ensure the good governance and wellbeing of their communities (if they can fund it). Big cities with considerable resources may use this power to great effect in both practical and democratic terms. However, their authority has commonly been circumscribed in various ways: implicitly by limits on revenue-raising and by ministerial oversight of municipal performance; and explicitly by the provisions of other legislation, as well as the over-riding functions and capacity of state and federal agencies in providing services and infrastructure (as will be seen shortly).

Another key factor limiting local government's role and effectiveness in metropolitan governance has been its continued fragmentation into numerous separate and 'on a par' municipalities (see Figure 25.1). Greater Sydney, for example, has 34 local government areas for a total population of about 5.4 million, Greater Melbourne 31 for 5.2 million, and Greater Perth 31 for just 2.1 million. Even very large metropolitan municipalities have no greater legal status or authority than their smaller counterparts. Yet local governments generally resist any differentiation of their roles according to scale and capacity, municipal mergers and mandatory cooperative entities at (sub) regional level. Despite enabling or supportive provisions in local government Acts, inter-municipal cooperation has tended to be tentative, patchy and intermittent (Sansom, 2019a). No multi-purpose 'upper tier' municipalities have been created, nor any directly elected regional or special-purpose bodies. Only South East Queensland has a dedicated regional Council of Mayors with the capacity to lobby effectively and partner with state and federal governments – as it did recently to secure the 2032 Olympics for Brisbane and its region.

Typically, municipalities have prioritised protecting their individual autonomy, regardless of any negative impacts on the status of local government as a whole and despite the way their individualism has enabled state and federal governments to 'divide and rule', often with negative consequences for local democracy. Moreover, while all municipalities have the power to establish locality based committees with delegated authority to undertake aspects of planning and service delivery, few have done so. Almost all have continued to resist the concept of creating 'lower-tier' bodies along the lines of Britain's parish, community and town councils, or New Zealand's community boards (Sansom, 2019b).

The effectiveness of big-city local government has also been constrained by state-imposed limits on revenue-raising and the spectre of ministerial oversight and intervention. NSW has had a system of 'rate-pegging' for more than four decades, under which annual increases in property tax ('rates') may not exceed a set limit without special approval from the state's pricing authority. Victoria introduced a similar system in 2015. South Australia attempted to do so in 2018 – the bill was defeated in the upper house of parliament – but settled instead on a form of statutory oversight of councils' long-term financial (and hence rating) strategies. This includes public reports by the state's pricing authority on whether those strategies were considered appropriate, which may well have a similar impact to rate-capping given councillors' sensitivity to ratepayer complaints. State governments have also placed limits on various fees and charges levied by municipalities, notably developer contributions (see below under 'Housing Supply').

Intervention by state governments has taken many forms, including wholesale re-drawing of big city boundaries, as occurred in Greater Melbourne and Geelong in the mid-1990s, Queensland in 2007 and Greater Sydney in 2016. Suspension and dismissal of elected councils have been a regular occurrence. For example, in late 2020 the NSW minister for local government suspended the councillors of the Central Coast municipality – one of the state's largest with a population of around 340,000 and a budget of some A$800 million per annum – and installed a single administrator with absolute control over the municipality's affairs. The minister followed up by convening a public inquiry, thus enabling the period of suspension to continue at least until late 2024. Under the NSW local government Act the minister may take such steps totally at their discretion, without parliamentary scrutiny, and without being obliged to follow the recommendations of the inquiry, after which they may simply dismiss the councillors and call a fresh election – the eventual outcome at Central Coast. Moreover, the Central Coast administrator proposed holding a referendum at the next election to reduce the number of councillors from 15 to 9, possibly without wards. This would increase the councillor–population ratio from 1:23,000 now to well over 1:40,000 if implemented (Sansom, 2021).

Urban planning and management

Recent trends in how urban development has been planned, regulated and managed have been perhaps the greatest threat to local democracy in Australia's big cities. Governments at all levels are under pressure to promote economic and population growth, as well as to ensure related provision of housing and infrastructure. Sometimes this has been self-inflicted by state and local leaders, anxious to gain political benefits from growth or to prevent investment going elsewhere. High rates of growth over many decades have meant that property development and the construction sector have become critical elements of state and big-city political economies, especially around housing. The advent of 'mega-projects' has underlined this trend.

Housing supply

Population growth, the reduced average size of households, competition for homes in more accessible and attractive locations, and rapidly rising house and apartment prices fuelled in part by the low interest rates of recent decades, have combined to generate demands for major increases in housing supply. Meanwhile, there has often been strong community and local government resistance to higher density redevelopment. This stance has been portrayed by powerful lobbies as an intolerable obstacle to achieving more housing, and state governments have responded to unrelenting pressure from the housing and property development sector with severe reductions in local planning autonomy and discretion (Sydney Morning Herald, 2021a). At the same time, councils' ability to levy developers to fund the new local infrastructure and services needed has been closely regulated and constrained in the guise of reducing housing costs – further limiting the resources and choices available to local communities and decision-makers.

Planning approvals

More broadly, the planning and approvals processes for all forms of urban development, especially larger projects deemed to be of 'state significance', have been centralised in state agencies and ministers' offices. The involvement of elected councillors, and hence their constituents, in local planning and decision-making processes has been progressively pared back by transferring some or all of their authority to appointed planning panels; by the imposition of blanket state or regional policies and codes; and by ministers or state agencies using their powers to 'call-in' and determine proposals themselves (Clark, 2021).

A related issue has been the limited role of municipalities in metropolitan planning agencies. In the mid-20th century local government was a dominant player in Melbourne's Metropolitan Board of Works and Sydney's Cumberland County Council. Both were replaced by state departments or agencies with boards appointed by ministers. In mid-2023, Melbourne had no dedicated metropolitan planning organisation and the project- and precinct-oriented Victorian Planning Authority did not include representatives of local government or civil society organisations as such, although some of the board members had considerable relevant experience. The same applied to the Greater Sydney (by then renamed 'Cities') Commission (which was abolished shortly after, and its responsibilities centralised in the state planning department). In Western Australia 2 of the 16 members of the Planning Commission were explicit local government representatives; while in South Australia, one of five Planning Commission members had extensive local government experience but there was no legislative requirement for this. Only in Queensland and Tasmania were there specific arrangements for local governments to play a strong role in strategic metropolitan planning – as opposed to simply being consulted about strategies and then required to 'fill in the detail' (see below).

Mega-projects

As big cities have grown bigger, federal and state governments have become increasingly preoccupied with multi-billion-dollar urban development and/or infrastructure schemes, usually undertaken with commercial partners (Terrill, Emslie and Moran, 2020). These were commonly touted as generating vitally important economic growth, jobs, housing, improvements to transport networks, and in some cases government revenues. Examples have included development precincts (such as Sydney's harbourside Barangaroo, East Perth and Melbourne's Docklands); new freeways (commonly privately operated tollways); metro and light rail systems; and the new Western Sydney airport with its associated rail link and 'Aerotropolis' development. Invariably, these 'mega-projects' have proceeded under special legislation and/or commercial-in-confidence provisions, leaving little or no scope for effective municipal, public or even parliamentary scrutiny – notwithstanding some form of community consultation at the outset. An exception has been when a well-resourced municipality becomes a partner in the project, such as light rail in the cities of Gold Coast and Sydney.

Intergovernment relations and City Deals

Local democracy in big cities needs to be reinforced by robust and productive intergovernment relations, both vertical and horizontal. Without such arrangements the ability of municipalities to function as part of the broader system of government, and to advocate on behalf of their constituents, has been and remains greatly diminished. Most states have had an intergovernmental agreement of some sort with the local government association, but these were usually couched in very general terms around regular high-level consultations on matters of mutual concern.

Other than City Deals (discussed next) only two arrangements have dealt specifically with intergovernment relations at a metropolitan or big-city scale. The first of these was the *Greater Hobart Act 2019*, which set out strategic objectives for a metropolitan region comprising the central city of Hobart and three other municipalities, and established a Greater Hobart Committee, whose members are the four mayors and four state ministers (those for economic development, infrastructure, housing, and community development). The committee has been supported by an advisory group of senior local and state government officials.

The second body was the South East Queensland (SEQ) Regional Planning Committee, which around 2000 demonstrated a close partnership (more or less of equals) between the state government and the then SEQ Regional Organisation of Councils (resourced and forcefully led by the City of Brisbane). However, recent years have seen a strengthening of state control. A Regional Planning Committee still exists, chaired by the Deputy Premier and comprising 5 ministers and 12 mayors, but this appears to be a significantly weaker form of partnership. On the other hand, and as noted earlier, the parallel Council of Mayors, led by the dominant City of Brisbane, has been an effective advocate for collective local and regional interests.

In 2016, the then federal government launched a program of City Deals based loosely on the British model of devolved metropolitan governance, but without the element of ongoing additional resources and powers for local government – since only the states can confer the latter. Instead, Australia's City Deals focused on identifying and implementing agreed packages of projects via a series of 10–20 year federal-state agreements. However, there were provisions for – and in some instances guarantees of – robust partnerships with local governments and non-government organisations, such as universities (Burton, 2018).

Nine City Deals have been signed to date. Reflecting political priorities, three were for regional cities with populations below the threshold of 250,000 adopted for this chapter. There has appeared to be strong local government involvement in five of the others (Adelaide, Geelong, Hobart, Perth and SEQ). However, federal interest in the Western Sydney deal has focused on the mega-projects of the airport and associated transport links, and the key processes there are dominated by the state government, with municipalities in at best a supporting role (Australian Government, no date). More broadly, the Labor federal government elected in 2022 has failed to act on its promise to transform City Deals into 'real partnerships', and is allowing them to lapse without any evident replacement.

Community engagement

In all big cities, Australian municipalities are subject to various pieces of legislation that mandate community consultation on most aspects of their activities, notably strategic, corporate and land-use planning, environmental management, public works and service delivery (Christensen, 2018). Several states have required municipalities to prepare community engagement policies or strategies setting out the scope and methods of consultation they will adopt. In Victoria, that extended to requiring the use where appropriate of 'deliberative' engagement techniques such as online panels and citizens' juries (Savini and Grant, 2020).

So, while performance in this respect has remained patchy, there remains considerable scope to strengthen local democracy in big cities, if municipalities individually and collectively take their engagement responsibilities seriously, especially by supporting community advocacy. Recent research has shown how local governments can enhance the flow of information, opportunities for participation and the quality of community deliberation about major development and transport projects. This can advance inclusivity, fairness and legitimacy in decision-making processes (de Vries, 2021).

Community consultation and engagement by state and federal agencies has appeared on occasion to be improving but also to have remained, perhaps necessarily, more arms-length. Opinions differ on the extent to which agencies have taken community views seriously. For example, mounting complaints by owners of smallholdings around the Western Sydney airport and the associated 'Aerotropolis' development that their interests had been ignored, led to the appointment of an Independent Community Commissioner whose report (2023) identified inadequate communication and engagement. By contrast, in 2016 the Victorian government commissioned a lengthy citizens' jury process to determine the future of local government in Geelong, following the council's dismissal on the grounds that it had become dysfunctional.

Also, in 2017 the Victorian government established 'Metropolitan Partnerships' for each of six sub-regions in Greater Melbourne (Victoria State Government, 2023). These comprised 10 appointed local citizens together with the chief executives of each municipality in the sub-region, plus a deputy secretary from a relevant state department. The concept was to 'bring together experts and leaders from all levels of government, business and the community to identify and progress issues that matter in their region of Melbourne [and to] inform the delivery of projects, programs and services to better meet the specific needs of their communities' (Victoria State Government, 2023). In 2021 the Partnerships were renewed for another four years, and it appeared that their advice was at least being given serious consideration. On the other hand, their existence reflected the fact that the state government saw itself as the critical metropolitan manager, and it could be argued that the role of the Partnerships has the potential to diminish the standing of elected local government and community democracy in metropolitan affairs.

Proposals for reform

In recent years a range of proposals have been put forward that would address some elements of the democratic deficit in metropolitan and big-city governance.

- The central-city councils of both Melbourne (CBD News, 2021) and Sydney (Sydney Morning Herald, 2021b) have argued strongly (and, as noted earlier, successfully in the case of Sydney) for the removal of the 'double vote' for businesses. Research into the City of Melbourne's broader property franchise (Ng et al., 2017) found that 'no persuasive case has been made for corporations, groups who own rateable land and non-resident occupiers being able to vote ... local government could enhance democracy through more participative and innovative mechanisms'. The City of Brisbane and other big-city councils in south-east Queensland have no property franchise but have appeared nonetheless responsive to business interests.

- The Committee for Sydney, a business-based advocacy group, has championed 'a greater role for local government because cities need strong and vocal advocates at a local level'. It noted that municipalities 'still don't have a secure or growing revenue base to support their work nor the financial autonomy needed to be accountable to their citizens. Most importantly, they still don't receive the respect or the responsibilities the Committee believes will deliver a better city for residents'. The Committee similarly advocated an expanded role for local councils in 'shaping' Greater Sydney and called for a metropolitan Council of Mayors. It specifically noted the lack of any democratic process in appointing the members of the then Greater Sydney Commission (Committee for Sydney, 2018).

- Similarly, the Western Sydney Leadership Dialogue (2018), also a business-based body, has called for 'real' reform and strengthening of local government, including popularly elected mayors with increased authority. It also (unsuccessfully) proposed moves to improve and expand the remit of the Western Sydney City Deal by addressing governance issues, including:

  > the unevenness of power between the three levels of government ... throughout the Western Sydney City Deal process, with very little information being made public when it comes to the criteria applied to priority projects (and how they were evaluated).

- Several commentators have proposed introducing some form of metropolitan government, on the basis that due to their broader responsibilities and constituencies the states and the Commonwealth cannot focus sufficiently on complex, place-based metropolitan issues. Summarising this case, Marcus Spiller (Tomlinson and Spiller, 2018) argued:

  > ... the third prerequisite for genuine metropolitan governance, after clarity of functional mandate and fiscal autonomy, is democratic accountability ... A minimalist approach in an Australian context would involve an electoral college in which groups of constituent local governments covering logical segments of the metropolis select, by ballot, one or more of their pooled councillors to sit in the metropolitan governing body. This could operate with or without direct popular election of a metropolitan mayor. Such a model was in place in the last iteration of the Melbourne and Metropolitan Board of Works before it was disbanded as a proto-metropolitan government ... in 1985. (p.238)

However, there have been no signs of any state moving in that direction.

Conclusion

Across several Australian metropolitan regions and other big cities local government's potential as a force for place-based democracy has been undermined by state governments making heavy-handed and persistent interventions in municipal affairs. This trend has been compounded by the sector's own failings – parochialism, resistance to necessary change and a preoccupation with municipalities' corporate and political standing, rather than making wholehearted efforts to strengthen local democracy and more effectively represent community concerns and aspirations.

State and federal governments have appeared largely unconcerned about the quality of local democracy. Their focus has been on economic growth, 'mega' infrastructure projects, housing supply and winning parliamentary seats. This may sometimes translate into place-based action and genuinely engaging with municipalities and communities, but as a general rule wholly on the upper tiers' terms. Meanwhile, local MPs have very limited opportunities to scrutinise ministerial decisions and the actions of state or Commonwealth agencies in metropolitan planning and management.

Intriguingly, some of the most cogent arguments for bolstering local democracy – or at least the role of local government, which is not necessarily the same thing – come from business groups (other than the development and construction lobbies). They are perhaps particularly conscious of the failure of central governments to address place-based issues and to balance top-down directives with local policies and initiatives that underpin and advance the economic prospects of cities and regions. Notably, business sees value in more authoritative, popularly elected mayors who can lead locally and also work together at a metropolitan scale.

State governments determined to run big cities themselves – directly or by decree – seem unlikely to change course. Meaningful devolution to local areas has simply not been on the table. The election of a federal Labor government in May 2022 may herald some renewed Commonwealth interest in improving civic affairs and support for municipalities to play a more influential role. But for now, democratic improvements are most likely to depend on local governments themselves making greater use of their power of general competence and taking steps to enhance the quality of democracy and community engagement within their own realm (and to their own advantage). Several mechanisms could advance their cause and that of their constituents – more popularly elected mayors with real authority, better representation of neighbourhoods below the municipal level, expanded inter-municipal cooperation, and even the establishment of upper-tier entities with potentially greater power and political clout. Without changes like these that might act as a circuit breaker on recent trends, the future for many big-city communities looks distinctly more authoritarian, dominated by the power of states and the influence of corporations with a vested interest in large-scale urban growth.

References

ALP (Australian Labor Party) (2019) 'Labor's plan for cities', document produced in Bill Shorten's period as leader but on the website of Antony Albanese. https://perma.cc/ZY7X-PD7K

Australian Bureau of Statistics (2023) 'Latest release – Regional population', Agency webpage, 20 April. https://perma.cc/PEP3-FRU9

Australian Government (no date) *Cities*, Department of Infrastructure, Transport, Regional Development, Communications and the Arts. https://perma.cc/735G-CZU5

Burton, Paul (2018) 'Spills and City Deals: What Turnbull's urban policy has achieved, and where we go from here', *The Conversation*, 27 August. https://perma.cc/LE83-Q6CB

CBD News (2021) '"It's time for a public review": Push for election overhaul', CBD News, 25 August. https://perma.cc/E6UC-JKLG

Christensen, Helen (2018) 'Legislating community engagement at the Australian local government level', *Commonwealth Journal of Local Governance*, Issue 21: December 2018. https://perma.cc/F585-EGUU

Clark, David (2021) 'Transparency needed now and into the future', *Government News*, 2 December. https://perma.cc/X2BQ-SDFA

Committee for Sydney (2018) *A New Era for Local Government*, July. https://perma.cc/74AN-WMXC

de Vries, Sarah (2021) 'Australian local government's contribution to good governance on major projects: Increasing information, participation and deliberation', *Commonwealth Journal of Local Governance*, Issue 24: June. $ https://doi.org/10.5130/cjlg.vi24.7637

Independent Community Commissioner, NSW (2023) 'Report on Western Sydney Aerotropolis', Report online. https://perma.cc/V969-4LGE

Independent Local Government Review Panel (NSW) (2013) 'Final Report: Revitalising Local Government', Report online. https://perma.cc/TMM9-5HBS

Ng, Yee-Fui; Coghill, Ken; Thornton-Smith, Paul; Poblet, Marta (2017) 'Democratic representation and the property franchise in Australian local government', *Australian Journal of Public Administration*, vol. 76, no. 2, pp. 221–36.

Nicholls, Luke and Spiller, Marcus (2020) 'A twenty-first century framework for Australian metropolitan governance', *Australian Planner*, vol. 56, no. 2, pp.158–69. $ https://doi.org/10.1080/07293682.2020.1750443

Sansom, Graham (2019a) *The Practice of Municipal Cooperation: Australian Perspectives and Comparisons with Canada*. IMFG Papers on Municipal Finance and Governance No. 44, Institute on Municipal Finance and Governance, University of Toronto. https://perma.cc/ZFK3-EVPL

Sansom, Graham (2019b) 'Is Australian local government ready for localism?', *Policy Quarterly*, vol. 15, no. 2, May. OA at: https://perma.cc/7F5Z-RPVB

Sansom, Graham (2021) *Not So Simple: The Origins and Implications of Central Coast Council's 'Financial Calamity'*. https://perma.cc/F7KM-DEPY

Sansom, Graham and Dawkins, Jeremy (2013) 'Australia: Perth and South East Queensland' in Slack, Enid and Chattopadhyay, Rupak (eds) *Governance and Finance of Large Metropolitan Areas in Federal Systems,* Toronto: Oxford University Press, Canada, for the Forum of Federations.

Savini, Emanuela and Grant, Bligh (2020) 'Legislating deliberative engagement: Is local government in Victoria willing and able?' *Australian Journal of Public Administration*, vol. 79, no.4, pp.514–30. $ https://doi.org/10.1111/1467-8500.12420

Sydney Morning Herald (2021a) '"Silence taken as acceptance": State will intervene in tardy councils over housing', *Sydney Morning Herald*, 15 December. https://perma.cc/X56K-59KV

Sydney Morning Herald (2021b) 'Cost to ratepayers of businesses voting in City of Sydney election nears $13m', *Sydney Morning Herald*, 12 July. OA at Brisbane Times. https://perma.cc/HB2R-BX44

Terrill, Marion; Emslie, Owain; and Moran, Greg (2020) *The Rise of Megaprojects: Counting the Costs*, Melbourne: Grattan Institute, November. https://perma.cc/BCT8-RL5T

Tomlinson, Richard and Spiller, Marcus (eds) (2018) *Australia's Metropolitan Imperative: An Agenda for Governance Reform*, Canberra: CSIRO Publishing, p.238.

Victoria State Government (2023) 'Metropolitan partnerships', Agency website. https://perma.cc/S7XX-YFKT

Western Sydney Leadership Dialogue (2018) 'Governance reform for growth: Ideas on how we plan, finance, build and govern the growth centres of Greater Western Sydney'. https://perma.cc/XW2Q-LC68

Wikipedia (2023) 'Western Australia mayoral elections', online encyclopedia webpage. https://perma.cc/E3CY-BMM8

26

Systems of local government

Su Fei Tan and Graham Sansom

All six Australian states and the Northern Territory have systems of elected local government that derive their existence, boundaries, functions and powers from their constitutions and state legislation. (The Australian Capital Territory (ACT) is effectively a city-state, with no separate local governments – see Chapter 24.) The federal constitution makes no mention of this pervasive local third tier of administration. Yet the 537 local governments across the country play significant national democratic roles in two important respects. First, municipal councils reflect people's aspirations for decentralised governance, so that the more than 5,000 locally elected members can represent the voice of communities, guiding decision-making, setting longer-term strategies for their areas and contributing to national agendas. Second, councils provide a mechanism for the responsive delivery of essential local and regional infrastructure and services.

Their roles and responsibilities vary to some extent from state to state. However, in general their core functions comprise the provision of local infrastructure and municipal services, spatial planning and development control, place and environmental management, recreation facilities, and (sometimes) potable water supply and sewerage services, plus various other aspects of community wellbeing. Compared to other developed countries this range of functions is quite limited.

What does democracy require of Australian local government?

- Democratic local government should be enabled and entrenched constitutionally and in relevant legislation.
- Local voting systems should accurately reflect levels of community support for candidates and should be accessible to new citizens wishing to run for election.
- Local government areas and institutions should effectively express local and community identities and reflect communities of place.
- Principles of subsidiarity should apply and, within the constraints set out by state legislation, local government should be an independent centre of decision-making with enough financial resources to be able to make meaningful choices on behalf of citizens.

How to cite this chapter:

Tan, Su Fei and Sansom, Graham (2024) 'Systems of local government', in: Evans, Mark; Dunleavy, Patrick and Phillimore, John (eds) *Australia's Evolving Democracy: A New Democratic Audit,* London: LSE Press, pp. 544–556. **https://doi.org/10.31389/lsepress.ada.z**. Licence: CC-BY-NC 4.0

- Councillors should understand their constituents and be involved in community engagement on a regular basis.
- Councillors should be subject to effective scrutiny and should be publicly answerable to local citizens and the media.

Recent developments

The chapter begins by reviewing two recent key developments – changes in local democracy, and the impact on municipalities of the COVID-19 pandemic. Next, the SWOT analysis summarises the overall strengths, weaknesses, opportunities and threats affecting local government. The later parts of the chapter look in more depth at three more detailed issues for local democratic quality.

Electoral democracy

Across Australia local government elections are conducted under a universal residential franchise. In most areas (except for the whole of Queensland) there are also supplementary voting rights for non-resident property owners, an internationally unusual provision in a liberal democracy. In most cases elections are conducted or overseen by independent electoral commissions, and where councillors are elected by means of wards, rather than across the local government area as a whole (so-called 'at large' elections), there are usually rules for the delineation of ward boundaries aimed at ensuring 'one vote, one value'. Compulsory voting (covered in Chapter 5) applies to local government elections in Queensland, New South Wales, Victoria, urban municipalities in the Northern Territory and, only since June 2022, Tasmania. Typically, compulsory voting has produced voter turnouts of 70–80 per cent or more. In South Australia and Western Australia voting in local government elections remains voluntary, with turnouts around 30–35 per cent. In Tasmania, however, even with voluntary voting, the turnout had climbed from similar levels to almost 60 per cent. This appeared to reflect a number of factors, including the introduction of universal mail-in local voting for all citizens in 1996 (Zvulun, 2010), greater media interest in local government (likely due in part to the popular election of all mayors and deputy mayors), a strong sense of regional and local identity, and effective pre-election awareness campaigns.

Local government councillors make up a significant proportion of elected members across all levels of government. Figure 26.1 shows the number of elected members by level of government and jurisdiction. In 2015, there were approximately 5,060 local councillors in Australia (this number has since decreased as a result of municipal amalgamations in New South Wales, and persistent pressures from state governments to reduce councillor numbers generally). Except for the City of Brisbane, local governments across Australia are limited by statute to no more than 15 councillors – and very few have even that many. This reflects the neoliberal 'board of directors' model of the role councillors should play (see below). As a result, councillor to population ratios are high by international standards and in large cities can reach 1:20,000 or more. Moreover, in all jurisdictions except Queensland councillors are nominally part-time and generally lack dedicated staff support.

Figure 26.1: Australian elected representatives at all levels of government

Area	Population (in 2021, millions)	Federal (2023)			All state/territory (2024)	Local (2015)
		House	Senate	Total		
New South Wales	8.07	46	12	68	135	1,494
Victoria	6.53	38	12	50	128	631
Queensland	5.16	30	12	42	93	530
Western Australia	2.66	16	12	28	95	1,252
South Australia	1.78	10	12	22	69	716
Tasmania	0.56	5	12	17	40	280
Northern Territory	0.23	2	2	4	25	157
Australian Capital Territory	0.45	3	2	5	25	
Total	**25**	**150**	**76**	**236**	**585**	**5,060**

Source: This figure updates a table from Su Fei Tan (2020) 'Local democracy at work: An analysis of local government representatives and democracy in NSW', from which the last column ('Local 2015') is taken. The House seat allocations are from the Australian Electoral Commission (AEC, 2023). The numbers for state legislators are from Wikipedia (2024a).

Note: Queensland and the two territories have no upper houses (and so fewer representatives). Green shading shows that ACT Assembly is both the territory and the local government.

There are approximately 10 times as many councillors as elected state politicians, and 20 times as many as federal legislators per state. These councillors represent a great diversity of places and communities and govern very different kinds of organisations, ranging from metropolitan municipalities with populations of several hundred thousand that offer a wide array of services and have substantial resources, to rural and remote local governments with very small populations living in geographically large areas. Councillors are also expected to play diverse and sometimes conflicting roles, including representing the interests of their individual ward electorates and the municipal community as a whole, strategic and corporate planning and policy-making, ensuring good governance, and scrutinising the performance of both each other and their organisation, in particular the chief executive.

The impact of COVID-19

Australian local governments were severely affected by the COVID-19 pandemic and their limited resources were stretched by efforts to support local economies and communities. Some state governments (but controversially not the federal government, which allocated billions to the private and community sectors) provided substantial financial assistance to help maintain employment within the sector. The pandemic obliged local governments to make far-reaching and costly changes to modes of service delivery and to close facilities where people gather, including customer service centres, libraries, child-care services, leisure facilities and community centres. Council meetings had to move online and wherever possible staff worked from home, requiring action to strengthen their IT infrastructure and improve communications skills. Large numbers of staff were re-assigned to other roles or required to take unpaid leave; some were retrenched.

In addition, many councils introduced programs to support local businesses and community wellbeing, including action to minimise the adverse impact of isolation and loneliness.

The outcomes of the pandemic also changed the demographic profile of local government areas. The Australian Bureau of Statistics (ABS, 2021) reported that in July, August and September of 2020 Australia's capital cities experienced their highest net loss of population due to internal migration since records began. As more people moved to working-from-home arrangements, some gained greater freedom of choice in where they could live. The high cost of living in the major metropolitan areas has long provided an incentive to consider moving to attractive coastal or rural locations, notably for retirees and people looking for lower-cost housing.

In addition, the pandemic also saw state governments flex their constitutional muscles in terms of their sweeping powers and autonomy in matters of public health. This in turn led to a more assertive stance generally in the states' relations with the Commonwealth, and in the exercise of their authority over local government and civil society.

Strengths, weaknesses, opportunities and threats (SWOT) analysis

Current strengths	Current weaknesses
Effective guarantees of democratic local government are included in the state constitutions of Queensland, Victoria and to a lesser extent South Australia.	There has been no constitutional protection for democratic local government at all in New South Wales. Even where local government's existence and democratic status are assured, state constitutions do not limit states' power to intervene in local affairs. There has been no recognition of local government in the Australian federal constitution.
Compulsory voting in local elections means that turnout has been high at local government elections in Queensland, New South Wales, Victoria, Tasmania and urban areas in the Northern Territory.	Voluntary voting in Western Australia and South Australia has resulted in low voter turnouts.
Independent electoral commissions conduct or oversee most local government elections and may also set ward boundaries.	States can shape or manipulate various aspects of local elections through local government Acts, for example, by maintaining/strengthening property based voting, determining the type of voting and numbers of councillors overall and per ward, and ruling out popularly elected mayors.
Councillors exhibit a strong sense of commitment to their communities and in most cases carry out their roles on a part-time, voluntary basis.	Councillors have not been very socially diverse, with older professional men markedly over-represented. Citizens from lower income socioeconomic groups, young people, women, Indigenous communities, ethnic minorities, people with disabilities, and so on, continue to be under-represented on councils.

Local governments have generally been responsive and creative in meeting their community's needs, reflecting the knowledge and understanding councillors have of their communities.	The sheer diversity of local governments has made it difficult to identify common strategic and policy objectives – particularly when it comes to engaging with state and federal governments. Also there may be tensions between councillors and their federal and state level counterparts.
In all states local government Acts provide for elected councillors to determine strategic plans and policies in consultation with their communities, to set budgets and to monitor organisational performance in the provision of infrastructure and services.	Democratic decision-making can be challenged by institutional structures that empower the Chief Executive Officer (CEO) as head of the organisation, often with only limited oversight by councillors of their day-to-day management. The legislated role of mayors has typically been quite limited. State ministers for local government have significant 'reserve powers' to intervene in councils' affairs.
Over the past 40 years Australian local government has generally enjoyed a sound working relationship with Commonwealth governments and, until recently, a regular 'seat at the table' in key federal forums.	The recent abolition of the Council of Australian Governments (COAG) and the establishment in its place of the 'National Cabinet' (from which local government was initially excluded and has only limited involvement) has weakened local government's capacity and engagement in intergovernment relations.
Future opportunities	**Future threats**
Under their powers of general competence, local governments have scope to fill policy and program vacuums. For example, many have demonstrated a keen interest and willingness to address challenges posed by climate change.	The adverse impacts of COVID-19 continued to threaten the financial sustainability of councils in 2022, as they lost income streams while providing costly support to their communities throughout the pandemic, with potential longer effects.
There are opportunities to further leverage municipalities' position as the level of government closest to the people, by developing stronger community engagement to reinforce local democracy and decision-making.	Community trust in and support for the institutions of local government remain relatively low and may be further weakened by perceptions of poor performance in meeting local needs, inappropriate behaviour by councillors, and under-representation of women, young people and minority groups.
Continuing reform and innovation processes under way across the Australian jurisdictions provide new opportunities to strengthen local democracy and representation, and to enhance local government's status, for example, by introducing compulsory voting in South and Western Australia, both states that already have postal voting for local elections.	The COVID-19 pandemic highlighted the re-assertion of states' primacy and control within their jurisdictions, perhaps weakening local government as a democratic force.
The election in May 2022 of a Labor federal government offered opportunities to restore and strengthen federal-local relations and local government's involvement in inter-government relations more broadly.	Failure to make the most of those opportunities and/or the return of a Liberal-National (conservative) government after only one or two terms could see a long-term decline in local government's status and role.

The rest of this chapter looks in more detail at the structural influences on local government when engaging with other tiers of policy-making; how councillors and mayors represent their communities; and the evolving agenda of possible reforms.

Local government and other tiers of government

Sub-state governments are not mentioned in the 1901 Australian federal constitution. In 1974 and 1988 referenda were held to remedy that omission, in 1988 with an explicit requirement for states to entrench systems of democratic local government. However, both fell well short of the required majority support. Nevertheless, to date lack of federal constitutional recognition has not prevented direct and indirect funding of municipalities by the Commonwealth (federal) government, nor inclusion of local government representatives in a range of intergovernment forums – with the proviso that both depend on the goodwill of the Commonwealth and states.

Local government does enjoy varying degrees of recognition and protection under state constitutions, although in most cases those constitutional provisions can be altered simply by an Act of state parliament without a referendum. The form of such recognition varies widely. Typically, constitutions require the establishment of elected local governments across all or part of the state and empower the state parliament to pass laws as it sees fit for the boundaries, institutions, election and operations of those entities. Some provide additional protections for local democracy. Queensland requires a referendum to be held before a bill may be passed that would abolish the system of local government as a whole, and in South Australia such a bill requires an absolute majority of both houses of parliament. Also in Queensland, dissolution of an individual local government area must be ratified by the Legislative Assembly (LA). Victoria's constitution defines local government as a 'distinct and essential tier' of government and dismissal of an elected council requires an Act of Parliament (importantly, a constitutional provision that may only be changed by referendum).

However, none of the state constitutions guarantees democratic local government wherever that may be the people's expressed wish, and the New South Wales' constitution envisages that municipal councils may be either elected or 'duly appointed'. Nowhere does local government enjoy specific constitutionally entrenched powers or revenues, while both local government Acts and other legislation (notably that governing land-use/development planning) often include provisions that limit the rights of communities to exercise meaningful control over their local affairs.

The effectiveness of democratic local government may be constrained by state-imposed limits on revenue-raising and the spectre of ministerial oversight and intervention (see Chapter 15). New South Wales has had a system of 'rate-pegging' (setting an annual limit on increases in local property taxes) for more than four decades; Victoria introduced a similar system of 'rate-capping' in 2015; and in 2021 South Australia introduced statutory oversight of councils' financial strategies.

The wide-ranging powers of state local government ministers to oversee and intervene in the affairs of municipalities can have both positive and negative effects on local democracy. Sometimes councils may become dysfunctional when councillors are irrevocably divided on key issues. In such cases intervention in the form of an advisor appointed by the minister, or a performance improvement order, or in extreme cases a short period of suspension with the appointment of a temporary administrator, may prove helpful. However, when such interventions become commonplace and procedural constraints on ministers are minimal or non-existent, democratic values are at risk.

Weaker federal engagement

Federal and state constitutions and laws have very little to say about intergovernmental relations. What emerged, however, in the late 20th century was a framework of ministerial councils and other intergovernment forums and mechanisms, mostly established administratively rather than by legislation. Local government became part of that framework during the 1980s, and from 1992–2020 the president of the Australian Local Government Association (ALGA) was a member of the peak Council of Australian Governments (COAG) alongside the prime minister (PM) and first ministers of the states and territories. Local government was also represented on numerous ministerial councils and intergovernment committees. However, in recent years its involvement diminished, particularly under conservative Coalition federal governments, with less federal-local cooperation on policy issues and the Commonwealth's focus firmly on grants for favoured projects as opposed to increased general-purpose funding.

In April 2020 COAG was summarily disbanded by then PM Morrison as part of his response to the COVID-19 pandemic (Hitch, 2020). Morrison claimed that COAG had been cumbersome and ineffectual; he wanted a streamlined operation with a narrower agenda – a 'National Cabinet' consisting only of first ministers, that would meet frequently (monthly or even fortnightly), mostly online and 'behind closed doors' with fewer advisors in attendance. ALGA was excluded, albeit with a seat on a new 'National Federation Reform Council', which would meet annually.

The return of a federal Labor government in May 2022 brought some significant improvements to local government's position. Prime Minister Albanese (a former federal minister for local government) announced that the ALGA would attend one of four National Cabinet meetings each year, with local government issues firmly on the agenda. Also, his government would re-establish the Australian Council of Local Government (an Albanese initiative in 2008, abolished by the Coalition in 2013) to facilitate closer Commonwealth-local relations. Much has depended, however, on local government's collective performance in formulating and developing coherent, evidence-based policy positions, as opposed to simply advocating its perceived need for increased federal support.

Reassertion of state primacy and control

The impact of COVID-19, weaker engagement with the Commonwealth and the abolition of COAG were accompanied by a re-assertion of state primacy and control over local government. As noted earlier, Victoria has joined New South Wales in capping annual rates increases (Essential Services Commission, Victoria, 2021) and South Australia introduced a somewhat similar arrangement (Drew, 2018; Riddle and Johns, 2020). Several states have implemented land-use planning 'reforms' that transfer decision-making authority from municipalities to state ministers and/or their appointees. Some have subjected councillors to more demanding codes of conduct and complaints procedures; while elected councils that exhibit failures (real or perceived) to deliver good governance may be exposed to additional avenues for state intervention, suspension or dismissal.

Having given democratic local government a significant degree of autonomy plus increased scope through powers of general competence, and watched the emergence of large, well-resourced metropolitan and regional municipalities (ironically, often created by state-imposed amalgamations), some state governments now appear concerned that their erstwhile 'underling' looms as a competitor for status and resources. Within a few decades Australia will have a string of local governments with populations around 400,000 or more, big budgets, extensive professional and technical resources, significant international links around issues such as climate change, and undoubted capacity to partner directly with the Commonwealth on major initiatives. Without controls, municipal rates and charges might impede increases in state revenues, while stronger local democracy might disrupt the states' ability to determine infrastructure and development priorities and to promote preferred business investment (de Vries, 2021).

Councillors and mayors representing communities

Research in New South Wales showed that councillors felt a strong sense of commitment to their communities (Tan, 2020). In interviews, councillors identified several different but often overlapping reasons for standing for election. The primary factor was the desire to make a difference and improve the place where they live. Many spoke of pride in their hometown or the influence of family as the main source of their motivation. Some came to the attention of their local mayor through their involvement in the community and were subsequently asked to stand for election.

Despite this deep level of commitment it must also be noted that, in terms of representative democracy, in most cases the collective profile of councillors has not reflected that of the communities they represent. There has not been a national census of councillors, and data from state agencies has not always been available. The studies that have been carried out indicate that councillors are predominantly older, male professionals. In the NSW study councillors interviewed tended to possess similar characteristics in terms of age, socioeconomic class, profession and levels of education. This can be partly attributed to the structural features of local government and the resultant demands on councillors who are expected to be part-time and to work on a largely voluntary basis (except in Queensland).

Women continue to be under-represented (Wong and Zierke, 2022). In Victoria, the 2020 local government elections saw 272 female councillors (44 per cent) elected, the highest percentage nationally, but still below the state's 50 per cent target. In Tasmania, following the 2018 local government elections women made up 38 per cent of mayors, 45 per cent of deputy mayors, and 40 per cent of councillors. In 2019, 41 per cent of councillors elected in Western Australia's local government elections were women. Prior to the December 2021 local elections, women represented less than a third of all councillors and mayors serving on councils in NSW, although that number subsequently rose to nearly 40 per cent. In South Australia, a record percentage of women stood for and were elected to local government in the 2018 elections, but the percentage of female councillors remained little more than a third.

Decision-making processes are another key issue for local democracy. Legislative frameworks for decision-making by local governments typically align well with ideals of deliberative democracy. These include the need to consider a diversity of interests, the imperative for elected representatives to find compromises and the requirement to make well-informed decisions through a process of deliberation. However, while formal decision-making happens at council meetings, chief executives evidently exercise a great deal of power in shaping decision-making because they provide the material required by part-time councillors to reach decisions. Moreover, the agenda and accompanying business papers for council meetings are often very lengthy, and the sheer volume of information councillors are expected to read makes it more difficult for them to reach decisions in the best interests of their community.

Tensions between representative and participatory democracy pose particular challenges at the local level. Local government is ideally placed for facilitating citizen involvement in decision-making (Christensen, 2019). Typically, councillors and staff have a deep understanding of their communities and strong ties with their constituents, and over recent years there has been a proliferation of community engagement practice in Australian local governments, for several reasons. First, there has been a quest for better and more democratic outcomes resulting from participatory processes, and to respond to increasing demands for engagement from citizens. Second, governments have sought increased legitimacy through these practices, in an environment of community activism and increasing distrust of government. Third, the advent of technology has made it easier and more cost-effective for governments to engage with their constituents and stakeholders.

Thus local governments' knowledge, understanding and close ties with their communities lend themselves to the implementation of participatory, democratic decision-making. However, how this aligns with the statutory role of councillors and the system of representative democracy varies from council to council. In some cases councillors are very supportive of the need for further community engagement and see these processes as a way for them to interact more deeply and meaningfully with their constituents. In other cases, they see wider participation as unnecessary and a challenge to their status as an elected representative of community interests.

Electing mayors (or not)

A related issue for debate concerns the status and election of mayors. Across Australia, mayors combine ceremonial, political and to some extent quasi-executive roles. All local government Acts now describe the mayor as the political leader of the council and the local community, with especially important representative responsibilities. In recent years, amendments to several Acts have given mayors some additional authority, but except for Queensland all fall well short of creating 'executive' mayors: management remains firmly in the hands of the chief executive. As a general rule, mayors cannot exercise power in their own right and many find it difficult to exercise strong, consistent leadership. Commonly, they are elected indirectly by their fellow councillors rather than by the people and must be re-elected every one or two years. In Queensland, Tasmania and the urban areas of the Northern Territory, all mayors are popularly elected, as are a majority in South Australia and around 20 per cent in each of New South Wales and Western Australia. The latter three states have allowed individual municipalities to determine how the mayor was elected, but popular election did not come with any enhanced role or authority. In Victoria, popular election of mayors has been specifically precluded, except for the City of Melbourne, where it has been mandatory – as for all capital city Lord Mayors.

Continuing processes of reform

In all states local government has been subject to seemingly continuous processes of reform. These have compounded since the 1980s in response to changing ideas and expectations about how government is meant to operate, notably as a result of the widespread adoption of 'new public management' models. The primary aim of most reforms in local government has been to increase efficiency and effectiveness in service provision. At the same time, local government's remit has expanded from a narrow focus on property-related services ('roads, rates and rubbish') to encompass varied roles in planning, environmental management, economic development and community wellbeing. However, this model of a diverse range of activities and service delivery being determined by a citizen-elected body and administered by a single administrative organisation has not been paralleled by still-siloed state or federal agencies. Perhaps as a result, the complexities and capabilities within local government are poorly understood and undervalued by central governments, and this hampers effective intergovernment relations.

State and territory governments all amended their local government Acts between 1989 and 1995. Since then Queensland introduced a new Act in 2009, the Northern Territory in 2019 and Victoria in 2020. Other states have made (or began making) substantial amendments to their Acts. A key outcome of legislative change has been the granting of 'powers of general competence' to local governments, giving them more discretion over the roles they play and operational matters. For example, the *Victorian Local Government Act 2020* defines the role of a council as being to provide good governance in its municipal district for the benefit and wellbeing of the municipal community (Wikipedia, 2024b). It then provides that a council may perform any duties or functions or exercise any powers conferred on it by any Act, as well as any other functions that the council determines are necessary to enable it to perform its role, including some to be undertaken outside its municipal district.

The impact of these reforms on the role of councillors and on local democracy has been significant. In the case of NSW, historically the *Local Government Act 1919* identified the mayor as the 'chief executive officer', and the 'town or shire clerk' was in effect the chief administrative officer. In addition, the chief engineer and the health and building inspector also had their powers described in the legislation. The *Local Government Act 1993* (influenced by 'new public management' policy objectives) altered this arrangement, abolishing the town clerk position and establishing a General Manager/CEO who became the elected council's sole employee, with powers to appoint all other staff and to manage the organisation and implement the council's plans and policies more or less as she or he sees fit (subject to achieving the desired outcomes). For example, while councillors have input into and formally adopt the required 10-year community strategic plan, it then falls to the chief executive (and their staff) to fine-tune and implement the programs and activities necessary to achieve the plan's goals and objectives. The role of being a councillor has thus changed from being in touch with the day-to-day functioning of the organisation to exercising 'arms-length' responsibilities for setting strategic and policy directions, adopting the budget and monitoring progress.

This shift in theory and practice has proved problematic. In a discussion of local government reform in the Northern Territory, Sanders (2013) documented the frustration and confusion experienced by councillors who, following a change in the legislation, were no longer able, nor were they permitted, to deal directly with staff. Instead, councillors were being told to direct their questions and concerns through council meetings to the central shire administration and that appropriate directives would then be passed on. This denied councillors the direct relationship that they were used to. They felt that the new legislation was not meeting their needs and should be changed so that councillors and staff 'can work together' to attend to problems on a day-to-day basis. Further research is needed to establish the extent to which such concerns persist, but anecdotal evidence suggests they may still be widespread.

Moreover, the separation between policy and administration may sit uncomfortably with the realities of local representation. The 2013 report of the NSW Independent Local Government Review Panel (2013) noted that the role of a councillor is divided into two parts: as a member of the collective 'governing body' and as an 'elected person'. The former was seen in terms of deliberative planning, resource allocation, policy development and performance monitoring, removed from everyday administration and akin to a board of directors. The latter involves community representation, leadership and communication: it is more clearly political and includes those functions that most councillors would regard as fundamental to meeting their constituents' expectations and being re-elected. The Panel's investigations suggested that amendments to the local government Act were necessary to explain these contrasting roles – and how they interrelate – more clearly. Legislative changes were also recommended to clarify the relationships between councillors, mayors and the chief executive. Amendments along these lines were subsequently implemented in 2016, but no research exists to confirm whether or not councillors fully understand the challenges and implications of reconciling their various responsibilities, as well as their relationships with the chief executive and senior management.

Amalgamations

Another set of actions that directly impacts local democracy has been the structural reform of areas to amalgamate local governments or make boundary changes. Australian state and territory governments have long criticised small (in population and/or area) municipalities and claimed that larger organisations would be more efficient and effective, hence able to deliver better quality and a wider range of services. Several rounds of sweeping amalgamations occurred in the 1990s and early 2000s, except in Western Australia (see Figure 26.2). More recently, in 2016 the NSW government reduced the number of local government areas again from 152 to 128. In 2024 the Australian Local Government Association had 537 member councils, but a few may not have joined it (ALGA, 2024). Whether amalgamations have indeed resulted in efficiencies and cost-savings has remained hotly contested (Drew, Kortt and Dollery, 2013). An alternative view has been that in selected cases they can enhance local government's 'strategic capacity' to play a stronger role on behalf of local communities in the wider system of government, and in that sense strengthen democracy (Aulich, Sansom and McKinlay, 2013).

Mergers of councils are often bitterly opposed by local residents and politicians affected. For example, responding to the announcement of amalgamations in NSW in 2015, the mayor of Woollahra in Sydney's affluent eastern suburbs said her council would fight a forced merger with neighbouring Randwick and Waverley. ABC News (2015) quoted her as saying: 'I don't think people in Woollahra are going to roll over … If we are forced [to amalgamate], that just reinforces the view that democracy is dead in New South Wales.' Woollahra subsequently took their case to the High Court (Visentin, 2017). Resistance to forced mergers was typically based on a desire to retain the local character of an area, plus fears that larger areas would mean less local representation and advocacy, a weaker locality-specific voice with regard to land use planning decisions, and poorer or less appropriate services.

Figure 26.2: The number of local councils in Australia, 1982–2012

State/Territory	1982	1990	1995	2008	2012
New South Wales	175	176	177	152	152 *
Victoria	211	210	184	79	79
Western Australia	138	138	144	142	139
South Australia	127	n/a	119	68	68
Queensland	134	134	125	73	73
Tasmania	49	46	29	29	29
Northern Territory	6	22	63	16	16
Total	840	726	841	559	556

Source: Dollery, Kortt and Grant (2013) Funding the Future: Financial Sustainability and Infrastructure Finance in Australian Local Government, Sydney: The Federation Press, p.218.

Note: * In 2016, amalgamations in NSW saw the number of councils reduced from 152 to 128.

The impact on local representation lies in the number of residents each councillor represents: amalgamated councils invariably have fewer elected members than the combined total of their predecessors. The consequences for local democracy are unclear, and there has been limited research on the subject (Aulich, Sansom and McKinlay, 2013). This can be attributed to several factors. First, the impact on local representation may not be that obvious or readily appreciated, and public concern may dissipate once a reduction in councillor numbers has been accepted as the new norm. Second, in some mergers specific measures were put in place to ensure that the perceived quality of local democracy was not unduly affected (for example, by implementing ward structures or establishing transition committees in affected communities). Third, the new, larger councils may have become more conscious of the importance of transparency and accountability and made improvements in these areas to offset their having fewer councillors.

Conclusion

Local government offers citizens valuable opportunities to engage in democratic politics on issues that closely concern them and to directly experience making a difference, providing a seedbed for advancing democratic processes, engagement and understanding. Improving current performance might start with councils and states making concerted efforts to encourage a more diverse range of candidates to stand for office, thus achieving a mix of elected representatives that better reflects their community in terms of age, gender, socioeconomic status, and so on. Building the capacity of councillors to fulfil an expansive vision of their roles, responsibilities and how they fit within the local government system could also be a key element. Since local government is required to operate within the frameworks and constraints established by state and, to a lesser extent, federal governments, enhancing the value that those governments place on local democracy also remains vital. Strengthening the local base of Australia's democratic life will require commitment and collaboration across all three levels.

References

ABC News (2015) 'NSW councils to merge under State Government plan for forced amalgamations', ABC News 17 December, webpage. https://perma.cc/ZTR5-5SHG

ABS (Australian Bureau of Statistics) (2021) 'Regional internal migration estimates'. Agency webpage. https://perma.cc/E6V6-NQ2M

AEC (Australian Electoral Commission) (2023) 'State/territory entitlement to electoral divisions', Webpage, 27 July. https://perma.cc/2UTY-ZT39

ALGA (Australian Local Government Association) (2024) 'About ALGA', Webpage. https://perma.cc/6KQK-S6CF

Aulich, Chris; Sansom, Graham; and McKinlay, Peter (2013) 'A fresh look at municipal consolidation in Australia', *Local Government Studies*, vol. 40, no. 1, pp.1–20. $ https://www.tandfonline.com/doi/pdf/10.1080/03003930.2013.775124

Christensen, Helen (2019) 'Legislating community engagement at the Australian local government level', *Commonwealth Journal of Local Governance*, vol. 21, Article ID 6515. $ https://doi.org/10.5130/cjlg.v0i21.6515

de Vries, Sarah (2021) 'Australian local government's contribution to good governance on major projects: Increasing information, participation and deliberation,' *Commonwealth Journal of Local Governance*, Issue 24. $ https://doi.org/10.5130/cjlg.vi24.7637

Dollery, Brian; Kortt, Michael; and Grant, Bligh (2013) *Funding the Future: Financial Sustainability and Infrastructure Finance in Australian Local Government*, Sydney: The Federation Press.

Drew, Joseph (2018) *Rate Capping in South Australia: Implications, Desirable Amendments, and Preparedness*. Report, University of Technology Sydney Centre for Local Government, Ultimo, NSW. https://perma.cc/3Q9B-CJG2

Drew, Joseph; Kortt, Michael A; and Dollery, Brian (2013) 'A cautionary tale: Council amalgamation in Tasmania and the Deloitte Access Economics Report', *Australian Journal of Public Administration*, vol. 72, no. 1, pp.55–65. $ https://doi.org/10.1111/1467-8500.12011

Essential Services Commission, Victoria (2021) 'Annual council rate caps'. Agency webpage. https://perma.cc/UN8R-78Z4

Hitch, Georgia (2020) 'Scott Morrison says National Cabinet here to stay, will replace COAG meetings in wake of coronavirus', *ABC News*, 29 May. https://perma.cc/2FXP-PLWN

Independent Local Government Review Panel (NSW) (2013) *Revitalising Local Government*, Final Report of the NSW Independent Local Government Review Panel. https://perma.cc/MM58-G3RB

Riddle, Tracy and Johns, Tyler (2020) 'South Australian inquiry into local government rate capping policies' Kelledy Jones Lawyers 'Local reporter' webpage. https://perma.cc/U6V2-HTBL

Sanders, Will (2013) 'Losing localism, constraining councillors: Why the Northern Territory supershires are struggling'. *Policy Studies*, vol. 34, no. 4, pp.474–90. $ https://perma.cc/7GVM-VW6N

Tan, Su Fei (2020) *Local Democracy at Work: An Analysis of Local Government Representatives and Democracy in NSW*. PhD Thesis, University of Technology Sydney. https://perma.cc/NF43-JG8F

Visentin, Lisa (2017) 'High Court to decide Woollahra Council's merger fight', *Sydney Morning Herald*, 12 May 2017. https://perma.cc/5RHR-QKA7

Wikipedia (2024a) 'Parliaments of the Australian States and Territories', Online encyclopedia webpage. https://perma.cc/XW45-PQRG

Wikipedia (2024b) '[Victoria] Local Government Act, 2020', Online encyclopedia webpage. https://perma.cc/52ZZ-CJAC

Wong, Cindy and Zierke, Merle (2022) 'Briefing: Embedding gender equality in local government', Local Government Information Unit. https://perma.cc/M6T3-7UY2

Zvulun, Jacky (2010) 'Postal voting and voter turnout in local elections: Lessons from New Zealand and Australia', *Lex Localis, Journal of Local Self-Government*, vol. 8, no. 2, pp.115–31. $ https://doi.org/10.4335/8.2.115-131(2010)

Challenges and Change

27. Political institutions in the Anthropocene 559
    Pierrick Chalaye and John S. Dryzek

28. Democratic resilience and change 574
    Patrick Dunleavy and Mark Evans

27

Political institutions in the Anthropocene

Pierrick Chalaye and John S. Dryzek

Human institutions developed during the unusually stable Holocene epoch of the past 12,000 years. Its successor is the Anthropocene, the emerging epoch in which we live, defined by human activity decisively affecting the parameters of the Earth system as a whole. As a result of human actions and interventions, the global environment will become more unstable and susceptible to potentially catastrophic state shifts. Our established human institutions must now adapt to Anthropocene conditions or be discarded. Existing dominant practices and institutions (such as states and markets) suffer from pathological path dependencies. They generate forms of feedback that reinforce their own indispensability but are themselves insensitive to the condition of the Earth system. This chapter explores what can be done, in Australia, the only continent in the world to be governed by a single (albeit federal) state.

What does the Anthropocene require of Australia's political institutions?

- The key antidote needed for established institutions to adapt their behaviours is ecological reflexivity (Dryzek and Pickering, 2019). Reflexivity means the capacity of an institution, structure, or set of ideas to reflect on its own performance and core commitments, and if necessary, transform itself in response. Ecological here means openness to feedback on the condition of the Earth system, and the capacity to anticipate and forestall potentially catastrophic state-shifts in that system.
- Ecological reflexivity is the first virtue needed for social institutions in the Anthropocene. It cannot be reduced to sustainability or more effective environmental policy, but requires instead deep recognition, reflection and response.
- Recognition means listening for changes in socioecological systems, monitoring human impacts on those systems and anticipating changes and impacts in the future.
- Reflection means learning from past success and failure, the capacity to rethink core values and practices and envisioning possible futures.

How to cite this chapter:

Chalaye, Pierrick and Dryzek, John (2024) 'Political institutions in the Anthropocene', in: Evans, Mark; Dunleavy, Patrick and Phillimore, John (eds) *Australia's Evolving Democracy: A New Democratic Audit*, London: LSE Press, pp.559–573. https://doi.org/10.31389/lsepress.ada.aa. Licence: CC-BY-NC 4.0

- Response means the rearticulation of core aims, values, and discourses, and reconfiguration of functions and practices.
- Reflexive institutions need to demonstrate that democracy and justice can be preserved (and advanced) in the Anthropocene. The contours of both democracy and justice will need to be re-thought.
- Planetary justice must also be addressed because of the inequality of suffering that follows from an unstable Earth system.

Before proceeding, we note that ecological reflexivity is not necessarily served equally well by different kinds of democracy. A deliberative approach that emphasises meaningful communication encompassing citizens and leaders about matters of common concern might on the face of it be expected to do better than approaches that stress majority rule or the reconciliation of different interests, because individual and collective reflection is one of its defining features. But even that would need to be demonstrated rather than asserted.

Aggregate indicators of environmental performance suggest that Australia starts from a particularly low point in comparison with other developed countries. On greenhouse gas (GHG) emissions per capita (Environmental Performance Index, 2017), Australia is equal worst of 180 countries surveyed by the World Economic Forum in 2020 (alongside eight petrostates). The OECD concluded in 2019 that the state of Australia's biodiversity is 'poor and worsening' (2019). But it is not obvious that countries performing much better than Australia in terms of such summary indicators could be judged any better in terms of the overall demands of the new epoch on all states. Therefore, we need to dig more deeply in this Anthropocene audit of Australia.

Recent developments

The first component of reflexivity is the 'recognition' of impacts, especially an acute sensitivity to destructive changes that may be irreversible. On the face of it, climate change in particular has been widely recognised in Australian politics (as it has been in most other countries) – although a significant minority who deny evidence of adverse climate change remain politically powerful. Recognition of other aspects of instability in the Earth system fares less well. Biodiversity per se is weakly conceptualised as an issue in Australia, although particular cases of sensitive biodiversity loss (such as the bleaching of the Great Barrier Reef, land clearance and catastrophic losses of wildlife and habitats in bushfires) are more likely to be acknowledged. Awareness of ocean acidification, land system changes and biochemical flows (phosphorus and nitrogen) is even less well developed.

Before the fact, many media commentators characterised the May 2019 election as a 'climate election'. But to what extent did this prove true? The unexpected win for the Liberal-National Coalition hinged on its strong performance in coal-producing rural electoral districts in Queensland, suggesting that inaction on climate change and support for expanded investment in coal worked in its favour. Matters played out very differently in urban electoral districts. Notably, in Warringah in Sydney, coal and climate change contributed to the defeat of former Prime Minister (PM) and leading climate change denier Tony Abbott (Coalition) by Zali Steggall (Independent) (Crowley, 2021).

In fact, a case could be made that the 2019 election led to no gains in reflection at all. Instead, it further solidified the pre-existing societal polarisation on climate issues between youth, urban residents and women – generally supportive of climate action – on the one hand; and older, male and rural Australians, who are more sceptical, on the other (Colvin and Jotzo, 2021). In conventional electoral politics, climate change is seen as a venue where partisan advantage can be sought or lost, rather than as a collective problem to be solved, suggesting there is something very wrong with Australia's adversarial party system when it comes to both the reflection and response aspects of reflexivity.

Climate change turned out to play a bigger and more positive role in the May 2022 federal election. It was one of the keys to the success of the six 'Teal' Independents and three Greens in lower house seats, and one independent in the Senate (see Chapter 5). All except one of these candidates unseated Liberals.

Shortly after the 2019 election, instability in the Earth system made itself felt in a big way with the unprecedented destruction and unhealthy air quality that persisted for months in several major cities caused by the 2019–2020 summer bushfires. But the Coalition government and its supporters did everything they could to dampen or suppress recognition of any link between the bushfires and climate change. National MPs, and some Liberals, instead blamed arson and increasing fuel loads, the latter allegedly resulting from the active role of the Greens in preventing hazard-reduction burns and land-clearing, even though the Greens had never been in government in any of the most affected states (Mocatta and Hawley, 2020).

From March 2020 onwards, the bushfire crisis was soon displaced from the public agenda in the COVID-19 pandemic, which further aided governmental suppression of environmental concern. Rather than the 'build back better' themes used by governments elsewhere, the Morrison Coalition government argued for a 'gas-led recovery', renewing its commitment to fossil fuels, ostensibly as a way to respond to the socioeconomic consequences of the COVID-19 pandemic. The shift placed Australia among the least green countries in this respect (O'Callaghan, 2021).

Changes in the structure and organisation of the federal government, as well as in the way portfolios are interpreted, have further impeded recognition and reflection. In the 2019 government reshuffle, Morrison separated the environment and energy portfolios. Responsibility for climate change is now largely under energy, but this did not resolve earlier failures to integrate climate concerns into energy policy (OECD, 2019 and IEA, 2018). In 2021 Environment Minister, Sussan Ley, announced that she had no responsibility for climate change mitigation (that is, reduction of emissions), only for resilience and adaptation (responding to the effects of climate change) (Murphy, 2021). Resilience might sound as though it could contribute to reflexivity, but it is an elastic concept that can also be interpreted as the ability to absorb punishment while maintaining unchanged the essential structure of social, economic and political systems.

Between 2021 and 2024 Grant King, a former head of natural gas firm Origin Energy and of the Business Council of Australia, was head of the Climate Change Authority (CCA), confirming the Morrison government's concern to slow or impede recognition of a climate crisis and Earth system instability. King's background was in the gas industry, and he was known for his criticism of investment in renewable energy. This is not an isolated case. Since 2013, the Commonwealth government has allocated key government positions to fossil fuel advocates. As a result, key climate and energy institutions set up before 2013 have been:

- either dismantled, as with the Australian Climate Commission
- deflected from their original mission, as with CCA, or
- marginalised and under-resourced, as with the Australian Renewable Energy Agency (ARENA), and the Clean Energy Finance Corporation (CEFC) (Climate Action Tracker, 2020).

The net consequence has been to promote what is called 'carbon lock-in' – that is, solidifying the reliance of the political economy on fossil fuels. Lock-in is the antithesis of reflexivity.

In line with this failure on climate issues, the Coalition government actively tried to suppress recognition of environmental damage on other fronts. A particularly prominent example was Australia's intense and ongoing lobbying of UNESCO on the status of the Great Barrier Reef, which in 2021 succeeded in preventing the Reef from being classified as 'endangered', forcing UNESCO to reverse a previous decision that was based on science rather than lobbying (Morrison et al., 2020).

Multiple reports have exposed a major decline in Australia's biodiversity and ecosystem integrity as well as the inadequacy of its environmental legal framework under the *Environmental Protection and Biodiversity Conservation (EPBC) Act 1999*. A 2020 Independent Review of the *EPBC Act* conducted by Professor Graeme Samuel identified numerous weaknesses and failures to protect biodiversity, but received minimal response from the government that commissioned it. The most obvious issues are the weakness of environmental impact assessments and the numerous exemptions for industry sectors (like native forest logging) from complying with them. But this has led to no reflection on institutional weaknesses, let alone any response in the form of proposals to strengthen environmental protection.

One reform that has been attempted (in amendments to the *EPBC Act* introduced to Parliament in 2020) is to fully delegate the approval of development projects to states. Labor, the Greens, and some independents are opposed to this 'single touch' change (also previously known as 'one-stop-shop reform'), and it is still pending at the time of writing. The government's intent is to reduce environmental obstacles to economic development. However, the result may not necessarily be bad for reflexivity, if the states are run by environmentally more progressive governments than at federal level. As of 2023 that has mostly been the case.

Most states and territories have not suppressed ecological concerns to the same extent as the Commonwealth government. For instance, despite the many problems with such a target (for example, its (over)reliance on carbon dioxide removal and offset techniques, such as mass tree planting and carbon capture devices), all states and territories have adopted a net zero GHG emissions target, including a legislated one in Victoria, where a 2017 Act specified net zero by 2050, before the federal government reluctantly and ambiguously embraced net zero by 2050 in 2021. In 2022, the new federal Labor government legislated net zero by 2050 and a 43 per cent reduction of GHG emissions compared to 2005 levels by 2030. However, in general, these targets and environmental policy in states and territories are still far from adequate, considering the depth of negative environmental change in Australia (Ward et al., 2021). This is especially the case when targets are not accompanied by policies that would make them plausible, and conflict with federal government practice. After the 2022 federal election, Labor Resources Minister Madeleine King continued to insist that new fossil fuel projects were necessary for the economy. In July 2022, PM Albanese agreed, arguing further that Australia should continue to develop coal exports because they yielded less emissions than alternative sources in other countries. All this suggested that symbolic commitments with no adequate policies that could achieve them would continue to dominate.

However, 2023 did see the most important federal climate legislation for over a decade (though that is a very low bar). The *Safeguard Mechanism (Crediting) Amendments Act 2023* required 5 per cent per year reductions to 2030 in GHG emissions for 215 major polluters. The Act was passed with support from independents and (reluctantly) the Greens – Greens leader Adam Bandt described dealing with the Labor government as 'like negotiating with the political wing of the coal and gas corporations' (Guardian, 2023). The Greens had unsuccessfully sought a commitment from Labor to ban new coal and gas projects.

With a continent-wide government, and unique eco-systems of its own, Australia has numerous advantages that could help it to respond positively to the challenges posed by the Anthropocene. In terms of ecological reflexivity, Australia is at a crossroads. On the one hand, the country has obvious current strengths – such as a deep socioecological history, a flexible federal system, and relatively strong though recently weakened environmental science institutes. There are also many opportunities to respond to ecological challenges – such as a great potential for developing renewable energy, an international context that pushes Australia towards climate action and has made some states fairly committed to renewable energy.

However, these strengths are counterbalanced by multiple and often structural weaknesses that undermine Australia's capacity to be ecologically reflexive. Australia is still moving towards a future that largely turns its back on ecological issues, a course that has not changed in recent decades. For example, recent cuts to environmental science programs, the anti-environmental radicalisation of parts of the media and political parties, and the lack of reflection on the ecological dimension of the COVID-19 crisis are all indicators that Australia does not intend to conceptualise ecological issues as opportunities to rethink its institutions or the principles that guide them.

Strengths, weaknesses, opportunities and threats (SWOT) analysis

Current strengths	Current weaknesses
Identity and environmental issues	
While not always drawn upon in public policy, Australia has a deep socioecological history embodied in the worldviews and knowledge systems of Aboriginal and Torres Strait Islander peoples. Fire management is a well-known case in point, but other areas such as agriculture (Pascoe, 2014), water and land management (Gammage, 2012), and the rights of nature are also prominent examples. Government support comes in 'Caring for Country' Indigenous land management programs.	A significant part of the Australian political class, associated with a wing of the Liberal Party and the National Party, holds a strong ideological position (described by Dryzek, 2021 as 'grey radicalism'). As a matter of core identity, this view rejects climate change and environmental concerns. Consequently, its exponents cannot be reached by economic (let alone environmental) argument and evidence. The power of grey radicalism impedes reflexivity, even getting to the point of denying recognition of environmental problems. Grey radicalism also rejects any relevance for Indigenous knowledge systems.

Institutions and agenda-setting	
A federal structure allows states/territories to initiate some environmental reforms and 'path-find' new solutions. States have generally been in advance of the federal government in responding to climate change.	Australia scores among the lowest countries in the OECD on the health of its ecosystems, forest management, fish stocks, climate mitigation, air pollution (Environment Performance Index 2020; Climate Council, 2019). It also scores among the highest on materials and resources consumption per capita (OECD, 2021). Despite this, there is no federal willingness to recognise the severity of problems or to initiate structural cross-sectoral reforms on these key issues. And there is only a limited response capacity at the state and territory level. Policy-making has often been 'disjointed' (Warren et al., 2016).
Australia has made some very limited progress in creating supplementary subnational governance structures that fit with ecosystem boundaries and bring together federal and multiple state governments to focus on making 'holistic' policies – notably in the Murray-Darling Basin Authority (MDBA) and the Great Barrier Reef Marine Park Authority (GBRMPA).	The boundaries of state and territories were mainly drawn in an imperial age, and thus are chiefly straight lines 'dividing the cake' of a whole continent in arbitrary ways. The MDBA and GBRMPA remain weak, vulnerable to subversion by 'vested interests' and, in the case of the MDBA, domination by conflict between state governments.
The courts have also shown some signs of forcing government to anticipate the consequences of its decisions more effectively. A notable 2021 decision of the Federal Court found that the federal minister for the environment had a duty of care to protect all young people threatened by climate change (though this decision was overturned in 2022).	A great deal of environmental policy depends on the detailed regulatory decisions of governments, which Australian courts in the 'Westminster system' and 'common law' tradition have been reluctant to overturn (see Chapter 3). Therefore, there are limits to what the courts can do.
Environmental science	
Leading scientific institutions such as the Commonwealth Scientific and Industrial Research Organisation (CSIRO) provide Australia with significant scientific capacity to recognise environmental problems and chart complex ecological transitions – for example, see CSIRO (2015).	Significant cuts in governmental funding have weakened Australia's scientific capacity, particularly in climate change and adaptation programs, and especially affecting CSIRO's scientific work (OECD, 2019).
Media landscape	
Social media now offer alternative platforms through which relatively diverse opinions can be expressed. This change has limited the negative impact of misinformation and related controversies, especially those fuelled in and by News Corp and other extreme conservative media (Stutzner et al., 2021). However, social media too can spread and amplify misinformation, such as climate change denialism (see Chapter 9).	Australia has a highly concentrated media landscape. Murdoch's News Corp owns more than 60 per cent of daily newspapers by circulation (including *The Australian* and the *Herald Sun*) – see Chapter 8. Until a seemingly coordinated change of position in late 2021, opposed by some of its most prominent columnists, it has consistently fuelled denial of climate change. It still supports the coal and other fossil fuel industries and excoriates environmentalists.

Discourse and framing	
There have been times in the past (notably under the Hawke government) when a positive-sum framing of environmental issues enabled cooperation encompassing a broad range of interests. For example, this period produced the Ecologically Sustainable Development process (1990–1991) and the establishment of Landcare (in Victoria 1986, nationally 1989). Historically, Australia was a pioneer in environmental conservation and has, at times, experienced strong coalitions on key socioenvironmental issues, such as Landcare.	A toxic and long-standing 'jobs versus environment' framing of environmental issues has been amplified by the adversarial two-party system. This false trade-off has prevented the emergence of a cross-sectoral and cross-party discourse on reconciling job creation and environmental protection via ecological modernisation. Many different environmental issues get systematically distorted through the prism of this framing.
International context	
As long as Donald Trump was president, Australia had some cover for its failure to act on climate change in particular. Since 2020, the Biden presidency has exhorted Australia to do more on reducing GHG emissions. If taken at face value, the 2015 Paris Agreement on climate change means that thermal coal has no economic future, so the Australian coal industry (which until recently accounted for a third of world coal exports) may be forced into decline.	The Australian government has been at best a passive (often even the 'least progressive') actor in current international environmental governance. Since 2019 it has been dragged reluctantly into compliance with emerging international norms and trade conditions.
Future opportunities	**Future threats**
Identity and environmental issues	
First Law (also known as the Law of 'country'), which conditions relationships between humans and between humans and non-human beings, is being incorporated into some local governance mechanisms on an experimental basis, as in the Kimberley region (Poelina, Taylor and Perdrisat, 2019). Expansion of this idea could heighten how receptive governance systems are to signs from the Earth system.	Persistent influence from the discourse of grey radicalism could further polarise public debate. It may prevent Australia from recognising, reflecting on and responding to the intensity of ongoing ecological changes (for example, changes to fire regimes or biodiversity collapses).
Institutions and agenda setting	
Even states governed by the Coalition show some degree of recognition of the need to act on climate change, biodiversity conservation and renewable energy. Others are more advanced. For instance, the Australian Capital Authority (ACT) and Tasmania are already 100 per cent powered with renewable energy. And all state governments at least recognise the need to move to renewables in due course, unlike the Commonwealth (Climate Council, 2019). In addition, major banks and corporations have increasingly become insistent on the need to act on climate change and sometimes other environmental issues included in Environmental and Social Governance (ESG) indicators (Ramsay and Freeburn, 2021). This suggests governance leadership is moving from the public to the private sector.	COVID-19 overshadowed environmental concerns in 2020–2021, and the Australian government did not interpret it as a systemic issue related to degraded human-nature relationship (O'Callaghan, 2021). To tackle issues such as climate change and biodiversity, the Commonwealth government remains solely committed to, even expanding, a flawed system of grants and subsidies. In practice, these have proved open to gaming, abuse or even deliberate misdirection (for example, massive funding to the Great Barrier Reef Foundation). Limited (if any) positive outcomes have been demonstrated for conservation.

Environmental science	
Australia's scientific institutions could have their funding restored and better engage in international (for example, UNFCCC, IPCC) and national governance bodies and institutions (for example, Australian Energy Regulator).	Further budget cuts in socioecological science would be particularly detrimental both for mitigating ongoing structural ecological changes or adapting to them.
Media landscape	
Other highly concentrated media landscapes have not proven fatal to climate change coverage. In the UK, the power of the Murdoch media empire did not prevent significant progress on climate change under successive Conservative governments since 2010. In 2021, News Corporation in Australia pivoted to at least recognise the reality of climate change. Could News Corporation change further in Australia, especially on the passing of Rupert Murdoch, and under any new generation of leadership?	Governmental attempts to 'regulate' the content of social media in response to legitimate concerns over misinformation could restrict the diversity of views expressed in these spaces. The Murdoch media empire may seek to replicate the success of its Fox News network in the USA – which used extremist programming to 'weaponise' grey radicalism (as part of culture war discourse), SKY News has already followed this approach in its 'Sky After Dark' evening programming.
Discourse and framing	
Australia can be inspired by the many places where ecological modernisation has already occurred, notably in Europe. Voters and politicians may recover their own temporary domestic experience with this discourse in the Hawke era (Curran, 2015). One possible central framing is the idea that Australia could be a 'renewable energy superpower', popularised by Ross Garnaut (2008), author of the landmark *Climate Change Review*.	The climate denialism narrative stresses that Australia should be 'proud' of its current efforts to tackle climate change relative to other nations (Murphy and Morton, 2021). This stance could become more pervasive and extend to other issues, further contributing to failure to recognise the need to act against catastrophic governmental failure.
International context	
UK and EU carbon tariffs (placed on goods whose embedded emissions would be taxed if they were produced in the country or Union in question) could induce Australian producers to reduce emissions. (In 2021, Minister for Energy and Emissions Reduction Angus Taylor declared the Australian government's opposition to such mechanisms, impeding the progress of a UK–Australia free trade deal.) Responding to the signals of the Paris Agreement, financial institutions are no longer funding coal projects. China's actions restricting imports of coal (in response to Australia aligning more with a USA-lead anti-China defence stance) could force the curtailing of coal mining in Queensland and elsewhere.	International environmental governance continues to have weak compliance mechanisms (compared to trade and finance governance). It also tends to focus on climate change and does not necessarily insist on the multi-faceted aspects of environmental change. Biodiversity loss, reef destruction, forest change (for example, in the fire regime but also structural changes in ecosystems), and water management are all interrelated issues.

The electoral politics of climate change

We have already suggested that there is something wrong with Australia's party system when it comes to processing issues, such as climate change. Here we go deeper into the recent history of this issue in electoral politics. In the mid-2000s both major parties accepted the need to do something on climate change mitigation. Indeed, both proposed an emissions trading scheme to curb GHG emissions at the 2007 election. Although the then Liberal PM John Howard was actually a climate sceptic, he reluctantly accepted the need to follow what seemed to be shifting public opinion in favour of action.

The newly elected Labor government under Kevin Rudd then introduced legislation for a Carbon Pollution Reduction Scheme (CPRS), with emissions trading at its heart, and in 2009 it seemingly had secured the support of the Liberals, now led by Malcolm Turnbull. The Greens were opposed, holding out for more ambitious GHG pollution reduction. However, in just over a year Turnbull quickly fell victim to a party caucus coup organised by the right wing and climate-denial wing of the Liberals (see Chapter 13). His replacement as leader was the virulent climate change denier Tony Abbott, meaning the tenuous bipartisan consensus of 2007 disintegrated, and the CPRS failed. Rudd then essentially withdrew from the fray. From that time on the parliamentary Liberal Party has been committed to inaction on climate change. (Their Coalition partners in the National Party represented regional rural areas in the main and were dominated by MPs who were climate change deniers.) Even when Turnbull returned to the leadership of the Liberals (becoming PM) in 2015–2018, it was on the condition that he accept the position of the far right on climate change, irrespective of his personal views on the issue (Mazengarb, 2020). In government, the Liberal Party leadership has generally paid lip service to the existence of climate change. But the Coalition government's only policy response has been a manifestly ineffective 'direct action' system of subsidies and grants for projects that would notionally reduce emissions. Then, 2021 saw a chaotic and internally divisive formal embrace by the government of the net zero by 2050 target for GHG emissions, but the symbolic commitment was accompanied by no signs that this would lead to any change in policies. It is conceivable that the symbolic commitment alone may further solidify the reluctance of financial institutions to back fossil fuel projects.

Within the Labor Party, Rudd's failure on climate change was arguably a contributing factor to his loss of credibility and so eventual demise as leader (see Chapters 6 and 13). His successor Julia Gillard faced her own problems. Needing the support of the Greens to govern after a very close 2010 election in the House of Representatives, her government introduced, and parliament passed, a carbon tax – even though she had promised before the election that this would not happen. It was misrepresented by the Coalition as 'a great big tax on everything', who promised its repeal at the next election in 2013, which they won. Thus, the only demonstrably successful GHG mitigation measure ever implemented at the Commonwealth level was duly repealed, and climate change had claimed its second, or perhaps third, party leader. The 2019 election, widely billed as a climate election, ironically led to the defeat of Tony Abbott (no longer leader of his party) in his electorate of Warringah, largely because of his locally unpopular position on climate change. But the results in coal-producing electorates in Queensland were widely credited with ensuring the survival of the Coalition government. Matters changed considerably in 2022 when the Coalition lost seats to Teal Independents in part because of its extreme position against climate action (see Chapter 5).

Considering the three components of ecological reflexivity, at some level there is widespread (but not universal) recognition that climate change is a problem that needs to be addressed. Reflection, if it does happen, is largely a matter for the individual politician. There is nothing institutionalised in electoral or party politics to embody such reflection – such as a parliamentary committee for the planetary future, or mandated consideration of existing 'State of the Environment' reporting. Reflection on the condition of the Earth system plays a much smaller role than contemplation of how climate change can be used to electoral advantage, or in intra-party manoeuvring – as when the Liberal Party's extreme right wing first ousted Malcom Turnbull as their leader. Response is also constrained by the way that the adversarial game for short-term advantage between and within parties dominates any consideration of what kind of policy might be most effective.

It would be tempting to conclude that the dismal history of the electoral politics of climate change in Australia shows that adversarial party politics cannot be conducive to ecological reflexivity. But this cannot be the whole story, because the equally adversarial system of the UK has managed to produce a cross-party consensus on the severity of climate change and the need to act – although one that falls short in its contemplation of change to the basic structure of the political economy. With all main parties in the UK generally supportive of climate policy, the country is recognised as a comparative leader in this arena. What then makes the difference? Part of the story may be that the coal industry has a presence and power in Australia that is missing in the UK, where the industry was dismantled under Conservative PM Margaret Thatcher in the 1980s – though as a union-busting exercise, which only as a by-product makes her an accidental environmental hero. The other and perhaps more important part of the comparative story may be that the UK is not a settler society with factions of dominant parties committed to a grey radical identity of the kind that was described earlier.

Biodiversity

Australia plays an important role in global biodiversity. It is a megadiverse country, which means that the majority of known species living in Australia are unique to the country (for example, 87 per cent of its mammal species or 93 per cent of its frog species). However, Australia's biodiversity is declining rapidly. Australia has one of highest extinction rates in the world and increasing numbers of species (for example, koalas) and ecosystems (for example, the Great Barrier Reef and Murray Darling floodplain forests and wetlands) are classified as endangered. This is primarily because of habitat destruction and fragmentation, invasive species (for example, feral cats), pollution, climate change, changes in fire regime, drought and overconsumption of resources (notably water).

In Australia's regulation apparatus, land-based threatened species are supposed to be the most protected entities. Yet since 1999, 85 per cent of them experienced significant habitat loss. More than 90 per cent of total habitat loss was not referred to or submitted for any assessment, despite a requirement to do so under Commonwealth environment laws. Many ecosystems are collapsing due to climate change and changes in fire regimes that have not been seriously addressed. For instance, large-scale conversion of alpine forest to shrubland was caused by repeated fires from 2003–2014. With such a record, and without commensurate governmental action, Australia is not far from being a global pariah for biodiversity.

Within this overall failure there are nonetheless some notable initiatives and programs on biodiversity conservation in Australia. These have included:

- Australia's marine protected area system, which covers 7.4 per cent of the Australian marine environment and is the second largest in the world

- Indigenous Protected Areas, which cover 36 per cent of Australia's total protected areas, including some that are formally owned by Traditional Custodians (for example, the recent landmark case of the Daintree tropical rainforest in Queensland)
- Caring for Country programs, which aim to provide Indigenous-led conservation programs and replace the employee/consultant regime with a regime based on self-determination
- Landcare programs, which try to reduce the environmental impact of farming practices
- the Atlas of Living, a citizen-science program on biodiversity data
- strategies for combatting invasive species, which have received long-term political and financial support.

However, all these initiatives (apart from the last) do not benefit from continued political and financial support by the government, in particular at federal level. They fall far short of the necessary recognition of biodiversity in holistic, systemic terms. Australian biodiversity policy remains not only weak (not very protective), but fragmented (across states), underfunded, and poorly implemented (Ward et al., 2019). There are many concerns here, including a lack of independent and transparent scientific advice and decision-making power in relation to development projects. The cumulative impacts on biodiversity are not considered, and many key biodiversity threats are excluded from regulatory frameworks – for instance, land clearing and climate change are not recognised as 'matters of national significance'. For threatened ecosystems to be protected under the *EPBC Act*, they must often meet limited and restrictive 'condition thresholds' (for example, minimum size of the area). And there is little evidence that major assessment reports on biodiversity have had any influence on biodiversity policy.

The review of the *Environment Protection and Biodiversity Conservation (EPBC) Act* presented by Graeme Samuels in 2020 can be seen as a landmark when it comes to recognition of systemic failings on the biodiversity front, but it led to little reflection on the systemic causes of these failings. Reacting to Samuels, the federal government has proposed a minimal set of changes, which includes systematically incentivising biodiversity offsets rather than applying a precautionary approach to avoid biodiversity destruction. Offsets are essentially licences to behave badly, with compensatory remediation to be applied somewhere else. They do not reduce the net level of biodiversity destruction. In addition, the review proposed an Environment Assurance Commissioner, but the role would be a toothless one, because they would not be allowed to investigate outcomes. As a result, none of the key factors contributing to systemic biodiversity loss has been seriously addressed.

The situation worsened after 2019, with the Morrison government trying to roll back environmental regulation. At the international level, unlike many other countries, Australia has neither committed to 'net biodiversity loss' targets, nor pledged to reverse biodiversity loss in the near future. Furthermore, Australia's 'Strategy for Nature', which is supposed to implement the Convention on Biological Diversity (CBD), has not been linked to a specific action plan with measurable targets and goals, as is the case for other countries such as France, Germany or Aotearoa-New Zealand.

Finally, an essential aspect of ecological reflexivity is the ability to rethink the relationship between humans and non-humans. However, in Australia, this relationship is primarily characterised by a discourse that presents a misleading antagonism between valuable 'natural' elements that should be protected, and 'resources' that are considered unlimited and can therefore be extracted or exploited. This dichotomy is a major obstacle to effectively recognising and responding to the structural sources of contemporary biodiversity declines, both tangible or material losses (for example, pollution, habitat destruction) and intangible or immaterial losses (for example, the values placed on non-humans).

From government to polycentric governance?

If electoral and party politics are failing to confront the Anthropocene effectively at the federal level in particular, is there any kind of politics that might fill the gap? At the global level, persistent failure to reach an effective multilateral agreement on climate change has led to a proliferation of independent governance initiatives. They have ranged from voluntary carbon markets to international networks of cities sharing technology and emissions reduction commitments, as well as product certification schemes, and transnational social movements (such as transition initiatives) promoting low-carbon local economies. Some of these initiatives have involved cooperation across national or subnational governments. Some involve corporate actors, and others environmental non-governmental organisations (NGOs). Some initiatives involve all three. They are celebrated as constituting what Ostrom (2019) calls 'polycentric' or what Hoffmann (2011) terms 'experimental' governance.

Can we discern any signs of such a response to persistent failure on the part of the federal government occurring within Australia? Hajer (2011) applauds a polycentric 'energetic society' within the Netherlands, involving experimentation, networking, and learning, so the idea can apply at the national level. And it is also true that if we were to look to polycentrism (rather than federal government policy) in our search for ecological reflexivity, there are some relevant initiatives, including:

+ Regional Forest Agreements (RFA). These have a somewhat chequered history. They began over 20 years ago as cooperative alternatives to impasse in forest governance, seeking agreements across traditionally hostile interests, such as timber corporations and environmentalists, but also involving input from scientists, local communities and Traditional Owners. They have struggled in the face of those interests on different sides who do not believe that any reconciliation of positions is possible.
+ The large banks (NAB, Westpac, ANZ, Commonwealth) have all seen the writing on the wall when it comes to coal, with first ethical investors and now increasingly investment markets as a whole asking about ESG commitments. The big banks are less willing to finance large new thermal coal projects (especially when, like the Carmichael coal mine, they are locally contested). Large corporations have also announced ambitious climate change intentions. In 2021, mining giant BHP committed to net zero emissions by 2050 – however, the Minerals Council of Australia to which BHP belongs remains obstructive.
+ The adoption of net zero emissions targets for GHGs has proven much easier at the state level than at the federal level.
+ Some smaller jurisdictions, such as the ACT and Tasmania, have led the way in securing 100 per cent of their electricity from renewable sources – although in Tasmania this has been enabled by hydroelectric power, which has brought its own forms of environmental destruction.
+ Local and state jurisdictions are more likely to adopt and implement some forms of rights for non-human nature – notably, the Victorian Environmental Water Holder (VEWH), created in 2011 to hold water rights in Victorian streams (O'Donnell and Talbot-Jones, 2017).
+ The national policy vacuum created by the abolition of the National Water Commission in 2005 is being partially filled by private initiatives. For example, in 2020 Watertrust Australia was established with tens of millions of dollars in funding from the Myer Foundation, the Ian Potter Foundation and other private sources. Its mission is to develop a cooperative and deliberative approach to the management of Australia's water resources.

- Local governments have in many cases recognised the urgent need to adapt to the consequences of climate change (such as increased fire dangers, more flooding and faster coastal erosion).

Even taken together, these sorts of initiatives do not add up to an adequate national response to environmental degradation in Australia. But how do they look in terms of progress towards ecological reflexivity? If they are to make any progress in this respect they would need to be joined in a system of experimentation and learning, as opposed to being just sporadic innovations that come and go without much connecting. This is a demanding requirement, but again we can see intimations in the global governance of climate change, where disparate polycentric innovations are increasingly linked to the more centralised United Nations Framework Convention on Climate Change (UNFCCC) process in what Bäckstrand et al. call 'hybrid multilateralism' (2017).

What Australia currently lacks is the integrated capacity and will at federal government level to play a role analogous to that of the UNFCCC in hybrid multilateralism, or the supportive national government in the Netherlands case, meaning that the coordination and learning would itself need to be organised from the bottom up. The Watertrust initiative noted above could help perform this function on water governance – but ecological reflexivity in the Anthropocene demands a whole of governance approach that would span across all ecological, social and economic sectors.

Learning in any such coordinated system would also benefit from what Braithwaite (2007) calls 'nodes of contestation' where critics can highlight problems. Otherwise, the system could slip into the easy complacency of mostly symbolic actions, such as commitments to net zero issued with no feasible plan of how they will be achieved. Such announcements may be reassuring, but they do not go far enough. Contestation here could come from social movement activism, environmentalist groups, and Indigenous organisations, among others. By providing grist for deliberation, such contestation would also be good for the deliberative aspect of democracy. Deliberation is also necessary as a mode of conflict resolution across deep difference of the sort that has undermined the potential of RFA.

Conclusion

No country's institutions are ready for the Anthropocene, but Australia is especially challenged. On many individual fronts, such as climate change, biodiversity loss and water management, there are few mechanisms to facilitate the country's overall ability to listen to, reflect upon and respond effectively to structural socioecological changes. All of this is before we get to consider the interlinked character of these different aspects of environmental change, which requires thinking in more holistic Earth system terms. There are some positives: Australia's deeper socioecological history, the fact that states, territories, and even banks and corporations are compensating for federal failure on some issues, the massive potential for renewable energy and significant scientific expertise. All of these could help Australia's democracy respond to the challenges posed by the Anthropocene. But it is an uphill struggle that starts from a low base.

References

Bäckstrand, K., Kuyper, J. W., Linnér, B. O., & Lövbrand, E. (2017) 'Non-state actors in global climate governance: from Copenhagen to Paris and beyond.' *Environmental Politics*, 26(4), 561–579. https://doi.org/10.1080/09644016.2017.1327485

Braithwaite, John (2007) 'Contestatory citizenship; deliberative denizenship', in Brennan, Geoffrey; Goodin, Robert E.; Jackson, Frank; and Smith, Michael (eds) *Common Minds: Themes from the Philosophy of Philip Pettit*. Oxford: Oxford University Press. $ https://perma.cc/EE27-R2AB

Climate Action Tracker (2020) *Scaling up Climate Action: Key Opportunities for Transitioning to a Zero Emissions Society*, Full Report, November. https://perma.cc/MG7X-DR7L

Climate Council (2019) 'State of play: Renewable energy leaders and losers', Sydney: Climate Council Report. https://perma.cc/YYF5-RX3T

Colvin, Rebecca and Jotzo, Frank (2021) 'Australian voters' attitudes to climate action and their social-political determinants', *PLOS ONE*, vol. 16, no. 3. https://doi.org/10.1371/journal.pone.0248268

Crowley, Kate (2021) 'Fighting the future: The politics of climate policy failure in Australia (2015–2020)', *WIREs Clim Change*, vol. 12, no. 5, e725. https://doi.org/10.1002/wcc.725

CSIRO (2015) 'Warmer, wetter, hotter, drier? How to choose between climate futures', blogpost, 9 April. https://www.csiro.au/en/news/All/Articles/2015/April/warmer-wetter-hotter-drier-how-to-choose-between-climate-futures

Curran, Giorel (2015) 'Political modernisation for ecologically sustainable development in Australia', *Australian Journal of Environmental Management*, vol. 22, no.1. $ https://doi.org/10.1080/14486563.2014.999359

Dryzek, John S. and Pickering, Jonathan (2019) *The Politics of the Anthropocene*, Oxford University Press. $ https://doi.org/10.1093/oso/9780198809616.001.0001

Dryzek, John S (2021) *The Politics of the Earth: Environmental Discourses*, 4th edn, Oxford University Press. $ https://perma.cc/2KLU-V34K

Environmental Performance Index (2017) 'Greenhouse gas emissions per capita', database. https://perma.cc/BP9V-KAEA

Environmental Performance Index (EPI) (2020) 'Australia', country scorecard. https://perma.cc/AST9-BPUD

Gammage, Bill (2012) *The Biggest Estate on Earth: How Aborigines Made Australia*, Sydney: Allen & Unwin. $ https://perma.cc/29PC-JRN4

Garnaut, Ross (2008) *The Garnaut Climate Change Review: Final report*, Cambridge: Cambridge University Press. https://www.researchgate.net/publication/227389894_The_Garnaut_Climate_Change_Review

Guardian (2023) 'Australia passes most significant climate law in a decade amid concern over fossil fuel exports', *The Guardian, Australia*, 30 March. Webpage. https://perma.cc/BW8M-4226

Hajer, Maarten (2011) *The Energetic Society – In Search of a Governance Philosophy for a Clean Economy*. The Hague: Netherlands Environmental Assessment Agency. https://perma.cc/UE9R-XXPX

Hoffmann, Matthew J. (2011) *Climate Governance at the Crossroads: Experimenting with a Global Response after Kyoto*. Oxford: Oxford University Press. $ https://doi.org/10.1093/acprof:oso/9780195390087.001.0001

IEA (2018) *Energy Policies of IEA Countries: Australia 2018 Review*, Paris: IEA. https://perma.cc/ZK4C-6ARY

Mazengarb, Michael (2020) 'Turnbull says his biggest leadership failure was on climate change', *Renew Economy*, 22 April blogpost. https://perma.cc/H4GY-PUQN

Mocatta, Gabi and Hawley, Erin (2020) 'Uncovering a climate catastrophe? Media coverage of Australia's Black Summer bushfires and the revelatory extent of the climate blame frame', *M/C Journal*, vol. 23, no. 4. https://doi.org/10.5204/mcj.1666

Morrison, Tiffany H.; Adger, W.N.; Brown, Katrina; Hettiarachchi, M.; Huchery, C.; Lemos, M.C.; and Hughes, T.P. (2020) 'Political dynamics and governance of World Heritage ecosystems', *Nature Sustainability* vol. 3, pp.947–55. https://doi.org/10.1038/s41893-020-0568-8

Murphy, Katharine (2021) 'Environment minister Sussan Ley says climate action not her portfolio in stoush with states', *The Guardian, Australia*, 16 April. https://perma.cc/CJ3V-QDWT

Murphy, Katherine and Morton, Adam (2021) 'Fact check: Angus Taylor's response to the landmark IPCC report'. *Guardian, Australia*, 10 August. https://perma.cc/KW7S-7WQA

O'Callaghan, Brian (2021) 'Are we building back better? Evidence from 2020 and pathways for inclusive green recovery spending', UN Environment Programme, 10 March. https://perma.cc/4NZ6-347S

O'Donnell, E. and Talbot-Jones, J. (2017) 'Legal rights for rivers: What does this actually mean?' *Australian Environment Review*, vol. 32, no. 6, pp. 159–162.

OECD (2019) *OECD Environmental Performance Reviews: Australia 2019*. Paris: OECD Publishing. https://doi.org/10.1787/9789264310452-en

OECD (2021) Data/Indicators/'Material Consumption'. Webpage. https://perma.cc/W85Z-R3U4

Ostrom, Elinor (2009) *A Polycentric Approach for Coping with Climate Change*, Washington, DC: World Bank, Open Knowledge repository. Policy Research working paper; no. WPS 5095. https://perma.cc/LL9Y-7T3K

Pascoe, Bruce (2014) *Dark Emu*. Broome: Magabala Books. $ https://perma.cc/TXJ8-2A89

Poelina, Anne; Taylor, Katherine S.; and Perdrisat, Ian. (2019) 'Martuwarra Fitzroy River Council: an Indigenous cultural approach to collaborative water governance', Australasian Journal of Environmental Management, vol. 26, no .3 'Special Issue: Indigenous water management', ed by Sue Jackson and Bradley Moggridge. $ https://doi.org/10.1080/14486563.2019.1651226

Ramsay, Ian and Freeburn, Lloyd (2021) 'Australian companies are facing more climate-focused ESG resolutions than ever before, and they are paying quiet dividends'. *The Conversation, Australia*, 8 November. https://perma.cc/4JJ8-FT8U

Stutzer, Roman, Rinscheid, Adrian, Oliveira, Thiago, D.; Loureiro, Pedro, Mendes; Kachi, Aya and Duygan, Mert (2021) 'Black coal, thin ice: The discursive legitimisation of Australian coal in the age of climate change', *Humanities and Social Science Communications*, vol. 8, no. 178. https://doi.org/10.1057/s41599-021-00827-5

Ward, Michelle S.; Barmand, Shayan; Watson, James; and Williams, Brooke (2021) 'Australia faces environmental crisis', *Science,* vol. 371, no. 6534, pp.1115–16. https://doi.org/10.1126/science.abg9225

Ward, Michelle S.; Simmonds, Jeremy S.; Reside, April E.; Watson, James E. M.; Rhodes, Jonathan R.; Possingham, Hugh P.; Trezise, James; Fletcher, Rachel; File, Lindsey; and Taylor, Martin (2019) 'Lots of loss with little scrutiny: The attrition of habitat critical for threatened species in Australia', *Conservation Science and Practice*, 8 September. https://doi.org/10.1111/csp2.117

Warren, Evan; Christoff, Peter; and Green, Donna (2016) 'Australia's sustainable energy transition: The disjointed politics of decarbonisation', *Environmental Innovation and Societal Transitions*, vol. 21. https://doi.org/10.1016/j.eist.2016.01.001

28

Democratic resilience and change

Patrick Dunleavy and Mark Evans

Most social scientists and political system actors in liberal democracies agree that in the last 25 years their political system has fallen on 'hard times' across the world. The number of liberal democracies has remained static or fallen back (depending on how loosely the term is used). Previously well-established 'strong' or 'mature' liberal democracies have fallen prey to 'democratic backsliding' by incumbents in a range of ways. Some have moved a long way now into the category of 'flawed' or systematically imperfect democracies (notably, the USA and Hungary). Some previously flawed democracies have collapsed into military regimes or semi-autocracies (such as Thailand, Myanmar) and the previous marginally democratic cases of Pakistan and Bangladesh (each for the nth time). What were once seen as 'semi-democratic' countries have retained their elections but become outright autocracies, actively promoting old-style 'power politics' via international aggression (as with Putin's Russia). And among autocracies there has been a tightening of overall control into strong dictatorships where previous small areas of protest freedoms from state control have been extirpated (as in China under President Xi, and in Belarus).

How can Australia's overall performance as a liberal democracy be assessed?

There are three key ways of accomplishing this task:

- Analysing how Australia fares *in comparison with other liberal democracies* using these main types of data:

  - Overall 'democracy index' rankings compiled by experts and driven by multiple sets of data and quantitative evidence.

  - Other separate comparisons using objective data that tap into aspects relevant to liberal democratic social outcome goals (like equality, good healthcare, etc.).

  - How Australian citizens themselves evaluate the degree of democracy domestically, compared with people in similar countries overseas.

How to cite this chapter:

Dunleavy, Patrick and Evans, Mark (2024) 'Democratic resilience and change', in: Evans, Mark; Dunleavy, Patrick and Phillimore, John (eds) *Australia's Evolving Democracy: A New Democratic Audit*, London: LSE Press, pp.574–602. https://doi.org/10.31389/lsepress.ada.ab. Licence: CC-BY-NC 4.0

- Looking at the evolution of domestic popular support for democracy *over time*, especially considering how far citizens have shown attitudes in opinion surveys that are consistent with maintaining a democratic 'civic culture'.
- Drawing out some key *qualitative* judgements made in the main Chapters 1 to 27 above.

One of the most discussed (but very US-centric books) in this literature has been Levitsky and Ziblatt's (2018) 'stages' model in *How Democracies Die*. They argued that democracy has historically been subverted most commonly by 'backsliding' carried out in stages that subtly impair its operation until an incumbent party or politicians can decisively seize power in ways that prevent their opponents ever coming back. First, incumbent power holders attack all integrity watchdogs, seeking to politicise them under government control. Next, they seek permanent power by targeting their opponents to exclude rival parties (using tax or business laws, for instance, as well as electoral restrictions), and changing the rules of the game – for example, using 'voter suppression' tactics to make it harder for opposition voters to get to the polls or enacting blanket bans via stealth on previous non-voters. Constituencies are rigged to 'gerrymander' results and free media are progressively taken over by incumbent party oligarchs, while state media become mouthpieces for the party in power only, abandoning any pretence of partisan impartiality. Lastly, populist intimidation tactics and extreme partisan rhetoric are used to portray all opposition groups as 'enemies of the state' and generate a 'spiral of silence' among opposition party supporters, faced only with the prospects of endless defeats from fraudulent elections.

At every move, the incumbents and their agents may stay just inside the law, while systematically acting against the whole spirit of democratic power-sharing and accountability and eroding 'the soft guardrails' of democracy (Levitsky and Ziblatt, 2018) and the dozens of the 'micro-institutions' across many legal and administrative fields that provide the foundations for democracy (Dunleavy, 2019). Considered individually any one of the incremental changes above may seem small scale, reversible or non-fundamental, but after decades of extreme polarisation, the increasing escalation of such tactics can seriously erode all respect for constitutional checks and balances.

However, the American political scientists Andrew Little and Amy Meng (2024) argued in a recent paper that the consensus picture of democratic decline has been overblown, and has been based on analysts' pessimism, rather than on hard facts:

> *Despite the general narrative that we are in a period of global democratic decline, there have been surprisingly few empirical studies to assess whether this is systematically true. Most existing studies of backsliding rely heavily, if not entirely, on subjective indicators which rely on expert coder judgement. We survey other more objective indicators of democracy (such as incumbent performance in elections), and find little evidence of global democratic decline over the last decade ... To explain the discrepancy between trends in subjective and objective indicators, the simplest explanation is that recent declines in average democracy scores are driven by changes in bias [among the 'experts' coding democratic performance]. While we cannot rule out the possibility that the world is experiencing major democratic backsliding almost exclusively in ways which require subjective judgement to detect, this claim is not justified by existing evidence.* (Little and Meng, 2023)

Yet on closer inspection this judgement appears highly complacent and over-claiming, because it is based on very few indicators, most of them basic statistics of an extraordinarily crude kind. For example, a central argument in the Little and Meng (2023) analysis is that if incumbents retained power 'backsliding' claims are supported, but if the incumbent lost an election then this provides a clear sign that no democratic backsliding has occurred. A moment's consideration of the American case suggests the poverty of this 'only objective numbers count' approach. In 2020, the Republican incumbent Donald Trump lost but then insisted that he had not lost, exerting huge pressure on his vice-president and other officials involved in the election certification to arbitrarily disallow packets of votes in several states so that he might be seen to have won. The 6 January 2021 assault on Congress by Trump's enraged supporters, and the presidents' encouragement of it, for which he was prosecuted in 2023–2024, capped his 'bad loser' antics. Trump subsequently waged a remorseless campaign alleging a 'fake' result that successfully persuaded a huge majority of Republican voters that he was indeed wrongly denied the presidency by some kind of vote-fixing conspiracy against him (for which no evidence was ever produced), a public opinion pattern that endured largely undimmed in the ensuing four years. At the time of writing, Trump is the Republican candidate for president (for the third time) and has made apparently undisguised promises to rig future elections in his party's favour if he wins and persecute his opponents. Trump's example was copied in a minor key in Brazil by Bolsonaro's 2023 denial that he had lost the presidential election there, which also led to violent demonstrations that wrecked the country's legislature.

The damage wreaked to American democracy by Trump was also vividly captured in a later article by Levitsky and Ziblatt (2021):

> Whether it is the [Senate] filibuster [to talk out legislation], funding the government, impeachment [of the President], or judicial nominations [especially to the USA's Supreme Court], our system of checks and balances works best when politicians on both sides of the aisle deploy their institutional prerogatives with restraint. In other words, when they avoid applying the letter of the law in ways contrary to the spirit of the law – what's sometimes called [playing] constitutional hardball. When contemporary democracies die, they usually do so via constitutional hardball. Democracy's primary assailants today are not generals or armed revolutionaries, but rather politicians – Hugo Chávez [in Venezuela], Vladimir Putin, Viktor Orbán [in Hungary], Recep Tayyip Erdoğan [in Turkey] – who eviscerate democracy's substance behind a carefully crafted veneer of legality and constitutionality.

In contrast to the USA, Australian democracy at the end of 2023 looks in a far better state. Very few incumbent dirty tricks and subversions of democracy have been detected in the preceding chapters. Isolated examples include the 2019 decision by the Liberal-National government to use 'sports rort' and community grants payments for partisan purposes, focusing them on marginal seats in the run up to that year's federal election, and their maintenance of government advertising including clear coalition policy themes and terminology right up to the last possible moment before the Prime Minister (PM) Scott Morrison announced the election date. Another disturbing example of playing fast and loose with constitutional powers was the secret move made by Morrison at the onset of the COVID-19 pandemic to appoint himself to five additional ministries including Treasury, Health, Industry and Home Affairs. The step was agreed by the Governor-General but never disclosed even to the PM's colleagues, let alone to parliament. When this unprecedented breach of collegial rule was discovered several years later, it raised acute alarm about the over-concentration of power in the premiers' hands. Many democracies have fallen in the past when top leaders gain 'decree' powers under the cloak of a national emergency to justify their edicts. Thankfully though, these cases seem to have been isolated instances. In 2022, abuses of government power for partisan ends at election time were not evident, and a peaceful transfer of power followed in the same way as ever after the election. Similarly, Morrison's 'portfolio grab' remained notional and was never actually operationalised, for then his colleagues would have had to be told. Perhaps, as his defenders argue, it was only a 'just-in-case' over-reaction taken to really tie down emergency powers at the highly disruptive and hard-to-predict onset of the pandemic.

However, even if there are few 'smoking gun' indications of democratic backsliding in Australia, it is worth looking broadly at how the political system has fared before reaching a more considered overall audit verdict. Political scientists, economists, and sociologists, and wider political commentators, the media, politicians and policy practitioners all take modern indices of democracy seriously as key windows into inherently complex assessments. Sometimes this approach may have risks, because although the wording of a given statement stays the same its *meaning* may change because the context in which people are answering has shifted markedly. However, on more general assessment questions the approach is still a useful one. Accordingly, the chapter begins by first considering how Australia compares in terms of quantitative measures with other liberal democracies. The second section looks at how quantitative indicators have moved that chart the health of democracy *within* Australia. The last section draws out a few overarching themes and conclusions from the detailed qualitative treatments in the previous chapters. For this summary chapter alone, we also do not use the SWOT analysis device employed in all the previous chapters, but provide a brief summing up in the Conclusion.

Comparing Australia with other liberal democracies

There are several different approaches to assessing countries' democratic performance comparatively, using statistical methods and metrics. Each has some limitations. Judgement scoring across multiple categories of political practices can create indices that sum up many different points of information into overall rankings of performance, relying either on 'expert' judgements by political and legal analysts or on quantitative survey data. Alternatively, using 'unobtrusive measures' of people's behaviour (what they do in real situations) is non-reactive – people cannot 'edit' how they are coded (as they can by altering their responses in surveys). However, the meaning of behaviours is often context-dependent, especially where countries are dissimilar. Finally, cross-country survey data relies on asking respondents in multiple countries questions with exactly the same wording at (roughly) the same time. However, the *meaning* of even the most carefully chosen words may still vary a good deal across country contexts, and shift over time. We use evidence derived from all three approaches to situate Australia against other liberal democratic countries.

Comparing indices of democracy based on objective data or expert judgements

Indices of democracy bring together a large number of separate assessments (or judgements) spanning across different aspects of political systems and civil rights regimes. Figure 28.1 shows a selection of the best-known and most internationally well-regarded overall indices of democratic quality covering Australia, and that are fairly recent and have reasonably sophisticated methodologies. The indices are arranged in a rough descending order of their influence. The Economist Intelligence Unit's (EIU) Democracy Index is perhaps the most widely quoted, although its methods are not entirely clear. The next three are produced by academic authors, with better explained methods. The democracy NGO International IDEA (2022) has an Index that has been adopted by the UN, which means that it tends to pull some punches on imperfect democracies. The Sustainable Governance Index (SGI) relies on asking experts to rate very precisely each country's performance on 60 measures – but has been criticised by a few 'objective data' exponents from the USA (see Little and Meng, 2024). The Varieties of Democracy (V-Dem) Index has gained ground in academia recently. The Zurich 'Democracy Barometer' assesses a smaller selection of established democracies and accords a lot of influence to the proportionality of the main electoral systems, which other measures more or less ignore, and where Australia tends not to perform well (see Chapter 5).

All the rankings have rated Australia as a well-established and relatively high-performing liberal democracy. Somewhat like other Westminster systems, such as the UK, it has not placed in the top positions (Dunleavy, 2018) – these ranks have been occupied by the Scandinavian countries and some European nations. The EIU ranks Australia joint 9th, just inside the top 10 countries, ahead of the UK in 16th place but behind New Zealand in 4th place. The SGI index also rates Australia as 9th in terms of democracy, but only 16th in terms of 'good governance'. The V-Dem measure has Australia lying 20th, with the UK ahead (14th) and New Zealand also (6th). In several indices, Australia has fared poorly because of its lack of clear civil rights safeguards and a complex rights regime (see Chapter 3), and because its emphasis has been on legislature representation, with public participation arrangements being less prominent.

However, the top-scoring countries also tend to be small or very small countries in population terms, especially the Scandinavian countries with some tiny additions (like Estonia). Arguably, smaller states are more straightforward to operate, and organising public participation and consultation is simpler. It might be somewhat easier to run a liberal democracy with (say) six million people than with Australia's current 26 million. It also might be simpler to run a country that is spatially compact like New Zealand or the UK than to run a whole continent spanning across radically differing regions, as Australia does. (However, some high-ranked Scandinavian countries like Sweden, Finland and Norway also have large spatial areas.)

Most comparative assessments of democracy carried out in 2020–2021 during the pandemic were inevitably focused heavily on the effects of the pandemic. Some measures, particularly travel restrictions within Australia imposed to limit the spread of the virus, were seen as unusual curtailments of freedom of assembly and movement (domestically and internationally) by indices (Gardner, 2024; and see Chapters 2 and 3). So too were emergency laws enacted through executive orders, without usual parliamentary scrutiny and accountability (see Chapters 11 and 12), and in some cases delayed elections. V-Dem found that although 'most democracies have acted responsibly in the face of the pandemic, nine register major, and 23 moderate, violations of international norms. The situation is worse in autocracies: 55 were involved in major or

Figure 28.1: Five overall quantitative index rankings of liberal democracies and how they rated Australia, 2017–2021

Name of index	Produced by	Rating of Australia	Australia's rank as a democracy	Lowest scoring elements	Methods used
Democracy Index	Economist Intelligence Unit (EIU) 2022	9 out of 10. Classed as a 'Full democracy'	9th	'Political participation' = 7.8 out of 10	Varied sources, not entirely clear
SGI Sustainable Governance Indicators	Berlin SGI, 2022	On quality of democracy (score 7.3 out of max 10) On good governance 7.3 out of 10	9th on democracy and 16th on good governance	Access to information (poor media fairness) 6.0 (out of 10) Civil rights 7.0 (out of 10)	Quantitative analysis of expert assessments, plus qualitative briefs on aspects
Varieties of Democracy	V-Dem at University of Gothenburg, 2023	0.81 out of 1 (81%) on the Liberal Democracy Index	11th (up from 20th in 2019)	'Participatory component' = 0.66 out of 1 (66%) 'Egalitarian component' = 0.84 (lowest democracy score) (84%)	Quantitative data analysis, aggregated into six components
Global State of Democracy	International IDEA, 2022	Range of 82% to 86% scores across four main indices. Also seen as a 'high performing democracy' for their 5th index, participatory engagement	Not given	21% on 'direct democracy'; 60% on 'social group equality'	Varied, but data-heavy
Democracy Barometer	Zurich University, 2020 (but using 2017 data)	3.76 out of 5 on an overall 'democratic quality' index, (highest 4.41)	22nd (in 2017)		Quantitative data analysis, aggregated into six components

Source: URL links to all sources are included in the second column (see also **References** section for full details).

moderate violations in response to the pandemic' (V-Dem, 2021, p.9). Australia's relatively high success in controlling COVID-19 was achieved at limited cost to rights (apart from restrictions on movement) as many earlier chapters have shown.

Quite a few other comparative classifications of democracy are orientated only towards assessing marginal or what the EIU terms 'flawed democracy' cases, such as those found in many developing countries. Designed to be inclusive and often used to assist aid agencies distribute funds, these measures simply do not work at all for established democracies, normally assigning

Figure 28.2: Some current quantitative index rankings of partial aspects of liberal democracy and how they rated Australia in 2020

Name of index, and who produces it	Aspect of democracy covered	Rating of Australia	Australia's rank in the world as a democracy	Methods used
Freedom House Index, 2023 See also (PEI, 2019b)	Freedom, political rights, civil rights	95 out of 100 (and thus 'free'); 'Freedom on the Net' score = 76/100	Joint 8th	25 indicators are scored 0–4 points by Freedom House analysts, for an aggregate score of maximum 100. Political rights score 38 out of possible 40; civil liberties 57 out of possible 60
Perceptions of Electoral Integrity (PEI) (2019a). Team at Harvard, Sydney University and University of East Anglia	How well-run, impartial and democratic are elections?	70% on overall PEI index	31st in first wave, revised to 14th in later waves	Uses multiple data indicators covering all aspects of election processes, from voter registration, regulating parties through to vote counting
Transparency International, 2022	Corruption, bribery, etc.	75 out of 100 (improving)	14th	Survey evidence of perceptions of corruption
InCise Index of Civil Service Effectiveness (2019). By Blavatnik School of Government, Oxford University, with UK think-tank, the Institute for Government (with UK civil service funding)	How well national bureaucracies operate, using objective indicators and expert judgements	Average score of 0.863 (mean 0.516); highest score on crisis and risk management	5th out of 38 countries assessed	116 metrics aggregated into 12 component scores

*Note: URL links to all sources are included in the first column (see also **References** section).*

them all 'perfect scores'. Other studies use simplistic typologies or are very dated. For instance, the Polity IV and V scores produced by a USA think-tank have given Australia a 'perfect' 10/10 score, alongside the USA, until 2016 (Center for Systemic Peace, 2024). (In the past, Polity was run from the same unit also running a separate atrocities dataset funded by the CI.)

In addition, *there are a range of more partial measures relevant to democracy assessment, covering a few or* single aspects of performance that are highly relevant to assessing democratic outcomes. Figure 28.2 shows how Australia compares with other countries on freedom of speech and media, the integrity and fairness of elections, perceptions of corruption and civil service effectiveness. These indicators cover areas that are threats of 'democratic backsliding' discussed earlier, with electoral laws or public administration services being run in partisan ways to favour incumbents.

Figure 28.3: Three current index rankings of the social outcomes or political equality aspects of liberal democracy, and how they rated Australia in 2020–2021

Name of index	Aspect covered	Rating of Australia	Australia's rank	Methods
Social Progress Index, 2022	Index of how society meets people's basic needs, creates wellbeing foundations and offers opportunities	88% (down slightly)	12th (up from 18th in 2019)	Index aggregated from 12 underlying indicators, then normalised
World Happiness Report, 2023	Happiness index citizens' own evaluation of their wellbeing	7.1 out of 10 (top country's score = 7.8)	11th (up from 19th in 2017)	Survey data on population happiness, then analysed using country statistics on healthy life expectation, social support, generosity, choices
OECD, 2019	Inequality after taxes and transfers (Gini coefficient)	9th in terms of overall Gini coefficient (Fig 10b)	21st (out of 37 OECD countries) on impact of state cash redistribution (Fig 10a)	Country statistics on income levels across social groups

Australia has scored well on most of these measures, ranking within the top 10 countries on the 'freedom' index, in its anti-corruption measures and in terms of its public service effectiveness. Some of these measures can also be questioned. On the Perceptions of Electoral Integrity (PEI, 2019a), Australia initially trailed in 31st place thanks to its weak laws and regulations on donations to political parties, donations transparency and its heavily biased and partisan print media – a pattern found in most Anglosphere liberal democracies (Young, 2011). Later this low PEI ranking was revised, and Australia was instead placed 14th in international terms. (PEI has been criticised as unstable and neglecting some deeper quality aspects of party competition and elections (Flavin and Shufeldt, 2019). Australia's strong showing on the Freedom House measure has been chiefly due to that measure assigning a lot of weight to market freedoms. The InCise 2019 index placed Australia 5th, behind only the UK (ranked top), Canada, New Zealand and Finland. However, this problematic measure was devised and funded with help from a British civil service think-tank – it appears to have privileged an Anglosphere and 'new public management' conception of public administration over European (somewhat more hierarchical and neo-Weberian) models. The relatively strong Transparency International ranking for Australia might also be queried. It seems appropriate for the federal civil service and politics, but perhaps puts too optimistic a gloss on recurring problems for Australian state politics, or for major business sectors like banking, in both of which significant corruption and malfeasance problems have surfaced in recent years.

A key aim of liberal democracy is to maximise the overall social welfare of citizens, and achieving some basic equality of social conditions across all citizens is widely acknowledged as an essential foundation for political equality. As a country with a developed economy and high per capita level of gross domestic product (GDP), Australia should do well to realise that goal, while in the Australian political tradition the concept of a 'fair go' is also important. Figure 28.3 shows three important indices.

Australia's performance here is rather disappointing. On the OECD index of social inequality (the widely used Gini coefficient), Australia was the 9th best-performing country. OECD (2019, Figure 5) does show that (along with New Zealand) Australia targets cash transfers most to people in the lowest income quintile (those needing it most). However, it ranked in the bottom third of countries for redistribution effects via cash payments (OECD, 2019, Figure 10 B. Gini coefficients).

In terms of wellbeing and reported happiness, Australia does rather better, but was only ranked 18th or 19th in the world despite the many advantages of its suburban lifestyle, and widely available environmental benefits (such as ready access to beaches and wilderness for leisure). The country's score on the Social Progress Index was strong in percentage terms, but again this score only just made the top 20 countries.

Comparing subjective ratings by citizens

Other evidence in the World Values Survey (WVS) shows how respondents rate their own country in terms of its democracy, freedom levels or performance. In over half of the established liberal democracies shown citizens rated their level of freedom higher than they rated the extent of democracy (Figure 28.4) shown by the blue dots on a white background here. American

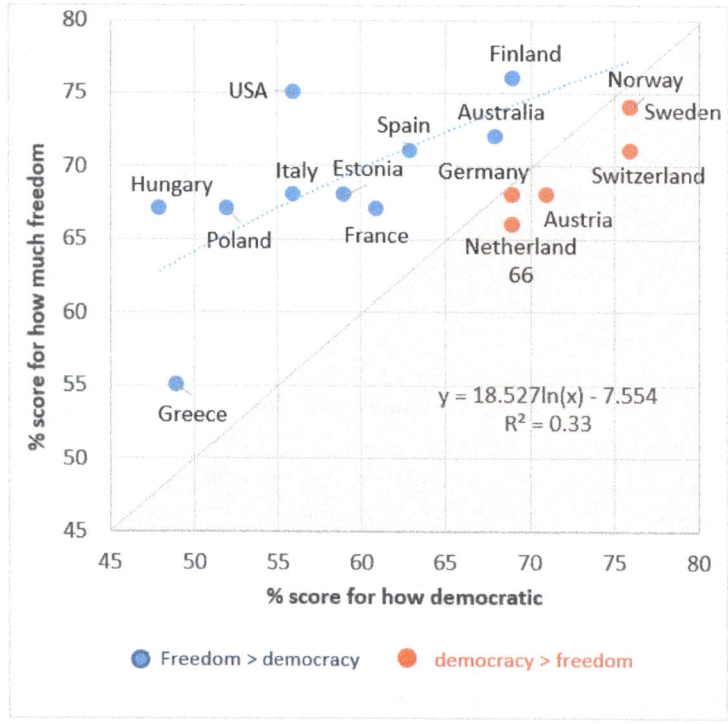

Figure 28.4: How citizens ranked their country in terms of how democratic it was, and how much freedom they had in 2017–2020

$y = 18.527\ln(x) - 7.554$
$R^2 = 0.33$

Source: Compiled by authors using data from World Values Survey Wave 7 responses (WVS, 2021).

Notes: The zero is suppressed here. The orange shaded part of the chart shows where respondents saw their country as being more democratic than it was free. The white-shaded part shows where respondents saw their country as being freer than it was democratic. The greater the right-angle distance of a country's dot from the orange-white boundary, the greater the disparity between freedom and democracy that respondents perceived. In Germany, for example, the disparity was almost zero. The dotted line shows the trend line for a regression across all the data, for which the equation is at bottom right.

Figure 28.5: How Australia respondents compared with those in other established liberal democracies in terms of social and political trust, in 2017–2020 data

Source: Evans, Jennings and Stoker (2020), *How does Australia Compare: What Makes a Leading Democracy?* Table 1.

Notes: Data are taken from the World Values Survey, 2017–2020 wave. In the blue shaded area, the levels of social trust are greater than the levels of political trust. In the white shaded areas, the level of political trust is greater than the level of social trust.

respondents especially rated their level of freedom as greater than their level of democracy. In a small number of countries, shown by the red dots on an orange background, democracy levels were rated above freedom levels. From the best fit trendline it is apparent that perceived freedom and democracy in this small set of countries were not that closely related – although the two cases of Greece (where both freedom and democracy levels are rated very low) and the USA explain much of this weakness.

By contrast, Australia lies close to the trendline in Figure 28.4, and somewhat above the parity line for the two dimensions. Thus, according to its WVS respondents Australia was slightly freer than it was democratic, but it did well on both dimensions. Its score ranked it as the 7th most democratic country of those shown (behind six affluent European countries) and the 4th freest country (behind only three Scandinavian countries and the USA). In response to another WVS question asking respondents if democracy was important, Australia's score was 86 per cent (out of a possible 100 per cent), ranking it 12th among liberal democracies, a relatively weak performance.

Closely related to perceptions of democracy is the level of 'trust' that citizens have in their state (Evans and Stoker, 2018). On 'trust' Australian respondents seem more sceptical and questioning of elites. The WVS asked how much respondents trusted other people in society, and how much they trusted political office-holders, and the results were somewhat less favourable for Australian democracy (Figure 28.5 shows). Over half of Australian respondents endorsed the statement that other people could generally be trusted, making the country the 7th or 8th most socially trusting. (The two 'Australia' dots in the Figure showing differences in the national averages over two waves of the survey, but they were very close together and consistent.) However, less than one in three respondents believed that Australian political leaders could generally be trusted, placing the country 14th out of the 17 countries in Figure 28.5. The 'parity line' in the chart shows where the two dimensions of trust were equally

Figure 28.6: How Australian respondents compared with those in three other liberal democracies in their level of confidence in political parties, government and healthcare after the onset of the COVID-19 pandemic in May and June 2020

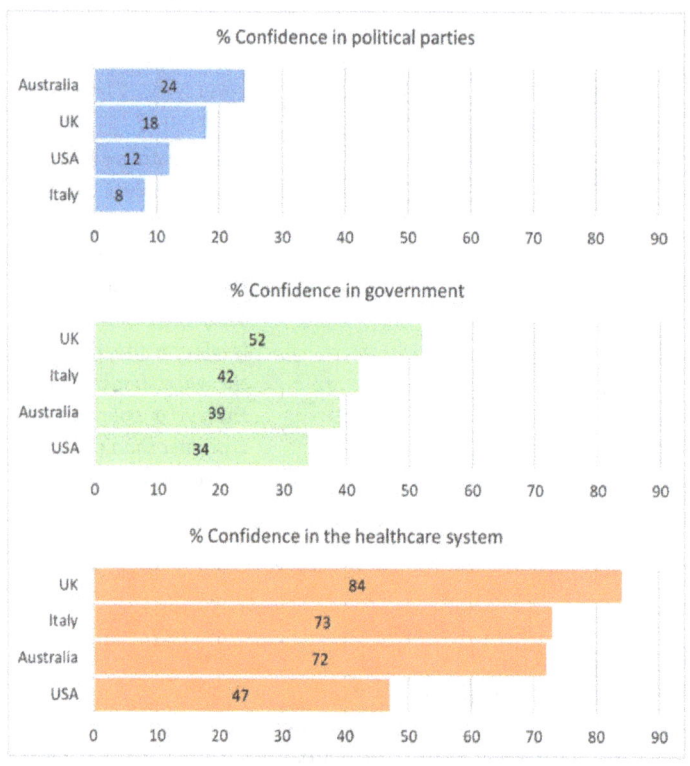

Source: Ipsos survey from May/June 2020, described in Jennings et al., 2021. The numbers inside bars add together respondents answering either 'a great deal of confidence' or 'quite a lot of confidence'.

developed. Given its moderate level of social trust Australia was well below the line on political trust – in fact only France and Denmark were further from parity.

The COVID-19 pandemic generally produced an upsurge of trust in democratic governments. At the height of the crisis (during May/June 2020), Figure 28.6 shows trust in different elements of the political system in Australia and three other established liberal democracies (the UK, USA and Italy). Citizens were least confident in the political parties to handle the pandemic well, moderately confident in government, and (as we would expect) most confident in their country's healthcare system. The Australian responses showed considerably more public confidence in political parties than other countries (albeit still at a low level). Confidence in Australian government was markedly less than the UK, but on a par with levels in Italy and the USA. Australia essentially tied second with Italy on trust in the healthcare system, and considerably behind the UK with its NHS, but beating by far the USA with its mostly private healthcare.

The same four-country comparison survey also recorded citizens' level of confidence in core institutions crucial for the long-running health of liberal democracies. Australian respondents' confidence in most public services (the health service, armed forces, police and universities) was high (75–80 per cent), similar to the levels in the other countries. Around 50–60 per cent of Australian respondents were confident about the federal government, the civil service and courts, again more or less on a par with other countries. However, confidence in the Australian press was much less, on a par with the dismal showing of political parties but not disastrous, unlike the UK public's view of their media (with only 7 per cent confident in them).

Figure 28.7: How Australian respondents rated the ease of finding government information and the quality of administrative services compared with other countries in a cross-national OECD survey, 2022

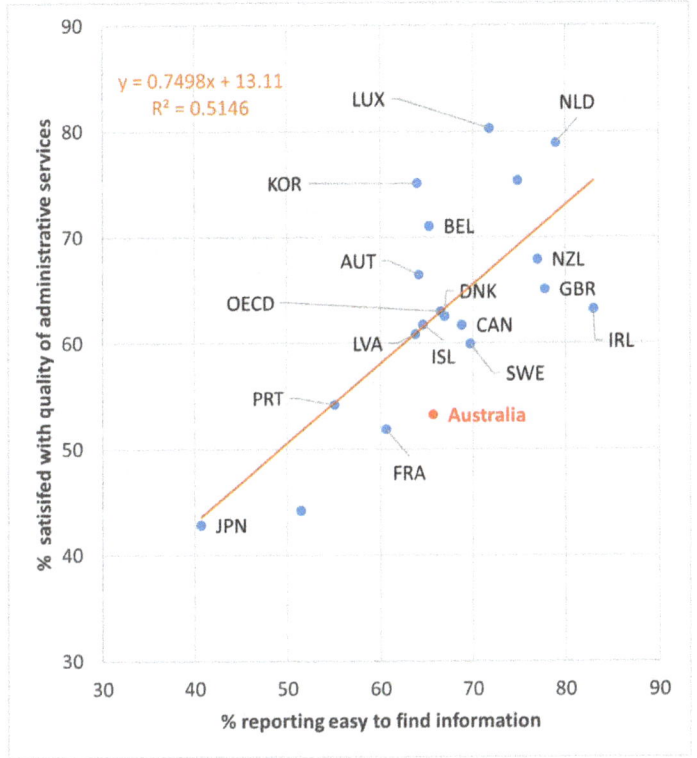

Source: OECD (2022) *Building Trust to Reinforce Democracy* 'Figure 5.2. Perception that information is easily available is positively linked with satisfaction with administrative services cross-nationally'. The brown line shows the trend line for a regression across all the data, for which the equation is at the top left.

A final aspect of effective liberal democratic arrangements concerns how easy it is to find government information, which we might expect to be associated with how satisfied citizens are with administrative services. Yet, Australia seems to be an exception to this pattern. Two-thirds of respondents in a cross-national OECD survey reported that it was 'easy to find information' on Australian government services, ranking it 12th out of the 20 nations shown in Figure 28.7. However, only just over half of respondents said they were satisfied with 'the quality of the administrative services', placing Australia third from bottom in Figure 28.7 and well below the trendline shown.

Ceiling effects are less evident when attention focuses on subjective responses gathered consistently across liberal democracies. Australia makes the top division of excellent performers on some indicators, but it is ranked a creditable but not stellar performer on others. Its rather similar rankings across a wide range of comparative indicators (coming from different authors and institutions) suggests that these measures have correctly gauged the country's basic position. Compared with other securely established liberal democracies, Australia is not quite in the top division, but sits well up within the closely following group of good but not outstanding political systems.

Do Australians have faith in democracy?

For decades now political scientists and other pollsters have gauged citizens' view of democracy within one country by asking how satisfied or dissatisfied they are with it. The Australian Election Survey (AES) asked this just after each federal election, a critical time for the public. Figure 28.8 shows that from 2001 to 2013 many more respondents said they were satisfied with democracy (the green dashed line) than said they were dissatisfied (the red dashed line). In 2016 and 2019 the gap between the two lines narrowed a lot (from 44 to just 19–20 per cent), and it would have been tempting then to identify a loss of faith in democracy. However, in 2022 far more people again said they were satisfied, and fewer were dissatisfied, pushing the net satisfaction balance back up to 40 per cent. Throughout this century the balance of satisfied minus dissatisfied respondents in the AES has been solidly in positive terrain, albeit substantially less so since 2010 than in earlier periods shown.

Some of the democratic decline literature has drawn on different kinds of data, where survey respondents are presented with pre-defined statements that the analysts judge are relevant to gauging faith in democracy. In the USA and many recently established democracies (like former communist countries in eastern Europe) such surveys have shown disturbing numbers of respondents willing to endorse anti-democracy statements. And in a 2017 cross-national survey, 28 per cent of Australia respondents who placed themselves on the political right agreed with the statement that: 'A system in which a strong leader can make decisions without interference from parliaments and the courts would be a good way of governing this country' (**Pew Research, 2017**). But only 16 per cent of centrist respondents and 8 per cent of those on the left gave this response.

We have no sure way of knowing if respondents recognise anti-democracy views when agreeing with statements, nor what salience they ascribe to them. 'Agree' questions may

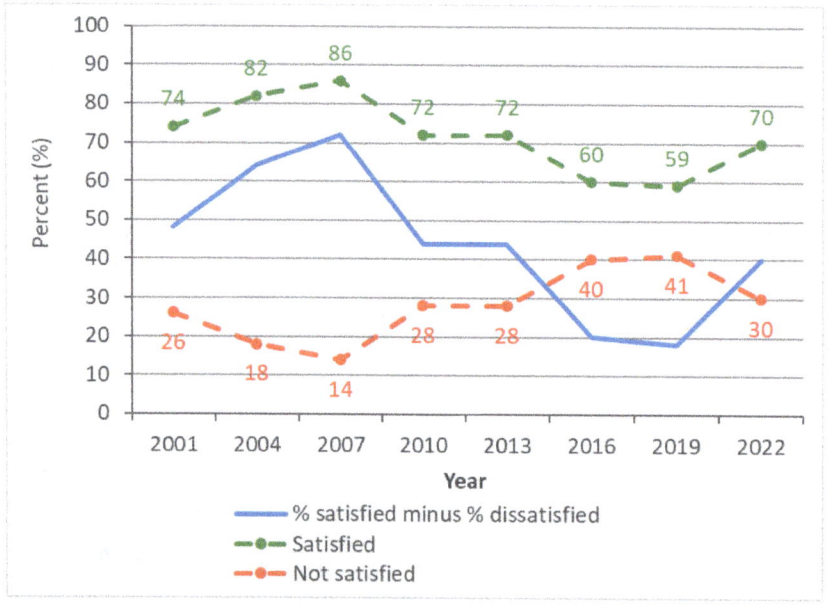

Figure 28.8: Respondents' satisfaction with democracy in successive Australian Election Study samples, 2001–2022

Source: **Cameron et al. 2022**, *The 2022 Australian Federal Election Study*, Figure 5.1.

Figure 28.9: Respondents' views about democracy in Lowy Institute surveys, 2012–2022

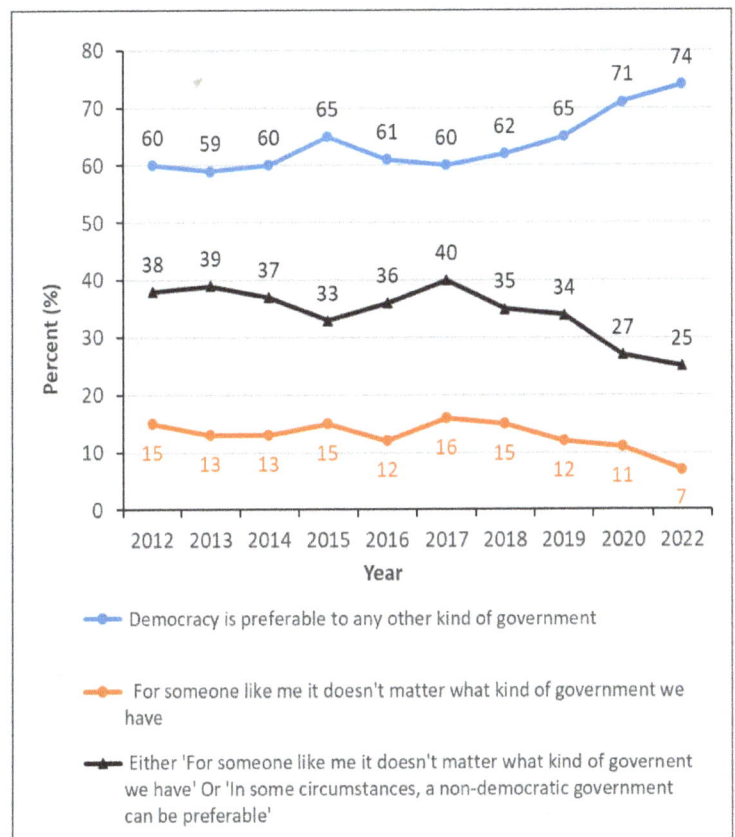

Source: Lowy Institute (2022) and various dates.

Note: Respondents were asked to choose one of the three statements in Figure 28.9.

capture a deeply held conviction motivating behaviours, or just an apathetic endorsement of a hypothetical statement asked out of the blue. However, we can take *changes* in such indicators over time to be capturing something, especially if they seem to show consistent trends.

Figure 28.9 shows a useful series from repeated Lowy Institute surveys over the last decade asking respondents to choose one of the three statements below the chart. From 2012–2019, a stable 'large majority' of three-fifths of respondents picked the first view that democracy is a better system than alternatives, and this percentage grew to nearly three-quarters of the sample in 2022. Similarly stable from 2012–2019 was the smaller fraction of between one in eight and one in 14 respondents who picked the 'indifference' statement that systems of government made no difference to 'someone like me'. A relatively stable quarter of people chose the last statement that 'in some circumstances a non-democratic government could be preferable'. Adding this last response to the bottom indifferent line gives a total for both 'non-democracy' responses, shown in Figure 28.9 by the black line. The vertical gap between the blue and black lines then shows the net balance of the pro-democracy responses. This difference was just 20 per cent points in 2017, but it has grown consistently since, and reached over 50 per cent points by 2022, exceeding anything earlier on.

Another approach to gauging democratic quality over time has asked respondents whether they trust key institutions, but here the results have not shown similarly benign patterns. Figure 28.10 shows that less than a third of respondents in the 2022 AES survey agreed that 'people

Figure 28.10: Australian respondents' trust in 'people in government', 2001–2022

Year	% People in government can be trusted	% People in government look after themselves	Trust balance (%)
2001	32	68	-36
2004	40	60	-20
2007	43	57	-14
2010	37	63	-26
2013	34	65	-31
2016	25	74	-49
2019	25	75	-50
2022	30	70	-40

Source: Cameron et al., 2022, *The 2022 Australian Federal Election – Results from the Australian Election Study.* See also Cameron and McAllister (2019).

Notes: The question asked was: 'In general, do you feel that the people in government are too often interested in looking after themselves, or do you feel that they can be trusted to do the right thing nearly all the time?' The trust balance is column 2 (trust) minus column 3 (look after themselves).

in government' can be trusted, while more than twice as many agreed that they 'look after themselves'. This level is slightly less adverse than ratings in the period 2016–2019, because during the COVID-19 pandemic more respondents said they trusted government (see Figure 28.6).

A final approach to assessment has asked more specifically about what respondents liked or disliked about 'Australian democracy'. Lists of possible prompts were provided and respondents asked to pick out their 'top ten' (Figure 28.11). Very similar (but unfortunately not quite identically phrased) questions were given to samples of Australian citizens, elites and federal politicians, and Figure 28.11 shows how these differently situated actors' lists of likes compared.

All three sets of actors included free and fair elections in their top three likes, and both citizens and politicians assigned importance to stable government, with citizens liking the two-party system, but also politicians finding a middle ground.

Figure 28.11: 'Top 10' responses by citizens, elites and federal politicians to the survey question: 'What do you like about Australian democracy?'

'What do you like about democracy in Australia?'		
Citizens in 2018	**Elites in 2016**	**Federal politicians 2019**
1. Stable government	1. Compulsory voting	1. Political participation (equality of access, ability to engage)
2. Free and fair elections	2. Social equality ('fair go')	2. Free and fair voting
3. Two-party system	3. Free and fair elections	3. Compulsory voting
4. Political choice	4. Free press	4. Stable government (ordered transitions)
5. Representative government	5. Freedom of speech and assembly	5. Freedom of speech
6. Politicians usually find a good middle ground on policy	6. Australia is relatively free from corruption	6. Open government (including freedom of information)
7. Big corporations and wealthy people don't have too much influence	7. Representative government	7. Strong institutions
	8. Rule of law	8. Rights protection (including minorities)
8. Political participation	9. Separation of powers	9. Constitutional checks and balances
9. Australia has experienced a good economy and lifestyle	10. Stable government	10. Free press
10. Good public services		

Sources: First column (Stoker, Evans and Halupka, 2018); second column (Evans, Stoker and Halupka, 2016); third column (Evans, Halupka and Stoker, 2019) also Evans, Halupka and Stoker (2018).

Figure 28.12: 'Top 10' responses by citizens, elites and federal politicians to the survey question: 'What do you dislike about Australian democracy?'

'What do you dislike about democracy in Australia?'

Citizens in 2018	Elites in 2016	Federal politicians 2019
1. We don't get much choice; political parties are too similar	1. Lack of action by governments of all persuasion on key public policy problems	1. Media misrepresentation (misinformation, pressure)
2. Big business has too much power	2. The decline in the quality of public policy debate	2. Integrity (political donations/corruption/political advertising)
3. The media has too much power	3. The personalisation of politics by the media and decline in media standards	3. Short-termism/three-year electoral cycle
4. Women are not well represented within politics	4. The poor behaviour of politicians	4. Dominance of party machines and two-party system
5. People from diverse cultures are not well represented within politics	5. Narrow parliamentary representativeness in gender, ethnic and class terms	5. Conflict-driven party politics (adversarial, combative, hyper partisanship)
6. Young people are not well represented within politics	6. Australians dislike adversarial politics	6. Over-representation of minorities
7. Too much compromise and not enough decisive action	7. The major political parties are undemocratic and broken	7. Public understanding/political literacy
8. Minor parties and independents hold too much power	8. Poor leadership	8. Power of vested interests
9. The battle between the two main political parties puts me off politics	9. Weak economic conditions in the global economy	9. Lack of responsiveness to constituents/poor public engagement
10. The media focuses too much on personalities and not enough on policy	10. The rise of the career politician	10. Centralisation of power

Sources: First column (Stoker, Evans and Halupka, 2018); second column (Evans, Stoker and Halupka, 2016); third column (Evans, Halupka and Stoker, 2019).

All actors included stable government in their top ten likes. Elites and politicians placed a free press and freedom of speech and assembly quite high, but these did not make the citizens' top ten. Citizens liked representative government and participation opportunities, as did elites. Politicians and elites liked checks and balances, rights protection, the rule of law and open government, but none of these made the citizen respondents' list. Good public services made the citizen list at the bottom, but not those of other actors.

Turning to dislikes about Australian democracy the citizen respondents essentially felt that their influence was hampered by that of the parties (using discretionary power in several ways), big business, the media (too much power and too much focus on personalities) and a lack of social diversity in politics (Figure 28.12). Elite responses often mirrored these complaints, but with more of an emphasis upon politicians' poor behaviour, narrow backgrounds and poor leadership. Federal politicians' dislikes about Australian democracy focused on over-adversarial conflicts, 'biased' media representations, lack of integrity, vested interests, not serving constituents, short-termism and the centralisation of power. Politicians also criticised citizens' limited understanding of politics.

Assessing Australian democracy in qualitative terms

The rich tapestry of analysis in earlier chapters continues the fundamental qualitative traditions of the democratic audit stream of work (see Chapter 1; and Beetham, 1999; Beetham and Weir, 1999; Sawer et al., 2009). Attempting to re-summarise them here could risk either being repetitive or blurring their focus on achieving balanced commentary with late-stage over-simplifications. Instead, we have sought to conclude by condensing out from the detailed qualitative audit analyses given in the 27 chapters some overall findings related to the quantitative measures discussed so far. We focus most on the key areas where democratic performance has been problematic or sub-optimal, and sketch in some potential feasible solutions, measures that might help to deepen citizens' democratic engagements and faith in the political system. We also briefly set these audit conclusions within a brief review of the generally difficult and perhaps darkening picture for liberal democracies within the Asia-Pacific region, where Australia's example has been (and can continue to be) so influential.

In the 21st century Australia has clearly not suffered from 'democratic backsliding', any greater polarisation of top two-party politics than normal in the past, nor any sustained rise of populist parties securing representation – although there have been recurrent but short-lived 'surge' outcomes in voting indicating varied levels of dissatisfaction with conventional political parties and politicians. Apart from occasional reactions to these wobbles, neither of the top two 'major' parties has adopted populist rhetoric and tactics that overtly call into question the civil rights of minorities. To the contrary, many past defects of elections management and the regulation of democratic competition at state level have been corrected and electoral integrity has been maintained and improved. The earlier chapters generally show that most of the diverse 'micro-institutions' needed across many sectors of regulation and public administration to support strong democracy (Dunleavy, 2019) are generally in place and in good health. (We consider some key exceptions to this picture at the end of the section.)

Similarly, although Australia has no integrated charter of human and civil rights, in recent years substantial improvements have been made in rectifying major rights-anomalies and defects affecting huge numbers of Australians – especially in equalising the position of gay and lesbian people; acknowledging and rectifying past institutional abuses of vulnerable social groups in the care of government agencies or civil society NGOs; delivering (albeit belatedly) on the rights of women to equal pay and equal representation in public and business life; and improving the still substantial remaining discrimination and disadvantagements suffered by Aboriginal 'bush' communities and other ethnic minorities. The failure of the Voice initiative at federal level could mark important setbacks for Indigenous people's cause. Yet even in this conjuncture, the wider picture of rights improvements has been positive and important.

Australia's counterpart 'Westminster systems' (including Canada, the UK, India and New Zealand) have all faced exceptional problems in managing the transition to multi-party politics that is arguably inevitable in the modern period. The first three have retained plurality rule ('first past the post' or FPTP) voting, and so the democratic costs of maintaining the 'stability' of national two-party dominance have been large, with very high levels of deviation from proportionality (DV scores). Huge threshold vote levels have been imposed on new party entrants before they can win any seats at all (let alone achieve proportional numbers of seats to votes), thereby artificially suppressing any smaller competitors. These features have insulated the 'major' parties in the UK, Canada and India from competition in ways that have produced repeated episodes of 'dominant party systems' where party competition becomes ineffectual because of incumbents' strong artificial advantages from the voting system (Dunleavy, 2010). This protection also allowed governments with an overall majority to push the limits of their country's constitutional feasibilities for narrow and overtly partisan ends (Innes, 2023; Bevan, 2023).

Australia has not joined New Zealand is shifting over wholly to proportional representation. Yet the unique emphasis of its voting processes, that everyone should vote and that every vote should count via the Alternative Vote (AV) aggregation process into the two-party preferred vote (TPP), has meant that barriers to new party entrants have been somewhat less. And the 'balancing' use of the Single Transferable Vote (STV) in upper house elections (with lower entry barriers and somewhat lower DV scores both federally and in the states) has also helped it to manage the modern transition to multi-party politics far better than its FPTP Westminster counterparts.

Yet the extensive advantagement of the top two parties vis-à-vis newer and smaller competitors has been a central fact of life across both federal and state government. At least Australian voters have had many opportunities to signal the diversification of their preferences (albeit often a little unavailingly, to short-lived 'surge' parties, or other parties with a somewhat episodic presence). And despite some limited populist themes being picked up occasionally by main party politicians (especially on the political right), new populist politics and parties have signally failed to take off in Australia, up to now. Nor have rich interventionists (like Clive Palmer) secured political representation, despite spending large sums on campaigning. After the COVID-19 pandemic, some analysts claimed a 'great reset', such that populist politics has declined in many democracies (Bennett Institute, 2022). But any such effect proved strictly temporary (Kampfner, 2023).

In terms of transitioning to more multi-party politics, the Greens have become fairly solidly established on the centre-left. Their winning three AV seats in Brisbane from Labor in 2022 may suggest that the Greens might yet be able to develop more local 'bastions' of support needed to regularly make the TPP count stage. Similarly, the ability of six Teal Independents in 2022 to pull some local Liberal votes with them into a new moderate political coalition (alongside local centre-left voters) may signal an end to the centre-right's previously lower level of fragmentation. In 2016 and 2019, hardline right-wing lobbies and factions in the coalition arguably 'held to ransom' the Liberal-National government's overall policy stance on climate change and women's rights. Initially, this had few electoral costs, given the comparatively greater fragmentation of Labor-Green voting (and Labor trade union 'brown' factions limiting their own party's climate policy). Yet voters in 2022 found ways to bypass the attempted vetoes of powerful factions inside both the top two parties and may be able to do so again in any similar conjuncture.

Where Australia's historic two-party predominance has never yet cracked is in terms of Labor's and the Liberal-National Coalition's monopoly of ministerial positions, both federally and at state level. On multiple occasions collective governmental power has now passed peacefully and consensually from one of the top two parties to its main rival with no problems, despite the occasional doom-laden coalition warnings of impending catastrophe should Labor win. Yet the transition to multi-party politics has only exceptionally and very rarely led to *even one* minister from outside Labor or the coalition ranks being appointed, still less a whole set of ministers entering a formal coalition government between two distinct parties. (The Liberal-Nationals' permanent coalition is really just a factional coordination of a single party entity and so does not count here.) The formal creation of a genuine coalition government, and the regular access of other parties' politicians to ministerial rank, of course will depend on future AV elections not delivering an overall majority to the leading 'major' party.

There have been some short-lived 'hung parliament' periods in federal and state lower houses where ministers have lacked a single-party majority. And the normal upper house pattern at federal level and in five states has been one where the governing party has no automatic or secure majority for new legislation (and sometimes even confidence votes). Yet (as in other Westminster systems) Australia's federal and state governments dispose of a considerable armoury of executive powers that prime ministers, state premiers and ministers (at both levels) can use in ways that are only weakly checked by legislatures, and usually 'after the fact'. From a democratic audit viewpoint, some of the most troubling scandals of modern Australian politics have their roots in ministers' ability to exploit executive powers for nakedly partisan ends in ways that clearly skate outside the rule of law (as with the 'sports rorts' and other 'pork barrelling' scandals, and media abuses of power during the 2019 election). Some episodes have infringed the civil rights of unpopular minorities in populist mode and thus the foundational political equality of a democratic polity. The populist 'anti-bludger' (or 'scrounger') politics of Liberal and National minsters in 2016–2020 was a key example, that led to the illegal pursuit of 'robodebt' policies (see Chapters 13 and 14). Rather similar has been the (for a long time bipartisan) Labor and Coalition elites' joint insistence on housing irregular asylum seekers and refugee migrants offshore, contrary to international treaty obligations. Thus, AV's weaknesses in ensuring the democratic accountability of ministers have created spaces where ministers' discretionary capabilities have been exploited in party competition. In some mitigation, both these cases were initially justified by ministers citing clear majority backing from 'public opinion'. And when malfeasance or rights infringements have been demonstrated, most such efforts at 'exploitative' politics have either proved limited in scope, or backfired, or proved short-lived (as with robodebt).

There are also strong defenders of advantaging the top two Australian parties vis-à-vis smaller rivals, citing Schumpeter's minimalist version of liberal democracy as just a polity where voters have a genuine choice between two competing and credible government teams. At both the federal and state levels, AV has a great track record of (almost) always awarding the most seats to the most popular party, and it enjoys enduring support among the Australian public, despite their equal recognition of the constraints that this has imposed on voters' ability to spur governments into action on some issues (see Figures 28.11 and 28.12). Critics argue that there can be severe policy consequences in letting the top two parties' ministers and elites indulge in internal factional appeasement rather than following national interest policies. A key example in 2016–2022 was arguably the Liberal-National governments' weak policies against climate change and their insistence on continuing to develop new coal and oil projects, despite the 2019–2020 bushfires wake-up call and many other signs of darkening Anthropocene-era changes (see Chapter 27). Australia's long-time lags in developing solar and wind power (belatedly being swiftly rectified in the 2020s), and Labor's 2023 decision to license new fossil fuel projects because of continuing energy security difficulties and trade union lobbying, seem to be other examples of 'faction appeasement' decisions.

Yet in another critically important area of national policy-making, defenders of the Schumpeterian/Westminster system's capacity for strong executive action and ability to respond to public opinion changes might have a strong counter-example. In the 2010s, many critics pointed out that Australia's international policies (and its wider cultural orientation and alignments) were bifurcating in unsustainable ways. Australian trade with many Asian countries developed phenomenally, with China becoming overwhelmingly its largest trading partner thanks to massive iron ore, coal and oil exports from Western Australia, the Northern Territory and Queensland. An influx of Chinese capital into Australia followed, especially in infrastructure facilities. At the same time, the 2000s and 2010s saw large increases in the regular in-migration of people from Asian countries, as 'white Australia' policies and the domination of UK and European in-migration were finally eclipsed, and an 'Asian century' loomed. Yet Australia's historic sociocultural attitudes of anxieties about (and distancing from) Asia persisted with considerable force (Walker, 1995; Sobocinska et al., 2012). And despite the shift in its economic dependencies, and opening up of immigration, critics argued that in the 21st century culturally Australia had become a 'stranded nation', situated within Asia but uncommitted to it (Walker, 2019).

Throughout these rapid changes Australia's defence and international policies were solidly and intimately tied into long-standing alliances, mainly with the USA. Under PM Menzies in 1965–1967 Australia backed the USA with force commitments in the Vietnam war (rather disastrously for its troops) when even the UK did not. And it formed part of the USA alliances that threw back the Iraqi invasion of Kuwait in 1991, invaded and occupied Iraq in 2003 (and again in 2005–2009) and intervened militarily twice in Afghanistan (with troops involved in 2001–2014 and 2015–2021). Although these recent interventions were on a far more restricted scale than those of the UK, Australia was still usually the third or fourth largest USA ally in terms of force commitments. American forces also operate major bases in the north of the country and are Australia's largest partner for annual joint exercises under the joint Pacific command structure. Defence links to the UK (in a far smaller way) have also been sustained by traditional monarchical and Commonwealth ties to the UK (re-emphasised by the failure of the 1999 republic referendum), plus links to two other countries included in the 'five Eyes' security and intelligence alliance (Canada and New Zealand). Some observers of Australia's long-run policy evolution linked this period of systematic ambivalence in its orientation to its alleged long-run 'cultural cringe' dependence on Anglosphere cultures from the USA and Britain, evident in its reluctance to release monarchical ties to the UK (reinforced by royal visits after 1999).

In the 2000s and 2010s many critics argued that Australia could not comfortably straddle two diverging horses at once – remaining militarily tied into USA-lead alliances when America was developing far more China-critical (even anti-China) policy stances on defence, intelligence, foreign policy and security issues. Federal PMs repeatedly denied that these difficulties were unmanageable. But in the late 2010s Australia regularly had to denounce actions taken by China to apparently 'punish' Australia for issuing pro-USA or critical statements on a series of incidents – including cyber-attacks on parliament and government agencies, sources attributed to China but not admitted. China also became increasingly and frankly authoritarian under President Xi, engaging in a period of aggressive 'wolf-warrior diplomacy' against the USA and its allies (Xiaolin, 2023), building up military forces in the South China Sea, and threatening the invasion of Taiwan with increasing frequency. Xi also offered a powerful non-democratic development pathway model, plus aid, to still developing countries across the Asia Pacific nations, including the Solomon Islands in return for a naval base there. Punitive Chinese measures were taken against Australia's wheat and wines imports when PM Scott Morrison ill-advisedly demanded an investigation into the origins of the COVID-19 pandemic, feeding populist suspicions that it was caused by a leak from a Chinese laboratory.

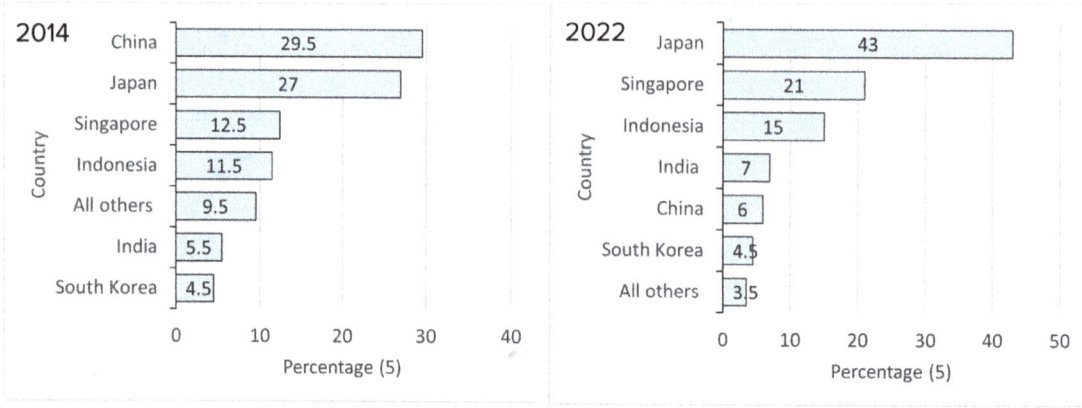

Figure 28.13: How Lowy survey respondents' perceptions of Australia's 'best friend in Asia' changed between 2014 and 2022

Source: Lowy Institute Poll, 2022.

At the same time, Australia made efforts in the Asian group of nations to encourage a focus on economic growth as the pathway to political liberalisation in Asia. Yet trends in the Asia-Pacific world region were not favourable for liberal democracy. Thailand and Burma previously made the EIU's 'badly flawed democracy' status but both dropped out following military take-overs. Vietnam's Communist system did not improve, but nor did it worsen on civil rights. Indian democracy has remained resilient but with substantial problems, with recent trends moving it towards a new BJP 'dominant party system', accompanied by some populist Hindu attacks on civil rights for Muslims and other ethnic minorities. Nearest of all to Australia is Indonesia, an overwhelmingly Islamic country where democratic processes have remained resilient, despite some threats from extreme jihadist movements. Previous conflicts over Indonesia government military reactions to East Timor's independence faded into the past.

These developments, especially the dire warnings about China's military build-up had a transformative effect on Australian public opinion, as Figure 28.13 demonstrates. In 2014–2016, three in ten respondents in Lowy Institute surveys saw China as Australia's 'best friend in Asia' – this came shortly after the then Labor government in 2012 inaugurated a turn towards Asia in economic and cultural terms. By 2022, that survey share fell to just one in 16 respondents, while the public recognition of Japan, Singapore and Indonesia as friendly nations soared.

Liberal-National politicians both fuelled and sought to capitalise on this dramatic *volte face* in public views. The strong executive powers under 'Westminster system' arrangements gave PM Scott Morrison a dramatic (if costly) way to signal a policy change and seek to wrongfoot his opponents. In August 2021, the PM suddenly announced the cancellation of an ongoing A$50 billion contract that Australia had signed with a French submarine manufacturer only in 2019. The French deal was originally announced in 2016 by PM Malcom Turnbull and involved converting a French nuclear-powered sub design to use conventional propulsion only. There were indications in 2021 that the project was running into some technical difficulties, which provided a thin pretext for the cancellation. Australia ended up paying A$2.4 billion for work already done by the French contractor, plus a penalty fee of A$750 million for its cancellation.

Instead, Morrison immediately followed up by announcing a new three-way USA, UK and Australian agreement (AUKUS) to develop a fleet of more powerful nuclear-powered submarines for Australia. This deal had been six months in development and kept completely secret, since it would be Australia's first nuclear-powered defence technology, outclassing all its neighbours (except China) in creating untrackable subs armed with long-range cruise missiles. In characteristic 'Westminster system' style, the PM gave the Labor opposition just 24 hours' notice of the AUKUS deal before it was announced in parliament. Equally characteristically, the Labor shadow cabinet used that short time to decide that they would support AUKUS, which the party and Albanese continued to do once he became PM.

Other announcements under Morrison of expanded cooperation with USA forces in training and bases made clear that the Coalition government meant AUKUS to signal both its decisive re-commitment to 'the West' in any military conflict with China, and a determination to remain militarily more advanced than any of its other Asia-Pacific neighbours. For instance, huge increases were touted in the Australian army's fire power from a reach of 60 miles away with conventional artillery (useful only for defence) to one of 600+ miles away with cruise missiles. Air force weaponry also attracted new investments for distance-handling of targets, along with other substantial boosts to the military budget and to a wide range of equipment. The AUKUS decision triggered strong denunciations from China of 'war mongering' but Australia went on to join the 'Quad' conference (with the USA, Japan and India), discussing other aspects of 'containing' perceived China threats. Dire forecasts followed of high costs for Australia from Chinese sanctions and the increase in 'new cold war' tensions (**Tricontinental Institute for Social Research, 2022**).

However, instead the *Economist* (**2023**) argued that China's actions had not worked and that 'The "lucky country" may be uniquely able to endure Chinese bullying'. Australia quickly found other Asian markets in Japan, South Korea and India for the agricultural products and liquid natural gas exports that China boycotted. Other observers also took a sanguine view, arguing that China's 'sound and fury' could not offset its strong economic needs for Australian basic resources and access to its product markets (**Herscovitch, 2023**; **Uren, 2023**). By 2023, China also rolled back generally on its previous 'wolf diplomacy' policies and scrapped most sanctions on Australian goods thereafter (**Collinson, 2023**; **Curran, 2022**). A cooling-off of overt diplomatic hostilities occurred under the new Labor government after PM Albanese met President Xi in person at a conference in June 2023. Some critics still took a less sanguine view, arguing that these small shifts 'can't undo fundamental differences' (**Zelinsky, 2023**). If China invades or intervenes militarily in Taiwan, American observers also argue that Australia would surely back USA counter-measures, even if this meant some form of outright war (**Brands, 2022**).

The AUKUS saga reminds us that for a polity to remain a liberal democracy it must also be effective as a state as well. And systems of party competition and elections do not just shape how citizens' preferences reach political elites but can also have important influences on governance and policy outcomes. Defenders of the status quo can argue that in privileging the top two parties, Australian democracy has not been perfect but has been resilient. That is a considerable virtue in these dark times for democracy worldwide, especially as the global region around Australia potentially threatens to become a far more turbulent geo-political environment than in the past.

Conclusions and reform priorities

The over-time and comparative data considered here clearly situate Australia as a long-established and solidly founded liberal democracy. Especially within the Indo-Pacific region Australia (alongside New Zealand) has been a very important local exemplar of how to run a pluralistic society and electoral governance in ways that have fostered long-term economic expansion and increased prosperity over time – as the non-stop stream of visitors from nearby countries to admire Parliament House in Canberra also demonstrates. At the same time, Australia (along with the UK) has not 'topped the table' in democratic terms, or even been in the top 10 countries for many decades. And it has experienced some substantial 'democratic malaise' problems, including declining trust in government in recent years. Both comparative and over time indicators of Australia's democratic performance have given rather variable or mixed pictures at times, often apparently responding to quite short-term factors. Although indices have turned up in 2022, previous data suggested some decline in democratic confidence over recent decades.

The qualitative analysis in the book's main chapters (Chapters 1 to 27) also demonstrate that Australia has been home to many lasting and worthwhile democratic innovations. Many benign outcomes have followed on from holding frequent elections with compulsory voting at both federal and state levels. For instance:

- voter turnout has consistently exceeded 90 per cent (albeit under compulsory voting)
- the electoral systems in the House of Representatives and Senate have different features, which help different parties secure representation
- modern Australian election processes overall have been rated as high in integrity
- citizens have been engaged in the electoral process, and although women's representation in the federal parliament has been low, it has increased over time
- Australia has generally avoided the extremes of partisan polarisation produced by strong populist policies securing significant voter support or being adopted by the top two parties, and partisan polarisation has been moderate
- 'democratic backsliding' has generally been ruled out by 'rule of law' principles, enforced by the courts and the High Court, together with the independence of most 'micro-institutions' regulating discrete aspects of elections and policy-making
- Australia has a vigorous interest group universe that in the modern period has been a force for increased social diversity, reduction of discrimination against minorities, and (along with social media) speedier and more complete citizen vigilance not just over government, but also over media and important civil society institutions.

Turning to the quality of democrat governance, Australia has enjoyed a very 'balanced' configuration of political control across the two houses of the legislature at federal level, and to a lesser extent in five of the six states, with PR-elected upper houses not bound by the same rigid discipline enforced by single-party governments in the AV-elected lower chambers. The relationship between the Commonwealth and states and territories has also been broadly cooperative, with state and territory control tending to shift against long-term parties in power at federal level in ways that can 'stabilise' policy-making. Thirty years of continuous economic growth have testified both to Australia's 'lucky country' situation in terms of resources and geographical placement, but also to regulatory systems and public services that have been highly rated in international terms and actively supported economic modernisation and improvements in societal diversity and rights regimes.

Nevertheless, there also remain significant challenges for elections and the quality of democracy in Australia, including:

+ the 'artificial' protection given to the top two parties, which has conferred a duopoly of government control on the top two parties at all levels of government. This situation has now lasted for decade after decade, denying all other parties experience of ministerial government, and despite voters' sharply weakening identification with the top parties
+ disproportional treatment of smaller parties in the House of Representatives
+ 'semi-permanent campaigning', produced by the short electoral cycle
+ the make-up of MPs and senators has not reflected the broader population in many respects
+ the highly biased and partisan press and private broadcasting control by a few 'oligarchs' like Rupert Murdoch and other tycoons has continuously raised important questions about democratic fairness and journalistic integrity at election times especially, with no amelioration of the situation
+ significant integrity question marks still exist, around the roles of money in party financing and its weak regulation.

In terms of the wider democratic representation of interests, there are multiple signs (recognised by most voters) that major problems remain:

+ Business has a political and governmental power that exceeds all other societal interests and is permanently at work shaping federal and state policies both through regular *de facto* resource suasion, political lobbying, partisan funding and control over policy-relevant information.
+ Australia's interest group and media processes have only recently worked to highlight minority disadvantagement and rectification of past wrongs. And in other fields (like climate change and the characterisation of irregular migration) active press and media disinformation campaigns have remained prominent and heavily biased.
+ Federal government policy has sometimes apparently lagged years behind Australia's opportunities and threats, partly because of veto power of factional blocs pushing minority sectional interests inside the top two governing parties, especially in environmental policies.
+ The weakness of rights regimes under 'Westminster system' arrangements and the relatively unconstrained executive powers enjoyed by incumbent governments have regularly tempted PMs, premiers and ministers to play hardball with their constitutional remit, threatening to impose unwarranted costs on unpopular or less politically protected minorities.

Reform priorities

The picture drawn here and in the previous chapters is a complex one, yet one that underlines the importance of established liberal democracies not sitting back complacently on their laurels, but instead committing to continued democratic developments and reforms to further improve how they operate. This imperative is made all the more pressing by rapid technological and socioeconomic developments in fields like social media, the use of data science and artificial intelligence in policy-making, the developing importance of robotics in the economy and within government, the continued worsening of climate change threats (like drought and desertification) in the Anthropocene era, and the changes in Indo-Pacific international relations. Australia's society and political situation will inevitably change radically in the next decade, and perhaps unrecognisably in the next three decades. Therefore, its liberal democracy will need to grow its capabilities to engage citizens and tackle 'wicked' problems accordingly (Head and Alford, 2015).

What then should the areas of urgent attention be? Australia has been among the best nations in the world at conducting elections. However, uncontrolled government advertising in the run-up to the 2019 and 2022 elections, problems with Australia's political funding and disclosure scheme, and growing concern about political donations made by vested interests have increasingly undermined Australia's claim to fully 'fair' elections. These factors mean that incumbent governments are placed at a significant advantage at election time. Improving regulations to counteract these issues is relatively straightforward.

Second, good democratic governance requires constant vigilance in the protection of civil rights (including minority rights) and duties. Although Australia has no integrated charter of human and civil rights, in recent years improvements have been made in rectifying major rights-anomalies and defects affecting large numbers of Australians (see Chapter 2). But an influential human rights monitoring report in 2021 still found that Australia remains 'strikingly poor at protecting the rights of those most at risk of rights abuses' such as children, Aboriginal and Torres Strait Islander youth, people with disabilities, people with low socioeconomic status, and refugees and asylum seekers (SBS News, 2021). Maintaining some continued progress on rights (albeit short of a charter of rights) is the essential counterpart of free elections and majority rule.

Third, good democratic governance depends upon public faith in and commitment to sustaining a democratic culture – as measured through levels of public satisfaction in democratic values and public trust in government. In general, Australians are great champions of democratic values, but they have become more distrusting of people in government and now have limited confidence in the ability of parties and governments of whatever form to address major public policy concerns. Rebuilding trust levels via responsible government and party campaigning practice is an effort that relies on party elites being willing to forego narrow party opportunism and cases where the public interest can be eroded by a 'hard line' pushing of self-restraint limits.

Fourth, the administrative and legal channels of citizen participation and inclusive parliamentary representation need to be strengthened, since Australia performs poorly in this regard, for instance by using citizens juries to monitor and evaluate key issue areas and direct democratic arrangements, such as participatory budgets at the local scale. To counter Australia's strong 'metropolitan dominance' in every state, there is also an urgent need for governments to connect more effectively with citizens in regional Australia and better address regional policy concerns.

Finally, good democratic governance relies on keeping governments responsible and accountable, responsive to the needs of the citizenry in service terms, and free from corruption. On the positive side, and with some misgivings, Australia's democratic institutions met the challenges posed by both the 2019–2020 bushfire and COVID-19 emergencies in an effective and adaptive manner. Its parliaments are comparatively dutiful and innovative custodians of democratic values and in the main hold executives effectively to account across states and territories. The system of justice and integrity agencies has been robust and fair, and the Australian public service has discharged its functions with professionalism and creativity.

However, the federation has become dominated by the Commonwealth executive wielding disproportionate political and economic power in Australia's democratic settlement, which undermines the effectiveness of traditional checks and balances through the separation of powers. And Australian government is still far from free of corruption – for instance, the extravagant remuneration of politicians after they leave office, (their 'vast post-service wealth') has opened a new frontier of acute concern (Peters and Burns, 2023). A lack of integrity in public office in both the public sector and politics has become culturally embedded and addressing it is an issue of significant political salience.

In sum, evidence from the Audit suggests that Australian democracy needs to find a way to renew itself in these five areas. It requires a period of democratic imagination, reflection and reinvention to restore and strengthen what Amartya Sen (1999) refers to as the 'protective power of democracy'. In general, there is still overwhelming support for representative democracy but with a focus on making the system of government even more representative of the people they serve, accountable and responsive to their constituents and underpinned by a cleaner integrity politics and more 'caring', 'collaborative' and 'evidence-based' policy-making.

Notes

We are grateful to Alice Park who undertook much of the research and early data collection into some relevant indices of democracy cited here and their evaluation.

References

Beetham, David (1999) 'The idea of democratic audit in comparative perspective', *Parliamentary Affairs*, vol. 52, no. 4, pp.567–81. $ https://doi.org/10.1093/pa/52.4.567

Beetham, David and Weir, Stuart (1999) 'Auditing democracy in Britain: Introducing the democratic criteria', in *Political Power and Democratic Control in Britain*, London: Routledge. Chapter 1, pp.3–21. $ https://www.routledge.com/Political-Power-and-Democratic-Control-in-Britain/Beetham-Weir/p/book/9780415096447

Bennett Institute (2022) *The Great Reset: Public Opinion, Populism, and the Pandemic,* Cambridge, United Kingdom: Centre for the Future of Democracy report. Written by Foa, R.S.; Romero-Vidal, X.; Klassen, A.J.; Fuenzalida Concha, J.; Quednau, M. and Fenner, L.S. https://perma.cc/PZ62-C3R3

Bevan, Gwyn (2023) *How Did Britain Come to This? A Century of Failures of Systemic Governance*, London: LSE Press. https://press.lse.ac.uk/site/books/m/10.31389/lsepress.hdb/

Brands, Hal (2022) 'Why Australia is gearing up for possible war with China', 9 November. *Bloomberg.com* webpage. https://perma.cc/8A6L-TX7D

Cameron, Sarah and McAllister, Ian (2019) *Trends in Australian Political Opinion: Results from the Australian Election Study 1987–2019*, Canberra: The Australian National University. https://perma.cc/6EJ6-SAUG

Cameron, Sarah McAllister, Ian; Jackman, Simon; and Sheppard, Jill (2022) *The 2022 Australian Federal Election – Results from the Australian Election Study*. Australian Election Study web report. Griffith University. https://perma.cc/2ULA-ZZMM

Center for Systemic Peace (2024) *Polity V*, webpage. https://perma.cc/YC2N-ZAVG

Collinson, Elena (2023) 'Euphoria to fear – Review of *Australia's China odyssey: From Euphoria to Fear*', Council of Foreign relations website, 30 May. https://perma.cc/H79E-96ZG

Curran, James (2022) *Australia's China Odyssey: From Euphoria to Fear*, Sydney: New South Wales Press. $ https://perma.cc/7GQC-HP24

Dunleavy, Patrick (2010) 'Rethinking dominant party systems', in Bogaards, Matthijs and Bouceck, Francoise (eds) *Dominant Political Parties and Democracy: Concepts, Measures, Cases and Comparisons*, London: Routledge, pp.14–62. OA at: https://perma.cc/7HS6-3J8S

Dunleavy, Patrick (2018) 'Auditing the UK's changing democracy', Ch.1, pp. 15-42 https://doi.org/10.31389/book1.a In Dunleavy, Patrick; Park, Alice and Taylor, Ros (eds) (2018) *The UK's Changing Democracy: The 2018 Democratic Audit*, London: LSE Press, Chapter 1, pp.17–41. https://doi.org/10.31389/book1

Dunleavy, Patrick (2019) 'Micro-institutions and liberal democracy'. *Political Insight*, 10(1), 35-39. https://doi.org/10.1177/2041905819838154

Economist (2023) 'Australia has faced down China's trade bans and emerged stronger', *The Economist*, 23 May. https://perma.cc/MW5B-53WL

Economist Intelligence Unit (EIU) (2022) *Democracy Index 2022*. Online Report. https://perma.cc/F9WE-CE24

Evans, Mark (2021) 'Scott Morrison's pandemic popularity boost has vanished, along with public trust in our politicians', *Guardian*, 15 November. https://perma.cc/AM3N-6QP4

Evans, Mark and Stoker, Gerry (2019) 'Does political trust matter?', in Elstub, Steven and Escobar, Óliver (eds) *Handbook of Democratic Innovation and Governance*, Chichester: Edward Elgar, Chapter 8, pp.120–34. $ https://perma.cc/W5LJ-BDKG

Evans, Mark; Stoker, Gerry; and Halupka, Max (2016) 'Now for the big question: Who do you trust to run the country?', *The Conversation*, 2 May. https://perma.cc/BPU9-FAYH

Evans, Mark; Halupka, Max; and Stoker, Gerry (2018) *How Australians Imagine Their Democracy: The 'Power of Us'*, Canberra: Museum of Australian Democracy. https://apo.org.au/sites/default/files/resource-files/2018-07/apo-nid193921.pdf

Evans, Mark; Halupka, Max; and Stoker, Gerry (2019) 'Trust and democracy in Australia', in Evans, Mark; Grattan, Michelle and McCaffrie, Brendan (eds) *From Turnbull to Morrison: Understanding The Trust Divide*, Melbourne: Melbourne University Press, Chapter 2, pp.17–35. $ https://perma.cc/6DF7-9WXB

Evans, Mark; Jennings, Will and Stoker, Gerry (2020) *How Does Australia Compare: What Makes A Leading Democracy? Two Paradoxes For Australian Democratic Governance*. Canberra: Democracy25 report No.6. https://perma.cc/K3J6-CBF8

Flavin, Patrick and Shufeldt, Gregory (2019) 'Comparing two measures of electoral integrity in the American States', *State Politics & Policy Quarterly*, Vol. 19, No. 1 (March 2019), pp. 83–100. $ https://www.jstor.org/stable/26973442

Freedom House Index (2023) Australia scores webpage. https://perma.cc/3LUW-9FFL

Gardner, Robyn (2024) 'Administrative Law / Regulatory & Policy Responses / Governance', Bibliography article with cross-national literature summaries on AustLII Community site. https://perma.cc/QNC4-STV4

Head, Brian and Alford, John (2015) 'Wicked problems: Implications for Public Policy and Management', *Administration & Society*, vol. 47, no. 6, pp. 701–729. DOI:10.1177/0095399713481601 Open access at: https://www.researchgate.net/publication/275573005_Wicked_Problems_Implications_for_Public_Policy_and_Management

Herscovitch, Benjamin (2023) 'China's sound and fury over Aukus will mean little for ties with Australia', *The Guardian, Australia,* 15 March, webpage. https://perma.cc/2N2Z-EGAG

InCiSE (Index of Civil Service Effectiveness) (2019) By Blavatnik School of Government, Oxford University, with UK think-tank, the Institute for Government. https://perma.cc/FSE9-VQGA

Innes, Abby (2023) *Late Soviet Britain: Why Materialist Utopias Fail*, Cambridge: Cambridge University Press. $ https://doi.org/10.1017/9781009373647

International IDEA (2022) 'Global state of democracy initiative', Web dataset. https://perma.cc/8V3E-YZLV

Jennings, Will; Valgarðsson, Viktor; Stoker, Gerry; Devine, Dan; Gaskell, Jen; and Evans, Mar (2021) *Report No 8: Political Trust and the COVID-19 Crisis: Pushing Populism to the Backburner? A Study of Public Opinion in Australia, Italy, the UK and the USA,* Canberra: Australia Democracy 2025, p.22. https://perma.cc/GS6X-T7Y5

Kampfner, John (2023) 'Right wing populism is set to sweep the west in 2024', *Foreign Affairs*, 26 December blogpost. https://perma.cc/M248-TLAV

Levitsky, Steven and Ziblatt, Daniel (2018) *How Democracies Die.* New York: Penguin Random House. https://perma.cc/2N7L-R2FZ

Levitksy, Steven and Ziblatt, Daniel (2021) 'The biggest threat to democracy is the GOP stealing the next election', *The Atlantic*, 9 July. https://perma.cc/84UY-TSSV

Little, Andrew T and Meng, Anne (2023) 'Subjective and objective measurement of democratic backsliding', *SSRN* ,17 January. Research paper online. https://perma.cc/X75C-M5XM

Little, Andrew T and Meng, Anne (2024) 'Measuring democratic backsliding'. *PS: Political Science & Politics.* Vol. 57, no. 2, pp. 149-161. https://doi.org/10.1017/S104909652300063X

Lowy Institute (2022) 'Lowy Institute poll 2022', by Natasha Kassam. https://poll.lowyinstitute.org/report/2022/

OECD (Organisation for Economic Cooperation and Development) (2019) 'Income redistribution through taxes and transfers across OECD countries', Economics Department Working Papers No. 1453 by Causa, Orsetta; and Hermansen, Mikkel. https://perma.cc/PR7T-H2PR

OECD (Organisation for Economic Cooperation and Development) (2022) *Building Trust to Reinforce Democracy.* Paris: Organization for Economic Co-operation and Development. Updated 13July. https://doi.org/10.1787/b407f99c-en

PEI (Perceptions of Electoral Integrity) (2019a) *Electoral Integrity Worldwide.* By Norris, Pippa and Grömping, Max. PEI 7.0 Report. https://perma.cc/Z9SN-DWWV

PEI (Perceptions of Electoral Integrity) (2019b) 'Freedom House Index', Webpage. https://perma.cc/M5JP-EX6H

Peters, B. Guy and Burns, John P. (2023) 'Debate: Politicians and their vast post-service wealth', *Public Money & Management*, vol. 43, no. 6, 4 May. $ https://doi.org/10.1080/09540962.2023.2198907

Pew Research (2017) 'Democracy widely supported, little backing for rule by strong leader or military', Pew Research webpage, 16 October. https://perma.cc/AQT4-FJCC

Sawer, Marian; Aljorenson, Norman; and Larkin, Phil (2009) *Australia – The State of Democracy*, Canberra: Federation Press.

SBS News (2021) 'Australia has delivered "strikingly poor" results on a new human rights scorecard', SBS webpage, 29 June. https://perma.cc/A7Q2-ET7X

Sen, Amartya Kumar (1999) 'Democracy as a universal value', *Journal of Democracy*, vol. 10, no.3, pp.3–17. https://perma.cc/B5Y7-FNU2

SGI (Sustainable Government Index) (2022) SGI webpage. https://perma.cc/A44J-XGES

Sobocinska, Agnieszka and Walker, David Robert (eds) (2012) *Australia's Asia: From Yellow Peril to Asian Century.* Perth: University of Western Australia Publishing.

Social Progress Index (2022) 'Global Index 2022: Results'. Social Progress Imperative Project webpage. https://perma.cc/PKP4-Q2QP

Stoker, G.; Evans, M. and Halupka, M. (2018) *Trust and Democracy in Australia –Democratic Decline and Renewal,* Canberra: Democracy 2025/Museum of Australian Democracy. Report No. 1. https://perma.cc/9MQJ-5BZE

Transparency International (2022) Project webpage. https://perma.cc/64E3-NEKA

Tricontinental Institute for Social Research (2022) 'Nothing good will come from the new cold war with Australia as a frontline state'. 8 December. Webpage. https://perma.cc/3CR5-RVP5

Uren, David (2023) 'Why China's coercion of Australia failed', *The Strategist*, Australian Strategic Policy Institute, 27 April, webpage. https://perma.cc/3BWV-U7KG

V-Dem (2021) *Autocratization Goes Viral: Democracy Report 2021,* V-Dem Institute, University of Gothenberg, report. https://perma.cc/UM2M-Y5CW

Varieties of Democracy (V-Dem) (2023) *Democracy Report 2023*. V-Dem Institute webpage at University of Gothenberg. https://perma.cc/YY9A-SFAX

Walker, David (1995) *Anxious Nation: Australia and the Rise of Asia 1850–1939*, Crawley, WA: University of Western Australia Press, 1999. $ https://perma.cc/QL8R-NUTA

Walker, David (2019) *Stranded Nation: White Australia in an Asian Region,* Crawley: UWA University of Western Australia Press. $ https://perma.cc/UG5P-PYUF

Wikipedia (2024) 'Gini coefficient', online encyclopaedia webpage. https://perma.cc/7USF-FGVH

World Happiness Report (2023) *World Happiness Report 2023,* webpage. https://perma.cc/U3TH-USM9

WVS (2021) World Values Survey Wave 7 webpage. https://perma.cc/VB2L-XBSX

Xiaolin, Duan (2023) 'Domestic sources of China's wolf-warrior diplomacy: Individual incentive, institutional changes and diversionary strategies'. *The Pacific Review*, vol. 37, no. 3, pp. 585–603. $ https://doi.org/10.1080/09512748.2023.2205163

Young, Sally (2011) *How Australia Decides: Election Reporting and the Media*, Cambridge: Cambridge University Press. $ https://perma.cc/C2UV-TKRG

Zelinsky, Misha (2023) 'The China-Australia relationship is still close to the rocks', *Foreign Policy*, 6 July blog. https://perma.cc/K83V-92E2

Zurich University (2020) 'Democracy Barometer', webpage. https://perma.cc/K2T9-BQRB

Index

A

AAT (Administrative Appeals Tribunal) 262–263, 356
Abbott, Tony... 179, 222, 234, 240, 277, 286, 333, 359
   climate change and environmental policies 560, 567
   First Nations peoples policy .. 56, 77
   gender equality issues 113
   politicisation of the executive..... 313, 314
   refugee and asylum seeker policies 61
   welfare reform 306
   see also Liberal-National Coalition
ABC (Australian Broadcasting Commission)..127, 168, 169, 170, 172–173, 174, 175, 184, 185, 268
   50/50 Project................................ 222
Abjorensen, Norman 346, 354, 355, 360
Aboriginal Advancement League 76
Aboriginal Affairs Action Plan, South Australia........................ 445
Aboriginal and Torres Strait Islander Agreement 2019-2028, ACT 525–526
Aboriginal and Torres Strait Islander Commission (ASTIC) 87
Aboriginal and Torres Strait Islander peoples
   in the APS (Australian Public Service).. 318
   current issues 43–44
   gender issues in employment.... 217
   gender-based violence 210, 221, 507, 509
   historical mistreatment of 34, 35, 37, 181, 590
   human rights and civil liberties .. 53, 54, 55, 62, 598
   Indigenous knowledge, environmental issues................... 563
   policing and imprisonment.... 57, 64, 424, 509, 526
   political exclusion of................ 36–37
   states.. 367
      Australian Capital Territory ...406, 519, 520, 525–526
      New South Wales.... 377, 379, 381
      Northern Territory.497, 502, 503, 507–511
      Queensland 406, 415, 418–419, 421, 423–424, 427
      South Australia...... 424, 434, 435, 445–446
      Tasmania 485, 493–494
      Victoria...........394, 398, 406, 408
      Western Australia 406, 463–464, 469, 470
   Torres Strait Islander practices in family law 424
   see also First Nations peoples; Voice to Parliament referendum, 2023
Aboriginal and Torres Strait Islander Peoples Act of Recognition Review Panel 2014 77
Aboriginal and Torres Strait Islanders Elected Body (ATSIEB), ACT 525
Aboriginal Community Assembly, Victoria 406
Aboriginal Land Rights Act (1976) 506
Aboriginal Languages Act 2017, New South Wales 379
Aboriginal Representative Body, Victoria 406
above-the-line voting, STV (Single Transferable Vote).... 46, 48, 270, 271, 458, 467, 490
ABS (Australian Bureau of Statistics)...... 220, 331–332, 353
ACCI (Australian Chamber of Commerce and Industry)....... 148
ACF (Australian Conservation Foundation).............................. 148
ACNA (Australian Charities and Not-for-Profits Commission) 261
ACT (Australian Capital Territory) *see* Australian Capital Territory
ACTPS (Australian Capital Territory Public Service)...... 520, 523, 524
ACTU (Australian Council of Trade Unions) 66, 148
Adelaide............................... 432, 437
   Greater Adelaide 530, 538
Adelaide Advertiser.................. 442
Administrative Appeals Tribunal (AAT) 262–263, 356
Advance SA party, South Australia 439
Advanced Strategic Research Agency (ASRA)....................... 314
advertising, government 184, 287, 311, 598
advisors........................ 42, 277, 289
   and the politicisation of the executive.................................. 313–314
advocacy groups........................ 147
   see also interest groups
AEC (Australian Electoral Commission) ... 109, 114, 115, 126, 136, 138, 153, 337, 510
AES (Australian Election Survey) 586–587, 588
Afghanistan....................... 295, 593
   Roberts-Smith defamation case.177, 178, 181, 184
AFP (Australian Federal Police) 184, 289, 522
Age, The 172

Roberts-Smith defamation case. 177, 178, 181, 184
AGO (Australian Geospatial-Intelligence Organisation)...295
AHPPC (Australian Health Protection Principal Committee) 348
AHRC (Australian Human Rights Commission).....55–56, 59, 214, 246, 356
AI (artificial intelligence)............152
Ai Group (Australian Industry Group) 148
Albanese, Anthony.123, 234, 263, 349, 457, 464–465, 550, 562
 APS reform 314, 321
 consensual style 236, 285
 foreign policy 297
 gender equality policies 220
 government reform agenda 308–309
 international relations policies ..595
 leadership selection............ 135–136
 media policy............................ 177
 and republicanism 81
 tax policy....................333
 Voice to Parliament referendum, 2023...57, 58, 79, 85, 86, 87–88, 91
ALGA (Australian Local Government Association)...348, 349, 352, 532, 550, 554
ALP (Australia Labor Party) see Labor Party
Aly, Anne.........................125
AMA (Australian Medical Association) 148
Amazon......................180
ANAO (Australian National Audit Office).....................338–339
ANC News...................443
Andrews, Daniel 394, 396, 397, 407
Andrews, Karen 61
Animal Justice party, Victoria . 403
ANMF (Australian Nursing and Midwifery Federation) 148
Anthropocene, the, environmental issues in 559–560, 571
 biodiversity................562, 568–569
 electoral politics...............561–562, 567–568
 polycentric governance 570–571
 recent developments........560–563
 SWOT analysis..................563–566
anti-terrorism laws....................... 90
ANZ 268
Anzac Hall 340–341
Apple 169, 180
APS (Australian Public Service)
............276, 293, 294, 297, 298, 301–303, 318, 321, 330, 598
 capability deficit...................314–316
 character of............................316–319
 consultants and outsourcing 310, 315
 COVID-19 pandemic 303, 304–305, 311, 312, 318
 criticisms of................................303
 cyber-security 311
 and democracy....................301–302
 digital modernisation ..310, 319, 320
 ethnic diversity 318
 gender equality and rights209, 215, 223, 311, 317
 IRAPS (Independent review of the Australian Public Service)......... 2019 .... 303, 305, 306, 312, 314
 politicisation of 313–316
 recent developments.........303–309
 reform 303–304, 308–309
 Royal Commission on the Robodebt Scheme 2023.288–289, 303–304, 306–308
 service delivery improvement 318–319
 staff numbers 303, 316–317
 SWOT analysis......................310–312
 values and standards of conduct 303
 see also Services Australia
APSC (Australian Public Service Commission)....... 276–277, 289, 309
ARENA (Australian Renewable Energy Agency) 562
artificial intelligence (AI)............152
ASD (Australian Signals Directorate)..............................295
Asia, Australia's relationship with 593–595
Asian Australians........ 54, 214, 318
ASIC (Australian Securities and Investments Commission)...268
ASIO (Australian Security and Intelligence Organisation)...247, 295
ASIS (Australian Secret Intelligence Service)..............295
ASRA (Advanced Strategic Research Agency) 314
ASTIC (Aboriginal and Torres Strait Islander Commission)...87
asylum seekers see refugees and asylum seekers
Atlas of Living 569
ATO (Australian Tax Office).....306
ATSIEB (Aboriginal and Torres Strait Islanders Elected Body), ACT 525
Attorney-General........................ 40

Audit Office, New South Wales 372
AUKUS (Australia, UK, USA) nuclear submarine deal......285, 289, 297, 595
austerity programs 294
Australia
 Westminster advisory system.....315
Australia Labor Party (ALP) see Labor Party
Australia Post.............................269
Australian Broadcasting Commission (ABC) see ABC (Australian Broadcasting Commission)
Australian Bureau of Statistics (ABS) 220, 331–332, 353
Australian Capital Television v Commonwealth 1992 75
Australian Capital Territory.....508, 514–515, 526, 544
 Aboriginal and Torres Strait Islander peoples 406, 519, 520, 525–526
 climate change and environmental policies 523, 565, 570
 Constitution and rights...............519, 524–526
 COVID-19 pandemic... 518–519, 523
 diversity in political representation 213, 214, 520, 521
 elected representatives at federal, state and local level....................546
 elections and party competition 516–518
 executive and Legislative Assembly (LA)............... 516–518, 521–524, 525
 human rights protection. 55, 60, 75, 380, 446
 land sales and purchases...........522
 local democracy............................530
 media 533
 party funding........................136
 public service............. 520, 523, 524
 recent developments...........516–519
 responsive government....522–523
 Senate representation.................257
 social and economic disadvantage 523
 SWOT analysis.................... 519–520
 transparency and accountability 522
 Voice to Parliament referendum, 2023................................ 84
Australian Capital Territory Public Service (ACTPS). 520, 523, 524
Australian Capital Territory (Self-Government) Act 1988 524
Australian Chamber of Commerce and Industry (ACCI) 148

Australian Charities and Not-for-Profits Commission (ACNA) . 261
Australian Climate Commission 562
Australian Communications and Media Authority 175, 182
Australian Competition and Consumer Commission 180, 353
  Digital Platforms Inquiry Report. 194
Australian Conservation Foundation (ACF).................... 148
Australian Conservatives, party funding 154
Australian Council of Trade Unions (ACTU)................... 66, 148
Australian Curriculum, Assessment and Reporting Authority 353
Australian Defence Force 295, 303
Australian democracy . 33, 34–35, 42–43
  Cabinet and Prime Minister roles 39–42
  governance institutions.......... 37–39
  historical development of...... 35–44
  influence of the Constitution 36–37
  performance assessment of 574–577
    faith in democracy 586–589
    international comparisons 577–585
    likes and dislikes 588–589
    qualitative assessments 590–595
    reform priorities 597–599
  political style of 38
  SWOT analysis......................... 43–44
Australian Election Survey (AES) 586–587, 588
Australian Electoral Commission (AEC) 109, 114, 115, 126, 136, 138, 153, 337, 510
Australian Energy Regulator.... 353
Australian Federal Police (AFP) 184, 289, 522
Australian Geospatial-Intelligence Organisation (AGO)............... 295
Australian Health Practitioner Regulatory Agency 353
Australian Health Protection Principal Committee (AHPPC) 348
Australian Human Rights Commission (AHRC) 55–56, 59, 214, 246, 356
Australian Human Rights Framework, 2010..................... 55

Australian Industry Group (Ai Group) 148
Australian Lawyers Alliance...... 65
Australian Local Government Association (ALGA) 348, 349, 352, 532, 550, 554
Australian Medical Association (AMA) 148
Australian Motoring Enthusiasts Party 271
Australian National Audit Office 308
Australian National Audit Office (ANAO) 338–339
Australian Nursing and Midwifery Federation (ANMF)................. 148
Australian Press Council.. 175, 182
Australian Public Service (APS) *see* APS (Australian Public Service)
Australian Public Service Commission (APSC) 276–277, 289, 309
Australian Red Cross 148
Australian Renewable Energy Agency (ARENA)..................... 562
Australian Secret Intelligence Service (ASIS) 295
Australian Securities and Investments Commission (ASIC)... 268
Australian Security and Intelligence Organisation (ASIO)............................... 247, 295
Australian Signals Directorate (ASD)... 295
Australian Tax Office (ATO) 306
Australian Taxation Office 291
Australian, The 170, 564
Australian War Memorial (AWM) 340–341
AV (Alternative Vote) 98, 123, 591, 592
  House of Representatives.... 35, 42, 44, 45, 48, 98, 99, 117, 231
  TPP (two-party preferred vote) 48, 99, 100–102, 112, 123, 124, 127, 369, 397, 438, 468, 499, 500, 502, 591
  states....................... 103, 107, 114, 596
    New South Wales. 367, 368–369, 376
    Northern Territory. 499, 500, 502
    South Australia................ 434, 436
    Tasmania 478, 482
    Victoria..................... 397, 399, 400
    Western Australia.. 456, 457, 466
AWM (Australian War Memorial) 340–341

B

Baby Boomers, media impartiality 200
Bach, Stanley.............................. 255
'back flips' (policy reversals)... 333
Bäckstrand, K............................. 571
Baird, Michael............................. 369
Baker, Barbara........................... 494
Banking Royal Commission 268–269
banks
  climate change and environmental policies 570
  corporate power 159
Barilaro, John 202
Barnett, Colin................... 456, 473
Barr, Andrew 521, 522–523
Bassi v Commissioner of Police (NSW) 62–63
BBC 172–173
Beetham, David 34, 160
below-the-line voting, STV (Single Transferable Vote).... 46, 48, 270–271, 467, 488, 490
benchmarking 353
Berejiklian, Gladys........... 369, 372, 373–374, 376, 381, 384, 385
Berry, Yvette 518
BHP 570
Biden, Joe 60, 297, 565
big cities *see* metropolitan regions/big cities, local democracy in
bills of rights.......................... 66–67
  Australia's lack of 38, 53, 70, 73, 74, 75, 176, 380, 446
  'British Bill of Rights'..................... 66
  Charter/Bill of Rights debate, New South Wales 380
biodiversity............. 560, 568–569
  see also environmental issues
Bishop, Julie 222
'Black Saturday', 2009 394
  see also bushfires
Bligh, Anna................................. 416
BLM (Black Lives Matter) ...62–63, 421
Blunt, David................................ 382
Bolsonaro, Jair 576
Bolte, Henry................................ 407
Bond, Alan.................................. 179
Boston Consulting Group........ 269
Boult, Andrew............................. 170
Bowen, Chris 136
Braithwaite, John 571
'branch stacking' 397, 405
Brandis, George.......................... 65
Brazil 576

Index

Brennan, Frank 65, 88
Bridgman, Peter 426
Brisbane
   City of Brisbane 531, 534, 538, 540, 545
   Greater Brisbane, South East Queensland 530, 531, 532, 535, 538
   Olympic Games 2032 .... 532, 535
broadcasting media *see* media, mainstream
Brooks, Adam 487
Brown v Tasmania 2017 75
Browne, Bill 107, 271–272
Bryce, Quentin 211
budgetary control 291–294
bureaucratisation of political parties 134
Burgess, Verona 314
Burns, John P. 161
bushfires 277, 285, 296–297, 561, 598
   New South Wales 374–375
   and social media 195
Business Council of Australia .. 160
businesses
   concentration of 152
   corporate executive pay 161
   CSR (corporate social responsibility) 152
   ESG (environmental and social governance) 152
   inter-firm transfers 161
   pay-as-you-go income tax 145
   tax avoidance industry 160
   see also corporate power
Business.gov.au 302
Butcher, John 305, 331
Buttfield, Nancy 222

C

Cabinet 235, 275–277, 279
   cabinet committees 276, 279, 281
   Expenditure Review Committee 281
   Service Delivery and Coordination Committee 281
   'collective responsibility' of 279, 450
   gender diversity 40
   'inner cabinets' 41
   role and powers of 37, 39–42
   South Australia 447, 449
   see also core executive
Cabinet Secretary 281
Calma, Tom 87
Cameron, Sarah 113, 114
Campbell, Kathryn 289
Canada
   COVID-19 pandemic 283
   electoral system 590–591
   federalism 355
   'Five Eyes' intelligence network 295, 593
   political appointees 313
Canberra
   AWM (Australian War Memorial) 340–341
   bushfires 296
Canberra Health Services Strategic Plan 2020-23, Australian Capital Territory .523
Canberra Times 533
   Roberts-Smith defamation case .177, 178, 181, 184
'car parks' rort .. 284, 311, 339, 576
'carbon lock-in' 562
carbon tax 127, 129, 158, 242, 285, 333, 347, 567
'Caring for Country' Indigenous land management programs 563, 569
Carr, Kim 332
Carson, Andrea 331
'cartel party' system 138
Cash, Michaelia 220, 525
CBD (Convention on Biological Diversity) 569
CCA (Climate Change Authority) 561, 562
CCCLM (Council of Capital City Lord Mayors) 532
CDCs (community development councils) 91–92
CEFC (Clean Energy Finance Corporation) 562
centralisation, of government 346–347
Centre for Aboriginal Economic Policy Research 79
Centrelink 288, 306, 307
CFFR (Council on Federal Financial Relations) 348
Channel Nine Network 179
Chant, Kerry 375
charities, historical mistreatment of minorities 34, 37, 151
Charles III, King (UK) 80, 81
Charlesworth, Hilary 223
Charter of Human Rights 57
Chartism, England 116
Chief Minister, Treasury and Economic Development Directorate (CMTEDD), Australian Capital Territory .524
childcare issues 208, 211, 217
children
   forced separation of First Nations children 37, 55
   'Home Children' imported from the UK 181
   rights of 90, 202–203
   Stolen Generation 55, 78
China 280
   Australia's relationship with 297, 593, 594–595
   climate change and environmental issues 566
   closure of border with, COVID-19 pandemic 282
   cyber-interference in elections .. 187
   threats to Taiwan 60
   trade dependence on 285
Chinese Australians
   in the APS (Australian Public Service) 318
   House of Representatives 245
   human rights and civil liberties ... 54
   New South Wales 381
   political representation 117, 125
Chiu, Osmond 380
Christian Democrats, New South Wales 369, 370, 371
churches, historical mistreatment of minorities 34, 37, 151, 181, 182
Churchill, Winston 341
CIA 295
cities *see* metropolitan regions/ big cities, local democracy in
Cities Commission, Greater Sydney 537
citizen-centred policy 327, 329, 330
City Deals 532, 538, 540
civic engagement, in policy-making 330, 331–332
civil liberties 33, 53–54
   COVID-19 pandemic 62–64
   detention of refugees 61
   recent developments 54–57
   rights deficit 66–67
   social rights 64–66
   SWOT analysis 59–60
   Voice to Parliament 57–59
civil rights 598
Civil Rights Act 2006 (Victoria) 60
civil service *see* APS (Australian Public Service)
civil society organisations, and policy-making 329, 336
Clean Energy Finance Corporation (CEFC) 562
Climate 200 .... 113, 130
climate change 48, 99, 100–102, 112, 122, 123, 124, 129, 130, 139, 285, 333
   and the Anthropocene 560–563, 565, 566, 567–568, 571
   Australian Capital Territory 523, 565, 570
   and bushfires 277

climate change denial 564, 366, 567
fossil fuel and mining industries 158, 159
House of Representatives 234–235
and the media 186
and the Murdoch media 179
policy failures and failures to act
.... 296–297
reform priorities 597–598
states' role in 347
Climate Change Authority (CCA)
.... 561, 562
Climate Change Review 566
Climate Change Strategy, Victoria
.... 408
'closure' motions, House of Representatives 242, 243
Clune, David 372
CMTEDD (Chief Minister, Treasury and Economic Development Directorate), Australian Capital Territory 524
COAG (Council of Australian Governments) 72, 262, 281, 282, 348, 349, 351–352, 353, 359, 532, 548, 550
Reform Council 353, 359
COAG Legislation Amendment Bill 356
coal industry *see* fossil fuel industry
Coaldrake, Peter 426
co-design 92, 329, 330, 348
Cody, Howard 482
Commission on the Rights of the Child (CRC) 202–203
Commissioner of Police (NSW) v Gibson (2020) 62
Commissioner of Police v Gray (2020) NSWSC 867 62
Committee for Sydney 540
Commonwealth
fiscal powers 351–352
and local government 550
and metropolitan regions/big cities
.... 531, 538
Reform of the Federation White Paper 2014 358
revenue and expenses 351
see also federalism, and democracy
Commonwealth Act 1977 506
Commonwealth Bank 268
Commonwealth departments and ministers 289–295
see also core executive
Commonwealth Grants Commission 464, 507–508
Commonwealth Scientific and Industrial Research Organisation (CSIRO) 564
Communications, Engagement and Education Strategy, New South Wales 384
Community Alliance party 516
community development councils (CDCs) 91–92
Community Sport Infrastructure Programme
'sports rort' 245, 278, 284, 286, 287, 311, 338–339, 576, 592
compulsory voting .. 35, 47–49, 97, 174, 596
local government 545
COMSEQ (Council of Mayors for South East Queensland) 532, 535
Consensus Statement on the Reform of the Tasmanian Constitution 492–493
Conservative governments, UK
.... 66
Conservatives, South Australia
.... 437, 439, 441
Constitution 34, 35, 70–71, 81, 232
amendment of 71, 72, 90
and citizen rights 38
and the core executive 276
and First Nations peoples 36–37, 56, 72, 73, 74, 76–80
'foreign alliance prohibition' 246
governance institutions 37–38
human rights protections and the High Court 72, 74–76
influence of 36–37
legislative federalism 357
and political parties 37
recent developments 71–72
and republicanism 72, 80–81
and the right to public protest 62
SWOT analysis 73–74
Constitution Act 1889 (Western Australia) 462, 463
Constitution Act 1902, New South Wales 379
Constitution Act 1934, South Australia 434, 435, 437, 444–445, 447
Constitution Act 1934, Tasmania
.... 485, 492–493
Constitution Act 1975 (Victoria)
.... 396
Constitution Acts Amendment Act 1899 (Western Australia)
.... 462
Constitutional and Electoral Legislation Amendment (Electoral Equality) Act 2021, Western Australia 458, 462
Conte, Guiseppe 283
Convention against Torture, Optional Protocol 56
Convention on Biological Diversity (CBD) 569
Convention on the Rights of Persons with Disabilities, Optional Protocol 56
Conversation, The 172
Cook, Roger 457, 460, 464
Cooper, William 58, 76
core executive .197–198, 275–277
Commonwealth departments and ministers 289–295
democracy 275–276
'disposable leaders' controversy
.... 285–286
'governance' scandals and standards of conduct 287–289
policy failures and failures to act
.... 296–297
recent developments 277, 281–285
SWOT analysis 278–280
see also cabinet; Commonwealth departments and ministers; executive; ministers; PM (Prime Minister)
corporate power 143–144, 152, 158–162, 597
media ownership and control
.... 178–183
political donations 153–155, 336
see also interest groups
corporate social responsibility (CSR) 152
corruption
anti-corruption agencies 329
Queensland Parliament and political system .. 418, 420, 421, 422, 425
reform priorities 598, 599
Western Australia 471–473
Corruption and Crime Commission, Western Australia
.... 471, 472–473
Corruption and Integrity Commission 308
Council of Australian Governments (COAG) *see* COAG (Council of Australian Governments)
Council of Capital City Lord Mayors (CCCLM) 532
Council of Mayors, Brisbane .. 531, 538
Council of Mayors for South East Queensland (COMSEQ) 532, 535

Council of Mayors, Sydney 540
Council on Federal Financial Relations (CFFR) 348
counter-terrorism legislation 57
Country Liberal Party, Northern Territory...... 499, 500, 501, 502, 504, 505, 506, 510, 511–512
see also Liberal Country League party; Liberal Party; Liberal-National Coalition
Court, Charles 462
Covid Emergency Response Act 2020 433
COVID-19 pandemic ... 73, 74, 122, 297, 550, 561, 565, 591, 598
  anti-lockdown protests..........63, 150
  anti-vaccination protests......63, 123, 150, 195
  closure of border with China 282
  conspiracy theories..............150, 195
  democratic impact of..........578–579
  economic stimulus payments........71
  exclusion of civil society groups 150–151
  fiscal impact of......................291, 292
  gender equality issues 208, 211, 218
  government responses.......281–282
  House of Representatives 232, 236, 238–239, 247
  human rights and civil liberties .. 60, 62–64
  labour shortages............................ 157
  and the media................174, 182, 183
  policy-making 330, 334
  public trust in government 109, 583
  Senate Committee........................244
  and social media........... 191, 195, 201
  states' responses........... 71, 347, 352
    Australian Capital Territory 518–519, 523
    New South Wales. 375–376, 379, 383–384, 518, 519
    Northern Territory..497, 501, 505, 509
    Queensland .. 419, 420, 422, 423, 426
    South Australia...... 433, 435, 449, 450
    Tasmania 482–483
    Victoria. 334, 347, 394–396, 398, 399, 403–404, 407, 410
    Western Australia 71–72, 334, 454–456, 461, 462, 464
  UK 283
  USA..283
  vaccination programme 71, 284, 305, 318, 395, 419, 518–519
  see also National Cabinet
Crabb, Annabel...........................222
Craven, Greg 88
CRC (Commission on the Rights of the Child) 202–203

Crime and Corruption Commission, Queensland..422, 425
Crisis Council of Cabinet, Victoria 407
Crommelin, Michael 358
crossbenchers
  Queensland................................... 417
  South Australia....................433, 448
CSIRO (Commonwealth Scientific and Industrial Research Organisation)........................564
CSR (corporate social responsibility) 152
culture, gender equality issues in 221–223
Cumberland County Council, Sydney 537
cyber-security.............. 187, 247, 311

D

DA (democratic audit)....... 34, 346, 354, 360
Dahlerup, Drude 223
data protection, COVID-19 pandemic.................................. 64
Davies, Mia............................... 457
Davis, David 395
Davis, Megan................................77
Daylight Saving Party, Western Australia 458, 468
de Brouwer, Gordon 307
Defence Intelligence Organisation (DIO) 295
defence policy..................593–594
  ASRA (Advanced Strategic Research Agency).........................314
  AUKUS (Australia, UK, USA) nuclear submarine deal. 285, 289, 297, 595
deindustrialisation.....................155
democracy
  Anthropocene...................... 559–560
  and the APS (Australian Public Service)...................................301–302
  Churchill on 341
  constitutional requirements ... 70–71
  core executive 275–276
  'democratic backsliding' 50, 114, 166, 450, 484, 574, 575–576, 577, 580, 590, 596
  federal legislature................231–232
  'flawed' 34, 574, 579, 594
  gender diversity and rights 206–207
  human rights and civil liberties protection 54
  interest groups 143–144
  international comparisons
    citizens' ratings 582–585
    objective indices/expert judg-

ments..................................578–582
  key principles and evaluation criteria............................ 33–34
  LAs (Legislative Assemblies) 368
  LCs (Legislative Councils)...........368
  local government................544–545
  and media...............................166–167
  metropolitan regions/big cities 529–530
  and policy-making 326–327
  political parties 120–121
  referenda in...............................84–85
  second/upper chambers ..253–254
  social media 191–192
  state government
    Australian Capital Territory 514–515
    New South Wales........... 367–368
    Northern Territory...........497–498
    Queensland 415–416
    South Australia................ 432–433
    Victoria.............................367–368
    Western Australia 453–454
  'strong democracy' principles ... 35
  voting systems.........................97–98
  see also Australian democracy; federalism, and democracy
Democracy Barometer....578, 579
democratic audit (DA)....... 34, 346, 354, 360
Democratic Labor Party (DLP) 266
Democratic Labor Party, Victoria 398
Democrats
  Australian Capital Territory . 516, 517, 518
  Senate..........................256, 257, 266
  South Australia ... 437, 439, 440, 441
Department of Defence, IDAHOBIT (International Day Against Homophobia, Biphobia, Intersexism and Transphobia)............................223
Department of Finance. 276, 293, 294
Department of Foreign Affairs and Trade (DFAT)....................276
Department of Home Affairs .. 348
Department of Human Services (DHS).....................291, 306, 307
Department of State Growth, Tasmania................................... 487
Department of the PM and Cabinet (DPM&C) 276, 295, 311, 509
departmental secretaries........290
departments, Commonwealth 289–295
Deputy PM (Prime Minister) 281
Despoja, Natashe Scott...........208
DFAT (Department of Foreign

Affairs and Trade) 276
DHS (Department of Human Services) 291, 306, 307
differently abled people
　human rights and civil liberties .. 54, 56
　see also disabilities, people with
Digital News Report: Australia 2021 (Park) 196, 200
Digital Platforms Inquiry Report (Australian Competition and Consumer Commission) 194
Digital Strategy 2019, Parliament 246
Digital Transformation Agency 310
Digital Transformation Office .. 294
DIO (Defence Intelligence Organisation) 295
disabilities, people with 54, 56, 149, 220–221, 598
discrimination, federal protection against... 56
DLP (Democratic Labor Party) 266
donations *see* political parties, finance and campaigning
'Dorothy Dixer' questions........240
'double dissolution'.. 104, 105, 116, 256, 260, 263, 266, 271
DPM&C (Department of the PM and Cabinet) 276, 295, 311, 509
Dreyfus, Mark 88
Druery, Glenn 271
Dryzek, John.............................158
Dufresne, Yannick 331
Dunleavy, Patrick..........................6
Dutton, Peter 57, 61, 85, 88, 91, 114, 123, 139, 223, 286
　see also Liberal Party; Liberal-National Coalition governments
DV (deviation from proportionality) score .. 590, 591
　House of Representatives .102–103, 117
　Senate......................... 106, 117

E

ecological reflexivity 559–560, 563, 567–468, 569, 571
Ecologically Sustainable Development process (1990-1991) 565
Economic Development Priorities 2022-25, Australian Capital Territory 523
Economics Committee, Senate 268
ECSA (Electoral Commission of South Australia)......................442

Edman, Phil 472
Edwards, Lindy...........................158
EIU (Economist Intelligence Unit) 34
　Democracy index....... 578, 579, 594
elections 97–98
　cyber-interference in 187
　electoral cycle 122, 285
　　House of Representatives 98, 116–117, 278, 597
　　Senate...........................116–117, 125
　electoral integrity 114–116
　gender issues 103
　JSCEM (Joint Standing Committee on Electoral Matters).................... 271
　local areas 110–113
　and the media........................116, 167
　policy promises/mandates 332–333
　quality of representation and citizens' political engagement 110–114
　recent developments............ 98–107
　small parties 102–103
　SWOT analysis........ 49–50, 107–109
　voter ID policy....................... 337
　voter registration issues................115
　see also House of Representatives; Senate; voting; voting systems; individual states
Electoral Act 1985, South Australia 442
Electoral Act 2004, Tasmania 485, 491
Electoral Act, Western Australia 465, 469
Electoral Boundaries Commission, Victoria............ 403
'electoral college' 135
Electoral Commission, Australian Capital Territory 524
Electoral Commission of South Australia (ECSA)..................... 442
Electoral District Boundaries Commissioners, South Australia 438
Electoral Legislation Amendment (Voter Identification) Bill 2022 337
Elfrink, Tim...............................184
Elizabeth II, Queen (UK)............. 81
Ellis, Felix 487
Emergency Management Act, South Australia...................... 433
emergency powers *see* COVID-19 pandemic
Emergency Relief National Coordination Group, Department of Social Services 281, 305
employment

gender equality and rights 217–219, 222–223
Enabling Act 1850, Tasmania . 492
Enhancing Online Safety Act 2015 201
Enoch, Leeanne 418
environmental and social governance (ESG) 152, 565
Environmental Assurance Commission 569
environmental issues 129, 139
　Indigenous knowledge 563
　see also Anthropocene, the, environmental issues in; climate change; global warming
EPBC (Environmental Protection and Biodiversity Conservation) Act 1999....................................562
　Independent Review, 2020 ...... 562, 569
e-petitions 246
　New South Wales 383–384
ERC (Expenditure Review Committee) 293, 294
Errington, Wayne D. 334–335
eSafety Commissioner..............201
ESG (environmental and social governance)................... 152, 565
EU (European Union), carbon tariffs......................................566
eugenics movement....................37
Evans, Mark.................................. 6
evidence-based policy.... 327, 329
executive 38, 232
　see also core executive
Executive Council, South Australia 446
Expenditure Review Committee (ERC) 293, 294
Expenditure Review Committee, Northern Territory........ 504, 505
Expert Panel on Constitutional Recognition of Indigenous Australians, 2012 77

F

Facebook.. 169, 180, 192, 193, 194, 195, 196, 198, 200, 328
　Facebook Messenger..................193
　see also Meta
Fair Work Act 267–268
'fake news' ..167, 182, 191, 192, 198
Family First party
　Queensland....................................417
　Senate.................................257, 266
　South Australia 436, 439, 441
　Tasmania 480
Farrer, Josie 463
Federal Court of Australia 338

federal government, powers and responsibilities of 38
federal legislature
and democracy.....................231–232
see also House of Representatives; Senate
federalism, and democracy 346–347, 353–354, 360
centralisation........................ 346–347
constitutional provisions and executive federalism..........350–354
independent agencies 353–354
legislative federalism......... 357–358
performance accountability 353
recent developments.................... 347
reform proposals.................358–360
SWOT analysis....................349–350
transparency and accountability 354–358
see also National Cabinet
Ferguson, Thomas 336
'financial initiative'............244–245
Financial Review 170, 172
Finkelstein Inquiry (2012)...........169
First Law (Law of 'country').......565
First Nations peoples
compulsory sterilisation 37
and the Constitution 36–37, 56, 72, 73, 74, 76–80
current issues 43–44
forced separation of children 37, 55
gender-based violence 221
and the Greens..............................134
historical mistreatment of34, 35, 37, 181, 590
human rights and civil liberties .. 53, 54, 55, 56, 90
interest groups 148–149, 150
policing and imprisonment of 57, 64
political exclusion of................ 36–37
political representation 109, 117, 125
New South Wales............. 377, 381
Queensland 418–419, 423–424
South Australia..................443, 446
Victoria...404
public support for constitutional voice for 57
trust of.. 89
voting rights 36–37
see also Aboriginal and Torres Islander peoples; Voice to Parliament referendum, 2023
First Nations Treaty Institute, Queensland 423
first past the post (FPTP) electoral systems... 45, 48, 103, 104, 482, 501, 590
First People's Assembly of Victoria (FPAV)........................406
First Secretaries Group............ 349
Fiscal Integrity and Transparency Act, Northern Territory 504

Fitzgerald Inquiry 1989, Queensland 421, 425
'Five Eyes' intelligence network 295, 593
Fletcher, Paul 269
Flew, Terry 181
FOI (Freedom of Information) 263, 280, 329
National Cabinet 355–357
RTI (Right to Information), Tasmania 489
Victoria 408
Food Standards Australia and New Zealand 353
'foreign alliance prohibition', Constitution...............................246
'Foreign Fighters' law................. 64
foreign policy...............................297
'Forgotten Australians'...............181
fossil fuel industry 129–130, 137, 158, 159, 160, 561–562, 564, 567, 568, 593
climate change 158, 159
political donations 137
Queensland......... 129, 160, 566, 567
UK 568
vehicles 296
Western Australia..........................474
see also mining industry
fossil fuel vehicles 296
FPAV (First People's Assembly of Victoria)......................................406
FPTP (first past the post) electoral systems... 45, 48, 103, 104, 482, 501, 590
'fracking' (hydraulic fracturing), Victoria 397
Franchise Act 1902 75
Fraser, Malcolm......................... 277
free press ... 166, 167, 169, 178, 183
see also media, mainstream; press media
Freedom House..........57, 580, 581
Freedom of Information Act, Northern Territory.................504
Freedom of Information (FOI) *see* FOI (Freedom of Information)
French, Robert............................. 88
Frewen, John................... 284, 305
Frydenberg, Josh 123

G

Gaetjens, Phil............................ 287
gambling industry, corporate power 159
Garnaut, Ross 566
GBRMPA (Great Barrier Reef Marine Park Authority) 564
Geelong, South East Queensland

....530, 531, 532, 535, 538, 539
'gender deafness' 222
Gender Equality Act 2020, Victoria 207, 405
Gender Equality Action Plan 2023, Labor 210
gender equality and rights 206–207, 223
Cabinet... 40
cultural barriers 222–223
and democracy...................206–207
employment sectors and money 217–218
gender pay gap.149, 206, 209, 210, 218–219
gender-based violence 210, 220–221, 245
media and culture....... 178, 221–223
parental leave....................... 219–220
political leadership 40, 207, 209, 211–214
public sector 215–216
recent developments.........207–208
SWOT analysis..................... 209–211
traditional gender roles...............222
gender identity, federal protection against discrimination 56
Generation X, news consumption 195, 196
Generation Y, news consumption 195, 196
Generation Z
news consumption 195, 196, 200
traditional gender roles...............222
Germany, COVID-19 pandemic 283
'gerrymandering' 114
South Australia 432
GetUp! 277, 332
GFC (global financial crisis) *see* global financial crisis (GFC), 2008–2010
GHG (greenhouse gas) emissions *see* climate change
Gibbs, Pearl Gambayani 58
Gilchrist, David 305
Gillard, Julia 135, 157, 158, 178, 207, 211, 222, 234, 242, 277, 286
climate change and environmental policies 333, 567
First Nations peoples policy 77
'misogyny' speech.......................240
policy promises analysis.............335
refugees and asylum seekers policy...338
see also Labor Party/governments
Gilmer, Elizabeth Meriwether ("Dorothy Dixer")..................240

global financial crisis (GFC), 2008–2010 ... 41, 266, 280, 294
   economic stimulus policy . 333–334
Global Gender Gap Report, World Economic Forum 206, 210
global warming .. 48, 99, 100–102, 112, 122, 123, 124, 129, 139
   see also climate change
globalisation 160
Goetz, Klaus H 263–264
Gold Coast 530, 531, 534, 537
Google 169, 179, 180, 194, 198
   Google Plus 193
   YouTube 193
Gorton, John 277
governance institutions 37–39
governance, international assessments of 316
Governor-General .. 37, 39, 42–43, 80, 260, 276, 290
Grant, Stan 58–59
Grant, Stan Jr. 89, 91
Great Barrier Reef 560, 562, 568–569
Great Barrier Reef Foundation 565
Great Barrier Reef Marine Park Authority (GBRMPA) 564
Great Barrier Reef Park Authority 353
Greater Hobart 530, 532, 538
Greater Hobart Act 2019 538
Greater Melbourne 530, 531, 532, 535, 537, 539
Greater Perth 530, 535
Greater Sydney Commission . 540
Green, Anthony 87, 480
greenhouse gas (GHG) emissions
   see climate change
Greens ... 39, 61, 122, 123, 124, 129, 139, 591
   2022 election 113
   climate change and environmental policies 561, 563, 567
   environmental issues 130, 562
   Fair Work Act 267
   finance and campaigning ... 127, 136, 137, 153, 154
      federal funding 138
   and First Nations peoples 134
   gender equality policies 207, 212, 213, 222
   House of Representatives 98–99, 100, 102, 233, 236
   leadership selection 135
   local district elections 112, 113
   local influence on policy 134
   and the media 172, 186
   membership and social representation 131–132

Senate 104, 105, 106, 107, 256, 257, 266, 271
states
   Australian Capital Territory 516, 517, 518, 520, 521, 523
   New South Wales. 368, 369, 370, 371, 382
   Northern Territory 499, 500
   Queensland 416, 417, 418, 427
   South Australia 433, 436, 437, 439, 440, 441
   Tasmania 480, 481, 482, 483, 486, 490, 491, 493
   Victoria. 396, 399, 400, 401, 402, 403
   Western Australia . 458, 466, 467, 470
Greiner, Nick 372
grey radicalism 563, 565, 566
group pluralism 144–147
group voting ticket (GVT) system
   see GVT (group voting ticket) system
Guardian 172
guillotine, House of Representatives 242, 243
Gummer, Michael 504, 505
gun laws 147
Gutwein, Peter 480, 485, 490
GVT (group voting ticket) system
   Victoria 398, 399, 410
   Western Australia 458

H

Ha v New South Wales 351
Haines, Helen 139
Hajer, Maarten 570
Hamer, Rupert 407
Hanson, Pauline 102, 139, 440, 466
Hanson-Young, Sarah 222
Hare-Clark PR voting system
   Australian Capital Territory . 516, 517, 521
   Tasmania ... 478, 481, 482, 483, 486, 489, 490
Harradine, Brian 266, 488
Harvey, Lisa 455
Hawke, Bob ... 71, 87, 116, 277, 506, 524
   see also Labor governments
Hazzard, Brad 374
Head, Brian 158
healthcare
   government expenditure on 293
   trade unions 156
Hehir, Grant 308
Henry Tax review 336
Herald Sun 564
Hewson, John 129

'Fightback' policy agenda 335
Higgins, Brittany 178, 208, 245, 287–288
High Court 38
   First Nations peoples issues . 79–80
   human rights protections 74–76
   media independence 176
   refugees and asylum seekers policy ruling 338
   right to public protest 62
   taxation decisions 351
Hobart
   Greater Hobart 530, 532, 538
Hodgman, Will 480, 490
Hoffmann, Matthew J. 570
Holgate, Christine 269
Holmes à Court, Simon 113, 130
Holmes, Brenton 330
Holmes, Catherine 288
'Home Children' imported from the UK 181
Honey, David 457
House of Assembly Restoration Bill 2020, Tasmania 493
House of Assembly, South Australia 433, 434, 435, 436–438, 440, 447, 448
House of Assembly, Tasmania ... 478, 480, 481, 482, 483, 485, 486–487, 489, 492, 493, 494
House of Representatives 231–232, 247
   backbenchers 234
   budget process and scrutiny 238, 244–245
   candidate selection 133
   chamber debates and scrutinising legislation 242–245
   Chinese Australians 245
   climate change issues 234–235
   'closure' motions 242, 243
   committees 238, 243–244
   communicating with the public 246–247
   COVID-19 pandemic 232, 236, 238–239, 246, 247
   digital communication 246–247
   diversity and representation 235, 245–246
   elected representatives by state 546
   elections and voting 97, 98–100, 110–111, 117, 596, 597
   AV (Alternative Vote) .. 35, 42, 44, 45, 48, 97, 98, 99, 117, 123, 124, 231
   DV (deviation from proportionality) score 102–103, 117
   electoral cycle 98, 116–117, 278, 597
   electoral district size 114–115
   fairness 100–103

TPP (two-party preferred vote) 48, 99, 100–102, 112, 123, 124
equalisation of districts 114–115
executive and two-party dominance 231, 232–236
First Nations people 239, 245
gender equality issues 209, 211, 212, 213, 245–246, 247
guillotine 242, 243
hung parliaments 42, 128, 231
Indian Australians 245
law-making powers 231
ministers 235
misogynistic behaviour 235
Question Time . 234, 237, 240–242, 246, 247
recent developments 232–236
session length 39, 126, 231, 242
Speaker 237, 240
Standing Orders 237
SWOT analysis 237–239
'whipping' votes 235
workplace culture 245–246
see also Parliament
housing supply, metropolitan regions/big cities 536–537
Howard, John 41, 134, 257, 266, 267, 525
climate change and environmental policies 567
'core' electoral promises .. 332–333
First Nations peoples policy .. 77, 87, 89
gun laws 147, 333
labour rights policies 66
trade union laws 155, 157
Work Choices policy 334
see also Liberal Party; Liberal-National Coalition
human rights 33, 53–54, 598
Charter/Bill of Rights debate, New South Wales 380
COVID-19 pandemic 62–64
detention of refugees 61
High Court 74–76
recent developments 54–57
rights deficit 66–67
social rights 64–66
states' legislation 55, 60, 75
SWOT analysis 59–60
Voice to Parliament 57–59
Human Rights Act 54–55
Human Rights Act 1998 (ACT) .. 60
Human Rights Act 2019 (Queensland) 60
Human Rights Act (UK) 66
Human Rights Education Grants Scheme 55
Human Rights Measurement Initiative, 2021 .... 54, 90
Human Rights (Parliamentary Scrutiny) Act 2011(Cth), The .. 55

hung parliaments 42, 592
House of Representatives ... 42, 128, 231
Hurley, David 80
Husic, Ed 125
hybrid multinationalism 571

I

Ian Potter Foundation 570
ICAC Act 2012, South Australia 448, 449
ICAC (Independent Commission Against Corruption) 177, 247
ICAC (Independent Commission Against Corruption), New South Wales ... 372–374, 377, 380–381
ICAC (Independent Commission Against Corruption), Northern Territory 504
ICAC (Independent Commission Against Corruption), South Australia 448–449
ICCPR (International Covenant on Civil and Political Rights), UN 54–55, 56, 59, 60
IDAHOBIT (International Day Against Homophobia, Biphobia, Intersexism and Transphobia) 223
IGIS (Inspector-General of Intelligence and Security) 295
immigration 593
anti-immigration policies 60
from Asian countries 109
'white Australia' policies 34, 54, 593
see also refugees and asylum seekers
imprisonment and policing, First Nations peoples 57, 64, 424, 509, 526
InCISE Index of Civil Service Effectiveness 580, 581
income tax, pay-as-you-go system 145
InDaily 443
independent agencies ('joint institutions') 353–354
Independent Broad-based Anti-Corruption Commission, Victoria 405
Independent Commission Against Corruption (ICAC) *see* ICAC (Independent Commission Against Corruption)
Independent Electoral Commission, New South Wales 381

Independent Local Government Review Panel (NSW) ... 535, 554
Independent Review of Tasmanian State Services ... 488
Independent Review of the Australian Public Service (IRAPS), 2019 ..... 303, 305, 306, 312, 314
India 590–591, 594, 595
Indian Australians
in the APS (Australian Public Service) 318
House of Representatives 245
New South Wales 381
political representation 117, 125
Indigenous knowledge, environmental issues 563
Indigenous languages 424
Indigenous Protected Areas ... 569
Indigenous Voice 56
Indigenous women
gender equality and rights 222–223
gender-based violence 221
Indonesia 594
informal voting 48
see also voting
information, ease of finding 585
'inner state' 295
Inspector-General for Emergency Management, Victoria 394
Inspector-General of Intelligence and Security (IGIS) 295
Instagram 193, 198, 200
see also Meta
Institute for Health and Welfare 353
Institute of Public Affairs (IPA) 316, 397
Integrity Commission, Australian Capital Territory . 520, 522, 524
intelligence services 184, 276
interest groups . 143–144, 148, 162, 596, 597
decline of large groups 155–157
empirics 147–151
factors affecting influence 146
group pluralism 144–147
and party funding 153–155
recent developments 144–151
SWOT analysis 151–152
see also corporate power
Intergovernmental Agreement on Federal Financial Relations, 2008 386
Intergovernmental Agreement on the Reform of Commonwealth-State Financial Relations 352
intergovernmental relations *see*

federalism, and democracy
International Civil Service
  Effectiveness Index................316
International Criminal Court.......61
International Day Against
  Homophobia, Biphobia,
  Intersexism and Transphobia
  (IDAHOBIT).............................223
International IDEA, Global State
  of Democracy................578, 579
international relations 593–595
  reform priorities............................598
internet metadata access....57, 60
internet platform companies,
  corporate power....................159
intersex status, federal protection
  against discrimination 56
Inter-State Commission 350
'investment theory' of political
  influence 336
IPA (Institute of Public Affairs) 397
Iran, cyber-interference in
  elections 187
IRAPS (Independent Review of
  the Australian Public Service)
  2019
  .... 303, 305, 306, 312, 314
Iraq 295, 593
Irving, Helen................................36
IT (information technology)....294,
  319, 320
  and COVID-19 pandemic 305
  cyber-security.................187, 247, 311
  Tasmania...489
  Victoria..................................408–409
Italy, COVID-19 pandemic........283
Ivison, Duncan............................58

J

Jacobs, Jack 58–59
Jacqui Lambie Network............271
Japan.......................295, 594, 595
Jenkins, Kate 207
Johnson, Boris............................283
'joint institutions' (independent
  agencies)......................353–354
Joint Select Committee on
  Constitutional Recognition of
  Aboriginal and Torres Strait
  Islander Peoples 2015 77
JPCHR 61
JSCEM (Joint Standing
  Committee on Electoral
  Matters).............................271, 337
judiciary..................................38, 232
  gender equality and rights.215–216
Justice Party, Victoria 403
Juukan Gorge caves destruction,

Rio Tinto..........................463–464

K

Kartinyeri v Commonwealth 1998
 76–77
Katter
  House of Representatives...........233
  party funding....................................154
Katter's Australia Party,
  Queensland 417, 418
Keating, Paul....80, 263, 266, 335
Kildea, Paul 355, 359
King, Grant 561
King, Madeleine.........................562
Kingswell v The Queen 1985 75
Kirkup, Zac 455

L

LA (Legislative Assembly)
  Australian Capital Territory 516–518,
  521–524, 525
  democratic requirements 368
  New South Wales 367, 368–369,
  381, 382, 383
  Northern Territory 497, 499–501,
  502, 504–505
  Queensland........ 415, 420, 423, 549
  Victoria 392, 397, 398, 399, 400,
  401, 403
  Western Australia....... 456, 457, 461,
  465–466, 468, 470
Labor Party/governments...39, 72,
  79, 81, 123, 124, 278, 286, 591
  APS reform 314, 321
  branches 132, 133
  Cabinet..40
  climate change and environmental
  policies 242, 285, 562, 563, 567,
  592
  election defeat, 2019 123
  electoral cycle reform............116–117
  environmental issues...........129, 562
  finance and campaigning 127,
  136–137, 153, 154, 296
  fiscal policy......................................293
  formation of 36
  Gender Equality Action Plan 2023
 210
  gender equality issues 245
  gender equality policies 108, 207,
  212, 213, 214
  government reform agenda
 308–309
  House of Representatives....98–99,
  100, 101, 103
    two-party dominance 231,
    232–236
  hung parliaments.............................42
  leadership selection process 41,
  135–136, 234
  local district elections.....110, 111, 112,
  113

local influence on policy 133, 134,
  328
and the media 167, 168, 172, 179, 186
membership and social
  representation 131–132
and the mining industry 160
ministerial positions 591–592
National Strategy to Achieve
  Gender Equality 223
political competition......128, 129, 139
politicisation of the executive....313,
  314
refugees and asylum seekers ...335
Senate 104, 105, 106, 107, 253, 256,
  257, 265
states
  Australian Capital Territory 516,
  517, 518, 520, 521, 523, 526
  New South Wales. 367, 368, 369,
  370, 371, 372, 380–381, 382, 384
  Northern Territory....................499,
  500, 501, 502, 504, 505, 506,
  510, 511–512
  Queensland....................... 415, 416,
  417, 418, 419, 420, 421, 422, 423,
  424, 425, 426, 427
  South Australia........................432,
  433, 435, 436, 437, 438, 439,
  441, 443, 444, 446, 447, 448
  Tasmania 480, 481, 482, 484,
  486, 490, 491
  Victoria..396, 397, 399, 400, 401,
  402, 403, 405, 407
  Western Australia..134, 453, 454,
  455, 456–457, 458, 459, 460,
  464–465, 466, 467, 468, 469,
  470, 473, 474
trade unions ..128, 136, 153, 154, 157
see also Gillard, Julia; Hawke, Bob;
  Rudd, Kevin; Voice to Parliament
  referendum, 2023
Labour government, UK 66
labour rights..................................66
Lambie, Jacquie.........................488
Lambie Network party, Tasmania
  ....480, 481
Landcare programs...................569
  Victoria...565
Langton, Marcia 87
Larkin, Phil......346, 354, 355, 360
Law Council 356
LC (Legislative Council).............107
  democratic requirements 368
  New South Wales 107, 367,
  370–371, 372, 375–376, 382, 383
  South Australia. 107, 267–268, 433,
  434, 436, 437, 438–440, 441, 443,
  445, 446
  states...107
  Tasmania ... 107, 478, 482, 483, 485,
  487, 492, 494
  Victoria 107, 392, 398, 399, 400,
  402, 403

Western Australia............................ 107, 358, 456–457, 457–459, 461, 462, 467–468, 469, 470, 472, 473
Leader of the Opposition, House of Representatives................ 240
'leadership spills'......277, 278, 285
Lee, Elizabeth.............................. 518
Lee, Jing... 443
Leeser, Julian.................................. 87
legal aid 67
Legal and Constitutional Affairs References Committee......... 332
Legalise Cannabis party
   South Australia 439
   Victoria 403
'legislation' committees, Senate 261
legislative federalism....... 357–358
Legislative Scrutiny Committee, Northern Territories 505
legislature............................... 38, 232
Levitsky, Steven 575, 576
Ley, Sussan 561
LGBTIQ+ people 590
   federal protection against discrimination............................. 56
   human rights and civil liberties ...34, 54
   interest groups 148, 150
   marriage equality 56, 62
   religious schools' discrimination against 65
   same-sex marriage....................... 223
   violence against 210
Liberal Country League party, South Australia........................ 436
liberal democracy see democracy
Liberal Democrats
   Senate..................................... 256, 257
   South Australia 439
   Victoria 403
Liberal Movement, South Australia 439
Liberal National Party of Queensland (LNP).415, 416, 417, 418, 419, 420, 421, 422, 425, 427
Liberal Party 41, 123, 591
   Cabinet.. 39, 40
   climate change and environmental policies 561, 563, 567, 568
   finance and campaigning 127, 136–137, 153, 154
   First Nations peoples policy 91
   gender equality issues 212, 213, 214, 245
   House of Representatives.......... 233
   leadership selection..................... 135
   local influence on policy 134, 328
   membership and social representation 131–132

   and the mining industry 160
   misogynistic behaviour 113, 122, 125, 128, 178
   NSW scandals...............................122
   party branches........................132, 133
   political competition.... 128–129, 139
   Senate... 253
   states
      Australian Capital Territory 516, 517, 518
      New South Wales.. 369, 370, 371, 381, 382
      Northern Territory.....................500
      South Australia.......................... 433, 436, 437, 438, 439, 441, 443, 444, 445–446, 448
      Tasmania 480, 481, 482, 483, 485, 486, 487, 490, 491
      Victoria.....................396, 405, 407
      Western Australia 456, 457, 458, 459, 462, 463, 465, 466, 467, 468, 469, 470, 472, 473
   voter suppression........................... 114
   see also Dutton, Peter; Howard, John; Liberal-National Coalition; Turnbull, Malcolm
Liberal-National Coalition.........122, 286, 518, 525, 591
   bushfires...............................296–297
   climate change and environmental policies 234, 347, 560–561, 591, 592
   COVID-19 pandemic policies 304–305, 561, 562, 576
   fiscal policy.................. 291, 292, 293
   gender equality issues 591
   gun laws 147
   House of Representatives.... 98, 99, 100, 101, 103
      two-party dominance 231, 232–236
   human rights protection................ 55
   international relations policies 594–595
   Internet platform companies 159, 180–181
   labour rights policies 66
   local district elections.....110, 111, 112, 113
   malapportionment......................... 114
   media 127, 167, 168, 172, 175, 179, 184
   ministerial positions 591–592
   misogynistic behaviour 122, 125, 128, 178
   party branches........................132, 133
   PM and deputy PM appointments 234, 278
   political competition.............129–130
   political donations 296
   politicisation of the executive.... 313, 314
   refugees and asylum seekers ... 335
   scandals, 2019–2021...................284

   Senate 104, 105, 106, 107, 255, 256, 257, 265, 271
   social media policy.......................201
   states
      New South Wales. 367, 368, 369, 370, 371, 376
      Queensland 415
      Victoria.395, 397, 399, 400, 402, 403
      Western Australia.459, 463, 466, 467
   and trade unions............151, 155, 157
   voter enrolment.............................510
   welfare reform 306–307
   Work Choices.............. 267, 268, 334
   see also Abbott, Tony; Dutton, Peter; Howard, John; Morrison, Scott; Turnbull, Malcolm
Lin, Jin 318
Lindblom, Charles E....................158
Little, Andrew 575
LNP (Liberal National Party of Queensland) .. 415, 416, 417, 418, 419, 420, 421, 422, 425, 427
Lobbying of Government Officials Act 2011 (LOGO Act), New South Wales............................. 373
local government... 544–545, 555
   amalgamations 554–555
   climate change and environmental policies 571
   councillors and mayors 545–546, 551–552
   COVID-19 pandemic.. 546–547, 548
   elected representatives by state 546
   electoral democracy 545–546
   intergovernmental relations 549–551
   recent developments......... 545–547
   reform 553, 555
   state primacy and control. 550–551
   SWOT analysis.................. 547–548
Local Government Act 1919, New South Wales.............................553
Local Government Act 1993, New South Wales.............................553
Local Government Act 2020, Victoria 405
Local Government Ministers Council 532
Love, Shane 457
Love v Commonwealth; Thoms v Commonwealth 2020............ 80
lower chamber see House of Representatives
Lower Hunter................................530
Lowy Institute surveys......587, 594
Lyons, Joseph..................................76

Index 615

M

Mabo v Queensland (No 2) 2020 80
Maddox, Graham 354
Maguire, Darryl 373
Maher, Kevin 446
Maiden, Samantha 178
Makarrata Commission 78, 86, 239
management consultants . 159, 161
Manlinauskas, Peter 433
Māori representation, New Zealand Parliament 214, 424
Marriage Act 1961 56
marriage equality 56, 62
Marshall, Steven 433, 445, 448
mass shootings 147
Masters, Chris, Roberts-Smith defamation case 177, 178, 181, 184
mayors ... 531, 532, 533, 534–535, 552
  Council of Mayors, Brisbane 531
  local government 552
  see also metropolitan regions/big cities, local democracy in
McAllister, Ian 122
McCloy v New South Wales 2015 75
McCormack, Tim 494
McCusker, Malcolm 458
McGowan, Cathy 139, 460
McGowan, Mark 134, 454, 456–457, 458, 465, 468, 473, 474
McKechnie, John 472–473
McKenzie, Bridget 287
McKenzie, Nick, Roberts-Smith defamation case 177, 178, 181, 184
McKenzie scandal ('sports rort') 245, 278, 284, 286, 287, 311, 338–339, 576, 592
McKinlay v Commonwealth 1975 .... 77, 78
MDBA (Murray-Darling Basin Authority) 564
'Me Too' movement 113, 178
media, mainstream 166–168, 186–187, 597
  broadcasting media
    commercial TV and radio 168, 173–174
    free competition 166
    hybrid state broadcasters 168
    impartiality 169
    online content 169–170, 174
    regulation of 166
    state broadcasters 167, 168
  climate change and environmental issues 564, 566
  corporate power 159
  cyber-interference 186
  and democracy 166–167
  and elections 109, 116, 167
  gender equality issues 178, 221–223
  independence and corporate control 178–183
  media freedom and government intervention 184
  online content 169, 176, 194, 195–197
  and policy-making 328
  and the political elite 185–186
  political leanings and influence . 171, 172, 178–179
  press media 170–172
    free press 166, 167, 169
    online content 169–170
  public trust 182, 183
  recent developments 169–174
  self-regulation 167, 182
  societal roles of 181–183
  SWOT analysis 175–177
  see also social media
'mediatisation' 185–186
Medicare 293
  PBS (Pharmaceutical Benefits Scheme) 154
mega-events, Olympic Games 2032, Brisbane 532, 535
mega-projects 537
Melbourne
  bushfires 296
  city council 534
  City of Melbourne 540, 552
  COVID-19 pandemic 394
  Greater Melbourne 530, 531, 532, 535, 537, 539
  media 172
Member of Parliament (Standards) Act 1978, Victoria 405
men
  gender equality issues in the media 221–222
  millennial males and traditional gender roles 222
  parental leave 219
Meng, Amy 575
Menzies, Robert 134, 593
Mercer, Trish 331
Merkel, Angela 283
Meta 179, 193
  see also WhatsApp
  see also Facebook; Instagram
Metcalfe, Andrew 314
Metropolitan Board of Works, Greater Melbourne 537
Metropolitan Partnerships, Greater Melbourne 532, 539
metropolitan regions/big cities, local democracy in 529–530, 541
  community engagement 539
  COVID-19 pandemic 533
  elected representation deficiencies 534–535
  intergovernment relations and City Deals 538
  municipal structure and roles 535–536
  recent developments 530–531
  reform proposals 540
  SWOT analysis 531–533
  urban planning and management 536–537
Mettam, Libby 457
MFF (Minister for Finance) 281, 293, 294
Michels, Robert 134
micro parties, Senate *see* crossbenchers
micro-institutions 126
Microsoft 180
Migration Act 1958 (Cth) 80
Migration Amendment (Clarifying International Obligation for Removal) Bill 2021 61
millennial males, traditional gender roles 222
Milligan, Louise 288
Minerals Council of Australia .. 570
Minerals Resource Rent Tax (MRRT) 336
mining industry .. 129, 137, 158, 160, 296, 336, 570
  Northern Territory 506
  political donations 137, 296
  Queensland 123, 129, 160, 415, 426, 427, 566
  South Australia 448
  Western Australia 160, 218, 455, 458, 459, 463, 474
  see also fossil fuel industry
Minister for Finance (MFF) 281, 293, 294
Minister of Foreign Affairs 276
Ministerial Councils 348, 349, 352, 354, 359
ministers 275–277
  junior minister 289
  ministerial effectiveness and portfolio reorganisations ... 290–291
  ministerial responsibility, South Australia 447–448
  tenure length 291
  two-party domination of ministerial positions 591–592
  wrongful dismissal accountability,

Senate..................................269
see also Cabinet; core executive
'Ministers' Meetings'.................348
misogynistic behaviour 208–209, 211, 287–288
    House of Representatives..........235
    Liberal Party ...113, 122, 125, 128, 178
    Liberal-National Coalition .. 122, 125, 128, 178
    'misogyny' speech, Julia Gillard 240
    National Party 122, 125, 128
Mlambo-Ngcuke, Phumzile......210
model law...............................358
monarchy..............................42–43
    and republicanism...................80–81
Morrison, Scott........... 65, 122, 123, 126, 136, 161, 180, 184, 195, 268, 269, 286, 287, 333, 335
    APS reform................................306
    AWM (Australian War Memorial) 340–341
    bushfires.............242, 277, 296–297, 374–375
    cabinet committees.....................281
    climate change policy.........129–130, 296, 569
    COVID-19 pandemic policies........71, 72, 282–284, 283, 284, 304–305, 550, 561, 576–577, 593
    First Nations peoples policy .56, 79, 87
    fiscal policy............................291, 292
    foreign policy...............................297
    gender equality issues...... 178, 208, 223
    international relations policies 594–595
    National Cabinet...................262–263
    politicisation of the executive.... 313, 314
    refugee and asylum seeker policies 61
    'robodebt' crisis..........................338
    social media policy.....................201
    voter ID policy.............................337
    voter suppression..........................114
    welfare reform....................306–307
    women's issues............................113
    see also Liberal-National Coalition governments
MRRT (Minerals Resource Rent Tax)..336
Ms Represented........................222
Mueller, Dennis..........................182
Muir, Ricky................................ 271
Mundine, Warren..........................87
Murdoch, Rupert...................... 170, 171, 172, 175, 179, 186, 397, 442, 564, 566, 597
Murphy, Brendan.......................282
Murray Darling Basin.................568
Murray Darling Basin Royal Commission............................448
Murray-Darling Basin Authority (MDBA)....................................564
Museum of Australian Democracy 92
Myer Foundation........................570
MySpace....................................193

N

Namadgi Agreement 2001......525
National Action Plan on Human Rights.. 55
National Anti-Corruption Commission.................. 309, 329
National Australia Bank...........268
National Cabinet....... 72, 233, 281, 282, 284, 348–349, 350, 359, 360, 407, 449, 532, 548, 550
    Reform Committees.....................348
    Terms of Reference....................360
    transparency issues............ 355–357
National Capital Authority (NCA) 340
National Co-Design Group.........79
National Commuter Car Park Fund ('car parks' rort) .. 284, 311, 339, 576
National Competition Council 353
National Competition Policy ... 353
National Congress of Australia's First Peoples......................55, 56
National Constitution Convention 2017..87
    see also Uluru Statement from the Heart, 2017
National Coordination Mechanism.............................348
National COVID Vaccine Taskforce.................................305
National Crisis Committee......295
National Disability Insurance Scheme (NDIS)...............149, 336
National Disability Insurance Service (NDIA)............... 290, 314
National Farmers' Federation . 148
National Federation Reform Council.................348, 349, 550
National Firearms Agreement. 147
National Human Rights Consultation Committee........ 55
national parks, Northern Territories..................................506
National Partnership agreements 353
National Party...............................41
    Cabinet................................... 39, 40
    climate change and environmental policies 561, 563, 567
    finance and campaigning ...136–137, 153, 154
    gender equality issues........ 212, 213
    House of Representatives..........233
    leadership selection......................135
    local influence on policy 134
    membership and social representation........................131–132
    misogynistic behaviour...... 122, 125, 128
    political competition.....................139
    states
        South Australia.................436, 437
        Western Australia.456, 458, 459, 460, 462, 463, 467, 468, 470
    see also Liberal-National Coalition
National School Chaplaincy Program....................................338
National Security Advisor........ 281, 295
National Security Agency, USA 295
National Security Committee .295
National Seniors Australia........148
National Summit on Women's Safety..246
National Transport Commission 353
National Water Commission .. 353, 570
Nationwide News v Wills 1992 .75
Native Title Act, Western Australia....................................463
'Nauru Files' (Guardian) 61
NCA (National Capital Authority) 340
NDIA (National Disability Insurance Service)........ 290, 314
NDIS (National Disability Insurance Scheme).......149, 336
Netherlands................................570
new policy proposals (NPPs).. 293
new public management (NPM) 308, 312, 314, 315, 320, 337
New South Wales............. 367, 388
    Aboriginal and Torres Strait Islander peoples 377, 379, 381
    bushfires............................277, 374–375
    Charter/Bill of Rights debate 380
    climate change and environmental policies 377, 384
    Constitution............... 379–380, 549
    core executive, premier and government.........................384–386
    corruption and malfeasance prevention 372–374, 380–381
    COVID-19 pandemic. 375–376, 379, 383–384, 518, 519
    cyber-security................................377
    diversity in political representation 377, 381, 382, 551

elected representatives at federal, state and local level 546
elections and voting 103, 458
   AV (Alternative Vote) 367, 368–369, 376
   electoral politics 368–371
   House of Representatives seats 367
   LA (Legislative Assembly) 367, 368–369, 381, 382, 383
   LC (Legislative Council) 107, 367, 370–371, 382, 383
     Public Accountability Committee 372, 375–376
   Liberal Party scandals 122
   local democracy 531, 535
   local government 545, 547, 549, 550, 551, 552, 553, 554, 555
   media 172
   Parliament and the Executive 382–384
   party funding 136
   police service 372
   political parties and community representation 380–382
   poverty and wealth 386
   public services 291, 384–385
     outcome-driven production 386–387
   recent developments 368–376
   and the right to public protest 62–63
   Senate seats 46, 263
   state election, 2022 114
   SWOT analysis 376–378
   tax revenue base 377
   trade relationship with China 377
   VFI (Vertical Fiscal Imbalance) 387
New Tax System (Commonwealth-state Financial Arrangements) Act, A 1999 352
New Zealand
   democracy indices 578
   electoral system 590–591
   'Five Eyes' intelligence network 295, 593
   Westminster advisory system 315
New Zealand Parliament 214
Newman, Campbell 420, 421, 425
News Corporation 170, 171, 172, 175, 179, 180, 184, 442, 564, 566
News Media and Digital Platforms Bargaining Code, 2021 .... 176, 180–181
News of the World 179
newspapers *see* media, mainstream
Ng, Yee-Fui 339
Ngo, Tung 443
Nine Entertainment Co. 180
Nine Media 170, 171, 172
Nine News 173
no confidence votes 41
No Pokies party, South Australia 439, 440
Noongar people 463
Northern Territory 497–498, 511–512
   Aboriginal and Torres Strait Islander peoples 497, 502, 503, 507
     disadvantagement of 509
     diversion of resources from 508–509
     electoral deficit in representation 510–511
     sexual abuse against women and children 507, 509
   child protection 57
   Commonwealth-State relations 506–507
   corruption 505
   COVID-19 pandemic 497, 501, 505, 509
   elected representatives at federal, state and local level 546
   elections
     AV (Alternative Vote) 499, 500, 502
   elections and party politics 499–501, 510–511
   Emergency Response ('Intervention') 506–507
   executive, Legislative Assembly and policy-making 504–506
   fossil fuel industry 593
   governance defects 507–511
   LA (Legislative Assembly) 497, 499–501, 502, 504–505
   local government 505–506, 545, 547, 552, 553–554, 555
   mining industry 506
   public services 497, 503, 506, 508
   recent developments 499–501
   size of electorate 115
   SWOT analysis 502–503
   urban 'bias' of policies 507–508
   women's voting rights 37
Northern Territory Electoral Commission (NTEC) 510
Northern Territory (Self Government) Act (1978) 506
Not Too Young to Run, Victoria 404–405
NPM (new public management) 308, 312, 314, 315, 320, 337
NPPs (new policy proposals) 293
NSW Review of Federal Financial Relations (Thodey) 387
NTEC (Northern Territory Electoral Commission) 510

O

OECD index of social inequality 581, 582
Office for Women 209
Office of Public Integrity (OPI), South Australia 448
Office of the Clerk Assistant (Procedure) 266
Office of the Gene Technology Regulator 353
Office of the Independent Assessor, Queensland 422
older people, interest groups . 148
One Nation Party 102, 139, 337
   finance and campaigning 136, 137
   Senate 256, 257, 271
   states
     Northern Territory 499
     Queensland 417, 418
     South Australia 433, 437, 439, 440
     Western Australia 458, 466, 467
Online Safety Bill 2021 .... 199, 201–202
Operation COVID Shield 284
OPI (Office of Public Integrity), South Australia 448
Optional Protocol to the Convention against Torture .. 56
Optional Protocol to the Convention on the Rights of Persons with Disabilities 56
Oquist, Ben 107, 271–272
Ostrom, Elinor 570

P

Packer, Kerry 179
Palaszczuk, Anastasia 416, 417, 418–419, 422, 423, 425, 427
Palawa people, Tasmania 494
Palmer, Clive 71–72, 127, 152, 455, 471, 473, 591
Palmer party, Tasmania 480
Palmer United
   Queensland 417
   Senate 256, 257
Palmer v Western Australia 2021 72
parental leave 219–220
Paris Agreement 2015 .... 565, 566
Park, Sora 196, 200
Parkin, Andrew 354–355
Parkinson, Martin 310, 314, 316
Parliament
   cyber-security 247
   Digital Strategy 2019 246
   and the media 185–186
   see also House of Representatives;

Senate Parliament House, Canberra ...185
Parliamentary Budget Office (PBO)............................. 244, 266
Parliamentary Joint Committee on Human Rights (PJCHR).... 59, 64–65, 244
Parliamentary Library...............266
participation, in policy-making 329, 330, 331–332
parties *see* political parties
Path to Treaty Commitment, Queensland 423, 424
Pathways to Politics for Women, Victoria......................................404
Patmore, P. 490
Patrick, Rex................72, 262–263, 355–356
Patrick v Secretary, Department of Prime Minister and cabinet 2021 72
pay-as-you-go system, income tax...145
PBO (Parliamentary Budget Office)............................ 244, 266
Pearson, Noel............................... 58
PEI (Perceptions of Electoral Integrity)......................... 580, 581
Pell, George 182
People's House *see* House of Representatives
Perceptions of Electoral Integrity (PEI) 580, 581
performance accountability.... 353
Performance Accountability and Measurement Act...................308
Perrottet, Dominic 374
Perth
  Greater Perth 530, 535
Peston, Robert............................153
Peters, B. Guy.............................161
Pharmaceutical Society of Australia.....................................154
Pharmacy Guild of Australia 154–155
Philippine Australians................125
Piper, Greg 382
PJCHR (Parliamentary Joint Committee on Human Rights) 59, 64–65, 244
PKKP (Puutu Kunti Kurrama and Pinikura) people............463–464
Planning Authority, Victoria 537
Planning Commission, Western Australia 537
pluralism
  group pluralism 144–147
PM and C (prime minister and cabinet) department 39, 41, 355, 356
PM (Prime Minister) 275–276
  budgetary control 294
  and cabinet committees 281
  'disposable leaders' controversy 285–286
  and the House of Representatives 231
  leadership conflicts 286
  'leadership spills' 277, 278, 285
  no confidence votes 41
  presidential style......................... 270
  rapid rotation of.......................... 277
  role and powers of ... 37, 38, 39–42, 278, 279, 290, 313
  security powers............................295
  see also core executive
PMBs (Private Member Bills) 266–267
PMO (PM's Office) 41, 276
Pocock, David 257
Police Commissioner, South Australia 433
Police Death and Disability Bill 2011, New South Wales381, 382
policing
  First Nations peoples.... 57, 64, 424, 509, 526
  police brutality 221
policy-making 326–327, 332, 341–342
  citizen participation and civil engagement........................... 331–332
  consistency with election promises or political values 332–333
  COVID-19 pandemic............330, 334
  and democracy.................... 326–327
  interests served by policy 336
  'legality' 338
  need for policy............................. 337
  party values and policy design . 335
  policy over-reach 333–334
  policy reversals ('back flips') 333
  politicisation of 313–314
  process... 331
  recent developments...................327
  Social Licence to Operate. 339–341
  SWOT analysis.....................328–330
  transparency and accountability 338–339
  'visionary' or 'reformist' policies 334–335
political competition, political parties 128–130
political engagement..........110–114
political parties... 37–38, 120–122, 139
  branches 132–133
  bureaucratisation of..................... 134
  candidate selection.......................133
  caucus meetings...........................41
  declining membership.................332
  democratic requirements 120–121
  diversity...128
  ethnic diversity 125
  finance and campaigning.... 121, 127, 134, 136–138, 152, 336, 597, 598
    federal funding 137–138
    interest groups..................153–155
  gender equality issues125, 211–212, 213
  internal democracy and governance 131–136
  leadership selection..... 121, 135–136
  local influence on policy.... 133–134, 328
  membership and social representation 126, 131–132
  online and social media activities 127
  political competition............. 128–130
  public trust in 125
  recent developments........... 122–123
  small parties 102–103, 130
  state government 368
  SWOT analysis.......................124–128
politicians
  accessibility of 145
  post-service compensation for leaders...................................... 161
pork-barrelling.........266, 339, 592
Porter, Christopher 287–288, 455
powers
  emergency powers (*see* COVID-19 pandemic)
  separation of.................................38
  three As (key powers)........... 40, 278
PR (proportional representation) 44, 101–102, 124, 591, 596
  Hare-Clark system
    Australian Capital Territory 516, 517, 521
  Tasmania 478, 481, 482, 483, 486, 489, 490
  see also STV (Single Transferable Vote)
'preference harvesting'....271, 398
'preferential voting'......................44
  see also AV (Alternative Vote), House of Representatives
press media *see* media, mainstream
Price, Jacinta Nampijinpa... 86–87
PriceWaterhouseCoopers (PwC) 159, 161, 289, 310
Prime Minister (PM) *see* PM (Prime Minister)
prisons
  and the COVID-19 pandemic 64
  policing and imprisonment of Aboriginal and Torres Strait Islander peoples ...57, 64, 424, 509, 526

Private Member Bills (PMBs) 266–267
Productivity Commission 294, 353
protest, right to, COVID-19 pandemic............................62–64
PSC (Public Sector Commission), Western Australia 471
Public Accountability Committee, New South Wales................. 372, 375–376
Public Health Act, South Australia 433
public officials, accessibility of 145
public sector
   gender diversity and rights 215–216
   operational issues 161
   trade unions 156
Public Sector Commission (PSC), Western Australia 471
Public Service Amendment Bill 2023 309
public services
   state government 368
   see also APS (Australian Public Service)
Public Services Act 1999 306, 321
Public Services Standards Commissioner 524
Puutu Kunti Kurrama and Pinikura (PKKP) people 463–464
PwC (PriceWaterhouseCoopers) 159, 161, 289, 310

Q

QPS (Queensland Public Service) 426
Queensland 415–416, 427–428
   Aboriginal and Torres Strait Islander peoples 406, 415, 418–419, 421, 423–424, 427
   climate change and environmental policies 426–427
   COVID-19 pandemic.. 419, 420, 422, 423, 426
   diversity in political representation 213, 214, 418–419, 423–425
   elected representatives at federal, state and local level 546
   elections, accountability and representation 416–419
   elections and voting......................103
   federal Parliament seats 417
   fossil fuel industry....... 129, 160, 566, 567, 593
   historical unenfranchisement of First Nations peoples...................... 36
   'How to Vote' cards..................48–49
   human rights protection......... 55, 75, 380, 425, 446
      Human Rights Act 2019............ 60
   LA (Legislative Assembly). 415, 420, 423, 549
   local government...... 420, 545, 547, 549, 552, 553, 555
   malapportionment in elections ... 114
   mining industry.... 123, 129, 160, 415, 426, 427, 566
   party funding..................................136
   public service.....420, 421, 425–426
   recent developments...........416–419
   scrutiny and diversity.........423–425
   social inequality............................. 427
   South-East Queensland 531, 532, 538
   strong government and democratic accountability.....................422–425
   structural adaptation..........426–427
   SWOT analysis......................420–421
   urban planning 537, 538
   Women's Safety and Justice Taskforce.......................................221
Queensland Independent Remuneration Tribunal.......... 417
Queensland Public Service (QPS) 426
Question Time, House of Representatives........... 234, 237, 240–242, 246, 247

R

R v Pearson; Ex parte Sipka 1993 75
racism
   in legislation 75
   and the Voice to Parliament referendum, 2023 .... 88, 91
   'white Australia' policies 34, 54, 593
   see also First Nations peoples
Randall, Don................................286
Rann, Mike..........................445, 448
Ratcliff, Shaun............................. 331
RBA (Reserve Bank of Australia) 276
Re Canavan 246
Re Gallagher.............................246
Red Cross 148
'references' committees, Senate 261
referenda
   in a democracy.........................84–85
   see also Voice to Parliament referendum, 2023
Referendum Council...................78
referral of powers......................357
Reform of the Federation White Paper 2014 358
refugees and asylum seekers 335, 592, 598
   detention of............................. 56, 61
   human rights and civil liberties .. 54, 90
   interest groups 150
   see also immigration
Regional Councils, Northern Territories..................................506
Regional Forest Agreements (RFA).. 570
religion, freedom of 65, 74, 75
Religious Discrimination Bill 2021 65
renewable energy. 347, 562, 563, 565, 566, 570, 592
Report on Government Services (Productivity Commission)... 353
republicanism 80–81
   1999 referendum 593
Reserve Bank of Australia (RBA) 276
Resource Super Profits Tax (RSPT)..336
Respect at Work Bill 2021 246
Respect@Work 207, 208, 209, 246
'responsible party government' 38
retail giants, corporate power of 159
retail pharmaceutical industry, political donations......... 137–138
Reuters Institute.......................... 174
Reynolds, Daniel.......................... 65
Reynolds, Linda.......................... 287
RFA (Regional Forest Agreements)..............................570
Rimmer, Ben................................358
Rio Tinto, Juukan Gorge caves destruction 463–464
Roberts-Smith, Ben, defamation case against media 177, 178, 181, 184
'robodebt' crisis 201, 280, 284, 288–289, 298, 311, 338, 592
Rockliff, Jeremy................. 481, 490
'rorting'.................................184, 287
   see also 'car parks' rort; 'sports rort'
Royal Commission into Misconduct in the Banking, Superannuation and Financial Services Industry (2019) 159
Royal Commission into the Robodebt Scheme 288–289, 303–304, 306–308
RSPT (Resource Super Profits Tax).. 336
RTI (Right to Information), Tasmania..................................489
Rudd, Kevin.40, 135, 157, 158, 175, 179, 234, 266, 267, 277, 286
   climate change and environmental

policies 333, 567
economic stimulus policy . 333–334
electoral promises...............332, 333
First Nations peoples policy ..56, 77
RSPT (Resource Super Profits Tax)
....336
Strategic Priorities and Budget
Committee..41
see also Labor Party/governments
'Rules for the Protection of
Juveniles Deprived of Their
Liberty' (UN).................................57
Russia, cyber-interference in
elections 187
Ryan, Scott...255
Rylah, Joan.................................... 487

S

SAAAC (South Australian
Aboriginal Advisory Council)
....445
SA-Best party, South Australia
.... 437, 439, 440, 441
*Safeguard Mechanism (Crediting)
Amendments Act 2023* 563
same-sex marriage....................223
Samuels, Graeme............ 562, 569
Sanders, Will 500, 553–554
'sandwich generation' 220
Saunders, Cheryl 357, 358
Savva, Niki 374
Sawer, Geoffrey 355
Sawer, Marian 346, 354, 355, 360
SBS (Special Broadcasting
Service) 168
Scrutiny of Delegated Legislation
Committee, Senate.................261
second chamber see Senate
security services..........................295
    covert surveillance 330
Sen, Amartya 599
Senate 39, 253–254, 272–273,
350
    assignment of seats 46
    'balance of power'.........................266
    Banking Royal Commission
   268–269
    budget process 244, 260
    candidate selection........................ 133
    committees
        Committee on COVID-19.........244
        committees ... 255, 259, 261–262
            Economics Committee........268
            Estimates Committee 269
            Environment and Communica-
            tions References Committee 269
    COVID-19 pandemic. 244, 258, 259
    crossbenchers. 255, 258, 266–267
    diversity of representation 259,
    264–265, 272

elected representatives by state
....546
elections and voting...............97, 98,
104–105, 116, 117, 253, 255–258,
263–267, 596
    allocation of seats....................263
    'double dissolution' 104, 105, 116,
    256, 260, 263, 266, 271
    DV (deviation from proportionali-
    ty) score 106, 117
    electoral cycle............116–117, 125
    fairness 105–106
    'preference harvesting' 271
    reforms.............................. 270–271
    STV (Single Transferable Vote)
    .... 35, 39, 42, 44, 45,
    46–47, 48, 97, 98, 104–105, 107,
    117, 253, 258, 270–271, 458, 467,
    488, 490
electoral cycle 597
First Nations senators.................272
gender diversity issues 207, 209,
211, 212, 213, 272
government in minority and the
Fair Work Act 267–268
hung parliaments 128
legislative process..............261–262
limitation of power........................280
ministers...255
National Cabinet 259, 262–263
political development and
character of 264–265
powers...................................260–263
public understanding of..... 271–272
purposes, powers and processes
....260–263
question time 261
recent developments..........255–258
role on 'democracy' issues
....267–269
session length 126
SWOT analysis....................258–259
tensions and reforms 270–272
wrongful dismissal accountability
....269
see also Parliament
separation of powers 38
SEQ (South-East Queensland)
Regional Organisation of
Councils 538
SEQ (South-East Queensland)
Regional Planning Committee
....538
Service Delivery and
Coordination Committee......281
Services Australia.. 291, 302, 306,
314, 318, 319
    see also APS (Australian Public
    Service)
Services NSW......... 291, 384–385,
386–387
Seven Network 178
Seven West Media 180

Sex Discrimination and Fair Work
(Respect at Work) Amendment
Bill 2021 207
Sex Discrimination Commissioner
....207
*Sex Discrimination (Sexual
Orientation Gender Identity,
and Intersex Status) Amedment
Act 2013 (Cth)*.......................... 56
sexism, in politics......................222
sexual misconduct within
government................178, 208, 245,
287–288
    see also misogynistic behaviour;
    women, political representation
sexual orientation, federal
protection against
discrimination 56
sexual violence, human rights
and civil liberties...................... 54
SGI (Sustainable Governance
Index)................................578, 579
Shanks, Jordan ('friendlyjordies')
....202
Shooters, Fishers and Farmers
party, NSW 369, 370, 371
Shorten, Bill....................... 135, 335
Sidoti, John 373
Simpkin, Luke 286
Singapore 295, 594
'single-issue' senators see
crossbenchers
Sky News.... 170, 173, 175, 177, 185,
397, 566
Smethurst, Annika 184
Smith, Tony.................................. 271
social housing, Queensland... 427
Social Licence to Operate
.... 339–341
social media...............168, 176, 185,
191–192, 203–204
    Australians' use of 195–197
    bushfires..195
    censorship 201–203
    and civic engagement................330
    climate change and environmental
    issues 564, 566
    and democracy......................191–192
    impartiality..................................200
    interest groups 149, 152
    polarising effect of...............194–195
    and policy-making 328
    public trust..................................182
    recent developments........... 193–197
    regulation of..................192, 193, 195
    SWOT analysis......................197–199
    Voice to Parliament referendum,
    2023.. 91
    and the Voice to Parliament
    referendum, 2023 423–424

and young Australians...... 202–203
see also media; News Media and Digital Platforms Bargaining Code, 2021
Social Progress Index....... 581, 582
social rights............................64–66
Religious Discrimination Bill 2021
.... 65
solar power 296
South Australia.........................432
   Aboriginal and Torres Strait Islander peoples 424, 434, 435, 445–446
   Commonwealth-state relations. 449
   Constitution 434
   constitutional issues........... 444–446
   consultation and deliberative democracy.............................. 446
   corruption 448–449
   COVID-19 pandemic. 433, 435, 449, 450
   diversity in political representation 213, 214, 435, 443–444, 551
   elected representatives at federal, state and local level 546
   elections and electoral systems 432, 434, 436–444
     AV (Alternative Vote)......434, 436
     electoral cycle............................ 117
     malapportionment of seats..... 114, 432, 437–438, 458
   executive and Parliament. 446–448
   Fair Work legislation 267–268
   House of Assembly .. 433, 434, 435, 436–438, 440, 447, 448
   human rights 446
   ICAC (Independent Commission Against Corruption)............ 448–449
   LC (Legislative Council)....... 107, 267–268, 433, 434, 436, 437, 438–440, 441, 443, 445, 446
   local government...... 545, 547, 549, 551, 552, 555
   media diversity 442–443
   mining industry.............................. 448
   ministerial responsibility ... 447–448
   parties and party system .. 440–442
   State Ombudsman........................ 448
   SWOT analysis.................... 434–435
   Voice to Parliament.............434, 435
   women's voting rights 37
South Australian Aboriginal Advisory Council (SAAAC) .. 445
South Australian Electoral Commission 434
South Korea 595
South West Native Title Settlement............................. 463
South-East Queensland (SEQ) Regional Organisation of Councils 538
South-East Queensland (SEQ) Regional Planning Committee

....538
Speaker, House of Representatives............ 237, 240
Special Broadcasting Service (SBS) 168
Specific Purpose Payment....... 353
Speirs, David................................ 448
Spiller, Marcus 540
'sports rort' 245, 278, 284, 286, 287, 311, 338–339, 576, 592
Standing Committee on Law and Justice, New South Wales... 380
Standing Orders, House of Representatives..................... 237
State Governor, South Australia
....446
State Ombudsman, South Australia 448
State Policies and Projects Act 1993, Tasmania 488
State Premiers, National Cabinet
.... 262, 281
state residency, discrimination based on....................................74
states
   abolition of...................................71
   climate change policies 347, 562, 565
   constitutions and local government 549
   COVID-19 pandemic...............71, 347
   delegation of development project approval to 562
   elected representatives by state 546
   elections and voting............ 103, 596
     AV (Alternative Vote) 103, 107, 114
     STV (Single Transferable Vote) 103, 107
   fiscal powers 351–352
   human rights protection.. 55, 60, 75
   LCs (Legislative Councils)............ 107
   political representation 131, 132, 213, 214
   powers and responsibilities of.....38
   resurgence of 347
   revenue and expenses.................351
   Senate representation................... 39
   service delivery 347
   state primacy and control. 550–551
   see also federalism, and democracy; individual states; National Cabinet
Stecker, Christian............. 263–264
Stokes, Kerry................................178
Stolen Generation 55, 78
Strategic Priorities and Budget Committee...............................41
'Strategy for Nature' 569
'strong democracy' principles.. 35

STV (Single Transferable Vote)
.... 253, 258
   above-the-line......... 46, 48, 270, 271, 458, 467, 490
   below-the-line........ 46, 48, 270–271, 467, 488, 490
   democratic requirements 98
   Senate..... 35, 39, 44, 45, 46–47, 48, 97, 98, 104–105, 107, 117, 591
   states....................................... 103, 107
     Australian Capital Territory (Hare-Clark system)............. 516, 517, 521
     New South Wales... 367, 370, 376
     South Australia...............434, 436
     Tasmania (Hare-Clark system) 478, 481, 483, 486, 487, 489, 490
     Victoria.............................. 398, 400
     Western Australia .. 457, 458, 461, 467, 469
Summit for Democracy 2021.... 60
Sunday Mail, The...................... 442
Sunday Telegraph 184
Sunshine Coast................. 530, 531
superannuation funds, corporate power 159
Supreme Court of New South Wales, right to public protest
.... 62–63
surveillance, covert...................330
Sustainable Governance Index (SGI).................................578, 579
SWOT analysis
   Anthropocene.................... 563–566
   APS (Australian Public Service)
  310–312
   Australian democracy............. 43–44
   Constitution 73–74
   core executive 278–280
   elections and voting systems
   .... 49–50, 107–109
   federalism, and democracy
   349–350
   gender equality and rights .209–211
   House of Representatives 237–239
   human rights and civil liberties
  59–60
   local government............... 547–548
   metropolitan regions/big cities
   531–533
   policy-making 328–330
   political parties 124–128
   Senate...................................258–259
   social media 197–199
   states
     Australian Capital Territory
     519–520
     New South Wales........... 376–378
     Northern Territory.......... 502–503
     Queensland 420–421
     South Australia................ 434–435
     Tasmania 483–485
     Victoria..............................397–399

Western Australia............459–461
Voice to Parliament referendum, 2023...................................... 90
Sydney 386
   bushfires...................................296
   city council................................534
   City of Sydney..............................540
   Greater Sydney .530, 531, 535, 537, 538, 540
   Western Sydney airport and 'Aeropolis' development....537, 539
Sydney Morning Herald....170, 172
   Roberts-Smith defamation case.177, 178, 181, 184

T

Taiwan 60, 593, 595
Tame, Grace................................208
Tasmania
   Aboriginal and Torres Strait Islander peoples 485, 493–494
   changing electoral policies 480–482
   climate change and environmental policies 565, 570
   Constitution................. 485, 491–493
   corruption 391, 484
   COVID-19 pandemic............482–483
   digital infrastructure 489
   diversity in political representation 213, 214, 551
   elected representatives at federal, state and local level 546
   elections, voting and party competition 103, 489–491
      AV (Alternative Vote)......478, 482
   House of Assembly... 478, 480, 481, 482, 483, 485, 486–487, 489, 492, 493, 494
   House of Representatives seats 488
   intergovernmental relations........488
   LC (Legislative Council)...... 107, 478, 482, 483, 485, 487, 492, 494
   local government....... 545, 547, 551, 552, 555
   Parliament and the executive 485–487
   public services............484, 488, 489
   responsible government and core executive............................. 487–488
   Senate seats 46, 263, 266, 488
   size of electorate 115
   STV (Single Transferable Vote) ..103
   SWOT analysis........................483–485
   urban planning 537
   VFI (Vertical Fiscal Imbalance)...488
Tasmanian Constitution Act ..492, 493
Tasmanian Integrity Commission (TIC)...391
Tasmanian State Service (TSS) 484, 488, 489

tax avoidance industry..............160
taxation
   Commonwealth and state powers 351–352
   pay-as-you-go system 145
Taylor, Angus 566
Teal Independents 87, 100, 101, 102, 105, 108, 113–114, 117, 123, 124, 130, 139, 178, 207, 208, 209, 211, 233, 235, 236, 257, 265, 561, 567, 591
Telstra 159, 266
Territory Alliance, Northern Territory........................... 499, 500
Territory Chief Ministers, National Cabinet............................. 262, 281
Thatcher, Margaret....................568
'think tanks'.................................161
Thodey, David 387
three As (key powers) 40, 278
TIC (Tasmanian Integrity Commission)............................391
TikTok 180, 193
Tobin, Andrew 426
torture................................... 56, 61
TPP (two-party perferred vote) 48, 99, 100–102, 112, 123, 124, 127, 369, 397, 438, 468, 499, 500, 502, 591
Trad, Jackie................416, 418, 425
trade associations 147
   party funding......................... 153, 154
trade unions
   declining membership.151, 155–157, 332
   and the Labor Party........ 36, 147, 153, 154, 157
   labour rights 66
   public attitudes towards......156–157
   scale of 148
Traditional Owners and First Peoples, Victoria 406
   see also Aboriginal and Torres Strait Islander peoples; First Nations peoples
transgender people 90
Transparency International 580, 581
Treasurer.......... 276, 281, 293, 294
Treasury 276, 293
Treaty Advancement Committee, Queensland 424
Treaty Authority, Victoria 406
trial by jury...................................74
Trudeau, Justin...........................283
Trump, Donald 103, 283, 296, 297, 565, 576
Truth Telling and Healing Inquiry, Queensland 423

TSS (Tasmanian State Service) 484, 488, 489
Turnbull, Malcolm ...136, 222, 234, 271, 277, 286, 294, 594
   climate change and environmental policies 567, 568
   First Nations peoples policy ..78, 87
   fiscal policy............................291–292
   policy.. 333
   politicisation of the executive....313, 314
   welfare reform 306
   see also Liberal Party; Liberal-National Coalition
Twomey, Anne..................356, 357

U

UDHR (Universal Declaration of Human Rights)......................... 59
Uhr, John.......................................261
UK
   AUKUS (Australia, UK, USA) nuclear submarine deal. 285, 289, 297, 595
   'British Bill of Rights'...................... 66
   carbon tariffs 566
   climate change and environmental policies 568
   COVID-19 pandemic......................283
   democracy indices 578
   electoral system.................. 590–591
   'Five Eyes' intelligence network 295, 593
   fossil fuel vehicles policy............296
   'Home Children' imported to Australia 181
   political appointees.......................313
   Westminster advisory system.....315
Ukraine, Russian invasion of, 2022 60
Uluru Statement from the Heart, 2017...44, 56, 78, 79, 86, 87, 89, 91, 239
UNESCO 562
Ungunmerr, Miriam-Rose.........406
uniform legislation 357
United Australia Party........ 102, 138
   Senate.. 271
United Nations
   Declaration of Human Rights (UDHR)...................................... 59
   and the detention of refugees and asylum seekers....................... 61
   Framework Convention on Climate Change (UNFCCC) 571
   Human Rights Committee (UNHRC) 54, 90
   'Rules for the Protection of Juveniles Deprived of Their Liberty' 57
   violence against Indigenous women...............................210

upper chamber *see* Senate
urban management and planning, metropolitan regions/big cities 536–537
USA
  AUKUS (Australia, UK, USA) nuclear submarine deal. 285, 289, 297, 595
  Australia's relationship with 297, 593, 595
  climate change policy 296, 297
  COVID-19 pandemic 283
  'democratic backsliding' 574, 576
  electoral cycle 98, 116
  'Five Eyes' network 295, 593
  FPTP (first past the post) electoral systems 103
  intelligence and security services 295
  mainstream media 176, 177
  renditions and torture, Iraq and Afghanistan 295
  Senate 253
  voter identity policies 337
  voter suppression 114

V

van Onselen, D.P. 334–335
Vanderstock and Anor v State of Victoria 351
V-Dem (Varieties of Democracy) Index 578–579
Veterans' Affairs 314
VFI (Vertical Fiscal Imbalance) 351, 358
  New South Wales 387
  Tasmania 488
  Victoria 408, 409
Victoria 392–393, 410
  Aboriginal and Torres Strait Islander peoples 394, 398, 406, 408
  bushfires 394, 410
  climate change and environmental policies 408, 562
  Constitution 396–397, 403–404, 549
  core executive and public services 407–409
  COVID-19 pandemic 334, 347, 394–396, 398, 399, 403–404, 407, 410
  diversity in political representation 404, 405, 551
  elected representatives at federal, state and local level 546
  elections and party politics 103, 397, 399–400
    AV (Alternative Vote) 397, 399, 400
      electoral cycle 117
  fossil fuel vehicles policy 296
  'fracking' ban 397

Gender Equality Act 2020 207
gender equality issues 210
human rights 55, 75, 380, 446
  Charter of Human Rights and Responsibilities 394–395, 396, 398, 409
  Civil Rights Act 2006 60
LA (Legislative Assembly). 392, 397, 398, 399, 400, 401, 403
Landcare 565
LC (Legislative Council) 107, 392, 398, 399, 400, 402, 403
local government 405, 545, 547, 549, 550, 551, 555
media alignments 397
metropolitan regions/big cities . 539
National Cabinet 348
Parliament 403–404
party funding 136
political parties . 396, 397, 399, 400, 401, 402, 403, 404–405
'pork-barrelling' 339
premiers since 1970s 407
Public Health and Wellbeing Amendment (Pandemic Management) Bill 2021 ("Pandemic Bill") 395
recent developments 393–397
Senate election, 2013 271
state election, 2022 114
SWOT analysis 397–399
urban planning 537
VFI (Vertical Fiscal Imbalance).. 408, 409
Victoria Public Accounts and Estimates Committee 404
Victorian Aboriginal Affairs Framework 2018–2023 408
Victorian Electoral Commission 403
Victorian Local Government Act 2020 553
Victorian Treaty Advancement Commission 406
Vietnam War 593
Vietnamese Australians 125
Vincent, Kelly 444
Vine 193
'Voice for Indi' 139
Voice to Parliament referendum, 2023 .... 44, 53, 72, 73, 78–79, 80, 81, 84–85, 89–90, 139, 239, 257–258, 379, 406, 419, 423–424, 445, 503, 590
  campaign 87–89
  future prospects 91–92
  implications of the 'No' vote . 89–90
  opinion polls 86, 87
  origins and lead-up ... 57–59, 85–87
  referendum result by seats ... 86, 87
  SWOT analysis 90
voluntary assisted dying

legislation 331, 425, 493, 525
voting
  compulsory 35, 47–49, 139, 596
    local government 545
  electoral integrity 114–116
  informal 48
  voter ID policy 337
  voter registration issues 115
  voter suppression 114
  see also elections
voting rights 74, 75
  First Nations peoples 36–37
  women 37
voting systems 97–98
  in democracy 97–98
  FPTP (first past the post) system 45, 48, 103, 104, 482, 501, 590
  GVT (group voting ticket) system 398, 399, 410, 458
  Hare-Clark system
    Australian Capital Territory 516, 517, 521
    Tasmania 478, 481, 482, 483, 486, 489, 490
  marking of preferences 47–48
  recent developments 98–107
  SWOT analysis 49–50, 107–109
  see also AV (Alternative Vote); elections; PR (proportional representation); STV (Single Transferable Vote)

W

Walsh, Pat 406
Ward, Gareth 373
Warner, Kate 494
water resources 570, 571
Watertrust Australia 570, 571
Watt Review 489
WeChat 193
Weir, Stuart 34
welfare payments, government expenditure on 293
West Australian, The 455, 460
Western Australia 453–454
  Aboriginal and Torres Strait Islander peoples 406, 463–464, 469, 470
  Commonwealth-State relations 453, 464–465
  Constitution 455, 462–465
  COVID-19 pandemic 71–72, 334, 454–456, 461, 462, 464
  diversity in political representation 460, 469–470, 551
  elected representatives at federal, state and local level 546
  fossil fuel industry 474, 593
  gender-based violence 221
  government accountability and public sector corruption issues 471–473

historical unenfranchisement of First Nations peoples..................... 36
LA (Legislative Assembly).456, 457, 461, 465–466, 468, 470
LC (Legislative Council)............... 107, 358, 456–457, 457–459, 461, 462, 467–468, 469, 470, 472, 473
 Standing Committee on Uniform Legislation and Statutes Review 358
local government....... 545, 547, 551, 552, 554, 555
Mark McGowan and Labor's political domination............ 456–457
media diversity 460
mining industry ..160, 218, 455, 458, 459, 463, 474
party competition, elections and representation 465–470
 AV (Alternative Vote)..... 456, 457, 466
 malapportionment of seats 457–459, 467
 SWOT analysis....................... 459-461
 urban planning 537
Western Australia Electoral Commission 469
Western Sydney City Deal 540
Western Sydney Leadership Dialogue 540
Westminster systems..... 11, 36, 38, 39, 40, 41, 42, 44, 70, 74, 103, 117, 235, 236, 254, 255, 276, 281, 287, 288, 289, 290, 291, 298, 306, 313, 314, 315, 316, 446, 447, 482, 485, 492, 493, 504, 511, 564, 578, 590, 591, 592, 594, 595, 597
Westpac 268
WFH (working from home)........ 211
WGEA (Workplace Gender Equality Agency).209, 219–220
WhatsApp............................ 193, 198
 see also Meta
'whipping' votes, House of Representatives..................... 235
'white Australia' policies.... 34, 54, 593
Whitlam, Gough 39, 179, 260
WHO (World Health Organization) 282
Whyte, Paul 471–472
Williams, George 65
Williams, John.................. 268, 269
Willumson, David M. 263–264
Wiradjuri nation............................ 58
'woke agenda'............................. 223
Wollongong-Shellharbour 530
women..123
 gender pay gap.149, 206, 209, 210, 218–219
 human rights and civil liberties .. 54, 590
 interest groups 148, 149
 legal rights..37
 parental leave...................... 219–220
 political representation 103, 117, 596
  Australian Capital Territory 213, 214, 520, 521
  House of Representatives 108
  local government 551
  New South Wales....377, 381, 382
  party membership and social representation 132
  political parties.......................... 125
  Queensland 213, 214, 418, 423
  Senate..108
  South Australia.........213, 214, 435, 443
  Victoria.............................. 404, 405
  Western Australia.. 460, 469, 470
 'sandwich generation' 220
 unpaid labour............... 211, 219–220
 voting rights 37
 see also Indigenous women; misogynistic behaviour
Women's Safety and Justice Taskforce, Queensland......... 221
Women's Safety Summit, 2021 208
Wood Royal Commission 372
Woollahra, Sydney 554
Work Choices legislation..........267, 268, 334
'workforce disincentive rate' ... 219
working from home (WFH) 211
Workplace Gender Equality Act 2012 209
Workplace Gender Equality Agency (WGEA) ..209, 219–220
Workplace Relations Act 1996. 66
World Bank.................................... 316
World Economic Forum, Global Gender Gap Report 206, 210
World Happiness Report 581, 582
World Health Organization (WHO) 282
World Values Survey (WVS) 582–583
Wran, Neville................................ 372
wrongful dismissal accountability, Senate 269
WVS (World Values Survey) 582–583
Wyatt, Ken 56

X

X (formerly Twitter)...169, 180, 192, 198, 200, 328
Xenophon, Nick 257, 266, 267–268
Xenophon/Centre Alliance, House of Representatives .. 233
Xenophone Team party, South Australia 439, 441
Xi Jinping.................. 297, 593, 595

Y

Yindyamarra Nguluway research program, Charles Sturt University.................................... 89
Yindyamarra Winhanganha 91
Yoorrook Justice Commission, Victoria 406
Young, Jeannette 419
young people
 media viewing habits.................... 174
 news sources.........................196–197
 political engagement.................... 92
 political representation
  South Australia.......................... 444
  Victoria.............................404–405
 social media 202–203
 youth detention, protection against abuse 57
Youth Justice Act 2005 (NT)......57
YouTube ...193, 195, 198, 200, 202

Z

Zempilas, Basil 457, 474
Ziblatt, Daniel 575, 576

www.ingramcontent.com/pod-product-compliance
Lightning Source LLC
Chambersburg PA
CBHW080352030426
42334CB00024B/2845